The Individual Investor's Guide to

Low-Load

Mutual Funds

The American Association
of Individual Investors

The Individual Investor's Guide to

Low-Load

Mutual Funds

The American Association
of Individual Investors

14th Edition

The *American Association of Individual Investors* is an independent, not-for-profit corporation formed in 1978 for the purpose of assisting individuals in becoming effective managers of their own assets through programs of education, information, and research.

Data in this guide was gathered directly from the funds. While the material in this *Guide* cannot be guaranteed to be error free, it has been obtained from sources believed to be reliable.

Preface

Inside the *Guide* are the information and performance statistics you will need to make well-informed decisions on your mutual fund investments. Our goal is to provide pertinent information, organized to minimize your time spent collecting and comparing information on the increasingly large universe of mutual funds.

The data for this *Guide* was gathered from each fund's prospectus and annual report, and from direct contact with each fund. We calculate all performance and risk statistics, and then verify our information. Our objective is full, accurate, and timely disclosure of investment information.

The 1995 edition of the *Low-Load Mutual Fund Guide* covers 877 mutual funds. There are 51 more funds in the *Guide* this year than last year.

John Bajkowski oversaw the development and production of the *Guide*. Mark Fister assisted in the calculation of the performance statistics; Marie Swick supervised the data collection and verification; and Michael Gutierrez and Susan Pawlick assisted in collecting data. Martha Crawford served as project editor for the *Guide* and Kurt Zauke designed the cover.

Chicago   John Markese, Ph.D.
March 1995   President

Table of Contents

Preface v
Chapter 1: How to Use This Guide 1
Chapter 2: Investing in Mutual Funds 2
   Diversification 2
   Avoiding Excessive Charges 3
   Sorting Out Charges 4
Chapter 3: Mutual Fund Categories 5
   Aggressive Growth Funds 6
   Growth Funds 6
   Growth and Income Funds 7
   Balanced Funds 7
   Bond Funds 8
   International Bond and Stock Funds 8
   Gold Funds 9
   Other Types of Funds 10
Chapter 4: Understanding Mutual Fund Statements 11
   The Prospectus 11
   Statement of Additional Information 16
   Annual, Semiannual, and Quarterly Reports 17
   Marketing Brochures and Advertisements 17
   Account Statements 18
Chapter 5: Understanding Risk 19
   A Look at Risk 19
   Standard Deviation 20
   Market Risk 20
   Beta 21
   Average Maturity 21
Chapter 6: Which Funds Were Included 23
   Size 23
   Loads 23
Chapter 7: A Key to Terms and Statistics 24
Chapter 8: Fund Performance Rankings 29
Chapter 9: Individual Fund Listings 57
Appendix A: Special Types of Funds 935
   Asset Allocation Funds 935
   Funds Investing in Funds 936
   Global Funds 936

Index Mutual Funds 937
Sector Funds 938
Small Capitalization Stock Funds 939
Socially Conscious Funds 941
State-Specific Tax-Exempt Bond Funds 941
Appendix B: Changes to the Funds 945
Fund Name Changes 945
Investment Category Changes 945
Funds Dropped from the Guide 946
Index 949

How to Use This Guide 1

Selecting a mutual fund, while less time-consuming than investing in individual securities, does require some homework. No one should put money into an investment that is not understood. This does not require a detailed investigation of the fund's investments, but it does require an understanding of the investment objectives and strategies, and the possible risks and returns.

This *Guide* is designed to provide you with that understanding. We have kept the chapters brief and to the point, so that individuals new to mutual fund investing will not be overwhelmed with unnecessary details.

Chapters 2 through 5 deal with the basics of investing in mutual funds—diversification; loads; the various categories of mutual funds and what they mean; how to read a mutual fund's prospectus and annual report, as well as any other information they send you; and how to evaluate the risk of a mutual fund.

Those who are familiar with mutual funds may want to skip directly to Chapter 6, which describes how the mutual funds were chosen for inclusion in the *Guide*. Chapter 7 is a key to the terms used in the performance tables and the mutual fund data pages, and includes an explanation of how the returns were calculated and what the different risk measures mean.

Chapter 8 presents the performance tables, which include the historical performance of different categories of mutual funds and their corresponding benchmarks. While past performance is no indication of future performance, it may indicate the quality and consistency of fund management. From this section, you should pick out several mutual funds that meet your investment objectives and risk tolerance. These funds can then be examined more closely in the mutual fund data pages.

Chapter 9 contains the individual fund listings. The funds are listed alphabetically; their ticker symbol and investment category are indicated at the top of the page after the fund's name. These pages provide 10 years of per share data, performance statistics along with risk measures, portfolio information, and shareholder services provided by the fund. Use the address and telephone numbers provided to call or write the funds to request a copy of the prospectus and annual report. You should read the prospectus carefully before investing.

At the back of the *Guide* is a list of special category funds that includes asset allocation, funds investing in other mutual funds, global, index, sector, small capitalization stocks, socially conscious, and state specific tax-exempt bond funds. And finally, there is a list of fund changes, including fund name changes, investment category changes, and funds that were dropped from the *Guide*.

Investing in Mutual Funds

2

A mutual fund is an investment company that pools investors' money to invest in securities. An open-end mutual fund continuously issues new shares when investors want to invest in the fund, and it redeems shares when investors want to sell. A mutual fund trades directly with its shareholders, and the share price of the fund represents the market value of the securities that the fund holds.

There are several advantages that mutual funds offer individual investors. They provide:

- Professional investment management at a low cost, even for small accounts;
- A diversified group of securities that only a large portfolio can provide;
- Information through prospectuses and annual reports that facilitates comparisons among funds;
- Special services such as check writing, dividend reinvestment plans, telephone switching, and periodic withdrawal and investment plans;
- Account statements that make it easy to track the value of your investment and that ease the paperwork at tax time.

Successful investing takes time and effort, and it requires special knowledge and relevant, up-to-date information. Investors must spend a considerable amount of energy searching for opportunities and monitoring each investment. Professional investment management is relatively cheap with mutual funds. The typical adviser charges about 0.5% annually for managing a fund's assets. For an individual making a $10,000 investment, that comes to only $50 a year.

Of course, mutual fund investing does not preclude investing in securities on your own. One useful strategy would be to invest in mutual funds and individual securities. The mutual funds would ensure your participation in overall market moves and lend diversification to your portfolio, while the individual securities would provide you with the opportunity to apply your specific investment analysis skills.

DIVERSIFICATION

If there is one ingredient to successful investing that is universally agreed upon, it is the benefit of diversification. This is a concept that is backed by a great deal of research, market experience, and common sense. Diversification reduces risk. Risk to investors is frequently defined as volatility of return—in other words, how much an investment's return might vary over a year. Investors prefer returns that are relatively predictable, and thus less volatile. On the other hand, they want returns that are high, but higher returns are accompanied by higher risks. Diversification eliminates some of the risk without reducing potential returns.

Mutual funds, because of their size and the laws governing their operation, provide investors with diversification that might be difficult for an individual to duplicate. This is true not only for common stock funds, but also for bond funds, municipal bond funds, gold funds, international bond and stock funds—in fact, for almost all mutual funds. Even the sector funds that invest only within one industry offer diversification within that industry. The degree of diversification will vary among funds, but most will provide investors with some amount of diversification.

AVOIDING EXCESSIVE CHARGES

This book is dedicated to no-load and low-load mutual funds. Investors should realize that:

- A load is a sales commission that goes to the seller of the fund shares;
- A load does not go to anyone responsible for managing the fund's assets and does not serve as an incentive for the fund manager to perform better;
- Funds with loads, on average, consistently underperform no-load funds when the load is taken into consideration in performance calculations;
- For every high-performing load fund, there exists a similar no-load or low-load fund that can be purchased more cheaply;
- Loads understate the real commission charged because they reduce the total amount being invested: $10,000 invested in a 6% front-end load fund results in a $600 sales charge and only a $9,400 investment in the fund;
- If a load fund is held over a long time period, the effect of the load, if paid up front, is not diminished as quickly as many people believe; if the money paid for the load had been working for you, as in a no-load fund, it would have been compounding over the whole time period.

The bottom line in any investment is how it performs for you, the investor, and that performance includes consideration of all loads, fees and expenses. There may be some load funds that will do even better factoring in the load, but you have no way of finding that fund in advance. The only guide you have is historical performance, which is not necessarily an indication of future performance. With a heavily loaded fund, you are starting your investment with a significant loss—the load. Avoid unnecessary charges whenever possible.

SORTING OUT CHARGES

It is best to stick with no-load or low-load funds, but they are becoming more difficult to distinguish from heavily loaded funds. The use of high front-end loads has declined, and funds are now turning to other kinds of charges. Some mutual funds sold by brokerage firms, for example, have lowered their front-end loads to 5%, and others have introduced back-end loads (deferred sales charges), which are sales commissions paid when exiting the fund. In both instances, the load is often accompanied by annual charges.

On the other hand, some no-load funds have found that to compete, they must market themselves much more aggressively. To do so, they have introduced charges of their own.

The result has been the introduction of low loads, redemption fees, and annual charges. Low loads—up to 3%—are sometimes added instead of the annual charges. In addition, some funds have instituted a charge for investing or withdrawing money.

Redemption fees work like back-end loads: You pay a percentage of the value of your fund when you get out. Loads are on the amount you have invested, while redemption fees are calculated against the value of your fund assets. Some funds have sliding scale redemption fees, so that the longer you remain invested, the lower the charge when you leave. Some funds use redemption fees to discourage short-term trading, a policy that is designed to protect longer-term investors. These funds usually have redemption fees that disappear after six months.

Probably the most confusing charge is the annual charge, the 12b-1 plan. The adoption of a 12b-1 plan by a fund permits the adviser to use fund assets to pay for distribution costs, including advertising, distribution of fund literature such as prospectuses and annual reports, and sales commissions paid to brokers. Some funds use 12b-1 plans as masked load charges: They levy very high rates on the fund and use the money to pay brokers to sell the fund. Since the charge is annual and based on the value of the investment, this can result in a total cost to a long-term investor that exceeds a high up-front sales load. A fee table is required in all prospectuses clarifying the impact of a 12b-1 plan and other charges.

The fee table makes the comparison of total expenses among funds easier. Selecting a fund based solely on expenses, including loads and charges, will not give you optimal results, but avoiding funds with high expenses and unnecessary charges is important for long-term performance.

Mutual Fund Categories 3

Mutual funds come in all shapes and sizes; there are over 850 funds covered in this book alone, each with its own characteristics. Many mutual funds, however, have shared investment objectives that generally lead to other characteristics that are similar.

These shared characteristics allow us to divide mutual funds into several broad categories. This chapter defines the mutual fund categories we used for this book. In this guide, the individual fund data pages appear alphabetically; the fund's category is indicated beneath the fund's name.

The following table summarizes some important characteristics of funds by category. Averages for expense ratio, income to assets, portfolio turnover, and portfolio composition illustrate some of the differences in the investment categories.

Investment Category	Expense Ratio (%)	Income to Assets (%)	Portfolio Turnover (%)	Portfolio Composition (%)				
				Stocks	Bonds	Conv't.	Other	Cash
Aggressive Growth	1.49	-0.32	132	88	0	1	0	11
Growth	1.20	0.77	95	86	1	1	0	12
Growth & Income	0.96	2.55	75	83	2	5	2	8
Balanced	0.98	3.60	91	48	34	5	4	9
Corporate Bond	0.70	6.26	117	0	87	4	2	7
Corp. High-Yield Bond	0.91	8.48	147	4	86	1	4	5
Government Bond	0.75	5.48	177	0	95	0	0	5
Mortgage-Backed Bond	0.71	6.51	196	0	93	0	0	7
General Bond	0.74	5.60	186	0	91	0	0	9
Tax-Exempt Bond	0.62	5.12	57	0	99	0	0	1
International Stock	1.46	0.62	85	89	2	1	2	6
International Bond	1.13	6.19	230	1	86	1	1	11
Gold	1.44	0.36	57	89	0	1	6	4
Domestic Equity Fund	1.20	1.03	100	86	1	2	1	10
Small Cap Stock	1.31	0.00	79	88	0	0	1	11
Domestic Taxable Bond	0.75	5.93	175	0	92	1	0	7

AGGRESSIVE GROWTH FUNDS

The investment objective of aggressive growth funds is maximum capital gains. They invest aggressively in common stocks and tend to stay fully invested over the market cycle. Sometimes, these funds will borrow money to purchase securities, and some may engage in trading stock options or take positions in stock index futures.

Aggressive growth funds typically provide low income distributions. This is because they tend to be fully invested in common stocks and do not earn a significant amount of interest income. In addition, the common stocks they invest in are generally growth-oriented stocks that pay little or no cash dividends.

Many aggressive growth funds concentrate their assets in particular industries or segments of the market, and their degree of diversification may not be as great as other types of funds. These investment strategies result in increased risk. Thus, they tend to perform better than the overall market during bull markets but fare worse during bear markets.

In general, long-term investors who need not be concerned with monthly or yearly variation in investment return will find investment in this class of funds rewarding. Because of the extreme volatility of return, however, risk-averse investors with a short-term investment horizon may find that these mutual funds lie well outside their comfort zones. During prolonged market declines, aggressive growth funds can sustain severe declines in net asset value.

Market timing is not a strategy we recommend, particularly over the short term. Although the transaction costs of switching in and out of no-load mutual funds are near zero, it can create significant tax liabilities. In addition, the ability to consistently time the market correctly in the short term, after adjusting for risk, costs, and taxes, has not been demonstrated. However, aggressive growth funds, with their high volatility and fully invested position, do make ideal vehicles for those who believe they know the next market move.

GROWTH FUNDS

The investment objective of growth funds is to obtain long-term growth of invested capital. They generally do not engage in speculative tactics such as using financial leverage. On occasion, these funds will use stock or index options or futures to reduce risk by hedging their portfolio positions.

Growth funds typically are more stable than aggressive growth funds. Generally, they invest in growth-oriented firms that are more mature and that pay cash dividends. You are likely to find companies such as Disney, PepsiCo, and McDonald's in the portfolios of growth funds.

The degree of concentration of assets is not as severe as with aggressive growth funds. Additionally, these funds tend to move from fully invested to partially invested positions over the market cycle. They build up cash positions during uncertain market environments.

In general, growth fund performance tends to mirror the market during bull and bear markets. Some growth funds have been able to perform relatively well during recent bear markets because their managers were able to change portfolio composition by a much greater degree or to maintain much higher cash positions than aggressive growth fund managers. However, higher cash positions can also cause the funds to underperform aggressive growth funds during bull markets.

Aggressive investors should consider holding both growth fund shares and aggressive growth fund shares in their overall portfolios. This is an especially appealing strategy for investors who hold aggressive growth mutual funds that invest in small stock growth firms. The portfolios of these funds complement the portfolios of growth funds, leading to greater overall diversification. The combination produces overall returns that will tend to be less volatile than an investment in only aggressive growth funds.

As with aggressive growth funds, these funds can sustain severe declines during prolonged bear markets. Since some portfolio managers of growth funds attempt to time the market over the longer market cycle, using these funds to move in and out of the market for timing purposes may be counterproductive.

GROWTH AND INCOME FUNDS

Growth and income funds generally invest in the common stocks and convertible securities of seasoned, well-established, cash-dividend-paying companies. The funds attempt to provide shareholders with significant income along with long-term growth. They generally attempt to avoid excessive fluctuations in return. One tends to find a high concentration of public utility common stocks and sometimes convertible securities in the portfolios of growth and income funds. The funds also provide higher income distributions, less variability in return, and greater diversification than growth and aggressive growth funds. Names such as equity-income, income, and total return have been attached to funds that have characteristics of growth and income funds. Because of the high current income offered by these kinds of funds, potential investors should keep the tax consequences in mind.

BALANCED FUNDS

The balanced fund category has become less distinct in recent years, and a significant overlap in fund objectives exists between growth and income funds and balanced funds. In general, the portfolios of balanced funds consist of investments in common stocks and substantial investments in bonds and convertible securities. The proportion of stocks and bonds that will be held is usually stated in the investment objective, but usually the portfolio manager has the option of allocating the proportions between some stated range. Some asset allocation funds—funds that have a wide latitude of portfolio composition change—can also be found in the balanced category. Balanced funds are generally less volatile than aggressive growth, growth, and growth and income funds. As with growth and income funds, balanced funds provide a high dividend yield.

BOND FUNDS

Bond mutual funds are attractive to investors because they provide diversification and liquidity, which may not be as readily attainable in direct bond investments.

Bond funds have portfolios with a wide range of average maturities. Many funds use their names to characterize their maturity structure. Generally, short term means that the portfolio has a weighted average maturity of less than three years. Intermediate implies an average maturity of three to 10 years, and long term is over 10 years. The longer the maturity, the greater the change in fund value when interest rates change. Longer-term bond funds are riskier than shorter-term funds, and they tend to offer higher yields.

Bond funds are principally categorized by the types of bonds they hold. Corporate bond funds invest generally at least 70% of assets in investment grade corporate bonds of various maturities; however, corporate high-yield bond funds provide high income and invest generally at least 70% of assets in corporate bonds rated below investment grade.

Government bond funds invest generally in the bonds of the U.S. government and its agencies, while mortgage-backed bond funds invest generally at least 70% of assets in mortgage-backed securities. General bond funds invest in a mix of government and agency bonds, corporate bonds, and mortgage-backed securities. Tax-exempt bond funds invest in bonds whose income is exempt from federal income tax. Some tax-exempt funds may invest in bonds whose income is also exempt from the income tax of a specific state.

INTERNATIONAL BOND AND STOCK FUNDS

International funds invest in bonds and stocks of foreign firms and governments. Some funds specialize in regions, such as the Pacific or Europe, and others invest worldwide. In addition, some funds—usually termed "global funds"—invest in both foreign and U.S. securities. We have two classifications of international funds—international stock funds and international bond funds—and we provide a portfolio breakdown by country.

International funds provide investors with added diversification. The most important factor when diversifying a portfolio is selecting assets that do not behave similarly to each other under similar economic scenarios. Within the U.S., investors can diversify by selecting securities of firms in different industries. In the international realm, investors take the diversification process one step further by holding securities of firms in different countries. The more independently these foreign markets move in relation to the U.S. stock market, the greater will be the diversification benefit, and the lower the risk.

In addition, international funds overcome some of the difficulties investors face in making foreign investments directly. For instance, individuals have to thoroughly understand the foreign brokerage process, be familiar with the various foreign marketplaces and their economies, be aware of currency fluctuation trends, and have access to reliable financial information. This can be a monumental task for the individual investor.

There are some risks to investing internationally. In addition to the risk inherent in investing in any security, there is an additional exchange rate risk. The return to a U.S. investor from a foreign security depends on both the security's return in its own currency and the rate at which that currency can be exchanged for U.S. dollars. Another uncertainty is political risk, which includes government restriction, taxation, or even total prohibition of the exchange of one currency into another. Of course, the more the mutual fund is diversified among various countries, the less the risk involved.

GOLD FUNDS

Gold mutual funds specialize in investments in both foreign and domestic companies that mine gold and other precious metals. Some funds also hold gold directly through investments in gold coins or bullion. Gold options are another method used to invest in the industry. Mutual fund investments in precious metals range from the conservative to the highly speculative.

Gold and other precious metals mutual funds allow investors interested in this area to invest in a more liquid and diversified vehicle than would be available through a direct purchase.

The appeal of gold and precious metals is that they have performed well during extreme inflationary periods. Over the short term, the price of gold moves in response to a variety of political, economic, and psychological forces. As world tension and anxiety rise, so may the price of gold. In periods of peace and stability, the price of gold may decline. Because gold may perform in an inverse relationship to stocks, bonds, and cash, it may be a stabilizing component in one's portfolio. Silver and platinum react in a similar fashion to gold.

Precious metals funds, like the metals themselves, are very volatile, often shooting from the bottom to the top and back to the bottom in fund rankings over the years. Investors should understand, however, that because most gold funds invest in the stock of gold mining companies, they are still subject to some stock market risk.

OTHER TYPES OF FUNDS

There are many specialized mutual funds that do not have their own categories. Instead, they will be found in one of the various categories mentioned above. These funds are classified by their investment objectives rather than by their investment strategies. For instance, several funds specialize in specific sectors or industries, but one industry-specific fund does not necessarily appear in the same category as another industry-specific sector fund. For example, a technology sector fund would likely appear in the aggressive growth category while a utility sector fund would be found in the growth and income category. Specialized funds include small company funds, "socially conscious" funds, index funds, funds investing in funds, and asset allocation funds.

Asset allocation funds, for example, are usually one of two types. Some allocation funds are designed to provide diversification among the various categories of investments and within each investment category. For example, an asset allocation fund may hold minimum percentages in stocks, bonds, cash, and international investments. The second asset allocation strategy used by some funds is to move money around according to what the fund managers believe to be optimal proportions given their expectations for the economy, interest rates, and other market factors. These latter asset allocation funds are market timing funds, distinctly different and with greater risk than the asset allocation funds striving solely for diversification. These market-timing asset allocation funds are the type noted as asset allocation funds in the book.

One other fund type deserves a special mention—the index fund. An example of an index fund is Vanguard's Index Trust—500, categorized as a growth and income fund. This fund is designed to match the Standard & Poor's 500 stock index and does so by investing in all 500 stocks in the S&P 500; the amounts invested in each stock are proportional to the firm's market value representation in the S&P 500. Statistics on this fund are quite useful for comparison with other funds, since the index represents a widely followed segment of the market. Index funds are available covering most major segments of the bond and stock markets, domestic and international. Because they are unmanaged, they make no research efforts to select particular stocks or bonds, nor do they make timing decisions. This passive management approach makes the cost of managing an index fund relatively low. A list of specialized funds is at the back of this *Guide*.

Understanding Mutual Fund Statements 4

One of the advantages of mutual fund investing is the wealth of information that mutual funds provide to fund investors and prospective investors. Taken together, the various reports provide investors with vital information concerning financial matters and how the fund is managed, both key elements in the selection process. In fact, mutual fund prospectuses, annual reports, and performance statistics are key sources of information most investors will need in the selection and monitoring process.

To new mutual fund investors, the information may seem overwhelming. However, regulations governing the industry have standardized the reports: Once you know where to look for information, the location will hold true for almost all funds.

There are basically five types of statements produced by the mutual fund: the prospectus; the statement of additional information; annual, semiannual, and quarterly reports; marketing brochures; and account statements. Actually, the second report—the statement of additional information—is part of the prospectus. However, the Securities and Exchange Commission allows mutual funds to simplify and streamline the prospectus, if they choose, by dividing it into two parts: Part A, which all prospective investors must receive if requested, and Part B—the statement of additional information—which the fund must send investors if they specifically request it. In practice, when most people (including the funds) refer to the prospectus, they are referring to Part A. For simplicity, that is what we will do here as well.

THE PROSPECTUS

The prospectus is the single most important document produced by the mutual fund, and it is must-reading for investors before investing. Current shareholders must be sent new prospectuses when they are updated, at least once every 14 months.

The prospectus is generally organized into sections, and although it must cover specific topics, the overall structure may differ somewhat among funds. The cover usually gives a quick synopsis of the fund: investment category, sales or redemption charges, minimum investment, retirement plans available, address and telephone number. More detailed descriptions are in the body of the prospectus.

Fee Table: All mutual fund prospectuses must include a table near the front that delineates all fees and charges to the investor. The table contains three sections: The first section lists all transaction charges to the investor, including all front-end and back-end loads and redemption fees; the second section lists all annual fund operating expenses, including management fees and any 12b-1 charges, as a percentage of net assets; and the third section is an illustration of the total cost of these fees and charges to an investor over time. The illustration assumes an initial investment of $1,000 and a 5% growth rate for the fund, and states the total dollar cost to an investor if he were to redeem his shares at the end of one year, three years, five years, and 10 years.

Selected Per Share Data and Ratios: One of the most important sections of

---

The Prospectus Fee Table: An Example

Expenses

The following tables are intended to assist you in understanding the various costs and expenses that an investor in the Funds may bear directly or indirectly. For a more complete explanation of the fees and expenses borne by the Funds, see the discussions under the prospectus headings "How to Purchase Shares" and "Management of the Funds", as well as the Statement of Additional Information incorporated by reference into this prospectus.

Shareholder Transaction Expenses

	Oakmark Fund	Oakmark International
Sales commissions to purchase shares (sales load)	None	None
Commissions to reinvest dividends	None	None
Deferred sales load	None	None
Redemption fees*	None	None
Fees to exchange shares**	None	None

Annual Fund Operating Expenses
(as a percentage of net assets)

	Oakmark Fund	Oakmark International
Investment management fees	1.00%	1.00%
12b-1 Fees	None	None
Other Expenses	0.32%	0.26%
Total Fund operating expenses	1.32%	1.26%

---

* If you request payment of redemption proceeds by wire, you must pay the cost of the wire (currently $5).

** There is no fee for an exchange between the Funds. There is a charge of $5 for an exchange from either Fund to Goldman Sachs - Institutional Liquid Assets Government Portfolio.

The following example illustrates the expenses that you would pay on a $1,000 investment in each Fund over various time periods assuming (1) a 5% annual rate of return, (2) the operating expense percentages listed in the table above remain the same through each of the periods, (3) reinvestment of all dividends and capital gain distributions, and (4) redemption at the end of each time period.

	1 Year	3 Years	5 Years	10 Years
Oakmark Fund	$13	$42	$72	$159
Oakmark International	13	40	69	152

This example should not be considered a representation of past or future expenses or performance. Actual expenses may be greater or less than those shown.

Source: Oakmark prospectus, March 1, 1994.

Selected Per Share Data and Ratios: An Example

500 PORTFOLIO

Year Ended December 31,

	1993	1992	1991	1990	1989	1988	1987	1986	1985	1984
Net Asset Value, Beginning of Year	$40.97	$39.32	$31.24	$33.64	$27.18	$24.65	$24.27	$22.99	$19.52	$19.70
Investment Operations										
Net Investment Income	1.13	1.12	1.15	1.17	1.20	1.08	.88	.89	.91	.88
Net Realized and Unrealized Gain (Loss) on Investments	2.89	1.75	8.20	(2.30)	7.21	2.87	.36	3.30	5.08	.30
Total from Investment Operations	4.02	2.87	9.35	(1.13)	8.41	3.95	1.24	4.19	5.99	1.18
Distributions										
Dividends from Net Investment Income	(1.13)	(1.12)	(1.15)	(1.17)	(1.20)	(1.10)	(.69)	(.89)	(.91)	(.88)
Distributions from Realized Capital Gains	(.03)	(.10)	(.12)	(.10)	(.75)	(.32)	(.17)	(2.02)	(1.61)	(.48)
Total Distributions	(1.16)	(1.22)	(1.27)	(1.27)	(1.95)	(1.42)	(.86)	(2.91)	(2.52)	(1.36)
Net Asset Value, End of Year	$43.83	$40.97	$39.32	$31.24	$33.64	$27.18	$24.65	$24.27	$22.99	$19.52
Total Return*	9.89%	7.42%	30.22%	(3.32)%	31.36%	16.22%	4.71%	18.06%	31.23%	6.21%
Ratios/Supplemental Data										
Net Assets, End of Year (Millions)	$8,273	$6,547	$4,345	$2,173	$1,804	$1,055	$826	$485	$394	$290
Ratio of Expenses to Average Net Assets	.19%	.19%	.20%	.22%	.21%	.22%	.26%	.28%	.28%	.27%
Ratio of Net Investment Income to Average Net Assets	2.65%	2.81%	3.07%	3.60%	3.62%	4.08%	3.15%	3.40%	4.09%	4.53%
Portfolio Turnover Rate	6%†	4%†	5%†	23%†	8%	10%	15%	29%	36%	14%

*Total return figures do not reflect the annual account maintenance fee of $10 or applicable portfolio transaction fees.
†Portfolio turn over rates excluding in-kind redemptions were 2%, 1%, 1% and 6%, respectively.

Source: Vanguard Index Trust—500 prospectus, April 4, 1994.

---

the prospectus contains the selected per share data and ratios, which provides statistics on income and capital changes per share of the fund. The per share figures are given for the life of the fund or 10 years, whichever is less. Also included are important statistical summaries of investment activities throughout each period. Occasionally these financial statements are only referred to in the prospectus and are actually contained in the annual report, which in this instance would accompany the prospectus.

The per share section summarizes the financial activity over the fund's fiscal year, which may or may not correspond to the calendar year, to arrive at the end-of-year net asset value for the fund. The financial activity summarized includes increases in net asset value due to dividend and interest payments received and capital gains from investment activity. Decreases in net asset value are due to capital losses from investment activity, investment expenses, and payouts to fund shareholders in the form of distributions.

Potential investors may want to note the line items in this section. *Investment income* represents the dividends and interest earned by the fund during its fiscal year. *Expenses* reflect such fund costs as the management fee, legal fees, and transfer agent fees. These expenses are given in detail in the statement of operations section of the annual report.

Net investment income is investment income less expenses. This line is important for investors to note because it reflects the level and stability of net income over the time period. A high net investment income would most likely be found in funds that have income rather than growth as their investment category. Since net investment income must be distributed to shareholders to avoid direct taxation of the fund, a high net investment income has the potential of translating into a high tax liability for the investor.

Net realized and unrealized gain (loss) on investments is the change in the value of investments that have been sold (realized) during the year or that continue to be held (unrealized) by the fund.

Distributions to fund shareholders are also detailed. These distributions will include dividends from net investment income for the current fiscal period. Tax law requires that income earned must be distributed in the calendar year earned. Also included in distributions will be any realized net capital gains.

The last line in the per share section will be the *net asset value* at the end of the year, which reflects the value of one share of the fund. It is calculated by determining the total assets of the fund and dividing by the number of mutual fund shares outstanding. The figure will change for a variety of reasons, including changes in investment income, expenses, gains, losses, and distributions. Depending upon the source of change, a decline in net asset value may or may not be due to poor performance. For instance, a decline in net asset value may be due to a distribution of net realized gains on securities.

The financial ratios at the bottom of the per share financial data are important indicators of fund performance and strategy. The *expense ratio* relates expenses incurred by the fund to average net assets. These expenses include the investment advisory fee, legal and accounting fees, and 12b-1 charges to the fund; they do not include fund brokerage costs, loads, or redemption fees. A high expense ratio detracts from your investment return. In general, common stock funds have higher expense ratios than bond funds, and smaller funds have higher expense ratios than larger funds. International funds also tend to have higher expense ratios than domestic funds. Index funds usually have the lowest expense ratios. The average expense ratio for common stock funds is 1.20%, and for bond funds about 0.75%.

The *ratio of net investment income to average net assets* is very similar to a dividend yield. This, too, should reflect the investment category of the fund. Common stock funds with income as a significant part of their investment objective would be expected to have a ratio in the 2% to 4% range under current market conditions, and aggressive growth funds would have a ratio closer to 0%. Bond funds would normally have ratios more than twice those of common stock funds.

The *portfolio turnover rate* is the lower of purchases or sales divided by average net assets. It reflects how frequently securities are bought and sold by the fund. For purposes of determining the turnover rate for common stock funds, fixed-income securities with a maturity of less than a year are excluded, as are all government securities, short- and long-term. For bond funds, however, long-term U.S. government bonds are included.

Investors should take note of the portfolio turnover rate, because the higher the turnover, the greater the brokerage costs incurred by the fund. Brokerage costs are not reflected in the expense ratio but instead are directly reflected as a decrease in net asset value. In addition, mutual funds with high turnover rates generally have higher capital gains distributions—a potential tax liability. Aggressive growth mutual funds are most likely to have high turnover rates. Some bond funds also have very high portfolio turnover rates. A 100% portfolio turnover rate indicates that the value of the portfolio was completely turned over in a year; a 200% portfolio turnover indicates that the value of the portfolio was completely turned over twice in a year. The portfolio turnover rate for the average mutual fund is around 100% but varies with market conditions and investment category.

Investment Objective/Policy: The investment objective section of the prospectus elaborates on the brief sentence or two from the prospectus cover. In this section, the fund describes the types of investments it will make—whether it is bonds, stocks, convertible securities, options, etc.—along with some general guidelines as to the proportions these securities will represent in the fund's portfolio. The investment objective statement usually indicates whether it will be oriented toward capital gains or income. In this section, the management will also briefly discuss its approach to market timing, risk assumption, and the anticipated level of portfolio turnover. Some prospectuses may indicate any investment restrictions they have placed on the fund, such as purchasing securities on margin, selling short, concentrating in firms or industries, trading foreign securities, and lending securities; this section may also state the allowable proportions in certain investment categories. The restrictions section is usually given in more detail in the statement of additional information.

Fund Management: The fund management section names the investment adviser and gives the advisory fee schedule. Most advisers charge a management fee on a sliding scale that decreases as assets under management increase. Occasionally, some portion of the fund adviser's fees are subject to the fund's performance relative to the market.

Some prospectuses will describe the fund's officers and directors with a short biography of affiliations and relevant experience. For most funds, however, this information is provided in more detail in the statement of additional information. The board of directors is elected by fund shareholders; the fund adviser is selected by the board of directors. The adviser is usually a firm operated by or affiliated with officers of the fund. Information on fund officers and directors is not critical to fund selection. In the prospectus the portfolio manager for the fund is named. The portfolio manager is responsible for the day-to-day investment decisions of the fund and is employed by the fund adviser. Who the portfolio manager is and how long the manager has been in the position can be useful in judging historical performance.

Other Important Sections: There are several other sections in a mutual fund prospectus that investors should be aware of. They will appear under various headings, depending upon the prospectus, but they are not difficult to find.

Mutual funds that have 12b-1 plans must describe them in the prospectus. Under SEC rules, a description of these plans must be prominently and clearly placed in the prospectus, usually in a section titled "Distribution Plan." The distribution plan details the marketing aspects of the fund and how it relates to fund expenses. For instance, advertising, distribution of fund literature, and any arrangements with brokers would be included in the marketing plan; the 12b-1 plan pays for these distribution expenses. The distribution plan section specifies the maximum annual 12b-1 charge that can be made. Funds often charge less than the maximum. The actual charge to the fund of a 12b-1 plan is listed at the front of the prospectus in the fee table.

The capital stock section, or fund share characteristics section, provides shareholders with a summary of their voting rights, participation in dividends and distributions, and the number of authorized and issued shares of the fund. Often, a separate section will discuss the tax treatment that will apply to fund distributions, which may include dividends, interest, and capital gains.

The how-to-buy-shares section gives the minimum initial investment and any subsequent minimums; it will also list load charges or fees. In addition, information on mail, wire, and telephone purchases is provided, along with distribution reinvestment options, automatic exchange, investment and withdrawal plans, and retirement options.

The how-to-redeem-shares section discusses telephone, written, and wire redemption options, including automatic withdrawal plans, with a special section on signature guarantees and other documents that may be needed. Also detailed are any fees for reinvestment or redemption. Shareholder services are usually outlined here, with emphasis on exchanges among funds in a family of funds. This will include any fees for exchanging, any limits on the number of exchanges allowed, and any exchange restrictions.

STATEMENT OF ADDITIONAL INFORMATION

This document elaborates on the prospectus. The investment objectives section is more in-depth, with a list and description of investment restrictions. The management section gives brief biographies of directors and officers, and provides the number of fund shares owned beneficially by the officers and directors named. The investment adviser section, while reiterating the major points made in the prospectus, gives all the expense items and contract provisions of the agreement between the adviser and the fund. If the fund has a 12b-1 plan, further details will likely be in the statement of additional information.

Many times, the statement of additional information will include much more information on the tax consequences of mutual fund distributions and investment. Conditions under which withholding for federal income tax will take place are also provided. The fund's financial statements are incorporated by reference to the annual report to shareholders and generally do not appear in the statement of additional information. Finally, the independent auditors give their opinion on the accuracy of the fund's financial statements.

ANNUAL, SEMIANNUAL, AND QUARTERLY REPORTS

All funds must send their shareholders audited annual and semiannual reports. Mutual funds are allowed to combine their prospectus and annual report; some do this, but many do not.

The annual report describes the fund activities over the past year and provides a listing of all investments of the fund at market value as of the end of the fiscal year. Sometimes the cost basis of each investment is also given. Looking in-depth at the individual securities held by the fund is probably a waste of time. However, it is helpful to be aware of the overall investment categories. For instance, investors should look at the percentage invested in common stocks, bonds, convertible bonds, and any other holdings. In addition, a look at the types of common stocks held and the percentage of fund assets by industry classification gives the investor some indication of how the portfolio will fare in various market environments.

The annual report will also have a balance sheet, which lists all assets and liabilities of the fund by general category. This holds little interest for investors.

The statement of operations, similar to an income statement, is of interest only in that the fund expenses are broken down. For most funds, the management fee is by far the largest expense; the expense ratio in the prospectus conveys much more useful information. The statement of changes in net assets is very close to the financial information provided in the prospectus, but the information is not on a per share basis. Per share information will, however, frequently be detailed in the annual report in a separate section. Footnotes to the financial statements elaborate on the entries, but other than any pending litigation against the fund, they are most often routine.

The quarterly or semiannual reports are current accounts of the investment portfolio and provide more timely views of the fund's investments than does the annual report.

MARKETING BROCHURES AND ADVERTISEMENTS

These will generally provide a brief description of the fund. However, the most important bit of information will be the telephone number to call to receive the fund prospectus and annual report, if you have not received them already.

The SEC has tightened and standardized the rules regarding mutual fund advertising. All mutual funds that use performance figures in their ads must now include one-, three-, five-, and 10-year total return figures. Bond funds that quote yields must use a standardized method for computing yield, and they must include total return figures as well. Finally, any applicable sales commissions must be mentioned in the advertisement.

ACCOUNT STATEMENTS

Mutual funds send out periodic account statements detailing reinvestment of dividend and capital gains distributions, new purchases or redemptions, and any other account activity such as service fees. This statement provides a running account balance by date with share accumulations, an account value to date, and a total of distributions made to date. These statements are invaluable for tax purposes and should be saved. The fund will also send out, in January, a Form 1099-DIV for any distributions made in the previous year and a Form 1099-B if any mutual fund shares were sold.

Understanding Risk 5

Risk tolerance refers to the level of volatility of an investment that an investor finds acceptable. The anticipated holding period of an investment is important because it should affect the investor's risk tolerance. Time is a form of diversification; longer holding periods provide greater diversification across different market environments. Investors who anticipate longer holding periods can take on more risk.

The liquidity needs of an investor similarly help define the types of funds that the investor should consider. Liquidity implies preservation of capital, and if liquidity is important, then mutual funds with smaller variations in value should be considered. A liquid mutual fund is one in which withdrawals from the fund can be made at any time with a reasonable certainty that the per share value will not have dropped sharply. Highly volatile aggressive growth funds are the least liquid, and short-term fixed-income funds are the most liquid.

A LOOK AT RISK

Risk is the most difficult concept for many investors to grasp, and yet much of the mutual fund investment decision depends on an understanding of risk. There are many different ways to categorize investment risk and numerous approaches to the measurement of risk. If we can assume that the volatility of the return on your mutual fund investment is the concern you grapple with when you think of risk, the task of making decisions about risk becomes easier.

Questions about how much value a mutual fund is likely to lose in a down market or how certain it is that a fund will be worth a given amount at the end of the year are the same concerns as volatility of return. Changes in the domestic and international economies, interest rates, exchange rates, corporate profits, consumer confidence, and general expectations all combine to move markets up and down, creating volatility, or risk.

Total risk for a mutual fund measures variation in return from all sources. As an example, variation in return for common stocks is caused by factors unique to the firm, industry variables, and conditions affecting all stocks. Market risk refers to the variables such as interest rates, inflation, and the business cycle that affect all stocks to some degree. In well-diversified portfolios of common stock, the firm and industry risk of the various stocks in the portfolio offset each other; thus, these portfolios tend to have lower total risk, and this total risk is usually composed almost entirely of market risk. For less diversified portfolios, funds that hold very few stocks, or sector funds that concentrate investment in one industry, total risk is usually higher and is composed of firm and industry risk in addition to market risk.

Risk levels based upon total risk are given for all funds with 36 months of performance data. The five categories (high, above average, average, below average, and low) serve as a way to compare the risk inherent in common stock funds, international funds, sector funds, bond funds, or any type of mutual fund. Shorter-term bond funds would be expected to have relatively low total risk while some of the concentrated, less-diversified, aggressive common stock funds would likely be ranked in the high total risk category.

The total risk measure will enable you to construct a portfolio of funds that reflects your risk tolerance and the holding period you anticipate for your portfolio. Portfolios for individuals with low risk tolerance and short holding periods should be composed predominantly of funds that are less volatile, with lower total risk. Individuals with high risk tolerances and longer holding periods can form appropriate portfolios by combining mutual funds with higher total risk.

STANDARD DEVIATION

Total risk is measured by the standard deviation statistic, a numerical measure of how much the return on a mutual fund has varied, no matter what the cause, from the historical average return of the fund. Higher standard deviations indicate higher total risk. The category risk rank measures the total risk of a fund to the average total risk for all funds in the same investment category. The rankings for category risk are high, above average, average, below average, and low. Funds ranked above average and high for category risk should produce returns above the average for the investment category.

The risk index indicates the magnitude of the standard deviation for a fund relative to the average standard deviation for funds in the category. A risk index of 1.2, for example, means that the standard deviation for a fund is 20% higher than the average standard deviation for the category.

MARKET RISK

Market risk is a part of total risk but measures only the sensitivity of the fund to movements in the general market. This is valuable information to the individual investor, particularly when combined with use of the total risk and category risk rank measures, to judge how a mutual fund will perform in different market situations. The market risk measure used for common stock funds is beta; for bond funds, average maturity is used.

BETA

Beta is a measure of the relative volatility inherent in a mutual fund investment. This volatility is compared to some measure of the market such as Standard & Poor's index of 500 common stocks. The market's beta is always 1.0 by definition, and a money market fund's beta is always 0. If you hold a mutual fund with a beta of 1.0, it will move, on average, in tandem with the market. If the market is up 10%, the fund will be up, on average, 10%, and if the market drops 10%, the fund will drop, on average, 10%. A mutual fund with a beta of 1.5 is 50% more volatile than the market: If the market is up 10%, the fund will be up, on average, 50% more, or 15%; conversely, if the market is down 10%, the fund, on average, will be down 15%. A negative beta, a rare occurrence, implies that the mutual fund moves in the opposite direction of the market's movement.

The higher the fund's beta, the greater the volatility of the investment in the fund and the less appropriate the fund would be for shorter holding periods or to meet liquidity needs. Remember that beta is a relative measure: A low beta only implies that the fund's movement is not volatile relative to the market. Its return, however, may be quite variable, resulting in high total risk. For instance, industry-specific sector fund moves may not be related to market volatility, but changes in the industry may cause the returns of these funds to fluctuate widely. For a well-diversified stock fund, beta is a very useful measure of risk, but for concentrated funds, beta only captures a portion of the variability that the fund may experience. Betas for gold funds, for example, can be very misleading. Gold funds often have relatively low betas, but these funds are extremely volatile. Their volatility stems from factors that do not affect the common stock market as much. In addition, the betas of gold funds sometimes change significantly from year to year.

AVERAGE MATURITY

For all bond funds, the average maturity of the bonds in the portfolio is reported as a market risk measure, rather than beta. The volatility of a bond fund is determined by how the fund reacts primarily to changes in interest rates, although high-yield (junk) bond funds and international bond funds can be affected significantly by factors other than interest rates. When interest rates rise, bond funds fall in value, and conversely, when interest rates fall, bond mutual funds rise in value. The longer the average maturity of the bond fund, the greater will be the variation in the return on the bond fund when interest rates change. Bond mutual fund investors with less risk tolerance and shorter holding periods should seek shorter maturity funds, and longer-term bond fund investors who are more risk tolerant will find funds with longer maturities a better match.

In the case where a bond fund holds mortgage-backed securities, average maturity may not capture the potential for decline in effective maturity when interest rates fall and mortgages are refinanced. Bond funds that hold corporate bonds and municipal bonds also face changing effective maturities when interest rates decline and bond issuers call bonds before maturity.

Which Funds Were Included $\qquad$ 6

The funds that appear in *The Individual Investor's Guide to Low-Load Mutual Funds* were selected from a large universe of funds. Following are the various screens we used to arrive at the final selection.

SIZE

Funds must appear on the National Association of Securities Dealers mutual fund list found in most major newspapers. Funds are required to have a minimum of $25 million in assets to qualify for inclusion in the *Guide*.

LOADS

The decision as to what constitutes a significant load is difficult, but we took this approach in the *Guide*:

- All funds with front-end loads, back-end loads, or redemption fees of 3% or less were included if the fund did not also have a 12b-1 charge. Funds with redemption fees that disappear after six months that also have 12b-1 charges appear in this *Guide*.
- Funds with 12b-1 plans and no front- or back-end loads were included in the *Guide*; we note, however, if the fund has a 12b-1 plan and what the maximum annual charge is. Investors should carefully assess these plans individually.

A Key to Terms and Statistics

Much of the information used in the mutual fund data pages and performance tables is from mutual fund reports (the prospectus and annual and quarterly reports) and our own solicitation of information from the fund. Other statistics, such as fund performance and risk, were calculated by AAII. All numbers are truncated rather than rounded.

When *na* appears in the performance tables or on the mutual fund page, it indicates that the number was not available or does not apply in that particular instance. For example, the 10-year annual return figure would not be available for funds that have been operating less than 10 years. For three-year annual return, category risk, standard deviation, total risk, and beta, funds operating less than three years would not have the number available. We do not compile the bull and bear ratings for funds not operating during the entire bull or bear market period. Dashes (—) are used generally during years when the fund was not in operation or did not have a complete calendar year of operations.

The following provides an explanation of the terms we have used in the performance tables and mutual fund data pages. The explanations are listed in the order in which the data and information appear on the mutual fund pages.

Fund Name: The funds are presented alphabetically by fund name.

Ticker: The ticker symbol for each fund is given in parentheses for those investors who may want to access on-line data with their computer or touch-tone phone. The ticker is four letters and is usually followed by an "X," indicating that this is a mutual fund. For example, the Acorn fund ticker symbol is ACRNX.

Investment Category: The fund's investment category is indicated at the top of the page next to the fund's ticker symbol. After evaluating the information and statistics, we placed all mutual funds in exclusive categories by investment category and type of investment. For more complete definitions of the mutual fund investment categories used in the *Guide*, see Chapter 3.

Fund Address and Telephone Number(s): The address and telephone number where investors can write or call to have specific questions answered or to obtain a copy of the prospectus.

Fund Inception Date: The day the fund was made available to the public for purchase.

Performance

Return (%): Return percentages for the periods below.

3yr Annual: Assuming an investment on January 1, 1992, the annual total return if held through December 31, 1994.

5yr Annual: Assuming an investment on January 1, 1990, the annual total return if held through December 31, 1994.

10yr Annual: Assuming an investment on January 1, 1985, the annual total return if held through December 31, 1994.

Bull: This return reflects the fund's performance in the most recent bull market, starting October 1, 1990, and continuing through January 31, 1994.

Bear: This return reflects the fund's performance in the most recent bear market, from February 1, 1994, through June 30, 1994.

Differ from category (+/−): The difference between the return for the fund and average return for all funds in the same investment category for the *3yr Annual, 5yr Annual, 10yr Annual, Bull,* and *Bear* periods. When the difference from category is negative, the fund underperformed the average fund in its investment category for the period by the percent indicated. The rankings, with possibilities of high, above average, average, below average, low, are relative to all other funds within the same investment category. A rank of high, for example, would indicate that the return is in the highest 20% for that time period of all funds in the investment category.

Total Risk: The total risk of a fund relative to the total risk of all funds in the *Guide* as measured over the last three years. A high total risk indicates that the fund was in the group that had the greatest volatility of return for all funds, and a low total risk puts it into the group with the lowest volatility of return. Possibilities are high, above average, average, below average, low.

Standard Deviation: A measure of total risk, expressed as an annual return, that indicates the degree of variation in return experienced relative to the average return for a fund as measured over the last three years. The higher the standard deviation, the greater the total risk of the fund. Standard deviation of any fund can be compared to any other fund.

Category Risk: The total risk of the fund relative to the average total risk for funds within the same investment category as measured over the last three years. High category risk would, for example, indicate one of the highest total risks in the investment category. The possibilities are high, above average, average, below average, low.

Risk Index: A numerical measure of relative category risk, the risk index is a ratio of the total risk of the fund to the average total risk of funds in the category as measured over the last three years. Ratios above 1.0 indicate higher than average risk and ratios below 1.0 indicate lower than average risk for the category.

Beta: A risk measure that relates the fund's volatility of returns to the market. The higher the beta of a fund, the higher the market risk of the fund. The figure is based on monthly returns for 36 months. A beta of 1.0 indicates that the fund's returns will on average be as volatile as the market and move in the same direction; a beta higher than 1.0 indicates that if the market rises or falls, the fund will rise or fall respectively but to a greater degree; a beta of less than 1.0 indicates that if the market rises or falls, the fund will rise or fall to a lesser degree. The S&P 500 index always has a beta of 1.0 because it is the measure we selected to represent the overall stock market. Beta is a meaningful figure of risk only for well-diversified common stock portfolios. For sector funds and other concentrated portfolios, beta is less useful than total risk as a measure of risk. Beta was not calculated for bond funds since they do not react in the same way to the factors that affect the stock market. For bond funds, the average maturity of the bond portfolio is more indicative of market risk than beta and is used in place of beta.

Avg Mat: For bond funds, average maturity in years is an indication of market risk. When interest rates rise, bond prices fall and when interest rates fall, bond prices rise. The longer the average maturity of the bonds held in the portfolio, the greater will be the sensitivity of the fund to interest rate changes and thus the greater the risk. The refinancing of mortgages and the calling of outstanding bonds can affect average maturity when interest rates decline. An *na* indicates that the mutual fund did not provide us with an average maturity figure.

Return (%): This is a total return figure, expressed as a percentage and was computed using monthly net asset values per share and shareholder distributions during the year. All distributions were assumed to have been reinvested on the reinvestment date (ex-dividend date or payable date). Rate of return is calculated on the basis of the calendar year. Return figures do not take into account front-end and back-end loads, redemption fees, or one-time or annual account charges, if any. The 12b-1 charge is reflected in the return figure.

Differ from Category (+/–): The difference between the return for the fund and average return for all funds in the same investment category for the time period.

Per Share Data

Dividends, Net Income ($): Per share income distributions for the calendar year.

Distrib'ns, Cap Gains ($): Per share distributions for the year from realized capital gains after netting out realized losses. These distributions vary each year with both the investment success of the fund and the amount of securities sold.

Net Asset Value ($): Net asset value is the sum of all securities held, based on their market value, divided by the number of mutual fund shares outstanding.

Expense Ratio (%): The sum of administrative fees plus adviser management fees and 12b-1 fees divided by the average net asset value of the fund, stated as a percentage. Brokerage costs incurred by the fund are not included in the expense ratio but are instead reflected directly in net asset value. Front-end loads, back-end loads, redemption fees, and account activity charges are not included in this ratio.

Net Income to Assets (%): The income of the fund from dividends and interest after expenses, divided by the average net asset value of the fund. This ratio is similar to a dividend yield and would be higher for income-oriented funds and lower for growth-oriented funds. The figure only reflects income and does not reflect capital gains or losses. It is not total return.

Portfolio Turnover (%): A measure of the trading activity of the fund, which is computed by dividing the lesser of purchases or sales for the year by the monthly average value of the securities owned by the fund during the year. Securities with maturities of less than one year are excluded from the calculation. The result is expressed as a percentage, with 100% implying a complete portfolio turnover within one year.

Total Assets (Millions $): Aggregate fund value in millions of dollars.

Portfolio

Portfolio Manager: The name of the portfolio manager(s) and the year when the manager(s) began managing the fund are noted, providing additional information useful in evaluating past performance. Funds managed by a committee are so noted. For some funds, a recent change in the portfolio manager(s) may indicate that the long-term annual performance figures and other performance classifications are less meaningful.

Investm't Category: Notes the investment category of the fund. Following this is the growth (capital gains) versus income emphasis of the fund, what the geographical distribution is, and any special emphasis of the fund. The possible choices in the section are below.

Growth versus Income Emphasis: Capital Gains, Capital Gains & Income, and Income.

Geographical Distribution: Domestic, Foreign, Country/Region.

Special Emphasis: Asset Allocation, Fund of Funds, Index, Sector, Small Cap, Socially Conscious, and State Specific.

Portfolio: This information was obtained directly from the fund's annual and quarterly reports. The portfolio composition classifies investments by type and gives the percentage of the total portfolio invested in each. Some funds employ leverage (borrowing) to buy securities, and this may result in the portfolio total percent invested exceeding 100%.

Largest Holdings: This may indicate industries, types of securities, government versus corporate bonds, for example, or in the case of international funds, the percentages held by country. For municipal bond funds the percentage held in general obligation bonds is indicated.

Unrealized Net Capital Gains: Indicates percentage of current portfolio that represents net unrealized capital gains (or losses) and potential capital gains distributions.

Shareholder Information

Minimum Investment and Minimum IRA Investment: The minimum initial and subsequent investments, by mail, in the fund are detailed. Minimum investment by telephone or by wire may be different. Often, funds will have a lower minimum IRA investment; this is also indicated.

Maximum Fees:

Load: The maximum load is given, if any, and whether the load is front-end or back-end is indicated.

12b-1: If a fund has a 12b-1 plan, the maximum amount that can be charged is given; service charges, if any, are included in the 12b-1 charge figure.

Other Charges: Charges, such as an annual account fee or an account start-up fee, are noted. Redemption fees are given along with the time period, if appropriate.

Distributions: The months in which income and capital gains distributions are made are indicated, when available.

Exchange: Number Per Year indicates the maximum number of exchanges allowed; Fee indicates any fees charged for exchanges; and Telephone indicates whether telephone exchanges with other funds in the family are permitted. If exchange privileges are allowed, we have indicated whether exchanges are available with a money market fund (money market fund available).

Services: Investor services provided by the fund are detailed. These include the availability for IRA and other pension plans; whether the fund allows for an automatic exchange between funds in the family (auto exchange); whether the fund allows for automatic investments through an investor's checking account (auto invest); and whether the fund allows the automatic and systematic withdrawal of money from the fund (auto withdraw). Since all funds have automatic reinvestment of distributions options, this service was not specifically noted.

Fund Performance Rankings

8

When choosing among mutual funds, most investors start with performance statistics: How well have the various mutual funds performed in the past? If past performance alone could perfectly predict future performance, selection would be easy.

What past performance can tell you is how well the fund's management has handled different market environments, how consistent the fund has been, and how well the fund has done relative to its risk level, relative to other similar funds, and relative to the market.

We present performance statistics in several different forms. First, we provide an overall picture, with the average performance of each mutual fund category for the last five years, along with benchmarks for large and small company domestic stocks, international stocks, bonds, and Treasury bills. The top 20 and bottom 20 mutual fund performers for 1994 are given as a recent reference of performance. The list changes each year and reflects the cyclical nature of financial markets and the changing success of individual mutual fund managers. Lists of the top 50 mutual funds ranked by annual return over the last 10 years, five years and three years are given for a long-term perspective on investment performance.

Since the performance of a fund must be judged relative to similar funds, we have also grouped the funds by investment category and ranked them according to their total return performance for 1994. To make the comparison easier, we have also provided other data. The fund's annual returns for the last three years, five years, and 10 years give a longer-term perspective on the performance of the fund; category and total risk ranks are also given to judge performance.

Key to Fund Categories Used in Performance Tables

AG-Aggressive Growth	**B-CHY**-Corp. High-Yield Bond	**IntIS**-International Stock
Grth-Growth	**B-Gov**-Government Bond	**IntIB**-International Bond
GI-Growth & Income	**B-MB**-Mortgage-Backed Bond	**Gld**-Gold
Bal-Balanced	**B-Gen**-General Bond	
B-Cor-Corporate Bond	**B-TE**-Tax-Exempt Bond	

Total Risk and Return Performance for Different Mutual Fund Categories

Fund Investment Category	Annual Return (%)					5yr	Bull	Bear	Std Dev	Total Risk
	1994	1993	1992	1991	1990					
Aggressive Growth	-0.7	19.5	11.0	52.1	-6.2	12.5	133.2	-10.8	14.1	high
Growth	-0.6	13.4	11.6	35.7	-5.7	9.6	92.1	-6.6	9.3	abv av
Growth & Income	-1.4	13.2	10.2	27.6	-6.0	7.9	75.8	-6.3	7.9	av
Balanced	-1.9	13.4	8.3	23.4	-0.5	8.0	65.0	-5.7	6.0	blw av
Corporate Bond	-2.4	11.4	8.9	17.1	4.8	7.8	49.8	-4.3	3.0	low
Corporate High-Yield Bond	-2.7	18.4	15.6	27.4	-5.1	9.3	79.3	-5.3	4.8	low
Government Bond	-4.8	10.9	6.4	15.3	6.2	6.7	51.2	-6.4	4.5	low
Mortgage-Backed Bond	-2.8	6.8	6.1	14.4	9.7	6.9	38.0	-4.4	3.2	low
General Bond	-2.0	9.2	6.6	14.6	7.2	6.9	41.0	-3.8	3.8	low
Tax-Exempt Bond	-5.2	11.7	8.3	11.3	6.3	6.1	41.8	-5.2	6.0	blw av
International Stock	-3.0	38.6	-2.9	13.1	-10.4	4.9	63.9	-7.0	12.7	high
International Bond	-6.3	13.4	4.7	16.0	11.5	8.6	60.3	-7.8	5.8	blw av
Gold	-11.5	86.9	-15.7	-4.8	-22.5	0.0	32.9	-10.0	25.9	high
Domestic Equity	-0.9	15.1	11.0	38.1	-6.0	9.9	99.3	-7.7	9.6	abv av
Small Capitalization Stock	-0.3	16.9	13.1	51.3	-8.8	12.7	124.3	-9.6	10.9	abv av
Domestic Taxable Bond	-3.0	10.0	7.2	15.8	6.2	7.1	47.2	-4.7	3.7	low
Index Comparisons										
S&P 500	1.3	10.0	7.6	30.4	-3.1	8.6	74.2	-6.5	7.9	av
Russell 2000*	-1.8	18.9	18.4	46.0	-19.5	10.1	122.7	-9.2	11.7	abv av
MS EAFE**	8.0	33.1	-12.1	12.5	-23.3	1.7	57.8	0.4	15.4	high
Salomon Corporate Bond†	-3.5	12.1	8.8	18.4	7.2	8.3	53.0	-6.2	4.6	low
Salomon High-Yield Corp. Bond†	-1.2	17.3	17.8	40.2	-8.1	11.9	96.4	-4.5	4.4	low
Salomon Treasury/Agency Bond†	-3.3	10.7	7.2	15.3	8.7	7.5	46.3	-5.3	4.3	low
Salomon Mortgage-Backed Bond†	-1.4	7.0	7.3	15.6	10.9	7.7	40.9	-3.5	3.1	low
Salomon Investm't-Grade Bond†	-2.8	9.8	7.5	15.9	9.0	7.7	46.0	-5.0	3.9	low
Treasury Bills	3.9	2.9	3.3	5.6	7.8	4.7	14.8	1.4	0.2	low

Return figures are averages for funds in each category

*Index of small company stocks; Source: Frank Russell Company

**Europe, Australia, Far East Index.; Source: Morgan Stanley

†Salomon Brothers Bond Indexes.; Source: Salomon Brothers

Total Risk & Return for Domestic Taxable Bond Mutual Funds by Maturity

Maturity Category	Annual Return (%)					5yr	Bull	Bear	Std Dev	Total Risk
	1994	1993	1992	1991	1990					
Short-Term Bond Funds	0.2	5.8	5.4	11.5	7.8	6.1	29.8	-1.4	2.2	low
Intermediate-Term Bond Funds	-2.7	10.8	8.2	17.7	5.0	7.5	51.2	-4.6	4.0	low
Long-Term Bond Funds	-5.8	12.5	7.4	16.4	6.4	7.2	54.4	-7.8	4.9	blw av

The Top 20 Performers: 1994

Type	Fund Name	Annual Return (%)				Category Risk	Total Risk
		1994	3yr	5yr	10yr		
AG	PBHG Emerging Growth	23.7	na	na	na	na	na
AG	Robertson Stephens Value + Growth	23.1	na	na	na	na	na
AG	Fidelity Sel Health Care	21.4	0.8	18.5	21.5	abv av	high
Grth	Montgomery Growth	20.9	na	na	na	na	na
AG	Fidelity Sel Computers	20.4	23.7	23.9	na	high	high
AG	Fidelity Sel Medical Delivery	19.8	3.1	17.8	na	high	high
Grth	Strong Growth	17.2	na	na	na	na	na
AG	Fidelity Sel Electronics	17.1	25.4	23.0	na	abv av	high
IntlS	Fidelity Japan	16.4	na	na	na	na	na
Grth	Janus Mercury	15.8	na	na	na	na	na
AG	T Rowe Price Science & Tech	15.7	19.5	21.9	na	high	high
AG	Fidelity Sel Dev'ping Communic'ns	15.1	21.1	na	na	abv av	high
IntlS	T Rowe Price Japan	15.0	6.3	na	na	high	high
Grth	Fidelity Sel Chemical	14.7	12.1	13.3	na	abv av	abv av
AG	Fidelity Sel Paper & Forest Prod	14.1	14.8	11.6	na	abv av	high
AG	Berger Small Company Growth	13.7	na	na	na	na	na
AG	Twentieth Century Giftrust	13.4	20.7	21.9	25.5	high	high
IntlS	Vanguard Int'l Equity Index—Pacific	12.9	7.7	na	na	high	high
AG	Crabbe Huson Special	11.7	26.0	19.4	na	high	high
Grth	Vanguard Primecap	11.4	12.7	13.1	15.5	abv av	abv av

The Bottom 20 Performers: 1994

Type	Fund Name	Annual Return (%)				Category Risk	Total Risk
		1994	3yr	5yr	10yr		
AG	American Heritage	-35.3	2.9	8.2	na	high	high
Gld	INVESCO Strat Port—Gold	-27.8	4.5	-3.9	1.9	abv av	high
B-Gov	Fundamental US Gov't Strat Income	-25.6	na	na	na	na	na
B-MB	Managers Interm Mortgage	-25.0	-2.6	na	na	high	abv av
IntlS	Fidelity Latin America	-23.1	na	na	na	na	na
AG	CGM Capital Development	-22.9	5.2	18.6	19.6	high	high
AG	Fidelity Sel Air Transportation	-21.7	2.9	4.1	na	abv av	high
IntlS	Fidelity Southeast Asia	-21.7	na	na	na	na	na
IntlS	Fifty-Nine Wall St Pacific Basin	-21.4	13.3	na	na	high	high
GI	Gintel ERISA	-21.2	-1.7	0.4	8.0	high	high
B-TE	NY Muni	-20.5	0.0	2.7	6.2	high	abv av
B-TE	Cal Muni	-19.9	0.0	2.6	6.4	high	av
IntlB	BB&K International Fixed-Income	-19.2	na	na	na	na	na
IntlS	T Rowe Price New Asia	-19.1	17.1	na	na	high	high
AG	Dreyfus Special Growth—Investor	-18.2	7.3	8.7	11.8	abv av	high
AG	Fidelity Sel Biotechnology	-18.1	-9.5	16.2	na	high	high
IntlS	Fidelity Emerging Markets	-17.9	16.4	na	na	high	high
B-Gov	Benham Target Mat Trust—2020	-17.6	6.5	6.2	na	high	high
AG	Fidelity Sel Broker & Invest Mgmt	-17.2	9.1	14.6	na	abv av	high
IntlS	Scudder Pacific Opportunities	-17.1	na	na	na	na	na

The Top 50 Performers: 10 Years, 1985-1994

Type	Fund Name	Annual Return (%)				Category Risk	Total Risk
		10yr	5yr	3yr	1994		
AG	Twentieth Century Giftrust	25.5	21.9	20.7	13.4	high	high
AG	Fidelity Sel Health Care	21.5	18.5	0.8	21.4	abv av	high
AG	INVESCO Strat Port—Health Sci	20.5	13.9	-7.2	0.9	high	high
Grth	Vanguard Spec Port—Health Care	19.9	15.5	6.4	9.5	high	high
AG	INVESCO Strat Port—Leisure	19.7	16.6	16.7	-4.9	blw av	high
AG	CGM Capital Development	19.6	18.6	5.2	-22.9	high	high
AG	Berger One Hundred	19.1	16.9	7.0	-6.6	av	high
IntlS	Fidelity Overseas	19.1	4.9	7.8	1.2	abv av	high
AG	INVESCO Strat Port—Tech	18.8	22.5	12.8	5.2	high	high
AG	Twentieth Century Ultra	18.7	19.3	5.9	-3.6	high	high
Grth	Fidelity Contrafund	18.5	17.5	11.6	-1.1	blw av	abv av
AG	Fidelity OTC Port	18.0	11.4	6.6	-2.6	low	abv av
Grth	Fidelity Magellan	17.9	12.0	9.4	-1.8	av	abv av
IntlS	T Rowe Price Int'l Stock	17.9	7.2	10.3	-0.7	av	high
AG	Fidelity Sel Leisure	17.3	9.3	14.7	-6.8	blw av	abv av
IntlS	Vanguard Int'l Growth	17.1	4.8	11.1	0.7	av	high
AG	Fidelity Growth Company	17.0	13.5	7.0	-2.2	low	abv av
IntlS	Vanguard Trustees' Equity—Int'l	16.8	3.8	7.8	5.2	blw av	abv av
Grth	Acorn	16.5	13.0	15.0	-7.4	high	abv av
GI	Safeco Equity	16.1	12.9	16.2	9.9	high	high
IntlS	Scudder International	16.1	5.5	8.8	-2.9	blw av	abv av
Grth	IAI Regional	15.8	8.8	4.3	0.6	blw av	av
Grth	Fidelity Retirement Growth	15.6	12.0	10.5	0.0	av	abv av
IntlS	Japan	15.6	-0.4	4.2	10.0	high	high
AG	SteinRoe Special	15.6	10.8	9.8	-3.3	low	abv av
AG	SIT Growth	15.5	11.3	1.8	-0.4	blw av	high
Grth	Vanguard Primecap	15.5	13.1	12.7	11.4	abv av	abv av
GI	Dodge & Cox Stock	15.4	9.7	11.3	5.1	abv av	av
Grth	Founders Growth	15.4	10.7	8.1	-3.3	high	high
GI	Mutual Beacon	15.4	11.5	16.8	5.6	low	blw av
AG	Twentieth Century Growth	15.4	9.7	-0.7	-1.5	blw av	abv av
AG	Heartland Value	15.2	16.3	19.8	1.7	av	high
Grth	Janus	15.1	10.6	5.4	-1.1	low	av
GI	Mutual Qualified	15.1	11.6	16.7	5.7	low	av
Grth	Meridian	14.9	16.5	9.5	0.5	high	abv av
AG	Twentieth Century Vista	14.9	9.5	2.6	4.6	abv av	high
Grth	Babson Enterprise	14.8	12.2	14.0	2.4	av	abv av
Bal	CGM Mutual	14.8	10.6	5.2	-9.7	high	abv av
AG	Founders Special	14.8	11.8	6.1	-4.9	av	high
Bal	INVESCO Industrial Income	14.8	10.8	4.2	-3.8	high	av
AG	INVESCO Dynamics	14.7	15.6	9.7	-1.9	av	high
GI	Mutual Shares	14.7	10.8	15.3	4.5	low	av
IntlS	INVESCO Int'l—Pacific Basin	14.6	1.9	8.8	4.6	high	high
Grth	William Blair Growth Shares	14.4	13.3	9.8	6.4	abv av	abv av
AG	Evergreen Limited Market—Class Y	14.3	7.8	2.5	-10.5	blw av	high
Grth	Columbia Growth	14.2	10.2	7.8	-0.6	abv av	abv av
GI	Neuberger & Berman Guardian	14.2	11.8	11.0	0.6	abv av	av
Grth	Scudder Capital Growth	14.2	6.5	5.0	-9.8	high	high
GI	Scudder Growth & Income	14.2	10.2	9.1	2.5	av	av
Grth	Value Line	14.1	9.5	2.2	-4.4	abv av	abv av

The Top 50 Performers: Five Years, 1990-1994

Type	Fund Name	Annual Return (%) 5yr	10yr	3yr	1994	Category Risk	Total Risk
AG	Fidelity Sel Computers	23.9	na	23.7	20.4	high	high
AG	Fidelity Sel Home Finance	23.5	na	27.3	2.6	abv av	high
AG	Fidelity Sel Electronics	23.0	na	25.4	17.1	abv av	high
AG	INVESCO Strat Port—Tech	22.5	18.8	12.8	5.2	high	high
AG	Fidelity Sel Technology	22.2	10.5	15.8	11.1	abv av	high
AG	PBHG Growth	21.9	na	25.4	4.7	high	high
AG	T Rowe Price Science & Tech	21.9	na	19.5	15.7	high	high
AG	Twentieth Century Giftrust	21.9	25.5	20.7	13.4	high	high
AG	Fidelity Sel Software & Comp	21.5	na	21.7	0.3	high	high
AG	Crabbe Huson Special	19.4	na	26.0	11.7	high	high
AG	Twentieth Century Ultra	19.3	18.7	5.9	-3.6	high	high
AG	Kaufmann	19.2	na	12.7	8.9	abv av	high
AG	Strong Common Stock	18.9	na	14.5	-0.4	low	abv av
Grth	Fidelity Low-Priced Stock	18.8	na	17.5	4.8	av	abv av
AG	CGM Capital Development	18.6	19.6	5.2	-22.9	high	high
AG	Fidelity Sel Health Care	18.5	21.5	0.8	21.4	abv av	high
Grth	Fidelity Blue Chip Growth	18.3	na	13.2	9.8	abv av	abv av
Grth	Regis ICM Small Company Port	18.1	na	18.6	3.4	abv av	abv av
Grth	INVESCO Strat Port—Financial	17.9	na	12.2	-5.8	high	abv av
AG	Fidelity Sel Medical Delivery	17.8	na	3.1	19.8	high	high
AG	Oberweis Emerging Growth	17.7	na	6.3	-3.5	high	high
Grth	Fidelity Contrafund	17.5	18.5	11.6	-1.1	blw av	abv av
AG	Wasatch Aggressive Equity	17.0	na	10.6	5.4	av	high
AG	Berger One Hundred	16.9	19.1	7.0	-6.6	av	high
Grth	Fidelity Sel Regional Banks	16.8	na	18.2	0.2	high	high
AG	Founders Discovery	16.7	na	5.5	-7.7	av	high
AG	INVESCO Strat Port—Leisure	16.6	19.7	16.7	-4.9	blw av	high
Grth	Meridian	16.5	14.9	9.5	0.5	high	abv av
AG	Fidelity Sel Automotive	16.4	na	18.7	-12.7	av	high
Grth	Brandywine	16.3	na	12.3	0.0	high	high
AG	Heartland Value	16.3	15.2	19.8	1.7	av	high
AG	Fidelity Sel Biotechnology	16.2	na	-9.5	-18.1	high	high
AG	Fidelity Sel Retailing	15.9	na	9.4	-5.0	blw av	high
AG	INVESCO Dynamics	15.6	14.7	9.7	-1.9	av	high
Grth	Vanguard Spec Port—Health Care	15.5	19.9	6.4	9.5	high	high
AG	Fidelity Sel Transportation	14.9	na	18.4	3.8	low	abv av
Bal	Evergreen Foundation—Class Y	14.8	na	11.1	-1.1	high	av
Grth	Crabbe Huson Equity	14.6	na	14.2	1.5	blw av	av
AG	Fidelity Sel Broker & Invest Mgmt	14.6	na	9.1	-17.2	abv av	high
Grth	Fidelity Sel Financial Services	14.6	13.6	17.3	-3.6	high	high
AG	Robertson Stephens Emerging Growth	14.4	na	4.0	7.9	high	high
AG	MIM Stock Appreciation	14.2	na	1.5	-10.4	av	high
Grth	Harbor Capital Appreciation	14.1	na	8.4	3.3	high	high
AG	INVESCO Strat Port—Health Sci	13.9	20.5	-7.2	0.9	high	high
Grth	Strong Discovery	13.8	na	5.5	-5.6	high	high
B-CHY	Fidelity Capital & Income	13.7	12.0	15.1	-4.6	high	blw av
GI	Fidelity Convertible Securities	13.7	na	12.1	-1.7	blw av	av
AG	Fidelity Growth Company	13.5	17.0	7.0	-2.2	low	abv av
Grth	Fidelity Sel Chemical	13.3	na	12.1	14.7	abv av	abv av
Grth	William Blair Growth Shares	13.3	14.4	9.8	6.4	abv av	abv av

The Top 50 Performers: Three Years, 1992-1994

Type	Fund Name	Annual Return (%)				Category Risk	Total Risk
		3yr	5yr	10yr	1994		
AG	Fidelity Sel Home Finance	27.3	23.5	na	2.6	abv av	high
Grth	Oakmark	26.1	na	na	3.3	abv av	abv av
AG	Crabbe Huson Special	26.0	19.4	na	11.7	high	high
AG	Fidelity Sel Electronics	25.4	23.0	na	17.1	abv av	high
AG	PBHG Growth	25.4	21.9	na	4.7	high	high
AG	Fidelity Sel Computers	23.7	23.9	na	20.4	high	high
AG	Fidelity Sel Software & Comp	21.7	21.5	na	0.3	high	high
AG	Fidelity Sel Dev'ping Communic'ns	21.1	na	na	15.1	abv av	high
AG	Twentieth Century Giftrust	20.7	21.9	25.5	13.4	high	high
AG	Fidelity Sel Multimedia	20.3	12.1	na	4.0	blw av	high
AG	Heartland Value	19.8	16.3	15.2	1.7	av	high
AG	T Rowe Price Science & Tech	19.5	21.9	na	15.7	high	high
AG	Fidelity Sel Automotive	18.7	16.4	na	-12.7	av	high
Grth	Regis ICM Small Company Port	18.6	18.1	na	3.4	abv av	abv av
AG	Fidelity Sel Transportation	18.4	14.9	na	3.8	low	abv av
AG	Lazard Small Cap Portfolio	18.3	na	na	2.0	blw av	abv av
Grth	Fidelity Sel Regional Banks	18.2	16.8	na	0.2	high	high
AG	Fidelity Sel Industrial Equipment	18.0	12.0	na	3.1	av	high
Gld	Fidelity Sel Precious Metals	17.7	5.5	7.9	-1.1	blw av	high
Grth	Fidelity Low-Priced Stock	17.5	18.8	na	4.8	av	abv av
Grth	Fidelity Sel Financial Services	17.3	14.6	13.6	-3.6	high	high
IntlS	T Rowe Price New Asia	17.1	na	na	-19.1	high	high
Grth	Fidelity Value	17.0	12.0	13.6	7.6	blw av	av
Grth	Longleaf Partners	17.0	13.3	na	8.9	low	av
GI	Mutual Beacon	16.8	11.5	15.4	5.6	low	blw av
Grth	Fidelity Capital Appreciation Port	16.7	8.0	na	2.5	av	abv av
AG	INVESCO Strat Port—Leisure	16.7	16.6	19.7	-4.9	blw av	high
GI	Mutual Qualified	16.7	11.6	15.1	5.7	low	av
GI	Warburg Pincus Growth and Income	16.5	13.2	na	7.5	high	abv av
IntlS	Fidelity Emerging Markets	16.4	na	na	-17.9	high	high
GI	Safeco Equity	16.2	12.9	16.1	9.9	high	high
Grth	Fidelity Sel Telecomm	15.9	11.2	na	4.3	high	abv av
AG	Fidelity Sel Technology	15.8	22.2	10.5	11.1	abv av	high
Grth	Berwyn	15.5	10.9	13.2	3.8	high	abv av
GI	Cohen & Steers Realty Shares	15.5	na	na	8.3	high	high
GI	Mutual Shares	15.3	10.8	14.7	4.5	low	av
IntlS	Harbor Int'l	15.2	10.8	na	5.4	abv av	high
B-CHY	Fidelity Capital & Income	15.1	13.7	12.0	-4.6	high	blw av
B-CHY	Fidelity Spartan High Income	15.1	na	na	3.1	abv av	blw av
Grth	Acorn	15.0	13.0	16.5	-7.4	high	abv av
AG	Fidelity Sel Paper & Forest Prod	14.8	11.6	na	14.1	abv av	high
AG	Baron Asset	14.7	10.5	na	7.4	low	abv av
AG	Fidelity Sel Leisure	14.7	9.3	17.3	-6.8	blw av	abv av
AG	Strong Common Stock	14.5	18.9	na	-0.4	low	abv av
Gld	US World Gold	14.5	0.9	na	-16.9	high	high
Grth	First Eagle Fund of America	14.4	8.3	na	-2.5	high	high
AG	INVESCO Emerging Growth	14.3	na	na	-3.7	av	high
Grth	Crabbe Huson Equity	14.2	14.6	na	1.5	blw av	av
IntlS	Fidelity Worldwide	14.2	na	na	2.9	low	abv av
Grth	Babson Enterprise	14.0	12.2	14.8	2.4	av	abv av

Aggressive Growth Funds
Ranked by 1994 Total Return

Fund Name	Annual Return (%)				Category Risk	Total Risk
	1994	3yr	5yr	10yr		
PBHG Emerging Growth	23.7	na	na	na	na	na
Robertson Stephens Value + Growth	23.1	na	na	na	na	na
Fidelity Sel Health Care	21.4	0.8	18.5	21.5	abv av	high
Fidelity Sel Computers	20.4	23.7	23.9	na	high	high
Fidelity Sel Medical Delivery	19.8	3.1	17.8	na	high	high
Fidelity Sel Electronics	17.1	25.4	23.0	na	abv av	high
T Rowe Price Science & Tech	15.7	19.5	21.9	na	high	high
Fidelity Sel Dev'ping Communic'ns	15.1	21.1	na	na	abv av	high
Fidelity Sel Paper & Forest Prod	14.1	14.8	11.6	na	abv av	high
Berger Small Company Growth	13.7	na	na	na	na	na
Twentieth Century Giftrust	13.4	20.7	21.9	25.5	high	high
Crabbe Huson Special	11.7	26.0	19.4	na	high	high
Fidelity Sel Technology	11.1	15.8	22.2	10.5	abv av	high
Janus Enterprise	8.9	na	na	na	na	na
Kaufmann	8.9	12.7	19.2	na	abv av	high
Fidelity Sel Industrial Materials	8.1	13.8	10.6	na	blw av	abv av
Robertson Stephens Emerging Growth	7.9	4.0	14.4	na	high	high
Baron Asset	7.4	14.7	10.5	na	low	abv av
Fairmont	7.2	12.2	9.1	9.0	av	high
Merger	7.1	9.9	9.4	na	low	low
Chesapeake Growth	6.9	na	na	na	na	na
Fidelity Sel Food & Agriculture	6.0	6.9	12.4	na	low	av
Janus Venture	5.4	7.3	12.7	na	low	abv av
Wasatch Aggressive Equity	5.4	10.6	17.0	na	av	high
INVESCO Strat Port—Tech	5.2	12.8	22.5	18.8	high	high
PBHG Growth	4.7	25.4	21.9	na	high	high
Twentieth Century Vista	4.6	2.6	9.5	14.9	abv av	high
Fidelity Sel Multimedia	4.0	20.3	12.1	na	blw av	high
Fidelity Fifty	3.9	na	na	na	na	na
Fidelity Sel Transportation	3.8	18.4	14.9	na	low	abv av
Fidelity Sel Industrial Equipment	3.1	18.0	12.0	na	av	high
Fidelity Sel Home Finance	2.6	27.3	23.5	na	abv av	high
Columbia Special	2.2	12.2	13.2	na	blw av	abv av
Lazard Small Cap Portfolio	2.0	18.3	na	na	blw av	abv av
Fidelity Sel Defense & Aerospace	1.7	9.4	9.6	6.2	low	abv av
Heartland Value	1.7	19.8	16.3	15.2	av	high
Value Line Special Situations	1.0	3.2	7.7	7.7	abv av	high
INVESCO Strat Port—Health Sci	0.9	-7.2	13.9	20.5	high	high
Fidelity New Millenium	0.8	na	na	na	na	na
Evergreen—Class Y	0.7	5.1	7.5	11.6	low	abv av
Fidelity Sel Energy Service	0.5	7.9	-0.4	na	high	high
Vanguard Explorer	0.5	9.4	12.7	10.1	blw av	abv av
Fidelity Sel Software & Comp	0.3	21.7	21.5	na	high	high
T Rowe Price New Horizons	0.3	10.6	13.2	11.9	av	high
IAI Emerging Growth	0.1	12.0	na	na	high	high
Galaxy Small Company Equity	0.0	7.4	na	na	abv av	high
SteinRoe Capital Opportunities	0.0	9.3	8.5	12.1	blw av	high
T Rowe Price OTC	0.0	10.5	8.2	10.8	low	abv av
Dreyfus New Leaders	-0.1	8.5	10.3	na	low	abv av
Fidelity Emerging Growth	-0.1	9.0	na	na	av	high

Aggressive Growth Funds
Ranked by 1994 Total Return

Fund Name	Annual Return (%)				Category Risk	Total Risk
	1994	3yr	5yr	10yr		
SIT Growth	-0.4	1.8	11.3	15.5	blw av	high
Strong Common Stock	-0.4	14.5	18.9	na	low	abv av
Vanguard Index Trust—Small Cap	-0.5	11.7	10.6	10.1	blw av	abv av
USAA Aggressive Growth	-0.7	-0.6	8.2	9.7	abv av	high
Caldwell & Orkin Aggressive Growth	-0.9	9.4	na	na	low	abv av
Warburg Pincus Emerging Grth	-1.4	9.2	12.9	na	av	high
Managers Capital Appreciation	-1.5	8.2	na	na	low	abv av
Twentieth Century Growth	-1.5	-0.7	9.7	15.4	blw av	abv av
Safeco Growth	-1.6	5.2	10.0	11.9	high	high
Neuberger & Berman Genesis	-1.8	8.9	8.9	na	low	abv av
INVESCO Dynamics	-1.9	9.7	15.6	14.7	av	high
Managers Special Equity	-1.9	9.9	na	na	low	abv av
Fidelity Growth Company	-2.2	7.0	13.5	17.0	low	abv av
Fidelity OTC Port	-2.6	6.6	11.4	18.0	low	abv av
Founders Frontier	-2.8	7.2	11.2	na	av	high
Schwab Small-Cap Index	-3.0	na	na	na	na	na
SteinRoe Special	-3.3	9.8	10.8	15.6	low	abv av
Oberweis Emerging Growth	-3.5	6.3	17.7	na	high	high
Loomis Sayles Growth	-3.6	2.9	na	na	blw av	abv av
Standish Small Capitalization Equity	-3.6	10.6	na	na	av	high
Twentieth Century Ultra	-3.6	5.9	19.3	18.7	high	high
INVESCO Emerging Growth	-3.7	14.3	na	na	av	high
Value Line Leveraged Growth	-3.7	2.9	9.4	13.5	blw av	abv av
GIT Equity—Special Growth	-3.9	5.5	4.4	12.4	low	abv av
Founders Special	-4.9	6.1	11.8	14.8	av	high
INVESCO Strat Port—Leisure	-4.9	16.7	16.6	19.7	blw av	high
Fidelity Sel Retailing	-5.0	9.4	15.9	na	blw av	high
Perritt Capital Growth	-5.0	2.0	4.2	na	low	abv av
Scudder Development	-5.3	0.3	12.0	11.8	abv av	high
Marshall Mid-Cap Stock	-5.6	na	na	na	na	na
Berger One Hundred	-6.6	7.0	16.9	19.1	av	high
Fidelity Sel Leisure	-6.8	14.7	9.3	17.3	blw av	abv av
Cappiello-Rushmore Emerging Growth	-6.9	na	na	na	na	na
Fidelity Sel Consumer Products	-7.0	7.9	na	na	blw av	abv av
INVESCO Strat Port—Energy	-7.2	-2.0	-5.4	4.7	abv av	high
Founders Discovery	-7.7	5.5	16.7	na	av	high
Loomis Sayles Small Cap	-8.3	8.9	na	na	na	high
Prudent Speculator	-8.9	-1.7	-0.6	na	high	high
Fidelity Sel Environ'l Serv	-9.5	-3.9	-1.4	na	av	high
WPG Tudor	-9.8	2.4	8.2	12.3	abv av	high
Montgomery Small Cap	-9.9	7.0	na	na	abv av	high
Fifty-Nine Wall St Small Company	-10.4	3.5	na	na	blw av	high
MIM Stock Appreciation	-10.4	1.5	14.2	na	av	high
Evergreen Limited Market—Class Y	-10.5	2.5	7.8	14.3	blw av	high
INVESCO Strat Port—Environm'l	-11.3	-11.7	na	na	abv av	high
Fidelity Sel Automotive	-12.7	18.7	16.4	na	av	high
Legg Mason Special Investment	-13.0	7.5	11.7	na	av	high
Salomon Brothers Capital	-14.1	1.7	5.0	9.2	blw av	high
Fidelity Sel Constr'n & Hous'g	-15.9	10.0	11.2	na	blw av	high
Bull & Bear Special Equities	-16.5	7.6	2.1	na	high	high

Aggressive Growth Funds
Ranked by 1994 Total Return

Fund Name	Annual Return (%)				Category Risk	Total Risk
	1994	3yr	5yr	10yr		
Fidelity Sel Broker & Invest Mgmt	-17.2	9.1	14.6	na	abv av	high
Fidelity Sel Biotechnology	-18.1	-9.5	16.2	na	high	high
Dreyfus Special Growth—Investor	-18.2	7.3	8.7	11.8	abv av	high
Fidelity Sel Air Transportation	-21.7	2.9	4.1	na	abv av	high
CGM Capital Development	-22.9	5.2	18.6	19.6	high	high
American Heritage	-35.3	2.9	8.2	na	high	high
Aggressive Growth Fund Average	**-0.7**	**8.9**	**12.5**	**14.0**	**av**	**high**

Growth Funds
Ranked by 1994 Total Return

Fund Name	Annual Return (%)				Category Risk	Total Risk
	1994	3yr	5yr	10yr		
Montgomery Growth	20.9	na	na	na	na	na
Strong Growth	17.2	na	na	na	na	na
Janus Mercury	15.8	na	na	na	na	na
Fidelity Sel Chemical	14.7	12.1	13.3	na	abv av	abv av
Vanguard Primecap	11.4	12.7	13.1	15.5	abv av	abv av
Fidelity Blue Chip Growth	9.8	13.2	18.3	na	abv av	abv av
Vanguard Spec Port—Health Care	9.5	6.4	15.5	19.9	high	high
Longleaf Partners	8.9	17.0	13.3	na	low	av
Yacktman	8.7	na	na	na	na	na
Fidelity Value	7.6	17.0	12.0	13.6	blw av	av
FAM Value	6.8	10.2	13.3	na	av	abv av
William Blair Growth Shares	6.4	9.8	13.3	14.4	abv av	abv av
IAI MidCap Growth	5.6	na	na	na	na	na
Armstrong Associates	5.3	8.9	7.4	9.8	av	abv av
T Rowe Price New Era	5.1	7.3	5.3	11.5	low	av
Fidelity Low-Priced Stock	4.8	17.5	18.8	na	av	abv av
Fidelity Sel Telecomm	4.3	15.9	11.2	na	high	abv av
Fidelity Dividend Growth	4.2	na	na	na	na	na
Lazard Equity	4.2	9.1	9.5	na	blw av	abv av
Berwyn	3.8	15.5	10.9	13.2	high	abv av
Vanguard US Growth	3.8	1.7	10.0	12.8	low	av
Longleaf Partners Small Cap	3.7	9.9	3.2	na	av	abv av
T Rowe Price Capital Appreciation	3.7	9.4	9.5	na	low	blw av
Dreyfus Appreciation	3.6	2.9	8.2	13.6	blw av	abv av
Mutual Discovery	3.5	na	na	na	na	na
Regis ICM Small Company Port	3.4	18.6	18.1	na	abv av	abv av
Harbor Capital Appreciation	3.3	8.4	14.1	na	high	high
Oakmark	3.3	26.1	na	na	abv av	abv av
USAA Growth	3.3	6.8	9.3	11.4	av	abv av
Royce Premier	3.2	12.4	na	na	low	blw av
Strong Opportunity	3.1	13.6	11.3	na	av	abv av
Fidelity Discipline Equity	3.0	9.9	12.3	na	blw av	abv av
Vanguard Index Trust—Growth Port	2.8	na	na	na	na	na
Flex Muirfield	2.6	5.8	9.5	na	low	blw av
Fidelity Capital Appreciation Port	2.5	16.7	8.0	na	av	abv av

Growth Funds
Ranked by 1994 Total Return

Fund Name	1994	3yr	5yr	10yr	Category Risk	Total Risk
Babson Enterprise	2.4	14.0	12.2	14.8	av	abv av
Brandywine Blue	2.3	13.7	na	na	high	high
Fontaine Capital Appreciation	2.3	3.9	5.8	na	low	av
Marshall Value Equity	2.0	na	na	na	na	na
Reich & Tang Equity	1.6	10.4	9.3	na	low	av
Scudder Value	1.6	na	na	na	na	na
Crabbe Huson Equity	1.5	14.2	14.6	na	blw av	
Legg Mason Value	1.2	7.8	7.0	10.9	abv av	abv av
Nicholas II	1.0	5.5	9.0	12.9	blw av	av
Neuberger & Berman Focus	0.8	12.4	10.7	13.0	av	abv av
Rightime	0.8	4.1	8.2	na	low	blw av
Salomon Brothers Opportunity	0.8	9.0	7.2	12.0	blw av	av
T Rowe Price Growth Stock	0.8	7.3	9.6	13.6	av	abv av
Fidelity Stock Selector	0.7	9.8	na	na	av	abv av
UMB Heartland Fund	0.7	5.7	na	na	low	blw av
Galaxy Equity Growth	0.6	4.0	na	na	low	av
IAI Regional	0.6	4.3	8.8	15.8	blw av	av
Maxus Equity	0.6	12.4	11.5	na	blw av	abv av
Meridian	0.5	9.5	16.5	14.9	high	abv av
Fidelity Sel Energy	0.4	5.3	2.2	8.4	high	high
Fremont Growth	0.4	na	na	na	na	na
Dreyfus Core Value - Investor	0.3	6.7	5.2	12.3	blw av	abv av
Fiduciary Capital Growth	0.3	9.6	9.6	10.1	blw av	av
Gradison McDonald Established Value	0.3	10.1	8.4	13.4	blw av	av
Fidelity Sel Regional Banks	0.2	18.2	16.8	na	high	high
Sound Shore	0.2	10.8	9.9	na	low	av
T Rowe Price Mid-Cap Growth	0.2	na	na	na	na	na
Vista Equity	0.2	4.6	na	na	low	av
Brandywine	0.0	12.3	16.3	na	high	high
Fidelity Retirement Growth	0.0	10.5	12.0	15.6	av	abv av
New Century Capital Port	0.0	4.6	8.2	na	av	abv av
Northeast Investors Growth	0.0	0.5	7.1	13.1	av	abv av
Vontobel US Value	0.0	7.1	na	na	blw av	av
Gabelli Asset	-0.1	11.8	9.4	na	low	av
SteinRoe Prime Equities	-0.1	7.4	10.0	na	low	av
Benham Equity Growth	-0.2	5.0	na	na	low	av
National Industries	-0.2	0.1	6.5	9.1	low	av
Fidelity Sel Insurance	-0.3	9.7	10.2	na	abv av	abv av
Tweedy Browne American Value	-0.5	na	na	na	na	na
Columbia Growth	-0.6	7.8	10.2	14.2	abv av	abv av
Flex Growth	-0.6	4.2	7.4	na	low	blw av
Merriman Capital Appreciation	-0.6	2.3	6.1	na	low	blw av
Pennsylvania Mutual	-0.7	8.6	8.3	12.0	low	blw av
Tocqueville	-0.7	12.4	10.1	na	low	av
Dreman High Return	-0.9	9.0	11.8	na	abv av	abv av
Seven Seas Series—Small Cap	-0.9	na	na	na	na	na
Wayne Hummer Growth	-0.9	4.2	8.9	12.1	low	av
Fidelity Contrafund	-1.1	11.6	17.5	18.5	blw av	abv av
Janus	-1.1	5.4	10.6	15.1	low	av
Preferred Growth	-1.1	na	na	na	na	na

Growth Funds
Ranked by 1994 Total Return

Fund Name	Annual Return (%)				Category	
	1994	3yr	5yr	10yr	Risk	Total Risk
Sentry	-1.1	4.0	8.8	12.2	low	av
Scudder Quality Growth	-1.3	1.7	na	na	abv av	abv av
T Rowe Price Small Cap Value	-1.3	13.6	11.8	na	blw av	av
L. Roy Papp Stock	-1.4	4.3	9.3	na	blw av	av
Safeco Northwest	-1.5	4.2	na	na	av	abv av
Skyline Special Equities II	-1.5	na	na	na	na	na
M.S.B. Fund	-1.6	9.4	7.3	11.6	blw av	av
Regis DSI Disciplined Value	-1.6	8.1	7.1	na	blw av	av
Vanguard Morgan Growth	-1.6	4.9	8.0	12.5	av	abv av
Vanguard Spec Port—Energy	-1.6	9.7	5.4	12.0	high	high
Vanguard Index Trust—Ext. Market	-1.7	8.1	9.0	na	av	abv av
Fidelity Magellan	-1.8	9.4	12.0	17.9	av	abv av
Portico Special Growth—Retail	-2.0	4.3	12.6	na	high	abv av
Volumetric	-2.0	3.4	7.2	na	av	abv av
Gradison McDonald Opportunity Value	-2.1	7.4	7.9	11.8	blw av	av
Clipper	-2.4	7.9	9.0	13.2	abv av	abv av
First Eagle Fund of America	-2.5	14.4	8.3	na	high	high
Selected Special Shares	-2.5	5.4	6.4	10.9	abv av	abv av
Lazard Special Equity Portfolio	-2.6	7.4	8.9	na	low	blw av
Nicholas	-2.8	5.0	9.4	12.7	low	av
Warburg Pincus Cap Appreciation	-2.8	6.5	7.6	na	av	abv av
Leeb Personal Finance	-3.0	1.9	na	na	low	low
Nicholas Limited Edition	-3.0	7.2	11.6	na	blw av	av
BayFunds Equity Port—Investment Shares	-3.2	na	na	na	na	na
Founders Growth	-3.3	8.1	10.7	15.4	high	high
Gabelli Growth	-3.3	3.9	8.1	na	av	abv av
American Pension Investors—Growth	-3.4	5.2	8.2	na	abv av	abv av
Fidelity Sel Financial Services	-3.6	17.3	14.6	13.6	high	high
Galaxy II Small Company Index—Retail	-3.6	6.3	na	na	av	abv av
Neuberger & Berman Manhattan	-3.6	7.6	8.4	13.9	high	high
Standish Equity	-3.7	8.3	na	na	abv av	abv av
SteinRoe Stock	-3.7	2.3	9.5	12.8	av	abv av
Century Shares Trust	-3.8	6.7	8.0	13.3	abv av	abv av
Dreyfus Peoples S&P MidCap Index	-3.9	6.8	na	na	av	abv av
Blanchard American Equity	-4.1	na	na	na	na	na
Babson Shadow Stock	-4.2	9.0	7.9	na	blw av	abv av
Value Line	-4.4	2.2	9.5	14.1	abv av	abv av
Eclipse Equity	-4.7	9.9	8.5	na	abv av	abv av
Matrix Growth	-4.8	2.9	6.9	na	blw av	av
Portico MidCore Growth—Retail	-5.3	na	na	na	na	na
Schroder US Equity	-5.3	7.1	10.2	12.2	abv av	abv av
SBSF	-5.6	6.6	7.0	11.4	low	av
Strong Discovery	-5.6	5.5	13.8	na	high	high
Marshall Stock	-5.7	na	na	na	na	na
INVESCO Strat Port—Financial	-5.8	12.2	17.9	na	high	abv av
Mathers	-5.8	-0.2	3.6	10.7	low	low
Monetta	-6.1	-0.1	11.5	na	abv av	abv av
Dreyfus Growth Opportunity	-6.3	-2.9	5.2	10.8	high	high
Twentieth Century Heritage	-6.3	7.5	8.9	na	high	abv av
Fidelity Trend	-6.6	9.0	9.0	13.4	abv av	abv av

Growth Funds
Ranked by 1994 Total Return

Fund Name	Annual Return (%)				Category Risk	Total Risk
	1994	3yr	5yr	10yr		
Janus Twenty	-6.7	-0.5	10.8	na	abv av	abv av
Schwartz Value	-6.7	na	na	na	na	na
Turner Growth Equity	-6.7	na	na	na	na	na
Fidelity Sel Natural Gas Port	-6.8	na	na	na	na	na
Dreyfus Capital Growth	-6.9	4.2	8.1	12.1	low	av
Babson Enterprise II	-7.3	9.1	na	na	abv av	abv av
Acorn	-7.4	15.0	13.0	16.5	high	abv av
T Rowe Price New America Growth	-7.4	6.1	11.1	na	high	high
Twentieth Century Select	-8.0	0.2	5.7	12.7	abv av	abv av
Ariel Appreciation	-8.3	3.8	7.9	na	av	abv av
INVESCO Growth	-8.8	3.4	9.2	11.6	abv av	abv av
IAI Value	-9.0	7.4	5.6	10.1	av	abv av
Scudder Capital Growth	-9.8	5.0	6.5	14.2	high	high
Weitz Value Port	-9.8	7.1	8.2	na	blw av	av
AARP Capital Growth	-10.0	2.9	5.2	12.6	high	abv av
Harbor Growth	-11.4	-0.5	6.6	na	high	high
MIM Stock Growth	-11.7	-4.0	1.1	na	av	abv av
Gintel	-16.4	2.0	2.7	8.6	high	high
Growth Fund Average	**-0.6**	**7.7**	**9.6**	**12.9**	**av**	**abv av**

Growth and Income Funds
Ranked by 1994 Total Return

Fund Name	Annual Return (%)				Category Risk	Total Risk
	1994	3yr	5yr	10yr		
Safeco Equity	9.9	16.2	12.9	16.1	high	high
Cohen & Steers Realty Shares	8.3	15.5	na	na	high	high
Warburg Pincus Growth and Income	7.5	16.5	13.2	na	high	abv av
Stratton Growth	7.1	6.7	6.7	11.0	low	av
Valley Forge	5.9	10.6	6.7	7.4	low	low
Mutual Qualified	5.7	16.7	11.6	15.1	low	av
Mutual Beacon	5.6	16.8	11.5	15.4	low	blw av
Gateway Index Plus	5.5	6.0	9.1	10.5	low	low
Dodge & Cox Stock	5.1	11.3	9.7	15.4	abv av	av
Mutual Shares	4.5	15.3	10.8	14.7	low	av
T Rowe Price Equity Income	4.5	11.0	9.8	na	low	blw av
INVESCO Value Trust—Value Equity	4.0	6.4	9.0	na	blw av	av
Twentieth Century Value	3.9	na	na	na	na	na
Galaxy Equity Value	3.5	8.7	8.9	na	blw av	av
Sequoia	3.3	7.7	10.9	14.0	abv av	abv av
Fidelity Equity-Income II	3.1	13.4	na	na	blw av	av
AARP Growth & Income	3.0	9.1	10.0	13.5	blw av	av
PRA Real Estate Securities	2.9	13.3	6.9	na	high	high
Greenspring	2.8	11.1	8.9	11.5	low	blw av
SIT Growth & Income	2.8	3.6	7.5	12.3	abv av	abv av

Growth and Income Funds
Ranked by 1994 Total Return

Fund Name	Annual Return (%)				Category Risk	Total Risk
	1994	3yr	5yr	10yr		
UMB Stock	2.7	6.7	8.2	11.3	low	blw av
Analytic Optioned Equity	2.5	5.1	5.9	9.3	low	low
Babson Value	2.5	13.2	10.6	13.9	av	av
Fidelity Fund	2.5	9.5	9.1	13.6	av	av
Scudder Growth & Income	2.5	9.1	10.2	14.2	av	av
Homestead Value	2.4	10.7	na	na	blw av	av
Fidelity Growth & Income	2.2	10.8	12.5	na	low	av
T Rowe Price Dividend Growth	2.1	na	na	na	na	na
Columbia Common Stock	2.0	9.3	na	na	av	av
Fidelity Real Estate Investment	2.0	11.1	11.7	na	high	abv av
Evergreen Growth & Income—Class Y	1.6	9.8	9.7	na	av	av
Regis C & B Equity	1.3	3.3	na	na	low	blw av
Seven Seas Series—S&P 500	1.3	na	na	na	na	na
T Rowe Price Spectrum Growth	1.3	9.5	na	na	abv av	av
USAA Growth & Income	1.2	na	na	na	na	na
Vanguard Index Trust—500	1.1	6.1	8.4	14.0	av	av
ASM	1.0	6.5	na	na	av	av
Fidelity Market Index	1.0	5.9	na	na	av	av
Portico Equity Index—Retail	1.0	5.6	8.1	na	blw av	av
Galaxy II Large Company Index—Retail	0.9	5.8	na	na	av	av
Managers Income Equity	0.9	7.6	na	na	blw av	av
T. Rowe Price Equity Index	0.9	5.8	na	na	blw av	av
Woodward Equity Index	0.9	na	na	na	na	na
T. Rowe Price Blue Chip Growth	0.8	na	na	na	na	na
Galaxy Equity Income	0.7	5.3	na	na	low	blw av
Dreyfus Peoples Index	0.6	5.8	7.9	na	av	av
Harbor Value	0.6	5.4	6.0	na	abv av	av
Neuberger & Berman Guardian	0.6	11.0	11.8	14.2	abv av	av
Founders Blue Chip	0.5	4.7	8.1	13.3	abv av	av
Bartlett Basic Value	0.4	7.3	7.0	10.5	blw av	av
Preferred Value	0.4	na	na	na	na	na
WPG Quantitative Equity	0.3	na	na	na	na	na
Corefund Equity Index	0.2	5.3	na	na	blw av	av
Fidelity Equity-Income	0.2	11.7	9.2	12.4	blw av	av
Portico Growth & Income—Retail	0.1	4.0	6.5	na	low	av
Dreman Contrarian	0.0	6.6	7.5	na	high	abv av
1784 Growth and Income	-0.1	na	na	na	na	na
Merriman Growth & Income	-0.1	0.4	4.6	na	low	low
Schwab 1000	-0.1	5.8	na	na	av	av
T Rowe Price Growth & Income	-0.1	9.1	8.7	10.8	blw av	av
Vanguard Index Trust—Tot Stock Mkt	-0.1	na	na	na	na	na
Vanguard Windsor	-0.1	11.5	8.5	13.2	high	abv av
Seven Seas Series Growth & Income	-0.2	na	na	na	na	na
Domini Social Equity	-0.3	5.9	na	na	av	av
Seven Seas Series—Matrix Equity	-0.3	na	na	na	na	na
Babson Growth	-0.5	6.1	6.4	11.9	blw av	av
Benham Income & Growth	-0.5	6.0	na	na	blw av	av
Reynolds Blue Chip Growth	-0.5	-1.9	5.1	na	high	abv av
Vanguard Quantitative Port	-0.6	6.5	8.9	na	av	av
USAA Income Stock	-0.7	6.0	8.4	na	blw av	av

Growth and Income Funds
Ranked by 1994 Total Return

Fund Name	Annual Return (%)				Category	
	1994	3yr	5yr	10yr	Risk	Total Risk
Vanguard Index Trust—Value Port	-0.7	na	na	na	na	na
Lindner	-0.8	10.2	7.9	12.2	blw av	av
Loomis Sayles Growth & Income	-0.8	8.1	na	na	abv av	abv av
Lindner Utility	-0.9	na	na	na	na	na
Vanguard Windsor II	-1.1	7.9	7.8	na	blw av	av
Salomon Brothers Investors	-1.2	6.9	8.1	11.5	abv av	abv av
Strong Total Return	-1.3	6.7	8.5	11.0	high	abv av
Vanguard Equity Income	-1.5	7.1	6.3	na	blw av	av
Marshall Equity Income	-1.6	na	na	na	na	na
Fidelity Convertible Securities	-1.7	12.1	13.7	na	blw av	av
MIM Stock Income	-1.8	0.8	3.4	na	blw av	av
Neuberger & Berman Partners	-1.8	10.3	9.2	13.3	high	abv av
Strong American Utilities	-2.6	na	na	na	na	na
Aquinas Equity Income	-2.9	na	na	na	na	na
Lexington Growth & Income	-3.1	7.2	6.6	11.3	abv av	av
Maxus Laureate	-3.2	na	na	na	na	na
Royce Equity Income Series	-3.2	9.3	7.5	na	low	blw av
Selected American Shares	-3.2	2.5	8.7	13.2	high	abv av
Hotchkis and Wiley Equity Income	-3.5	8.3	7.0	na	abv av	av
Vanguard Trustees' Equity—US	-3.9	6.2	6.8	11.1	high	abv av
Legg Mason American Leading Cos	-4.1	na	na	na	na	na
Dreyfus	-4.2	2.4	5.8	10.9	av	av
Schafer Value	-4.2	12.0	12.2	na	abv av	abv av
IAI Growth & Income	-4.7	2.8	5.1	11.3	av	av
Charter Capital Blue Chip Growth	-4.8	-2.9	5.5	6.2	high	abv av
Janus Growth & Income	-4.8	2.2	na	na	high	abv av
Dreyfus Growth & Income	-5.1	10.5	na	na	low	av
Fidelity Utilities	-5.1	6.7	8.4	na	abv av	abv av
Value Line Convertible	-5.2	7.3	8.9	na	low	blw av
US All American Equity	-5.3	3.2	4.3	6.8	blw av	av
WPG Growth & Income	-5.4	5.6	8.2	12.4	abv av	abv av
Vanguard Convertible Securities	-5.6	8.4	9.4	na	av	av
Amana Income	-6.4	2.0	4.9	na	blw av	av
Evergreen Total Return—Class Y	-6.4	5.1	6.0	10.0	low	av
SBSF Convertible Securities	-6.4	7.7	8.6	na	low	blw av
Legg Mason Total Return	-7.1	6.5	7.1	na	abv av	abv av
Dreyfus Third Century	-7.4	-0.2	7.2	11.0	abv av	abv av
Fidelity Sel Utilities Growth	-7.4	4.8	6.9	12.9	abv av	av
Copley	-7.6	6.1	6.6	10.1	high	abv av
Vanguard Preferred Stock	-7.9	4.1	7.7	10.7	low	low
Philadelphia	-8.5	8.7	3.8	9.6	av	av
Vanguard Spec Port—Utilities Income	-8.5	na	na	na	na	na
Galaxy II Utility Index—Retail	-8.6	na	na	na	na	na
Berger One Hundred & One	-9.0	5.6	11.7	12.3	abv av	abv av
Rushmore American Gas Index	-9.7	5.4	1.6	na	high	abv av
INVESCO Strat Port—Utilities	-9.9	6.5	6.8	na	av	av
Benham Utilities Income	-10.0	na	na	na	na	na
US Income	-10.2	4.5	3.5	8.3	high	abv av
US Real Estate	-11.6	-2.4	2.9	na	high	high
Stratton Monthly Dividend Shares	-12.1	1.0	6.0	9.2	abv av	av

Growth and Income Funds
Ranked by 1994 Total Return

Fund Name	Annual Return (%)				Category	
	1994	3yr	5yr	10yr	Risk	Total Risk
Dreyfus Edison Electric Index	-12.7	1.1	na	na	high	abv av
America's Utility	-13.0	na	na	na	na	na
Cappiello-Rushmore Utility Income	-13.3	na	na	na	na	na
Gintel ERISA	-21.2	-1.7	0.4	8.0	high	high
Growth and Income Fund Average	**-1.4**	**7.1**	**7.9**	**11.7**	**av**	**av**

Balanced Funds
Ranked by 1994 Total Return

Fund Name	Annual Return (%)				Category	
	1994	3yr	5yr	10yr	Risk	Total Risk
Dreyfus Balanced	3.9	na	na	na	na	na
Pax World	2.6	0.7	6.3	10.2	blw av	blw av
INVESCO Value Trust—Total Return	2.5	8.1	9.5	na	av	blw av
Northeast Investors Trust	2.2	14.0	11.2	11.3	blw av	blw av
Dodge & Cox Balanced	1.9	9.3	9.7	13.9	abv av	blw av
Fidelity Puritan	1.8	12.6	10.7	13.7	abv av	blw av
Dreyfus Asset Allocation—Total Return	1.6	na	na	na	na	na
Bascom Hill Balanced	1.0	4.5	5.7	na	blw av	blw av
Hotchkis and Wiley Balanced Income	0.7	7.4	8.2	na	low	blw av
Columbia Balanced	0.0	7.3	na	na	blw av	blw av
Eclipse Balanced	0.0	9.4	9.9	na	av	blw av
Janus Balanced	0.0	na	na	na	na	na
Twentieth Century Balanced	0.0	0.2	8.5	na	high	av
Primary Trend	-0.1	3.7	5.5	na	high	av
Vanguard Star	-0.2	6.9	7.9	na	blw av	blw av
Vanguard Wellington	-0.4	6.8	7.9	12.4	abv av	blw av
Crabbe Huson Asset Allocation	-0.8	9.5	9.6	na	av	blw av
Regis C & B Balanced	-0.9	3.6	8.5	na	low	low
USAA Cornerstone	-0.9	9.2	6.5	12.3	high	av
Berwyn Income	-1.0	12.0	11.5	na	av	blw av
Safeco Income	-1.0	7.4	6.4	11.1	abv av	blw av
Evergreen Foundation—Class Y	-1.1	11.1	14.8	na	high	av
Fidelity Asset Manager—Income	-1.3	na	na	na	na	na
IAI Balanced	-1.4	na	na	na	na	na
Strong Asset Allocation	-1.5	5.1	7.4	9.2	low	low
Vanguard Balanced Index	-1.5	na	na	na	na	na
Founders Balanced	-1.9	8.2	8.1	10.4	abv av	blw av
Regis Sterling Partners Balanced	-1.9	5.4	na	na	blw av	blw av
T Rowe Price Spectrum Income	-1.9	5.9	na	na	low	low
T Rowe Price Balanced	-2.0	6.1	9.3	12.5	av	blw av
Jurika & Voyles Balanced	-2.2	na	na	na	na	na
Vanguard Asset Allocation	-2.2	6.0	8.6	na	high	av
Scudder Balanced	-2.3	na	na	na	na	na
Galaxy Asset Allocation	-2.4	3.9	na	na	blw av	blw av
Preferred Asset Allocation	-2.5	na	na	na	na	na
USAA Balanced	-2.6	5.1	6.1	na	low	blw av
Evergreen American Retirement—Class Y	-2.8	7.4	7.9	na	av	blw av
Permanent Port	-2.8	4.7	3.6	6.3	low	blw av

Balanced Funds
Ranked by 1994 Total Return

Fund Name	Annual Return (%)				Category Risk	Total Risk
	1994	3yr	5yr	10yr		
Merriman Asset Allocation	-2.9	5.7	6.0	na	low	blw av
Aquinas Balanced	-3.0	na	na	na	na	na
Lindner Dividend	-3.3	10.3	9.8	11.6	low	low
MIM Bond Income	-3.6	1.9	4.1	na	blw av	blw av
INVESCO Industrial Income	-3.8	4.2	10.8	14.8	high	av
SteinRoe Total Return	-4.1	5.1	8.1	11.0	av	blw av
Portico Balanced—Retail	-4.2	na	na	na	na	na
Value Line Income	-4.3	1.7	6.6	10.3	abv av	blw av
Maxus Income	-4.4	3.8	6.3	na	low	low
Vanguard Wellesley Income	-4.4	6.0	8.4	11.7	abv av	blw av
Lepercq-Istel	-5.0	4.3	4.4	7.9	high	av
USAA Income	-5.2	4.1	7.7	9.9	blw av	blw av
Fidelity Balanced	-5.3	6.8	8.9	na	blw av	blw av
Fidelity Asset Manager	-6.5	9.0	11.0	na	abv av	blw av
Fidelity Asset Manager—Growth	-7.3	11.6	na	na	high	av
BB&K Diversa	-9.3	4.7	3.8	na	abv av	blw av
CGM Mutual	-9.7	5.2	10.6	14.8	high	abv av
Balanced Fund Average	**-1.9**	**6.4**	**8.0**	**11.3**	**av**	**blw av**

Corporate Bond Funds
Ranked by 1994 Total Return

Fund Name	Annual Return (%)				Category Risk	Total Risk
	1994	3yr	5yr	10yr		
Strong Advantage	3.4	6.5	7.3	na	low	low
Permanent Port—Versatile Bond	2.5	3.9	na	na	low	low
Janus Short-Term Bond	0.3	na	na	na	na	na
Homestead Short-Term Bond	0.0	4.2	na	na	blw av	low
Vanguard Short-Term Corporate	0.0	4.6	7.2	8.4	blw av	low
INVESCO Income—Sel Income	-1.2	6.7	8.6	9.9	av	low
Janus Flexible Income	-2.9	7.8	8.5	na	abv av	low
SteinRoe Income	-3.8	5.9	8.1	na	abv av	low
Loomis Sayles Bond	-4.0	10.2	na	na	high	blw av
Fidelity Short-Term Bond	-4.1	3.9	6.2	na	av	low
Vanguard Interm Term Corporate	-4.2	na	na	na	na	na
Fidelity Spartan Short-Term Income	-4.6	na	na	na	na	na
Fidelity Spartan Investment Grade	-5.1	na	na	na	na	na
Vanguard Long Term Corp Bond	-5.3	5.9	8.8	10.4	high	blw av
CGM Fixed Income	-8.0	na	na	na	na	na
Corporate Bond Fund Average	**-2.4**	**5.9**	**7.8**	**9.5**	**av**	**low**

Corporate High-Yield Bond Funds
Ranked by 1994 Total Return

Fund Name	Annual Return (%)				Category Risk	Total Risk
	1994	3yr	5yr	10yr		
Fidelity Spartan High Income	3.1	15.1	na	na	abv av	blw av
Nicholas Income	-0.1	7.5	8.5	9.2	low	low
Vanguard High Yield Corporate	-1.6	9.9	10.0	10.5	abv av	blw av
Safeco High Yield Bond	-2.2	9.1	9.2	na	low	low
GIT Income—Maximum	-2.7	7.8	7.8	8.0	av	low
Value Line Aggressive Income	-4.1	8.5	9.3	na	blw av	low
Fidelity Capital & Income	-4.6	15.1	13.7	12.0	high	blw av
INVESCO Income—High Yield	-4.9	7.9	8.2	10.1	blw av	low
T Rowe Price High Yield	-8.0	8.7	8.4	9.6	high	blw av
Corp. High-Yield Bond Fund Average	**-2.7**	**9.9**	**9.3**	**9.9**	**av**	**low**

Government Bond Funds
Ranked by 1994 Total Return

Fund Name	Annual Return (%)				Category Risk	Total Risk
	1994	3yr	5yr	10yr		
Eaton Vance Short-Term Treasury	3.4	2.9	na	na	low	low
Permanent Treasury Bill	3.3	2.8	4.1	na	low	low
Capstone Gov't Income	1.1	2.6	2.6	7.0	low	low
Benham Target Mat Trust—1995	0.7	4.9	7.9	na	blw av	low
Bernstein Gov't Short Duration	0.4	3.4	6.0	na	low	low
Benham Short-Term Treasury & Agency	0.1	na	na	na	na	na
Seven Seas Short Term Gov't Securities	0.1	na	na	na	na	na
Columbia US Gov't Securities	0.0	3.8	6.6	na	low	low
Dreyfus 100% US Treasury Short Term	-0.3	4.4	6.4	na	blw av	low
Vanguard Admiral Short US Treas	-0.3	na	na	na	na	na
Twentieth Century US Gov't Short Term	-0.4	2.6	5.3	6.8	low	low
Vanguard Short-Term US Treasury	-0.6	4.1	na	na	low	low
Dreyfus Short Interm Gov't	-0.7	4.4	7.3	na	blw av	low
Fidelity Short-Interm Gov't	-1.3	2.8	na	na	low	low
INVESCO Value Trust—Interm Gov't	-1.5	4.3	7.1	na	blw av	low
Warburg Pincus Interm Mat Gov't	-1.7	4.1	7.1	na	av	low
IAI Gov't	-2.2	3.8	na	na	blw av	low
Benham Treasury Note	-2.3	3.9	6.8	na	blw av	low
T Rowe Price US Treasury Interm	-2.3	3.8	6.9	na	av	low
Janus Interm Gov't Securities	-2.4	1.5	na	na	blw av	low
Prudential Gov't Securities Interm Term	-2.5	3.5	6.3	8.1	blw av	low
Schwab Short/Interm Gov't Bond	-2.8	3.5	na	na	blw av	low
GIT Income—Gov't Port	-3.6	3.6	6.3	8.5	av	low
Galaxy II U.S. Treasury Index Retail	-3.6	4.2	na	na	av	low
Dreyfus 100% US Treasury Interm Term	-3.9	4.5	7.4	na	av	low
Vanguard Admiral Interm US Treas	-4.2	na	na	na	na	na
Vanguard Interm-Term US Treasury	-4.3	4.7	na	na	abv av	blw av
Bull & Bear US Gov't Securities	-4.7	3.3	6.5	na	av	low
Fidelity Gov't Securities	-5.3	4.7	7.8	9.0	abv av	blw av
T Rowe Price US Treasury Long Term	-5.7	4.0	6.9	na	abv av	blw av

Government Bond Funds
Ranked by 1994 Total Return

Fund Name	Annual Return (%)				Category	
	1994	3yr	5yr	10yr	Risk	Total Risk
Benham Target Mat Trust—2000	-6.8	5.2	8.3	na	high	av
Vanguard Admiral Long US Treas	-6.8	na	na	na	na	na
CA Investment Trust US Gov't	-6.9	5.3	8.3	na	abv av	blw av
INVESCO Income—US Gov't Sec	-7.0	2.6	6.0	na	abv av	blw av
Vanguard Long-Term US Treasury	-7.0	5.2	7.6	na	high	av
Rushmore US Gov't Interm-Term	-7.3	3.5	6.5	na	abv av	blw av
Founders Gov't Securities	-7.4	2.1	5.0	na	abv av	blw av
Scudder U.S. Government Zero Coupon 2000	-7.9	4.9	7.7	na	high	av
Benham Target Mat Trust—2005	-8.8	6.6	8.8	na	high	abv av
WPG Gov't Securities	-8.8	2.3	5.8	na	av	low
Dreyfus 100% US Treasury Long Term	-9.1	4.4	7.5	na	abv av	av
Benham Long-Term Treasury & Agency	-9.2	na	na	na	na	na
Rushmore US Gov't Long-Term	-9.9	3.2	6.0	na	high	av
Benham Target Mat Trust—2010	-11.5	7.0	8.2	na	high	abv av
Fidelity Spartan Long-Term Gov't	-12.2	3.4	na	na	high	av
Benham Target Mat Trust—2015	-14.0	6.5	7.4	na	high	high
Benham Target Mat Trust—2020	-17.6	6.5	6.2	na	high	high
Fundamental US Gov't Strat Income	-25.6	na	na	na	na	na
Government Bond Fund Average	**-4.8**	**4.0**	**6.7**	**7.8**	**av**	**low**

Mortgage-Backed Bond Funds
Ranked by 1994 Total Return

Fund Name	Annual Return (%)				Category	
	1994	3yr	5yr	10yr	Risk	Total Risk
Smith Breedon Short Dur U.S. Gov't Series	4.1	na	na	na	na	na
Fidelity Mortgage Securities	1.9	4.6	7.5	9.0	low	low
SIT US Gov't Securities	1.7	4.8	7.5	na	low	low
Montgomery Short Gov't Bond	1.1	na	na	na	na	na
USAA GNMA Trust	0.0	4.3	na	na	av	low
T Rowe Price Adjustable Rate US Gov't	-0.6	1.9	na	na	low	low
Fidelity Spartan Ltd Maturity Gov't	-0.9	3.6	6.3	na	low	low
Vanguard GNMA	-0.9	3.8	7.6	9.4	av	low
Dreyfus Investors GNMA	-1.0	4.8	7.2	na	abv av	low
Benham Adjustable Rate Gov't	-1.1	2.5	na	na	low	low
Fidelity Spartan Ginnie Mae	-1.5	3.6	na	na	blw av	low
AARP GNMA & US Treasury	-1.6	3.5	6.8	na	blw av	low
Benham GNMA Income	-1.6	4.1	7.5	na	blw av	low
Smith Breedon Interm Dur US Gov't Series	-1.6	na	na	na	na	na
T Rowe Price GNMA	-1.6	3.5	7.0	na	blw av	low
Fidelity Ginnie Mae	-1.9	3.5	6.8	na	blw av	low
Lexington GNMA Income	-2.0	3.6	7.0	8.7	abv av	low
Standish Securitized	-2.1	3.8	7.6	na	high	low
Selected US Gov't Income	-2.4	3.4	6.4	na	abv av	low
Eaton Vance Classic Gov't Obligations	-2.6	na	na	na	na	na

Mortgage-Backed Bond Funds
Ranked by 1994 Total Return

Fund Name	Annual Return (%)				Category Risk	Total Risk
	1994	3yr	5yr	10yr		
Dreyfus GNMA	-2.7	3.4	6.8	na	av	low
Marshall Government Income	-2.7	na	na	na	na	na
Scudder GNMA	-3.1	3.1	6.8	na	abv av	low
Fidelity Spartan Gov't Income	-3.5	3.4	6.8	na	abv av	low
1784 US Gov't Medium Term Income	-3.7	na	na	na	na	na
Safeco GNMA	-4.2	3.0	6.4	na	abv av	low
Managers Short Gov't	-6.0	0.4	na	na	av	low
Value Line Adjustable Rate US Gov't	-9.9	na	na	na	na	na
Value Line US Gov't Securities	-10.6	1.4	6.0	8.4	high	low
Managers Interm Mortgage	-25.0	-2.6	na	na	high	abv av
Mortgage-Backed Bond Fund Average	**-2.8**	**3.1**	**6.9**	**8.8**	**av**	**low**

General Bond Funds
Ranked by 1994 Total Return

Fund Name	Annual Return (%)				Category Risk	Total Risk
	1994	3yr	5yr	10yr		
Hotchkis and Wiley Low Duration	5.2	na	na	na	na	na
Seven Seas Yield Plus	4.0	na	na	na	na	na
Harbor Short Duration	2.7	na	na	na	na	na
IAI Reserve	2.7	3.1	5.1	na	low	low
Pacifica Asset Preservation	2.3	3.8	na	na	low	low
Vista Short-Term Bond	2.3	3.9	na	na	low	low
Consolidated Standish Short Asset Resv	2.2	3.8	5.9	na	low	low
Neuberger & Berman Ultra Short Bond	2.2	3.0	4.9	na	low	low
Marshall Short-Term Income	1.8	na	na	na	na	na
Blanchard Short Term Bond	1.0	na	na	na	na	na
Portico Short Term Bond Market—Retail	0.9	4.7	6.9	na	low	low
Bernstein Short Duration Plus	0.5	4.0	6.4	na	low	low
Dreyfus Short Term Income	0.1	na	na	na	na	na
SteinRoe Limited Maturity Income	0.0	na	na	na	na	na
Galaxy Short Term Bond	-0.3	3.9	na	na	low	low
Neuberger & Berman Ltd Maturity Bond	-0.3	3.8	6.3	na	low	low
Connecticut Mutual Inv Acts Income	-0.4	4.6	6.8	na	low	low
Fidelity Spartan Short Intermediate Gov't	-0.5	na	na	na	na	na
Preferred Short-Term Gov't Securities	-0.6	na	na	na	na	na
Warburg Pincus Fixed Income	-0.6	5.6	7.2	na	av	low
William Blair Income Shares	-0.7	4.6	na	na	blw av	low
Flex Bond	-0.9	3.4	6.6	na	av	low
Vanguard Short-Term Federal	-0.9	4.0	6.6	na	blw av	low
Regis DSI Limited Maturity Bond	-1.1	3.2	6.4	na	blw av	low
Strong Income	-1.3	8.0	6.2	na	high	low
Strong Short-Term Bond	-1.6	4.6	6.7	na	blw av	low
AmSouth Limited Maturity	-1.8	3.7	6.2	na	blw av	low
Legg Mason US Gov't Interm Port	-1.9	3.5	6.7	na	blw av	low
Morgan Grenfell Fixed Income	-1.9	na	na	na	na	na
Fidelity Interm Bond	-2.0	5.1	7.4	9.1	av	low

General Bond Funds
Ranked by 1994 Total Return

Fund Name	Annual Return (%)				Category Risk	Total Risk
	1994	3yr	5yr	10yr		
Babson Bond Trust—Port S	-2.1	4.3	7.0	na	blw av	low
Portico Interm Bond Market—Retail	-2.1	na	na	na	na	na
Brundage Story & Rose Short/Interm	-2.2	4.0	na	na	blw av	low
T Rowe Price New Income	-2.2	3.9	7.1	8.8	av	low
BayFunds Bond Port-Investment Shares	-2.3	na	na	na	na	na
Lazard Strategic Yield Portfolio	-2.3	6.1	na	na	high	low
Preferred Fixed Income	-2.3	na	na	na	na	na
Wayne Hummer Income	-2.4	na	na	na	na	na
SteinRoe Interm Bond	-2.5	4.6	7.1	9.5	av	low
Vanguard Total Bond Market Port	-2.6	4.5	7.4	na	av	low
Bartlett Fixed Income	-2.8	3.5	6.1	na	blw av	low
Dodge & Cox Income	-2.8	5.2	8.1	na	abv av	low
Merriman Flexible Bond	-2.8	5.1	6.9	na	abv av	low
Scudder Short-Term Bond	-2.8	3.5	6.8	8.9	blw av	low
T Rowe Price Short-Term Bond	-2.9	2.8	5.5	7.0	low	low
Aquinas Fixed Income	-3.0	na	na	na	na	na
Marshall Intermediate Bond	-3.0	na	na	na	na	na
Portico Bond IMMDEX—Retail	-3.0	4.9	7.8	na	abv av	low
UMB Bond	-3.0	3.8	6.4	8.0	blw av	low
Bernstein Interm Duration	-3.1	4.5	7.4	na	av	low
SteinRoe Gov't Income	-3.1	3.3	6.5	na	av	low
Vista Bond	-3.1	4.6	na	na	av	low
AmSouth Bond	-3.2	4.3	6.9	na	abv av	low
Babson Bond Trust—Port L	-3.2	5.0	7.5	9.3	av	low
Columbia Fixed Income Securities	-3.3	4.8	7.8	9.4	abv av	low
BayFunds Short-Term Yield-Investm't Shares	-3.4	na	na	na	na	na
Strong Gov't Securities	-3.4	5.9	8.5	na	abv av	low
Galaxy Interm Bond	-3.7	2.8	5.9	na	abv av	low
Harbor Bond	-3.7	5.6	8.7	na	av	low
AARP High Quality Bond	-4.4	4.0	6.9	8.2	high	low
Twentieth Century Long-Term Bond	-4.4	3.5	6.7	na	abv av	low
Scudder Income	-4.5	4.7	7.8	9.6	high	blw av
Legg Mason Investment Grade	-4.8	4.1	6.7	na	abv av	low
Standish Fixed Income	-4.8	5.2	8.4	na	high	blw av
IAI Bond	-4.9	4.4	7.4	9.2	high	blw av
Fidelity Investment Grade	-5.3	5.9	8.4	9.6	high	blw av
Blanchard Flexible Income	-5.5	na	na	na	na	na
Dreyfus A Bonds Plus	-6.1	5.2	7.7	9.7	high	blw av
Galaxy High Quality Bond	-6.4	4.0	na	na	high	blw av
Managers Bond	-7.2	3.7	na	na	high	blw av
Managers Short & Interm Bond	-8.3	3.4	na	na	av	low
Heartland U.S. Government Securities	-9.6	5.4	8.5	na	high	av
General Bond Fund Average	**-2.0**	**4.3**	**6.9**	**8.9**	**av**	**low**

Tax-Exempt Bond Funds
Ranked by 1994 Total Return

Fund Name	Annual Return (%)				Category Risk	Total Risk
	1994	3yr	5yr	10yr		
Twentieth Century Tax-Exempt Short	2.4	na	na	na	na	na
Calvert Tax-Free Reserves Ltd Trm—Class A	2.3	3.8	4.8	5.9	low	low
Vanguard Short-Term Muni Bond	1.6	3.3	4.7	5.4	low	low
Pacifica Short Term CA Tax-Free	1.1	na	na	na	na	na
Dupree Kentucky Tax-Free Short to Medium	1.0	4.4	5.5	na	low	low
USAA Tax Exempt Short-Term	0.8	4.0	5.1	5.9	low	low
SIT Minnesota Tax Free Income	0.6	na	na	na	na	na
T Rowe Price MD Short-Term Tax-Free	0.6	na	na	na	na	na
Fifty-Nine Wall St Tax-Free Short/Interm	0.3	na	na	na	na	na
T Rowe Price Tax-Free Short-Interm	0.3	4.1	5.2	5.8	low	low
Vanguard Limited-Term Muni Bond	0.0	4.2	5.8	na	low	low
Fidelity Spartan Short-Interm Muni	-0.1	4.3	5.6	na	low	low
Dreyfus Short-Interm Municipal	-0.3	4.2	5.5	na	low	low
Warburg Pincus NY Muni Bond	-0.5	5.5	6.3	na	low	low
Benham CA Tax-Free Short-Term	-0.6	na	na	na	na	na
SIT Tax Free Income	-0.6	5.7	6.7	na	low	low
Strong High Yield Municipal Bond	-1.0	na	na	na	na	na
Morgan Grenfell Muni Bond	-1.1	7.5	na	na	low	low
Schwab Short/Intermediate Tax-Free	-1.1	na	na	na	na	na
Evergreen Short-Interm Muni—Class Y	-1.4	4.3	na	na	low	low
Portico Tax-Exempt Interm Bond—Retail	-1.6	na	na	na	na	na
Strong Short-Term Muni Bond	-1.6	4.0	na	na	low	low
Babson Tax-Free Income—Port S	-1.7	3.6	5.3	6.4	low	low
Evergreen Short Interm Muni CA—Class Y	-1.7	na	na	na	na	na
Schwab CA Short/Interm Tax-Free	-2.0	na	na	na	na	na
Twentieth Century Tax-Exempt Interm	-2.0	4.5	5.9	na	low	low
Vanguard Interm-Term Muni Bond	-2.1	5.9	7.3	9.1	blw av	low
Bernstein Diversified Muni Port	-2.4	4.0	5.7	na	low	low
Bernstein NY Muni Port	-2.5	4.1	5.8	na	low	low
Oregon Municipal Bond	-2.6	4.3	5.8	na	low	low
T Rowe Price Tax-Free Insured Interm	-2.6	na	na	na	na	na
Dupree KY Tax-Free Income	-2.9	6.0	7.2	8.7	low	low
1784 Tax-Exempt Med-Term Income	-3.0	na	na	na	na	na
Bernstein CA Muni Port	-3.1	3.8	na	na	low	low
Eaton Vance Classic Nat'l Ltd Maturity TF	-3.1	na	na	na	na	na
SteinRoe Interm Muni	-3.4	4.9	6.5	na	blw av	low
Benham Nat'l Tax-Free Interm Term	-3.5	4.4	6.3	7.5	blw av	low
Scudder Medium Term Tax Free	-3.5	5.2	6.8	na	low	low
Benham CA Tax-Free Interm	-3.7	4.4	6.1	7.1	blw av	low
Standish Mass Interm Tax-Exempt	-3.8	na	na	na	na	na
Neuberger & Berman Muni Securities	-3.9	3.9	5.5	na	low	low
SteinRoe High Yield Muni	-4.0	3.7	5.7	9.4	blw av	blw av
USAA Tax Exempt Interm-Term	-4.0	5.0	6.5	8.0	blw av	low
Fidelity Spartan NY Interm Muni	-4.2	na	na	na	na	na
T Rowe Price Tax-Free High Yield	-4.3	5.7	7.2	na	blw av	blw av
Dreyfus Interm Muni Bond	-4.4	4.9	6.5	8.1	blw av	blw av
Strong Muni Bond	-4.5	6.1	7.2	na	av	blw av
Vanguard Penn Tax-Free Insur Long	-4.5	5.8	7.2	na	av	blw av
Columbia Muni Bond	-4.6	3.9	6.0	8.5	low	low
Fidelity Spartan CA Interm Muni	-4.6	na	na	na	na	na

Tax-Exempt Bond Funds

Ranked by 1994 Total Return

Fund Name	Annual Return (%)				Category Risk	Total Risk
	1994	3yr	5yr	10yr		
Dreyfus Conn Interm Muni Bond	-4.7	na	na	na	na	na
Fidelity Limited Term Muni	-4.7	4.9	6.5	8.1	blw av	blw av
Vanguard Florida Insured Tax Free	-4.7	na	na	na	na	na
First Hawaii Muni Bond	-4.8	4.5	6.0	na	blw av	blw av
Dreyfus Florida Interm Muni	-4.9	na	na	na	na	na
Fremont CA Interm Tax-Free	-4.9	3.9	na	na	low	low
Fidelity Spartan Intermediate Municipal	-5.0	na	na	na	na	na
Fidelity Spartan Penn Muni High Yield	-5.0	5.4	7.1	na	av	blw av
Rushmore Virginia Tax-Free	-5.0	4.6	5.8	6.8	blw av	blw av
T Rowe Price Maryland Tax-Free	-5.0	5.1	6.5	na	blw av	blw av
T Rowe Price Virginia Tax-Free Bond	-5.0	5.2	na	na	av	blw av
Vanguard High-Yield Muni Bond	-5.0	5.5	7.3	9.9	abv av	blw av
Dreyfus NY Tax-Exempt Interm	-5.1	4.9	6.4	na	blw av	blw av
Vanguard Ohio Tax Free Insur Long	-5.1	5.4	na	na	abv av	blw av
Dreyfus NJ Interm Muni Bond	-5.2	na	na	na	na	na
Rushmore Maryland Tax-Free	-5.2	4.6	5.3	7.1	blw av	blw av
US Tax Free	-5.2	4.3	5.7	7.6	av	blw av
Vanguard NJ Tax Free Insured Long	-5.2	5.4	7.0	na	abv av	blw av
Benham CA Tax-Free High-Yield	-5.3	5.3	6.5	na	blw av	blw av
Galaxy Tax-Exempt Bond	-5.3	4.9	na	na	av	blw av
SteinRoe Managed Muni	-5.3	4.4	6.4	9.9	blw av	blw av
1784 Mass Tax-Exempt Income	-5.4	na	na	na	na	na
Dreyfus CA Interm Muni Bond	-5.4	na	na	na	na	na
Fidelity Ohio Tax-Free High Yield	-5.5	4.9	6.7	na	blw av	blw av
INVESCO Tax-Free Long-Term Bond	-5.5	4.8	6.7	9.8	av	blw av
Scudder Ohio Tax-Free	-5.5	4.9	6.6	na	av	blw av
T Rowe Price Tax-Free Income	-5.5	5.2	6.7	8.1	av	blw av
Twentieth Century Tax-Exempt Long	-5.6	4.4	6.2	na	blw av	blw av
Vanguard Insured Long-Term Muni	-5.6	5.2	7.0	9.5	high	av
Vanguard NY Insured Tax Free	-5.6	5.4	7.0	na	abv av	blw av
Fidelity Spartan NJ Muni High Yield	-5.7	5.0	6.8	na	av	blw av
T Rowe Price CA Tax-Free Bond	-5.7	4.9	6.5	na	av	blw av
Vanguard CA Tax-Free Insured Long	-5.7	5.1	6.6	na	high	av
Vanguard Long-Term Muni Bond	-5.7	5.3	7.2	9.7	high	av
Fidelity Aggressive Tax-Free	-5.8	5.3	7.0	na	blw av	blw av
T Rowe Price NY Tax-Free	-5.8	5.5	6.8	na	av	blw av
Fidelity Minnesota Tax-Free	-5.9	4.4	5.7	na	blw av	blw av
Scudder Penn Tax Free	-5.9	5.1	6.6	na	av	blw av
Dreyfus Mass Tax-Exempt Bond	-6.0	4.3	6.2	na	blw av	blw av
Dreyfus NJ Muni Bond	-6.0	4.9	6.8	na	av	blw av
Fidelity Mass Tax-Free High Yield	-6.0	5.0	6.7	8.7	blw av	blw av
Scudder Managed Muni Bond	-6.0	5.0	6.8	9.0	abv av	blw av
Benham Nat'l Tax-Free Long-Term	-6.1	5.4	7.1	8.5	high	av
Fidelity Spartan Aggressive Municipal	-6.1	na	na	na	na	na
Scudder Mass Tax-Free	-6.1	5.9	7.2	na	abv av	blw av
T Rowe Price NJ Tax-Free	-6.1	5.4	na	na	abv av	blw av
AARP Insured Tax Free General Bond	-6.2	4.6	6.5	8.0	abv av	blw av
USAA Tax-Exempt Virginia Bond	-6.3	4.6	na	na	av	blw av
Dreyfus Mass Interm Muni Bond	-6.4	na	na	na	na	na
Heartland Wisconsin Tax Free	-6.4	na	na	na	na	na

Tax-Exempt Bond Funds
Ranked by 1994 Total Return

Fund Name	Annual Return (%)				Category Risk	Total Risk
	1994	3yr	5yr	10yr		
Strong Insured Muni Bond	-6.4	6.0	na	na	high	av
Benham CA Tax-Free Insured	-6.5	4.9	6.5	na	high	av
Benham CA Tax-Free Long-Term	-6.5	4.7	6.5	8.3	abv av	blw av
Lexington Tax-Exempt Bond Trust	-6.5	3.3	5.2	na	av	blw av
Dreyfus NY Insured Tax-Exempt	-6.6	4.0	6.1	na	av	blw av
Fidelity Spartan Florida Muni Income	-6.7	na	na	na	na	na
Value Line Tax Exempt High Yield	-6.8	3.8	6.0	8.1	abv av	blw av
Dreyfus NY Tax-Exempt	-6.9	4.4	6.2	8.3	av	blw av
Dreyfus Muni Bond	-7.0	4.3	6.2	8.5	av	blw av
Fidelity Spartan Conn Tax-Free High-Yield	-7.0	4.3	6.0	na	abv av	blw av
General CA Muni Bond	-7.0	4.7	6.5	na	abv av	blw av
Schwab Long-Term Tax-Free	-7.0	na	na	na	na	na
Dreyfus CA Tax Exempt Bond	-7.1	3.4	5.4	7.8	av	blw av
General NY Muni Bond	-7.1	5.2	7.2	7.8	abv av	blw av
Galaxy NY Muni Bond	-7.2	4.0	na	na	abv av	blw av
Scudder NY Tax Free	-7.2	4.9	6.6	8.2	high	av
General Muni Bond	-7.3	4.8	7.3	9.1	abv av	blw av
Scudder CA Tax Free	-7.3	4.8	6.7	8.8	high	av
Babson Tax-Free Income—Port L	-7.4	4.0	6.0	8.6	av	blw av
Fidelity High Yield Tax Free Port	-7.4	4.2	6.2	9.0	av	blw av
Fidelity Michigan Tax-Free High Yield	-7.5	4.8	6.3	na	av	blw av
Fidelity Spartan Maryland Muni Income	-7.5	na	na	na	na	na
Fidelity Insured Tax-Free	-7.7	4.2	6.2	na	high	av
Janus Federal Tax-Exempt	-7.7	na	na	na	na	na
Value Line NY Tax-Exempt Trust	-7.7	4.8	6.5	na	high	av
Eaton Vance Classic National Municipals	-7.9	na	na	na	na	na
Evergreen National Tax-Free—Class Y	-7.9	na	na	na	na	na
Fidelity NY Tax-Free Insured	-7.9	4.0	6.1	na	abv av	blw av
USAA Tax Exempt Long-Term	-7.9	4.0	6.1	8.7	av	blw av
Fidelity NY Tax-Free High Yield	-8.0	4.1	6.1	8.5	abv av	blw av
Galaxy Connecticut Municipal Bond	-8.0	na	na	na	na	na
Fidelity Spartan Muni Income	-8.1	4.4	na	na	abv av	blw av
GIT Tax-Free Virginia Port	-8.2	3.4	5.2	na	av	blw av
Safeco Muni Bond	-8.2	3.9	6.3	9.5	high	av
Fidelity Spartan NY Muni High Yield	-8.3	4.3	na	na	high	av
Scudder High Yield Tax-Free	-8.3	4.9	6.8	na	high	av
Cal Tax-Free Income	-8.6	4.5	6.4	na	high	av
Dreyfus Insured Muni Bond	-8.6	3.4	5.7	na	high	av
Fidelity Muni Bond	-8.6	4.0	6.1	8.8	high	av
Fidelity CA Tax-Free High Yield	-8.8	3.9	5.7	7.9	abv av	blw av
GIT Tax-Free National Port	-8.8	3.2	5.0	7.8	abv av	blw av
Schwab CA Long-Term Tax-Free	-8.9	na	na	na	na	na
Fidelity Spartan CA Muni High Yield	-9.0	4.1	6.3	na	abv av	blw av
USAA Tax Exempt NY Bond	-9.0	3.9	na	na	high	av
Safeco CA Tax-Free Income	-9.1	3.5	5.9	8.9	high	av
USAA Tax Exempt CA Bond	-9.3	3.4	5.8	na	high	av
Bull & Bear Muni Income	-9.7	1.9	4.5	8.2	high	av
USAA Florida Tax-Free Income	-10.0	na	na	na	na	na
Fidelity CA Tax-Free Insured	-10.2	3.7	5.7	na	high	av
Cal Muni	-19.9	0.0	2.6	6.4	high	av

Tax-Exempt Bond Funds
Ranked by 1994 Total Return

| Fund Name | Annual Return (%) | | | | Category | |
	1994	3yr	5yr	10yr	Risk	Total Risk
NY Muni	-20.5	0.0	2.7	6.2	high	abv av
Tax-Exempt Bond Fund Average	**-5.2**	**4.5**	**6.1**	**8.1**	**av**	**blw av**

International Stock Funds
Ranked by 1994 Total Return

| Fund Name | Annual Return (%) | | | | Category | |
	1994	3yr	5yr	10yr	Risk	Total Risk
Fidelity Japan	16.4	na	na	na	na	na
T Rowe Price Japan	15.0	6.3	na	na	high	high
Vanguard Int'l Equity Index—Pacific	12.9	7.7	na	na	high	high
Japan	10.0	4.2	-0.4	15.6	high	high
Fidelity European Capital Appreciation	6.8	na	na	na	na	na
Fidelity Europe	6.2	9.6	5.5	na	av	high
Harbor Int'l	5.4	15.2	10.8	na	abv av	high
Vanguard Trustees' Equity—Int'l	5.2	7.8	3.8	16.8	blw av	abv av
INVESCO Int'l—Pacific Basin	4.6	8.8	1.9	14.6	high	high
Tweedy Browne Global Value	4.3	na	na	na	na	na
Nomura Pacific Basin	4.2	8.5	3.8	na	high	high
T Rowe Price European Stock	4.0	7.7	na	na	blw av	high
Bernstein Int'l Value	3.8	na	na	na	na	na
Schwab International Index	3.8	na	na	na	na	na
Janus Worldwide	3.6	13.1	na	na	low	abv av
Dreyfus/Laurel International—Investor	3.5	4.9	0.0	na	abv av	high
Preferred Int'l	3.2	na	na	na	na	na
Fidelity Worldwide	2.9	14.2	na	na	low	abv av
USAA International	2.6	12.7	8.0	na	blw av	abv av
Managers International Equity	2.0	13.7	na	na	low	abv av
Lexington Global	1.8	9.0	4.4	na	low	abv av
Vanguard Int'l Equity Index—Europe	1.8	8.3	na	na	av	high
Babson-Stewart Ivory Int'l	1.3	9.9	6.7	na	blw av	abv av
Fidelity Overseas	1.2	7.8	4.9	19.1	abv av	high
Fidelity Diversified Int'l	1.0	5.9	na	na	abv av	high
Brinson Non-U.S. Equity	0.9	na	na	na	na	na
Vanguard Int'l Growth	0.7	11.1	4.8	17.1	av	high
USAA World Growth	0.6	na	na	na	na	na
INVESCO Int'l—Int'l Growth	0.5	3.9	0.5	na	abv av	high
IAI Int'l	0.4	9.5	5.8	na	av	high
Lazard International Equity Portfolio	0.2	7.0	na	na	abv av	high
Warburg Pincus Int'l Equity	0.1	13.1	10.7	na	abv av	high
William Blair International Growth	0.0	na	na	na	na	na
International Equity	-0.2	11.7	5.2	na	av	high
Bartlett Value Int'l	-0.5	8.6	5.9	na	blw av	high
Regis TS & W International Equity	-0.7	na	na	na	na	na
T Rowe Price Int'l Stock	-0.7	10.3	7.2	17.9	av	high
Strong Int'l Stock	-1.5	na	na	na	na	na
Wright Int'l Blue Chip Equity	-1.6	6.6	5.7	na	blw av	abv av
Loomis Sayles International Equity	-1.7	8.9	na	na	blw av	high

International Stock Funds
Ranked by 1994 Total Return

Fund Name	Annual Return (%)				Category Risk	Total Risk
	1994	3yr	5yr	10yr		
Brinson Global	-1.8	na	na	na	na	na
Founders World Wide Growth	-2.1	8.8	13.1	na	blw av	abv av
Columbia Int'l Stock	-2.4	na	na	na	na	na
Galaxy International Equity	-2.5	7.8	na	na	low	abv av
Fidelity Int'l Growth & Income	-2.8	8.2	5.8	na	low	abv av
Fidelity Pacific-Basin	-2.8	13.7	3.8	na	high	high
Hotchkis and Wiley International	-2.9	11.2	na	na	abv av	high
SIT International Growth	-2.9	13.9	na	na	av	high
Scudder International	-2.9	8.8	5.5	16.1	blw av	abv av
INVESCO Int'l—European	-3.0	3.7	3.9	na	abv av	high
Acorn Int'l	-3.7	na	na	na	na	na
Fifty-Nine Wall St European	-4.0	9.4	na	na	av	high
Fremont Global	-4.1	6.4	7.0	na	low	blw av
Scudder Global	-4.2	9.5	7.5	na	low	av
Twentieth Century Int'l Equity	-4.7	12.5	na	na	blw av	abv av
Strong Asia Pacific	-5.2	na	na	na	na	na
Vontobel EuroPacific	-5.3	9.1	na	na	av	high
Dreyfus International Equity	-5.4	na	na	na	na	na
Standish International Equity	-6.9	5.0	3.2	na	abv av	high
Blanchard Global Growth	-7.5	5.0	3.7	na	low	av
T Rowe Price Int'l Discovery	-7.6	7.9	4.1	na	abv av	high
Harbor International Growth	-7.7	na	na	na	na	na
Montgomery Emerging Markets	-7.7	na	na	na	na	na
Scudder Global Small Company	-7.7	8.4	na	na	low	abv av
Oakmark Int'l	-9.0	na	na	na	na	na
Scudder Latin America	-9.4	na	na	na	na	na
US Global Resources	-9.6	1.3	-1.6	5.1	low	abv av
Fidelity Global Balanced	-11.4	na	na	na	na	na
Fidelity Canada	-11.9	2.3	3.5	na	blw av	abv av
BB&K International Equity	-12.5	na	na	na	na	na
Bull & Bear US & Overseas	-13.1	2.3	3.7	na	blw av	abv av
Montgomery International Small Cap	-13.2	na	na	na	na	na
Montgomery Global Communic'ns	-13.4	na	na	na	na	na
Lexington Worldwide Emerging Mkts	-13.8	13.4	na	na	high	high
Evergreen Global Real Estate—Class Y	-14.0	12.7	5.5	na	abv av	high
T Rowe Price Latin America	-15.9	na	na	na	na	na
Scudder Pacific Opportunities	-17.1	na	na	na	na	na
Fidelity Emerging Markets	-17.9	16.4	na	na	high	high
T Rowe Price New Asia	-19.1	17.1	na	na	high	high
Fifty-Nine Wall St Pacific Basin	-21.4	13.3	na	na	high	high
Fidelity Southeast Asia	-21.7	na	na	na	na	na
Fidelity Latin America	-23.1	na	na	na	na	na
International Stock Fund Average	**-3.0**	**9.1**	**4.9**	**15.2**	**av**	**high**

International Bond Funds
Ranked by 1994 Total Return

Fund Name	Annual Return (%)				Category Risk	Total Risk
	1994	3yr	5yr	10yr		
Flex Short Term Global Income	2.1	na	na	na	na	na
Benham European Gov't Bond	1.5	na	na	na	na	na
Scudder Short-Term Global Income	-1.0	3.6	na	na	low	low
Legg Mason Global Gov't Trust	-1.6	na	na	na	na	na
T Rowe Price International Bond	-1.8	6.4	10.4	na	abv av	av
Morgan Grenfell Global Fixed Income	-2.4	na	na	na	na	na
T Rowe Price Global Gov't Bond	-3.0	3.6	na	na	blw av	low
T Rowe Price Short-Term Global Inc	-3.0	na	na	na	na	na
Brinson Global Bond	-3.4	na	na	na	na	na
Blanchard Short-Term Global Inc	-4.6	2.3	na	na	low	low
Warburg Pincus Global Fixed Income	-5.4	4.9	na	na	av	blw av
Fidelity Short Term World Income	-5.9	3.5	na	na	blw av	low
Standish Global Fixed Income	-7.0	na	na	na	na	na
Scudder Emerging Markets Inc	-8.0	na	na	na	na	na
Scudder International Bond	-8.5	4.4	11.0	na	av	blw av
Loomis Sayles Global Bond	-8.7	1.7	na	na	high	av
Bull & Bear Global Income	-13.4	6.9	6.9	5.4	abv av	av
Fidelity Global Bond	-16.3	2.1	6.1	na	high	av
Fidelity New Markets Income	-16.4	na	na	na	na	na
BB&K International Fixed-Income	-19.2	na	na	na	na	na
International Bond Fund Average	**-6.3**	**3.9**	**8.6**	**5.4**	**av**	**blw av**

Gold Funds
Ranked by 1994 Total Return

Fund Name	Annual Return (%)				Category Risk	Total Risk
	1994	3yr	5yr	10yr		
Fidelity Sel Precious Metals	-1.1	17.7	5.5	7.9	blw av	high
US Gold Shares	-2.6	2.3	-9.8	-1.7	high	high
Vanguard Spec Port—Gold & PM	-5.4	13.7	4.2	10.5	low	high
Lexington GoldFund	-7.0	11.3	0.5	9.0	av	high
Scudder Gold	-7.4	10.3	0.8	na	low	high
USAA Gold	-9.3	9.7	-1.5	2.6	blw av	high
Bull & Bear Gold Investors Ltd	-13.8	10.2	0.6	6.7	av	high
Blanchard Precious Metals	-14.9	11.5	0.9	na	abv av	high
Fidelity Sel American Gold	-15.4	13.5	2.6	na	low	high
Benham Gold Equities Index	-16.7	11.2	-0.2	na	high	high
US World Gold	-16.9	14.5	0.9	na	high	high
INVESCO Strat Port—Gold	-27.8	4.5	-3.9	1.9	abv av	high
Gold Fund Average	**-11.5**	**10.8**	**0.0**	**5.2**	**av**	**high**

Small Capitalization Stock Funds
Ranked by 1994 Total Return

Fund Name	Annual Return (%)				Category Risk	Total Risk
	1994	3yr	5yr	10yr		
PBHG Emerging Growth	23.7	na	na	na	na	na
Robertson Stephens Value + Growth	23.1	na	na	na	na	na
Berger Small Company Growth	13.7	na	na	na	na	na
Twentieth Century Giftrust	13.4	20.7	21.9	25.5	high	high
Crabbe Huson Special	11.7	26.0	19.4	na	high	high
Kaufmann	8.9	12.7	19.2	na	abv av	high
Robertson Stephens Emerging Growth	7.9	4.0	14.4	na	high	high
FAM Value	6.8	10.2	13.3	na	av	abv av
Janus Venture	5.4	7.3	12.7	na	low	abv av
Fidelity Low-Priced Stock	4.8	17.5	18.8	na	av	abv av
PBHG Growth	4.7	25.4	21.9	na	high	high
Twentieth Century Vista	4.6	2.6	9.5	14.9	abv av	high
Tweedy Browne Global Value	4.3	na	na	na	na	na
Longleaf Partners Small Cap	3.7	9.9	3.2	na	av	abv av
Mutual Discovery	3.5	na	na	na	na	na
Regis ICM Small Company Port	3.4	18.6	18.1	na	abv av	abv av
Royce Premier	3.2	12.4	na	na	low	blw av
Babson Enterprise	2.4	14.0	12.2	14.8	av	abv av
Columbia Special	2.2	12.2	13.2	na	blw av	abv av
Lazard Small Cap Portfolio	2.0	18.3	na	na	blw av	abv av
Heartland Value	1.7	19.8	16.3	15.2	av	high
Nicholas II	1.0	5.5	9.0	12.9	blw av	av
Fidelity New Millenium	0.8	na	na	na	na	na
Evergreen—Class Y	0.7	5.1	7.5	11.6	low	abv av
UMB Heartland Fund	0.7	5.7	na	na	low	blw av
Meridian	0.5	9.5	16.5	14.9	high	abv av
Vanguard Explorer	0.5	9.4	12.7	10.1	blw av	abv av
T Rowe Price New Horizons	0.3	10.6	13.2	11.9	av	high
IAI Emerging Growth	0.1	12.0	na	na	high	high
Galaxy Small Company Equity	0.0	7.4	na	na	abv av	high
T Rowe Price OTC	0.0	10.5	8.2	10.8	low	abv av
Dreyfus New Leaders	-0.1	8.5	10.3	na	low	abv av
Fidelity Emerging Growth	-0.1	9.0	na	na	av	high
SIT Growth	-0.4	1.8	11.3	15.5	blw av	high
Vanguard Index Trust—Small Cap	-0.5	11.7	10.6	10.1	blw av	abv av
Pennsylvania Mutual	-0.7	8.6	8.3	12.0	low	blw av
USAA Aggressive Growth	-0.7	-0.6	8.2	9.7	abv av	high
Caldwell & Orkin Aggressive Growth	-0.9	9.4	na	na	low	abv av
Seven Seas Series—Small Cap	-0.9	na	na	na	na	na
T Rowe Price Small Cap Value	-1.3	13.6	11.8	na	blw av	av
Warburg Pincus Emerging Grth	-1.4	9.2	12.9	na	av	high
Skyline Special Equities II	-1.5	na	na	na	na	na
Vanguard Index Trust—Ext. Market	-1.7	8.1	9.0	na	av	abv av
Neuberger & Berman Genesis	-1.8	8.9	8.9	na	low	abv av
Managers Special Equity	-1.9	9.9	na	na	low	abv av
Gradison McDonald Opportunity Value	-2.1	7.4	7.9	11.8	blw av	av
Lazard Special Equity Portfolio	-2.6	7.4	8.9	na	low	blw av
Founders Frontier	-2.8	7.2	11.2	na	av	high
Nicholas Limited Edition	-3.0	7.2	11.6	na	blw av	abv av
Schwab Small-Cap Index	-3.0	na	na	na	na	na

Small Capitalization Stock Funds
Ranked by 1994 Total Return

Fund Name	Annual Return (%)				Category Risk	Total Risk
	1994	3yr	5yr	10yr		
Oberweis Emerging Growth	-3.5	6.3	17.7	na	high	high
Galaxy II Small Company Index—Retail	-3.6	6.3	na	na	av	abv av
Standish Small Capitalization Equity	-3.6	10.6	na	na	av	high
Twentieth Century Ultra	-3.6	5.9	19.3	18.7	high	high
Acorn Int'l	-3.7	na	na	na	na	na
INVESCO Emerging Growth	-3.7	14.3	na	na	av	high
GIT Equity—Special Growth	-3.9	5.5	4.4	12.4	low	abv av
Babson Shadow Stock	-4.2	9.0	7.9	na	blw av	abv av
Eclipse Equity	-4.7	9.9	8.5	na	abv av	abv av
Perritt Capital Growth	-5.0	2.0	4.2	na	low	abv av
Scudder Development	-5.3	0.3	12.0	11.8	abv av	high
Strong Discovery	-5.6	5.5	13.8	na	high	high
Monetta	-6.1	-0.1	11.5	na	abv av	abv av
Schwartz Value	-6.7	na	na	na	na	na
Cappiello-Rushmore Emerging Growth	-6.9	na	na	na	na	na
Acorn	-7.4	15.0	13.0	16.5	high	abv av
T Rowe Price Int'l Discovery	-7.6	7.9	4.1	na	abv av	high
Founders Discovery	-7.7	5.5	16.7	na	av	high
Scudder Global Small Company	-7.7	8.4	na	na	low	abv av
Loomis Sayles Small Cap	-8.3	8.9	na	na	av	high
Prudent Speculator	-8.9	-1.7	-0.6	na	high	high
Montgomery Small Cap	-9.9	7.0	na	na	abv av	high
Fifty-Nine Wall St Small Company	-10.4	3.5	na	na	blw av	high
Evergreen Limited Market—Class Y	-10.5	2.5	7.8	14.3	blw av	high
Legg Mason Special Investment	-13.0	7.5	11.7	na	av	high
Montgomery International Small Cap	-13.2	na	na	na	na	na
Small Capitalization Fund Average	**-0.3**	**9.6**	**12.7**	**15.0**	**av**	**abv av**

Individual Fund Listings 9

1784 Growth and Income
(SEGWX)
Growth & Income

680 East Swedesford Road
Wayne, PA 19087
(800) 252-1784

PERFORMANCE

fund inception date: 6/7/93

	3yr Annual	5yr Annual	10yr Annual	Bull	Bear
Return (%)	na	na	na	na	-8.2
Differ from Category (+/-)	na	na	na	na	-1.9 blw av

Total Risk	Standard Deviation	Category Risk	Risk Index	Beta
na	na	na	na	na

	1994	1993	1992	1991	1990	1989	1988	1987	1986	1985
Return (%)	-0.1	—	—	—	—	—	—	—	—	—
Differ from category (+/-) . . .	1.3	—	—	—	—	—	—	—	—	—

PER SHARE DATA

	1994	1993	1992	1991	1990	1989	1988	1987	1986	1985
Dividends, Net Income ($) .	0.11	—	—	—	—	—	—	—	—	—
Distrib'ns, Cap Gain ($) . . .	0.09	—	—	—	—	—	—	—	—	—
Net Asset Value ($)	10.47	—	—	—	—	—	—	—	—	—
Expense Ratio (%).	0.35	—	—	—	—	—	—	—	—	—
Net Income to Assets (%). .	1.23	—	—	—	—	—	—	—	—	—
Portfolio Turnover (%).	na	—	—	—	—	—	—	—	—	—
Total Assets (Millions $) . . .	193	—	—	—	—	—	—	—	—	—

PORTFOLIO (as of 5/31/94)

Portfolio Manager: committee

Investm't Category: Growth & Income

Cap Gain	Asset Allocation
✔ Cap & Income	Fund of Funds
Income	Index
	Sector
✔ Domestic	Small Cap
Foreign	Socially Conscious
Country/Region	State Specific

Portfolio: stocks 94% bonds 0%
convertibles 0% other 0% cash 6%

Largest Holdings: consumer non-durable—retail 16%, technology 16%

Unrealized Net Capital Gains: 3% of portfolio value

SHAREHOLDER INFORMATION

Minimum Investment
Initial: $1,000   Subsequent: $250

Minimum IRA Investment
Initial: $250   Subsequent: $250

Maximum Fees
Load: none   12b-1: 0.25%
Other: none

Distributions
Income: quarterly   Capital Gains: Dec

Exchange Options
Number Per Year: no limit   Fee: none
Telephone: yes (money market fund available)

Services
IRA, pension, auto invest, auto withdraw

1784 Mass Tax-Exempt Income (SEMAX)

680 East Swedesford Road
Wayne, PA 19087
(800) 252-1784

Tax-Exempt Bond

PERFORMANCE

fund inception date: 6/14/93

	3yr Annual	5yr Annual	10yr Annual	Bull	Bear
Return (%)	na	na	na	na	-5.3
Differ from Category (+/-)	na	na	na	na	-0.1 av

Total Risk	Standard Deviation	Category Risk	Risk Index	Avg Mat
na	na	na	na	8.7 yrs

	1994	1993	1992	1991	1990	1989	1988	1987	1986	1985
Return (%)	-5.4	—	—	—	—	—	—	—	—	—
Differ from category (+/-)	-0.2	—	—	—	—	—	—	—	—	—

PER SHARE DATA

	1994	1993	1992	1991	1990	1989	1988	1987	1986	1985
Dividends, Net Income ($)	0.48	—	—	—	—	—	—	—	—	—
Distrib'ns, Cap Gain ($)	0.00	—	—	—	—	—	—	—	—	—
Net Asset Value ($)	9.35	—	—	—	—	—	—	—	—	—
Expense Ratio (%)	0.33	—	—	—	—	—	—	—	—	—
Net Income to Assets (%)	5.10	—	—	—	—	—	—	—	—	—
Portfolio Turnover (%)	na	—	—	—	—	—	—	—	—	—
Total Assets (Millions $)	55	—	—	—	—	—	—	—	—	—

PORTFOLIO (as of 5/31/94)

Portfolio Manager: Susan Sanderson - 1993

Investm't Category: Tax-Exempt Bond

Cap Gain	Asset Allocation
Cap & Income	Fund of Funds
✔ Income	Index
	Sector
✔ Domestic	Small Cap
Foreign	Socially Conscious
Country/Region	✔ State Specific

Portfolio: stocks 0%   bonds 89%
convertibles 0%   other 0%   cash 11%

Largest Holdings: general obligation 26%

Unrealized Net Capital Gains: -4% of portfolio value

SHAREHOLDER INFORMATION

Minimum Investment
Initial: $1,000   Subsequent: $250

Minimum IRA Investment
Initial: na   Subsequent: na

Maximum Fees
Load: none   12b-1: 0.25%
Other: none

Distributions
Income: monthly   Capital Gains: Dec

Exchange Options
Number Per Year: no limit   Fee: none
Telephone: yes (money market fund available)

Services
auto invest, auto withdraw

1784 Tax-Exempt Med-Term Income (SETMX)

680 East Swedesford Road
Wayne, PA 19087
(800) 252-1784

Tax-Exempt Bond

PERFORMANCE

fund inception date: 6/14/93

	3yr Annual	5yr Annual	10yr Annual	Bull	Bear
Return (%)	na	na	na	na	-3.8
Differ from Category (+/-)	na	na	na	na	1.4 abv av

Total Risk	Standard Deviation	Category Risk	Risk Index	Avg Mat
na	na	na	na	7.4 yrs

	1994	1993	1992	1991	1990	1989	1988	1987	1986	1985
Return (%)	-3.0	—	—	—	—	—	—	—	—	—
Differ from category (+/-) . . .	2.2	—	—	—	—	—	—	—	—	—

PER SHARE DATA

	1994	1993	1992	1991	1990	1989	1988	1987	1986	1985
Dividends, Net Income ($) .	0.48	—	—	—	—	—	—	—	—	—
Distrib'ns, Cap Gain ($) . . .	0.00	—	—	—	—	—	—	—	—	—
Net Asset Value ($)	9.56	—	—	—	—	—	—	—	—	—
Expense Ratio (%).	0.32	—	—	—	—	—	—	—	—	—
Net Income to Assets (%). .	5.06	—	—	—	—	—	—	—	—	—
Portfolio Turnover (%)	na	—	—	—	—	—	—	—	—	—
Total Assets (Millions $)	90	—	—	—	—	—	—	—	—	—

PORTFOLIO (as of 5/31/94)

Portfolio Manager: David Thompson - 1993

Investm't Category: Tax-Exempt Bond

Cap Gain	Asset Allocation
Cap & Income	Fund of Funds
✔ Income	Index
	Sector
✔ Domestic	Small Cap
Foreign	Socially Conscious
Country/Region	State Specific

Portfolio: stocks 0%   bonds 95%
convertibles 0%   other 0%   cash 5%

Largest Holdings: general obligation 34%

Unrealized Net Capital Gains: -2% of portfolio value

SHAREHOLDER INFORMATION

Minimum Investment
Initial: $1,000   Subsequent: $250

Minimum IRA Investment
Initial: na   Subsequent: na

Maximum Fees
Load: none   12b-1: 0.25%
Other: none

Distributions
Income: monthly   Capital Gains: Dec

Exchange Options
Number Per Year: no limit   Fee: none
Telephone: yes (money market fund available)

Services
auto invest, auto withdraw

1784 US Gov't Medium Term Income (SEGTX)

680 East Swedesford Road
Wayne, PA 19087
(800) 252-1784

Mortgage-Backed Bond

PERFORMANCE

fund inception date: 6/7/93

	3yr Annual	5yr Annual	10yr Annual	Bull	Bear
Return (%)	na	na	na	na	-5.1
Differ from Category (+/-)	na	na	na	na	-0.7 blw av

Total Risk	Standard Deviation	Category Risk	Risk Index	Avg Mat
na	na	na	na	3.3 yrs

	1994	1993	1992	1991	1990	1989	1988	1987	1986	1985
Return (%)	-3.7	—	—	—	—	—	—	—	—	—
Differ from category (+/-)	-0.9	—	—	—	—	—	—	—	—	—

PER SHARE DATA

	1994	1993	1992	1991	1990	1989	1988	1987	1986	1985
Dividends, Net Income ($)	0.57	—	—	—	—	—	—	—	—	—
Distrib'ns, Cap Gain ($)	0.00	—	—	—	—	—	—	—	—	—
Net Asset Value ($)	9.06	—	—	—	—	—	—	—	—	—
Expense Ratio (%)	0.31	—	—	—	—	—	—	—	—	—
Net Income to Assets (%)	6.08	—	—	—	—	—	—	—	—	—
Portfolio Turnover (%)	na	—	—	—	—	—	—	—	—	—
Total Assets (Millions $)	109	—	—	—	—	—	—	—	—	—

PORTFOLIO (as of 5/31/94)

Portfolio Manager: committee

Investm't Category: Mortgage-Backed Bond

Cap Gain	Asset Allocation
Cap & Income	Fund of Funds
✔ Income	Index
	Sector
✔ Domestic	Small Cap
Foreign	Socially Conscious
Country/Region	State Specific

Portfolio: stocks 0%   bonds 92%
convertibles 0%   other 0%   cash 8%

Largest Holdings: mortgage-backed 62%,
U.S. government 24%

Unrealized Net Capital Gains: -5% of portfolio value

SHAREHOLDER INFORMATION

Minimum Investment
Initial: $1,000   Subsequent: $250

Minimum IRA Investment
Initial: $250   Subsequent: $250

Maximum Fees
Load: none   12b-1: 0.25%
Other: none

Distributions
Income: monthly   Capital Gains: Dec

Exchange Options
Number Per Year: no limit   Fee: none
Telephone: yes (money market fund available)

Services
IRA, pension, auto invest, auto withdraw

AARP Capital Growth

(ACGFX)

Growth

P.O. Box 2540
Boston, MA 02208
(800) 253-2277, (617) 439-4640

PERFORMANCE
fund inception date: 11/30/84

	3yr Annual	5yr Annual	10yr Annual	Bull	Bear
Return (%)	2.9	5.2	12.6	89.5	-11.4
Differ from Category (+/-)	-4.8 low	-4.4 low	-0.3 av	-2.6 av	-4.8 low

Total Risk	Standard Deviation	Category Risk	Risk Index	Beta
abv av	11.6%	high	1.2	1.1

	1994	1993	1992	1991	1990	1989	1988	1987	1986	1985
Return (%)	-10.0	15.8	4.7	40.5	-15.7	33.4	27.3	0.2	15.8	29.4
Differ from category (+/-) . .	-9.4	2.4	-6.9	4.8	-10.0	7.3	9.3	-1.6	1.2	0.2

PER SHARE DATA

	1994	1993	1992	1991	1990	1989	1988	1987	1986	1985
Dividends, Net Income ($) .	0.01	0.05	0.14	0.23	0.59	0.19	0.09	0.15	0.19	0.09
Distrib'ns, Cap Gain ($) . . .	0.64	2.90	1.21	0.94	1.79	1.93	0.42	1.23	0.91	0.19
Net Asset Value ($)	30.15	34.24	32.09	31.94	23.57	30.83	24.72	19.84	21.19	19.21
Expense Ratio (%).	0.97	1.05	1.13	1.17	1.11	1.16	1.23	1.24	1.44	1.50
Net Income to Assets (%). .	0.02	0.22	0.61	0.90	2.00	0.89	0.37	0.62	1.27	1.95
Portfolio Turnover (%).	79	100	89	100	83	64	45	54	46	41
Total Assets (Millions $) . . .	631	662	424	242	160	180	91	116	55	20

PORTFOLIO (as of 9/30/94)

Portfolio Manager: J. Cox - 1984, S. Aronoff - 1989, W. Gadsden - 1989

Investm't Category: Growth

✔ Cap Gain	Asset Allocation
Cap & Income	Fund of Funds
Income	Index
	Sector
✔ Domestic	Small Cap
✔ Foreign	Socially Conscious
Country/Region	State Specific

Portfolio: stocks 92%   bonds 0%
convertibles 2%   other 0%   cash 6%

Largest Holdings: cable television 12%, telephone/communications 8%

Unrealized Net Capital Gains: 2% of portfolio value

SHAREHOLDER INFORMATION

Minimum Investment
Initial: $500   Subsequent: $0

Minimum IRA Investment
Initial: $250   Subsequent: $0

Maximum Fees
Load: none   12b-1: none
Other: none

Distributions
Income: Dec   Capital Gains: Dec

Exchange Options
Number Per Year: 8   Fee: none
Telephone: yes (money market fund available)

Services
IRA, pension, auto invest, auto withdraw

62   *Guide to Low-Load Mutual Funds*

AARP GNMA & US
Treasury (AGNMX)

Mortgage-Backed Bond

P.O. Box 2540
Boston, MA 02208
(800) 253-2277, (617) 439-4640

PERFORMANCE   fund inception date: 11/30/84

	3yr Annual	5yr Annual	10yr Annual	Bull	Bear
Return (%)	3.5	6.8	na	36.3	-4.0
Differ from Category (+/-)	0.4 av	-0.1 blw av	na	-1.7 blw av	0.4 av

Total Risk	Standard Deviation	Category Risk	Risk Index	Avg Mat
low	3.0%	blw av	0.9	6.6 yrs

	1994	1993	1992	1991	1990	1989	1988	1987	1986	1985
Return (%).............	-1.6	5.9	6.5	14.3	9.7	11.6	7.0	1.9	11.4	—
Differ from category (+/-) ..	1.2	-0.9	0.4	-0.1	0.0	-0.9	-0.1	0.1	0.2	—

PER SHARE DATA

	1994	1993	1992	1991	1990	1989	1988	1987	1986	1985
Dividends, Net Income ($).	0.94	1.09	1.21	1.25	1.30	1.30	1.36	1.34	1.48	—
Distrib'ns, Cap Gain ($) ...	0.00	0.00	0.00	0.00	0.00	0.00	0.00	0.00	0.01	—
Net Asset Value ($)	14.56	15.77	15.93	16.13	15.28	15.18	14.82	15.14	16.19	—
Expense Ratio (%)	0.66	0.70	0.72	0.74	0.79	0.79	0.81	0.88	0.90	—
Net Income to Assets (%) .	6.09	7.15	7.69	8.23	8.71	8.76	9.09	8.76	9.49	—
Portfolio Turnover (%)	114	105	74	87	61	48	85	51	61	—
Total Assets (Millions $)..	5,248	6,641	5,231	3,310	2,582	2,518	2,838	2,828	1,905	—

PORTFOLIO (as of 9/30/94)

Portfolio Manager: David H. Glen - 1985,
Robert E. Pruyne - 1984

Investm't Category: Mortgage-Backed Bond
Cap Gain	Asset Allocation
Cap & Income	Fund of Funds
✔ Income	Index
	Sector
✔ Domestic	Small Cap
Foreign	Socially Conscious
Country/Region	State Specific

Portfolio: stocks 0%   bonds 71%
convertibles 0%   other 0%   cash 29%

Largest Holdings: mortgage-backed 71%

Unrealized Net Capital Gains: -1% of portfolio value

SHAREHOLDER INFORMATION

Minimum Investment
Initial: $500   Subsequent: $0

Minimum IRA Investment
Initial: $250   Subsequent: $0

Maximum Fees
Load: none   12b-1: none
Other: none

Distributions
Income: monthly   Capital Gains: Dec

Exchange Options
Number Per Year: 8   Fee: none
Telephone: yes (money market fund available)

Services
IRA, pension, auto invest, auto withdraw

AARP Growth & Income
(AGIFX)
Growth & Income

P.O. Box 2540
Boston, MA 02208
(800) 253-2277, (617) 439-4640

PERFORMANCE

fund inception date: 11/30/84

	3yr Annual	5yr Annual	10yr Annual	Bull	Bear
Return (%)	9.1	10.0	13.5	79.9	-3.8
Differ from Category (+/-)	2.0 abv av	2.1 high	1.8 abv av	4.1 av	2.5 high

Total Risk	Standard Deviation	Category Risk	Risk Index	Beta
av	7.7%	blw av	0.9	0.8

	1994	1993	1992	1991	1990	1989	1988	1987	1986	1985
Return (%)	3.0	15.6	9.2	26.4	-2.0	26.6	10.9	0.8	19.5	30.2
Differ from category (+/-) ...	4.4	2.4	-1.0	-1.2	4.0	5.2	-6.1	0.2	3.7	4.5

PER SHARE DATA

	1994	1993	1992	1991	1990	1989	1988	1987	1986	1985
Dividends, Net Income ($) .	0.97	0.84	0.92	1.01	1.22	1.06	1.03	0.95	0.70	0.32
Distrib'ns, Cap Gain ($) ...	1.23	0.21	0.30	0.48	0.13	0.00	0.00	0.77	0.88	0.09
Net Asset Value ($)	31.74	32.94	29.41	28.08	23.45	25.36	20.90	19.79	21.28	19.18
Expense Ratio (%)........	0.76	0.84	0.91	0.96	1.03	1.04	1.06	1.08	1.21	1.50
Net Income to Assets (%)..	3.00	3.08	3.84	4.61	4.76	4.19	4.52	3.81	4.55	5.62
Portfolio Turnover (%).....	31	17	36	54	58	55	61	43	37	12
Total Assets (Millions $) ..	2,298	1,713	748	392	248	236	228	358	99	26

PORTFOLIO (as of 9/30/94)

Portfolio Manager: B. Thorndik - 1984, R. Hoffman - 1990, K. Millard - 1991

Investm't Category: Growth & Income
Cap Gain	Asset Allocation
✔ Cap & Income	Fund of Funds
Income	Index
	Sector
✔ Domestic	Small Cap
✔ Foreign	Socially Conscious
Country/Region	State Specific

Portfolio: stocks 81%   bonds 0%
convertibles 9%   other 0%   cash 10%

Largest Holdings: pharmaceuticals 11%, banks 6%

Unrealized Net Capital Gains: 10% of portfolio value

SHAREHOLDER INFORMATION

Minimum Investment
Initial: $500   Subsequent: $0

Minimum IRA Investment
Initial: $250   Subsequent: $0

Maximum Fees
Load: none   12b-1: none
Other: none

Distributions
Income: quarterly   Capital Gains: Dec

Exchange Options
Number Per Year: 8   Fee: none
Telephone: yes (money market fund available)

Services
IRA, pension, auto invest, auto withdraw

AARP High Quality Bond

(AGBFX)

General Bond

P.O. Box 2540
Boston, MA 02208
(800) 253-2277, (617) 439-4640

PERFORMANCE

fund inception date: 1/1/85

	3yr Annual	5yr Annual	10yr Annual	Bull	Bear
Return (%)	4.0	6.9	8.2	45.8	-6.6
Differ from Category (+/-)	-0.3 blw av	0.0 av	-0.7 low	4.8 abv av	-2.8 low

Total Risk	Standard Deviation	Category Risk	Risk Index	Avg Mat
low	4.8%	high	1.2	12.2 yrs

	1994	1993	1992	1991	1990	1989	1988	1987	1986	1985
Return (%)	-4.4	10.9	6.2	15.4	7.5	12.2	8.0	1.1	11.6	15.7
Differ from category (+/-)	-2.4	1.7	-0.4	0.8	0.3	0.8	0.6	-1.1	-2.6	-3.7

PER SHARE DATA

	1994	1993	1992	1991	1990	1989	1988	1987	1986	1985
Dividends, Net Income ($)	0.86	0.92	1.01	1.07	1.17	1.22	1.25	1.35	1.34	1.42
Distrib'ns, Cap Gain ($)	0.00	0.38	0.18	0.00	0.00	0.00	0.00	0.00	0.23	0.05
Net Asset Value ($)	14.92	16.51	16.07	16.29	15.12	15.20	14.68	14.77	15.96	15.77
Expense Ratio (%)	0.95	1.01	1.13	1.17	1.14	1.16	1.17	1.18	1.30	1.50
Net Income to Assets (%)	5.31	5.64	6.40	7.26	7.86	8.33	8.55	7.81	8.86	9.86
Portfolio Turnover (%)	63	100	63	90	47	58	24	193	62	53
Total Assets (Millions $)	529	623	384	201	151	129	124	108	88	45

PORTFOLIO (as of 9/30/94)

Portfolio Manager: S. Wohler - 1990, William Hutchinson - 1987

Investm't Category: General Bond

Cap Gain	Asset Allocation
Cap & Income	Fund of Funds
✔ Income	Index
	Sector
✔ Domestic	Small Cap
Foreign	Socially Conscious
Country/Region	State Specific

Portfolio: stocks 0%   bonds 79%
convertibles 0%   other 0%   cash 21%

Largest Holdings: U.S. government and agencies 28%, mortgage-backed 21%

Unrealized Net Capital Gains: -3% of portfolio value

SHAREHOLDER INFORMATION

Minimum Investment
Initial: $500   Subsequent: $0

Minimum IRA Investment
Initial: $250   Subsequent: $0

Maximum Fees
Load: none   12b-1: none
Other: none

Distributions
Income: monthly   Capital Gains: Dec

Exchange Options
Number Per Year: 8   Fee: none
Telephone: yes (money market fund available)

Services
IRA, pension, auto invest, auto withdraw

AARP Insured Tax Free General Bond (AITGX)

P.O. Box 2540
Boston, MA 02208
(800) 253-2277, (617) 439-4640

Tax-Exempt Bond

	3yr Annual	5yr Annual	10yr Annual	Bull	Bear
Return (%)	4.6	6.5	8.0	46.2	-6.3
Differ from Category (+/-)	0.1 av	0.4 av	-0.1 blw av	4.4 abv av	-1.1 blw av

Total Risk	Standard Deviation	Category Risk	Risk Index	Avg Mat
blw av	6.7%	abv av	1.1	12.3 yrs

	1994	1993	1992	1991	1990	1989	1988	1987	1986	1985
Return (%)	-6.2	12.6	8.5	12.2	6.3	10.7	12.2	-1.4	16.8	10.2
Differ from category (+/-)	-1.0	0.9	0.2	0.9	0.0	1.7	2.0	-0.1	0.4	-7.2

PER SHARE DATA

	1994	1993	1992	1991	1990	1989	1988	1987	1986	1985
Dividends, Net Income ($)	0.86	0.88	0.93	0.98	1.04	1.07	1.08	1.08	1.04	0.86
Distrib'ns, Cap Gain ($)	0.00	0.40	0.43	0.17	0.00	0.25	0.00	0.00	0.20	0.06
Net Asset Value ($)	16.54	18.54	17.62	17.52	16.68	16.70	16.31	15.55	16.89	15.57
Expense Ratio (%)	0.68	0.72	0.74	0.77	0.80	0.84	0.92	1.00	1.13	1.29
Net Income to Assets (%)	4.80	4.90	5.31	5.92	6.29	6.52	6.95	6.58	6.40	6.11
Portfolio Turnover (%)	38	47	62	32	48	149	164	135	135	90
Total Assets (Millions $)	1,748	2,123	1,488	1,067	771	527	313	238	129	62

PORTFOLIO (as of 9/30/94)

Portfolio Manager: D. Carleton - 1988, P. Condon - 1989

Investm't Category: Tax-Exempt Bond

Cap Gain	Asset Allocation
Cap & Income	Fund of Funds
✔ Income	Index
	Sector
✔ Domestic	Small Cap
Foreign	Socially Conscious
Country/Region	State Specific

Portfolio: stocks 0%   bonds 100%
convertibles 0%   other 0%   cash 0%

Largest Holdings: general obligation 24%

Unrealized Net Capital Gains: -1% of portfolio value

SHAREHOLDER INFORMATION

Minimum Investment
Initial: $500   Subsequent: $0

Minimum IRA Investment
Initial: na   Subsequent: na

Maximum Fees
Load: none   12b-1: none
Other: none

Distributions
Income: monthly   Capital Gains: Dec

Exchange Options
Number Per Year: 8   Fee: none
Telephone: yes (money market fund available)

Services
auto invest, auto withdraw

Acorn (ACRNX)
Growth

227 West Monroe
Chicago, IL 60606
(800) 922-6769

this fund is closed to new investors

fund inception date: 6/10/70

PERFORMANCE

	3yr Annual	5yr Annual	10yr Annual	Bull	Bear
Return (%)	15.0	13.0	16.5	155.3	-9.4
Differ from Category (+/-)	7.3 high	3.4 high	3.6 high	63.2 high	-2.8 blw av

Total Risk	Standard Deviation	Category Risk	Risk Index	Beta
abv av	11.6%	high	1.2	0.9

	1994	1993	1992	1991	1990	1989	1988	1987	1986	1985
Return (%)	-7.4	32.3	24.2	47.3	-17.5	24.9	24.6	4.4	16.8	31.5
Differ from category (+/-)	-6.8	18.9	12.6	11.6	-11.8	-1.2	6.6	2.6	2.2	2.3

PER SHARE DATA

	1994	1993	1992	1991	1990	1989	1988	1987	1986	1985
Dividends, Net Income ($)	0.11	0.06	0.14	0.10	0.13	0.11	0.16	0.15	0.10	0.10
Distrib'ns, Cap Gain ($)	0.56	0.59	0.35	0.15	0.44	0.36	0.64	1.08	1.21	0.37
Net Asset Value ($)	12.24	13.95	11.06	9.32	6.51	8.58	7.27	6.48	7.45	7.56
Expense Ratio (%)	0.63	0.65	0.67	0.72	0.82	0.73	0.80	0.82	0.79	0.78
Net Income to Assets (%)	0.58	0.30	0.72	1.30	1.60	1.59	1.52	1.85	1.71	1.73
Portfolio Turnover (%)	19	20	25	25	36	26	36	52	34	32
Total Assets (Millions $)	1,982	2,044	1,450	1,150	767	855	563	418	414	317

PORTFOLIO (as of 6/30/94)

Portfolio Manager: Ralph Wanger - 1970

Investm't Category: Growth

✔ Cap Gain	Asset Allocation
Cap & Income	Fund of Funds
Income	Index
	Sector
✔ Domestic	✔ Small Cap
✔ Foreign	Socially Conscious
Country/Region	State Specific

Portfolio: stocks 93% bonds 0%
convertibles 0% other 0% cash 7%

Largest Holdings: broadcasting & CATV 6%, gaming equipment 4%

Unrealized Net Capital Gains: 35% of portfolio value

SHAREHOLDER INFORMATION

Minimum Investment
Initial: $1,000   Subsequent: $100

Minimum IRA Investment
Initial: $200   Subsequent: $100

Maximum Fees
Load: 2.00% redemption 12b-1: none
Other: redemption fee applies for 60 days

Distributions
Income: Jul, Dec   Capital Gains: Jul, Dec

Exchange Options
Number Per Year: no limit   Fee: none
Telephone: yes (money market fund available)

Services
IRA, auto exchange, auto invest, auto withdraw

Acorn Int'l (ACINX)

International Stock

227 West Monroe
Chicago, IL 60606
(800) 922-6769

this fund is closed to new investors

PERFORMANCE

fund inception date: 9/23/92

	3yr Annual	5yr Annual	10yr Annual	Bull	Bear
Return (%)	na	na	na	na	-6.4
Differ from Category (+/-)	na	na	na	na	0.6 av

Total Risk	Standard Deviation	Category Risk	Risk Index	Beta
na	na	na	na	na

	1994	1993	1992	1991	1990	1989	1988	1987	1986	1985
Return (%)	-3.7	49.1	—	—	—	—	—	—	—	—
Differ from category (+/-) . .	-0.7	10.5	—	—	—	—	—	—	—	—

PER SHARE DATA

	1994	1993	1992	1991	1990	1989	1988	1987	1986	1985
Dividends, Net Income ($) .	0.09	0.00	—	—	—	—	—	—	—	—
Distrib'ns, Cap Gain ($) . . .	0.01	0.00	—	—	—	—	—	—	—	—
Net Asset Value ($)	15.24	15.94	—	—	—	—	—	—	—	—
Expense Ratio (%).	1.20	1.20	—	—	—	—	—	—	—	—
Net Income to Assets (%). .	0.60	0.10	—	—	—	—	—	—	—	—
Portfolio Turnover (%).	20	19	—	—	—	—	—	—	—	—
Total Assets (Millions $) . .	1,364	954	—	—	—	—	—	—	—	—

PORTFOLIO (as of 6/30/94)

Portfolio Manager: Ralph Wanger - 1992

Investm't Category: International Stock

✔ Cap Gain
    Cap & Income
    Income
    Domestic
✔ Foreign
    Country/Region

    Asset Allocation
    Fund of Funds
    Index
    Sector
✔ Small Cap
    Socially Conscious
    State Specific

Portfolio: stocks 83% bonds 0%
convertibles 0% other 0% cash 17%

Largest Holdings: Japan 11%, United Kingdom 5%

Unrealized Net Capital Gains: 8% of portfolio value

SHAREHOLDER INFORMATION

Minimum Investment
Initial: $1,000   Subsequent: $100

Minimum IRA Investment
Initial: $200   Subsequent: $100

Maximum Fees
Load: 2.00% redemption   12b-1: none
Other: redemption fee applies for 60 days

Distributions
Income: Jul, Dec   Capital Gains: Jul, Dec

Exchange Options
Number Per Year: no limit   Fee: none
Telephone: yes (money market fund available)

Services
IRA, pension, auto exchange, auto invest, auto withdraw

Amana Income (AMANX)

Growth & Income

1300 N. State Street
Bellingham, WA 98225
(800) 728-8762

PERFORMANCE

fund inception date: 6/23/86

	3yr Annual	5yr Annual	10yr Annual	Bull	Bear
Return (%)	2.0	4.9	na	51.1	-11.0
Differ from Category (+/-)	-5.1 low	-3.0 low	na	-24.7 low	-4.7 low

Total Risk	Standard Deviation	Category Risk	Risk Index	Beta
av	7.8%	blw av	0.9	0.9

	1994	1993	1992	1991	1990	1989	1988	1987	1986	1985
Return (%).	-6.4	11.6	1.8	23.6	-3.3	18.3	13.4	-7.5	—	—
Differ from category (+/-) . .	-5.0	-1.6	-8.4	-4.0	2.7	-3.1	-3.6	-8.1	—	—

PER SHARE DATA

	1994	1993	1992	1991	1990	1989	1988	1987	1986	1985
Dividends, Net Income ($).	0.35	0.30	0.32	0.29	0.42	0.42	0.36	0.36	—	—
Distrib'ns, Cap Gain ($) . . .	0.19	0.14	0.00	0.00	0.00	0.00	0.00	0.51	—	—
Net Asset Value ($)	11.81	13.19	12.21	12.30	10.19	10.98	9.65	8.84	—	—
Expense Ratio (%)	1.58	1.58	1.58	1.66	1.76	1.88	2.07	1.81	—	—
Net Income to Assets (%) .	2.22	2.65	2.75	3.73	3.67	3.85	3.17	3.53	—	—
Portfolio Turnover (%)	21	28	18	28	18	70	65	54	—	—
Total Assets (Millions $).	9	10	6	5	4	3	3	3	—	—

PORTFOLIO (as of 5/31/94)

Portfolio Manager: Nicholas Kaiser - 1986

Investm't Category: Growth & Income

Cap Gain	Asset Allocation
✔ Cap & Income	Fund of Funds
Income	Index
	Sector
✔ Domestic	Small Cap
✔ Foreign	✔ Socially Conscious
Country/Region	State Specific

Portfolio: stocks 100% bonds 0%
convertibles 0%   other 0%   cash 0%

Largest Holdings: telecommunication services 11%, electric utilities 10%

Unrealized Net Capital Gains: 7% of portfolio value

SHAREHOLDER INFORMATION

Minimum Investment
Initial: $100   Subsequent: $25

Minimum IRA Investment
Initial: $25   Subsequent: $25

Maximum Fees
Load: none   12b-1: none
Other: none

Distributions
Income: May, Dec   Capital Gains: Dec

Exchange Options
Number Per Year: no limit   Fee: none
Telephone: yes (money market fund available)

Services
IRA, auto exchange, auto invest, auto withdraw

America's Utility (AMUTX)
Growth & Income

901 East Byrd Street
P.O. Box 26501
Richmond, VA 23261
(800) 487-3863, (804) 649-1315

PERFORMANCE

fund inception date: 5/5/92

	3yr Annual	5yr Annual	10yr Annual	Bull	Bear
Return (%)	na	na	na	na	-13.2
Differ from Category (+/-)	na	na	na	na	-6.9 low

Total Risk	Standard Deviation	Category Risk	Risk Index	Beta
na	na	na	na	na

	1994	1993	1992	1991	1990	1989	1988	1987	1986	1985
Return (%)	-13.0	13.3	—	—	—	—	—	—	—	—
Differ from category (+/-) .	-11.6	0.1	—	—	—	—	—	—	—	—

PER SHARE DATA

	1994	1993	1992	1991	1990	1989	1988	1987	1986	1985
Dividends, Net Income ($) .	0.96	0.92	—	—	—	—	—	—	—	—
Distrib'ns, Cap Gain ($) . . .	0.00	0.40	—	—	—	—	—	—	—	—
Net Asset Value ($)	19.50	23.54	—	—	—	—	—	—	—	—
Expense Ratio (%).	1.21	1.21	—	—	—	—	—	—	—	—
Net Income to Assets (%). .	4.60	4.19	—	—	—	—	—	—	—	—
Portfolio Turnover (%)	12	21	—	—	—	—	—	—	—	—
Total Assets (Millions $) . . .	123	131	—	—	—	—	—	—	—	—

PORTFOLIO (as of 6/30/94)

Portfolio Manager: Julie Cannell - 1992

Investm't Category: Growth & Income

Cap Gain	Asset Allocation
✔ Cap & Income	Fund of Funds
Income	Index
	✔ Sector
✔ Domestic	Small Cap
Foreign	Socially Conscious
Country/Region	State Specific

Portfolio: stocks 83%   bonds 0%
convertibles 0%   other 0%   cash 17%

Largest Holdings: public utility—electric 63%, telecommunications 19%

Unrealized Net Capital Gains: -15% of portfolio value

SHAREHOLDER INFORMATION

Minimum Investment
Initial: $1,000   Subsequent: $250

Minimum IRA Investment
Initial: $20   Subsequent: $20

Maximum Fees
Load: none   12b-1: none
Other: none

Distributions
Income: quarterly   Capital Gains: Dec

Exchange Options
Number Per Year: none   Fee:
Telephone:

Services
IRA, pension

American Heritage
(AHERX)
Aggressive Growth

1370 Avenue of the Americas
31st Floor
New York, NY 10019
(800) 828-5050, (212) 397-3900

PERFORMANCE   fund inception date: 6/1/81

	3yr Annual	5yr Annual	10yr Annual	Bull	Bear
Return (%)	2.9	8.2	na	220.3	-28.2
Differ from Category (+/-)	-6.0 low	-4.3 low	na	87.1 high	-17.4 low

Total Risk	Standard Deviation	Category Risk	Risk Index	Beta
high	18.1%	high	1.2	1.0

	1994	1993	1992	1991	1990	1989	1988	1987	1986	1985
Return (%).............	-35.3	41.3	19.2	96.5	-30.7	-2.8	1.9	-19.8	—	—
Differ from category (+/-) .	-34.6	21.8	8.2	44.4	-24.5	-29.6	-13.3	-17.6	—	—

PER SHARE DATA

	1994	1993	1992	1991	1990	1989	1988	1987	1986	1985
Dividends, Net Income ($).	0.14	0.07	0.08	0.16	0.00	0.00	0.00	0.09	—	—
Distrib'ns, Cap Gain ($) ...	0.00	0.00	0.00	0.22	0.00	0.00	0.00	0.00	—	—
Net Asset Value ($)	0.85	1.53	1.13	1.02	0.72	1.04	1.07	1.05	—	—
Expense Ratio (%)	2.41	2.10	2.20	6.79	11.04	13.02	11.90	11.80	—	—
Net Income to Assets (%) .	3.40	-0.46	21.50	-3.72	5.80	-8.00	-8.70	-9.30	—	—
Portfolio Turnover (%)	434	278	776	607	76	81	189	287	—	—
Total Assets (Millions $).....	57	150	27	2	1	1	1	1	—	—

PORTFOLIO (as of 5/31/94)

Portfolio Manager: Heiko Thieme - 1990

Investm't Category: Aggressive Growth

✔ Cap Gain	Asset Allocation
Cap & Income	Fund of Funds
Income	Index
	Sector
✔ Domestic	Small Cap
Foreign	Socially Conscious
Country/Region	State Specific

Portfolio: stocks 98% bonds 1%
convertibles 1% other 0% cash 0%

Largest Holdings: biotechnology 14%, consumer products 10%

Unrealized Net Capital Gains: -14% of portfolio value

SHAREHOLDER INFORMATION

Minimum Investment
Initial: $5,000   Subsequent: $1,000

Minimum IRA Investment
Initial: $2,000   Subsequent: $0

Maximum Fees
Load: none   12b-1: none
Other: none

Distributions
Income: Dec   Capital Gains: Dec

Exchange Options
Number Per Year: none   Fee:
Telephone:

Services
IRA, pension, auto withdraw

American Pension Investors—Growth (APITX)

Growth

P.O. Box 2529
2303 Yorktown Ave.
Lynchburg, VA 24501
(800) 544-6060, (804) 846-1361

PERFORMANCE

fund inception date: 6/1/85

	3yr Annual	5yr Annual	10yr Annual	Bull	Bear
Return (%)	5.2	8.2	na	113.6	-10.9
Differ from Category (+/-)	-2.5 blw av	-1.4 blw av	na	21.5 high	-4.3 low

Total Risk	Standard Deviation	Category Risk	Risk Index	Beta
abv av	11.3%	abv av	1.2	1.0

	1994	1993	1992	1991	1990	1989	1988	1987	1986	1985
Return (%)	-3.4	18.2	1.9	45.9	-12.6	15.6	25.9	-7.6	13.1	—
Differ from category (+/-) . .	-2.8	4.8	-9.7	10.2	-6.9	-10.5	7.9	-9.4	-1.5	—

PER SHARE DATA

	1994	1993	1992	1991	1990	1989	1988	1987	1986	1985
Dividends, Net Income ($) .	0.00	0.00	0.00	0.00	0.00	0.08	0.15	0.06	0.56	—
Distrib'ns, Cap Gain ($) . . .	1.11	0.58	0.38	0.95	0.00	2.05	0.00	1.88	0.65	—
Net Asset Value ($)	11.28	12.83	11.34	11.49	8.53	9.76	10.25	8.26	10.74	—
Expense Ratio (%).	2.24	2.05	1.97	2.38	2.60	2.66	2.74	2.41	2.59	—
Net Income to Assets (%).	-1.75	-1.56	-1.24	0.02	0.36	0.78	0.82	1.11	2.00	—
Portfolio Turnover (%)	90	157	99	206	118	163	165	190	169	—
Total Assets (Millions $)	50	49	40	30	32	32	27	19	4	—

PORTFOLIO (as of 5/31/94)

Portfolio Manager: David Basten - 1985

Investm't Category: Growth
- ✔ Cap Gain
- Cap & Income
- Income
- ✔ Domestic
- ✔ Foreign
- Country/Region
- Asset Allocation
- ✔ Fund of Funds
- Index
- Sector
- Small Cap
- Socially Conscious
- State Specific

Portfolio: stocks 100% bonds 0%
convertibles 0% other 0% cash 0%

Largest Holdings: small company growth funds 28%, capital appreciation funds 27%

Unrealized Net Capital Gains: 5% of portfolio value

SHAREHOLDER INFORMATION

Minimum Investment
Initial: $500   Subsequent: $100

Minimum IRA Investment
Initial: $500   Subsequent: $100

Maximum Fees
Load: none   12b-1: 1.00%
Other: none

Distributions
Income: Dec   Capital Gains: Dec

Exchange Options
Number Per Year: no limit   Fee: none
Telephone: none

Services
IRA, pension, auto invest, auto withdraw

AmSouth Bond (AOBDX)

General Bond

1900 East Dublin-Granville Rd.
Columbus, OH 43229
(800) 451-8382

PERFORMANCE

fund inception date: 12/1/88

	3yr Annual	5yr Annual	10yr Annual	Bull	Bear
Return (%)	4.3	6.9	na	43.8	-4.6
Differ from Category (+/-)	0.0 av	0.0 av	na	2.8 abv av	-0.8 blw av

Total Risk	Standard Deviation	Category Risk	Risk Index	Avg Mat
low	4.3%	abv av	1.1	6.4 yrs

	1994	1993	1992	1991	1990	1989	1988	1987	1986	1985
Return (%)	-3.2	9.8	6.8	15.3	6.9	12.6	—	—	—	—
Differ from category (+/-)	-1.2	0.6	0.2	0.7	-0.3	1.2	—	—	—	—

PER SHARE DATA

	1994	1993	1992	1991	1990	1989	1988	1987	1986	1985
Dividends, Net Income ($)	0.70	0.69	0.72	0.74	0.78	0.72	—	—	—	—
Distrib'ns, Cap Gain ($)	0.04	0.03	0.33	0.05	0.01	0.03	—	—	—	—
Net Asset Value ($)	10.08	11.17	10.84	11.11	10.37	10.48	—	—	—	—
Expense Ratio (%)	0.78	0.78	0.82	0.93	0.84	1.10	—	—	—	—
Net Income to Assets (%)	6.31	6.37	6.94	7.26	7.82	7.47	—	—	—	—
Portfolio Turnover (%)	30	14	240	181	53	na	—	—	—	—
Total Assets (Millions $)	90	67	60	26	17	4	—	—	—	—

PORTFOLIO (as of 7/31/94)

Portfolio Manager: not specified

Investm't Category: General Bond

Cap Gain	Asset Allocation
Cap & Income	Fund of Funds
✔ Income	Index
	Sector
✔ Domestic	Small Cap
✔ Foreign	Socially Conscious
Country/Region	State Specific

Portfolio: stocks 0%　bonds 97%
convertibles 0%　other 0%　cash 3%

Largest Holdings: corporate 46%, U.S. government 41%

Unrealized Net Capital Gains: -1% of portfolio value

SHAREHOLDER INFORMATION

Minimum Investment
Initial: $1,000　　Subsequent: $0

Minimum IRA Investment
Initial: $1,000　　Subsequent: $0

Maximum Fees
Load: 3.00% front　　12b-1: none
Other: none

Distributions
Income: monthly　　Capital Gains: Dec

Exchange Options
Number Per Year: no limit　　Fee: none
Telephone: yes (money market fund available)

Services
IRA, pension, auto invest

AmSouth Limited Maturity (AOLMX)

General Bond

1900 East Dublin-Granville Rd.
Columbus, OH 43229
(800) 451-8382

PERFORMANCE

	3yr Annual	5yr Annual	10yr Annual	Bull	Bear
Return (%)	3.7	6.2	na	32.2	-3.1
Differ from Category (+/-)	-0.6 blw av	-0.7 low	na	-8.8 low	0.7 abv av

Total Risk	Standard Deviation	Category Risk	Risk Index	Avg Mat
low	2.5%	blw av	0.6	2.9 yrs

	1994	1993	1992	1991	1990	1989	1988	1987	1986	1985
Return (%)	-1.8	7.1	6.0	11.9	8.5	—	—	—	—	—
Differ from category (+/-)	0.2	-2.1	-0.6	-2.7	1.3	—	—	—	—	—

PER SHARE DATA

	1994	1993	1992	1991	1990	1989	1988	1987	1986	1985
Dividends, Net Income ($)	0.55	0.56	0.67	0.73	0.77	—	—	—	—	—
Distrib'ns, Cap Gain ($)	0.00	0.13	0.08	0.08	0.00	—	—	—	—	—
Net Asset Value ($)	9.89	10.63	10.57	10.69	10.31	—	—	—	—	—
Expense Ratio (%)	0.79	0.69	0.68	0.85	1.02	—	—	—	—	—
Net Income to Assets (%)	5.05	5.67	6.78	7.19	7.23	—	—	—	—	—
Portfolio Turnover (%)	48	141	35	85	119	—	—	—	—	—
Total Assets (Millions $)	47	59	38	11	5	—	—	—	—	—

PORTFOLIO (as of 7/31/94)

Portfolio Manager: not specified

Investm't Category: General Bond

Cap Gain	Asset Allocation
Cap & Income	Fund of Funds
✔ Income	Index
	Sector
✔ Domestic	Small Cap
✔ Foreign	Socially Conscious
Country/Region	State Specific

Portfolio: stocks 0% bonds 98%
convertibles 0% other 0% cash 2%

Largest Holdings: corporate 93%, U.S. government 4%

Unrealized Net Capital Gains: -3% of portfolio value

SHAREHOLDER INFORMATION

Minimum Investment
Initial: $1,000   Subsequent: $0

Minimum IRA Investment
Initial: $1,000   Subsequent: $0

Maximum Fees
Load: 3.00% front   12b-1: none
Other: none

Distributions
Income: monthly   Capital Gains: Dec

Exchange Options
Number Per Year: no limit   Fee: none
Telephone: yes (money market fund available)

Services
IRA, pension, auto invest

Analytic Optioned Equity
(ANALX)
Growth & Income

2222 Martin St.
Suite 230
Irvine, CA 92715
(800) 374-2633, (714) 833-0294

	3yr Annual	5yr Annual	10yr Annual	Bull	Bear
Return (%)	5.1	5.9	9.3	42.3	-3.5
Differ from Category (+/-)	-2.0 blw av	-2.0 low	-2.4 low	-33.5 low	2.8 high

Total Risk	Standard Deviation	Category Risk	Risk Index	Beta
low	4.8%	low	0.6	0.6

	1994	1993	1992	1991	1990	1989	1988	1987	1986	1985
Return (%)	2.5	6.7	6.1	13.3	1.4	17.7	15.6	4.2	10.6	16.5
Differ from category (+/-) . .	3.9	-6.5	-4.1	-14.3	7.4	-3.7	-1.4	3.6	-5.2	-9.2

PER SHARE DATA

	1994	1993	1992	1991	1990	1989	1988	1987	1986	1985
Dividends, Net Income ($).	0.31	0.33	0.29	0.40	0.48	0.51	0.42	0.46	0.45	0.48
Distrib'ns, Cap Gain ($) . . .	0.82	0.49	0.78	0.80	0.78	0.66	0.66	2.48	2.20	1.20
Net Asset Value ($)	11.12	11.96	11.97	12.29	11.92	13.00	12.06	11.38	13.70	14.85
Expense Ratio (%)	1.01	1.07	1.02	1.10	1.11	1.09	1.13	1.17	1.18	1.23
Net Income to Assets (%) .	4.81	3.51	2.33	3.05	3.68	3.74	3.44	2.68	2.90	3.30
Portfolio Turnover (%)	44	36	82	76	72	61	66	84	64	54
Total Assets (Millions $).	48	77	92	100	106	107	102	75	76	85

PORTFOLIO (as of 6/30/94)

Portfolio Manager: Charles Dobson - 1978

Investm't Category: Growth & Income

Cap Gain	Asset Allocation
✔ Cap & Income	Fund of Funds
Income	Index
	Sector
✔ Domestic	Small Cap
Foreign	Socially Conscious
Country/Region	State Specific

Portfolio: stocks 91% bonds 7%
convertibles 0% other 2% cash 0%

Largest Holdings: telecommunication utilities 10%, oil/gas international 6%

Unrealized Net Capital Gains: 3% of portfolio value

SHAREHOLDER INFORMATION

Minimum Investment
Initial: $5,000   Subsequent: $0

Minimum IRA Investment
Initial: $0   Subsequent: $0

Maximum Fees
Load: none   12b-1: none
Other: none

Distributions
Income: quarterly   Capital Gains: Dec

Exchange Options
Number Per Year: no limit   Fee: none
Telephone: yes (money market fund not available)

Services
IRA, pension, auto withdraw

Aquinas Balanced (AQBLX)

Balanced

5310 Harvest Hill Road
Suite 248
Dallas, TX 75230
(214) 233-6655

	3yr Annual	5yr Annual	10yr Annual	Bull	Bear
Return (%)	na	na	na	na	-7.4
Differ from Category (+/-)	na	na	na	na	-1.7 blw av

Total Risk	Standard Deviation	Category Risk	Risk Index	Beta
na	na	na	na	na

	1994	1993	1992	1991	1990	1989	1988	1987	1986	1985
Return (%)	-3.0	—	—	—	—	—	—	—	—	—
Differ from category (+/-)	-1.1	—	—	—	—	—	—	—	—	—

PER SHARE DATA

	1994	1993	1992	1991	1990	1989	1988	1987	1986	1985
Dividends, Net Income ($)	0.26	—	—	—	—	—	—	—	—	—
Distrib'ns, Cap Gain ($)	0.00	—	—	—	—	—	—	—	—	—
Net Asset Value ($)	9.43	—	—	—	—	—	—	—	—	—
Expense Ratio (%)	1.40	—	—	—	—	—	—	—	—	—
Net Income to Assets (%)	2.71	—	—	—	—	—	—	—	—	—
Portfolio Turnover (%)	na	—	—	—	—	—	—	—	—	—
Total Assets (Millions $)	30	—	—	—	—	—	—	—	—	—

PORTFOLIO (as of 6/30/94)

Portfolio Manager: not specified

Investm't Category: Balanced

Cap Gain	Asset Allocation
✔ Cap & Income	Fund of Funds
Income	Index
	Sector
✔ Domestic	Small Cap
Foreign	Socially Conscious
Country/Region	State Specific

Portfolio: stocks 55% bonds 36%
convertibles 2% other 0% cash 7%

Largest Holdings: corporate bonds 16%, mortgage-backed bonds 10%

Unrealized Net Capital Gains: -5% of portfolio value

SHAREHOLDER INFORMATION

Minimum Investment
Initial: $1,000   Subsequent: $250

Minimum IRA Investment
Initial: $500   Subsequent: $50

Maximum Fees
Load: none   12b-1: none
Other: none

Distributions
Income: quarterly   Capital Gains: Dec

Exchange Options
Number Per Year: 4   Fee: none
Telephone: yes (money market fund not available)

Services
IRA, pension, auto invest, auto withdraw

Aquinas Equity Income
(AQEIX)
Growth & Income

5310 Harvest Hill Road
Suite 248
Dallas, TX 75230
(214) 233-6655

	3yr Annual	5yr Annual	10yr Annual	Bull	Bear
Return (%)	na	na	na	na	-5.1
Differ from Category (+/-)	na	na	na	na	1.2 abv av

Total Risk	Standard Deviation	Category Risk	Risk Index	Beta
na	na	na	na	na

	1994	1993	1992	1991	1990	1989	1988	1987	1986	1985
Return (%)	-2.9	—	—	—	—	—	—	—	—	—
Differ from category (+/-)	-1.5	—	—	—	—	—	—	—	—	—

PER SHARE DATA

	1994	1993	1992	1991	1990	1989	1988	1987	1986	1985
Dividends, Net Income ($)	0.32	—	—	—	—	—	—	—	—	—
Distrib'ns, Cap Gain ($)	0.00	—	—	—	—	—	—	—	—	—
Net Asset Value ($)	9.39	—	—	—	—	—	—	—	—	—
Expense Ratio (%)	1.39	—	—	—	—	—	—	—	—	—
Net Income to Assets (%)	3.47	—	—	—	—	—	—	—	—	—
Portfolio Turnover (%)	na	—	—	—	—	—	—	—	—	—
Total Assets (Millions $)	32	—	—	—	—	—	—	—	—	—

PORTFOLIO (as of 6/30/94)

Portfolio Manager: not available

Investm't Category: Growth & Income

Cap Gain	Asset Allocation
✔ Cap & Income	Fund of Funds
Income	Index
	Sector
✔ Domestic	Small Cap
Foreign	Socially Conscious
Country/Region	State Specific

Portfolio: stocks 96% bonds 0% convertibles 0% other 0% cash 4%

Largest Holdings: drugs 14%, telecommunications 14%

Unrealized Net Capital Gains: -6% of portfolio value

SHAREHOLDER INFORMATION

Minimum Investment
Initial: $1,000   Subsequent: $250

Minimum IRA Investment
Initial: $500   Subsequent: $50

Maximum Fees
Load: none   12b-1: none
Other: none

Distributions
Income: quarterly   Capital Gains: Dec

Exchange Options
Number Per Year: 4   Fee: none
Telephone: yes (money market fund not available)

Services
IRA, pension, auto invest, auto withdraw

Aquinas Fixed Income

(AQFIX)

General Bond

5310 Harvest Hill Road
Suite 248
Dallas, TX 75230
(214) 233-6655

PERFORMANCE
fund inception date: 1/3/94

	3yr Annual	5yr Annual	10yr Annual	Bull	Bear
Return (%)	na	na	na	na	-5.0
Differ from Category (+/-)	na	na	na	na	-1.2 blw av

Total Risk	Standard Deviation		Category Risk	Risk Index	Avg Mat
na	na		na	na	11.6 yrs

	1994	1993	1992	1991	1990	1989	1988	1987	1986	1985
Return (%)	-3.0	—	—	—	—	—	—	—	—	—
Differ from category (+/-)	-1.0	—	—	—	—	—	—	—	—	—

PER SHARE DATA

	1994	1993	1992	1991	1990	1989	1988	1987	1986	1985
Dividends, Net Income ($)	0.45	—	—	—	—	—	—	—	—	—
Distrib'ns, Cap Gain ($)	0.00	—	—	—	—	—	—	—	—	—
Net Asset Value ($)	9.24	—	—	—	—	—	—	—	—	—
Expense Ratio (%)	1.00	—	—	—	—	—	—	—	—	—
Net Income to Assets (%)	4.37	—	—	—	—	—	—	—	—	—
Portfolio Turnover (%)	na	—	—	—	—	—	—	—	—	—
Total Assets (Millions $)	28	—	—	—	—	—	—	—	—	—

PORTFOLIO (as of 6/30/94)

Portfolio Manager: not specified

Investm't Category: General Bond

Cap Gain	Asset Allocation
Cap & Income	Fund of Funds
✔ Income	Index
	Sector
✔ Domestic	Small Cap
✔ Foreign	Socially Conscious
Country/Region	State Specific

Portfolio: stocks 0%   bonds 88%
convertibles 0%   other 0%   cash 12%

Largest Holdings: corporate 37%, mortgage-backed 24%

Unrealized Net Capital Gains: -4% of portfolio value

SHAREHOLDER INFORMATION

Minimum Investment
Initial: $1,000   Subsequent: $250

Minimum IRA Investment
Initial: $500   Subsequent: $50

Maximum Fees
Load: none   12b-1: none
Other: none

Distributions
Income: monthly   Capital Gains: Dec

Exchange Options
Number Per Year: 4   Fee: none
Telephone: yes (money market fund not available)

Services
IRA, pension, auto invest, auto withdraw

Ariel Appreciation
(CAAPX)
Growth

307 North Michigan Avenue
Suite 500
Chicago, IL 60601
(800) 292-7435

fund inception date: 12/1/89

	3yr Annual	5yr Annual	10yr Annual	Bull	Bear
Return (%)	3.8	7.9	na	87.3	-5.4
Differ from Category (+/-)	-3.9 low	-1.7 blw av	na	-4.8 av	1.2 abv av

Total Risk	Standard Deviation	Category Risk	Risk Index	Beta
abv av	9.2%	av	0.9	0.8

	1994	1993	1992	1991	1990	1989	1988	1987	1986	1985
Return (%)	-8.3	7.9	13.2	33.1	-1.5	—	—	—	—	—
Differ from category (+/-)	-7.7	-5.5	1.6	-2.6	4.2	—	—	—	—	—

PER SHARE DATA

	1994	1993	1992	1991	1990	1989	1988	1987	1986	1985
Dividends, Net Income ($)	0.06	0.40	0.06	0.19	0.24	—	—	—	—	—
Distrib'ns, Cap Gain ($)	1.40	0.00	0.02	0.00	0.00	—	—	—	—	—
Net Asset Value ($)	19.51	22.89	21.60	19.15	14.53	—	—	—	—	—
Expense Ratio (%)	1.35	1.37	1.44	1.50	0.70	—	—	—	—	—
Net Income to Assets (%)	0.17	0.33	0.57	1.61	2.33	—	—	—	—	—
Portfolio Turnover (%)	12	56	na	20	4	—	—	—	—	—
Total Assets (Millions $)	128	219	146	76	23	—	—	—	—	—

PORTFOLIO (as of 9/30/94)

Portfolio Manager: Eric McKissack—1989

Investm't Category: Growth
- ✔ Cap Gain
- Cap & Income
- Income
- Asset Allocation
- Fund of Funds
- Index
- Sector
- ✔ Domestic
- Foreign
- Country/Region
- Small Cap
- Socially Conscious
- State Specific

Portfolio: stocks 100% bonds 0%
convertibles 0% other 0% cash 0%

Largest Holdings: healthcare 13%, financial services 9%

Unrealized Net Capital Gains: 13% of portfolio value

SHAREHOLDER INFORMATION

Minimum Investment
Initial: $1,000 Subsequent: $50

Minimum IRA Investment
Initial: $250 Subsequent: $50

Maximum Fees
Load: none 12b-1: 0.25%
Other: none

Distributions
Income: Dec Capital Gains: Dec

Exchange Options
Number Per Year: 5 Fee: none
Telephone: yes (money market fund available)

Services
IRA, pension, auto invest, auto withdraw

Armstrong Associates

(ARMSX)
Growth

750 N. Saint Paul
Suite 1300
Dallas, TX 75201-3250
(214) 720-9101

	3yr Annual	5yr Annual	10yr Annual	Bull	Bear
Return (%)	8.9	7.4	9.8	56.6	-9.6
Differ from Category (+/-)	1.2 abv av	-2.2 blw av	-3.1 low	-35.5 low	-3.0 low

Total Risk	Standard Deviation	Category Risk	Risk Index	Beta
abv av	9.4%	av	1.0	1.0

	1994	1993	1992	1991	1990	1989	1988	1987	1986	1985
Return (%)	5.3	15.0	6.7	18.7	-6.6	14.2	15.5	-0.4	11.5	21.1
Differ from category (+/-)	5.9	1.6	-4.9	-17.0	-0.9	-11.9	-2.5	-2.2	-3.1	-8.1

PER SHARE DATA

	1994	1993	1992	1991	1990	1989	1988	1987	1986	1985
Dividends, Net Income ($)	0.04	0.00	0.02	0.15	0.23	0.24	0.11	0.14	0.16	0.24
Distrib'ns, Cap Gain ($)	0.59	0.17	0.01	0.03	0.17	0.54	0.23	1.91	0.51	0.00
Net Asset Value ($)	8.52	8.69	7.70	7.24	6.26	7.14	6.94	6.30	7.99	7.76
Expense Ratio (%)	1.90	1.80	1.90	1.90	1.80	1.90	2.00	1.70	1.60	1.70
Net Income to Assets (%)	0.00	0.20	0.80	2.30	2.90	3.00	1.30	1.00	1.60	3.10
Portfolio Turnover (%)	15	17	35	24	44	46	20	51	54	53
Total Assets (Millions $)	10	10	9	9	10	10	10	12	11	10

PORTFOLIO (as of 6/30/94)

Portfolio Manager: C.K. Lawson - 1967

Investm't Category: Growth

✔ Cap Gain	Asset Allocation
Cap & Income	Fund of Funds
Income	Index
	Sector
✔ Domestic	Small Cap
Foreign	Socially Conscious
Country/Region	State Specific

Portfolio: stocks 90%   bonds 0%
convertibles 0%   other 0%   cash 10%

Largest Holdings: telecommunications 14%, industrial conglomerate 11%

Unrealized Net Capital Gains: 24% of portfolio value

SHAREHOLDER INFORMATION

Minimum Investment
Initial: $250   Subsequent: $0

Minimum IRA Investment
Initial: $250   Subsequent: $0

Maximum Fees
Load: none   12b-1: none
Other: none

Distributions
Income: Dec   Capital Gains: Dec

Exchange Options
Number Per Year: none   Fee:
Telephone:

Services
IRA, pension, auto invest, auto withdraw

ASM (ASMUX)
Growth & Income

15438 N. Florida Avenue
Suite 107
Tampa, FL 33613
(800) 445-2763, (813) 963-3150

PERFORMANCE
fund inception date: 3/4/91

	3yr Annual	5yr Annual	10yr Annual	Bull	Bear
Return (%)	6.5	na	na	na	-9.2
Differ from Category (+/-)	-0.6 av	na	na	na	-2.9 low

Total Risk	Standard Deviation	Category Risk	Risk Index	Beta
av	8.4%	av	1.0	0.9

	1994	1993	1992	1991	1990	1989	1988	1987	1986	1985
Return (%).	1.0	13.3	5.6	—	—	—	—	—	—	—
Differ from category (+/-) . .	2.4	0.1	-4.6	—	—	—	—	—	—	—

PER SHARE DATA

	1994	1993	1992	1991	1990	1989	1988	1987	1986	1985
Dividends, Net Income ($).	0.25	0.45	0.43	—	—	—	—	—	—	—
Distrib'ns, Cap Gain ($) . . .	0.17	0.00	0.00	—	—	—	—	—	—	—
Net Asset Value ($)	9.59	9.91	9.15	—	—	—	—	—	—	—
Expense Ratio (%)	0.75	0.75	0.75	—	—	—	—	—	—	—
Net Income to Assets (%) .	2.17	3.35	2.41	—	—	—	—	—	—	—
Portfolio Turnover (%) . .	1,193	642	405	—	—	—	—	—	—	—
Total Assets (Millions $).	6	14	7	—	—	—	—	—	—	—

PORTFOLIO (as of 4/30/94)

Portfolio Manager: Steven H. Adler - 1991

Investm't Category: Growth & Income
Cap Gain	Asset Allocation
✔ Cap & Income	Fund of Funds
Income	✔ Index
	Sector
✔ Domestic	Small Cap
Foreign	Socially Conscious
Country/Region	State Specific

Portfolio: stocks 100%   bonds 0%
convertibles 0%   other 0%   cash 0%

Largest Holdings: Dow Jones industrial average

Unrealized Net Capital Gains: 0% of portfolio value

SHAREHOLDER INFORMATION

Minimum Investment
Initial: $1,000   Subsequent: $100

Minimum IRA Investment
Initial: $500   Subsequent: $100

Maximum Fees
Load: 0.75% redemption   12b-1: none
Other: redemption fee applies if more than 6/yr

Distributions
Income: quarterly   Capital Gains: Dec

Exchange Options
Number Per Year: no limit   Fee: none
Telephone: yes (money market fund available)

Services
IRA, auto invest

Individual Fund Listings   81

Babson Bond Trust—Port L (BABIX)

General Bond

Three Crown Center
2440 Pershing Rd., #G-15
Kansas City, MO 64108
(800) 422-2766, (816) 471-5200

PERFORMANCE

fund inception date: 8/2/45

	3yr Annual	5yr Annual	10yr Annual	Bull	Bear
Return (%)	5.0	7.5	9.3	45.4	-5.2
Differ from Category (+/-)	0.7 abv av	0.6 abv av	0.4 av	4.4 abv av	-1.4 blw av

Total Risk	Standard Deviation	Category Risk	Risk Index	Avg Mat
low	4.2%	av	1.1	13.2 yrs

	1994	1993	1992	1991	1990	1989	1988	1987	1986	1985
Return (%)	-3.2	11.1	7.8	15.0	7.7	13.1	7.1	1.9	13.8	20.6
Differ from category (+/-) . .	-1.2	1.9	1.2	0.4	0.5	1.7	-0.3	-0.3	-0.4	1.2

PER SHARE DATA

	1994	1993	1992	1991	1990	1989	1988	1987	1986	1985
Dividends, Net Income ($) .	0.11	0.12	0.12	0.13	0.13	0.14	0.16	0.16	0.16	0.16
Distrib'ns, Cap Gain ($) . . .	0.00	0.05	0.01	0.00	0.00	0.00	0.00	0.00	0.00	0.00
Net Asset Value ($)	1.47	1.63	1.62	1.63	1.54	1.56	1.51	1.56	1.69	1.63
Expense Ratio (%).	na	0.98	0.99	0.98	0.97	0.97	0.97	0.97	1.00	1.00
Net Income to Assets (%). . .	na	7.00	7.67	8.42	8.81	9.19	9.99	9.29	7.75	8.82
Portfolio Turnover (%).	na	80	54	75	51	51	42	54	46	32
Total Assets (Millions $) . . .	138	160	142	115	91	78	66	65	20	16

PORTFOLIO (as of 5/31/94)

Portfolio Manager: Edward Martin - 1984

Investm't Category: General Bond
Cap Gain	Asset Allocation
Cap & Income	Fund of Funds
✔ Income	Index
	Sector
✔ Domestic	Small Cap
Foreign	Socially Conscious
Country/Region	State Specific

Portfolio: stocks 0% bonds 98%
convertibles 0% other 0% cash 2%

Largest Holdings: corporate 60%, U.S. government 19%

Unrealized Net Capital Gains: -3% of portfolio value

SHAREHOLDER INFORMATION

Minimum Investment
Initial: $500   Subsequent: $50

Minimum IRA Investment
Initial: $250   Subsequent: $50

Maximum Fees
Load: none   12b-1: none
Other: none

Distributions
Income: monthly   Capital Gains: Dec

Exchange Options
Number Per Year: no limit   Fee: none
Telephone: yes (money market fund available)

Services
IRA, pension, auto exchange, auto invest, auto withdraw

Babson Bond Trust—Port S (BBDSX)

General Bond

Three Crown Center
2440 Pershing Rd., #G-15
Kansas City, MO 64108
(800) 422-2766, (816) 471-5200

PERFORMANCE

fund inception date: 4/19/88

	3yr Annual	5yr Annual	10yr Annual	Bull	Bear
Return (%)	4.3	7.0	na	38.5	-3.7
Differ from Category (+/-)	0.0 av	0.1 av	na	-2.5 blw av	0.1 av

Total Risk	Standard Deviation	Category Risk	Risk Index	Avg Mat
low	3.2%	blw av	0.8	9.9 yrs

	1994	1993	1992	1991	1990	1989	1988	1987	1986	1985
Return (%)	-2.1	8.4	6.9	14.4	8.0	10.8	—	—	—	—
Differ from category (+/-)	-0.1	-0.8	0.3	-0.2	0.8	-0.6	—	—	—	—

PER SHARE DATA

	1994	1993	1992	1991	1990	1989	1988	1987	1986	1985
Dividends, Net Income ($)	0.70	0.71	0.75	0.80	0.85	0.82	—	—	—	—
Distrib'ns, Cap Gain ($)	0.00	0.16	0.06	0.02	0.00	0.00	—	—	—	—
Net Asset Value ($)	9.42	10.33	10.34	10.45	9.90	9.98	—	—	—	—
Expense Ratio (%)	na	0.68	0.65	0.66	0.78	0.91	—	—	—	—
Net Income to Assets (%)	na	6.80	7.22	7.98	8.65	8.28	—	—	—	—
Portfolio Turnover (%)	na	147	47	60	35	27	—	—	—	—
Total Assets (Millions $)	28	37	31	14	7	5	—	—	—	—

PORTFOLIO (as of 5/31/94)

Portfolio Manager: Edward Martin - 1988

Investm't Category: General Bond

Cap Gain	Asset Allocation
Cap & Income	Fund of Funds
✔ Income	Index
	Sector
✔ Domestic	Small Cap
Foreign	Socially Conscious
Country/Region	State Specific

Portfolio: stocks 0%   bonds 100%
convertibles 0%   other 0%   cash 0%

Largest Holdings: corporate 62%, U.S. government 25%

Unrealized Net Capital Gains: -4% of portfolio value

SHAREHOLDER INFORMATION

Minimum Investment
Initial: $500   Subsequent: $50

Minimum IRA Investment
Initial: $250   Subsequent: $50

Maximum Fees
Load: none   12b-1: none
Other: none

Distributions
Income: monthly   Capital Gains: Dec

Exchange Options
Number Per Year: no limit   Fee: none
Telephone: yes (money market fund available)

Services
IRA, pension, auto exchange, auto invest, auto withdraw

Babson Enterprise

(BABEX)

Growth

Three Crown Center
2440 Pershing Rd., #G-15
Kansas City, MO 64108
(800) 422-2766, (816) 471-5200

this fund is closed to new investors

PERFORMANCE

fund inception date: 12/2/83

	3yr Annual	5yr Annual	10yr Annual	Bull	Bear
Return (%)	14.0	12.2	14.8	119.8	-4.3
Differ from Category (+/-)	6.3 high	2.6 high	1.9 high	27.7 high	2.3 abv av

Total Risk	Standard Deviation	Category Risk	Risk Index	Beta
abv av	9.6%	av	1.0	0.6

	1994	1993	1992	1991	1990	1989	1988	1987	1986	1985
Return (%)	2.4	16.2	24.5	43.0	-15.8	22.4	32.4	-9.1	9.0	38.6
Differ from category (+/-) . . .	3.0	2.8	12.9	7.3	-10.1	-3.7	14.4	-10.9	-5.6	9.4

PER SHARE DATA

	1994	1993	1992	1991	1990	1989	1988	1987	1986	1985
Dividends, Net Income ($) .	0.04	0.05	0.09	0.08	0.13	0.19	0.06	0.08	0.05	0.00
Distrib'ns, Cap Gain ($) . . .	1.69	1.11	2.33	0.76	0.31	0.69	0.76	1.68	1.73	0.00
Net Asset Value ($)	15.15	16.51	15.22	14.19	10.55	13.06	11.39	9.22	12.12	12.78
Expense Ratio (%).	na	1.09	1.11	1.17	1.22	1.24	1.37	1.35	1.37	1.58
Net Income to Assets (%). . .	na	0.33	0.57	0.66	1.08	1.74	0.50	0.23	0.42	0.62
Portfolio Turnover (%).	na	17	28	15	10	15	41	24	32	38
Total Assets (Millions $) . . .	190	216	178	121	76	87	52	36	47	34

PORTFOLIO (as of 5/31/94)

Portfolio Manager: Peter Schliemann - 1983

Investm't Category: Growth

✔ Cap Gain	Asset Allocation
Cap & Income	Fund of Funds
Income	Index
	Sector
✔ Domestic	✔ Small Cap
Foreign	Socially Conscious
Country/Region	State Specific

Portfolio: stocks 98% bonds 0%
convertibles 0% other 0% cash 2%

Largest Holdings: consumer cyclical 23%,
capital goods 23%

Unrealized Net Capital Gains: 14% of portfolio value

SHAREHOLDER INFORMATION

Minimum Investment
Initial: $1,000   Subsequent: $100

Minimum IRA Investment
Initial: $250   Subsequent: $100

Maximum Fees
Load: none   12b-1: none
Other: none

Distributions
Income: Dec   Capital Gains: Dec

Exchange Options
Number Per Year: no limit   Fee: none
Telephone: yes (money market fund available)

Services
IRA, pension, auto exchange, auto invest, auto
withdraw

Babson Enterprise II
(BAETX)
Growth

Three Crown Center
2440 Pershing Rd., #G-15
Kansas City, MO 64108
(800) 422-2766, (816) 471-5200

PERFORMANCE

fund inception date: 8/5/91

	3yr Annual	5yr Annual	10yr Annual	Bull	Bear
Return (%)	9.1	na	na	na	-7.8
Differ from Category (+/-)	1.4 abv av	na	na	na	-1.2 blw av

Total Risk	Standard Deviation	Category Risk	Risk Index	Beta
abv av	10.3%	abv av	1.1	0.8

	1994	1993	1992	1991	1990	1989	1988	1987	1986	1985
Return (%).	-7.3	19.7	17.2	—	—	—	—	—	—	—
Differ from category (+/-) . .	-6.7	6.3	5.6	—	—	—	—	—	—	—

PER SHARE DATA

	1994	1993	1992	1991	1990	1989	1988	1987	1986	1985
Dividends, Net Income ($).	0.02	0.00	0.00	—	—	—	—	—	—	—
Distrib'ns, Cap Gain ($) . . .	0.09	0.33	0.03	—	—	—	—	—	—	—
Net Asset Value ($)	16.19	17.60	14.97	—	—	—	—	—	—	—
Expense Ratio (%)	na	1.60	1.83	—	—	—	—	—	—	—
Net Income to Assets (%) . . .	na	-0.14	-0.11	—	—	—	—	—	—	—
Portfolio Turnover (%)	na	18	14	—	—	—	—	—	—	—
Total Assets (Millions $).	36	30	11	—	—	—	—	—	—	—

PORTFOLIO (as of 5/31/94)

Portfolio Manager: Peter Schliemann - 1991,
Lance James - 1991

Investm't Category: Growth

✔ Cap Gain	Asset Allocation
Cap & Income	Fund of Funds
Income	Index
	Sector
✔ Domestic	Small Cap
Foreign	Socially Conscious
Country/Region	State Specific

Portfolio: stocks 95% bonds 0%
convertibles 0% other 0% cash 5%

Largest Holdings: consumer cyclical 28%,
capital goods 25%

Unrealized Net Capital Gains: 10% of portfolio value

SHAREHOLDER INFORMATION

Minimum Investment
Initial: $1,000   Subsequent: $100

Minimum IRA Investment
Initial: $250   Subsequent: $100

Maximum Fees
Load: none   12b-1: none
Other: none

Distributions
Income: Dec   Capital Gains: Dec

Exchange Options
Number Per Year: no limit   Fee: none
Telephone: yes (money market fund available)

Services
IRA, pension, auto exchange, auto invest, auto withdraw

Babson Growth (BABSX)

Growth & Income

Three Crown Center
2440 Pershing Rd., #G-15
Kansas City, MO 64108
(800) 422-2766, (816) 471-5200

PERFORMANCE

fund inception date: 3/9/60

	3yr Annual	5yr Annual	10yr Annual	Bull	Bear
Return (%)	6.1	6.4	11.9	69.6	-5.8
Differ from Category (+/-)	-1.0 av	-1.5 blw av	0.2 av	-6.2 blw av	0.5 av

Total Risk	Standard Deviation	Category Risk	Risk Index	Beta
av	7.5%	blw av	0.9	0.9

	1994	1993	1992	1991	1990	1989	1988	1987	1986	1985
Return (%)	-0.5	10.2	9.1	26.0	-9.4	22.1	15.9	3.4	18.8	29.6
Differ from category (+/-) . . .	0.9	-3.0	-1.1	-1.6	-3.4	0.7	-1.1	2.8	3.0	3.9

PER SHARE DATA

	1994	1993	1992	1991	1990	1989	1988	1987	1986	1985
Dividends, Net Income ($)	0.20	0.19	0.20	0.22	0.27	0.29	0.31	0.46	0.35	0.40
Distrib'ns, Cap Gain ($) . . .	0.81	0.55	0.33	0.04	0.55	1.46	2.14	1.51	1.97	1.85
Net Asset Value ($)	11.97	13.08	12.58	12.02	9.75	11.61	10.97	11.59	12.95	12.88
Expense Ratio (%).	0.86	0.86	0.86	0.86	0.86	0.86	0.81	0.74	0.75	0.76
Net Income to Assets (%). .	1.54	1.54	1.69	2.26	2.28	2.53	2.21	2.12	2.65	3.23
Portfolio Turnover (%)	10	13	12	22	23	33	26	14	20	35
Total Assets (Millions $) . . .	226	246	232	236	259	266	238	289	253	215

PORTFOLIO (as of 6/30/94)

Portfolio Manager: David Kirk - 1986

Investm't Category: Growth & Income

Cap Gain	Asset Allocation
✔ Cap & Income	Fund of Funds
Income	Index
	Sector
✔ Domestic	Small Cap
Foreign	Socially Conscious
Country/Region	State Specific

Portfolio: stocks 97%   bonds 0%
convertibles 0%   other 0%   cash 3%

Largest Holdings: consumer cyclical 18%, consumer staples 16%

Unrealized Net Capital Gains: 30% of portfolio value

SHAREHOLDER INFORMATION

Minimum Investment
Initial: $500   Subsequent: $50

Minimum IRA Investment
Initial: $250   Subsequent: $50

Maximum Fees
Load: none   12b-1: none
Other: none

Distributions
Income: Jun, Dec   Capital Gains: Jun, Dec

Exchange Options
Number Per Year: no limit   Fee: none
Telephone: yes (money market fund available)

Services
IRA, pension, auto exchange, auto invest, auto withdraw

Babson Shadow Stock
(SHSTX)
Growth

Three Crown Center
2440 Pershing Rd., #G-15
Kansas City, MO 64108
(800) 422-2766, (816) 471-5200

PERFORMANCE

fund inception date: 9/10/87

	3yr Annual	5yr Annual	10yr Annual	Bull	Bear
Return (%)	9.0	7.9	na	102.1	-8.2
Differ from Category (+/-)	1.3 abv av	-1.7 blw av	na	10.0 abv av	-1.6 blw av

Total Risk	Standard Deviation	Category Risk	Risk Index	Beta
abv av	8.8%	blw av	0.9	0.5

	1994	1993	1992	1991	1990	1989	1988	1987	1986	1985
Return (%)	-4.2	15.2	17.4	39.9	-19.3	11.2	22.4	—	—	—
Differ from category (+/-)	-3.6	1.8	5.8	4.2	-13.6	-14.9	4.4	—	—	—

PER SHARE DATA

	1994	1993	1992	1991	1990	1989	1988	1987	1986	1985
Dividends, Net Income ($)	0.09	0.10	0.09	0.09	0.09	0.17	0.12	—	—	—
Distrib'ns, Cap Gain ($)	2.15	1.02	0.06	0.00	0.00	0.27	0.10	—	—	—
Net Asset Value ($)	9.52	12.32	11.72	10.11	7.29	9.14	8.60	—	—	—
Expense Ratio (%)	1.28	1.25	1.26	1.31	1.29	1.33	1.51	—	—	—
Net Income to Assets (%)	0.50	1.05	0.87	1.20	1.49	1.39	1.57	—	—	—
Portfolio Turnover (%)	43	15	23	0	16	15	7	—	—	—
Total Assets (Millions $)	33	36	26	22	25	26	16	—	—	—

PORTFOLIO (as of 6/30/94)

Portfolio Manager: Peter Schliemann - 1987, Nick Whitridge - 1987

Investm't Category: Growth
✔ Cap Gain	Asset Allocation
Cap & Income	Fund of Funds
Income	Index
	Sector
✔ Domestic	✔ Small Cap
Foreign	Socially Conscious
Country/Region	State Specific

Portfolio: stocks 98%   bonds 0%
convertibles 0%   other 0%   cash 2%

Largest Holdings: financial 19%, consumer cyclical 15%

Unrealized Net Capital Gains: 5% of portfolio value

SHAREHOLDER INFORMATION

Minimum Investment
Initial: $2,500   Subsequent: $100

Minimum IRA Investment
Initial: $250   Subsequent: $100

Maximum Fees
Load: none   12b-1: none
Other: none

Distributions
Income: Jun, Dec   Capital Gains: Jun, Dec

Exchange Options
Number Per Year: no limit   Fee: none
Telephone: yes (money market fund available)

Services
IRA, pension, auto exchange, auto invest, auto withdraw

Babson-Stewart Ivory Int'l (BAINX)

International Stock

Three Crown Center
2440 Pershing Rd., #G-15
Kansas City, MO 64108
(800) 422-2766, (816) 471-5200

PERFORMANCE   **fund inception date: 4/1/88**

	3yr Annual	5yr Annual	10yr Annual	Bull	Bear
Return (%)	9.9	6.7	na	70.1	-2.6
Differ from Category (+/-)	0.8 abv av	1.8 abv av	na	6.2 abv av	4.4 high

Total Risk	Standard Deviation	Category Risk	Risk Index	Beta
abv av	12.0%	blw av	0.9	0.6

	1994	1993	1992	1991	1990	1989	1988	1987	1986	1985
Return (%)	1.3	33.4	-1.7	15.0	-9.3	26.9	—	—	—	—
Differ from category (+/-)	4.3	-5.2	1.2	1.9	1.1	4.4	—	—	—	—

PER SHARE DATA

	1994	1993	1992	1991	1990	1989	1988	1987	1986	1985
Dividends, Net Income ($)	0.04	0.06	0.14	0.12	0.07	0.07	—	—	—	—
Distrib'ns, Cap Gain ($)	0.92	0.33	0.03	0.00	0.15	0.28	—	—	—	—
Net Asset Value ($)	15.45	16.20	12.43	12.81	11.24	12.63	—	—	—	—
Expense Ratio (%)	1.32	1.57	1.58	1.75	1.75	2.68	—	—	—	—
Net Income to Assets (%)	0.34	0.88	1.16	1.10	0.36	0.62	—	—	—	—
Portfolio Turnover (%)	60	49	44	52	42	40	—	—	—	—
Total Assets (Millions $)	55	43	18	12	11	4	—	—	—	—

PORTFOLIO (as of 6/30/94)

Portfolio Manager: John Wright - 1988

Investm't Category: International Stock

✔ Cap Gain
  Cap & Income
  Income

  Asset Allocation
  Fund of Funds
  Index
  Sector

  Domestic
✔ Foreign
  Country/Region

  Small Cap
  Socially Conscious
  State Specific

Portfolio: stocks 97%   bonds 0%
convertibles 0%   other 0%   cash 3%

Largest Holdings: Japan 26%, United Kingdom 16%

Unrealized Net Capital Gains: 16% of portfolio value

SHAREHOLDER INFORMATION

Minimum Investment
Initial: $2,500   Subsequent: $100

Minimum IRA Investment
Initial: $250   Subsequent: $100

Maximum Fees
Load: none   12b-1: none
Other: none

Distributions
Income: Jun   Capital Gains: Jun

Exchange Options
Number Per Year: no limit   Fee: none
Telephone: yes (money market fund available)

Services
IRA, pension, auto exchange, auto invest, auto withdraw

Babson Tax-Free Income—Port L (BALTX)

Tax-Exempt Bond

Three Crown Center
2440 Pershing Rd., #G-15
Kansas City, MO 64108
(800) 422-2766, (816) 471-5200

PERFORMANCE

fund inception date: 2/22/80

	3yr Annual	5yr Annual	10yr Annual	Bull	Bear
Return (%)	4.0	6.0	8.6	44.6	-6.9
Differ from Category (+/-)	-0.5 blw av	-0.1 blw av	0.5 abv av	2.8 av	-1.7 low

Total Risk	Standard Deviation	Category Risk	Risk Index	Avg Mat
blw av	6.2%	av	1.0	16.0 yrs

	1994	1993	1992	1991	1990	1989	1988	1987	1986	1985
Return (%)	-7.4	12.2	8.3	12.2	6.2	8.7	11.6	-1.8	18.4	20.4
Differ from category (+/-)	-2.2	0.5	0.0	0.9	-0.1	-0.3	1.4	-0.5	2.0	3.0

PER SHARE DATA

	1994	1993	1992	1991	1990	1989	1988	1987	1986	1985
Dividends, Net Income ($)	0.42	0.45	0.49	0.53	0.55	0.60	0.64	0.62	0.68	0.72
Distrib'ns, Cap Gain ($)	0.02	0.41	0.36	0.03	0.00	0.00	0.00	0.19	0.63	0.00
Net Asset Value ($)	8.16	9.28	9.05	9.17	8.70	8.73	8.60	8.31	9.30	9.02
Expense Ratio (%)	1.02	1.00	0.99	0.98	1.00	0.99	1.00	0.99	1.00	1.00
Net Income to Assets (%)	4.73	5.03	5.73	6.22	6.47	7.51	7.54	6.80	7.75	8.82
Portfolio Turnover (%)	53	126	128	116	121	172	168	123	46	32
Total Assets (Millions $)	26	33	30	29	28	26	21	22	20	16

PORTFOLIO (as of 6/30/94)

Portfolio Manager: Joel Vernick - 1987

Investm't Category: Tax-Exempt Bond

Cap Gain	Asset Allocation
Cap & Income	Fund of Funds
✔ Income	Index
	Sector
✔ Domestic	Small Cap
Foreign	Socially Conscious
Country/Region	State Specific

Portfolio: stocks 0%   bonds 100%
convertibles 0%   other 0%   cash 0%

Largest Holdings: general obligation 34%

Unrealized Net Capital Gains: -1% of portfolio value

SHAREHOLDER INFORMATION

Minimum Investment
Initial: $1,000   Subsequent: $100

Minimum IRA Investment
Initial: na   Subsequent: na

Maximum Fees
Load: none   12b-1: none
Other: none

Distributions
Income: monthly   Capital Gains: Jun, Dec

Exchange Options
Number Per Year: no limit   Fee: none
Telephone: yes (money market fund available)

Services
auto exchange, auto invest, auto withdraw

Babson Tax-Free Income—Port S (BASTX)

Tax-Exempt Bond

Three Crown Center
2440 Pershing Rd., #G-15
Kansas City, MO 64108
(800) 422-2766, (816) 471-5200

PERFORMANCE

fund inception date: 2/22/80

	3yr Annual	5yr Annual	10yr Annual	Bull	Bear
Return (%)	3.6	5.3	6.4	29.0	-2.6
Differ from Category (+/-)	-0.9 low	-0.8 low	-1.7 low	-12.8 low	2.6 high

Total Risk	Standard Deviation	Category Risk	Risk Index	Avg Mat
low	2.8%	low	0.4	5.4 yrs

	1994	1993	1992	1991	1990	1989	1988	1987	1986	1985
Return (%)	-1.7	6.7	6.3	9.4	6.5	6.9	5.3	3.5	10.4	11.0
Differ from category (+/-) . . .	3.5	-5.0	-2.0	-1.9	0.2	-2.1	-4.9	4.8	-6.0	-6.4

PER SHARE DATA

	1994	1993	1992	1991	1990	1989	1988	1987	1986	1985
Dividends, Net Income ($) .	0.45	0.48	0.52	0.57	0.60	0.65	0.66	0.62	0.67	0.70
Distrib'ns, Cap Gain ($) . . .	0.01	0.06	0.11	0.14	0.00	0.00	0.03	0.09	0.07	0.00
Net Asset Value ($)	10.40	11.05	10.87	10.84	10.58	10.51	10.45	10.59	10.93	10.60
Expense Ratio (%).	1.02	1.00	1.00	0.99	0.99	0.99	1.00	0.99	1.00	1.00
Net Income to Assets (%). .	4.22	4.58	5.14	5.57	5.82	6.48	6.01	5.91	6.47	6.87
Portfolio Turnover (%)	21	47	81	98	74	115	131	66	35	37
Total Assets (Millions $)	28	31	22	18	18	18	16	16	13	10

PORTFOLIO (as of 6/30/94)

Portfolio Manager: Joel Vernick - 1987

Investm't Category: Tax-Exempt Bond

Cap Gain	Asset Allocation
Cap & Income	Fund of Funds
✔ Income	Index
	Sector
✔ Domestic	Small Cap
Foreign	Socially Conscious
Country/Region	State Specific

Portfolio: stocks 0%   bonds 100%
convertibles 0%   other 0%   cash 0%

Largest Holdings: general obligation 40%

Unrealized Net Capital Gains: 0% of portfolio value

SHAREHOLDER INFORMATION

Minimum Investment
Initial: $1,000   Subsequent: $100

Minimum IRA Investment
Initial: na   Subsequent: na

Maximum Fees
Load: none   12b-1: none
Other: none

Distributions
Income: monthly   Capital Gains: Jun, Dec

Exchange Options
Number Per Year: no limit   Fee: none
Telephone: yes (money market fund available)

Services
auto exchange, auto invest, auto withdraw

Babson Value (BVALX)

Growth & Income

Three Crown Center
2440 Pershing Rd., #G-15
Kansas City, MO 64108
(800) 422-2766, (816) 471-5200

PERFORMANCE

fund inception date: 12/21/84

	3yr Annual	5yr Annual	10yr Annual	Bull	Bear
Return (%)	13.2	10.6	13.9	105.3	-3.6
Differ from Category (+/-)	6.1 high	2.7 high	2.2 high	29.5 high	2.7 high

Total Risk	Standard Deviation	Category Risk	Risk Index	Beta
av	8.2%	av	1.0	0.8

	1994	1993	1992	1991	1990	1989	1988	1987	1986	1985
Return (%)	2.5	22.8	15.3	28.9	-11.3	18.2	18.9	3.1	20.8	26.4
Differ from category (+/-)	3.9	9.6	5.1	1.3	-5.3	-3.2	1.9	2.5	5.0	0.7

PER SHARE DATA

	1994	1993	1992	1991	1990	1989	1988	1987	1986	1985
Dividends, Net Income ($)	0.47	0.54	0.62	0.71	0.71	0.51	0.76	0.66	0.87	0.00
Distrib'ns, Cap Gain ($)	0.60	0.91	0.33	0.00	0.00	0.04	0.08	0.04	0.18	0.00
Net Asset Value ($)	24.78	25.22	21.75	19.67	15.85	18.68	16.27	14.38	14.64	13.04
Expense Ratio (%)	na	1.00	1.01	1.01	1.04	1.06	1.11	1.08	1.20	0.93
Net Income to Assets (%)	na	2.30	3.10	3.82	4.44	4.10	3.87	3.31	3.60	4.79
Portfolio Turnover (%)	na	26	17	31	6	17	24	52	27	13
Total Assets (Millions $)	122	45	34	25	22	20	10	14	6	2

PORTFOLIO (as of 5/31/94)

Portfolio Manager: Roland Whitridge - 1984

Investm't Category: Growth & Income

Cap Gain	Asset Allocation
✔ Cap & Income	Fund of Funds
Income	Index
	Sector
✔ Domestic	Small Cap
Foreign	Socially Conscious
Country/Region	State Specific

Portfolio: stocks 90% bonds 0%
convertibles 2% other 0% cash 8%

Largest Holdings: financial services 10%, retail 9%

Unrealized Net Capital Gains: 15% of portfolio value

SHAREHOLDER INFORMATION

Minimum Investment
Initial: $1,000   Subsequent: $100

Minimum IRA Investment
Initial: $250   Subsequent: $100

Maximum Fees
Load: none   12b-1: none
Other: none

Distributions
Income: quarterly   Capital Gains: Dec

Exchange Options
Number Per Year: no limit   Fee: none
Telephone: yes (money market fund available)

Services
IRA, pension, auto exchange, auto invest, auto withdraw

Baron Asset (BARAX)

Aggressive Growth

450 Park Ave.
New York, NY 10022
(800) 992-2766, (212) 759-7700

PERFORMANCE

fund inception date: 6/12/87

	3yr Annual	5yr Annual	10yr Annual	Bull	Bear
Return (%)	14.7	10.5	na	111.3	-5.3
Differ from Category (+/-)	5.8 high	-2.0 blw av	na	-21.9 blw av	5.5 high

Total Risk	Standard Deviation	Category Risk	Risk Index	Beta
abv av	10.9%	low	0.7	0.8

	1994	1993	1992	1991	1990	1989	1988	1987	1986	1985
Return (%)	7.4	23.4	13.8	34.0	-18.4	24.9	34.4	—	—	—
Differ from category (+/-)	8.1	3.9	2.8	-18.1	-12.2	-1.9	19.2	—	—	—

PER SHARE DATA

	1994	1993	1992	1991	1990	1989	1988	1987	1986	1985
Dividends, Net Income ($)	0.00	0.00	0.00	0.04	0.20	0.16	0.05	—	—	—
Distrib'ns, Cap Gain ($)	0.66	0.77	0.16	0.00	0.00	1.25	0.65	—	—	—
Net Asset Value ($)	22.01	21.11	17.73	15.71	11.75	14.66	12.87	—	—	—
Expense Ratio (%)	1.60	1.80	1.70	1.70	1.80	2.10	2.50	—	—	—
Net Income to Assets (%)	-0.70	-0.70	-0.50	0.50	1.50	1.30	0.50	—	—	—
Portfolio Turnover (%)	55	108	96	143	98	149	242	—	—	—
Total Assets (Millions $)	3	62	44	47	40	48	12	—	—	—

PORTFOLIO (as of 9/30/94)

Portfolio Manager: Ron Baron - 1987

Investm't Category: Aggressive Growth

✔ Cap Gain	Asset Allocation
Cap & Income	Fund of Funds
Income	Index
	Sector
✔ Domestic	Small Cap
Foreign	Socially Conscious
Country/Region	State Specific

Portfolio: stocks 94% bonds 5%
convertibles 0% other 0% cash 1%

Largest Holdings: business services 20%, communications 13%

Unrealized Net Capital Gains: 26% of portfolio value

SHAREHOLDER INFORMATION

Minimum Investment
Initial: $2,000   Subsequent: $0

Minimum IRA Investment
Initial: $2,000   Subsequent: $0

Maximum Fees
Load: none   12b-1: 0.25%
Other: none

Distributions
Income: Dec   Capital Gains: Dec

Exchange Options
Number Per Year: none   Fee:
Telephone:

Services
IRA, auto invest

Bartlett Basic Value

(MBBVX)

Growth & Income

36 E. Fourth St.
Suite 400
Cincinnati, OH 45202
(800) 800-4612, (513) 621-4612

PERFORMANCE   fund inception date: 5/5/83

	3yr Annual	5yr Annual	10yr Annual	Bull	Bear
Return (%)	7.3	7.0	10.5	74.0	-4.8
Differ from Category (+/-)	0.2 av	-0.9 blw av	-1.2 blw av	-1.8 av	1.5 abv av

Total Risk	Standard Deviation	Category Risk	Risk Index	Beta
av	7.6%	blw av	0.9	0.8

	1994	1993	1992	1991	1990	1989	1988	1987	1986	1985
Return (%)...............	0.4	11.6	10.2	25.9	-9.6	11.6	26.2	-3.7	13.6	25.2
Differ from category (+/-) ..	1.8	-1.6	0.0	-1.7	-3.6	-9.8	9.2	-4.3	-2.2	-0.5

PER SHARE DATA

	1994	1993	1992	1991	1990	1989	1988	1987	1986	1985
Dividends, Net Income ($).	0.24	0.22	0.32	0.39	0.52	0.84	0.52	0.45	0.45	0.55
Distrib'ns, Cap Gain ($) ...	1.03	0.14	0.28	0.00	0.00	0.18	1.15	0.39	1.41	0.18
Net Asset Value ($)	14.10	15.28	14.02	13.28	10.87	12.58	12.18	11.01	12.20	12.37
Expense Ratio (%)	1.22	1.21	1.22	1.21	1.19	1.23	1.57	1.28	1.56	1.78
Net Income to Assets (%) .	1.68	2.14	2.77	3.87	4.81	4.57	2.75	3.49	4.05	6.01
Portfolio Turnover (%)	30	43	49	92	77	99	97	58	82	36
Total Assets (Millions $).....	92	97	89	96	106	100	81	91	52	22

PORTFOLIO (as of 9/30/94)

Portfolio Manager: James Miller - 1983, Woodrow Uible - 1983

Investm't Category: Growth & Income

✔ Cap Gain   Asset Allocation
  Cap & Income   Fund of Funds
  Income   Index
       Sector
✔ Domestic   Small Cap
✔ Foreign   Socially Conscious
  Country/Region   State Specific

Portfolio: stocks 86%   bonds 5%
convertibles 1%   other 1%   cash 7%

Largest Holdings: financial services 18%, energy 8%

Unrealized Net Capital Gains: 14% of portfolio value

SHAREHOLDER INFORMATION

Minimum Investment
Initial: $5,000   Subsequent: $100

Minimum IRA Investment
Initial: $250   Subsequent: $100

Maximum Fees
Load: none   12b-1: none
Other: none

Distributions
Income: quarterly   Capital Gains: Dec

Exchange Options
Number Per Year: no limit   Fee: none
Telephone: yes (money market fund available)

Services
IRA, pension, auto exchange, auto invest, auto withdraw

Bartlett Fixed Income

(BFXFX)

General Bond

36 E. Fourth St.
Suite 400
Cincinnati, OH 45202
(800) 800-4612, (513) 621-4612

PERFORMANCE

fund inception date: 4/22/86

	3yr Annual	5yr Annual	10yr Annual	Bull	Bear
Return (%)	3.5	6.1	na	37.2	-3.8
Differ from Category (+/-)	-0.8 low	-0.8 low	na	-3.8 blw av	0.0 av

Total Risk	Standard Deviation	Category Risk	Risk Index	Avg Mat
low	3.2%	blw av	0.8	6.0 yrs

	1994	1993	1992	1991	1990	1989	1988	1987	1986	1985
Return (%)	-2.8	6.9	6.9	14.3	6.0	12.5	7.6	2.7	—	—
Differ from category (+/-) . .	-0.8	-2.3	0.3	-0.3	-1.2	1.1	0.2	0.5	—	—

PER SHARE DATA

	1994	1993	1992	1991	1990	1989	1988	1987	1986	1985
Dividends, Net Income ($) .	0.52	0.49	0.62	0.70	0.75	0.84	0.84	0.85	—	—
Distrib'ns, Cap Gain ($) . . .	0.00	0.17	0.00	0.00	0.00	0.00	0.00	0.00	—	—
Net Asset Value ($)	9.48	10.29	10.25	10.19	9.57	9.76	9.46	9.58	—	—
Expense Ratio (%).	1.00	1.00	1.00	1.00	1.00	1.00	1.00	0.93	—	—
Net Income to Assets (%). .	5.31	5.81	6.85	7.68	8.56	8.95	8.56	8.57	—	—
Portfolio Turnover (%). . . .	154	175	126	165	95	104	205	192	—	—
Total Assets (Millions $)	90	123	148	159	157	159	157	145	—	—

PORTFOLIO (as of 9/30/94)

Portfolio Manager: Dale Rabiner - 1986

Investm't Category: General Bond

Cap Gain	Asset Allocation
Cap & Income	Fund of Funds
✔ Income	Index
	Sector
✔ Domestic	Small Cap
✔ Foreign	Socially Conscious
Country/Region	State Specific

Portfolio: stocks 0% bonds 90%
convertibles 6% other 0% cash 4%

Largest Holdings: corporate 33%, mortgage-backed 31%

Unrealized Net Capital Gains: -2% of portfolio value

SHAREHOLDER INFORMATION

Minimum Investment
Initial: $5,000   Subsequent: $100

Minimum IRA Investment
Initial: $250   Subsequent: $100

Maximum Fees
Load: none   12b-1: none
Other: none

Distributions
Income: monthly   Capital Gains: Dec

Exchange Options
Number Per Year: no limit   Fee: none
Telephone: yes (money market fund available)

Services
IRA, pension, auto exchange, auto invest, auto withdraw

Bartlett Value Int'l

(BVLIX)

International Stock

36 E. Fourth St.
Suite 400
Cincinnati, OH 45202
(800) 800-4612, (513) 621-4612

fund inception date: 10/6/89

PERFORMANCE

	3yr Annual	5yr Annual	10yr Annual	Bull	Bear
Return (%)	8.6	5.9	na	73.0	-7.2
Differ from Category (+/-)	-0.5 av	1.0 abv av	na	9.1 abv av	-0.2 av

Total Risk	Standard Deviation	Category Risk	Risk Index	Beta
high	12.3%	blw av	0.9	0.9

	1994	1993	1992	1991	1990	1989	1988	1987	1986	1985
Return (%)...............	-0.5	31.3	-1.8	21.4	-14.5	—	—	—	—	—
Differ from category (+/-) ..	2.5	-7.3	1.1	8.3	-4.1	—	—	—	—	—

PER SHARE DATA

	1994	1993	1992	1991	1990	1989	1988	1987	1986	1985
Dividends, Net Income ($).	0.08	0.07	0.11	0.22	0.28	—	—	—	—	—
Distrib'ns, Cap Gain ($) ...	0.62	0.00	0.00	0.02	0.17	—	—	—	—	—
Net Asset Value ($)	11.60	12.33	9.45	9.73	8.22	—	—	—	—	—
Expense Ratio (%)	1.85	2.00	2.00	1.99	1.41	—	—	—	—	—
Net Income to Assets (%) .	1.17	1.13	1.79	3.31	1.80	—	—	—	—	—
Portfolio Turnover (%)	28	19	27	39	155	—	—	—	—	—
Total Assets (Millions $).....	56	44	22	24	21	—	—	—	—	—

PORTFOLIO (as of 9/30/94)

Portfolio Manager: Madelynn Matlock - 1989

Investm't Category: International Stock

✔ Cap Gain	Asset Allocation
Cap & Income	Fund of Funds
Income	Index
	Sector
Domestic	Small Cap
✔ Foreign	Socially Conscious
Country/Region	State Specific

Portfolio: stocks 91% bonds 0%
convertibles 3% other 1% cash 5%

Largest Holdings: France 10%, Japan 9%

Unrealized Net Capital Gains: 10% of portfolio value

SHAREHOLDER INFORMATION

Minimum Investment
Initial: $5,000   Subsequent: $100

Minimum IRA Investment
Initial: $250   Subsequent: $100

Maximum Fees
Load: none   12b-1: none
Other: none

Distributions
Income: quarterly   Capital Gains: Dec

Exchange Options
Number Per Year: no limit   Fee: none
Telephone: yes (money market fund available)

Services
IRA, pension, auto exchange, auto invest, auto withdraw

Bascom Hill Balanced
(BHBFX)
Balanced

6411 Mineral Point Road
Madison, WI 53705
(800) 767-0300, (608) 273-2020

PERFORMANCE   fund inception date: 12/18/86

	3yr Annual	5yr Annual	10yr Annual	Bull	Bear
Return (%)	4.5	5.7	na	51.9	-2.2
Differ from Category (+/-)	-1.9 blw av	-2.3 low	na	-13.1 blw av	3.5 high

Total Risk	Standard Deviation	Category Risk	Risk Index	Beta
blw av	5.7%	blw av	0.9	0.6

	1994	1993	1992	1991	1990	1989	1988	1987	1986	1985
Return (%)	1.0	4.2	8.4	25.0	-7.3	12.1	7.7	3.6	—	—
Differ from category (+/-) . . .	2.9	-9.2	0.1	1.6	-6.8	-5.2	-4.1	1.2	—	—

PER SHARE DATA

	1994	1993	1992	1991	1990	1989	1988	1987	1986	1985
Dividends, Net Income ($) .	0.98	1.04	0.72	0.78	1.00	1.18	0.91	0.60	—	—
Distrib'ns, Cap Gain ($) . . .	1.47	1.23	0.52	0.00	0.00	0.46	0.00	0.00	—	—
Net Asset Value ($)	20.16	22.37	23.65	23.00	19.04	21.62	20.76	20.13	—	—
Expense Ratio (%).	na	1.24	1.90	1.94	1.96	2.00	2.00	2.00	—	—
Net Income to Assets (%). . .	na	2.53	2.53	3.33	5.00	5.60	4.90	4.80	—	—
Portfolio Turnover (%)	na	76	71	64	71	47	0	0	—	—
Total Assets (Millions $)	9	13	15	15	13	14	9	5	—	—

PORTFOLIO (as of 6/30/94)

Portfolio Manager: Frank Burgess - 1986

Investm't Category: Balanced
Cap Gain	✔ Asset Allocation
✔ Cap & Income	Fund of Funds
Income	Index
	Sector
✔ Domestic	Small Cap
Foreign	Socially Conscious
Country/Region	State Specific

Portfolio: stocks 33%   bonds 36%
convertibles 0%   other 0%   cash 31%

Largest Holdings: U.S. government 17%, corporate bonds 14%

Unrealized Net Capital Gains: 0% of portfolio value

SHAREHOLDER INFORMATION

Minimum Investment
Initial: $1,000   Subsequent: $100

Minimum IRA Investment
Initial: $1,000   Subsequent: $100

Maximum Fees
Load: none   12b-1: none
Other: none

Distributions
Income: quarterly   Capital Gains: Dec

Exchange Options
Number Per Year: none   Fee:
Telephone:

Services
IRA

BayFunds Bond Port— Investment Shares (BFBPX)

P.O. Box 665
Waltham, MA 02254
(800) 229-3863

General Bond

PERFORMANCE

fund inception date: 2/1/93

	3yr Annual	5yr Annual	10yr Annual	Bull	Bear
Return (%)	na	na	na	na	-4.2
Differ from Category (+/-)	na	na	na	na	-0.4 av

Total Risk	Standard Deviation	Category Risk	Risk Index	Avg Mat
na	na	na	na	6.5 yrs

	1994	1993	1992	1991	1990	1989	1988	1987	1986	1985
Return (%).	-2.3	—	—	—	—	—	—	—	—	—
Differ from category (+/-) . .	-0.3	—	—	—	—	—	—	—	—	—

PER SHARE DATA

	1994	1993	1992	1991	1990	1989	1988	1987	1986	1985
Dividends, Net Income ($).	0.49	—	—	—	—	—	—	—	—	—
Distrib'ns, Cap Gain ($) . . .	0.00	—	—	—	—	—	—	—	—	—
Net Asset Value ($)	9.41	—	—	—	—	—	—	—	—	—
Expense Ratio (%)	1.13	—	—	—	—	—	—	—	—	—
Net Income to Assets (%) .	4.84	—	—	—	—	—	—	—	—	—
Portfolio Turnover (%)	na	—	—	—	—	—	—	—	—	—
Total Assets (Millions $).	5	—	—	—	—	—	—	—	—	—

PORTFOLIO (as of 6/30/94)

Portfolio Manager: Rick Vincent - 1993

Investm't Category: General Bond

Cap Gain	Asset Allocation
Cap & Income	Fund of Funds
✔ Income	Index
	Sector
✔ Domestic	Small Cap
Foreign	Socially Conscious
Country/Region	State Specific

Portfolio: stocks 0%   bonds 98%
convertibles 0%   other 0%   cash 2%

Largest Holdings: U.S. government and agencies 59%, corporate 21%

Unrealized Net Capital Gains: -3% of portfolio value

SHAREHOLDER INFORMATION

Minimum Investment
Initial: $2,500   Subsequent: $100

Minimum IRA Investment
Initial: $500   Subsequent: $0

Maximum Fees
Load: none   12b-1: none
Other: none

Distributions
Income: monthly   Capital Gains: Dec

Exchange Options
Number Per Year: no limit   Fee: none
Telephone: yes (money market fund available)

Services
IRA, pension, auto invest

BayFunds Equity Port— Investment Shares (BFEPX)

P.O. Box 665
Waltham, MA 02254
(800) 229-3863

Growth

PERFORMANCE
fund inception date: 2/1/93

	3yr Annual	5yr Annual	10yr Annual	Bull	Bear
Return (%)	na	na	na	na	-8.8
Differ from Category (+/-)	na	na	na	na	-2.2 blw av

Total Risk	Standard Deviation	Category Risk	Risk Index	Beta
na	na	na	na	na

	1994	1993	1992	1991	1990	1989	1988	1987	1986	1985
Return (%)	-3.2	—	—	—	—	—	—	—	—	—
Differ from category (+/-) . .	-2.6	—	—	—	—	—	—	—	—	—

PER SHARE DATA

	1994	1993	1992	1991	1990	1989	1988	1987	1986	1985
Dividends, Net Income ($) .	0.09	—	—	—	—	—	—	—	—	—
Distrib'ns, Cap Gain ($) . . .	0.00	—	—	—	—	—	—	—	—	—
Net Asset Value ($)	10.54	—	—	—	—	—	—	—	—	—
Expense Ratio (%).	1.25	—	—	—	—	—	—	—	—	—
Net Income to Assets (%) . .	0.74	—	—	—	—	—	—	—	—	—
Portfolio Turnover (%)	na	—	—	—	—	—	—	—	—	—
Total Assets (Millions $)	28	—	—	—	—	—	—	—	—	—

PORTFOLIO (as of 6/30/94)

Portfolio Manager: Geraldine Carroll - 1993

Investm't Category: Growth
- ✔ Cap Gain
- Cap & Income
- Income
- ✔ Domestic
- Foreign
- Country/Region
- Asset Allocation
- Fund of Funds
- Index
- Sector
- Small Cap
- Socially Conscious
- State Specific

Portfolio: stocks 91% bonds 0%
convertibles 0% other 0% cash 9%

Largest Holdings: banks 7%, international oil 4%

Unrealized Net Capital Gains: 0% of portfolio value

SHAREHOLDER INFORMATION

Minimum Investment
Initial: $2,500   Subsequent: $100

Minimum IRA Investment
Initial: $500   Subsequent: $0

Maximum Fees
Load: none   12b-1: none
Other: none

Distributions
Income: quarterly   Capital Gains: Dec

Exchange Options
Number Per Year: no limit   Fee: none
Telephone: yes (money market fund available)

Services
IRA, pension, auto invest

BayFunds Short-Term Yield—Investment Shares

P.O. Box 665
Waltham, MA 02254
(800) 229-3863

(BFSTX) *General Bond*

PERFORMANCE

fund inception date: 2/1/93

	3yr Annual	5yr Annual	10yr Annual	Bull	Bear
Return (%)	na	na	na	na	-3.7
Differ from Category (+/-)	na	na	na	na	0.1 av

Total Risk	Standard Deviation	Category Risk	Risk Index	Avg Mat
na	na	na	na	1.5 yrs

	1994	1993	1992	1991	1990	1989	1988	1987	1986	1985
Return (%)	-3.4	—	—	—	—	—	—	—	—	—
Differ from category (+/-)	-1.4	—	—	—	—	—	—	—	—	—

PER SHARE DATA

	1994	1993	1992	1991	1990	1989	1988	1987	1986	1985
Dividends, Net Income ($)	0.43	—	—	—	—	—	—	—	—	—
Distrib'ns, Cap Gain ($)	0.00	—	—	—	—	—	—	—	—	—
Net Asset Value ($)	9.15	—	—	—	—	—	—	—	—	—
Expense Ratio (%)	0.77	—	—	—	—	—	—	—	—	—
Net Income to Assets (%)	4.47	—	—	—	—	—	—	—	—	—
Portfolio Turnover (%)	na	—	—	—	—	—	—	—	—	—
Total Assets (Millions $)	34	—	—	—	—	—	—	—	—	—

PORTFOLIO (as of 6/30/94)

Portfolio Manager: Eric Letendre - 1993

Investm't Category: General Bond

Cap Gain	Asset Allocation
Cap & Income	Fund of Funds
✔ Income	Index
	Sector
✔ Domestic	Small Cap
Foreign	Socially Conscious
Country/Region	State Specific

Portfolio: stocks 0%   bonds 81%
convertibles 0%   other 0%   cash 19%

Largest Holdings: corporate 40%, U.S. government 21%

Unrealized Net Capital Gains: -1% of portfolio value

SHAREHOLDER INFORMATION

Minimum Investment
Initial: $2,500   Subsequent: $100

Minimum IRA Investment
Initial: $500   Subsequent: $0

Maximum Fees
Load: none   12b-1: none
Other: none

Distributions
Income: monthly   Capital Gains: Dec

Exchange Options
Number Per Year: no limit   Fee: none
Telephone: yes (money market fund available)

Services
IRA, pension, auto invest

BB&K Diversa (DVERX)

Balanced

2755 Campus Drive
San Mateo, CA 94403
(800) 224-5273

PERFORMANCE

fund inception date: 12/2/86

	3yr Annual	5yr Annual	10yr Annual	Bull	Bear
Return (%)	4.7	3.8	na	51.9	-9.7
Differ from Category (+/-)	-1.7 blw av	-4.2 low	na	-13.1 blw av	-4.0 low

Total Risk	Standard Deviation	Category Risk	Risk Index	Beta
blw av	6.7%	abv av	1.1	0.5

	1994	1993	1992	1991	1990	1989	1988	1987	1986	1985
Return (%)	-9.3	21.5	4.4	15.8	-9.5	12.7	6.6	8.5	—	—
Differ from category (+/-) . .	-7.4	8.1	-3.9	-7.6	-9.0	-4.6	-5.2	6.1	—	—

PER SHARE DATA

	1994	1993	1992	1991	1990	1989	1988	1987	1986	1985
Dividends, Net Income ($) .	0.31	0.30	0.30	0.46	0.30	0.45	0.46	0.51	—	—
Distrib'ns, Cap Gain ($) . . .	0.00	0.00	0.00	0.00	0.00	0.00	0.00	0.13	—	—
Net Asset Value ($)	11.64	13.18	11.11	10.94	9.85	11.20	10.35	10.14	—	—
Expense Ratio (%).	1.82	1.70	1.90	1.54	1.46	1.34	1.26	1.02	—	—
Net Income to Assets (%). .	2.03	2.88	2.75	3.01	3.60	5.24	5.13	2.45	—	—
Portfolio Turnover (%). . . .	137	96	94	254	235	100	89	66	—	—
Total Assets (Millions $)	41	51	50	57	79	103	105	91	—	—

PORTFOLIO (as of 9/30/94)

Portfolio Manager: Richard L. Holbrook - 1992, Arthur Micheletti - 1992

Investm't Category: Balanced

Cap Gain	✔ Asset Allocation
✔ Cap & Income	Fund of Funds
Income	Index
	Sector
✔ Domestic	Small Cap
✔ Foreign	Socially Conscious
Country/Region	State Specific

Portfolio: stocks 56%   bonds 27%
convertibles 0%   other 9%   cash 8%

Largest Holdings: foreign government bonds 16%, U.S. government bonds 10%

Unrealized Net Capital Gains: 5% of portfolio value

SHAREHOLDER INFORMATION

Minimum Investment
Initial: $5,000   Subsequent: $100

Minimum IRA Investment
Initial: $5,000   Subsequent: $100

Maximum Fees
Load: none   12b-1: none
Other: none

Distributions
Income: quarterly   Capital Gains: Dec

Exchange Options
Number Per Year: no limit   Fee: none
Telephone: yes (money market fund not available)

Services
IRA, pension, auto withdraw

BB&K International Equity (BBIEX)

2755 Campus Drive
San Mateo, CA 94403
(800) 224-5273

International Stock

PERFORMANCE

fund inception date: 10/1/93

	3yr Annual	5yr Annual	10yr Annual	Bull	Bear
Return (%)	na	na	na	na	-9.6
Differ from Category (+/-)	na	na	na	na	-2.6 blw av

Total Risk	Standard Deviation	Category Risk	Risk Index	Beta
na	na	na	na	na

	1994	1993	1992	1991	1990	1989	1988	1987	1986	1985
Return (%)	-12.5	—	—	—	—	—	—	—	—	—
Differ from category (+/-)	-9.5	—	—	—	—	—	—	—	—	—

PER SHARE DATA

	1994	1993	1992	1991	1990	1989	1988	1987	1986	1985
Dividends, Net Income ($)	0.00	—	—	—	—	—	—	—	—	—
Distrib'ns, Cap Gain ($)	0.00	—	—	—	—	—	—	—	—	—
Net Asset Value ($)	5.70	—	—	—	—	—	—	—	—	—
Expense Ratio (%)	1.39	—	—	—	—	—	—	—	—	—
Net Income to Assets (%)	0.29	—	—	—	—	—	—	—	—	—
Portfolio Turnover (%)	176	—	—	—	—	—	—	—	—	—
Total Assets (Millions $)	148	—	—	—	—	—	—	—	—	—

PORTFOLIO (as of 9/30/94)

Portfolio Manager: Richard L. Holbrook - 1993

Investm't Category: International Stock
✔ Cap Gain   Asset Allocation
   Cap & Income   Fund of Funds
   Income   Index
                   Sector
   Domestic   Small Cap
✔ Foreign   Socially Conscious
   Country/Region State Specific

Portfolio: stocks 84%   bonds 0%
convertibles 1%   other 0%   cash 15%

Largest Holdings: Japan 14%, United Kingdom 13%

Unrealized Net Capital Gains: 9% of portfolio value

SHAREHOLDER INFORMATION

Minimum Investment
Initial: $5,000   Subsequent: $100

Minimum IRA Investment
Initial: $5,000   Subsequent: $100

Maximum Fees
Load: none   12b-1: none
Other: none

Distributions
Income: Dec   Capital Gains: Dec

Exchange Options
Number Per Year: no limit   Fee: none
Telephone: yes (money market fund not available)

Services
IRA, pension, auto withdraw

BB&K International Fixed-Income (BBIFX)

International Bond

2755 Campus Drive
San Mateo, CA 94403
(800) 224-5273

PERFORMANCE

fund inception date: 10/1/93

	3yr Annual	5yr Annual	10yr Annual	Bull	Bear
Return (%)	na	na	na	na	-18.9
Differ from Category (+/-)	na	na	na	na	-11.1 low

Total Risk	Standard Deviation	Category Risk	Risk Index	Avg Mat
na	na	na	na	6.3 yrs

	1994	1993	1992	1991	1990	1989	1988	1987	1986	1985
Return (%)	-19.2	—	—	—	—	—	—	—	—	—
Differ from category (+/-) .	-12.9	—	—	—	—	—	—	—	—	—

PER SHARE DATA

	1994	1993	1992	1991	1990	1989	1988	1987	1986	1985
Dividends, Net Income ($) .	0.65	—	—	—	—	—	—	—	—	—
Distrib'ns, Cap Gain ($) . . .	0.00	—	—	—	—	—	—	—	—	—
Net Asset Value ($)	7.81	—	—	—	—	—	—	—	—	—
Expense Ratio (%).	1.12	—	—	—	—	—	—	—	—	—
Net Income to Assets (%). .	5.87	—	—	—	—	—	—	—	—	—
Portfolio Turnover (%). . . .	319	—	—	—	—	—	—	—	—	—
Total Assets (Millions $) . . .	104	—	—	—	—	—	—	—	—	—

PORTFOLIO (as of 9/30/94)

Portfolio Manager: Arthur Micheletti - 1992

Investm't Category: International Bond

Cap Gain	Asset Allocation
Cap & Income	Fund of Funds
✔ Income	Index
	Sector
Domestic	Small Cap
✔ Foreign	Socially Conscious
Country/Region	State Specific

Portfolio: stocks 0%   bonds 86%
convertibles 0%   other 0%   cash 14%

Largest Holdings: Germany 23%, Japan 15%

Unrealized Net Capital Gains: 0% of portfolio value

SHAREHOLDER INFORMATION

Minimum Investment
Initial: $5,000   Subsequent: $100

Minimum IRA Investment
Initial: $5,000   Subsequent: $100

Maximum Fees
Load: none   12b-1: none
Other: none

Distributions
Income: quarterly   Capital Gains: Dec

Exchange Options
Number Per Year: no limit   Fee: none
Telephone: yes (money market fund not available)

Services
IRA, pension, auto withdraw

Benham Adjustable Rate Gov't (BARGX)

1665 Charleston Rd.
Mountain View, CA 94043
(800) 321-8321, (415) 965-4222

Mortgage-Backed Bond

PERFORMANCE

fund inception date: 9/3/91

	3yr Annual	5yr Annual	10yr Annual	Bull	Bear
Return (%)	2.5	na	na	na	-1.1
Differ from Category (+/-)	-0.6 low	na	na	na	3.3 high

Total Risk	Standard Deviation	Category Risk	Risk Index	Avg Mat
low	1.3%	low	0.4	na

	1994	1993	1992	1991	1990	1989	1988	1987	1986	1985
Return (%)	-1.1	3.5	5.2	—	—	—	—	—	—	—
Differ from category (+/-)	1.7	-3.3	-0.9	—	—	—	—	—	—	—

PER SHARE DATA

	1994	1993	1992	1991	1990	1989	1988	1987	1986	1985
Dividends, Net Income ($)	0.47	0.56	0.60	—	—	—	—	—	—	—
Distrib'ns, Cap Gain ($)	0.00	0.00	0.00	—	—	—	—	—	—	—
Net Asset Value ($)	9.26	9.84	10.05	—	—	—	—	—	—	—
Expense Ratio (%)	0.56	0.45	0.00	—	—	—	—	—	—	—
Net Income to Assets (%)	4.53	5.66	7.02	—	—	—	—	—	—	—
Portfolio Turnover (%)	na	82	82	—	—	—	—	—	—	—
Total Assets (Millions $)	446	1,102	886	—	—	—	—	—	—	—

PORTFOLIO (as of 9/30/94)

Portfolio Manager: Randy Merk - 1991

Investm't Category: Mortgage-Backed Bond

Cap Gain	Asset Allocation
Cap & Income	Fund of Funds
✔ Income	Index
	Sector
✔ Domestic	Small Cap
Foreign	Socially Conscious
Country/Region	State Specific

Portfolio: stocks 0% bonds 99%
convertibles 0% other 0% cash 1%

Largest Holdings: mortgage-backed 95%

Unrealized Net Capital Gains: -3% of portfolio value

SHAREHOLDER INFORMATION

Minimum Investment
Initial: $1,000   Subsequent: $100

Minimum IRA Investment
Initial: $1,000   Subsequent: $25

Maximum Fees
Load: none   12b-1: none
Other: none

Distributions
Income: monthly   Capital Gains: Dec

Exchange Options
Number Per Year: 6   Fee: none
Telephone: yes (money market fund available)

Services
IRA, pension, auto exchange, auto invest, auto withdraw

Benham CA Tax-Free High-Yield (BCHYX)

Tax-Exempt Bond

1665 Charleston Rd.
Mountain View, CA 94043
(800) 321-8321, (415) 965-4222

PERFORMANCE

fund inception date: 12/30/86

	3yr Annual	5yr Annual	10yr Annual	Bull	Bear
Return (%)	5.3	6.5	na	43.3	-5.0
Differ from Category (+/-)	0.8 high	0.4 av	na	1.5 av	0.2 abv av

Total Risk	Standard Deviation	Category Risk	Risk Index	Avg Mat
blw av	5.4%	blw av	0.9	20.5 yrs

	1994	1993	1992	1991	1990	1989	1988	1987	1986	1985
Return (%)	-5.3	13.1	9.1	10.9	5.6	9.6	12.4	-11.0	—	—
Differ from category (+/-) . .	-0.1	1.4	0.8	-0.4	-0.7	0.6	2.2	-9.7	—	—

PER SHARE DATA

	1994	1993	1992	1991	1990	1989	1988	1987	1986	1985
Dividends, Net Income ($) .	0.56	0.57	0.57	0.59	0.61	0.65	0.65	0.68	—	—
Distrib'ns, Cap Gain ($) . . .	0.00	0.12	0.00	0.00	0.00	0.00	0.00	0.00	—	—
Net Asset Value ($)	8.54	9.60	9.12	8.90	8.58	8.72	8.57	8.23	—	—
Expense Ratio (%).	0.51	0.55	0.56	0.50	0.24	0.00	0.00	0.00	—	—
Net Income to Assets (%). .	6.02	6.14	6.54	6.79	7.23	7.67	7.85	7.50	—	—
Portfolio Turnover (%)	42	27	33	47	104	50	143	57	—	—
Total Assets (Millions $)	96	116	80	66	45	33	13	8	—	—

PORTFOLIO (as of 8/31/94)

Portfolio Manager: G. David MacEwen - 1991

Investm't Category: Tax-Exempt Bond

Cap Gain	Asset Allocation
Cap & Income	Fund of Funds
✔ Income	Index
	Sector
✔ Domestic	Small Cap
Foreign	Socially Conscious
Country/Region	✔ State Specific

Portfolio: stocks 0% bonds 100%
convertibles 0% other 0% cash 0%

Largest Holdings: general obligation 0%

Unrealized Net Capital Gains: 1% of portfolio value

SHAREHOLDER INFORMATION

Minimum Investment
Initial: $1,000   Subsequent: $100

Minimum IRA Investment
Initial: na   Subsequent: na

Maximum Fees
Load: none   12b-1: none
Other: none

Distributions
Income: monthly   Capital Gains: Dec

Exchange Options
Number Per Year: 6   Fee: none
Telephone: yes (money market fund available)

Services
auto exchange, auto invest, auto withdraw

Benham CA Tax-Free Insured (BCINX)

1665 Charleston Rd.
Mountain View, CA 94043
(800) 321-8321, (415) 965-4222

Tax-Exempt Bond

fund inception date: 12/30/86

PERFORMANCE

	3yr Annual	5yr Annual	10yr Annual	Bull	Bear
Return (%)	4.9	6.5	na	47.8	-7.1
Differ from Category (+/-)	0.4 abv av	0.4 av	na	6.0 high	-1.9 low

Total Risk	Standard Deviation	Category Risk	Risk Index	Avg Mat
av	6.9%	high	1.1	17.1 yrs

	1994	1993	1992	1991	1990	1989	1988	1987	1986	1985
Return (%).	-6.5	13.4	9.1	11.2	6.7	10.3	10.1	-6.0	—	—
Differ from category (+/-) . .	-1.3	1.7	0.8	-0.1	0.4	1.3	-0.1	-4.7	—	—

PER SHARE DATA

	1994	1993	1992	1991	1990	1989	1988	1987	1986	1985
Dividends, Net Income ($).	0.52	0.54	0.57	0.57	0.59	0.59	0.63	0.65	—	—
Distrib'ns, Cap Gain ($) . . .	0.00	0.28	0.10	0.00	0.00	0.00	0.00	0.00	—	—
Net Asset Value ($)	9.23	10.43	9.94	9.74	9.30	9.29	8.98	8.75	—	—
Expense Ratio (%)	0.49	0.52	0.55	0.59	0.61	0.66	0.00	0.00	—	—
Net Income to Assets (%) .	5.20	5.37	5.90	6.18	6.43	6.62	7.39	7.11	—	—
Portfolio Turnover (%)	47	60	54	38	117	74	145	21	—	—
Total Assets (Millions $). . . .	161	223	146	95	60	43	30	13	—	—

PORTFOLIO (as of 8/31/94)

Portfolio Manager: G. David MacEwen - 1991

Investm't Category: Tax-Exempt Bond

Cap Gain	Asset Allocation
Cap & Income	Fund of Funds
✔ Income	Index
	Sector
✔ Domestic	Small Cap
Foreign	Socially Conscious
Country/Region	✔ State Specific

Portfolio: stocks 0%   bonds 100%
convertibles 0%   other 0%   cash 0%

Largest Holdings: general obligation 8%

Unrealized Net Capital Gains: 0% of portfolio value

SHAREHOLDER INFORMATION

Minimum Investment
Initial: $1,000   Subsequent: $100

Minimum IRA Investment
Initial: na   Subsequent: na

Maximum Fees
Load: none   12b-1: none
Other: none

Distributions
Income: monthly   Capital Gains: Dec

Exchange Options
Number Per Year: 6   Fee: none
Telephone: yes (money market fund available)

Services
auto exchange, auto invest, auto withdraw

Benham CA Tax-Free Interm (BCITX)

1665 Charleston Rd.
Mountain View, CA 94043
(800) 321-8321, (415) 965-4222

Tax-Exempt Bond

PERFORMANCE

fund inception date: 11/9/83

	3yr Annual	5yr Annual	10yr Annual	Bull	Bear
Return (%)	4.4	6.1	7.1	36.8	-4.2
Differ from Category (+/-)	-0.1 av	0.0 blw av	-1.0 low	-5.0 low	1.0 abv av

Total Risk	Standard Deviation	Category Risk	Risk Index	Avg Mat
low	4.8%	blw av	0.8	6.9 yrs

	1994	1993	1992	1991	1990	1989	1988	1987	1986	1985
Return (%)	-3.7	10.6	7.0	10.3	6.9	7.9	5.8	0.8	12.5	13.9
Differ from category (+/-)	1.5	-1.1	-1.3	-1.0	0.6	-1.1	-4.4	2.1	-3.9	-3.5

PER SHARE DATA

	1994	1993	1992	1991	1990	1989	1988	1987	1986	1985
Dividends, Net Income ($)	0.53	0.55	0.58	0.60	0.62	0.63	0.63	0.63	0.67	0.69
Distrib'ns, Cap Gain ($)	0.00	0.09	0.02	0.00	0.00	0.00	0.00	0.00	0.00	0.00
Net Asset Value ($)	10.43	11.38	10.88	10.74	10.30	10.23	10.08	10.12	10.67	10.10
Expense Ratio (%)	0.48	0.50	0.52	0.55	0.58	0.60	0.64	0.67	0.74	0.96
Net Income to Assets (%)	4.82	5.05	5.50	5.84	6.08	6.25	6.19	5.92	6.71	7.11
Portfolio Turnover (%)	43	26	49	29	20	40	47	52	23	48
Total Assets (Millions $)	393	469	305	242	191	167	157	167	124	56

PORTFOLIO (as of 8/31/94)

Portfolio Manager: G. David MacEwen - 1991

Investm't Category: Tax-Exempt Bond

Cap Gain	Asset Allocation
Cap & Income	Fund of Funds
✔ Income	Index
	Sector
✔ Domestic	Small Cap
Foreign	Socially Conscious
Country/Region	✔ State Specific

Portfolio: stocks 0%   bonds 100%
convertibles 0%   other 0%   cash 0%

Largest Holdings: general obligation 0%

Unrealized Net Capital Gains: 1% of portfolio value

SHAREHOLDER INFORMATION

Minimum Investment
Initial: $1,000   Subsequent: $100

Minimum IRA Investment
Initial: na   Subsequent: na

Maximum Fees
Load: none   12b-1: none
Other: none

Distributions
Income: monthly   Capital Gains: Dec

Exchange Options
Number Per Year: 6   Fee: none
Telephone: yes (money market fund available)

Services
auto exchange, auto invest, auto withdraw

Benham CA Tax-Free Long-Term (BCLTX)

Tax-Exempt Bond

1665 Charleston Rd.
Mountain View, CA 94043
(800) 321-8321, (415) 965-4222

PERFORMANCE

fund inception date: 11/9/83

	3yr Annual	5yr Annual	10yr Annual	Bull	Bear
Return (%)	4.7	6.5	8.3	46.9	-6.4
Differ from Category (+/-)	0.2 av	0.4 av	0.2 av	5.1 abv av	-1.2 blw av

Total Risk	Standard Deviation	Category Risk	Risk Index	Avg Mat
blw av	6.5%	abv av	1.0	17.9 yrs

	1994	1993	1992	1991	1990	1989	1988	1987	1986	1985
Return (%)	-6.5	13.7	8.1	11.8	6.5	9.7	10.4	-4.5	19.2	17.8
Differ from category (+/-)	-1.3	2.0	-0.2	0.5	0.2	0.7	0.2	-3.2	2.8	0.4

PER SHARE DATA

	1994	1993	1992	1991	1990	1989	1988	1987	1986	1985
Dividends, Net Income ($)	0.62	0.65	0.68	0.70	0.71	0.73	0.74	0.76	0.80	0.85
Distrib'ns, Cap Gain ($)	0.06	0.43	0.27	0.00	0.00	0.00	0.00	0.00	0.09	0.00
Net Asset Value ($)	10.21	11.63	11.21	11.28	10.75	10.78	10.51	10.21	11.49	10.43
Expense Ratio (%)	0.48	0.49	0.52	0.55	0.57	0.58	0.63	0.65	0.74	0.95
Net Income to Assets (%)	5.51	5.76	6.14	6.48	6.64	6.98	7.19	6.87	7.70	8.58
Portfolio Turnover (%)	61	55	72	38	74	78	35	82	47	91
Total Assets (Millions $)	249	324	276	247	197	178	143	180	196	83

PORTFOLIO (as of 8/31/94)

Portfolio Manager: G. David MacEwen - 1991

Investm't Category: Tax-Exempt Bond

Cap Gain	Asset Allocation
Cap & Income	Fund of Funds
✔ Income	Index
	Sector
✔ Domestic	Small Cap
Foreign	Socially Conscious
Country/Region	✔ State Specific

Portfolio: stocks 0% bonds 100%
convertibles 0% other 0% cash 0%

Largest Holdings: general obligation 0%

Unrealized Net Capital Gains: 1% of portfolio value

SHAREHOLDER INFORMATION

Minimum Investment
Initial: $1,000   Subsequent: $100

Minimum IRA Investment
Initial: na   Subsequent: na

Maximum Fees
Load: none   12b-1: none
Other: none

Distributions
Income: monthly   Capital Gains: Dec

Exchange Options
Number Per Year: 6   Fee: none
Telephone: yes (money market fund available)

Services
auto exchange, auto invest, auto withdraw

Benham CA Tax-Free Short-Term (BCSTX)

1665 Charleston Rd.
Mountain View, CA 94043
(800) 321-8321, (415) 965-4222

Tax-Exempt Bond

	3yr Annual	5yr Annual	10yr Annual	Bull	Bear
Return (%)	na	na	na	na	-1.3
Differ from Category (+/-)	na	na	na	na	3.9 high

Total Risk	Standard Deviation	Category Risk	Risk Index	Avg Mat
na	na	na	na	2.7 yrs

	1994	1993	1992	1991	1990	1989	1988	1987	1986	1985
Return (%)	-0.6	5.9	—	—	—	—	—	—	—	—
Differ from category (+/-) . . .	4.6	-5.8	—	—	—	—	—	—	—	—

PER SHARE DATA

	1994	1993	1992	1991	1990	1989	1988	1987	1986	1985
Dividends, Net Income ($) .	0.39	0.38	—	—	—	—	—	—	—	—
Distrib'ns, Cap Gain ($) . . .	0.00	0.04	—	—	—	—	—	—	—	—
Net Asset Value ($)	9.90	10.35	—	—	—	—	—	—	—	—
Expense Ratio (%).	0.51	0.36	—	—	—	—	—	—	—	—
Net Income to Assets (%). .	3.68	3.76	—	—	—	—	—	—	—	—
Portfolio Turnover (%).	65	54	—	—	—	—	—	—	—	—
Total Assets (Millions $) . . .	106	125	—	—	—	—	—	—	—	—

PORTFOLIO (as of 8/31/94)

Portfolio Manager: G. David MacEwen - 1992

Investm't Category: Tax-Exempt Bond

Cap Gain	Asset Allocation
Cap & Income	Fund of Funds
✔ Income	Index
	Sector
✔ Domestic	Small Cap
Foreign	Socially Conscious
Country/Region	✔ State Specific

Portfolio: stocks 0% bonds 100%
convertibles 0% other 0% cash 0%

Largest Holdings: general obligation 0%

Unrealized Net Capital Gains: 0% of portfolio value

SHAREHOLDER INFORMATION

Minimum Investment
Initial: $1,000   Subsequent: $100

Minimum IRA Investment
Initial: na   Subsequent: na

Maximum Fees
Load: none   12b-1: none
Other: none

Distributions
Income: Monthly   Capital Gains: Dec

Exchange Options
Number Per Year: 6   Fee: none
Telephone: yes (money market fund available)

Services
auto exchange, auto invest, auto withdraw

Benham Equity Growth
(BEQGX)
Growth

1665 Charleston Rd.
Mountain View, CA 94043
(800) 321-8321, (415) 965-4222

PERFORMANCE

fund inception date: 5/9/91

	3yr Annual	5yr Annual	10yr Annual	Bull	Bear
Return (%)	5.0	na	na	na	-5.5
Differ from Category (+/-)	-2.7 blw av	na	na	na	1.1 av

Total Risk	Standard Deviation	Category Risk	Risk Index	Beta
av	7.9%	low	0.8	0.9

	1994	1993	1992	1991	1990	1989	1988	1987	1986	1985
Return (%).............	-0.2	11.4	4.1	—	—	—	—	—	—	—
Differ from category (+/-) ..	0.4	-2.0	-7.5	—	—	—	—	—	—	—

PER SHARE DATA

	1994	1993	1992	1991	1990	1989	1988	1987	1986	1985
Dividends, Net Income ($).	0.30	0.23	0.33	—	—	—	—	—	—	—
Distrib'ns, Cap Gain ($) ...	0.26	0.66	0.02	—	—	—	—	—	—	—
Net Asset Value ($)	11.53	12.12	11.68	—	—	—	—	—	—	—
Expense Ratio (%)	0.75	0.75	0.75	—	—	—	—	—	—	—
Net Income to Assets (%) .	2.11	2.04	2.33	—	—	—	—	—	—	—
Portfolio Turnover (%)	na	96	114	—	—	—	—	—	—	—
Total Assets (Millions $).....	97	96	74	—	—	—	—	—	—	—

PORTFOLIO (as of 6/30/94)

Portfolio Manager: Steve Colton - 1991

Investm't Category: Growth
- ✔ Cap Gain
- Cap & Income
- Income
- Asset Allocation
- Fund of Funds
- Index
- Sector
- ✔ Domestic
- Foreign
- Country/Region
- Small Cap
- Socially Conscious
- State Specific

Portfolio: stocks 99% bonds 0%
convertibles 0% other 0% cash 1%

Largest Holdings: utilities—telephone 10%, major regional banks 8%

Unrealized Net Capital Gains: 1% of portfolio value

SHAREHOLDER INFORMATION

Minimum Investment
Initial: $1,000   Subsequent: $100

Minimum IRA Investment
Initial: $1,000   Subsequent: $100

Maximum Fees
Load: none   12b-1: none
Other: none

Distributions
Income: quarterly   Capital Gains: Dec

Exchange Options
Number Per Year: 6   Fee: none
Telephone: yes (money market fund available)

Services
IRA, pension, auto exchange, auto invest, auto withdraw

Benham European Gov't Bond (BEGBX)

International Bond

1665 Charleston Rd.
Mountain View, CA 94043
(800) 321-8321, (415) 965-4222

PERFORMANCE

fund inception date: 2/5/92

	3yr Annual	5yr Annual	10yr Annual	Bull	Bear
Return (%)	na	na	na	na	-1.0
Differ from Category (+/-)	na	na	na	na	6.8 high

Total Risk	Standard Deviation	Category Risk	Risk Index	Avg Mat
na	na	na	na	6.6 yrs

	1994	1993	1992	1991	1990	1989	1988	1987	1986	1985
Return (%)	1.5	11.6	—	—	—	—	—	—	—	—
Differ from category (+/-)	7.8	-1.8	—	—	—	—	—	—	—	—

PER SHARE DATA

	1994	1993	1992	1991	1990	1989	1988	1987	1986	1985
Dividends, Net Income ($)	0.60	0.11	—	—	—	—	—	—	—	—
Distrib'ns, Cap Gain ($)	0.01	0.26	—	—	—	—	—	—	—	—
Net Asset Value ($)	10.36	10.82	—	—	—	—	—	—	—	—
Expense Ratio (%)	0.87	0.85	—	—	—	—	—	—	—	—
Net Income to Assets (%)	5.88	6.27	—	—	—	—	—	—	—	—
Portfolio Turnover (%)	na	310	—	—	—	—	—	—	—	—
Total Assets (Millions $)	193	354	—	—	—	—	—	—	—	—

PORTFOLIO (as of 6/30/94)

Portfolio Manager: Jeff Tyler - 1992

Investm't Category: International Bond

Cap Gain	Asset Allocation
Cap & Income	Fund of Funds
✔ Income	Index
	Sector
Domestic	Small Cap
✔ Foreign	Socially Conscious
✔ Country/Region	State Specific

Portfolio: stocks 0% bonds 100%
convertibles 0% other 0% cash 0%

Largest Holdings: Germany 30%, France 23%

Unrealized Net Capital Gains: -1% of portfolio value

SHAREHOLDER INFORMATION

Minimum Investment
Initial: $1,000   Subsequent: $100

Minimum IRA Investment
Initial: $1,000   Subsequent: $25

Maximum Fees
Load: none   12b-1: none
Other: none

Distributions
Income: quarterly   Capital Gains: Dec

Exchange Options
Number Per Year: 6   Fee: none
Telephone: yes (money market fund available)

Services
IRA, pension, auto exchange, auto invest, auto withdraw

Benham GNMA Income
(BGNMX)
Mortgage-Backed Bond

1665 Charleston Rd.
Mountain View, CA 94043
(800) 321-8321, (415) 965-4222

PERFORMANCE

fund inception date: 9/23/85

	3yr Annual	5yr Annual	10yr Annual	Bull	Bear
Return (%)	4.1	7.5	na	40.4	-3.5
Differ from Category (+/-)	1.0 high	0.6 abv av	na	2.4 high	0.9 abv av

Total Risk	Standard Deviation	Category Risk	Risk Index	Avg Mat
low	3.1%	blw av	0.9	na

	1994	1993	1992	1991	1990	1989	1988	1987	1986	1985
Return (%)	-1.6	6.5	7.6	15.5	10.1	13.8	8.5	2.7	11.3	—
Differ from category (+/-)	1.2	-0.3	1.5	1.1	0.4	1.3	1.4	0.9	0.1	—

PER SHARE DATA

	1994	1993	1992	1991	1990	1989	1988	1987	1986	1985
Dividends, Net Income ($)	0.68	0.70	0.81	0.86	0.89	0.90	0.88	0.88	1.02	—
Distrib'ns, Cap Gain ($)	0.00	0.01	0.00	0.00	0.00	0.00	0.00	0.07	0.00	—
Net Asset Value ($)	9.90	10.76	10.78	10.80	10.15	10.08	9.69	9.76	10.44	—
Expense Ratio (%)	0.57	0.56	0.62	0.72	0.75	0.75	0.73	0.74	0.29	—
Net Income to Assets (%)	6.74	7.31	8.18	8.85	9.04	9.11	8.94	8.79	10.52	—
Portfolio Turnover (%)	na	70	97	207	433	497	497	566	264	—
Total Assets (Millions $)	952	1,261	724	409	290	253	259	393	169	—

PORTFOLIO (as of 9/30/94)

Portfolio Manager: Randall Merk - 1987

Investm't Category: Mortgage-Backed Bond

Cap Gain	Asset Allocation
Cap & Income	Fund of Funds
✔ Income	Index
	Sector
✔ Domestic	Small Cap
Foreign	Socially Conscious
Country/Region	State Specific

Portfolio: stocks 0% bonds 94%
convertibles 0% other 0% cash 6%

Largest Holdings: mortgage-backed 90%,
U.S. government 4%

Unrealized Net Capital Gains: -3% of portfolio value

SHAREHOLDER INFORMATION

Minimum Investment
Initial: $1,000   Subsequent: $100

Minimum IRA Investment
Initial: $1,000   Subsequent: $25

Maximum Fees
Load: none   12b-1: none
Other: none

Distributions
Income: monthly   Capital Gains: Dec

Exchange Options
Number Per Year: 6   Fee: none
Telephone: yes (money market fund available)

Services
IRA, pension, auto exchange, auto invest, auto withdraw

Benham Gold Equities Index (BGEIX)

1665 Charleston Rd.
Mountain View, CA 94043
(800) 321-8321, (415) 965-4222

Gold

PERFORMANCE

fund inception date: 8/17/88

	3yr Annual	5yr Annual	10yr Annual	Bull	Bear
Return (%)	11.2	-0.2	na	30.2	-14.0
Differ from Category (+/-)	0.4 av	-0.2 blw av	na	-2.7 blw av	-4.0 low

Total Risk	Standard Deviation	Category Risk	Risk Index	Beta
high	28.1%	high	1.0	0.4

	1994	1993	1992	1991	1990	1989	1988	1987	1986	1985
Return (%)	-16.7	81.2	-8.6	-11.2	-19.4	29.9	—	—	—	—
Differ from category (+/-) . .	-5.2	-5.7	7.1	-6.4	3.1	5.2	—	—	—	—

PER SHARE DATA

	1994	1993	1992	1991	1990	1989	1988	1987	1986	1985
Dividends, Net Income ($) .	0.02	0.01	0.01	0.02	0.05	0.05	—	—	—	—
Distrib'ns, Cap Gain ($) . . .	0.03	0.00	0.00	0.00	0.03	0.00	—	—	—	—
Net Asset Value ($)	11.33	13.67	7.55	8.28	9.35	11.71	—	—	—	—
Expense Ratio (%)	0.60	0.72	0.75	0.75	0.96	1.00	—	—	—	—
Net Income to Assets (%) . .	0.25	0.23	0.23	0.30	0.01	0.36	—	—	—	—
Portfolio Turnover (%)	na	28	53	56	21	34	—	—	—	—
Total Assets (Millions $) . . .	570	636	164	124	104	62	—	—	—	—

PORTFOLIO (as of 6/30/94)

Portfolio Manager: Bill Martin - 1992

Investm't Category: Gold

✔ Cap Gain   Asset Allocation
   Cap & Income   Fund of Funds
   Income   ✔ Index
       ✔ Sector
✔ Domestic   Small Cap
✔ Foreign   Socially Conscious
   Country/Region   State Specific

Portfolio: stocks 100%   bonds 0%
convertibles 0%   other 0%   cash 0%

Largest Holdings: Benham North American Gold Equities Index

Unrealized Net Capital Gains: 6% of portfolio value

SHAREHOLDER INFORMATION

Minimum Investment
Initial: $1,000   Subsequent: $100

Minimum IRA Investment
Initial: $1,000   Subsequent: $25

Maximum Fees
Load: none   12b-1: none
Other: none

Distributions
Income: Jun, Dec   Capital Gains: Dec

Exchange Options
Number Per Year: 6   Fee: none
Telephone: yes (money market fund available)

Services
IRA, pension, auto exchange, auto invest, auto withdraw

Benham Income & Growth (BIGRX)

Growth & Income

1665 Charleston Rd.
Mountain View, CA 94043
(800) 321-8321, (415) 965-4222

PERFORMANCE

fund inception date: 5/9/91

	3yr Annual	5yr Annual	10yr Annual	Bull	Bear
Return (%)	6.0	na	na	na	-6.4
Differ from Category (+/-)	-1.1 blw av	na	na	na	-0.1 av

Total Risk	Standard Deviation	Category Risk	Risk Index	Beta
av	7.4%	blw av	0.9	0.9

	1994	1993	1992	1991	1990	1989	1988	1987	1986	1985
Return (%).............	-0.5	11.3	7.8	—	—	—	—	—	—	—
Differ from category (+/-) ..	0.9	-1.9	-2.4	—	—	—	—	—	—	—

PER SHARE DATA

	1994	1993	1992	1991	1990	1989	1988	1987	1986	1985
Dividends, Net Income ($).	0.43	0.42	0.42	—	—	—	—	—	—	—
Distrib'ns, Cap Gain ($) ...	0.64	0.19	0.03	—	—	—	—	—	—	—
Net Asset Value ($)	13.92	15.08	14.11	—	—	—	—	—	—	—
Expense Ratio (%)	0.75	0.75	0.75	—	—	—	—	—	—	—
Net Income to Assets (%) .	2.92	2.90	3.16	—	—	—	—	—	—	—
Portfolio Turnover (%)	na	31	63	—	—	—	—	—	—	—
Total Assets (Millions $)....	224	232	141	—	—	—	—	—	—	—

PORTFOLIO (as of 6/30/94)

Portfolio Manager: Steve Colton - 1991

Investm't Category: Growth & Income
- Cap Gain
- ✔ Cap & Income
- Income
- ✔ Domestic
- Foreign
- Country/Region
- Asset Allocation
- Fund of Funds
- Index
- Sector
- Small Cap
- Socially Conscious
- State Specific

Portfolio: stocks 99%   bonds 0%
convertibles 0%   other 0%   cash 1%

Largest Holdings: telephone utilities 10%, electric company utilities 8%

Unrealized Net Capital Gains: 0% of portfolio value

SHAREHOLDER INFORMATION

Minimum Investment
Initial: $1,000   Subsequent: $100

Minimum IRA Investment
Initial: $1,000   Subsequent: $25

Maximum Fees
Load: none   12b-1: none
Other: none

Distributions
Income: monthly   Capital Gains: Dec

Exchange Options
Number Per Year: 6   Fee: none
Telephone: yes (money market fund available)

Services
IRA, pension, auto exchange, auto invest, auto withdraw

Benham Long-Term Treasury & Agency

(BLAGX) *Government Bond*

1665 Charleston Rd.
Mountain View, CA 94043
(800) 321-8321, (415) 965-4222

PERFORMANCE

fund inception date: 9/8/92

	3yr Annual	5yr Annual	10yr Annual	Bull	Bear
Return (%)	na	na	na	na	-12.2
Differ from Category (+/-)	na	na	na	na	-5.8 low

Total Risk	Standard Deviation	Category Risk	Risk Index	Avg Mat
na	na	na	na	21.1 yrs

	1994	1993	1992	1991	1990	1989	1988	1987	1986	1985
Return (%)	-9.2	17.6	—	—	—	—	—	—	—	—
Differ from category (+/-)	-4.4	6.7	—	—	—	—	—	—	—	—

PER SHARE DATA

	1994	1993	1992	1991	1990	1989	1988	1987	1986	1985
Dividends, Net Income ($)	0.59	0.66	—	—	—	—	—	—	—	—
Distrib'ns, Cap Gain ($)	0.00	0.59	—	—	—	—	—	—	—	—
Net Asset Value ($)	8.69	10.22	—	—	—	—	—	—	—	—
Expense Ratio (%)	0.68	0.00	—	—	—	—	—	—	—	—
Net Income to Assets (%)	6.64	7.18	—	—	—	—	—	—	—	—
Portfolio Turnover (%)	na	56	—	—	—	—	—	—	—	—
Total Assets (Millions $)	28	23	—	—	—	—	—	—	—	—

PORTFOLIO (as of 9/30/94)

Portfolio Manager: David Schroeder - 1992

Investm't Category: Government Bond

Cap Gain	Asset Allocation
Cap & Income	Fund of Funds
✔ Income	Index
	Sector
✔ Domestic	Small Cap
Foreign	Socially Conscious
Country/Region	State Specific

Portfolio: stocks 0%   bonds 100%
convertibles 0%   other 0%   cash 0%

Largest Holdings: U.S. government 100%

Unrealized Net Capital Gains: -4% of portfolio value

SHAREHOLDER INFORMATION

Minimum Investment
Initial: $1,000   Subsequent: $100

Minimum IRA Investment
Initial: $1,000   Subsequent: $25

Maximum Fees
Load: none   12b-1: none
Other: none

Distributions
Income: monthly   Capital Gains: Dec

Exchange Options
Number Per Year: 6   Fee: none
Telephone: yes (money market fund available)

Services
IRA, pension, auto exchange, auto invest, auto withdraw

Benham Nat'l Tax-Free Interm Term (BNTIX)

1665 Charleston Rd.
Mountain View, CA 94043
(800) 321-8321, (415) 965-4222

Tax-Exempt Bond

fund inception date: 7/31/84

	3yr Annual	5yr Annual	10yr Annual	Bull	Bear
Return (%)	4.4	6.3	7.5	38.3	-4.1
Differ from Category (+/-)	-0.1 av	0.2 av	-0.6 blw av	-3.5 blw av	1.1 abv av

Total Risk	Standard Deviation		Category Risk	Risk Index		Avg Mat
low	4.8%		blw av	0.8		6.1 yrs

	1994	1993	1992	1991	1990	1989	1988	1987	1986	1985
Return (%).	-3.5	10.1	7.1	11.6	6.8	8.2	6.6	2.2	14.2	12.5
Differ from category (+/-) . .	1.7	-1.6	-1.2	0.3	0.5	-0.8	-3.6	3.5	-2.2	-4.9

PER SHARE DATA

	1994	1993	1992	1991	1990	1989	1988	1987	1986	1985
Dividends, Net Income ($).	0.50	0.51	0.54	0.58	0.62	0.62	0.64	0.63	0.68	0.74
Distrib'ns, Cap Gain ($) . . .	0.04	0.11	0.11	0.12	0.01	0.00	0.00	0.00	0.00	0.00
Net Asset Value ($)	10.19	11.11	10.67	10.58	10.14	10.10	9.92	9.91	10.32	9.66
Expense Ratio (%)	0.67	0.72	0.65	0.50	0.50	0.50	0.50	0.50	0.27	0.00
Net Income to Assets (%) .	4.61	4.81	5.38	5.97	6.12	6.36	6.34	6.27	7.41	8.26
Portfolio Turnover (%)	46	36	85	55	142	49	54	26	44	77
Total Assets (Millions $).	62	76	44	34	25	21	20	20	12	3

PORTFOLIO (as of 5/31/94)

Portfolio Manager: G. David MacEwen - 1991

Investm't Category: Tax-Exempt Bond

Cap Gain	Asset Allocation
Cap & Income	Fund of Funds
✔ Income	Index
	Sector
✔ Domestic	Small Cap
Foreign	Socially Conscious
Country/Region	State Specific

Portfolio: stocks 0% bonds 100%
convertibles 0% other 0% cash 0%

Largest Holdings: general obligation 24%

Unrealized Net Capital Gains: 1% of portfolio value

SHAREHOLDER INFORMATION

Minimum Investment
Initial: $1,000 Subsequent: $100

Minimum IRA Investment
Initial: na Subsequent: na

Maximum Fees
Load: none 12b-1: none
Other: none

Distributions
Income: monthly Capital Gains: Dec

Exchange Options
Number Per Year: 6 Fee: none
Telephone: yes (money market fund available)

Services
auto exchange, auto invest, auto withdraw

Benham Nat'l Tax-Free Long-Term (BTFLX)

Tax-Exempt Bond

1665 Charleston Rd.
Mountain View, CA 94043
(800) 321-8321, (415) 965-4222

PERFORMANCE

fund inception date: 7/31/84

	3yr Annual	5yr Annual	10yr Annual	Bull	Bear
Return (%)	5.4	7.1	8.5	50.5	-6.5
Differ from Category (+/-)	0.9 high	1.0 high	0.4 av	8.7 high	-1.3 blw av

Total Risk	Standard Deviation	Category Risk	Risk Index	Avg Mat
av	6.9%	high	1.1	15.6 yrs

	1994	1993	1992	1991	1990	1989	1988	1987	1986	1985
Return (%)	-6.1	14.2	9.2	12.9	6.7	9.6	11.2	-6.7	18.7	19.1
Differ from category (+/-) ..	-0.9	2.5	0.9	1.6	0.4	0.6	1.0	-5.4	2.3	1.7

PER SHARE DATA

	1994	1993	1992	1991	1990	1989	1988	1987	1986	1985
Dividends, Net Income ($)	0.61	0.63	0.64	0.69	0.72	0.74	0.77	0.80	0.89	0.97
Distrib'ns, Cap Gain ($) ...	0.06	0.24	0.29	0.23	0.09	0.05	0.00	0.00	0.00	0.00
Net Asset Value ($)	10.70	12.10	11.38	11.31	10.88	11.00	10.78	10.41	12.00	10.90
Expense Ratio (%)........	0.67	0.72	0.65	0.50	0.50	0.50	0.50	0.50	0.26	0.00
Net Income to Assets (%)..	5.16	5.40	6.00	6.57	6.58	7.14	7.27	7.11	8.61	9.70
Portfolio Turnover (%).....	39	105	148	150	215	69	76	102	57	32
Total Assets (Millions $)	45	66	42	35	44	33	25	24	22	7

PORTFOLIO (as of 5/31/94)

Portfolio Manager: G. David MacEwen - 1991

Investm't Category: Tax-Exempt Bond

Cap Gain	Asset Allocation
Cap & Income	Fund of Funds
✔ Income	Index
	Sector
✔ Domestic	Small Cap
Foreign	Socially Conscious
Country/Region	State Specific

Portfolio: stocks 0% bonds 100%
convertibles 0% other 0% cash 0%

Largest Holdings: general obligation 0%

Unrealized Net Capital Gains: 2% of portfolio value

SHAREHOLDER INFORMATION

Minimum Investment
Initial: $1,000   Subsequent: $100

Minimum IRA Investment
Initial: na   Subsequent: na

Maximum Fees
Load: none   12b-1: none
Other: none

Distributions
Income: monthly   Capital Gains: Dec

Exchange Options
Number Per Year: 6   Fee: none
Telephone: yes (money market fund available)

Services
auto exchange, auto invest, auto withdraw

Benham Short-Term Treasury & Agency (BSTAX)

Government Bond

1665 Charleston Rd.
Mountain View, CA 94043
(800) 321-8321, (415) 965-4222

PERFORMANCE

fund inception date: 9/8/92

	3yr Annual	5yr Annual	10yr Annual	Bull	Bear
Return (%)	na	na	na	na	-1.1
Differ from Category (+/-)	na	na	na	na	5.3 high

Total Risk	Standard Deviation	Category Risk	Risk Index	Avg Mat
na	na	na	na	1.9 yrs

	1994	1993	1992	1991	1990	1989	1988	1987	1986	1985
Return (%)	0.1	5.3	—	—	—	—	—	—	—	—
Differ from category (+/-)	4.9	-5.6	—	—	—	—	—	—	—	—

PER SHARE DATA

	1994	1993	1992	1991	1990	1989	1988	1987	1986	1985
Dividends, Net Income ($)	0.44	0.38	—	—	—	—	—	—	—	—
Distrib'ns, Cap Gain ($)	0.00	0.04	—	—	—	—	—	—	—	—
Net Asset Value ($)	9.57	10.00	—	—	—	—	—	—	—	—
Expense Ratio (%)	0.68	0.00	—	—	—	—	—	—	—	—
Net Income to Assets (%)	4.69	4.50	—	—	—	—	—	—	—	—
Portfolio Turnover (%)	na	157	—	—	—	—	—	—	—	—
Total Assets (Millions $)	30	24	—	—	—	—	—	—	—	—

PORTFOLIO (as of 9/30/94)

Portfolio Manager: David Schroeder

Investm't Category: Government Bond

Cap Gain	Asset Allocation
Cap & Income	Fund of Funds
✔ Income	Index
	Sector
✔ Domestic	Small Cap
Foreign	Socially Conscious
Country/Region	State Specific

Portfolio: stocks 0%   bonds 100%
convertibles 0%   other 0%   cash 0%

Largest Holdings: U.S. government & agencies 100%

Unrealized Net Capital Gains: -1% of portfolio value

SHAREHOLDER INFORMATION

Minimum Investment
Initial: $1,000   Subsequent: $100

Minimum IRA Investment
Initial: $1,000   Subsequent: $25

Maximum Fees
Load: none   12b-1: none
Other: none

Distributions
Income: monthly   Capital Gains: Dec

Exchange Options
Number Per Year: 6   Fee: none
Telephone: yes (money market fund available)

Services
IRA, pension, auto exchange, auto invest, auto withdraw

Benham Target Mat Trust—1995 (BTMFX)

1665 Charleston Rd.
Mountain View, CA 94043
(800) 321-8321, (415) 965-4222

Government Bond

PERFORMANCE

fund inception date: 3/25/85

	3yr Annual	5yr Annual	10yr Annual	Bull	Bear
Return (%)	4.9	7.9	na	42.2	-1.1
Differ from Category (+/-)	0.9 high	1.2 high	na	-9.0 av	5.3 high

Total Risk	Standard Deviation	Category Risk	Risk Index	Avg Mat
low	3.1%	blw av	0.6	1.1 yrs

	1994	1993	1992	1991	1990	1989	1988	1987	1986	1985
Return (%)	0.7	6.9	7.3	16.1	9.2	15.3	7.8	-3.8	26.3	—
Differ from category (+/-)	5.5	-4.0	0.9	0.8	3.0	0.8	-0.1	-1.7	5.7	—

PER SHARE DATA

	1994	1993	1992	1991	1990	1989	1988	1987	1986	1985
Dividends, Net Income ($)	0.00	0.00	0.00	0.00	0.00	0.00	0.00	0.00	0.00	—
Distrib'ns, Cap Gain ($)	0.00	0.00	0.00	0.00	0.00	0.00	0.00	0.00	0.00	—
Net Asset Value ($)	95.29	94.57	88.43	82.40	70.94	64.96	56.33	52.22	54.33	—
Expense Ratio (%)	0.61	0.59	0.62	0.65	0.70	0.70	0.70	0.70	0.70	—
Net Income to Assets (%)	4.47	5.22	6.39	7.35	7.74	7.95	8.09	7.70	7.29	—
Portfolio Turnover (%)	177	139	140	110	121	95	108	86	89	—
Total Assets (Millions $)	80	80	95	92	58	39	16	7	5	—

PORTFOLIO (as of 9/30/94)

Portfolio Manager: David Schroeder - 1990

Investm't Category: Government Bond
Cap Gain	Asset Allocation
Cap & Income	Fund of Funds
✔ Income	Index
	Sector
✔ Domestic	Small Cap
Foreign	Socially Conscious
Country/Region	State Specific

Portfolio: stocks 0%   bonds 100%
convertibles 0%   other 0%   cash 0%

Largest Holdings: U.S. government 100%

Unrealized Net Capital Gains: 0% of portfolio value

SHAREHOLDER INFORMATION

Minimum Investment
Initial: $1,000   Subsequent: $100

Minimum IRA Investment
Initial: $1,000   Subsequent: $25

Maximum Fees
Load: none   12b-1: none
Other: none

Distributions
Income: Dec   Capital Gains: Dec

Exchange Options
Number Per Year: 6   Fee: none
Telephone: yes (money market fund available)

Services
IRA, pension, auto exchange, auto invest, auto withdraw

Benham Target Mat Trust—2000 (BTMTX)

Government Bond

1665 Charleston Rd.
Mountain View, CA 94043
(800) 321-8321, (415) 965-4222

PERFORMANCE

fund inception date: 3/25/85

	3yr Annual	5yr Annual	10yr Annual	Bull	Bear
Return (%)	5.2	8.3	na	69.2	-8.4
Differ from Category (+/-)	1.2 high	1.6 high	na	18.0 high	-2.0 blw av

Total Risk	Standard Deviation	Category Risk	Risk Index	Avg Mat
av	7.3%	high	1.6	6.0 yrs

	1994	1993	1992	1991	1990	1989	1988	1987	1986	1985
Return (%)	-6.8	15.4	8.4	20.6	6.3	19.8	11.4	-5.9	32.3	—
Differ from category (+/-)	-2.0	4.5	2.0	5.3	0.1	5.3	3.5	-3.8	11.7	—

PER SHARE DATA

	1994	1993	1992	1991	1990	1989	1988	1987	1986	1985
Dividends, Net Income ($)	0.00	0.00	0.00	0.00	0.00	0.00	0.00	0.00	0.00	—
Distrib'ns, Cap Gain ($)	0.00	0.00	0.00	0.00	0.00	0.00	0.00	0.00	0.00	—
Net Asset Value ($)	66.60	71.53	61.95	57.11	47.33	44.52	37.16	33.33	35.44	—
Expense Ratio (%)	0.59	0.60	0.66	0.66	0.70	0.70	0.70	0.70	0.70	—
Net Income to Assets (%)	5.74	5.94	6.90	7.67	7.84	7.81	8.33	8.08	7.34	—
Portfolio Turnover (%)	89	76	93	67	79	49	163	73	39	—
Total Assets (Millions $)	255	288	190	90	53	35	14	6	5	—

PORTFOLIO (as of 9/30/94)

Portfolio Manager: David Schroeder - 1990

Investm't Category: Government Bond

Cap Gain	Asset Allocation
Cap & Income	Fund of Funds
✔ Income	Index
	Sector
✔ Domestic	Small Cap
Foreign	Socially Conscious
Country/Region	State Specific

Portfolio: stocks 0% bonds 100%
convertibles 0% other 0% cash 0%

Largest Holdings: U. S. government 100%

Unrealized Net Capital Gains: -4% of portfolio value

SHAREHOLDER INFORMATION

Minimum Investment
Initial: $1,000   Subsequent: $100

Minimum IRA Investment
Initial: $1,000   Subsequent: $25

Maximum Fees
Load: none   12b-1: none
Other: none

Distributions
Income: Dec   Capital Gains: Dec

Exchange Options
Number Per Year: 6   Fee: none
Telephone: yes (money market fund available)

Services
IRA, pension, auto exchange, auto invest, auto withdraw

Benham Target Mat Trust—2005 (BTFIX)

Government Bond

1665 Charleston Rd.
Mountain View, CA 94043
(800) 321-8321, (415) 965-4222

PERFORMANCE

fund inception date: 3/25/85

	3yr Annual	5yr Annual	10yr Annual	Bull	Bear
Return (%)	6.6	8.8	na	88.6	-12.6
Differ from Category (+/-)	2.6 high	2.1 high	na	37.4 high	-6.2 low

Total Risk	Standard Deviation	Category Risk	Risk Index	Avg Mat
abv av	10.1%	high	2.2	10.9 yrs

	1994	1993	1992	1991	1990	1989	1988	1987	1986	1985
Return (%)	-8.8	21.5	9.5	21.4	3.5	23.8	14.4	-10.3	42.2	—
Differ from category (+/-) . .	-4.0	10.6	3.1	6.1	-2.7	9.3	6.5	-8.2	21.6	—

PER SHARE DATA

	1994	1993	1992	1991	1990	1989	1988	1987	1986	1985
Dividends, Net Income ($) .	0.00	0.00	0.00	0.00	0.00	0.00	0.00	0.00	0.00	—
Distrib'ns, Cap Gain ($) . . .	0.00	0.00	0.00	0.00	0.00	0.00	0.00	0.00	0.00	—
Net Asset Value ($)	46.07	50.57	41.60	37.97	31.26	30.18	24.36	21.28	23.74	—
Expense Ratio (%).	0.64	0.62	0.63	0.70	0.70	0.70	0.70	0.70	0.70	—
Net Income to Assets (%). .	6.37	6.44	7.27	7.80	7.93	7.66	8.44	8.31	7.25	—
Portfolio Turnover (%).	68	49	64	85	186	72	27	68	50	—
Total Assets (Millions $) . . .	101	130	169	161	46	25	9	4	3	—

PORTFOLIO (as of 9/30/94)

Portfolio Manager: David Schroeder - 1990

Investm't Category: Government Bond

Cap Gain	Asset Allocation
Cap & Income	Fund of Funds
✔ Income	Index
	Sector
✔ Domestic	Small Cap
Foreign	Socially Conscious
Country/Region	State Specific

Portfolio: stocks 0%   bonds 100%
convertibles 0%   other 0%   cash 0%

Largest Holdings: U. S. government 100%

Unrealized Net Capital Gains: 1% of portfolio value

SHAREHOLDER INFORMATION

Minimum Investment
Initial: $1,000   Subsequent: $100

Minimum IRA Investment
Initial: $1,000   Subsequent: $25

Maximum Fees
Load: none   12b-1: none
Other: none

Distributions
Income: Dec   Capital Gains: Dec

Exchange Options
Number Per Year: 6   Fee: none
Telephone: yes (money market fund available)

Services
IRA, pension, auto exchange, auto invest, auto withdraw

Benham Target Mat Trust—2010 (BTTNX)

Government Bond

1665 Charleston Rd.
Mountain View, CA 94043
(800) 321-8321, (415) 965-4222

PERFORMANCE

fund inception date: 3/25/85

	3yr Annual	5yr Annual	10yr Annual	Bull	Bear
Return (%)	7.0	8.2	na	102.4	-16.9
Differ from Category (+/-)	3.0 high	1.5 high	na	51.2 high	-10.5 low

Total Risk	Standard Deviation	Category Risk	Risk Index	Avg Mat
abv av	12.0%	high	2.6	15.6 yrs

	1994	1993	1992	1991	1990	1989	1988	1987	1986	1985
Return (%)	-11.5	26.2	9.7	21.0	0.2	28.0	15.7	-15.2	54.4	—
Differ from category (+/-)	-6.7	15.3	3.3	5.7	-6.0	13.5	7.8	-13.1	33.8	—

PER SHARE DATA

	1994	1993	1992	1991	1990	1989	1988	1987	1986	1985
Dividends, Net Income ($)	0.00	0.00	0.00	0.00	0.00	0.00	0.00	0.00	0.00	—
Distrib'ns, Cap Gain ($)	0.00	0.00	0.00	0.00	0.00	0.00	0.00	0.00	0.00	—
Net Asset Value ($)	32.98	37.29	29.53	26.90	22.22	22.16	17.31	14.96	17.65	—
Expense Ratio (%)	0.68	0.66	0.70	0.70	0.70	0.70	0.70	0.70	0.70	—
Net Income to Assets (%)	6.35	6.32	7.20	7.73	7.82	7.34	8.11	8.13	6.71	—
Portfolio Turnover (%)	35	131	95	131	191	88	259	84	91	—
Total Assets (Millions $)	55	61	56	48	37	42	10	9	5	—

PORTFOLIO (as of 9/30/94)

Portfolio Manager: David Schroeder - 1990

Investm't Category: Government Bond

Cap Gain	Asset Allocation
Cap & Income	Fund of Funds
✔ Income	Index
	Sector
✔ Domestic	Small Cap
Foreign	Socially Conscious
Country/Region	State Specific

Portfolio: stocks 0% bonds 100%
convertibles 0% other 0% cash 0%

Largest Holdings: U. S. government 100%

Unrealized Net Capital Gains: -7% of portfolio value

SHAREHOLDER INFORMATION

Minimum Investment
Initial: $1,000   Subsequent: $100

Minimum IRA Investment
Initial: $1,000   Subsequent: $25

Maximum Fees
Load: none   12b-1: none
Other: none

Distributions
Income: Dec   Capital Gains: Dec

Exchange Options
Number Per Year: 6   Fee: none
Telephone: yes (money market fund available)

Services
IRA, pension, auto exchange, auto invest, auto withdraw

Benham Target Mat Trust—2015 (BTFTX)

1665 Charleston Rd.
Mountain View, CA 94043
(800) 321-8321, (415) 965-4222

Government Bond

PERFORMANCE

fund inception date: 9/1/86

	3yr Annual	5yr Annual	10yr Annual	Bull	Bear
Return (%)	6.5	7.4	na	112.3	-19.5
Differ from Category (+/-)	2.5 high	0.7 abv av	na	61.1 high	-13.1 low

Total Risk	Standard Deviation	Category Risk	Risk Index	Avg Mat
high	14.4%	high	3.2	20.8 yrs

	1994	1993	1992	1991	1990	1989	1988	1987	1986	1985
Return (%)	-14.0	30.5	7.7	22.4	-3.3	33.4	11.0	-20.1	—	—
Differ from category (+/-) . .	-9.2	19.6	1.3	7.1	-9.5	18.9	3.1	-18.0	—	—

PER SHARE DATA

	1994	1993	1992	1991	1990	1989	1988	1987	1986	1985
Dividends, Net Income ($) .	0.00	0.00	0.00	0.00	0.00	0.00	0.00	0.00	—	—
Distrib'ns, Cap Gain ($) . . .	0.00	0.00	0.00	0.00	0.00	0.00	0.00	0.00	—	—
Net Asset Value ($)	24.11	28.06	21.50	19.95	16.29	16.86	12.63	11.37	—	—
Expense Ratio (%).	0.68	0.63	0.62	0.61	0.70	0.70	0.70	0.70	—	—
Net Income to Assets (%). .	5.97	6.28	7.04	7.79	7.74	7.02	7.97	7.99	—	—
Portfolio Turnover (%).	64	138	103	40	81	48	188	509	—	—
Total Assets (Millions $) . . .	123	76	131	222	296	234	12	2	—	—

PORTFOLIO (as of 9/30/94)

Portfolio Manager: David Schroeder - 1990

Investm't Category: Government Bond

Cap Gain	Asset Allocation
Cap & Income	Fund of Funds
✔ Income	Index
	Sector
✔ Domestic	Small Cap
Foreign	Socially Conscious
Country/Region	State Specific

Portfolio: stocks 0% bonds 100%
convertibles 0% other 0% cash 0%

Largest Holdings: U. S. government 100%

Unrealized Net Capital Gains: 3% of portfolio value

SHAREHOLDER INFORMATION

Minimum Investment
Initial: $1,000   Subsequent: $100

Minimum IRA Investment
Initial: $1,000   Subsequent: $25

Maximum Fees
Load: none   12b-1: none
Other: none

Distributions
Income: Dec   Capital Gains: Dec

Exchange Options
Number Per Year: 6   Fee: none
Telephone: yes (money market fund available)

Services
IRA, pension, auto exchange, auto invest, auto withdraw

Benham Target Mat Trust—2020 (BTTTX)

1665 Charleston Rd.
Mountain View, CA 94043
(800) 321-8321, (415) 965-4222

Government Bond

PERFORMANCE

fund inception date: 12/29/89

	3yr Annual	5yr Annual	10yr Annual	Bull	Bear
Return (%)	6.5	6.2	na	113.0	-21.7
Differ from Category (+/-)	2.5 high	-0.5 blw av	na	61.8 high	-15.3 low

Total Risk	Standard Deviation	Category Risk	Risk Index	Avg Mat
high	16.8%	high	3.7	25.5 yrs

	1994	1993	1992	1991	1990	1989	1988	1987	1986	1985
Return (%)	-17.6	35.6	8.3	17.3	-4.5	—	—	—	—	—
Differ from category (+/-)	-12.8	24.7	1.9	2.0	-10.7	—	—	—	—	—

PER SHARE DATA

	1994	1993	1992	1991	1990	1989	1988	1987	1986	1985
Dividends, Net Income ($)	0.00	0.00	0.00	0.00	0.00	—	—	—	—	—
Distrib'ns, Cap Gain ($)	0.00	0.00	0.00	0.00	0.00	—	—	—	—	—
Net Asset Value ($)	16.27	19.76	14.57	13.45	11.46	—	—	—	—	—
Expense Ratio (%)	0.70	0.70	0.66	0.67	0.70	—	—	—	—	—
Net Income to Assets (%)	6.28	6.10	7.19	7.50	7.79	—	—	—	—	—
Portfolio Turnover (%)	116	178	144	151	189	—	—	—	—	—
Total Assets (Millions $)	125	48	42	88	53	—	—	—	—	—

PORTFOLIO (as of 9/30/94)

Portfolio Manager: David Schroeder - 1990

Investm't Category: Government Bond

Cap Gain	Asset Allocation
Cap & Income	Fund of Funds
✔ Income	Index
	Sector
✔ Domestic	Small Cap
Foreign	Socially Conscious
Country/Region	State Specific

Portfolio: stocks 0%   bonds 100%
convertibles 0%   other 0%   cash 0%

Largest Holdings: U. S. government 100%

Unrealized Net Capital Gains: -7% of portfolio value

SHAREHOLDER INFORMATION

Minimum Investment
Initial: $1,000   Subsequent: $100

Minimum IRA Investment
Initial: $1,000   Subsequent: $25

Maximum Fees
Load: none   12b-1: none
Other: none

Distributions
Income: Dec   Capital Gains: Dec

Exchange Options
Number Per Year: 6   Fee: none
Telephone: yes (money market fund available)

Services
IRA, pension, auto exchange, auto invest, auto withdraw

Benham Treasury Note
(CPTNX)

Government Bond

1665 Charleston Rd.
Mountain View, CA 94043
(800) 321-8321, (415) 965-4222

PERFORMANCE

fund inception date: 5/16/80

	3yr Annual	5yr Annual	10yr Annual	Bull	Bear
Return (%)	3.9	6.8	na	37.7	-3.7
Differ from Category (+/-)	-0.1 av	0.1 av	na	-13.5 blw av	2.7 av

Total Risk	Standard Deviation	Category Risk	Risk Index	Avg Mat
low	3.4%	blw av	0.7	2.9 yrs

	1994	1993	1992	1991	1990	1989	1988	1987	1986	1985
Return (%)	-2.3	7.9	6.5	13.7	9.2	11.9	5.2	-1.0	—	—
Differ from category (+/-) . . .	2.5	-3.0	0.1	-1.6	3.0	-2.6	-2.7	1.1	—	—

PER SHARE DATA

	1994	1993	1992	1991	1990	1989	1988	1987	1986	1985
Dividends, Net Income ($) .	0.51	0.49	0.60	0.72	0.75	0.77	0.74	0.73	—	—
Distrib'ns, Cap Gain ($) . . .	0.00	0.28	0.48	0.00	0.00	0.00	0.00	0.19	—	—
Net Asset Value ($)	9.76	10.51	10.46	10.85	10.22	10.09	9.74	9.97	—	—
Expense Ratio (%).	0.53	0.53	0.59	0.73	0.75	0.75	0.75	0.93	—	—
Net Income to Assets (%). .	5.04	5.18	6.55	7.49	7.66	7.67	7.36	6.26	—	—
Portfolio Turnover (%)	na	299	149	70	217	386	465	396	—	—
Total Assets (Millions $) . . .	296	387	303	159	97	72	54	43	—	—

PORTFOLIO (as of 9/30/94)

Portfolio Manager: Jeff Tyler - 1988

Investm't Category: Government Bond

Cap Gain	Asset Allocation
Cap & Income	Fund of Funds
✔ Income	Index
	Sector
✔ Domestic	Small Cap
Foreign	Socially Conscious
Country/Region	State Specific

Portfolio: stocks 0%   bonds 100%
convertibles 0%   other 0%   cash 0%

Largest Holdings: U.S. government 100%

Unrealized Net Capital Gains: -2% of portfolio value

SHAREHOLDER INFORMATION

Minimum Investment
Initial: $1,000   Subsequent: $100

Minimum IRA Investment
Initial: $1,000   Subsequent: $25

Maximum Fees
Load: none   12b-1: none
Other: none

Distributions
Income: monthly   Capital Gains: Dec

Exchange Options
Number Per Year: 6   Fee: none
Telephone: yes (money market fund available)

Services
IRA, pension, auto exchange, auto invest, auto withdraw

Benham Utilities Income
(BULIX)
Growth & Income

1665 Charleston Rd.
Mountain View, CA 94043
(800) 321-8321, (415) 965-4222

PERFORMANCE

fund inception date: 3/3/93

	3yr Annual	5yr Annual	10yr Annual	Bull	Bear
Return (%)	na	na	na	na	-9.9
Differ from Category (+/-)	na	na	na	na	-3.6 low

Total Risk	Standard Deviation	Category Risk	Risk Index	Beta
na	na	na	na	na

	1994	1993	1992	1991	1990	1989	1988	1987	1986	1985
Return (%)	-10.0	—	—	—	—	—	—	—	—	—
Differ from category (+/-)	-8.6	—	—	—	—	—	—	—	—	—

PER SHARE DATA

	1994	1993	1992	1991	1990	1989	1988	1987	1986	1985
Dividends, Net Income ($)	0.44	—	—	—	—	—	—	—	—	—
Distrib'ns, Cap Gain ($)	0.00	—	—	—	—	—	—	—	—	—
Net Asset Value ($)	8.79	—	—	—	—	—	—	—	—	—
Expense Ratio (%)	0.75	—	—	—	—	—	—	—	—	—
Net Income to Assets (%)	4.47	—	—	—	—	—	—	—	—	—
Portfolio Turnover (%)	na	—	—	—	—	—	—	—	—	—
Total Assets (Millions $)	152	—	—	—	—	—	—	—	—	—

PORTFOLIO (as of 6/30/94)

Portfolio Manager: Steve Colton - 1993

Investm't Category: Growth & Income

Cap Gain	Asset Allocation
✔ Cap & Income	Fund of Funds
Income	Index
	Sector
✔ Domestic	Small Cap
Foreign	Socially Conscious
Country/Region	State Specific

Portfolio: stocks 94%   bonds 6%
convertibles 0%   other 0%   cash 0%

Largest Holdings: electric utilities 41%, telephone utilities 35%

Unrealized Net Capital Gains: -12% of portfolio value

SHAREHOLDER INFORMATION

Minimum Investment
Initial: $1,000   Subsequent: $100

Minimum IRA Investment
Initial: $1,000   Subsequent: $25

Maximum Fees
Load: none   12b-1: none
Other: none

Distributions
Income: monthly   Capital Gains: Dec

Exchange Options
Number Per Year: 6   Fee: none
Telephone: yes (money market fund available)

Services
IRA, pension, auto exchange, auto invest, auto withdraw

Berger One Hundred
(BEONX)
Aggressive Growth

P.O. Box 5005
Denver, CO 80217
(800) 333-1001, (303) 329-0200

	3yr Annual	5yr Annual	10yr Annual	Bull	Bear
Return (%)	7.0	16.9	19.1	185.8	-16.2
Differ from Category (+/-)	-1.9 blw av	4.4 abv av	5.1 high	52.6 high	-5.4 low

Total Risk	Standard Deviation	Category Risk	Risk Index	Beta
high	14.8%	av	1.0	1.1

	1994	1993	1992	1991	1990	1989	1988	1987	1986	1985
Return (%)	-6.6	21.1	8.5	88.8	-5.4	48.2	1.6	15.6	20.0	25.8
Differ from category (+/-) . .	-5.9	1.6	-2.5	36.7	0.8	21.4	-13.6	17.8	8.2	-6.5

PER SHARE DATA

	1994	1993	1992	1991	1990	1989	1988	1987	1986	1985
Dividends, Net Income ($) .	0.00	0.00	0.00	0.00	0.00	0.01	0.00	0.00	0.00	0.00
Distrib'ns, Cap Gain ($) . . .	0.00	0.00	0.00	0.17	0.59	0.89	0.08	1.58	0.39	0.00
Net Asset Value ($)	15.69	16.81	13.87	12.78	6.87	7.98	5.99	5.97	6.57	5.79
Expense Ratio (%).	1.70	1.69	1.89	2.24	2.13	1.62	1.72	1.61	1.71	2.00
Net Income to Assets (%).	-0.74	-1.00	-0.75	-1.06	-0.71	-0.54	-0.57	-0.27	-0.47	-0.59
Portfolio Turnover (%).	64	74	51	78	145	83	166	106	122	130
Total Assets (Millions $) . .	2,113	1,610	384	77	13	14	11	12	10	8

PORTFOLIO (as of 9/30/94)

Portfolio Manager: Rodney Linafelter - 1990

Investm't Category: Aggressive Growth

✔ Cap Gain
    Cap & Income
    Income

    Asset Allocation
    Fund of Funds
    Index
    Sector

✔ Domestic
✔ Foreign
    Country/Region

    Small Cap
    Socially Conscious
    State Specific

Portfolio: stocks 91%   bonds 0%
convertibles 0%   other 0%   cash 9%

Largest Holdings: computer software 7%, electronic—semiconductors 6%

Unrealized Net Capital Gains: 14% of portfolio value

SHAREHOLDER INFORMATION

Minimum Investment
Initial: $250   Subsequent: $50

Minimum IRA Investment
Initial: $250   Subsequent: $50

Maximum Fees
Load: none   12b-1: 0.25%
Other: none

Distributions
Income: Dec   Capital Gains: Dec

Exchange Options
Number Per Year: 4   Fee: none
Telephone: yes (money market fund available)

Services
IRA, pension, auto exchange, auto invest, auto withdraw

Berger One Hundred & One (BEOOX)

Growth & Income

P.O. Box 5005
Denver, CO 80217
(800) 333-1001, (303) 329-0200

PERFORMANCE

fund inception date: 1/1/66

	3yr Annual	5yr Annual	10yr Annual	Bull	Bear
Return (%)	5.6	11.7	12.3	134.7	-10.9
Differ from Category (+/-)	-1.5 blw av	3.8 high	0.6 av	58.9 high	-4.6 low

Total Risk	Standard Deviation	Category Risk	Risk Index	Beta
abv av	9.1%	abv av	1.1	0.8

	1994	1993	1992	1991	1990	1989	1988	1987	1986	1985
Return (%).	-9.0	23.5	4.8	60.9	-7.9	20.2	5.3	-2.8	15.1	29.1
Differ from category (+/-) . .	-7.6	10.3	-5.4	33.3	-1.9	-1.2	-11.7	-3.4	-0.7	3.4

PER SHARE DATA

	1994	1993	1992	1991	1990	1989	1988	1987	1986	1985
Dividends, Net Income ($).	0.13	0.09	0.05	0.23	0.12	0.24	0.35	0.41	0.30	0.18
Distrib'ns, Cap Gain ($) . . .	0.00	0.00	0.00	0.75	0.00	0.00	0.00	0.68	1.50	0.15
Net Asset Value ($)	10.71	11.92	9.72	9.32	6.47	7.16	6.17	6.19	7.49	8.08
Expense Ratio (%)	1.81	2.10	2.56	2.66	2.48	2.00	2.00	1.79	1.96	2.00
Net Income to Assets (%) .	1.19	1.05	1.05	1.99	1.74	5.09	3.48	4.04	3.65	2.42
Portfolio Turnover (%)	23	62	42	143	139	132	159	241	187	166
Total Assets (Millions $). . . .	368	183	33	4	4	2	2	3	3	2

PORTFOLIO (as of 9/30/94)

Portfolio Manager: Rodney Linafelter - 1990

Investm't Category: Growth & Income

Cap Gain	Asset Allocation
✔ Cap & Income	Fund of Funds
Income	Index
	Sector
✔ Domestic	Small Cap
✔ Foreign	Socially Conscious
Country/Region	State Specific

Portfolio:	stocks 76%	bonds 0%
convertibles 14%	other 0%	cash 10%

Largest Holdings: diversified operations 7%, telecommunications services 4%

Unrealized Net Capital Gains: 4% of portfolio value

SHAREHOLDER INFORMATION

Minimum Investment
Initial: $250   Subsequent: $50

Minimum IRA Investment
Initial: $250   Subsequent: $50

Maximum Fees
Load: none   12b-1: 0.25%
Other: none

Distributions
Income: quarterly   Capital Gains: Dec

Exchange Options
Number Per Year: 4   Fee: none
Telephone: yes (money market fund available)

Services
IRA, pension, auto exchange, auto invest, auto withdraw

Berger Small Company Growth (BESCX)

P.O. Box 5005
Denver, CO 80217
(800) 333-1001, (303) 329-0200

Aggressive Growth

PERFORMANCE

fund inception date: 12/31/93

	3yr Annual	5yr Annual	10yr Annual	Bull	Bear
Return (%)	na	na	na	na	-8.8
Differ from Category (+/-)	na	na	na	na	2.0 abv av

Total Risk	Standard Deviation	Category Risk	Risk Index	Beta
na	na	na	na	na

	1994	1993	1992	1991	1990	1989	1988	1987	1986	1985
Return (%)	13.7	—	—	—	—	—	—	—	—	—
Differ from category (+/-) . .	14.4	—	—	—	—	—	—	—	—	—

PER SHARE DATA

	1994	1993	1992	1991	1990	1989	1988	1987	1986	1985
Dividends, Net Income ($) .	0.00	—	—	—	—	—	—	—	—	—
Distrib'ns, Cap Gain ($) . . .	0.00	—	—	—	—	—	—	—	—	—
Net Asset Value ($)	2.84	—	—	—	—	—	—	—	—	—
Expense Ratio (%).	2.05	—	—	—	—	—	—	—	—	—
Net Income to Assets (%). .	0.32	—	—	—	—	—	—	—	—	—
Portfolio Turnover (%)	na	—	—	—	—	—	—	—	—	—
Total Assets (Millions $) . . .	291	—	—	—	—	—	—	—	—	—

PORTFOLIO (as of 9/30/94)

Portfolio Manager: William R. Keithler - 1993

Investm't Category: Aggressive Growth

✔ Cap Gain	Asset Allocation
Cap & Income	Fund of Funds
Income	Index
	Sector
✔ Domestic	✔ Small Cap
✔ Foreign	Socially Conscious
Country/Region	State Specific

Portfolio: stocks 86% bonds 0%
convertibles 0% other 0% cash 14%

Largest Holdings: computer software 10%, electronic—semiconductors 7%

Unrealized Net Capital Gains: 11% of portfolio value

SHAREHOLDER INFORMATION

Minimum Investment
Initial: $250 Subsequent: $50

Minimum IRA Investment
Initial: $250 Subsequent: $50

Maximum Fees
Load: none 12b-1: 0.25%
Other: none

Distributions
Income: Nov Capital Gains: Nov

Exchange Options
Number Per Year: 4 Fee: none
Telephone: yes (money market fund available)

Services
IRA, pension, auto exchange, auto invest, auto withdraw

Bernstein CA Muni Port
(SNCAX)
Tax-Exempt Bond

767 Fifth Ave.
New York, NY 10153
(212) 756-4097

PERFORMANCE

fund inception date: 8/6/90

	3yr Annual	5yr Annual	10yr Annual	Bull	Bear
Return (%)	3.8	na	na	32.3	-3.4
Differ from Category (+/-)	-0.7 low	na	na	-9.5 low	1.8 high

Total Risk	Standard Deviation	Category Risk	Risk Index	Avg Mat
low	3.8%	low	0.6	6.7 yrs

	1994	1993	1992	1991	1990	1989	1988	1987	1986	1985
Return (%).............	-3.1	8.2	6.8	9.3	—	—	—	—	—	—
Differ from category (+/-)..	2.1	-3.5	-1.5	-2.0	—	—	—	—	—	—

PER SHARE DATA

	1994	1993	1992	1991	1990	1989	1988	1987	1986	1985
Dividends, Net Income ($).	0.62	0.60	0.65	0.67	—	—	—	—	—	—
Distrib'ns, Cap Gain ($) ...	0.00	0.03	0.07	0.01	—	—	—	—	—	—
Net Asset Value ($).....	12.73	13.78	13.32	13.17	—	—	—	—	—	—
Expense Ratio (%)	0.70	0.73	0.77	0.79	—	—	—	—	—	—
Net Income to Assets (%) .	4.51	4.36	4.96	5.40	—	—	—	—	—	—
Portfolio Turnover (%)	24	23	53	49	—	—	—	—	—	—
Total Assets (Millions $)....	160	163	83	50	—	—	—	—	—	—

PORTFOLIO (as of 9/30/94)

Portfolio Manager: committee

Investm't Category: Tax-Exempt Bond
Cap Gain	Asset Allocation
Cap & Income	Fund of Funds
✔ Income	Index
	Sector
✔ Domestic	Small Cap
Foreign	Socially Conscious
Country/Region	✔ State Specific

Portfolio: stocks 0% bonds 95%
convertibles 0% other 0% cash 5%

Largest Holdings: general obligation 5%

Unrealized Net Capital Gains: 0% of portfolio value

SHAREHOLDER INFORMATION

Minimum Investment
Initial: $25,000   Subsequent: $5,000

Minimum IRA Investment
Initial: na   Subsequent: na

Maximum Fees
Load: none   12b-1: none
Other: none

Distributions
Income: monthly   Capital Gains: Dec

Exchange Options
Number Per Year: no limit   Fee: none
Telephone: yes (money market fund not available)

Services
auto withdraw

Bernstein Diversified Muni Port (SNDPX)

767 Fifth Ave.
New York, NY 10153
(212) 756-4097

Tax-Exempt Bond

PERFORMANCE

fund inception date: 1/9/89

	3yr Annual	5yr Annual	10yr Annual	Bull	Bear
Return (%)	4.0	5.7	na	32.7	-3.3
Differ from Category (+/-)	-0.5 blw av	-0.4 low	na	-9.1 low	1.9 high

Total Risk	Standard Deviation	Category Risk	Risk Index	Avg Mat
low	3.8%	low	0.6	6.9 yrs

	1994	1993	1992	1991	1990	1989	1988	1987	1986	1985
Return (%)	-2.4	8.4	6.5	10.1	6.8	—	—	—	—	—
Differ from category (+/-) . . .	2.8	-3.3	-1.8	-1.2	0.5	—	—	—	—	—

PER SHARE DATA

	1994	1993	1992	1991	1990	1989	1988	1987	1986	1985
Dividends, Net Income ($) .	0.62	0.62	0.69	0.73	0.74	—	—	—	—	—
Distrib'ns, Cap Gain ($) . . .	0.00	0.07	0.11	0.03	0.01	—	—	—	—	—
Net Asset Value ($)	12.74	13.70	13.29	13.25	12.75	—	—	—	—	—
Expense Ratio (%).	0.67	0.69	0.69	0.71	0.75	—	—	—	—	—
Net Income to Assets (%). .	4.57	4.64	5.33	5.69	5.83	—	—	—	—	—
Portfolio Turnover (%).	34	34	48	34	47	—	—	—	—	—
Total Assets (Millions $) . . .	504	487	302	210	158	—	—	—	—	—

PORTFOLIO (as of 9/30/94)

Portfolio Manager: committee

Investm't Category: Tax-Exempt Bond
Cap Gain	Asset Allocation
Cap & Income	Fund of Funds
✔ Income	Index
	Sector
✔ Domestic	Small Cap
Foreign	Socially Conscious
Country/Region	State Specific

Portfolio: stocks 0%   bonds 96%
convertibles 0%   other 0%   cash 4%

Largest Holdings: general obligation 19%

Unrealized Net Capital Gains: 0% of portfolio value

SHAREHOLDER INFORMATION

Minimum Investment
Initial: $25,000   Subsequent: $5,000

Minimum IRA Investment
Initial: na   Subsequent: na

Maximum Fees
Load: none   12b-1: none
Other: none

Distributions
Income: monthly   Capital Gains: Dec

Exchange Options
Number Per Year: no limit   Fee: none
Telephone: yes (money market fund not available)

Services
auto withdraw

Bernstein Gov't Short Duration (SNGSX)

767 Fifth Ave.
New York, NY 10153
(212) 756-4097

Government Bond

PERFORMANCE
fund inception date: 1/3/89

	3yr Annual	5yr Annual	10yr Annual	Bull	Bear
Return (%)	3.4	6.0	na	27.0	-0.8
Differ from Category (+/-)	-0.6 blw av	-0.7 low	na	-24.2 low	5.6 high

Total Risk	Standard Deviation	Category Risk	Risk Index	Avg Mat
low	1.6%	low	0.3	1.7 yrs

	1994	1993	1992	1991	1990	1989	1988	1987	1986	1985
Return (%)	0.4	4.6	5.3	11.2	8.9	9.3	—	—	—	—
Differ from category (+/-)	5.2	-6.3	-1.1	-4.1	2.7	-5.2	—	—	—	—

PER SHARE DATA

	1994	1993	1992	1991	1990	1989	1988	1987	1986	1985
Dividends, Net Income ($)	0.56	0.42	0.59	0.81	0.95	0.95	—	—	—	—
Distrib'ns, Cap Gain ($)	0.00	0.15	0.47	0.20	0.06	0.08	—	—	—	—
Net Asset Value ($)	12.15	12.66	12.65	13.03	12.67	12.60	—	—	—	—
Expense Ratio (%)	0.68	0.68	0.68	0.70	0.72	0.85	—	—	—	—
Net Income to Assets (%)	3.85	3.40	5.02	6.67	7.52	7.82	—	—	—	—
Portfolio Turnover (%)	213	130	221	176	171	141	—	—	—	—
Total Assets (Millions $)	143	189	255	212	160	138	—	—	—	—

PORTFOLIO (as of 9/30/94)

Portfolio Manager: committee

Investm't Category: Government Bond
Cap Gain	Asset Allocation
Cap & Income	Fund of Funds
✔ Income	Index
	Sector
✔ Domestic	Small Cap
✔ Foreign	Socially Conscious
Country/Region	State Specific

Portfolio: stocks 0%   bonds 100%
convertibles 0%   other 0%   cash 0%

Largest Holdings: U. S. government 100%

Unrealized Net Capital Gains: 0% of portfolio value

SHAREHOLDER INFORMATION

Minimum Investment
Initial: $25,000   Subsequent: $5,000

Minimum IRA Investment
Initial: $25,000   Subsequent: $5,000

Maximum Fees
Load: none   12b-1: none
Other: none

Distributions
Income: monthly   Capital Gains: Dec

Exchange Options
Number Per Year: no limit   Fee: none
Telephone: yes (money market fund not available)

Services
IRA, pension, auto withdraw

Bernstein Int'l Value

(SNIVX)

International Stock

767 Fifth Ave.
New York, NY 10153
(212) 756-4097

PERFORMANCE   fund inception date: 6/22/92

	3yr Annual	5yr Annual	10yr Annual	Bull	Bear
Return (%)	na	na	na	na	-0.2
Differ from Category (+/-)	na	na	na	na	6.8 high

Total Risk	Standard Deviation	Category Risk	Risk Index	Beta
na	na	na	na	na

	1994	1993	1992	1991	1990	1989	1988	1987	1986	1985
Return (%)	3.8	34.5	—	—	—	—	—	—	—	—
Differ from category (+/-) . . .	6.8	-4.1	—	—	—	—	—	—	—	—

PER SHARE DATA

	1994	1993	1992	1991	1990	1989	1988	1987	1986	1985
Dividends, Net Income ($) .	0.11	0.02	—	—	—	—	—	—	—	—
Distrib'ns, Cap Gain ($) . . .	0.63	0.12	—	—	—	—	—	—	—	—
Net Asset Value ($)	15.43	15.59	—	—	—	—	—	—	—	—
Expense Ratio (%).	1.39	1.53	—	—	—	—	—	—	—	—
Net Income to Assets (%). .	1.13	1.27	—	—	—	—	—	—	—	—
Portfolio Turnover (%)	23	21	—	—	—	—	—	—	—	—
Total Assets (Millions $) . .	1,429	705	—	—	—	—	—	—	—	—

PORTFOLIO (as of 9/30/94)

Portfolio Manager: committee

Investm't Category: International Stock

✔ Cap Gain	Asset Allocation
Cap & Income	Fund of Funds
Income	Index
	Sector
Domestic	Small Cap
✔ Foreign	Socially Conscious
Country/Region	State Specific

Portfolio: stocks 96%   bonds 0%
convertibles 0%   other 0%   cash 4%

Largest Holdings: Japan 36%, Germany 15%

Unrealized Net Capital Gains: 6% of portfolio value

SHAREHOLDER INFORMATION

Minimum Investment
Initial: $25,000   Subsequent: $5,000

Minimum IRA Investment
Initial: $25,000   Subsequent: $5,000

Maximum Fees
Load: none   12b-1: none
Other: none

Distributions
Income: Dec   Capital Gains: Dec

Exchange Options
Number Per Year: no limit   Fee: none
Telephone: yes (money market fund not available)

Services
IRA, pension, auto withdraw

Bernstein Interm Duration (SNIDX)

General Bond

767 Fifth Ave.
New York, NY 10153
(212) 756-4097

PERFORMANCE

fund inception date: 1/17/89

	3yr Annual	5yr Annual	10yr Annual	Bull	Bear
Return (%)	4.5	7.4	na	45.8	-4.6
Differ from Category (+/-)	0.2 av	0.5 abv av	na	4.8 abv av	-0.8 blw av

Total Risk	Standard Deviation	Category Risk	Risk Index	Avg Mat
low	3.9%	av	1.0	13.2 yrs

	1994	1993	1992	1991	1990	1989	1988	1987	1986	1985
Return (%)	-3.1	10.3	6.9	16.9	7.1	—	—	—	—	—
Differ from category (+/-) . .	-1.1	1.1	0.3	2.3	-0.1	—	—	—	—	—

PER SHARE DATA

	1994	1993	1992	1991	1990	1989	1988	1987	1986	1985
Dividends, Net Income ($).	0.70	0.75	0.78	0.97	0.95	—	—	—	—	—
Distrib'ns, Cap Gain ($) . . .	0.00	0.21	0.58	0.16	0.02	—	—	—	—	—
Net Asset Value ($)	12.37	13.49	13.12	13.57	12.65	—	—	—	—	—
Expense Ratio (%)	0.65	0.66	0.67	0.68	0.71	—	—	—	—	—
Net Income to Assets (%) .	5.14	5.59	6.64	7.80	7.77	—	—	—	—	—
Portfolio Turnover (%)	203	60	150	81	119	—	—	—	—	—
Total Assets (Millions $). . . .	842	728	524	375	241	—	—	—	—	—

PORTFOLIO (as of 9/30/94)

Portfolio Manager: committee

Investm't Category: General Bond

Cap Gain	Asset Allocation
Cap & Income	Fund of Funds
✔ Income	Index
	Sector
✔ Domestic	Small Cap
✔ Foreign	Socially Conscious
Country/Region	State Specific

Portfolio:	stocks 0%	bonds 98%
convertibles 0%	other 0%	cash 2%

Largest Holdings: U. S. government 76%, mortgage-backed 16%

Unrealized Net Capital Gains: -3% of portfolio value

SHAREHOLDER INFORMATION

Minimum Investment
Initial: $25,000   Subsequent: $5,000

Minimum IRA Investment
Initial: $25,000   Subsequent: $5,000

Maximum Fees
Load: none   12b-1: none
Other: none

Distributions
Income: monthly   Capital Gains: Dec

Exchange Options
Number Per Year: no limit   Fee: none
Telephone: yes (money market fund not available)

Services
IRA, pension, auto withdraw

Bernstein NY Muni Port
(SNNYX)
Tax-Exempt Bond

767 Fifth Ave.
New York, NY 10153
(212) 756-4097

PERFORMANCE

fund inception date: 1/9/89

	3yr Annual	5yr Annual	10yr Annual	Bull	Bear
Return (%)	4.1	5.8	na	33.3	-3.1
Differ from Category (+/-)	-0.4 blw av	-0.3 blw av	na	-8.5 low	2.1 high

Total Risk	Standard Deviation	Category Risk	Risk Index	Avg Mat
low	3.9%	low	0.6	6.2 yrs

	1994	1993	1992	1991	1990	1989	1988	1987	1986	1985
Return (%)	-2.5	8.5	6.8	10.4	6.6	—	—	—	—	—
Differ from category (+/-) . . .	2.7	-3.2	-1.5	-0.9	0.3	—	—	—	—	—

PER SHARE DATA

	1994	1993	1992	1991	1990	1989	1988	1987	1986	1985
Dividends, Net Income ($) .	0.64	0.66	0.73	0.74	0.75	—	—	—	—	—
Distrib'ns, Cap Gain ($) . . .	0.00	0.07	0.13	0.02	0.01	—	—	—	—	—
Net Asset Value ($)	12.72	13.71	13.32	13.29	12.77	—	—	—	—	—
Expense Ratio (%).	0.67	0.69	0.69	0.70	0.74	—	—	—	—	—
Net Income to Assets (%). .	4.78	4.91	5.55	5.79	5.94	—	—	—	—	—
Portfolio Turnover (%)	22	34	43	30	36	—	—	—	—	—
Total Assets (Millions $) . . .	376	365	239	191	158	—	—	—	—	—

PORTFOLIO (as of 9/30/94)

Portfolio Manager: committee

Investm't Category: Tax-Exempt Bond

Cap Gain	Asset Allocation
Cap & Income	Fund of Funds
✔ Income	Index
	Sector
✔ Domestic	Small Cap
Foreign	Socially Conscious
Country/Region	✔ State Specific

Portfolio: stocks 0% bonds 95%
convertibles 0% other 0% cash 5%

Largest Holdings: general obligation 9%

Unrealized Net Capital Gains: 0% of portfolio value

SHAREHOLDER INFORMATION

Minimum Investment
Initial: $25,000   Subsequent: $5,000

Minimum IRA Investment
Initial: na   Subsequent: na

Maximum Fees
Load: none   12b-1: none
Other: none

Distributions
Income: monthly   Capital Gains: Dec

Exchange Options
Number Per Year: no limit   Fee: none
Telephone: yes (money market fund not available)

Services
auto withdraw

Bernstein Short Duration Plus (SNSDX)

767 Fifth Ave.
New York, NY 10153
(212) 756-4097

General Bond

fund inception date: 12/12/88

PERFORMANCE

	3yr Annual	5yr Annual	10yr Annual	Bull	Bear
Return (%)	4.0	6.4	na	29.9	-0.7
Differ from Category (+/-)	-0.3 blw av	-0.5 blw av	na	-11.1 low	3.1 high

Total Risk	Standard Deviation	Category Risk	Risk Index	Avg Mat
low	1.6%	low	0.4	2.8 yrs

	1994	1993	1992	1991	1990	1989	1988	1987	1986	1985
Return (%)	0.5	5.4	6.1	12.3	8.0	9.5	—	—	—	—
Differ from category (+/-)	2.5	-3.8	-0.5	-2.3	0.8	-1.9	—	—	—	—

PER SHARE DATA

	1994	1993	1992	1991	1990	1989	1988	1987	1986	1985
Dividends, Net Income ($)	0.59	0.58	0.68	0.90	0.94	0.98	—	—	—	—
Distrib'ns, Cap Gain ($)	0.00	0.16	0.35	0.14	0.07	0.11	—	—	—	—
Net Asset Value ($)	12.14	12.66	12.72	12.97	12.52	12.56	—	—	—	—
Expense Ratio (%)	0.65	0.66	0.66	0.67	0.68	0.75	—	—	—	—
Net Income to Assets (%)	4.30	4.52	5.75	7.42	7.67	7.91	—	—	—	—
Portfolio Turnover (%)	285	112	170	140	155	133	—	—	—	—
Total Assets (Millions $)	507	508	536	435	391	335	—	—	—	—

PORTFOLIO (as of 9/30/94)

Portfolio Manager: committee

Investm't Category: General Bond

Cap Gain	Asset Allocation
Cap & Income	Fund of Funds
✔ Income	Index
	Sector
✔ Domestic	Small Cap
✔ Foreign	Socially Conscious
Country/Region	State Specific

Portfolio: stocks 0%   bonds 99%
convertibles 0%   other 0%   cash 1%

Largest Holdings: U.S. government 88%, corporate 6%

Unrealized Net Capital Gains: 0% of portfolio value

SHAREHOLDER INFORMATION

Minimum Investment
Initial: $25,000   Subsequent: $5,000

Minimum IRA Investment
Initial: $25,000   Subsequent: $5,000

Maximum Fees
Load: none   12b-1: none
Other: none

Distributions
Income: monthly   Capital Gains: Dec

Exchange Options
Number Per Year: no limit   Fee: none
Telephone: yes (money market fund not available)

Services
IRA, pension, auto withdraw

Berwyn (BERWX)

Growth

1189 Lancaster Ave.
Berwyn, PA 19312
(800) 824-2249, (302) 324-4495

PERFORMANCE

fund inception date: 5/1/84

	3yr Annual	5yr Annual	10yr Annual	Bull	Bear
Return (%)	15.5	10.9	13.2	122.6	-8.0
Differ from Category (+/-)	7.8 high	1.3 abv av	0.3 av	30.5 high	-1.4 blw av

Total Risk	Standard Deviation	Category Risk	Risk Index	Beta
abv av	12.0%	high	1.2	0.9

	1994	1993	1992	1991	1990	1989	1988	1987	1986	1985
Return (%)	3.8	22.9	20.6	43.5	-23.8	16.4	21.5	2.8	14.6	23.5
Differ from category (+/-) ...	4.4	9.5	9.0	7.8	-18.1	-9.7	3.5	1.0	0.0	-5.7

PER SHARE DATA

	1994	1993	1992	1991	1990	1989	1988	1987	1986	1985
Dividends, Net Income ($) .	0.01	0.00	0.04	0.11	0.13	0.09	0.08	0.16	0.09	0.05
Distrib'ns, Cap Gain ($) ...	0.78	0.58	1.31	0.27	0.72	0.80	0.47	1.85	0.12	0.00
Net Asset Value ($)	17.55	17.67	14.85	13.46	9.66	13.82	12.63	10.85	12.41	11.03
Expense Ratio (%)........	1.35	1.37	1.38	1.38	1.46	1.42	1.45	1.52	1.66	2.00
Net Income to Assets (%).	-0.20	-0.18	0.28	0.91	1.11	0.70	0.60	0.50	1.10	1.42
Portfolio Turnover (%).....	24	24	45	33	24	25	20	43	17	24
Total Assets (Millions $)	63	48	31	19	12	14	11	8	6	3

PORTFOLIO (as of 6/30/94)

Portfolio Manager: Robert E. Killen - 1984

Investm't Category: Growth

✔ Cap Gain	Asset Allocation
Cap & Income	Fund of Funds
Income	Index
	Sector
✔ Domestic	Small Cap
✔ Foreign	Socially Conscious
Country/Region	State Specific

Portfolio: stocks 96% bonds 0%
convertibles 0%   other 1%   cash 3%

Largest Holdings: steel & steel products 10%, manufacture of machinery 7%

Unrealized Net Capital Gains: 14% of portfolio value

SHAREHOLDER INFORMATION

Minimum Investment
Initial: $10,000   Subsequent: $1,000

Minimum IRA Investment
Initial: $1,000   Subsequent: $250

Maximum Fees
Load: 1.00% redemption   12b-1: none
Other: redemption fee applies for 1 year

Distributions
Income: Dec   Capital Gains: Dec

Exchange Options
Number Per Year: 4   Fee: none
Telephone: yes (money market fund available)

Services
IRA, auto invest, auto withdraw

Berwyn Income (BERIX)

Balanced

1189 Lancaster Ave.
Berwyn, PA 19312
(800) 824-2249, (302) 324-4495

PERFORMANCE

fund inception date: 9/1/87

	3yr Annual	5yr Annual	10yr Annual	Bull	Bear
Return (%)	12.0	11.5	na	87.9	-5.3
Differ from Category (+/-)	5.6 high	3.5 high	na	22.9 high	0.4 av

Total Risk	Standard Deviation	Category Risk	Risk Index	Beta
blw av	6.1%	av	1.0	0.4

	1994	1993	1992	1991	1990	1989	1988	1987	1986	1985
Return (%).	-1.0	16.9	21.7	22.9	-0.1	11.8	11.3	—	—	—
Differ from category (+/-) . .	0.9	3.5	13.4	-0.5	0.4	-5.5	-0.5	—	—	—

PER SHARE DATA

	1994	1993	1992	1991	1990	1989	1988	1987	1986	1985
Dividends, Net Income ($).	0.73	0.65	0.70	0.93	0.83	0.79	0.77	—	—	—
Distrib'ns, Cap Gain ($) . . .	0.03	0.68	0.55	0.05	0.04	0.06	0.05	—	—	—
Net Asset Value ($)	10.74	11.63	11.12	10.20	9.14	10.03	9.75	—	—	—
Expense Ratio (%)	1.00	1.07	1.34	1.34	1.46	1.50	1.75	—	—	—
Net Income to Assets (%) .	6.30	6.15	6.14	8.40	8.59	8.00	8.29	—	—	—
Portfolio Turnover (%)	28	83	46	14	14	3	17	—	—	—
Total Assets (Millions $).	55	31	12	5	3	3	2	—	—	—

PORTFOLIO (as of 6/30/94)

Portfolio Manager: Edward A. Killen - 1994

Investm't Category: Balanced

Cap Gain	✔ Asset Allocation
✔ Cap & Income	Fund of Funds
Income	Index
	Sector
✔ Domestic	Small Cap
✔ Foreign	Socially Conscious
Country/Region	State Specific

Portfolio: stocks 15% bonds 31%
convertibles 44% other 0% cash 10%

Largest Holdings: computer & peripheral 10%, commercial aircraft & aerospace 9%

Unrealized Net Capital Gains: -4% of portfolio value

SHAREHOLDER INFORMATION

Minimum Investment
Initial: $10,000   Subsequent: $1,000

Minimum IRA Investment
Initial: $1,000   Subsequent: $250

Maximum Fees
Load: none   12b-1: none
Other: none

Distributions
Income: quarterly   Capital Gains: Dec

Exchange Options
Number Per Year: 4   Fee: none
Telephone: yes (money market fund available)

Services
IRA, auto invest, auto withdraw

Blanchard American Equity (BLAEX)

Growth

41 Madison Avenue
24th Floor
New York, NY 10010
(800) 922-7771

PERFORMANCE

fund inception date: 11/9/92

	3yr Annual	5yr Annual	10yr Annual	Bull	Bear
Return (%)	na	na	na	na	-11.5
Differ from Category (+/-)	na	na	na	na	-4.9 low

Total Risk	Standard Deviation	Category Risk	Risk Index	Beta
na	na	na	na	na

	1994	1993	1992	1991	1990	1989	1988	1987	1986	1985
Return (%)	-4.1	-1.2	—	—	—	—	—	—	—	—
Differ from category (+/-)	-3.5	-14.6	—	—	—	—	—	—	—	—

PER SHARE DATA

	1994	1993	1992	1991	1990	1989	1988	1987	1986	1985
Dividends, Net Income ($)	0.00	0.00	—	—	—	—	—	—	—	—
Distrib'ns, Cap Gain ($)	0.23	0.00	—	—	—	—	—	—	—	—
Net Asset Value ($)	9.23	9.87	—	—	—	—	—	—	—	—
Expense Ratio (%)	3.00	3.13	—	—	—	—	—	—	—	—
Net Income to Assets (%)	-2.04	-1.66	—	—	—	—	—	—	—	—
Portfolio Turnover (%)	97	49	—	—	—	—	—	—	—	—
Total Assets (Millions $)	10	19	—	—	—	—	—	—	—	—

PORTFOLIO (as of 4/30/94)

Portfolio Manager: Jeffrey Miller - 1992

Investm't Category: Growth

✔ Cap Gain	Asset Allocation
Cap & Income	Fund of Funds
Income	Index
	Sector
✔ Domestic	Small Cap
Foreign	Socially Conscious
Country/Region	State Specific

Portfolio:	stocks 93%	bonds 0%
convertibles 0%	other 0%	cash 7%

Largest Holdings: financial services 14%, computer software & services 10%

Unrealized Net Capital Gains: 1% of portfolio value

SHAREHOLDER INFORMATION

Minimum Investment
Initial: $3,000   Subsequent: $200

Minimum IRA Investment
Initial: $2,000   Subsequent: $200

Maximum Fees
Load: none   12b-1: 0.50%
Other: none

Distributions
Income: Dec   Capital Gains: Dec

Exchange Options
Number Per Year: no limit   Fee: none
Telephone: yes (money market fund available)

Services
IRA, pension, auto invest, auto withdraw

Blanchard Flexible Income (BLFIX)

General Bond

41 Madison Avenue
24th Floor
New York, NY 10010
(800) 922-7771

	3yr Annual	5yr Annual	10yr Annual	Bull	Bear
Return (%)	na	na	na	na	-5.6
Differ from Category (+/-)	na	na	na	na	-1.8 blw av

Total Risk	Standard Deviation	Category Risk	Risk Index	Avg Mat
na	na	na	na	6.0 yrs

	1994	1993	1992	1991	1990	1989	1988	1987	1986	1985
Return (%)	-5.5	13.8	—	—	—	—	—	—	—	—
Differ from category (+/-)	-3.5	4.6	—	—	—	—	—	—	—	—

PER SHARE DATA

	1994	1993	1992	1991	1990	1989	1988	1987	1986	1985
Dividends, Net Income ($)	0.32	0.42	—	—	—	—	—	—	—	—
Distrib'ns, Cap Gain ($)	0.00	0.07	—	—	—	—	—	—	—	—
Net Asset Value ($)	4.55	5.15	—	—	—	—	—	—	—	—
Expense Ratio (%)	1.30	0.20	—	—	—	—	—	—	—	—
Net Income to Assets (%)	7.10	9.02	—	—	—	—	—	—	—	—
Portfolio Turnover (%)	346	129	—	—	—	—	—	—	—	—
Total Assets (Millions $)	272	686	—	—	—	—	—	—	—	—

PORTFOLIO (as of 4/30/94)

Portfolio Manager: Jack Burks - 1992

Investm't Category: General Bond

Cap Gain	Asset Allocation
Cap & Income	Fund of Funds
✔ Income	Index
	Sector
✔ Domestic	Small Cap
✔ Foreign	Socially Conscious
Country/Region	State Specific

Portfolio: stocks 0%   bonds 91%
convertibles 0%   other 1%   cash 8%

Largest Holdings: corporate 40%, foreign government and agencies 25%

Unrealized Net Capital Gains: -2% of portfolio value

SHAREHOLDER INFORMATION

Minimum Investment
Initial: $3,000   Subsequent: $200

Minimum IRA Investment
Initial: $2,000   Subsequent: $200

Maximum Fees
Load: none   12b-1: 0.25%
Other: none

Distributions
Income: monthly   Capital Gains: Dec

Exchange Options
Number Per Year: no limit   Fee: none
Telephone: yes (money market fund available)

Services
IRA, pension, auto invest, auto withdraw

Blanchard Global Growth (BGGFX)

International Stock

41 Madison Avenue
24th Floor
New York, NY 10010
(800) 922-7771

PERFORMANCE

fund inception date: 7/28/86

	3yr Annual	5yr Annual	10yr Annual	Bull	Bear
Return (%)	5.0	3.7	na	47.6	-8.9
Differ from Category (+/-)	-4.1 low	-1.2 blw av	na	-16.3 blw av	-1.9 blw av

Total Risk	Standard Deviation	Category Risk	Risk Index	Beta
av	7.5%	low	0.5	0.7

	1994	1993	1992	1991	1990	1989	1988	1987	1986	1985
Return (%)	-7.5	24.4	0.7	10.7	-6.3	15.6	7.5	16.3	—	—
Differ from category (+/-) . .	-4.5	-14.2	3.6	-2.4	4.1	-6.9	-6.9	1.9	—	—

PER SHARE DATA

	1994	1993	1992	1991	1990	1989	1988	1987	1986	1985
Dividends, Net Income ($) .	0.00	0.00	0.30	0.31	0.21	0.38	0.10	0.11	—	—
Distrib'ns, Cap Gain ($) . . .	0.22	1.28	0.19	0.00	0.21	0.51	0.18	0.65	—	—
Net Asset Value ($)	9.47	10.48	9.47	9.89	9.22	10.28	9.69	9.29	—	—
Expense Ratio (%).	2.61	2.40	2.31	2.36	2.28	2.29	2.28	3.10	—	—
Net Income to Assets (%). .	0.67	1.72	2.31	2.84	2.86	2.27	1.42	0.34	—	—
Portfolio Turnover (%). . . .	166	138	109	78	88	85	119	69	—	—
Total Assets (Millions $)	93	96	127	193	233	244	246	149	—	—

PORTFOLIO (as of 4/30/94)

Portfolio Manager: committee

Investm't Category: International Stock
✔ Cap Gain ✔ Asset Allocation
Cap & Income Fund of Funds
Income Index
Sector
✔ Domestic Small Cap
✔ Foreign Socially Conscious
Country/Region State Specific

Portfolio: stocks 61% bonds 39%
convertibles 0% other 0% cash 0%

Largest Holdings: United States 43%, Netherlands 11%

Unrealized Net Capital Gains: 1% of portfolio value

SHAREHOLDER INFORMATION

Minimum Investment
Initial: $3,000 Subsequent: $200

Minimum IRA Investment
Initial: $2,000 Subsequent: $200

Maximum Fees
Load: none 12b-1: 0.75%
Other: none

Distributions
Income: Dec Capital Gains: Dec

Exchange Options
Number Per Year: no limit Fee: none
Telephone: yes (money market fund available)

Services
IRA, pension, auto invest, auto withdraw

Blanchard Precious Metals (BLPMX)

Gold

41 Madison Avenue
24th Floor
New York, NY 10010
(800) 922-7771

PERFORMANCE

fund inception date: 6/22/88

	3yr Annual	5yr Annual	10yr Annual	Bull	Bear
Return (%)	11.5	0.9	na	40.0	-7.6
Differ from Category (+/-)	0.7 abv av	0.9 abv av	na	7.1 abv av	2.4 abv av

Total Risk	Standard Deviation	Category Risk	Risk Index	Beta
high	26.4%	abv av	1.0	0.3

	1994	1993	1992	1991	1990	1989	1988	1987	1986	1985
Return (%)	-14.9	100.4	-18.4	-2.3	-22.8	8.0	—	—	—	—
Differ from category (+/-)	-3.4	13.5	-2.7	2.5	-0.3	-16.7	—	—	—	—

PER SHARE DATA

	1994	1993	1992	1991	1990	1989	1988	1987	1986	1985
Dividends, Net Income ($)	0.00	0.00	0.00	0.00	0.00	0.03	—	—	—	—
Distrib'ns, Cap Gain ($)	1.18	0.00	0.00	0.00	0.00	0.11	—	—	—	—
Net Asset Value ($)	6.99	9.64	4.81	5.90	6.04	7.83	—	—	—	—
Expense Ratio (%)	2.46	2.65	3.09	3.05	2.95	3.99	—	—	—	—
Net Income to Assets (%)	-1.21	-1.79	-1.57	-1.28	-0.40	0.77	—	—	—	—
Portfolio Turnover (%)	174	73	62	57	56	20	—	—	—	—
Total Assets (Millions $)	77	72	20	24	31	25	—	—	—	—

PORTFOLIO (as of 4/30/94)

Portfolio Manager: Peter Cavelti - 1988

Investm't Category: Gold

✔ Cap Gain   Asset Allocation
   Cap & Income   Fund of Funds
   Income   Index
   ✔ Sector
✔ Domestic   Small Cap
✔ Foreign   Socially Conscious
   Country/Region   State Specific

Portfolio: stocks 67%   bonds 0%
convertibles 0%   other 33%   cash 0%

Largest Holdings: Canadian metal mining companies 41%, gold bullion 28%

Unrealized Net Capital Gains: -2% of portfolio value

SHAREHOLDER INFORMATION

Minimum Investment
Initial: $3,000   Subsequent: $200

Minimum IRA Investment
Initial: $2,000   Subsequent: $200

Maximum Fees
Load: none   12b-1: 0.75%
Other: none

Distributions
Income: Dec   Capital Gains: Dec

Exchange Options
Number Per Year: no limit   Fee: none
Telephone: yes (money market fund available)

Services
IRA, pension, auto invest, auto withdraw

Blanchard Short Term Bond (BSTBX)

General Bond

41 Madison Avenue
24th Floor
New York, NY 10010
(800) 922-7771

PERFORMANCE

fund inception date: 4/16/93

	3yr Annual	5yr Annual	10yr Annual	Bull	Bear
Return (%)	na	na	na	na	-0.8
Differ from Category (+/-)	na	na	na	na	3.0 high

Total Risk	Standard Deviation	Category Risk	Risk Index	Avg Mat
na	na	na	na	2.1 yrs

	1994	1993	1992	1991	1990	1989	1988	1987	1986	1985
Return (%)	1.0	—	—	—	—	—	—	—	—	—
Differ from category (+/-) ...	3.0	—	—	—	—	—	—	—	—	—

PER SHARE DATA

	1994	1993	1992	1991	1990	1989	1988	1987	1986	1985
Dividends, Net Income ($) .	0.15	—	—	—	—	—	—	—	—	—
Distrib'ns, Cap Gain ($) ...	0.00	—	—	—	—	—	—	—	—	—
Net Asset Value ($)	2.88	—	—	—	—	—	—	—	—	—
Expense Ratio (%)........	0.63	—	—	—	—	—	—	—	—	—
Net Income to Assets (%)..	5.64	—	—	—	—	—	—	—	—	—
Portfolio Turnover (%)....	212	—	—	—	—	—	—	—	—	—
Total Assets (Millions $)	24	—	—	—	—	—	—	—	—	—

PORTFOLIO (as of 4/30/94)

Portfolio Manager: committee

Investm't Category: General Bond

Cap Gain	Asset Allocation
Cap & Income	Fund of Funds
✔ Income	Index
	Sector
✔ Domestic	Small Cap
✔ Foreign	Socially Conscious
Country/Region	State Specific

Portfolio: stocks 0% bonds 88%
convertibles 0% other 1% cash 11%

Largest Holdings: U.S. government & agencies 45%, corporate 27%

Unrealized Net Capital Gains: -1% of portfolio value

SHAREHOLDER INFORMATION

Minimum Investment
Initial: $3,000   Subsequent: $200

Minimum IRA Investment
Initial: $2,000   Subsequent: $200

Maximum Fees
Load: none   12b-1: 0.25%
Other: none

Distributions
Income: monthly   Capital Gains: Dec

Exchange Options
Number Per Year: no limit   Fee: none
Telephone: yes (money market fund available)

Services
IRA, pension, auto invest, auto withdraw

Blanchard Short-Term Global Inc (BSGIX)

International Bond

41 Madison Avenue
24th Floor
New York, NY 10010
(800) 922-7771

PERFORMANCE

fund inception date: 1/8/91

	3yr Annual	5yr Annual	10yr Annual	Bull	Bear
Return (%)	2.3	na	na	na	-2.5
Differ from Category (+/-)	-1.6 blw av	na	na	na	5.3 high

Total Risk	Standard Deviation	Category Risk	Risk Index	Avg Mat
low	2.6%	low	0.5	1.5 yrs

	1994	1993	1992	1991	1990	1989	1988	1987	1986	1985
Return (%)	-4.6	8.5	3.5	—	—	—	—	—	—	—
Differ from category (+/-)	1.7	-4.9	-1.2	—	—	—	—	—	—	—

PER SHARE DATA

	1994	1993	1992	1991	1990	1989	1988	1987	1986	1985
Dividends, Net Income ($)	0.11	0.12	0.14	—	—	—	—	—	—	—
Distrib'ns, Cap Gain ($)	0.00	0.00	0.00	—	—	—	—	—	—	—
Net Asset Value ($)	1.68	1.87	1.84	—	—	—	—	—	—	—
Expense Ratio (%)	1.44	1.44	1.32	—	—	—	—	—	—	—
Net Income to Assets (%)	6.41	6.97	8.50	—	—	—	—	—	—	—
Portfolio Turnover (%)	327	610	412	—	—	—	—	—	—	—
Total Assets (Millions $)	305	632	1,241	—	—	—	—	—	—	—

PORTFOLIO (as of 4/30/94)

Portfolio Manager: Robert McHenry - 1991

Investm't Category: International Bond

Cap Gain	Asset Allocation
Cap & Income	Fund of Funds
✔ Income	Index
	Sector
✔ Domestic	Small Cap
✔ Foreign	Socially Conscious
Country/Region	State Specific

Portfolio: stocks 0% bonds 65%
convertibles 0% other 0% cash 35%

Largest Holdings: United States 29%, Italy 13%

Unrealized Net Capital Gains: -1% of portfolio value

SHAREHOLDER INFORMATION

Minimum Investment
Initial: $3,000 Subsequent: $200

Minimum IRA Investment
Initial: $2,000 Subsequent: $200

Maximum Fees
Load: none 12b-1: 0.25%
Other: none

Distributions
Income: monthly Capital Gains: Dec

Exchange Options
Number Per Year: no limit Fee: none
Telephone: yes (money market fund available)

Services
IRA, pension, auto invest, auto withdraw

Brandywine (BRWIX)

Growth

3908 Kennett Pike
Greenville, DE 19807
(800) 656-3017, (302) 656-6200

PERFORMANCE

fund inception date: 12/1/85

	3yr Annual	5yr Annual	10yr Annual	Bull	Bear
Return (%)	12.3	16.3	na	131.4	-10.3
Differ from Category (+/-)	4.6 high	6.7 high	na	39.3 high	-3.7 low

Total Risk	Standard Deviation	Category Risk	Risk Index	Beta
high	13.5%	high	1.4	1.0

	1994	1993	1992	1991	1990	1989	1988	1987	1986	1985
Return (%)	0.0	22.5	15.6	49.1	0.6	32.8	17.6	2.6	16.3	—
Differ from category (+/-) . . .	0.6	9.1	4.0	13.4	6.3	6.7	-0.4	0.8	1.7	—

PER SHARE DATA

	1994	1993	1992	1991	1990	1989	1988	1987	1986	1985
Dividends, Net Income ($) .	0.00	0.00	0.01	0.13	0.28	0.03	0.04	0.00	0.03	—
Distrib'ns, Cap Gain ($) . . .	1.45	2.87	0.54	2.11	1.00	0.68	0.00	0.88	0.00	—
Net Asset Value ($)	23.50	24.97	22.74	20.17	15.17	16.40	12.87	10.97	11.61	—
Expense Ratio (%).	1.10	1.10	1.10	1.09	1.12	1.13	1.20	1.20	1.30	—
Net Income to Assets (%). .	0.10	-0.10	0.20	1.49	0.93	0.23	0.34	-0.18	0.70	—
Portfolio Turnover (%). . . .	190	150	189	188	158	91	107	147	58	—
Total Assets (Millions $) . .	2,299	1,500	695	528	272	170	123	128	57	—

PORTFOLIO (as of 9/30/94)

Portfolio Manager: not specified

Investm't Category: Growth

✔ Cap Gain	Asset Allocation
Cap & Income	Fund of Funds
Income	Index
	Sector
✔ Domestic	Small Cap
✔ Foreign	Socially Conscious
Country/Region	State Specific

Portfolio: stocks 67% bonds 0%
convertibles 0% other 0% cash 33%

Largest Holdings: healthcare 10%, semiconductors 7%

Unrealized Net Capital Gains: 7% of portfolio value

SHAREHOLDER INFORMATION

Minimum Investment
Initial: $25,000   Subsequent: $1,000

Minimum IRA Investment
Initial: $25,000   Subsequent: $1,000

Maximum Fees
Load: none   12b-1: none
Other: none

Distributions
Income: Oct, Dec   Capital Gains: Oct, Dec

Exchange Options
Number Per Year: none   Fee:
Telephone:

Services
IRA, auto withdraw

Brandywine Blue (BLUEX)
Growth

3908 Kennett Pike
Greenville, DE 19807
(800) 656-3017, (302) 656-6200

fund inception date: 1/10/91

PERFORMANCE

	3yr Annual	5yr Annual	10yr Annual	Bull	Bear
Return (%)	13.7	na	na	na	-8.3
Differ from Category (+/-)	6.0 high	na	na	na	-1.7 blw av

Total Risk	Standard Deviation	Category Risk	Risk Index	Beta
high	12.7%	high	1.3	1.0

	1994	1993	1992	1991	1990	1989	1988	1987	1986	1985
Return (%)..............	2.3	27.2	13.1	—	—	—	—	—	—	—
Differ from category (+/-) ..	2.9	13.8	1.5	—	—	—	—	—	—	—

PER SHARE DATA

	1994	1993	1992	1991	1990	1989	1988	1987	1986	1985
Dividends, Net Income ($).	0.00	0.00	0.00	—	—	—	—	—	—	—
Distrib'ns, Cap Gain ($) ...	0.11	2.33	0.00	—	—	—	—	—	—	—
Net Asset Value ($)	17.05	16.77	15.08	—	—	—	—	—	—	—
Expense Ratio (%)	1.90	2.00	2.00	—	—	—	—	—	—	—
Net Income to Assets (%) .	-0.40	-0.60	-0.30	—	—	—	—	—	—	—
Portfolio Turnover (%)	220	144	191	—	—	—	—	—	—	—
Total Assets (Millions $).....	32	23	4	—	—	—	—	—	—	—

PORTFOLIO (as of 9/30/94)

Portfolio Manager: Foster Friess - 1991

Investm't Category: Growth

✔ Cap Gain   Asset Allocation
  Cap & Income   Fund of Funds
  Income   Index
                    Sector
✔ Domestic   Small Cap
  Foreign   Socially Conscious
  Country/Region   State Specific

Portfolio: stocks 72%   bonds 0%
convertibles 0%   other 0%   cash 28%

Largest Holdings: healthcare 11%, semi-conductors & related 10%

Unrealized Net Capital Gains: 7% of portfolio value

SHAREHOLDER INFORMATION

Minimum Investment
Initial: $100,000   Subsequent: $1,000

Minimum IRA Investment
Initial: $100,000   Subsequent: $1,000

Maximum Fees
Load: none   12b-1: none
Other: none

Distributions
Income: Oct, Dec   Capital Gains: Oct, Dec

Exchange Options
Number Per Year: none   Fee:
Telephone:

Services
IRA, auto withdraw

Brinson Global (BPGLX)

International Stock

209 South LaSalle Street
Chicago, IL 60604
(312) 220-7100

	3yr Annual	5yr Annual	10yr Annual	Bull	Bear
Return (%)	na	na	na	na	-4.8
Differ from Category (+/-)	na	na	na	na	2.2 abv av

Total Risk	Standard Deviation	Category Risk	Risk Index	Beta
na	na	na	na	na

	1994	1993	1992	1991	1990	1989	1988	1987	1986	1985
Return (%)	-1.8	11.1	—	—	—	—	—	—	—	—
Differ from category (+/-) .	1.2	-27.5	—	—	—	—	—	—	—	—

PER SHARE DATA

	1994	1993	1992	1991	1990	1989	1988	1987	1986	1985
Dividends, Net Income ($) .	0.18	0.27	—	—	—	—	—	—	—	—
Distrib'ns, Cap Gain ($) . .	0.09	0.27	—	—	—	—	—	—	—	—
Net Asset Value ($)	10.31	10.79	—	—	—	—	—	—	—	—
Expense Ratio (%).	1.10	1.05	—	—	—	—	—	—	—	—
Net Income to Assets (%). .	3.25	3.56	—	—	—	—	—	—	—	—
Portfolio Turnover (%). . . .	231	149	—	—	—	—	—	—	—	—
Total Assets (Millions $) . . .	317	252	—	—	—	—	—	—	—	—

PORTFOLIO (as of 6/30/94)

Portfolio Manager: committee

Investm't Category: International Stock

Cap Gain	✔ Asset Allocation
✔ Cap & Income	Fund of Funds
Income	Index
	Sector
✔ Domestic	Small Cap
✔ Foreign	Socially Conscious
Country/Region	State Specific

Portfolio: stocks 67%   bonds 28%
convertibles 0%   other 0%   cash 5%

Largest Holdings: United States 86%, Germany 3%

Unrealized Net Capital Gains: 0% of portfolio value

SHAREHOLDER INFORMATION

Minimum Investment
Initial: $100,000   Subsequent: $2,500

Minimum IRA Investment
Initial: $100,000   Subsequent: $2,500

Maximum Fees
Load: none   12b-1: none
Other: none

Distributions
Income: June, Dec   Capital Gains: Dec

Exchange Options
Number Per Year: no limit   Fee: none
Telephone: yes (money market fund not available)

Services
IRA

Brinson Global Bond
(BPGBX)
International Bond

209 South LaSalle Street
Chicago, IL 60604
(312) 220-7100

fund inception date: 7/30/93

	3yr Annual	5yr Annual	10yr Annual	Bull	Bear
Return (%)	na	na	na	na	-5.1
Differ from Category (+/-)	na	na	na	na	2.7 av

Total Risk	Standard Deviation	Category Risk	Risk Index	Avg Mat
na	na	na	na	8.6 yrs

	1994	1993	1992	1991	1990	1989	1988	1987	1986	1985
Return (%)	-3.4	—	—	—	—	—	—	—	—	—
Differ from category (+/-)	2.9	—	—	—	—	—	—	—	—	—

PER SHARE DATA

	1994	1993	1992	1991	1990	1989	1988	1987	1986	1985
Dividends, Net Income ($)	0.10	—	—	—	—	—	—	—	—	—
Distrib'ns, Cap Gain ($)	0.00	—	—	—	—	—	—	—	—	—
Net Asset Value ($)	9.61	—	—	—	—	—	—	—	—	—
Expense Ratio (%)	0.90	—	—	—	—	—	—	—	—	—
Net Income to Assets (%)	4.91	—	—	—	—	—	—	—	—	—
Portfolio Turnover (%)	na	—	—	—	—	—	—	—	—	—
Total Assets (Millions $)	47	—	—	—	—	—	—	—	—	—

PORTFOLIO (as of 6/30/94)

Portfolio Manager: committee

Investm't Category: International Bond

Cap Gain	Asset Allocation
Cap & Income	Fund of Funds
✔ Income	Index
	Sector
✔ Domestic	Small Cap
✔ Foreign	Socially Conscious
Country/Region	State Specific

Portfolio: stocks 0% bonds 94%
convertibles 0% other 0% cash 6%

Largest Holdings: United States 32%, Germany 13%

Unrealized Net Capital Gains: -1% of portfolio value

SHAREHOLDER INFORMATION

Minimum Investment
Initial: $100,000   Subsequent: $2,500

Minimum IRA Investment
Initial: $100,000   Subsequent: $2,500

Maximum Fees
Load: none   12b-1: none
Other: none

Distributions
Income: June, Dec   Capital Gains: Dec

Exchange Options
Number Per Year: no limit   Fee: none
Telephone: yes (money market fund not available)

Services
IRA

Brinson Non-U.S. Equity

(BNUEX)

International Stock

209 South LaSalle Street
Chicago, IL 60604
(312) 220-7100

PERFORMANCE
fund inception date: 8/31/93

	3yr Annual	5yr Annual	10yr Annual	Bull	Bear
Return (%)	na	na	na	na	-5.6
Differ from Category (+/-)	na	na	na	na	1.4 abv av

Total Risk	Standard Deviation	Category Risk	Risk Index	Beta
na	na	na	na	na

	1994	1993	1992	1991	1990	1989	1988	1987	1986	1985
Return (%)	0.9	—	—	—	—	—	—	—	—	—
Differ from category (+/-) . . .	3.9	—	—	—	—	—	—	—	—	—

PER SHARE DATA

	1994	1993	1992	1991	1990	1989	1988	1987	1986	1985
Dividends, Net Income ($) .	0.05	—	—	—	—	—	—	—	—	—
Distrib'ns, Cap Gain ($) . . .	0.00	—	—	—	—	—	—	—	—	—
Net Asset Value ($)	9.68	—	—	—	—	—	—	—	—	—
Expense Ratio (%).	1.00	—	—	—	—	—	—	—	—	—
Net Income to Assets (%). .	1.88	—	—	—	—	—	—	—	—	—
Portfolio Turnover (%).	na	—	—	—	—	—	—	—	—	—
Total Assets (Millions $) . . .	113	—	—	—	—	—	—	—	—	—

PORTFOLIO (as of 6/30/94)

Portfolio Manager: committee

Investm't Category: International Stock

✔ Cap Gain	Asset Allocation
Cap & Income	Fund of Funds
Income	Index
	Sector
Domestic	Small Cap
✔ Foreign	Socially Conscious
Country/Region	State Specific

Portfolio: stocks 94% bonds 0%
convertibles 0% other 0% cash 6%

Largest Holdings: Japan 35%, United Kingdom 16%

Unrealized Net Capital Gains: 4% of portfolio value

SHAREHOLDER INFORMATION

Minimum Investment
Initial: $100,000   Subsequent: $2,500

Minimum IRA Investment
Initial: $100,000   Subsequent: $2,500

Maximum Fees
Load: none   12b-1: none
Other: none

Distributions
Income: June, Dec   Capital Gains: Dec

Exchange Options
Number Per Year: no limit   Fee: none
Telephone: yes (money market fund not available)

Services
IRA

Brundage Story & Rose
Short/Interm (BRSFX)
General Bond

312 Walnut Street
21st Floor
Cincinnati, OH 45202
(800) 543-8721, (513) 629-2000

PERFORMANCE

fund inception date: 1/2/91

	3yr Annual	5yr Annual	10yr Annual	Bull	Bear
Return (%)	4.0	na	na	na	-3.3
Differ from Category (+/-)	-0.3 blw av	na	na	na	0.5 abv av

Total Risk	Standard Deviation	Category Risk	Risk Index	Avg Mat
low	3.1%	blw av	0.8	10.0 yrs

	1994	1993	1992	1991	1990	1989	1988	1987	1986	1985
Return (%)..............	-2.2	8.3	6.4	13.2	—	—	—	—	—	—
Differ from category (+/-) ..	-0.2	-0.9	-0.2	-1.4	—	—	—	—	—	—

PER SHARE DATA

	1994	1993	1992	1991	1990	1989	1988	1987	1986	1985
Dividends, Net Income ($).	0.60	0.63	0.69	0.68	—	—	—	—	—	—
Distrib'ns, Cap Gain ($) ...	0.00	0.04	0.00	0.00	—	—	—	—	—	—
Net Asset Value ($)	9.92	10.76	10.56	10.59	—	—	—	—	—	—
Expense Ratio (%)	0.50	0.50	0.50	0.50	—	—	—	—	—	—
Net Income to Assets (%) .	5.32	5.95	6.50	7.05	—	—	—	—	—	—
Portfolio Turnover (%)	49	29	24	12	—	—	—	—	—	—
Total Assets (Millions $).....	33	73	32	12	—	—	—	—	—	—

PORTFOLIO (as of 5/31/94)

Portfolio Manager: Dean Benner - 1991

Investm't Category: General Bond

Cap Gain	Asset Allocation
Cap & Income	Fund of Funds
✔ Income	Index
	Sector
✔ Domestic	Small Cap
Foreign	Socially Conscious
Country/Region	State Specific

Portfolio: stocks 0% bonds 99%
convertibles 0% other 0% cash 1%

Largest Holdings: mortgage-backed 39%, corporate 31%

Unrealized Net Capital Gains: -2% of portfolio value

SHAREHOLDER INFORMATION

Minimum Investment
Initial: $1,000   Subsequent: $0

Minimum IRA Investment
Initial: $250   Subsequent: $0

Maximum Fees
Load: none   12b-1: 0.25%
Other: none

Distributions
Income: monthly   Capital Gains: Dec

Exchange Options
Number Per Year: no limit   Fee: none
Telephone: yes (money market fund available)

Services
IRA, pension, auto invest, auto withdraw

Bull & Bear Global Income (BBGLX)

International Bond

11 Hanover Square
New York, NY 10005
(800) 847-4200, (212) 363-1100

PERFORMANCE

fund inception date: 9/1/83

	3yr Annual	5yr Annual	10yr Annual	Bull	Bear
Return (%)	6.9	6.9	5.4	66.7	-14.8
Differ from Category (+/-)	3.0 high	-1.7 blw av	0.0 high	6.4 abv av	-7.0 low

Total Risk	Standard Deviation	Category Risk	Risk Index	Avg Mat
av	7.4%	abv av	1.2	10.4 yrs

	1994	1993	1992	1991	1990	1989	1988	1987	1986	1985
Return (%)	-13.4	24.9	13.1	17.9	-3.0	-3.0	4.9	-6.4	5.9	20.9
Differ from category (+/-) . .	-7.1	11.5	8.4	1.9	-14.5	-5.2	2.5	-19.8	0.0	0.0

PER SHARE DATA

	1994	1993	1992	1991	1990	1989	1988	1987	1986	1985
Dividends, Net Income ($) .	0.66	0.72	0.75	0.75	0.96	1.20	1.29	1.62	1.84	1.93
Distrib'ns, Cap Gain ($) . . .	0.00	0.00	0.00	0.00	0.00	0.00	0.00	0.00	0.00	0.00
Net Asset Value ($)	7.97	9.94	8.59	8.29	7.71	8.93	10.43	11.19	13.57	14.55
Expense Ratio (%).	1.98	1.95	1.93	1.95	1.72	1.68	1.71	1.50	1.37	1.16
Net Income to Assets (%). .	6.58	7.44	9.25	10.08	10.99	12.08	11.96	12.40	13.45	13.86
Portfolio Turnover (%). . . .	223	172	206	555	134	122	124	85	77	127
Total Assets (Millions $)	40	57	44	43	51	83	124	206	113	33

PORTFOLIO (as of 6/30/94)

Portfolio Manager: Clifford McCarthy - 1990

Investm't Category: International Bond

Cap Gain	Asset Allocation
Cap & Income	Fund of Funds
✔ Income	Index
	Sector
✔ Domestic	Small Cap
✔ Foreign	Socially Conscious
Country/Region	State Specific

Portfolio: stocks 1% bonds 89%
convertibles 0% other 3% cash 7%

Largest Holdings: United States 30%, South Africa 10%

Unrealized Net Capital Gains: -6% of portfolio value

SHAREHOLDER INFORMATION

Minimum Investment
Initial: $1,000   Subsequent: $100

Minimum IRA Investment
Initial: $500   Subsequent: $100

Maximum Fees
Load: none   12b-1: 0.50%
Other: none

Distributions
Income: monthly   Capital Gains: Dec

Exchange Options
Number Per Year: no limit   Fee: none
Telephone: yes (money market fund available)

Services
IRA, pension, auto invest, auto withdraw

Bull & Bear Gold Investors Ltd (BBGIX)

Gold

11 Hanover Square
New York, NY 10005
(800) 847-4200, (212) 363-1100

PERFORMANCE   fund inception date: 11/1/74

	3yr Annual	5yr Annual	10yr Annual	Bull	Bear
Return (%)	10.2	0.6	6.7	35.6	-13.3
Differ from Category (+/-)	-0.6 blw av	0.6 av	1.5 av	2.7 av	-3.3 blw av

Total Risk	Standard Deviation	Category Risk	Risk Index	Beta
high	25.6%	av	0.9	0.4

	1994	1993	1992	1991	1990	1989	1988	1987	1986	1985
Return (%)	-13.8	87.6	-17.1	-1.1	-22.1	19.3	-13.5	30.3	35.0	2.5
Differ from category (+/-)	-2.3	0.7	-1.4	3.7	0.4	-5.4	5.4	-1.6	-2.6	9.9

PER SHARE DATA

	1994	1993	1992	1991	1990	1989	1988	1987	1986	1985
Dividends, Net Income ($)	0.00	0.00	0.00	0.05	0.04	0.13	0.03	0.00	0.03	0.12
Distrib'ns, Cap Gain ($)	1.45	0.11	0.00	0.00	0.00	0.00	0.00	1.39	0.00	0.00
Net Asset Value ($)	14.50	18.52	9.93	11.99	12.18	15.69	13.26	15.37	12.86	9.55
Expense Ratio (%)	2.57	3.01	2.96	2.59	2.62	2.46	2.33	2.46	2.39	1.74
Net Income to Assets (%)	-0.68	-0.29	-0.63	0.34	0.65	0.17	0.10	-0.21	0.18	1.08
Portfolio Turnover (%)	129	156	97	95	65	60	52	66	32	30
Total Assets (Millions $)	37	53	25	33	40	38	48	62	20	21

PORTFOLIO (as of 6/30/94)

Portfolio Manager: Bassett S. Winmill - 1994

Investm't Category: Gold

✔ Cap Gain	Asset Allocation
Cap & Income	Fund of Funds
Income	Index
	✔ Sector
✔ Domestic	Small Cap
✔ Foreign	Socially Conscious
Country/Region	State Specific

Portfolio: stocks 89%   bonds 0%
convertibles 7%   other 2%   cash 2%

Largest Holdings: N. American gold mining cos. 37%, S. African gold mining cos. 34%

Unrealized Net Capital Gains: 13% of portfolio value

SHAREHOLDER INFORMATION

Minimum Investment
Initial: $1,000   Subsequent: $100

Minimum IRA Investment
Initial: $500   Subsequent: $100

Maximum Fees
Load: none   12b-1: 1.00%
Other: none

Distributions
Income: Dec   Capital Gains: Dec

Exchange Options
Number Per Year: no limit   Fee: none
Telephone: yes (money market fund available)

Services
IRA, pension, auto invest, auto withdraw

Bull & Bear Muni Income

(BBMIX)

Tax-Exempt Bond

11 Hanover Square
New York, NY 10005
(800) 847-4200, (212) 363-1100

	3yr Annual	5yr Annual	10yr Annual	Bull	Bear
Return (%)	1.9	4.5	8.2	39.8	-9.6
Differ from Category (+/-)	-2.6 low	-1.6 low	0.1 av	-2.0 blw av	-4.4 low

Total Risk	Standard Deviation	Category Risk	Risk Index	Avg Mat
av	6.9%	high	1.1	11.5 yrs

	1994	1993	1992	1991	1990	1989	1988	1987	1986	1985
Return (%)	-9.7	10.5	6.0	13.6	3.8	8.9	11.6	-0.9	19.6	22.4
Differ from category (+/-) . .	-4.5	-1.2	-2.3	2.3	-2.5	-0.1	1.4	0.4	3.2	5.0

PER SHARE DATA

	1994	1993	1992	1991	1990	1989	1988	1987	1986	1985
Dividends, Net Income ($) .	0.68	0.76	0.89	1.03	1.01	1.14	1.19	1.26	1.31	1.39
Distrib'ns, Cap Gain ($) . . .	0.00	0.45	0.32	0.86	0.00	0.52	0.00	0.00	0.58	0.00
Net Asset Value ($)	15.25	17.63	17.06	17.27	16.92	17.29	17.44	16.74	18.17	16.88
Expense Ratio (%).	1.61	1.61	1.60	1.60	1.50	1.35	1.27	1.18	1.18	1.02
Net Income to Assets (%). .	4.28	4.25	5.19	5.86	5.94	6.35	7.11	7.18	7.29	8.70
Portfolio Turnover (%)	na	74	320	511	172	188	70	62	60	46
Total Assets (Millions $)	15	22	21	20	21	21	19	16	21	11

PORTFOLIO (as of 6/30/94)

Portfolio Manager: Cliff McCarthy - 1990

Investm't Category: Tax-Exempt Bond
Cap Gain	Asset Allocation
Cap & Income	Fund of Funds
✔ Income	Index
	Sector
✔ Domestic	Small Cap
Foreign	Socially Conscious
Country/Region	State Specific

Portfolio: stocks 0%   bonds 88%
convertibles 0%   other 0%   cash 12%

Largest Holdings: general obligation 30%

Unrealized Net Capital Gains: -3% of portfolio value

SHAREHOLDER INFORMATION

Minimum Investment
Initial: $1,000   Subsequent: $100

Minimum IRA Investment
Initial: na   Subsequent: na

Maximum Fees
Load: none   12b-1: 0.50%
Other: none

Distributions
Income: monthly   Capital Gains: Dec

Exchange Options
Number Per Year: no limit   Fee: none
Telephone: yes (money market fund available)

Services
auto exchange, auto invest, auto withdraw

Bull & Bear Special Equities (BBSEX)

Aggressive Growth

11 Hanover Square
New York, NY 10005
(800) 847-4200, (212) 363-1100

PERFORMANCE

fund inception date: 3/20/86

	3yr Annual	5yr Annual	10yr Annual	Bull	Bear
Return (%)	7.6	2.1	na	87.6	-22.7
Differ from Category (+/-)	-1.3 av	-10.4 low	na	-45.6 low	-11.9 low

Total Risk	Standard Deviation	Category Risk	Risk Index	Beta
high	18.8%	high	1.3	1.2

	1994	1993	1992	1991	1990	1989	1988	1987	1986	1985
Return (%)	-16.5	16.3	28.3	40.5	-36.3	42.2	22.7	-6.4	—	—
Differ from category (+/-) .	-15.8	-3.2	17.3	-11.6	-30.1	15.4	7.5	-4.2	—	—

PER SHARE DATA

	1994	1993	1992	1991	1990	1989	1988	1987	1986	1985
Dividends, Net Income ($).	0.00	0.00	0.00	0.00	0.00	0.00	0.00	0.00	—	—
Distrib'ns, Cap Gain ($) . . .	0.19	5.64	0.00	0.00	0.00	4.05	1.15	0.00	—	—
Net Asset Value ($)	19.11	23.13	24.88	19.38	13.79	21.68	18.17	15.75	—	—
Expense Ratio (%)	2.95	2.74	3.07	2.83	3.10	3.50	2.94	3.01	—	—
Net Income to Assets (%) .	-2.77	-2.73	-2.78	-2.11	-3.19	-3.23	-1.49	-0.82	—	—
Portfolio Turnover (%)	na	256	261	384	475	433	514	751	—	—
Total Assets (Millions $).	45	70	68	17	9	6	3	2	—	—

PORTFOLIO (as of 6/30/94)

Portfolio Manager: Brett B. Sneed - 1988

Investm't Category: Aggressive Growth

✔ Cap Gain	Asset Allocation
Cap & Income	Fund of Funds
Income	Index
	Sector
✔ Domestic	Small Cap
✔ Foreign	Socially Conscious
Country/Region	State Specific

Portfolio: stocks 80% bonds 0%
convertibles 0% other 0% cash 20%

Largest Holdings: financial services 13%, communications products and equipment 9%

Unrealized Net Capital Gains: -9% of portfolio value

SHAREHOLDER INFORMATION

Minimum Investment
Initial: $1,000 Subsequent: $100

Minimum IRA Investment
Initial: $500 Subsequent: $100

Maximum Fees
Load: none 12b-1: 1.00%
Other: none

Distributions
Income: Dec Capital Gains: Dec

Exchange Options
Number Per Year: no limit Fee: none
Telephone: yes (money market fund available)

Services
IRA, pension, auto invest, auto withdraw

Bull & Bear US & Overseas (BBOSX)

International Stock

11 Hanover Square
New York, NY 10005
(800) 847-4200, (212) 363-1100

PERFORMANCE

	3yr Annual	5yr Annual	10yr Annual	Bull	Bear
Return (%)	2.3	3.7	na	54.6	-11.2
Differ from Category (+/-)	-6.8 low	-1.2 blw av	na	-9.3 blw av	-4.2 blw av

Total Risk	Standard Deviation	Category Risk	Risk Index	Beta
abv av	11.9%	blw av	0.9	0.8

	1994	1993	1992	1991	1990	1989	1988	1987	1986	1985
Return (%)	-13.1	26.7	-2.6	22.6	-8.5	15.5	3.7	—	—	—
Differ from category (+/-) .	-10.1	-11.9	0.3	9.5	1.9	-7.0	-10.7	—	—	—

PER SHARE DATA

	1994	1993	1992	1991	1990	1989	1988	1987	1986	1985
Dividends, Net Income ($) .	0.49	0.00	0.00	0.00	0.00	0.02	0.02	—	—	—
Distrib'ns, Cap Gain ($) . . .	0.00	0.90	0.57	0.96	0.11	0.44	0.00	—	—	—
Net Asset Value ($)	7.08	8.71	7.59	8.38	7.62	8.46	7.72	—	—	—
Expense Ratio (%)	3.50	3.55	3.56	3.56	3.50	3.50	3.02	—	—	—
Net Income to Assets (%) .	-1.96	-2.36	0.51	0.90	-0.09	-1.29	0.44	—	—	—
Portfolio Turnover (%)	na	182	175	208	270	178	140	—	—	—
Total Assets (Millions $)	8	11	9	1	1	1	1	—	—	—

PORTFOLIO (as of 6/30/94)

Portfolio Manager: Brett B. Sneed - 1994

Investm't Category: International Stock

Cap Gain	Asset Allocation
✔ Cap & Income	Fund of Funds
Income	Index
	Sector
✔ Domestic	Small Cap
✔ Foreign	Socially Conscious
Country/Region	State Specific

Portfolio: stocks 95%   bonds 0%
convertibles 0%   other 0%   cash 5%

Largest Holdings: Japan 16%, United States 15%

Unrealized Net Capital Gains: 2% of portfolio value

SHAREHOLDER INFORMATION

Minimum Investment
Initial: $1,000   Subsequent: $100

Minimum IRA Investment
Initial: $500   Subsequent: $100

Maximum Fees
Load: none   12b-1: 1.00%
Other: none

Distributions
Income: Dec   Capital Gains: Dec

Exchange Options
Number Per Year: no limit   Fee: none
Telephone: yes (money market fund available)

Services
IRA, pension, auto invest, auto withdraw

Bull & Bear US Gov't Securities (BBUSX)

Government Bond

11 Hanover Square
New York, NY 10005
(800) 847-4200, (212) 363-1100

PERFORMANCE

fund inception date: 3/7/86

	3yr Annual	5yr Annual	10yr Annual	Bull	Bear
Return (%)	3.3	6.5	na	40.8	-4.8
Differ from Category (+/-)	-0.7 blw av	-0.2 blw av	na	-10.4 av	1.6 av

Total Risk	Standard Deviation	Category Risk	Risk Index	Avg Mat
low	4.6%	av	1.0	3.4 yrs

	1994	1993	1992	1991	1990	1989	1988	1987	1986	1985
Return (%).	-4.7	10.2	5.2	15.1	7.8	10.3	4.5	5.4	—	—
Differ from category (+/-) . .	0.1	-0.7	-1.2	-0.2	1.6	-4.2	-3.4	7.5	—	—

PER SHARE DATA

	1994	1993	1992	1991	1990	1989	1988	1987	1986	1985
Dividends, Net Income ($).	0.65	0.70	0.90	0.96	1.02	1.14	1.38	1.46	—	—
Distrib'ns, Cap Gain ($) . . .	0.00	0.00	0.00	0.00	0.00	0.00	0.00	0.00	—	—
Net Asset Value ($)	14.22	15.60	14.80	14.95	13.88	13.87	13.65	14.38	—	—
Expense Ratio (%)	1.85	1.91	1.86	1.86	1.99	1.74	1.96	2.06	—	—
Net Income to Assets (%) .	4.16	5.38	6.40	7.14	7.86	8.87	9.95	9.40	—	—
Portfolio Turnover (%)	261	176	140	407	279	217	174	185	—	—
Total Assets (Millions $).	15	21	26	31	33	38	64	47	—	—

PORTFOLIO (as of 6/30/94)

Portfolio Manager: Cliff McCarthy - 1990

Investm't Category: Government Bond

Cap Gain	Asset Allocation
Cap & Income	Fund of Funds
✔ Income	Index
	Sector
✔ Domestic	Small Cap
Foreign	Socially Conscious
Country/Region	State Specific

Portfolio: stocks 0%   bonds 100%
convertibles 0%   other 0%   cash 0%

Largest Holdings: U.S. government 85%, mortgage-backed 15%

Unrealized Net Capital Gains: -3% of portfolio value

SHAREHOLDER INFORMATION

Minimum Investment
Initial: $1,000   Subsequent: $100

Minimum IRA Investment
Initial: $500   Subsequent: $100

Maximum Fees
Load: none   12b-1: 0.25%
Other: none

Distributions
Income: monthly   Capital Gains: Dec

Exchange Options
Number Per Year: no limit   Fee: none
Telephone: yes (money market fund available)

Services
IRA, pension, auto invest, auto withdraw

CA Investment Trust US Gov't (CAUSX)

44 Montgomery St., Suite 2100
San Francisco, CA 94104
(800) 225-8778, (415) 398-2727

Government Bond

PERFORMANCE

fund inception date: 12/4/85

	3yr Annual	5yr Annual	10yr Annual	Bull	Bear
Return (%)	5.3	8.3	na	58.0	-8.9
Differ from Category (+/-)	1.3 high	1.6 high	na	6.8 abv av	-2.5 blw av

Total Risk	Standard Deviation	Category Risk	Risk Index	Avg Mat
blw av	6.7%	abv av	1.4	18.5 yrs

	1994	1993	1992	1991	1990	1989	1988	1987	1986	1985
Return (%)	-6.9	15.7	8.4	17.4	8.5	13.4	7.2	1.2	11.9	—
Differ from category (+/-) . .	-2.1	4.8	2.0	2.1	2.3	-1.1	-0.7	3.3	-8.7	—

PER SHARE DATA

	1994	1993	1992	1991	1990	1989	1988	1987	1986	1985
Dividends, Net Income ($) .	0.67	0.70	0.72	0.82	0.81	0.85	0.88	0.95	0.82	—
Distrib'ns, Cap Gain ($) . . .	0.00	0.05	0.05	0.00	0.00	0.00	0.00	0.00	0.00	—
Net Asset Value ($)	9.84	11.29	10.43	10.38	9.61	9.64	9.29	9.49	10.33	—
Expense Ratio (%).	0.62	0.52	0.38	0.60	0.60	0.61	0.59	0.34	0.04	—
Net Income to Assets (%). .	6.10	6.55	7.12	8.73	8.64	9.18	9.24	8.27	9.66	—
Portfolio Turnover (%). . . .	129	52	122	53	78	78	110	115	278	—
Total Assets (Millions $)	26	35	80	21	12	11	10	13	10	—

PORTFOLIO (as of 8/31/94)

Portfolio Manager: Phillip McClanahan - 1985

Investm't Category: Government Bond

Cap Gain	Asset Allocation
Cap & Income	Fund of Funds
✔ Income	Index
	Sector
✔ Domestic	Small Cap
Foreign	Socially Conscious
Country/Region	State Specific

Portfolio: stocks 0% bonds 99%
convertibles 0% other 0% cash 1%

Largest Holdings: U.S. government 51%,
mortgage-backed 41%

Unrealized Net Capital Gains: 0% of portfolio value

SHAREHOLDER INFORMATION

Minimum Investment
Initial: $10,000   Subsequent: $250

Minimum IRA Investment
Initial: $0   Subsequent: $0

Maximum Fees
Load: none   12b-1: none
Other: none

Distributions
Income: monthly   Capital Gains: Dec

Exchange Options
Number Per Year: no limit   Fee: none
Telephone: yes (money market fund available)

Services
IRA, pension, auto exchange, auto invest, auto withdraw

Cal Muni (CAMFX)
Tax-Exempt Bond

90 Washington St.
New York, NY 10006
(800) 322-6864, (212) 635-3005

PERFORMANCE

fund inception date: 9/29/84

	3yr Annual	5yr Annual	10yr Annual	Bull	Bear
Return (%)	0.0	2.6	6.4	40.7	-13.7
Differ from Category (+/-)	-4.5 low	-3.5 low	-1.7 low	-1.1 blw av	-8.5 low

Total Risk	Standard Deviation	Category Risk	Risk Index	Avg Mat
av	8.3%	high	1.3	15.7 yrs

	1994	1993	1992	1991	1990	1989	1988	1987	1986	1985
Return (%).	-19.9	16.7	7.2	8.8	4.3	8.0	12.2	1.4	9.6	22.1
Differ from category (+/-) .	-14.7	5.0	-1.1	-2.5	-2.0	-1.0	2.0	2.7	-6.8	4.7

PER SHARE DATA

	1994	1993	1992	1991	1990	1989	1988	1987	1986	1985
Dividends, Net Income ($).	0.55	0.56	0.60	0.58	0.55	0.53	0.61	0.66	0.76	0.81
Distrib'ns, Cap Gain ($) . . .	0.00	0.20	0.00	0.00	0.00	0.22	0.05	0.17	1.66	0.00
Net Asset Value ($)	7.10	9.49	8.81	8.80	8.64	8.82	8.87	8.52	9.23	10.67
Expense Ratio (%)	3.31	2.16	1.63	2.38	2.48	2.49	1.55	1.61	2.33	3.02
Net Income to Assets (%) .	7.06	6.04	6.87	6.58	6.36	5.95	6.88	7.66	7.16	7.78
Portfolio Turnover (%)	na	51	19	47	43	86	58	32	34	288
Total Assets (Millions $). . . .	10	16	12	10	10	11	10	8	4	11

PORTFOLIO (as of 6/30/94)

Portfolio Manager: Lance Brofman - 1984

Investm't Category: Tax-Exempt Bond
Cap Gain	Asset Allocation
Cap & Income	Fund of Funds
✔ Income	Index
	Sector
✔ Domestic	Small Cap
Foreign	Socially Conscious
Country/Region	✔ State Specific

Portfolio: stocks 0% bonds 100%
convertibles 0% other 0% cash 0%

Largest Holdings: general obligation 0%

Unrealized Net Capital Gains: -9% of portfolio value

SHAREHOLDER INFORMATION

Minimum Investment
Initial: $1,000   Subsequent: $100

Minimum IRA Investment
Initial: na   Subsequent: na

Maximum Fees
Load: none   12b-1: 0.50%
Other: none

Distributions
Income: monthly   Capital Gains: Dec

Exchange Options
Number Per Year: no limit   Fee: none
Telephone: yes (money market fund available)

Services
auto invest, auto withdraw

Cal Tax-Free Income
(CFNTX)
Tax-Exempt Bond

44 Montgomery St., Suite 2100
San Francisco, CA 94104
(800) 225-8778, (415) 398-2727

PERFORMANCE

fund inception date: 12/4/85

	3yr Annual	5yr Annual	10yr Annual	Bull	Bear
Return (%)	4.5	6.4	na	47.9	-8.1
Differ from Category (+/-)	0.0 av	0.3 av	na	6.1 high	-2.9 low

Total Risk	Standard Deviation	Category Risk	Risk Index	Avg Mat
av	7.6%	high	1.2	18.0 yrs

	1994	1993	1992	1991	1990	1989	1988	1987	1986	1985
Return (%)	-8.6	14.7	8.8	12.1	6.7	9.9	11.3	-1.2	22.7	—
Differ from category (+/-) . .	-3.4	3.0	0.5	0.8	0.4	0.9	1.1	0.1	6.3	—

PER SHARE DATA

	1994	1993	1992	1991	1990	1989	1988	1987	1986	1985
Dividends, Net Income ($) .	0.63	0.68	0.72	0.74	0.76	0.79	0.80	0.89	0.80	—
Distrib'ns, Cap Gain ($) . . .	0.20	0.29	0.08	0.00	0.00	0.00	0.00	0.00	0.00	—
Net Asset Value ($)	11.23	13.18	12.36	12.13	11.52	11.54	11.25	10.86	11.90	—
Expense Ratio (%).	0.60	0.60	0.60	0.60	0.59	0.60	0.61	0.39	0.03	—
Net Income to Assets (%). .	5.09	5.41	5.98	6.43	6.67	7.06	7.43	7.22	8.01	—
Portfolio Turnover (%)	31	25	45	44	42	48	102	87	50	—
Total Assets (Millions $) . . .	185	279	217	137	86	70	39	37	21	—

PORTFOLIO (as of 8/31/94)

Portfolio Manager: Phillip McClanahan - 1985

Investm't Category: Tax-Exempt Bond

Cap Gain	Asset Allocation
Cap & Income	Fund of Funds
✔ Income	Index
	Sector
✔ Domestic	Small Cap
Foreign	Socially Conscious
Country/Region	✔ State Specific

Portfolio: stocks 0%   bonds 100%
convertibles 0%   other 0%   cash 0%

Largest Holdings: general obligation 9%

Unrealized Net Capital Gains: 0% of portfolio value

SHAREHOLDER INFORMATION

Minimum Investment
Initial: $10,000   Subsequent: $250

Minimum IRA Investment
Initial: na   Subsequent: na

Maximum Fees
Load: none   12b-1: none
Other: none

Distributions
Income: monthly   Capital Gains: Dec

Exchange Options
Number Per Year: no limit   Fee: none
Telephone: yes (money market fund available)

Services
auto exchange, auto invest, auto withdraw

Caldwell & Orkin Aggressive Growth

(COAGX) *Aggressive Growth*

2050 Tower Place
3340 Peachtree Road
Atlanta, GA 30326
(800) 237-7073

	3yr Annual	5yr Annual	10yr Annual	Bull	Bear
Return (%)	9.4	na	na	na	-2.1
Differ from Category (+/-)	0.5 av	na	na	na	8.7 high

Total Risk	Standard Deviation	Category Risk	Risk Index	Beta
abv av	11.0%	low	0.7	0.6

	1994	1993	1992	1991	1990	1989	1988	1987	1986	1985
Return (%)	-0.9	14.9	15.2	—	—	—	—	—	—	—
Differ from category (+/-) . .	-0.2	-4.6	4.2	—	—	—	—	—	—	—

PER SHARE DATA

	1994	1993	1992	1991	1990	1989	1988	1987	1986	1985
Dividends, Net Income ($).	0.26	0.04	0.00	—	—	—	—	—	—	—
Distrib'ns, Cap Gain ($) . . .	0.22	2.69	0.51	—	—	—	—	—	—	—
Net Asset Value ($)	11.71	12.31	13.17	—	—	—	—	—	—	—
Expense Ratio (%)	1.21	1.30	1.64	—	—	—	—	—	—	—
Net Income to Assets (%) .	0.44	-0.01	-0.76	—	—	—	—	—	—	—
Portfolio Turnover (%)	292	223	50	—	—	—	—	—	—	—
Total Assets (Millions $).	35	19	12	—	—	—	—	—	—	—

PORTFOLIO (as of 4/30/94)

Portfolio Manager: Michael B. Orkin - 1992

Investm't Category: Aggressive Growth

✔ Cap Gain	Asset Allocation
Cap & Income	Fund of Funds
Income	Index
	Sector
✔ Domestic	✔ Small Cap
Foreign	Socially Conscious
Country/Region	State Specific

Portfolio: stocks 32%   bonds 0%
convertibles 0%   other 0%   cash 68%

Largest Holdings: retail drug stores 3%, electrical connectors and equipment 3%

Unrealized Net Capital Gains: 0% of portfolio value

SHAREHOLDER INFORMATION

Minimum Investment
Initial: $10,000   Subsequent: $1,000

Minimum IRA Investment
Initial: $2,000   Subsequent: $1,000

Maximum Fees
Load: none   12b-1: none
Other: none

Distributions
Income: Dec   Capital Gains: Dec

Exchange Options
Number Per Year: no limit   Fee: none
Telephone: none

Services
IRA, pension

Calvert Tax-Free Reserves Ltd Term— Class A (CTFLX) *Tax-Exempt Bond*

4550 Montgomery Avenue
Suite 1000 North
Bethesda, MD 20814
(800) 368-2748, (301) 951-4820

PERFORMANCE

fund inception date: 4/2/81

	3yr Annual	5yr Annual	10yr Annual	Bull	Bear
Return (%)	3.8	4.8	5.9	19.0	0.7
Differ from Category (+/-)	-0.7 low	-1.3 low	-2.2 low	-22.8 low	5.9 high

Total Risk	Standard Deviation	Category Risk	Risk Index	Avg Mat
low	0.4%	low	0.0	0.7 yrs

	1994	1993	1992	1991	1990	1989	1988	1987	1986	1985
Return (%)	2.3	4.0	5.0	6.4	6.4	7.2	6.9	3.6	8.5	8.6
Differ from category (+/-) . . .	7.5	-7.7	-3.3	-4.9	0.1	-1.8	-3.3	4.9	-7.9	-8.8

PER SHARE DATA

	1994	1993	1992	1991	1990	1989	1988	1987	1986	1985
Dividends, Net Income ($) .	0.38	0.38	0.50	0.63	0.67	0.68	0.61	0.60	0.65	0.70
Distrib'ns, Cap Gain ($) . . .	0.00	0.00	0.00	0.00	0.00	0.00	0.00	0.00	0.04	0.03
Net Asset Value ($)	10.59	10.72	10.68	10.65	10.61	10.61	10.55	10.45	10.67	10.48
Expense Ratio (%).	0.65	0.67	0.71	0.73	0.77	0.78	0.81	0.76	0.81	0.88
Net Income to Assets (%). .	3.41	3.59	4.58	5.99	6.35	6.35	5.71	5.59	6.00	6.65
Portfolio Turnover (%).	na	14	5	1	12	21	68	52	67	90
Total Assets (Millions $) . . .	547	678	568	294	152	133	145	148	189	77

PORTFOLIO (as of 6/30/94)

Portfolio Manager: Reno Martini - 1982

Investm't Category: Tax-Exempt Bond

Cap Gain	Asset Allocation
Cap & Income	Fund of Funds
✔ Income	Index
	Sector
✔ Domestic	Small Cap
Foreign	Socially Conscious
Country/Region	State Specific

Portfolio: stocks 0% bonds 100%
convertibles 0% other 0% cash 0%

Largest Holdings: general obligation 9%

Unrealized Net Capital Gains: 0% of portfolio value

SHAREHOLDER INFORMATION

Minimum Investment
Initial: $2,000   Subsequent: $250

Minimum IRA Investment
Initial: na   Subsequent: na

Maximum Fees
Load: 2.00% front   12b-1: none
Other: none

Distributions
Income: monthly   Capital Gains: Dec

Exchange Options
Number Per Year: 8   Fee: none
Telephone: yes (money market fund available)

Services
auto exchange, auto invest, auto withdraw

Cappiello-Rushmore Emerging Growth (CREGX)

4922 Fairmont Ave.
Bethesda, MD 20814
(800) 622-1386, (301) 657-1500

Aggressive Growth

PERFORMANCE

fund inception date: 10/1/92

	3yr Annual	5yr Annual	10yr Annual	Bull	Bear
Return (%)	na	na	na	na	-22.0
Differ from Category (+/-)	na	na	na	na	-11.2 low

Total Risk	Standard Deviation	Category Risk	Risk Index	Beta
na	na	na	na	na

	1994	1993	1992	1991	1990	1989	1988	1987	1986	1985
Return (%)	-6.9	22.5	—	—	—	—	—	—	—	—
Differ from category (+/-)	-6.2	3.0	—	—	—	—	—	—	—	—

PER SHARE DATA

	1994	1993	1992	1991	1990	1989	1988	1987	1986	1985
Dividends, Net Income ($)	0.00	0.00	—	—	—	—	—	—	—	—
Distrib'ns, Cap Gain ($)	0.00	0.14	—	—	—	—	—	—	—	—
Net Asset Value ($)	11.65	12.52	—	—	—	—	—	—	—	—
Expense Ratio (%)	1.50	1.50	—	—	—	—	—	—	—	—
Net Income to Assets (%)	-0.85	-0.63	—	—	—	—	—	—	—	—
Portfolio Turnover (%)	128	67	—	—	—	—	—	—	—	—
Total Assets (Millions $)	19	12	—	—	—	—	—	—	—	—

PORTFOLIO (as of 6/30/94)

Portfolio Manager: Frank Cappiello - 1992

Investm't Category: Aggressive Growth

✔ Cap Gain	Asset Allocation
Cap & Income	Fund of Funds
Income	Index
	Sector
✔ Domestic	✔ Small Cap
Foreign	Socially Conscious
Country/Region	State Specific

Portfolio: stocks 96% bonds 0%
convertibles 0% other 0% cash 4%

Largest Holdings: healthcare 19%, semiconductors/components 8%

Unrealized Net Capital Gains: -12% of portfolio value

SHAREHOLDER INFORMATION

Minimum Investment
Initial: $2,500 Subsequent: $0

Minimum IRA Investment
Initial: $500 Subsequent: $0

Maximum Fees
Load: none 12b-1: none
Other: none

Distributions
Income: Dec Capital Gains: Dec

Exchange Options
Number Per Year: no limit Fee: none
Telephone: yes (money market fund available)

Services
IRA, pension, auto invest

Cappiello-Rushmore
Utility Income (CRUTX)

4922 Fairmont Ave.
Bethesda, MD 20814
(800) 622-1386, (301) 657-1500

Growth & Income

PERFORMANCE

fund inception date: 10/1/92

	3yr Annual	5yr Annual	10yr Annual	Bull	Bear
Return (%)	na	na	na	na	-14.9
Differ from Category (+/-)	na	na	na	na	-8.6 low

Total Risk	Standard Deviation	Category Risk	Risk Index	Beta
na	na	na	na	na

	1994	1993	1992	1991	1990	1989	1988	1987	1986	1985
Return (%)	-13.3	6.1	—	—	—	—	—	—	—	—
Differ from category (+/-)	-11.9	-7.1	—	—	—	—	—	—	—	—

PER SHARE DATA

	1994	1993	1992	1991	1990	1989	1988	1987	1986	1985
Dividends, Net Income ($)	0.45	0.37	—	—	—	—	—	—	—	—
Distrib'ns, Cap Gain ($)	0.00	0.01	—	—	—	—	—	—	—	—
Net Asset Value ($)	8.62	10.47	—	—	—	—	—	—	—	—
Expense Ratio (%)	1.05	1.05	—	—	—	—	—	—	—	—
Net Income to Assets (%)	5.21	3.31	—	—	—	—	—	—	—	—
Portfolio Turnover (%)	26	15	—	—	—	—	—	—	—	—
Total Assets (Millions $)	19	11	—	—	—	—	—	—	—	—

PORTFOLIO (as of 6/30/94)

Portfolio Manager: Frank Cappiello - 1992

Investm't Category: Growth & Income
Cap Gain	Asset Allocation
✔ Cap & Income	Fund of Funds
Income	Index
	✔ Sector
✔ Domestic	Small Cap
Foreign	Socially Conscious
Country/Region	State Specific

Portfolio: stocks 90% bonds 0%
convertibles 0% other 0% cash 10%

Largest Holdings: gas & electric 75%, telephone 9%

Unrealized Net Capital Gains: -22% of portfolio value

SHAREHOLDER INFORMATION

Minimum Investment
Initial: $2,500   Subsequent: $0

Minimum IRA Investment
Initial: $500   Subsequent: $0

Maximum Fees
Load: none   12b-1: none
Other: none

Distributions
Income: quarterly   Capital Gains: Dec

Exchange Options
Number Per Year: no limit   Fee: none
Telephone: yes (money market fund available)

Services
IRA, pension, auto invest

Capstone Gov't Income
(CGVIX)
Government Bond

5847 San Felipe
Suite 4100
Houston, TX 77057
(800) 262-6631

PERFORMANCE

fund inception date: 6/4/68

	3yr Annual	5yr Annual	10yr Annual	Bull	Bear
Return (%)	2.6	2.6	7.0	14.1	-0.4
Differ from Category (+/-)	-1.4 low	-4.1 low	-0.8 blw av	-37.1 low	6.0 high

Total Risk	Standard Deviation	Category Risk	Risk Index	Avg Mat
low	1.2%	low	0.2	0.9 yrs

	1994	1993	1992	1991	1990	1989	1988	1987	1986	1985
Return (%)	1.1	3.3	3.5	6.5	-1.0	7.2	11.7	3.7	16.1	20.4
Differ from category (+/-) . .	5.9	-7.6	-2.9	-8.8	-7.2	-7.3	3.8	5.8	-4.5	1.9

PER SHARE DATA

	1994	1993	1992	1991	1990	1989	1988	1987	1986	1985
Dividends, Net Income ($).	0.13	0.10	0.10	0.18	0.45	0.48	0.44	0.53	0.48	0.48
Distrib'ns, Cap Gain ($) . . .	0.00	0.00	0.00	0.00	0.00	0.00	0.00	0.00	0.00	0.00
Net Asset Value ($)	4.73	4.80	4.74	4.67	4.55	5.05	5.17	5.03	5.36	5.06
Expense Ratio (%)	0.85	0.93	0.96	1.67	1.40	1.24	1.29	1.29	1.52	1.72
Net Income to Assets (%) .	3.92	3.64	4.69	5.29	9.06	8.75	8.51	8.90	9.18	10.32
Portfolio Turnover (%)	na	596	633	754	82	70	100	102	186	236
Total Assets (Millions $). . . .	58	90	30	38	18	20	25	23	19	12

PORTFOLIO (as of 6/30/94)

Portfolio Manager: Edward Jaroski - 1987, Howard Potter - 1991

Investm't Category: Government Bond
Cap Gain	Asset Allocation
Cap & Income	Fund of Funds
✔ Income	Index
	Sector
✔ Domestic	Small Cap
Foreign	Socially Conscious
Country/Region	State Specific

Portfolio: stocks 0%   bonds 80%
convertibles 0%   other 0%   cash 20%

Largest Holdings: U.S. government 80%

Unrealized Net Capital Gains: -1% of portfolio value

SHAREHOLDER INFORMATION

Minimum Investment
Initial: $10,000   Subsequent: $0

Minimum IRA Investment
Initial: $10,000   Subsequent: $0

Maximum Fees
Load: none   12b-1: 0.20%
Other: none

Distributions
Income: Dec   Capital Gains: Dec

Exchange Options
Number Per Year: 12   Fee: none
Telephone: yes (money market fund available)

Services
IRA, pension, auto invest, auto withdraw

Century Shares Trust
(CENSX)
Growth

One Liberty Square
Boston, MA 02109
(800) 321-1928, (617) 482-3060

PERFORMANCE

fund inception date: 3/1/28

	3yr Annual	5yr Annual	10yr Annual	Bull	Bear
Return (%)	6.7	8.0	13.3	97.2	-7.4
Differ from Category (+/-)	-1.0 av	-1.6 blw av	0.4 av	5.1 abv av	-0.8 blw av

Total Risk	Standard Deviation	Category Risk	Risk Index	Beta
abv av	10.2%	abv av	1.1	0.7

	1994	1993	1992	1991	1990	1989	1988	1987	1986	1985
Return (%)	-3.8	-0.3	26.9	31.5	-7.8	41.6	15.6	-8.0	9.6	43.4
Differ from category (+/-) . .	-3.2	-13.7	15.3	-4.2	-2.1	15.5	-2.4	-9.8	-5.0	14.2

PER SHARE DATA

	1994	1993	1992	1991	1990	1989	1988	1987	1986	1985
Dividends, Net Income ($)	0.45	0.45	0.42	0.47	0.51	0.50	0.54	0.50	0.51	0.54
Distrib'ns, Cap Gain ($) . . .	0.88	1.10	0.56	0.57	0.58	0.71	1.90	1.61	1.11	0.91
Net Asset Value ($)	21.77	24.04	25.68	21.03	16.82	19.42	14.62	14.76	18.30	18.22
Expense Ratio (%).	1.02	0.82	0.84	0.95	1.03	0.94	0.87	0.81	0.77	0.84
Net Income to Assets (%). .	1.77	1.72	1.84	2.28	2.82	2.78	3.45	2.60	2.57	3.14
Portfolio Turnover (%)	na	19	5	0	3	3	3	2	6	6
Total Assets (Millions $) . . .	206	241	260	158	130	151	110	109	140	123

PORTFOLIO (as of 6/30/94)

Portfolio Manager: Allan W. Fulkerson - 1976

Investm't Category: Growth

✔ Cap Gain	Asset Allocation
Cap & Income	Fund of Funds
Income	Index
	✔ Sector
✔ Domestic	Small Cap
Foreign	Socially Conscious
Country/Region	State Specific

Portfolio: stocks 96% bonds 0%
convertibles 3% other 0% cash 1%

Largest Holdings: insurance 88%, banking institutions 6%

Unrealized Net Capital Gains: 50% of portfolio value

SHAREHOLDER INFORMATION

Minimum Investment
Initial: $500   Subsequent: $25

Minimum IRA Investment
Initial: $500   Subsequent: $25

Maximum Fees
Load: none   12b-1: none
Other: none

Distributions
Income: Jun, Dec   Capital Gains: Dec

Exchange Options
Number Per Year: none   Fee:
Telephone:

Services
IRA, pension, auto invest, auto withdraw

CGM Capital Development (LOMCX)

P.O. Box 449
Boston, MA 02117
(800) 345-4048, (617) 859-7714

Aggressive Growth

this fund is closed to new investors

	3yr Annual	5yr Annual	10yr Annual	Bull	Bear
Return (%)	5.2	18.6	19.6	270.3	-21.9
Differ from Category (+/-)	-3.7 blw av	6.1 high	5.6 high	137.1 high	-11.1 low

Total Risk	Standard Deviation	Category Risk	Risk Index	Beta
high	17.3%	high	1.2	1.5

	1994	1993	1992	1991	1990	1989	1988	1987	1986	1985
Return (%)	-22.9	28.6	17.4	99.2	1.3	17.8	-0.2	15.8	28.4	46.2
Differ from category (+/-)	-22.2	9.1	6.4	47.1	7.5	-9.0	-15.4	18.0	16.6	13.9

PER SHARE DATA

	1994	1993	1992	1991	1990	1989	1988	1987	1986	1985
Dividends, Net Income ($)	0.07	0.07	0.20	0.06	0.10	0.34	0.62	0.14	0.16	0.18
Distrib'ns, Cap Gain ($)	0.71	7.51	2.68	11.05	0.00	0.00	0.02	10.09	7.46	0.00
Net Asset Value ($)	20.58	27.71	27.43	25.80	18.53	18.37	15.87	16.56	23.12	25.02
Expense Ratio (%)	0.84	0.85	0.86	0.88	0.94	0.92	0.92	0.82	0.74	0.79
Net Income to Assets (%)	0.15	0.23	0.79	0.21	0.40	1.26	3.89	0.70	0.45	0.66
Portfolio Turnover (%)	153	143	163	272	226	254	301	187	208	209
Total Assets (Millions $)	401	523	395	326	176	190	194	231	210	170

PORTFOLIO (as of 6/30/94)

Portfolio Manager: G. Kenneth Heebner - 1976

Investm't Category: Aggressive Growth

✔ Cap Gain	Asset Allocation
Cap & Income	Fund of Funds
Income	Index
	Sector
✔ Domestic	Small Cap
Foreign	Socially Conscious
Country/Region	State Specific

Portfolio: stocks 100% bonds 0%
convertibles 0% other 0% cash 0%

Largest Holdings: basic materials 17%, metals & mining 16%

Unrealized Net Capital Gains: 0% of portfolio value

SHAREHOLDER INFORMATION

Minimum Investment
Initial: $2,500   Subsequent: $50

Minimum IRA Investment
Initial: $1,000   Subsequent: $50

Maximum Fees
Load: none   12b-1: none
Other: none

Distributions
Income: Dec   Capital Gains: Dec

Exchange Options
Number Per Year: 4   Fee: none
Telephone: yes (money market fund available)

Services
IRA, pension, auto exchange, auto invest, auto withdraw

CGM Fixed Income
(CFXIX)
Corporate Bond

P.O. Box 449
Boston, MA 02117
(800) 345-4048, (617) 859-7714

PERFORMANCE

fund inception date: 3/17/92

	3yr Annual	5yr Annual	10yr Annual	Bull	Bear
Return (%)	na	na	na	na	-8.9
Differ from Category (+/-)	na	na	na	na	-4.6 low

Total Risk	Standard Deviation	Category Risk	Risk Index	Avg Mat
na	na	na	na	11.6 yrs

	1994	1993	1992	1991	1990	1989	1988	1987	1986	1985
Return (%)	-8.0	18.9	—	—	—	—	—	—	—	—
Differ from category (+/-) . .	-5.6	7.5	—	—	—	—	—	—	—	—

PER SHARE DATA

	1994	1993	1992	1991	1990	1989	1988	1987	1986	1985
Dividends, Net Income ($) .	0.73	0.67	—	—	—	—	—	—	—	—
Distrib'ns, Cap Gain ($) . . .	0.00	0.32	—	—	—	—	—	—	—	—
Net Asset Value ($)	9.57	11.17	—	—	—	—	—	—	—	—
Expense Ratio (%).	0.85	0.85	—	—	—	—	—	—	—	—
Net Income to Assets (%). .	6.73	6.30	—	—	—	—	—	—	—	—
Portfolio Turnover (%). . . .	156	149	—	—	—	—	—	—	—	—
Total Assets (Millions $)	28	32	—	—	—	—	—	—	—	—

PORTFOLIO (as of 6/30/94)

Portfolio Manager: Janis H. Saul - 1993, G. Kenneth Heebner - 1993

Investm't Category: Corporate Bond

Cap Gain	Asset Allocation
Cap & Income	Fund of Funds
✔ Income	Index
	Sector
✔ Domestic	Small Cap
✔ Foreign	Socially Conscious
Country/Region	State Specific

Portfolio: stocks 0%   bonds 73%
convertibles 25%   other 0%   cash 2%

Largest Holdings: airline bonds 13%, chemical bonds 10%

Unrealized Net Capital Gains: -4% of portfolio value

SHAREHOLDER INFORMATION

Minimum Investment
Initial: $2,500   Subsequent: $50

Minimum IRA Investment
Initial: $1,000   Subsequent: $50

Maximum Fees
Load: none   12b-1: none
Other: none

Distributions
Income: monthly   Capital Gains: Dec

Exchange Options
Number Per Year: 4   Fee: none
Telephone: yes (money market fund available)

Services
IRA, pension, auto exchange, auto invest, auto withdraw

CGM Mutual (LOMMX)

Balanced

P.O. Box 449
Boston, MA 02117
(800) 345-4048, (617) 859-7714

PERFORMANCE   fund inception date: 11/5/29

	3yr Annual	5yr Annual	10yr Annual	Bull	Bear
Return (%)	5.2	10.6	14.8	103.7	-9.8
Differ from Category (+/-)	-1.2 blw av	2.6 high	3.5 high	38.7 high	-4.1 low

Total Risk	Standard Deviation	Category Risk	Risk Index	Beta
abv av	9.1%	high	1.5	0.9

	1994	1993	1992	1991	1990	1989	1988	1987	1986	1985
Return (%).............	-9.7	21.8	6.0	40.8	1.1	21.5	3.1	13.6	25.2	34.5
Differ from category (+/-) ..	-7.8	8.4	-2.3	17.4	1.6	4.2	-8.7	11.2	7.8	10.2

PER SHARE DATA

	1994	1993	1992	1991	1990	1989	1988	1987	1986	1985
Dividends, Net Income ($).	1.04	0.86	0.93	0.97	0.88	1.02	1.10	1.06	0.94	1.08
Distrib'ns, Cap Gain ($) ...	0.00	1.93	1.42	2.64	0.05	0.86	0.00	4.52	2.75	0.00
Net Asset Value ($)	25.05	28.88	26.02	26.80	21.64	22.34	19.94	20.40	22.86	21.53
Expense Ratio (%)	0.91	0.93	0.93	0.93	0.97	0.97	1.01	0.94	0.84	0.86
Net Income to Assets (%) .	4.23	3.45	3.74	3.80	4.00	4.26	5.25	3.69	3.81	5.10
Portfolio Turnover (%)	174	97	121	201	159	218	218	197	127	186
Total Assets (Millions $)..	1,630	947	549	402	296	312	293	303	203	121

PORTFOLIO (as of 6/30/94)

Portfolio Manager: G. Kenneth Heebner - 1981

Investm't Category: Balanced

Cap Gain	✔ Asset Allocation
✔ Cap & Income	Fund of Funds
Income	Index
	Sector
✔ Domestic	Small Cap
Foreign	Socially Conscious
Country/Region	State Specific

Portfolio: stocks 73% bonds 27%
convertibles 0% other 0% cash 0%

Largest Holdings: bonds—corporate 27%, stocks—real estate investment trusts 25%

Unrealized Net Capital Gains: -5% of portfolio value

SHAREHOLDER INFORMATION

Minimum Investment
Initial: $2,500   Subsequent: $50

Minimum IRA Investment
Initial: $1,000   Subsequent: $50

Maximum Fees
Load: none   12b-1: none
Other: none

Distributions
Income: quarterly   Capital Gains: Dec

Exchange Options
Number Per Year: 4   Fee: none
Telephone: yes (money market fund available)

Services
IRA, pension, auto exchange, auto invest, auto withdraw

CharterCapital Blue Chip Growth (CCBGX)

4920 W. Vliet St.
Milwaukee, WI 53208
(414) 257-1842

Growth & Income

PERFORMANCE

fund inception date: 8/1/84

	3yr Annual	5yr Annual	10yr Annual	Bull	Bear
Return (%)	-2.9	5.5	6.2	63.3	-5.8
Differ from Category (+/-)	-10.0 low	-2.4 low	-5.5 low	-12.5 blw av	0.5 av

Total Risk	Standard Deviation	Category Risk	Risk Index	Beta
abv av	9.5%	high	1.2	0.8

	1994	1993	1992	1991	1990	1989	1988	1987	1986	1985
Return (%)	-4.8	1.8	-5.6	45.7	-1.6	9.1	1.8	-4.9	16.0	13.5
Differ from category (+/-) . .	-3.4	-11.4	-15.8	18.1	4.4	-12.3	-15.2	-5.5	0.2	-12.2

PER SHARE DATA

	1994	1993	1992	1991	1990	1989	1988	1987	1986	1985
Dividends, Net Income ($) .	0.16	0.00	0.00	0.00	0.16	0.36	0.36	0.38	0.41	0.29
Distrib'ns, Cap Gain ($) . . .	0.00	0.00	0.00	0.00	0.00	0.00	0.00	1.56	0.72	0.18
Net Asset Value ($)	12.31	13.10	12.86	13.63	9.35	9.67	9.19	9.38	11.50	10.87
Expense Ratio (%).	2.24	2.18	2.15	2.28	2.29	2.07	1.73	1.73	1.87	1.95
Net Income to Assets (%). .	0.68	-0.13	-0.60	-0.39	1.61	2.95	2.65	1.74	3.41	3.99
Portfolio Turnover (%).	39	295	166	112	314	194	226	107	232	179
Total Assets (Millions $)	6	9	12	13	8	12	25	40	30	24

PORTFOLIO (as of 6/30/94)

Portfolio Manager: Lauren Toll - 1988, F. John Mirek - 1993

Investm't Category: Growth & Income

Cap Gain	Asset Allocation
✔ Cap & Income	Fund of Funds
Income	Index
	Sector
✔ Domestic	Small Cap
Foreign	Socially Conscious
Country/Region	State Specific

Portfolio: stocks 42% bonds 7%
convertibles 3% other 0% cash 48%

Largest Holdings: capital goods 12%, utilities 11%

Unrealized Net Capital Gains: -1% of portfolio value

SHAREHOLDER INFORMATION

Minimum Investment
Initial: $50   Subsequent: $50

Minimum IRA Investment
Initial: $250   Subsequent: $50

Maximum Fees
Load: none   12b-1: none
Other: none

Distributions
Income: Dec   Capital Gains: Dec

Exchange Options
Number Per Year: none   Fee:
Telephone:

Services
IRA, pension, auto withdraw

Chesapeake Growth
(CPGRX)
Aggressive Growth

P.O. Box 69
105 N. Washington
Rocky Mount, NC 27802
(800) 525-3863

	3yr Annual	5yr Annual	10yr Annual	Bull	Bear
Return (%)	na	na	na	na	-13.6
Differ from Category (+/-)	na	na	na	na	-2.8 blw av

Total Risk	Standard Deviation	Category Risk	Risk Index	Beta
na	na	na	na	na

	1994	1993	1992	1991	1990	1989	1988	1987	1986	1985
Return (%)	6.9	33.3	—	—	—	—	—	—	—	—
Differ from category (+/-)	7.6	13.8	—	—	—	—	—	—	—	—

PER SHARE DATA

	1994	1993	1992	1991	1990	1989	1988	1987	1986	1985
Dividends, Net Income ($)	0.00	0.21	—	—	—	—	—	—	—	—
Distrib'ns, Cap Gain ($)	0.00	0.00	—	—	—	—	—	—	—	—
Net Asset Value ($)	14.03	13.11	—	—	—	—	—	—	—	—
Expense Ratio (%)	1.49	1.54	—	—	—	—	—	—	—	—
Net Income to Assets (%)	-0.79	-0.47	—	—	—	—	—	—	—	—
Portfolio Turnover (%)	66	45	—	—	—	—	—	—	—	—
Total Assets (Millions $)	235	69	—	—	—	—	—	—	—	—

PORTFOLIO (as of 8/31/94)

Portfolio Manager: Gardner - 1993, Lewis - 1993

Investm't Category: Aggressive Growth

✔ Cap Gain	Asset Allocation
Cap & Income	Fund of Funds
Income	Index
	Sector
✔ Domestic	Small Cap
✔ Foreign	Socially Conscious
Country/Region	State Specific

Portfolio: stocks 93% bonds 0%
convertibles 0% other 0% cash 7%

Largest Holdings: insurance—life and health 10%, computer software & services 10%

Unrealized Net Capital Gains: 9% of portfolio value

SHAREHOLDER INFORMATION

Minimum Investment
Initial: $25,000   Subsequent: $500

Minimum IRA Investment
Initial: $25,000   Subsequent: $500

Maximum Fees
Load: 3.00% front   12b-1: none
Other: none

Distributions
Income: quarterly   Capital Gains: Oct

Exchange Options
Number Per Year: no limit   Fee: none
Telephone: none

Services
IRA, auto invest, auto withdraw

Clipper (CFIMX)
Growth

9601 Wilshire Blvd., Suite 800
Beverly Hills, CA 90210
(800) 776-5033, (310) 247-3940

PERFORMANCE

fund inception date: 2/28/84

	3yr Annual	5yr Annual	10yr Annual	Bull	Bear
Return (%)	7.9	9.0	13.2	98.8	-8.1
Differ from Category (+/-)	0.2 av	-0.6 av	0.3 av	6.7 abv av	-1.5 blw av

Total Risk	Standard Deviation	Category Risk	Risk Index	Beta
abv av	10.3%	abv av	1.1	1.1

	1994	1993	1992	1991	1990	1989	1988	1987	1986	1985
Return (%)	-2.4	11.1	15.9	32.5	-7.5	22.1	19.6	2.8	18.7	26.4
Differ from category (+/-) . .	-1.8	-2.3	4.3	-3.2	-1.8	-4.0	1.6	1.0	4.1	-2.8

PER SHARE DATA

	1994	1993	1992	1991	1990	1989	1988	1987	1986	1985
Dividends, Net Income ($) .	0.71	0.75	0.96	1.18	1.14	1.00	0.95	3.28	0.00	0.84
Distrib'ns, Cap Gain ($) . . .	2.00	6.73	3.02	1.97	0.21	1.55	1.68	5.88	1.41	0.38
Net Asset Value ($)	46.09	50.02	51.74	48.10	38.80	43.45	37.74	33.76	41.55	36.17
Expense Ratio (%).	1.13	1.11	1.12	1.15	1.15	1.17	1.24	1.25	1.28	1.50
Net Income to Assets (%). .	1.45	1.41	2.02	2.67	2.71	2.54	2.44	4.00	4.26	5.19
Portfolio Turnover (%).	40	64	46	42	23	26	33	140	40	15
Total Assets (Millions $) . . .	247	280	210	161	125	128	86	76	73	35

PORTFOLIO (as of 6/30/94)

Portfolio Manager: James H. Gipson - 1984, Michael Sandler - 1994

Investm't Category: Growth
✔ Cap Gain   Asset Allocation
   Cap & Income   Fund of Funds
   Income   Index
                    Sector
✔ Domestic   Small Cap
✔ Foreign   Socially Conscious
   Country/Region   State Specific

Portfolio: stocks 98%   bonds 0%
convertibles 0%   other 0%   cash 2%

Largest Holdings: mortgage finance 18%, securities industry 17%

Unrealized Net Capital Gains: 4% of portfolio value

SHAREHOLDER INFORMATION

Minimum Investment
Initial: $5,000   Subsequent: $1,000

Minimum IRA Investment
Initial: $2,000   Subsequent: $200

Maximum Fees
Load: none   12b-1: none
Other: none

Distributions
Income: Dec   Capital Gains: Dec

Exchange Options
Number Per Year: none   Fee:
Telephone:

Services
IRA, auto invest, auto withdraw

Cohen & Steers Realty Shares (CSRSX)

Growth & Income

757 Third Ave.
New York, NY 10017
(212) 832-3232

PERFORMANCE

fund inception date: 7/1/91

	3yr Annual	5yr Annual	10yr Annual	Bull	Bear
Return (%)	15.5	na	na	na	5.6
Differ from Category (+/-)	8.4 high	na	na	na	11.9 high

Total Risk	Standard Deviation	Category Risk	Risk Index	Beta
high	12.7%	high	1.6	0.3

	1994	1993	1992	1991	1990	1989	1988	1987	1986	1985
Return (%)	8.3	18.7	20.0	—	—	—	—	—	—	—
Differ from category (+/-) . .	9.7	5.5	9.8	—	—	—	—	—	—	—

PER SHARE DATA

	1994	1993	1992	1991	1990	1989	1988	1987	1986	1985
Dividends, Net Income ($) .	1.66	1.51	1.80	—	—	—	—	—	—	—
Distrib'ns, Cap Gain ($) . . .	0.00	1.68	0.23	—	—	—	—	—	—	—
Net Asset Value ($)	32.90	31.92	29.58	—	—	—	—	—	—	—
Expense Ratio (%)	1.10	1.18	1.25	—	—	—	—	—	—	—
Net Income to Assets (%) .	5.44	4.57	5.92	—	—	—	—	—	—	—
Portfolio Turnover (%)	51	65	15	—	—	—	—	—	—	—
Total Assets (Millions $)	458	167	50	—	—	—	—	—	—	—

PORTFOLIO (as of 6/30/94)

Portfolio Manager: Martin Cohen - 1991, Robert Steers - 1991

Investm't Category: Growth & Income
Cap Gain	Asset Allocation
✔ Cap & Income	Fund of Funds
Income	Index
	✔ Sector
✔ Domestic	Small Cap
✔ Foreign	Socially Conscious
Country/Region	State Specific

Portfolio: stocks 93% bonds 0%
convertibles 0% other 0% cash 7%

Largest Holdings: shopping center/community center 31%, apartment 25%

Unrealized Net Capital Gains: 1% of portfolio value

SHAREHOLDER INFORMATION

Minimum Investment
Initial: $10,000   Subsequent: $500

Minimum IRA Investment
Initial: na   Subsequent: na

Maximum Fees
Load: none   12b-1: none
Other: none

Distributions
Income: quarterly   Capital Gains: Dec

Exchange Options
Number Per Year: none   Fee:
Telephone:

Services

Columbia Balanced

(CBALX)

Balanced

1301 S.W. Fifth Ave.
P.O. Box 1350
Portland, OR 97207
(800) 547-1707, (503) 222-3600

PERFORMANCE

fund inception date: 10/1/91

	3yr Annual	5yr Annual	10yr Annual	Bull	Bear
Return (%)	7.3	na	na	na	-5.0
Differ from Category (+/-)	0.9 abv av	na	na	na	0.7 av

Total Risk	Standard Deviation	Category Risk	Risk Index	Beta
blw av	5.6%	blw av	0.9	0.6

	1994	1993	1992	1991	1990	1989	1988	1987	1986	1985
Return (%)	0.0	13.6	8.8	—	—	—	—	—	—	—
Differ from category (+/-) . . .	1.9	0.2	0.5	—	—	—	—	—	—	—

PER SHARE DATA

	1994	1993	1992	1991	1990	1989	1988	1987	1986	1985
Dividends, Net Income ($) .	0.64	0.57	0.57	—	—	—	—	—	—	—
Distrib'ns, Cap Gain ($) . . .	0.00	0.59	0.08	—	—	—	—	—	—	—
Net Asset Value ($)	17.28	17.91	16.80	—	—	—	—	—	—	—
Expense Ratio (%).	0.72	0.73	0.81	—	—	—	—	—	—	—
Net Income to Assets (%). .	3.49	3.32	4.08	—	—	—	—	—	—	—
Portfolio Turnover (%). . . .	104	107	138	—	—	—	—	—	—	—
Total Assets (Millions $) . . .	249	187	90	—	—	—	—	—	—	—

PORTFOLIO (as of 6/30/94)

Portfolio Manager: Mike Powers - 1991

Investm't Category: Balanced

Cap Gain	✔ Asset Allocation
✔ Cap & Income	Fund of Funds
Income	Index
	Sector
✔ Domestic	Small Cap
✔ Foreign	Socially Conscious
Country/Region	State Specific

Portfolio: stocks 50% bonds 40%
convertibles 1% other 0% cash 9%

Largest Holdings: mortgage-backed bonds 14%, U.S. government bonds 13%

Unrealized Net Capital Gains: 0% of portfolio value

SHAREHOLDER INFORMATION

Minimum Investment
Initial: $1,000   Subsequent: $100

Minimum IRA Investment
Initial: $1,000   Subsequent: $100

Maximum Fees
Load: none   12b-1: none
Other: none

Distributions
Income: quarterly   Capital Gains: Dec

Exchange Options
Number Per Year: 4   Fee: none
Telephone: yes (money market fund available)

Services
IRA, pension, auto exchange, auto invest, auto withdraw

Columbia Common Stock (CMSTX)

Growth & Income

1301 S.W. Fifth Ave.
P.O. Box 1350
Portland, OR 97207
(800) 547-1707, (503) 222-3600

PERFORMANCE

fund inception date: 10/1/91

	3yr Annual	5yr Annual	10yr Annual	Bull	Bear
Return (%)	9.3	na	na	na	-5.5
Differ from Category (+/-)	2.2 abv av	na	na	na	0.8 abv av

Total Risk	Standard Deviation	Category Risk	Risk Index	Beta
av	8.0%	av	1.0	0.9

	1994	1993	1992	1991	1990	1989	1988	1987	1986	1985
Return (%)	2.0	16.4	9.9	—	—	—	—	—	—	—
Differ from category (+/-)	3.4	3.2	-0.3	—	—	—	—	—	—	—

PER SHARE DATA

	1994	1993	1992	1991	1990	1989	1988	1987	1986	1985
Dividends, Net Income ($)	0.25	0.21	0.24	—	—	—	—	—	—	—
Distrib'ns, Cap Gain ($)	0.19	0.84	0.17	—	—	—	—	—	—	—
Net Asset Value ($)	15.16	15.29	14.04	—	—	—	—	—	—	—
Expense Ratio (%)	0.84	0.84	0.86	—	—	—	—	—	—	—
Net Income to Assets (%)	1.73	1.48	1.97	—	—	—	—	—	—	—
Portfolio Turnover (%)	62	90	68	—	—	—	—	—	—	—
Total Assets (Millions $)	124	102	51	—	—	—	—	—	—	—

PORTFOLIO (as of 6/30/94)

Portfolio Manager: Terry L. Chambers - 1991

Investm't Category: Growth & Income
- Cap Gain
- ✔ Cap & Income
- Income
- ✔ Domestic
- ✔ Foreign
- Country/Region
- Asset Allocation
- Fund of Funds
- Index
- Sector
- Small Cap
- Socially Conscious
- State Specific

Portfolio: stocks 90% bonds 0%
convertibles 2% other 0% cash 8%

Largest Holdings: energy 9%, entertainment & media 8%

Unrealized Net Capital Gains: 2% of portfolio value

SHAREHOLDER INFORMATION

Minimum Investment
Initial: $1,000   Subsequent: $100

Minimum IRA Investment
Initial: $1,000   Subsequent: $100

Maximum Fees
Load: none   12b-1: none
Other: none

Distributions
Income: quarterly   Capital Gains: Dec

Exchange Options
Number Per Year: 4   Fee: none
Telephone: yes (money market fund available)

Services
IRA, pension, auto exchange, auto invest, auto withdraw

Columbia Fixed Income Securities (CFISX)

General Bond

1301 S.W. Fifth Ave.
P.O. Box 1350
Portland, OR 97207
(800) 547-1707, (503) 222-3600

PERFORMANCE

fund inception date: 2/25/83

	3yr Annual	5yr Annual	10yr Annual	Bull	Bear
Return (%)	4.8	7.8	9.4	48.1	-5.3
Differ from Category (+/-)	0.5 abv av	0.9 high	0.5 abv av	7.1 abv av	-1.5 blw av

Total Risk	Standard Deviation	Category Risk	Risk Index	Avg Mat
low	4.5%	abv av	1.1	6.4 yrs

	1994	1993	1992	1991	1990	1989	1988	1987	1986	1985
Return (%)	-3.3	10.4	7.9	16.8	8.2	14.3	7.7	1.3	12.3	20.1
Differ from category (+/-)	-1.3	1.2	1.3	2.2	1.0	2.9	0.3	-0.9	-1.9	0.7

PER SHARE DATA

	1994	1993	1992	1991	1990	1989	1988	1987	1986	1985
Dividends, Net Income ($)	0.83	0.85	0.95	1.00	1.03	1.04	1.04	1.03	1.21	1.39
Distrib'ns, Cap Gain ($)	0.00	0.36	0.40	0.18	0.00	0.00	0.00	0.27	0.00	0.00
Net Asset Value ($)	12.16	13.44	13.28	13.59	12.72	12.75	12.11	12.23	13.37	13.05
Expense Ratio (%)	0.66	0.66	0.66	0.69	0.73	0.74	0.77	0.82	0.79	0.88
Net Income to Assets (%)	6.16	6.14	7.03	7.63	8.20	8.27	8.44	8.21	9.15	11.03
Portfolio Turnover (%)	161	118	196	159	132	114	133	114	97	94
Total Assets (Millions $)	252	300	263	207	134	111	103	100	124	83

PORTFOLIO (as of 6/30/94)

Portfolio Manager: committee

Investm't Category: General Bond

Cap Gain	Asset Allocation
Cap & Income	Fund of Funds
✔ Income	Index
	Sector
✔ Domestic	Small Cap
Foreign	Socially Conscious
Country/Region	State Specific

Portfolio: stocks 0%   bonds 97%
convertibles 0%   other 0%   cash 3%

Largest Holdings: mortgage-backed 31%, U.S. government 28%

Unrealized Net Capital Gains: -3% of portfolio value

SHAREHOLDER INFORMATION

Minimum Investment
Initial: $1,000   Subsequent: $100

Minimum IRA Investment
Initial: $1,000   Subsequent: $100

Maximum Fees
Load: none   12b-1: none
Other: none

Distributions
Income: monthly   Capital Gains: Dec

Exchange Options
Number Per Year: 4   Fee: none
Telephone: yes (money market fund available)

Services
IRA, pension, auto exchange, auto invest, auto withdraw

Columbia Growth (CLMBX)

Growth

1301 S.W. Fifth Ave.
P.O. Box 1350
Portland, OR 97207
(800) 547-1707, (503) 222-3600

PERFORMANCE   fund inception date: 8/16/67

	3yr Annual	5yr Annual	10yr Annual	Bull	Bear
Return (%)	7.8	10.2	14.2	84.2	-8.7
Differ from Category (+/-)	0.1 av	0.6 abv av	1.3 abv av	-7.9 av	-2.1 blw av

Total Risk	Standard Deviation	Category Risk	Risk Index	Beta
abv av	10.5%	abv av	1.1	1.0

	1994	1993	1992	1991	1990	1989	1988	1987	1986	1985
Return (%).	-0.6	13.0	11.8	34.2	-3.3	29.0	10.8	14.7	6.9	32.0
Differ from category (+/-) . .	0.0	-0.4	0.2	-1.5	2.4	2.9	-7.2	12.9	-7.7	2.8

PER SHARE DATA

	1994	1993	1992	1991	1990	1989	1988	1987	1986	1985
Dividends, Net Income ($).	0.26	0.18	0.20	0.39	0.48	0.54	0.52	0.61	0.40	0.33
Distrib'ns, Cap Gain ($) . . .	1.11	3.02	2.98	2.44	0.46	3.40	0.64	5.33	6.48	0.00
Net Asset Value ($)	24.84	26.38	26.18	26.26	21.68	23.40	21.21	20.19	22.88	28.02
Expense Ratio (%)	0.83	0.82	0.86	0.90	0.96	0.96	1.04	1.04	1.00	1.06
Net Income to Assets (%) .	0.92	0.66	0.77	1.50	2.08	2.14	2.33	1.46	0.78	1.81
Portfolio Turnover (%)	90	105	116	164	172	166	179	197	130	92
Total Assets (Millions $). . . .	591	611	518	432	271	267	204	194	200	250

PORTFOLIO (as of 6/30/94)

Portfolio Manager: Alec MacMillan - 1992

Investm't Category: Growth

✔ Cap Gain	Asset Allocation
Cap & Income	Fund of Funds
Income	Index
	Sector
✔ Domestic	Small Cap
Foreign	Socially Conscious
Country/Region	State Specific

Portfolio: stocks 96%   bonds 0%
convertibles 0%   other 0%   cash 4%

Largest Holdings: consumer non-durables 16%, technology 13%

Unrealized Net Capital Gains: 2% of portfolio value

SHAREHOLDER INFORMATION

Minimum Investment
Initial: $1,000   Subsequent: $100

Minimum IRA Investment
Initial: $1,000   Subsequent: $100

Maximum Fees
Load: none   12b-1: none
Other: none

Distributions
Income: Dec   Capital Gains: Dec

Exchange Options
Number Per Year: 4   Fee: none
Telephone: yes (money market fund available)

Services
IRA, pension, auto exchange, auto invest, auto withdraw

Columbia Int'l Stock
(CMISX)
International Stock

1301 S.W. Fifth Ave.
P.O. Box 1350
Portland, OR 97207
(800) 547-1707, (503) 222-3600

PERFORMANCE

fund inception date: 9/10/92

	3yr Annual	5yr Annual	10yr Annual	Bull	Bear
Return (%)	na	na	na	na	-3.2
Differ from Category (+/-)	na	na	na	na	3.8 high

Total Risk	Standard Deviation	Category Risk	Risk Index	Beta
na	na	na	na	na

	1994	1993	1992	1991	1990	1989	1988	1987	1986	1985
Return (%)	-2.4	33.3	—	—	—	—	—	—	—	—
Differ from category (+/-) . . .	0.6	-5.3	—	—	—	—	—	—	—	—

PER SHARE DATA

	1994	1993	1992	1991	1990	1989	1988	1987	1986	1985
Dividends, Net Income ($) .	0.00	0.00	—	—	—	—	—	—	—	—
Distrib'ns, Cap Gain ($) . . .	0.21	0.31	—	—	—	—	—	—	—	—
Net Asset Value ($)	12.43	12.96	—	—	—	—	—	—	—	—
Expense Ratio (%).	1.71	1.71	—	—	—	—	—	—	—	—
Net Income to Assets (%).	-0.31	-0.62	—	—	—	—	—	—	—	—
Portfolio Turnover (%). . . .	156	144	—	—	—	—	—	—	—	—
Total Assets (Millions $) . . .	118	73	—	—	—	—	—	—	—	—

PORTFOLIO (as of 6/30/94)

Portfolio Manager: James McAlear - 1992

Investm't Category: International Stock

✔ Cap Gain	Asset Allocation
Cap & Income	Fund of Funds
Income	Index
	Sector
✔ Domestic	Small Cap
✔ Foreign	Socially Conscious
Country/Region	State Specific

Portfolio: stocks 94% bonds 0%
convertibles 3% other 0% cash 3%

Largest Holdings: Japan 54%, France 7%

Unrealized Net Capital Gains: 9% of portfolio value

SHAREHOLDER INFORMATION

Minimum Investment
Initial: $1,000   Subsequent: $100

Minimum IRA Investment
Initial: $1,000   Subsequent: $100

Maximum Fees
Load: none   12b-1: none
Other: none

Distributions
Income: Dec   Capital Gains: Dec

Exchange Options
Number Per Year: 4   Fee: none
Telephone: yes (money market fund available)

Services
IRA, pension, auto exchange, auto invest, auto withdraw

Columbia Muni Bond
(CMBFX)
Tax-Exempt Bond

1301 S.W. Fifth Ave.
P.O. Box 1350
Portland, OR 97207
(800) 547-1707, (503) 222-3600

PERFORMANCE   fund inception date: 7/2/84

	3yr Annual	5yr Annual	10yr Annual	Bull	Bear
Return (%)	3.9	6.0	8.5	38.1	-5.1
Differ from Category (+/-)	-0.6 low	-0.1 blw av	0.4 av	-3.7 blw av	0.1 abv av

Total Risk	Standard Deviation	Category Risk	Risk Index	Avg Mat
low	4.7%	low	0.7	14.4 yrs

	1994	1993	1992	1991	1990	1989	1988	1987	1986	1985
Return (%)	-4.6	10.7	6.4	11.7	6.8	8.9	10.2	1.2	16.7	19.7
Differ from category (+/-)	0.6	-1.0	-1.9	0.4	0.5	-0.1	0.0	2.5	0.3	2.3

PER SHARE DATA

	1994	1993	1992	1991	1990	1989	1988	1987	1986	1985
Dividends, Net Income ($)	0.64	0.66	0.69	0.72	0.75	0.76	0.77	0.77	0.83	0.88
Distrib'ns, Cap Gain ($)	0.00	0.08	0.12	0.03	0.01	0.01	0.03	0.00	0.00	0.00
Net Asset Value ($)	11.48	12.71	12.17	12.22	11.65	11.64	11.42	11.11	11.75	10.82
Expense Ratio (%)	0.58	0.58	0.59	0.59	0.60	0.61	0.63	0.66	0.65	0.76
Net Income to Assets (%)	5.20	5.25	5.69	6.07	6.50	6.59	6.71	6.84	7.17	8.51
Portfolio Turnover (%)	23	9	18	15	7	11	10	21	3	17
Total Assets (Millions $)	339	430	342	285	208	167	141	119	118	58

PORTFOLIO (as of 6/30/94)

Portfolio Manager: Thomas Thomsen - 1984

Investm't Category: Tax-Exempt Bond

Cap Gain	Asset Allocation
Cap & Income	Fund of Funds
✔ Income	Index
	Sector
✔ Domestic	Small Cap
Foreign	Socially Conscious
Country/Region	State Specific

Portfolio: stocks 0%   bonds 99%
convertibles 0%   other 0%   cash 1%

Largest Holdings: general obligation 40%

Unrealized Net Capital Gains: 1% of portfolio value

SHAREHOLDER INFORMATION

Minimum Investment
Initial: $1,000   Subsequent: $100

Minimum IRA Investment
Initial: na   Subsequent: na

Maximum Fees
Load: none   12b-1: none
Other: none

Distributions
Income: monthly   Capital Gains: Dec

Exchange Options
Number Per Year: 4   Fee: none
Telephone: yes (money market fund available)

Services
auto exchange, auto invest, auto withdraw

Columbia Special (CLSPX)

Aggressive Growth

1301 S.W. Fifth Ave.
P.O. Box 1350
Portland, OR 97207
(800) 547-1707, (503) 222-3600

PERFORMANCE

fund inception date: 11/20/85

	3yr Annual	5yr Annual	10yr Annual	Bull	Bear
Return (%)	12.2	13.2	na	149.0	-7.2
Differ from Category (+/-)	3.3 abv av	0.7 av	na	15.8 abv av	3.6 abv av

Total Risk	Standard Deviation	Category Risk	Risk Index	Beta
abv av	11.8%	blw av	0.8	0.9

	1994	1993	1992	1991	1990	1989	1988	1987	1986	1985
Return (%)	2.2	21.6	13.6	50.4	-12.3	31.9	42.5	3.0	15.8	—
Differ from category (+/-) . . .	2.9	2.1	2.6	-1.7	-6.1	5.1	27.3	5.2	4.0	—

PER SHARE DATA

	1994	1993	1992	1991	1990	1989	1988	1987	1986	1985
Dividends, Net Income ($) .	0.07	0.01	0.00	0.00	0.02	0.01	0.00	0.00	0.00	—
Distrib'ns, Cap Gain ($) . . .	1.19	3.32	1.04	0.77	0.00	1.05	1.87	0.00	0.25	—
Net Asset Value ($)	18.69	19.51	18.79	17.45	12.12	13.85	11.32	9.26	8.99	—
Expense Ratio (%).	1.11	1.12	1.19	1.22	1.32	1.35	1.38	1.44	1.54	—
Net Income to Assets (%). .	0.31	0.01	-0.25	-0.16	0.05	0.18	0.06	-0.63	-0.47	—
Portfolio Turnover (%). . . .	125	154	117	115	147	124	244	333	203	—
Total Assets (Millions $) . . .	889	773	471	264	122	96	31	21	20	—

PORTFOLIO (as of 6/30/94)

Portfolio Manager: Robert Unger - 1994

Investm't Category: Aggressive Growth

✔ Cap Gain	Asset Allocation
Cap & Income	Fund of Funds
Income	Index
	Sector
✔ Domestic	✔ Small Cap
✔ Foreign	Socially Conscious
Country/Region	State Specific

Portfolio: stocks 87%   bonds 0%
convertibles 0%   other 0%   cash 13%

Largest Holdings: consumer non-durable 13%, machinery & capital spending 12%

Unrealized Net Capital Gains: 1% of portfolio value

SHAREHOLDER INFORMATION

Minimum Investment
Initial: $2,000   Subsequent: $100

Minimum IRA Investment
Initial: $2,000   Subsequent: $100

Maximum Fees
Load: none   12b-1: none
Other: none

Distributions
Income: Dec   Capital Gains: Dec

Exchange Options
Number Per Year: 4   Fee: none
Telephone: yes (money market fund available)

Services
IRA, pension, auto exchange, auto invest, auto withdraw

Columbia US Gov't Securities (CUGGX)

Government Bond

1301 S.W. Fifth Ave.
P.O. Box 1350
Portland, OR 97207
(800) 547-1707, (503) 222-3600

PERFORMANCE

fund inception date: 10/14/86

	3yr Annual	5yr Annual	10yr Annual	Bull	Bear
Return (%)	3.8	6.6	na	31.5	-1.2
Differ from Category (+/-)	-0.2 av	-0.1 av	na	-19.7 low	5.2 high

Total Risk	Standard Deviation	Category Risk	Risk Index	Avg Mat
low	2.4%	low	0.5	1.5 yrs

	1994	1993	1992	1991	1990	1989	1988	1987	1986	1985
Return (%)	0.0	5.9	5.8	12.7	9.2	9.6	5.3	4.1	—	—
Differ from category (+/-)	4.8	-5.0	-0.6	-2.6	3.0	-4.9	-2.6	6.2	—	—

PER SHARE DATA

	1994	1993	1992	1991	1990	1989	1988	1987	1986	1985
Dividends, Net Income ($)	0.37	0.32	0.39	0.53	0.61	0.63	0.56	0.52	—	—
Distrib'ns, Cap Gain ($)	0.00	0.16	0.21	0.46	0.00	0.00	0.00	0.00	—	—
Net Asset Value ($)	7.99	8.36	8.35	8.47	8.43	8.30	8.17	8.30	—	—
Expense Ratio (%)	0.76	0.75	0.76	0.76	0.85	0.85	0.85	0.85	—	—
Net Income to Assets (%)	3.83	3.74	4.60	6.18	7.33	7.66	6.88	6.34	—	—
Portfolio Turnover (%)	215	254	289	309	222	159	394	147	—	—
Total Assets (Millions $)	33	36	35	35	23	13	9	7	—	—

PORTFOLIO (as of 6/30/94)

Portfolio Manager: Thomas Thomsen - 1986

Investm't Category: Government Bond

Cap Gain	Asset Allocation
Cap & Income	Fund of Funds
✔ Income	Index
	Sector
✔ Domestic	Small Cap
Foreign	Socially Conscious
Country/Region	State Specific

Portfolio: stocks 0%   bonds 100%
convertibles 0%   other 0%   cash 0%

Largest Holdings: U.S. government 100%

Unrealized Net Capital Gains: -1% of portfolio value

SHAREHOLDER INFORMATION

Minimum Investment
Initial: $1,000   Subsequent: $100

Minimum IRA Investment
Initial: $1,000   Subsequent: $100

Maximum Fees
Load: none   12b-1: none
Other: none

Distributions
Income: monthly   Capital Gains: Dec

Exchange Options
Number Per Year: 4   Fee: none
Telephone: yes (money market fund available)

Services
IRA, pension, auto exchange, auto invest, auto withdraw

Connecticut Mutual Inv Acts Income (CINAX)

140 Garden Street
Hartford, CT 06154
(800) 322-2642

General Bond

PERFORMANCE

fund inception date: 9/16/85

	3yr Annual	5yr Annual	10yr Annual	Bull	Bear
Return (%)	4.6	6.8	na	33.2	-2.2
Differ from Category (+/-)	0.3 abv av	-0.1 av	na	-7.8 blw av	1.6 abv av

Total Risk	Standard Deviation	Category Risk	Risk Index	Avg Mat
low	2.3%	low	0.6	3.6 yrs

	1994	1993	1992	1991	1990	1989	1988	1987	1986	1985
Return (%)	-0.4	7.9	6.5	14.1	6.3	9.5	6.7	2.0	—	—
Differ from category (+/-) . . .	1.6	-1.3	-0.1	-0.5	-0.9	-1.9	-0.7	-0.2	—	—

PER SHARE DATA

	1994	1993	1992	1991	1990	1989	1988	1987	1986	1985
Dividends, Net Income ($) .	0.68	0.65	0.78	0.81	0.94	0.88	0.85	0.76	—	—
Distrib'ns, Cap Gain ($) . . .	0.00	0.00	0.00	0.00	0.00	0.00	0.00	0.51	—	—
Net Asset Value ($)	9.14	9.86	9.75	9.91	9.44	9.79	9.77	9.97	—	—
Expense Ratio (%).	0.63	0.63	0.63	1.12	1.24	1.27	1.24	1.27	—	—
Net Income to Assets (%). .	6.96	6.56	8.09	8.44	9.78	8.93	8.43	7.32	—	—
Portfolio Turnover (%).	65	146	109	50	90	52	150	231	—	—
Total Assets (Millions $)	46	49	38	22	19	18	16	15	—	—

PORTFOLIO (as of 6/30/94)

Portfolio Manager: Stephen Libera - 1979

Investm't Category: General Bond

Cap Gain	Asset Allocation
Cap & Income	Fund of Funds
✔ Income	Index
	Sector
✔ Domestic	Small Cap
Foreign	Socially Conscious
Country/Region	State Specific

Portfolio: stocks 0% bonds 96%
convertibles 0% other 0% cash 4%

Largest Holdings: corporate 67%, mortgage-backed 16%

Unrealized Net Capital Gains: 4% of portfolio value

SHAREHOLDER INFORMATION

Minimum Investment
Initial: $1,000 Subsequent: $0

Minimum IRA Investment
Initial: $0 Subsequent: $0

Maximum Fees
Load: 2.00% front 12b-1: none
Other: none

Distributions
Income: monthly Capital Gains: Aug, Dec

Exchange Options
Number Per Year: 12 Fee: $5
Telephone: yes (money market fund available)

Services
IRA, pension, auto invest, auto withdraw

Consolidated Standish Short Asset Resv (STARX)

General Bond

One Financial Center
Boston, MA 02111
(617) 350-6100

	3yr Annual	5yr Annual	10yr Annual	Bull	Bear
Return (%)	3.8	5.9	na	23.7	-0.4
Differ from Category (+/-)	-0.5 blw av	-1.0 low	na	-17.3 low	3.4 high

Total Risk	Standard Deviation	Category Risk	Risk Index	Avg Mat
low	1.1%	low	0.2	0.8 yrs

	1994	1993	1992	1991	1990	1989	1988	1987	1986	1985
Return (%)	2.2	5.0	4.3	9.4	8.9	—	—	—	—	—
Differ from category (+/-)	4.2	-4.2	-2.3	-5.2	1.7	—	—	—	—	—

PER SHARE DATA

	1994	1993	1992	1991	1990	1989	1988	1987	1986	1985
Dividends, Net Income ($)	1.01	1.16	1.34	1.47	1.66	—	—	—	—	—
Distrib'ns, Cap Gain ($)	0.00	0.00	0.02	0.11	0.01	—	—	—	—	—
Net Asset Value ($)	19.22	19.79	19.96	20.46	20.20	—	—	—	—	—
Expense Ratio (%)	0.17	0.33	0.37	0.38	0.45	—	—	—	—	—
Net Income to Assets (%)	2.57	5.82	6.60	7.17	8.17	—	—	—	—	—
Portfolio Turnover (%)	na	182	167	134	128	—	—	—	—	—
Total Assets (Millions $)	275	263	289	266	105	—	—	—	—	—

PORTFOLIO (as of 6/30/94)

Portfolio Manager: Jennifer Pline - 1989

Investm't Category: General Bond

Cap Gain	Asset Allocation
Cap & Income	Fund of Funds
✔ Income	Index
	Sector
✔ Domestic	Small Cap
Foreign	Socially Conscious
Country/Region	State Specific

Portfolio: stocks 0% bonds 93%
convertibles 0% other 0% cash 7%

Largest Holdings: asset-backed 28%, corporate 15%

Unrealized Net Capital Gains: 1% of portfolio value

SHAREHOLDER INFORMATION

Minimum Investment
Initial: $1,000,000   Subsequent: $100,000

Minimum IRA Investment
Initial: $1,000,000   Subsequent: $100,000

Maximum Fees
Load: none   12b-1: none
Other: none

Distributions
Income: monthly   Capital Gains: Dec

Exchange Options
Number Per Year: none   Fee:
Telephone:

Services
IRA

Copley (COPLX)

Growth & Income

315 Pleasant St., 5th Fl.
P.O. Box 3287
Fall River, MA 02722
(508) 674-8459

PERFORMANCE

fund inception date: 9/1/78

	3yr Annual	5yr Annual	10yr Annual	Bull	Bear
Return (%)	6.1	6.6	10.1	56.9	-8.7
Differ from Category (+/-)	-1.0 av	-1.3 blw av	-1.6 low	-18.9 low	-2.4 low

Total Risk	Standard Deviation	Category Risk	Risk Index	Beta
abv av	9.8%	high	1.2	0.5

	1994	1993	1992	1991	1990	1989	1988	1987	1986	1985
Return (%)	-7.6	10.1	17.6	17.1	-1.5	17.8	19.8	-8.2	17.7	24.6
Differ from category (+/-) . .	-6.2	-3.1	7.4	-10.5	4.5	-3.6	2.8	-8.8	1.9	-1.1

PER SHARE DATA

	1994	1993	1992	1991	1990	1989	1988	1987	1986	1985
Dividends, Net Income ($) .	0.00	0.00	0.00	0.00	0.00	0.00	0.00	0.00	0.00	0.00
Distrib'ns, Cap Gain ($) . . .	0.00	0.00	0.00	0.00	0.00	0.00	0.00	0.00	0.00	0.00
Net Asset Value ($)	19.71	21.35	19.38	16.47	14.06	14.28	12.12	10.11	11.02	9.36
Expense Ratio (%).	1.10	1.14	1.38	1.50	1.86	1.38	1.72	1.43	1.47	1.50
Net Income to Assets (%). .	3.72	5.93	4.86	5.34	5.81	6.45	5.58	5.20	7.26	7.90
Portfolio Turnover (%).	25	5	7	16	3	24	10	16	19	29
Total Assets (Millions $)	73	70	32	28	29	21	26	34	21	8

PORTFOLIO (as of 8/31/94)

Portfolio Manager: Irving Levine - 1978

Investm't Category: Growth & Income

Cap Gain	Asset Allocation
✔ Cap & Income	Fund of Funds
Income	Index
	Sector
✔ Domestic	Small Cap
Foreign	Socially Conscious
Country/Region	State Specific

Portfolio: stocks 95% bonds 0%
convertibles 0% other 5% cash 0%

Largest Holdings: electric & gas 19%, electric
power companies 18%

Unrealized Net Capital Gains: 13% of portfolio value

SHAREHOLDER INFORMATION

Minimum Investment
Initial: $1,000   Subsequent: $100

Minimum IRA Investment
Initial: $100   Subsequent: $100

Maximum Fees
Load: none   12b-1: none
Other: none

Distributions
Income: none   Capital Gains: none

Exchange Options
Number Per Year: none   Fee:
Telephone:

Services
IRA, pension, auto withdraw

Corefund Equity Index
(VEIFX)
Growth & Income

680 E. Swedesford Rd.
Wayne, PA 19087
(800) 355-2673

	3yr Annual	5yr Annual	10yr Annual	Bull	Bear
Return (%)	5.3	na	na	na	-6.5
Differ from Category (+/-)	-1.8 blw av	na	na	na	-0.2 av

Total Risk	Standard Deviation	Category Risk	Risk Index	Beta
av	7.8%	blw av	0.9	1.0

	1994	1993	1992	1991	1990	1989	1988	1987	1986	1985
Return (%)............	0.2	9.3	6.7	—	—	—	—	—	—	—
Differ from category (+/-) ..	1.6	-3.9	-3.5	—	—	—	—	—	—	—

PER SHARE DATA

	1994	1993	1992	1991	1990	1989	1988	1987	1986	1985
Dividends, Net Income ($).	0.55	0.56	0.48	—	—	—	—	—	—	—
Distrib'ns, Cap Gain ($) ...	0.99	0.00	0.40	—	—	—	—	—	—	—
Net Asset Value ($)	20.11	21.61	20.30	—	—	—	—	—	—	—
Expense Ratio (%)	0.35	0.49	0.57	—	—	—	—	—	—	—
Net Income to Assets (%) .	2.63	2.82	2.66	—	—	—	—	—	—	—
Portfolio Turnover (%)	13	4	27	—	—	—	—	—	—	—
Total Assets (Millions $).....	78	77	20	—	—	—	—	—	—	—

PORTFOLIO (as of 6/30/94)

Portfolio Manager: not specified

Investm't Category: Growth & Income
Cap Gain	Asset Allocation
✔ Cap & Income	Fund of Funds
Income	✔ Index
	Sector
✔ Domestic	Small Cap
Foreign	Socially Conscious
Country/Region	State Specific

Portfolio: stocks 97% bonds 0%
convertibles 0% other 0% cash 3%

Largest Holdings: S&P 500 composite price index

Unrealized Net Capital Gains: 7% of portfolio value

SHAREHOLDER INFORMATION

Minimum Investment
Initial: $500 Subsequent: $0

Minimum IRA Investment
Initial: $500 Subsequent: $0

Maximum Fees
Load: none 12b-1: none
Other: none

Distributions
Income: quarterly Capital Gains: Jun, Dec

Exchange Options
Number Per Year: no limit Fee: none
Telephone: yes (money market fund available)

Services
IRA, pension, auto invest, auto withdraw

Crabbe Huson Asset Allocation (CHAAX)

Balanced

121 S.W. Morrison St.
Suite 1410
Portland, OR 97204
(800) 541-9732, (503) 295-0919

PERFORMANCE

fund inception date: 1/31/89

	3yr Annual	5yr Annual	10yr Annual	Bull	Bear
Return (%)	9.5	9.6	na	74.0	-5.7
Differ from Category (+/-)	3.1 high	1.6 abv av	na	9.0 abv av	0.0 av

Total Risk	Standard Deviation	Category Risk	Risk Index	Beta
blw av	6.0%	av	1.0	0.6

	1994	1993	1992	1991	1990	1989	1988	1987	1986	1985
Return (%)	-0.8	18.2	12.1	21.2	-0.7	—	—	—	—	—
Differ from category (+/-) . . .	1.1	4.8	3.8	-2.2	-0.2	—	—	—	—	—

PER SHARE DATA

	1994	1993	1992	1991	1990	1989	1988	1987	1986	1985
Dividends, Net Income ($) .	0.32	0.22	0.32	0.47	0.46	—	—	—	—	—
Distrib'ns, Cap Gain ($) . . .	0.47	0.72	0.30	0.19	0.00	—	—	—	—	—
Net Asset Value ($)	12.17	13.07	11.87	11.15	9.78	—	—	—	—	—
Expense Ratio (%).	1.47	1.46	1.52	1.76	1.90	—	—	—	—	—
Net Income to Assets (%). .	1.94	1.85	3.02	3.97	4.51	—	—	—	—	—
Portfolio Turnover (%)	na	116	155	158	162	—	—	—	—	—
Total Assets (Millions $) . . .	107	7	55	24	13	—	—	—	—	—

PORTFOLIO (as of 4/30/94)

Portfolio Manager: Richard Huson - 1989

Investm't Category: Balanced
- Cap Gain
- ✔ Cap & Income
- Income
- ✔ Asset Allocation
- Fund of Funds
- Index
- Sector
- ✔ Domestic
- ✔ Foreign
- Country/Region
- Small Cap
- Socially Conscious
- State Specific

Portfolio: stocks 48% bonds 38%
convertibles 0% other 2% cash 12%

Largest Holdings: bonds—U.S. gov't & agency 33%, stocks—energy & energy serv 5%

Unrealized Net Capital Gains: 2% of portfolio value

SHAREHOLDER INFORMATION

Minimum Investment
Initial: $2,000 Subsequent: $500

Minimum IRA Investment
Initial: $2,000 Subsequent: $500

Maximum Fees
Load: none 12b-1: 0.25%
Other: none

Distributions
Income: quarterly Capital Gains: Dec

Exchange Options
Number Per Year: 10 Fee: none
Telephone: yes (money market fund available)

Services
IRA, pension, auto invest, auto withdraw

Crabbe Huson Equity

(CHEYX)

Growth

121 S.W. Morrison St.
Suite 1410
Portland, OR 97204
(800) 541-9732, (503) 295-0919

PERFORMANCE

fund inception date: 1/31/89

	3yr Annual	5yr Annual	10yr Annual	Bull	Bear
Return (%)	14.2	14.6	na	122.6	-4.7
Differ from Category (+/-)	6.5 high	5.0 high	na	30.5 high	1.9 abv av

Total Risk	Standard Deviation	Category Risk	Risk Index	Beta
av	8.0%	blw av	0.8	0.8

	1994	1993	1992	1991	1990	1989	1988	1987	1986	1985
Return (%)	1.5	25.9	16.4	35.0	-1.5	—	—	—	—	—
Differ from category (+/-)	2.1	12.5	4.8	-0.7	4.2	—	—	—	—	—

PER SHARE DATA

	1994	1993	1992	1991	1990	1989	1988	1987	1986	1985
Dividends, Net Income ($)	0.15	0.07	0.15	0.13	0.34	—	—	—	—	—
Distrib'ns, Cap Gain ($)	0.25	0.79	0.55	0.83	0.00	—	—	—	—	—
Net Asset Value ($)	15.69	15.84	13.27	12.00	9.64	—	—	—	—	—
Expense Ratio (%)	1.49	1.49	1.55	1.84	1.93	—	—	—	—	—
Net Income to Assets (%)	0.78	0.67	1.57	1.60	2.56	—	—	—	—	—
Portfolio Turnover (%)	na	114	180	171	265	—	—	—	—	—
Total Assets (Millions $)	155	41	13	5	2	—	—	—	—	—

PORTFOLIO (as of 4/30/94)

Portfolio Manager: R. Huson - 1989, S. Laveson - 1989, J. Maack - 1989

Investm't Category: Growth

✔ Cap Gain	Asset Allocation
Cap & Income	Fund of Funds
Income	Index
	Sector
✔ Domestic	Small Cap
✔ Foreign	Socially Conscious
Country/Region	State Specific

Portfolio: stocks 73% bonds 0%
convertibles 0% other 2% cash 25%

Largest Holdings: consumer products 9%, energy & energy services 9%

Unrealized Net Capital Gains: 3% of portfolio value

SHAREHOLDER INFORMATION

Minimum Investment
Initial: $2,000   Subsequent: $500

Minimum IRA Investment
Initial: $2,000   Subsequent: $500

Maximum Fees
Load: none   12b-1: 0.25%
Other: none

Distributions
Income: Dec   Capital Gains: Dec

Exchange Options
Number Per Year: 10   Fee: none
Telephone: yes (money market fund available)

Services
IRA, pension, auto invest, auto withdraw

Crabbe Huson Special

(CHSPX)

Aggressive Growth

121 S.W. Morrison St.
Suite 1410
Portland, OR 97204
(800) 541-9732, (503) 295-0919

PERFORMANCE

fund inception date: 4/9/87

	3yr Annual	5yr Annual	10yr Annual	Bull	Bear
Return (%)	26.0	19.4	na	153.5	-4.9
Differ from Category (+/-)	17.1 high	6.9 high	na	20.3 abv av	5.9 high

Total Risk	Standard Deviation	Category Risk	Risk Index	Beta
high	18.0%	high	1.2	1.0

	1994	1993	1992	1991	1990	1989	1988	1987	1986	1985
Return (%)	11.7	34.5	33.3	17.0	3.8	17.2	19.4	—	—	—
Differ from category (+/-) . .	12.4	15.0	22.3	-35.1	10.0	-9.6	4.2	—	—	—

PER SHARE DATA

	1994	1993	1992	1991	1990	1989	1988	1987	1986	1985
Dividends, Net Income ($) .	0.04	0.33	0.00	0.05	0.16	0.26	0.00	—	—	—
Distrib'ns, Cap Gain ($) . . .	0.45	0.00	0.00	3.74	0.68	1.40	0.00	—	—	—
Net Asset Value ($)	13.34	12.40	9.47	7.10	9.45	9.92	9.87	—	—	—
Expense Ratio (%).	1.48	1.57	1.74	1.92	2.00	2.00	3.94	—	—	—
Net Income to Assets (%).	-0.40	-0.73	-0.25	0.32	1.55	1.96	3.34	—	—	—
Portfolio Turnover (%).	na	73	102	256	314	275	155	—	—	—
Total Assets (Millions $) . . .	346	29	5	3	2	3	4	—	—	—

PORTFOLIO (as of 4/30/94)

Portfolio Manager: James Crabbe - 1990

Investm't Category: Aggressive Growth

✔ Cap Gain	Asset Allocation
Cap & Income	Fund of Funds
Income	Index
	Sector
✔ Domestic	✔ Small Cap
✔ Foreign	Socially Conscious
Country/Region	State Specific

Portfolio: stocks 84% bonds 4%
convertibles 0% other 0% cash 12%

Largest Holdings: electronics and technology 21%, financial services 15%

Unrealized Net Capital Gains: 1% of portfolio value

SHAREHOLDER INFORMATION

Minimum Investment
Initial: $2,000   Subsequent: $500

Minimum IRA Investment
Initial: $2,000   Subsequent: $500

Maximum Fees
Load: none   12b-1: 0.25%
Other: none

Distributions
Income: Dec   Capital Gains: Dec

Exchange Options
Number Per Year: 10   Fee: none
Telephone: yes (money market fund available)

Services
IRA, pension, auto invest, auto withdraw

Dodge & Cox Balanced
(DODBX)
Balanced

One Sansome St., 35th Fl.
San Francisco, CA 94104
(800) 621-3979, (415) 981-1710

PERFORMANCE

fund inception date: 1/1/31

	3yr Annual	5yr Annual	10yr Annual	Bull	Bear
Return (%)	9.3	9.7	13.9	73.6	-5.1
Differ from Category (+/-)	2.9 high	1.7 abv av	2.6 high	8.6 abv av	0.6 av

Total Risk	Standard Deviation	Category Risk	Risk Index	Beta
blw av	6.3%	abv av	1.0	0.7

	1994	1993	1992	1991	1990	1989	1988	1987	1986	1985
Return (%).	1.9	15.9	10.5	20.7	0.9	23.0	11.5	7.1	18.8	32.4
Differ from category (+/-) . .	3.8	2.5	2.2	-2.7	1.4	5.7	-0.3	4.7	1.4	8.1

PER SHARE DATA

	1994	1993	1992	1991	1990	1989	1988	1987	1986	1985
Dividends, Net Income ($).	1.79	1.67	1.73	1.76	1.81	1.76	1.68	1.70	1.62	1.70
Distrib'ns, Cap Gain ($) . . .	0.33	1.06	0.07	0.29	0.33	0.71	0.46	2.67	3.56	0.37
Net Asset Value ($)	45.21	46.40	42.44	40.09	35.03	36.85	32.09	30.72	32.62	31.93
Expense Ratio (%)	0.58	0.60	0.63	0.65	0.70	0.72	0.77	0.72	0.73	0.75
Net Income to Assets (%) .	3.74	3.67	4.27	4.78	5.24	4.98	5.19	4.69	4.86	6.03
Portfolio Turnover (%)	4	15	6	10	10	12	9	15	14	26
Total Assets (Millions $). . . .	725	487	269	179	83	51	39	34	28	25

PORTFOLIO (as of 6/30/94)

Portfolio Manager: committee

Investm't Category: Balanced

Cap Gain	Asset Allocation
✔ Cap & Income	Fund of Funds
Income	Index
	Sector
✔ Domestic	Small Cap
Foreign	Socially Conscious
Country/Region	State Specific

Portfolio: stocks 57% bonds 37%
convertibles 0% other 0% cash 6%

Largest Holdings: bonds—mortgage backed
15%, stocks—finance 12%

Unrealized Net Capital Gains: 6% of portfolio value

SHAREHOLDER INFORMATION

Minimum Investment
Initial: $2,500   Subsequent: $100

Minimum IRA Investment
Initial: $1,000   Subsequent: $100

Maximum Fees
Load: none   12b-1: none
Other: none

Distributions
Income: quarterly   Capital Gains: Mar, Dec

Exchange Options
Number Per Year: none   Fee:
Telephone:

Services
IRA, auto invest, auto withdraw

Dodge & Cox Income
(DODIX)
General Bond

One Sansome St., 35th Fl.
San Francisco, CA 94104
(800) 621-3979, (415) 981-1710

PERFORMANCE

	3yr Annual	5yr Annual	10yr Annual	Bull	Bear
Return (%)	5.2	8.1	na	51.2	-5.3
Differ from Category (+/-)	0.9 high	1.2 high	na	10.2 high	-1.5 blw av

Total Risk	Standard Deviation	Category Risk	Risk Index	Avg Mat
low	4.7%	abv av	1.2	12.4 yrs

	1994	1993	1992	1991	1990	1989	1988	1987	1986	1985
Return (%)	-2.8	11.3	7.7	17.9	7.4	14.0	—	—	—	—
Differ from category (+/-) . .	-0.8	2.1	1.1	3.3	0.2	2.6	—	—	—	—

PER SHARE DATA

	1994	1993	1992	1991	1990	1989	1988	1987	1986	1985
Dividends, Net Income ($) .	0.76	0.78	0.82	0.82	0.81	0.69	—	—	—	—
Distrib'ns, Cap Gain ($) . . .	0.05	0.17	0.09	0.03	0.01	0.01	—	—	—	—
Net Asset Value ($)	10.74	11.89	11.55	11.59	10.61	10.68	—	—	—	—
Expense Ratio (%).	0.53	0.60	0.62	0.64	0.69	0.66	—	—	—	—
Net Income to Assets (%). .	6.60	6.50	7.14	7.63	7.99	7.85	—	—	—	—
Portfolio Turnover (%).	17	26	12	15	13	3	—	—	—	—
Total Assets (Millions $) . . .	195	180	136	96	52	33	—	—	—	—

PORTFOLIO (as of 6/30/94)

Portfolio Manager: committee

Investm't Category: General Bond

Cap Gain	Asset Allocation
Cap & Income	Fund of Funds
✔ Income	Index
	Sector
✔ Domestic	Small Cap
Foreign	Socially Conscious
Country/Region	State Specific

Portfolio: stocks 0%   bonds 99%
convertibles 0%   other 0%   cash 1%

Largest Holdings: mortgage-backed 35%,
U.S. government 21%

Unrealized Net Capital Gains: -2% of portfolio value

SHAREHOLDER INFORMATION

Minimum Investment
Initial: $2,500   Subsequent: $100

Minimum IRA Investment
Initial: $1,000   Subsequent: $100

Maximum Fees
Load: none   12b-1: none
Other: none

Distributions
Income: quarterly   Capital Gains: Mar, Dec

Exchange Options
Number Per Year: none   Fee:
Telephone:

Services
IRA, auto invest, auto withdraw

Dodge & Cox Stock
(DODGX)
Growth & Income

One Sansome St., 35th Fl.
San Francisco, CA 94104
(800) 621-3979, (415) 981-1710

PERFORMANCE — fund inception date: 1/1/65

	3yr Annual	5yr Annual	10yr Annual	Bull	Bear
Return (%)	11.3	9.7	15.4	85.2	-5.3
Differ from Category (+/-)	4.2 high	1.8 abv av	3.7 high	9.4 abv av	1.0 abv av

Total Risk	Standard Deviation	Category Risk	Risk Index	Beta
av	8.7%	abv av	1.1	1.0

	1994	1993	1992	1991	1990	1989	1988	1987	1986	1985
Return (%)	5.1	18.3	10.8	21.4	-5.0	26.9	13.7	11.9	18.3	37.8
Differ from category (+/-)	6.5	5.1	0.6	-6.2	1.0	5.5	-3.3	11.3	2.5	12.1

PER SHARE DATA

	1994	1993	1992	1991	1990	1989	1988	1987	1986	1985
Dividends, Net Income ($)	1.15	1.04	1.11	1.24	1.35	1.23	1.07	1.04	0.94	1.01
Distrib'ns, Cap Gain ($)	0.89	2.84	0.16	0.87	0.28	0.82	1.11	1.57	3.90	1.23
Net Asset Value ($)	53.94	53.23	48.37	44.85	38.79	42.57	35.26	32.94	31.66	30.95
Expense Ratio (%)	0.61	0.62	0.64	0.64	0.65	0.65	0.69	0.65	0.66	0.68
Net Income to Assets (%)	2.00	1.95	2.43	2.87	3.47	3.12	3.09	2.68	2.95	3.80
Portfolio Turnover (%)	4	15	7	5	7	4	10	12	10	22
Total Assets (Millions $)	543	449	336	281	173	152	82	68	45	39

PORTFOLIO (as of 6/30/94)

Portfolio Manager: committee

Investm't Category: Growth & Income

Cap Gain	Asset Allocation
✔ Cap & Income	Fund of Funds
Income	Index
	Sector
✔ Domestic	Small Cap
Foreign	Socially Conscious
Country/Region	State Specific

Portfolio: stocks 94% bonds 0%
convertibles 0% other 0% cash 6%

Largest Holdings: finance 21%, consumer 18%

Unrealized Net Capital Gains: 21% of portfolio value

SHAREHOLDER INFORMATION

Minimum Investment
Initial: $2,500   Subsequent: $100

Minimum IRA Investment
Initial: $1,000   Subsequent: $100

Maximum Fees
Load: none   12b-1: none
Other: none

Distributions
Income: quarterly   Capital Gains: Mar, Dec

Exchange Options
Number Per Year: none   Fee:
Telephone:

Services
IRA, auto invest, auto withdraw

Domini Social Equity

(DSEFX)

Growth & Income

6 St. James Avenue
Boston, MA 02116
(800) 762-6814

	3yr Annual	5yr Annual	10yr Annual	Bull	Bear
Return (%)	5.9	na	na	na	-6.6
Differ from Category (+/-)	-1.2 blw av	na	na	na	-0.3 av

Total Risk	Standard Deviation	Category Risk	Risk Index	Beta
av	7.9%	av	1.0	0.9

	1994	1993	1992	1991	1990	1989	1988	1987	1986	1985
Return (%)	-0.3	6.5	12.1	—	—	—	—	—	—	—
Differ from category (+/-)	1.1	-6.7	1.9	—	—	—	—	—	—	—

PER SHARE DATA

	1994	1993	1992	1991	1990	1989	1988	1987	1986	1985
Dividends, Net Income ($)	0.20	0.14	0.13	—	—	—	—	—	—	—
Distrib'ns, Cap Gain ($)	0.08	0.07	0.02	—	—	—	—	—	—	—
Net Asset Value ($)	12.10	12.43	11.87	—	—	—	—	—	—	—
Expense Ratio (%)	0.75	0.75	0.75	—	—	—	—	—	—	—
Net Income to Assets (%)	1.67	1.41	1.53	—	—	—	—	—	—	—
Portfolio Turnover (%)	8	4	3	—	—	—	—	—	—	—
Total Assets (Millions $)	34	26	7	—	—	—	—	—	—	—

PORTFOLIO (as of 7/31/94)

Portfolio Manager: not specified

Investm't Category: Growth & Income

Cap Gain	Asset Allocation
✔ Cap & Income	Fund of Funds
Income	Index
	Sector
✔ Domestic	Small Cap
Foreign	✔ Socially Conscious
Country/Region	State Specific

Portfolio: stocks 99% bonds 0%
convertibles 0% other 0% cash 1%

Largest Holdings: financial 11%, food & beverage 9%

Unrealized Net Capital Gains: 3% of portfolio value

SHAREHOLDER INFORMATION

Minimum Investment
Initial: $1,000 Subsequent: $0

Minimum IRA Investment
Initial: $250 Subsequent: $0

Maximum Fees
Load: none 12b-1: 0.25%
Other: none

Distributions
Income: June, Dec Capital Gains: Dec

Exchange Options
Number Per Year: none Fee:
Telephone:

Services
IRA, pension, auto invest, auto withdraw

Dreman Contrarian

(DRCPX)

Growth & Income

10 Exchange Place
Suite 2050
Jersey City, NJ 07302
(800) 533-1608

PERFORMANCE

fund inception date: 3/18/88

	3yr Annual	5yr Annual	10yr Annual	Bull	Bear
Return (%)	6.6	7.5	na	81.9	-5.5
Differ from Category (+/-)	-0.5 av	-0.4 av	na	6.1 abv av	0.8 abv av

Total Risk	Standard Deviation	Category Risk	Risk Index	Beta
abv av	9.6%	high	1.2	1.1

	1994	1993	1992	1991	1990	1989	1988	1987	1986	1985
Return (%)	0.0	8.9	11.3	26.5	-6.0	18.2	—	—	—	—
Differ from category (+/-)	1.4	-4.3	1.1	-1.1	0.0	-3.2	—	—	—	—

PER SHARE DATA

	1994	1993	1992	1991	1990	1989	1988	1987	1986	1985
Dividends, Net Income ($)	0.28	0.20	0.26	0.27	0.26	0.29	—	—	—	—
Distrib'ns, Cap Gain ($)	1.16	0.84	0.00	0.11	0.28	0.81	—	—	—	—
Net Asset Value ($)	12.18	13.62	13.50	12.38	10.11	11.34	—	—	—	—
Expense Ratio (%)	1.25	1.25	1.25	1.25	1.25	1.25	—	—	—	—
Net Income to Assets (%)	1.92	1.64	2.04	2.35	2.46	2.59	—	—	—	—
Portfolio Turnover (%)	na	16	28	36	37	45	—	—	—	—
Total Assets (Millions $)	12	17	14	14	11	9	—	—	—	—

PORTFOLIO (as of 6/30/94)

Portfolio Manager: David Dreman - 1988

Investm't Category: Growth & Income

Cap Gain	Asset Allocation
✔ Cap & Income	Fund of Funds
Income	Index
	Sector
✔ Domestic	Small Cap
Foreign	Socially Conscious
Country/Region	State Specific

Portfolio: stocks 100% bonds 0%
convertibles 0% other 0% cash 0%

Largest Holdings: financial services 12%, banks/regional 8%

Unrealized Net Capital Gains: 19% of portfolio value

SHAREHOLDER INFORMATION

Minimum Investment
Initial: $1,000   Subsequent: $100

Minimum IRA Investment
Initial: $1,000   Subsequent: $100

Maximum Fees
Load: none   12b-1: none
Other: none

Distributions
Income: quarterly   Capital Gains: Dec

Exchange Options
Number Per Year: no limit   Fee: none
Telephone: yes (money market fund available)

Services
IRA, pension, auto invest, auto withdraw

Dreman High Return

(DRHRX)

Growth

10 Exchange Place
Suite 2050
Jersey City, NJ 07302
(800) 533-1608

PERFORMANCE

fund inception date: 3/18/88

	3yr Annual	5yr Annual	10yr Annual	Bull	Bear
Return (%)	9.0	11.8	na	137.3	-4.5
Differ from Category (+/-)	1.3 abv av	2.2 abv av	na	45.2 high	2.1 abv av

Total Risk	Standard Deviation	Category Risk	Risk Index	Beta
abv av	10.3%	abv av	1.1	1.1

	1994	1993	1992	1991	1990	1989	1988	1987	1986	1985
Return (%)	-0.9	9.2	19.7	47.5	-8.6	18.4	—	—	—	—
Differ from category (+/-) . .	-0.3	-4.2	8.1	11.8	-2.9	-7.7	—	—	—	—

PER SHARE DATA

	1994	1993	1992	1991	1990	1989	1988	1987	1986	1985
Dividends, Net Income ($) .	0.24	0.21	0.24	0.30	0.35	0.43	—	—	—	—
Distrib'ns, Cap Gain ($) . . .	0.00	0.25	0.12	0.20	0.07	2.26	—	—	—	—
Net Asset Value ($)	15.11	15.50	14.62	12.53	8.85	10.14	—	—	—	—
Expense Ratio (%).	1.25	1.25	1.25	1.25	1.25	1.25	—	—	—	—
Net Income to Assets (%). .	1.56	1.47	1.88	2.52	3.61	3.83	—	—	—	—
Portfolio Turnover (%)	na	14	13	37	204	156	—	—	—	—
Total Assets (Millions $)	34	29	14	7	3	3	—	—	—	—

PORTFOLIO (as of 6/30/94)

Portfolio Manager: David Dreman - 1988

Investm't Category: Growth

✔ Cap Gain	Asset Allocation
Cap & Income	Fund of Funds
Income	Index
	Sector
✔ Domestic	Small Cap
Foreign	Socially Conscious
Country/Region	State Specific

Portfolio: stocks 99% bonds 0%
convertibles 0% other 0% cash 1%

Largest Holdings: banks/regional 16%, financial services 11%

Unrealized Net Capital Gains: 14% of portfolio value

SHAREHOLDER INFORMATION

Minimum Investment
Initial: $1,000   Subsequent: $100

Minimum IRA Investment
Initial: $1,000   Subsequent: $100

Maximum Fees
Load: none   12b-1: none
Other: none

Distributions
Income: quarterly   Capital Gains: Dec

Exchange Options
Number Per Year: no limit   Fee: none
Telephone: yes (money market fund available)

Services
IRA, pension, auto invest, auto withdraw

Dreyfus (DREVX)
Growth & Income

200 Park Ave.
New York, NY 10166
(800) 645-6561, (718) 895-1206

PERFORMANCE   fund inception date: 5/24/51

	3yr Annual	5yr Annual	10yr Annual	Bull	Bear
Return (%)	2.4	5.8	10.9	58.3	-8.4
Differ from Category (+/-)	-4.7 low	-2.1 low	-0.8 blw av	-17.5 blw av	-2.1 blw av

Total Risk	Standard Deviation	Category Risk	Risk Index	Beta
av	8.0%	av	1.0	0.9

	1994	1993	1992	1991	1990	1989	1988	1987	1986	1985
Return (%).	-4.2	6.3	5.5	28.0	-3.3	23.6	8.7	8.6	16.3	25.0
Differ from category (+/-) . .	-2.8	-6.9	-4.7	0.4	2.7	2.2	-8.3	8.0	0.5	-0.7

PER SHARE DATA

	1994	1993	1992	1991	1990	1989	1988	1987	1986	1985
Dividends, Net Income ($).	0.22	0.33	0.24	0.35	0.51	0.59	0.46	0.77	0.59	0.49
Distrib'ns, Cap Gain ($) . . .	0.40	0.66	0.34	0.28	0.37	0.36	0.16	2.57	2.70	0.98
Net Asset Value ($)	11.93	13.10	13.27	13.14	10.80	12.07	10.55	10.28	12.55	13.86
Expense Ratio (%)	na	0.74	0.74	0.78	0.77	0.75	0.77	0.71	0.74	0.75
Net Income to Assets (%) . . .	na	1.67	2.08	2.65	4.20	4.73	4.62	3.51	3.77	4.24
Portfolio Turnover (%)	na	39	55	80	99	104	179	110	149	83
Total Assets (Millions $). .	2,445	3,082	3,148	2,998	2,526	2,537	2,262	2,369	2,308	2,165

PORTFOLIO (as of 6/30/94)

Portfolio Manager: Wolodymyr Wronskyj - 1986

Investm't Category: Growth & Income
Cap Gain	Asset Allocation
✔ Cap & Income	Fund of Funds
Income	Index
	Sector
✔ Domestic	Small Cap
✔ Foreign	Socially Conscious
Country/Region	State Specific

Portfolio: stocks 90% bonds 0%
convertibles 0% other 0% cash 10%

Largest Holdings: financial 16%, consumer cyclical 16%

Unrealized Net Capital Gains: 20% of portfolio value

SHAREHOLDER INFORMATION

Minimum Investment
Initial: $2,500   Subsequent: $100

Minimum IRA Investment
Initial: $750   Subsequent: $0

Maximum Fees
Load: none   12b-1: none
Other: none

Distributions
Income: quarterly   Capital Gains: Dec

Exchange Options
Number Per Year: no limit   Fee: none
Telephone: yes (money market fund available)

Services
IRA, pension, auto exchange, auto invest, auto withdraw

Dreyfus 100% US Treasury Interm Term

200 Park Ave.
New York, NY 10166
(800) 645-6561, (718) 895-1206

(DRGIX) *Government Bond*

PERFORMANCE

fund inception date: 3/27/87

	3yr Annual	5yr Annual	10yr Annual	Bull	Bear
Return (%)	4.5	7.4	na	44.6	-4.5
Differ from Category (+/-)	0.5 abv av	0.7 abv av	na	-6.6 av	1.9 av

Total Risk	Standard Deviation	Category Risk	Risk Index	Avg Mat
low	4.5%	av	1.0	4.4 yrs

	1994	1993	1992	1991	1990	1989	1988	1987	1986	1985
Return (%)	-3.9	11.0	7.1	15.2	8.5	12.8	5.7	—	—	—
Differ from category (+/-)	0.9	0.1	0.7	-0.1	2.3	-1.7	-2.2	—	—	—

PER SHARE DATA

	1994	1993	1992	1991	1990	1989	1988	1987	1986	1985
Dividends, Net Income ($)	0.91	0.95	1.00	1.07	1.13	1.14	1.16	—	—	—
Distrib'ns, Cap Gain ($)	0.00	0.00	0.00	0.00	0.00	0.00	0.00	—	—	—
Net Asset Value ($)	12.16	13.60	13.12	13.22	12.48	12.59	12.22	—	—	—
Expense Ratio (%)	0.88	0.73	0.52	0.62	0.80	0.80	0.47	—	—	—
Net Income to Assets (%)	7.09	6.92	7.68	8.44	9.15	9.16	9.18	—	—	—
Portfolio Turnover (%)	na	333	116	22	4	6	21	—	—	—
Total Assets (Millions $)	185	253	231	183	71	61	62	—	—	—

PORTFOLIO (as of 6/30/94)

Portfolio Manager: Gerald Thunelius - 1994

Investm't Category: Government Bond
- Cap Gain
- Cap & Income
- ✔ Income
- ✔ Domestic
- Foreign
- Country/Region
- Asset Allocation
- Fund of Funds
- Index
- Sector
- Small Cap
- Socially Conscious
- State Specific

Portfolio: stocks 0% bonds 88%
convertibles 0% other 0% cash 12%

Largest Holdings: U.S. government 88%

Unrealized Net Capital Gains: -3% of portfolio value

SHAREHOLDER INFORMATION

Minimum Investment
Initial: $2,500 Subsequent: $100

Minimum IRA Investment
Initial: na Subsequent: na

Maximum Fees
Load: none 12b-1: none
Other: none

Distributions
Income: monthly Capital Gains: Dec

Exchange Options
Number Per Year: no limit Fee: none
Telephone: yes (money market fund available)

Services
auto exchange, auto invest, auto withdraw

Dreyfus 100% US Treasury Long Term

(DRGBX) *Government Bond*

200 Park Ave.
New York, NY 10166
(800) 645-6561, (718) 895-1206

PERFORMANCE

fund inception date: 3/27/87

	3yr Annual	5yr Annual	10yr Annual	Bull	Bear
Return (%)	4.4	7.5	na	61.7	-8.7
Differ from Category (+/-)	0.4 abv av	0.8 abv av	na	10.5 abv av	-2.3 blw av

Total Risk	Standard Deviation	Category Risk	Risk Index	Avg Mat
av	7.0%	abv av	1.5	16.1 yrs

	1994	1993	1992	1991	1990	1989	1988	1987	1986	1985
Return (%)	-9.1	16.5	7.5	18.2	7.0	16.2	8.1	—	—	—
Differ from category (+/-)	-4.3	5.6	1.1	2.9	0.8	1.7	0.2	—	—	—

PER SHARE DATA

	1994	1993	1992	1991	1990	1989	1988	1987	1986	1985
Dividends, Net Income ($)	1.01	1.03	1.07	1.13	1.17	1.17	1.17	—	—	—
Distrib'ns, Cap Gain ($)	0.00	0.00	0.00	0.00	0.00	0.00	0.00	—	—	—
Net Asset Value ($)	13.26	15.68	14.37	14.42	13.26	13.56	12.74	—	—	—
Expense Ratio (%)	0.95	0.78	0.56	0.25	0.00	0.00	0.00	—	—	—
Net Income to Assets (%)	6.86	6.65	7.63	8.34	9.05	8.79	9.04	—	—	—
Portfolio Turnover (%)	na	420	97	21	31	40	19	—	—	—
Total Assets (Millions $)	123	211	239	217	43	24	10	—	—	—

PORTFOLIO (as of 6/30/94)

Portfolio Manager: Gerald Thunelius - 1994

Investm't Category: Government Bond

Cap Gain	Asset Allocation
Cap & Income	Fund of Funds
✔ Income	Index
	Sector
✔ Domestic	Small Cap
Foreign	Socially Conscious
Country/Region	State Specific

Portfolio: stocks 0%   bonds 91%
convertibles 0%   other 0%   cash 9%

Largest Holdings: U.S. government 91%

Unrealized Net Capital Gains: -4% of portfolio value

SHAREHOLDER INFORMATION

Minimum Investment
Initial: $2,500   Subsequent: $100

Minimum IRA Investment
Initial: na   Subsequent: na

Maximum Fees
Load: none   12b-1: none
Other: none

Distributions
Income: monthly   Capital Gains: Dec

Exchange Options
Number Per Year: no limit   Fee: none
Telephone: yes (money market fund available)

Services
auto exchange, auto invest, auto withdraw

Dreyfus 100% US Treasury Short Term

200 Park Ave.
New York, NY 10166
(800) 645-6561, (718) 895-1206

(DRTSX) *Government Bond*

PERFORMANCE

fund inception date: 9/10/87

	3yr Annual	5yr Annual	10yr Annual	Bull	Bear
Return (%)	4.4	6.4	na	36.7	-1.2
Differ from Category (+/-)	0.4 abv av	-0.3 blw av	na	-14.5 blw av	5.2 high

Total Risk	Standard Deviation	Category Risk	Risk Index	Avg Mat
low	2.6%	blw av	0.5	2.0 yrs

	1994	1993	1992	1991	1990	1989	1988	1987	1986	1985
Return (%)	-0.3	7.0	7.0	12.9	6.2	12.8	7.8	—	—	—
Differ from category (+/-) . . .	4.5	-3.9	0.6	-2.4	0.0	-1.7	-0.1	—	—	—

PER SHARE DATA

	1994	1993	1992	1991	1990	1989	1988	1987	1986	1985
Dividends, Net Income ($) .	1.14	1.25	1.35	1.13	1.14	1.19	1.20	—	—	—
Distrib'ns, Cap Gain ($) . . .	0.00	0.00	0.00	0.00	0.00	0.00	0.00	—	—	—
Net Asset Value ($)	14.55	15.75	15.91	16.18	15.40	15.62	14.96	—	—	—
Expense Ratio (%)	0.29	0.11	0.03	0.00	0.00	0.00	0.00	—	—	—
Net Income to Assets (%) . .	7.86	7.82	8.34	8.60	7.50	7.84	7.75	—	—	—
Portfolio Turnover (%)	na	322	138	60	0	0	0	—	—	—
Total Assets (Millions $) . . .	172	190	144	29	2	2	4	—	—	—

PORTFOLIO (as of 6/30/94)

Portfolio Manager: Gerald Thunelius - 1994

Investm't Category: Government Bond

Cap Gain	Asset Allocation
Cap & Income	Fund of Funds
✔ Income	Index
	Sector
✔ Domestic	Small Cap
Foreign	Socially Conscious
Country/Region	State Specific

Portfolio: stocks 0%   bonds 93%
convertibles 0%   other 0%   cash 7%

Largest Holdings: U.S. government 93%

Unrealized Net Capital Gains: -4% of portfolio value

SHAREHOLDER INFORMATION

Minimum Investment
Initial: $2,500   Subsequent: $100

Minimum IRA Investment
Initial: na   Subsequent: na

Maximum Fees
Load: none   12b-1: none
Other: none

Distributions
Income: monthly   Capital Gains: Dec

Exchange Options
Number Per Year: no limit   Fee: none
Telephone: yes (money market fund available)

Services
auto exchange, auto invest, auto withdraw

Dreyfus A Bonds Plus
(DRBDX)
General Bond

200 Park Ave.
New York, NY 10166
(800) 645-6561, (718) 895-1206

	3yr Annual	5yr Annual	10yr Annual	Bull	Bear
Return (%)	5.2	7.7	9.7	58.6	-8.1
Differ from Category (+/-)	0.9 high	0.8 abv av	0.8 high	17.6 high	-4.3 low

Total Risk	Standard Deviation	Category Risk	Risk Index	Avg Mat
blw av	5.8%	high	1.5	11.8 yrs

	1994	1993	1992	1991	1990	1989	1988	1987	1986	1985
Return (%).............	-6.1	14.9	8.2	18.7	4.7	14.2	9.0	-0.3	14.1	23.2
Differ from category (+/-) ...	-4.1	5.7	1.6	4.1	-2.5	2.8	1.6	-2.5	-0.1	3.8

PER SHARE DATA

	1994	1993	1992	1991	1990	1989	1988	1987	1986	1985
Dividends, Net Income ($).	0.94	1.00	1.07	1.11	1.15	1.19	1.19	1.34	1.34	1.42
Distrib'ns, Cap Gain ($) ...	0.07	0.58	0.21	0.00	0.00	0.00	0.00	0.22	0.25	0.00
Net Asset Value ($).....	13.24	15.18	14.62	14.74	13.44	13.98	13.34	13.36	14.99	14.61
Expense Ratio (%).......	0.90	0.93	0.88	0.85	0.86	0.94	0.88	0.84	0.87	0.94
Net Income to Assets (%) .	6.30	7.07	7.88	8.59	8.52	8.90	8.87	8.72	10.34	11.85
Portfolio Turnover (%)	93	81	67	26	40	66	49	79	61	20
Total Assets (Millions $)....	484	638	447	340	300	262	254	320	222	123

PORTFOLIO (as of 9/30/94)

Portfolio Manager: Gariti Kono - 1994

Investm't Category: General Bond

Cap Gain	Asset Allocation
Cap & Income	Fund of Funds
✔ Income	Index
	Sector
✔ Domestic	Small Cap
✔ Foreign	Socially Conscious
Country/Region	State Specific

Portfolio: stocks 0% bonds 96%
convertibles 0% other 0% cash 4%

Largest Holdings: corporate 80%, mortgage-backed 16%

Unrealized Net Capital Gains: -4% of portfolio value

SHAREHOLDER INFORMATION

Minimum Investment
Initial: $2,500   Subsequent: $100

Minimum IRA Investment
Initial: $750   Subsequent: $0

Maximum Fees
Load: none   12b-1: none
Other: none

Distributions
Income: monthly   Capital Gains: Dec

Exchange Options
Number Per Year: no limit   Fee: none
Telephone: yes (money market fund available)

Services
IRA, pension, auto exchange, auto invest, auto withdraw

Dreyfus Appreciation
(DGAGX)
Growth

200 Park Ave.
New York, NY 10166
(800) 645-6561, (718) 895-1206

PERFORMANCE

fund inception date: 1/18/84

	3yr Annual	5yr Annual	10yr Annual	Bull	Bear
Return (%)	2.9	8.2	13.6	62.8	-7.3
Differ from Category (+/-)	-4.8 low	-1.4 blw av	0.7 abv av	-29.3 low	-0.7 av

Total Risk	Standard Deviation	Category Risk	Risk Index	Beta
abv av	9.0%	blw av	0.9	1.0

	1994	1993	1992	1991	1990	1989	1988	1987	1986	1985
Return (%)	3.6	0.7	4.6	38.4	-1.8	27.2	16.6	4.5	15.1	35.3
Differ from category (+/-)	4.2	-12.7	-7.0	2.7	3.9	1.1	-1.4	2.7	0.5	6.1

PER SHARE DATA

	1994	1993	1992	1991	1990	1989	1988	1987	1986	1985
Dividends, Net Income ($)	0.28	0.27	0.13	0.20	0.24	0.17	0.17	0.14	0.02	0.12
Distrib'ns, Cap Gain ($)	0.01	0.06	0.08	0.25	0.78	0.69	0.08	0.96	0.10	0.01
Net Asset Value ($)	15.17	14.92	15.15	14.67	10.95	12.20	10.28	9.03	9.67	8.51
Expense Ratio (%)	na	1.07	1.14	1.30	1.24	1.18	1.74	1.63	1.50	1.51
Net Income to Assets (%)	na	1.66	1.46	1.69	2.21	1.38	1.41	0.65	0.65	1.15
Portfolio Turnover (%)	na	9	3	13	179	130	137	179	183	198
Total Assets (Millions $)	233	241	208	81	40	46	41	40	27	5

PORTFOLIO (as of 6/30/94)

Portfolio Manager: not specified

Investm't Category: Growth

✔ Cap Gain	Asset Allocation
Cap & Income	Fund of Funds
Income	Index
	Sector
✔ Domestic	Small Cap
✔ Foreign	Socially Conscious
Country/Region	State Specific

Portfolio: stocks 96% bonds 0%
convertibles 0% other 0% cash 4%

Largest Holdings: food, beverage & tobacco 21%, health care & related products 14%

Unrealized Net Capital Gains: 5% of portfolio value

SHAREHOLDER INFORMATION

Minimum Investment
Initial: $2,500   Subsequent: $100

Minimum IRA Investment
Initial: $750   Subsequent: $0

Maximum Fees
Load: none   12b-1: 0.20%
Other: none

Distributions
Income: Dec   Capital Gains: Dec

Exchange Options
Number Per Year: no limit   Fee: none
Telephone: yes (money market fund available)

Services
IRA, pension, auto exchange, auto invest, auto withdraw

Dreyfus Asset Allocation—Total Return

200 Park Ave.
New York, NY 10166
(800) 645-6561, (718) 895-1206

(DRAAX) *Balanced*

PERFORMANCE   **fund inception date: 7/1/93**

	3yr Annual	5yr Annual	10yr Annual	Bull	Bear
Return (%)	na	na	na	na	-4.3
Differ from Category (+/-)	na	na	na	na	1.4 abv av

Total Risk	Standard Deviation	Category Risk	Risk Index	Beta
na	na	na	na	na

	1994	1993	1992	1991	1990	1989	1988	1987	1986	1985
Return (%)..............	1.6	—	—	—	—	—	—	—	—	—
Differ from category (+/-) ..	3.5	—	—	—	—	—	—	—	—	—

PER SHARE DATA

	1994	1993	1992	1991	1990	1989	1988	1987	1986	1985
Dividends, Net Income ($).	0.37	—	—	—	—	—	—	—	—	—
Distrib'ns, Cap Gain ($) . . .	0.05	—	—	—	—	—	—	—	—	—
Net Asset Value ($)	12.48	—	—	—	—	—	—	—	—	—
Expense Ratio (%)	na	—	—	—	—	—	—	—	—	—
Net Income to Assets (%) . . .	na	—	—	—	—	—	—	—	—	—
Portfolio Turnover (%)	na	—	—	—	—	—	—	—	—	—
Total Assets (Millions $).	49	—	—	—	—	—	—	—	—	—

PORTFOLIO (as of 4/30/94)

Portfolio Manager: Ernest Wiggins - 1994

Investm't Category: Balanced
Cap Gain	✔ Asset Allocation
✔ Cap & Income	Fund of Funds
Income	Index
	Sector
✔ Domestic	Small Cap
Foreign	Socially Conscious
Country/Region	State Specific

Portfolio: stocks 61% bonds 15%
convertibles 0% other 0% cash 24%

Largest Holdings: bonds—U.S. government 15%, stocks—oil & gas production 7%

Unrealized Net Capital Gains: -2% of portfolio value

SHAREHOLDER INFORMATION

Minimum Investment
Initial: $2,500   Subsequent: $100

Minimum IRA Investment
Initial: $750   Subsequent: $0

Maximum Fees
Load: none   12b-1: 0.50%
Other: none

Distributions
Income: Dec   Capital Gains: Dec

Exchange Options
Number Per Year: no limit   Fee: none
Telephone: yes (money market fund available)

Services
IRA, pension, auto exchange, auto invest, auto withdraw

Dreyfus Balanced

(DRBAX)

Balanced

200 Park Ave.
New York, NY 10166
(800) 645-6561, (718) 895-1206

PERFORMANCE

fund inception date: 9/30/92

	3yr Annual	5yr Annual	10yr Annual	Bull	Bear
Return (%)	na	na	na	na	-2.8
Differ from Category (+/-)	na	na	na	na	2.9 high

Total Risk	Standard Deviation	Category Risk	Risk Index	Beta
na	na	na	na	na

	1994	1993	1992	1991	1990	1989	1988	1987	1986	1985
Return (%)	3.9	10.8	—	—	—	—	—	—	—	—
Differ from category (+/-) . . .	5.8	-2.6	—	—	—	—	—	—	—	—

PER SHARE DATA

	1994	1993	1992	1991	1990	1989	1988	1987	1986	1985
Dividends, Net Income ($) .	0.46	0.40	—	—	—	—	—	—	—	—
Distrib'ns, Cap Gain ($) . . .	0.13	0.14	—	—	—	—	—	—	—	—
Net Asset Value ($)	13.39	13.46	—	—	—	—	—	—	—	—
Expense Ratio (%).	0.69	na	—	—	—	—	—	—	—	—
Net Income to Assets (%). .	3.26	na	—	—	—	—	—	—	—	—
Portfolio Turnover (%)	58	na	—	—	—	—	—	—	—	—
Total Assets (Millions $)	91	59	—	—	—	—	—	—	—	—

PORTFOLIO (as of 8/31/94)

Portfolio Manager: Peter Santoriello - 1992

Investm't Category: Balanced

Cap Gain	Asset Allocation
✔ Cap & Income	Fund of Funds
Income	Index
	Sector
✔ Domestic	Small Cap
Foreign	Socially Conscious
Country/Region	State Specific

Portfolio: stocks 41% bonds 48%
convertibles 0% other 0% cash 11%

Largest Holdings: bonds—U.S. government
& agencies 21%, stocks—pharmaceuticals 8%

Unrealized Net Capital Gains: 3% of portfolio value

SHAREHOLDER INFORMATION

Minimum Investment
Initial: $2,500   Subsequent: $100

Minimum IRA Investment
Initial: $750   Subsequent: $0

Maximum Fees
Load: none   12b-1: none
Other: none

Distributions
Income: quarterly   Capital Gains: Dec

Exchange Options
Number Per Year: no limit   Fee: none
Telephone: yes (money market fund available)

Services
IRA, pension, auto exchange, auto invest, auto withdraw

Dreyfus CA Interm Muni Bond (DCIMX)

200 Park Ave.
New York, NY 10166
(800) 645-6561, (718) 895-1206

Tax-Exempt Bond

PERFORMANCE

fund inception date: 4/20/92

	3yr Annual	5yr Annual	10yr Annual	Bull	Bear
Return (%)	na	na	na	na	-5.4
Differ from Category (+/-)	na	na	na	na	-0.2 av

Total Risk	Standard Deviation	Category Risk	Risk Index	Avg Mat
na	na	na	na	7.8 yrs

	1994	1993	1992	1991	1990	1989	1988	1987	1986	1985
Return (%)	-5.4	14.4	—	—	—	—	—	—	—	—
Differ from category (+/-) . .	-0.2	2.7	—	—	—	—	—	—	—	—

PER SHARE DATA

	1994	1993	1992	1991	1990	1989	1988	1987	1986	1985
Dividends, Net Income ($).	0.67	0.73	—	—	—	—	—	—	—	—
Distrib'ns, Cap Gain ($) . . .	0.00	0.00	—	—	—	—	—	—	—	—
Net Asset Value ($)	12.54	13.97	—	—	—	—	—	—	—	—
Expense Ratio (%)	0.04	0.00	—	—	—	—	—	—	—	—
Net Income to Assets (%) .	5.25	5.61	—	—	—	—	—	—	—	—
Portfolio Turnover (%)	6	6	—	—	—	—	—	—	—	—
Total Assets (Millions $). . . .	237	305	—	—	—	—	—	—	—	—

PORTFOLIO (as of 9/30/94)

Portfolio Manager: Laurence Troutman - 1992

Investm't Category: Tax-Exempt Bond

Cap Gain	Asset Allocation
Cap & Income	Fund of Funds
✔ Income	Index
	Sector
✔ Domestic	Small Cap
Foreign	Socially Conscious
Country/Region	✔ State Specific

Portfolio: stocks 0% bonds 92%
convertibles 0% other 0% cash 8%

Largest Holdings: general obligation 12%

Unrealized Net Capital Gains: -1% of portfolio value

SHAREHOLDER INFORMATION

Minimum Investment
Initial: $2,500   Subsequent: $100

Minimum IRA Investment
Initial: na   Subsequent: na

Maximum Fees
Load: none   12b-1: none
Other: none

Distributions
Income: monthly   Capital Gains: Nov

Exchange Options
Number Per Year: no limit   Fee: none
Telephone: yes (money market fund available)

Services
auto exchange, auto invest, auto withdraw

Dreyfus CA Tax Exempt Bond (DRCAX)

Tax-Exempt Bond

200 Park Ave.
New York, NY 10166
(800) 645-6561, (718) 895-1206

PERFORMANCE

fund inception date: 7/26/83

	3yr Annual	5yr Annual	10yr Annual	Bull	Bear
Return (%)	3.4	5.4	7.8	38.2	-5.9
Differ from Category (+/-)	-1.1 low	-0.7 low	-0.3 blw av	-3.6 blw av	-0.7 av

Total Risk	Standard Deviation	Category Risk	Risk Index	Avg Mat
blw av	5.9%	av	0.9	21.8 yrs

	1994	1993	1992	1991	1990	1989	1988	1987	1986	1985
Return (%)	-7.1	11.8	6.6	10.3	6.7	8.5	9.6	-1.6	17.7	18.0
Differ from category (+/-)	-1.9	0.1	-1.7	-1.0	0.4	-0.5	-0.6	-0.3	1.3	0.6

PER SHARE DATA

	1994	1993	1992	1991	1990	1989	1988	1987	1986	1985
Dividends, Net Income ($)	0.82	0.86	0.90	0.96	1.02	1.04	1.05	1.06	1.10	1.13
Distrib'ns, Cap Gain ($)	0.05	0.17	0.15	0.04	0.00	0.00	0.00	0.00	0.00	0.00
Net Asset Value ($)	13.61	15.56	14.86	14.96	14.50	14.58	14.42	14.15	15.47	14.13
Expense Ratio (%)	0.70	0.69	0.68	0.69	0.69	0.70	0.71	0.70	0.72	0.75
Net Income to Assets (%)	5.46	5.88	6.32	6.82	7.10	7.32	7.37	7.08	7.85	8.75
Portfolio Turnover (%)	28	41	46	56	35	40	60	32	19	27
Total Assets (Millions $)	1,433	1,843	1,751	1,630	1,497	1,385	1,175	1,175	973	529

PORTFOLIO (as of 5/31/94)

Portfolio Manager: Larry Troutman - 1986

Investm't Category: Tax-Exempt Bond

Cap Gain	Asset Allocation
Cap & Income	Fund of Funds
✔ Income	Index
	Sector
✔ Domestic	Small Cap
Foreign	Socially Conscious
Country/Region	✔ State Specific

Portfolio: stocks 0%   bonds 94%
convertibles 0%   other 0%   cash 6%

Largest Holdings: general obligation 12%

Unrealized Net Capital Gains: 2% of portfolio value

SHAREHOLDER INFORMATION

Minimum Investment
Initial: $2,500   Subsequent: $100

Minimum IRA Investment
Initial: na   Subsequent: na

Maximum Fees
Load: none   12b-1: none
Other: none

Distributions
Income: monthly   Capital Gains: Nov

Exchange Options
Number Per Year: no limit   Fee: none
Telephone: yes (money market fund available)

Services
auto exchange, auto invest, auto withdraw

Dreyfus Capital Growth

(DRLEX)

Growth

200 Park Ave.
New York, NY 10166
(800) 645-6561, (718) 895-1206

	3yr Annual	5yr Annual	10yr Annual	Bull	Bear
Return (%)	4.2	8.1	12.1	78.3	-10.2
Differ from Category (+/-)	-3.5 blw av	-1.5 blw av	-0.8 blw av	-13.8 blw av	-3.6 low

Total Risk	Standard Deviation	Category Risk	Risk Index	Beta
av	6.9%	low	0.7	0.7

	1994	1993	1992	1991	1990	1989	1988	1987	1986	1985
Return (%)	-6.9	14.7	6.2	32.6	-1.4	20.4	1.8	11.1	19.3	30.5
Differ from category (+/-)	-6.3	1.3	-5.4	-3.1	4.3	-5.7	-16.2	9.3	4.7	1.3

PER SHARE DATA

	1994	1993	1992	1991	1990	1989	1988	1987	1986	1985
Dividends, Net Income ($)	0.44	0.80	0.24	0.39	0.76	0.70	0.64	0.41	0.52	0.78
Distrib'ns, Cap Gain ($)	0.23	2.22	1.37	1.37	0.00	0.00	0.00	3.66	4.73	1.94
Net Asset Value ($)	14.56	16.38	16.98	17.50	14.62	15.61	13.55	13.94	16.23	18.07
Expense Ratio (%)	1.12	1.06	1.07	1.14	1.34	1.58	1.31	1.23	1.01	1.20
Net Income to Assets (%)	2.10	1.24	1.74	2.13	3.97	5.32	3.91	1.98	2.69	4.12
Portfolio Turnover (%)	158	102	141	81	89	124	111	123	141	82
Total Assets (Millions $)	552	618	521	494	401	484	472	631	486	407

PORTFOLIO (as of 9/30/94)

Portfolio Manager: Howard Stein - 1969

Investm't Category: Growth

✔ Cap Gain	Asset Allocation
Cap & Income	Fund of Funds
Income	Index
	Sector
✔ Domestic	Small Cap
✔ Foreign	Socially Conscious
Country/Region	State Specific

Portfolio: stocks 56% bonds 27%
convertibles 0% other 0% cash 17%

Largest Holdings: consumer staples 18%, basic industries 6%

Unrealized Net Capital Gains: 4% of portfolio value

SHAREHOLDER INFORMATION

Minimum Investment
Initial: $2,500   Subsequent: $100

Minimum IRA Investment
Initial: $750   Subsequent: $0

Maximum Fees
Load: 3.00% front   12b-1: none
Other: none

Distributions
Income: Dec   Capital Gains: Dec

Exchange Options
Number Per Year: 2   Fee: none
Telephone: yes (money market fund available)

Services
IRA, pension, auto exchange, auto invest, auto withdraw

Dreyfus Conn Interm Muni Bond (DCTIX)

200 Park Ave.
New York, NY 10166
(800) 645-6561, (718) 895-1206

Tax-Exempt Bond

PERFORMANCE

fund inception date: 6/26/92

	3yr Annual	5yr Annual	10yr Annual	Bull	Bear
Return (%)	na	na	na	na	-4.8
Differ from Category (+/-)	na	na	na	na	0.4 abv av

Total Risk	Standard Deviation	Category Risk	Risk Index	Avg Mat
na	na	na	na	9.2 yrs

	1994	1993	1992	1991	1990	1989	1988	1987	1986	1985
Return (%)	-4.7	12.7	—	—	—	—	—	—	—	—
Differ from category (+/-)	0.5	1.0	—	—	—	—	—	—	—	—

PER SHARE DATA

	1994	1993	1992	1991	1990	1989	1988	1987	1986	1985
Dividends, Net Income ($)	0.66	0.68	—	—	—	—	—	—	—	—
Distrib'ns, Cap Gain ($)	0.00	0.01	—	—	—	—	—	—	—	—
Net Asset Value ($)	12.47	13.77	—	—	—	—	—	—	—	—
Expense Ratio (%)	0.01	0.00	—	—	—	—	—	—	—	—
Net Income to Assets (%)	5.07	5.21	—	—	—	—	—	—	—	—
Portfolio Turnover (%)	11	37	—	—	—	—	—	—	—	—
Total Assets (Millions $)	124	137	—	—	—	—	—	—	—	—

PORTFOLIO (as of 9/30/94)

Portfolio Manager: Stephen Kris - 1992

Investm't Category: Tax-Exempt Bond

Cap Gain	Asset Allocation
Cap & Income	Fund of Funds
✔ Income	Index
	Sector
✔ Domestic	Small Cap
Foreign	Socially Conscious
Country/Region	✔ State Specific

Portfolio: stocks 0% bonds 100%
convertibles 0% other 0% cash 0%

Largest Holdings: general obligation 50%

Unrealized Net Capital Gains: -2% of portfolio value

SHAREHOLDER INFORMATION

Minimum Investment
Initial: $2,500   Subsequent: $100

Minimum IRA Investment
Initial: na   Subsequent: na

Maximum Fees
Load: none   12b-1: none
Other: none

Distributions
Income: monthly   Capital Gains: Dec

Exchange Options
Number Per Year: no limit   Fee: none
Telephone: yes (money market fund available)

Services
auto exchange, auto invest, auto withdraw

Dreyfus Core Value - Investor (BCCAX)

Growth

P.O. Box 9692
Providence, RI 02940
(800) 548-2868

PERFORMANCE

fund inception date: 2/6/47

	3yr Annual	5yr Annual	10yr Annual	Bull	Bear
Return (%)	6.7	5.2	12.3	65.6	-5.5
Differ from Category (+/-)	-1.0 av	-4.4 low	-0.6 av	-26.5 low	1.1 av

Total Risk	Standard Deviation	Category Risk	Risk Index	Beta
abv av	8.8%	blw av	0.9	1.0

	1994	1993	1992	1991	1990	1989	1988	1987	1986	1985
Return (%)	0.3	16.4	4.0	22.8	-13.4	24.9	19.5	0.2	22.5	34.9
Differ from category (+/-)	0.9	3.0	-7.6	-12.9	-7.7	-1.2	1.5	-1.6	7.9	5.7

PER SHARE DATA

	1994	1993	1992	1991	1990	1989	1988	1987	1986	1985
Dividends, Net Income ($)	0.40	0.30	0.36	0.50	0.55	0.55	0.59	1.32	0.50	0.74
Distrib'ns, Cap Gain ($)	2.97	1.50	2.64	0.57	0.06	7.60	1.88	5.36	5.79	1.56
Net Asset Value ($)	24.55	27.80	25.46	27.40	23.20	27.49	28.65	26.07	32.40	32.11
Expense Ratio (%)	1.11	1.15	1.22	1.20	1.26	1.23	1.31	0.95	0.95	0.96
Net Income to Assets (%)	1.33	1.10	1.33	1.61	1.96	2.75	2.14	2.16	2.65	3.60
Portfolio Turnover (%)	na	75	66	157	180	111	24	46	37	59
Total Assets (Millions $)	318	444	423	509	475	640	543	432	452	369

PORTFOLIO (as of 6/30/94)

Portfolio Manager: Guy Scott - 1991

Investm't Category: Growth

✔ Cap Gain
Cap & Income
Income

Asset Allocation
Fund of Funds
Index
Sector
Small Cap
Socially Conscious
State Specific

✔ Domestic
✔ Foreign
Country/Region

Portfolio: stocks 90% bonds 0%
convertibles 2% other 0% cash 8%

Largest Holdings: financial services 17%, consumer services 12%

Unrealized Net Capital Gains: 6% of portfolio value

SHAREHOLDER INFORMATION

Minimum Investment
Initial: $1,000   Subsequent: $0

Minimum IRA Investment
Initial: $500   Subsequent: $0

Maximum Fees
Load: none   12b-1: 0.25%
Other: none

Distributions
Income: quarterly   Capital Gains: Dec

Exchange Options
Number Per Year: no limit   Fee: none
Telephone: yes (money market fund available)

Services
IRA, pension, auto exchange, auto invest, auto withdraw

Dreyfus Edison Electric Index (DEEIX)

Growth & Income

200 Park Ave.
New York, NY 10166
(800) 645-6561, (718) 895-1206

PERFORMANCE

fund inception date: 12/6/91

	3yr Annual	5yr Annual	10yr Annual	Bull	Bear
Return (%)	1.1	na	na	na	-16.3
Differ from Category (+/-)	-6.0 low	na	na	na	-10.0 low

Total Risk	Standard Deviation	Category Risk	Risk Index	Beta
abv av	10.4%	high	1.3	0.6

	1994	1993	1992	1991	1990	1989	1988	1987	1986	1985
Return (%)	-12.7	10.4	7.4	—	—	—	—	—	—	—
Differ from category (+/-) .	-11.3	-2.8	-2.8	—	—	—	—	—	—	—

PER SHARE DATA

	1994	1993	1992	1991	1990	1989	1988	1987	1986	1985
Dividends, Net Income ($) .	0.73	0.67	0.66	—	—	—	—	—	—	—
Distrib'ns, Cap Gain ($) . . .	0.00	0.21	0.01	—	—	—	—	—	—	—
Net Asset Value ($)	11.28	13.78	13.26	—	—	—	—	—	—	—
Expense Ratio (%).	na	0.75	0.24	—	—	—	—	—	—	—
Net Income to Assets (%). . .	na	4.80	5.31	—	—	—	—	—	—	—
Portfolio Turnover (%)	na	14	3	—	—	—	—	—	—	—
Total Assets (Millions $)	71	107	37	—	—	—	—	—	—	—

PORTFOLIO (as of 4/30/94)

Portfolio Manager: not specified

Investm't Category: Growth & Income

Cap Gain	Asset Allocation
✔ Cap & Income	Fund of Funds
Income	✔ Index
	✔ Sector
✔ Domestic	Small Cap
Foreign	Socially Conscious
Country/Region	State Specific

Portfolio: stocks 100% bonds 0%
convertibles 0% other 0% cash 0%

Largest Holdings: Edison Electric Institute index

Unrealized Net Capital Gains: -12% of portfolio value

SHAREHOLDER INFORMATION

Minimum Investment
Initial: $2,500   Subsequent: $100

Minimum IRA Investment
Initial: $750   Subsequent: $0

Maximum Fees
Load: none   12b-1: none
Other: none

Distributions
Income: quarterly   Capital Gains: Dec

Exchange Options
Number Per Year: no limit   Fee: none
Telephone: none

Services
IRA, pension, auto invest

Dreyfus Florida Interm Muni (DFLIX)

Tax-Exempt Bond

200 Park Ave.
New York, NY 10166
(800) 645-6561, (718) 895-1206

	3yr Annual	5yr Annual	10yr Annual	Bull	Bear
Return (%)	na	na	na	na	-4.9
Differ from Category (+/-)	na	na	na	na	0.3 abv av

Total Risk	Standard Deviation	Category Risk	Risk Index	Avg Mat
na	na	na	na	8.7 yrs

	1994	1993	1992	1991	1990	1989	1988	1987	1986	1985
Return (%)	-4.9	12.8	—	—	—	—	—	—	—	—
Differ from category (+/-)	0.3	1.1	—	—	—	—	—	—	—	—

PER SHARE DATA

	1994	1993	1992	1991	1990	1989	1988	1987	1986	1985
Dividends, Net Income ($)	0.65	0.71	—	—	—	—	—	—	—	—
Distrib'ns, Cap Gain ($)	0.01	0.01	—	—	—	—	—	—	—	—
Net Asset Value ($)	12.52	13.85	—	—	—	—	—	—	—	—
Expense Ratio (%)	0.43	0.20	—	—	—	—	—	—	—	—
Net Income to Assets (%)	4.98	5.20	—	—	—	—	—	—	—	—
Portfolio Turnover (%)	na	13	—	—	—	—	—	—	—	—
Total Assets (Millions $)	409	529	—	—	—	—	—	—	—	—

PORTFOLIO (as of 6/30/94)

Portfolio Manager: Stephen Kris - 1992

Investm't Category: Tax-Exempt Bond

Cap Gain	Asset Allocation
Cap & Income	Fund of Funds
✔ Income	Index
	Sector
✔ Domestic	Small Cap
Foreign	Socially Conscious
Country/Region	✔ State Specific

Portfolio: stocks 0%   bonds 100%
convertibles 0%   other 0%   cash 0%

Largest Holdings: general obligation 23%

Unrealized Net Capital Gains: 0% of portfolio value

SHAREHOLDER INFORMATION

Minimum Investment
Initial: $2,500   Subsequent: $100

Minimum IRA Investment
Initial: na   Subsequent: na

Maximum Fees
Load: none   12b-1: none
Other: none

Distributions
Income: monthly   Capital Gains: Aug

Exchange Options
Number Per Year: no limit   Fee: none
Telephone: yes (money market fund available)

Services
auto exchange, auto invest, auto withdraw

Dreyfus GNMA
(DRGMX)
Mortgage-Backed Bond

200 Park Ave.
New York, NY 10166
(800) 645-6561, (718) 895-1206

PERFORMANCE

fund inception date: 5/29/85

	3yr Annual	5yr Annual	10yr Annual	Bull	Bear
Return (%)	3.4	6.8	na	37.3	-3.7
Differ from Category (+/-)	0.3 blw av	-0.1 blw av	na	-0.7 av	0.7 av

Total Risk	Standard Deviation	Category Risk	Risk Index	Avg Mat
low	3.2%	av	1.0	18.3 yrs

	1994	1993	1992	1991	1990	1989	1988	1987	1986	1985
Return (%)	-2.7	7.1	6.3	14.4	9.7	11.5	6.3	2.4	9.7	—
Differ from category (+/-) . . .	0.1	0.3	0.2	0.0	0.0	-1.0	-0.8	0.6	-1.5	—

PER SHARE DATA

	1994	1993	1992	1991	1990	1989	1988	1987	1986	1985
Dividends, Net Income ($)	0.94	1.03	1.13	1.23	1.29	1.29	1.30	1.45	1.48	—
Distrib'ns, Cap Gain ($) . . .	0.00	0.00	0.00	0.00	0.00	0.00	0.00	0.03	0.00	—
Net Asset Value ($)	13.79	15.15	15.12	15.32	14.54	14.49	14.21	14.59	15.70	—
Expense Ratio (%).	0.95	0.94	0.95	0.97	0.97	0.99	1.01	1.01	0.96	—
Net Income to Assets (%). .	6.54	7.20	8.05	8.81	8.98	8.89	8.98	8.87	10.27	—
Portfolio Turnover (%). . . .	211	155	61	26	272	473	288	257	245	—
Total Assets (Millions $) . .	1,426	1,801	1,575	1,583	1,496	1,616	1,981	2,397	1,738	—

PORTFOLIO (as of 4/30/94)

Portfolio Manager: Garitt Kono - 1992

Investm't Category: Mortgage-Backed Bond

Cap Gain	Asset Allocation
Cap & Income	Fund of Funds
✔ Income	Index
	Sector
✔ Domestic	Small Cap
Foreign	Socially Conscious
Country/Region	State Specific

Portfolio: stocks 0% bonds 82%
convertibles 0% other 0% cash 18%

Largest Holdings: mortgage-backed 82%

Unrealized Net Capital Gains: -1% of portfolio value

SHAREHOLDER INFORMATION

Minimum Investment
Initial: $2,500   Subsequent: $100

Minimum IRA Investment
Initial: $750   Subsequent: $0

Maximum Fees
Load: none   12b-1: 0.20%
Other: none

Distributions
Income: monthly   Capital Gains: Dec

Exchange Options
Number Per Year: no limit   Fee: none
Telephone: yes (money market fund available)

Services
IRA, pension, auto exchange, auto invest, auto
withdraw

Dreyfus Growth & Income (DGRIX)

Growth & Income

200 Park Ave.
New York, NY 10166
(800) 645-6561, (718) 895-1206

PERFORMANCE

fund inception date: 12/31/91

	3yr Annual	5yr Annual	10yr Annual	Bull	Bear
Return (%)	10.5	na	na	na	-9.1
Differ from Category (+/-)	3.4 abv av	na	na	na	-2.8 low

Total Risk	Standard Deviation	Category Risk	Risk Index	Beta
av	7.3%	low	0.9	0.7

	1994	1993	1992	1991	1990	1989	1988	1987	1986	1985
Return (%)	-5.1	18.5	20.1	—	—	—	—	—	—	—
Differ from category (+/-)	-3.7	5.3	9.9	—	—	—	—	—	—	—

PER SHARE DATA

	1994	1993	1992	1991	1990	1989	1988	1987	1986	1985
Dividends, Net Income ($)	0.36	0.36	0.27	—	—	—	—	—	—	—
Distrib'ns, Cap Gain ($)	0.17	0.04	0.00	—	—	—	—	—	—	—
Net Asset Value ($)	15.63	17.04	14.73	—	—	—	—	—	—	—
Expense Ratio (%)	1.14	1.24	1.02	—	—	—	—	—	—	—
Net Income to Assets (%)	2.18	2.92	2.30	—	—	—	—	—	—	—
Portfolio Turnover (%)	97	85	127	—	—	—	—	—	—	—
Total Assets (Millions $)	1,617	1,263	99	—	—	—	—	—	—	—

PORTFOLIO (as of 10/31/94)

Portfolio Manager: Richard Hoey - 1992

Investm't Category: Growth & Income
Cap Gain	Asset Allocation
✔ Cap & Income	Fund of Funds
Income	Index
	Sector
✔ Domestic	Small Cap
✔ Foreign	Socially Conscious
Country/Region	State Specific

Portfolio: stocks 54% bonds 0%
convertibles 19% other 0% cash 27%

Largest Holdings: basic & process industries 13%, energy 8%

Unrealized Net Capital Gains: 2% of portfolio value

SHAREHOLDER INFORMATION

Minimum Investment
Initial: $2,500   Subsequent: $100

Minimum IRA Investment
Initial: $750   Subsequent: $0

Maximum Fees
Load: none   12b-1: none
Other: none

Distributions
Income: quarterly   Capital Gains: Dec

Exchange Options
Number Per Year: no limit   Fee: none
Telephone: yes (money market fund available)

Services
IRA, pension, auto exchange, auto invest, auto withdraw

Dreyfus Growth Opportunity (DREQX)

Growth

200 Park Ave.
New York, NY 10166
(800) 645-6561, (718) 895-1206

	3yr Annual	5yr Annual	10yr Annual	Bull	Bear
Return (%)	-2.9	5.2	10.8	61.9	-8.9
Differ from Category (+/-)	-10.6 low	-4.4 low	-2.1 low	-30.2 low	-2.3 blw av

Total Risk	Standard Deviation	Category Risk	Risk Index	Beta
high	12.4%	high	1.3	1.1

	1994	1993	1992	1991	1990	1989	1988	1987	1986	1985
Return (%)	-6.3	1.7	-4.2	51.4	-6.5	14.7	17.8	6.7	15.2	30.6
Differ from category (+/-) . .	-5.7	-11.7	-15.8	15.7	-0.8	-11.4	-0.2	4.9	0.6	1.4

PER SHARE DATA

	1994	1993	1992	1991	1990	1989	1988	1987	1986	1985
Dividends, Net Income ($) .	0.09	0.00	0.01	0.13	0.28	0.46	0.41	0.43	0.21	0.21
Distrib'ns, Cap Gain ($) . . .	1.85	2.60	0.00	0.00	0.02	0.81	0.03	2.07	2.60	0.34
Net Asset Value ($)	8.18	10.74	13.14	13.73	9.16	10.12	9.94	8.81	10.50	11.59
Expense Ratio (%)	1.09	1.00	0.95	0.98	1.00	1.04	0.91	0.95	0.98	1.02
Net Income to Assets (%) .	-0.14	0.11	0.85	2.32	3.13	3.50	3.69	1.62	1.87	2.04
Portfolio Turnover (%)	195	90	57	147	126	83	129	73	56	44
Total Assets (Millions $) . . .	361	490	632	512	526	571	492	516	477	441

PORTFOLIO (as of 2/28/94)

Portfolio Manager: Ernest G. Wiggins Jr. - 1994

Investm't Category: Growth
✔ Cap Gain   Asset Allocation
  Cap & Income   Fund of Funds
  Income   Index
     Sector
✔ Domestic   Small Cap
✔ Foreign   Socially Conscious
  Country/Region   State Specific

Portfolio: stocks 90%   bonds 0%
convertibles 0%   other 0%   cash 10%

Largest Holdings: healthcare 20%, energy 13%

Unrealized Net Capital Gains: 6% of portfolio value

SHAREHOLDER INFORMATION

Minimum Investment
Initial: $2,500   Subsequent: $100

Minimum IRA Investment
Initial: $750   Subsequent: $0

Maximum Fees
Load: none   12b-1: none
Other: none

Distributions
Income: Dec   Capital Gains: Dec

Exchange Options
Number Per Year: no limit   Fee: none
Telephone: yes (money market fund available)

Services
IRA, pension, auto exchange, auto invest, auto withdraw

Dreyfus Insured Muni Bond (DTBDX)

200 Park Ave.
New York, NY 10166
(800) 645-6561, (718) 895-1206

Tax-Exempt Bond

fund inception date: 6/25/85

PERFORMANCE

	3yr Annual	5yr Annual	10yr Annual	Bull	Bear
Return (%)	3.4	5.7	na	42.9	-7.9
Differ from Category (+/-)	-1.1 low	-0.4 low	na	1.1 av	-2.7 low

Total Risk	Standard Deviation	Category Risk	Risk Index	Avg Mat
av	7.1%	high	1.1	23.2 yrs

	1994	1993	1992	1991	1990	1989	1988	1987	1986	1985
Return (%).	-8.6	12.5	7.7	11.3	7.0	8.7	10.1	-1.9	17.0	—
Differ from category (+/-) . .	-3.4	0.8	-0.6	0.0	0.7	-0.3	-0.1	-0.6	0.6	—

PER SHARE DATA

	1994	1993	1992	1991	1990	1989	1988	1987	1986	1985
Dividends, Net Income ($).	0.95	1.03	1.08	1.11	1.16	1.17	1.19	1.21	1.28	—
Distrib'ns, Cap Gain ($) . . .	0.00	0.71	0.21	0.00	0.00	0.00	0.00	0.00	0.00	—
Net Asset Value ($)	16.51	19.08	18.54	18.46	17.63	17.60	17.30	16.83	18.40	—
Expense Ratio (%)	0.93	0.94	0.96	0.96	0.99	1.00	0.90	0.84	0.73	—
Net Income to Assets (%) .	5.25	5.69	6.07	6.50	6.63	6.96	7.11	6.78	7.60	—
Portfolio Turnover (%)	34	80	51	62	67	68	96	75	51	—
Total Assets (Millions $). . . .	215	290	241	219	191	186	177	198	144	—

PORTFOLIO (as of 4/30/94)

Portfolio Manager: Lawrence Troutman - 1985

Investm't Category: Tax-Exempt Bond

Cap Gain	Asset Allocation
Cap & Income	Fund of Funds
✔ Income	Index
	Sector
✔ Domestic	Small Cap
Foreign	Socially Conscious
Country/Region	State Specific

Portfolio: stocks 0% bonds 93%
convertibles 0% other 0% cash 7%

Largest Holdings: general obligation 7%

Unrealized Net Capital Gains: 0% of portfolio value

SHAREHOLDER INFORMATION

Minimum Investment
Initial: $2,500　　　Subsequent: $100

Minimum IRA Investment
Initial: na　　　Subsequent: na

Maximum Fees
Load: none　　　12b-1: 0.20%
Other: none

Distributions
Income: monthly　　　Capital Gains: Nov

Exchange Options
Number Per Year: no limit　　Fee: none
Telephone: yes (money market fund available)

Services
auto exchange, auto invest, auto withdraw

Dreyfus Interm Muni Bond (DITEX)

Tax-Exempt Bond

200 Park Ave.
New York, NY 10166
(800) 645-6561, (718) 895-1206

PERFORMANCE

fund inception date: 8/11/83

	3yr Annual	5yr Annual	10yr Annual	Bull	Bear
Return (%)	4.9	6.5	8.1	40.5	-4.4
Differ from Category (+/-)	0.4 abv av	0.4 av	0.0 blw av	-1.3 blw av	0.8 abv av

Total Risk	Standard Deviation	Category Risk	Risk Index	Avg Mat
blw av	5.0%	blw av	0.8	9.8 yrs

	1994	1993	1992	1991	1990	1989	1988	1987	1986	1985
Return (%)	-4.4	11.4	8.7	11.1	6.7	8.7	8.0	1.1	15.4	16.0
Differ from category (+/-) . . .	0.8	-0.3	0.4	-0.2	0.4	-0.3	-2.2	2.4	-1.0	-1.4

PER SHARE DATA

	1994	1993	1992	1991	1990	1989	1988	1987	1986	1985
Dividends, Net Income ($) .	0.75	0.77	0.84	0.90	0.94	0.96	0.97	0.97	1.01	1.02
Distrib'ns, Cap Gain ($) . . .	0.06	0.16	0.31	0.08	0.00	0.00	0.00	0.00	0.00	0.00
Net Asset Value ($)	13.14	14.60	13.97	13.95	13.48	13.54	13.37	13.30	14.12	13.16
Expense Ratio (%).	0.70	0.71	0.70	0.69	0.71	0.71	0.73	0.71	0.75	0.81
Net Income to Assets (%). .	5.22	5.68	6.47	6.84	7.01	7.27	7.21	7.07	7.76	8.23
Portfolio Turnover (%)	36	60	48	31	40	34	49	50	34	21
Total Assets (Millions $) . .	1,449	1,836	1,406	1,237	1,113	1,056	1,015	1,090	920	548

PORTFOLIO (as of 5/31/94)

Portfolio Manager: Monica Wieboldt - 1985

Investm't Category: Tax-Exempt Bond

Cap Gain	Asset Allocation
Cap & Income	Fund of Funds
✔ Income	Index
	Sector
✔ Domestic	Small Cap
Foreign	Socially Conscious
Country/Region	State Specific

Portfolio: stocks 0%   bonds 95%
convertibles 0%   other 0%   cash 5%

Largest Holdings: general obligation 12%

Unrealized Net Capital Gains: 2% of portfolio value

SHAREHOLDER INFORMATION

Minimum Investment
Initial: $2,500   Subsequent: $100

Minimum IRA Investment
Initial: na   Subsequent: na

Maximum Fees
Load: none   12b-1: none
Other: none

Distributions
Income: monthly   Capital Gains: Nov

Exchange Options
Number Per Year: no limit   Fee: none
Telephone: yes (money market fund available)

Services
auto exchange, auto invest, auto withdraw

Dreyfus International Equity (DITFX)

International Stock

200 Park Ave.
New York, NY 10166
(800) 645-6561, (718) 895-1206

PERFORMANCE

fund inception date: 6/29/93

	3yr Annual	5yr Annual	10yr Annual	Bull	Bear
Return (%)	na	na	na	na	-7.5
Differ from Category (+/-)	na	na	na	na	-0.5 av

Total Risk	Standard Deviation	Category Risk	Risk Index	Beta
na	na	na	na	na

	1994	1993	1992	1991	1990	1989	1988	1987	1986	1985
Return (%)	-5.4	—	—	—	—	—	—	—	—	—
Differ from category (+/-) . .	-2.4	—	—	—	—	—	—	—	—	—

PER SHARE DATA

	1994	1993	1992	1991	1990	1989	1988	1987	1986	1985
Dividends, Net Income ($)	0.03	—	—	—	—	—	—	—	—	—
Distrib'ns, Cap Gain ($)	0.25	—	—	—	—	—	—	—	—	—
Net Asset Value ($)	14.28	—	—	—	—	—	—	—	—	—
Expense Ratio (%)	na	—	—	—	—	—	—	—	—	—
Net Income to Assets (%)	na	—	—	—	—	—	—	—	—	—
Portfolio Turnover (%)	na	—	—	—	—	—	—	—	—	—
Total Assets (Millions $)	158	—	—	—	—	—	—	—	—	—

PORTFOLIO (as of 5/31/94)

Portfolio Manager: Paul D.A. Nix - 1993

Investm't Category: International Stock

✔ Cap Gain   Asset Allocation
  Cap & Income   Fund of Funds
  Income   Index
                  Sector
  Domestic   Small Cap
✔ Foreign   Socially Conscious
  Country/Region State Specific

Portfolio:	stocks 94%	bonds 0%
convertibles 2%	other 1%	cash 3%

Largest Holdings: Japan 25%, United Kingdom 13%

Unrealized Net Capital Gains: 3% of portfolio value

SHAREHOLDER INFORMATION

Minimum Investment
Initial: $2,500   Subsequent: $100

Minimum IRA Investment
Initial: $750   Subsequent: $0

Maximum Fees
Load: none   12b-1: 0.50%
Other: none

Distributions
Income: Dec   Capital Gains: Dec

Exchange Options
Number Per Year: no limit   Fee: none
Telephone: yes (money market fund available)

Services
IRA, pension, auto exchange, auto invest, auto withdraw

Dreyfus Investors GNMA
(DIGFX)
Mortgage-Backed Bond

200 Park Ave.
New York, NY 10166
(800) 645-6561, (718) 895-1206

PERFORMANCE

fund inception date: 8/5/87

	3yr Annual	5yr Annual	10yr Annual	Bull	Bear
Return (%)	4.8	7.2	na	36.0	-2.8
Differ from Category (+/-)	1.7 high	0.3 abv av	na	-2.0 low	1.6 abv av

Total Risk	Standard Deviation	Category Risk	Risk Index	Avg Mat
low	3.6%	abv av	1.1	14.0 yrs

	1994	1993	1992	1991	1990	1989	1988	1987	1986	1985
Return (%)	-1.0	8.7	6.9	13.2	8.5	8.4	10.5	—	—	—
Differ from category (+/-) . . .	1.8	1.9	0.8	-1.2	-1.2	-4.1	3.4	—	—	—

PER SHARE DATA

	1994	1993	1992	1991	1990	1989	1988	1987	1986	1985
Dividends, Net Income ($)	1.07	1.11	1.16	1.06	1.20	1.22	1.34	—	—	—
Distrib'ns, Cap Gain ($) . . .	0.00	0.00	0.00	0.00	0.00	0.00	0.00	—	—	—
Net Asset Value ($)	14.15	15.39	15.20	15.34	14.55	14.55	14.59	—	—	—
Expense Ratio (%).	0.00	0.00	0.00	0.00	0.00	0.00	0.00	—	—	—
Net Income to Assets (%). .	7.20	7.15	7.70	7.78	8.29	8.64	8.97	—	—	—
Portfolio Turnover (%).	na	34	31	40	0	288	1,026	—	—	—
Total Assets (Millions $)	44	54	45	25	3	3	2	—	—	—

PORTFOLIO (as of 6/30/94)

Portfolio Manager: Garitt Kono - 1992

Investm't Category: Mortgage-Backed Bond

Cap Gain	Asset Allocation
Cap & Income	Fund of Funds
✔ Income	Index
	Sector
✔ Domestic	Small Cap
Foreign	Socially Conscious
Country/Region	State Specific

Portfolio: stocks 0% bonds 94%
convertibles 0% other 0% cash 6%

Largest Holdings: mortgage-backed 85%,
U.S. government 9%

Unrealized Net Capital Gains: -2% of portfolio value

SHAREHOLDER INFORMATION

Minimum Investment
Initial: $2,500   Subsequent: $100

Minimum IRA Investment
Initial: na   Subsequent: na

Maximum Fees
Load: none   12b-1: none
Other: none

Distributions
Income: monthly   Capital Gains: Dec

Exchange Options
Number Per Year: no limit   Fee: none
Telephone: yes (money market fund available)

Services
auto exchange, auto invest, auto withdraw

Dreyfus/Laurel International—Investor

P.O. Box 9692
Providence, RI 02940
(800) 548-2868

(BINTX) *International Stock*

PERFORMANCE

fund inception date: 10/12/88

	3yr Annual	5yr Annual	10yr Annual	Bull	Bear
Return (%)	4.9	0.0	na	36.3	-3.2
Differ from Category (+/-)	-4.2 low	-4.9 low	na	-27.6 low	3.8 high

Total Risk	Standard Deviation	Category Risk	Risk Index	Beta
high	14.1%	abv av	1.1	0.7

	1994	1993	1992	1991	1990	1989	1988	1987	1986	1985
Return (%)	3.5	24.5	-10.3	6.6	-18.5	15.4	—	—	—	—
Differ from category (+/-)	6.5	-14.1	-7.4	-6.5	-8.1	-7.1	—	—	—	—

PER SHARE DATA

	1994	1993	1992	1991	1990	1989	1988	1987	1986	1985
Dividends, Net Income ($)	0.19	0.00	0.00	0.07	0.17	0.18	—	—	—	—
Distrib'ns, Cap Gain ($)	0.00	0.00	0.00	0.14	0.22	0.09	—	—	—	—
Net Asset Value ($)	12.94	12.68	10.18	11.36	10.85	13.79	—	—	—	—
Expense Ratio (%)	1.84	1.79	1.87	1.63	1.63	1.76	—	—	—	—
Net Income to Assets (%)	0.74	0.46	0.24	0.97	1.50	1.52	—	—	—	—
Portfolio Turnover (%)	114	202	110	145	28	47	—	—	—	—
Total Assets (Millions $)	5	5	11	30	31	25	—	—	—	—

PORTFOLIO (as of 8/31/94)

Portfolio Manager: Sandor Cseh - 1994, D. Kirk Henry - 1994

Investm't Category: International Stock
- ✔ Cap Gain
- Cap & Income
- Income
- Domestic
- ✔ Foreign
- Country/Region
- Asset Allocation
- Fund of Funds
- Index
- Sector
- Small Cap
- Socially Conscious
- State Specific

Portfolio: stocks 71% bonds 0%
convertibles 1% other 25% cash 13%

Largest Holdings: France 15%, Germany 12%

Unrealized Net Capital Gains: 2% of portfolio value

SHAREHOLDER INFORMATION

Minimum Investment
Initial: $1,000 Subsequent: $100

Minimum IRA Investment
Initial: $500 Subsequent: $0

Maximum Fees
Load: none 12b-1: 0.25%
Other: none

Distributions
Income: Jun, Dec Capital Gains: Dec

Exchange Options
Number Per Year: 8 Fee: none
Telephone: yes (money market fund available)

Services
IRA, pension, auto exchange, auto invest, auto withdraw

Dreyfus Mass Interm Muni Bond (DMAIX)

Tax-Exempt Bond

200 Park Ave.
New York, NY 10166
(800) 645-6561, (718) 895-1206

PERFORMANCE

fund inception date: 6/26/92

	3yr Annual	5yr Annual	10yr Annual	Bull	Bear
Return (%)	na	na	na	na	-5.3
Differ from Category (+/-)	na	na	na	na	-0.1 av

Total Risk	Standard Deviation	Category Risk	Risk Index	Avg Mat
na	na	na	na	8.3 yrs

	1994	1993	1992	1991	1990	1989	1988	1987	1986	1985
Return (%)	-6.4	12.5	—	—	—	—	—	—	—	—
Differ from category (+/-)	-1.2	0.8	—	—	—	—	—	—	—	—

PER SHARE DATA

	1994	1993	1992	1991	1990	1989	1988	1987	1986	1985
Dividends, Net Income ($)	0.62	0.68	—	—	—	—	—	—	—	—
Distrib'ns, Cap Gain ($)	0.02	0.00	—	—	—	—	—	—	—	—
Net Asset Value ($)	12.22	13.72	—	—	—	—	—	—	—	—
Expense Ratio (%)	0.41	0.00	—	—	—	—	—	—	—	—
Net Income to Assets (%)	4.84	5.17	—	—	—	—	—	—	—	—
Portfolio Turnover (%)	2	9	—	—	—	—	—	—	—	—
Total Assets (Millions $)	67	89	—	—	—	—	—	—	—	—

PORTFOLIO (as of 9/30/94)

Portfolio Manager: Laurence Troutman - 1992

Investm't Category: Tax-Exempt Bond

Cap Gain	Asset Allocation
Cap & Income	Fund of Funds
✔ Income	Index
	Sector
✔ Domestic	Small Cap
Foreign	Socially Conscious
Country/Region	✔ State Specific

Portfolio: stocks 0%   bonds 100%
convertibles 0%   other 0%   cash 0%

Largest Holdings: general obligation 44%

Unrealized Net Capital Gains: -4% of portfolio value

SHAREHOLDER INFORMATION

Minimum Investment
Initial: $2,500   Subsequent: $100

Minimum IRA Investment
Initial: na   Subsequent: na

Maximum Fees
Load: none   12b-1: none
Other: none

Distributions
Income: monthly   Capital Gains: Nov

Exchange Options
Number Per Year: no limit   Fee: none
Telephone: yes (money market fund available)

Services
auto exchange, auto invest, auto withdraw

Dreyfus Mass Tax-Exempt Bond (DMEBX)

200 Park Ave.
New York, NY 10166
(800) 645-6561, (718) 895-1206

Tax-Exempt Bond

PERFORMANCE

fund inception date: 6/11/85

	3yr Annual	5yr Annual	10yr Annual	Bull	Bear
Return (%)	4.3	6.2	na	43.4	-6.2
Differ from Category (+/-)	-0.2 blw av	0.1 av	na	1.6 av	-1.0 blw av

Total Risk	Standard Deviation	Category Risk	Risk Index	Avg Mat
blw av	5.6%	blw av	0.9	21.2 yrs

	1994	1993	1992	1991	1990	1989	1988	1987	1986	1985
Return (%)	-6.0	12.4	7.4	12.6	6.0	7.7	10.5	-3.4	17.9	—
Differ from category (+/-)	-0.8	0.7	-0.9	1.3	-0.3	-1.3	0.3	-2.1	1.5	—

PER SHARE DATA

	1994	1993	1992	1991	1990	1989	1988	1987	1986	1985
Dividends, Net Income ($)	0.90	0.94	0.97	1.03	1.09	1.08	1.09	1.09	1.17	—
Distrib'ns, Cap Gain ($)	0.00	0.45	0.00	0.00	0.00	0.00	0.00	0.00	0.00	—
Net Asset Value ($)	15.21	17.13	16.51	16.30	15.44	15.62	15.54	15.09	16.75	—
Expense Ratio (%)	0.80	0.81	0.84	0.81	0.83	0.83	0.79	0.64	0.26	—
Net Income to Assets (%)	5.30	5.83	6.30	6.87	6.92	7.06	7.18	6.75	7.66	—
Portfolio Turnover (%)	29	85	68	50	55	18	71	39	103	—
Total Assets (Millions $)	147	192	157	121	108	99	84	82	54	—

PORTFOLIO (as of 5/31/94)

Portfolio Manager: Lawrence Troutman - 1986

Investm't Category: Tax-Exempt Bond
Cap Gain	Asset Allocation
Cap & Income	Fund of Funds
✔ Income	Index
	Sector
✔ Domestic	Small Cap
Foreign	Socially Conscious
Country/Region	✔ State Specific

Portfolio: stocks 0%   bonds 95%
convertibles 0%   other 0%   cash 5%

Largest Holdings: general obligation 12%

Unrealized Net Capital Gains: 2% of portfolio value

SHAREHOLDER INFORMATION

Minimum Investment
Initial: $2,500   Subsequent: $100

Minimum IRA Investment
Initial: na   Subsequent: na

Maximum Fees
Load: none   12b-1: none
Other: none

Distributions
Income: monthly   Capital Gains: Dec

Exchange Options
Number Per Year: no limit   Fee: none
Telephone: yes (money market fund available)

Services
auto exchange, auto invest, auto withdraw

Dreyfus Muni Bond

(DRTAX)

Tax-Exempt Bond

200 Park Ave.
New York, NY 10166
(800) 645-6561, (718) 895-1206

PERFORMANCE

fund inception date: 10/4/76

	3yr Annual	5yr Annual	10yr Annual	Bull	Bear
Return (%)	4.3	6.2	8.5	42.7	-6.6
Differ from Category (+/-)	-0.2 blw av	0.1 av	0.4 av	0.9 av	-1.4 blw av

Total Risk	Standard Deviation	Category Risk	Risk Index	Avg Mat
blw av	6.1%	av	1.0	22.5 yrs

	1994	1993	1992	1991	1990	1989	1988	1987	1986	1985
Return (%)	-7.0	12.6	8.4	11.9	6.4	9.3	11.5	-1.7	17.3	19.4
Differ from category (+/-) . .	-1.8	0.9	0.1	0.6	0.1	0.3	1.3	-0.4	0.9	2.0

PER SHARE DATA

	1994	1993	1992	1991	1990	1989	1988	1987	1986	1985
Dividends, Net Income ($) .	0.74	0.78	0.82	0.86	0.90	0.91	0.91	0.92	0.98	1.02
Distrib'ns, Cap Gain ($) . . .	0.07	0.33	0.28	0.00	0.00	0.00	0.00	0.00	0.00	0.00
Net Asset Value ($)	11.63	13.36	12.87	12.92	12.35	12.48	12.27	11.86	13.01	11.97
Expense Ratio (%).	0.68	0.69	0.68	0.67	0.67	0.68	0.71	0.68	0.69	0.69
Net Income to Assets (%). .	5.80	5.96	6.49	7.05	7.23	7.41	7.68	7.34	8.16	9.11
Portfolio Turnover (%). . . .	36	45	68	36	28	36	51	67	53	27
Total Assets (Millions $) . .	3,630	4,675	4,273	4,082	3,594	3,486	3,245	3,528	3,648	2,724

PORTFOLIO (as of 8/31/94)

Portfolio Manager: Richard Moynihan - 1976

Investm't Category: Tax-Exempt Bond

Cap Gain	Asset Allocation
Cap & Income	Fund of Funds
✔ Income	Index
	Sector
✔ Domestic	Small Cap
Foreign	Socially Conscious
Country/Region	State Specific

Portfolio: stocks 0% bonds 96%
convertibles 0% other 0% cash 4%

Largest Holdings: general obligation 8%

Unrealized Net Capital Gains: 1% of portfolio value

SHAREHOLDER INFORMATION

Minimum Investment
Initial: $2,500   Subsequent: $100

Minimum IRA Investment
Initial: na   Subsequent: na

Maximum Fees
Load: none   12b-1: none
Other: none

Distributions
Income: monthly   Capital Gains: Dec

Exchange Options
Number Per Year: no limit   Fee: none
Telephone: yes (money market fund available)

Services
auto exchange, auto invest, auto withdraw

Dreyfus New Leaders
(DNLDX)
Aggressive Growth

200 Park Ave.
New York, NY 10166
(800) 645-6561, (718) 895-1206

PERFORMANCE   fund inception date: 1/29/85

	3yr Annual	5yr Annual	10yr Annual	Bull	Bear
Return (%)	8.5	10.3	na	96.1	-5.5
Differ from Category (+/-)	-0.4 av	-2.2 blw av	na	-37.1 blw av	5.3 high

Total Risk	Standard Deviation	Category Risk	Risk Index	Beta
abv av	9.7%	low	0.6	0.7

	1994	1993	1992	1991	1990	1989	1988	1987	1986	1985
Return (%).	-0.1	17.0	9.4	45.3	-11.8	31.2	23.3	-5.1	12.4	—
Differ from category (+/-) . .	0.6	-2.5	-1.6	-6.8	-5.6	4.4	8.1	-2.9	0.6	—

PER SHARE DATA

	1994	1993	1992	1991	1990	1989	1988	1987	1986	1985
Dividends, Net Income ($).	0.08	0.07	0.14	0.22	0.48	0.38	0.22	0.17	0.01	—
Distrib'ns, Cap Gain ($) . . .	2.61	3.34	2.93	2.74	1.08	1.09	0.00	0.00	0.01	—
Net Asset Value ($)	31.33	34.13	32.17	32.29	24.25	29.27	23.41	19.16	20.34	—
Expense Ratio (%)	na	1.22	1.21	1.29	1.42	1.37	1.50	1.41	1.30	—
Net Income to Assets (%) . . .	na	0.19	0.43	0.76	1.31	1.60	0.90	0.35	0.66	—
Portfolio Turnover (%)	na	127	119	108	129	114	120	177	195	—
Total Assets (Millions $). . . .	391	349	234	194	102	196	112	80	65	—

PORTFOLIO (as of 6/30/94)

Portfolio Manager: Thomas Frank - 1985

Investm't Category: Aggressive Growth

✔ Cap Gain	Asset Allocation
Cap & Income	Fund of Funds
Income	Index
	Sector
✔ Domestic	✔ Small Cap
✔ Foreign	Socially Conscious
Country/Region	State Specific

Portfolio: stocks 80%   bonds 0%
convertibles 0%   other 0%   cash 20%

Largest Holdings: financial 15%, healthcare 13%

Unrealized Net Capital Gains: 4% of portfolio value

SHAREHOLDER INFORMATION

Minimum Investment
Initial: $2,500   Subsequent: $100

Minimum IRA Investment
Initial: $750   Subsequent: $0

Maximum Fees
Load: 1.00% redemption   12b-1: 0.25%
Other: redemption fee applies for 6 mos

Distributions
Income: Dec   Capital Gains: Dec

Exchange Options
Number Per Year: no limit   Fee: none
Telephone: yes (money market fund available)

Services
IRA, pension, auto exchange, auto invest, auto withdraw

Dreyfus NJ Interm Muni Bond (DNJIX)

200 Park Ave.
New York, NY 10166
(800) 645-6561, (718) 895-1206

Tax-Exempt Bond

PERFORMANCE
fund inception date: 6/26/92

	3yr Annual	5yr Annual	10yr Annual	Bull	Bear
Return (%)	na	na	na	na	-5.3
Differ from Category (+/-)	na	na	na	na	-0.1 av

Total Risk	Standard Deviation	Category Risk	Risk Index	Avg Mat
na	na	na	na	8.4 yrs

	1994	1993	1992	1991	1990	1989	1988	1987	1986	1985
Return (%)	-5.2	12.4	—	—	—	—	—	—	—	—
Differ from category (+/-) . . .	0.0	0.7	—	—	—	—	—	—	—	—

PER SHARE DATA

	1994	1993	1992	1991	1990	1989	1988	1987	1986	1985
Dividends, Net Income ($) .	0.65	0.68	—	—	—	—	—	—	—	—
Distrib'ns, Cap Gain ($) . . .	0.00	0.00	—	—	—	—	—	—	—	—
Net Asset Value ($)	12.56	13.93	—	—	—	—	—	—	—	—
Expense Ratio (%).	0.06	0.00	—	—	—	—	—	—	—	—
Net Income to Assets (%). .	4.97	5.27	—	—	—	—	—	—	—	—
Portfolio Turnover (%)	5	na	—	—	—	—	—	—	—	—
Total Assets (Millions $) . . .	212	240	—	—	—	—	—	—	—	—

PORTFOLIO (as of 9/30/94)

Portfolio Manager: Stephen Kris - 1992

Investm't Category: Tax-Exempt Bond

Cap Gain	Asset Allocation
Cap & Income	Fund of Funds
✔ Income	Index
	Sector
✔ Domestic	Small Cap
Foreign	Socially Conscious
Country/Region	✔ State Specific

Portfolio: stocks 0% bonds 100%
convertibles 0% other 0% cash 0%

Largest Holdings: general obligation 47%

Unrealized Net Capital Gains: -2% of portfolio value

SHAREHOLDER INFORMATION

Minimum Investment
Initial: $2,500   Subsequent: $100

Minimum IRA Investment
Initial: na   Subsequent: na

Maximum Fees
Load: none   12b-1: none
Other: none

Distributions
Income: monthly   Capital Gains: Nov

Exchange Options
Number Per Year: no limit   Fee: none
Telephone: yes (money market fund available)

Services
auto exchange, auto invest, auto withdraw

Dreyfus NJ Muni Bond
(DRNJX)
Tax-Exempt Bond

200 Park Ave.
New York, NY 10166
(800) 645-6561, (718) 895-1206

PERFORMANCE   fund inception date: 11/6/87

	3yr Annual	5yr Annual	10yr Annual	Bull	Bear
Return (%)	4.9	6.8	na	44.9	-5.8
Differ from Category (+/-)	0.4 abv av	0.7 abv av	na	3.1 abv av	-0.6 av

Total Risk	Standard Deviation	Category Risk	Risk Index	Avg Mat
blw av	6.0%	av	1.0	20.3 yrs

	1994	1993	1992	1991	1990	1989	1988	1987	1986	1985
Return (%)	-6.0	12.9	8.7	11.9	7.9	9.1	12.6	—	—	—
Differ from category (+/-) . .	-0.8	1.2	0.4	0.6	1.6	0.1	2.4	—	—	—

PER SHARE DATA

	1994	1993	1992	1991	1990	1989	1988	1987	1986	1985
Dividends, Net Income ($) .	0.77	0.79	0.80	0.81	0.83	0.83	0.88	—	—	—
Distrib'ns, Cap Gain ($) . . .	0.02	0.02	0.20	0.04	0.00	0.04	0.00	—	—	—
Net Asset Value ($)	12.41	14.03	13.17	13.06	12.47	12.36	12.16	—	—	—
Expense Ratio (%)	0.79	0.72	0.73	0.75	0.77	0.82	0.39	—	—	—
Net Income to Assets (%) .	5.84	5.74	6.06	6.36	6.74	6.77	7.36	—	—	—
Portfolio Turnover (%)	na	6	34	23	25	35	61	—	—	—
Total Assets (Millions $)	577	724	614	516	350	257	175	—	—	—

PORTFOLIO (as of 6/30/94)

Portfolio Manager: Samuel Weinstock - 1988

Investm't Category: Tax-Exempt Bond

Cap Gain	Asset Allocation
Cap & Income	Fund of Funds
✔ Income	Index
	Sector
✔ Domestic	Small Cap
Foreign	Socially Conscious
Country/Region	✔ State Specific

Portfolio: stocks 0%   bonds 99%
convertibles 0%   other 0%   cash 1%

Largest Holdings: general obligation 14%

Unrealized Net Capital Gains: 4% of portfolio value

SHAREHOLDER INFORMATION

Minimum Investment
Initial: $2,500   Subsequent: $100

Minimum IRA Investment
Initial: na   Subsequent: na

Maximum Fees
Load: none   12b-1: 0.25%
Other: none

Distributions
Income: monthly   Capital Gains: Dec

Exchange Options
Number Per Year: no limit   Fee: none
Telephone: yes (money market fund available)

Services
auto exchange, auto invest, auto withdraw

Dreyfus NY Insured Tax-Exempt (DNYBX)

200 Park Ave.
New York, NY 10166
(800) 645-6561, (718) 895-1206

Tax-Exempt Bond

PERFORMANCE

fund inception date: 2/18/87

	3yr Annual	5yr Annual	10yr Annual	Bull	Bear
Return (%)	4.0	6.1	na	43.9	-6.5
Differ from Category (+/-)	-0.5 blw av	0.0 blw av	na	2.1 av	-1.3 blw av

Total Risk	Standard Deviation	Category Risk	Risk Index	Avg Mat
blw av	6.0%	av	1.0	24.6 yrs

	1994	1993	1992	1991	1990	1989	1988	1987	1986	1985
Return (%)	-6.6	11.0	8.5	13.0	5.9	8.7	11.3	—	—	—
Differ from category (+/-) . .	-1.4	-0.7	0.2	1.7	-0.4	-0.3	1.1	—	—	—

PER SHARE DATA

	1994	1993	1992	1991	1990	1989	1988	1987	1986	1985
Dividends, Net Income ($) .	0.59	0.60	0.63	0.65	0.72	0.71	0.73	—	—	—
Distrib'ns, Cap Gain ($) . . .	0.00	0.22	0.04	0.00	0.00	0.00	0.00	—	—	—
Net Asset Value ($)	10.66	12.04	11.60	11.33	10.64	10.75	10.56	—	—	—
Expense Ratio (%).	0.98	0.96	0.90	0.88	0.50	0.50	0.23	—	—	—
Net Income to Assets (%). .	5.15	5.01	5.49	6.01	6.74	6.64	7.00	—	—	—
Portfolio Turnover (%).	na	19	16	16	63	54	32	—	—	—
Total Assets (Millions $) . . .	151	197	180	148	92	66	45	—	—	—

PORTFOLIO (as of 6/30/94)

Portfolio Manager: Lawrence Troutman - 1987

Investm't Category: Tax-Exempt Bond

Cap Gain	Asset Allocation
Cap & Income	Fund of Funds
✔ Income	Index
	Sector
✔ Domestic	Small Cap
Foreign	Socially Conscious
Country/Region	✔ State Specific

Portfolio: stocks 0%   bonds 100%
convertibles 0%   other 0%   cash 0%

Largest Holdings: general obligation 9%

Unrealized Net Capital Gains: 4% of portfolio value

SHAREHOLDER INFORMATION

Minimum Investment
Initial: $2,500   Subsequent: $100

Minimum IRA Investment
Initial: na   Subsequent: na

Maximum Fees
Load: none   12b-1: 0.25%
Other: none

Distributions
Income: monthly   Capital Gains: Dec

Exchange Options
Number Per Year: no limit   Fee: none
Telephone: yes (money market fund available)

Services
auto exchange, auto invest, auto withdraw

Dreyfus NY Tax-Exempt
(DRNYX)
Tax-Exempt Bond

200 Park Ave.
New York, NY 10166
(800) 645-6561, (718) 895-1206

PERFORMANCE

fund inception date: 7/26/83

	3yr Annual	5yr Annual	10yr Annual	Bull	Bear
Return (%)	4.4	6.2	8.3	44.1	-6.1
Differ from Category (+/-)	-0.1 av	0.1 av	0.2 av	2.3 av	-0.9 blw av

Total Risk	Standard Deviation	Category Risk	Risk Index	Avg Mat
blw av	6.0%	av	1.0	19.8 yrs

	1994	1993	1992	1991	1990	1989	1988	1987	1986	1985
Return (%)	-6.9	12.6	8.8	12.4	5.5	8.9	10.1	-2.6	17.0	20.6
Differ from category (+/-)	-1.7	0.9	0.5	1.1	-0.8	-0.1	-0.1	-1.3	0.6	3.2

PER SHARE DATA

	1994	1993	1992	1991	1990	1989	1988	1987	1986	1985
Dividends, Net Income ($)	0.85	0.90	0.98	1.03	1.05	1.06	1.07	1.08	1.12	1.16
Distrib'ns, Cap Gain ($)	0.10	0.37	0.22	0.00	0.00	0.00	0.00	0.00	0.00	0.00
Net Asset Value ($)	14.09	16.15	15.51	15.40	14.67	14.94	14.73	14.39	15.89	14.59
Expense Ratio (%)	0.71	0.70	0.69	0.70	0.70	0.69	0.72	0.71	0.71	0.76
Net Income to Assets (%)	5.49	6.03	6.69	7.08	7.12	7.34	7.41	7.04	7.83	8.74
Portfolio Turnover (%)	35	51	40	26	31	38	57	38	14	28
Total Assets (Millions $)	1,702	2,145	1,898	1,752	1,681	1,643	1,463	1,538	1,245	652

PORTFOLIO (as of 5/31/94)

Portfolio Manager: Monica Wieboldt - 1985

Investm't Category: Tax-Exempt Bond

Cap Gain	Asset Allocation
Cap & Income	Fund of Funds
✔ Income	Index
	Sector
✔ Domestic	Small Cap
Foreign	Socially Conscious
Country/Region	✔ State Specific

Portfolio: stocks 0% bonds 94%
convertibles 0% other 0% cash 6%

Largest Holdings: general obligation 17%

Unrealized Net Capital Gains: 3% of portfolio value

SHAREHOLDER INFORMATION

Minimum Investment
Initial: $2,500   Subsequent: $100

Minimum IRA Investment
Initial: na   Subsequent: na

Maximum Fees
Load: none   12b-1: none
Other: none

Distributions
Income: monthly   Capital Gains: Dec

Exchange Options
Number Per Year: no limit   Fee: none
Telephone: yes (money market fund available)

Services
auto exchange, auto invest, auto withdraw

Dreyfus NY Tax-Exempt Interm (DRNIX)

200 Park Ave.
New York, NY 10166
(800) 645-6561, (718) 895-1206

Tax-Exempt Bond

PERFORMANCE

fund inception date: 6/12/87

	3yr Annual	5yr Annual	10yr Annual	Bull	Bear
Return (%)	4.9	6.4	na	41.7	-4.4
Differ from Category (+/-)	0.4 abv av	0.3 av	na	-0.1 blw av	0.8 abv av

Total Risk	Standard Deviation	Category Risk	Risk Index	Avg Mat
blw av	5.1%	blw av	0.8	9.0 yrs

	1994	1993	1992	1991	1990	1989	1988	1987	1986	1985
Return (%)	-5.1	11.5	9.3	11.1	6.0	9.2	9.5	—	—	—
Differ from category (+/-) . . .	0.1	-0.2	1.0	-0.2	-0.3	0.2	-0.7	—	—	—

PER SHARE DATA

	1994	1993	1992	1991	1990	1989	1988	1987	1986	1985
Dividends, Net Income ($) .	0.86	0.90	0.97	1.03	1.11	1.11	1.09	—	—	—
Distrib'ns, Cap Gain ($) . . .	0.00	0.03	0.11	0.08	0.06	0.00	0.00	—	—	—
Net Asset Value ($)	16.89	18.69	17.63	17.15	16.48	16.68	16.32	—	—	—
Expense Ratio (%).	0.89	0.85	0.85	0.60	0.30	0.24	0.00	—	—	—
Net Income to Assets (%). .	4.81	5.25	5.95	6.48	6.75	6.80	6.58	—	—	—
Portfolio Turnover (%)	20	17	29	56	38	7	1	—	—	—
Total Assets (Millions $) . . .	338	416	174	113	94	58	25	—	—	—

PORTFOLIO (as of 5/31/94)

Portfolio Manager: Monica Wieboldt - 1987

Investm't Category: Tax-Exempt Bond

Cap Gain	Asset Allocation
Cap & Income	Fund of Funds
✔ Income	Index
	Sector
✔ Domestic	Small Cap
Foreign	Socially Conscious
Country/Region	✔ State Specific

Portfolio: stocks 0%   bonds 99%
convertibles 0%   other 0%   cash 1%

Largest Holdings: general obligation 15%

Unrealized Net Capital Gains: 1% of portfolio value

SHAREHOLDER INFORMATION

Minimum Investment
Initial: $2,500   Subsequent: $100

Minimum IRA Investment
Initial: na   Subsequent: na

Maximum Fees
Load: none   12b-1: 0.25%
Other: none

Distributions
Income: monthly   Capital Gains: Nov

Exchange Options
Number Per Year: no limit   Fee: none
Telephone: yes (money market fund available)

Services
auto exchange, auto invest, auto withdraw

Dreyfus Peoples Index
(PEOPX)
Growth & Income

200 Park Ave.
New York, NY 10166
(800) 645-6561, (718) 895-1206

	3yr Annual	5yr Annual	10yr Annual	Bull	Bear
Return (%)	5.8	7.9	na	72.3	-6.8
Differ from Category (+/-)	-1.3 blw av	0.0 av	na	-3.5 av	-0.5 blw av

Total Risk	Standard Deviation	Category Risk	Risk Index	Beta
av	7.9%	av	1.0	1.0

	1994	1993	1992	1991	1990	1989	1988	1987	1986	1985
Return (%)	0.6	9.5	7.7	29.8	-5.1	—	—	—	—	—
Differ from category (+/-)	2.0	-3.7	-2.5	2.2	0.9	—	—	—	—	—

PER SHARE DATA

	1994	1993	1992	1991	1990	1989	1988	1987	1986	1985
Dividends, Net Income ($)	0.42	0.31	0.40	0.38	0.22	—	—	—	—	—
Distrib'ns, Cap Gain ($)	1.33	0.66	0.04	0.00	0.00	—	—	—	—	—
Net Asset Value ($)	14.29	15.93	15.43	14.73	11.64	—	—	—	—	—
Expense Ratio (%)	na	0.39	0.00	0.00	0.00	—	—	—	—	—
Net Income to Assets (%)	na	2.36	3.04	3.45	3.46	—	—	—	—	—
Portfolio Turnover (%)	na	3	3	1	1	—	—	—	—	—
Total Assets (Millions $)	209	295	93	69	29	—	—	—	—	—

PORTFOLIO (as of 4/30/94)

Portfolio Manager: Geraldine Hom - 1990

Investm't Category: Growth & Income

Cap Gain	Asset Allocation
✔ Cap & Income	Fund of Funds
Income	✔ Index
	Sector
✔ Domestic	Small Cap
Foreign	Socially Conscious
Country/Region	State Specific

Portfolio: stocks 95%   bonds 0%
convertibles 0%   other 0%   cash 5%

Largest Holdings: S&P 500 composite stock price index

Unrealized Net Capital Gains: 8% of portfolio value

SHAREHOLDER INFORMATION

Minimum Investment
Initial: $2,500   Subsequent: $100

Minimum IRA Investment
Initial: $750   Subsequent: $0

Maximum Fees
Load: 1.00% redemption   12b-1: none
Other: redemption fee applies for 6 mos

Distributions
Income: Dec   Capital Gains: Dec

Exchange Options
Number Per Year: no limit   Fee: none
Telephone: none

Services
IRA, pension, auto invest

Dreyfus Peoples S&P MidCap Index (PESPX)

200 Park Ave.
New York, NY 10166
(800) 645-6561, (718) 895-1206

Growth

PERFORMANCE

fund inception date: 6/19/91

	3yr Annual	5yr Annual	10yr Annual	Bull	Bear
Return (%)	6.8	na	na	na	-9.6
Differ from Category (+/-)	-0.9 av	na	na	na	-3.0 low

Total Risk	Standard Deviation	Category Risk	Risk Index	Beta
abv av	9.8%	av	1.0	1.0

	1994	1993	1992	1991	1990	1989	1988	1987	1986	1985
Return (%)	-3.9	13.5	11.9	—	—	—	—	—	—	—
Differ from category (+/-) . .	-3.3	0.1	0.3	—	—	—	—	—	—	—

PER SHARE DATA

	1994	1993	1992	1991	1990	1989	1988	1987	1986	1985
Dividends, Net Income ($) .	0.28	0.27	0.27	—	—	—	—	—	—	—
Distrib'ns, Cap Gain ($) . . .	0.75	0.56	0.26	—	—	—	—	—	—	—
Net Asset Value ($)	15.48	17.19	15.87	—	—	—	—	—	—	—
Expense Ratio (%).	na	0.09	0.00	—	—	—	—	—	—	—
Net Income to Assets (%). . .	na	1.97	2.22	—	—	—	—	—	—	—
Portfolio Turnover (%).	na	16	16	—	—	—	—	—	—	—
Total Assets (Millions $)	79	74	46	—	—	—	—	—	—	—

PORTFOLIO (as of 4/30/94)

Portfolio Manager: not specified

Investm't Category: Growth

✔ Cap Gain	Asset Allocation
Cap & Income	Fund of Funds
Income	✔ Index
	Sector
✔ Domestic	Small Cap
Foreign	Socially Conscious
Country/Region	State Specific

Portfolio: stocks 100% bonds 0%
convertibles 0% other 0% cash 0%

Largest Holdings: S&P MidCap 400 index

Unrealized Net Capital Gains: 6% of portfolio value

SHAREHOLDER INFORMATION

Minimum Investment
Initial: $2,500   Subsequent: $100

Minimum IRA Investment
Initial: $750   Subsequent: $0

Maximum Fees
Load: 1.00% redemption   12b-1: none
Other: redemption fee applies for 6 mos

Distributions
Income: Dec   Capital Gains: Dec

Exchange Options
Number Per Year: no limit   Fee: none
Telephone: none

Services
IRA, pension, auto invest

Dreyfus Short Interm Gov't (DSIGX)

Government Bond

200 Park Ave.
New York, NY 10166
(800) 645-6561, (718) 895-1206

PERFORMANCE

fund inception date: 4/16/87

	3yr Annual	5yr Annual	10yr Annual	Bull	Bear
Return (%)	4.4	7.3	na	35.7	-1.6
Differ from Category (+/-)	0.4 abv av	0.6 abv av	na	-15.5 low	4.8 high

Total Risk	Standard Deviation	Category Risk	Risk Index	Avg Mat
low	2.8%	blw av	0.6	2.3 yrs

	1994	1993	1992	1991	1990	1989	1988	1987	1986	1985
Return (%)..............	-0.7	7.3	7.0	13.4	10.0	11.2	5.6	—	—	—
Differ from category (+/-) ..	4.1	-3.6	0.6	-1.9	3.8	-3.3	-2.3	—	—	—

PER SHARE DATA

	1994	1993	1992	1991	1990	1989	1988	1987	1986	1985
Dividends, Net Income ($).	0.76	0.78	0.82	0.84	0.99	1.02	0.95	—	—	—
Distrib'ns, Cap Gain ($) ...	0.00	0.06	0.27	0.21	0.00	0.00	0.00	—	—	—
Net Asset Value ($)	10.53	11.37	11.39	11.69	11.28	11.20	11.03	—	—	—
Expense Ratio (%)	0.42	0.40	0.35	0.49	0.00	0.00	0.00	—	—	—
Net Income to Assets (%) .	6.78	6.75	7.00	7.41	8.90	9.24	8.56	—	—	—
Portfolio Turnover (%)	na	317	226	132	25	17	89	—	—	—
Total Assets (Millions $)....	473	556	334	144	63	32	18	—	—	—

PORTFOLIO (as of 5/31/94)

Portfolio Manager: Gerald Thunelius - 1994

Investm't Category: Government Bond

Cap Gain	Asset Allocation
Cap & Income	Fund of Funds
✔ Income	Index
	Sector
✔ Domestic	Small Cap
Foreign	Socially Conscious
Country/Region	State Specific

Portfolio: stocks 0%   bonds 93%
convertibles 0%   other 0%   cash 7%

Largest Holdings: U. S. government and agencies 83%, mortgage-backed 10%

Unrealized Net Capital Gains: -2% of portfolio value

SHAREHOLDER INFORMATION

Minimum Investment
Initial: $2,500   Subsequent: $100

Minimum IRA Investment
Initial: $750   Subsequent: $0

Maximum Fees
Load: none   12b-1: none
Other: none

Distributions
Income: monthly   Capital Gains: Dec

Exchange Options
Number Per Year: no limit   Fee: none
Telephone: yes (money market fund available)

Services
IRA, pension, auto exchange, auto invest, auto withdraw

Dreyfus Short Term Income (DSTIX)

200 Park Ave.
New York, NY 10166
(800) 645-6561, (718) 895-1206

General Bond

PERFORMANCE

fund inception date: 8/18/92

	3yr Annual	5yr Annual	10yr Annual	Bull	Bear
Return (%)	na	na	na	na	-1.9
Differ from Category (+/-)	na	na	na	na	1.9 high

Total Risk	Standard Deviation	Category Risk	Risk Index	Avg Mat
na	na	na	na	2.6 yrs

	1994	1993	1992	1991	1990	1989	1988	1987	1986	1985
Return (%)	0.1	9.1	—	—	—	—	—	—	—	—
Differ from category (+/-)	2.1	-0.1	—	—	—	—	—	—	—	—

PER SHARE DATA

	1994	1993	1992	1991	1990	1989	1988	1987	1986	1985
Dividends, Net Income ($)	0.83	0.91	—	—	—	—	—	—	—	—
Distrib'ns, Cap Gain ($)	0.00	0.00	—	—	—	—	—	—	—	—
Net Asset Value ($)	11.60	12.42	—	—	—	—	—	—	—	—
Expense Ratio (%)	0.24	na	—	—	—	—	—	—	—	—
Net Income to Assets (%)	6.79	7.58	—	—	—	—	—	—	—	—
Portfolio Turnover (%)	74	na	—	—	—	—	—	—	—	—
Total Assets (Millions $)	223	325	—	—	—	—	—	—	—	—

PORTFOLIO (as of 7/31/94)

Portfolio Manager: Gerald Thunelius - 1994

Investm't Category: General Bond

Cap Gain	Asset Allocation
Cap & Income	Fund of Funds
✔ Income	Index
	Sector
✔ Domestic	Small Cap
✔ Foreign	Socially Conscious
Country/Region	State Specific

Portfolio:	stocks 0%	bonds 91%
convertibles 0%	other 0%	cash 9%

Largest Holdings: corporate 77%, U.S. government 5%

Unrealized Net Capital Gains: -2% of portfolio value

SHAREHOLDER INFORMATION

Minimum Investment
Initial: $2,500   Subsequent: $100

Minimum IRA Investment
Initial: $750   Subsequent: $0

Maximum Fees
Load: none   12b-1: 0.20%
Other: none

Distributions
Income: monthly   Capital Gains: Dec

Exchange Options
Number Per Year: no limit   Fee: none
Telephone: yes (money market fund available)

Services
IRA, pension, auto exchange, auto invest, auto withdraw

Dreyfus Short-Interm Municipal (DSIBX)

Tax-Exempt Bond

200 Park Ave.
New York, NY 10166
(800) 645-6561, (718) 895-1206

PERFORMANCE

fund inception date: 4/30/87

	3yr Annual	5yr Annual	10yr Annual	Bull	Bear
Return (%)	4.2	5.5	na	26.5	-1.0
Differ from Category (+/-)	-0.3 blw av	-0.6 low	na	-15.3 low	4.2 high

Total Risk	Standard Deviation	Category Risk	Risk Index	Avg Mat
low	1.7%	low	0.2	2.1 yrs

	1994	1993	1992	1991	1990	1989	1988	1987	1986	1985
Return (%)	-0.3	6.6	6.7	8.2	6.6	6.5	5.7	—	—	—
Differ from category (+/-)	4.9	-5.1	-1.6	-3.1	0.3	-2.5	-4.5	—	—	—

PER SHARE DATA

	1994	1993	1992	1991	1990	1989	1988	1987	1986	1985
Dividends, Net Income ($)	0.57	0.57	0.66	0.71	0.78	0.78	0.75	—	—	—
Distrib'ns, Cap Gain ($)	0.00	0.01	0.02	0.00	0.00	0.00	0.00	—	—	—
Net Asset Value ($)	12.70	13.31	13.05	12.88	12.58	12.55	12.54	—	—	—
Expense Ratio (%)	0.74	0.75	0.72	0.59	0.50	0.43	0.00	—	—	—
Net Income to Assets (%)	4.35	4.76	5.42	6.07	6.29	6.01	5.81	—	—	—
Portfolio Turnover (%)	34	31	64	67	100	126	63	—	—	—
Total Assets (Millions $)	427	575	188	77	64	60	47	—	—	—

PORTFOLIO (as of 3/31/94)

Portfolio Manager: Samuel Weinstock - 1987

Investm't Category: Tax-Exempt Bond

Cap Gain	Asset Allocation
Cap & Income	Fund of Funds
✔ Income	Index
	Sector
✔ Domestic	Small Cap
Foreign	Socially Conscious
Country/Region	State Specific

Portfolio: stocks 0% bonds 100%
convertibles 0% other 0% cash 0%

Largest Holdings: general obligation 20%

Unrealized Net Capital Gains: 0% of portfolio value

SHAREHOLDER INFORMATION

Minimum Investment
Initial: $2,500   Subsequent: $100

Minimum IRA Investment
Initial: na   Subsequent: na

Maximum Fees
Load: none   12b-1: 0.10%
Other: none

Distributions
Income: monthly   Capital Gains: Dec

Exchange Options
Number Per Year: no limit   Fee: none
Telephone: yes (money market fund available)

Services
auto exchange, auto invest, auto withdraw

Dreyfus Special Growth—Investor (BOSSX)

P.O. Box 9692
Providence, RI 02940
(800) 548-2868

Aggressive Growth

PERFORMANCE

	3yr Annual	5yr Annual	10yr Annual	Bull	Bear
Return (%)	7.3	8.7	11.8	121.1	-11.7
Differ from Category (+/-)	-1.6 av	-3.8 blw av	-2.2 blw av	-12.1 av	-0.9 av

Total Risk	Standard Deviation	Category Risk	Risk Index	Beta
high	15.3%	abv av	1.0	1.1

	1994	1993	1992	1991	1990	1989	1988	1987	1986	1985
Return (%)	-18.2	20.0	26.1	29.2	-4.8	18.8	21.4	-3.8	7.6	34.8
Differ from category (+/-) .	-17.5	0.5	15.1	-22.9	1.4	-8.0	6.2	-1.6	-4.2	2.5

PER SHARE DATA

	1994	1993	1992	1991	1990	1989	1988	1987	1986	1985
Dividends, Net Income ($) .	0.00	0.00	0.19	0.00	0.03	0.25	0.34	0.81	0.31	0.35
Distrib'ns, Cap Gain ($) . . .	0.05	1.79	1.62	2.82	0.00	2.37	0.00	4.10	4.96	0.00
Net Asset Value ($)	14.64	17.97	16.45	14.59	13.56	14.28	14.27	12.02	17.21	20.95
Expense Ratio (%).	1.54	1.73	1.57	1.70	1.62	1.72	1.58	1.49	1.32	1.35
Net Income to Assets (%).	-0.53	-1.09	-0.71	-0.34	0.19	0.82	2.70	3.25	1.16	1.96
Portfolio Turnover (%)	na	94	112	141	222	184	183	322	192	257
Total Assets (Millions $) . . .	64	118	64	42	44	40	35	31	35	53

PORTFOLIO (as of 6/30/94)

Portfolio Manager: Guy Scott - 1990

Investm't Category: Aggressive Growth
✔ Cap Gain   Asset Allocation
  Cap & Income   Fund of Funds
  Income   Index
                    Sector
✔ Domestic   Small Cap
✔ Foreign   Socially Conscious
  Country/Region   State Specific

Portfolio: stocks 86%   bonds 0%
convertibles 1%   other 0%   cash 13%

Largest Holdings: energy 24%, consumer services 17%

Unrealized Net Capital Gains: -3% of portfolio value

SHAREHOLDER INFORMATION

Minimum Investment
Initial: $1,000   Subsequent: $0

Minimum IRA Investment
Initial: $500   Subsequent: $0

Maximum Fees
Load: none   12b-1: 0.25%
Other: none

Distributions
Income: Dec   Capital Gains: Dec

Exchange Options
Number Per Year: 12   Fee: none
Telephone: yes (money market fund available)

Services
IRA, pension, auto exchange, auto invest, auto withdraw

Dreyfus Third Century

(DRTHX)

Growth & Income

200 Park Ave.
New York, NY 10166
(800) 645-6561, (718) 895-1206

PERFORMANCE

fund inception date: 3/29/72

	3yr Annual	5yr Annual	10yr Annual	Bull	Bear
Return (%)	-0.2	7.2	11.0	70.9	-10.5
Differ from Category (+/-)	-7.3 low	-0.7 blw av	-0.7 blw av	-4.9 blw av	-4.2 low

Total Risk	Standard Deviation	Category Risk	Risk Index	Beta
abv av	9.0%	abv av	1.1	0.8

	1994	1993	1992	1991	1990	1989	1988	1987	1986	1985
Return (%)	-7.4	5.2	1.9	38.0	3.4	17.3	23.2	2.6	4.5	29.7
Differ from category (+/-)	-6.0	-8.0	-8.3	10.4	9.4	-4.1	6.2	2.0	-11.3	4.0

PER SHARE DATA

	1994	1993	1992	1991	1990	1989	1988	1987	1986	1985
Dividends, Net Income ($)	0.07	0.04	0.05	0.08	0.12	0.18	0.30	0.36	0.31	0.21
Distrib'ns, Cap Gain ($)	1.01	0.61	0.06	0.22	0.23	0.19	0.26	1.27	0.96	0.51
Net Asset Value ($)	6.53	8.26	8.48	8.42	6.33	6.45	5.82	5.18	6.51	7.50
Expense Ratio (%)	1.17	1.11	1.08	1.04	1.05	1.04	1.02	0.99	0.97	1.01
Net Income to Assets (%)	0.52	0.48	0.83	1.10	3.19	4.71	2.94	2.95	3.72	3.39
Portfolio Turnover (%)	71	67	48	73	163	53	37	33	63	44
Total Assets (Millions $)	347	517	443	266	196	169	153	170	176	174

PORTFOLIO (as of 5/31/94)

Portfolio Manager: Maceo Sloan - 1994

Investm't Category: Growth & Income
Cap Gain	Asset Allocation
✔ Cap & Income	Fund of Funds
Income	Index
	Sector
✔ Domestic	Small Cap
Foreign	✔ Socially Conscious
Country/Region	State Specific

Portfolio: stocks 68% bonds 0%
convertibles 0% other 0% cash 32%

Largest Holdings: finance 15%, technology 9%

Unrealized Net Capital Gains: 13% of portfolio value

SHAREHOLDER INFORMATION

Minimum Investment
Initial: $2,500   Subsequent: $100

Minimum IRA Investment
Initial: $750   Subsequent: $0

Maximum Fees
Load: none   12b-1: none
Other: none

Distributions
Income: Dec   Capital Gains: Dec

Exchange Options
Number Per Year: no limit   Fee: none
Telephone: yes (money market fund available)

Services
IRA, pension, auto exchange, auto invest, auto withdraw

Dupree KY Tax-Free Income (KYTFX)

Tax-Exempt Bond

P.O. Box 1149
Lexington, KY 40589
(800) 866-0614, (606) 254-7741

PERFORMANCE

fund inception date: 7/1/79

	3yr Annual	5yr Annual	10yr Annual	Bull	Bear
Return (%)	6.0	7.2	8.7	41.5	-5.0
Differ from Category (+/-)	1.5 high	1.1 high	0.6 abv av	-0.3 blw av	0.2 abv av

Total Risk	Standard Deviation	Category Risk	Risk Index	Avg Mat
low	4.6%	low	0.7	12.8 yrs

	1994	1993	1992	1991	1990	1989	1988	1987	1986	1985
Return (%)	-2.9	12.6	9.0	10.6	7.3	10.7	10.3	-0.9	16.8	15.8
Differ from category (+/-) . . .	2.3	0.9	0.7	-0.7	1.0	1.7	0.1	0.4	0.4	-1.6

PER SHARE DATA

	1994	1993	1992	1991	1990	1989	1988	1987	1986	1985
Dividends, Net Income ($) .	0.40	0.42	0.43	0.45	0.46	0.47	0.47	0.48	0.53	0.56
Distrib'ns, Cap Gain ($) . . .	0.00	0.05	0.00	0.00	0.00	0.00	0.00	0.00	0.00	0.00
Net Asset Value ($)	7.09	7.72	7.28	7.09	6.83	6.80	6.58	6.41	6.96	6.43
Expense Ratio (%).	0.69	0.67	0.71	0.75	0.76	0.78	0.81	0.79	0.78	0.76
Net Income to Assets (%). .	5.82	5.79	6.28	6.63	6.82	7.44	7.40	7.32	8.39	9.31
Portfolio Turnover (%)	30	31	12	18	36	44	87	54	28	30
Total Assets (Millions $) . . .	246	271	169	114	88	73	61	62	36	19

PORTFOLIO (as of 6/30/94)

Portfolio Manager: William Griggs - 1989

Investm't Category: Tax-Exempt Bond

Cap Gain	Asset Allocation
Cap & Income	Fund of Funds
✔ Income	Index
	Sector
✔ Domestic	Small Cap
Foreign	Socially Conscious
Country/Region	✔ State Specific

Portfolio: stocks 0%   bonds 100%
convertibles 0%   other 0%   cash 0%

Largest Holdings: general obligation 0%

Unrealized Net Capital Gains: 1% of portfolio value

SHAREHOLDER INFORMATION

Minimum Investment
Initial: $100   Subsequent: $100

Minimum IRA Investment
Initial: na   Subsequent: na

Maximum Fees
Load: none   12b-1: none
Other: none

Distributions
Income: quarterly   Capital Gains: Jun, Dec

Exchange Options
Number Per Year: no limit   Fee: none
Telephone: yes (money market fund not available)

Services
auto exchange, auto invest, auto withdraw

Dupree KY Tax-Free Short to Medium (KYSMX)

Tax-Exempt Bond

P.O. Box 1149
Lexington, KY 40589
(800) 866-0614, (606) 254-7741

PERFORMANCE

fund inception date: 9/15/87

	3yr Annual	5yr Annual	10yr Annual	Bull	Bear
Return (%)	4.4	5.5	na	25.1	-1.4
Differ from Category (+/-)	-0.1 av	-0.6 low	na	-16.7 low	3.8 high

Total Risk	Standard Deviation	Category Risk	Risk Index	Avg Mat
low	1.8%	low	0.3	2.8 yrs

	1994	1993	1992	1991	1990	1989	1988	1987	1986	1985
Return (%).............	1.0	5.6	6.8	7.2	6.8	7.4	5.1	—	—	—
Differ from category (+/-) ..	6.2	-6.1	-1.5	-4.1	0.5	-1.6	-5.1	—	—	—

PER SHARE DATA

	1994	1993	1992	1991	1990	1989	1988	1987	1986	1985
Dividends, Net Income ($).	0.20	0.22	0.25	0.27	0.29	0.30	0.28	—	—	—
Distrib'ns, Cap Gain ($) ...	0.00	0.00	0.00	0.00	0.00	0.00	0.00	—	—	—
Net Asset Value ($)	5.15	5.30	5.23	5.13	5.04	5.00	4.94	—	—	—
Expense Ratio (%)	0.72	0.76	0.76	0.76	0.76	0.75	0.75	—	—	—
Net Income to Assets (%) .	3.92	4.37	4.96	5.58	5.79	5.88	5.48	—	—	—
Portfolio Turnover (%)	17	22	29	26	58	41	103	—	—	—
Total Assets (Millions $).....	61	70	34	13	6	7	3	—	—	—

PORTFOLIO (as of 6/30/94)

Portfolio Manager: William Griggs - 1989

Investm't Category: Tax-Exempt Bond

Cap Gain	Asset Allocation
Cap & Income	Fund of Funds
✔ Income	Index
	Sector
✔ Domestic	Small Cap
Foreign	Socially Conscious
Country/Region	✔ State Specific

Portfolio: stocks 0%   bonds 100%
convertibles 0%   other 0%   cash 0%

Largest Holdings: general obligation 0%

Unrealized Net Capital Gains: 0% of portfolio value

SHAREHOLDER INFORMATION

Minimum Investment
Initial: $100   Subsequent: $100

Minimum IRA Investment
Initial: na   Subsequent: na

Maximum Fees
Load: none   12b-1: none
Other: none

Distributions
Income: monthly   Capital Gains: Dec

Exchange Options
Number Per Year: no limit   Fee: none
Telephone: yes (money market fund not available)

Services
auto exchange, auto invest, auto withdraw

Eaton Vance Classic Gov't Obligations (ECGOX)

Mortgage-Backed Bond

24 Federal Street
Boston, MA 02110
(800) 225-6265, (617) 482-8260

PERFORMANCE

fund inception date: 11/1/93

	3yr Annual	5yr Annual	10yr Annual	Bull	Bear
Return (%)	na	na	na	na	-3.6
Differ from Category (+/-)	na	na	na	na	0.8 av

Total Risk	Standard Deviation	Category Risk	Risk Index	Avg Mat
na	na	na	na	na

	1994	1993	1992	1991	1990	1989	1988	1987	1986	1985
Return (%)	-2.6	—	—	—	—	—	—	—	—	—
Differ from category (+/-) . . .	0.2	—	—	—	—	—	—	—	—	—

PER SHARE DATA

	1994	1993	1992	1991	1990	1989	1988	1987	1986	1985
Dividends, Net Income ($) .	0.71	—	—	—	—	—	—	—	—	—
Distrib'ns, Cap Gain ($) . . .	0.00	—	—	—	—	—	—	—	—	—
Net Asset Value ($)	8.98	—	—	—	—	—	—	—	—	—
Expense Ratio (%).	2.60	—	—	—	—	—	—	—	—	—
Net Income to Assets (%). .	6.41	—	—	—	—	—	—	—	—	—
Portfolio Turnover (%)	na	—	—	—	—	—	—	—	—	—
Total Assets (Millions $)	39	—	—	—	—	—	—	—	—	—

PORTFOLIO (as of 6/30/94)

Portfolio Manager: Susan Schiff - 1993

Investm't Category: Mortgage-Backed Bond

Cap Gain	Asset Allocation
Cap & Income	Fund of Funds
✔ Income	Index
	Sector
✔ Domestic	Small Cap
Foreign	Socially Conscious
Country/Region	State Specific

Portfolio: stocks 0%   bonds 99%
convertibles 0%   other 0%   cash 1%

Largest Holdings: mortgage-backed 85%, U.S. government 14%

Unrealized Net Capital Gains: -1% of portfolio value

SHAREHOLDER INFORMATION

Minimum Investment
Initial: $1,000   Subsequent: $50

Minimum IRA Investment
Initial: $50   Subsequent: $50

Maximum Fees
Load: none   12b-1: 1.00%
Other: none

Distributions
Income: monthly   Capital Gains: Dec

Exchange Options
Number Per Year: no limit   Fee: none
Telephone: yes (money market fund not available)

Services
IRA, pension, auto invest, auto withdraw

Eaton Vance Classic Nat'l Ltd Maturity TF (EZNAX)

24 Federal Street
Boston, MA 02110
(800) 225-6265, (617) 482-8260

Tax-Exempt Bond

PERFORMANCE

fund inception date: 12/8/93

	3yr Annual	5yr Annual	10yr Annual	Bull	Bear
Return (%)	na	na	na	na	-3.3
Differ from Category (+/-)	na	na	na	na	1.9 high

Total Risk	Standard Deviation	Category Risk	Risk Index	Avg Mat
na	na	na	na	6.7 yrs

	1994	1993	1992	1991	1990	1989	1988	1987	1986	1985
Return (%)	-3.1	—	—	—	—	—	—	—	—	—
Differ from category (+/-)	2.1	—	—	—	—	—	—	—	—	—

PER SHARE DATA

	1994	1993	1992	1991	1990	1989	1988	1987	1986	1985
Dividends, Net Income ($)	0.45	—	—	—	—	—	—	—	—	—
Distrib'ns, Cap Gain ($)	0.00	—	—	—	—	—	—	—	—	—
Net Asset Value ($)	9.26	—	—	—	—	—	—	—	—	—
Expense Ratio (%)	1.51	—	—	—	—	—	—	—	—	—
Net Income to Assets (%)	3.96	—	—	—	—	—	—	—	—	—
Portfolio Turnover (%)	na	—	—	—	—	—	—	—	—	—
Total Assets (Millions $)	21	—	—	—	—	—	—	—	—	—

PORTFOLIO (as of 9/30/94)

Portfolio Manager: Raymond E. Hender - 1993

Investm't Category: Tax-Exempt Bond

Cap Gain	Asset Allocation
Cap & Income	Fund of Funds
✔ Income	Index
	Sector
✔ Domestic	Small Cap
Foreign	Socially Conscious
Country/Region	State Specific

Portfolio: stocks 0%   bonds 100%
convertibles 0%   other 0%   cash 0%

Largest Holdings: general obligation 13%

Unrealized Net Capital Gains: -1% of portfolio value

SHAREHOLDER INFORMATION

Minimum Investment
Initial: $1,000   Subsequent: $50

Minimum IRA Investment
Initial: na   Subsequent: na

Maximum Fees
Load: none   12b-1: 1.00%
Other: none

Distributions
Income: monthly   Capital Gains: Dec

Exchange Options
Number Per Year: no limit   Fee: none
Telephone: yes (money market fund available)

Services
auto invest, auto withdraw

Eaton Vance Classic National Municipals

24 Federal Street
Boston, MA 02110
(800) 225-6265, (617) 482-8260

(ECHMX) *Tax-Exempt Bond*

PERFORMANCE

fund inception date: 12/3/93

	3yr Annual	5yr Annual	10yr Annual	Bull	Bear
Return (%)	na	na	na	na	-7.2
Differ from Category (+/-)	na	na	na	na	-2.0 low

Total Risk	Standard Deviation	Category Risk	Risk Index	Avg Mat
na	na	na	na	25.2 yrs

	1994	1993	1992	1991	1990	1989	1988	1987	1986	1985
Return (%)	-7.9	—	—	—	—	—	—	—	—	—
Differ from category (+/-)	-2.7	—	—	—	—	—	—	—	—	—

PER SHARE DATA

	1994	1993	1992	1991	1990	1989	1988	1987	1986	1985
Dividends, Net Income ($)	0.61	—	—	—	—	—	—	—	—	—
Distrib'ns, Cap Gain ($)	0.00	—	—	—	—	—	—	—	—	—
Net Asset Value ($)	8.62	—	—	—	—	—	—	—	—	—
Expense Ratio (%)	1.59	—	—	—	—	—	—	—	—	—
Net Income to Assets (%)	4.80	—	—	—	—	—	—	—	—	—
Portfolio Turnover (%)	na	—	—	—	—	—	—	—	—	—
Total Assets (Millions $)	37	—	—	—	—	—	—	—	—	—

PORTFOLIO (as of 3/31/94)

Portfolio Manager: Thomas Metzold - 1993

Investm't Category: Tax-Exempt Bond

Cap Gain	Asset Allocation
Cap & Income	Fund of Funds
✔ Income	Index
	Sector
✔ Domestic	Small Cap
Foreign	Socially Conscious
Country/Region	State Specific

Portfolio: stocks 0%   bonds 100%
convertibles 0%   other 0%   cash 0%

Largest Holdings: general obligation 2%

Unrealized Net Capital Gains: 0% of portfolio value

SHAREHOLDER INFORMATION

Minimum Investment
Initial: $1,000   Subsequent: $50

Minimum IRA Investment
Initial: na   Subsequent: na

Maximum Fees
Load: none   12b-1: 1.00%
Other: none

Distributions
Income: monthly   Capital Gains: Dec

Exchange Options
Number Per Year: no limit   Fee: none
Telephone: yes (money market fund available)

Services
auto invest, auto withdraw

Eaton Vance Short-Term Treasury (EVTYX)

24 Federal Street
Boston, MA 02110
(800) 225-6265, (617) 482-8260

Government Bond

PERFORMANCE

fund inception date: 2/4/91

	3yr Annual	5yr Annual	10yr Annual	Bull	Bear
Return (%)	2.9	na	na	na	1.2
Differ from Category (+/-)	-1.1 blw av	na	na	na	7.6 high

Total Risk	Standard Deviation	Category Risk	Risk Index	Avg Mat
low	0.2%	low	0.0	1.0 yrs

	1994	1993	1992	1991	1990	1989	1988	1987	1986	1985
Return (%)	3.4	2.3	3.1	—	—	—	—	—	—	—
Differ from category (+/-)	8.2	-8.6	-3.3	—	—	—	—	—	—	—

PER SHARE DATA

	1994	1993	1992	1991	1990	1989	1988	1987	1986	1985
Dividends, Net Income ($)	0.00	0.00	0.00	—	—	—	—	—	—	—
Distrib'ns, Cap Gain ($)	0.00	0.00	0.00	—	—	—	—	—	—	—
Net Asset Value ($)	57.52	55.58	54.30	—	—	—	—	—	—	—
Expense Ratio (%)	0.60	0.60	0.60	—	—	—	—	—	—	—
Net Income to Assets (%)	2.59	2.48	3.01	—	—	—	—	—	—	—
Portfolio Turnover (%)	0	0	0	—	—	—	—	—	—	—
Total Assets (Millions $)	1	41	5	—	—	—	—	—	—	—

PORTFOLIO (as of 6/30/94)

Portfolio Manager: Michael Terry - 1991

Investm't Category: Government Bond
Cap Gain	Asset Allocation
Cap & Income	Fund of Funds
✔ Income	Index
	Sector
✔ Domestic	Small Cap
Foreign	Socially Conscious
Country/Region	State Specific

Portfolio: stocks 0% bonds 100%
convertibles 0% other 0% cash 0%

Largest Holdings: U.S. government 100%

Unrealized Net Capital Gains: 0% of portfolio value

SHAREHOLDER INFORMATION

Minimum Investment
Initial: $5,000 Subsequent: $50

Minimum IRA Investment
Initial: $50 Subsequent: $50

Maximum Fees
Load: none 12b-1: 0.25%
Other: none

Distributions
Income: monthly Capital Gains: Dec

Exchange Options
Number Per Year: no limit Fee: none
Telephone: yes (money market fund not available)

Services
IRA, pension, auto invest, auto withdraw

Eclipse Balanced
(EBALX)
Balanced

P.O. Box 2196
Peachtree City, GA 30269
(800) 872-2710, (404) 631-0414

PERFORMANCE

fund inception date: 5/1/89

	3yr Annual	5yr Annual	10yr Annual	Bull	Bear
Return (%)	9.4	9.9	na	72.1	-4.9
Differ from Category (+/-)	3.0 high	1.9 high	na	7.1 abv av	0.8 abv av

Total Risk	Standard Deviation	Category Risk	Risk Index	Beta
blw av	5.9%	av	0.9	0.6

	1994	1993	1992	1991	1990	1989	1988	1987	1986	1985
Return (%)	0.0	17.0	12.0	20.9	1.4	—	—	—	—	—
Differ from category (+/-) . . .	1.9	3.6	3.7	-2.5	1.9	—	—	—	—	—

PER SHARE DATA

	1994	1993	1992	1991	1990	1989	1988	1987	1986	1985
Dividends, Net Income ($) .	0.56	0.64	0.73	0.71	0.76	—	—	—	—	—
Distrib'ns, Cap Gain ($) . . .	0.31	1.04	0.93	0.00	0.00	—	—	—	—	—
Net Asset Value ($)	17.76	18.63	17.37	17.02	14.69	—	—	—	—	—
Expense Ratio (%).	0.80	0.69	0.52	0.66	1.00	—	—	—	—	—
Net Income to Assets (%). .	3.12	3.42	4.31	5.03	5.42	—	—	—	—	—
Portfolio Turnover (%)	na	65	95	101	120	—	—	—	—	—
Total Assets (Millions $)	27	21	14	10	4	—	—	—	—	—

PORTFOLIO (as of 6/30/94)

Portfolio Manager: Wesley G. McCain - 1989

Investm't Category: Balanced

Cap Gain	Asset Allocation
✔ Cap & Income	Fund of Funds
Income	Index
	Sector
✔ Domestic	Small Cap
✔ Foreign	Socially Conscious
Country/Region	State Specific

Portfolio: stocks 59% bonds 38%
convertibles 0% other 0% cash 3%

Largest Holdings: bonds—finance 15%,
stocks—electronic technology 12%

Unrealized Net Capital Gains: 0% of portfolio value

SHAREHOLDER INFORMATION

Minimum Investment
Initial: $1,000 Subsequent: $0

Minimum IRA Investment
Initial: $1,000 Subsequent: $0

Maximum Fees
Load: none 12b-1: none
Other: none

Distributions
Income: quarterly Capital Gains: Dec

Exchange Options
Number Per Year: no limit Fee: none
Telephone: yes (money market fund available)

Services
IRA, pension, auto invest, auto withdraw

Eclipse Equity
(EEQFX)
Growth

P.O. Box 2196
Peachtree City, GA 30269
(800) 872-2710, (404) 631-0414

PERFORMANCE   fund inception date: 1/31/87

	3yr Annual	5yr Annual	10yr Annual	Bull	Bear
Return (%)	9.9	8.5	na	98.4	-10.4
Differ from Category (+/-)	2.2 abv av	-1.1 av	na	6.3 abv av	-3.8 low

Total Risk	Standard Deviation	Category Risk	Risk Index	Beta
abv av	10.0%	abv av	1.0	0.9

	1994	1993	1992	1991	1990	1989	1988	1987	1986	1985
Return (%)	-4.7	17.0	19.3	31.1	-13.6	16.3	12.7	—	—	—
Differ from category (+/-) . .	-4.1	3.6	7.7	-4.6	-7.9	-9.8	-5.3	—	—	—

PER SHARE DATA

	1994	1993	1992	1991	1990	1989	1988	1987	1986	1985
Dividends, Net Income ($).	0.03	0.08	0.15	0.16	0.32	0.28	0.41	—	—	—
Distrib'ns, Cap Gain ($) . . .	0.87	2.02	0.65	0.00	0.00	0.64	0.00	—	—	—
Net Asset Value ($)	11.83	13.35	13.20	11.73	9.07	10.86	10.12	—	—	—
Expense Ratio (%)	1.11	1.12	1.15	1.18	1.18	1.09	1.12	—	—	—
Net Income to Assets (%) .	0.14	0.55	1.17	1.48	2.57	2.40	4.05	—	—	—
Portfolio Turnover (%)	na	101	111	119	154	46	31	—	—	—
Total Assets (Millions $). . . .	195	197	163	149	110	184	161	—	—	—

PORTFOLIO (as of 6/30/94)

Portfolio Manager: Wesley McCain - 1987

Investm't Category: Growth

✔ Cap Gain
   Cap & Income
   Income

   Asset Allocation
   Fund of Funds
   Index
   Sector

✔ Domestic
✔ Foreign
   Country/Region

✔ Small Cap
   Socially Conscious
   State Specific

Portfolio: stocks 92%   bonds 0%
convertibles 0%   other 0%   cash 8%

Largest Holdings: retail 13%, electronic technology 9%

Unrealized Net Capital Gains: 0% of portfolio value

SHAREHOLDER INFORMATION

Minimum Investment
Initial: $1,000   Subsequent: $0

Minimum IRA Investment
Initial: $1,000   Subsequent: $0

Maximum Fees
Load: none   12b-1: none
Other: none

Distributions
Income: Dec   Capital Gains: Dec

Exchange Options
Number Per Year: no limit   Fee: none
Telephone: yes (money market fund available)

Services
IRA, pension, auto invest, auto withdraw

Evergreen American Retirement—Class Y

(EAMRX) *Balanced*

2500 Westchester Ave.
Purchase, NY 10577
(800) 235-0064, (914) 694-2020

	3yr Annual	5yr Annual	10yr Annual	Bull	Bear
Return (%)	7.4	7.9	na	62.8	-5.8
Differ from Category (+/-)	1.0 abv av	-0.1 blw av	na	-2.2 av	-0.1 blw av

Total Risk	Standard Deviation	Category Risk	Risk Index	Beta
blw av	5.8%	av	0.9	0.6

	1994	1993	1992	1991	1990	1989	1988	1987	1986	1985
Return (%)	-2.8	14.0	11.8	18.7	-0.4	13.4	—	—	—	—
Differ from category (+/-)	-0.9	0.6	3.5	-4.7	0.1	-3.9	—	—	—	—

PER SHARE DATA

	1994	1993	1992	1991	1990	1989	1988	1987	1986	1985
Dividends, Net Income ($)	0.60	0.60	0.61	0.60	0.60	0.59	—	—	—	—
Distrib'ns, Cap Gain ($)	0.00	0.27	0.17	0.22	0.16	0.42	—	—	—	—
Net Asset Value ($)	10.67	11.60	10.95	10.52	9.59	10.41	—	—	—	—
Expense Ratio (%)	1.30	1.36	1.51	1.50	1.50	1.88	—	—	—	—
Net Income to Assets (%)	5.43	5.13	6.23	5.91	6.04	5.49	—	—	—	—
Portfolio Turnover (%)	na	92	151	97	33	152	—	—	—	—
Total Assets (Millions $)	37	37	24	16	12	12	—	—	—	—

PORTFOLIO (as of 6/30/94)

Portfolio Manager: Irene D. O'Neill - 1988

Investm't Category: Balanced

Cap Gain	Asset Allocation
✔ Cap & Income	Fund of Funds
Income	Index
	Sector
✔ Domestic	Small Cap
Foreign	Socially Conscious
Country/Region	State Specific

Portfolio: stocks 52%   bonds 24%
convertibles 19%   other 1%   cash 4%

Largest Holdings: stocks—energy 8%, stocks—banks 8%

Unrealized Net Capital Gains: 0% of portfolio value

SHAREHOLDER INFORMATION

Minimum Investment
Initial: $1,000   Subsequent: $0

Minimum IRA Investment
Initial: $1,000   Subsequent: $0

Maximum Fees
Load: none   12b-1: none
Other: none

Distributions
Income: quarterly   Capital Gains: Dec

Exchange Options
Number Per Year: no limit   Fee: $5 (first 4 free)
Telephone: yes (money market fund available)

Services
IRA, pension, auto exchange, auto invest, auto withdraw

Evergreen—Class Y
(EVGRX)
Aggressive Growth

2500 Westchester Ave.
Purchase, NY 10577
(800) 235-0064, (914) 694-2020

PERFORMANCE
fund inception date: 10/18/71

	3yr Annual	5yr Annual	10yr Annual	Bull	Bear
Return (%)	5.1	7.5	11.6	86.1	-4.7
Differ from Category (+/-)	-3.8 blw av	-5.0 low	-2.4 blw av	-47.1 low	6.1 high

Total Risk	Standard Deviation	Category Risk	Risk Index	Beta
abv av	9.3%	low	0.6	0.9

	1994	1993	1992	1991	1990	1989	1988	1987	1986	1985
Return (%)	0.7	6.2	8.7	40.0	-11.7	15.0	22.9	-2.9	12.9	35.4
Differ from category (+/-)	1.4	-13.3	-2.3	-12.1	-5.5	-11.8	7.7	-0.7	1.1	3.1

PER SHARE DATA

	1994	1993	1992	1991	1990	1989	1988	1987	1986	1985
Dividends, Net Income ($)	0.07	0.09	0.07	0.17	0.18	0.36	0.21	0.38	0.14	0.17
Distrib'ns, Cap Gain ($)	2.16	0.61	0.62	0.69	0.26	0.61	0.56	1.68	1.66	0.41
Net Asset Value ($)	12.03	14.20	14.03	13.54	10.34	12.21	11.49	9.98	12.47	12.67
Expense Ratio (%)	1.22	1.12	1.13	1.15	1.15	1.11	1.03	1.03	1.04	1.08
Net Income to Assets (%)	0.40	0.60	0.56	1.45	1.83	2.46	1.70	1.32	1.41	1.73
Portfolio Turnover (%)	19	21	32	35	39	40	42	46	48	59
Total Assets (Millions $)	454	629	722	754	525	867	751	808	638	334

PORTFOLIO (as of 9/30/94)

Portfolio Manager: Stephen Lieber - 1971

Investm't Category: Aggressive Growth
- ✔ Cap Gain
- Cap & Income
- Income
- Asset Allocation
- Fund of Funds
- Index
- Sector

- ✔ Domestic
- Foreign
- Country/Region
- ✔ Small Cap
- Socially Conscious
- State Specific

Portfolio: stocks 99%   bonds 0%
convertibles 0%   other 0%   cash 1%

Largest Holdings: banks 22%, healthcare products & services 18%

Unrealized Net Capital Gains: 33% of portfolio value

SHAREHOLDER INFORMATION

Minimum Investment
Initial: $1,000   Subsequent: $0

Minimum IRA Investment
Initial: $1,000   Subsequent: $0

Maximum Fees
Load: none   12b-1: none
Other: none

Distributions
Income: Dec   Capital Gains: Dec

Exchange Options
Number Per Year: no limit   Fee: $5 (first 4 free)
Telephone: yes (money market fund available)

Services
IRA, pension, auto exchange, auto invest, auto withdraw

Evergreen Foundation—Class Y (EFONX)

2500 Westchester Ave.
Purchase, NY 10577
(800) 235-0064, (914) 694-2020

Balanced

PERFORMANCE

fund inception date: 1/2/90

	3yr Annual	5yr Annual	10yr Annual	Bull	Bear
Return (%)	11.1	14.8	na	115.3	-5.8
Differ from Category (+/-)	4.7 high	6.8 high	na	50.3 high	-0.1 blw av

Total Risk	Standard Deviation	Category Risk	Risk Index	Beta
av	7.5%	high	1.2	0.8

	1994	1993	1992	1991	1990	1989	1988	1987	1986	1985
Return (%)	-1.1	15.7	19.9	36.3	6.5	—	—	—	—	—
Differ from category (+/-) . . .	0.8	2.3	11.6	12.9	7.0	—	—	—	—	—

PER SHARE DATA

	1994	1993	1992	1991	1990	1989	1988	1987	1986	1985
Dividends, Net Income ($) .	0.42	0.31	0.24	0.33	1.17	—	—	—	—	—
Distrib'ns, Cap Gain ($) . . .	0.28	0.41	0.63	0.97	0.52	—	—	—	—	—
Net Asset Value ($)	12.27	13.12	11.98	10.75	8.95	—	—	—	—	—
Expense Ratio (%)	1.17	1.20	1.40	1.20	0.00	—	—	—	—	—
Net Income to Assets (%) . .	3.21	2.80	2.93	2.86	15.07	—	—	—	—	—
Portfolio Turnover (%)	na	60	127	178	131	—	—	—	—	—
Total Assets (Millions $) . . .	331	246	64	11	2	—	—	—	—	—

PORTFOLIO (as of 6/30/94)

Portfolio Manager: Stephen A. Lieber - 1990

Investm't Category: Balanced

Cap Gain	✔ Asset Allocation
✔ Cap & Income	Fund of Funds
Income	Index
	Sector
✔ Domestic	Small Cap
Foreign	Socially Conscious
Country/Region	State Specific

Portfolio: stocks 57% bonds 27%
convertibles 3% other 0% cash 13%

Largest Holdings: bonds—U.S. government
& agencies 27%, stocks—finance & insurance 9%

Unrealized Net Capital Gains: -2% of portfolio value

SHAREHOLDER INFORMATION

Minimum Investment
Initial: $1,000   Subsequent: $0

Minimum IRA Investment
Initial: $1,000   Subsequent: $0

Maximum Fees
Load: none   12b-1: none
Other: none

Distributions
Income: quarterly   Capital Gains: Dec

Exchange Options
Number Per Year: no limit   Fee: $5 (first 4 free)
Telephone: yes (money market fund available)

Services
IRA, pension, auto exchange, auto invest, auto withdraw

Evergreen Global Real Estate—Class Y (EGLRX)

2500 Westchester Ave.
Purchase, NY 10577
(800) 235-0064, (914) 694-2020

International Stock

PERFORMANCE
fund inception date: 2/1/89

	3yr Annual	5yr Annual	10yr Annual	Bull	Bear
Return (%)	12.7	5.5	na	94.3	-10.1
Differ from Category (+/-)	3.6 abv av	0.6 av	na	30.4 high	-3.1 blw av

Total Risk	Standard Deviation	Category Risk	Risk Index	Beta
high	14.2%	abv av	1.1	0.7

	1994	1993	1992	1991	1990	1989	1988	1987	1986	1985
Return (%)	-14.0	51.4	10.1	13.0	-19.2	—	—	—	—	—
Differ from category (+/-)	-11.0	12.8	13.0	-0.1	-8.8	—	—	—	—	—

PER SHARE DATA

	1994	1993	1992	1991	1990	1989	1988	1987	1986	1985
Dividends, Net Income ($)	0.10	0.00	0.00	0.00	0.00	—	—	—	—	—
Distrib'ns, Cap Gain ($)	0.52	0.18	0.23	0.00	0.00	—	—	—	—	—
Net Asset Value ($)	12.06	14.75	9.86	9.16	8.10	—	—	—	—	—
Expense Ratio (%)	1.54	1.56	2.00	2.00	2.00	—	—	—	—	—
Net Income to Assets (%)	0.74	0.03	-0.10	-0.27	-0.39	—	—	—	—	—
Portfolio Turnover (%)	na	88	245	207	325	—	—	—	—	—
Total Assets (Millions $)	97	142	8	7	6	—	—	—	—	—

PORTFOLIO (as of 6/30/94)

Portfolio Manager: Samual Lieber - 1989

Investm't Category: International Stock
- ✔ Cap Gain
- Cap & Income
- Income
- Domestic ✔
- Foreign ✔
- Country/Region
- Asset Allocation
- Fund of Funds
- Index
- ✔ Sector
- Small Cap
- Socially Conscious
- State Specific

Portfolio: stocks 98% bonds 0%
convertibles 1% other 1% cash 0%

Largest Holdings: United States 36%, Japan 15%

Unrealized Net Capital Gains: 0% of portfolio value

SHAREHOLDER INFORMATION

Minimum Investment
Initial: $1,000 Subsequent: $0

Minimum IRA Investment
Initial: $1,000 Subsequent: $0

Maximum Fees
Load: none 12b-1: none
Other: none

Distributions
Income: Dec Capital Gains: Dec

Exchange Options
Number Per Year: no limit Fee: $5 (first 4 free)
Telephone: yes (money market fund available)

Services
IRA, pension, auto exchange, auto invest, auto withdraw

Evergreen Growth & Income—Class Y (EVVTX)

2500 Westchester Ave.
Purchase, NY 10577
(800) 235-0064, (914) 694-2020

Growth & Income

PERFORMANCE

fund inception date: 10/15/86

	3yr Annual	5yr Annual	10yr Annual	Bull	Bear
Return (%)	9.8	9.7	na	83.7	-5.8
Differ from Category (+/-)	2.7 abv av	1.8 abv av	na	7.9 abv av	0.5 av

Total Risk	Standard Deviation	Category Risk	Risk Index	Beta
av	8.4%	av	1.0	0.9

	1994	1993	1992	1991	1990	1989	1988	1987	1986	1985
Return (%)	1.6	14.4	13.8	25.8	-4.4	25.4	24.5	-4.3	—	—
Differ from category (+/-) . . .	3.0	1.2	3.6	-1.8	1.6	4.0	7.5	-4.9	—	—

PER SHARE DATA

	1994	1993	1992	1991	1990	1989	1988	1987	1986	1985
Dividends, Net Income ($) .	0.14	0.14	0.15	0.19	0.30	0.52	0.19	0.24	—	—
Distrib'ns, Cap Gain ($) . . .	1.01	0.68	0.46	0.31	0.47	0.76	0.86	0.00	—	—
Net Asset Value ($)	14.52	15.41	14.18	12.99	10.72	12.03	10.62	9.38	—	—
Expense Ratio (%).	1.37	1.26	1.33	1.41	1.50	1.54	1.56	1.76	—	—
Net Income to Assets (%). .	0.94	0.99	1.18	1.55	2.62	4.13	1.70	1.90	—	—
Portfolio Turnover (%)	na	28	30	23	41	53	41	48	—	—
Total Assets (Millions $)	73	77	64	48	36	32	24	22	—	—

PORTFOLIO (as of 6/30/94)

Portfolio Manager: Edmund H. Nicklin - 1986

Investm't Category: Growth & Income

Cap Gain	Asset Allocation
✔ Cap & Income	Fund of Funds
Income	Index
	Sector
✔ Domestic	Small Cap
Foreign	Socially Conscious
Country/Region	State Specific

Portfolio:	stocks 95%	bonds 2%
convertibles 0%	other 0%	cash 3%

Largest Holdings: business equipment & services 15%, banks & thrifts 9%

Unrealized Net Capital Gains: 22% of portfolio value

SHAREHOLDER INFORMATION

Minimum Investment
Initial: $1,000   Subsequent: $0

Minimum IRA Investment
Initial: $1,000   Subsequent: $0

Maximum Fees
Load: none   12b-1: none
Other: none

Distributions
Income: Dec   Capital Gains: Dec

Exchange Options
Number Per Year: no limit   Fee: $5 (first 4 free)
Telephone: yes (money market fund available)

Services
IRA, pension, auto exchange, auto invest, auto withdraw

Evergreen Limited Market—Class Y (EVLMX)

2500 Westchester Ave.
Purchase, NY 10577
(800) 235-0064, (914) 694-2020

Aggressive Growth

PERFORMANCE
fund inception date: 6/1/83

	3yr Annual	5yr Annual	10yr Annual	Bull	Bear
Return (%)	2.5	7.8	14.3	94.4	-9.1
Differ from Category (+/-)	-6.4 low	-4.7 low	0.3 av	-38.8 blw av	1.7 abv av

Total Risk	Standard Deviation	Category Risk	Risk Index	Beta
high	12.9%	blw av	0.9	0.7

	1994	1993	1992	1991	1990	1989	1988	1987	1986	1985
Return (%).	-10.5	9.5	10.1	51.0	-10.4	20.8	26.0	-3.2	14.9	53.9
Differ from category (+/-) . .	-9.8	-10.0	-0.9	-1.1	-4.2	-6.0	10.8	-1.0	3.1	21.6

PER SHARE DATA

	1994	1993	1992	1991	1990	1989	1988	1987	1986	1985
Dividends, Net Income ($).	0.00	0.00	0.00	0.14	0.53	0.36	0.05	0.00	0.00	0.00
Distrib'ns, Cap Gain ($) . . .	3.68	1.27	1.69	1.00	0.58	3.67	0.28	0.95	2.62	1.17
Net Asset Value ($)	15.70	21.70	20.99	20.63	14.46	17.37	17.79	14.38	15.74	15.82
Expense Ratio (%)	1.26	1.24	1.25	1.32	1.33	1.30	1.47	1.44	1.44	1.67
Net Income to Assets (%) .	-0.33	-0.07	0.22	3.32	2.25	0.86	0.01	-0.20	-0.10	-0.05
Portfolio Turnover (%)	89	29	55	59	46	45	47	43	56	69
Total Assets (Millions $). . . .	81	104	62	46	38	37	23	21	19	9

PORTFOLIO (as of 5/31/94)

Portfolio Manager: Derrick E. Wenger - 1993

Investm't Category: Aggressive Growth

✔ Cap Gain   Asset Allocation
   Cap & Income   Fund of Funds
   Income   Index
       Sector
✔ Domestic   ✔ Small Cap
   Foreign   Socially Conscious
   Country/Region   State Specific

Portfolio: stocks 99%   bonds 0%
convertibles 0%   other 0%   cash 1%

Largest Holdings: consumer products 21%, banks 14%

Unrealized Net Capital Gains: 6% of portfolio value

SHAREHOLDER INFORMATION

Minimum Investment
Initial: $1,000   Subsequent: $0

Minimum IRA Investment
Initial: $1,000   Subsequent: $0

Maximum Fees
Load: none   12b-1: none
Other: none

Distributions
Income: Dec   Capital Gains: Dec

Exchange Options
Number Per Year: no limit   Fee: $5 (first 4 free)
Telephone: yes (money market fund available)

Services
IRA, pension, auto exchange, auto invest, auto withdraw

Evergreen National Tax-Free—Class Y (EINSX)

2500 Westchester Ave.
Purchase, NY 10577
(800) 235-0064, (914) 694-2020

Tax-Exempt Bond

PERFORMANCE

fund inception date: 12/31/92

	3yr Annual	5yr Annual	10yr Annual	Bull	Bear
Return (%)	na	na	na	na	-8.0
Differ from Category (+/-)	na	na	na	na	-2.8 low

Total Risk	Standard Deviation	Category Risk	Risk Index	Avg Mat
na	na	na	na	17.1 yrs

	1994	1993	1992	1991	1990	1989	1988	1987	1986	1985
Return (%)	-7.9	16.0	—	—	—	—	—	—	—	—
Differ from category (+/-)	-2.7	4.3	—	—	—	—	—	—	—	—

PER SHARE DATA

	1994	1993	1992	1991	1990	1989	1988	1987	1986	1985
Dividends, Net Income ($)	0.51	0.58	—	—	—	—	—	—	—	—
Distrib'ns, Cap Gain ($)	0.00	0.16	—	—	—	—	—	—	—	—
Net Asset Value ($)	9.46	10.82	—	—	—	—	—	—	—	—
Expense Ratio (%)	0.29	0.00	—	—	—	—	—	—	—	—
Net Income to Assets (%)	5.07	5.51	—	—	—	—	—	—	—	—
Portfolio Turnover (%)	135	166	—	—	—	—	—	—	—	—
Total Assets (Millions $)	21	38	—	—	—	—	—	—	—	—

PORTFOLIO (as of 8/31/94)

Portfolio Manager: James Colby - 1992

Investm't Category: Tax-Exempt Bond
- Cap Gain
- Cap & Income
- ✔ Income
- ✔ Domestic
- Foreign
- Country/Region
- Asset Allocation
- Fund of Funds
- Index
- Sector
- Small Cap
- Socially Conscious
- State Specific

Portfolio: stocks 0%   bonds 89%
convertibles 0%   other 0%   cash 11%

Largest Holdings: general obligation 6%

Unrealized Net Capital Gains: -1% of portfolio value

SHAREHOLDER INFORMATION

Minimum Investment
Initial: $1,000   Subsequent: $0

Minimum IRA Investment
Initial: na   Subsequent: na

Maximum Fees
Load: none   12b-1: none
Other: none

Distributions
Income: monthly   Capital Gains: Dec

Exchange Options
Number Per Year: no limit   Fee: $5 (first 4 free)
Telephone: yes (money market fund not available)

Services
auto exchange, auto invest, auto withdraw

Evergreen Short Interm Muni CA—Class Y (EMUCX)

2500 Westchester Ave.
Purchase, NY 10577
(800) 235-0064, (914) 694-2020

Tax-Exempt Bond

PERFORMANCE

fund inception date: 10/16/92

	3yr Annual	5yr Annual	10yr Annual	Bull	Bear
Return (%)	na	na	na	na	-2.2
Differ from Category (+/-)	na	na	na	na	3.0 high

Total Risk	Standard Deviation	Category Risk	Risk Index	Avg Mat
na	na	na	na	3.6 yrs

	1994	1993	1992	1991	1990	1989	1988	1987	1986	1985
Return (%)	-1.7	7.7	—	—	—	—	—	—	—	—
Differ from category (+/-)	3.5	-4.0	—	—	—	—	—	—	—	—

PER SHARE DATA

	1994	1993	1992	1991	1990	1989	1988	1987	1986	1985
Dividends, Net Income ($)	0.42	0.44	—	—	—	—	—	—	—	—
Distrib'ns, Cap Gain ($)	0.03	0.01	—	—	—	—	—	—	—	—
Net Asset Value ($)	9.78	10.41	—	—	—	—	—	—	—	—
Expense Ratio (%)	0.52	0.30	—	—	—	—	—	—	—	—
Net Income to Assets (%)	4.20	3.96	—	—	—	—	—	—	—	—
Portfolio Turnover (%)	12	37	—	—	—	—	—	—	—	—
Total Assets (Millions $)	25	30	—	—	—	—	—	—	—	—

PORTFOLIO (as of 8/31/94)

Portfolio Manager: Steven Shachat - 1992

Investm't Category: Tax-Exempt Bond
- Cap Gain
- Cap & Income
- ✔ Income
- ✔ Domestic
- Foreign
- Country/Region
- Asset Allocation
- Fund of Funds
- Index
- Sector
- Small Cap
- Socially Conscious
- ✔ State Specific

Portfolio: stocks 0% bonds 93%
convertibles 0% other 0% cash 7%

Largest Holdings: general obligation 5%

Unrealized Net Capital Gains: 0% of portfolio value

SHAREHOLDER INFORMATION

Minimum Investment
Initial: $1,000   Subsequent: $100

Minimum IRA Investment
Initial: na   Subsequent: na

Maximum Fees
Load: none   12b-1: none
Other: none

Distributions
Income: monthly   Capital Gains: Dec

Exchange Options
Number Per Year: no limit   Fee: $5 (first 4 free)
Telephone: yes (money market fund available)

Services
auto exchange, auto invest, auto withdraw

Evergreen Short-Interm Muni—Class Y (EMUNX)

2500 Westchester Ave.
Purchase, NY 10577
(800) 235-0064, (914) 694-2020

Tax-Exempt Bond

PERFORMANCE
fund inception date: 11/18/91

	3yr Annual	5yr Annual	10yr Annual	Bull	Bear
Return (%)	4.3	na	na	na	-2.1
Differ from Category (+/-)	-0.2 blw av	na	na	na	3.1 high

Total Risk	Standard Deviation	Category Risk	Risk Index	Avg Mat
low	2.5%	low	0.4	3.0 yrs

	1994	1993	1992	1991	1990	1989	1988	1987	1986	1985
Return (%)	-1.4	7.2	7.3	—	—	—	—	—	—	—
Differ from category (+/-) . . .	3.8	-4.5	-1.0	—	—	—	—	—	—	—

PER SHARE DATA

	1994	1993	1992	1991	1990	1989	1988	1987	1986	1985
Dividends, Net Income ($) .	0.46	0.49	0.49	—	—	—	—	—	—	—
Distrib'ns, Cap Gain ($) . . .	0.00	0.05	0.00	—	—	—	—	—	—	—
Net Asset Value ($)	9.97	10.58	10.38	—	—	—	—	—	—	—
Expense Ratio (%).	0.58	0.40	0.17	—	—	—	—	—	—	—
Net Income to Assets (%). .	4.54	4.73	4.85	—	—	—	—	—	—	—
Portfolio Turnover (%).	32	37	57	—	—	—	—	—	—	—
Total Assets (Millions $)	44	63	54	—	—	—	—	—	—	—

PORTFOLIO (as of 8/31/94)

Portfolio Manager: Steven Shachat - 1991

Investm't Category: Tax-Exempt Bond
Cap Gain	Asset Allocation
Cap & Income	Fund of Funds
✔ Income	Index
	Sector
✔ Domestic	Small Cap
Foreign	Socially Conscious
Country/Region	State Specific

Portfolio: stocks 0% bonds 98%
convertibles 0% other 0% cash 2%

Largest Holdings: general obligation 21%

Unrealized Net Capital Gains: 0% of portfolio value

SHAREHOLDER INFORMATION

Minimum Investment
Initial: $1,000 Subsequent: $100

Minimum IRA Investment
Initial: na Subsequent: na

Maximum Fees
Load: none 12b-1: none
Other: none

Distributions
Income: monthly Capital Gains: Dec

Exchange Options
Number Per Year: no limit Fee: $5 (first 4 free)
Telephone: yes (money market fund available)

Services
auto exchange, auto invest, auto withdraw

Evergreen Total Return—Class Y (EVTRX)

Growth & Income

2500 Westchester Ave.
Purchase, NY 10577
(800) 235-0064, (914) 694-2020

PERFORMANCE

fund inception date: 9/7/78

	3yr Annual	5yr Annual	10yr Annual	Bull	Bear
Return (%)	5.1	6.0	10.0	65.1	-7.7
Differ from Category (+/-)	-2.0 blw av	-1.9 low	-1.7 low	-10.7 blw av	-1.4 blw av

Total Risk	Standard Deviation	Category Risk	Risk Index	Beta
av	7.1%	low	0.9	0.8

	1994	1993	1992	1991	1990	1989	1988	1987	1986	1985
Return (%).............	-6.4	12.9	10.0	22.9	-6.2	16.8	15.7	-7.9	20.1	29.8
Differ from category (+/-) ..	-5.0	-0.3	-0.2	-4.7	-0.2	-4.6	-1.3	-8.5	4.3	4.1

PER SHARE DATA

	1994	1993	1992	1991	1990	1989	1988	1987	1986	1985
Dividends, Net Income ($).	1.08	1.08	1.08	1.08	1.08	1.09	1.08	1.33	1.09	0.97
Distrib'ns, Cap Gain ($) ...	0.25	1.20	0.46	0.00	0.00	0.00	0.02	0.88	1.11	0.98
Net Asset Value ($)	17.03	19.62	19.43	19.12	16.49	18.76	17.01	15.66	19.18	17.87
Expense Ratio (%)	1.21	1.18	1.21	1.23	1.18	1.02	1.01	1.02	1.11	1.31
Net Income to Assets (%) .	5.57	5.65	5.73	5.90	5.64	6.36	5.80	5.68	6.06	6.18
Portfolio Turnover (%)	na	164	137	137	89	86	81	44	65	82
Total Assets (Millions $)....	943	1,180	1,032	1,151	1,292	1,312	1,355	1,636	408	83

PORTFOLIO (as of 9/30/94)

Portfolio Manager: Nola M. Falcone - 1978

Investm't Category: Growth & Income

Cap Gain	Asset Allocation
✔ Cap & Income	Fund of Funds
Income	Index
	Sector
✔ Domestic	Small Cap
Foreign	Socially Conscious
Country/Region	State Specific

Portfolio: stocks 75%   bonds 1%
convertibles 24%   other 0%   cash 0%

Largest Holdings: electric utilities 15%, banks 11%

Unrealized Net Capital Gains: -9% of portfolio value

SHAREHOLDER INFORMATION

Minimum Investment
Initial: $1,000   Subsequent: $0

Minimum IRA Investment
Initial: $1,000   Subsequent: $0

Maximum Fees
Load: none   12b-1: none
Other: none

Distributions
Income: quarterly   Capital Gains: Dec

Exchange Options
Number Per Year: no limit   Fee: $5 (first 4 free)
Telephone: yes (money market fund available)

Services
IRA, pension, auto exchange, auto invest, auto withdraw

Fairmont (FAIMX)

Aggressive Growth

1346 S. Third St.
Louisville, KY 40208
(800) 262-9936, (502) 636-5633

PERFORMANCE

fund inception date: 9/2/81

	3yr Annual	5yr Annual	10yr Annual	Bull	Bear
Return (%)	12.2	9.1	9.0	114.3	-1.7
Differ from Category (+/-)	3.3 abv av	-3.4 blw av	-5.0 low	-18.9 blw av	9.1 high

Total Risk	Standard Deviation	Category Risk	Risk Index	Beta
high	14.8%	av	1.0	1.0

	1994	1993	1992	1991	1990	1989	1988	1987	1986	1985
Return (%)	7.2	15.5	14.0	40.5	-22.1	6.8	3.1	-7.7	14.0	32.1
Differ from category (+/-) . . .	7.9	-4.0	3.0	-11.6	-15.9	-20.0	-12.1	-5.5	2.2	-0.2

PER SHARE DATA

	1994	1993	1992	1991	1990	1989	1988	1987	1986	1985
Dividends, Net Income ($) .	0.00	0.00	0.00	0.09	0.30	0.21	0.24	0.18	0.19	0.26
Distrib'ns, Cap Gain ($) . . .	0.00	0.00	0.00	0.00	0.00	0.00	0.00	0.08	3.85	0.93
Net Asset Value ($)	24.06	22.43	19.41	17.02	12.17	16.02	15.19	14.96	16.50	18.08
Expense Ratio (%)	1.75	1.78	1.79	1.79	1.68	1.37	1.25	1.18	1.48	2.05
Net Income to Assets (%) .	-1.11	-0.66	-0.85	0.51	1.53	1.01	1.30	0.91	1.22	1.41
Portfolio Turnover (%)	230	155	132	115	128	90	158	145	129	123
Total Assets (Millions $)	22	19	17	17	16	43	64	79	60	24

PORTFOLIO (as of 6/30/94)

Portfolio Manager: Morton H. Sachs - 1981

Investm't Category: Aggressive Growth

✔ Cap Gain	Asset Allocation
Cap & Income	Fund of Funds
Income	Index
	Sector
✔ Domestic	Small Cap
Foreign	Socially Conscious
Country/Region	State Specific

Portfolio: stocks 92% bonds 0%
convertibles 0% other 0% cash 8%

Largest Holdings: banking 20%, healthcare management 10%

Unrealized Net Capital Gains: 8% of portfolio value

SHAREHOLDER INFORMATION

Minimum Investment
Initial: $1,000   Subsequent: $0

Minimum IRA Investment
Initial: $1,000   Subsequent: $0

Maximum Fees
Load: none   12b-1: none
Other: none

Distributions
Income: Dec   Capital Gains: Dec

Exchange Options
Number Per Year: no limit   Fee: none
Telephone: none

Services
IRA, pension

FAM Value (FAMVX)

Growth

118 North Grand Street
P.O. Box 399
Cobleskill, NY 12043
(800) 932-3271

PERFORMANCE

fund inception date: 1/1/187

	3yr Annual	5yr Annual	10yr Annual	Bull	Bear
Return (%)	10.2	13.3	na	98.7	-3.7
Differ from Category (+/-)	2.5 abv av	3.7 high	na	6.6 abv av	2.9 high

Total Risk	Standard Deviation	Category Risk	Risk Index	Beta
abv av	9.7%	av	1.0	0.6

	1994	1993	1992	1991	1990	1989	1988	1987	1986	1985
Return (%)	6.8	0.2	25.0	47.6	-5.3	20.3	35.5	-17.1	—	—
Differ from category (+/-)	7.4	-13.2	13.4	11.9	0.4	-5.8	17.5	-18.9	—	—

PER SHARE DATA

	1994	1993	1992	1991	1990	1989	1988	1987	1986	1985
Dividends, Net Income ($)	0.12	0.09	0.10	0.08	0.08	0.06	0.25	0.10	—	—
Distrib'ns, Cap Gain ($)	0.63	0.05	0.48	0.82	0.02	0.06	0.00	0.02	—	—
Net Asset Value ($)	21.04	20.40	20.50	16.87	12.06	12.85	10.78	8.14	—	—
Expense Ratio (%)	1.37	1.39	1.50	1.49	1.53	1.51	1.48	1.54	—	—
Net Income to Assets (%)	0.47	0.57	0.81	0.66	0.72	0.56	2.89	1.47	—	—
Portfolio Turnover (%)	na	5	10	14	9	15	12	16	—	—
Total Assets (Millions $)	209	217	45	14	6	5	2	1	—	—

PORTFOLIO (as of 6/30/94)

Portfolio Manager: Thomas Putnam - 1987, Diane VanBuren - 1987

Investm't Category: Growth
- ✔ Cap Gain
- Cap & Income
- Income
- Asset Allocation
- Fund of Funds
- Index
- Sector
- ✔ Domestic
- Foreign
- Country/Region
- ✔ Small Cap
- Socially Conscious
- State Specific

Portfolio: stocks 100% bonds 0% convertibles 0% other 0% cash 0%

Largest Holdings: insurance 25%, banking 16%

Unrealized Net Capital Gains: 0% of portfolio value

SHAREHOLDER INFORMATION

Minimum Investment
Initial: $2,000   Subsequent: $100

Minimum IRA Investment
Initial: $100   Subsequent: $50

Maximum Fees
Load: none   12b-1: none
Other: none

Distributions
Income: Dec   Capital Gains: Dec

Exchange Options
Number Per Year: none   Fee:
Telephone:

Services
IRA, pension, auto invest

Fidelity Aggressive Tax-Free (FATFX)

Tax-Exempt Bond

82 Devonshire St.
Boston, MA 02109
(800) 544-8888, (801) 534-1910

PERFORMANCE

fund inception date: 9/13/85

	3yr Annual	5yr Annual	10yr Annual	Bull	Bear
Return (%)	5.3	7.0	na	44.1	-5.6
Differ from Category (+/-)	0.8 high	0.9 high	na	2.3 av	-0.4 av

Total Risk	Standard Deviation	Category Risk	Risk Index	Avg Mat
blw av	5.4%	blw av	0.9	20.5 yrs

	1994	1993	1992	1991	1990	1989	1988	1987	1986	1985
Return (%)	-5.8	13.7	9.1	11.7	7.4	9.5	13.4	1.3	17.6	—
Differ from category (+/-) . .	-0.6	2.0	0.8	0.4	1.1	0.5	3.2	2.6	1.2	—

PER SHARE DATA

	1994	1993	1992	1991	1990	1989	1988	1987	1986	1985
Dividends, Net Income ($) .	0.77	0.78	0.83	0.86	0.88	0.88	0.90	0.90	0.92	—
Distrib'ns, Cap Gain ($) . . .	0.05	0.34	0.13	0.06	0.00	0.00	0.00	0.00	0.00	—
Net Asset Value ($)	10.81	12.34	11.88	11.80	11.43	11.49	11.33	10.82	11.56	—
Expense Ratio (%).	0.64	0.64	0.64	0.69	0.66	0.69	0.73	0.74	0.65	—
Net Income to Assets (%). .	6.52	6.37	7.01	7.46	7.79	7.68	7.98	8.06	8.17	—
Portfolio Turnover (%)	45	54	43	30	46	46	46	68	17	—
Total Assets (Millions $) . . .	793	948	761	654	551	546	456	353	394	—

PORTFOLIO (as of 6/30/94)

Portfolio Manager: Ann Punzak - 1985

Investm't Category: Tax-Exempt Bond

Cap Gain	Asset Allocation
Cap & Income	Fund of Funds
✔ Income	Index
	Sector
✔ Domestic	Small Cap
Foreign	Socially Conscious
Country/Region	State Specific

Portfolio: stocks 0% bonds 100%
convertibles 0% other 0% cash 0%

Largest Holdings: general obligation 6%

Unrealized Net Capital Gains: -1% of portfolio value

SHAREHOLDER INFORMATION

Minimum Investment
Initial: $2,500   Subsequent: $250

Minimum IRA Investment
Initial: na   Subsequent: na

Maximum Fees
Load: 1.00% redemption   12b-1: none
Other: redemption fee applies for 6 mos

Distributions
Income: monthly   Capital Gains: Feb, Dec

Exchange Options
Number Per Year: 4   Fee: none
Telephone: yes (money market fund available)

Services
auto exchange, auto invest, auto withdraw

Fidelity Asset Manager

(FASMX)

Balanced

82 Devonshire St.
Boston, MA 02109
(800) 544-8888, (801) 534-1910

	3yr Annual	5yr Annual	10yr Annual	Bull	Bear
Return (%)	9.0	11.0	na	92.2	-9.1
Differ from Category (+/-)	2.6 abv av	3.0 high	na	27.2 high	-3.4 low

Total Risk	Standard Deviation	Category Risk	Risk Index	Beta
blw av	6.5%	abv av	1.0	0.6

	1994	1993	1992	1991	1990	1989	1988	1987	1986	1985
Return (%)	-6.5	23.2	12.7	23.6	5.3	15.2	—	—	—	—
Differ from category (+/-)	-4.6	9.8	4.4	0.2	5.8	-2.1	—	—	—	—

PER SHARE DATA

	1994	1993	1992	1991	1990	1989	1988	1987	1986	1985
Dividends, Net Income ($)	0.40	0.59	0.48	0.45	0.65	0.38	—	—	—	—
Distrib'ns, Cap Gain ($)	0.17	0.43	0.19	0.50	0.00	0.24	—	—	—	—
Net Asset Value ($)	13.83	15.40	13.37	12.46	10.87	10.94	—	—	—	—
Expense Ratio (%)	1.04	1.09	1.17	1.17	1.17	1.58	—	—	—	—
Net Income to Assets (%)	3.63	4.28	5.58	5.74	5.89	5.88	—	—	—	—
Portfolio Turnover (%)	109	98	134	134	105	167	—	—	—	—
Total Assets (Millions $)	11,075	8,958	2,762	743	316	245	—	—	—	—

PORTFOLIO (as of 9/30/94)

Portfolio Manager: Bob Beckwitt - 1988

Investm't Category: Balanced

Cap Gain	✔ Asset Allocation
✔ Cap & Income	Fund of Funds
Income	Index
	Sector
✔ Domestic	Small Cap
✔ Foreign	Socially Conscious
Country/Region	State Specific

Portfolio: stocks 39%   bonds 34%
convertibles 1%   other 2%   cash 24%

Largest Holdings: U.S. government bonds 15%, foreign government bonds 6%

Unrealized Net Capital Gains: 1% of portfolio value

SHAREHOLDER INFORMATION

Minimum Investment
Initial: $2,500   Subsequent: $250

Minimum IRA Investment
Initial: $500   Subsequent: $250

Maximum Fees
Load: none   12b-1: none
Other: none

Distributions
Income: quarterly   Capital Gains: Dec

Exchange Options
Number Per Year: 4   Fee: none
Telephone: yes (money market fund available)

Services
IRA, pension, auto exchange, auto invest, auto withdraw

Fidelity Asset Manager— Growth (FASGX)

82 Devonshire St.
Boston, MA 02109
(800) 544-8888, (801) 534-1910

Balanced

PERFORMANCE

fund inception date: 12/1/91

	3yr Annual	5yr Annual	10yr Annual	Bull	Bear
Return (%)	11.6	na	na	na	-10.0
Differ from Category (+/-)	5.2 high	na	na	na	-4.3 low

Total Risk	Standard Deviation	Category Risk	Risk Index	Beta
av	8.5%	high	1.4	0.8

	1994	1993	1992	1991	1990	1989	1988	1987	1986	1985
Return (%)	-7.3	26.3	19.0	—	—	—	—	—	—	—
Differ from category (+/-) . .	-5.4	12.9	10.7	—	—	—	—	—	—	—

PER SHARE DATA

	1994	1993	1992	1991	1990	1989	1988	1987	1986	1985
Dividends, Net Income ($) .	0.19	0.09	0.15	—	—	—	—	—	—	—
Distrib'ns, Cap Gain ($) . . .	0.17	0.51	0.08	—	—	—	—	—	—	—
Net Asset Value ($)	12.84	14.25	11.77	—	—	—	—	—	—	—
Expense Ratio (%).	1.15	1.19	1.64	—	—	—	—	—	—	—
Net Income to Assets (%). .	2.64	3.02	3.50	—	—	—	—	—	—	—
Portfolio Turnover (%). . . .	104	97	693	—	—	—	—	—	—	—
Total Assets (Millions $) . .	2,852	1,717	94	—	—	—	—	—	—	—

PORTFOLIO (as of 9/30/94)

Portfolio Manager: Bob Beckwitt - 1991

Investm't Category: Balanced

Cap Gain	✔ Asset Allocation
✔ Cap & Income	Fund of Funds
Income	Index
	Sector
✔ Domestic	Small Cap
✔ Foreign	Socially Conscious
Country/Region	State Specific

Portfolio: stocks 47%   bonds 26%
convertibles 0%   other 4%   cash 23%

Largest Holdings: bonds—U.S. government 12%, stocks—finance 7%

Unrealized Net Capital Gains: 1% of portfolio value

SHAREHOLDER INFORMATION

Minimum Investment
Initial: $2,500   Subsequent: $250

Minimum IRA Investment
Initial: $500   Subsequent: $250

Maximum Fees
Load: none   12b-1: none
Other: none

Distributions
Income: Dec   Capital Gains: Dec

Exchange Options
Number Per Year: 4   Fee: none
Telephone: yes (money market fund available)

Services
IRA, pension, auto exchange, auto invest, auto withdraw

Fidelity Asset Manager— Income (FASIX)

82 Devonshire St.
Boston, MA 02109
(800) 544-8888, (801) 534-1910

Balanced

PERFORMANCE

fund inception date: 10/1/92

	3yr Annual	5yr Annual	10yr Annual	Bull	Bear
Return (%)	na	na	na	na	-3.8
Differ from Category (+/-)	na	na	na	na	1.9 high

Total Risk	Standard Deviation	Category Risk	Risk Index	Beta
na	na	na	na	na

	1994	1993	1992	1991	1990	1989	1988	1987	1986	1985
Return (%).	-1.3	15.3	—	—	—	—	—	—	—	—
Differ from category (+/-) . .	0.6	1.9	—	—	—	—	—	—	—	—

PER SHARE DATA

	1994	1993	1992	1991	1990	1989	1988	1987	1986	1985
Dividends, Net Income ($).	0.49	0.49	—	—	—	—	—	—	—	—
Distrib'ns, Cap Gain ($) . . .	0.00	0.08	—	—	—	—	—	—	—	—
Net Asset Value ($)	10.42	11.06	—	—	—	—	—	—	—	—
Expense Ratio (%)	0.71	0.65	—	—	—	—	—	—	—	—
Net Income to Assets (%) .	4.92	5.19	—	—	—	—	—	—	—	—
Portfolio Turnover (%)	83	47	—	—	—	—	—	—	—	—
Total Assets (Millions $). . . .	476	284	—	—	—	—	—	—	—	—

PORTFOLIO (as of 9/30/94)

Portfolio Manager: Bob Beckwitt - 1992

Investm't Category: Balanced
Cap Gain	✔ Asset Allocation
✔ Cap & Income	Fund of Funds
Income	Index
	Sector
✔ Domestic	Small Cap
✔ Foreign	Socially Conscious
Country/Region	State Specific

Portfolio: stocks 15% bonds 62%
convertibles 1% other 3% cash 19%

Largest Holdings: U.S. government bonds 28%, finance bonds 14%

Unrealized Net Capital Gains: -1% of portfolio value

SHAREHOLDER INFORMATION

Minimum Investment
Initial: $2,500   Subsequent: $250

Minimum IRA Investment
Initial: $500   Subsequent: $250

Maximum Fees
Load: none   12b-1: none
Other: none

Distributions
Income: monthly   Capital Gains: Sep, Dec

Exchange Options
Number Per Year: 4   Fee: none
Telephone: yes (money market fund available)

Services
IRA, pension, auto exchange, auto invest, auto withdraw

Fidelity Balanced
(FBALX)
Balanced

82 Devonshire St.
Boston, MA 02109
(800) 544-8888, (801) 534-1910

PERFORMANCE

fund inception date: 11/6/86

	3yr Annual	5yr Annual	10yr Annual	Bull	Bear
Return (%)	6.8	8.9	na	76.4	-7.4
Differ from Category (+/-)	0.4 av	0.9 abv av	na	11.4 abv av	-1.7 blw av

Total Risk	Standard Deviation	Category Risk	Risk Index	Beta
blw av	5.7%	blw av	0.9	0.4

	1994	1993	1992	1991	1990	1989	1988	1987	1986	1985
Return (%)	-5.3	19.2	7.9	26.7	-0.4	19.7	15.7	1.9	—	—
Differ from category (+/-) ..	-3.4	5.8	-0.4	3.3	0.1	2.4	3.9	-0.5		

PER SHARE DATA

	1994	1993	1992	1991	1990	1989	1988	1987	1986	1985
Dividends, Net Income ($) .	0.40	0.60	0.66	0.60	0.68	1.00	0.68	0.60	—	—
Distrib'ns, Cap Gain ($) ...	0.00	0.64	0.36	0.45	0.00	0.22	0.00	0.07	—	—
Net Asset Value ($)	12.29	13.39	12.29	12.35	10.63	11.37	10.55	9.72	—	—
Expense Ratio (%)........	1.01	0.93	0.96	0.98	0.97	1.13	1.30	1.19	—	—
Net Income to Assets (%)..	4.09	5.07	5.68	5.93	6.74	8.90	6.29	6.03	—	—
Portfolio Turnover (%)....	157	162	242	238	223	168	213	161	—	—
Total Assets (Millions $)..	4,999	4,638	1,366	458	268	146	125	167	—	—

PORTFOLIO (as of 7/31/94)

Portfolio Manager: Bob Haber - 1988

Investm't Category: Balanced
Cap Gain	✔ Asset Allocation
✔ Cap & Income	Fund of Funds
Income	Index
	Sector
✔ Domestic	Small Cap
Foreign	Socially Conscious
Country/Region	State Specific

Portfolio: stocks 28%   bonds 49%
convertibles 15%   other 2%   cash 6%

Largest Holdings: stocks—finance 13%,
bonds—U.S. government and agencies 13%

Unrealized Net Capital Gains: -1% of portfolio value

SHAREHOLDER INFORMATION

Minimum Investment
Initial: $2,500   Subsequent: $250

Minimum IRA Investment
Initial: $500   Subsequent: $250

Maximum Fees
Load: none   12b-1: none
Other: none

Distributions
Income: quarterly   Capital Gains: Sep, Dec

Exchange Options
Number Per Year: 4   Fee: none
Telephone: yes (money market fund available)

Services
IRA, pension, auto exchange, auto invest, auto withdraw

Fidelity Blue Chip Growth (FBGRX)

Growth

82 Devonshire St.
Boston, MA 02109
(800) 544-8888, (801) 534-1910

PERFORMANCE

fund inception date: 12/31/87

	3yr Annual	5yr Annual	10yr Annual	Bull	Bear
Return (%)	13.2	18.3	na	132.4	-2.4
Differ from Category (+/-)	5.5 high	8.7 high	na	40.3 high	4.2 high

Total Risk	Standard Deviation	Category Risk	Risk Index	Beta
abv av	9.9%	abv av	1.0	1.0

	1994	1993	1992	1991	1990	1989	1988	1987	1986	1985
Return (%)	9.8	24.5	6.1	54.8	3.5	36.2	5.9	—	—	—
Differ from category (+/-) .	10.4	11.1	-5.5	19.1	9.2	10.1	-12.1	—	—	—

PER SHARE DATA

	1994	1993	1992	1991	1990	1989	1988	1987	1986	1985
Dividends, Net Income ($).	0.00	0.01	0.14	0.08	0.15	0.12	0.03	—	—	—
Distrib'ns, Cap Gain ($) . . .	0.58	4.12	0.62	0.00	0.00	0.17	0.00	—	—	—
Net Asset Value ($)	25.95	24.17	22.83	22.25	14.43	14.09	10.56	—	—	—
Expense Ratio (%)	1.22	1.25	1.27	1.26	1.26	1.56	2.74	—	—	—
Net Income to Assets (%) .	0.21	0.46	0.55	0.80	1.14	0.97	0.14	—	—	—
Portfolio Turnover (%)	271	319	71	99	68	83	40	—	—	—
Total Assets (Millions $). .	3,287	1,069	476	219	131	54	41	—	—	—

PORTFOLIO (as of 7/31/94)

Portfolio Manager: Michael Gordon - 1993

Investm't Category: Growth

✔ Cap Gain   Asset Allocation
  Cap & Income   Fund of Funds
  Income   Index
                   Sector
✔ Domestic   Small Cap
✔ Foreign   Socially Conscious
  Country/Region   State Specific

Portfolio: stocks 97%   bonds 0%
convertibles 0%   other 0%   cash 3%

Largest Holdings: technology 31%, energy 15%

Unrealized Net Capital Gains: 4% of portfolio value

SHAREHOLDER INFORMATION

Minimum Investment
Initial: $2,500   Subsequent: $250

Minimum IRA Investment
Initial: $500   Subsequent: $250

Maximum Fees
Load: 3.00% front   12b-1: none
Other: none

Distributions
Income: Sep   Capital Gains: Sep

Exchange Options
Number Per Year: 4   Fee: none
Telephone: yes (money market fund available)

Services
IRA, pension, auto exchange, auto invest, auto withdraw

Fidelity CA Tax-Free High Yield (FCTFX)

82 Devonshire St.
Boston, MA 02109
(800) 544-8888, (801) 534-1910

Tax-Exempt Bond

PERFORMANCE

fund inception date: 7/7/84

	3yr Annual	5yr Annual	10yr Annual	Bull	Bear
Return (%)	3.9	5.7	7.9	42.3	-7.6
Differ from Category (+/-)	-0.6 low	-0.4 low	-0.2 blw av	0.5 blw av	-2.4 low

Total Risk	Standard Deviation	Category Risk	Risk Index	Avg Mat
blw av	6.4%	abv av	1.0	20.0 yrs

	1994	1993	1992	1991	1990	1989	1988	1987	1986	1985
Return (%)	-8.8	13.4	8.7	10.1	6.9	9.6	11.7	-3.6	17.5	16.5
Differ from category (+/-) . .	-3.6	1.7	0.4	-1.2	0.6	0.6	1.5	-2.3	1.1	-0.9

PER SHARE DATA

	1994	1993	1992	1991	1990	1989	1988	1987	1986	1985
Dividends, Net Income ($)	0.69	0.72	0.74	0.75	0.75	0.76	0.75	0.77	0.80	0.93
Distrib'ns, Cap Gain ($) . . .	0.15	0.27	0.00	0.00	0.00	0.00	0.00	0.06	0.05	0.00
Net Asset Value ($)	10.50	12.42	11.86	11.62	11.26	11.26	10.99	10.54	11.80	10.81
Expense Ratio (%).	0.56	0.60	0.59	0.58	0.60	0.61	0.73	0.68	0.72	1.00
Net Income to Assets (%). .	6.10	6.17	6.52	6.71	6.73	7.05	7.15	6.68	7.75	9.53
Portfolio Turnover (%).	32	32	23	15	34	21	52	46	16	14
Total Assets (Millions $) . . .	443	592	529	523	514	494	399	461	323	30

PORTFOLIO (as of 8/31/94)

Portfolio Manager: John F. Haley Jr. - 1985

Investm't Category: Tax-Exempt Bond

Cap Gain	Asset Allocation
Cap & Income	Fund of Funds
✔ Income	Index
	Sector
✔ Domestic	Small Cap
Foreign	Socially Conscious
Country/Region	✔ State Specific

Portfolio: stocks 0%   bonds 100%
convertibles 0%   other 0%   cash 0%

Largest Holdings: general obligation 6%

Unrealized Net Capital Gains: 0% of portfolio value

SHAREHOLDER INFORMATION

Minimum Investment
Initial: $2,500   Subsequent: $250

Minimum IRA Investment
Initial: na   Subsequent: na

Maximum Fees
Load: none   12b-1: none
Other: none

Distributions
Income: monthly   Capital Gains: Apr, Dec

Exchange Options
Number Per Year: 4   Fee: none
Telephone: yes (money market fund available)

Services
auto exchange, auto invest, auto withdraw

Fidelity CA Tax-Free Insured (FCXIX)

Tax-Exempt Bond

82 Devonshire St.
Boston, MA 02109
(800) 544-8888, (801) 534-1910

PERFORMANCE

fund inception date: 9/18/86

	3yr Annual	5yr Annual	10yr Annual	Bull	Bear
Return (%)	3.7	5.7	na	45.5	-8.7
Differ from Category (+/-)	-0.8 low	-0.4 low	na	3.7 abv av	-3.5 low

Total Risk	Standard Deviation	Category Risk	Risk Index	Avg Mat
av	7.3%	high	1.2	20.3 yrs

	1994	1993	1992	1991	1990	1989	1988	1987	1986	1985
Return (%).............	-10.2	13.8	9.1	10.9	7.0	8.7	11.6	-4.5	—	—
Differ from category (+/-) ..	-5.0	2.1	0.8	-0.4	0.7	-0.3	1.4	-3.2	—	—

PER SHARE DATA

	1994	1993	1992	1991	1990	1989	1988	1987	1986	1985
Dividends, Net Income ($).	0.56	0.59	0.60	0.60	0.61	0.62	0.61	0.61	—	—
Distrib'ns, Cap Gain ($) ...	0.17	0.20	0.00	0.00	0.00	0.00	0.00	0.00	—	—
Net Asset Value ($)......	9.23	11.07	10.45	10.15	9.72	9.68	9.49	9.07	—	—
Expense Ratio (%)	0.61	0.63	0.66	0.72	0.75	0.83	0.65	0.45	—	—
Net Income to Assets (%) .	5.56	5.72	6.06	6.30	6.38	6.54	6.70	6.27	—	—
Portfolio Turnover (%)	28	27	19	14	10	32	76	28	—	—
Total Assets (Millions $)....	197	312	178	114	87	69	43	35	—	—

PORTFOLIO (as of 8/31/94)

Portfolio Manager: John F. Haley Jr. - 1986

Investm't Category: Tax-Exempt Bond

Cap Gain	Asset Allocation
Cap & Income	Fund of Funds
✔ Income	Index
	Sector
✔ Domestic	Small Cap
Foreign	Socially Conscious
Country/Region	✔ State Specific

Portfolio: stocks 0% bonds 100%
convertibles 0% other 0% cash 0%

Largest Holdings: general obligation 9%

Unrealized Net Capital Gains: -2% of portfolio value

SHAREHOLDER INFORMATION

Minimum Investment
Initial: $2,500 Subsequent: $250

Minimum IRA Investment
Initial: na Subsequent: na

Maximum Fees
Load: none 12b-1: none
Other: none

Distributions
Income: monthly Capital Gains: Apr, Dec

Exchange Options
Number Per Year: 4 Fee: none
Telephone: yes (money market fund available)

Services
auto exchange, auto invest, auto withdraw

Fidelity Canada (FICDX)

International Stock

82 Devonshire St.
Boston, MA 02109
(800) 544-8888, (801) 534-1910

	3yr Annual	5yr Annual	10yr Annual	Bull	Bear
Return (%)	2.3	3.5	na	55.2	-13.1
Differ from Category (+/-)	-6.8 low	-1.4 low	na	-8.7 blw av	-6.1 low

Total Risk	Standard Deviation	Category Risk	Risk Index	Beta
abv av	11.9%	blw av	0.9	0.9

	1994	1993	1992	1991	1990	1989	1988	1987	1986	1985
Return (%)	-11.9	25.4	-2.8	17.6	-5.4	26.9	19.4	—	—	—
Differ from category (+/-)..	-8.9	-13.2	0.1	4.5	5.0	4.4	5.0	—	—	—

PER SHARE DATA

	1994	1993	1992	1991	1990	1989	1988	1987	1986	1985
Dividends, Net Income ($) .	0.01	0.00	0.02	0.00	0.06	0.01	0.12	—	—	—
Distrib'ns, Cap Gain ($) ...	0.00	0.04	0.00	0.92	0.85	0.68	0.15	—	—	—
Net Asset Value ($)	16.00	18.19	14.53	14.98	13.53	15.29	12.59	—	—	—
Expense Ratio (%)........	1.74	2.00	2.00	2.01	2.05	2.06	2.02	—	—	—
Net Income to Assets (%).	-0.47	-0.66	-0.11	0.17	0.34	0.16	4.24	—	—	—
Portfolio Turnover (%).....	47	131	55	68	164	152	401	—	—	—
Total Assets (Millions $) ...	332	104	21	23	17	24	10	—	—	—

PORTFOLIO (as of 4/30/94)

Portfolio Manager: George Domolky - 1987

Investm't Category: International Stock

✔ Cap Gain	Asset Allocation
Cap & Income	Fund of Funds
Income	Index
	Sector
Domestic	Small Cap
✔ Foreign	Socially Conscious
✔ Country/Region	State Specific

Portfolio: stocks 97% bonds 0%
convertibles 2% other 0% cash 1%

Largest Holdings: Canada 94%, United States 5%

Unrealized Net Capital Gains: 1% of portfolio value

SHAREHOLDER INFORMATION

Minimum Investment
Initial: $2,500   Subsequent: $250

Minimum IRA Investment
Initial: $500   Subsequent: $250

Maximum Fees
Load: 3.00% front   12b-1: none
Other: none

Distributions
Income: Dec   Capital Gains: Dec

Exchange Options
Number Per Year: 2   Fee: none
Telephone: yes (money market fund available)

Services
IRA, pension, auto exchange, auto invest, auto withdraw

Fidelity Capital & Income
(FAGIX)
Corporate High-Yield Bond

82 Devonshire St.
Boston, MA 02109
(800) 544-8888, (801) 534-1910

PERFORMANCE

fund inception date: 11/1/77

	3yr Annual	5yr Annual	10yr Annual	Bull	Bear
Return (%)	15.1	13.7	12.0	111.0	-5.0
Differ from Category (+/-)	5.2 high	4.4 high	2.1 high	31.7 high	0.3 abv av

Total Risk	Standard Deviation	Category Risk	Risk Index	Avg Mat
blw av	6.3%	high	1.3	6.3 yrs

	1994	1993	1992	1991	1990	1989	1988	1987	1986	1985
Return (%)	-4.6	24.8	28.0	29.8	-3.8	-3.1	12.5	1.2	18.0	25.5
Differ from category (+/-)	-1.9	6.4	12.4	2.4	1.3	-4.5	0.4	0.1	3.7	2.3

PER SHARE DATA

	1994	1993	1992	1991	1990	1989	1988	1987	1986	1985
Dividends, Net Income ($)	0.80	0.83	0.66	0.74	0.76	1.08	1.01	1.05	1.10	1.15
Distrib'ns, Cap Gain ($)	0.00	0.00	0.00	0.00	0.00	0.00	0.00	0.28	0.31	0.00
Net Asset Value ($)	8.63	9.86	8.61	7.28	6.23	7.26	8.56	8.53	9.72	9.51
Expense Ratio (%)	0.97	0.91	0.80	0.81	0.81	0.77	0.88	0.78	0.80	0.83
Net Income to Assets (%)	6.78	7.45	9.77	11.26	12.70	11.96	11.38	10.99	11.30	12.54
Portfolio Turnover (%)	100	102	132	108	95	72	68	116	104	157
Total Assets (Millions $)	2,039	2,744	1,580	952	1,062	1,741	1,530	1,720	1,645	782

PORTFOLIO (as of 4/30/94)

Portfolio Manager: David Breazzano - 1991

Investm't Category: Corp. High-Yield Bond

Cap Gain	Asset Allocation
✔ Cap & Income	Fund of Funds
Income	Index
	Sector
✔ Domestic	Small Cap
✔ Foreign	Socially Conscious
Country/Region	State Specific

Portfolio: stocks 11% bonds 72%
convertibles 2% other 10% cash 5%

Largest Holdings: media & leisure 11%, construction & real estate 9%

Unrealized Net Capital Gains: 1% of portfolio value

SHAREHOLDER INFORMATION

Minimum Investment
Initial: $2,500   Subsequent: $250

Minimum IRA Investment
Initial: $500   Subsequent: $100

Maximum Fees
Load: 1.50% redemption   12b-1: none
Other: redemption fee applies for 1 year

Distributions
Income: monthly   Capital Gains: Jun, Dec

Exchange Options
Number Per Year: 4   Fee: none
Telephone: yes (money market fund available)

Services
IRA, pension, auto exchange, auto invest, auto withdraw

Fidelity Capital Appreciation Port (FDCAX)

Growth

82 Devonshire St.
Boston, MA 02109
(800) 544-8888, (801) 534-1910

PERFORMANCE

fund inception date: 11/26/86

	3yr Annual	5yr Annual	10yr Annual	Bull	Bear
Return (%)	16.7	8.0	na	90.1	-8.0
Differ from Category (+/-)	9.0 high	-1.6 blw av	na	-2.0 av	-1.4 blw av

Total Risk	Standard Deviation	Category Risk	Risk Index	Beta
abv av	9.1%	av	0.9	0.6

	1994	1993	1992	1991	1990	1989	1988	1987	1986	1985
Return (%)	2.5	33.4	16.3	9.9	-15.6	26.9	37.6	19.2	—	—
Differ from category (+/-) . . .	3.1	20.0	4.7	-25.8	-9.9	0.8	19.6	17.4	—	—

PER SHARE DATA

	1994	1993	1992	1991	1990	1989	1988	1987	1986	1985
Dividends, Net Income ($) .	0.17	0.10	0.18	0.62	0.17	0.24	0.13	0.02	—	—
Distrib'ns, Cap Gain ($) . . .	1.85	1.06	0.60	2.13	0.01	1.22	0.00	0.82	—	—
Net Asset Value ($)	15.31	16.92	13.57	12.34	13.84	16.63	14.29	10.48	—	—
Expense Ratio (%).	1.24	0.86	0.71	0.83	1.14	1.14	1.36	1.25	—	—
Net Income to Assets (%). .	0.89	0.93	1.63	3.87	1.61	1.84	1.35	0.56	—	—
Portfolio Turnover (%). . . .	107	120	99	72	56	73	120	203	—	—
Total Assets (Millions $) . .	1,623	1,411	1,009	1,110	1,354	2,155	1,436	867	—	—

PORTFOLIO (as of 4/30/94)

Portfolio Manager: Tom Sweeney - 1986

Investm't Category: Growth

✔ Cap Gain
  Cap & Income
  Income
  Asset Allocation
  Fund of Funds
  Index
  Sector
✔ Domestic
  Small Cap
✔ Foreign
  Socially Conscious
  Country/Region
  State Specific

Portfolio: stocks 93% bonds 0%
convertibles 0% other 0% cash 7%

Largest Holdings: transportation 17%, basic industries 16%

Unrealized Net Capital Gains: 3% of portfolio value

SHAREHOLDER INFORMATION

Minimum Investment
Initial: $2,500   Subsequent: $250

Minimum IRA Investment
Initial: $500   Subsequent: $250

Maximum Fees
Load: 3.00% front   12b-1: none
Other: none

Distributions
Income: Dec   Capital Gains: Dec

Exchange Options
Number Per Year: 4   Fee: none
Telephone: yes (money market fund available)

Services
IRA, pension, auto exchange, auto invest, auto withdraw

Fidelity Contrafund
(FCNTX)

Growth

82 Devonshire St.
Boston, MA 02109
(800) 544-8888, (801) 534-1910

PERFORMANCE

fund inception date: 5/17/67

	3yr Annual	5yr Annual	10yr Annual	Bull	Bear
Return (%)	11.6	17.5	18.5	148.8	-7.7
Differ from Category (+/-)	3.9 abv av	7.9 high	5.6 high	56.7 high	-1.1 blw av

Total Risk	Standard Deviation	Category Risk	Risk Index	Beta
abv av	9.0%	blw av	0.9	0.9

	1994	1993	1992	1991	1990	1989	1988	1987	1986	1985
Return (%).............	-1.1	21.4	15.8	54.9	3.9	43.1	21.0	-1.9	13.1	27.0
Differ from category (+/-) ..	-0.5	8.0	4.2	19.2	9.6	17.0	3.0	-3.7	-1.5	-2.2

PER SHARE DATA

	1994	1993	1992	1991	1990	1989	1988	1987	1986	1985
Dividends, Net Income ($).	0.00	0.18	0.20	0.11	0.09	0.25	0.32	0.00	0.25	0.25
Distrib'ns, Cap Gain ($) ...	0.22	2.25	1.92	1.06	0.00	1.07	0.00	0.43	2.15	0.00
Net Asset Value ($)	30.28	30.84	27.47	25.60	17.35	16.78	12.65	10.72	11.29	12.16
Expense Ratio (%)	1.03	1.06	0.87	0.89	1.06	0.95	0.98	0.92	0.88	0.95
Net Income to Assets (%) .	0.64	0.46	1.19	1.00	3.02	4.01	3.01	1.26	1.68	3.84
Portfolio Turnover (%)	275	255	297	217	320	266	250	196	190	135
Total Assets (Millions $)..	8,682	6,345	1,986	1,000	332	298	106	86	84	86

PORTFOLIO (as of 6/30/94)

Portfolio Manager: Will Danoff - 1990

Investm't Category: Growth

✔ Cap Gain	Asset Allocation
Cap & Income	Fund of Funds
Income	Index
	Sector
✔ Domestic	Small Cap
✔ Foreign	Socially Conscious
Country/Region	State Specific

Portfolio: stocks 85% bonds 1%
convertibles 1% other 0% cash 13%

Largest Holdings: technology 19%, energy 9%

Unrealized Net Capital Gains: 0% of portfolio value

SHAREHOLDER INFORMATION

Minimum Investment
Initial: $2,500   Subsequent: $250

Minimum IRA Investment
Initial: $500   Subsequent: $250

Maximum Fees
Load: 3.00% front   12b-1: none
Other: none

Distributions
Income: Dec   Capital Gains: Dec

Exchange Options
Number Per Year: 4   Fee: none
Telephone: yes (money market fund available)

Services
IRA, pension, auto exchange, auto invest, auto withdraw

Fidelity Convertible Securities (FCVSX)

82 Devonshire St.
Boston, MA 02109
(800) 544-8888, (801) 534-1910

Growth & Income

PERFORMANCE

fund inception date: 1/5/87

	3yr Annual	5yr Annual	10yr Annual	Bull	Bear
Return (%)	12.1	13.7	na	117.1	-7.8
Differ from Category (+/-)	5.0 high	5.8 high	na	41.3 high	-1.5 blw av

Total Risk	Standard Deviation	Category Risk	Risk Index	Beta
av	7.7%	blw av	0.9	0.6

	1994	1993	1992	1991	1990	1989	1988	1987	1986	1985
Return (%)	-1.7	17.7	22.0	38.7	-2.8	26.2	15.8	—	—	—
Differ from category (+/-) . .	-0.3	4.5	11.8	11.1	3.2	4.8	-1.2	—	—	—

PER SHARE DATA

	1994	1993	1992	1991	1990	1989	1988	1987	1986	1985
Dividends, Net Income ($) .	0.80	0.73	0.67	0.64	0.62	0.77	0.72	—	—	—
Distrib'ns, Cap Gain ($) . . .	0.00	1.09	0.40	0.37	0.00	0.00	0.00	—	—	—
Net Asset Value ($)	15.36	16.45	15.55	13.67	10.65	11.60	9.83	—	—	—
Expense Ratio (%).	0.87	0.92	0.96	1.17	1.31	1.38	1.60	—	—	—
Net Income to Assets (%). .	4.55	4.62	4.82	4.99	5.63	7.48	6.20	—	—	—
Portfolio Turnover (%)	401	312	258	152	223	207	191	—	—	—
Total Assets (Millions $) . . .	891	1,057	412	126	57	60	45	—	—	—

PORTFOLIO (as of 5/31/94)

Portfolio Manager: Andrew Offit - 1992

Investm't Category: Growth & Income

Cap Gain	Asset Allocation
✔ Cap & Income	Fund of Funds
Income	Index
	Sector
✔ Domestic	Small Cap
✔ Foreign	Socially Conscious
Country/Region	State Specific

Portfolio: stocks 19% bonds 1%
convertibles 70% other 0% cash 10%

Largest Holdings: health 15%, technology 14%

Unrealized Net Capital Gains: 0% of portfolio value

SHAREHOLDER INFORMATION

Minimum Investment
Initial: $2,500   Subsequent: $250

Minimum IRA Investment
Initial: $500   Subsequent: $250

Maximum Fees
Load: none   12b-1: none
Other: none

Distributions
Income: quarterly   Capital Gains: Dec

Exchange Options
Number Per Year: 4   Fee: none
Telephone: yes (money market fund available)

Services
IRA, pension, auto exchange, auto invest, auto withdraw

Fidelity Discipline Equity

(FDEQX)

Growth

82 Devonshire St.
Boston, MA 02109
(800) 544-8888, (801) 534-1910

	3yr Annual	5yr Annual	10yr Annual	Bull	Bear
Return (%)	9.9	12.3	na	102.5	-6.6
Differ from Category (+/-)	2.2 abv av	2.7 high	na	10.4 abv av	0.0 av

Total Risk	Standard Deviation	Category Risk	Risk Index	Beta
abv av	9.0%	blw av	0.9	1.0

	1994	1993	1992	1991	1990	1989	1988	1987	1986	1985
Return (%)	3.0	13.9	13.2	36.0	-0.7	36.3	—	—	—	—
Differ from category (+/-)	3.6	0.5	1.6	0.3	5.0	10.2	—	—	—	—

PER SHARE DATA

	1994	1993	1992	1991	1990	1989	1988	1987	1986	1985
Dividends, Net Income ($)	0.25	0.21	0.19	0.23	0.30	0.13	—	—	—	—
Distrib'ns, Cap Gain ($)	0.52	1.04	0.99	1.32	0.00	0.13	—	—	—	—
Net Asset Value ($)	17.94	18.18	17.07	16.14	13.11	13.52	—	—	—	—
Expense Ratio (%)	1.09	1.09	1.16	1.19	1.24	1.94	—	—	—	—
Net Income to Assets (%)	1.07	1.39	1.79	2.05	2.29	2.04	—	—	—	—
Portfolio Turnover (%)	143	279	255	210	171	118	—	—	—	—
Total Assets (Millions $)	1,160	790	341	154	96	71	—	—	—	—

PORTFOLIO (as of 4/30/94)

Portfolio Manager: Brad Lewis - 1988

Investm't Category: Growth

✔ Cap Gain	Asset Allocation
Cap & Income	Fund of Funds
Income	Index
	Sector
✔ Domestic	Small Cap
✔ Foreign	Socially Conscious
Country/Region	State Specific

Portfolio: stocks 85%   bonds 0%
convertibles 0%   other 0%   cash 15%

Largest Holdings: finance 12%, utilities 11%

Unrealized Net Capital Gains: 6% of portfolio value

SHAREHOLDER INFORMATION

Minimum Investment
Initial: $2,500   Subsequent: $250

Minimum IRA Investment
Initial: $500   Subsequent: $250

Maximum Fees
Load: none   12b-1: none
Other: none

Distributions
Income: Dec   Capital Gains: Dec

Exchange Options
Number Per Year: 4   Fee: none
Telephone: yes (money market fund available)

Services
IRA, pension, auto exchange, auto invest, auto withdraw

Fidelity Diversified Int'l

(FDIVX)

International Stock

82 Devonshire St.
Boston, MA 02109
(800) 544-8888, (801) 534-1910

fund inception date: 12/30/91

	3yr Annual	5yr Annual	10yr Annual	Bull	Bear
Return (%)	5.9	na	na	na	-4.7
Differ from Category (+/-)	-3.2 low	na	na	na	2.3 abv av

Total Risk	Standard Deviation	Category Risk	Risk Index	Beta
high	13.2%	abv av	1.0	0.8

	1994	1993	1992	1991	1990	1989	1988	1987	1986	1985
Return (%)	1.0	36.6	-13.8	—	—	—	—	—	—	—
Differ from category (+/-)	4.0	-2.0	-10.9	—	—	—	—	—	—	—

PER SHARE DATA

	1994	1993	1992	1991	1990	1989	1988	1987	1986	1985
Dividends, Net Income ($)	0.03	0.01	0.10	—	—	—	—	—	—	—
Distrib'ns, Cap Gain ($)	0.39	0.10	0.00	—	—	—	—	—	—	—
Net Asset Value ($)	11.30	11.60	8.57	—	—	—	—	—	—	—
Expense Ratio (%)	1.36	1.47	2.00	—	—	—	—	—	—	—
Net Income to Assets (%)	0.44	0.84	1.38	—	—	—	—	—	—	—
Portfolio Turnover (%)	99	56	56	—	—	—	—	—	—	—
Total Assets (Millions $)	306	247	36	—	—	—	—	—	—	—

PORTFOLIO (as of 4/30/94)

Portfolio Manager: Greg Fraser - 1991

Investm't Category: International Stock

✔ Cap Gain	Asset Allocation
Cap & Income	Fund of Funds
Income	Index
	Sector
Domestic	Small Cap
✔ Foreign	Socially Conscious
Country/Region	State Specific

Portfolio: stocks 90% bonds 1%
convertibles 0% other 2% cash 7%

Largest Holdings: Japan 28%, France 10%

Unrealized Net Capital Gains: 8% of portfolio value

SHAREHOLDER INFORMATION

Minimum Investment
Initial: $2,500   Subsequent: $250

Minimum IRA Investment
Initial: $500   Subsequent: $250

Maximum Fees
Load: 3.00% front   12b-1: none
Other: none

Distributions
Income: Dec   Capital Gains: Dec

Exchange Options
Number Per Year: 4   Fee: none
Telephone: yes (money market fund available)

Services
IRA, pension, auto exchange, auto invest, auto withdraw

Fidelity Dividend Growth
(FDGFX)
Growth

82 Devonshire St.
Boston, MA 02109
(800) 544-8888, (801) 534-1910

PERFORMANCE
fund inception date: 4/28/93

	3yr Annual	5yr Annual	10yr Annual	Bull	Bear
Return (%)	na	na	na	na	-9.4
Differ from Category (+/-)	na	na	na	na	-2.8 blw av

Total Risk	Standard Deviation	Category Risk	Risk Index	Beta
na	na	na	na	na

	1994	1993	1992	1991	1990	1989	1988	1987	1986	1985
Return (%)	4.2	—	—	—	—	—	—	—	—	—
Differ from category (+/-)	4.8	—	—	—	—	—	—	—	—	—

PER SHARE DATA

	1994	1993	1992	1991	1990	1989	1988	1987	1986	1985
Dividends, Net Income ($)	0.01	—	—	—	—	—	—	—	—	—
Distrib'ns, Cap Gain ($)	0.24	—	—	—	—	—	—	—	—	—
Net Asset Value ($)	12.37	—	—	—	—	—	—	—	—	—
Expense Ratio (%)	1.40	—	—	—	—	—	—	—	—	—
Net Income to Assets (%)	0.13	—	—	—	—	—	—	—	—	—
Portfolio Turnover (%)	291	—	—	—	—	—	—	—	—	—
Total Assets (Millions $)	102	—	—	—	—	—	—	—	—	—

PORTFOLIO (as of 7/31/94)

Portfolio Manager: Fergus Shiel - 1994

Investm't Category: Growth
- ✔ Cap Gain
-   Cap & Income
-   Income
- ✔ Domestic
-   Foreign
-   Country/Region

-   Asset Allocation
-   Fund of Funds
-   Index
-   Sector
-   Small Cap
-   Socially Conscious
-   State Specific

Portfolio: stocks 99% bonds 0%
convertibles 0% other 0% cash 1%

Largest Holdings: technology 16%, utilities 10%

Unrealized Net Capital Gains: 3% of portfolio value

SHAREHOLDER INFORMATION

Minimum Investment
Initial: $2,500   Subsequent: $250

Minimum IRA Investment
Initial: $500   Subsequent: $250

Maximum Fees
Load: none   12b-1: none
Other: none

Distributions
Income: Sep, Dec   Capital Gains: Sep, Dec

Exchange Options
Number Per Year: 4   Fee: none
Telephone: yes (money market fund available)

Services
IRA, pension, auto exchange, auto invest, auto withdraw

Fidelity Emerging Growth (FDEGX)

Aggressive Growth

82 Devonshire St.
Boston, MA 02109
(800) 544-8888, (801) 534-1910

PERFORMANCE

fund inception date: 12/28/90

	3yr Annual	5yr Annual	10yr Annual	Bull	Bear
Return (%)	9.0	na	na	na	-15.4
Differ from Category (+/-)	0.1 av	na	na	na	-4.6 blw av

Total Risk	Standard Deviation	Category Risk	Risk Index	Beta
high	14.2%	av	1.0	1.2

	1994	1993	1992	1991	1990	1989	1988	1987	1986	1985
Return (%)	-0.1	19.8	8.3	67.0	—	—	—	—	—	—
Differ from category (+/-) ...	0.6	0.3	-2.7	14.9	—	—	—	—	—	—

PER SHARE DATA

	1994	1993	1992	1991	1990	1989	1988	1987	1986	1985
Dividends, Net Income ($) .	0.00	0.00	0.02	0.00	—	—	—	—	—	—
Distrib'ns, Cap Gain ($) ...	0.31	3.57	0.14	0.39	—	—	—	—	—	—
Net Asset Value ($)	16.99	17.33	17.58	16.38	—	—	—	—	—	—
Expense Ratio (%)........	1.11	1.19	1.09	1.37	—	—	—	—	—	—
Net Income to Assets (%).	-0.57	-0.20	0.56	-0.10	—	—	—	—	—	—
Portfolio Turnover (%)....	204	332	531	326	—	—	—	—	—	—
Total Assets (Millions $) ...	635	641	614	530	—	—	—	—	—	—

PORTFOLIO (as of 5/31/94)

Portfolio Manager: Larry Greenberg - 1993

Investm't Category: Aggressive Growth

✔ Cap Gain	Asset Allocation
Cap & Income	Fund of Funds
Income	Index
	Sector
✔ Domestic	✔ Small Cap
✔ Foreign	Socially Conscious
Country/Region	State Specific

Portfolio: stocks 92% bonds 0%
convertibles 0% other 0% cash 8%

Largest Holdings: computer services & software 14%, communications equipment 12%

Unrealized Net Capital Gains: 2% of portfolio value

SHAREHOLDER INFORMATION

Minimum Investment
Initial: $2,500 Subsequent: $250

Minimum IRA Investment
Initial: $500 Subsequent: $250

Maximum Fees
Load: 3.00% front 12b-1: none
Other: 0.75% redemption fee (90 days)

Distributions
Income: Feb, Dec Capital Gains: Feb, Dec

Exchange Options
Number Per Year: 4 Fee: none
Telephone: yes (money market fund available)

Services
IRA, pension, auto exchange, auto invest, auto withdraw

Fidelity Emerging Markets (FEMKX)

International Stock

82 Devonshire St.
Boston, MA 02109
(800) 544-8888, (801) 534-1910

PERFORMANCE

fund inception date: 11/1/90

	3yr Annual	5yr Annual	10yr Annual	Bull	Bear
Return (%)	16.4	na	na	na	-17.0
Differ from Category (+/-)	7.3 high	na	na	na	-10.0 low

Total Risk	Standard Deviation	Category Risk	Risk Index	Beta
high	19.7%	high	1.5	1.0

	1994	1993	1992	1991	1990	1989	1988	1987	1986	1985
Return (%)	-17.9	81.7	5.8	6.7	—	—	—	—	—	—
Differ from category (+/-) .	-14.9	43.1	8.7	-6.4	—	—	—	—	—	—

PER SHARE DATA

	1994	1993	1992	1991	1990	1989	1988	1987	1986	1985
Dividends, Net Income ($).	0.04	0.05	0.08	0.08	—	—	—	—	—	—
Distrib'ns, Cap Gain ($) . . .	0.00	0.00	0.15	0.14	—	—	—	—	—	—
Net Asset Value ($)	16.13	19.70	10.87	10.49	—	—	—	—	—	—
Expense Ratio (%)	1.55	1.91	2.60	2.60	—	—	—	—	—	—
Net Income to Assets (%) .	0.33	0.44	0.90	1.34	—	—	—	—	—	—
Portfolio Turnover (%)	215	57	159	45	—	—	—	—	—	—
Total Assets (Millions $). .	1,508	1,675	13	6	—	—	—	—	—	—

PORTFOLIO (as of 4/30/94)

Portfolio Manager: Richard Hazelwood - 1993

Investm't Category: International Stock

✔ Cap Gain	Asset Allocation
Cap & Income	Fund of Funds
Income	Index
	Sector
Domestic	Small Cap
✔ Foreign	Socially Conscious
Country/Region	State Specific

Portfolio: stocks 80% bonds 5%
convertibles 6% other 1% cash 8%

Largest Holdings: Malaysia 18%, Mexico 17%

Unrealized Net Capital Gains: 0% of portfolio value

SHAREHOLDER INFORMATION

Minimum Investment
Initial: $2,500   Subsequent: $250

Minimum IRA Investment
Initial: $500   Subsequent: $250

Maximum Fees
Load: 3.00% front   12b-1: none
Other: 1.50% redemption fee (90 days)

Distributions
Income: Dec   Capital Gains: Dec

Exchange Options
Number Per Year: 4   Fee: none
Telephone: yes (money market fund available)

Services
IRA, pension, auto exchange, auto invest, auto withdraw

Fidelity Equity-Income

(FEQIX)

Growth & Income

82 Devonshire St.
Boston, MA 02109
(800) 544-8888, (801) 534-1910

PERFORMANCE

fund inception date: 5/16/66

	3yr Annual	5yr Annual	10yr Annual	Bull	Bear
Return (%)	11.7	9.2	12.4	98.7	-4.9
Differ from Category (+/-)	4.6 high	1.3 abv av	0.7 abv av	22.9 high	1.4 abv av

Total Risk	Standard Deviation	Category Risk	Risk Index	Beta
av	7.6%	blw av	0.9	0.9

	1994	1993	1992	1991	1990	1989	1988	1987	1986	1985
Return (%)	0.2	21.3	14.6	29.4	-13.9	18.6	22.4	-1.6	16.8	25.0
Differ from category (+/-) . . .	1.6	8.1	4.4	1.8	-7.9	-2.8	5.4	-2.2	1.0	-0.7

PER SHARE DATA

	1994	1993	1992	1991	1990	1989	1988	1987	1986	1985
Dividends, Net Income ($)	0.98	1.15	1.08	1.20	1.55	1.75	1.51	1.51	1.70	1.70
Distrib'ns, Cap Gain ($) . . .	2.22	0.12	0.00	0.00	0.30	1.16	0.00	3.92	3.08	0.52
Net Asset Value ($)	30.70	33.84	29.01	26.31	21.34	26.90	25.20	21.85	27.29	27.51
Expense Ratio (%).	0.73	0.67	0.68	0.70	0.71	0.63	0.66	0.65	0.66	0.72
Net Income to Assets (%). .	3.52	4.02	4.80	6.20	6.10	6.50	5.50	5.80	7.10	7.90
Portfolio Turnover (%)	48	84	111	107	92	68	120	110	118	123
Total Assets (Millions $) . .	7,412	6,582	4,422	3,941	4,751	4,401	3,683	3,818	2,362	1,351

PORTFOLIO (as of 7/31/94)

Portfolio Manager: Stephen Peterson - 1993

Investm't Category: Growth & Income

Cap Gain	Asset Allocation
✔ Cap & Income	Fund of Funds
Income	Index
	Sector
✔ Domestic	Small Cap
Foreign	Socially Conscious
Country/Region	State Specific

Portfolio: stocks 76% bonds 7%
convertibles 13% other 1% cash 3%

Largest Holdings: finance 16%, utilities 10%

Unrealized Net Capital Gains: 11% of portfolio value

SHAREHOLDER INFORMATION

Minimum Investment
Initial: $2,500   Subsequent: $250

Minimum IRA Investment
Initial: $500   Subsequent: $250

Maximum Fees
Load: 2.00% front   12b-1: none
Other: none

Distributions
Income: quarterly   Capital Gains: Mar, Dec

Exchange Options
Number Per Year: 4   Fee: none
Telephone: yes (money market fund available)

Services
IRA, pension, auto exchange, auto invest, auto withdraw

Fidelity Equity-Income II
(FEQTX)
Growth & Income

82 Devonshire St.
Boston, MA 02109
(800) 544-8888, (801) 534-1910

PERFORMANCE
fund inception date: 8/21/90

	3yr Annual	5yr Annual	10yr Annual	Bull	Bear
Return (%)	13.4	na	na	132.1	-2.9
Differ from Category (+/-)	6.3 high	na	na	56.3 high	3.4 high

Total Risk	Standard Deviation	Category Risk	Risk Index	Beta
av	7.5%	blw av	0.9	0.8

	1994	1993	1992	1991	1990	1989	1988	1987	1986	1985
Return (%)	3.1	18.8	19.0	46.5	—	—	—	—	—	—
Differ from category (+/-)	4.5	5.6	8.8	18.9	—	—	—	—	—	—

PER SHARE DATA

	1994	1993	1992	1991	1990	1989	1988	1987	1986	1985
Dividends, Net Income ($)	0.39	0.45	0.38	0.46	—	—	—	—	—	—
Distrib'ns, Cap Gain ($)	0.88	0.73	0.36	0.17	—	—	—	—	—	—
Net Asset Value ($)	17.72	18.41	16.51	14.52	—	—	—	—	—	—
Expense Ratio (%)	0.84	0.88	1.01	1.52	—	—	—	—	—	—
Net Income to Assets (%)	2.48	2.69	3.09	3.83	—	—	—	—	—	—
Portfolio Turnover (%)	81	55	89	206	—	—	—	—	—	—
Total Assets (Millions $)	7,697	4,992	1,942	292	—	—	—	—	—	—

PORTFOLIO (as of 5/31/94)

Portfolio Manager: Brian Posner - 1992

Investm't Category: Growth & Income

Cap Gain	Asset Allocation
✔ Cap & Income	Fund of Funds
Income	Index
	Sector
✔ Domestic	Small Cap
✔ Foreign	Socially Conscious
Country/Region	State Specific

Portfolio: stocks 77% bonds 4%
convertibles 5% other 0% cash 14%

Largest Holdings: finance 22%, energy 13%

Unrealized Net Capital Gains: 3% of portfolio value

SHAREHOLDER INFORMATION

Minimum Investment
Initial: $2,500   Subsequent: $250

Minimum IRA Investment
Initial: $500   Subsequent: $250

Maximum Fees
Load: none   12b-1: none
Other: none

Distributions
Income: quarterly   Capital Gains: Jan, Dec

Exchange Options
Number Per Year: 4   Fee: none
Telephone: yes (money market fund available)

Services
IRA, pension, auto exchange, auto invest, auto withdraw

Fidelity Europe (FIEUX)

International Stock

82 Devonshire St.
Boston, MA 02109
(800) 544-8888, (801) 534-1910

PERFORMANCE

fund inception date: 10/1/86

	3yr Annual	5yr Annual	10yr Annual	Bull	Bear
Return (%)	9.6	5.5	na	42.5	-7.2
Differ from Category (+/-)	0.5 abv av	0.6 av	na	-21.4 low	-0.2 av

Total Risk	Standard Deviation	Category Risk	Risk Index	Beta
high	12.6%	av	0.9	0.8

	1994	1993	1992	1991	1990	1989	1988	1987	1986	1985
Return (%)	6.2	27.1	-2.5	4.1	-4.5	32.3	5.8	14.9	—	—
Differ from category (+/-) . . .	9.2	-11.5	0.4	-9.0	5.9	9.8	-8.6	0.5	—	—

PER SHARE DATA

	1994	1993	1992	1991	1990	1989	1988	1987	1986	1985
Dividends, Net Income ($) .	0.20	0.08	0.29	0.51	0.38	0.19	0.28	0.01	—	—
Distrib'ns, Cap Gain ($) . . .	0.11	0.00	0.00	0.00	0.00	0.00	0.00	0.00	—	—
Net Asset Value ($)	20.00	19.12	15.10	15.79	15.67	16.81	12.85	12.41	—	—
Expense Ratio (%).	1.31	1.25	1.22	1.31	1.45	1.89	2.66	1.91	—	—
Net Income to Assets (%). .	0.34	1.44	2.38	2.83	2.87	1.67	0.97	0.48	—	—
Portfolio Turnover (%)	61	76	95	80	148	160	180	241	—	—
Total Assets (Millions $) . . .	487	499	431	297	389	97	102	131	—	—

PORTFOLIO (as of 4/30/94)

Portfolio Manager: Sally Walden - 1992

Investm't Category: International Stock

✔ Cap Gain	Asset Allocation
Cap & Income	Fund of Funds
Income	Index
	Sector
Domestic	Small Cap
✔ Foreign	Socially Conscious
✔ Country/Region	State Specific

Portfolio: stocks 94% bonds 0% convertibles 0% other 3% cash 3%

Largest Holdings: United Kingdom 24%, Germany 11%

Unrealized Net Capital Gains: 16% of portfolio value

SHAREHOLDER INFORMATION

Minimum Investment
Initial: $2,500   Subsequent: $250

Minimum IRA Investment
Initial: $500   Subsequent: $250

Maximum Fees
Load: 3.00% front   12b-1: none
Other: none

Distributions
Income: Dec   Capital Gains: Dec

Exchange Options
Number Per Year: 4   Fee: none
Telephone: yes (money market fund available)

Services
IRA, pension, auto exchange, auto invest, auto withdraw

Fidelity European Capital Appreciation (FECAX)

82 Devonshire St.
Boston, MA 02109
(800) 544-8888, (801) 534-1910

International Stock

PERFORMANCE

fund inception date: 12/24/93

	3yr Annual	5yr Annual	10yr Annual	Bull	Bear
Return (%)	na	na	na	na	-4.8
Differ from Category (+/-)	na	na	na	na	2.2 abv av

Total Risk	Standard Deviation	Category Risk	Risk Index	Beta
na	na	na	na	na

	1994	1993	1992	1991	1990	1989	1988	1987	1986	1985
Return (%).	6.8	—	—	—	—	—	—	—	—	—
Differ from category (+/-) . .	9.8	—	—	—	—	—	—	—	—	—

PER SHARE DATA

	1994	1993	1992	1991	1990	1989	1988	1987	1986	1985
Dividends, Net Income ($).	0.00	—	—	—	—	—	—	—	—	—
Distrib'ns, Cap Gain ($) . . .	0.00	—	—	—	—	—	—	—	—	—
Net Asset Value ($)	10.72	—	—	—	—	—	—	—	—	—
Expense Ratio (%)	1.70	—	—	—	—	—	—	—	—	—
Net Income to Assets (%) .	0.01	—	—	—	—	—	—	—	—	—
Portfolio Turnover (%)	294	—	—	—	—	—	—	—	—	—
Total Assets (Millions $). . . .	291	—	—	—	—	—	—	—	—	—

PORTFOLIO (as of 4/30/94)

Portfolio Manager: Kevin McCarey - 1993

Investm't Category: International Stock

✔ Cap Gain	Asset Allocation
Cap & Income	Fund of Funds
Income	Index
	Sector
Domestic	Small Cap
✔ Foreign	Socially Conscious
✔ Country/Region	State Specific

Portfolio: stocks 82% bonds 0%
convertibles 0% other 4% cash 14%

Largest Holdings: Netherlands 16%, France 15%

Unrealized Net Capital Gains: 3% of portfolio value

SHAREHOLDER INFORMATION

Minimum Investment
Initial: $2,500   Subsequent: $250

Minimum IRA Investment
Initial: $500   Subsequent: $250

Maximum Fees
Load: 3.00% front   12b-1: none
Other: none

Distributions
Income: Dec   Capital Gains: Dec

Exchange Options
Number Per Year: 4   Fee: none
Telephone: yes (money market fund available)

Services
IRA, pension, auto exchange, auto invest, auto withdraw

Fidelity Fifty (FFTYX)

Aggressive Growth

82 Devonshire St.
Boston, MA 02109
(800) 544-8888, (801) 534-1910

PERFORMANCE

fund inception date: 9/17/93

	3yr Annual	5yr Annual	10yr Annual	Bull	Bear
Return (%)	na	na	na	na	-7.3
Differ from Category (+/-)	na	na	na	na	3.5 abv av

Total Risk	Standard Deviation	Category Risk	Risk Index	Beta
na	na	na	na	na

	1994	1993	1992	1991	1990	1989	1988	1987	1986	1985
Return (%)	3.9	—	—	—	—	—	—	—	—	—
Differ from category (+/-)	4.6	—	—	—	—	—	—	—	—	—

PER SHARE DATA

	1994	1993	1992	1991	1990	1989	1988	1987	1986	1985
Dividends, Net Income ($)	0.02	—	—	—	—	—	—	—	—	—
Distrib'ns, Cap Gain ($)	0.10	—	—	—	—	—	—	—	—	—
Net Asset Value ($)	10.88	—	—	—	—	—	—	—	—	—
Expense Ratio (%)	1.58	—	—	—	—	—	—	—	—	—
Net Income to Assets (%)	0.23	—	—	—	—	—	—	—	—	—
Portfolio Turnover (%)	320	—	—	—	—	—	—	—	—	—
Total Assets (Millions $)	60	—	—	—	—	—	—	—	—	—

PORTFOLIO (as of 6/30/94)

Portfolio Manager: Scott Stewart - 1993

Investm't Category: Aggressive Growth

✔ Cap Gain	Asset Allocation
Cap & Income	Fund of Funds
Income	Index
	Sector
✔ Domestic	Small Cap
✔ Foreign	Socially Conscious
Country/Region	State Specific

Portfolio: stocks 78% bonds 0%
convertibles 0% other 0% cash 22%

Largest Holdings: technology 13%, health 11%

Unrealized Net Capital Gains: -1% of portfolio value

SHAREHOLDER INFORMATION

Minimum Investment
Initial: $2,500   Subsequent: $250

Minimum IRA Investment
Initial: $500   Subsequent: $250

Maximum Fees
Load: 3.00% front   12b-1: none
Other: none

Distributions
Income: Aug, Dec   Capital Gains: Aug, Dec

Exchange Options
Number Per Year: 4   Fee: none
Telephone: yes (money market fund available)

Services
IRA, pension, auto exchange, auto invest, auto withdraw

Fidelity Fund (FFIDX)

Growth & Income

82 Devonshire St.
Boston, MA 02109
(800) 544-8888, (801) 534-1910

PERFORMANCE

fund inception date: 4/30/30

	3yr Annual	5yr Annual	10yr Annual	Bull	Bear
Return (%)	9.5	9.1	13.6	75.1	-6.5
Differ from Category (+/-)	2.4 abv av	1.2 abv av	1.9 abv av	-0.7 av	-0.2 av

Total Risk	Standard Deviation	Category Risk	Risk Index	Beta
av	8.0%	av	1.0	0.9

	1994	1993	1992	1991	1990	1989	1988	1987	1986	1985
Return (%).	2.5	18.3	8.4	24.1	-5.0	28.8	17.8	3.2	15.5	28.0
Differ from category (+/-) . .	3.9	5.1	-1.8	-3.5	1.0	7.4	0.8	2.6	-0.3	2.3

PER SHARE DATA

	1994	1993	1992	1991	1990	1989	1988	1987	1986	1985
Dividends, Net Income ($).	0.33	0.44	0.48	0.50	0.74	0.68	0.56	0.48	0.66	0.72
Distrib'ns, Cap Gain ($) . . .	0.94	2.55	0.58	1.15	0.00	1.17	0.00	2.72	4.08	0.10
Net Asset Value ($)	18.48	19.27	18.94	18.47	16.30	17.93	15.42	13.58	16.05	18.08
Expense Ratio (%)	0.65	0.66	0.67	0.68	0.66	0.64	0.67	0.67	0.60	0.66
Net Income to Assets (%) .	1.85	2.94	2.37	2.84	4.04	3.76	3.69	2.75	3.48	4.25
Portfolio Turnover (%)	207	261	151	267	259	191	175	211	214	215
Total Assets (Millions $). .	1,886	1,669	1,354	1,320	1,064	1,087	892	870	780	761

PORTFOLIO (as of 6/30/94)

Portfolio Manager: Beth Terrana - 1993

Investm't Category: Growth & Income

Cap Gain	Asset Allocation
✔ Cap & Income	Fund of Funds
Income	Index
	Sector
✔ Domestic	Small Cap
✔ Foreign	Socially Conscious
Country/Region	State Specific

Portfolio: stocks 81% bonds 1%
convertibles 5% other 1% cash 12%

Largest Holdings: energy 9%, technology 9%

Unrealized Net Capital Gains: 0% of portfolio value

SHAREHOLDER INFORMATION

Minimum Investment
Initial: $2,500   Subsequent: $250

Minimum IRA Investment
Initial: $500   Subsequent: $250

Maximum Fees
Load: none   12b-1: none
Other: none

Distributions
Income: quarterly   Capital Gains: Feb, Dec

Exchange Options
Number Per Year: 4   Fee: none
Telephone: yes (money market fund available)

Services
IRA, pension, auto exchange, auto invest, auto withdraw

Fidelity Ginnie Mae
(FGMNX)
Mortgage-Backed Bond

82 Devonshire St.
Boston, MA 02109
(800) 544-8888, (801) 534-1910

PERFORMANCE

fund inception date: 11/8/85

	3yr Annual	5yr Annual	10yr Annual	Bull	Bear
Return (%)	3.5	6.8	na	36.6	-4.4
Differ from Category (+/-)	0.4 av	-0.1 blw av	na	-1.4 blw av	0.0 blw av

Total Risk	Standard Deviation	Category Risk	Risk Index	Avg Mat
low	3.1%	blw av	0.9	9.2 yrs

	1994	1993	1992	1991	1990	1989	1988	1987	1986	1985
Return (%)	-1.9	6.1	6.6	13.5	10.4	13.8	7.1	1.1	13.0	—
Differ from category (+/-)	0.9	-0.7	0.5	-0.9	0.7	1.3	0.0	-0.7	1.8	—

PER SHARE DATA

	1994	1993	1992	1991	1990	1989	1988	1987	1986	1985
Dividends, Net Income ($)	0.64	0.62	0.75	0.83	0.85	0.85	0.84	0.87	0.95	—
Distrib'ns, Cap Gain ($)	0.02	0.25	0.00	0.00	0.00	0.00	0.00	0.00	0.01	—
Net Asset Value ($)	9.99	10.86	11.07	11.10	10.56	10.38	9.91	10.05	10.81	—
Expense Ratio (%)	0.82	0.80	0.80	0.83	0.83	0.85	0.87	0.79	0.75	—
Net Income to Assets (%)	7.03	7.26	7.73	8.24	8.71	9.03	8.57	8.28	9.13	—
Portfolio Turnover (%)	303	259	114	125	96	291	361	177	106	—
Total Assets (Millions $)	704	893	914	797	658	651	722	869	652	—

PORTFOLIO (as of 7/31/94)

Portfolio Manager: Bob Ives - 1993

Investm't Category: Mortgage-Backed Bond

Cap Gain	Asset Allocation
Cap & Income	Fund of Funds
✔ Income	Index
	Sector
✔ Domestic	Small Cap
✔ Foreign	Socially Conscious
Country/Region	State Specific

Portfolio: stocks 0% bonds 94%
convertibles 0% other 0% cash 6%

Largest Holdings: mortgage-backed 94%

Unrealized Net Capital Gains: -3% of portfolio value

SHAREHOLDER INFORMATION

Minimum Investment
Initial: $2,500   Subsequent: $250

Minimum IRA Investment
Initial: $500   Subsequent: $250

Maximum Fees
Load: none   12b-1: none
Other: none

Distributions
Income: monthly   Capital Gains: Sep, Dec

Exchange Options
Number Per Year: 4   Fee: none
Telephone: yes (money market fund available)

Services
IRA, pension, auto exchange, auto invest, auto withdraw

Fidelity Global Balanced
(FGBLX)
International Stock

82 Devonshire St.
Boston, MA 02109
(800) 544-8888, (801) 534-1910

PERFORMANCE
fund inception date: 2/1/93

	3yr Annual	5yr Annual	10yr Annual	Bull	Bear
Return (%)	na	na	na	na	-14.0
Differ from Category (+/-)	na	na	na	na	-7.0 low

Total Risk	Standard Deviation	Category Risk	Risk Index	Beta
na	na	na	na	na

	1994	1993	1992	1991	1990	1989	1988	1987	1986	1985
Return (%)	-11.4	—	—	—	—	—	—	—	—	—
Differ from category (+/-)	-8.4	—	—	—	—	—	—	—	—	—

PER SHARE DATA

	1994	1993	1992	1991	1990	1989	1988	1987	1986	1985
Dividends, Net Income ($)	0.10	—	—	—	—	—	—	—	—	—
Distrib'ns, Cap Gain ($)	0.00	—	—	—	—	—	—	—	—	—
Net Asset Value ($)	11.56	—	—	—	—	—	—	—	—	—
Expense Ratio (%)	1.67	—	—	—	—	—	—	—	—	—
Net Income to Assets (%)	2.56	—	—	—	—	—	—	—	—	—
Portfolio Turnover (%)	226	—	—	—	—	—	—	—	—	—
Total Assets (Millions $)	236	—	—	—	—	—	—	—	—	—

PORTFOLIO (as of 7/31/94)

Portfolio Manager: Bob Haber - 1993

Investm't Category: International Stock

Cap Gain	✔ Asset Allocation
✔ Cap & Income	Fund of Funds
Income	Index
	Sector
✔ Domestic	Small Cap
✔ Foreign	Socially Conscious
Country/Region	State Specific

Portfolio: stocks 37% bonds 39%
convertibles 22% other 1% cash 1%

Largest Holdings: United States 24%, Argentina 17%

Unrealized Net Capital Gains: -4% of portfolio value

SHAREHOLDER INFORMATION

Minimum Investment
Initial: $2,500   Subsequent: $250

Minimum IRA Investment
Initial: $500   Subsequent: $250

Maximum Fees
Load: none   12b-1: none
Other: none

Distributions
Income: quarterly   Capital Gains: Sep, Dec

Exchange Options
Number Per Year: 4   Fee: none
Telephone: yes (money market fund available)

Services
IRA, pension, auto exchange, auto invest, auto withdraw

Fidelity Global Bond

(FGBDX)

International Bond

82 Devonshire St.
Boston, MA 02109
(800) 544-8888, (801) 534-1910

PERFORMANCE

fund inception date: 12/30/86

	3yr Annual	5yr Annual	10yr Annual	Bull	Bear
Return (%)	2.1	6.1	na	51.5	-17.2
Differ from Category (+/-)	-1.8 low	-2.5 low	na	-8.8 low	-9.4 low

Total Risk	Standard Deviation	Category Risk	Risk Index	Avg Mat
av	7.8%	high	1.3	9.6 yrs

	1994	1993	1992	1991	1990	1989	1988	1987	1986	1985
Return (%)	-16.3	21.9	4.3	12.7	12.2	7.9	3.6	19.1	—	—
Differ from category (+/-) .	-10.0	8.5	-0.4	-3.3	0.7	5.7	1.2	5.7	—	—

PER SHARE DATA

	1994	1993	1992	1991	1990	1989	1988	1987	1986	1985
Dividends, Net Income ($) .	0.69	0.86	1.08	0.90	1.05	0.49	0.90	0.69	—	—
Distrib'ns, Cap Gain ($) . . .	0.02	0.25	0.00	0.00	0.00	0.00	0.00	0.00	—	—
Net Asset Value ($)	9.88	12.61	11.34	11.90	11.38	11.08	10.72	11.21	—	—
Expense Ratio (%).	1.20	1.15	1.23	1.35	1.40	1.50	1.14	0.95	—	—
Net Income to Assets (%). .	6.17	7.84	8.02	7.92	7.82	7.56	7.61	7.14	—	—
Portfolio Turnover (%). . . .	289	172	81	228	154	150	227	297	—	—
Total Assets (Millions $) . . .	382	687	332	160	126	57	59	44	—	—

PORTFOLIO (as of 6/30/94)

Portfolio Manager: John Kelly - 1993

Investm't Category: International Bond

Cap Gain	Asset Allocation
✔ Cap & Income	Fund of Funds
Income	Index
	Sector
✔ Domestic	Small Cap
✔ Foreign	Socially Conscious
Country/Region	State Specific

Portfolio: stocks 0% bonds 66%
convertibles 6% other 6% cash 22%

Largest Holdings: Argentina 18%, Mexico 12%

Unrealized Net Capital Gains: -3% of portfolio value

SHAREHOLDER INFORMATION

Minimum Investment
Initial: $2,500   Subsequent: $250

Minimum IRA Investment
Initial: $500   Subsequent: $250

Maximum Fees
Load: none   12b-1: none
Other: none

Distributions
Income: monthly   Capital Gains: Dec

Exchange Options
Number Per Year: 4   Fee: none
Telephone: yes (money market fund available)

Services
IRA, pension, auto exchange, auto invest, auto withdraw

Fidelity Gov't Securities
(FGOVX)
Government Bond

82 Devonshire St.
Boston, MA 02109
(800) 544-8888, (801) 534-1910

PERFORMANCE
fund inception date: 4/4/79

	3yr Annual	5yr Annual	10yr Annual	Bull	Bear
Return (%)	4.7	7.8	9.0	50.7	-7.0
Differ from Category (+/-)	0.7 abv av	1.1 high	1.2 high	-0.5 abv av	-0.6 av

Total Risk	Standard Deviation	Category Risk	Risk Index	Avg Mat
blw av	5.2%	abv av	1.6	10.8 yrs

	1994	1993	1992	1991	1990	1989	1988	1987	1986	1985
Return (%)	-5.3	12.3	7.9	15.9	9.5	12.6	6.3	1.0	14.6	17.7
Differ from category (+/-)	-0.5	1.4	1.5	0.6	3.3	-1.9	-1.6	3.1	-6.0	-0.8

PER SHARE DATA

	1994	1993	1992	1991	1990	1989	1988	1987	1986	1985
Dividends, Net Income ($)	0.62	0.67	0.73	0.80	0.83	0.79	0.84	0.85	0.91	0.98
Distrib'ns, Cap Gain ($)	0.02	0.31	0.25	0.00	0.00	0.00	0.00	0.00	0.00	0.00
Net Asset Value ($)	9.17	10.34	10.10	10.30	9.64	9.61	9.27	9.52	10.28	9.80
Expense Ratio (%)	0.69	0.69	0.70	0.70	0.66	0.73	0.79	0.87	0.84	0.81
Net Income to Assets (%)	6.26	6.64	7.31	8.23	8.84	8.29	8.87	8.68	8.72	10.46
Portfolio Turnover (%)	402	311	219	257	302	312	283	253	138	137
Total Assets (Millions $)	611	744	581	522	469	560	568	683	752	270

PORTFOLIO (as of 9/30/94)

Portfolio Manager: Curtis Hollingsworth - 1990

Investm't Category: Government Bond

Cap Gain	Asset Allocation
Cap & Income	Fund of Funds
✔ Income	Index
	Sector
✔ Domestic	Small Cap
Foreign	Socially Conscious
Country/Region	State Specific

Portfolio: stocks 0% bonds 100%
convertibles 0% other 0% cash 0%

Largest Holdings: U. S. government & agencies 100%

Unrealized Net Capital Gains: -5% of portfolio value

SHAREHOLDER INFORMATION

Minimum Investment
Initial: $2,500   Subsequent: $250

Minimum IRA Investment
Initial: $500   Subsequent: $250

Maximum Fees
Load: none   12b-1: none
Other: none

Distributions
Income: monthly   Capital Gains: Feb

Exchange Options
Number Per Year: 4   Fee: none
Telephone: yes (money market fund available)

Services
IRA, pension, auto exchange, auto invest, auto withdraw

Fidelity Growth & Income (FGRIX)

82 Devonshire St.
Boston, MA 02109
(800) 544-8888, (801) 534-1910

Growth & Income

PERFORMANCE

fund inception date: 12/30/85

	3yr Annual	5yr Annual	10yr Annual	Bull	Bear
Return (%)	10.8	12.5	na	109.6	-5.7
Differ from Category (+/-)	3.7 high	4.6 high	na	33.8 high	0.6 abv av

Total Risk	Standard Deviation	Category Risk	Risk Index	Beta
av	7.3%	low	0.9	0.8

	1994	1993	1992	1991	1990	1989	1988	1987	1986	1985
Return (%)	2.2	19.5	11.5	41.8	-6.7	29.6	22.9	5.7	34.9	—
Differ from category (+/-)	3.6	6.3	1.3	14.2	-0.7	8.2	5.9	5.1	19.1	—

PER SHARE DATA

	1994	1993	1992	1991	1990	1989	1988	1987	1986	1985
Dividends, Net Income ($)	0.40	0.52	0.57	0.38	0.58	0.75	0.62	0.45	0.16	—
Distrib'ns, Cap Gain ($)	1.24	0.77	2.40	0.64	0.22	1.27	0.00	1.35	0.00	—
Net Asset Value ($)	21.09	22.22	19.71	20.49	15.22	17.17	14.85	12.60	13.33	—
Expense Ratio (%)	0.82	0.83	0.86	0.87	0.87	0.89	1.02	1.09	1.21	—
Net Income to Assets (%)	2.09	2.67	2.49	2.62	3.43	4.76	3.69	2.96	3.12	—
Portfolio Turnover (%)	92	87	221	215	108	97	135	165	69	—
Total Assets (Millions $)	9,344	7,642	4,199	2,686	1,910	1,428	1,188	1,629	365	—

PORTFOLIO (as of 7/31/94)

Portfolio Manager: Steven Kaye - 1993

Investm't Category: Growth & Income

Cap Gain	Asset Allocation
✔ Cap & Income	Fund of Funds
Income	Index
	Sector
✔ Domestic	Small Cap
✔ Foreign	Socially Conscious
Country/Region	State Specific

Portfolio: stocks 79% bonds 4%
convertibles 4% other 0% cash 13%

Largest Holdings: finance 9%, energy 8%

Unrealized Net Capital Gains: 7% of portfolio value

SHAREHOLDER INFORMATION

Minimum Investment
Initial: $2,500   Subsequent: $250

Minimum IRA Investment
Initial: $500   Subsequent: $250

Maximum Fees
Load: 3.00% front   12b-1: none
Other: none

Distributions
Income: quarterly   Capital Gains: Sep, Dec

Exchange Options
Number Per Year: 4   Fee: none
Telephone: yes (money market fund available)

Services
IRA, pension, auto exchange, auto invest, auto withdraw

Fidelity Growth Company (FDGRX)

Aggressive Growth

82 Devonshire St.
Boston, MA 02109
(800) 544-8888, (801) 534-1910

PERFORMANCE

fund inception date: 1/17/83

	3yr Annual	5yr Annual	10yr Annual	Bull	Bear
Return (%)	7.0	13.5	17.0	124.6	-9.9
Differ from Category (+/-)	-1.9 blw av	1.0 abv av	3.0 abv av	-8.6 av	0.9 av

Total Risk	Standard Deviation	Category Risk	Risk Index	Beta
abv av	10.9%	low	0.7	1.0

	1994	1993	1992	1991	1990	1989	1988	1987	1986	1985
Return (%)	-2.2	16.1	7.9	48.3	3.5	41.6	16.0	-1.6	13.0	39.9
Differ from category (+/-)	-1.5	-3.4	-3.1	-3.8	9.7	14.8	0.8	0.6	1.2	7.6

PER SHARE DATA

	1994	1993	1992	1991	1990	1989	1988	1987	1986	1985
Dividends, Net Income ($)	0.22	0.07	0.09	0.08	0.00	0.14	0.11	0.01	0.07	0.07
Distrib'ns, Cap Gain ($)	0.92	2.92	1.48	1.73	0.00	2.00	0.00	0.83	4.65	0.00
Net Asset Value ($)	27.26	29.06	27.64	27.09	19.60	18.92	15.00	13.02	14.11	16.83
Expense Ratio (%)	1.08	1.07	1.09	1.07	1.14	0.95	1.03	1.02	1.11	1.18
Net Income to Assets (%)	0.41	0.43	0.52	0.75	1.51	1.42	0.70	0.00	0.23	0.55
Portfolio Turnover (%)	143	159	250	174	189	269	257	212	120	129
Total Assets (Millions $)	2,993	2,512	1,752	1,133	535	283	129	112	180	147

PORTFOLIO (as of 5/31/94)

Portfolio Manager: Bob Stansky - 1987

Investm't Category: Aggressive Growth

✔ Cap Gain	Asset Allocation
Cap & Income	Fund of Funds
Income	Index
	Sector
✔ Domestic	Small Cap
✔ Foreign	Socially Conscious
Country/Region	State Specific

Portfolio: stocks 89% bonds 0%
convertibles 0% other 1% cash 10%

Largest Holdings: technology 27%, retail & wholesale 11%

Unrealized Net Capital Gains: 4% of portfolio value

SHAREHOLDER INFORMATION

Minimum Investment
Initial: $2,500 Subsequent: $250

Minimum IRA Investment
Initial: $500 Subsequent: $250

Maximum Fees
Load: 3.00% front 12b-1: none
Other: none

Distributions
Income: Jan, Dec Capital Gains: Jan, Dec

Exchange Options
Number Per Year: 4 Fee: none
Telephone: yes (money market fund available)

Services
IRA, pension, auto exchange, auto invest, auto withdraw

Fidelity High Yield Tax Free Port (FHIGX)

82 Devonshire St.
Boston, MA 02109
(800) 544-8888, (801) 534-1910

Tax-Exempt Bond

PERFORMANCE

fund inception date: 12/1/77

	3yr Annual	5yr Annual	10yr Annual	Bull	Bear
Return (%)	4.2	6.2	9.0	42.8	-6.5
Differ from Category (+/-)	-0.3 blw av	0.1 av	0.9 abv av	1.0 av	-1.3 blw av

Total Risk	Standard Deviation	Category Risk	Risk Index	Avg Mat
blw av	5.9%	av	0.9	19.0 yrs

	1994	1993	1992	1991	1990	1989	1988	1987	1986	1985
Return (%)	-7.4	13.1	8.3	10.1	8.4	11.3	12.2	-2.8	18.8	21.4
Differ from category (+/-) . .	-2.2	1.4	0.0	-1.2	2.1	2.3	2.0	-1.5	2.4	4.0

PER SHARE DATA

	1994	1993	1992	1991	1990	1989	1988	1987	1986	1985
Dividends, Net Income ($) .	0.75	0.76	0.81	0.83	0.86	0.89	0.90	0.93	0.99	1.04
Distrib'ns, Cap Gain ($) . . .	0.00	0.50	0.19	0.16	0.23	0.39	0.01	0.12	0.44	0.00
Net Asset Value ($)	11.25	12.95	12.60	12.58	12.36	12.44	12.36	11.87	13.29	12.44
Expense Ratio (%).	0.56	0.56	0.57	0.56	0.57	0.58	0.60	0.71	0.57	0.56
Net Income to Assets (%). .	6.17	5.85	6.40	6.72	6.96	7.10	7.48	7.38	7.63	8.83
Portfolio Turnover (%).	50	53	47	44	58	71	47	80	49	57
Total Assets (Millions $) . .	1,671	2,164	2,075	1,996	1,785	1,738	1,574	1,610	2,449	1,600

PORTFOLIO (as of 5/31/94)

Portfolio Manager: Anne Punzak - 1993

Investm't Category: Tax-Exempt Bond

Cap Gain	Asset Allocation
Cap & Income	Fund of Funds
✔ Income	Index
	Sector
✔ Domestic	Small Cap
Foreign	Socially Conscious
Country/Region	State Specific

Portfolio: stocks 0%   bonds 100%
convertibles 0%   other 0%   cash 0%

Largest Holdings: general obligation 13%

Unrealized Net Capital Gains: 0% of portfolio value

SHAREHOLDER INFORMATION

Minimum Investment
Initial: $2,500   Subsequent: $250

Minimum IRA Investment
Initial: na   Subsequent: na

Maximum Fees
Load: none   12b-1: none
Other: none

Distributions
Income: monthly   Capital Gains: Dec

Exchange Options
Number Per Year: 4   Fee: none
Telephone: yes (money market fund available)

Services
auto exchange, auto invest, auto withdraw

Fidelity Insured Tax-Free
(FMUIX)
Tax-Exempt Bond

82 Devonshire St.
Boston, MA 02109
(800) 544-8888, (801) 534-1910

PERFORMANCE   fund inception date: 11/13/85

	3yr Annual	5yr Annual	10yr Annual	Bull	Bear
Return (%)	4.2	6.2	na	44.3	-7.8
Differ from Category (+/-)	-0.3 blw av	0.1 av	na	2.5 av	-2.6 low

Total Risk	Standard Deviation	Category Risk	Risk Index	Avg Mat
av	6.9%	high	1.1	18.8 yrs

	1994	1993	1992	1991	1990	1989	1988	1987	1986	1985
Return (%)	-7.7	13.8	7.9	11.5	7.0	9.4	11.1	-2.0	18.4	—
Differ from category (+/-)	-2.5	2.1	-0.4	0.2	0.7	0.4	0.9	-0.7	2.0	—

PER SHARE DATA

	1994	1993	1992	1991	1990	1989	1988	1987	1986	1985
Dividends, Net Income ($)	0.63	0.65	0.69	0.70	0.71	0.72	0.71	0.72	0.74	—
Distrib'ns, Cap Gain ($)	0.12	0.28	0.11	0.00	0.00	0.00	0.00	0.01	0.00	—
Net Asset Value ($)	10.69	12.37	11.72	11.63	11.09	11.05	10.78	10.36	11.33	—
Expense Ratio (%)	0.59	0.61	0.63	0.65	0.67	0.70	0.70	0.62	0.60	—
Net Income to Assets (%)	5.34	5.31	5.91	6.23	6.52	6.57	6.64	6.73	6.52	—
Portfolio Turnover (%)	71	78	69	62	66	51	35	57	23	—
Total Assets (Millions $)	318	448	371	303	199	175	154	145	146	—

PORTFOLIO (as of 6/30/94)

Portfolio Manager: Gary Wickwire - 1993

Investm't Category: Tax-Exempt Bond

Cap Gain	Asset Allocation
Cap & Income	Fund of Funds
✔ Income	Index
	Sector
✔ Domestic	Small Cap
Foreign	Socially Conscious
Country/Region	State Specific

Portfolio: stocks 0%   bonds 100%
convertibles 0%   other 0%   cash 0%

Largest Holdings: general obligation 12%

Unrealized Net Capital Gains: -4% of portfolio value

SHAREHOLDER INFORMATION

Minimum Investment
Initial: $2,500   Subsequent: $250

Minimum IRA Investment
Initial: na   Subsequent: na

Maximum Fees
Load: none   12b-1: none
Other: none

Distributions
Income: monthly   Capital Gains: Feb, Dec

Exchange Options
Number Per Year: 4   Fee: none
Telephone: yes (money market fund available)

Services
auto exchange, auto invest, auto withdraw

Fidelity Interm Bond

(FTHRX)

General Bond

82 Devonshire St.
Boston, MA 02109
(800) 544-8888, (801) 534-1910

PERFORMANCE

fund inception date: 5/23/75

	3yr Annual	5yr Annual	10yr Annual	Bull	Bear
Return (%)	5.1	7.4	9.1	42.9	-4.2
Differ from Category (+/-)	0.8 abv av	0.5 abv av	0.2 av	1.9 av	-0.4 av

Total Risk	Standard Deviation	Category Risk	Risk Index	Avg Mat
low	3.7%	av	0.9	6.7 yrs

	1994	1993	1992	1991	1990	1989	1988	1987	1986	1985
Return (%)	-2.0	11.9	6.0	14.4	7.5	11.7	7.2	1.9	13.0	20.7
Differ from category (+/-) . . .	0.0	2.7	-0.6	-0.2	0.3	0.3	-0.2	-0.3	-1.2	1.3

PER SHARE DATA

	1994	1993	1992	1991	1990	1989	1988	1987	1986	1985
Dividends, Net Income ($) .	0.64	0.75	0.78	0.77	0.82	0.89	0.87	1.61	0.66	0.74
Distrib'ns, Cap Gain ($) . . .	0.09	0.09	0.05	0.00	0.00	0.00	0.00	0.10	0.22	0.00
Net Asset Value ($)	9.83	10.78	10.41	10.62	10.00	10.10	9.87	10.04	11.55	11.03
Expense Ratio (%).	0.64	0.61	0.63	0.66	0.72	0.62	0.87	0.86	0.75	0.79
Net Income to Assets (%). .	6.88	7.44	7.45	8.05	8.57	9.35	8.76	9.17	9.27	10.73
Portfolio Turnover (%).	81	51	80	73	82	101	59	67	101	68
Total Assets (Millions $) . .	2,127	1,838	1,235	878	661	528	504	370	367	244

PORTFOLIO (as of 4/30/94)

Portfolio Manager: Michael Gray - 1987

Investm't Category: General Bond

Cap Gain	Asset Allocation
Cap & Income	Fund of Funds
✔ Income	Index
	Sector
✔ Domestic	Small Cap
✔ Foreign	Socially Conscious
Country/Region	State Specific

Portfolio: stocks 0% bonds 87%
convertibles 0% other 0% cash 13%

Largest Holdings: U.S. government & agencies 34%, corporate 26%

Unrealized Net Capital Gains: -1% of portfolio value

SHAREHOLDER INFORMATION

Minimum Investment
Initial: $2,500   Subsequent: $250

Minimum IRA Investment
Initial: $500   Subsequent: $100

Maximum Fees
Load: none   12b-1: none
Other: none

Distributions
Income: monthly   Capital Gains: Jun, Dec

Exchange Options
Number Per Year: 4   Fee: none
Telephone: yes (money market fund available)

Services
IRA, pension, auto exchange, auto invest, auto withdraw

Fidelity Int'l Growth & Income (FIGRX)

82 Devonshire St.
Boston, MA 02109
(800) 544-8888, (801) 534-1910

International Stock

PERFORMANCE

fund inception date: 12/31/86

	3yr Annual	5yr Annual	10yr Annual	Bull	Bear
Return (%)	8.2	5.8	na	60.0	-6.3
Differ from Category (+/-)	-0.9 blw av	0.9 abv av	na	-3.9 av	0.7 av

Total Risk	Standard Deviation	Category Risk	Risk Index	Beta
abv av	11.0%	low	0.8	0.7

	1994	1993	1992	1991	1990	1989	1988	1987	1986	1985
Return (%)	-2.8	35.0	-3.3	8.0	-3.2	19.1	11.5	8.3	—	—
Differ from category (+/-)	0.2	-3.6	-0.4	-5.1	7.2	-3.4	-2.9	-6.1		

PER SHARE DATA

	1994	1993	1992	1991	1990	1989	1988	1987	1986	1985
Dividends, Net Income ($)	0.00	0.06	0.32	0.17	0.43	0.16	0.20	0.09	—	—
Distrib'ns, Cap Gain ($)	0.53	0.05	0.00	0.00	0.00	0.00	0.00	0.00	—	—
Net Asset Value ($)	16.53	17.57	13.09	13.87	13.00	13.88	11.79	10.75	—	—
Expense Ratio (%)	1.26	1.52	1.62	1.89	1.98	1.92	2.58	2.72	—	—
Net Income to Assets (%)	1.56	0.87	2.78	2.86	2.31	1.98	1.08	1.23	—	—
Portfolio Turnover (%)	184	24	76	117	102	147	112	158	—	—
Total Assets (Millions $)	1,272	1,061	60	50	35	26	32	41	—	—

PORTFOLIO (as of 4/30/94)

Portfolio Manager: Rick Mace - 1993

Investm't Category: International Stock

Cap Gain	Asset Allocation
✔ Cap & Income	Fund of Funds
Income	Index
	Sector
✔ Domestic	Small Cap
✔ Foreign	Socially Conscious
Country/Region	State Specific

Portfolio: stocks 49% bonds 25%
convertibles 5% other 3% cash 18%

Largest Holdings: Japan 37%, United States 10%

Unrealized Net Capital Gains: 1% of portfolio value

SHAREHOLDER INFORMATION

Minimum Investment
Initial: $2,500   Subsequent: $250

Minimum IRA Investment
Initial: $500   Subsequent: $250

Maximum Fees
Load: none   12b-1: none
Other: none

Distributions
Income: Dec   Capital Gains: Dec

Exchange Options
Number Per Year: 4   Fee: none
Telephone: yes (money market fund available)

Services
IRA, pension, auto exchange, auto invest, auto withdraw

Fidelity Investment Grade (FBNDX)

General Bond

82 Devonshire St.
Boston, MA 02109
(800) 544-8888, (801) 534-1910

PERFORMANCE

fund inception date: 8/6/71

	3yr Annual	5yr Annual	10yr Annual	Bull	Bear
Return (%)	5.9	8.4	9.6	56.4	-7.1
Differ from Category (+/-)	1.6 high	1.5 high	0.7 high	15.4 high	-3.3 low

Total Risk	Standard Deviation	Category Risk	Risk Index	Avg Mat
blw av	4.9%	high	1.2	10.7 yrs

	1994	1993	1992	1991	1990	1989	1988	1987	1986	1985
Return (%)	-5.3	16.1	8.3	18.9	6.0	13.0	7.8	0.1	13.5	21.1
Differ from category (+/-) . .	-3.3	6.9	1.7	4.3	-1.2	1.6	0.4	-2.1	-0.7	1.7

PER SHARE DATA

	1994	1993	1992	1991	1990	1989	1988	1987	1986	1985
Dividends, Net Income ($) .	0.50	0.56	0.56	0.59	0.60	0.61	0.60	0.63	0.69	0.77
Distrib'ns, Cap Gain ($) . . .	0.12	0.00	0.00	0.00	0.00	0.00	0.00	0.00	0.00	0.00
Net Asset Value ($)	6.85	7.89	7.30	7.28	6.67	6.88	6.65	6.73	7.36	7.12
Expense Ratio (%).	0.74	0.68	0.70	0.67	0.70	0.66	0.76	0.69	0.67	0.79
Net Income to Assets (%). .	6.94	7.74	8.29	8.84	8.76	8.91	8.95	9.17	10.53	12.22
Portfolio Turnover (%).	61	74	77	101	103	128	118	127	243	164
Total Assets (Millions $) . . .	995	1,044	943	455	359	334	316	384	250	166

PORTFOLIO (as of 4/30/94)

Portfolio Manager: Michael Gray - 1987

Investm't Category: General Bond

Cap Gain	Asset Allocation
Cap & Income	Fund of Funds
✔ Income	Index
	Sector
✔ Domestic	Small Cap
✔ Foreign	Socially Conscious
Country/Region	State Specific

Portfolio: stocks 0%   bonds 90%
convertibles 0%   other 2%   cash 8%

Largest Holdings: corporate 38%, U.S. government & agencies 25%

Unrealized Net Capital Gains: 0% of portfolio value

SHAREHOLDER INFORMATION

Minimum Investment
Initial: $2,500   Subsequent: $250

Minimum IRA Investment
Initial: $500   Subsequent: $100

Maximum Fees
Load: none   12b-1: none
Other: none

Distributions
Income: monthly   Capital Gains: Jun, Dec

Exchange Options
Number Per Year: 4   Fee: none
Telephone: yes (money market fund available)

Services
IRA, pension, auto exchange, auto invest, auto withdraw

Fidelity Japan (FJAPX)

International Stock

82 Devonshire St.
Boston, MA 02109
(800) 544-8888, (801) 534-1910

PERFORMANCE   fund inception date: 9/15/92

	3yr Annual	5yr Annual	10yr Annual	Bull	Bear
Return (%)	na	na	na	na	14.7
Differ from Category (+/-)	na	na	na	na	21.7 high

Total Risk	Standard Deviation		Category Risk	Risk Index	Beta
na	na		na	na	na

	1994	1993	1992	1991	1990	1989	1988	1987	1986	1985
Return (%)	16.4	20.4	—	—	—	—	—	—	—	—
Differ from category (+/-)	19.4	-18.2	—	—	—	—	—	—	—	—

PER SHARE DATA

	1994	1993	1992	1991	1990	1989	1988	1987	1986	1985
Dividends, Net Income ($)	0.00	0.00	—	—	—	—	—	—	—	—
Distrib'ns, Cap Gain ($)	0.36	0.39	—	—	—	—	—	—	—	—
Net Asset Value ($)	13.15	11.61	—	—	—	—	—	—	—	—
Expense Ratio (%)	1.66	1.71	—	—	—	—	—	—	—	—
Net Income to Assets (%)	-0.26	-0.77	—	—	—	—	—	—	—	—
Portfolio Turnover (%)	206	257	—	—	—	—	—	—	—	—
Total Assets (Millions $)	389	97	—	—	—	—	—	—	—	—

PORTFOLIO (as of 4/30/94)

Portfolio Manager: Shigeki Makino - 1994

Investm't Category: International Stock
- ✔ Cap Gain
- Cap & Income
- Income
- Domestic
- ✔ Foreign
- ✔ Country/Region
- Asset Allocation
- Fund of Funds
- Index
- Sector
- Small Cap
- Socially Conscious
- State Specific

Portfolio: stocks 78%   bonds 0%
convertibles 0%   other 0%   cash 22%

Largest Holdings: Japan 78%

Unrealized Net Capital Gains: 5% of portfolio value

SHAREHOLDER INFORMATION

Minimum Investment
Initial: $2,500   Subsequent: $250

Minimum IRA Investment
Initial: $500   Subsequent: $250

Maximum Fees
Load: 3.00% front   12b-1: none
Other: 1% redemption fee (90 days)

Distributions
Income: Dec   Capital Gains: Dec

Exchange Options
Number Per Year: 4   Fee: none
Telephone: yes (money market fund available)

Services
IRA, pension, auto exchange, auto invest, auto withdraw

Fidelity Latin America
(FLATX)

82 Devonshire St.
Boston, MA 02109
(800) 544-8888, (801) 534-1910

International Stock

PERFORMANCE

fund inception date: 4/19/93

	3yr Annual	5yr Annual	10yr Annual	Bull	Bear
Return (%)	na	na	na	na	-24.3
Differ from Category (+/-)	na	na	na	na	-17.3 low

Total Risk	Standard Deviation	Category Risk	Risk Index	Beta
na	na	na	na	na

	1994	1993	1992	1991	1990	1989	1988	1987	1986	1985
Return (%)	-23.1	—	—	—	—	—	—	—	—	—
Differ from category (+/-) .	-20.1	—	—	—	—	—	—	—	—	—

PER SHARE DATA

	1994	1993	1992	1991	1990	1989	1988	1987	1986	1985
Dividends, Net Income ($) .	0.00	—	—	—	—	—	—	—	—	—
Distrib'ns, Cap Gain ($) . . .	0.00	—	—	—	—	—	—	—	—	—
Net Asset Value ($)	12.37	—	—	—	—	—	—	—	—	—
Expense Ratio (%).	1.54	—	—	—	—	—	—	—	—	—
Net Income to Assets (%). .	0.41	—	—	—	—	—	—	—	—	—
Portfolio Turnover (%)	126	—	—	—	—	—	—	—	—	—
Total Assets (Millions $) . . .	616	—	—	—	—	—	—	—	—	—

PORTFOLIO (as of 4/30/94)

Portfolio Manager: Patti Satterthwaite - 1993

Investm't Category: International Stock

Cap Gain	Asset Allocation
✔ Cap & Income	Fund of Funds
Income	Index
	Sector
Domestic	Small Cap
✔ Foreign	Socially Conscious
✔ Country/Region	State Specific

Portfolio: stocks 85%   bonds 6%
convertibles 0%   other 0%   cash 9%

Largest Holdings: Mexico 42%, Brazil 18%

Unrealized Net Capital Gains: -6% of portfolio value

SHAREHOLDER INFORMATION

Minimum Investment
Initial: $2,500   Subsequent: $250

Minimum IRA Investment
Initial: $500   Subsequent: $250

Maximum Fees
Load: 3.00% front   12b-1: none
Other: 1.50% redemption fee (90 days)

Distributions
Income: Dec   Capital Gains: Dec

Exchange Options
Number Per Year: 4   Fee: none
Telephone: yes (money market fund available)

Services
IRA, pension, auto exchange, auto invest, auto withdraw

Fidelity Limited Term Muni (FLTMX)

82 Devonshire St.
Boston, MA 02109
(800) 544-8888, (801) 534-1910

Tax-Exempt Bond

PERFORMANCE

fund inception date: 4/15/77

	3yr Annual	5yr Annual	10yr Annual	Bull	Bear
Return (%)	4.9	6.5	8.1	40.4	-5.3
Differ from Category (+/-)	0.4 abv av	0.4 av	0.0 blw av	-1.4 blw av	-0.1 av

Total Risk	Standard Deviation	Category Risk	Risk Index	Avg Mat
blw av	5.1%	blw av	0.8	9.0 yrs

	1994	1993	1992	1991	1990	1989	1988	1987	1986	1985
Return (%)	-4.7	12.2	8.1	11.1	6.9	7.8	8.2	1.1	15.1	17.3
Differ from category (+/-)	0.5	0.5	-0.2	-0.2	0.6	-1.2	-2.0	2.4	-1.3	-0.1

PER SHARE DATA

	1994	1993	1992	1991	1990	1989	1988	1987	1986	1985
Dividends, Net Income ($)	0.51	0.52	0.57	0.60	0.61	0.62	0.60	0.58	0.62	0.64
Distrib'ns, Cap Gain ($)	0.02	0.24	0.10	0.15	0.05	0.00	0.00	0.00	0.00	0.00
Net Asset Value ($)	8.99	9.99	9.60	9.52	9.27	9.31	9.23	9.10	9.58	8.88
Expense Ratio (%)	0.54	0.57	0.64	0.68	0.67	0.66	0.67	0.74	0.68	0.71
Net Income to Assets (%)	5.31	5.19	5.94	6.41	6.63	6.70	6.51	6.29	6.55	7.41
Portfolio Turnover (%)	45	111	50	42	72	55	30	59	30	73
Total Assets (Millions $)	881	1,192	976	696	468	443	441	459	580	315

PORTFOLIO (as of 6/30/94)

Portfolio Manager: David Murphy - 1989

Investm't Category: Tax-Exempt Bond

Cap Gain	Asset Allocation
Cap & Income	Fund of Funds
✔ Income	Index
	Sector
✔ Domestic	Small Cap
Foreign	Socially Conscious
Country/Region	State Specific

Portfolio: stocks 0% bonds 100%
convertibles 0% other 0% cash 0%

Largest Holdings: general obligation 24%

Unrealized Net Capital Gains: 0% of portfolio value

SHAREHOLDER INFORMATION

Minimum Investment
Initial: $2,500   Subsequent: $250

Minimum IRA Investment
Initial: na   Subsequent: na

Maximum Fees
Load: none   12b-1: none
Other: none

Distributions
Income: monthly   Capital Gains: Feb, Dec

Exchange Options
Number Per Year: 4   Fee: none
Telephone: yes (money market fund available)

Services
auto exchange, auto invest, auto withdraw

Fidelity Low-Priced Stock (FLPSX)

82 Devonshire St.
Boston, MA 02109
(800) 544-8888, (801) 534-1910

Growth

PERFORMANCE

fund inception date: 12/27/89

	3yr Annual	5yr Annual	10yr Annual	Bull	Bear
Return (%)	17.5	18.8	na	154.9	-5.3
Differ from Category (+/-)	9.8 high	9.2 high	na	62.8 high	1.3 abv av

Total Risk	Standard Deviation	Category Risk	Risk Index	Beta
abv av	9.8%	av	1.0	0.7

	1994	1993	1992	1991	1990	1989	1988	1987	1986	1985
Return (%)	4.8	20.2	28.9	46.2	0.0	—	—	—	—	—
Differ from category (+/-)	5.4	6.8	17.3	10.5	5.7	—	—	—	—	—

PER SHARE DATA

	1994	1993	1992	1991	1990	1989	1988	1987	1986	1985
Dividends, Net Income ($)	0.09	0.16	0.10	0.15	0.14	—	—	—	—	—
Distrib'ns, Cap Gain ($)	2.05	1.62	0.69	0.60	0.26	—	—	—	—	—
Net Asset Value ($)	16.00	17.30	15.96	13.05	9.47	—	—	—	—	—
Expense Ratio (%)	1.13	1.12	1.20	1.36	1.92	—	—	—	—	—
Net Income to Assets (%)	0.51	1.00	1.27	2.14	3.77	—	—	—	—	—
Portfolio Turnover (%)	54	47	82	84	126	—	—	—	—	—
Total Assets (Millions $)	2,354	2,030	928	256	116	—	—	—	—	—

PORTFOLIO (as of 7/31/94)

Portfolio Manager: Joel Tillinghast - 1989

Investm't Category: Growth

✔ Cap Gain	Asset Allocation
Cap & Income	Fund of Funds
Income	Index
	Sector
✔ Domestic	✔ Small Cap
✔ Foreign	Socially Conscious
Country/Region	State Specific

Portfolio: stocks 76% bonds 0%
convertibles 1% other 0% cash 23%

Largest Holdings: finance 12%, technology 8%

Unrealized Net Capital Gains: 8% of portfolio value

SHAREHOLDER INFORMATION

Minimum Investment
Initial: $2,500 Subsequent: $250

Minimum IRA Investment
Initial: $500 Subsequent: $250

Maximum Fees
Load: 3.00% front 12b-1: none
Other: 1.50% redemption fee (90 days)

Distributions
Income: Sep, Dec Capital Gains: Sep, Dec

Exchange Options
Number Per Year: 4 Fee: none
Telephone: yes (money market fund available)

Services
IRA, pension, auto exchange, auto invest, auto withdraw

Fidelity Magellan

(FMAGX)

Growth

82 Devonshire St.
Boston, MA 02109
(800) 544-8888, (801) 534-1910

fund inception date: 5/2/63

PERFORMANCE

	3yr Annual	5yr Annual	10yr Annual	Bull	Bear
Return (%)	9.4	12.0	17.9	114.2	-9.5
Differ from Category (+/-)	1.7 abv av	2.4 abv av	5.0 high	22.1 high	-2.9 blw av

Total Risk	Standard Deviation	Category Risk	Risk Index	Beta
abv av	9.3%	av	1.0	1.0

	1994	1993	1992	1991	1990	1989	1988	1987	1986	1985
Return (%)	-1.8	24.6	7.0	41.0	-4.5	34.5	22.7	1.0	23.7	43.1
Differ from category (+/-)	-1.2	11.2	-4.6	5.3	1.2	8.4	4.7	-0.8	9.1	13.9

PER SHARE DATA

	1994	1993	1992	1991	1990	1989	1988	1987	1986	1985
Dividends, Net Income ($)	0.13	0.75	1.25	1.30	0.83	1.24	0.90	0.72	0.46	0.65
Distrib'ns, Cap Gain ($)	2.64	6.50	8.82	5.43	2.42	3.82	0.00	9.02	6.84	1.78
Net Asset Value ($)	66.80	70.85	63.01	68.61	53.93	59.85	48.32	40.10	48.69	45.21
Expense Ratio (%)	0.96	1.00	1.05	1.06	1.03	1.08	1.14	1.08	1.08	1.12
Net Income to Assets (%)	0.50	2.11	1.57	2.47	2.54	2.13	1.33	1.18	1.95	2.79
Portfolio Turnover (%)	137	155	172	135	82	87	101	96	96	126
Total Assets (Millions $)	36,441	31,088	19,825	14,807	13,162	9,626	8,438	9,889	6,086	2,363

PORTFOLIO (as of 9/30/94)

Portfolio Manager: Jeff Vinik - 1992

Investm't Category: Growth
- ✔ Cap Gain
- Cap & Income
- Income
- ✔ Domestic
- ✔ Foreign
- Country/Region
- Asset Allocation
- Fund of Funds
- Index
- Sector
- Small Cap
- Socially Conscious
- State Specific

Portfolio: stocks 96%   bonds 1%
convertibles 0%   other 1%   cash 2%

Largest Holdings: electronics 11%, computers & office equipment 8%

Unrealized Net Capital Gains: 12% of portfolio value

SHAREHOLDER INFORMATION

Minimum Investment
Initial: $2,500   Subsequent: $250

Minimum IRA Investment
Initial: $500   Subsequent: $250

Maximum Fees
Load: 3.00% front   12b-1: none
Other: none

Distributions
Income: Dec   Capital Gains: Dec

Exchange Options
Number Per Year: 4   Fee: none
Telephone: yes (money market fund available)

Services
IRA, pension, auto exchange, auto invest, auto withdraw

Fidelity Market Index

(FSMKX)

Growth & Income

82 Devonshire St.
Boston, MA 02109
(800) 544-8888, (801) 534-1910

PERFORMANCE

fund inception date: 3/6/90

	3yr Annual	5yr Annual	10yr Annual	Bull	Bear
Return (%)	5.9	na	na	72.5	-6.6
Differ from Category (+/-)	-1.2 blw av	na	na	-3.3 av	-0.3 av

Total Risk	Standard Deviation	Category Risk	Risk Index	Beta
av	7.9%	av	1.0	1.0

	1994	1993	1992	1991	1990	1989	1988	1987	1986	1985
Return (%)	1.0	9.6	7.3	30.3	—	—	—	—	—	—
Differ from category (+/-) . . .	2.4	-3.6	-2.9	2.7	—	—	—	—	—	—

PER SHARE DATA

	1994	1993	1992	1991	1990	1989	1988	1987	1986	1985
Dividends, Net Income ($) .	0.80	0.80	0.81	0.83	—	—	—	—	—	—
Distrib'ns, Cap Gain ($) . . .	0.00	0.18	0.00	0.07	—	—	—	—	—	—
Net Asset Value ($)	34.15	34.60	32.49	31.07	—	—	—	—	—	—
Expense Ratio (%).	0.45	0.44	0.35	0.28	—	—	—	—	—	—
Net Income to Assets (%). .	2.38	2.54	2.84	3.52	—	—	—	—	—	—
Portfolio Turnover (%)	3	0	1	1	—	—	—	—	—	—
Total Assets (Millions $) . . .	306	300	230	112	—	—	—	—	—	—

PORTFOLIO (as of 4/30/94)

Portfolio Manager: Jennifer Farrelly - 1994

Investm't Category: Growth & Income

Cap Gain	Asset Allocation
✔ Cap & Income	Fund of Funds
Income	✔ Index
	Sector
✔ Domestic	Small Cap
Foreign	Socially Conscious
Country/Region	State Specific

Portfolio: stocks 99% bonds 0%
convertibles 0% other 0% cash 1%

Largest Holdings: S&P 500 composite stock price index

Unrealized Net Capital Gains: 17% of portfolio value

SHAREHOLDER INFORMATION

Minimum Investment
Initial: $2,500   Subsequent: $250

Minimum IRA Investment
Initial: $500   Subsequent: $100

Maximum Fees
Load: 0.50% redemption   12b-1: none
Other: redemption fee applies for 6 mos

Distributions
Income: quarterly   Capital Gains: Jun, Dec

Exchange Options
Number Per Year: 4   Fee: none
Telephone: yes (money market fund available)

Services
IRA, pension, auto exchange, auto invest, auto withdraw

Fidelity Mass Tax-Free High Yield (FDMMX)

82 Devonshire St.
Boston, MA 02109
(800) 544-8888, (801) 534-1910

Tax-Exempt Bond

PERFORMANCE

fund inception date: 11/10/83

	3yr Annual	5yr Annual	10yr Annual	Bull	Bear
Return (%)	5.0	6.7	8.7	44.3	-5.5
Differ from Category (+/-)	0.5 abv av	0.6 abv av	0.6 abv av	2.5 av	-0.3 av

Total Risk	Standard Deviation	Category Risk	Risk Index	Avg Mat
blw av	5.7%	blw av	0.9	19.9 yrs

	1994	1993	1992	1991	1990	1989	1988	1987	1986	1985
Return (%).	-6.0	12.9	9.2	11.3	7.3	9.2	10.6	-1.2	16.8	19.6
Differ from category (+/-) . .	-0.8	1.2	0.9	0.0	1.0	0.2	0.4	0.1	0.4	2.2

PER SHARE DATA

	1994	1993	1992	1991	1990	1989	1988	1987	1986	1985
Dividends, Net Income ($).	0.70	0.71	0.73	0.76	0.80	0.80	0.80	0.80	0.82	0.91
Distrib'ns, Cap Gain ($) . . .	0.23	0.26	0.07	0.08	0.11	0.00	0.00	0.03	0.00	0.00
Net Asset Value ($)	10.48	12.13	11.64	11.41	11.04	11.16	10.98	10.68	11.66	10.72
Expense Ratio (%)	0.54	0.55	0.57	0.56	0.57	0.56	0.61	0.64	0.64	0.76
Net Income to Assets (%) .	6.16	6.19	6.43	7.05	7.20	7.33	7.56	6.85	782.00	9.01
Portfolio Turnover (%)	29	42	18	29	31	26	25	36	13	12
Total Assets (Millions $). . . .	993	1,378	1,235	842	737	663	580	642	500	203

PORTFOLIO (as of 7/31/94)

Portfolio Manager: Guy Wickwire - 1983

Investm't Category: Tax-Exempt Bond

Cap Gain	Asset Allocation
Cap & Income	Fund of Funds
✔ Income	Index
	Sector
✔ Domestic	Small Cap
Foreign	Socially Conscious
Country/Region	✔ State Specific

Portfolio: stocks 0%   bonds 100%
convertibles 0%   other 0%   cash 0%

Largest Holdings: general obligation 12%

Unrealized Net Capital Gains: 1% of portfolio value

SHAREHOLDER INFORMATION

Minimum Investment
Initial: $2,500   Subsequent: $250

Minimum IRA Investment
Initial: na   Subsequent: na

Maximum Fees
Load: none   12b-1: none
Other: none

Distributions
Income: monthly   Capital Gains: Sep, Dec

Exchange Options
Number Per Year: 4   Fee: none
Telephone: yes (money market fund available)

Services
auto exchange, auto invest, auto withdraw

Fidelity Michigan Tax-Free High Yield (FMHTX)

82 Devonshire St.
Boston, MA 02109
(800) 544-8888, (801) 534-1910

Tax-Exempt Bond

PERFORMANCE

fund inception date: 11/12/85

	3yr Annual	5yr Annual	10yr Annual	Bull	Bear
Return (%)	4.8	6.3	na	45.9	-6.6
Differ from Category (+/-)	0.3 av	0.2 av	na	4.1 abv av	-1.4 blw av

Total Risk	Standard Deviation	Category Risk	Risk Index	Avg Mat
blw av	6.2%	av	1.0	18.2 yrs

	1994	1993	1992	1991	1990	1989	1988	1987	1986	1985
Return (%)	-7.5	13.8	9.5	12.0	5.1	10.2	13.0	-2.8	19.0	—
Differ from category (+/-) . .	-2.3	2.1	1.2	0.7	-1.2	1.2	2.8	-1.5	2.6	—

PER SHARE DATA

	1994	1993	1992	1991	1990	1989	1988	1987	1986	1985
Dividends, Net Income ($) .	0.69	0.71	0.73	0.74	0.76	0.76	0.75	0.77	0.79	—
Distrib'ns, Cap Gain ($) . . .	0.17	0.24	0.02	0.00	0.00	0.00	0.00	0.04	0.00	—
Net Asset Value ($)	10.58	12.34	11.71	11.41	10.89	11.10	10.79	10.25	11.38	—
Expense Ratio (%).	0.58	0.59	0.61	0.62	0.64	0.69	0.75	0.72	0.60	—
Net Income to Assets (%). .	5.85	5.79	6.36	6.73	6.98	6.92	7.12	7.25	7.03	—
Portfolio Turnover (%).	18	33	15	12	18	19	24	44	24	—
Total Assets (Millions $) . . .	434	560	464	379	279	234	171	128	127	—

PORTFOLIO (as of 6/30/94)

Portfolio Manager: Maureen Newman - 1994

Investm't Category: Tax-Exempt Bond

Cap Gain	Asset Allocation
Cap & Income	Fund of Funds
✔ Income	Index
	Sector
✔ Domestic	Small Cap
Foreign	Socially Conscious
Country/Region	✔ State Specific

Portfolio: stocks 0% bonds 100%
convertibles 0% other 0% cash 0%

Largest Holdings: general obligation 12%

Unrealized Net Capital Gains: 0% of portfolio value

SHAREHOLDER INFORMATION

Minimum Investment
Initial: $2,500 Subsequent: $250

Minimum IRA Investment
Initial: na Subsequent: na

Maximum Fees
Load: none 12b-1: none
Other: none

Distributions
Income: monthly Capital Gains: Feb, Dec

Exchange Options
Number Per Year: 4 Fee: none
Telephone: yes (money market fund available)

Services
auto exchange, auto invest, auto withdraw

Fidelity Minnesota Tax-Free (FIMIX)

Tax-Exempt Bond

82 Devonshire St.
Boston, MA 02109
(800) 544-8888, (801) 534-1910

PERFORMANCE

fund inception date: 11/21/85

	3yr Annual	5yr Annual	10yr Annual	Bull	Bear
Return (%)	4.4	5.7	na	38.0	-5.9
Differ from Category (+/-)	-0.1 av	-0.4 low	na	-3.8 low	-0.7 av

Total Risk	Standard Deviation	Category Risk	Risk Index	Avg Mat
blw av	5.5%	blw av	0.9	19.8 yrs

	1994	1993	1992	1991	1990	1989	1988	1987	1986	1985
Return (%)	-5.9	12.4	7.6	8.4	7.2	9.2	12.6	-3.8	17.0	—
Differ from category (+/-)	-0.7	0.7	-0.7	-2.9	0.9	0.2	2.4	-2.5	0.6	—

PER SHARE DATA

	1994	1993	1992	1991	1990	1989	1988	1987	1986	1985
Dividends, Net Income ($)	0.63	0.65	0.67	0.69	0.70	0.71	0.71	0.72	0.77	—
Distrib'ns, Cap Gain ($)	0.08	0.00	0.00	0.00	0.00	0.00	0.00	0.03	0.00	—
Net Asset Value ($)	10.14	11.52	10.85	10.73	10.55	10.52	10.31	9.82	10.99	—
Expense Ratio (%)	0.60	0.61	0.67	0.72	0.76	0.80	0.82	0.79	0.60	—
Net Income to Assets (%)	5.79	5.85	6.25	6.47	6.72	6.84	7.06	7.04	7.05	—
Portfolio Turnover (%)	39	37	12	14	29	25	31	63	23	—
Total Assets (Millions $)	277	339	281	222	167	131	100	79	93	—

PORTFOLIO (as of 6/30/94)

Portfolio Manager: Steve Harvey - 1993

Investm't Category: Tax-Exempt Bond

Cap Gain	Asset Allocation
Cap & Income	Fund of Funds
✔ Income	Index
	Sector
✔ Domestic	Small Cap
Foreign	Socially Conscious
Country/Region	✔ State Specific

Portfolio: stocks 0% bonds 100%
convertibles 0% other 0% cash 0%

Largest Holdings: general obligation 11%

Unrealized Net Capital Gains: -2% of portfolio value

SHAREHOLDER INFORMATION

Minimum Investment
Initial: $2,500   Subsequent: $250

Minimum IRA Investment
Initial: na   Subsequent: na

Maximum Fees
Load: none   12b-1: none
Other: none

Distributions
Income: monthly   Capital Gains: Feb, Dec

Exchange Options
Number Per Year: 4   Fee: none
Telephone: yes (money market fund available)

Services
auto exchange, auto invest, auto withdraw

Fidelity Mortgage Securities (FMSFX)

Mortgage-Backed Bond

82 Devonshire St.
Boston, MA 02109
(800) 544-8888, (801) 534-1910

PERFORMANCE

fund inception date: 12/31/84

	3yr Annual	5yr Annual	10yr Annual	Bull	Bear
Return (%)	4.6	7.5	9.0	35.4	-0.7
Differ from Category (+/-)	1.5 high	0.6 abv av	0.2 abv av	-2.6 low	3.7 high

Total Risk	Standard Deviation	Category Risk	Risk Index	Avg Mat
low	2.4%	low	0.7	7.6 yrs

	1994	1993	1992	1991	1990	1989	1988	1987	1986	1985
Return (%)	1.9	6.6	5.4	13.6	10.3	13.6	6.6	2.6	11.2	19.6
Differ from category (+/-) . . .	4.7	-0.2	-0.7	-0.8	0.6	1.1	-0.5	0.8	0.0	0.0

PER SHARE DATA

	1994	1993	1992	1991	1990	1989	1988	1987	1986	1985
Dividends, Net Income ($) .	0.62	0.63	0.75	0.82	0.83	0.84	0.82	0.90	1.00	1.15
Distrib'ns, Cap Gain ($) . . .	0.05	0.07	0.00	0.00	0.00	0.00	0.00	0.00	0.03	0.00
Net Asset Value ($)	10.26	10.73	10.73	10.91	10.38	10.21	9.77	9.94	10.58	10.48
Expense Ratio (%).	0.79	0.76	0.80	0.82	0.82	0.88	0.90	0.80	0.75	0.75
Net Income to Assets (%). .	6.73	7.18	7.57	8.39	8.78	8.72	8.96	8.79	9.13	11.53
Portfolio Turnover (%). . . .	563	278	146	209	110	271	245	160	106	72
Total Assets (Millions $) . . .	349	377	441	410	388	421	485	603	652	140

PORTFOLIO (as of 7/31/94)

Portfolio Manager: Kevin Grant - 1993

Investm't Category: Mortgage-Backed Bond

Cap Gain	Asset Allocation
Cap & Income	Fund of Funds
✔ Income	Index
	Sector
✔ Domestic	Small Cap
✔ Foreign	Socially Conscious
Country/Region	State Specific

Portfolio: stocks 0% bonds 84%
convertibles 0% other 0% cash 16%

Largest Holdings: mortgage-backed 84%

Unrealized Net Capital Gains: 0% of portfolio value

SHAREHOLDER INFORMATION

Minimum Investment
Initial: $2,500   Subsequent: $250

Minimum IRA Investment
Initial: $500   Subsequent: $250

Maximum Fees
Load: none   12b-1: none
Other: none

Distributions
Income: monthly   Capital Gains: Sep, Dec

Exchange Options
Number Per Year: 4   Fee: none
Telephone: yes (money market fund available)

Services
IRA, pension, auto exchange, auto invest, auto withdraw

Fidelity Muni Bond

(FMBDX)

Tax-Exempt Bond

82 Devonshire St.
Boston, MA 02109
(800) 544-8888, (801) 534-1910

PERFORMANCE
fund inception date: 8/19/76

	3yr Annual	5yr Annual	10yr Annual	Bull	Bear
Return (%)	4.0	6.1	8.8	44.8	-7.3
Differ from Category (+/-)	-0.5 blw av	0.0 blw av	0.7 abv av	3.0 abv av	-2.1 low

Total Risk	Standard Deviation	Category Risk	Risk Index	Avg Mat
av	6.8%	high	1.1	20.0 yrs

	1994	1993	1992	1991	1990	1989	1988	1987	1986	1985
Return (%)	-8.6	13.1	8.9	11.9	6.8	9.5	12.2	-1.5	19.5	20.0
Differ from category (+/-)	-3.4	1.4	0.6	0.6	0.5	0.5	2.0	-0.2	3.1	2.6

PER SHARE DATA

	1994	1993	1992	1991	1990	1989	1988	1987	1986	1985
Dividends, Net Income ($)	0.45	0.49	0.52	0.53	0.54	0.56	0.56	0.55	0.55	0.58
Distrib'ns, Cap Gain ($)	0.14	0.41	0.18	0.07	0.00	0.00	0.00	0.00	0.00	0.00
Net Asset Value ($)	7.36	8.69	8.50	8.47	8.13	8.13	7.95	7.60	8.28	7.42
Expense Ratio (%)	0.54	0.49	0.49	0.50	0.50	0.50	0.51	0.57	0.51	0.46
Net Income to Assets (%)	5.54	5.51	6.11	6.35	6.71	6.90	7.11	7.03	6.90	8.06
Portfolio Turnover (%)	91	74	53	33	49	64	46	72	72	145
Total Assets (Millions $)	1,005	1,273	1,192	1,163	1,071	1,053	984	903	1,141	906

PORTFOLIO (as of 6/30/94)

Portfolio Manager: Gary Swayze - 1985

Investm't Category: Tax-Exempt Bond

Cap Gain	Asset Allocation
Cap & Income	Fund of Funds
✔ Income	Index
	Sector
✔ Domestic	Small Cap
Foreign	Socially Conscious
Country/Region	State Specific

Portfolio: stocks 0% bonds 100%
convertibles 0% other 0% cash 0%

Largest Holdings: general obligation 11%

Unrealized Net Capital Gains: -3% of portfolio value

SHAREHOLDER INFORMATION

Minimum Investment
Initial: $2,500   Subsequent: $250

Minimum IRA Investment
Initial: na   Subsequent: na

Maximum Fees
Load: none   12b-1: none
Other: none

Distributions
Income: monthly   Capital Gains: Feb, Dec

Exchange Options
Number Per Year: 4   Fee: none
Telephone: yes (money market fund available)

Services
auto exchange, auto invest, auto withdraw

Fidelity New Markets Income (FNMIX)

International Bond

82 Devonshire St.
Boston, MA 02109
(800) 544-8888, (801) 534-1910

PERFORMANCE

fund inception date: 5/4/93

	3yr Annual	5yr Annual	10yr Annual	Bull	Bear
Return (%)	na	na	na	na	-27.1
Differ from Category (+/-)	na	na	na	na	-19.3 low

Total Risk	Standard Deviation	Category Risk	Risk Index	Avg Mat
na	na	na	na	10.7 yrs

	1994	1993	1992	1991	1990	1989	1988	1987	1986	1985
Return (%)	-16.4	—	—	—	—	—	—	—	—	—
Differ from category (+/-) .	-10.1	—	—	—	—	—	—	—	—	—

PER SHARE DATA

	1994	1993	1992	1991	1990	1989	1988	1987	1986	1985
Dividends, Net Income ($) .	0.57	—	—	—	—	—	—	—	—	—
Distrib'ns, Cap Gain ($) ...	0.20	—	—	—	—	—	—	—	—	—
Net Asset Value ($)	10.20	—	—	—	—	—	—	—	—	—
Expense Ratio (%)	1.28	—	—	—	—	—	—	—	—	—
Net Income to Assets (%)..	5.17	—	—	—	—	—	—	—	—	—
Portfolio Turnover (%)	472	—	—	—	—	—	—	—	—	—
Total Assets (Millions $) ...	179	—	—	—	—	—	—	—	—	—

PORTFOLIO (as of 6/30/94)

Portfolio Manager: Rob Citrone - 1993

Investm't Category: International Bond

Cap Gain	Asset Allocation
Cap & Income	Fund of Funds
✔ Income	Index
	Sector
✔ Domestic	Small Cap
✔ Foreign	Socially Conscious
Country/Region	State Specific

Portfolio: stocks 10% bonds 86%
convertibles 3% other 1% cash 0%

Largest Holdings: Brazil 27%, Argentina 23%

Unrealized Net Capital Gains: -13% of portfolio value

SHAREHOLDER INFORMATION

Minimum Investment
Initial: $2,500   Subsequent: $250

Minimum IRA Investment
Initial: $500   Subsequent: $250

Maximum Fees
Load: none   12b-1: none
Other: none

Distributions
Income: Dec   Capital Gains: Dec

Exchange Options
Number Per Year: 4   Fee: none
Telephone: yes (money market fund available)

Services
IRA, pension, auto exchange, auto invest, auto withdraw

Fidelity New Millenium
(FMILX)
Aggressive Growth

82 Devonshire St.
Boston, MA 02109
(800) 544-8888, (801) 534-1910

	3yr Annual	5yr Annual	10yr Annual	Bull	Bear
Return (%)	na	na	na	na	-9.1
Differ from Category (+/-)	na	na	na	na	1.7 abv av

Total Risk	Standard Deviation	Category Risk	Risk Index	Beta
na	na	na	na	na

	1994	1993	1992	1991	1990	1989	1988	1987	1986	1985
Return (%)	0.8	24.6	—	—	—	—	—	—	—	—
Differ from category (+/-)	1.5	5.1	—	—	—	—	—	—	—	—

PER SHARE DATA

	1994	1993	1992	1991	1990	1989	1988	1987	1986	1985
Dividends, Net Income ($)	0.00	0.01	—	—	—	—	—	—	—	—
Distrib'ns, Cap Gain ($)	0.28	0.25	—	—	—	—	—	—	—	—
Net Asset Value ($)	12.11	12.30	—	—	—	—	—	—	—	—
Expense Ratio (%)	1.32	1.32	—	—	—	—	—	—	—	—
Net Income to Assets (%)	0.00	-0.10	—	—	—	—	—	—	—	—
Portfolio Turnover (%)	185	204	—	—	—	—	—	—	—	—
Total Assets (Millions $)	319	271	—	—	—	—	—	—	—	—

PORTFOLIO (as of 5/31/94)

Portfolio Manager: Neal Miller - 1992

Investm't Category: Aggressive Growth

✔ Cap Gain	Asset Allocation
Cap & Income	Fund of Funds
Income	Index
	Sector
✔ Domestic	✔ Small Cap
✔ Foreign	Socially Conscious
Country/Region	State Specific

Portfolio: stocks 93% bonds 0%
convertibles 0% other 0% cash 7%

Largest Holdings: technology 19%, media & leisure 9%

Unrealized Net Capital Gains: 2% of portfolio value

SHAREHOLDER INFORMATION

Minimum Investment
Initial: $2,500   Subsequent: $250

Minimum IRA Investment
Initial: $500   Subsequent: $250

Maximum Fees
Load: 3.00% front   12b-1: none
Other: none

Distributions
Income: Dec   Capital Gains: Dec

Exchange Options
Number Per Year: 4   Fee: none
Telephone: yes (money market fund available)

Services
IRA, pension, auto exchange, auto invest, auto withdraw

Fidelity NY Tax-Free High Yield (FTFMX)

82 Devonshire St.
Boston, MA 02109
(800) 544-8888, (801) 534-1910

Tax-Exempt Bond

PERFORMANCE

fund inception date: 7/10/84

	3yr Annual	5yr Annual	10yr Annual	Bull	Bear
Return (%)	4.1	6.1	8.5	44.7	-7.3
Differ from Category (+/-)	-0.4 blw av	0.0 blw av	0.4 av	2.9 abv av	-2.1 low

Total Risk	Standard Deviation	Category Risk	Risk Index	Avg Mat
blw av	6.7%	abv av	1.1	20.0 yrs

	1994	1993	1992	1991	1990	1989	1988	1987	1986	1985
Return (%)	-8.0	12.8	8.9	13.3	5.0	9.2	11.9	-2.4	16.7	20.8
Differ from category (+/-)	-2.8	1.1	0.6	2.0	-1.3	0.2	1.7	-1.1	0.3	3.4

PER SHARE DATA

	1994	1993	1992	1991	1990	1989	1988	1987	1986	1985
Dividends, Net Income ($)	0.67	0.72	0.77	0.78	0.80	0.81	0.79	0.80	0.82	0.92
Distrib'ns, Cap Gain ($)	0.24	0.46	0.00	0.00	0.00	0.00	0.00	0.10	0.17	0.00
Net Asset Value ($)	11.04	12.97	12.57	12.28	11.56	11.78	11.55	11.06	12.26	11.41
Expense Ratio (%)	0.58	0.61	0.61	0.59	0.61	0.63	0.67	0.60	0.67	1.00
Net Income to Assets (%)	5.61	6.08	6.52	6.81	6.87	6.99	7.10	6.76	7.61	9.05
Portfolio Turnover (%)	43	45	30	45	34	49	64	51	62	8
Total Assets (Millions $)	380	482	412	386	381	368	312	352	202	28

PORTFOLIO (as of 7/31/94)

Portfolio Manager: Norm Lind - 1993

Investm't Category: Tax-Exempt Bond

Cap Gain	Asset Allocation
Cap & Income	Fund of Funds
✔ Income	Index
	Sector
✔ Domestic	Small Cap
Foreign	Socially Conscious
Country/Region	✔ State Specific

Portfolio: stocks 0%   bonds 100%
convertibles 0%   other 0%   cash 0%

Largest Holdings: general obligation 12%

Unrealized Net Capital Gains: -1% of portfolio value

SHAREHOLDER INFORMATION

Minimum Investment
Initial: $2,500   Subsequent: $250

Minimum IRA Investment
Initial: na   Subsequent: na

Maximum Fees
Load: none   12b-1: none
Other: none

Distributions
Income: monthly   Capital Gains: Jun, Dec

Exchange Options
Number Per Year: 4   Fee: none
Telephone: yes (money market fund available)

Services
auto exchange, auto invest, auto withdraw

Fidelity NY Tax-Free Insured (FNTIX)

82 Devonshire St.
Boston, MA 02109
(800) 544-8888, (801) 534-1910

Tax-Exempt Bond

PERFORMANCE

fund inception date: 10/11/85

	3yr Annual	5yr Annual	10yr Annual	Bull	Bear
Return (%)	4.0	6.1	na	43.9	-7.1
Differ from Category (+/-)	-0.5 blw av	0.0 blw av	na	2.1 av	-1.9 low

Total Risk	Standard Deviation	Category Risk	Risk Index	Avg Mat
blw av	6.6%	abv av	1.1	19.3 yrs

	1994	1993	1992	1991	1990	1989	1988	1987	1986	1985
Return (%)	-7.9	12.8	8.5	12.4	6.1	9.0	11.2	-3.1	17.3	—
Differ from category (+/-)	-2.7	1.1	0.2	1.1	-0.2	0.0	1.0	-1.8	0.9	—

PER SHARE DATA

	1994	1993	1992	1991	1990	1989	1988	1987	1986	1985
Dividends, Net Income ($)	0.63	0.65	0.68	0.69	0.70	0.70	0.69	0.70	0.71	—
Distrib'ns, Cap Gain ($)	0.15	0.31	0.00	0.00	0.00	0.00	0.00	0.00	0.01	—
Net Asset Value ($)	10.50	12.24	11.73	11.46	10.84	10.89	10.65	10.22	11.28	—
Expense Ratio (%)	0.59	0.61	0.62	0.64	0.65	0.65	0.67	0.60	0.60	—
Net Income to Assets (%)	5.48	5.73	6.17	6.45	6.47	6.55	6.72	6.31	6.81	—
Portfolio Turnover (%)	48	39	17	33	18	31	29	30	8	—
Total Assets (Millions $)	300	409	309	247	206	180	155	172	63	—

PORTFOLIO (as of 7/31/94)

Portfolio Manager: David Murphy - 1992

Investm't Category: Tax-Exempt Bond

Cap Gain	Asset Allocation
Cap & Income	Fund of Funds
✔ Income	Index
	Sector
✔ Domestic	Small Cap
Foreign	Socially Conscious
Country/Region	✔ State Specific

Portfolio: stocks 0% bonds 100%
convertibles 0% other 0% cash 0%

Largest Holdings: general obligation 0%

Unrealized Net Capital Gains: -1% of portfolio value

SHAREHOLDER INFORMATION

Minimum Investment
Initial: $2,500   Subsequent: $250

Minimum IRA Investment
Initial: na   Subsequent: na

Maximum Fees
Load: none   12b-1: none
Other: none

Distributions
Income: monthly   Capital Gains: Jun, Dec

Exchange Options
Number Per Year: 4   Fee: none
Telephone: yes (money market fund available)

Services
auto exchange, auto invest, auto withdraw

Fidelity Ohio Tax-Free High Yield (FOHFX)

82 Devonshire St.
Boston, MA 02109
(800) 544-8888, (801) 534-1910

Tax-Exempt Bond

PERFORMANCE

fund inception date: 11/15/85

	3yr Annual	5yr Annual	10yr Annual	Bull	Bear
Return (%)	4.9	6.7	na	43.8	-5.5
Differ from Category (+/-)	0.4 abv av	0.6 abv av	na	2.0 av	-0.3 av

Total Risk	Standard Deviation	Category Risk	Risk Index	Avg Mat
blw av	5.7%	blw av	0.9	17.9 yrs

	1994	1993	1992	1991	1990	1989	1988	1987	1986	1985
Return (%)	-5.5	12.5	8.6	11.4	7.4	9.9	12.9	-2.3	16.4	—
Differ from category (+/-) . .	-0.3	0.8	0.3	0.1	1.1	0.9	2.7	-1.0	0.0	—

PER SHARE DATA

	1994	1993	1992	1991	1990	1989	1988	1987	1986	1985
Dividends, Net Income ($)	0.66	0.69	0.72	0.72	0.72	0.73	0.72	0.74	0.77	—
Distrib'ns, Cap Gain ($) . . .	0.19	0.25	0.00	0.00	0.00	0.00	0.00	0.00	0.00	—
Net Asset Value ($)	10.52	12.02	11.55	11.32	10.84	10.79	10.50	9.97	10.97	—
Expense Ratio (%).	0.58	0.57	0.61	0.64	0.66	0.71	0.73	0.79	0.60	—
Net Income to Assets (%). .	5.74	5.67	6.31	6.53	6.82	6.79	7.08	7.09	7.01	—
Portfolio Turnover (%)	18	41	20	11	12	22	23	36	32	—
Total Assets (Millions $) . . .	349	456	385	328	242	201	153	117	107	—

PORTFOLIO (as of 6/30/94)

Portfolio Manager: Steve Harvey - 1994

Investm't Category: Tax-Exempt Bond

Cap Gain	Asset Allocation
Cap & Income	Fund of Funds
✔ Income	Index
	Sector
✔ Domestic	Small Cap
Foreign	Socially Conscious
Country/Region	✔ State Specific

Portfolio: stocks 0% bonds 100%
convertibles 0% other 0% cash 0%

Largest Holdings: general obligation 23%

Unrealized Net Capital Gains: 0% of portfolio value

SHAREHOLDER INFORMATION

Minimum Investment
Initial: $2,500   Subsequent: $250

Minimum IRA Investment
Initial: na   Subsequent: na

Maximum Fees
Load: none   12b-1: none
Other: none

Distributions
Income: monthly   Capital Gains: Feb, Dec

Exchange Options
Number Per Year: 4   Fee: none
Telephone: yes (money market fund available)

Services
auto exchange, auto invest, auto withdraw

Fidelity OTC Port
(FOCPX)

82 Devonshire St.
Boston, MA 02109
(800) 544-8888, (801) 534-1910

Aggressive Growth

PERFORMANCE

fund inception date: 12/31/84

	3yr Annual	5yr Annual	10yr Annual	Bull	Bear
Return (%)	6.6	11.4	18.0	107.5	-11.5
Differ from Category (+/-)	-2.3 blw av	-1.1 av	4.0 abv av	-25.7 blw av	-0.7 av

Total Risk	Standard Deviation	Category Risk	Risk Index	Beta
abv av	10.0%	low	0.7	0.7

	1994	1993	1992	1991	1990	1989	1988	1987	1986	1985
Return (%).............	-2.6	8.3	14.9	49.1	-4.7	30.3	22.8	1.5	11.3	68.6
Differ from category (+/-) ..	-1.9	-11.2	3.9	-3.0	1.5	3.5	7.6	3.7	-0.5	36.3

PER SHARE DATA

	1994	1993	1992	1991	1990	1989	1988	1987	1986	1985
Dividends, Net Income ($).	0.21	0.10	0.25	0.12	0.05	0.51	0.30	0.02	0.02	0.01
Distrib'ns, Cap Gain ($) ...	0.00	3.42	2.24	2.51	0.58	2.41	0.00	1.93	1.27	0.45
Net Asset Value ($)	23.27	24.14	25.65	24.78	18.54	20.14	17.68	14.64	16.47	15.93
Expense Ratio (%)	0.88	1.08	1.17	1.29	1.35	1.32	1.42	1.36	1.31	1.50
Net Income to Assets (%) .	0.48	0.53	0.59	1.00	2.30	2.02	0.90	0.12	0.57	0.51
Portfolio Turnover (%)	222	213	245	198	212	118	193	191	132	122
Total Assets (Millions $)..	1,381	1,306	1,037	864	697	772	933	1,274	784	74

PORTFOLIO (as of 7/31/94)

Portfolio Manager: Abigail Johnson - 1994

Investm't Category: Aggressive Growth
- ✔ Cap Gain
- Cap & Income
- Income
- Asset Allocation
- Fund of Funds
- Index
- Sector
- ✔ Domestic
- Foreign
- Country/Region
- Small Cap
- Socially Conscious
- State Specific

Portfolio: stocks 76% bonds 0%
convertibles 0% other 0% cash 24%

Largest Holdings: technology 23%, finance 12%

Unrealized Net Capital Gains: 2% of portfolio value

SHAREHOLDER INFORMATION

Minimum Investment
Initial: $2,500   Subsequent: $250

Minimum IRA Investment
Initial: $500   Subsequent: $250

Maximum Fees
Load: 3.00% front   12b-1: none
Other: none

Distributions
Income: Sep   Capital Gains: Sep

Exchange Options
Number Per Year: 4   Fee: none
Telephone: yes (money market fund available)

Services
IRA, pension, auto exchange, auto invest, auto withdraw

Fidelity Overseas
(FOSFX)
International Stock

82 Devonshire St.
Boston, MA 02109
(800) 544-8888, (801) 534-1910

PERFORMANCE

fund inception date: 12/4/84

	3yr Annual	5yr Annual	10yr Annual	Bull	Bear
Return (%)	7.8	4.9	19.1	51.5	-4.0
Differ from Category (+/-)	-1.3 blw av	0.0 av	3.9 high	-12.4 blw av	3.0 abv av

Total Risk	Standard Deviation	Category Risk	Risk Index	Beta
high	13.4%	abv av	1.0	0.6

	1994	1993	1992	1991	1990	1989	1988	1987	1986	1985
Return (%)	1.2	40.0	-11.4	8.6	-6.6	16.9	8.2	18.3	69.2	78.6
Differ from category (+/-) . . .	4.2	1.4	-8.5	-4.5	3.8	-5.6	-6.2	3.9	10.2	36.2

PER SHARE DATA

	1994	1993	1992	1991	1990	1989	1988	1987	1986	1985
Dividends, Net Income ($) .	0.00	0.43	0.37	0.44	0.68	0.28	0.58	0.00	0.00	0.00
Distrib'ns, Cap Gain ($) . . .	0.47	0.00	2.10	1.16	0.86	1.06	0.00	9.41	2.14	0.13
Net Asset Value ($)	27.30	27.43	19.90	25.26	24.79	28.20	25.30	23.92	28.68	18.25
Expense Ratio (%).	1.28	1.27	1.52	1.53	1.26	1.06	1.38	1.71	1.57	1.72
Net Income to Assets (%). .	0.61	1.00	1.78	2.19	1.34	1.06	1.21	-0.53	-0.32	0.73
Portfolio Turnover (%)	67	64	122	132	96	100	115	122	107	63
Total Assets (Millions $) . .	2,194	1,515	801	969	1,011	876	1,149	1,393	1,766	119

PORTFOLIO (as of 4/30/94)

Portfolio Manager: John R. Hickling - 1993

Investm't Category: International Stock

✔ Cap Gain	Asset Allocation
Cap & Income	Fund of Funds
Income	Index
	Sector
Domestic	Small Cap
✔ Foreign	Socially Conscious
Country/Region	State Specific

Portfolio: stocks 77% bonds 2%
convertibles 0% other 5% cash 16%

Largest Holdings: Japan 20%, United States 16%

Unrealized Net Capital Gains: 15% of portfolio value

SHAREHOLDER INFORMATION

Minimum Investment
Initial: $2,500   Subsequent: $250

Minimum IRA Investment
Initial: $500   Subsequent: $250

Maximum Fees
Load: 3.00% front   12b-1: none
Other: none

Distributions
Income: Dec   Capital Gains: Dec

Exchange Options
Number Per Year: 4   Fee: none
Telephone: yes (money market fund available)

Services
IRA, pension, auto exchange, auto invest, auto withdraw

Fidelity Pacific-Basin

(FPBFX)

International Stock

82 Devonshire St.
Boston, MA 02109
(800) 544-8888, (801) 534-1910

PERFORMANCE — fund inception date: 10/1/86

	3yr Annual	5yr Annual	10yr Annual	Bull	Bear
Return (%)	13.7	3.8	na	81.7	-1.5
Differ from Category (+/-)	4.6 high	-1.1 blw av	na	17.8 high	5.5 high

Total Risk	Standard Deviation	Category Risk	Risk Index	Beta
high	17.2%	high	1.3	0.7

	1994	1993	1992	1991	1990	1989	1988	1987	1986	1985
Return (%)	-2.8	63.9	-7.6	12.5	-27.1	11.4	10.4	24.9	—	—
Differ from category (+/-)	0.2	25.3	-4.7	-0.6	-16.7	-11.1	-4.0	10.5	—	—

PER SHARE DATA

	1994	1993	1992	1991	1990	1989	1988	1987	1986	1985
Dividends, Net Income ($)	0.02	0.13	0.11	0.00	0.16	0.01	0.09	0.15	—	—
Distrib'ns, Cap Gain ($)	2.02	0.27	0.00	0.00	0.00	0.63	0.02	0.00	—	—
Net Asset Value ($)	16.19	18.80	11.74	12.83	11.40	15.87	14.82	13.52	—	—
Expense Ratio (%)	1.59	1.59	1.84	1.88	1.59	1.40	1.80	2.10	—	—
Net Income to Assets (%)	-0.19	0.15	0.65	0.12	0.88	-0.18	0.04	-0.83	—	—
Portfolio Turnover (%)	169	77	105	143	118	133	228	324	—	—
Total Assets (Millions $)	475	500	116	95	86	111	136	159	—	—

PORTFOLIO (as of 4/30/94)

Portfolio Manager: Simon Fraser - 1993

Investm't Category: International Stock

✔ Cap Gain	Asset Allocation
Cap & Income	Fund of Funds
Income	Index
	Sector
Domestic	Small Cap
✔ Foreign	Socially Conscious
✔ Country/Region	State Specific

Portfolio: stocks 93% bonds 0%
convertibles 3% other 0% cash 4%

Largest Holdings: Japan 38%, Malaysia 11%

Unrealized Net Capital Gains: 11% of portfolio value

SHAREHOLDER INFORMATION

Minimum Investment
Initial: $2,500   Subsequent: $250

Minimum IRA Investment
Initial: $500   Subsequent: $250

Maximum Fees
Load: 3.00% front   12b-1: none
Other: none

Distributions
Income: Dec   Capital Gains: Dec

Exchange Options
Number Per Year: 4   Fee: none
Telephone: yes (money market fund available)

Services
IRA, pension, auto exchange, auto invest, auto withdraw

Fidelity Puritan

(FPURX)

Balanced

82 Devonshire St.
Boston, MA 02109
(800) 544-8888, (801) 534-1910

PERFORMANCE

fund inception date: 4/16/47

	3yr Annual	5yr Annual	10yr Annual	Bull	Bear
Return (%)	12.6	10.7	13.7	93.6	-3.8
Differ from Category (+/-)	6.2 high	2.7 high	2.4 high	28.6 high	1.9 high

Total Risk	Standard Deviation	Category Risk	Risk Index	Beta
blw av	6.7%	abv av	1.1	0.7

	1994	1993	1992	1991	1990	1989	1988	1987	1986	1985
Return (%)	1.8	21.4	15.4	24.4	-6.3	19.5	18.8	-1.7	20.7	28.7
Differ from category (+/-) . . .	3.7	8.0	7.1	1.0	-5.8	2.2	7.0	-4.1	3.3	4.4

PER SHARE DATA

	1994	1993	1992	1991	1990	1989	1988	1987	1986	1985
Dividends, Net Income ($)	0.54	0.72	0.82	0.80	0.80	0.99	0.91	0.94	0.92	0.97
Distrib'ns, Cap Gain ($) . . .	0.71	1.36	0.69	0.00	0.00	0.54	0.00	0.77	0.76	1.16
Net Asset Value ($)	14.81	15.75	14.74	14.14	12.05	13.70	12.76	11.53	13.34	12.52
Expense Ratio (%).	0.79	0.74	0.64	0.66	0.65	0.64	0.72	0.70	0.63	0.61
Net Income to Assets (%). .	4.00	4.89	6.23	5.94	6.30	7.41	6.58	6.40	7.50	8.40
Portfolio Turnover (%).	74	76	102	108	58	77	88	63	85	133
Total Assets (Millions $) .	11,769	8,934	5,577	4,943	4,768	4,948	4,283	4,955	2,206	1,083

PORTFOLIO (as of 7/31/94)

Portfolio Manager: Richard Fentin - 1987

Investm't Category: Balanced

Cap Gain	Asset Allocation
✔ Cap & Income	Fund of Funds
Income	Index
	Sector
✔ Domestic	Small Cap
✔ Foreign	Socially Conscious
Country/Region	State Specific

Portfolio: stocks 62% bonds 30%
convertibles 4% other 3% cash 1%

Largest Holdings: stocks—basic industries
9%, stocks—energy 8%

Unrealized Net Capital Gains: 5% of portfolio value

SHAREHOLDER INFORMATION

Minimum Investment
Initial: $2,500   Subsequent: $250

Minimum IRA Investment
Initial: $500   Subsequent: $250

Maximum Fees
Load: 2.00% front   12b-1: none
Other: none

Distributions
Income: quarterly   Capital Gains: Sep, Dec

Exchange Options
Number Per Year: 4   Fee: none
Telephone: yes (money market fund available)

Services
IRA, pension, auto exchange, auto invest, auto withdraw

Fidelity Real Estate Investment (FRESX)

82 Devonshire St.
Boston, MA 02109
(800) 544-8888, (801) 534-1910

Growth & Income

	3yr Annual	5yr Annual	10yr Annual	Bull	Bear
Return (%)	11.1	11.7	na	98.8	1.6
Differ from Category (+/-)	4.0 high	3.8 high	na	23.0 high	7.9 high

Total Risk	Standard Deviation	Category Risk	Risk Index	Beta
abv av	11.8%	high	1.4	0.4

	1994	1993	1992	1991	1990	1989	1988	1987	1986	1985
Return (%).............	2.0	12.5	19.5	39.1	-8.6	13.7	10.3	-7.6	—	—
Differ from category (+/-) ..	3.4	-0.7	9.3	11.5	-2.6	-7.7	-6.7	-8.2	—	—

PER SHARE DATA

	1994	1993	1992	1991	1990	1989	1988	1987	1986	1985
Dividends, Net Income ($).	0.63	0.60	0.43	0.49	0.51	0.54	0.59	0.60	—	—
Distrib'ns, Cap Gain ($) ...	0.00	0.00	0.00	0.00	0.00	0.00	0.00	0.00	—	—
Net Asset Value ($).....	13.20	13.57	12.60	10.94	8.26	9.59	8.92	8.62	—	—
Expense Ratio (%)	1.18	1.16	1.24	1.47	1.39	1.28	1.50	1.50	—	—
Net Income to Assets (%) .	4.92	5.81	5.84	8.45	7.11	6.87	6.26	7.17	—	—
Portfolio Turnover (%)	78	82	84	49	70	42	89	6	—	—
Total Assets (Millions $)....	555	409	76	45	50	63	71	86	—	—

PORTFOLIO (as of 7/31/94)

Portfolio Manager: Barry Greenfield - 1986

Investm't Category: Growth & Income
Cap Gain	Asset Allocation
✔ Cap & Income	Fund of Funds
Income	Index
	✔ Sector
✔ Domestic	Small Cap
Foreign	Socially Conscious
Country/Region	State Specific

Portfolio: stocks 91%   bonds 0%
convertibles 3%   other 0%   cash 6%

Largest Holdings: apartment REITs 26%, shopping center REITs 26%

Unrealized Net Capital Gains: 4% of portfolio value

SHAREHOLDER INFORMATION

Minimum Investment
Initial: $2,500   Subsequent: $250

Minimum IRA Investment
Initial: $500   Subsequent: $250

Maximum Fees
Load: none   12b-1: none
Other: none

Distributions
Income: quarterly   Capital Gains: Mar, Dec

Exchange Options
Number Per Year: 4   Fee: none
Telephone: yes (money market fund available)

Services
IRA, pension, auto exchange, auto invest, auto withdraw

Fidelity Retirement Growth (FDFFX)

Growth

82 Devonshire St.
Boston, MA 02109
(800) 544-8888, (801) 534-1910

PERFORMANCE

fund inception date: 3/25/83

	3yr Annual	5yr Annual	10yr Annual	Bull	Bear
Return (%)	10.5	12.0	15.6	116.0	-6.1
Differ from Category (+/-)	2.8 abv av	2.4 abv av	2.7 high	23.9 high	0.5 av

Total Risk	Standard Deviation	Category Risk	Risk Index	Beta
abv av	9.3%	av	1.0	0.9

	1994	1993	1992	1991	1990	1989	1988	1987	1986	1985
Return (%)	0.0	22.1	10.5	45.5	-10.1	30.4	15.5	9.3	14.1	28.9
Differ from category (+/-)	0.6	8.7	-1.1	9.8	-4.4	4.3	-2.5	7.5	-0.5	-0.3

PER SHARE DATA

	1994	1993	1992	1991	1990	1989	1988	1987	1986	1985
Dividends, Net Income ($)	0.22	0.14	0.16	0.20	0.11	0.38	0.21	0.37	0.35	0.24
Distrib'ns, Cap Gain ($)	1.68	1.75	3.53	1.04	0.57	0.00	0.00	6.68	0.98	0.15
Net Asset Value ($)	16.24	18.14	16.44	18.23	13.45	15.66	12.31	10.84	16.31	15.63
Expense Ratio (%)	1.12	1.05	1.02	0.83	0.98	0.92	1.09	0.97	1.07	1.14
Net Income to Assets (%)	0.87	0.80	1.01	1.56	2.34	2.51	1.79	1.25	1.11	2.86
Portfolio Turnover (%)	73	101	138	119	127	139	156	171	161	100
Total Assets (Millions $)	3,184	2,970	2,166	1,577	1,292	1,448	1,244	993	915	600

PORTFOLIO (as of 5/31/94)

Portfolio Manager: Harris Leviton - 1992

Investm't Category: Growth

✔ Cap Gain	Asset Allocation
Cap & Income	Fund of Funds
Income	Index
	Sector
✔ Domestic	Small Cap
✔ Foreign	Socially Conscious
Country/Region	State Specific

Portfolio: stocks 74% bonds 0%
convertibles 5% other 1% cash 20%

Largest Holdings: technology 12%, basic industries 9%

Unrealized Net Capital Gains: 8% of portfolio value

SHAREHOLDER INFORMATION

Minimum Investment
Initial: $500   Subsequent: $250

Minimum IRA Investment
Initial: $500   Subsequent: $250

Maximum Fees
Load: none   12b-1: none
Other: none

Distributions
Income: Jan, Dec   Capital Gains: Jan, Dec

Exchange Options
Number Per Year: 4   Fee: none
Telephone: yes (money market fund available)

Services
IRA, pension, auto exchange, auto invest, auto withdraw

Fidelity Sel Air Transportation (FSAIX)

82 Devonshire St.
Boston, MA 02109
(800) 544-8888, (801) 534-1910

Aggressive Growth

PERFORMANCE

fund inception date: 12/16/85

	3yr Annual	5yr Annual	10yr Annual	Bull	Bear
Return (%)	2.9	4.1	na	117.7	-16.1
Differ from Category (+/-)	-6.0 low	-8.4 low	na	-15.5 av	-5.3 low

Total Risk	Standard Deviation	Category Risk	Risk Index	Beta
high	16.3%	abv av	1.1	1.2

	1994	1993	1992	1991	1990	1989	1988	1987	1986	1985
Return (%)	-21.7	30.8	6.5	37.0	-18.1	26.3	29.0	-20.6	13.7	—
Differ from category (+/-)	-21.0	11.3	-4.5	-15.1	-11.9	-0.5	13.8	-18.4	1.9	—

PER SHARE DATA

	1994	1993	1992	1991	1990	1989	1988	1987	1986	1985
Dividends, Net Income ($)	0.00	0.00	0.00	0.00	0.00	0.00	0.00	0.02	0.00	
Distrib'ns, Cap Gain ($)	1.09	0.27	0.36	0.25	0.00	0.57	0.00	1.04	0.00	
Net Asset Value ($)	12.43	17.09	13.27	12.81	9.54	11.66	9.68	7.50	10.81	
Expense Ratio (%)	2.50	2.48	2.51	2.48	2.55	2.52	2.62	1.58	1.92	
Net Income to Assets (%)	-1.39	-0.90	-1.04	-0.34	-0.03	-0.18	-0.75	0.36	-0.60	
Portfolio Turnover (%)	133	96	261	106	143	115	340	611	1,125	
Total Assets (Millions $)	7	16	6	4	4	11	2	4	1	—

PORTFOLIO (as of 8/31/94)

Portfolio Manager: Jason Weiner - 1994

Investm't Category: Aggressive Growth
- ✔ Cap Gain
- Cap & Income
- Income
- Asset Allocation
- Fund of Funds
- Index
- ✔ Sector
- Small Cap
- ✔ Domestic
- ✔ Foreign
- Country/Region
- Socially Conscious
- State Specific

Portfolio: stocks 85% bonds 0%
convertibles 0% other 0% cash 15%

Largest Holdings: major national air transportation 49%, regional air transportation 17%

Unrealized Net Capital Gains: 2% of portfolio value

SHAREHOLDER INFORMATION

Minimum Investment
Initial: $2,500   Subsequent: $250

Minimum IRA Investment
Initial: $500   Subsequent: $250

Maximum Fees
Load: 3.00% front   12b-1: none
Other: $7.50 redemption fee (30 days or more), 0.75% fee (less than 30 days)

Distributions
Income: Apr, Dec   Capital Gains: Apr, Dec

Exchange Options
Number Per Year: no limit   Fee: $7.50
Telephone: yes (money market fund available)

Services: IRA, pension, auto exchange, auto invest, auto withdraw

Fidelity Sel American Gold (FSAGX)

Gold

82 Devonshire St.
Boston, MA 02109
(800) 544-8888, (801) 534-1910

PERFORMANCE

fund inception date: 12/16/85

	3yr Annual	5yr Annual	10yr Annual	Bull	Bear
Return (%)	13.5	2.6	na	44.8	-10.5
Differ from Category (+/-)	2.7 abv av	2.6 high	na	11.9 abv av	-0.5 av

Total Risk	Standard Deviation	Category Risk	Risk Index	Beta
high	23.9%	low	0.9	0.3

	1994	1993	1992	1991	1990	1989	1988	1987	1986	1985
Return (%)	-15.4	78.6	-3.0	-6.1	-17.2	22.0	-12.4	40.5	18.0	—
Differ from category (+/-) . .	-3.9	-8.3	12.7	-1.3	5.3	-2.7	6.5	8.6	-19.6	—

PER SHARE DATA

	1994	1993	1992	1991	1990	1989	1988	1987	1986	1985
Dividends, Net Income ($) .	0.00	0.00	0.00	0.00	0.00	0.00	0.00	0.06	0.00	—
Distrib'ns, Cap Gain ($) . . .	0.00	0.00	0.00	0.00	0.00	0.00	0.00	0.18	0.00	—
Net Asset Value ($)	19.91	23.55	13.18	13.60	14.49	17.50	14.34	16.38	11.83	—
Expense Ratio (%).	1.37	1.59	1.75	1.75	1.85	2.03	2.33	1.21	1.50	—
Net Income to Assets (%).	-0.20	-0.44	-0.47	-0.29	-0.38	-0.61	0.06	1.13	0.81	—
Portfolio Turnover (%).	17	30	40	38	68	56	89	78	52	—
Total Assets (Millions $) . . .	314	364	130	164	195	175	206	435	5	—

PORTFOLIO (as of 8/31/94)

Portfolio Manager: Malcolm MacNaught - 1985

Investm't Category: Gold
- ✔ Cap Gain
- Cap & Income
- Income
- ✔ Domestic
- ✔ Foreign
- Country/Region
- Asset Allocation
- Fund of Funds
- Index
- ✔ Sector
- Small Cap
- Socially Conscious
- State Specific

Portfolio: stocks 84% bonds 0%
convertibles 2% other 7% cash 7%

Largest Holdings: Canadian gold mining cos. 56%, United States mining cos. 19%.

Unrealized Net Capital Gains: 15% of portfolio value

SHAREHOLDER INFORMATION

Minimum Investment
Initial: $2,500   Subsequent: $250

Minimum IRA Investment
Initial: $500   Subsequent: $250

Maximum Fees
Load: 3.00% front   12b-1: none
Other: $7.50 redemption fee (30 days or more), 0.75% fee (less than 30 days)

Distributions
Income: Apr, Dec   Capital Gains: Apr, Dec

Exchange Options
Number Per Year: no limit   Fee: $7.50
Telephone: yes (money market fund available)

Services: IRA, pension, auto exchange, auto invest, auto withdraw

Fidelity Sel Automotive

(FSAVX)

Aggressive Growth

82 Devonshire St.
Boston, MA 02109
(800) 544-8888, (801) 534-1910

PERFORMANCE

fund inception date: 6/30/86

	3yr Annual	5yr Annual	10yr Annual	Bull	Bear
Return (%)	18.7	16.4	na	199.6	-14.2
Differ from Category (+/-)	9.8 high	3.9 abv av	na	66.4 high	-3.4 blw av

Total Risk	Standard Deviation	Category Risk	Risk Index	Beta
high	14.2%	av	1.0	1.0

	1994	1993	1992	1991	1990	1989	1988	1987	1986	1985
Return (%)	-12.7	35.3	41.6	37.3	-6.7	4.1	20.0	6.5	—	—
Differ from category (+/-)	-12.0	15.8	30.6	-14.8	-0.5	-22.7	4.8	8.7	—	—

PER SHARE DATA

	1994	1993	1992	1991	1990	1989	1988	1987	1986	1985
Dividends, Net Income ($)	0.05	0.05	0.06	0.00	0.18	0.41	0.00	0.04	—	—
Distrib'ns, Cap Gain ($)	2.26	1.26	0.36	0.70	0.00	0.00	0.00	0.46	—	—
Net Asset Value ($)	19.36	24.91	19.49	14.07	10.80	11.74	11.67	9.72	—	—
Expense Ratio (%)	1.83	1.57	2.48	2.25	2.42	2.63	2.49	1.63	—	—
Net Income to Assets (%)	0.42	0.72	0.36	2.06	1.84	1.22	0.91	1.90	—	—
Portfolio Turnover (%)	47	140	29	219	121	149	311	284	—	—
Total Assets (Millions $)	64	194	178	1	1	1	8	5	—	—

PORTFOLIO (as of 8/31/94)

Portfolio Manager: Brenda Reed - 1994

Investm't Category: Aggressive Growth
- ✔ Cap Gain
- Cap & Income
- Income
- ✔ Domestic
- ✔ Foreign
- Country/Region

- Asset Allocation
- Fund of Funds
- Index
- ✔ Sector
- Small Cap
- Socially Conscious
- State Specific

Portfolio: stocks 89%   bonds 0%
convertibles 0%   other 0%   cash 11%

Largest Holdings: auto & truck parts 41%, motor vehicles & car bodies 21%

Unrealized Net Capital Gains: 0% of portfolio value

SHAREHOLDER INFORMATION

Minimum Investment
Initial: $2,500   Subsequent: $250

Minimum IRA Investment
Initial: $500   Subsequent: $250

Maximum Fees
Load: 3.00% front   12b-1: none
Other: $7.50 redemption fee (30 days or more), 0.75% fee (less than 30 days)

Distributions
Income: Apr, Dec   Capital Gains: Apr, Dec

Exchange Options
Number Per Year: no limit   Fee: $7.50
Telephone: yes (money market fund available)

Services: IRA, pension, auto exchange, auto invest, auto withdraw

Fidelity Sel Biotechnology (FBIOX)

82 Devonshire St.
Boston, MA 02109
(800) 544-8888, (801) 534-1910

Aggressive Growth

PERFORMANCE

fund inception date: 12/16/85

	3yr Annual	5yr Annual	10yr Annual	Bull	Bear
Return (%)	-9.5	16.2	na	116.5	-22.2
Differ from Category (+/-)	-18.4 low	3.7 abv av	na	-16.7 av	-11.4 low

Total Risk	Standard Deviation	Category Risk	Risk Index	Beta
high	19.6%	high	1.3	1.1

	1994	1993	1992	1991	1990	1989	1988	1987	1986	1985
Return (%)	-18.1	0.7	-10.3	99.0	44.3	43.9	4.1	-3.3	3.4	—
Differ from category (+/-) .	-17.4	-18.8	-21.3	46.9	50.5	17.1	-11.1	-1.1	-8.4	—

PER SHARE DATA

	1994	1993	1992	1991	1990	1989	1988	1987	1986	1985
Dividends, Net Income ($) .	0.00	0.00	0.00	0.02	0.00	0.00	0.00	0.00	0.00	—
Distrib'ns, Cap Gain ($) . . .	0.00	0.00	3.89	2.52	0.67	0.24	0.00	0.28	0.00	—
Net Asset Value ($)	23.41	28.61	28.41	36.42	19.94	14.30	10.10	9.70	10.35	—
Expense Ratio (%).	1.54	1.50	1.50	1.63	2.07	2.21	2.51	1.38	1.41	—
Net Income to Assets (%) .	-0.41	-0.37	-0.34	0.24	-0.31	-0.43	-1.31	-0.41	0.74	—
Portfolio Turnover (%)	68	79	160	166	290	80	205	431	937	—
Total Assets (Millions $) . . .	396	589	679	482	70	46	47	75	39	—

PORTFOLIO (as of 8/31/94)

Portfolio Manager: Karen Firestone - 1992

Investm't Category: Aggressive Growth

✔ Cap Gain	Asset Allocation
Cap & Income	Fund of Funds
Income	Index
	✔ Sector
✔ Domestic	Small Cap
✔ Foreign	Socially Conscious
Country/Region	State Specific

Portfolio: stocks 73% bonds 0%
convertibles 0% other 0% cash 27%

Largest Holdings: biotechnology 43%, drugs 20%

Unrealized Net Capital Gains: 2% of portfolio value

SHAREHOLDER INFORMATION

Minimum Investment
Initial: $2,500   Subsequent: $250

Minimum IRA Investment
Initial: $500   Subsequent: $250

Maximum Fees
Load: 3.00% front   12b-1: none
Other: $7.50 redemption fee (30 days or more), 0.75% fee (less than 30 days)

Distributions
Income: Apr, Dec   Capital Gains: Apr, Dec

Exchange Options
Number Per Year: no limit   Fee: $7.50
Telephone: yes (money market fund available)

Services: IRA, pension, auto exchange, auto invest, auto withdraw

Fidelity Sel Broker & Invest Mgmt (FSLBX)

82 Devonshire St.
Boston, MA 02109
(800) 544-8888, (801) 534-1910

Aggressive Growth

PERFORMANCE

fund inception date: 7/29/85

	3yr Annual	5yr Annual	10yr Annual	Bull	Bear
Return (%)	9.1	14.6	na	209.8	-10.9
Differ from Category (+/-)	0.2 av	2.1 abv av	na	76.6 high	-0.1 av

Total Risk	Standard Deviation	Category Risk	Risk Index	Beta
high	16.7%	abv av	1.1	1.1

	1994	1993	1992	1991	1990	1989	1988	1987	1986	1985
Return (%)............	-17.2	49.3	5.1	82.2	-16.1	14.0	18.5	-36.8	9.5	—
Differ from category (+/-) .	-16.5	29.8	-5.9	30.1	-9.9	-12.8	3.3	-34.6	-2.3	—

PER SHARE DATA

	1994	1993	1992	1991	1990	1989	1988	1987	1986	1985
Dividends, Net Income ($).	0.00	0.01	0.00	0.01	0.09	0.16	0.09	0.03	0.02	—
Distrib'ns, Cap Gain ($) ...	0.00	1.47	0.00	0.00	0.00	0.00	0.00	1.15	0.02	—
Net Asset Value ($).....	15.14	18.30	13.34	12.69	6.97	8.42	7.52	6.42	12.12	—
Expense Ratio (%)	2.49	2.21	2.17	2.50	2.50	2.54	2.58	1.67	1.52	—
Net Income to Assets (%) .	-0.47	0.02	0.16	0.94	0.91	1.18	0.09	0.69	1.39	—
Portfolio Turnover (%)	60	111	254	62	142	185	447	603	347	—
Total Assets (Millions $).....	21	84	17	11	2	4	4	13	42	—

PORTFOLIO (as of 8/31/94)

Portfolio Manager: Arieh Coll - 1993

Investm't Category: Aggressive Growth

✔ Cap Gain	Asset Allocation
Cap & Income	Fund of Funds
Income	Index
	✔ Sector
✔ Domestic	Small Cap
✔ Foreign	Socially Conscious
Country/Region	State Specific

Portfolio: stocks 82% bonds 0%
convertibles 0% other 2% cash 16%

Largest Holdings: security & commodity brokers 43%, investment advice 14%

Unrealized Net Capital Gains: 3% of portfolio value

SHAREHOLDER INFORMATION

Minimum Investment
Initial: $2,500 Subsequent: $250

Minimum IRA Investment
Initial: $500 Subsequent: $250

Maximum Fees
Load: 3.00% front 12b-1: none
Other: $7.50 redemption fee (30 days or more), 0.75% fee (less than 30 days)

Distributions
Income: Apr, Dec Capital Gains: Apr, Dec

Exchange Options
Number Per Year: no limit Fee: $7.50
Telephone: yes (money market fund available)

Services: IRA, pension, auto exchange, auto invest, auto withdraw

Fidelity Sel Chemical
(FSCHX)
Growth

82 Devonshire St.
Boston, MA 02109
(800) 544-8888, (801) 534-1910

PERFORMANCE   fund inception date: 7/29/85

	3yr Annual	5yr Annual	10yr Annual	Bull	Bear
Return (%)	12.1	13.3	na	106.5	2.6
Differ from Category (+/-)	4.4 high	3.7 high	na	14.4 abv av	9.2 high

Total Risk	Standard Deviation	Category Risk	Risk Index	Beta
abv av	10.7%	abv av	1.1	1.0

	1994	1993	1992	1991	1990	1989	1988	1987	1986	1985
Return (%)	14.7	12.7	8.9	38.6	-4.1	17.3	20.9	14.8	26.8	—
Differ from category (+/-) . .	15.3	-0.7	-2.7	2.9	1.6	-8.8	2.9	13.0	12.2	—

PER SHARE DATA

	1994	1993	1992	1991	1990	1989	1988	1987	1986	1985
Dividends, Net Income ($)	0.22	0.23	0.31	0.18	0.10	0.16	0.00	0.00	0.00	—
Distrib'ns, Cap Gain ($) . . .	0.60	3.05	3.36	0.71	0.60	1.13	0.00	0.04	0.06	—
Net Asset Value ($)	32.91	29.42	29.16	30.20	22.49	24.14	21.70	17.94	15.66	—
Expense Ratio (%).	1.52	1.89	2.16	2.50	2.37	2.24	1.93	1.52	1.50	—
Net Income to Assets (%). .	1.29	1.21	0.40	1.21	1.65	1.27	1.61	1.03	1.24	—
Portfolio Turnover (%)	39	214	87	87	99	117	179	170	125	—
Total Assets (Millions $) . . .	167	26	39	20	21	44	118	86	45	—

PORTFOLIO (as of 8/31/94)

Portfolio Manager: Jeffrey Feinberg - 1995

Investm't Category: Growth

✔ Cap Gain	Asset Allocation
Cap & Income	Fund of Funds
Income	Index
	✔ Sector
✔ Domestic	Small Cap
✔ Foreign	Socially Conscious
Country/Region	State Specific

Portfolio: stocks 94% bonds 0%
convertibles 0% other 0% cash 6%

Largest Holdings: chemicals 55%, plastics, resins & elastomers 9%

Unrealized Net Capital Gains: 9% of portfolio value

SHAREHOLDER INFORMATION

Minimum Investment
Initial: $2,500   Subsequent: $250

Minimum IRA Investment
Initial: $500   Subsequent: $250

Maximum Fees
Load: 3.00% front   12b-1: none
Other: $7.50 redemption fee (30 days or more), 0.75% fee (less than 30 days)

Distributions
Income: Apr, Dec   Capital Gains: Apr, Dec

Exchange Options
Number Per Year: no limit   Fee: $7.50
Telephone: yes (money market fund available)

Services: IRA, pension, auto exchange, auto invest, auto withdraw

Fidelity Sel Computers
(FDCPX)
Aggressive Growth

82 Devonshire St.
Boston, MA 02109
(800) 544-8888, (801) 534-1910

	3yr Annual	5yr Annual	10yr Annual	Bull	Bear
Return (%)	23.7	23.9	na	173.5	-5.9
Differ from Category (+/-)	14.8 high	11.4 high	na	40.3 abv av	4.9 abv av

Total Risk	Standard Deviation	Category Risk	Risk Index	Beta
high	18.7%	high	1.3	1.1

	1994	1993	1992	1991	1990	1989	1988	1987	1986	1985
Return (%)	20.4	28.8	21.9	30.7	18.4	6.8	-5.0	-6.3	7.8	—
Differ from category (+/-) .	21.1	9.3	10.9	-21.4	24.6	-20.0	-20.2	-4.1	-4.0	—

PER SHARE DATA

	1994	1993	1992	1991	1990	1989	1988	1987	1986	1985
Dividends, Net Income ($).	0.00	0.00	0.00	0.27	0.12	0.00	0.00	0.01	0.00	—
Distrib'ns, Cap Gain ($) . . .	0.00	1.80	0.00	0.22	0.00	0.00	0.00	0.33	0.04	—
Net Asset Value ($)	29.33	24.35	20.44	16.76	13.20	11.25	10.53	11.09	12.21	—
Expense Ratio (%)	1.70	1.81	2.17	2.26	2.64	2.56	2.62	1.58	1.68	—
Net Income to Assets (%) .	-1.15	-0.98	-0.18	2.94	-0.94	-1.18	-0.75	0.32	-0.05	—
Portfolio Turnover (%)	332	254	568	695	596	466	284	259	269	—
Total Assets (Millions $). . . .	175	60	32	29	27	15	23	118	24	—

PORTFOLIO (as of 8/31/94)

Portfolio Manager: Harry Lange - 1992

Investm't Category: Aggressive Growth
- ✔ Cap Gain
-   Cap & Income
-   Income
-   Asset Allocation
-   Fund of Funds
-   Index
- ✔ Sector
- ✔ Domestic
- ✔ Foreign
-   Country/Region
-   Small Cap
-   Socially Conscious
-   State Specific

Portfolio: stocks 87%   bonds 0%
convertibles 6%   other 0%   cash 7%

Largest Holdings: semiconductors 35%, mini & micro computers 11%

Unrealized Net Capital Gains: 10% of portfolio value

SHAREHOLDER INFORMATION

Minimum Investment
Initial: $2,500   Subsequent: $250

Minimum IRA Investment
Initial: $500   Subsequent: $250

Maximum Fees
Load: 3.00% front   12b-1: none
Other: $7.50 redemption fee (30 days or more), 0.75% fee (less than 30 days)

Distributions
Income: Apr, Dec   Capital Gains: Apr, Dec

Exchange Options
Number Per Year: no limit   Fee: $7.50
Telephone: yes (money market fund available)

Services: IRA, pension, auto exchange, auto invest, auto withdraw

Fidelity Sel Construction and Housing (FSHOX)

82 Devonshire St.
Boston, MA 02109
(800) 544-8888, (801) 534-1910

Aggressive Growth

PERFORMANCE

fund inception date: 9/29/86

	3yr Annual	5yr Annual	10yr Annual	Bull	Bear
Return (%)	+10.0	11.2	na	167.9	-14.9
Differ from Category (+/-)	1.1 abv av	-1.3 av	na	34.7 abv av	-4.1 blw av

Total Risk	Standard Deviation	Category Risk	Risk Index	Beta
high	12.8%	blw av	0.9	0.9

	1994	1993	1992	1991	1990	1989	1988	1987	1986	1985
Return (%)	-15.9	33.6	18.7	41.3	-9.6	16.5	29.1	-12.4	—	—
Differ from category (+/-) .	-15.2	14.1	7.7	-10.8	-3.4	-10.3	13.9	-10.2	—	—

PER SHARE DATA

	1994	1993	1992	1991	1990	1989	1988	1987	1986	1985
Dividends, Net Income ($) .	0.00	0.00	0.00	0.00	0.16	0.08	0.06	0.00	—	—
Distrib'ns, Cap Gain ($) . . .	0.52	0.22	0.01	0.88	1.27	1.62	0.27	0.13	—	—
Net Asset Value ($)	15.95	19.59	14.84	12.51	9.55	11.89	11.65	9.28	—	—
Expense Ratio (%).	1.54	2.02	2.50	2.48	2.41	2.56	2.70	1.46	—	—
Net Income to Assets (%). .	0.08	0.20	-0.49	0.08	-0.03	1.16	-0.41	0.57	—	—
Portfolio Turnover (%)	29	60	183	137	185	225	330	590	—	—
Total Assets (Millions $)	17	64	26	4	1	1	3	6	—	—

PORTFOLIO (as of 8/31/94)

Portfolio Manager: Bill Bower - 1994

Investm't Category: Aggressive Growth
- ✔ Cap Gain
- Cap & Income
- Income
- Asset Allocation
- Fund of Funds
- Index
- ✔ Sector
- ✔ Domestic
- ✔ Foreign
- Country/Region
- Small Cap
- Socially Conscious
- State Specific

Portfolio: stocks 96% bonds 0%
convertibles 0% other 0% cash 4%

Largest Holdings: cement 23%, operative builders 13%

Unrealized Net Capital Gains: 5% of portfolio value

SHAREHOLDER INFORMATION

Minimum Investment
Initial: $2,500 Subsequent: $250

Minimum IRA Investment
Initial: $500 Subsequent: $250

Maximum Fees
Load: 3.00% front 12b-1: none
Other: $7.50 redemption fee (30 days or more), 0.75% fee (less than 30 days)

Distributions
Income: Apr, Dec Capital Gains: Apr, Dec

Exchange Options
Number Per Year: no limit Fee: $7.50
Telephone: yes (money market fund available)

Services: IRA, pension, auto exchange, auto invest, auto withdraw

Fidelity Sel Consumer Products (FSCPX)

82 Devonshire St.
Boston, MA 02109
(800) 544-8888, (801) 534-1910

Aggressive Growth

PERFORMANCE

fund inception date: 6/29/90

	3yr Annual	5yr Annual	10yr Annual	Bull	Bear
Return (%)	7.9	na	na	111.3	-12.0
Differ from Category (+/-)	-1.0 av	na	na	-21.9 blw av	-1.2 blw av

Total Risk	Standard Deviation	Category Risk	Risk Index	Beta
abv av	11.4%	blw av	0.8	1.1

	1994	1993	1992	1991	1990	1989	1988	1987	1986	1985
Return (%)...............	-7.0	24.6	8.5	38.5	—	—	—	—	—	—
Differ from category (+/-) ..	-6.3	5.1	-2.5	-13.6	—	—	—	—	—	—

PER SHARE DATA

	1994	1993	1992	1991	1990	1989	1988	1987	1986	1985
Dividends, Net Income ($).	0.00	0.00	0.00	0.00	—	—	—	—	—	—
Distrib'ns, Cap Gain ($) ...	0.60	1.40	0.97	0.22	—	—	—	—	—	—
Net Asset Value ($).....	13.70	15.41	13.51	13.38	—	—	—	—	—	—
Expense Ratio (%)	2.49	2.47	2.48	2.43	—	—	—	—	—	—
Net Income to Assets (%) .	-1.17	-0.80	-0.56	0.62	—	—	—	—	—	—
Portfolio Turnover (%)	96	215	140	108	—	—	—	—	—	—
Total Assets (Millions $)......	7	9	7	1	—	—	—	—	—	—

PORTFOLIO (as of 8/31/94)

Portfolio Manager: Mary English - 1994

Investm't Category: Aggressive Growth

✔ Cap Gain   Asset Allocation
   Cap & Income   Fund of Funds
   Income   Index
                 ✔ Sector
✔ Domestic   Small Cap
✔ Foreign   Socially Conscious
   Country/Region   State Specific

Portfolio: stocks 91%   bonds 0%
convertibles 0%   other 0%   cash 9%

Largest Holdings: conglomerates 9%, hotels, motels & tourist courts 4.5%

Unrealized Net Capital Gains: 9% of portfolio value

SHAREHOLDER INFORMATION

Minimum Investment
Initial: $2,500   Subsequent: $250

Minimum IRA Investment
Initial: $500   Subsequent: $250

Maximum Fees
Load: 3.00% front   12b-1: none
Other: $7.50 redemption fee (30 days or more), 0.75% fee (less than 30 days)

Distributions
Income: Apr, Dec   Capital Gains: Apr, Dec

Exchange Options
Number Per Year: no limit   Fee: $7.50
Telephone: yes (money market fund available)

Services: IRA, pension, auto exchange, auto invest, auto withdraw

Fidelity Sel Defense & Aerospace (FSDAX)

Aggressive Growth

82 Devonshire St.
Boston, MA 02109
(800) 544-8888, (801) 534-1910

PERFORMANCE

fund inception date: 5/8/84

	3yr Annual	5yr Annual	10yr Annual	Bull	Bear
Return (%)	9.4	9.6	6.2	86.3	-5.6
Differ from Category (+/-)	0.5 av	-2.9 blw av	-7.8 low	-46.9 low	5.2 abv av

Total Risk	Standard Deviation	Category Risk	Risk Index	Beta
abv av	10.7%	low	0.7	0.9

	1994	1993	1992	1991	1990	1989	1988	1987	1986	1985
Return (%)	1.7	28.8	0.0	26.9	-4.5	8.8	4.3	-23.1	4.8	26.3
Differ from category (+/-)	2.4	9.3	-11.0	-25.2	1.7	-18.0	-10.9	-20.9	-7.0	-6.0

PER SHARE DATA

	1994	1993	1992	1991	1990	1989	1988	1987	1986	1985
Dividends, Net Income ($)	0.00	0.10	0.00	0.06	0.12	0.00	0.00	0.00	0.03	0.10
Distrib'ns, Cap Gain ($)	0.27	0.62	0.00	0.00	0.00	0.00	0.00	0.46	0.20	0.00
Net Asset Value ($)	18.32	18.27	14.75	14.75	11.67	12.35	11.35	10.88	14.79	14.31
Expense Ratio (%)	2.48	2.48	2.46	2.49	2.43	2.53	2.33	1.54	1.60	1.50
Net Income to Assets (%)	-0.49	-0.14	-0.10	0.78	0.34	-0.39	-0.91	0.16	0.33	1.13
Portfolio Turnover (%)	148	87	32	162	96	62	162	264	280	271
Total Assets (Millions $)	3	2	1	3	1	1	2	4	11	10

PORTFOLIO (as of 8/31/94)

Portfolio Manager: Bill Rubin - 1994

Investm't Category: Aggressive Growth
- ✔ Cap Gain
- Cap & Income
- Income
- ✔ Domestic
- ✔ Foreign
- Country/Region
- Asset Allocation
- Fund of Funds
- Index
- ✔ Sector
- Small Cap
- Socially Conscious
- State Specific

Portfolio: stocks 99% bonds 0%
convertibles 0% other 0% cash 1%

Largest Holdings: conglomerates 26%, defense electronics 13%

Unrealized Net Capital Gains: 1% of portfolio value

SHAREHOLDER INFORMATION

Minimum Investment
Initial: $2,500   Subsequent: $250

Minimum IRA Investment
Initial: $500   Subsequent: $250

Maximum Fees
Load: 3.00% front   12b-1: none
Other: $7.50 redemption fee (30 days or more), 0.75% fee (less than 30 days)

Distributions
Income: Apr, Dec   Capital Gains: Apr, Dec

Exchange Options
Number Per Year: no limit   Fee: $7.50
Telephone: yes (money market fund available)

Services: IRA, pension, auto exchange, auto invest, auto withdraw

Fidelity Sel Dev'ping Communic'ns (FSDCX)

82 Devonshire St.
Boston, MA 02109
(800) 544-8888, (801) 534-1910

Aggressive Growth

fund inception date: 6/29/90

	3yr Annual	5yr Annual	10yr Annual	Bull	Bear
Return (%)	21.1	na	na	235.8	-16.5
Differ from Category (+/-)	12.2 high	na	na	102.6 high	-5.7 low

Total Risk	Standard Deviation	Category Risk	Risk Index	Beta
high	16.7%	abv av	1.1	1.6

	1994	1993	1992	1991	1990	1989	1988	1987	1986	1985
Return (%).............	15.1	31.7	17.2	61.3	—	—	—	—	—	—
Differ from category (+/-) .	15.8	12.2	6.2	9.2	—	—	—	—	—	—

PER SHARE DATA

	1994	1993	1992	1991	1990	1989	1988	1987	1986	1985
Dividends, Net Income ($).	0.00	0.00	0.00	0.00	—	—	—	—	—	—
Distrib'ns, Cap Gain ($) . . .	1.67	1.47	0.03	0.79	—	—	—	—	—	—
Net Asset Value ($)	20.24	19.24	15.91	13.60	—	—	—	—	—	—
Expense Ratio (%)	1.57	1.88	2.50	2.50	—	—	—	—	—	—
Net Income to Assets (%) .	-1.02	-0.59	-0.61	-1.23	—	—	—	—	—	—
Portfolio Turnover (%)	262	77	25	469	—	—	—	—	—	—
Total Assets (Millions $). . . .	276	245	39	7	—	—	—	—	—	—

PORTFOLIO (as of 8/31/94)

Portfolio Manager: Paul Antico - 1993

Investm't Category: Aggressive Growth
- ✔ Cap Gain
- Cap & Income
- Income
- Asset Allocation
- Fund of Funds
- Index
- ✔ Sector
- ✔ Domestic
- ✔ Foreign
- Country/Region
- Small Cap
- Socially Conscious
- State Specific

Portfolio:	stocks 92%	bonds 0%
convertibles 0%	other 0%	cash 8%

Largest Holdings: cellular & communication services 24%, telephone equipment 17%

Unrealized Net Capital Gains: 10% of portfolio value

SHAREHOLDER INFORMATION

Minimum Investment
Initial: $2,500   Subsequent: $250

Minimum IRA Investment
Initial: $500   Subsequent: $250

Maximum Fees
Load: 3.00% front   12b-1: none
Other: $7.50 redemption fee (30 days or more), 0.75% fee (less than 30 days)

Distributions
Income: Apr, Dec   Capital Gains: Apr, Dec

Exchange Options
Number Per Year: no limit   Fee: $7.50
Telephone: yes (money market fund available)

Services: IRA, pension, auto exchange, auto invest, auto withdraw

Fidelity Sel Electronics

(FSELX)

Aggressive Growth

82 Devonshire St.
Boston, MA 02109
(800) 544-8888, (801) 534-1910

fund inception date: 7/29/85

PERFORMANCE

	3yr Annual	5yr Annual	10yr Annual	Bull	Bear
Return (%)	25.4	23.0	na	175.7	-2.4
Differ from Category (+/-)	16.5 high	10.5 high	na	42.5 abv av	8.4 high

Total Risk	Standard Deviation	Category Risk	Risk Index	Beta
high	15.8%	abv av	1.1	1.0

	1994	1993	1992	1991	1990	1989	1988	1987	1986	1985
Return (%)	17.1	32.0	27.4	35.2	5.8	15.6	-8.4	-13.4	-23.8	—
Differ from category (+/-) . .	17.8	12.5	16.4	-16.9	12.0	-11.2	-23.6	-11.2	-35.6	—

PER SHARE DATA

	1994	1993	1992	1991	1990	1989	1988	1987	1986	1985
Dividends, Net Income ($) .	0.00	0.00	0.00	0.00	0.01	0.00	0.00	0.00	0.00	—
Distrib'ns, Cap Gain ($) . . .	0.00	2.75	0.00	0.00	0.00	0.00	0.00	0.00	0.00	—
Net Asset Value ($)	18.49	15.78	14.12	11.08	8.19	7.75	6.70	7.32	8.46	—
Expense Ratio (%).	1.71	1.69	2.16	2.26	2.57	2.79	2.54	1.61	1.77	—
Net Income to Assets (%).	-0.89	-0.50	-1.07	-0.45	-0.02	-1.51	-1.02	0.05	0.85	—
Portfolio Turnover (%). . . .	312	293	299	268	378	697	686	511	326	—
Total Assets (Millions $) . . .	156	45	34	18	26	8	12	16	10	—

PORTFOLIO (as of 8/31/94)

Portfolio Manager: Harry Lange - 1994

Investm't Category: Aggressive Growth

✔ Cap Gain	Asset Allocation
Cap & Income	Fund of Funds
Income	Index
	✔ Sector
✔ Domestic	Small Cap
✔ Foreign	Socially Conscious
Country/Region	State Specific

Portfolio: stocks 89%   bonds 0%
convertibles 5%   other 0%   cash 6%

Largest Holdings: semiconductors 51%, electronics and electronic components 4%

Unrealized Net Capital Gains: 9% of portfolio value

SHAREHOLDER INFORMATION

Minimum Investment
Initial: $2,500   Subsequent: $250

Minimum IRA Investment
Initial: $500   Subsequent: $250

Maximum Fees
Load: 3.00% front   12b-1: none
Other: $7.50 redemption fee (30 days or more), 0.75% fee (less than 30 days)

Distributions
Income: Apr, Dec   Capital Gains: Apr, Dec

Exchange Options
Number Per Year: no limit   Fee: $7.50
Telephone: yes (money market fund available)

Services: IRA, pension, auto exchange, auto invest, auto withdraw

Fidelity Sel Energy
(FSENX)
Growth

82 Devonshire St.
Boston, MA 02109
(800) 544-8888, (801) 534-1910

PERFORMANCE

fund inception date: 7/14/81

	3yr Annual	5yr Annual	10yr Annual	Bull	Bear
Return (%)	5.3	2.2	8.4	9.4	-0.4
Differ from Category (+/-)	-2.4 blw av	-7.4 low	-4.5 low	-82.7 low	6.2 high

Total Risk	Standard Deviation	Category Risk	Risk Index	Beta
high	15.1%	high	1.6	1.1

	1994	1993	1992	1991	1990	1989	1988	1987	1986	1985
Return (%)	0.4	19.1	-2.3	0.0	-4.4	42.8	15.9	-1.7	5.4	17.9
Differ from category (+/-)	1.0	5.7	-13.9	-35.7	1.3	16.7	-2.1	-3.5	-9.2	-11.3

PER SHARE DATA

	1994	1993	1992	1991	1990	1989	1988	1987	1986	1985
Dividends, Net Income ($)	0.11	0.03	0.27	0.16	0.15	0.07	0.32	0.03	0.00	0.63
Distrib'ns, Cap Gain ($)	0.51	0.57	0.00	0.02	1.43	0.22	0.00	0.27	0.00	0.00
Net Asset Value ($)	15.87	16.43	14.32	14.95	15.13	17.47	12.44	11.01	11.53	10.93
Expense Ratio (%)	1.79	1.71	1.78	1.79	1.94	1.77	2.09	1.50	1.54	1.35
Net Income to Assets (%)	0.53	1.88	1.16	0.99	1.69	2.48	1.72	3.31	5.11	4.33
Portfolio Turnover (%)	98	72	81	61	74	168	183	226	167	163
Total Assets (Millions $)	96	82	77	92	83	80	109	104	33	52

PORTFOLIO (as of 8/31/94)

Portfolio Manager: Albert Ruback - 1994

Investm't Category: Growth

✔ Cap Gain	Asset Allocation
Cap & Income	Fund of Funds
Income	Index
	✔ Sector
✔ Domestic	Small Cap
✔ Foreign	Socially Conscious
Country/Region	State Specific

Portfolio: stocks 94% bonds 0%
convertibles 0% other 0% cash 6%

Largest Holdings: crude petroleum & gas 37%, oil & gas exploration 30%

Unrealized Net Capital Gains: 5% of portfolio value

SHAREHOLDER INFORMATION

Minimum Investment
Initial: $2,500 Subsequent: $250

Minimum IRA Investment
Initial: $500 Subsequent: $250

Maximum Fees
Load: 3.00% front 12b-1: none
Other: $7.50 redemption fee (30 days or more), 0.75% fee (less than 30 days)

Distributions
Income: Apr, Dec Capital Gains: Apr, Dec

Exchange Options
Number Per Year: no limit Fee: $7.50
Telephone: yes (money market fund available)

Services: IRA, pension, auto exchange, auto invest, auto withdraw

Fidelity Sel Energy Service (FSESX)

82 Devonshire St.
Boston, MA 02109
(800) 544-8888, (801) 534-1910

Aggressive Growth

PERFORMANCE

fund inception date: 12/16/85

	3yr Annual	5yr Annual	10yr Annual	Bull	Bear
Return (%)	7.9	-0.4	na	-17.2	4.2
Differ from Category (+/-)	-1.0 av	-12.9 low	na	-150.4 low	15.0 high

Total Risk	Standard Deviation	Category Risk	Risk Index	Beta
high	17.0%	high	1.2	0.7

	1994	1993	1992	1991	1990	1989	1988	1987	1986	1985
Return (%)	0.5	20.9	3.4	-23.4	1.7	59.4	-0.3	-11.7	-15.7	—
Differ from category (+/-)	1.2	1.4	-7.6	-75.5	7.9	32.6	-15.5	-9.5	-27.5	—

PER SHARE DATA

	1994	1993	1992	1991	1990	1989	1988	1987	1986	1985
Dividends, Net Income ($)	0.02	0.05	0.00	0.00	0.02	0.00	0.00	0.00	0.00	—
Distrib'ns, Cap Gain ($)	0.48	0.00	0.00	0.00	0.00	0.00	0.00	0.00	0.00	—
Net Asset Value ($)	11.14	11.61	9.64	9.32	12.18	11.99	7.52	7.55	8.56	—
Expense Ratio (%)	1.74	1.76	2.07	1.82	2.29	2.53	2.71	1.49	1.51	—
Net Income to Assets (%)	0.36	0.13	-1.13	-0.02	-0.42	-0.45	-1.06	1.03	2.57	—
Portfolio Turnover (%)	330	236	89	62	128	78	461	575	54	—
Total Assets (Millions $)	50	40	41	73	61	44	33	19	1	—

PORTFOLIO (as of 8/31/94)

Portfolio Manager: Dan Pickering - 1994

Investm't Category: Aggressive Growth
- ✔ Cap Gain
- Cap & Income
- Income
- ✔ Domestic
- ✔ Foreign
- Country/Region
- Asset Allocation
- Fund of Funds
- Index
- ✔ Sector
- Small Cap
- Socially Conscious
- State Specific

Portfolio: stocks 95% bonds 3%
convertibles 2% other 0% cash 0%

Largest Holdings: oil & gas services 59%, drilling 15%

Unrealized Net Capital Gains: -8% of portfolio value

SHAREHOLDER INFORMATION

Minimum Investment
Initial: $2,500   Subsequent: $250

Minimum IRA Investment
Initial: $500   Subsequent: $250

Maximum Fees
Load: 3.00% front   12b-1: none
Other: $7.50 redemption fee (30 days or more), 0.75% fee (less than 30 days)

Distributions
Income: Apr, Dec   Capital Gains: Apr, Dec

Exchange Options
Number Per Year: no limit   Fee: $7.50
Telephone: yes (money market fund available)

Services: IRA, pension, auto exchange, auto invest, auto withdraw

Fidelity Sel Environ'l Serv
(FSLEX)

82 Devonshire St.
Boston, MA 02109
(800) 544-8888, (801) 534-1910

Aggressive Growth

PERFORMANCE

fund inception date: 6/29/89

	3yr Annual	5yr Annual	10yr Annual	Bull	Bear
Return (%)	-3.9	-1.4	na	23.4	-14.8
Differ from Category (+/-)	-12.8 low	-13.9 low	na	-109.8 low	-4.0 blw av

Total Risk	Standard Deviation	Category Risk	Risk Index	Beta
high	14.7%	av	1.0	1.1

	1994	1993	1992	1991	1990	1989	1988	1987	1986	1985
Return (%)	-9.5	-0.6	-1.3	7.6	-2.4	—	—	—	—	—
Differ from category (+/-)	-8.8	-20.1	-12.3	-44.5	3.8	—	—	—	—	—

PER SHARE DATA

	1994	1993	1992	1991	1990	1989	1988	1987	1986	1985
Dividends, Net Income ($)	0.00	0.00	0.00	0.00	0.00	—	—	—	—	—
Distrib'ns, Cap Gain ($)	0.00	0.00	0.39	0.42	0.00	—	—	—	—	—
Net Asset Value ($)	10.13	11.20	11.27	11.84	11.42	—	—	—	—	—
Expense Ratio (%)	1.88	1.99	2.03	2.03	2.25	—	—	—	—	—
Net Income to Assets (%)	-1.32	-0.70	-0.74	-0.30	0.16	—	—	—	—	—
Portfolio Turnover (%)	95	176	130	122	72	—	—	—	—	—
Total Assets (Millions $)	32	49	65	100	101	—	—	—	—	—

PORTFOLIO (as of 8/31/94)

Portfolio Manager: Philip Barton - 1993

Investm't Category: Aggressive Growth
- ✔ Cap Gain
- Cap & Income
- Income
- Asset Allocation
- Fund of Funds
- Index
- ✔ Sector
- ✔ Domestic
- ✔ Foreign
- Country/Region
- Small Cap
- Socially Conscious
- State Specific

Portfolio: stocks 95%   bonds 0%
convertibles 0%   other 0%   cash 5%

Largest Holdings: refuse systems 19%, pollution equipment & design 15%

Unrealized Net Capital Gains: -6% of portfolio value

SHAREHOLDER INFORMATION

Minimum Investment
Initial: $2,500   Subsequent: $250

Minimum IRA Investment
Initial: $500   Subsequent: $250

Maximum Fees
Load: 3.00% front   12b-1: none
Other: $7.50 redemption fee (30 days or more), 0.75% fee (less than 30 days)

Distributions
Income: Apr, Dec   Capital Gains: Apr, Dec

Exchange Options
Number Per Year: no limit   Fee: $7.50
Telephone: yes (money market fund available)

Services: IRA, pension, auto exchange, auto invest, auto withdraw

Fidelity Sel Financial Services (FIDSX)

Growth

82 Devonshire St.
Boston, MA 02109
(800) 544-8888, (801) 534-1910

PERFORMANCE

fund inception date: 12/1/81

	3yr Annual	5yr Annual	10yr Annual	Bull	Bear
Return (%)	17.3	14.6	13.6	228.2	-2.8
Differ from Category (+/-)	9.6 high	5.0 high	0.7 abv av	136.1 high	3.8 high

Total Risk	Standard Deviation	Category Risk	Risk Index	Beta
high	14.1%	high	1.5	1.2

	1994	1993	1992	1991	1990	1989	1988	1987	1986	1985
Return (%)	-3.6	17.5	42.8	61.6	-24.3	19.3	12.0	-16.5	15.0	41.2
Differ from category (+/-) . .	-3.0	4.1	31.2	25.9	-18.6	-6.8	-6.0	-18.3	0.4	12.0

PER SHARE DATA

	1994	1993	1992	1991	1990	1989	1988	1987	1986	1985
Dividends, Net Income ($)	0.59	0.20	0.51	0.35	0.52	0.33	0.81	0.12	0.21	0.29
Distrib'ns, Cap Gain ($) . . .	4.13	7.32	3.38	0.00	0.00	0.19	0.00	1.54	0.33	0.00
Net Asset Value ($)	43.12	49.79	48.83	37.14	23.22	31.39	26.73	24.57	31.56	27.86
Expense Ratio (%).	1.63	1.54	1.85	2.49	2.22	1.07	2.47	1.57	1.26	1.50
Net Income to Assets (%). .	1.24	0.86	1.49	2.22	2.03	3.53	1.58	1.65	3.05	4.17
Portfolio Turnover (%)	74	100	164	237	308	186	81	40	136	170
Total Assets (Millions $)	94	128	91	35	21	32	28	56	234	68

PORTFOLIO (as of 8/31/94)

Portfolio Manager: Louis Salemy - 1994

Investm't Category: Growth
- ✔ Cap Gain
- Cap & Income
- Income
- ✔ Domestic
- ✔ Foreign
- Country/Region
- Asset Allocation
- Fund of Funds
- Index
- ✔ Sector
- Small Cap
- Socially Conscious
- State Specific

Portfolio: stocks 94% bonds 0%
convertibles 0% other 0% cash 6%

Largest Holdings: national commercial banks 31%, Federal Reserve state banks 17%

Unrealized Net Capital Gains: 9% of portfolio value

SHAREHOLDER INFORMATION

Minimum Investment
Initial: $2,500   Subsequent: $250

Minimum IRA Investment
Initial: $500   Subsequent: $250

Maximum Fees
Load: 3.00% front   12b-1: none
Other: $7.50 redemption fee (30 days or more), 0.75% fee (less than 30 days)

Distributions
Income: Apr, Dec   Capital Gains: Apr, Dec

Exchange Options
Number Per Year: no limit   Fee: $7.50
Telephone: yes (money market fund available)

Services: IRA, pension, auto exchange, auto invest, auto withdraw

Fidelity Sel Food & Agriculture (FDFAX)

Aggressive Growth

82 Devonshire St.
Boston, MA 02109
(800) 544-8888, (801) 534-1910

PERFORMANCE   **fund inception date: 7/29/85**

	3yr Annual	5yr Annual	10yr Annual	Bull	Bear
Return (%)	6.9	12.4	na	76.4	-6.2
Differ from Category (+/-)	-2.0 blw av	-0.1 av	na	-56.8 low	4.6 abv av

Total Risk	Standard Deviation	Category Risk	Risk Index	Beta
av	8.3%	low	0.5	0.8

	1994	1993	1992	1991	1990	1989	1988	1987	1986	1985
Return (%).............	6.0	8.8	6.0	34.0	9.3	38.8	26.7	7.5	22.5	—
Differ from category (+/-)..	6.7	-10.7	-5.0	-18.1	15.5	12.0	11.5	9.7	10.7	—

PER SHARE DATA

	1994	1993	1992	1991	1990	1989	1988	1987	1986	1985
Dividends, Net Income ($).	0.08	0.08	0.10	0.11	0.27	0.04	0.05	0.03	0.00	—
Distrib'ns, Cap Gain ($) ...	1.85	2.68	1.57	1.59	0.79	2.17	0.00	0.55	0.00	—
Net Asset Value ($)	30.60	30.75	30.93	30.86	24.39	23.29	18.42	14.57	14.10	—
Expense Ratio (%)	1.71	1.67	1.83	2.22	2.53	2.50	2.45	1.67	1.75	—
Net Income to Assets (%) .	0.18	0.21	0.46	0.85	0.82	0.48	-0.41	0.71	1.70	—
Portfolio Turnover (%)	129	515	63	124	267	248	215	608	576	—
Total Assets (Millions $).....	85	175	108	64	25	15	9	11	9	—

PORTFOLIO (as of 8/31/94)

Portfolio Manager: Bill Mankivsky - 1993

Investm't Category: Aggressive Growth
- ✔ Cap Gain
- Cap & Income
- Income
- ✔ Domestic
- ✔ Foreign
- Country/Region
- Asset Allocation
- Fund of Funds
- Index
- ✔ Sector
- Small Cap
- Socially Conscious
- State Specific

Portfolio:	stocks 84%	bonds 0%
convertibles 0%	other 0%	cash 16%

Largest Holdings: meat & fish 15%, tobacco manufacturers 10%

Unrealized Net Capital Gains: 9% of portfolio value

SHAREHOLDER INFORMATION

Minimum Investment
Initial: $2,500   Subsequent: $250

Minimum IRA Investment
Initial: $500   Subsequent: $250

Maximum Fees
Load: 3.00% front   12b-1: none
Other: $7.50 redemption fee (30 days or more), 0.75% fee (less than 30 days)

Distributions
Income: Apr, Dec   Capital Gains: Apr, Dec

Exchange Options
Number Per Year: no limit   Fee: $7.50
Telephone: yes (money market fund available)

Services: IRA, pension, auto exchange, auto invest, auto withdraw

Fidelity Sel Health Care

(FSPHX)

Aggressive Growth

82 Devonshire St.
Boston, MA 02109
(800) 544-8888, (801) 534-1910

PERFORMANCE

fund inception date: 7/14/81

	3yr Annual	5yr Annual	10yr Annual	Bull	Bear
Return (%)	0.8	18.5	21.5	83.7	-1.3
Differ from Category (+/-)	-8.1 low	6.0 high	7.5 high	-49.5 low	9.5 high

Total Risk	Standard Deviation	Category Risk	Risk Index	Beta
high	16.3%	abv av	1.1	1.0

	1994	1993	1992	1991	1990	1989	1988	1987	1986	1985
Return (%)	21.4	2.4	-17.4	83.6	24.3	42.4	8.8	-0.6	21.9	59.4
Differ from category (+/-) . .	22.1	-17.1	-28.4	31.5	30.5	15.6	-6.4	1.6	10.1	27.1

PER SHARE DATA

	1994	1993	1992	1991	1990	1989	1988	1987	1986	1985
Dividends, Net Income ($) .	0.62	0.07	0.16	0.34	0.20	0.13	0.28	0.00	0.00	0.05
Distrib'ns, Cap Gain ($) . . .	5.74	0.00	8.51	8.81	5.67	0.84	0.00	0.92	0.36	0.00
Net Asset Value ($)	70.80	63.62	62.19	85.95	52.98	47.58	34.13	31.62	32.78	27.15
Expense Ratio (%)	1.38	1.46	1.44	1.53	1.74	1.41	1.64	1.39	1.29	1.26
Net Income to Assets (%) . .	0.81	0.24	-0.02	1.28	1.61	0.95	0.06	-0.01	0.53	0.56
Portfolio Turnover (%)	214	112	154	159	126	114	122	213	217	159
Total Assets (Millions $) . . .	796	560	838	624	217	210	208	341	251	145

PORTFOLIO (as of 8/31/94)

Portfolio Manager: Charles Mangum - 1992

Investm't Category: Aggressive Growth

✔ Cap Gain	Asset Allocation
Cap & Income	Fund of Funds
Income	Index
	✔ Sector
✔ Domestic	Small Cap
✔ Foreign	Socially Conscious
Country/Region	State Specific

Portfolio: stocks 87%   bonds 0%
convertibles 1%   other 0%   cash 12%

Largest Holdings: drugs 49%, medical supplies & appliances 11%

Unrealized Net Capital Gains: 7% of portfolio value

SHAREHOLDER INFORMATION

Minimum Investment
Initial: $2,500   Subsequent: $250

Minimum IRA Investment
Initial: $500   Subsequent: $250

Maximum Fees
Load: 3.00% front   12b-1: none
Other: $7.50 redemption fee (30 days or more), 0.75% fee (less than 30 days)

Distributions
Income: Apr, Dec   Capital Gains: Apr, Dec

Exchange Options
Number Per Year: no limit   Fee: $7.50
Telephone: yes (money market fund available)

Services: IRA, pension, auto exchange, auto invest, auto withdraw

Fidelity Sel Home Finance (FSVLX)

82 Devonshire St.
Boston, MA 02109
(800) 544-8888, (801) 534-1910

Aggressive Growth

PERFORMANCE

fund inception date: 12/16/85

	3yr Annual	5yr Annual	10yr Annual	Bull	Bear
Return (%)	27.3	23.5	na	287.5	7.9
Differ from Category (+/-)	18.4 high	11.0 high	na	154.3 high	18.7 high

Total Risk	Standard Deviation	Category Risk	Risk Index	Beta
high	15.5%	abv av	1.1	0.9

	1994	1993	1992	1991	1990	1989	1988	1987	1986	1985
Return (%)	2.6	27.2	57.8	64.6	-15.0	9.3	18.4	-7.9	27.5	—
Differ from category (+/-)	3.3	7.7	46.8	12.5	-8.8	-17.5	3.2	-5.7	15.7	—

PER SHARE DATA

	1994	1993	1992	1991	1990	1989	1988	1987	1986	1985
Dividends, Net Income ($)	0.12	0.01	0.01	0.14	0.14	0.04	0.13	0.00	0.00	—
Distrib'ns, Cap Gain ($)	3.60	1.40	0.28	0.00	0.00	0.49	0.00	3.50	0.00	—
Net Asset Value ($)	21.33	24.44	20.35	13.09	8.05	9.65	9.30	7.96	12.88	—
Expense Ratio (%)	1.39	1.55	2.08	2.50	2.53	2.56	2.57	1.53	1.54	—
Net Income to Assets (%)	0.72	0.61	0.40	1.78	0.83	1.13	0.17	-0.05	5.76	—
Portfolio Turnover (%)	94	61	134	159	282	216	456	335	312	—
Total Assets (Millions $)	130	156	49	8	5	5	6	24	36	—

PORTFOLIO (as of 8/31/94)

Portfolio Manager: David Ellison - 1985

Investm't Category: Aggressive Growth

✔ Cap Gain   Asset Allocation
  Cap & Income   Fund of Funds
  Income   Index
              ✔ Sector
✔ Domestic   Small Cap
✔ Foreign   Socially Conscious
  Country/Region State Specific

Portfolio:	stocks 73%	bonds 0%
convertibles 0%	other 0%	cash 27%

Largest Holdings: savings banks and savings & loans 29%, federal charter savings banks 23%

Unrealized Net Capital Gains: 12% of portfolio value

SHAREHOLDER INFORMATION

Minimum Investment
Initial: $2,500   Subsequent: $250

Minimum IRA Investment
Initial: $500   Subsequent: $250

Maximum Fees
Load: 3.00% front   12b-1: none
Other: $7.50 redemption fee (30 days or more), 0.75% fee (less than 30 days)

Distributions
Income: Apr, Dec   Capital Gains: Apr, Dec

Exchange Options
Number Per Year: no limit   Fee: $7.50
Telephone: yes (money market fund available)

Services: IRA, pension, auto exchange, auto invest, auto withdraw

Fidelity Sel Industrial Equipment (FSCGX)

82 Devonshire St.
Boston, MA 02109
(800) 544-8888, (801) 534-1910

Aggressive Growth

PERFORMANCE

fund inception date: 9/29/86

	3yr Annual	5yr Annual	10yr Annual	Bull	Bear
Return (%)	18.0	12.0	na	120.7	-10.7
Differ from Category (+/-)	9.1 high	-0.5 av	na	-12.5 av	0.1 av

Total Risk	Standard Deviation	Category Risk	Risk Index	Beta
high	13.3%	av	0.9	0.9

	1994	1993	1992	1991	1990	1989	1988	1987	1986	1985
Return (%)	3.1	43.3	11.3	26.8	-15.5	17.9	4.8	-9.2	—	—
Differ from category (+/-) . . .	3.8	23.8	0.3	-25.3	-9.3	-8.9	-10.4	-7.0	—	—

PER SHARE DATA

	1994	1993	1992	1991	1990	1989	1988	1987	1986	1985
Dividends, Net Income ($) .	0.00	0.01	0.00	0.11	0.09	0.00	0.00	0.00	—	—
Distrib'ns, Cap Gain ($) . . .	0.17	0.40	0.00	0.00	0.00	0.00	0.00	0.23	—	—
Net Asset Value ($)	19.57	19.14	13.65	12.26	9.76	11.63	9.86	9.40	—	—
Expense Ratio (%)	1.69	2.49	2.49	2.52	2.59	2.58	2.65	1.70	—	—
Net Income to Assets (%) .	-0.24	0.15	-0.57	0.09	1.06	-0.66	-0.37	0.38	—	—
Portfolio Turnover (%)	157	407	167	43	132	164	407	514	—	—
Total Assets (Millions $) . . .	104	85	7	1	3	2	5	2	—	—

PORTFOLIO (as of 8/31/94)

Portfolio Manager: Robert Bertelson - 1994

Investm't Category: Aggressive Growth

✔ Cap Gain	Asset Allocation
Cap & Income	Fund of Funds
Income	Index
	✔ Sector
✔ Domestic	Small Cap
✔ Foreign	Socially Conscious
Country/Region	State Specific

Portfolio: stocks 95% bonds 0%
convertibles 0% other 0% cash 5%

Largest Holdings: general industrial machinery 28%, construction equipment 16%

Unrealized Net Capital Gains: -1% of portfolio value

SHAREHOLDER INFORMATION

Minimum Investment
Initial: $2,500   Subsequent: $250

Minimum IRA Investment
Initial: $500   Subsequent: $250

Maximum Fees
Load: 3.00% front   12b-1: none
Other: $7.50 redemption fee (30 days or more), 0.75% fee (less than 30 days)

Distributions
Income: Apr, Dec   Capital Gains: Apr, Dec

Exchange Options
Number Per Year: no limit   Fee: $7.50
Telephone: yes (money market fund available)

Services: IRA, pension, auto exchange, auto invest, auto withdraw

Fidelity Sel Industrial Materials (FSDPX)

82 Devonshire St.
Boston, MA 02109
(800) 544-8888, (801) 534-1910

Aggressive Growth

fund inception date: 9/29/86

PERFORMANCE

	3yr Annual	5yr Annual	10yr Annual	Bull	Bear
Return (%)	13.8	10.6	na	117.1	-1.3
Differ from Category (+/-)	4.9 abv av	-1.9 blw av	na	-16.1 av	9.5 high

Total Risk	Standard Deviation	Category Risk	Risk Index	Beta
abv av	11.4%	blw av	0.8	1.1

	1994	1993	1992	1991	1990	1989	1988	1987	1986	1985
Return (%).............	8.1	21.3	12.3	35.8	-17.1	4.4	10.8	15.6	—	—
Differ from category (+/-) ..	8.8	1.8	1.3	-16.3	-10.9	-22.4	-4.4	17.8	—	—

PER SHARE DATA

	1994	1993	1992	1991	1990	1989	1988	1987	1986	1985
Dividends, Net Income ($).	0.18	0.06	0.08	0.06	0.34	0.00	0.21	0.02	—	—
Distrib'ns, Cap Gain ($) ...	0.00	0.00	0.00	0.00	0.00	0.00	0.00	0.01	—	—
Net Asset Value ($)	21.96	20.47	16.92	15.13	11.19	13.86	13.27	12.17	—	—
Expense Ratio (%)	1.61	2.02	2.47	2.49	2.59	2.68	2.43	1.56	—	—
Net Income to Assets (%) .	1.18	0.86	0.25	1.30	1.22	-0.54	0.53	0.15	—	—
Portfolio Turnover (%)	106	273	222	148	250	289	455	414	—	—
Total Assets (Millions $)....	180	36	22	2	3	8	42	27	—	—

PORTFOLIO (as of 8/31/94)

Portfolio Manager: Douglas Chase - 1994

Investm't Category: Aggressive Growth
✔ Cap Gain	Asset Allocation
Cap & Income	Fund of Funds
Income	Index
	✔ Sector
✔ Domestic	Small Cap
✔ Foreign	Socially Conscious
Country/Region	State Specific

Portfolio: stocks 99% bonds 0%
convertibles 0% other 0% cash 1%

Largest Holdings: chemicals 32%, paper 21%

Unrealized Net Capital Gains: 6% of portfolio value

SHAREHOLDER INFORMATION

Minimum Investment
Initial: $2,500   Subsequent: $250

Minimum IRA Investment
Initial: $500   Subsequent: $250

Maximum Fees
Load: 3.00% front   12b-1: none
Other: $7.50 redemption fee (30 days or more), 0.75% fee (less than 30 days)

Distributions
Income: Apr, Dec   Capital Gains: Apr, Dec

Exchange Options
Number Per Year: no limit   Fee: $7.50
Telephone: yes (money market fund available)

Services: IRA, pension, auto exchange, auto invest, auto withdraw

Fidelity Sel Insurance
(FSPCX)
Growth

82 Devonshire St.
Boston, MA 02109
(800) 544-8888, (801) 534-1910

PERFORMANCE
fund inception date: 12/16/85

	3yr Annual	5yr Annual	10yr Annual	Bull	Bear
Return (%)	9.7	10.2	na	107.6	-4.1
Differ from Category (+/-)	2.0 abv av	0.6 abv av	na	15.5 abv av	2.5 abv av

Total Risk	Standard Deviation	Category Risk	Risk Index	Beta
abv av	11.3%	abv av	1.2	0.8

	1994	1993	1992	1991	1990	1989	1988	1987	1986	1985
Return (%)	-0.3	8.1	22.5	36.6	-9.8	37.8	17.4	-12.1	7.6	—
Differ from category (+/-) ...	0.3	-5.3	10.9	0.9	-4.1	11.7	-0.6	-13.9	-7.0	—

PER SHARE DATA

	1994	1993	1992	1991	1990	1989	1988	1987	1986	1985
Dividends, Net Income ($) .	0.00	0.01	0.03	0.26	0.00	0.15	0.09	0.14	0.00	—
Distrib'ns, Cap Gain ($) ...	0.00	1.96	1.71	0.00	0.00	0.00	0.00	0.00	0.00	—
Net Asset Value ($)	19.96	20.03	20.33	18.30	13.60	15.08	11.05	9.49	10.97	—
Expense Ratio (%)........	2.13	2.49	2.47	2.49	2.50	2.53	2.48	1.63	1.51	—
Net Income to Assets (%)..	0.33	-0.26	0.22	1.58	1.15	0.98	0.28	0.53	1.34	—
Portfolio Turnover (%)....	148	81	112	98	158	95	174	718	299	—
Total Assets (Millions $)....	10	18	2	2	2	3	3	7	5	—

PORTFOLIO (as of 8/31/94)

Portfolio Manager: Bob Chow - 1993

Investm't Category: Growth

✔ Cap Gain	Asset Allocation
Cap & Income	Fund of Funds
Income	Index
	✔ Sector
✔ Domestic	Small Cap
✔ Foreign	Socially Conscious
Country/Region	State Specific

Portfolio: stocks 88% bonds 0%
convertibles 0% other 0% cash 12%

Largest Holdings: property—casualty & reinsurance 71%, insurance carriers 7%

Unrealized Net Capital Gains: 5% of portfolio value

SHAREHOLDER INFORMATION

Minimum Investment
Initial: $2,500   Subsequent: $250

Minimum IRA Investment
Initial: $500   Subsequent: $250

Maximum Fees
Load: 3.00% front   12b-1: none
Other: $7.50 redemption fee (30 days or more), 0.75% fee (less than 30 days)

Distributions
Income: Apr, Dec   Capital Gains: Apr, Dec

Exchange Options
Number Per Year: no limit   Fee: $7.50
Telephone: yes (money market fund available)

Services: IRA, pension, auto exchange, auto invest, auto withdraw

Fidelity Sel Leisure
(FDLSX)
Aggressive Growth

82 Devonshire St.
Boston, MA 02109
(800) 544-8888, (801) 534-1910

PERFORMANCE

fund inception date: 5/8/84

	3yr Annual	5yr Annual	10yr Annual	Bull	Bear
Return (%)	14.7	9.3	17.3	142.6	-11.5
Differ from Category (+/-)	5.8 high	-3.2 blw av	3.3 abv av	9.4 abv av	-0.7 av

Total Risk	Standard Deviation	Category Risk	Risk Index	Beta
abv av	11.1%	blw av	0.7	1.0

	1994	1993	1992	1991	1990	1989	1988	1987	1986	1985
Return (%)	-6.8	39.5	16.2	32.9	-22.2	31.2	26.0	5.6	15.7	56.4
Differ from category (+/-)	-6.1	20.0	5.2	-19.2	-16.0	4.4	10.8	7.8	3.9	24.1

PER SHARE DATA

	1994	1993	1992	1991	1990	1989	1988	1987	1986	1985
Dividends, Net Income ($)	0.00	0.00	0.00	0.00	0.23	0.07	0.00	0.00	0.01	0.03
Distrib'ns, Cap Gain ($)	3.93	3.26	0.00	0.00	0.00	2.03	0.40	2.03	0.04	0.00
Net Asset Value ($)	38.27	45.22	35.09	30.19	22.71	29.52	24.13	19.49	20.51	17.76
Expense Ratio (%)	1.51	1.90	2.21	2.27	1.96	1.73	1.96	1.55	1.41	1.50
Net Income to Assets (%)	-0.42	-0.39	-0.28	0.34	0.86	0.50	-0.13	-0.16	0.48	1.16
Portfolio Turnover (%)	82	109	45	75	124	249	229	148	148	243
Total Assets (Millions $)	61	115	40	40	49	91	56	72	207	27

PORTFOLIO (as of 8/31/94)

Portfolio Manager: Deborah Wheeler - 1992

Investm't Category: Aggressive Growth
- ✔ Cap Gain
- Cap & Income
- Income
- Asset Allocation
- Fund of Funds
- Index
- ✔ Sector
- ✔ Domestic
- ✔ Foreign
- Country/Region
- Small Cap
- Socially Conscious
- State Specific

Portfolio: stocks 87%   bonds 1%
convertibles 0%   other 0%   cash 12%

Largest Holdings: television broadcasting 13%, hotels, motels & tourist courts 11%

Unrealized Net Capital Gains: 4% of portfolio value

SHAREHOLDER INFORMATION

Minimum Investment
Initial: $2,500   Subsequent: $250

Minimum IRA Investment
Initial: $500   Subsequent: $250

Maximum Fees
Load: 3.00% front   12b-1: none
Other: $7.50 redemption fee (30 days or more), 0.75% fee (less than 30 days)

Distributions
Income: Apr, Dec   Capital Gains: Apr, Dec

Exchange Options
Number Per Year: no limit   Fee: $7.50
Telephone: yes (money market fund available)

Services: IRA, pension, auto exchange, auto invest, auto withdraw

Fidelity Sel Medical Delivery (FSHCX)

Aggressive Growth

82 Devonshire St.
Boston, MA 02109
(800) 544-8888, (801) 534-1910

PERFORMANCE

fund inception date: 6/30/86

	3yr Annual	5yr Annual	10yr Annual	Bull	Bear
Return (%)	3.1	17.8	na	109.9	-4.3
Differ from Category (+/-)	-5.8 blw av	5.3 high	na	-23.3 blw av	6.5 high

Total Risk	Standard Deviation	Category Risk	Risk Index	Beta
high	19.2%	high	1.3	0.9

	1994	1993	1992	1991	1990	1989	1988	1987	1986	1985
Return (%)	19.8	5.5	-13.1	77.8	16.2	58.0	15.7	-12.0	—	—
Differ from category (+/-) ..	20.5	-14.0	-24.1	25.7	22.4	31.2	0.5	-9.8	—	—

PER SHARE DATA

	1994	1993	1992	1991	1990	1989	1988	1987	1986	1985
Dividends, Net Income ($)	0.07	0.00	0.00	0.00	0.00	0.05	0.00	0.02	—	—
Distrib'ns, Cap Gain ($) ...	0.88	0.00	1.55	1.24	0.39	0.26	0.00	0.36	—	—
Net Asset Value ($)	21.87	19.10	18.10	22.76	13.65	12.09	7.85	6.78	—	—
Expense Ratio (%)........	1.44	1.77	1.69	1.94	2.16	2.48	2.48	1.49	—	—
Net Income to Assets (%)..	0.10	-0.89	-0.71	-0.07	1.43	0.59	-0.65	0.62	—	—
Portfolio Turnover (%)....	205	155	181	165	253	92	264	221	—	—
Total Assets (Millions $) ...	247	148	129	131	23	20	3	3	—	—

PORTFOLIO (as of 8/31/94)

Portfolio Manager: Stephen Binder - 1994

Investm't Category: Aggressive Growth

✔ Cap Gain	Asset Allocation
Cap & Income	Fund of Funds
Income	Index
	✔ Sector
✔ Domestic	Small Cap
✔ Foreign	Socially Conscious
Country/Region	State Specific

Portfolio: stocks 83% bonds 0%
convertibles 0% other 0% cash 17%

Largest Holdings: hospitals 28%, HMOs & outpatient care 26%

Unrealized Net Capital Gains: 12% of portfolio value

SHAREHOLDER INFORMATION

Minimum Investment
Initial: $2,500   Subsequent: $250

Minimum IRA Investment
Initial: $500   Subsequent: $250

Maximum Fees
Load: 3.00% front   12b-1: none
Other: $7.50 redemption fee (30 days or more), 0.75% fee (less than 30 days)

Distributions
Income: Apr, Dec   Capital Gains: Apr, Dec

Exchange Options
Number Per Year: no limit   Fee: $7.50
Telephone: yes (money market fund available)

Services: IRA, pension, auto exchange, auto invest, auto withdraw

Fidelity Sel Multimedia
(FBMPX)
Aggressive Growth

82 Devonshire St.
Boston, MA 02109
(800) 544-8888, (801) 534-1910

PERFORMANCE

fund inception date: 6/30/86

	3yr Annual	5yr Annual	10yr Annual	Bull	Bear
Return (%)	20.3	12.1	na	165.6	-6.0
Differ from Category (+/-)	11.4 high	-0.4 av	na	32.4 abv av	4.8 abv av

Total Risk	Standard Deviation	Category Risk	Risk Index	Beta
high	12.1%	blw av	0.8	1.1

	1994	1993	1992	1991	1990	1989	1988	1987	1986	1985
Return (%)..............	4.0	37.9	21.4	37.8	-26.2	32.5	26.8	19.9	—	—
Differ from category (+/-) ..	4.7	18.4	10.4	-14.3	-20.0	5.7	11.6	22.1	—	—

PER SHARE DATA

	1994	1993	1992	1991	1990	1989	1988	1987	1986	1985
Dividends, Net Income ($).	0.00	0.00	0.00	0.00	0.00	0.00	0.00	0.01	—	—
Distrib'ns, Cap Gain ($) ...	3.21	0.64	0.23	0.00	0.00	2.57	0.75	0.78	—	—
Net Asset Value ($)	21.23	23.84	17.82	14.86	10.78	14.61	12.98	10.87	—	—
Expense Ratio (%)	1.88	2.49	2.49	2.53	2.51	2.66	2.48	1.50	—	—
Net Income to Assets (%) .	-0.79	-0.52	-1.22	-0.43	-0.14	-1.01	-0.52	0.25	—	—
Portfolio Turnover (%)	84	70	111	150	75	437	325	224	—	—
Total Assets (Millions $).....	26	66	8	5	7	45	17	7	—	—

PORTFOLIO (as of 8/31/94)

Portfolio Manager: Stephen DuFour - 1993

Investm't Category: Aggressive Growth
- ✔ Cap Gain
- Cap & Income
- Income
- ✔ Domestic
- ✔ Foreign
- Country/Region

- Asset Allocation
- Fund of Funds
- Index
- ✔ Sector
- Small Cap
- Socially Conscious
- State Specific

Portfolio: stocks 91%   bonds 0%
convertibles 0%   other 0%   cash 9%

Largest Holdings: newspapers 15%, cable TV operators 14%

Unrealized Net Capital Gains: 5% of portfolio value

SHAREHOLDER INFORMATION

Minimum Investment
Initial: $2,500   Subsequent: $250

Minimum IRA Investment
Initial: $500   Subsequent: $250

Maximum Fees
Load: 3.00% front   12b-1: none
Other: $7.50 redemption fee (30 days or more), 0.75% fee (less than 30 days)

Distributions
Income: Apr, Dec   Capital Gains: Apr, Dec

Exchange Options
Number Per Year: no limit   Fee: $7.50
Telephone: yes (money market fund available)

Services: IRA, pension, auto exchange, auto invest, auto withdraw

Fidelity Sel Natural Gas Port (FSNGX)

82 Devonshire St.
Boston, MA 02109
(800) 544-8888, (801) 534-1910

Growth

PERFORMANCE

fund inception date: 4/21/93

	3yr Annual	5yr Annual	10yr Annual	Bull	Bear
Return (%)	na	na	na	na	-0.1
Differ from Category (+/-)	na	na	na	na	6.5 high

Total Risk	Standard Deviation	Category Risk	Risk Index	Beta
na	na	na	na	na

	1994	1993	1992	1991	1990	1989	1988	1987	1986	1985
Return (%)	-6.8	—	—	—	—	—	—	—	—	—
Differ from category (+/-) . .	-6.2	—	—	—	—	—	—	—	—	—

PER SHARE DATA

	1994	1993	1992	1991	1990	1989	1988	1987	1986	1985
Dividends, Net Income ($) .	0.02	—	—	—	—	—	—	—	—	—
Distrib'ns, Cap Gain ($) . . .	0.00	—	—	—	—	—	—	—	—	—
Net Asset Value ($)	8.70	—	—	—	—	—	—	—	—	—
Expense Ratio (%).	1.75	—	—	—	—	—	—	—	—	—
Net Income to Assets (%) .	-0.07	—	—	—	—	—	—	—	—	—
Portfolio Turnover (%). . . .	162	—	—	—	—	—	—	—	—	—
Total Assets (Millions $)	79	—	—	—	—	—	—	—	—	—

PORTFOLIO (as of 8/31/94)

Portfolio Manager: Michael Tempero - 1994

Investm't Category: Growth

✔ Cap Gain	Asset Allocation
Cap & Income	Fund of Funds
Income	Index
	✔ Sector
✔ Domestic	Small Cap
✔ Foreign	Socially Conscious
Country/Region	State Specific

Portfolio: stocks 90% bonds 0%
convertibles 0% other 0% cash 10%

Largest Holdings: crude petroleum & gas 38%, gas transmission 14%

Unrealized Net Capital Gains: -4% of portfolio value

SHAREHOLDER INFORMATION

Minimum Investment
Initial: $2,500   Subsequent: $250

Minimum IRA Investment
Initial: $500   Subsequent: $250

Maximum Fees
Load: 3.00% front   12b-1: none
Other: $7.50 redemption fee (30 days or more), 0.75% fee (less than 30 days)

Distributions
Income: Apr, Dec   Capital Gains: Apr, Dec

Exchange Options
Number Per Year: no limit   Fee: $7.50
Telephone: yes (money market fund available)

Services: IRA, pension, auto exchange, auto invest, auto withdraw

Fidelity Sel Paper and Forest Prod (FSPFX)

82 Devonshire St.
Boston, MA 02109
(800) 544-8888, (801) 534-1910

Aggressive Growth

fund inception date: 6/30/86

	3yr Annual	5yr Annual	10yr Annual	Bull	Bear
Return (%)	14.8	11.6	na	128.9	-10.5
Differ from Category (+/-)	5.9 high	-0.9 av	na	-4.3 av	0.3 av

Total Risk	Standard Deviation	Category Risk	Risk Index	Beta
high	16.0%	abv av	1.1	0.9

	1994	1993	1992	1991	1990	1989	1988	1987	1986	1985
Return (%).	14.1	18.5	12.0	34.7	-15.1	4.0	6.7	3.9	—	—
Differ from category (+/-) .	14.8	-1.0	1.0	-17.4	-8.9	-22.8	-8.5	6.1	—	—

PER SHARE DATA

	1994	1993	1992	1991	1990	1989	1988	1987	1986	1985
Dividends, Net Income ($).	0.00	0.01	0.09	0.30	0.17	0.15	0.03	0.04	—	—
Distrib'ns, Cap Gain ($) . . .	1.17	0.00	0.00	0.00	0.00	0.00	0.00	1.04	—	—
Net Asset Value ($)	19.36	18.08	15.26	13.70	10.41	12.47	12.13	11.39		
Expense Ratio (%)	2.00	2.21	2.05	2.49	2.57	2.54	2.52	1.29		
Net Income to Assets (%) .	-0.22	0.49	0.92	1.73	0.92	0.07	-0.20	1.61		
Portfolio Turnover (%)	181	222	421	171	221	154	209	466		
Total Assets (Millions $).	76	49	28	12	5	9	15	110		

PORTFOLIO (as of 8/31/94)

Portfolio Manager: Scott Offen - 1993

Investm't Category: Aggressive Growth
- ✔ Cap Gain
- Cap & Income
- Income
- Asset Allocation
- Fund of Funds
- Index
- ✔ Sector
- ✔ Domestic
- Small Cap
- ✔ Foreign
- Socially Conscious
- Country/Region
- State Specific

Portfolio: stocks 98% bonds 0%
convertibles 0% other 0% cash 2%

Largest Holdings: paper & allied products 87%, paper containers 5%

Unrealized Net Capital Gains: 10% of portfolio value

SHAREHOLDER INFORMATION

Minimum Investment
Initial: $2,500   Subsequent: $250

Minimum IRA Investment
Initial: $500   Subsequent: $250

Maximum Fees
Load: 3.00% front   12b-1: none
Other: $7.50 redemption fee (30 days or more), 0.75% fee (less than 30 days)

Distributions
Income: Apr, Dec   Capital Gains: Apr, Dec

Exchange Options
Number Per Year: no limit   Fee: $7.50
Telephone: yes (money market fund available)

Services: IRA, pension, auto exchange, auto invest, auto withdraw

Fidelity Sel Precious Metals (FDPMX)

Gold

82 Devonshire St.
Boston, MA 02109
(800) 544-8888, (801) 534-1910

PERFORMANCE

fund inception date: 7/14/81

	3yr Annual	5yr Annual	10yr Annual	Bull	Bear
Return (%)	17.7	5.5	7.9	46.0	-3.2
Differ from Category (+/-)	6.9 high	5.5 high	2.7 abv av	13.1 high	6.8 high

Total Risk	Standard Deviation	Category Risk	Risk Index	Beta
high	25.5%	blw av	0.9	0.3

	1994	1993	1992	1991	1990	1989	1988	1987	1986	1985
Return (%)	-1.1	111.6	-21.8	1.5	-21.0	32.1	-23.8	37.5	32.9	-10.5
Differ from category (+/-)	10.4	24.7	-6.1	6.3	1.5	7.4	-4.9	5.6	-4.7	-3.1

PER SHARE DATA

	1994	1993	1992	1991	1990	1989	1988	1987	1986	1985
Dividends, Net Income ($)	0.23	0.21	0.17	0.10	0.15	0.18	0.46	0.07	0.10	0.39
Distrib'ns, Cap Gain ($)	0.00	0.00	0.00	0.00	0.00	0.00	0.00	0.12	0.00	0.00
Net Asset Value ($)	17.68	18.13	8.67	11.31	11.24	14.44	11.06	15.14	11.15	8.49
Expense Ratio (%)	1.48	1.73	1.81	1.79	1.93	1.88	2.02	1.50	1.48	1.11
Net Income to Assets (%)	1.33	1.12	0.92	1.52	1.01	2.18	2.42	3.44	4.16	3.65
Portfolio Turnover (%)	30	36	44	41	98	72	86	84	65	46
Total Assets (Millions $)	453	466	130	155	192	180	242	647	116	189

PORTFOLIO (as of 8/31/94)

Portfolio Manager: Malcolm MacNaught - 1981

Investm't Category: Gold
- ✔ Cap Gain
- Cap & Income
- Income
- ✔ Domestic
- ✔ Foreign
- Country/Region
- Asset Allocation
- Fund of Funds
- Index
- ✔ Sector
- Small Cap
- Socially Conscious
- State Specific

Portfolio: stocks 85% bonds 0% convertibles 0% other 3% cash 12%

Largest Holdings: South African gold mining cos. 34%, Canadian gold mining cos. 19%

Unrealized Net Capital Gains: 21% of portfolio value

SHAREHOLDER INFORMATION

Minimum Investment
Initial: $2,500   Subsequent: $250

Minimum IRA Investment
Initial: $500   Subsequent: $250

Maximum Fees
Load: 3.00% front   12b-1: none
Other: $7.50 redemption fee (30 days or more), 0.75% fee (less than 30 days)

Distributions
Income: Dec   Capital Gains: Dec

Exchange Options
Number Per Year: no limit   Fee: $7.50
Telephone: yes (money market fund available)

Services: IRA, pension, auto exchange, auto invest, auto withdraw

Fidelity Sel Regional Banks (FSRBX)

Growth

82 Devonshire St.
Boston, MA 02109
(800) 544-8888, (801) 534-1910

	3yr Annual	5yr Annual	10yr Annual	Bull	Bear
Return (%)	18.2	16.8	na	243.0	3.0
Differ from Category (+/-)	10.5 high	7.2 high	na	150.9 high	9.6 high

Total Risk	Standard Deviation	Category Risk	Risk Index	Beta
high	14.2%	high	1.5	1.0

	1994	1993	1992	1991	1990	1989	1988	1987	1986	1985
Return (%)	0.2	11.1	48.5	65.7	-20.6	26.6	25.7	-3.0	—	—
Differ from category (+/-) . .	0.8	-2.3	36.9	30.0	-14.9	0.5	7.7	-4.8	—	—

PER SHARE DATA

	1994	1993	1992	1991	1990	1989	1988	1987	1986	1985
Dividends, Net Income ($)	0.26	0.15	0.11	0.15	0.15	0.11	0.20	0.06	—	—
Distrib'ns, Cap Gain ($) . . .	1.01	3.92	0.81	0.53	0.00	0.65	0.47	0.15	—	—
Net Asset Value ($)	16.28	17.49	19.44	13.75	8.74	11.21	9.45	8.05	—	—
Expense Ratio (%)	1.50	1.49	1.77	2.51	2.55	2.53	2.48	1.63	—	—
Net Income to Assets (%) .	1.78	1.06	1.80	2.34	1.74	2.24	1.61	2.10	—	—
Portfolio Turnover (%)	101	63	89	110	411	352	291	227	—	—
Total Assets (Millions $)	108	116	156	24	5	17	9	2	—	—

PORTFOLIO (as of 8/31/94)

Portfolio Manager: Louis Salemy - 1994

Investm't Category: Growth
- ✔ Cap Gain
- Cap & Income
- Income
- ✔ Domestic
- ✔ Foreign
- Country/Region
- Asset Allocation
- Fund of Funds
- Index
- ✔ Sector
- Small Cap
- Socially Conscious
- State Specific

Portfolio: stocks 97%   bonds 0%
convertibles 0%   other 0%   cash 3%

Largest Holdings: Northeast banks 22%, Midwest banks 20%

Unrealized Net Capital Gains: 8% of portfolio value

SHAREHOLDER INFORMATION

Minimum Investment
Initial: $2,500   Subsequent: $250

Minimum IRA Investment
Initial: $500   Subsequent: $250

Maximum Fees
Load: 3.00% front   12b-1: none
Other: $7.50 redemption fee (30 days or more), 0.75% fee (less than 30 days)

Distributions
Income: Apr, Dec   Capital Gains: Apr, Dec

Exchange Options
Number Per Year: no limit   Fee: $7.50
Telephone: yes (money market fund available)

Services: IRA, pension, auto exchange, auto invest, auto withdraw

Fidelity Sel Retailing

(FSRPX)

Aggressive Growth

82 Devonshire St.
Boston, MA 02109
(800) 544-8888, (801) 534-1910

PERFORMANCE

	3yr Annual	5yr Annual	10yr Annual	Bull	Bear
Return (%)	9.4	15.9	na	153.4	-1.3
Differ from Category (+/-)	0.5 av	3.4 abv av	na	20.2 abv av	9.5 high

Total Risk	Standard Deviation	Category Risk	Risk Index	Beta
high	13.2%	blw av	0.9	0.6

	1994	1993	1992	1991	1990	1989	1988	1987	1986	1985
Return (%)	-5.0	13.0	22.0	68.1	-5.0	29.5	38.7	-7.3	14.1	—
Differ from category (+/-)	-4.3	-6.5	11.0	16.0	1.2	2.7	23.5	-5.1	2.3	—

PER SHARE DATA

	1994	1993	1992	1991	1990	1989	1988	1987	1986	1985
Dividends, Net Income ($)	0.00	0.00	0.00	0.00	0.00	0.16	0.03	0.23	0.00	—
Distrib'ns, Cap Gain ($)	0.00	2.63	1.17	0.50	0.03	2.57	0.18	0.76	0.00	—
Net Asset Value ($)	23.88	25.14	24.64	21.28	12.98	13.70	12.74	9.34	11.19	—
Expense Ratio (%)	1.79	1.77	1.87	2.54	2.50	2.51	2.47	1.54	1.67	—
Net Income to Assets (%)	-0.46	-0.44	-0.13	-0.34	2.13	0.48	0.13	0.39	0.63	—
Portfolio Turnover (%)	513	171	205	115	212	290	294	596	812	—
Total Assets (Millions $)	35	68	48	18	8	9	15	9	3	—

PORTFOLIO (as of 8/31/94)

Portfolio Manager: Jeff Feinberg - 1994

Investm't Category: Aggressive Growth
- ✔ Cap Gain
- Cap & Income
- Income
- Asset Allocation
- Fund of Funds
- Index
- ✔ Sector
- ✔ Domestic
- ✔ Foreign
- Country/Region
- Small Cap
- Socially Conscious
- State Specific

Portfolio: stocks 85%   bonds 0%
convertibles 0%   other 1%   cash 14%

Largest Holdings: general apparel stores 14%, department stores 13%

Unrealized Net Capital Gains: 6% of portfolio value

SHAREHOLDER INFORMATION

Minimum Investment
Initial: $2,500   Subsequent: $250

Minimum IRA Investment
Initial: $500   Subsequent: $250

Maximum Fees
Load: 3.00% front   12b-1: none
Other: $7.50 redemption fee (30 days or more), 0.75% fee (less than 30 days)

Distributions
Income: Apr, Dec   Capital Gains: Apr, Dec

Exchange Options
Number Per Year: no limit   Fee: $7.50
Telephone: yes (money market fund available)

Services: IRA, pension, auto exchange, auto invest, auto withdraw

Fidelity Sel Software & Comp (FSCSX)

Aggressive Growth

82 Devonshire St.
Boston, MA 02109
(800) 544-8888, (801) 534-1910

fund inception date: 7/29/85

PERFORMANCE

	3yr Annual	5yr Annual	10yr Annual	Bull	Bear
Return (%)	21.7	21.5	na	234.9	-25.3
Differ from Category (+/-)	12.8 high	9.0 high	na	101.7 high	-14.5 low

Total Risk	Standard Deviation	Category Risk	Risk Index	Beta
high	20.9%	high	1.4	1.3

	1994	1993	1992	1991	1990	1989	1988	1987	1986	1985
Return (%)..............	0.3	32.7	35.5	45.8	0.8	12.0	9.0	9.4	13.8	—
Differ from category (+/-) ..	1.0	13.2	24.5	-6.3	7.0	-14.8	-6.2	11.6	2.0	—

PER SHARE DATA

	1994	1993	1992	1991	1990	1989	1988	1987	1986	1985
Dividends, Net Income ($).	0.00	0.00	0.00	0.00	0.00	0.00	0.00	0.00	0.00	—
Distrib'ns, Cap Gain ($) ...	0.33	6.48	0.00	2.50	0.00	0.86	0.00	0.68	0.00	—
Net Asset Value ($)	27.29	27.55	26.43	19.50	15.32	15.19	14.34	13.15	12.65	—
Expense Ratio (%)	1.50	1.64	1.98	2.50	2.56	2.63	2.51	1.51	1.65	—
Net Income to Assets (%) .	-1.15	-0.37	-1.30	-0.84	-1.30	-1.51	-0.61	0.08	-0.35	—
Portfolio Turnover (%)	176	402	348	326	284	434	134	220	193	—
Total Assets (Millions $)....	211	162	89	17	10	14	23	103	17	—

PORTFOLIO (as of 8/31/94)

Portfolio Manager: John Hurley - 1994

Investm't Category: Aggressive Growth

✔ Cap Gain	Asset Allocation
Cap & Income	Fund of Funds
Income	Index
	✔ Sector
✔ Domestic	Small Cap
✔ Foreign	Socially Conscious
Country/Region	State Specific

Portfolio: stocks 89% bonds 0%
convertibles 0% other 2% cash 9%

Largest Holdings: datacommunications equip 17%, prepackaged computer software 24%

Unrealized Net Capital Gains: 2% of portfolio value

SHAREHOLDER INFORMATION

Minimum Investment
Initial: $2,500   Subsequent: $250

Minimum IRA Investment
Initial: $500   Subsequent: $250

Maximum Fees
Load: 3.00% front   12b-1: none
Other: $7.50 redemption fee (30 days or more), 0.75% fee (less than 30 days)

Distributions
Income: Apr, Dec   Capital Gains: Apr, Dec

Exchange Options
Number Per Year: no limit   Fee: $7.50
Telephone: yes (money market fund available)

Services: IRA, pension, auto exchange, auto invest, auto withdraw

Fidelity Sel Technology
(FSPTX)
Aggressive Growth

82 Devonshire St.
Boston, MA 02109
(800) 544-8888, (801) 534-1910

PERFORMANCE

fund inception date: 7/14/81

	3yr Annual	5yr Annual	10yr Annual	Bull	Bear
Return (%)	15.8	22.2	10.5	192.9	-10.7
Differ from Category (+/-)	6.9 high	9.7 high	-3.5 blw av	59.7 high	0.1 av

Total Risk	Standard Deviation	Category Risk	Risk Index	Beta
high	15.6%	abv av	1.1	1.2

	1994	1993	1992	1991	1990	1989	1988	1987	1986	1985
Return (%)	11.1	28.6	8.7	58.9	10.5	16.9	-2.6	-11.7	-7.4	7.5
Differ from category (+/-)	11.8	9.1	-2.3	6.8	16.7	-9.9	-17.8	-9.5	-19.2	-24.8

PER SHARE DATA

	1994	1993	1992	1991	1990	1989	1988	1987	1986	1985
Dividends, Net Income ($)	0.00	0.13	0.00	0.16	0.00	0.00	0.00	0.00	0.00	0.39
Distrib'ns, Cap Gain ($)	1.50	3.70	2.75	0.00	0.00	0.00	0.00	0.80	0.08	0.00
Net Asset Value ($)	41.36	38.73	33.79	33.92	21.46	19.42	16.60	17.06	20.27	21.99
Expense Ratio (%)	1.57	1.64	1.72	1.83	2.09	1.86	1.76	1.44	1.26	1.04
Net Income to Assets (%)	-0.91	0.52	-0.84	0.61	-0.76	-0.67	-0.71	-0.21	-0.21	1.24
Portfolio Turnover (%)	125	259	353	442	327	397	140	73	85	126
Total Assets (Millions $)	227	174	105	117	78	105	137	296	318	565

PORTFOLIO (as of 8/31/94)

Portfolio Manager: Harry Lange - 1993

Investm't Category: Aggressive Growth
✔ Cap Gain   Asset Allocation
  Cap & Income   Fund of Funds
  Income   Index
                    ✔ Sector
✔ Domestic   Small Cap
✔ Foreign   Socially Conscious
  Country/Region   State Specific

Portfolio: stocks 90%   bonds 0%
convertibles 4%   other 1%   cash 5%

Largest Holdings: semiconductors 29%, pre-packaged computer software 13%

Unrealized Net Capital Gains: 14% of portfolio value

SHAREHOLDER INFORMATION

Minimum Investment
Initial: $2,500   Subsequent: $250

Minimum IRA Investment
Initial: $500   Subsequent: $250

Maximum Fees
Load: 3.00% front   12b-1: none
Other: $7.50 redemption fee (30 days or more), 0.75% fee (less than 30 days)

Distributions
Income: Apr, Dec   Capital Gains: Apr, Dec

Exchange Options
Number Per Year: no limit   Fee: $7.50
Telephone: yes (money market fund available)

Services: IRA, pension, auto exchange, auto invest, auto withdraw

Fidelity Sel Telecomm
(FSTCX)
Growth

82 Devonshire St.
Boston, MA 02109
(800) 544-8888, (801) 534-1910

PERFORMANCE

fund inception date: 7/29/85

	3yr Annual	5yr Annual	10yr Annual	Bull	Bear
Return (%)	15.9	11.2	na	128.4	-5.1
Differ from Category (+/-)	8.2 high	1.6 abv av	na	36.3 high	1.5 abv av

Total Risk	Standard Deviation	Category Risk	Risk Index	Beta
abv av	11.6%	high	1.2	1.1

	1994	1993	1992	1991	1990	1989	1988	1987	1986	1985
Return (%).............	4.3	29.7	15.3	30.8	-16.3	50.8	27.7	15.2	19.8	—
Differ from category (+/-) ..	4.9	16.3	3.7	-4.9	-10.6	24.7	9.7	13.4	5.2	—

PER SHARE DATA

	1994	1993	1992	1991	1990	1989	1988	1987	1986	1985
Dividends, Net Income ($).	0.53	0.20	0.18	0.28	0.43	0.12	0.12	0.02	0.00	—
Distrib'ns, Cap Gain ($) ...	1.07	4.18	0.48	0.00	0.00	0.98	0.03	0.36	0.00	—
Net Asset Value ($)	37.48	37.54	32.51	28.79	22.23	27.11	18.73	14.78	13.18	—
Expense Ratio (%)	1.52	1.74	1.90	1.97	1.85	2.12	2.48	1.52	1.51	—
Net Income to Assets (%) .	0.80	1.16	1.32	1.35	1.83	1.63	1.64	1.12	2.00	—
Portfolio Turnover (%)	152	115	20	262	341	224	162	284	237	—
Total Assets (Millions $)....	363	414	78	55	77	116	36	11	4	—

PORTFOLIO (as of 8/31/94)

Portfolio Manager: David Felman - 1994

Investm't Category: Growth

✔ Cap Gain	Asset Allocation
Cap & Income	Fund of Funds
Income	Index
	✔ Sector
✔ Domestic	Small Cap
✔ Foreign	Socially Conscious
Country/Region	State Specific

Portfolio: stocks 88% bonds 0%
convertibles 0% other 4% cash 8%

Largest Holdings: telephone services 50%, cellular & communication services 9%

Unrealized Net Capital Gains: 4% of portfolio value

SHAREHOLDER INFORMATION

Minimum Investment
Initial: $2,500   Subsequent: $250

Minimum IRA Investment
Initial: $500   Subsequent: $250

Maximum Fees
Load: 3.00% front   12b-1: none
Other: $7.50 redemption fee (30 days or more), 0.75% fee (less than 30 days)

Distributions
Income: Apr, Dec   Capital Gains: Apr, Dec

Exchange Options
Number Per Year: no limit   Fee: $7.50
Telephone: yes (money market fund available)

Services: IRA, pension, auto exchange, auto invest, auto withdraw

Fidelity Sel Transportation (FSRFX)

82 Devonshire St.
Boston, MA 02109
(800) 544-8888, (801) 534-1910

Aggressive Growth

PERFORMANCE

fund inception date: 9/29/86

	3yr Annual	5yr Annual	10yr Annual	Bull	Bear
Return (%)	18.4	14.9	na	173.4	-2.5
Differ from Category (+/-)	9.5 high	2.4 abv av	na	40.2 abv av	8.3 high

Total Risk	Standard Deviation	Category Risk	Risk Index	Beta
abv av	10.4%	low	0.7	0.9

	1994	1993	1992	1991	1990	1989	1988	1987	1986	1985
Return (%)	3.8	29.3	23.7	54.1	-21.5	28.4	38.4	-17.4	—	—
Differ from category (+/-) . . .	4.5	9.8	12.7	2.0	-15.3	1.6	23.2	-15.2	—	—

PER SHARE DATA

	1994	1993	1992	1991	1990	1989	1988	1987	1986	1985
Dividends, Net Income ($) .	0.00	0.00	0.00	0.04	0.00	0.00	0.00	0.00	—	—
Distrib'ns, Cap Gain ($) . . .	2.19	1.96	0.36	0.00	0.50	2.32	0.00	0.13	—	—
Net Asset Value ($)	19.29	20.76	17.64	14.55	9.47	12.58	11.63	8.40	—	—
Expense Ratio (%)	2.21	2.48	2.43	2.39	2.50	2.50	2.41	1.60	—	—
Net Income to Assets (%) .	-0.72	-0.53	-0.34	0.52	-0.20	-0.33	-0.59	0.01	—	—
Portfolio Turnover (%)	224	116	423	187	156	172	255	218	—	—
Total Assets (Millions $)	11	10	3	1	1	3	1	1	—	—

PORTFOLIO (as of 8/31/94)

Portfolio Manager: Stephen DuFour - 1994

Investm't Category: Aggressive Growth
- ✔ Cap Gain   Asset Allocation
- Cap & Income   Fund of Funds
- Income   Index
-     ✔ Sector
- ✔ Domestic   Small Cap
- ✔ Foreign   Socially Conscious
- Country/Region   State Specific

Portfolio: stocks 88%   bonds 0%
convertibles 0%   other 0%   cash 12%

Largest Holdings: local & long distance trucking 19%, railroads 11%

Unrealized Net Capital Gains: 6% of portfolio value

SHAREHOLDER INFORMATION

Minimum Investment
Initial: $2,500   Subsequent: $250

Minimum IRA Investment
Initial: $500   Subsequent: $250

Maximum Fees
Load: 3.00% front   12b-1: none
Other: $7.50 redemption fee (30 days or more), 0.75% fee (less than 30 days)

Distributions
Income: Apr, Dec   Capital Gains: Apr, Dec

Exchange Options
Number Per Year: no limit   Fee: $7.50
Telephone: yes (money market fund available)

Services: IRA, pension, auto exchange, auto invest, auto withdraw

Fidelity Sel Utilities Growth (FSUTX)

Growth & Income

82 Devonshire St.
Boston, MA 02109
(800) 544-8888, (801) 534-1910

PERFORMANCE

fund inception date: 12/10/81

	3yr Annual	5yr Annual	10yr Annual	Bull	Bear
Return (%)	4.8	6.9	12.9	68.0	-7.5
Differ from Category (+/-)	-2.3 blw av	-1.0 blw av	1.2 abv av	-7.8 blw av	-1.2 blw av

Total Risk	Standard Deviation	Category Risk	Risk Index	Beta
av	8.7%	abv av	1.1	0.7

	1994	1993	1992	1991	1990	1989	1988	1987	1986	1985
Return (%).............	-7.4	12.5	10.5	21.0	0.5	39.0	16.4	-9.2	24.0	31.7
Differ from category (+/-) ..	-6.0	-0.7	0.3	-6.6	6.5	17.6	-0.6	-9.8	8.2	6.0

PER SHARE DATA

	1994	1993	1992	1991	1990	1989	1988	1987	1986	1985
Dividends, Net Income ($).	1.05	1.13	1.33	1.69	0.60	0.81	1.42	0.45	0.22	0.48
Distrib'ns, Cap Gain ($) ...	0.67	4.94	1.70	1.19	0.58	0.00	0.00	0.84	0.14	0.00
Net Asset Value ($)	33.08	37.58	38.80	38.01	34.02	35.05	25.90	23.49	27.31	22.30
Expense Ratio (%)	1.37	1.42	1.51	1.65	1.67	1.21	1.94	1.45	1.42	1.50
Net Income to Assets (%) .	3.15	3.71	4.58	4.75	3.93	5.33	4.71	4.88	6.31	7.14
Portfolio Turnover (%)	23	34	45	45	75	75	143	161	96	52
Total Assets (Millions $)....	202	279	206	197	124	84	85	99	86	56

PORTFOLIO (as of 8/31/94)

Portfolio Manager: John Muresianu - 1992

Investm't Category: Growth & Income
Cap Gain	Asset Allocation
✔ Cap & Income	Fund of Funds
Income	Index
	✔ Sector
✔ Domestic	Small Cap
✔ Foreign	Socially Conscious
Country/Region	State Specific

Portfolio: stocks 95% bonds 0%
convertibles 0% other 1% cash 4%

Largest Holdings: telephone services 39%, electric power 16%

Unrealized Net Capital Gains: 0% of portfolio value

SHAREHOLDER INFORMATION

Minimum Investment
Initial: $2,500   Subsequent: $250

Minimum IRA Investment
Initial: $500   Subsequent: $250

Maximum Fees
Load: 3.00% front   12b-1: none
Other: $7.50 redemption fee (30 days or more), 0.75% fee (less than 30 days)

Distributions
Income: Apr, Dec   Capital Gains: Apr, Dec

Exchange Options
Number Per Year: no limit   Fee: $7.50
Telephone: yes (money market fund available)

Services: IRA, pension, auto exchange, auto invest, auto withdraw

Fidelity Short-Interm Gov't (FFXSX)

82 Devonshire St.
Boston, MA 02109
(800) 544-8888, (801) 534-1910

Government Bond

PERFORMANCE

fund inception date: 9/13/91

	3yr Annual	5yr Annual	10yr Annual	Bull	Bear
Return (%)	2.8	na	na	na	-2.9
Differ from Category (+/-)	-1.2 low	na	na	na	3.5 abv av

Total Risk	Standard Deviation	Category Risk	Risk Index	Avg Mat
low	2.3%	low	0.5	4.1 yrs

	1994	1993	1992	1991	1990	1989	1988	1987	1986	1985
Return (%)	-1.3	5.2	4.6	—	—	—	—	—	—	—
Differ from category (+/-) . . .	3.5	-5.7	-1.8	—	—	—	—	—	—	—

PER SHARE DATA

	1994	1993	1992	1991	1990	1989	1988	1987	1986	1985
Dividends, Net Income ($) .	0.59	0.59	0.65	—	—	—	—	—	—	—
Distrib'ns, Cap Gain ($) . . .	0.00	0.00	0.07	—	—	—	—	—	—	—
Net Asset Value ($)	9.14	9.86	9.93	—	—	—	—	—	—	—
Expense Ratio (%).	0.95	0.61	0.28	—	—	—	—	—	—	—
Net Income to Assets (%). .	6.80	7.19	7.91	—	—	—	—	—	—	—
Portfolio Turnover (%). . . .	184	348	419	—	—	—	—	—	—	—
Total Assets (Millions $) . . .	151	152	173	—	—	—	—	—	—	—

PORTFOLIO (as of 9/30/94)

Portfolio Manager: Curtis Hollingsworth - 1991

Investm't Category: Government Bond

Cap Gain	Asset Allocation
Cap & Income	Fund of Funds
✔ Income	Index
	Sector
✔ Domestic	Small Cap
Foreign	Socially Conscious
Country/Region	State Specific

Portfolio: stocks 0%   bonds 98%
convertibles 0%   other 0%   cash 2%

Largest Holdings: U. S. government 68%, mortgage-backed 30%

Unrealized Net Capital Gains: -3% of portfolio value

SHAREHOLDER INFORMATION

Minimum Investment
Initial: $2,500   Subsequent: $250

Minimum IRA Investment
Initial: $500   Subsequent: $250

Maximum Fees
Load: none   12b-1: none
Other: none

Distributions
Income: monthly   Capital Gains: Nov, Dec

Exchange Options
Number Per Year: 4   Fee: none
Telephone: yes (money market fund available)

Services
IRA, pension, auto exchange, auto invest, auto withdraw

Fidelity Short-Term Bond (FSHBX)

Corporate Bond

82 Devonshire St.
Boston, MA 02109
(800) 544-8888, (801) 534-1910

PERFORMANCE

fund inception date: 9/15/86

	3yr Annual	5yr Annual	10yr Annual	Bull	Bear
Return (%)	3.9	6.2	na	36.1	-3.8
Differ from Category (+/-)	-2.0 low	-1.6 low	na	-13.7 blw av	0.5 abv av

Total Risk	Standard Deviation	Category Risk	Risk Index	Avg Mat
low	2.8%	av	0.9	2.0 yrs

	1994	1993	1992	1991	1990	1989	1988	1987	1986	1985
Return (%)	-4.1	9.1	7.3	14.0	5.7	10.5	5.7	3.9	—	—
Differ from category (+/-) . .	-1.7	-2.3	-1.6	-3.1	0.9	1.2	-3.4	1.8	—	—

PER SHARE DATA

	1994	1993	1992	1991	1990	1989	1988	1987	1986	1985
Dividends, Net Income ($).	0.57	0.66	0.75	0.82	0.81	0.80	0.82	0.83	—	—
Distrib'ns, Cap Gain ($) . . .	0.00	0.00	0.00	0.00	0.00	0.00	0.00	0.00	—	—
Net Asset Value ($)	8.60	9.55	9.38	9.45	9.05	9.34	9.21	9.50	—	—
Expense Ratio (%)	0.80	0.77	0.86	0.83	0.83	0.89	0.88	0.90	—	—
Net Income to Assets (%) .	6.70	7.68	8.23	8.65	8.28	8.77	8.77	8.40	—	—
Portfolio Turnover (%)	73	63	87	164	148	171	251	149	—	—
Total Assets (Millions $). .	1,514	2,476	983	235	197	236	382	137	—	—

PORTFOLIO (as of 4/30/94)

Portfolio Manager: Donald G. Taylor - 1989

Investm't Category: Corporate Bond

Cap Gain	Asset Allocation
Cap & Income	Fund of Funds
✔ Income	Index
	Sector
✔ Domestic	Small Cap
✔ Foreign	Socially Conscious
Country/Region	State Specific

Portfolio: stocks 0%   bonds 82%
convertibles 0%   other 8%   cash 10%

Largest Holdings: banks 16%, credit & other finance 12%

Unrealized Net Capital Gains: -3% of portfolio value

SHAREHOLDER INFORMATION

Minimum Investment
Initial: $2,500   Subsequent: $250

Minimum IRA Investment
Initial: $500   Subsequent: $100

Maximum Fees
Load: none   12b-1: none
Other: none

Distributions
Income: monthly   Capital Gains: Jun, Dec

Exchange Options
Number Per Year: 4   Fee: none
Telephone: yes (money market fund available)

Services
IRA, pension, auto exchange, auto invest, auto withdraw

Fidelity Short Term World Income (FSHWX)

International Bond

82 Devonshire St.
Boston, MA 02109
(800) 544-8888, (801) 534-1910

PERFORMANCE

fund inception date: 10/4/91

	3yr Annual	5yr Annual	10yr Annual	Bull	Bear
Return (%)	3.5	na	na	na	-6.1
Differ from Category (+/-)	-0.4 blw av	na	na	na	1.7 av

Total Risk	Standard Deviation	Category Risk	Risk Index	Avg Mat
low	4.2%	blw av	0.7	1.4 yrs

	1994	1993	1992	1991	1990	1989	1988	1987	1986	1985
Return (%)	-5.9	12.4	4.9	—	—	—	—	—	—	—
Differ from category (+/-) . . .	0.4	-1.0	0.2	—	—	—	—	—	—	—

PER SHARE DATA

	1994	1993	1992	1991	1990	1989	1988	1987	1986	1985
Dividends, Net Income ($) .	0.70	0.67	0.72	—	—	—	—	—	—	—
Distrib'ns, Cap Gain ($) . . .	0.00	0.00	0.00	—	—	—	—	—	—	—
Net Asset Value ($)	8.90	10.19	9.69	—	—	—	—	—	—	—
Expense Ratio (%).	1.07	1.00	1.09	—	—	—	—	—	—	—
Net Income to Assets (%). .	7.16	8.00	9.04	—	—	—	—	—	—	—
Portfolio Turnover (%). . . .	113	160	154	—	—	—	—	—	—	—
Total Assets (Millions $) . . .	265	419	649	—	—	—	—	—	—	—

PORTFOLIO (as of 6/30/94)

Portfolio Manager: Scott Kuldell - 1994

Investm't Category: International Bond

Cap Gain	Asset Allocation
Cap & Income	Fund of Funds
✔ Income	Index
	Sector
✔ Domestic	Small Cap
✔ Foreign	Socially Conscious
Country/Region	State Specific

Portfolio: stocks 0% bonds 69%
convertibles 0% other 8% cash 23%

Largest Holdings: Mexico 24%, United States 19%

Unrealized Net Capital Gains: -5% of portfolio value

SHAREHOLDER INFORMATION

Minimum Investment
Initial: $2,500   Subsequent: $250

Minimum IRA Investment
Initial: $500   Subsequent: $250

Maximum Fees
Load: none   12b-1: none
Other: none

Distributions
Income: monthly   Capital Gains: Dec

Exchange Options
Number Per Year: 4   Fee: none
Telephone: yes (money market fund available)

Services
IRA, pension, auto exchange, auto invest, auto withdraw

Fidelity Southeast Asia
(FSEAX)

International Stock

82 Devonshire St.
Boston, MA 02109
(800) 544-8888, (801) 534-1910

PERFORMANCE

fund inception date: 4/19/93

	3yr Annual	5yr Annual	10yr Annual	Bull	Bear
Return (%)	na	na	na	na	-16.3
Differ from Category (+/-)	na	na	na	na	-9.3 low

Total Risk	Standard Deviation	Category Risk	Risk Index	Beta
na	na	na	na	na

	1994	1993	1992	1991	1990	1989	1988	1987	1986	1985
Return (%)	-21.7	—	—	—	—	—	—	—	—	—
Differ from category (+/-)	-18.7	—	—	—	—	—	—	—	—	—

PER SHARE DATA

	1994	1993	1992	1991	1990	1989	1988	1987	1986	1985
Dividends, Net Income ($)	0.00	—	—	—	—	—	—	—	—	—
Distrib'ns, Cap Gain ($)	0.00	—	—	—	—	—	—	—	—	—
Net Asset Value ($)	12.84	—	—	—	—	—	—	—	—	—
Expense Ratio (%)	1.55	—	—	—	—	—	—	—	—	—
Net Income to Assets (%)	0.09	—	—	—	—	—	—	—	—	—
Portfolio Turnover (%)	212	—	—	—	—	—	—	—	—	—
Total Assets (Millions $)	660	—	—	—	—	—	—	—	—	—

PORTFOLIO (as of 4/30/94)

Portfolio Manager: Allan Liu - 1993

Investm't Category: International Stock

✔ Cap Gain	Asset Allocation
Cap & Income	Fund of Funds
Income	Index
	Sector
Domestic	Small Cap
✔ Foreign	Socially Conscious
✔ Country/Region	State Specific

Portfolio: stocks 88% bonds 1%
convertibles 4% other 0% cash 7%

Largest Holdings: Hong Kong 33%, Malaysia 18%

Unrealized Net Capital Gains: -5% of portfolio value

SHAREHOLDER INFORMATION

Minimum Investment
Initial: $2,500   Subsequent: $250

Minimum IRA Investment
Initial: $500   Subsequent: $250

Maximum Fees
Load: 3.00% front   12b-1: none
Other: 1.50% redemption fee (90 days)

Distributions
Income: Dec   Capital Gains: Dec

Exchange Options
Number Per Year: 4   Fee: none
Telephone: yes (money market fund available)

Services
IRA, pension, auto exchange, auto invest, auto withdraw

Fidelity Spartan Aggressive Municipal

82 Devonshire St.
Boston, MA 02109
(800) 544-8888, (801) 534-1910

(SPAMX) *Tax-Exempt Bond*

PERFORMANCE   fund inception date: 4/29/93

	3yr Annual	5yr Annual	10yr Annual	Bull	Bear
Return (%)	na	na	na	na	-5.9
Differ from Category (+/-)	na	na	na	na	-0.7 av

Total Risk	Standard Deviation	Category Risk	Risk Index	Avg Mat
na	na	na	na	20.1 yrs

	1994	1993	1992	1991	1990	1989	1988	1987	1986	1985
Return (%)	-6.1	—	—	—	—	—	—	—	—	—
Differ from category (+/-) . .	-0.9	—	—	—	—	—	—	—	—	—

PER SHARE DATA

	1994	1993	1992	1991	1990	1989	1988	1987	1986	1985
Dividends, Net Income ($) .	0.60	—	—	—	—	—	—	—	—	—
Distrib'ns, Cap Gain ($) . . .	0.00	—	—	—	—	—	—	—	—	—
Net Asset Value ($)	9.23	—	—	—	—	—	—	—	—	—
Expense Ratio (%).	0.60	—	—	—	—	—	—	—	—	—
Net Income to Assets (%). .	6.03	—	—	—	—	—	—	—	—	—
Portfolio Turnover (%).	64	—	—	—	—	—	—	—	—	—
Total Assets (Millions $)	57	—	—	—	—	—	—	—	—	—

PORTFOLIO (as of 8/31/94)

Portfolio Manager: Maureen Newman - 1994

Investm't Category: Tax-Exempt Bond
Cap Gain	Asset Allocation
Cap & Income	Fund of Funds
✔ Income	Index
	Sector
✔ Domestic	Small Cap
Foreign	Socially Conscious
Country/Region	State Specific

Portfolio: stocks 0%   bonds 100%
convertibles 0%   other 0%   cash 0%

Largest Holdings: general obligations 0%

Unrealized Net Capital Gains: -2% of portfolio value

SHAREHOLDER INFORMATION

Minimum Investment
Initial: $10,000   Subsequent: $100

Minimum IRA Investment
Initial: na   Subsequent: na

Maximum Fees
Load: 1.00% redemption   12b-1: none
Other: Redemption fee applies for 6 months

Distributions
Income: monthly   Capital Gains: Oct, Dec

Exchange Options
Number Per Year: 4   Fee: none
Telephone: yes (money market fund available)

Services
auto exchange, auto invest, auto withdraw

Fidelity Spartan CA Interm Muni (FSCMX)

82 Devonshire St.
Boston, MA 02109
(800) 544-8888, (801) 534-1910

Tax-Exempt Bond

PERFORMANCE

fund inception date: 12/30/93

	3yr Annual	5yr Annual	10yr Annual	Bull	Bear
Return (%)	na	na	na	na	-5.0
Differ from Category (+/-)	na	na	na	na	0.2 abv av

Total Risk	Standard Deviation	Category Risk	Risk Index	Avg Mat
na	na	na	na	10.3 yrs

	1994	1993	1992	1991	1990	1989	1988	1987	1986	1985
Return (%).............	-4.6	—	—	—	—	—	—	—	—	—
Differ from category (+/-) ..	0.6	—	—	—	—	—	—	—	—	—

PER SHARE DATA

	1994	1993	1992	1991	1990	1989	1988	1987	1986	1985
Dividends, Net Income ($).	0.47	—	—	—	—	—	—	—	—	—
Distrib'ns, Cap Gain ($) ...	0.00	—	—	—	—	—	—	—	—	—
Net Asset Value ($)	9.07	—	—	—	—	—	—	—	—	—
Expense Ratio (%)	0.55	—	—	—	—	—	—	—	—	—
Net Income to Assets (%) .	4.97	—	—	—	—	—	—	—	—	—
Portfolio Turnover (%)	44	—	—	—	—	—	—	—	—	—
Total Assets (Millions $).....	38	—	—	—	—	—	—	—	—	—

PORTFOLIO (as of 8/31/94)

Portfolio Manager: David Murphy - 1993

Investm't Category: Tax-Exempt Bond

Cap Gain	Asset Allocation
Cap & Income	Fund of Funds
✔ Income	Index
	Sector
✔ Domestic	Small Cap
Foreign	Socially Conscious
Country/Region	✔ State Specific

Portfolio: stocks 0%   bonds 100%
convertibles 0%   other 0%   cash 0%

Largest Holdings: general obligation 0%

Unrealized Net Capital Gains: -1% of portfolio value

SHAREHOLDER INFORMATION

Minimum Investment
Initial: $10,000   Subsequent: $1,000

Minimum IRA Investment
Initial: na   Subsequent: na

Maximum Fees
Load: none   12b-1: none
Other: none

Distributions
Income: monthly   Capital Gains: Apr, Dec

Exchange Options
Number Per Year: 4   Fee: $5.00
Telephone: yes (money market fund available)

Services
auto exchange, auto invest, auto withdraw

Fidelity Spartan CA Muni High Yield (FSCAX)

Tax-Exempt Bond

82 Devonshire St.
Boston, MA 02109
(800) 544-8888, (801) 534-1910

PERFORMANCE

fund inception date: 11/29/89

	3yr Annual	5yr Annual	10yr Annual	Bull	Bear
Return (%)	4.1	6.3	na	46.9	-7.7
Differ from Category (+/-)	-0.4 blw av	0.2 av	na	5.1 abv av	-2.5 low

Total Risk	Standard Deviation	Category Risk	Risk Index	Avg Mat
blw av	6.5%	abv av	1.0	21.0 yrs

	1994	1993	1992	1991	1990	1989	1988	1987	1986	1985
Return (%)	-9.0	14.0	8.8	11.6	8.1	—	—	—	—	—
Differ from category (+/-)	-3.8	2.3	0.5	0.3	1.8	—	—	—	—	—

PER SHARE DATA

	1994	1993	1992	1991	1990	1989	1988	1987	1986	1985
Dividends, Net Income ($)	0.61	0.64	0.66	0.68	0.72	—	—	—	—	—
Distrib'ns, Cap Gain ($)	0.18	0.39	0.06	0.00	0.00	—	—	—	—	—
Net Asset Value ($)	9.46	11.23	10.79	10.61	10.15	—	—	—	—	—
Expense Ratio (%)	0.55	0.40	0.36	0.19	0.00	—	—	—	—	—
Net Income to Assets (%)	5.92	6.07	6.36	7.02	7.42	—	—	—	—	—
Portfolio Turnover (%)	29	26	13	15	5	—	—	—	—	—
Total Assets (Millions $)	371	599	479	282	107	—	—	—	—	—

PORTFOLIO (as of 8/31/94)

Portfolio Manager: John F. Haley Jr. - 1989

Investm't Category: Tax-Exempt Bond

Cap Gain	Asset Allocation
Cap & Income	Fund of Funds
✔ Income	Index
	Sector
✔ Domestic	Small Cap
Foreign	Socially Conscious
Country/Region	✔ State Specific

Portfolio: stocks 0% bonds 100%
convertibles 0% other 0% cash 0%

Largest Holdings: general obligation 0%

Unrealized Net Capital Gains: 0% of portfolio value

SHAREHOLDER INFORMATION

Minimum Investment
Initial: $10,000   Subsequent: $1,000

Minimum IRA Investment
Initial: na   Subsequent: na

Maximum Fees
Load: 0.50% redemption   12b-1: none
Other: redemption fee applies for 6 months

Distributions
Income: monthly   Capital Gains: Jun, Dec

Exchange Options
Number Per Year: 4   Fee: $5
Telephone: yes (money market fund available)

Services
auto exchange, auto invest, auto withdraw

Fidelity Spartan Conn Tax-Free High-Yield

82 Devonshire St.
Boston, MA 02109
(800) 544-8888, (801) 534-1910

(FICNX) *Tax-Exempt Bond*

PERFORMANCE

fund inception date: 10/29/87

	3yr Annual	5yr Annual	10yr Annual	Bull	Bear
Return (%)	4.3	6.0	na	42.4	-6.4
Differ from Category (+/-)	-0.2 blw av	-0.1 blw av	na	0.6 av	-1.2 blw av

Total Risk	Standard Deviation	Category Risk	Risk Index	Avg Mat
blw av	6.3%	abv av	1.0	19.4 yrs

	1994	1993	1992	1991	1990	1989	1988	1987	1986	1985
Return (%)	-7.0	12.9	8.2	10.5	6.6	10.4	10.1	—	—	—
Differ from category (+/-)	-1.8	1.2	-0.1	-0.8	0.3	1.4	-0.1	—	—	—

PER SHARE DATA

	1994	1993	1992	1991	1990	1989	1988	1987	1986	1985
Dividends, Net Income ($)	0.64	0.68	0.69	0.68	0.69	0.70	0.71	—	—	—
Distrib'ns, Cap Gain ($)	0.11	0.33	0.00	0.00	0.04	0.02	0.00	—	—	—
Net Asset Value ($)	10.15	11.70	11.28	11.09	10.68	10.72	10.39	—	—	—
Expense Ratio (%)	0.55	0.55	0.55	0.55	0.62	0.54	0.11	—	—	—
Net Income to Assets (%)	5.68	5.81	6.21	6.34	6.51	6.62	7.10	—	—	—
Portfolio Turnover (%)	15	45	11	6	18	8	11	—	—	—
Total Assets (Millions $)	312	449	414	347	252	180	74	—	—	—

PORTFOLIO (as of 5/31/94)

Portfolio Manager: Maureen Newman - 1994

Investm't Category: Tax-Exempt Bond

Cap Gain	Asset Allocation
Cap & Income	Fund of Funds
✔ Income	Index
	Sector
✔ Domestic	Small Cap
Foreign	Socially Conscious
Country/Region	✔ State Specific

Portfolio: stocks 0%   bonds 100%
convertibles 0%   other 0%   cash 0%

Largest Holdings: general obligation 23%

Unrealized Net Capital Gains: 1% of portfolio value

SHAREHOLDER INFORMATION

Minimum Investment
Initial: $10,000   Subsequent: $1,000

Minimum IRA Investment
Initial: na   Subsequent: na

Maximum Fees
Load: 0.50% redemption   12b-1: none
Other: redemption fee applies for 6 months

Distributions
Income: monthly   Capital Gains: Jan, Dec

Exchange Options
Number Per Year: 4   Fee: $5
Telephone: yes (money market fund available)

Services
auto exchange, auto invest, auto withdraw

Fidelity Spartan Florida Muni Income (FFLIX)

82 Devonshire St.
Boston, MA 02109
(800) 544-8888, (801) 534-1910

Tax-Exempt Bond

PERFORMANCE

fund inception date: 3/16/92

	3yr Annual	5yr Annual	10yr Annual	Bull	Bear
Return (%)	na	na	na	na	-6.6
Differ from Category (+/-)	na	na	na	na	-1.4 blw av

Total Risk	Standard Deviation	Category Risk	Risk Index	Avg Mat
na	na	na	na	18.8 yrs

	1994	1993	1992	1991	1990	1989	1988	1987	1986	1985
Return (%)	-6.7	14.8	—	—	—	—	—	—	—	—
Differ from category (+/-)	-1.5	3.1	—	—	—	—	—	—	—	—

PER SHARE DATA

	1994	1993	1992	1991	1990	1989	1988	1987	1986	1985
Dividends, Net Income ($)	0.59	0.61	—	—	—	—	—	—	—	—
Distrib'ns, Cap Gain ($)	0.00	0.20	—	—	—	—	—	—	—	—
Net Asset Value ($)	9.99	11.33	—	—	—	—	—	—	—	—
Expense Ratio (%)	0.54	0.25	—	—	—	—	—	—	—	—
Net Income to Assets (%)	5.49	5.52	—	—	—	—	—	—	—	—
Portfolio Turnover (%)	49	50	—	—	—	—	—	—	—	—
Total Assets (Millions $)	339	445	—	—	—	—	—	—	—	—

PORTFOLIO (as of 11/30/94)

Portfolio Manager: Anne Punzak - 1992

Investm't Category: Tax-Exempt Bond

Cap Gain	Asset Allocation
Cap & Income	Fund of Funds
✔ Income	Index
	Sector
✔ Domestic	Small Cap
Foreign	Socially Conscious
Country/Region	✔ State Specific

Portfolio: stocks 0% bonds 100%
convertibles 0% other 0% cash 0%

Largest Holdings: general obligation 13%

Unrealized Net Capital Gains: -9% of portfolio value

SHAREHOLDER INFORMATION

Minimum Investment
Initial: $10,000   Subsequent: $1,000

Minimum IRA Investment
Initial: na   Subsequent: na

Maximum Fees
Load: 0.50% redemption   12b-1: none
Other: redemption fee applies for 6 months

Distributions
Income: monthly   Capital Gains: Dec

Exchange Options
Number Per Year: no limit   Fee: $5
Telephone: yes (money market fund available)

Services
auto exchange, auto invest, auto withdraw

Fidelity Spartan Ginnie Mae (SGNMX)

Mortgage-Backed Bond

82 Devonshire St.
Boston, MA 02109
(800) 544-8888, (801) 534-1910

fund inception date: 12/27/90

PERFORMANCE

	3yr Annual	5yr Annual	10yr Annual	Bull	Bear
Return (%)	3.6	na	na	na	-4.1
Differ from Category (+/-)	0.5 av	na	na	na	0.3 blw av

Total Risk	Standard Deviation	Category Risk	Risk Index	Avg Mat
low	3.1%	blw av	0.9	9.3 yrs

	1994	1993	1992	1991	1990	1989	1988	1987	1986	1985
Return (%)	-1.5	6.2	6.4	13.7	—	—	—	—	—	—
Differ from category (+/-)	1.3	-0.6	0.3	-0.7	—	—	—	—	—	—

PER SHARE DATA

	1994	1993	1992	1991	1990	1989	1988	1987	1986	1985
Dividends, Net Income ($)	0.62	0.56	0.76	0.85	—	—	—	—	—	—
Distrib'ns, Cap Gain ($)	0.00	0.07	0.24	0.02	—	—	—	—	—	—
Net Asset Value ($)	9.32	10.10	10.11	10.46	—	—	—	—	—	—
Expense Ratio (%)	0.65	0.41	0.17	0.25	—	—	—	—	—	—
Net Income to Assets (%)	7.36	7.63	8.09	8.69	—	—	—	—	—	—
Portfolio Turnover (%)	285	241	168	41	—	—	—	—	—	—
Total Assets (Millions $)	347	566	838	423	—	—	—	—	—	—

PORTFOLIO (as of 8/31/94)

Portfolio Manager: Bob Ives - 193

Investm't Category: Mortgage-Backed Bond
Cap Gain	Asset Allocation
Cap & Income	Fund of Funds
✔ Income	Index
	Sector
✔ Domestic	Small Cap
✔ Foreign	Socially Conscious
Country/Region	State Specific

Portfolio: stocks 0% bonds 99%
convertibles 0% other 0% cash 1%

Largest Holdings: mortgage-backed 99%

Unrealized Net Capital Gains: -3% of portfolio value

SHAREHOLDER INFORMATION

Minimum Investment
Initial: $10,000   Subsequent: $1,000

Minimum IRA Investment
Initial: $10,000   Subsequent: $1,000

Maximum Fees
Load: none   12b-1: none
Other: $5 account close-out fee

Distributions
Income: monthly   Capital Gains: Oct, Dec

Exchange Options
Number Per Year: 4   Fee: $5
Telephone: yes (money market fund available)

Services
IRA, pension, auto exchange, auto invest, auto withdraw

Fidelity Spartan Gov't Income (SPGVX)

82 Devonshire St.
Boston, MA 02109
(800) 544-8888, (801) 534-1910

Mortgage-Backed Bond

PERFORMANCE

fund inception date: 12/20/88

	3yr Annual	5yr Annual	10yr Annual	Bull	Bear
Return (%)	3.4	6.8	na	41.9	-6.1
Differ from Category (+/-)	0.3 blw av	-0.1 blw av	na	3.9 high	-1.7 low

Total Risk	Standard Deviation	Category Risk	Risk Index	Avg Mat
low	3.8%	abv av	1.1	9.7 yrs

	1994	1993	1992	1991	1990	1989	1988	1987	1986	1985
Return (%)	-3.5	7.3	7.1	15.1	9.1	15.2	—	—	—	—
Differ from category (+/-) . .	-0.7	0.5	1.0	0.7	-0.6	2.7	—	—	—	—

PER SHARE DATA

	1994	1993	1992	1991	1990	1989	1988	1987	1986	1985
Dividends, Net Income ($)	0.71	0.61	0.76	0.83	0.85	0.94	—	—	—	—
Distrib'ns, Cap Gain ($) . . .	0.00	0.26	0.42	0.04	0.04	0.03	—	—	—	—
Net Asset Value ($)	9.59	10.68	10.78	11.21	10.56	10.54	—	—	—	—
Expense Ratio (%).	0.65	0.65	0.65	0.53	0.16	0.65	—	—	—	—
Net Income to Assets (%). .	6.79	7.11	7.77	8.35	9.02	9.26	—	—	—	—
Portfolio Turnover (%)	354	170	59	96	68	277	—	—	—	—
Total Assets (Millions $) . . .	231	380	483	431	283	21	—	—	—	—

PORTFOLIO (as of 4/30/94)

Portfolio Manager: Bob Ives - 1993

Investm't Category: Mortgage-Backed Bond

Cap Gain	Asset Allocation
Cap & Income	Fund of Funds
✔ Income	Index
	Sector
✔ Domestic	Small Cap
Foreign	Socially Conscious
Country/Region	State Specific

Portfolio: stocks 0% bonds 90%
convertibles 0% other 0% cash 10%

Largest Holdings: mortgage-backed 62%,
U.S. government & agencies 28%

Unrealized Net Capital Gains: -3% of portfolio value

SHAREHOLDER INFORMATION

Minimum Investment
Initial: $10,000   Subsequent: $1,000

Minimum IRA Investment
Initial: $10,000   Subsequent: $1,000

Maximum Fees
Load: none   12b-1: none
Other: $5 account close-out fee

Distributions
Income: monthly   Capital Gains: Jun, Dec

Exchange Options
Number Per Year: 4   Fee: $5
Telephone: yes (money market fund available)

Services
IRA, pension, auto exchange, auto invest, auto withdraw

Fidelity Spartan High Income (SPHIX)

Corporate High-Yield Bond

82 Devonshire St.
Boston, MA 02109
(800) 544-8888, (801) 534-1910

PERFORMANCE

fund inception date: 8/29/90

	3yr Annual	5yr Annual	10yr Annual	Bull	Bear
Return (%)	15.1	na	na	110.0	-3.1
Differ from Category (+/-)	5.2 high	na	na	30.7 high	2.2 high

Total Risk	Standard Deviation	Category Risk	Risk Index	Avg Mat
blw av	4.9%	abv av	1.0	5.3 yrs

	1994	1993	1992	1991	1990	1989	1988	1987	1986	1985
Return (%)	3.1	21.8	21.4	34.3	—	—	—	—	—	—
Differ from category (+/-)	5.8	3.4	5.8	6.9	—	—	—	—	—	—

PER SHARE DATA

	1994	1993	1992	1991	1990	1989	1988	1987	1986	1985
Dividends, Net Income ($)	1.00	1.13	1.25	1.30	—	—	—	—	—	—
Distrib'ns, Cap Gain ($)	0.08	0.79	0.37	0.32	—	—	—	—	—	—
Net Asset Value ($)	11.46	12.17	11.65	11.00	—	—	—	—	—	—
Expense Ratio (%)	0.75	0.70	0.70	0.70	—	—	—	—	—	—
Net Income to Assets (%)	8.07	9.57	11.43	11.98	—	—	—	—	—	—
Portfolio Turnover (%)	213	136	99	72	—	—	—	—	—	—
Total Assets (Millions $)	617	671	371	101	—	—	—	—	—	—

PORTFOLIO (as of 4/30/94)

Portfolio Manager: David Glancy - 1993

Investm't Category: Corp. High-Yield Bond
Cap Gain | Asset Allocation
✔ Cap & Income | Fund of Funds
Income | Index
| Sector
✔ Domestic | Small Cap
✔ Foreign | Socially Conscious
Country/Region | State Specific

Portfolio: stocks 5% bonds 70%
convertibles 3% other 12% cash 10%

Largest Holdings: lodging & gaming 11%, broadcasting 8%

Unrealized Net Capital Gains: 0% of portfolio value

SHAREHOLDER INFORMATION

Minimum Investment
Initial: $10,000   Subsequent: $1,000

Minimum IRA Investment
Initial: $10,000   Subsequent: $1,000

Maximum Fees
Load: 1.00% redemption   12b-1: none
Other: redemption fee applies for 9 months

Distributions
Income: monthly   Capital Gains: Jun, Dec

Exchange Options
Number Per Year: 4   Fee: $5
Telephone: yes (money market fund available)

Services
IRA, pension, auto exchange, auto invest, auto withdraw

Fidelity Spartan
Intermediate Municipal

82 Devonshire St.
Boston, MA 02109
(800) 544-8888, (801) 534-1910

(FSIMX) *Tax-Exempt Bond*

PERFORMANCE

fund inception date: 4/26/93

	3yr Annual	5yr Annual	10yr Annual	Bull	Bear
Return (%)	na	na	na	na	-5.2
Differ from Category (+/-)	na	na	na	na	0.0 abv av

Total Risk	Standard Deviation	Category Risk	Risk Index	Avg Mat
na	na	na	na	9.3 yrs

	1994	1993	1992	1991	1990	1989	1988	1987	1986	1985
Return (%)	-5.0	—	—	—	—	—	—	—	—	—
Differ from category (+/-) . . .	0.2	—	—	—	—	—	—	—	—	—

PER SHARE DATA

	1994	1993	1992	1991	1990	1989	1988	1987	1986	1985
Dividends, Net Income ($)	0.51	—	—	—	—	—	—	—	—	—
Distrib'ns, Cap Gain ($) . . .	0.00	—	—	—	—	—	—	—	—	—
Net Asset Value ($)	9.41	—	—	—	—	—	—	—	—	—
Expense Ratio (%). . , ...	0.20	—	—	—	—	—	—	—	—	—
Net Income to Assets (%). .	5.09	—	—	—	—	—	—	—	—	—
Portfolio Turnover (%).	69	—	—	—	—	—	—	—	—	—
Total Assets (Millions $) . . .	205	—	—	—	—	—	—	—	—	—

PORTFOLIO (as of 8/31/94)

Portfolio Manager: David Murphy - 1993

Investm't Category: Tax-Exempt Bond

Cap Gain	Asset Allocation
Cap & Income	Fund of Funds
✔ Income	Index
	Sector
✔ Domestic	Small Cap
Foreign	Socially Conscious
Country/Region	State Specific

Portfolio:	stocks 0%	bonds 100%
convertibles 0%	other 0%	cash 0%

Largest Holdings: general obligation 17%

Unrealized Net Capital Gains: -3% of portfolio value

SHAREHOLDER INFORMATION

Minimum Investment
Initial: $10,000   Subsequent: $1,000

Minimum IRA Investment
Initial: na   Subsequent: na

Maximum Fees
Load: none   12b-1: none
Other: none

Distributions
Income: monthly   Capital Gains: Oct, Dec

Exchange Options
Number Per Year: 4   Fee: $5
Telephone: yes (money market fund available)

Services
auto exchange, auto invest, auto withdraw

Fidelity Spartan Investment Grade (FSIBX)

82 Devonshire St.
Boston, MA 02109
(800) 544-8888, (801) 534-1910

Corporate Bond

PERFORMANCE

fund inception date: 10/1/92

	3yr Annual	5yr Annual	10yr Annual	Bull	Bear
Return (%)	na	na	na	na	-8.2
Differ from Category (+/-)	na	na	na	na	-3.9 low

Total Risk	Standard Deviation	Category Risk	Risk Index	Avg Mat
na	na	na	na	17.6 yrs

	1994	1993	1992	1991	1990	1989	1988	1987	1986	1985
Return (%)	-5.1	15.7	—	—	—	—	—	—	—	—
Differ from category (+/-)	-2.7	4.3	—	—	—	—	—	—	—	—

PER SHARE DATA

	1994	1993	1992	1991	1990	1989	1988	1987	1986	1985
Dividends, Net Income ($)	0.70	0.78	—	—	—	—	—	—	—	—
Distrib'ns, Cap Gain ($)	0.03	0.01	—	—	—	—	—	—	—	—
Net Asset Value ($)	9.40	10.68	—	—	—	—	—	—	—	—
Expense Ratio (%)	0.65	0.65	—	—	—	—	—	—	—	—
Net Income to Assets (%)	6.90	7.58	—	—	—	—	—	—	—	—
Portfolio Turnover (%)	44	55	—	—	—	—	—	—	—	—
Total Assets (Millions $)	118	122	—	—	—	—	—	—	—	—

PORTFOLIO (as of 9/30/94)

Portfolio Manager: Michael Gray - 1992

Investm't Category: Corporate Bond

Cap Gain	Asset Allocation
Cap & Income	Fund of Funds
✔ Income	Index
	Sector
✔ Domestic	Small Cap
✔ Foreign	Socially Conscious
Country/Region	State Specific

Portfolio: stocks 0% bonds 88%
convertibles 0% other 0% cash 12%

Largest Holdings: finance 21%, U.S. government 13%

Unrealized Net Capital Gains: -8% of portfolio value

SHAREHOLDER INFORMATION

Minimum Investment
Initial: $10,000   Subsequent: $1,000

Minimum IRA Investment
Initial: $10,000   Subsequent: $1,000

Maximum Fees
Load: none   12b-1: none
Other: $5 account close-out fee

Distributions
Income: monthly   Capital Gains: Jun, Dec

Exchange Options
Number Per Year: 4   Fee: $5
Telephone: yes (money market fund available)

Services
IRA, pension, auto exchange, auto invest, auto withdraw

Fidelity Spartan Long-Term Gov't (SLTGX)

Government Bond

82 Devonshire St.
Boston, MA 02109
(800) 544-8888, (801) 534-1910

PERFORMANCE

fund inception date: 9/28/90

	3yr Annual	5yr Annual	10yr Annual	Bull	Bear
Return (%)	3.4	na	na	67.5	-15.4
Differ from Category (+/-)	-0.6 blw av	na	na	16.3 high	-9.0 low

Total Risk	Standard Deviation	Category Risk	Risk Index	Avg Mat
av	8.1%	high	1.8	22.0 yrs

	1994	1993	1992	1991	1990	1989	1988	1987	1986	1985
Return (%)	-12.2	16.6	8.0	17.3	—	—	—	—	—	—
Differ from category (+/-)	-7.4	5.7	1.6	2.0						

PER SHARE DATA

	1994	1993	1992	1991	1990	1989	1988	1987	1986	1985
Dividends, Net Income ($)	0.52	0.84	0.84	0.74	—	—	—	—	—	—
Distrib'ns, Cap Gain ($)	0.11	0.52	0.18	0.08	—	—	—	—	—	—
Net Asset Value ($)	10.27	12.40	11.82	11.92	—	—	—	—	—	—
Expense Ratio (%)	0.65	0.65	0.65	0.65	—	—	—	—	—	—
Net Income to Assets (%)	4.60	7.35	7.30	7.26	—	—	—	—	—	—
Portfolio Turnover (%)	750	135	335	256	—	—	—	—	—	—
Total Assets (Millions $)	71	71	63	34	—	—	—	—	—	—

PORTFOLIO (as of 7/31/94)

Portfolio Manager: Curt Hollingsworth - 1993

Investm't Category: Government Bond

Cap Gain	Asset Allocation
Cap & Income	Fund of Funds
✔ Income	Index
	Sector
✔ Domestic	Small Cap
✔ Foreign	Socially Conscious
Country/Region	State Specific

Portfolio: stocks 0%   bonds 100%
convertibles 0%   other 0%   cash 0%

Largest Holdings: U.S. government & agencies 100%

Unrealized Net Capital Gains: 1% of portfolio value

SHAREHOLDER INFORMATION

Minimum Investment
Initial: $10,000   Subsequent: $1,000

Minimum IRA Investment
Initial: $10,000   Subsequent: $1,000

Maximum Fees
Load: none   12b-1: none
Other: $5 account close-out fee

Distributions
Income: quarterly   Capital Gains: Dec

Exchange Options
Number Per Year: 4   Fee: $5
Telephone: yes (money market fund available)

Services
IRA, pension, auto exchange, auto invest, auto withdraw

Fidelity Spartan Ltd Maturity Gov't (FSTGX)

Mortgage-Backed Bond

82 Devonshire St.
Boston, MA 02109
(800) 544-8888, (801) 534-1910

PERFORMANCE

fund inception date: 5/2/88

	3yr Annual	5yr Annual	10yr Annual	Bull	Bear
Return (%)	3.6	6.3	na	31.2	-2.8
Differ from Category (+/-)	0.5 av	-0.6 low	na	-6.8 low	1.6 abv av

Total Risk	Standard Deviation	Category Risk	Risk Index	Avg Mat
low	2.1%	low	0.6	4.3 yrs

	1994	1993	1992	1991	1990	1989	1988	1987	1986	1985
Return (%)	-0.9	6.4	5.7	11.9	9.1	10.3	—	—	—	—
Differ from category (+/-)	1.9	-0.4	-0.4	-2.5	-0.6	-2.2	—	—	—	—

PER SHARE DATA

	1994	1993	1992	1991	1990	1989	1988	1987	1986	1985
Dividends, Net Income ($)	0.55	0.58	0.60	0.82	0.82	0.82	—	—	—	—
Distrib'ns, Cap Gain ($)	0.00	0.23	0.05	0.06	0.02	0.00	—	—	—	—
Net Asset Value ($)	9.35	10.00	10.17	10.25	9.99	9.96	—	—	—	—
Expense Ratio (%)	0.65	0.65	0.61	0.50	0.83	0.68	—	—	—	—
Net Income to Assets (%)	7.37	8.05	8.24	8.63	8.28	8.20	—	—	—	—
Portfolio Turnover (%)	391	324	330	288	270	806	—	—	—	—
Total Assets (Millions $)	830	1,389	1,770	881	132	126	—	—	—	—

PORTFOLIO (as of 7/31/94)

Portfolio Manager: Curtis Hollingsworth - 1988

Investm't Category: Mortgage-Backed Bond

Cap Gain	Asset Allocation
Cap & Income	Fund of Funds
✔ Income	Index
	Sector
✔ Domestic	Small Cap
✔ Foreign	Socially Conscious
Country/Region	State Specific

Portfolio: stocks 0%   bonds 95%
convertibles 0%   other 0%   cash 5%

Largest Holdings: mortgage-backed 49%, U.S. government & agencies 46%

Unrealized Net Capital Gains: 0% of portfolio value

SHAREHOLDER INFORMATION

Minimum Investment
Initial: $10,000   Subsequent: $1,000

Minimum IRA Investment
Initial: $10,000   Subsequent: $1,000

Maximum Fees
Load: none   12b-1: none
Other: $5 account close-out fee

Distributions
Income: monthly   Capital Gains: Sep, Dec

Exchange Options
Number Per Year: 4   Fee: $5
Telephone: yes (money market fund available)

Services
IRA, pension, auto invest, auto withdraw

Fidelity Spartan Maryland Muni Income (SMDMX)

82 Devonshire St.
Boston, MA 02109
(800) 544-8888, (801) 534-1910

Tax-Exempt Bond

PERFORMANCE

fund inception date: 4/22/93

	3yr Annual	5yr Annual	10yr Annual	Bull	Bear
Return (%)	na	na	na	na	-6.8
Differ from Category (+/-)	na	na	na	na	-1.6 blw av

Total Risk	Standard Deviation	Category Risk	Risk Index	Avg Mat
na	na	na	na	17.5 yrs

	1994	1993	1992	1991	1990	1989	1988	1987	1986	1985
Return (%)	-7.5	—	—	—	—	—	—	—	—	—
Differ from category (+/-)	-2.3	—	—	—	—	—	—	—	—	—

PER SHARE DATA

	1994	1993	1992	1991	1990	1989	1988	1987	1986	1985
Dividends, Net Income ($)	0.55	—	—	—	—	—	—	—	—	—
Distrib'ns, Cap Gain ($)	0.00	—	—	—	—	—	—	—	—	—
Net Asset Value ($)	9.07	—	—	—	—	—	—	—	—	—
Expense Ratio (%)	0.03	—	—	—	—	—	—	—	—	—
Net Income to Assets (%)	5.46	—	—	—	—	—	—	—	—	—
Portfolio Turnover (%)	64	—	—	—	—	—	—	—	—	—
Total Assets (Millions $)	35	—	—	—	—	—	—	—	—	—

PORTFOLIO (as of 8/31/94)

Portfolio Manager: Steven Harvey - 1993

Investm't Category: Tax-Exempt Bond

Cap Gain	Asset Allocation
Cap & Income	Fund of Funds
✔ Income	Index
	Sector
✔ Domestic	Small Cap
Foreign	Socially Conscious
Country/Region	✔ State Specific

Portfolio: stocks 0% bonds 100%
convertibles 0% other 0% cash 0%

Largest Holdings: general obligation 22%

Unrealized Net Capital Gains: -5% of portfolio value

SHAREHOLDER INFORMATION

Minimum Investment
Initial: $10,000   Subsequent: $1,000

Minimum IRA Investment
Initial: na   Subsequent: na

Maximum Fees
Load: 0.50% redemption   12b-1: none
Other: redemption fee applies for 6 months

Distributions
Income: monthly   Capital Gains: Oct, Dec

Exchange Options
Number Per Year: 4   Fee: $5
Telephone: yes (money market fund available)

Services
auto exchange, auto invest, auto withdraw

Fidelity Spartan Muni Income (FSMIX)

82 Devonshire St.
Boston, MA 02109
(800) 544-8888, (801) 534-1910

Tax-Exempt Bond

PERFORMANCE

fund inception date: 6/4/90

	3yr Annual	5yr Annual	10yr Annual	Bull	Bear
Return (%)	4.4	na	na	46.9	-7.3
Differ from Category (+/-)	-0.1 av	na	na	5.1 abv av	-2.1 low

Total Risk	Standard Deviation	Category Risk	Risk Index	Avg Mat
blw av	6.4%	abv av	1.0	19.7 yrs

	1994	1993	1992	1991	1990	1989	1988	1987	1986	1985
Return (%)	-8.1	14.3	8.3	12.6	—	—	—	—	—	—
Differ from category (+/-)	-2.9	2.6	0.0	1.3	—	—	—	—	—	—

PER SHARE DATA

	1994	1993	1992	1991	1990	1989	1988	1987	1986	1985
Dividends, Net Income ($)	0.61	0.64	0.69	0.72	—	—	—	—	—	—
Distrib'ns, Cap Gain ($)	0.08	0.55	0.07	0.04	—	—	—	—	—	—
Net Asset Value ($)	9.37	10.93	10.64	10.55	—	—	—	—	—	—
Expense Ratio (%)	0.55	0.47	0.36	0.23	—	—	—	—	—	—
Net Income to Assets (%)	5.76	6.09	6.68	7.24	—	—	—	—	—	—
Portfolio Turnover (%)	48	50	62	78	—	—	—	—	—	—
Total Assets (Millions $)	535	863	870	551	—	—	—	—	—	—

PORTFOLIO (as of 8/31/94)

Portfolio Manager: Norman Lind - 1990

Investm't Category: Tax-Exempt Bond

Cap Gain	Asset Allocation
Cap & Income	Fund of Funds
✔ Income	Index
	Sector
✔ Domestic	Small Cap
Foreign	Socially Conscious
Country/Region	State Specific

Portfolio: stocks 0%   bonds 100%
convertibles 0%   other 0%   cash 0%

Largest Holdings: general obligation 0%

Unrealized Net Capital Gains: -3% of portfolio value

SHAREHOLDER INFORMATION

Minimum Investment
Initial: $10,000   Subsequent: $1,000

Minimum IRA Investment
Initial: na   Subsequent: na

Maximum Fees
Load: 0.50% redemption   12b-1: none
Other: redemption fee applies for 6 months

Distributions
Income: monthly   Capital Gains: Oct, Dec

Exchange Options
Number Per Year: 4   Fee: $5
Telephone: yes (money market fund available)

Services
auto exchange, auto invest, auto withdraw

Fidelity Spartan NJ Muni High Yield (FNJHX)

82 Devonshire St.
Boston, MA 02109
(800) 544-8888, (801) 534-1910

Tax-Exempt Bond

PERFORMANCE

fund inception date: 1/1/88

	3yr Annual	5yr Annual	10yr Annual	Bull	Bear
Return (%)	5.0	6.8	na	45.5	-6.3
Differ from Category (+/-)	0.5 abv av	0.7 abv av	na	3.7 abv av	-1.1 blw av

Total Risk	Standard Deviation	Category Risk	Risk Index	Avg Mat
blw av	6.1%	av	1.0	17.5 yrs

	1994	1993	1992	1991	1990	1989	1988	1987	1986	1985
Return (%)	-5.7	13.0	8.7	12.3	7.1	10.3	10.8	—	—	—
Differ from category (+/-)	-0.5	1.3	0.4	1.0	0.8	1.3	0.6	—	—	—

PER SHARE DATA

	1994	1993	1992	1991	1990	1989	1988	1987	1986	1985
Dividends, Net Income ($)	0.63	0.64	0.70	0.69	0.67	0.71	0.74	—	—	—
Distrib'ns, Cap Gain ($)	0.00	0.15	0.16	0.08	0.00	0.08	0.00	—	—	—
Net Asset Value ($)	10.51	11.82	11.18	11.10	10.61	10.56	10.31	—	—	—
Expense Ratio (%)	0.55	0.55	0.51	0.52	0.65	0.56	0.00	—	—	—
Net Income to Assets (%)	5.56	5.52	6.22	6.44	6.47	6.76	7.52	—	—	—
Portfolio Turnover (%)	6	25	33	42	82	90	140	—	—	—
Total Assets (Millions $)	325	428	343	290	210	159	90	—	—	—

PORTFOLIO (as of 5/31/94)

Portfolio Manager: David L. Murphy - 1991

Investm't Category: Tax-Exempt Bond

Cap Gain	Asset Allocation
Cap & Income	Fund of Funds
✔ Income	Index
	Sector
✔ Domestic	Small Cap
Foreign	Socially Conscious
Country/Region	✔ State Specific

Portfolio: stocks 0% bonds 100%
convertibles 0% other 0% cash 0%

Largest Holdings: general obligation 15%

Unrealized Net Capital Gains: 3% of portfolio value

SHAREHOLDER INFORMATION

Minimum Investment
Initial: $10,000   Subsequent: $1,000

Minimum IRA Investment
Initial: na   Subsequent: na

Maximum Fees
Load: 0.50% redemption   12b-1: none
Other: redemption fee applies for 6 months, $5 close-out fee

Distributions
Income: monthly   Capital Gains: Jan, Dec

Exchange Options
Number Per Year: 4   Fee: $5
Telephone: yes (money market fund available)

Services
auto exchange, auto invest, auto withdraw

Fidelity Spartan NY Interm Muni (FSNMX)

82 Devonshire St.
Boston, MA 02109
(800) 544-8888, (801) 534-1910

Tax-Exempt Bond

PERFORMANCE

fund inception date: 12/29/93

	3yr Annual	5yr Annual	10yr Annual	Bull	Bear
Return (%)	na	na	na	na	-4.3
Differ from Category (+/-)	na	na	na	na	0.9 abv av

Total Risk	Standard Deviation	Category Risk	Risk Index	Avg Mat
na	na	na	na	9.4 yrs

	1994	1993	1992	1991	1990	1989	1988	1987	1986	1985
Return (%).	-4.2	—	—	—	—	—	—	—	—	—
Differ from category (+/-) . .	1.0	—	—	—	—	—	—	—	—	—

PER SHARE DATA

	1994	1993	1992	1991	1990	1989	1988	1987	1986	1985
Dividends, Net Income ($).	0.47	—	—	—	—	—	—	—	—	—
Distrib'ns, Cap Gain ($) . . .	0.00	—	—	—	—	—	—	—	—	—
Net Asset Value ($)	9.12	—	—	—	—	—	—	—	—	—
Expense Ratio (%)	0.00	—	—	—	—	—	—	—	—	—
Net Income to Assets (%) .	4.98	—	—	—	—	—	—	—	—	—
Portfolio Turnover (%)	23	—	—	—	—	—	—	—	—	—
Total Assets (Millions $).	31	—	—	—	—	—	—	—	—	—

PORTFOLIO (as of 7/31/94)

Portfolio Manager: David Murphy - 1993

Investm't Category: Tax-Exempt Bond

Cap Gain	Asset Allocation
Cap & Income	Fund of Funds
✔ Income	Index
	Sector
✔ Domestic	Small Cap
Foreign	Socially Conscious
Country/Region	✔ State Specific

Portfolio: stocks 0%   bonds 100%
convertibles 0%   other 0%   cash 0%

Largest Holdings: general obligation 13%

Unrealized Net Capital Gains: -2% of portfolio value

SHAREHOLDER INFORMATION

Minimum Investment
Initial: $10,000   Subsequent: $1,000

Minimum IRA Investment
Initial: na   Subsequent: na

Maximum Fees
Load: none   12b-1: none
Other: none

Distributions
Income: monthly   Capital Gains: Mar, Dec

Exchange Options
Number Per Year: 4   Fee: $5
Telephone: yes (money market fund available)

Services
auto exchange, auto invest, auto withdraw

Fidelity Spartan NY Muni High Yield (FSNYX)

82 Devonshire St.
Boston, MA 02109
(800) 544-8888, (801) 534-1910

Tax-Exempt Bond

PERFORMANCE

fund inception date: 2/3/90

	3yr Annual	5yr Annual	10yr Annual	Bull	Bear
Return (%)	4.3	na	na	48.1	-7.5
Differ from Category (+/-)	-0.2 blw av	na	na	6.3 high	-2.3 low

Total Risk	Standard Deviation	Category Risk	Risk Index	Avg Mat
av	6.9%	high	1.1	21.5 yrs

	1994	1993	1992	1991	1990	1989	1988	1987	1986	1985
Return (%)	-8.3	13.3	9.4	14.4	—	—	—	—	—	—
Differ from category (+/-) . .	-3.1	1.6	1.1	3.1	—	—	—	—	—	—

PER SHARE DATA

	1994	1993	1992	1991	1990	1989	1988	1987	1986	1985
Dividends, Net Income ($)	0.61	0.62	0.66	0.68	—	—	—	—	—	—
Distrib'ns, Cap Gain ($) . . .	0.28	0.28	0.11	0.02	—	—	—	—	—	—
Net Asset Value ($)	9.50	11.31	10.80	10.60	—	—	—	—	—	—
Expense Ratio (%).	0.55	0.48	0.38	0.19	—	—	—	—	—	—
Net Income to Assets (%). .	5.82	6.03	6.51	7.21	—	—	—	—	—	—
Portfolio Turnover (%).	49	35	21	40	—	—	—	—	—	—
Total Assets (Millions $) . . .	284	442	292	163	—	—	—	—	—	—

PORTFOLIO (as of 7/31/94)

Portfolio Manager: Norm Lind - 1993

Investm't Category: Tax-Exempt Bond

Cap Gain	Asset Allocation
Cap & Income	Fund of Funds
✔ Income	Index
	Sector
✔ Domestic	Small Cap
Foreign	Socially Conscious
Country/Region	✔ State Specific

Portfolio: stocks 0%   bonds 100%
convertibles 0%   other 0%   cash 0%

Largest Holdings: general obligation 12%

Unrealized Net Capital Gains: -2% of portfolio value

SHAREHOLDER INFORMATION

Minimum Investment
Initial: $10,000   Subsequent: $1,000

Minimum IRA Investment
Initial: na   Subsequent: na

Maximum Fees
Load: 0.50% redemption   12b-1: none
Other: redemption fee applies for 6 months; $5 close-out fee

Distributions
Income: monthly   Capital Gains: Jun, Dec

Exchange Options
Number Per Year: 4   Fee: $5
Telephone: yes (money market fund available)

Services
auto exchange, auto invest, auto withdraw

Fidelity Spartan Penn Muni High Yield (FPXTX)

82 Devonshire St.
Boston, MA 02109
(800) 544-8888, (801) 534-1910

Tax-Exempt Bond

PERFORMANCE

fund inception date: 8/6/86

	3yr Annual	5yr Annual	10yr Annual	Bull	Bear
Return (%)	5.4	7.1	na	47.0	-5.3
Differ from Category (+/-)	0.9 high	1.0 high	na	5.2 abv av	-0.1 av

Total Risk	Standard Deviation	Category Risk	Risk Index	Avg Mat
blw av	5.8%	av	0.9	18.9 yrs

	1994	1993	1992	1991	1990	1989	1988	1987	1986	1985
Return (%)	-5.0	13.1	9.1	12.4	7.2	9.8	14.3	-5.8	—	—
Differ from category (+/-)	0.2	1.4	0.8	1.1	0.9	0.8	4.1	-4.5	—	—

PER SHARE DATA

	1994	1993	1992	1991	1990	1989	1988	1987	1986	1985
Dividends, Net Income ($)	0.65	0.68	0.69	0.70	0.70	0.68	0.66	0.70	—	—
Distrib'ns, Cap Gain ($)	0.31	0.14	0.00	0.00	0.00	0.00	0.00	0.00	—	—
Net Asset Value ($)	9.62	11.13	10.59	10.37	9.88	9.90	9.66	9.06	—	—
Expense Ratio (%)	0.55	0.55	0.55	0.55	0.60	0.78	0.84	0.63	—	—
Net Income to Assets (%)	6.14	6.31	6.65	6.96	7.22	6.90	7.05	7.28	—	—
Portfolio Turnover (%)	39	38	8	6	8	23	31	54	—	—
Total Assets (Millions $)	241	303	242	199	143	104	63	42	—	—

PORTFOLIO (as of 6/30/94)

Portfolio Manager: Steve Harvey - 1993

Investm't Category: Tax-Exempt Bond

Cap Gain	Asset Allocation
Cap & Income	Fund of Funds
✔ Income	Index
	Sector
✔ Domestic	Small Cap
Foreign	Socially Conscious
Country/Region	✔ State Specific

Portfolio: stocks 0% bonds 100%
convertibles 0% other 0% cash 0%

Largest Holdings: general obligation 15%

Unrealized Net Capital Gains: 0% of portfolio value

SHAREHOLDER INFORMATION

Minimum Investment
Initial: $10,000 Subsequent: $1,000

Minimum IRA Investment
Initial: na Subsequent: na

Maximum Fees
Load: 0.50% redemption 12b-1: none
Other: redemption fee applies for 6 months

Distributions
Income: monthly Capital Gains: Feb, Dec

Exchange Options
Number Per Year: 4 Fee: $5
Telephone: yes (money market fund available)

Services
auto exchange, auto invest, auto withdraw

Fidelity Spartan Short Intermediate Gov't (SPSIX)

82 Devonshire St.
Boston, MA 02109
(800) 544-8888, (801) 534-1910

General Bond

	3yr Annual	5yr Annual	10yr Annual	Bull	Bear
Return (%)	na	na	na	na	-2.9
Differ from Category (+/-)	na	na	na	na	0.9 abv av

Total Risk	Standard Deviation		Category Risk	Risk Index	Avg Mat
na	na		na	na	4.6 yrs

	1994	1993	1992	1991	1990	1989	1988	1987	1986	1985
Return (%)	-0.5	5.6	—	—	—	—	—	—	—	—
Differ from category (+/-) ...	1.5	-3.6	—	—	—	—	—	—	—	—

PER SHARE DATA

	1994	1993	1992	1991	1990	1989	1988	1987	1986	1985
Dividends, Net Income ($) .	0.62	0.66	—	—	—	—	—	—	—	—
Distrib'ns, Cap Gain ($) ...	0.00	0.01	—	—	—	—	—	—	—	—
Net Asset Value ($)	9.23	9.91	—	—	—	—	—	—	—	—
Expense Ratio (%).	0.10	0.02	—	—	—	—	—	—	—	—
Net Income to Assets (%)..	7.33	7.28	—	—	—	—	—	—	—	—
Portfolio Turnover (%).	271	587	—	—	—	—	—	—	—	—
Total Assets (Millions $)	48	65	—	—	—	—	—	—	—	—

PORTFOLIO (as of 4/30/94)

Portfolio Manager: Curt Hollingsworth - 1992

Investm't Category: General Bond

Cap Gain	Asset Allocation
Cap & Income	Fund of Funds
✔ Income	Index
	Sector
✔ Domestic	Small Cap
Foreign	Socially Conscious
Country/Region	State Specific

Portfolio: stocks 0%   bonds 81%
convertibles 0%   other 0%   cash 19%

Largest Holdings: mortgage-backed 53%, U.S. government 28%

Unrealized Net Capital Gains: -3% of portfolio value

SHAREHOLDER INFORMATION

Minimum Investment
Initial: $10,000   Subsequent: $1,000

Minimum IRA Investment
Initial: $10,000   Subsequent: $1,000

Maximum Fees
Load: none   12b-1: none
Other: $5 account close-out fee

Distributions
Income: monthly   Capital Gains: Jun, Dec

Exchange Options
Number Per Year: 4   Fee: $5
Telephone: yes (money market fund available)

Services
IRA, pension, auto exchange, auto invest, auto withdraw

Fidelity Spartan Short-Interm Muni (FSTFX)

82 Devonshire St.
Boston, MA 02109
(800) 544-8888, (801) 534-1910

Tax-Exempt Bond

PERFORMANCE

fund inception date: 12/24/86

	3yr Annual	5yr Annual	10yr Annual	Bull	Bear
Return (%)	4.3	5.6	na	27.3	-1.6
Differ from Category (+/-)	-0.2 blw av	-0.5 low	na	-14.5 low	3.6 high

Total Risk	Standard Deviation	Category Risk	Risk Index	Avg Mat
low	2.3%	low	0.3	3.3 yrs

	1994	1993	1992	1991	1990	1989	1988	1987	1986	1985
Return (%).	-0.1	7.1	6.1	8.8	6.4	6.2	4.8	0.2	—	—
Differ from category (+/-) . .	5.1	-4.6	-2.2	-2.5	0.1	-2.8	-5.4	1.5	—	—

PER SHARE DATA

	1994	1993	1992	1991	1990	1989	1988	1987	1986	1985
Dividends, Net Income ($).	0.44	0.45	0.49	0.56	0.56	0.54	0.52	0.43	—	—
Distrib'ns, Cap Gain ($) . . .	0.00	0.01	0.00	0.00	0.00	0.00	0.00	0.00	—	—
Net Asset Value ($)	9.66	10.11	9.88	9.78	9.52	9.49	9.45	9.51	—	—
Expense Ratio (%)	0.47	0.55	0.55	0.55	0.60	0.58	0.35	0.60	—	—
Net Income to Assets (%) .	4.45	4.55	4.95	5.68	5.90	5.69	5.48	4.58	—	—
Portfolio Turnover (%)	44	56	28	59	75	82	96	180	—	—
Total Assets (Millions $). . . .	913	1,204	659	244	59	58	77	59	—	—

PORTFOLIO (as of 8/31/94)

Portfolio Manager: David Murphy - 1989

Investm't Category: Tax-Exempt Bond

Cap Gain	Asset Allocation
Cap & Income	Fund of Funds
✔ Income	Index
	Sector
✔ Domestic	Small Cap
Foreign	Socially Conscious
Country/Region	State Specific

Portfolio: stocks 0%   bonds 100%
convertibles 0%   other 0%   cash 0%

Largest Holdings: general obligation 22%

Unrealized Net Capital Gains: 0% of portfolio value

SHAREHOLDER INFORMATION

Minimum Investment
Initial: $10,000   Subsequent: $1,000

Minimum IRA Investment
Initial: na   Subsequent: na

Maximum Fees
Load: none   12b-1: none
Other: none

Distributions
Income: monthly   Capital Gains: Oct, Dec

Exchange Options
Number Per Year: 4   Fee: $5
Telephone: yes (money market fund available)

Services
auto exchange, auto invest, auto withdraw

Fidelity Spartan Short-Term Income (FTBDX)

82 Devonshire St.
Boston, MA 02109
(800) 544-8888, (801) 534-1910

Corporate Bond

PERFORMANCE

fund inception date: 10/1/92

	3yr Annual	5yr Annual	10yr Annual	Bull	Bear
Return (%)	na	na	na	na	-4.0
Differ from Category (+/-)	na	na	na	na	0.3 av

Total Risk	Standard Deviation	Category Risk	Risk Index	Avg Mat
na	na	na	na	2.2 yrs

	1994	1993	1992	1991	1990	1989	1988	1987	1986	1985
Return (%)	-4.6	9.0	—	—	—	—	—	—	—	—
Differ from category (+/-) . .	-2.2	-2.4	—	—	—	—	—	—	—	—

PER SHARE DATA

	1994	1993	1992	1991	1990	1989	1988	1987	1986	1985
Dividends, Net Income ($) .	0.60	0.72	—	—	—	—	—	—	—	—
Distrib'ns, Cap Gain ($) . . .	0.00	0.01	—	—	—	—	—	—	—	—
Net Asset Value ($)	8.92	9.97	—	—	—	—	—	—	—	—
Expense Ratio (%).	0.54	0.20	—	—	—	—	—	—	—	—
Net Income to Assets (%). .	6.42	7.32	—	—	—	—	—	—	—	—
Portfolio Turnover (%).	97	112	—	—	—	—	—	—	—	—
Total Assets (Millions $) . . .	610	1,529	—	—	—	—	—	—	—	—

PORTFOLIO (as of 9/30/94)

Portfolio Manager: Donald G. Taylor - 1992

Investm't Category: Corporate Bond

Cap Gain	Asset Allocation
Cap & Income	Fund of Funds
✔ Income	Index
	Sector
✔ Domestic	Small Cap
✔ Foreign	Socially Conscious
Country/Region	State Specific

Portfolio: stocks 0%   bonds 78%
convertibles 0%   other 1%   cash 21%

Largest Holdings: banks 15%, credit & other finance 7%

Unrealized Net Capital Gains: -4% of portfolio value

SHAREHOLDER INFORMATION

Minimum Investment
Initial: $10,000   Subsequent: $1,000

Minimum IRA Investment
Initial: $10,000   Subsequent: $1,000

Maximum Fees
Load: none   12b-1: none
Other: $5 account close-out fee

Distributions
Income: monthly   Capital Gains: Dec

Exchange Options
Number Per Year: 4   Fee: $5
Telephone: yes (money market fund available)

Services
IRA, pension, auto exchange, auto invest, auto withdraw

Fidelity Stock Selector

(FDSSX)

Growth

82 Devonshire St.
Boston, MA 02109
(800) 544-8888, (801) 534-1910

PERFORMANCE

fund inception date: 9/28/90

	3yr Annual	5yr Annual	10yr Annual	Bull	Bear
Return (%)	9.8	na	na	124.4	-6.0
Differ from Category (+/-)	2.1 abv av	na	na	32.3 high	0.6 av

Total Risk	Standard Deviation	Category Risk	Risk Index	Beta
abv av	9.8%	av	1.0	1.0

	1994	1993	1992	1991	1990	1989	1988	1987	1986	1985
Return (%)	0.7	13.9	15.4	45.9	—	—	—	—	—	—
Differ from category (+/-)	1.3	0.5	3.8	10.2	—	—	—	—	—	—

PER SHARE DATA

	1994	1993	1992	1991	1990	1989	1988	1987	1986	1985
Dividends, Net Income ($)	0.15	0.24	0.10	0.08	—	—	—	—	—	—
Distrib'ns, Cap Gain ($)	0.81	1.06	0.32	0.47	—	—	—	—	—	—
Net Asset Value ($)	17.91	18.75	17.61	15.63	—	—	—	—	—	—
Expense Ratio (%)	1.12	1.10	1.22	1.43	—	—	—	—	—	—
Net Income to Assets (%)	1.06	1.52	1.43	1.20	—	—	—	—	—	—
Portfolio Turnover (%)	238	192	268	317	—	—	—	—	—	—
Total Assets (Millions $)	786	650	260	99	—	—	—	—	—	—

PORTFOLIO (as of 4/30/94)

Portfolio Manager: Brad Lewis - 1990

Investm't Category: Growth

✔ Cap Gain	Asset Allocation
Cap & Income	Fund of Funds
Income	Index
	Sector
✔ Domestic	Small Cap
✔ Foreign	Socially Conscious
Country/Region	State Specific

Portfolio: stocks 91% bonds 0%
convertibles 0% other 0% cash 9%

Largest Holdings: banks 10%, autos, tires, & accessories 9%

Unrealized Net Capital Gains: 6% of portfolio value

SHAREHOLDER INFORMATION

Minimum Investment
Initial: $2,500   Subsequent: $250

Minimum IRA Investment
Initial: $500   Subsequent: $250

Maximum Fees
Load: none   12b-1: none
Other: none

Distributions
Income: Dec   Capital Gains: Dec

Exchange Options
Number Per Year: 4   Fee: none
Telephone: yes (money market fund available)

Services
IRA, pension, auto exchange, auto invest, auto withdraw

Fidelity Trend

(FTRNX)

Growth

82 Devonshire St.
Boston, MA 02109
(800) 544-8888, (801) 534-1910

PERFORMANCE

fund inception date: 6/16/58

	3yr Annual	5yr Annual	10yr Annual	Bull	Bear
Return (%)	9.0	9.0	13.4	112.5	-11.5
Differ from Category (+/-)	1.3 abv av	-0.6 av	0.5 abv av	20.4 abv av	-4.9 low

Total Risk	Standard Deviation	Category Risk	Risk Index	Beta
abv av	11.4%	abv av	1.2	1.2

	1994	1993	1992	1991	1990	1989	1988	1987	1986	1985
Return (%)	-6.6	19.1	16.7	36.2	-12.6	31.6	24.3	-4.1	13.2	28.2
Differ from category (+/-) . .	-6.0	5.7	5.1	0.5	-6.9	5.5	6.3	-5.9	-1.4	-1.0

PER SHARE DATA

	1994	1993	1992	1991	1990	1989	1988	1987	1986	1985
Dividends, Net Income ($) .	0.16	0.27	0.44	0.48	0.24	0.63	0.52	0.44	0.61	0.79
Distrib'ns, Cap Gain ($) . . .	3.89	5.06	3.23	1.79	0.14	4.22	1.06	6.20	10.64	1.25
Net Asset Value ($)	50.99	59.08	54.19	49.63	38.25	44.22	37.43	31.40	39.83	45.02
Expense Ratio (%).	1.03	0.92	0.56	0.53	0.61	0.58	0.47	0.49	0.52	0.52
Net Income to Assets (%). .	0.28	0.43	1.14	1.43	1.51	1.76	2.01	1.49	2.00	2.40
Portfolio Turnover (%).	35	50	47	57	48	67	49	128	71	62
Total Assets (Millions $) . .	1,193	1,396	1,115	892	702	889	702	599	669	712

PORTFOLIO (as of 6/30/94)

Portfolio Manager: Alan Leifer - 1987

Investm't Category: Growth

✔ Cap Gain	Asset Allocation
Cap & Income	Fund of Funds
Income	Index
	Sector
✔ Domestic	Small Cap
✔ Foreign	Socially Conscious
Country/Region	State Specific

Portfolio: stocks 97%   bonds 0%
convertibles 1%   other 0%   cash 2%

Largest Holdings: finance 14%, energy 10%

Unrealized Net Capital Gains: 12% of portfolio value

SHAREHOLDER INFORMATION

Minimum Investment
Initial: $2,500   Subsequent: $250

Minimum IRA Investment
Initial: $500   Subsequent: $250

Maximum Fees
Load: none   12b-1: none
Other: none

Distributions
Income: Feb, Dec   Capital Gains: Feb, Dec

Exchange Options
Number Per Year: 4   Fee: none
Telephone: yes (money market fund available)

Services
IRA, pension, auto exchange, auto invest, auto withdraw

Fidelity Utilities
(FIUIX)
Growth & Income

82 Devonshire St.
Boston, MA 02109
(800) 544-8888, (801) 534-1910

PERFORMANCE   fund inception date: 11/27/87

	3yr Annual	5yr Annual	10yr Annual	Bull	Bear
Return (%)	6.7	8.4	na	78.0	-7.6
Differ from Category (+/-)	-0.4 av	0.5 av	na	2.2 av	-1.3 blw av

Total Risk	Standard Deviation	Category Risk	Risk Index	Beta
abv av	8.9%	abv av	1.1	0.8

	1994	1993	1992	1991	1990	1989	1988	1987	1986	1985
Return (%).............	-5.1	15.6	10.9	21.1	1.8	25.9	14.7	—	—	—
Differ from category (+/-) ..	-3.7	2.4	0.7	-6.5	7.8	4.5	-2.3	—	—	—

PER SHARE DATA

	1994	1993	1992	1991	1990	1989	1988	1987	1986	1985
Dividends, Net Income ($).	0.54	0.52	0.60	0.63	0.69	0.76	0.52	—	—	—
Distrib'ns, Cap Gain ($) ...	0.80	0.22	0.38	0.18	0.30	0.31	0.03	—	—	—
Net Asset Value ($)	13.06	15.18	13.79	13.38	11.79	12.60	10.93	—	—	—
Expense Ratio (%)	0.88	0.87	0.95	0.94	1.02	1.47	2.00	—	—	—
Net Income to Assets (%) .	3.86	4.57	5.11	5.93	6.19	6.14	5.36	—	—	—
Portfolio Turnover (%)	122	73	39	43	61	10	0	—	—	—
Total Assets (Millions $)..	1,079	1,462	647	220	157	129	31	—	—	—

PORTFOLIO (as of 7/31/94)

Portfolio Manager: John Mureslanu - 1992

Investm't Category: Growth & Income
Cap Gain	Asset Allocation
✔ Cap & Income	Fund of Funds
Income	Index
	✔ Sector
✔ Domestic	Small Cap
✔ Foreign	Socially Conscious
Country/Region	State Specific

Portfolio: stocks 78% bonds 1%
convertibles 2% other 1% cash 18%

Largest Holdings: telephone services 27%, electric utilities 23%

Unrealized Net Capital Gains: 6% of portfolio value

SHAREHOLDER INFORMATION

Minimum Investment
Initial: $2,500 Subsequent: $250

Minimum IRA Investment
Initial: $500 Subsequent: $250

Maximum Fees
Load: none 12b-1: none
Other: none

Distributions
Income: quarterly Capital Gains: Mar, Dec

Exchange Options
Number Per Year: 4 Fee: none
Telephone: yes (money market fund available)

Services
IRA, pension, auto exchange, auto invest, auto withdraw

Fidelity Value

(FDVLX)

Growth

82 Devonshire St.
Boston, MA 02109
(800) 544-8888, (801) 534-1910

PERFORMANCE

	3yr Annual	5yr Annual	10yr Annual	Bull	Bear
Return (%)	17.0	12.0	13.6	106.8	-1.2
Differ from Category (+/-)	9.3 high	2.4 abv av	0.7 abv av	14.7 abv av	5.4 high

Total Risk	Standard Deviation	Category Risk	Risk Index	Beta
av	8.2%	blw av	0.8	0.8

	1994	1993	1992	1991	1990	1989	1988	1987	1986	1985
Return (%)	7.6	22.9	21.1	26.1	-12.8	22.9	29.0	-8.6	14.7	22.0
Differ from category (+/-)	8.2	9.5	9.5	-9.6	-7.1	-3.2	11.0	-10.4	0.1	-7.2

PER SHARE DATA

	1994	1993	1992	1991	1990	1989	1988	1987	1986	1985
Dividends, Net Income ($)	0.17	0.34	0.23	0.85	1.17	0.30	0.48	0.15	0.00	0.42
Distrib'ns, Cap Gain ($)	2.28	2.80	0.15	0.00	0.00	2.85	0.00	0.37	1.99	0.00
Net Asset Value ($)	40.81	40.23	35.35	29.50	24.10	28.99	26.14	20.63	23.06	21.76
Expense Ratio (%)	1.11	1.11	1.00	0.98	1.06	1.13	1.11	1.07	1.07	1.13
Net Income to Assets (%)	1.29	1.43	2.01	2.93	4.55	1.45	4.74	1.02	2.20	3.43
Portfolio Turnover (%)	475	117	81	137	165	386	480	442	281	246
Total Assets (Millions $)	3,720	1,695	331	124	92	139	135	92	143	101

PORTFOLIO (as of 4/30/94)

Portfolio Manager: Jeff Ubben - 1992

Investm't Category: Growth

✔ Cap Gain
  Cap & Income
  Income

  Asset Allocation
  Fund of Funds
  Index
  Sector

✔ Domestic
✔ Foreign
  Country/Region

  Small Cap
  Socially Conscious
  State Specific

Portfolio: stocks 87%   bonds 3%
convertibles 3%   other 0%   cash 7%

Largest Holdings: chemicals & plastics 7%, oil & gas 7%

Unrealized Net Capital Gains: 2% of portfolio value

SHAREHOLDER INFORMATION

Minimum Investment
Initial: $2,500   Subsequent: $250

Minimum IRA Investment
Initial: $500   Subsequent: $250

Maximum Fees
Load: none   12b-1: none
Other: none

Distributions
Income: Dec   Capital Gains: Dec

Exchange Options
Number Per Year: 4   Fee: none
Telephone: yes (money market fund available)

Services
IRA, pension, auto exchange, auto invest, auto withdraw

Fidelity Worldwide
(FWWFX)
International Stock

82 Devonshire St.
Boston, MA 02109
(800) 544-8888, (801) 534-1910

fund inception date: 5/30/90

	3yr Annual	5yr Annual	10yr Annual	Bull	Bear
Return (%)	14.2	na	na	76.4	-4.0
Differ from Category (+/-)	5.1 high	na	na	12.5 abv av	3.0 abv av

Total Risk	Standard Deviation	Category Risk	Risk Index	Beta
abv av	10.2%	low	0.8	0.9

	1994	1993	1992	1991	1990	1989	1988	1987	1986	1985
Return (%)	2.9	36.5	6.2	7.8	—	—	—	—	—	—
Differ from category (+/-)	5.9	-2.1	9.1	-5.3	—	—	—	—	—	—

PER SHARE DATA

	1994	1993	1992	1991	1990	1989	1988	1987	1986	1985
Dividends, Net Income ($)	0.07	0.10	0.26	0.10	—	—	—	—	—	—
Distrib'ns, Cap Gain ($)	0.66	0.15	0.00	0.00	—	—	—	—	—	—
Net Asset Value ($)	12.68	13.03	9.73	9.41	—	—	—	—	—	—
Expense Ratio (%)	1.40	1.40	1.51	1.69	—	—	—	—	—	—
Net Income to Assets (%)	0.83	1.99	2.02	2.19	—	—	—	—	—	—
Portfolio Turnover (%)	58	57	130	129	—	—	—	—	—	—
Total Assets (Millions $)	703	336	103	105	—	—	—	—	—	—

PORTFOLIO (as of 4/30/94)

Portfolio Manager: Penelope Dobkin - 1990

Investm't Category: International Stock

✔ Cap Gain	Asset Allocation
Cap & Income	Fund of Funds
Income	Index
	Sector
✔ Domestic	Small Cap
✔ Foreign	Socially Conscious
Country/Region	State Specific

Portfolio: stocks 76% bonds 3%
convertibles 2% other 3% cash 16%

Largest Holdings: United States 30%, Japan 14%

Unrealized Net Capital Gains: 6% of portfolio value

SHAREHOLDER INFORMATION

Minimum Investment
Initial: $2,500   Subsequent: $250

Minimum IRA Investment
Initial: $500   Subsequent: $250

Maximum Fees
Load: 3.00% front   12b-1: none
Other: none

Distributions
Income: Dec   Capital Gains: Dec

Exchange Options
Number Per Year: 4   Fee: none
Telephone: yes (money market fund available)

Services
IRA, pension, auto exchange, auto invest, auto withdraw

Fiduciary Capital Growth
(FCGFX)
Growth

225 E. Mason St.
Milwaukee, WI 53202
(414) 226-4555

PERFORMANCE

fund inception date: 12/18/81

	3yr Annual	5yr Annual	10yr Annual	Bull	Bear
Return (%)	9.6	9.6	10.1	96.0	-6.7
Differ from Category (+/-)	1.9 abv av	0.0 av	-2.8 low	3.9 abv av	-0.1 av

Total Risk	Standard Deviation	Category Risk	Risk Index	Beta
av	8.2%	blw av	0.8	0.7

	1994	1993	1992	1991	1990	1989	1988	1987	1986	1985
Return (%)	0.3	14.6	14.4	36.2	-11.6	17.9	18.7	-8.9	0.0	29.9
Differ from category (+/-) ...	0.9	1.2	2.8	0.5	-5.9	-8.2	0.7	-10.7	-14.6	0.7

PER SHARE DATA

	1994	1993	1992	1991	1990	1989	1988	1987	1986	1985
Dividends, Net Income ($) .	0.04	0.05	0.11	0.16	0.23	0.20	0.03	0.14	0.10	0.19
Distrib'ns, Cap Gain ($) ...	1.88	1.30	1.86	1.23	0.92	0.00	0.00	3.45	3.68	0.03
Net Asset Value ($)	17.76	19.63	18.33	17.87	14.23	17.54	15.04	12.69	17.90	21.42
Expense Ratio (%)........	1.20	1.20	1.30	1.50	1.40	1.30	1.30	1.10	1.20	1.30
Net Income to Assets (%)..	0.30	0.04	0.60	1.20	1.10	0.80	0.30	0.60	0.40	1.20
Portfolio Turnover (%).....	20	33	59	63	55	42	43	83	56	37
Total Assets (Millions $)	39	48	38	31	20	40	42	55	51	41

PORTFOLIO (as of 9/30/94)

Portfolio Manager: Ted Kellner - 1981, Don Wilson - 1981

Investm't Category: Growth
- ✔ Cap Gain
- Cap & Income
- Income
- ✔ Domestic
- ✔ Foreign
- Country/Region

- Asset Allocation
- Fund of Funds
- Index
- Sector
- Small Cap
- Socially Conscious
- State Specific

Portfolio: stocks 83%   bonds 5%
convertibles 0%   other 0%   cash 12%

Largest Holdings: software/service 13%, retail trade 10%

Unrealized Net Capital Gains: 12% of portfolio value

SHAREHOLDER INFORMATION

Minimum Investment
Initial: $1,000   Subsequent: $100

Minimum IRA Investment
Initial: $1,000   Subsequent: $100

Maximum Fees
Load: none   12b-1: none
Other: none

Distributions
Income: Oct, Dec   Capital Gains: Oct, Dec

Exchange Options
Number Per Year: 5   Fee: none
Telephone: none

Services
IRA, pension, auto invest, auto withdraw

Fifty-Nine Wall St European (FNEEX)

International Stock

6 St. James Avenue
Boston, MA 02116
(212) 493-8100

fund inception date: 11/1/90

PERFORMANCE

	3yr Annual	5yr Annual	10yr Annual	Bull	Bear
Return (%)	9.4	na	na	na	-12.1
Differ from Category (+/-)	0.3 av	na	na	na	-5.1 blw av

Total Risk	Standard Deviation	Category Risk	Risk Index	Beta
high	12.5%	av	0.9	1.0

	1994	1993	1992	1991	1990	1989	1988	1987	1986	1985
Return (%).............	-4.0	27.1	7.5	9.2	—	—	—	—	—	—
Differ from category (+/-) ..	-1.0	-11.5	10.4	-3.9	—	—	—	—	—	—

PER SHARE DATA

	1994	1993	1992	1991	1990	1989	1988	1987	1986	1985
Dividends, Net Income ($).	0.00	1.48	0.36	0.21	—	—	—	—	—	—
Distrib'ns, Cap Gain ($) ...	2.41	0.06	1.92	0.03	—	—	—	—	—	—
Net Asset Value ($)	27.91	31.66	26.19	26.48	—	—	—	—	—	—
Expense Ratio (%)	1.36	1.50	1.50	1.50	—	—	—	—	—	—
Net Income to Assets (%) .	0.24	1.28	1.71	1.54	—	—	—	—	—	—
Portfolio Turnover (%)	na	37	50	58	—	—	—	—	—	—
Total Assets (Millions $)....	101	3	27	14	—	—	—	—	—	—

PORTFOLIO (as of 4/30/94)

Portfolio Manager: John Nielsen - 1990, Henry Frantzen - 1992

Investm't Category: International Stock
- ✔ Cap Gain
- Cap & Income
- Income
- Domestic
- ✔ Foreign
- ✔ Country/Region
- Asset Allocation
- Fund of Funds
- Index
- Sector
- Small Cap
- Socially Conscious
- State Specific

Portfolio: stocks 100% bonds 0%
convertibles 0% other 0% cash 0%

Largest Holdings: United Kingdom 38%, Germany 15%

Unrealized Net Capital Gains: 5% of portfolio value

SHAREHOLDER INFORMATION

Minimum Investment
Initial: $25,000   Subsequent: $25,000

Minimum IRA Investment
Initial: na   Subsequent: na

Maximum Fees
Load: none   12b-1: none
Other: none

Distributions
Income: Dec   Capital Gains: Dec

Exchange Options
Number Per Year: none Fee:
Telephone:

Services

Fifty-Nine Wall St Pacific Basin (FNPEX)

6 St. James Avenue
Boston, MA 02116
(212) 493-8100

International Stock

PERFORMANCE

fund inception date: 11/1/90

	3yr Annual	5yr Annual	10yr Annual	Bull	Bear
Return (%)	13.3	na	na	na	-14.4
Differ from Category (+/-)	4.2 high	na	na	na	-7.4 low

Total Risk	Standard Deviation	Category Risk	Risk Index	Beta
high	19.9%	high	1.5	0.8

	1994	1993	1992	1991	1990	1989	1988	1987	1986	1985
Return (%)	-21.4	74.9	6.1	13.6	—	—	—	—	—	—
Differ from category (+/-)	-18.4	36.3	9.0	0.5	—	—	—	—	—	—

PER SHARE DATA

	1994	1993	1992	1991	1990	1989	1988	1987	1986	1985
Dividends, Net Income ($)	0.00	0.71	0.02	0.35	—	—	—	—	—	—
Distrib'ns, Cap Gain ($)	5.58	0.71	0.96	0.22	—	—	—	—	—	—
Net Asset Value ($)	30.36	46.10	27.29	26.63	—	—	—	—	—	—
Expense Ratio (%)	1.44	1.50	1.50	1.50	—	—	—	—	—	—
Net Income to Assets (%)	0.00	0.62	0.43	0.64	—	—	—	—	—	—
Portfolio Turnover (%)	na	79	84	56	—	—	—	—	—	—
Total Assets (Millions $)	101	2	31	20	—	—	—	—	—	—

PORTFOLIO (as of 4/30/94)

Portfolio Manager: John Nielsen - 1990, Henry Frantzen - 1992

Investm't Category: International Stock
- ✔ Cap Gain
-   Cap & Income
-   Income
-   Domestic
- ✔ Foreign
- ✔ Country/Region
-   Asset Allocation
-   Fund of Funds
-   Index
-   Sector
-   Small Cap
-   Socially Conscious
-   State Specific

Portfolio: stocks 99%   bonds 0%
convertibles 1%   other 0%   cash 0%

Largest Holdings: Hong Kong 42%, Japan 10%

Unrealized Net Capital Gains: 8% of portfolio value

SHAREHOLDER INFORMATION

Minimum Investment
Initial: $25,000   Subsequent: $25,000

Minimum IRA Investment
Initial: na   Subsequent: na

Maximum Fees
Load: none   12b-1: none
Other: none

Distributions
Income: Dec   Capital Gains: Dec

Exchange Options
Number Per Year: none   Fee:
Telephone:

Services

Fifty-Nine Wall St Small Company (FNSMX)

Aggressive Growth

6 St. James Avenue
Boston, MA 02116
(212) 493-8100

PERFORMANCE

fund inception date: 4/1/91

	3yr Annual	5yr Annual	10yr Annual	Bull	Bear
Return (%)	3.5	na	na	na	-13.4
Differ from Category (+/-)	-5.4 blw av	na	na	na	-2.6 blw av

Total Risk	Standard Deviation	Category Risk	Risk Index	Beta
high	12.5%	blw av	0.8	0.9

	1994	1993	1992	1991	1990	1989	1988	1987	1986	1985
Return (%)	-10.4	12.1	10.6	—	—	—	—	—	—	—
Differ from category (+/-)	-9.7	-7.4	-0.4	—	—	—	—	—	—	—

PER SHARE DATA

	1994	1993	1992	1991	1990	1989	1988	1987	1986	1985
Dividends, Net Income ($)	0.07	0.00	0.01	—	—	—	—	—	—	—
Distrib'ns, Cap Gain ($)	0.00	0.88	0.12	—	—	—	—	—	—	—
Net Asset Value ($)	11.12	12.50	11.96	—	—	—	—	—	—	—
Expense Ratio (%)	1.10	1.10	1.10	—	—	—	—	—	—	—
Net Income to Assets (%)	0.26	0.04	0.16	—	—	—	—	—	—	—
Portfolio Turnover (%)	na	116	67	—	—	—	—	—	—	—
Total Assets (Millions $)	33	3	20	—	—	—	—	—	—	—

PORTFOLIO (as of 4/30/94)

Portfolio Manager: D Murphy - 1991, J. Nielsen - 1991, C. Mellon -1993

Investm't Category: Aggressive Growth
- ✔ Cap Gain
- Cap & Income
- Income
- ✔ Domestic
- Foreign
- Country/Region
- Asset Allocation
- Fund of Funds
- Index
- Sector
- ✔ Small Cap
- Socially Conscious
- State Specific

Portfolio: stocks 100% bonds 0%
convertibles 0% other 0% cash 0%

Largest Holdings: finance 14%, health services 11%

Unrealized Net Capital Gains: 8% of portfolio value

SHAREHOLDER INFORMATION

Minimum Investment
Initial: $25,000 Subsequent: $25,000

Minimum IRA Investment
Initial: na Subsequent: na

Maximum Fees
Load: none 12b-1: none
Other: none

Distributions
Income: Dec Capital Gains: Dec

Exchange Options
Number Per Year: none Fee:
Telephone:

Services

Fifty-Nine Wall St Tax-Free Short/Interm (FNSIX)

Tax-Exempt Bond

6 St. James Avenue
Boston, MA 02116
(212) 493-8100

PERFORMANCE

fund inception date: 7/23/92

	3yr Annual	5yr Annual	10yr Annual	Bull	Bear
Return (%)	na	na	na	na	-1.1
Differ from Category (+/-)	na	na	na	na	4.1 high

Total Risk	Standard Deviation	Category Risk	Risk Index	Avg Mat
na	na	na	na	2.8 yrs

	1994	1993	1992	1991	1990	1989	1988	1987	1986	1985
Return (%)	0.3	5.9	—	—	—	—	—	—	—	—
Differ from category (+/-) . . .	5.5	-5.8	—	—	—	—	—	—	—	—

PER SHARE DATA

	1994	1993	1992	1991	1990	1989	1988	1987	1986	1985
Dividends, Net Income ($) .	0.35	0.35	—	—	—	—	—	—	—	—
Distrib'ns, Cap Gain ($) . . .	0.00	0.00	—	—	—	—	—	—	—	—
Net Asset Value ($)	10.02	10.34	—	—	—	—	—	—	—	—
Expense Ratio (%).	0.70	0.70	—	—	—	—	—	—	—	—
Net Income to Assets (%). .	3.32	3.42	—	—	—	—	—	—	—	—
Portfolio Turnover (%)	26	na	—	—	—	—	—	—	—	—
Total Assets (Millions $)	53	64	—	—	—	—	—	—	—	—

PORTFOLIO (as of 6/30/94)

Portfolio Manager: Barbara Brinkly - 1992, Eugene Rainis - 1992

Investm't Category: Tax-Exempt Bond

Cap Gain	Asset Allocation
Cap & Income	Fund of Funds
✔ Income	Index
	Sector
✔ Domestic	Small Cap
Foreign	Socially Conscious
Country/Region	State Specific

Portfolio: stocks 0% bonds 100%
convertibles 0% other 0% cash 0%

Largest Holdings: general obligations 5%

Unrealized Net Capital Gains: -1% of portfolio value

SHAREHOLDER INFORMATION

Minimum Investment
Initial: $10,000 Subsequent: $1,000

Minimum IRA Investment
Initial: na Subsequent: na

Maximum Fees
Load: none 12b-1: none
Other: none

Distributions
Income: monthly Capital Gains: Dec

Exchange Options
Number Per Year: none Fee:
Telephone:

Services

First Eagle Fund of America (FEAFX)

Growth

45 Broadway, 27th Fl.
New York, NY 10006
(800) 451-3623, (212) 943-9200

PERFORMANCE

fund inception date: 4/10/87

	3yr Annual	5yr Annual	10yr Annual	Bull	Bear
Return (%)	14.4	8.3	na	90.1	-9.5
Differ from Category (+/-)	6.7 high	-1.3 blw av	na	-2.0 av	-2.9 blw av

Total Risk	Standard Deviation	Category Risk	Risk Index	Beta
high	12.1%	high	1.3	1.2

	1994	1993	1992	1991	1990	1989	1988	1987	1986	1985
Return (%)	-2.5	23.8	24.3	20.9	-17.5	26.6	22.7	—	—	—
Differ from category (+/-)	-1.9	10.4	12.7	-14.8	-11.8	0.5	4.7	—	—	—

PER SHARE DATA

	1994	1993	1992	1991	1990	1989	1988	1987	1986	1985
Dividends, Net Income ($)	0.00	0.00	0.00	0.08	0.29	0.11	0.00	—	—	—
Distrib'ns, Cap Gain ($)	2.00	1.62	1.17	0.74	0.00	1.40	0.34	—	—	—
Net Asset Value ($)	12.70	15.04	13.48	11.85	10.51	13.11	11.56	—	—	—
Expense Ratio (%)	1.90	2.90	3.00	2.00	1.10	2.00	3.30	—	—	—
Net Income to Assets (%)	-0.70	-1.50	-1.00	0.80	1.30	1.30	0.20	—	—	—
Portfolio Turnover (%)	110	141	145	92	72	52	55	—	—	—
Total Assets (Millions $)	105	109	77	74	67	84	54	—	—	—

PORTFOLIO (as of 10/31/94)

Portfolio Manager: Harold J. Levy - 1987, David L. Cohen - 1989

Investm't Category: Growth
- ✔ Cap Gain
- Cap & Income
- Income
- ✔ Domestic
- ✔ Foreign
- Country/Region
- Asset Allocation
- Fund of Funds
- Index
- Sector
- Small Cap
- Socially Conscious
- State Specific

Portfolio: stocks 89% bonds 0%
convertibles 1% other 2% cash 8%

Largest Holdings: medical 22%, industrial products 20%

Unrealized Net Capital Gains: 10% of portfolio value

SHAREHOLDER INFORMATION

Minimum Investment
Initial: $5,000   Subsequent: $1,000

Minimum IRA Investment
Initial: $2,000   Subsequent: $1,000

Maximum Fees
Load: none   12b-1: none
Other: none

Distributions
Income: Nov   Capital Gains: Nov

Exchange Options
Number Per Year: none   Fee:
Telephone:

Services
IRA, pension

First Hawaii Muni Bond

(SURFX)

Tax-Exempt Bond

1270 Queen Emma St., Suite 607
Honolulu, HI 96813
(808) 599-2400

PERFORMANCE
fund inception date: 12/1/88

	3yr Annual	5yr Annual	10yr Annual	Bull	Bear
Return (%)	4.5	6.0	na	39.5	-4.2
Differ from Category (+/-)	0.0 av	-0.1 blw av	na	-2.3 blw av	1.0 abv av

Total Risk	Standard Deviation	Category Risk	Risk Index	Avg Mat
blw av	4.9%	blw av	0.8	14.5 yrs

	1994	1993	1992	1991	1990	1989	1988	1987	1986	1985
Return (%)	-4.8	10.4	8.6	10.5	6.2	9.2	—	—	—	—
Differ from category (+/-) . . .	0.4	-1.3	0.3	-0.8	-0.1	0.2	—	—	—	—

PER SHARE DATA

	1994	1993	1992	1991	1990	1989	1988	1987	1986	1985
Dividends, Net Income ($) .	0.56	0.58	0.60	0.61	0.62	0.66	—	—	—	—
Distrib'ns, Cap Gain ($) . . .	0.09	0.06	0.02	0.00	0.09	0.00	—	—	—	—
Net Asset Value ($)	10.18	11.37	10.89	10.61	10.18	10.28	—	—	—	—
Expense Ratio (%).	0.95	0.95	0.95	0.91	0.83	0.54	—	—	—	—
Net Income to Assets (%). .	5.01	5.21	5.67	6.05	6.16	6.40	—	—	—	—
Portfolio Turnover (%).	40	28	18	7	47	22	—	—	—	—
Total Assets (Millions $)	46	58	39	26	15	7	—	—	—	—

PORTFOLIO (as of 9/30/94)

Portfolio Manager: Louis Davanzo - 1991

Investm't Category: Tax-Exempt Bond

Cap Gain	Asset Allocation
Cap & Income	Fund of Funds
✔ Income	Index
	Sector
✔ Domestic	Small Cap
Foreign	Socially Conscious
Country/Region	✔ State Specific

Portfolio: stocks 0%   bonds 100%
convertibles 0%   other 0%   cash 0%

Largest Holdings: general obligation 17%

Unrealized Net Capital Gains: 0% of portfolio value

SHAREHOLDER INFORMATION

Minimum Investment
Initial: $1,000   Subsequent: $100

Minimum IRA Investment
Initial: na   Subsequent: na

Maximum Fees
Load: none   12b-1: 0.25%
Other: none

Distributions
Income: monthly   Capital Gains: Nov

Exchange Options
Number Per Year: no limit   Fee: none
Telephone: yes (money market fund not available)

Services
auto exchange, auto invest, auto withdraw

Flex Bond (FLXBX)

General Bond

6000 Memorial Dr.
P.O. Box 7177
Dublin, OH 43017
(800) 325-3539, (614) 766-7000

	3yr Annual	5yr Annual	10yr Annual	Bull	Bear
Return (%)	3.4	6.6	na	34.6	-3.1
Differ from Category (+/-)	-0.9 low	-0.3 blw av	na	-6.4 blw av	0.7 abv av

Total Risk	Standard Deviation	Category Risk	Risk Index	Avg Mat
low	4.1%	av	1.0	0.2 yrs

	1994	1993	1992	1991	1990	1989	1988	1987	1986	1985
Return (%)	-0.9	8.2	3.2	15.3	8.3	8.7	2.7	-0.6	12.5	—
Differ from category (+/-)	1.1	-1.0	-3.4	0.7	1.1	-2.7	-4.7	-2.8	-1.7	—

PER SHARE DATA

	1994	1993	1992	1991	1990	1989	1988	1987	1986	1985
Dividends, Net Income ($)	0.72	0.85	1.00	1.23	1.33	1.55	1.49	1.66	1.88	—
Distrib'ns, Cap Gain ($)	0.00	0.00	0.00	0.00	0.00	0.00	0.00	0.31	0.17	—
Net Asset Value ($)	19.25	20.18	19.46	19.84	18.37	18.24	18.25	19.22	21.31	—
Expense Ratio (%)	1.00	0.99	1.00	0.94	0.99	0.81	0.83	0.75	0.78	—
Net Income to Assets (%)	3.51	4.25	5.13	6.59	7.33	8.54	7.85	8.31	8.74	—
Portfolio Turnover (%)	na	na	101	214	500	0	188	258	150	—
Total Assets (Millions $)	12	13	11	9	6	5	6	13	13	—

PORTFOLIO (as of 6/30/94)

Portfolio Manager: Robert Kincheloe - 1994

Investm't Category: General Bond

Cap Gain	Asset Allocation
Cap & Income	Fund of Funds
✔ Income	Index
	Sector
✔ Domestic	Small Cap
Foreign	Socially Conscious
Country/Region	State Specific

Portfolio: stocks 0% bonds 59%
convertibles 0% other 0% cash 41%

Largest Holdings: mortgage-backed 57%,
U.S. government 2%

Unrealized Net Capital Gains: 0% of portfolio value

SHAREHOLDER INFORMATION

Minimum Investment
Initial: $2,500   Subsequent: $100

Minimum IRA Investment
Initial: $500   Subsequent: $100

Maximum Fees
Load: none   12b-1: 0.20%
Other: none

Distributions
Income: monthly   Capital Gains: Dec

Exchange Options
Number Per Year: no limit   Fee: none
Telephone: yes (money market fund available)

Services
IRA, pension, auto invest, auto withdraw

Flex Growth (FLCGX)

Growth

6000 Memorial Dr.
P.O. Box 7177
Dublin, OH 43017
(800) 325-3539, (614) 766-7000

PERFORMANCE

fund inception date: 3/20/85

	3yr Annual	5yr Annual	10yr Annual	Bull	Bear
Return (%)	4.2	7.4	na	51.7	-6.9
Differ from Category (+/-)	-3.5 blw av	-2.2 blw av	na	-40.4 low	-0.3 av

Total Risk	Standard Deviation	Category Risk	Risk Index	Beta
blw av	6.6%	low	0.7	0.5

	1994	1993	1992	1991	1990	1989	1988	1987	1986	1985
Return (%)	-0.6	7.2	6.3	21.4	4.3	10.1	-5.7	7.5	11.8	—
Differ from category (+/-) . . .	0.0	-6.2	-5.3	-14.3	10.0	-16.0	-23.7	5.7	-2.8	—

PER SHARE DATA

	1994	1993	1992	1991	1990	1989	1988	1987	1986	1985
Dividends, Net Income ($) .	0.27	0.16	0.11	0.34	0.57	0.32	0.78	0.05	0.28	—
Distrib'ns, Cap Gain ($) . . .	0.00	0.00	0.00	0.00	0.00	0.00	0.19	0.00	1.15	—
Net Asset Value ($)	13.08	13.45	12.70	12.05	10.21	10.33	9.67	11.27	10.52	—
Expense Ratio (%).	1.59	1.51	1.51	1.42	1.46	1.55	1.50	1.48	1.49	—
Net Income to Assets (%). .	0.81	1.31	1.31	2.98	4.90	2.63	2.06	1.79	2.32	—
Portfolio Turnover (%)	na	na	39	265	436	50	313	326	152	—
Total Assets (Millions $)	21	26	26	33	25	30	5	13	10	—

PORTFOLIO (as of 6/30/94)

Portfolio Manager: Philip Voelker - 1989, Robert Meeder Jr. - 1992

Investm't Category: Growth

✔ Cap Gain	Asset Allocation
Cap & Income	Fund of Funds
Income	Index
	Sector
✔ Domestic	Small Cap
Foreign	Socially Conscious
Country/Region	State Specific

Portfolio: stocks 0%   bonds 0%
convertibles 0%   other 0%   cash 100%

Largest Holdings: mortgage-backed bonds 52%, repurchase agreements 42%

Unrealized Net Capital Gains: 0% of portfolio value

SHAREHOLDER INFORMATION

Minimum Investment
Initial: $2,500   Subsequent: $100

Minimum IRA Investment
Initial: $500   Subsequent: $100

Maximum Fees
Load: none   12b-1: 0.20%
Other: none

Distributions
Income: quarterly   Capital Gains: Dec

Exchange Options
Number Per Year: no limit   Fee: none
Telephone: yes (money market fund available)

Services
IRA, pension, auto invest, auto withdraw

Flex Muirfield (FLMFX)

Growth

6000 Memorial Dr.
P.O. Box 7177
Dublin, OH 43017
(800) 325-3539, (614) 766-7000

PERFORMANCE

fund inception date: 8/10/88

	3yr Annual	5yr Annual	10yr Annual	Bull	Bear
Return (%)	5.8	9.5	na	61.9	-2.6
Differ from Category (+/-)	-1.9 blw av	-0.1 av	na	-30.2 low	4.0 high

Total Risk	Standard Deviation	Category Risk	Risk Index	Beta
blw av	5.8%	low	0.6	0.5

	1994	1993	1992	1991	1990	1989	1988	1987	1986	1985
Return (%)	2.6	8.1	6.9	29.8	2.4	13.9	—	—	—	—
Differ from category (+/-)	3.2	-5.3	-4.7	-5.9	8.1	-12.2	—	—	—	—

PER SHARE DATA

	1994	1993	1992	1991	1990	1989	1988	1987	1986	1985
Dividends, Net Income ($)	0.14	0.02	0.06	0.27	0.10	0.08	—	—	—	—
Distrib'ns, Cap Gain ($)	0.02	1.31	0.52	0.00	0.64	0.11	—	—	—	—
Net Asset Value ($)	5.34	5.36	6.25	6.43	5.22	5.84	—	—	—	—
Expense Ratio (%)	1.25	1.26	1.40	1.50	1.52	1.53	—	—	—	—
Net Income to Assets (%)	2.05	-0.13	1.05	1.25	4.46	1.65	—	—	—	—
Portfolio Turnover (%)	na	na	324	107	649	202	—	—	—	—
Total Assets (Millions $)	81	81	55	43	30	26	—	—	—	—

PORTFOLIO (as of 6/30/94)

Portfolio Manager: Robert Meeder Jr. - 1988

Investm't Category: Growth

✔ Cap Gain	Asset Allocation
Cap & Income	✔ Fund of Funds
Income	Index
	Sector
✔ Domestic	Small Cap
Foreign	Socially Conscious
Country/Region	State Specific

Portfolio:	stocks 0%	bonds 0%
convertibles 0%	other 0%	cash 100%

Largest Holdings: U.S. government 49%, repurchase agreements 47%

Unrealized Net Capital Gains: 0% of portfolio value

SHAREHOLDER INFORMATION

Minimum Investment
Initial: $2,500   Subsequent: $100

Minimum IRA Investment
Initial: $500   Subsequent: $100

Maximum Fees
Load: none   12b-1: 0.20%
Other: none

Distributions
Income: quarterly   Capital Gains: Dec

Exchange Options
Number Per Year: no limit   Fee: none
Telephone: yes (money market fund available)

Services
IRA, pension, auto invest, auto withdraw

Flex Short Term Global Income (FLGIX)

International Bond

6000 Memorial Dr.
P.O. Box 7177
Dublin, OH 43017
(800) 325-3539, (614) 766-7000

PERFORMANCE

fund inception date: 5/27/92

	3yr Annual	5yr Annual	10yr Annual	Bull	Bear
Return (%)	na	na	na	na	0.5
Differ from Category (+/-)	na	na	na	na	8.3 high

Total Risk	Standard Deviation	Category Risk	Risk Index	Avg Mat
na	na	na	na	0.2 yrs

	1994	1993	1992	1991	1990	1989	1988	1987	1986	1985
Return (%)	2.1	0.0	—	—	—	—	—	—	—	—
Differ from category (+/-)	8.4	-13.4	—	—	—	—	—	—	—	—

PER SHARE DATA

	1994	1993	1992	1991	1990	1989	1988	1987	1986	1985
Dividends, Net Income ($)	0.29	0.35	—	—	—	—	—	—	—	—
Distrib'ns, Cap Gain ($)	0.00	0.00	—	—	—	—	—	—	—	—
Net Asset Value ($)	9.32	9.41	—	—	—	—	—	—	—	—
Expense Ratio (%)	0.97	0.82	—	—	—	—	—	—	—	—
Net Income to Assets (%)	3.05	4.42	—	—	—	—	—	—	—	—
Portfolio Turnover (%)	na	na	—	—	—	—	—	—	—	—
Total Assets (Millions $)	3	14	—	—	—	—	—	—	—	—

PORTFOLIO (as of 6/30/94)

Portfolio Manager: Joseph Zarr - 1992

Investm't Category: International Bond

Cap Gain	Asset Allocation
Cap & Income	Fund of Funds
✔ Income	Index
	Sector
✔ Domestic	Small Cap
✔ Foreign	Socially Conscious
Country/Region	State Specific

Portfolio: stocks 0%   bonds 48%
convertibles 0%   other 0%   cash 52%

Largest Holdings: France 19%, United States 14%

Unrealized Net Capital Gains: 0% of portfolio value

SHAREHOLDER INFORMATION

Minimum Investment
Initial: $2,500   Subsequent: $100

Minimum IRA Investment
Initial: $500   Subsequent: $100

Maximum Fees
Load: none   12b-1: 0.20%
Other: none

Distributions
Income: monthly   Capital Gains: Dec

Exchange Options
Number Per Year: no limit   Fee: none
Telephone: yes (money market fund available)

Services
IRA, pension, auto invest, auto withdraw

Fontaine Capital Appreciation (FAPPX)

Growth

210 W. Pennsylvania Ave.
Suite 240
Towson, MD 21204
(800) 247-1550, (410) 825-7894

PERFORMANCE

fund inception date: 9/28/89

	3yr Annual	5yr Annual	10yr Annual	Bull	Bear
Return (%)	3.9	5.8	na	27.0	-4.7
Differ from Category (+/-)	-3.8 low	-3.8 low	na	-65.1 low	1.9 abv av

Total Risk	Standard Deviation	Category Risk	Risk Index	Beta
av	7.3%	low	0.7	0.4

	1994	1993	1992	1991	1990	1989	1988	1987	1986	1985
Return (%)	2.3	14.0	-3.9	11.8	6.1	—	—	—	—	—
Differ from category (+/-)	2.9	0.6	-15.5	-23.9	11.8	—	—	—	—	—

PER SHARE DATA

	1994	1993	1992	1991	1990	1989	1988	1987	1986	1985
Dividends, Net Income ($)	0.18	0.14	0.12	0.64	0.40	—	—	—	—	—
Distrib'ns, Cap Gain ($)	0.07	0.07	0.63	0.20	0.04	—	—	—	—	—
Net Asset Value ($)	10.75	10.75	9.60	10.78	10.40	—	—	—	—	—
Expense Ratio (%)	1.50	1.50	1.50	1.50	1.50	—	—	—	—	—
Net Income to Assets (%)	2.31	1.15	3.12	4.14	5.26	—	—	—	—	—
Portfolio Turnover (%)	233	131	129	79	288	—	—	—	—	—
Total Assets (Millions $)	5	7	15	16	4	—	—	—	—	—

PORTFOLIO (as of 6/30/94)

Portfolio Manager: Richard H. Fontaine - 1989

Investm't Category: Growth

Cap Gain	Asset Allocation
✔ Cap & Income	Fund of Funds
Income	Index
	Sector
✔ Domestic	Small Cap
✔ Foreign	Socially Conscious
Country/Region	State Specific

Portfolio: stocks 58% bonds 40%
convertibles 0% other 2% cash 0%

Largest Holdings: office automation 12%, gold mining 11%

Unrealized Net Capital Gains: -6% of portfolio value

SHAREHOLDER INFORMATION

Minimum Investment
Initial: $1,000   Subsequent: $100

Minimum IRA Investment
Initial: $250   Subsequent: $100

Maximum Fees
Load: none   12b-1: none
Other: none

Distributions
Income: Dec   Capital Gains: Dec

Exchange Options
Number Per Year: 8   Fee: none
Telephone: none

Services
IRA, pension

Founders Balanced

(FRINX)

Balanced

Founders Financial Center
2930 E. Third Ave.
Denver, CO 80206
(800) 525-2440, (303) 394-4404

	3yr Annual	5yr Annual	10yr Annual	Bull	Bear
Return (%)	8.2	8.1	10.4	68.2	-3.4
Differ from Category (+/-)	1.8 abv av	0.1 av	-0.9 blw av	3.2 av	2.3 high

Total Risk	Standard Deviation	Category Risk	Risk Index	Beta
blw av	6.4%	abv av	1.0	0.6

	1994	1993	1992	1991	1990	1989	1988	1987	1986	1985
Return (%)	-1.9	21.8	6.0	22.8	-4.9	25.3	11.0	1.8	14.5	12.7
Differ from category (+/-)	0.0	8.4	-2.3	-0.6	-4.4	8.0	-0.8	-0.6	-2.9	-11.6

PER SHARE DATA

	1994	1993	1992	1991	1990	1989	1988	1987	1986	1985
Dividends, Net Income ($)	0.20	0.21	0.28	0.31	0.35	0.32	0.38	0.41	0.33	0.40
Distrib'ns, Cap Gain ($)	0.00	0.96	0.09	0.33	0.00	0.32	0.00	0.87	0.44	0.16
Net Asset Value ($)	8.56	8.93	8.30	8.19	7.22	7.97	6.89	6.55	7.65	7.38
Expense Ratio (%)	1.33	1.34	1.88	1.73	1.65	1.52	1.64	1.66	1.59	1.50
Net Income to Assets (%)	2.04	2.30	3.57	4.01	4.63	4.19	5.39	4.03	4.44	5.88
Portfolio Turnover (%)	283	251	96	133	103	85	182	133	178	126
Total Assets (Millions $)	95	74	32	19	14	15	13	17	12	9

PORTFOLIO (as of 6/30/94)

Portfolio Manager: Pat Adams - 1993

Investm't Category: Balanced

Cap Gain	Asset Allocation
✔ Cap & Income	Fund of Funds
Income	Index
	Sector
✔ Domestic	Small Cap
✔ Foreign	Socially Conscious
Country/Region	State Specific

Portfolio: stocks 52%   bonds 19%
convertibles 6%   other 4%   cash 19%

Largest Holdings: stocks—retail 11%,
bonds—financial services 8%

Unrealized Net Capital Gains: -1% of portfolio value

SHAREHOLDER INFORMATION

Minimum Investment
Initial: $1,000   Subsequent: $100

Minimum IRA Investment
Initial: $500   Subsequent: $100

Maximum Fees
Load: none   12b-1: 0.25%
Other: none

Distributions
Income: quarterly   Capital Gains: Dec

Exchange Options
Number Per Year: 4   Fee: none
Telephone: yes (money market fund available)

Services
IRA, pension, auto exchange, auto invest, auto withdraw

Founders Blue Chip
(FRMUX)
Growth & Income

Founders Financial Center
2930 E. Third Ave.
Denver, CO 80206
(800) 525-2440, (303) 394-4404

PERFORMANCE

fund inception date: 7/5/38

	3yr Annual	5yr Annual	10yr Annual	Bull	Bear
Return (%)	4.7	8.1	13.3	61.5	-6.4
Differ from Category (+/-)	-2.4 blw av	0.2 av	1.6 abv av	-14.3 blw av	-0.1 av

Total Risk	Standard Deviation	Category Risk	Risk Index	Beta
av	8.5%	abv av	1.0	0.9

	1994	1993	1992	1991	1990	1989	1988	1987	1986	1985
Return (%)	0.5	14.4	-0.2	28.3	0.4	35.6	10.0	1.9	17.3	31.9
Differ from category (+/-)	1.9	1.2	-10.4	0.7	6.4	14.2	-7.0	1.3	1.5	6.2

PER SHARE DATA

	1994	1993	1992	1991	1990	1989	1988	1987	1986	1985
Dividends, Net Income ($)	0.06	0.04	0.08	0.11	0.17	0.16	0.19	0.24	0.29	0.38
Distrib'ns, Cap Gain ($)	0.31	1.38	0.66	0.74	0.51	1.04	0.25	1.71	3.22	1.85
Net Asset Value ($)	6.16	6.49	6.91	7.67	6.67	7.32	6.31	6.14	7.87	9.75
Expense Ratio (%)	1.24	1.22	1.23	1.10	1.07	0.98	1.00	0.87	0.74	0.70
Net Income to Assets (%)	0.61	0.57	1.13	1.52	2.35	2.03	2.81	2.11	2.64	3.69
Portfolio Turnover (%)	242	212	103	95	82	64	58	56	42	18
Total Assets (Millions $)	312	306	290	290	234	232	173	240	175	138

PORTFOLIO (as of 6/30/94)

Portfolio Manager: Pat Adams - 1993

Investm't Category: Growth & Income

Cap Gain	Asset Allocation
✔ Cap & Income	Fund of Funds
Income	Index
	Sector
✔ Domestic	Small Cap
✔ Foreign	Socially Conscious
Country/Region	State Specific

Portfolio: stocks 74% bonds 0%
convertibles 4% other 5% cash 17%

Largest Holdings: retail 14%, telecommunications & equipment 7%

Unrealized Net Capital Gains: 0% of portfolio value

SHAREHOLDER INFORMATION

Minimum Investment
Initial: $1,000　　　　Subsequent: $100

Minimum IRA Investment
Initial: $500　　　　Subsequent: $100

Maximum Fees
Load: none　　　　12b-1: 0.25%
Other: none

Distributions
Income: Dec　　　　Capital Gains: Dec

Exchange Options
Number Per Year: 4　　　Fee: none
Telephone: yes (money market fund available)

Services
IRA, pension, auto exchange, auto invest, auto withdraw

Founders Discovery

(FDISX)

Aggressive Growth

Founders Financial Center
2930 E. Third Ave.
Denver, CO 80206
(800) 525-2440, (303) 394-4404

PERFORMANCE

fund inception date: 12/31/89

	3yr Annual	5yr Annual	10yr Annual	Bull	Bear
Return (%)	5.5	16.7	na	136.4	-17.6
Differ from Category (+/-)	-3.4 blw av	4.2 abv av	na	3.2 av	-6.8 low

Total Risk	Standard Deviation	Category Risk	Risk Index	Beta
high	14.1%	av	1.0	0.8

	1994	1993	1992	1991	1990	1989	1988	1987	1986	1985
Return (%)	-7.7	10.8	15.1	62.4	13.1	—	—	—	—	—
Differ from category (+/-) . .	-7.0	-8.7	4.1	10.3	19.3	—	—	—	—	—

PER SHARE DATA

	1994	1993	1992	1991	1990	1989	1988	1987	1986	1985
Dividends, Net Income ($) .	0.00	0.00	0.06	0.00	0.10	—	—	—	—	—
Distrib'ns, Cap Gain ($) . . .	0.00	0.52	0.18	0.68	0.00	—	—	—	—	—
Net Asset Value ($)	19.88	21.55	19.93	17.52	11.22	—	—	—	—	—
Expense Ratio (%).	1.63	1.65	1.85	1.77	2.03	—	—	—	—	—
Net Income to Assets (%).	-0.97	-0.97	-0.67	-0.55	1.68	—	—	—	—	—
Portfolio Turnover (%)	102	99	111	165	271	—	—	—	—	—
Total Assets (Millions $) . . .	187	226	152	47	7	—	—	—	—	—

PORTFOLIO (as of 6/30/94)

Portfolio Manager: Michael Haines - 1989

Investm't Category: Aggressive Growth

✔ Cap Gain	Asset Allocation
Cap & Income	Fund of Funds
Income	Index
	Sector
✔ Domestic	✔ Small Cap
✔ Foreign	Socially Conscious
Country/Region	State Specific

Portfolio: stocks 71%   bonds 0%
convertibles 0%   other 0%   cash 29%

Largest Holdings: computer software 7%, healthcare services 6%

Unrealized Net Capital Gains: 0% of portfolio value

SHAREHOLDER INFORMATION

Minimum Investment
Initial: $1,000   Subsequent: $100

Minimum IRA Investment
Initial: $500   Subsequent: $100

Maximum Fees
Load: none   12b-1: 0.25%
Other: none

Distributions
Income: Dec   Capital Gains: Dec

Exchange Options
Number Per Year: 4   Fee: none
Telephone: yes (money market fund available)

Services
IRA, pension, auto exchange, auto invest, auto withdraw

Founders Frontier
(FOUNX)
Aggressive Growth

Founders Financial Center
2930 E. Third Ave.
Denver, CO 80206
(800) 525-2440, (303) 394-4404

PERFORMANCE

fund inception date: 1/22/87

	3yr Annual	5yr Annual	10yr Annual	Bull	Bear
Return (%)	7.2	11.2	na	109.7	-14.6
Differ from Category (+/-)	-1.7 av	-1.3 av	na	-23.5 blw av	-3.8 blw av

Total Risk	Standard Deviation	Category Risk	Risk Index	Beta
high	13.5%	av	0.9	1.2

	1994	1993	1992	1991	1990	1989	1988	1987	1986	1985
Return (%)	-2.8	16.5	8.9	49.3	-7.4	44.2	29.2	—	—	—
Differ from category (+/-)	-2.1	-3.0	-2.1	-2.8	-1.2	17.4	14.0	—	—	—

PER SHARE DATA

	1994	1993	1992	1991	1990	1989	1988	1987	1986	1985
Dividends, Net Income ($)	0.00	0.00	0.00	0.01	0.16	0.05	0.00	—	—	—
Distrib'ns, Cap Gain ($)	0.65	1.20	1.31	0.93	0.08	0.84	0.78	—	—	—
Net Asset Value ($)	26.50	27.94	25.03	24.21	16.87	18.49	13.45	—	—	—
Expense Ratio (%)	1.63	1.66	1.83	1.68	1.71	1.46	1.89	—	—	—
Net Income to Assets (%)	-0.58	-0.75	-0.58	0.05	0.78	0.38	-0.43	—	—	—
Portfolio Turnover (%)	105	109	155	158	207	198	312	—	—	—
Total Assets (Millions $)	249	254	146	103	39	50	9	—	—	—

PORTFOLIO (as of 6/30/94)

Portfolio Manager: Michael Haines - 1987

Investm't Category: Aggressive Growth

✔ Cap Gain	Asset Allocation
Cap & Income	Fund of Funds
Income	Index
	Sector
✔ Domestic	✔ Small Cap
✔ Foreign	Socially Conscious
Country/Region	State Specific

Portfolio:	stocks 73%	bonds 0%
convertibles 0%	other 0%	cash 27%

Largest Holdings: semiconductors & equip 11%, telecommunications & equip 7%

Unrealized Net Capital Gains: 2% of portfolio value

SHAREHOLDER INFORMATION

Minimum Investment
Initial: $1,000   Subsequent: $100

Minimum IRA Investment
Initial: $500   Subsequent: $100

Maximum Fees
Load: none   12b-1: 0.25%
Other: none

Distributions
Income: Dec   Capital Gains: Dec

Exchange Options
Number Per Year: 4   Fee: none
Telephone: yes (money market fund available)

Services
IRA, pension, auto exchange, auto invest, auto withdraw

Founders Gov't Securities (FGVSX)

Government Bond

Founders Financial Center
2930 E. Third Ave.
Denver, CO 80206
(800) 525-2440, (303) 394-4404

PERFORMANCE

fund inception date: 3/1/88

	3yr Annual	5yr Annual	10yr Annual	Bull	Bear
Return (%)	2.1	5.0	na	40.7	-7.9
Differ from Category (+/-)	-1.9 low	-1.7 low	na	-10.5 av	-1.5 blw av

Total Risk	Standard Deviation	Category Risk	Risk Index	Avg Mat
blw av	5.0%	abv av	1.1	5.9 yrs

	1994	1993	1992	1991	1990	1989	1988	1987	1986	1985
Return (%)	-7.4	9.2	5.3	14.8	4.4	13.3	—	—	—	—
Differ from category (+/-) . .	-2.6	-1.7	-1.1	-0.5	-1.8	-1.2	—	—	—	—

PER SHARE DATA

	1994	1993	1992	1991	1990	1989	1988	1987	1986	1985
Dividends, Net Income ($) .	0.50	0.46	0.51	0.60	0.69	0.79	—	—	—	—
Distrib'ns, Cap Gain ($) . . .	0.00	0.64	0.32	0.18	0.00	0.00	—	—	—	—
Net Asset Value ($)	8.78	10.02	10.19	10.48	9.85	10.13	—	—	—	—
Expense Ratio (%).	1.31	1.18	1.18	1.12	1.03	0.65	—	—	—	—
Net Income to Assets (%). .	5.53	4.33	4.83	5.89	7.15	7.90	—	—	—	—
Portfolio Turnover (%). . . .	352	429	204	261	103	195	—	—	—	—
Total Assets (Millions $)	21	31	25	18	7	7	—	—	—	—

PORTFOLIO (as of 6/30/94)

Portfolio Manager: Montgomery Cleworth - 1993

Investm't Category: Government Bond

Cap Gain	Asset Allocation
Cap & Income	Fund of Funds
✔ Income	Index
	Sector
✔ Domestic	Small Cap
Foreign	Socially Conscious
Country/Region	State Specific

Portfolio: stocks 0%   bonds 100%
convertibles 0%   other 0%   cash 0%

Largest Holdings: U.S. government and agencies 81%, mortgage-backed 19%

Unrealized Net Capital Gains: -4% of portfolio value

SHAREHOLDER INFORMATION

Minimum Investment
Initial: $1,000   Subsequent: $100

Minimum IRA Investment
Initial: $500   Subsequent: $100

Maximum Fees
Load: none   12b-1: 0.25%
Other: none

Distributions
Income: monthly   Capital Gains: Dec

Exchange Options
Number Per Year: 4   Fee: none
Telephone: yes (money market fund available)

Services
IRA, pension, auto exchange, auto invest, auto withdraw

Founders Growth

(FRGRX)

Growth

Founders Financial Center
2930 E. Third Ave.
Denver, CO 80206
(800) 525-2440, (303) 394-4404

	3yr Annual	5yr Annual	10yr Annual	Bull	Bear
Return (%)	8.1	10.7	15.4	114.2	-16.1
Differ from Category (+/-)	0.4 av	1.1 abv av	2.5 high	22.1 high	-9.5 low

Total Risk	Standard Deviation	Category Risk	Risk Index	Beta
high	14.0%	high	1.5	1.3

	1994	1993	1992	1991	1990	1989	1988	1987	1986	1985
Return (%)	-3.3	25.5	4.3	47.3	-10.6	41.7	4.8	10.0	19.7	28.7
Differ from category (+/-)	-2.7	12.1	-7.3	11.6	-4.9	15.6	-13.2	8.2	5.1	-0.5

PER SHARE DATA

	1994	1993	1992	1991	1990	1989	1988	1987	1986	1985
Dividends, Net Income ($)	0.00	0.00	0.01	0.07	0.13	0.07	0.15	0.13	0.10	0.17
Distrib'ns, Cap Gain ($)	0.34	0.85	1.16	0.87	0.01	1.27	0.00	1.61	1.35	0.00
Net Asset Value ($)	11.63	12.38	10.54	11.22	8.27	9.41	7.61	7.41	8.30	8.14
Expense Ratio (%)	1.30	1.32	1.54	1.45	1.45	1.28	1.38	1.25	1.27	1.17
Net Income to Assets (%)	-0.30	-0.15	0.06	0.65	1.53	0.77	1.74	0.99	1.19	2.49
Portfolio Turnover (%)	149	131	216	161	178	167	179	147	142	186
Total Assets (Millions $)	310	343	145	141	88	112	53	58	61	42

PORTFOLIO (as of 6/30/94)

Portfolio Manager: Edward F. Keely - 1993

Investm't Category: Growth

✔ Cap Gain	Asset Allocation
Cap & Income	Fund of Funds
Income	Index
	Sector
✔ Domestic	Small Cap
✔ Foreign	Socially Conscious
Country/Region	State Specific

Portfolio: stocks 76%   bonds 0%
convertibles 0%   other 0%   cash 24%

Largest Holdings: retail 10%, leisure & recreation 8%

Unrealized Net Capital Gains: -2% of portfolio value

SHAREHOLDER INFORMATION

Minimum Investment
Initial: $1,000   Subsequent: $100

Minimum IRA Investment
Initial: $500   Subsequent: $100

Maximum Fees
Load: none   12b-1: 0.25%
Other: none

Distributions
Income: Dec   Capital Gains: Dec

Exchange Options
Number Per Year: 4   Fee: none
Telephone: yes (money market fund available)

Services
IRA, pension, auto exchange, auto invest, auto withdraw

Founders Special
(FRSPX)
Aggressive Growth

Founders Financial Center
2930 E. Third Ave.
Denver, CO 80206
(800) 525-2440, (303) 394-4404

PERFORMANCE   fund inception date: 9/8/61

	3yr Annual	5yr Annual	10yr Annual	Bull	Bear
Return (%)	6.1	11.8	14.8	137.5	-14.7
Differ from Category (+/-)	-2.8 blw av	-0.7 av	0.8 av	4.3 av	-3.9 blw av

Total Risk	Standard Deviation	Category Risk	Risk Index	Beta
high	13.7%	av	0.9	1.3

	1994	1993	1992	1991	1990	1989	1988	1987	1986	1985
Return (%)	-4.9	16.0	8.2	63.6	-10.4	39.3	13.1	5.3	18.7	15.1
Differ from category (+/-) . .	-4.2	-3.5	-2.8	11.5	-4.2	12.5	-2.1	7.5	6.9	-17.2

PER SHARE DATA

	1994	1993	1992	1991	1990	1989	1988	1987	1986	1985
Dividends, Net Income ($) .	0.00	0.00	0.00	0.04	0.10	0.15	0.04	0.03	0.06	0.05
Distrib'ns, Cap Gain ($) . . .	0.28	1.33	0.46	0.57	0.81	0.81	0.31	0.72	0.69	0.00
Net Asset Value ($)	7.01	7.67	7.76	7.59	5.03	6.64	5.47	5.14	5.59	5.34
Expense Ratio (%).	1.35	1.33	1.23	1.15	1.20	1.06	1.12	1.14	1.06	1.02
Net Income to Assets (%).	-0.48	-0.14	-.05	0.76	1.54	1.95	0.59	0.45	0.73	0.85
Portfolio Turnover (%)	296	285	223	102	146	151	160	210	138	192
Total Assets (Millions $) . . .	300	433	457	226	58	95	63	66	70	95

PORTFOLIO (as of 6/30/94)

Portfolio Manager: Charles Hooper - 1991

Investm't Category: Aggressive Growth

✔ Cap Gain	Asset Allocation
Cap & Income	Fund of Funds
Income	Index
	Sector
✔ Domestic	Small Cap
✔ Foreign	Socially Conscious
Country/Region	State Specific

Portfolio:	stocks 90%	bonds 0%
convertibles 0%	other 0%	cash 10%

Largest Holdings: computer software 12%, retail 6%

Unrealized Net Capital Gains: -8% of portfolio value

SHAREHOLDER INFORMATION

Minimum Investment
Initial: $1,000   Subsequent: $100

Minimum IRA Investment
Initial: $500   Subsequent: $100

Maximum Fees
Load: none   12b-1: 0.25%
Other: none

Distributions
Income: Dec   Capital Gains: Dec

Exchange Options
Number Per Year: 4   Fee: none
Telephone: yes (money market fund available)

Services
IRA, pension, auto exchange, auto invest, auto withdraw

Founders World Wide Growth (FWWGX)

International Stock

Founders Financial Center
2930 E. Third Ave.
Denver, CO 80206
(800) 525-2440, (303) 394-4404

PERFORMANCE

fund inception date: 12/31/89

	3yr Annual	5yr Annual	10yr Annual	Bull	Bear
Return (%)	8.8	13.1	na	93.5	-9.8
Differ from Category (+/-)	-0.3 av	8.2 high	na	29.6 high	-2.8 blw av

Total Risk	Standard Deviation	Category Risk	Risk Index	Beta
abv av	11.9%	blw av	0.9	0.9

	1994	1993	1992	1991	1990	1989	1988	1987	1986	1985
Return (%)	-2.1	29.8	1.5	34.8	6.6	—	—	—	—	—
Differ from category (+/-)	0.9	-8.8	4.4	21.7	17.0	—	—	—	—	—

PER SHARE DATA

	1994	1993	1992	1991	1990	1989	1988	1987	1986	1985
Dividends, Net Income ($)	0.00	0.00	0.00	0.03	0.29	—	—	—	—	—
Distrib'ns, Cap Gain ($)	0.46	0.41	0.00	0.04	0.00	—	—	—	—	—
Net Asset Value ($)	17.09	17.94	14.13	13.92	10.38	—	—	—	—	—
Expense Ratio (%)	1.70	1.80	2.06	1.90	2.10	—	—	—	—	—
Net Income to Assets (%)	-0.11	-0.19	0.01	0.38	3.21	—	—	—	—	—
Portfolio Turnover (%)	116	117	152	84	170	—	—	—	—	—
Total Assets (Millions $)	104	85	37	20	6	—	—	—	—	—

PORTFOLIO (as of 6/30/94)

Portfolio Manager: Michael Gerding - 1990

Investm't Category: International Stock

✔ Cap Gain	Asset Allocation
Cap & Income	Fund of Funds
Income	Index
	Sector
✔ Domestic	Small Cap
✔ Foreign	Socially Conscious
Country/Region	State Specific

Portfolio: stocks 82% bonds 0%
convertibles 1% other 3% cash 14%

Largest Holdings: United States 12%, Japan 11%

Unrealized Net Capital Gains: 7% of portfolio value

SHAREHOLDER INFORMATION

Minimum Investment
Initial: $1,000   Subsequent: $100

Minimum IRA Investment
Initial: $500   Subsequent: $100

Maximum Fees
Load: none   12b-1: 0.25%
Other: none

Distributions
Income: Dec   Capital Gains: Dec

Exchange Options
Number Per Year: 4   Fee: none
Telephone: yes (money market fund available)

Services
IRA, pension, auto exchange, auto invest, auto withdraw

Fremont CA Interm Tax-Free (FCATX)

50 Fremont St., Suite 3600
San Francisco, CA 94105
(800) 548-4539, (415) 768-9000

Tax-Exempt Bond

PERFORMANCE

fund inception date: 11/16/90

	3yr Annual	5yr Annual	10yr Annual	Bull	Bear
Return (%)	3.9	na	na	na	-4.7
Differ from Category (+/-)	-0.6 low	na	na	na	0.5 abv av

Total Risk	Standard Deviation	Category Risk	Risk Index	Avg Mat
low	4.7%	low	0.7	8.5 yrs

	1994	1993	1992	1991	1990	1989	1988	1987	1986	1985
Return (%)	-4.9	9.9	7.2	10.7	—	—	—	—	—	—
Differ from category (+/-) . . .	0.3	-1.8	-1.1	-0.6	—	—	—	—	—	—

PER SHARE DATA

	1994	1993	1992	1991	1990	1989	1988	1987	1986	1985
Dividends, Net Income ($) .	0.52	0.55	0.56	0.60	—	—	—	—	—	—
Distrib'ns, Cap Gain ($) . . .	0.00	0.09	0.02	0.07	—	—	—	—	—	—
Net Asset Value ($)	10.03	11.09	10.69	10.53	—	—	—	—	—	—
Expense Ratio (%).	0.49	0.50	0.54	0.35	—	—	—	—	—	—
Net Income to Assets (%). .	4.83	5.05	5.38	5.88	—	—	—	—	—	—
Portfolio Turnover (%)	7	26	18	39	—	—	—	—	—	—
Total Assets (Millions $)	54	62	44	34	—	—	—	—	—	—

PORTFOLIO (as of 4/30/94)

Portfolio Manager: William M. Feeney - 1990

Investm't Category: Tax-Exempt Bond

Cap Gain	Asset Allocation
Cap & Income	Fund of Funds
✔ Income	Index
	Sector
✔ Domestic	Small Cap
Foreign	Socially Conscious
Country/Region	✔ State Specific

Portfolio: stocks 0%   bonds 97%
convertibles 0%   other 0%   cash 3%

Largest Holdings: general obligation 16%

Unrealized Net Capital Gains: 0% of portfolio value

SHAREHOLDER INFORMATION

Minimum Investment
Initial: $2,000   Subsequent: $200

Minimum IRA Investment
Initial: na   Subsequent: na

Maximum Fees
Load: none   12b-1: none
Other: none

Distributions
Income: monthly   Capital Gains: Oct

Exchange Options
Number Per Year: no limit   Fee: none
Telephone: yes (money market fund available)

Services
auto exchange, auto invest, auto withdraw

Fremont Global (FMAFX)

International Stock

50 Fremont St., Suite 3600
San Francisco, CA 94105
(800) 548-4539, (415) 768-9000

PERFORMANCE

fund inception date: 11/18/88

	3yr Annual	5yr Annual	10yr Annual	Bull	Bear
Return (%)	6.4	7.0	na	60.3	-7.1
Differ from Category (+/-)	-2.7 blw av	2.1 high	na	-3.6 av	-0.1 av

Total Risk	Standard Deviation	Category Risk	Risk Index	Beta
blw av	6.1%	low	0.4	0.6

	1994	1993	1992	1991	1990	1989	1988	1987	1986	1985
Return (%)	-4.1	19.5	5.2	18.6	-1.7	15.9	—	—	—	—
Differ from category (+/-)	-1.1	-19.1	8.1	5.5	8.7	-6.6	—	—	—	—

PER SHARE DATA

	1994	1993	1992	1991	1990	1989	1988	1987	1986	1985
Dividends, Net Income ($)	0.13	0.32	0.43	0.36	0.53	0.48	—	—	—	—
Distrib'ns, Cap Gain ($)	0.13	0.07	0.16	0.04	0.03	0.14	—	—	—	—
Net Asset Value ($)	12.79	13.62	11.74	11.74	10.25	11.02	—	—	—	—
Expense Ratio (%)	0.95	0.99	1.09	1.12	1.10	1.02	—	—	—	—
Net Income to Assets (%)	2.39	2.89	3.41	4.34	5.01	5.30	—	—	—	—
Portfolio Turnover (%)	35	40	50	81	36	51	—	—	—	—
Total Assets (Millions $)	436	214	102	74	55	44	—	—	—	—

PORTFOLIO (as of 4/30/94)

Portfolio Manager: P. F. Landini - 1988, D. L. Redo - 1988, J. Rhodes - 1988

Investm't Category: International Stock
Cap Gain	✔ Asset Allocation
✔ Cap & Income	Fund of Funds
Income	Index
	Sector
✔ Domestic	Small Cap
✔ Foreign	Socially Conscious
Country/Region	State Specific

Portfolio: stocks 56% bonds 25%
convertibles 0% other 2% cash 17%

Largest Holdings: international stocks 39%, U.S. stocks 15%

Unrealized Net Capital Gains: 5% of portfolio value

SHAREHOLDER INFORMATION

Minimum Investment
Initial: $2,000   Subsequent: $200

Minimum IRA Investment
Initial: $1,000   Subsequent: $0

Maximum Fees
Load: none   12b-1: none
Other: none

Distributions
Income: quarterly   Capital Gains: Oct, Dec

Exchange Options
Number Per Year: no limit   Fee: none
Telephone: yes (money market fund available)

Services
IRA, pension, auto exchange, auto invest, auto withdraw

Fremont Growth

(FEQFX)

Growth

50 Fremont St., Suite 3600
San Francisco, CA 94105
(800) 548-4539, (415) 768-9000

PERFORMANCE   fund inception date: 8/14/92

	3yr Annual	5yr Annual	10yr Annual	Bull	Bear
Return (%)	na	na	na	na	-9.9
Differ from Category (+/-)	na	na	na	na	-3.3 low

Total Risk	Standard Deviation	Category Risk	Risk Index	Beta
na	na	na	na	na

	1994	1993	1992	1991	1990	1989	1988	1987	1986	1985
Return (%)	0.4	6.4	—	—	—	—	—	—	—	—
Differ from category (+/-) . . .	1.0	-7.0	—	—	—	—	—	—	—	—

PER SHARE DATA

	1994	1993	1992	1991	1990	1989	1988	1987	1986	1985
Dividends, Net Income ($) .	0.22	0.16	—	—	—	—	—	—	—	—
Distrib'ns, Cap Gain ($) . . .	0.90	0.00	—	—	—	—	—	—	—	—
Net Asset Value ($)	10.11	11.18	—	—	—	—	—	—	—	—
Expense Ratio (%).	0.85	0.87	—	—	—	—	—	—	—	—
Net Income to Assets (%). .	1.60	1.19	—	—	—	—	—	—	—	—
Portfolio Turnover (%).	51	44	—	—	—	—	—	—	—	—
Total Assets (Millions $)	23	42	—	—	—	—	—	—	—	—

PORTFOLIO (as of 4/30/94)

Portfolio Manager: Andrew Pang - 1992,
Eugene Sit - 1992

Investm't Category: Growth

✔ Cap Gain	Asset Allocation
Cap & Income	Fund of Funds
Income	Index
	Sector
✔ Domestic	Small Cap
✔ Foreign	Socially Conscious
Country/Region	State Specific

Portfolio: stocks 87% bonds 0%
convertibles 0% other 5% cash 8%

Largest Holdings: technology 13%, financial
services 12%

Unrealized Net Capital Gains: 4% of portfolio value

SHAREHOLDER INFORMATION

Minimum Investment
Initial: $2,000   Subsequent: $200

Minimum IRA Investment
Initial: $1,000   Subsequent: $0

Maximum Fees
Load: none   12b-1: none
Other: none

Distributions
Income: quarterly   Capital Gains: Oct, Dec

Exchange Options
Number Per Year: no limit   Fee: none
Telephone: yes (money market fund available)

Services
IRA, pension, auto exchange, auto invest, auto
withdraw

Fundamental US Gov't Strat Income (FUSIX)

90 Washington St.
New York, NY 10006
(800) 322-6864, (212) 635-3005

Government Bond

PERFORMANCE

fund inception date: 3/3/92

	3yr Annual	5yr Annual	10yr Annual	Bull	Bear
Return (%)	na	na	na	na	-18.6
Differ from Category (+/-)	na	na	na	na	-12.2 low

Total Risk	Standard Deviation	Category Risk	Risk Index	Avg Mat
na	na	na	na	14.7 yrs

	1994	1993	1992	1991	1990	1989	1988	1987	1986	1985
Return (%).	-25.6	8.1	—	—	—	—	—	—	—	—
Differ from category (+/-) .	-20.8	-2.8	—	—	—	—	—	—	—	—

PER SHARE DATA

	1994	1993	1992	1991	1990	1989	1988	1987	1986	1985
Dividends, Net Income ($).	0.14	0.16	—	—	—	—	—	—	—	—
Distrib'ns, Cap Gain ($) . . .	0.00	0.01	—	—	—	—	—	—	—	—
Net Asset Value ($)	1.37	2.01	—	—	—	—	—	—	—	—
Expense Ratio (%)	2.12	1.44	—	—	—	—	—	—	—	—
Net Income to Assets (%) .	9.27	7.85	—	—	—	—	—	—	—	—
Portfolio Turnover (%)	na	90	—	—	—	—	—	—	—	—
Total Assets (Millions $).	19	62	—	—	—	—	—	—	—	—

PORTFOLIO (as of 6/30/94)

Portfolio Manager: committee

Investm't Category: Government Bond

Cap Gain	Asset Allocation
Cap & Income	Fund of Funds
✔ Income	Index
	Sector
✔ Domestic	Small Cap
Foreign	Socially Conscious
Country/Region	State Specific

Portfolio: stocks 0% bonds 100%
convertibles 0% other 0% cash 0%

Largest Holdings: U.S. government & agencies 78%, mortgage-backed 22%

Unrealized Net Capital Gains: -44% of portfolio value

SHAREHOLDER INFORMATION

Minimum Investment
Initial: $2,500 Subsequent: $100

Minimum IRA Investment
Initial: $2,000 Subsequent: $100

Maximum Fees
Load: none 12b-1: 0.25%
Other: none

Distributions
Income: monthly Capital Gains: Dec

Exchange Options
Number Per Year: no limit Fee: none
Telephone: yes (money market fund available)

Services
IRA, pension, auto invest, auto withdraw

Gabelli Asset (GABAX)

Growth

One Corporate Center
Rye, NY 10580
(800) 422-3554, (914) 921-5100

fund inception date: 3/3/86

PERFORMANCE

	3yr Annual	5yr Annual	10yr Annual	Bull	Bear
Return (%)	11.8	9.4	na	83.1	-6.5
Differ from Category (+/-)	4.1 abv av	-0.2 av	na	-9.0 av	0.1 av

Total Risk	Standard Deviation	Category Risk	Risk Index	Beta
av	7.6%	low	0.8	0.8

	1994	1993	1992	1991	1990	1989	1988	1987	1986	1985
Return (%)	-0.1	21.8	14.8	18.1	-4.9	26.1	31.1	16.1	—	—
Differ from category (+/-)	0.5	8.4	3.2	-17.6	0.8	0.0	13.1	14.3	—	—

PER SHARE DATA

	1994	1993	1992	1991	1990	1989	1988	1987	1986	1985
Dividends, Net Income ($)	0.26	0.17	0.25	0.39	0.77	0.56	0.38	0.09	—	—
Distrib'ns, Cap Gain ($)	0.79	0.76	0.50	0.12	0.00	0.72	1.23	0.41	—	—
Net Asset Value ($)	22.21	23.30	19.88	17.96	15.63	17.26	14.69	12.61	—	—
Expense Ratio (%)	1.33	1.31	1.31	1.30	1.20	1.26	1.31	1.26	—	—
Net Income to Assets (%)	0.94	0.82	1.42	2.34	4.51	4.17	2.04	1.19	—	—
Portfolio Turnover (%)	na	16	14	20	56	49	47	90	—	—
Total Assets (Millions $)	981	948	633	484	343	360	143	77	—	—

PORTFOLIO (as of 9/30/94)

Portfolio Manager: Mario J. Gabelli - 1986

Investm't Category: Growth

✔ Cap Gain	Asset Allocation
Cap & Income	Fund of Funds
Income	Index
	Sector
✔ Domestic	Small Cap
✔ Foreign	Socially Conscious
Country/Region	State Specific

Portfolio: stocks 80%   bonds 1%
convertibles 3%   other 0%   cash 16%

Largest Holdings: consumer products & services 10%, industrial equipment & supplies 10%

Unrealized Net Capital Gains: 16% of portfolio value

SHAREHOLDER INFORMATION

Minimum Investment
Initial: $1,000   Subsequent: $0

Minimum IRA Investment
Initial: $1,000   Subsequent: $0

Maximum Fees
Load: none   12b-1: 0.25%
Other: none

Distributions
Income: Dec   Capital Gains: Dec

Exchange Options
Number Per Year: no limit   Fee: none
Telephone: yes (money market fund available)

Services
IRA, pension, auto invest, auto withdraw

Gabelli Growth (GABGX)

Growth

One Corporate Center
Rye, NY 10580
(800) 422-3554, (914) 921-5100

	3yr Annual	5yr Annual	10yr Annual	Bull	Bear
Return (%)	3.9	8.1	na	68.3	-10.0
Differ from Category (+/-)	-3.8 low	-1.5 blw av	na	-23.8 blw av	-3.4 low

Total Risk	Standard Deviation	Category Risk	Risk Index	Beta
abv av	9.2%	av	0.9	1.0

	1994	1993	1992	1991	1990	1989	1988	1987	1986	1985
Return (%)	-3.3	11.2	4.4	34.3	-1.9	40.1	39.1	—	—	—
Differ from category (+/-)	-2.7	-2.2	-7.2	-1.4	3.8	14.0	21.1	—	—	—

PER SHARE DATA

	1994	1993	1992	1991	1990	1989	1988	1987	1986	1985
Dividends, Net Income ($)	0.09	0.09	0.09	0.15	0.39	0.17	0.20	—	—	—
Distrib'ns, Cap Gain ($)	2.70	0.67	0.56	0.42	0.07	0.48	0.33	—	—	—
Net Asset Value ($)	19.68	23.26	21.59	21.28	16.27	17.07	12.65	—	—	—
Expense Ratio (%)	1.41	1.41	1.41	1.45	1.50	1.85	2.30	—	—	—
Net Income to Assets (%)	0.17	0.22	0.46	0.97	2.67	2.24	0.72	—	—	—
Portfolio Turnover (%)	na	80	46	50	75	48	82	—	—	—
Total Assets (Millions $)	483	696	625	423	203	113	12	—	—	—

PORTFOLIO (as of 6/30/94)

Portfolio Manager: Mario J. Gabelli - 1994

Investm't Category: Growth

✔ Cap Gain	Asset Allocation
Cap & Income	Fund of Funds
Income	Index
	Sector
✔ Domestic	Small Cap
✔ Foreign	Socially Conscious
Country/Region	State Specific

Portfolio: stocks 98%   bonds 0%
convertibles 1%   other 1%   cash 0%

Largest Holdings: telecommunications 11%, industrial equipment & supplies 10%

Unrealized Net Capital Gains: 10% of portfolio value

SHAREHOLDER INFORMATION

Minimum Investment
Initial: $1,000   Subsequent: $0

Minimum IRA Investment
Initial: $1,000   Subsequent: $0

Maximum Fees
Load: none   12b-1: 0.25%
Other: none

Distributions
Income: Dec   Capital Gains: Dec

Exchange Options
Number Per Year: no limit   Fee: none
Telephone: yes (money market fund available)

Services
IRA, pension, auto invest, auto withdraw

Galaxy Asset Allocation
(GAAAX)
Balanced

440 Lincoln St.
Worcester, MA 01653
(800) 628-0414

PERFORMANCE · fund inception date: 12/30/91

	3yr Annual	5yr Annual	10yr Annual	Bull	Bear
Return (%)	3.9	na	na	na	-7.1
Differ from Category (+/-)	-2.5 low	na	na	na	-1.4 blw av

Total Risk	Standard Deviation	Category Risk	Risk Index	Beta
blw av	5.5%	blw av	0.9	0.6

	1994	1993	1992	1991	1990	1989	1988	1987	1986	1985
Return (%)	-2.4	8.0	6.5	—	—	—	—	—	—	—
Differ from category (+/-) . .	-0.5	-5.4	-1.8	—	—	—	—	—	—	—

PER SHARE DATA

	1994	1993	1992	1991	1990	1989	1988	1987	1986	1985
Dividends, Net Income ($) .	0.29	0.25	0.20	—	—	—	—	—	—	—
Distrib'ns, Cap Gain ($) . . .	0.00	0.00	0.00	—	—	—	—	—	—	—
Net Asset Value ($)	10.48	11.04	10.45	—	—	—	—	—	—	—
Expense Ratio (%)	1.18	1.14	1.11	—	—	—	—	—	—	—
Net Income to Assets (%). .	2.47	2.59	2.80	—	—	—	—	—	—	—
Portfolio Turnover (%).	na	7	2	—	—	—	—	—	—	—
Total Assets (Millions $)	67	112	11	—	—	—	—	—	—	—

PORTFOLIO (as of 4/30/94)

Portfolio Manager: Fred E. Thompson - 1991

Investm't Category: Balanced

Cap Gain	✔ Asset Allocation
✔ Cap & Income	Fund of Funds
Income	Index
	Sector
✔ Domestic	Small Cap
✔ Foreign	Socially Conscious
Country/Region	State Specific

Portfolio: stocks 58% bonds 30%
convertibles 0% other 2% cash 10%

Largest Holdings: bonds—U. S. gov't and agencies 26%, stocks—consumer staples 12%

Unrealized Net Capital Gains: 0% of portfolio value

SHAREHOLDER INFORMATION

Minimum Investment
Initial: $2,500 Subsequent: $100

Minimum IRA Investment
Initial: $500 Subsequent: $100

Maximum Fees
Load: none 12b-1: 0.25%
Other: none

Distributions
Income: quarterly Capital Gains: Dec

Exchange Options
Number Per Year: 3 Fee: none
Telephone: yes (money market fund available)

Services
IRA, pension, auto invest, auto withdraw

Galaxy Connecticut Municipal Bond (GACTX)

440 Lincoln St.
Worcester, MA 01653
(800) 628-0414

Tax-Exempt Bond

PERFORMANCE

fund inception date: 3/16/93

	3yr Annual	5yr Annual	10yr Annual	Bull	Bear
Return (%)	na	na	na	na	-7.0
Differ from Category (+/-)	na	na	na	na	-1.8 low

Total Risk	Standard Deviation	Category Risk	Risk Index	Avg Mat
na	na	na	na	12.6 yrs

	1994	1993	1992	1991	1990	1989	1988	1987	1986	1985
Return (%)	-8.0	—	—	—	—	—	—	—	—	—
Differ from category (+/-) ..	-2.8	—	—	—	—	—	—	—	—	—

PER SHARE DATA

	1994	1993	1992	1991	1990	1989	1988	1987	1986	1985
Dividends, Net Income ($) .	0.46	—	—	—	—	—	—	—	—	—
Distrib'ns, Cap Gain ($)	0.00	—	—	—	—	—	—	—	—	—
Net Asset Value ($)	9.11	—	—	—	—	—	—	—	—	—
Expense Ratio (%)	0.05	—	—	—	—	—	—	—	—	—
Net Income to Assets (%) ..	4.66	—	—	—	—	—	—	—	—	—
Portfolio Turnover (%)	na	—	—	—	—	—	—	—	—	—
Total Assets (Millions $)	16	—	—	—	—	—	—	—	—	—

PORTFOLIO (as of 4/30/94)

Portfolio Manager: Steve Woodruf - 1993

Investm't Category: Tax-Exempt Bond

Cap Gain	Asset Allocation
Cap & Income	Fund of Funds
✔ Income	Index
	Sector
✔ Domestic	Small Cap
Foreign	Socially Conscious
Country/Region	✔ State Specific

Portfolio: stocks 0% bonds 94%
convertibles 0% other 0% cash 6%

Largest Holdings: na

Unrealized Net Capital Gains: -5% of portfolio value

SHAREHOLDER INFORMATION

Minimum Investment
Initial: $2,500   Subsequent: $100

Minimum IRA Investment
Initial: na   Subsequent: na

Maximum Fees
Load: none   12b-1: 0.25%
Other: none

Distributions
Income: monthly   Capital Gains: Dec

Exchange Options
Number Per Year: 3   Fee: none
Telephone: yes (money market fund available)

Services
auto invest, auto withdraw

Galaxy Equity Growth

(GAEGX)

Growth

440 Lincoln St.
Worcester, MA 01653
(800) 628-0414

PERFORMANCE

fund inception date: 12/4/90

	3yr Annual	5yr Annual	10yr Annual	Bull	Bear
Return (%)	4.0	na	na	na	-6.3
Differ from Category (+/-)	-3.7 low	na	na	na	0.3 av

Total Risk	Standard Deviation	Category Risk	Risk Index	Beta
av	7.5%	low	0.8	0.9

	1994	1993	1992	1991	1990	1989	1988	1987	1986	1985
Return (%)	0.6	5.3	6.1	30.3	—	—	—	—	—	—
Differ from category (+/-) . . .	1.2	-8.1	-5.5	-5.4	—	—	—	—	—	—

PER SHARE DATA

	1994	1993	1992	1991	1990	1989	1988	1987	1986	1985
Dividends, Net Income ($) .	0.17	0.17	0.16	0.20	—	—	—	—	—	—
Distrib'ns, Cap Gain ($) . . .	0.17	0.15	0.00	0.00	—	—	—	—	—	—
Net Asset Value ($)	13.62	13.87	13.47	12.85	—	—	—	—	—	—
Expense Ratio (%)	0.90	0.97	0.95	0.83	—	—	—	—	—	—
Net Income to Assets (%). .	1.26	1.20	1.37	1.46	—	—	—	—	—	—
Portfolio Turnover (%).	na	16	22	16	—	—	—	—	—	—
Total Assets (Millions $)	68	435	225	92	—	—	—	—	—	—

PORTFOLIO (as of 4/30/94)

Portfolio Manager: Robert G. Armknecht - 1990

Investm't Category: Growth

✔ Cap Gain	Asset Allocation
Cap & Income	Fund of Funds
Income	Index
	Sector
✔ Domestic	Small Cap
✔ Foreign	Socially Conscious
Country/Region	State Specific

Portfolio: stocks 87% bonds 0%
convertibles 0% other 0% cash 13%

Largest Holdings: consumer staples 21%, technology 14%

Unrealized Net Capital Gains: 9% of portfolio value

SHAREHOLDER INFORMATION

Minimum Investment
Initial: $2,500   Subsequent: $100

Minimum IRA Investment
Initial: $500   Subsequent: $100

Maximum Fees
Load: none   12b-1: 0.25%
Other: none

Distributions
Income: quarterly   Capital Gains: Dec

Exchange Options
Number Per Year: 3   Fee: none
Telephone: yes (money market fund available)

Services
IRA, pension, auto invest, auto withdraw

Galaxy Equity Income
(GAEIX)
Growth & Income

440 Lincoln St.
Worcester, MA 01653
(800) 628-0414

PERFORMANCE

fund inception date: 12/14/90

	3yr Annual	5yr Annual	10yr Annual	Bull	Bear
Return (%)	5.3	na	na	na	-4.0
Differ from Category (+/-)	-1.8 blw av	na	na	na	2.3 high

Total Risk	Standard Deviation	Category Risk	Risk Index	Beta
blw av	6.1%	low	0.7	0.7

	1994	1993	1992	1991	1990	1989	1988	1987	1986	1985
Return (%)	0.7	8.0	7.4	22.3	—	—	—	—	—	—
Differ from category (+/-)	2.1	-5.2	-2.8	-5.3	—	—	—	—	—	—

PER SHARE DATA

	1994	1993	1992	1991	1990	1989	1988	1987	1986	1985
Dividends, Net Income ($)	0.30	0.30	0.28	0.35	—	—	—	—	—	—
Distrib'ns, Cap Gain ($)	0.21	0.25	0.04	0.20	—	—	—	—	—	—
Net Asset Value ($)	12.17	12.58	12.16	11.63	—	—	—	—	—	—
Expense Ratio (%)	1.03	1.16	1.03	0.85	—	—	—	—	—	—
Net Income to Assets (%)	2.48	2.34	2.84	2.72	—	—	—	—	—	—
Portfolio Turnover (%)	na	27	18	77	—	—	—	—	—	—
Total Assets (Millions $)	60	129	21	7	—	—	—	—	—	—

PORTFOLIO (as of 4/30/94)

Portfolio Manager: J. Edward Klisiewicz - 1990

Investm't Category: Growth & Income
- Cap Gain
- ✔ Cap & Income
- Income
- ✔ Domestic
- ✔ Foreign
- Country/Region
- Asset Allocation
- Fund of Funds
- Index
- Sector
- Small Cap
- Socially Conscious
- State Specific

Portfolio: stocks 88% bonds 4%
convertibles 0% other 1% cash 7%

Largest Holdings: consumer staples 20%, consumer cyclicals 12%

Unrealized Net Capital Gains: 3% of portfolio value

SHAREHOLDER INFORMATION

Minimum Investment
Initial: $2,500   Subsequent: $100

Minimum IRA Investment
Initial: $500   Subsequent: $100

Maximum Fees
Load: none   12b-1: 0.25%
Other: none

Distributions
Income: quarterly   Capital Gains: Dec

Exchange Options
Number Per Year: 3   Fee: none
Telephone: yes (money market fund available)

Services
IRA, pension, auto invest, auto withdraw

Galaxy Equity Value
(GALEX)
Growth & Income

440 Lincoln St.
Worcester, MA 01653
(800) 628-0414

	3yr Annual	5yr Annual	10yr Annual	Bull	Bear
Return (%)	8.7	8.9	na	71.0	-5.4
Differ from Category (+/-)	1.6 abv av	1.0 abv av	na	-4.8 blw av	0.9 abv av

Total Risk	Standard Deviation	Category Risk	Risk Index	Beta
av	7.6%	blw av	0.9	0.8

	1994	1993	1992	1991	1990	1989	1988	1987	1986	1985
Return (%)	3.5	14.7	8.2	23.3	-3.1	16.9	—	—	—	—
Differ from category (+/-)	4.9	1.5	-2.0	-4.3	2.9	-4.5	—	—	—	—

PER SHARE DATA

	1994	1993	1992	1991	1990	1989	1988	1987	1986	1985
Dividends, Net Income ($)	0.19	0.18	0.24	0.37	0.39	0.38	—	—	—	—
Distrib'ns, Cap Gain ($)	1.21	0.28	0.42	0.43	0.34	0.70	—	—	—	—
Net Asset Value ($)	11.88	12.84	11.60	11.35	9.90	10.98	—	—	—	—
Expense Ratio (%)	1.03	0.97	0.94	0.94	0.95	0.97	—	—	—	—
Net Income to Assets (%)	1.29	1.52	2.24	3.25	3.66	3.25	—	—	—	—
Portfolio Turnover (%)	na	50	136	40	94	44	—	—	—	—
Total Assets (Millions $)	73	190	134	100	93	92	—	—	—	—

PORTFOLIO (as of 4/30/94)

Portfolio Manager: G. Jay Evans - 1992

Investm't Category: Growth & Income

Cap Gain	Asset Allocation
✔ Cap & Income	Fund of Funds
Income	Index
	Sector
✔ Domestic	Small Cap
✔ Foreign	Socially Conscious
Country/Region	State Specific

Portfolio: stocks 86%   bonds 0%
convertibles 0%   other 0%   cash 14%

Largest Holdings: technology 17%, consumer cyclicals 15%

Unrealized Net Capital Gains: 6% of portfolio value

SHAREHOLDER INFORMATION

Minimum Investment
Initial: $2,500   Subsequent: $100

Minimum IRA Investment
Initial: $500   Subsequent: $100

Maximum Fees
Load: none   12b-1: 0.25%
Other: none

Distributions
Income: quarterly   Capital Gains: Dec

Exchange Options
Number Per Year: 3   Fee: none
Telephone: yes (money market fund available)

Services
IRA, pension, auto invest, auto withdraw

Galaxy High Quality Bond (GAHQX)

440 Lincoln St.
Worcester, MA 01653
(800) 628-0414

General Bond

fund inception date: 12/14/90

	3yr Annual	5yr Annual	10yr Annual	Bull	Bear
Return (%)	4.0	na	na	na	-7.7
Differ from Category (+/-)	-0.3 blw av	na	na	na	-3.9 low

Total Risk	Standard Deviation	Category Risk	Risk Index	Avg Mat
blw av	5.6%	high	1.4	14.0 yrs

	1994	1993	1992	1991	1990	1989	1988	1987	1986	1985
Return (%)	-6.4	12.8	6.7	15.1	—	—	—	—	—	—
Differ from category (+/-) ..	-4.4	3.6	0.1	0.5	—	—	—	—	—	—

PER SHARE DATA

	1994	1993	1992	1991	1990	1989	1988	1987	1986	1985
Dividends, Net Income ($) .	0.65	0.65	0.69	0.71	—	—	—	—	—	—
Distrib'ns, Cap Gain ($)....	0.00	0.27	0.16	0.08	—	—	—	—	—	—
Net Asset Value ($).......	9.55	10.89	10.49	10.65	—	—	—	—	—	—
Expense Ratio (%)........	0.78	0.76	0.87	0.95	—	—	—	—	—	—
Net Income to Assets (%) ..	5.81	5.98	6.55	7.25	—	—	—	—	—	—
Portfolio Turnover (%)	na	128	121	145	—	—	—	—	—	—
Total Assets (Millions $)	25	161	109	58	—	—	—	—	—	—

PORTFOLIO (as of 4/30/94)

Portfolio Manager: Kenneth W. Thomae - 1990

Investm't Category: General Bond
Cap Gain	Asset Allocation
Cap & Income	Fund of Funds
✔ Income	Index
	Sector
✔ Domestic	Small Cap
Foreign	Socially Conscious
Country/Region	State Specific

Portfolio: stocks 0%   bonds 98%
convertibles 0%   other 0%   cash 2%

Largest Holdings: U. S. government & agencies 74%, corporate 20%

Unrealized Net Capital Gains: -3% of portfolio value

SHAREHOLDER INFORMATION

Minimum Investment
Initial: $2,500   Subsequent: $100

Minimum IRA Investment
Initial: $500   Subsequent: $100

Maximum Fees
Load: none   12b-1: 0.25%
Other: none

Distributions
Income: monthly   Capital Gains: Dec

Exchange Options
Number Per Year: 3   Fee: none
Telephone: yes (money market fund available)

Services
IRA, pension, auto invest, auto withdraw

Galaxy II Large Company Index—Retail (ILCIX)

440 Lincoln St.
Worcester, MA 01653
(800) 628-0414

Growth & Income

PERFORMANCE

fund inception date: 10/1/90

	3yr Annual	5yr Annual	10yr Annual	Bull	Bear
Return (%)	5.8	na	na	na	-6.6
Differ from Category (+/-)	-1.3 blw av	na	na	na	-0.3 av

Total Risk	Standard Deviation	Category Risk	Risk Index	Beta
av	7.9%	av	1.0	1.0

	1994	1993	1992	1991	1990	1989	1988	1987	1986	1985
Return (%)	0.9	9.6	7.0	29.0	—	—	—	—	—	—
Differ from category (+/-) . . .	2.3	-3.6	-3.2	1.4	—	—	—	—	—	—

PER SHARE DATA

	1994	1993	1992	1991	1990	1989	1988	1987	1986	1985
Dividends, Net Income ($) .	0.37	0.36	0.32	0.32	—	—	—	—	—	—
Distrib'ns, Cap Gain ($) . . .	0.33	0.03	0.00	0.01	—	—	—	—	—	—
Net Asset Value ($)	14.46	15.02	14.06	13.45	—	—	—	—	—	—
Expense Ratio (%)	0.40	0.40	0.40	0.40	—	—	—	—	—	—
Net Income to Assets (%). .	2.41	2.57	2.79	3.45	—	—	—	—	—	—
Portfolio Turnover (%)	3	0	0	0	—	—	—	—	—	—
Total Assets (Millions $) . . .	137	133	87	17	—	—	—	—	—	—

PORTFOLIO (as of 3/31/94)

Portfolio Manager: Jay Evans - 1994

Investm't Category: Growth & Income
Cap Gain	Asset Allocation
✔ Cap & Income	Fund of Funds
Income	✔ Index
	Sector
✔ Domestic	Small Cap
Foreign	Socially Conscious
Country/Region	State Specific

Portfolio: stocks 94%   bonds 0%
convertibles 0%   other 0%   cash 6%

Largest Holdings: S&P 500 composite stock price index

Unrealized Net Capital Gains: 10% of portfolio value

SHAREHOLDER INFORMATION

Minimum Investment
Initial: $2,500   Subsequent: $100

Minimum IRA Investment
Initial: $500   Subsequent: $100

Maximum Fees
Load: none   12b-1: none
Other: none

Distributions
Income: quarterly   Capital Gains: Dec

Exchange Options
Number Per Year: 3   Fee: none
Telephone: yes (money market fund available)

Services
IRA, pension, auto invest, auto withdraw

Galaxy II Small Company Index—Retail (ISCIX)

440 Lincoln St.
Worcester, MA 01653
(800) 628-0414

Growth

PERFORMANCE

fund inception date: 10/1/90

	3yr Annual	5yr Annual	10yr Annual	Bull	Bear
Return (%)	6.3	na	na	na	-9.2
Differ from Category (+/-)	-1.4 blw av	na	na	na	-2.6 blw av

Total Risk	Standard Deviation	Category Risk	Risk Index	Beta
abv av	9.5%	av	1.0	0.9

	1994	1993	1992	1991	1990	1989	1988	1987	1986	1985
Return (%)	-3.6	11.3	12.2	45.6	—	—	—	—	—	—
Differ from category (+/-) . .	-3.0	-2.1	0.6	9.9	—	—	—	—	—	—

PER SHARE DATA

	1994	1993	1992	1991	1990	1989	1988	1987	1986	1985
Dividends, Net Income ($) .	0.27	0.24	0.24	0.09	—	—	—	—	—	—
Distrib'ns, Cap Gain ($)	0.83	0.33	0.06	0.22	—	—	—	—	—	—
Net Asset Value ($)	16.38	18.16	16.84	15.27	—	—	—	—	—	—
Expense Ratio (%)	0.40	0.40	0.40	0.40	—	—	—	—	—	—
Net Income to Assets (%) . .	1.55	1.80	2.26	2.98	—	—	—	—	—	—
Portfolio Turnover (%)	17	4	6	—	—	—	—	—	—	—
Total Assets (Millions $) . . .	230	213	116	16	—	—	—	—	—	—

PORTFOLIO (as of 3/31/94)

Portfolio Manager: Jay Evans - 1994

Investm't Category: Growth
- ✔ Cap Gain
- Cap & Income
- Income
- Asset Allocation
- Fund of Funds
- ✔ Index
- Sector
- ✔ Domestic
- Foreign
- Country/Region
- ✔ Small Cap
- Socially Conscious
- State Specific

Portfolio: stocks 94%   bonds 0%
convertibles 0%   other 0%   cash 6%

Largest Holdings: Small stock index

Unrealized Net Capital Gains: 10% of portfolio value

SHAREHOLDER INFORMATION

Minimum Investment
Initial: $2,500   Subsequent: $100

Minimum IRA Investment
Initial: $500   Subsequent: $100

Maximum Fees
Load: none   12b-1: none
Other: none

Distributions
Income: Dec   Capital Gains: Dec

Exchange Options
Number Per Year: 3   Fee: none
Telephone: yes (money market fund available)

Services
IRA, pension, auto invest, auto withdraw

Galaxy II U.S. Treasury Index—Retail (IUTIX)

440 Lincoln St.
Worcester, MA 01653
(800) 628-0414

Government Bond

PERFORMANCE

fund inception date: 6/4/91

	3yr Annual	5yr Annual	10yr Annual	Bull	Bear
Return (%)	4.2	na	na	na	-5.5
Differ from Category (+/-)	0.2 abv av	na	na	na	0.9 av

Total Risk	Standard Deviation	Category Risk	Risk Index	Avg Mat
low	4.3%	av	0.9	8.1 yrs

	1994	1993	1992	1991	1990	1989	1988	1987	1986	1985
Return (%)	-3.6	10.2	6.7	—	—	—	—	—	—	—
Differ from category (+/-)	1.2	-0.7	0.3	—	—	—	—	—	—	—

PER SHARE DATA

	1994	1993	1992	1991	1990	1989	1988	1987	1986	1985
Dividends, Net Income ($)	0.62	0.59	0.63	—	—	—	—	—	—	—
Distrib'ns, Cap Gain ($)	0.18	0.34	0.13	—	—	—	—	—	—	—
Net Asset Value ($)	9.63	10.83	10.68	—	—	—	—	—	—	—
Expense Ratio (%)	0.40	0.40	0.40	—	—	—	—	—	—	—
Net Income to Assets (%)	5.21	5.87	6.40	—	—	—	—	—	—	—
Portfolio Turnover (%)	74	34	56	—	—	—	—	—	—	—
Total Assets (Millions $)	104	145	102	—	—	—	—	—	—	—

PORTFOLIO (as of 3/31/94)

Portfolio Manager: Jay Evans - 1994

Investm't Category: Government Bond
Cap Gain	Asset Allocation
Cap & Income	Fund of Funds
✔ Income	✔ Index
	Sector
✔ Domestic	Small Cap
Foreign	Socially Conscious
Country/Region	State Specific

Portfolio: stocks 0% bonds 100%
convertibles 0% other 0% cash 0%

Largest Holdings: U.S. Treasury index

Unrealized Net Capital Gains: 0% of portfolio value

SHAREHOLDER INFORMATION

Minimum Investment
Initial: $25,000   Subsequent: $100

Minimum IRA Investment
Initial: $500   Subsequent: $100

Maximum Fees
Load: none   12b-1: none
Other: none

Distributions
Income: monthly   Capital Gains: Dec

Exchange Options
Number Per Year: 3   Fee: none
Telephone: yes (money market fund available)

Services
IRA, pension, auto invest, auto withdraw

Galaxy II Utility Index—Retail (IUTLX)

Growth & Income

440 Lincoln St.
Worcester, MA 01653
(800) 628-0414

fund inception date: 1/5/93

	3yr Annual	5yr Annual	10yr Annual	Bull	Bear
Return (%)	na	na	na	na	-8.8
Differ from Category (+/-)	na	na	na	na	-2.5 low

Total Risk	Standard Deviation	Category Risk	Risk Index	Beta
na	na	na	na	na

	1994	1993	1992	1991	1990	1989	1988	1987	1986	1985
Return (%)	-8.6	—	—	—	—	—	—	—	—	—
Differ from category (+/-)	-7.2	—	—	—	—	—	—	—	—	—

PER SHARE DATA

	1994	1993	1992	1991	1990	1989	1988	1987	1986	1985
Dividends, Net Income ($)	0.59	—	—	—	—	—	—	—	—	—
Distrib'ns, Cap Gain ($)	0.00	—	—	—	—	—	—	—	—	—
Net Asset Value ($)	9.43	—	—	—	—	—	—	—	—	—
Expense Ratio (%)	0.40	—	—	—	—	—	—	—	—	—
Net Income to Assets (%)	4.08	—	—	—	—	—	—	—	—	—
Portfolio Turnover (%)	19	—	—	—	—	—	—	—	—	—
Total Assets (Millions $)	53	—	—	—	—	—	—	—	—	—

PORTFOLIO (as of 3/31/94)

Portfolio Manager: Jay Evans - 1994

Investm't Category: Growth & Income
Cap Gain	Asset Allocation
✔ Cap & Income	Fund of Funds
Income	✔ Index
	✔ Sector
✔ Domestic	Small Cap
Foreign	Socially Conscious
Country/Region	State Specific

Portfolio: stocks 97% bonds 0%
convertibles 0% other 0% cash 3%

Largest Holdings: Utility index

Unrealized Net Capital Gains: -10% of portfolio value

SHAREHOLDER INFORMATION

Minimum Investment
Initial: $2,500   Subsequent: $100

Minimum IRA Investment
Initial: $500   Subsequent: $100

Maximum Fees
Load: none   12b-1: none
Other: none

Distributions
Income: quarterly   Capital Gains: Dec

Exchange Options
Number Per Year: 3   Fee: none
Telephone: yes (money market fund available)

Services
IRA, pension, auto invest, auto withdraw

Galaxy Interm Bond
(GALBX)
General Bond

440 Lincoln St.
Worcester, MA 01653
(800) 628-0414

	3yr Annual	5yr Annual	10yr Annual	Bull	Bear
Return (%)	2.8	5.9	na	38.7	-5.8
Differ from Category (+/-)	-1.5 low	-1.0 low	na	-2.3 av	-2.0 low

Total Risk	Standard Deviation	Category Risk	Risk Index	Avg Mat
low	4.5%	abv av	1.1	8.3 yrs

	1994	1993	1992	1991	1990	1989	1988	1987	1986	1985
Return (%)	-3.7	5.4	7.1	15.7	5.8	11.5	—	—	—	—
Differ from category (+/-). .	-1.7	-3.8	0.5	1.1	-1.4	0.1	—	—	—	—

PER SHARE DATA

	1994	1993	1992	1991	1990	1989	1988	1987	1986	1985
Dividends, Net Income ($) .	0.57	0.63	0.69	0.74	0.75	0.84	—	—	—	—
Distrib'ns, Cap Gain ($) . . .	0.00	0.11	0.10	0.00	0.00	0.00	—	—	—	—
Net Asset Value ($)	9.58	10.54	10.70	10.75	9.98	10.17	—	—	—	—
Expense Ratio (%)	0.82	0.80	0.80	0.96	0.98	0.99	—	—	—	—
Net Income to Assets (%). .	5.42	6.03	6.52	7.25	7.69	8.19	—	—	—	—
Portfolio Turnover (%).	na	153	103	150	162	112	—	—	—	—
Total Assets (Millions $)	84	434	199	100	81	71	—	—	—	—

PORTFOLIO (as of 4/30/94)

Portfolio Manager: Bruce R. Barton - 1988

Investm't Category: General Bond

Cap Gain	Asset Allocation
Cap & Income	Fund of Funds
✔ Income	Index
	Sector
✔ Domestic	Small Cap
Foreign	Socially Conscious
Country/Region	State Specific

Portfolio: stocks 0%   bonds 95%
convertibles 0%   other 0%   cash 5%

Largest Holdings: mortgage-backed 46%, corporate 34%

Unrealized Net Capital Gains: -3% of portfolio value

SHAREHOLDER INFORMATION

Minimum Investment
Initial: $2,500   Subsequent: $100

Minimum IRA Investment
Initial: $500   Subsequent: $100

Maximum Fees
Load: none   12b-1: 0.25%
Other: none

Distributions
Income: monthly   Capital Gains: Dec

Exchange Options
Number Per Year: 3   Fee: none
Telephone: yes (money market fund available)

Services
IRA, pension, auto invest, auto withdraw

Galaxy International Equity (GAIEX)

International Stock

440 Lincoln St.
Worcester, MA 01653
(800) 628-0414

PERFORMANCE

fund inception date: 12/30/91

	3yr Annual	5yr Annual	10yr Annual	Bull	Bear
Return (%)	7.8	na	na	na	-5.0
Differ from Category (+/-)	-1.3 blw av	na	na	na	2.0 abv av

Total Risk	Standard Deviation	Category Risk	Risk Index	Beta
abv av	11.4%	low	0.9	0.7

	1994	1993	1992	1991	1990	1989	1988	1987	1986	1985
Return (%)	-2.5	31.6	-2.2	—	—	—	—	—	—	—
Differ from category (+/-)	0.5	-7.0	0.7	—	—	—	—	—	—	—

PER SHARE DATA

	1994	1993	1992	1991	1990	1989	1988	1987	1986	1985
Dividends, Net Income ($)	0.02	0.01	0.06	—	—	—	—	—	—	—
Distrib'ns, Cap Gain ($)	0.16	0.00	0.00	—	—	—	—	—	—	—
Net Asset Value ($)	12.26	12.77	9.71	—	—	—	—	—	—	—
Expense Ratio (%)	1.51	1.57	1.61	—	—	—	—	—	—	—
Net Income to Assets (%)	0.48	0.37	1.19	—	—	—	—	—	—	—
Portfolio Turnover (%)	na	29	21	—	—	—	—	—	—	—
Total Assets (Millions $)	32	56	12	—	—	—	—	—	—	—

PORTFOLIO (as of 4/30/94)

Portfolio Manager: Jim Knauf - 1991

Investm't Category: International Stock

✔ Cap Gain	Asset Allocation
Cap & Income	Fund of Funds
Income	Index
	Sector
✔ Domestic	Small Cap
✔ Foreign	Socially Conscious
Country/Region	State Specific

Portfolio: stocks 91% bonds 0%
convertibles 0% other 2% cash 7%

Largest Holdings: Japan 31%, United Kingdom 7%

Unrealized Net Capital Gains: 7% of portfolio value

SHAREHOLDER INFORMATION

Minimum Investment
Initial: $2,500   Subsequent: $100

Minimum IRA Investment
Initial: $500   Subsequent: $100

Maximum Fees
Load: none   12b-1: 0.25%
Other: none

Distributions
Income: Dec   Capital Gains: Dec

Exchange Options
Number Per Year: 3   Fee: none
Telephone: yes (money market fund available)

Services
IRA, pension, auto invest, auto withdraw

Galaxy NY Muni Bond
(GANYX)

Tax-Exempt Bond

440 Lincoln St.
Worcester, MA 01653
(800) 628-0414

PERFORMANCE

fund inception date: 12/30/91

	3yr Annual	5yr Annual	10yr Annual	Bull	Bear
Return (%)	4.0	na	na	na	-6.3
Differ from Category (+/-)	-0.5 blw av	na	na	na	-1.1 blw av

Total Risk	Standard Deviation	Category Risk	Risk Index	Avg Mat
blw av	6.6%	abv av	1.1	14.0 yrs

	1994	1993	1992	1991	1990	1989	1988	1987	1986	1985
Return (%)	-7.2	12.3	8.2	—	—	—	—	—	—	—
Differ from category (+/-) . .	-2.0	0.6	-0.1	—	—	—	—	—	—	—

PER SHARE DATA

	1994	1993	1992	1991	1990	1989	1988	1987	1986	1985
Dividends, Net Income ($) .	0.49	0.49	0.47	—	—	—	—	—	—	—
Distrib'ns, Cap Gain ($) . . .	0.00	0.00	0.00	—	—	—	—	—	—	—
Net Asset Value ($)	9.81	11.10	10.34	—	—	—	—	—	—	—
Expense Ratio (%)	0.90	0.87	0.65	—	—	—	—	—	—	—
Net Income to Assets (%). .	4.42	4.54	5.22	—	—	—	—	—	—	—
Portfolio Turnover (%).	na	3	19	—	—	—	—	—	—	—
Total Assets (Millions $)	39	72	20	—	—	—	—	—	—	—

PORTFOLIO (as of 4/30/94)

Portfolio Manager: Maria C. Schwenzer - 1991

Investm't Category: Tax-Exempt Bond
Cap Gain	Asset Allocation
Cap & Income	Fund of Funds
✔ Income	Index
	Sector
✔ Domestic	Small Cap
Foreign	Socially Conscious
Country/Region	✔ State Specific

Portfolio: stocks 0%   bonds 96%
convertibles 0%   other 0%   cash 4%

Largest Holdings: na

Unrealized Net Capital Gains: -2% of portfolio value

SHAREHOLDER INFORMATION

Minimum Investment
Initial: $2,500   Subsequent: $100

Minimum IRA Investment
Initial: na   Subsequent: na

Maximum Fees
Load: none   12b-1: 0.25%
Other: none

Distributions
Income: monthly   Capital Gains: Dec

Exchange Options
Number Per Year: 3   Fee: none
Telephone: yes (money market fund available)

Services
auto invest, auto withdraw

Galaxy Short Term Bond
(GASTX)
General Bond

440 Lincoln St.
Worcester, MA 01653
(800) 628-0414

PERFORMANCE

fund inception date: 12/31/91

	3yr Annual	5yr Annual	10yr Annual	Bull	Bear
Return (%)	3.9	na	na	na	-2.1
Differ from Category (+/-)	-0.4 blw av	na	na	na	1.7 abv av

Total Risk	Standard Deviation	Category Risk	Risk Index	Avg Mat
low	2.1%	low	0.5	2.3 yrs

	1994	1993	1992	1991	1990	1989	1988	1987	1986	1985
Return (%)	-0.3	6.4	5.8	—	—	—	—	—	—	—
Differ from category (+/-)	1.7	-2.8	-0.8	—	—	—	—	—	—	—

PER SHARE DATA

	1994	1993	1992	1991	1990	1989	1988	1987	1986	1985
Dividends, Net Income ($)	0.45	0.46	0.51	—	—	—	—	—	—	—
Distrib'ns, Cap Gain ($)	0.00	0.06	0.01	—	—	—	—	—	—	—
Net Asset Value ($)	9.68	10.17	10.05	—	—	—	—	—	—	—
Expense Ratio (%)	0.89	0.86	0.90	—	—	—	—	—	—	—
Net Income to Assets (%)	4.32	4.51	5.77	—	—	—	—	—	—	—
Portfolio Turnover (%)	na	100	114	—	—	—	—	—	—	—
Total Assets (Millions $)	30	88	57	—	—	—	—	—	—	—

PORTFOLIO (as of 4/30/94)

Portfolio Manager: Ken Thomae - 1991

Investm't Category: General Bond

Cap Gain	Asset Allocation
Cap & Income	Fund of Funds
✔ Income	Index
	Sector
✔ Domestic	Small Cap
✔ Foreign	Socially Conscious
Country/Region	State Specific

Portfolio: stocks 0%   bonds 97%
convertibles 0%   other 0%   cash 3%

Largest Holdings: U.S. government & agencies 79%, corporate 18%

Unrealized Net Capital Gains: -1% of portfolio value

SHAREHOLDER INFORMATION

Minimum Investment
Initial: $2,500   Subsequent: $100

Minimum IRA Investment
Initial: $500   Subsequent: $100

Maximum Fees
Load: none   12b-1: 0.25%
Other: none

Distributions
Income: monthly   Capital Gains: Dec

Exchange Options
Number Per Year: 3   Fee: none
Telephone: yes (money market fund available)

Services
IRA, pension, auto invest, auto withdraw

Galaxy Small Company Equity (GASEX)

440 Lincoln St.
Worcester, MA 01653
(800) 628-0414

Aggressive Growth

	3yr Annual	5yr Annual	10yr Annual	Bull	Bear
Return (%)	7.4	na	na	na	-13.5
Differ from Category (+/-)	-1.5 av	na	na	na	-2.7 blw av

Total Risk	Standard Deviation	Category Risk	Risk Index	Beta
high	15.3%	abv av	1.0	1.2

	1994	1993	1992	1991	1990	1989	1988	1987	1986	1985
Return (%)	0.0	22.7	1.1	—	—	—	—	—	—	—
Differ from category (+/-)	0.7	3.2	-9.9	—	—	—	—	—	—	—

PER SHARE DATA

	1994	1993	1992	1991	1990	1989	1988	1987	1986	1985
Dividends, Net Income ($)	0.00	0.00	0.00	—	—	—	—	—	—	—
Distrib'ns, Cap Gain ($)	0.19	0.05	0.00	—	—	—	—	—	—	—
Net Asset Value ($)	12.16	12.37	10.12	—	—	—	—	—	—	—
Expense Ratio (%)	1.29	1.18	1.06	—	—	—	—	—	—	—
Net Income to Assets (%)	-0.41	-0.66	-0.63	—	—	—	—	—	—	—
Portfolio Turnover (%)	na	57	87	—	—	—	—	—	—	—
Total Assets (Millions $)	27	65	29	—	—	—	—	—	—	—

PORTFOLIO (as of 4/30/94)

Portfolio Manager: Steve Barbaro - 1991

Investm't Category: Aggressive Growth
- ✔ Cap Gain
- Cap & Income
- Income
- ✔ Domestic
- ✔ Foreign
- Country/Region
- Asset Allocation
- Fund of Funds
- Index
- Sector
- ✔ Small Cap
- Socially Conscious
- State Specific

Portfolio: stocks 75%   bonds 1%
convertibles 0%   other 0%   cash 24%

Largest Holdings: technology 19%, consumer staples 14%

Unrealized Net Capital Gains: 9% of portfolio value

SHAREHOLDER INFORMATION

Minimum Investment
Initial: $2,500   Subsequent: $100

Minimum IRA Investment
Initial: $500   Subsequent: $100

Maximum Fees
Load: none   12b-1: 0.25%
Other: none

Distributions
Income: quarterly   Capital Gains: Dec

Exchange Options
Number Per Year: 3   Fee: none
Telephone: yes (money market fund available)

Services
IRA, pension, auto invest, auto withdraw

Galaxy Tax-Exempt Bond (GABDX)

Tax-Exempt Bond

440 Lincoln St.
Worcester, MA 01653
(800) 628-0414

PERFORMANCE

fund inception date: 12/30/91

	3yr Annual	5yr Annual	10yr Annual	Bull	Bear
Return (%)	4.9	na	na	na	-5.4
Differ from Category (+/-)	0.4 abv av	na	na	na	-0.2 av

Total Risk	Standard Deviation	Category Risk	Risk Index	Avg Mat
blw av	6.1%	av	1.0	11.9 yrs

	1994	1993	1992	1991	1990	1989	1988	1987	1986	1985
Return (%)	-5.3	11.9	9.2	—	—	—	—	—	—	—
Differ from category (+/-)	-0.1	0.2	0.9	—	—	—	—	—	—	—

PER SHARE DATA

	1994	1993	1992	1991	1990	1989	1988	1987	1986	1985
Dividends, Net Income ($)	0.53	0.54	0.44	—	—	—	—	—	—	—
Distrib'ns, Cap Gain ($)	0.00	0.09	0.00	—	—	—	—	—	—	—
Net Asset Value ($)	9.95	11.07	10.47	—	—	—	—	—	—	—
Expense Ratio (%)	0.86	0.64	0.42	—	—	—	—	—	—	—
Net Income to Assets (%)	4.82	5.00	5.03	—	—	—	—	—	—	—
Portfolio Turnover (%)	na	38	11	—	—	—	—	—	—	—
Total Assets (Millions $)	31	145	15	—	—	—	—	—	—	—

PORTFOLIO (as of 4/30/94)

Portfolio Manager: Mary M. McGoldrick - 1991

Investm't Category: Tax-Exempt Bond

Cap Gain	Asset Allocation
Cap & Income	Fund of Funds
✔ Income	Index
	Sector
✔ Domestic	Small Cap
Foreign	Socially Conscious
Country/Region	State Specific

Portfolio: stocks 0% bonds 99%
convertibles 0% other 1% cash 0%

Largest Holdings: na

Unrealized Net Capital Gains: 0% of portfolio value

SHAREHOLDER INFORMATION

Minimum Investment
Initial: $2,500   Subsequent: $100

Minimum IRA Investment
Initial: na   Subsequent: na

Maximum Fees
Load: none   12b-1: 0.25%
Other: none

Distributions
Income: monthly   Capital Gains: Dec

Exchange Options
Number Per Year: 3   Fee: none
Telephone: yes (money market fund available)

Services
auto invest, auto withdraw

Gateway Index Plus
(GATEX)
Growth & Income

400 TechneCenter Dr.
Suite 220
Milford, OH 45150
(800) 354-6339, (513) 248-2700

PERFORMANCE

fund inception date: 12/7/77

	3yr Annual	5yr Annual	10yr Annual	Bull	Bear
Return (%)	6.0	9.1	10.5	47.3	-2.9
Differ from Category (+/-)	-1.1 blw av	1.2 abv av	-1.2 blw av	-28.5 low	3.4 high

Total Risk	Standard Deviation	Category Risk	Risk Index	Beta
low	4.0%	low	0.5	0.4

	1994	1993	1992	1991	1990	1989	1988	1987	1986	1985
Return (%)	5.5	7.4	5.1	17.7	10.1	19.4	19.7	-5.6	12.6	15.9
Differ from category (+/-). . .	6.9	-5.8	-5.1	-9.9	16.1	-2.0	2.7	-6.2	-3.2	-9.8

PER SHARE DATA

	1994	1993	1992	1991	1990	1989	1988	1987	1986	1985
Dividends, Net Income ($) .	0.27	0.29	0.28	0.30	0.41	0.37	0.21	0.33	0.34	0.46
Distrib'ns, Cap Gain ($) . . .	0.97	0.51	0.23	0.51	3.00	0.43	0.00	1.92	1.46	1.22
Net Asset Value ($)	15.48	15.85	15.51	15.24	13.64	15.49	13.67	11.60	14.63	14.69
Expense Ratio (%)	1.22	1.11	1.11	1.22	1.34	1.40	2.08	1.48	1.49	1.50
Net Income to Assets (%). .	1.60	1.58	1.96	2.17	2.59	2.21	1.75	1.83	2.23	2.81
Portfolio Turnover (%).	na	17	15	31	79	30	10	175	85	96
Total Assets (Millions $). . .	164	205	213	81	38	32	27	27	45	28

PORTFOLIO (as of 6/30/94)

Portfolio Manager: Peter Thayer - 1977

Investm't Category: Growth & Income
Cap Gain	Asset Allocation
✔ Cap & Income	Fund of Funds
Income	Index
	Sector
✔ Domestic	Small Cap
Foreign	Socially Conscious
Country/Region	State Specific

Portfolio: stocks 100% bonds 0%
convertibles 0% other 0% cash 0%

Largest Holdings: technology 15%, industrial cyclical 14%

Unrealized Net Capital Gains: 1% of portfolio value

SHAREHOLDER INFORMATION

Minimum Investment
Initial: $1,000   Subsequent: $100

Minimum IRA Investment
Initial: $1,000   Subsequent: $100

Maximum Fees
Load: none   12b-1: none
Other: none

Distributions
Income: quarterly   Capital Gains: Dec

Exchange Options
Number Per Year: no limit   Fee: none
Telephone: yes (money market fund available)

Services
IRA, pension, auto invest, auto withdraw

General CA Muni Bond
(GCABX)
Tax-Exempt Bond

200 Park Ave.
New York, NY 10166
(800) 645-6561, (718) 895-1206

PERFORMANCE   fund inception date: 10/10/89

	3yr Annual	5yr Annual	10yr Annual	Bull	Bear
Return (%)	4.7	6.5	na	44.2	-6.7
Differ from Category (+/-)	0.2 av	0.4 av	na	2.4 av	-1.5 blw av

Total Risk	Standard Deviation	Category Risk	Risk Index	Avg Mat
blw av	6.4%	abv av	1.0	21.4 yrs

	1994	1993	1992	1991	1990	1989	1988	1987	1986	1985
Return (%)	-7.0	13.6	8.6	10.9	7.7	—	—	—	—	—
Differ from category (+/-) . .	-1.8	1.9	0.3	-0.4	1.4	—	—	—	—	—

PER SHARE DATA

	1994	1993	1992	1991	1990	1989	1988	1987	1986	1985
Dividends, Net Income ($)	0.76	0.81	0.84	0.88	0.93	—	—	—	—	—
Distrib'ns, Cap Gain ($)	0.08	0.06	0.08	0.00	0.00	—	—	—	—	—
Net Asset Value ($)	12.36	14.19	13.28	13.11	12.66	—	—	—	—	—
Expense Ratio (%)	0.76	0.64	0.37	0.21	0.00	—	—	—	—	—
Net Income to Assets (%) . .	5.72	5.96	6.47	7.06	7.35	—	—	—	—	—
Portfolio Turnover (%)	29	30	24	3	10	—	—	—	—	—
Total Assets (Millions $) . . .	296	697	374	272	98	—	—	—	—	—

PORTFOLIO (as of 9/30/94)

Portfolio Manager: Paul Disdier - 1989

Investm't Category: Tax-Exempt Bond

Cap Gain	Asset Allocation
Cap & Income	Fund of Funds
✔ Income	Index
	Sector
✔ Domestic	Small Cap
Foreign	Socially Conscious
Country/Region	✔ State Specific

Portfolio: stocks 0%   bonds 100%
convertibles 0%   other 0%   cash 0%

Largest Holdings: general obligation 4% (as of 3/31/94)

Unrealized Net Capital Gains: 0% of portfolio value

SHAREHOLDER INFORMATION

Minimum Investment
Initial: $2,500   Subsequent: $100

Minimum IRA Investment
Initial: na   Subsequent: na

Maximum Fees
Load: none   12b-1: 0.25%
Other: none

Distributions
Income: monthly   Capital Gains: Nov

Exchange Options
Number Per Year: no limit   Fee: none
Telephone: yes (money market fund available)

Services
auto exchange, auto invest, auto withdraw

General Muni Bond

(GMBDX)

Tax-Exempt Bond

200 Park Ave.
New York, NY 10166
(800) 645-6561, (718) 895-1206

PERFORMANCE

fund inception date: 3/21/84

	3yr Annual	5yr Annual	10yr Annual	Bull	Bear
Return (%)	4.8	7.3	9.1	49.7	-6.8
Differ from Category (+/-)	0.3 av	1.2 high	1.0 high	7.9 high	-1.6 blw av

Total Risk	Standard Deviation	Category Risk	Risk Index	Avg Mat
blw av	6.6%	abv av	1.1	20.6 yrs

	1994	1993	1992	1991	1990	1989	1988	1987	1986	1985
Return (%)	-7.3	13.3	9.8	14.6	7.6	11.4	12.5	-5.5	17.1	21.0
Differ from category (+/-) . .	-2.1	1.6	1.5	3.3	1.3	2.4	2.3	-4.2	0.7	3.6

PER SHARE DATA

	1994	1993	1992	1991	1990	1989	1988	1987	1986	1985
Dividends, Net Income ($) .	0.86	0.91	0.99	1.06	1.09	1.01	0.96	0.98	1.07	1.17
Distrib'ns, Cap Gain ($) . . .	0.12	0.23	0.15	0.04	0.00	0.00	0.00	0.25	0.00	0.00
Net Asset Value ($)	13.72	15.84	15.02	14.76	13.90	13.97	13.48	12.87	14.89	13.69
Expense Ratio (%)	0.82	0.41	0.01	0.00	0.28	0.80	0.80	0.77	0.41	0.00
Net Income to Assets (%) . .	5.71	6.46	7.30	7.83	7.58	7.27	7.30	7.22	8.66	9.57
Portfolio Turnover (%)	59	64	38	50	110	218	67	105	87	71
Total Assets (Millions $) . . .	826	1,251	720	309	109	35	37	63	39	5

PORTFOLIO (as of 2/28/94)

Portfolio Manager: Paul Disdier - 1988

Investm't Category: Tax-Exempt Bond

Cap Gain	Asset Allocation
Cap & Income	Fund of Funds
✔ Income	Index
	Sector
✔ Domestic	Small Cap
Foreign	Socially Conscious
Country/Region	State Specific

Portfolio: stocks 0%   bonds 100%
convertibles 0%   other 0%   cash 0%

Largest Holdings: general obligation 6%

Unrealized Net Capital Gains: 6% of portfolio value

SHAREHOLDER INFORMATION

Minimum Investment
Initial: $2,500   Subsequent: $100

Minimum IRA Investment
Initial: na   Subsequent: na

Maximum Fees
Load: none   12b-1: 0.20%
Other: none

Distributions
Income: monthly   Capital Gains: Jun, Nov

Exchange Options
Number Per Year: no limit   Fee: none
Telephone: yes (money market fund available)

Services
auto exchange, auto invest, auto withdraw

General NY Muni Bond

(GNYMX)

Tax-Exempt Bond

200 Park Ave.
New York, NY 10166
(800) 645-6561, (718) 895-1206

	3yr Annual	5yr Annual	10yr Annual	Bull	Bear
Return (%)	5.2	7.2	7.8	50.1	-6.0
Differ from Category (+/-)	0.7 abv av	1.1 high	-0.3 blw av	8.3 high	-0.8 av

Total Risk	Standard Deviation	Category Risk	Risk Index	Avg Mat
blw av	6.5%	abv av	1.0	19.3 yrs

	1994	1993	1992	1991	1990	1989	1988	1987	1986	1985
Return (%)	-7.1	14.0	10.0	14.0	6.6	6.5	5.9	1.3	14.1	14.8
Differ from category (+/-) . .	-1.9	2.3	1.7	2.7	0.3	-2.5	-4.3	2.6	-2.3	-2.6

PER SHARE DATA

	1994	1993	1992	1991	1990	1989	1988	1987	1986	1985
Dividends, Net Income ($) .	1.13	1.15	1.22	1.29	1.36	1.05	1.01	1.04	1.18	1.29
Distrib'ns, Cap Gain ($)	0.12	0.30	0.27	0.00	0.00	0.00	0.00	0.00	0.00	0.00
Net Asset Value ($)	18.40	21.14	19.85	19.44	18.25	18.43	18.31	18.25	19.05	17.77
Expense Ratio (%)	0.73	0.69	0.62	0.36	0.07	1.32	1.10	0.89	0.46	0.21
Net Income to Assets (%) . .	5.54	5.64	6.32	6.95	7.36	5.60	5.49	5.66	6.44	7.47
Portfolio Turnover (%)	na	23	43	19	60	27	32	67	37	31
Total Assets (Millions $) . . .	293	400	284	209	103	38	47	53	56	13

PORTFOLIO (as of 4/30/94)

Portfolio Manager: Monica Wieboldt - 1988

Investm't Category: Tax-Exempt Bond

Cap Gain	Asset Allocation
Cap & Income	Fund of Funds
✔ Income	Index
	Sector
✔ Domestic	Small Cap
Foreign	Socially Conscious
Country/Region	✔ State Specific

Portfolio: stocks 0%   bonds 98%
convertibles 0%   other 0%   cash 2%

Largest Holdings: general obligation 11%

Unrealized Net Capital Gains: 2% of portfolio value

SHAREHOLDER INFORMATION

Minimum Investment
Initial: $2,500   Subsequent: $100

Minimum IRA Investment
Initial: na   Subsequent: na

Maximum Fees
Load: none   12b-1: 0.20%
Other: none

Distributions
Income: monthly   Capital Gains: Dec

Exchange Options
Number Per Year: no limit   Fee: none
Telephone: yes (money market fund available)

Services
auto exchange, auto invest, auto withdraw

Gintel (GINLX)

Growth

6 Greenwich Office Park
Greenwich, CT 06831
(800) 243-5808, (203) 622-6400

PERFORMANCE

fund inception date: 6/10/81

	3yr Annual	5yr Annual	10yr Annual	Bull	Bear
Return (%)	2.0	2.7	8.6	54.7	-17.2
Differ from Category (+/-)	-5.7 low	-6.9 low	-4.3 low	-37.4 low	-10.6 low

Total Risk	Standard Deviation	Category Risk	Risk Index	Beta
high	13.5%	high	1.4	1.1

	1994	1993	1992	1991	1990	1989	1988	1987	1986	1985
Return (%)	-16.4	2.0	24.6	15.5	-6.6	23.8	29.3	-14.1	20.8	20.0
Differ from category (+/-) .	-15.8	-11.4	13.0	-20.2	-0.9	-2.3	11.3	-15.9	6.2	-9.2

PER SHARE DATA

	1994	1993	1992	1991	1990	1989	1988	1987	1986	1985
Dividends, Net Income ($) .	0.05	0.51	0.10	0.31	0.49	1.44	0.00	0.32	0.29	0.32
Distrib'ns, Cap Gain ($) . . .	0.12	1.14	0.25	0.94	0.00	0.00	0.00	1.02	6.15	0.74
Net Asset Value ($)	12.46	15.11	16.45	13.48	12.75	14.18	12.70	9.82	12.71	15.97
Expense Ratio (%)	na	2.20	1.70	1.40	1.50	1.40	1.60	1.30	1.20	1.20
Net Income to Assets (%)	na	-0.30	0.90	1.90	3.10	7.40	2.50	1.30	1.60	2.30
Portfolio Turnover (%)	na	50	56	66	75	65	85	111	77	25
Total Assets (Millions $)	88	138	165	77	79	95	83	121	130	116

PORTFOLIO (as of 6/30/94)

Portfolio Manager: R. Gintel - 1981, C. Godman - 1992

Investm't Category: Growth

✔ Cap Gain	Asset Allocation
Cap & Income	Fund of Funds
Income	Index
	Sector
✔ Domestic	Small Cap
✔ Foreign	Socially Conscious
Country/Region	State Specific

Portfolio: stocks 80% bonds 0%
convertibles 0% other 0% cash 20%

Largest Holdings: mortgage investments 17%, radio frequency electronics 10%

Unrealized Net Capital Gains: 0% of portfolio value

SHAREHOLDER INFORMATION

Minimum Investment
Initial: $5,000   Subsequent: $0

Minimum IRA Investment
Initial: $5,000   Subsequent: $0

Maximum Fees
Load: none   12b-1: none
Other: none

Distributions
Income: Dec   Capital Gains: Dec

Exchange Options
Number Per Year: no limit   Fee: none
Telephone: yes (money market fund available)

Services
IRA, pension, auto invest, auto withdraw

Gintel ERISA (GINTX)

Growth & Income

6 Greenwich Office Park
Greenwich, CT 06831
(800) 243-5808, (203) 622-6400

PERFORMANCE

	3yr Annual	5yr Annual	10yr Annual	Bull	Bear
Return (%)	-1.7	0.4	8.0	43.3	-18.9
Differ from Category (+/-)	-8.8 low	-7.5 low	-3.7 low	-32.5 low	-12.6 low

Total Risk	Standard Deviation	Category Risk	Risk Index	Beta
high	12.7%	high	1.6	1.1

	1994	1993	1992	1991	1990	1989	1988	1987	1986	1985
Return (%)	-21.2	5.3	14.4	13.5	-5.1	15.4	21.9	-0.9	22.3	24.0
Differ from category (+/-)	-19.8	-7.9	4.2	-14.1	0.9	-6.0	4.9	-1.5	6.5	-1.7

PER SHARE DATA

	1994	1993	1992	1991	1990	1989	1988	1987	1986	1985
Dividends, Net Income ($)	0.45	2.27	0.64	0.84	1.36	3.44	0.00	2.00	1.08	1.10
Distrib'ns, Cap Gain ($)	0.00	5.53	0.00	0.91	0.00	5.99	0.00	13.41	1.47	1.88
Net Asset Value ($)	22.70	29.41	35.38	31.49	29.29	32.31	36.34	29.79	45.29	39.48
Expense Ratio (%)	na	2.20	1.70	1.50	1.60	1.30	1.30	1.20	1.30	1.30
Net Income to Assets (%)	na	1.00	1.50	2.40	3.50	5.90	2.50	2.90	1.80	3.00
Portfolio Turnover (%)	na	99	80	97	97	85	100	109	69	100
Total Assets (Millions $)	30	51	56	73	79	86	81	75	89	85

PORTFOLIO (as of 6/30/94)

Portfolio Manager: R. Gintel - 1982, C. Godman - 1992

Investm't Category: Growth & Income

Cap Gain	Asset Allocation
✔ Cap & Income	Fund of Funds
Income	Index
	Sector
✔ Domestic	Small Cap
Foreign	Socially Conscious
Country/Region	State Specific

Portfolio: stocks 88% bonds 0%
convertibles 0% other 0% cash 12%

Largest Holdings: apparel 11%, mortgage investments 11%

Unrealized Net Capital Gains: -3% of portfolio value

SHAREHOLDER INFORMATION

Minimum Investment
Initial: $10,000   Subsequent: $0

Minimum IRA Investment
Initial: $2,000   Subsequent: $0

Maximum Fees
Load: none   12b-1: none
Other: none

Distributions
Income: Dec   Capital Gains: Dec

Exchange Options
Number Per Year: no limit   Fee: none
Telephone: yes (money market fund available)

Services
IRA, pension, auto invest, auto withdraw

GIT Equity—Special Growth (GTSGX)

Aggressive Growth

1655 N. Fort Myer Dr.
Suite 1000
Arlington, VA 22209
(800) 336-3063, (703) 528-6500

PERFORMANCE

fund inception date: 7/21/83

	3yr Annual	5yr Annual	10yr Annual	Bull	Bear
Return (%)	5.5	4.4	12.4	64.5	-3.9
Differ from Category (+/-)	-3.4 blw av	-8.1 low	-1.6 av	-68.7 low	6.9 high

Total Risk	Standard Deviation	Category Risk	Risk Index	Beta
abv av	9.3%	low	0.6	0.6

	1994	1993	1992	1991	1990	1989	1988	1987	1986	1985
Return (%)	-3.9	14.8	6.7	25.7	-15.8	26.3	23.5	-2.0	15.1	47.1
Differ from category (+/-) . .	-3.2	-4.7	-4.3	-26.4	-9.6	-0.5	8.3	0.2	3.3	14.8

PER SHARE DATA

	1994	1993	1992	1991	1990	1989	1988	1987	1986	1985
Dividends, Net Income ($) .	0.10	0.17	0.12	0.21	0.33	0.40	0.11	0.23	0.12	0.09
Distrib'ns, Cap Gain ($) . . .	2.79	0.99	0.13	0.21	0.00	0.57	1.06	1.99	0.25	0.00
Net Asset Value ($)	17.65	21.37	19.64	18.64	15.16	18.40	15.38	13.43	16.03	14.23
Expense Ratio (%)	1.45	1.35	1.39	1.40	1.47	1.50	1.50	1.50	1.35	1.09
Net Income to Assets (%). .	0.75	0.44	0.95	1.82	2.59	2.24	0.73	0.92	1.38	1.29
Portfolio Turnover (%).	7	13	24	6	15	27	29	8	35	30
Total Assets (Millions $)	30	39	59	51	37	18	16	20	10	2

PORTFOLIO (as of 9/30/94)

Portfolio Manager: Richard Carney - 1983

Investm't Category: Aggressive Growth

✔ Cap Gain	Asset Allocation
Cap & Income	Fund of Funds
Income	Index
	Sector
✔ Domestic	✔ Small Cap
✔ Foreign	Socially Conscious
Country/Region	State Specific

Portfolio: stocks 77%   bonds 0%
convertibles 0%   other 0%   cash 23%

Largest Holdings: drugs & healthcare 9%, computer services 7%

Unrealized Net Capital Gains: 21% of portfolio value

SHAREHOLDER INFORMATION

Minimum Investment
Initial: $2,500   Subsequent: $0

Minimum IRA Investment
Initial: $500   Subsequent: $0

Maximum Fees
Load: none   12b-1: none
Other: none

Distributions
Income: Mar, Dec   Capital Gains: Mar, Dec

Exchange Options
Number Per Year: no limit   Fee: none
Telephone: yes (money market fund available)

Services
IRA, pension, auto invest, auto withdraw

GIT Income—Gov't Port

(GTTAX)

Government Bond

1655 N. Fort Myer Dr.
Suite 1000
Arlington, VA 22209
(800) 336-3063, (703) 528-6500

PERFORMANCE

fund inception date: 7/21/83

	3yr Annual	5yr Annual	10yr Annual	Bull	Bear
Return (%)	3.6	6.3	8.5	40.3	-4.5
Differ from Category (+/-)	-0.4 av	-0.4 blw av	0.7 abv av	-10.9 blw av	1.9 av

Total Risk	Standard Deviation	Category Risk	Risk Index	Avg Mat
low	4.7%	av	1.0	8.9 yrs

	1994	1993	1992	1991	1990	1989	1988	1987	1986	1985
Return (%)	-3.6	9.6	5.3	13.8	7.1	11.1	7.1	-1.0	13.6	24.8
Differ from category (+/-)	1.2	-1.3	-1.1	-1.5	0.9	-3.4	-0.8	1.1	-7.0	6.3

PER SHARE DATA

	1994	1993	1992	1991	1990	1989	1988	1987	1986	1985
Dividends, Net Income ($)	0.35	0.39	0.56	0.66	0.73	0.81	0.79	0.87	0.95	1.05
Distrib'ns, Cap Gain ($)	0.00	0.77	0.53	0.04	0.04	0.00	0.25	0.22	0.00	0.00
Net Asset Value ($)	9.30	10.01	10.21	10.77	10.12	10.21	9.95	10.28	11.51	11.01
Expense Ratio (%)	1.54	1.52	1.53	1.65	1.51	1.50	1.47	1.41	1.12	0.89
Net Income to Assets (%)	3.53	4.78	6.28	7.13	7.76	7.94	8.18	7.99	9.82	11.78
Portfolio Turnover (%)	287	357	123	116	86	45	36	31	26	63
Total Assets (Millions $)	7	3	7	6	6	7	6	9	8	4

PORTFOLIO (as of 9/30/94)

Portfolio Manager: John Edwards - 1988

Investm't Category: Government Bond

Cap Gain	Asset Allocation
Cap & Income	Fund of Funds
✔ Income	Index
	Sector
✔ Domestic	Small Cap
Foreign	Socially Conscious
Country/Region	State Specific

Portfolio: stocks 0% bonds 90%
convertibles 0% other 0% cash 10%

Largest Holdings: U.S. government 90%

Unrealized Net Capital Gains: -5% of portfolio value

SHAREHOLDER INFORMATION

Minimum Investment
Initial: $2,500   Subsequent: $0

Minimum IRA Investment
Initial: $500   Subsequent: $0

Maximum Fees
Load: none   12b-1: none
Other: none

Distributions
Income: monthly   Capital Gains: Dec

Exchange Options
Number Per Year: no limit   Fee: none
Telephone: yes (money market fund available)

Services
IRA, pension, auto invest, auto withdraw

GIT Income—Maximum
(GITMX)
Corporate High-Yield Bond

1655 N. Fort Myer Dr.
Suite 1000
Arlington, VA 22209
(800) 336-3063, (703) 528-6500

PERFORMANCE

fund inception date: 7/21/83

	3yr Annual	5yr Annual	10yr Annual	Bull	Bear
Return (%)	7.8	7.8	8.0	64.7	-6.2
Differ from Category (+/-)	-2.1 low	-1.5 low	-1.9 low	-14.6 low	-0.9 low

Total Risk	Standard Deviation	Category Risk	Risk Index	Avg Mat
low	4.8%	av	1.0	6.6 yrs

	1994	1993	1992	1991	1990	1989	1988	1987	1986	1985
Return (%)	-2.7	15.0	12.0	25.6	-7.5	2.8	10.0	-2.7	10.5	22.0
Differ from category (+/-) . . .	0.0	-3.4	-3.6	-1.8	-2.4	1.4	-2.1	-3.8	-3.8	-1.2

PER SHARE DATA

	1994	1993	1992	1991	1990	1989	1988	1987	1986	1985
Dividends, Net Income ($) .	0.60	0.62	0.69	0.69	0.82	0.89	0.86	0.96	1.10	1.17
Distrib'ns, Cap Gain ($) . . .	0.00	0.00	0.00	0.00	0.00	0.00	0.00	0.00	0.00	0.00
Net Asset Value ($)	6.85	7.66	7.23	7.09	6.24	7.59	8.24	8.30	9.48	9.59
Expense Ratio (%)	1.52	1.52	1.54	1.66	1.51	1.50	1.45	1.39	1.10	0.93
Net Income to Assets (%). . . .	8.02	9.26	9.95	11.57	11.16	10.45	10.48	10.87	12.23	13.75
Portfolio Turnover (%). . . .	251	73	124	54	93	80	78	127	47	66
Total Assets (Millions $)	6	7	6	5	7	10	11	17	12	7

PORTFOLIO (as of 9/30/94)

Portfolio Manager: John Edwards - 1988

Investm't Category: Corp. High-Yield Bond

Cap Gain	Asset Allocation
✔ Cap & Income	Fund of Funds
Income	Index
	Sector
✔ Domestic	Small Cap
Foreign	Socially Conscious
Country/Region	State Specific

Portfolio: stocks 0% bonds 96%
convertibles 0% other 0% cash 4%

Largest Holdings: automotive 10%, chemical 10%

Unrealized Net Capital Gains: -4% of portfolio value

SHAREHOLDER INFORMATION

Minimum Investment
Initial: $2,500 Subsequent: $0

Minimum IRA Investment
Initial: $500 Subsequent: $0

Maximum Fees
Load: none 12b-1: none
Other: none

Distributions
Income: monthly Capital Gains: Dec

Exchange Options
Number Per Year: no limit Fee: none
Telephone: yes (money market fund available)

Services
IRA, pension, auto invest, auto withdraw

GIT Tax-Free National Port (GTFHX)

Tax-Exempt Bond

1655 N. Fort Myer Dr.
Suite 1000
Arlington, VA 22209
(800) 336-3063, (703) 528-6500

PERFORMANCE

fund inception date: 12/30/82

	3yr Annual	5yr Annual	10yr Annual	Bull	Bear
Return (%)	3.2	5.0	7.8	39.7	-8.1
Differ from Category (+/-)	-1.3 low	-1.1 low	-0.3 blw av	-2.1 blw av	-2.9 low

Total Risk	Standard Deviation	Category Risk	Risk Index	Avg Mat
blw av	6.4%	abv av	1.0	14.7 yrs

	1994	1993	1992	1991	1990	1989	1988	1987	1986	1985
Return (%)	-8.8	11.7	8.1	10.2	5.3	7.2	8.5	0.2	19.3	19.0
Differ from category (+/-)	-3.6	0.0	-0.2	-1.1	-1.0	-1.8	-1.7	1.5	2.9	1.6

PER SHARE DATA

	1994	1993	1992	1991	1990	1989	1988	1987	1986	1985
Dividends, Net Income ($)	0.41	0.51	0.61	0.62	0.68	0.72	0.74	0.80	0.85	0.88
Distrib'ns, Cap Gain ($)	0.00	0.94	0.21	0.00	0.00	0.00	0.00	0.08	0.65	0.17
Net Asset Value ($)	9.55	10.92	11.12	11.06	10.62	10.75	10.72	10.58	11.45	10.90
Expense Ratio (%)	1.23	1.10	1.17	1.24	1.24	1.19	1.16	0.99	1.16	1.29
Net Income to Assets (%)	3.98	4.83	5.47	5.95	6.54	6.78	7.15	7.18	7.60	8.54
Portfolio Turnover (%)	175	212	114	91	41	58	77	66	117	173
Total Assets (Millions $)	31	41	41	40	40	41	40	45	43	34

PORTFOLIO (as of 9/30/94)

Portfolio Manager: Dan Gillespie - 1994

Investm't Category: Tax-Exempt Bond

Cap Gain	Asset Allocation
Cap & Income	Fund of Funds
✔ Income	Index
	Sector
✔ Domestic	Small Cap
Foreign	Socially Conscious
Country/Region	State Specific

Portfolio: stocks 0% bonds 100%
convertibles 0% other 0% cash 0%

Largest Holdings: general obligation 8%

Unrealized Net Capital Gains: -2% of portfolio value

SHAREHOLDER INFORMATION

Minimum Investment
Initial: $2,500   Subsequent: $0

Minimum IRA Investment
Initial: na   Subsequent: na

Maximum Fees
Load: none   12b-1: none
Other: none

Distributions
Income: monthly   Capital Gains: Nov

Exchange Options
Number Per Year: no limit   Fee: none
Telephone: yes (money market fund available)

Services
auto invest, auto withdraw

GIT Tax-Free Virginia Port (GTVAX)

Tax-Exempt Bond

1655 N. Fort Myer Dr.
Suite 1000
Arlington, VA 22209
(800) 336-3063, (703) 528-6500

PERFORMANCE

fund inception date: 10/13/89

	3yr Annual	5yr Annual	10yr Annual	Bull	Bear
Return (%)	3.4	5.2	na	38.8	-7.9
Differ from Category (+/-)	-1.1 low	-0.9 low	na	-3.0 blw av	-2.7 low

Total Risk	Standard Deviation	Category Risk	Risk Index	Avg Mat
blw av	6.0%	av	1.0	14.9 yrs

	1994	1993	1992	1991	1990	1989	1988	1987	1986	1985
Return (%)	-8.2	12.4	7.5	9.8	5.9	7.3	8.2	—	—	—
Differ from category (+/-). .	-3.0	0.7	-0.8	-1.5	-0.4	-1.7	-2.0	—	—	—

PER SHARE DATA

	1994	1993	1992	1991	1990	1989	1988	1987	1986	1985
Dividends, Net Income ($) .	0.47	0.55	0.58	0.61	0.62	0.63	0.68	—	—	—
Distrib'ns, Cap Gain ($) . . .	0.00	0.59	0.12	0.12	0.00	0.00	0.14	—	—	—
Net Asset Value ($)	10.34	11.78	11.54	11.41	11.08	11.07	10.92	—	—	—
Expense Ratio (%)	1.18	1.10	1.13	1.18	1.25	1.22	0.72	—	—	—
Net Income to Assets (%). .	4.23	4.80	5.20	5.47	5.69	5.71	6.41	—	—	—
Portfolio Turnover (%). . . .	104	80	74	73	11	34	58	—	—	—
Total Assets (Millions $). . . .	32	44	37	31	25	20	19	—	—	—

PORTFOLIO (as of 9/30/94)

Portfolio Manager: Dan Gillespie - 1994

Investm't Category: Tax-Exempt Bond

Cap Gain	Asset Allocation
Cap & Income	Fund of Funds
✔ Income	Index
	Sector
✔ Domestic	Small Cap
Foreign	Socially Conscious
Country/Region	✔ State Specific

Portfolio: stocks 0% bonds 100%
convertibles 0% other 0% cash 0%

Largest Holdings: general obligation 22%

Unrealized Net Capital Gains: -1% of portfolio value

SHAREHOLDER INFORMATION

Minimum Investment
Initial: $2,500   Subsequent: $0

Minimum IRA Investment
Initial: na   Subsequent: na

Maximum Fees
Load: none   12b-1: none
Other: none

Distributions
Income: monthly   Capital Gains: Nov

Exchange Options
Number Per Year: no limit   Fee: none
Telephone: yes (money market fund available)

Services
auto invest, auto withdraw

Gradison McDonald Established Value (GETGX)

580 Walnut St.
Cincinnati, OH 45202
(800) 869-5999, (513) 579-5700

Growth

PERFORMANCE

fund inception date: 8/16/83

	3yr Annual	5yr Annual	10yr Annual	Bull	Bear
Return (%)	10.1	8.4	13.4	76.6	-5.5
Differ from Category (+/-)	2.4 abv av	-1.2 blw av	0.5 abv av	-15.5 blw av	1.1 av

Total Risk	Standard Deviation	Category Risk	Risk Index	Beta
av	8.4%	blw av	0.9	0.8

	1994	1993	1992	1991	1990	1989	1988	1987	1986	1985
Return (%)	0.3	20.7	10.2	22.2	-8.0	16.0	15.1	12.4	22.0	28.7
Differ from category (+/-)	0.9	7.3	-1.4	-13.5	-2.3	-10.1	-2.9	10.6	7.4	-0.5

PER SHARE DATA

	1994	1993	1992	1991	1990	1989	1988	1987	1986	1985
Dividends, Net Income ($)	0.34	0.22	0.31	0.45	0.37	0.72	0.50	0.68	0.33	0.29
Distrib'ns, Cap Gain ($)	0.66	1.00	0.27	0.27	0.41	0.51	0.31	1.26	1.18	0.00
Net Asset Value ($)	21.77	22.71	19.87	18.60	15.85	18.07	16.64	15.18	15.21	13.73
Expense Ratio (%)	1.22	1.28	1.31	1.39	1.40	1.45	1.57	1.61	1.72	2.00
Net Income to Assets (%)	1.15	1.48	2.12	3.10	4.14	3.34	2.67	2.50	2.63	2.68
Portfolio Turnover (%)	38	28	68	74	64	50	26	76	79	70
Total Assets (Millions $)	260	244	176	150	135	102	69	54	30	12

PORTFOLIO (as of 4/30/94)

Portfolio Manager: William Leugers - 1983

Investm't Category: Growth

✔ Cap Gain	Asset Allocation
Cap & Income	Fund of Funds
Income	Index
	Sector
✔ Domestic	Small Cap
Foreign	Socially Conscious
Country/Region	State Specific

Portfolio: stocks 66% bonds 0%
convertibles 0% other 0% cash 34%

Largest Holdings: industrial products 10%, financial services 9%

Unrealized Net Capital Gains: 19% of portfolio value

SHAREHOLDER INFORMATION

Minimum Investment
Initial: $1,000   Subsequent: $50

Minimum IRA Investment
Initial: $1,000   Subsequent: $50

Maximum Fees
Load: none   12b-1: 0.25%
Other: none

Distributions
Income: quarterly   Capital Gains: May, Nov

Exchange Options
Number Per Year: no limit   Fee: none
Telephone: yes (money market fund available)

Services
IRA, pension, auto invest, auto withdraw

Gradison McDonald Opportunity Value (GOGFX)

580 Walnut St.
Cincinnati, OH 45202
(800) 869-5999, (513) 579-5700

Growth

PERFORMANCE   fund inception date: 8/16/83

	3yr Annual	5yr Annual	10yr Annual	Bull	Bear
Return (%)	7.4	7.9	11.8	91.9	-4.3
Differ from Category (+/-)	-0.3 av	-1.7 blw av	-1.1 blw av	-0.2 av	2.3 abv av

Total Risk	Standard Deviation	Category Risk	Risk Index	Beta
av	8.7%	blw av	0.9	0.6

	1994	1993	1992	1991	1990	1989	1988	1987	1986	1985
Return (%)	-2.1	11.0	14.3	35.9	-13.0	23.1	23.5	-5.3	12.9	28.0
Differ from category (+/-) . .	-1.5	-2.4	2.7	0.2	-7.3	-3.0	5.5	-7.1	-1.7	-1.2

PER SHARE DATA

	1994	1993	1992	1991	1990	1989	1988	1987	1986	1985
Dividends, Net Income ($) .	0.12	0.07	0.10	0.27	0.25	0.33	0.27	0.12	0.11	0.03
Distrib'ns, Cap Gain ($) . . .	0.44	0.80	0.64	0.68	0.07	0.26	0.63	0.13	0.73	0.00
Net Asset Value ($)	17.43	18.38	17.37	15.90	12.45	14.67	12.40	10.77	11.64	10.99
Expense Ratio (%)	1.38	1.44	1.49	1.61	1.52	1.84	1.83	1.73	2.00	2.00
Net Income to Assets (%). .	0.47	0.61	1.32	2.03	2.47	1.84	1.22	0.90	0.26	0.29
Portfolio Turnover (%).	40	39	64	64	37	36	74	65	83	99
Total Assets (Millions $). . . .	82	88	47	29	23	20	18	20	14	4

PORTFOLIO (as of 4/30/94)

Portfolio Manager: William Leugers - 1983

Investm't Category: Growth

✔ Cap Gain
  Cap & Income
  Income

  Asset Allocation
  Fund of Funds
  Index
  Sector
✔ Small Cap
  Socially Conscious
  State Specific

✔ Domestic
  Foreign
  Country/Region

Portfolio: stocks 66% bonds 0%
convertibles 0% other 0% cash 34%

Largest Holdings: electronics 11%, health-care 8%

Unrealized Net Capital Gains: 18% of port-folio value

SHAREHOLDER INFORMATION

Minimum Investment
Initial: $1,000   Subsequent: $50

Minimum IRA Investment
Initial: $1,000   Subsequent: $50

Maximum Fees
Load: none   12b-1: 0.25%
Other: none

Distributions
Income: May, Dec   Capital Gains: May, Dec

Exchange Options
Number Per Year: no limit   Fee: none
Telephone: yes (money market fund available)

Services
IRA, pension, auto invest, auto withdraw

Greenspring (GRSPX)

Growth & Income

2330 West Joppa Road
Suite 110
Lutherville, MD 21093
(800) 366-3863, (410) 823-5353

PERFORMANCE   fund inception date: 7/1/83

	3yr Annual	5yr Annual	10yr Annual	Bull	Bear
Return (%)	11.1	8.9	11.5	58.9	0.1
Differ from Category (+/-)	4.0 high	1.0 abv av	-0.2 av	-16.9 blw av	6.4 high

Total Risk	Standard Deviation	Category Risk	Risk Index	Beta
blw av	4.9%	low	0.6	0.4

	1994	1993	1992	1991	1990	1989	1988	1987	1986	1985
Return (%)	2.8	14.6	16.5	19.3	-6.5	10.6	15.9	9.1	15.9	20.1
Differ from category (+/-) . . .	4.2	1.4	6.3	-8.3	-0.5	-10.8	-1.1	8.5	0.1	-5.6

PER SHARE DATA

	1994	1993	1992	1991	1990	1989	1988	1987	1986	1985
Dividends, Net Income ($) .	0.51	0.40	0.51	0.52	0.68	0.79	1.25	1.65	0.73	1.13
Distrib'ns, Cap Gain ($)	0.45	1.41	0.72	0.07	0.00	0.18	0.04	1.26	1.47	0.04
Net Asset Value ($)	13.39	13.96	13.78	12.91	11.32	12.83	12.49	11.89	13.61	13.85
Expense Ratio (%)	1.35	1.31	1.48	1.33	1.31	1.27	1.29	1.36	1.46	1.49
Net Income to Assets (%) . .	3.62	2.78	3.68	3.79	4.82	6.23	11.13	8.57	5.55	5.96
Portfolio Turnover (%)	na	121	100	70	90	106	199	929	502	350
Total Assets (Millions $)	50	30	20	19	19	22	21	18	14	13

PORTFOLIO (as of 6/30/94)

Portfolio Manager: Charles vK. Carlson - 1987

Investm't Category: Growth & Income

Cap Gain	Asset Allocation
✔ Cap & Income	Fund of Funds
Income	Index
	Sector
✔ Domestic	Small Cap
Foreign	Socially Conscious
Country/Region	State Specific

Portfolio: stocks 43%   bonds 15%
convertibles 10%   other 10%   cash 22%

Largest Holdings: real estate 14%, insurance 8%

Unrealized Net Capital Gains: 4% of portfolio value

SHAREHOLDER INFORMATION

Minimum Investment
Initial: $1,000   Subsequent: $100

Minimum IRA Investment
Initial: $1,000   Subsequent: $100

Maximum Fees
Load: none   12b-1: none
Other: none

Distributions
Income: Jul, Dec   Capital Gains: Dec

Exchange Options
Number Per Year: none Fee:
Telephone:

Services
IRA, pension, auto withdraw

Harbor Bond (HABDX)

General Bond

One SeaGate
Toledo, OH 43666
(800) 422-1050, (419) 247-2477

PERFORMANCE
fund inception date: 12/29/87

	3yr Annual	5yr Annual	10yr Annual	Bull	Bear
Return (%)	5.6	8.7	na	55.9	-5.1
Differ from Category (+/-)	1.3 high	1.8 high	na	14.9 high	-1.3 blw av

Total Risk	Standard Deviation	Category Risk	Risk Index	Avg Mat
low	4.1%	av	1.0	7.4 yrs

	1994	1993	1992	1991	1990	1989	1988	1987	1986	1985
Return (%)	-3.7	12.4	9.1	19.6	7.9	13.6	7.1	—	—	—
Differ from category (+/-) . .	-1.7	3.2	2.5	5.0	0.7	2.2	-0.3	—	—	—

PER SHARE DATA

	1994	1993	1992	1991	1990	1989	1988	1987	1986	1985
Dividends, Net Income ($) .	0.61	0.65	0.74	0.86	0.85	0.83	0.67	—	—	—
Distrib'ns, Cap Gain ($) . . .	0.00	0.50	0.25	0.26	0.00	0.09	0.07	—	—	—
Net Asset Value ($)	10.28	11.31	11.10	11.11	10.29	10.36	9.96	—	—	—
Expense Ratio (%)	0.80	0.72	0.77	0.86	1.22	1.21	1.55	—	—	—
Net Income to Assets (%) . .	5.82	6.19	7.30	8.12	8.30	8.20	7.42	—	—	—
Portfolio Turnover (%)	207	119	53	58	91	91	124	—	—	—
Total Assets (Millions $) . . .	167	174	65	40	24	21	11	—	—	—

PORTFOLIO (as of 4/30/94)

Portfolio Manager: William Gross - 1987

Investm't Category: General Bond

Cap Gain	Asset Allocation
Cap & Income	Fund of Funds
✔ Income	Index
	Sector
✔ Domestic	Small Cap
✔ Foreign	Socially Conscious
Country/Region	State Specific

Portfolio: stocks 0% bonds 79%
convertibles 0% other 0% cash 21%

Largest Holdings: corporate 38%, mortgage-backed 28%

Unrealized Net Capital Gains: -1% of portfolio value

SHAREHOLDER INFORMATION

Minimum Investment
Initial: $2,000   Subsequent: $500

Minimum IRA Investment
Initial: $500   Subsequent: $100

Maximum Fees
Load: none   12b-1: none
Other: none

Distributions
Income: quarterly   Capital Gains: Dec

Exchange Options
Number Per Year: no limit   Fee: none
Telephone: yes (money market fund available)

Services
IRA, pension, auto invest, auto withdraw

Harbor Capital Appreciation (HACAX)

Growth

One SeaGate
Toledo, OH 43666
(800) 422-1050, (419) 247-2477

PERFORMANCE

fund inception date: 12/29/87

	3yr Annual	5yr Annual	10yr Annual	Bull	Bear
Return (%)	8.4	14.1	na	122.9	-11.0
Differ from Category (+/-)	0.7 av	4.5 high	na	30.8 high	-4.4 low

Total Risk	Standard Deviation	Category Risk	Risk Index	Beta
high	12.1%	high	1.3	1.2

	1994	1993	1992	1991	1990	1989	1988	1987	1986	1985
Return (%)	3.3	12.1	9.9	54.7	-1.7	24.1	15.2	—	—	—
Differ from category (+/-)	3.9	-1.3	-1.7	19.0	4.0	-2.0	-2.8	—	—	—

PER SHARE DATA

	1994	1993	1992	1991	1990	1989	1988	1987	1986	1985
Dividends, Net Income ($)	0.04	0.03	0.02	0.04	0.14	0.21	0.18	—	—	—
Distrib'ns, Cap Gain ($)	0.17	1.13	2.03	0.98	0.86	1.18	0.38	—	—	—
Net Asset Value ($)	16.71	16.37	15.65	16.11	11.09	12.31	11.05	—	—	—
Expense Ratio (%)	0.85	0.86	0.91	0.89	0.88	0.92	0.99	—	—	—
Net Income to Assets (%)	0.06	0.24	0.12	0.47	1.18	1.77	1.48	—	—	—
Portfolio Turnover (%)	86	93	69	90	162	75	48	—	—	—
Total Assets (Millions $)	239	150	77	80	55	60	46	—	—	—

PORTFOLIO (as of 4/30/94)

Portfolio Manager: Spiros Segalas - 1990

Investm't Category: Growth

✔ Cap Gain	Asset Allocation
Cap & Income	Fund of Funds
Income	Index
	Sector
✔ Domestic	Small Cap
Foreign	Socially Conscious
Country/Region	State Specific

Portfolio: stocks 96% bonds 0%
convertibles 0% other 0% cash 4%

Largest Holdings: software & services 15%, drugs & healthcare supplies 9%

Unrealized Net Capital Gains: 13% of portfolio value

SHAREHOLDER INFORMATION

Minimum Investment
Initial: $2,000   Subsequent: $500

Minimum IRA Investment
Initial: $500   Subsequent: $100

Maximum Fees
Load: none   12b-1: none
Other: none

Distributions
Income: Dec   Capital Gains: Dec

Exchange Options
Number Per Year: no limit   Fee: none
Telephone: yes (money market fund available)

Services
IRA, auto exchange, auto invest, auto withdraw

Harbor Growth (HAGWX)

Growth

One SeaGate
Toledo, OH 43666
(800) 422-1050, (419) 247-2477

PERFORMANCE

fund inception date: 11/19/86

	3yr Annual	5yr Annual	10yr Annual	Bull	Bear
Return (%)	-0.5	6.6	na	92.3	-13.8
Differ from Category (+/-)	-8.2 low	-3.0 low	na	0.2 av	-7.2 low

Total Risk	Standard Deviation	Category Risk	Risk Index	Beta
high	13.9%	high	1.4	1.1

	1994	1993	1992	1991	1990	1989	1988	1987	1986	1985
Return (%)	-11.4	18.3	-6.3	50.4	-6.6	22.9	14.2	2.9	—	—
Differ from category (+/-).	-10.8	4.9	-17.9	14.7	-0.9	-3.2	-3.8	1.1	—	—

PER SHARE DATA

	1994	1993	1992	1991	1990	1989	1988	1987	1986	1985
Dividends, Net Income ($) .	0.00	0.02	0.01	0.04	0.08	0.11	0.12	0.10	—	—
Distrib'ns, Cap Gain ($) . . .	0.32	0.00	1.36	2.31	0.94	0.49	0.00	0.79	—	—
Net Asset Value ($)	11.97	13.88	11.74	14.02	10.94	12.81	10.91	9.65	—	—
Expense Ratio (%)	0.89	0.90	0.90	0.91	0.94	1.03	1.06	1.33	—	—
Net Income to Assets (%).	-0.04	0.11	0.14	0.32	0.74	0.75	1.14	0.72	—	—
Portfolio Turnover (%). . . .	115	170	83	98	96	104	53	56	—	—
Total Assets (Millions $). . .	134	189	191	211	123	139	116	99	—	—

PORTFOLIO (as of 4/30/94)

Portfolio Manager: Arthur E. Nicholas - 1993

Investm't Category: Growth

✔ Cap Gain	Asset Allocation
Cap & Income	Fund of Funds
Income	Index
	Sector
✔ Domestic	Small Cap
Foreign	Socially Conscious
Country/Region	State Specific

Portfolio: stocks 95% bonds 0%
convertibles 0% other 0% cash 5%

Largest Holdings: drugs & healthcare 12%, computer & office equipment 12%

Unrealized Net Capital Gains: 6% of portfolio value

SHAREHOLDER INFORMATION

Minimum Investment
Initial: $2,000   Subsequent: $500

Minimum IRA Investment
Initial: $500   Subsequent: $100

Maximum Fees
Load: none   12b-1: none
Other: none

Distributions
Income: Dec   Capital Gains: Dec

Exchange Options
Number Per Year: no limit   Fee: none
Telephone: yes (money market fund available)

Services
IRA, auto exchange, auto invest, auto withdraw

Harbor Int'l (HAINX)

International Stock

One SeaGate
Toledo, OH 43666
(800) 422-1050, (419) 247-2477

this fund is closed to new investors

PERFORMANCE

fund inception date: 12/29/87

	3yr Annual	5yr Annual	10yr Annual	Bull	Bear
Return (%)	15.2	10.8	na	91.1	-8.6
Differ from Category (+/-)	6.1 high	5.9 high	na	27.2 high	-1.6 blw av

Total Risk	Standard Deviation	Category Risk	Risk Index	Beta
high	13.9%	abv av	1.0	1.1

	1994	1993	1992	1991	1990	1989	1988	1987	1986	1985
Return (%)	5.4	45.4	0.0	21.3	-9.7	36.8	37.7	—	—	—
Differ from category (+/-) . . .	8.4	6.8	2.9	8.2	0.7	14.3	23.3	—	—	—

PER SHARE DATA

	1994	1993	1992	1991	1990	1989	1988	1987	1986	1985
Dividends, Net Income ($) .	0.25	0.21	0.22	0.21	0.34	0.17	0.10	—	—	—
Distrib'ns, Cap Gain ($)	0.94	0.00	0.18	0.00	0.34	0.73	0.76	—	—	—
Net Asset Value ($)	24.45	24.32	16.87	17.28	14.42	16.74	12.90	—	—	—
Expense Ratio (%)	1.16	1.20	1.28	1.35	1.40	1.15	1.78	—	—	—
Net Income to Assets (%) . .	0.34	1.28	1.98	1.76	2.82	1.56	0.87	—	—	—
Portfolio Turnover (%)	28	15	25	19	28	21	27	—	—	—
Total Assets (Millions $) . .	2,953	2,609	701	206	64	29	10	—	—	—

PORTFOLIO (as of 4/30/94)

Portfolio Manager: Hakan Castegren - 1987

Investm't Category: International Stock

✔ Cap Gain	Asset Allocation
Cap & Income	Fund of Funds
Income	Index
	Sector
Domestic	Small Cap
✔ Foreign	Socially Conscious
Country/Region	State Specific

Portfolio: stocks 95% bonds 0%
convertibles 0% other 0% cash 5%

Largest Holdings: United Kingdom 13%, Switzerland 11%

Unrealized Net Capital Gains: 18% of portfolio value

SHAREHOLDER INFORMATION

Minimum Investment
Initial: $2,000   Subsequent: $500

Minimum IRA Investment
Initial: $500   Subsequent: $100

Maximum Fees
Load: none   12b-1: none
Other: none

Distributions
Income: Dec   Capital Gains: Dec

Exchange Options
Number Per Year: no limit   Fee: none
Telephone: yes (money market fund available)

Services
IRA, auto exchange, auto invest, auto withdraw

Harbor International Growth (HAIGX)

One SeaGate
Toledo, OH 43666
(800) 422-1050, (419) 247-2477

International Stock

PERFORMANCE

fund inception date: 11/1/93

	3yr Annual	5yr Annual	10yr Annual	Bull	Bear
Return (%)	na	na	na	na	-14.0
Differ from Category (+/-)	na	na	na	na	-7.0 low

Total Risk	Standard Deviation	Category Risk	Risk Index	Beta
na	na	na	na	na

	1994	1993	1992	1991	1990	1989	1988	1987	1986	1985
Return (%)	-7.7	—	—	—	—	—	—	—	—	—
Differ from category (+/-)	-4.7	—	—	—	—	—	—	—	—	—

PER SHARE DATA

	1994	1993	1992	1991	1990	1989	1988	1987	1986	1985
Dividends, Net Income ($)	0.06	—	—	—	—	—	—	—	—	—
Distrib'ns, Cap Gain ($)	0.00	—	—	—	—	—	—	—	—	—
Net Asset Value ($)	10.27	—	—	—	—	—	—	—	—	—
Expense Ratio (%)	0.97	—	—	—	—	—	—	—	—	—
Net Income to Assets (%)	0.94	—	—	—	—	—	—	—	—	—
Portfolio Turnover (%)	18	—	—	—	—	—	—	—	—	—
Total Assets (Millions $)	69	—	—	—	—	—	—	—	—	—

PORTFOLIO (as of 4/30/94)

Portfolio Manager: Howard Moss - 1993

Investm't Category: International Stock

✔ Cap Gain
  Cap & Income
  Income

  Asset Allocation
  Fund of Funds
  Index
  Sector
  Small Cap
  Socially Conscious
  State Specific

  Domestic
✔ Foreign
  Country/Region

Portfolio: stocks 95% bonds 0%
convertibles 0% other 0% cash 5%

Largest Holdings: banks 22%, pharmaceuticals 18%

Unrealized Net Capital Gains: -5% of portfolio value

SHAREHOLDER INFORMATION

Minimum Investment
Initial: $2,000   Subsequent: $500

Minimum IRA Investment
Initial: $500   Subsequent: $100

Maximum Fees
Load: none   12b-1: none
Other: none

Distributions
Income: Dec   Capital Gains: Dec

Exchange Options
Number Per Year: no limit   Fee: none
Telephone: yes (money market fund available)

Services
IRA, auto exchange, auto invest, auto withdraw

Harbor Short Duration

(HASDX)

General Bond

One SeaGate
Toledo, OH 43666
(800) 422-1050, (419) 247-2477

	3yr Annual	5yr Annual	10yr Annual	Bull	Bear
Return (%)	na	na	na	na	0.0
Differ from Category (+/-)	na	na	na	na	3.8 high

Total Risk	Standard Deviation	Category Risk	Risk Index	Avg Mat
na	na	na	na	0.9 yrs

	1994	1993	1992	1991	1990	1989	1988	1987	1986	1985
Return (%)	2.7	4.4	—	—	—	—	—	—	—	—
Differ from category (+/-)	4.7	-4.8	—	—	—	—	—	—	—	—

PER SHARE DATA

	1994	1993	1992	1991	1990	1989	1988	1987	1986	1985
Dividends, Net Income ($)	0.78	1.15	—	—	—	—	—	—	—	—
Distrib'ns, Cap Gain ($)	0.00	0.00	—	—	—	—	—	—	—	—
Net Asset Value ($)	8.71	9.25	—	—	—	—	—	—	—	—
Expense Ratio (%)	0.40	0.43	—	—	—	—	—	—	—	—
Net Income to Assets (%)	4.26	4.19	—	—	—	—	—	—	—	—
Portfolio Turnover (%)	1,597	1,212	—	—	—	—	—	—	—	—
Total Assets (Millions $)	101	118	—	—	—	—	—	—	—	—

PORTFOLIO (as of 10/31/94)

Portfolio Manager: Adnan Akant - 1992

Investm't Category: General Bond

Cap Gain	Asset Allocation
Cap & Income	Fund of Funds
✔ Income	Index
	Sector
✔ Domestic	Small Cap
Foreign	Socially Conscious
Country/Region	State Specific

Portfolio: stocks 0%   bonds 99%
convertibles 0%   other 0%   cash 1%

Largest Holdings: U. S. government 69%, asset-backed 17%

Unrealized Net Capital Gains: 0% of portfolio value

SHAREHOLDER INFORMATION

Minimum Investment
Initial: $2,000   Subsequent: $500

Minimum IRA Investment
Initial: $500   Subsequent: $100

Maximum Fees
Load: none   12b-1: none
Other: none

Distributions
Income: monthly   Capital Gains: Dec

Exchange Options
Number Per Year: no limit   Fee: none
Telephone: yes (money market fund available)

Services
IRA, auto exchange, auto invest, auto withdraw

Harbor Value (HAVLX)

Growth & Income

One SeaGate
Toledo, OH 43666
(800) 422-1050, (419) 247-2477

PERFORMANCE

fund inception date: 12/29/87

	3yr Annual	5yr Annual	10yr Annual	Bull	Bear
Return (%)	5.4	6.0	na	59.0	-5.1
Differ from Category (+/-)	-1.7 blw av	-1.9 low	na	-16.8 blw av	1.2 abv av

Total Risk	Standard Deviation	Category Risk	Risk Index	Beta
av	8.6%	abv av	1.0	1.0

	1994	1993	1992	1991	1990	1989	1988	1987	1986	1985
Return (%)	0.6	8.3	7.4	21.2	-5.5	29.8	19.7	—	—	—
Differ from category (+/-) . . .	2.0	-4.9	-2.8	-6.4	0.5	8.4	2.7	—	—	—

PER SHARE DATA

	1994	1993	1992	1991	1990	1989	1988	1987	1986	1985
Dividends, Net Income ($) .	0.36	0.32	0.38	0.46	0.52	0.51	0.35	—	—	—
Distrib'ns, Cap Gain ($) . . .	1.07	1.10	0.15	0.35	0.43	0.80	0.44	—	—	—
Net Asset Value ($)	11.88	13.21	13.50	13.06	11.46	13.14	11.16	—	—	—
Expense Ratio (%)	0.96	0.88	0.84	0.93	1.01	1.02	1.40	—	—	—
Net Income to Assets (%). .	2.42	2.48	3.11	3.61	3.96	3.91	3.36	—	—	—
Portfolio Turnover (%). . . .	79	50	20	33	31	40	44	—	—	—
Total Assets (Millions $) . . .	56	62	64	43	23	23	12	—	—	—

PORTFOLIO (as of 4/30/94)

Portfolio Manager: Gregory M. DePrince - 1994

Investm't Category: Growth & Income

Cap Gain	Asset Allocation
✔ Cap & Income	Fund of Funds
Income	Index
	Sector
✔ Domestic	Small Cap
Foreign	Socially Conscious
Country/Region	State Specific

Portfolio: stocks 97% bonds 0%
convertibles 0% other 0% cash 3%

Largest Holdings: banking 13%, petroleum 13%

Unrealized Net Capital Gains: 1% of portfolio value

SHAREHOLDER INFORMATION

Minimum Investment
Initial: $2,000   Subsequent: $500

Minimum IRA Investment
Initial: $500   Subsequent: $100

Maximum Fees
Load: none   12b-1: none
Other: none

Distributions
Income: quarterly   Capital Gains: Dec

Exchange Options
Number Per Year: no limit   Fee: none
Telephone: yes (money market fund available)

Services
IRA, auto exchange, auto invest, auto withdraw

Heartland U.S. Government Securities

790 North Milwaukee Street
Milwaukee, WI 53202
(800) 432-7856, (414) 347-7777

(HRUSX) *General Bond*

PERFORMANCE

fund inception date: 4/9/87

	3yr Annual	5yr Annual	10yr Annual	Bull	Bear
Return (%)	5.4	8.5	na	63.8	-10.3
Differ from Category (+/-)	1.1 high	1.6 high	na	22.8 high	-6.5 low

Total Risk	Standard Deviation	Category Risk	Risk Index	Avg Mat
av	6.8%	high	1.7	10.3 yrs

	1994	1993	1992	1991	1990	1989	1988	1987	1986	1985
Return (%)	-9.6	17.7	10.0	16.9	9.9	11.3	6.4	—	—	—
Differ from category (+/-) ..	-7.6	8.5	3.4	2.3	2.7	-0.1	-1.0	—	—	—

PER SHARE DATA

	1994	1993	1992	1991	1990	1989	1988	1987	1986	1985
Dividends, Net Income ($) .	0.59	0.56	0.66	0.69	0.73	0.77	0.76	—	—	—
Distrib'ns, Cap Gain ($)....	0.00	0.61	0.34	0.25	0.00	0.00	0.00	—	—	—
Net Asset Value ($).......	8.91	10.50	9.93	9.97	9.39	9.25	9.04	—	—	—
Expense Ratio (%)........	1.02	1.06	0.92	0.92	0.86	0.89	0.95	—	—	—
Net Income to Assets (%) ..	6.05	5.09	6.71	7.06	7.98	8.45	8.25	—	—	—
Portfolio Turnover (%)	na	200	149	185	127	142	136	—	—	—
Total Assets (Millions $)	64	66	28	29	16	11	12	—	—	—

PORTFOLIO (as of 9/30/94)

Portfolio Manager: Pat Retzer - 1987

Investm't Category: General Bond

Cap Gain	Asset Allocation
Cap & Income	Fund of Funds
✔ Income	Index
	Sector
✔ Domestic	Small Cap
Foreign	Socially Conscious
Country/Region	State Specific

Portfolio: stocks 0%   bonds 99%
convertibles 0%   other 0%   cash 1%

Largest Holdings: U.S. government 51%, corporate 24%

Unrealized Net Capital Gains: -6% of portfolio value

SHAREHOLDER INFORMATION

Minimum Investment
Initial: $1,000   Subsequent: $100

Minimum IRA Investment
Initial: $500   Subsequent: $100

Maximum Fees
Load: none   12b-1: 0.25%
Other: none

Distributions
Income: monthly   Capital Gains: Dec

Exchange Options
Number Per Year: 4   Fee: none
Telephone: yes (money market fund available)

Services
IRA, pension, auto invest, auto withdraw

Heartland Value (HRTVX)

Aggressive Growth

790 North Milwaukee Street
Milwaukee, WI 53202
(800) 432-7856, (414) 347-7777

PERFORMANCE

fund inception date: 12/28/84

	3yr Annual	5yr Annual	10yr Annual	Bull	Bear
Return (%)	19.8	16.3	15.2	176.8	-4.5
Differ from Category (+/-)	10.9 high	3.8 abv av	1.2 abv av	43.6 abv av	6.3 high

Total Risk	Standard Deviation	Category Risk	Risk Index	Beta
high	13.5%	av	0.9	0.7

	1994	1993	1992	1991	1990	1989	1988	1987	1986	1985
Return (%)	1.7	18.7	42.4	49.3	-17.0	6.6	27.0	-8.4	10.9	41.3
Differ from category (+/-) . . .	2.4	-0.8	31.4	-2.8	-10.8	-20.2	11.8	-6.2	-0.9	9.0

PER SHARE DATA

	1994	1993	1992	1991	1990	1989	1988	1987	1986	1985
Dividends, Net Income ($) .	0.00	0.00	0.00	0.00	0.02	0.14	0.13	0.14	0.09	0.00
Distrib'ns, Cap Gain ($) . . .	0.88	1.02	2.47	0.85	0.12	1.34	0.43	1.04	0.83	0.00
Net Asset Value ($)	22.72	23.22	20.41	16.06	11.32	13.82	14.35	11.74	14.01	13.46
Expense Ratio (%)	1.49	1.51	1.48	1.69	1.74	1.65	1.71	1.51	1.66	2.47
Net Income to Assets (%).	-0.69	-0.71	-0.49	-0.54	0.14	0.86	0.85	0.43	0.71	0.24
Portfolio Turnover (%).	na	51	76	79	76	88	50	78	89	64
Total Assets (Millions $). . .	338	186	48	29	19	30	28	27	28	11

PORTFOLIO (as of 6/30/94)

Portfolio Manager: Bill Nasgovitz - 1984, Hugh Denison - 1984

Investm't Category: Aggressive Growth
- ✔ Cap Gain
- Cap & Income
- Income
- ✔ Domestic
- ✔ Foreign
- Country/Region
- Asset Allocation
- Fund of Funds
- Index
- Sector
- ✔ Small Cap
- Socially Conscious
- State Specific

Portfolio: stocks 89% bonds 0%
convertibles 0% other 0% cash 11%

Largest Holdings: healthcare 11%, insurance 11%

Unrealized Net Capital Gains: 4% of portfolio value

SHAREHOLDER INFORMATION

Minimum Investment
Initial: $1,000   Subsequent: $100

Minimum IRA Investment
Initial: $500   Subsequent: $100

Maximum Fees
Load: none   12b-1: 0.25%
Other: none

Distributions
Income: Dec   Capital Gains: Dec

Exchange Options
Number Per Year: 4   Fee: none
Telephone: yes (money market fund available)

Services
IRA, pension, auto invest, auto withdraw

Heartland Wisconsin Tax Free (HRWIX)

790 North Milwaukee Street
Milwaukee, WI 53202
(800) 432-7856, (414) 347-7777

Tax-Exempt Bond

	3yr Annual	5yr Annual	10yr Annual	Bull	Bear
Return (%)	na	na	na	na	-6.2
Differ from Category (+/-)	na	na	na	na	-1.0 blw av

Total Risk	Standard Deviation	Category Risk	Risk Index	Avg Mat
na	na	na	na	20.9 yrs

	1994	1993	1992	1991	1990	1989	1988	1987	1986	1985
Return (%)	-6.4	10.7	—	—	—	—	—	—	—	—
Differ from category (+/-)	-1.2	-1.0	—	—	—	—	—	—	—	—

PER SHARE DATA

	1994	1993	1992	1991	1990	1989	1988	1987	1986	1985
Dividends, Net Income ($)	0.51	0.49	—	—	—	—	—	—	—	—
Distrib'ns, Cap Gain ($)	0.00	0.02	—	—	—	—	—	—	—	—
Net Asset Value ($)	9.21	10.38	—	—	—	—	—	—	—	—
Expense Ratio (%)	0.84	0.84	—	—	—	—	—	—	—	—
Net Income to Assets (%)	4.91	4.81	—	—	—	—	—	—	—	—
Portfolio Turnover (%)	na	6	—	—	—	—	—	—	—	—
Total Assets (Millions $)	101	99	—	—	—	—	—	—	—	—

PORTFOLIO (as of 6/30/94)

Portfolio Manager: Patrick Retzer - 1992

Investm't Category: Tax-Exempt Bond

Cap Gain	Asset Allocation
Cap & Income	Fund of Funds
✔ Income	Index
	Sector
✔ Domestic	Small Cap
Foreign	Socially Conscious
Country/Region	✔ State Specific

Portfolio: stocks 0%   bonds 100%
convertibles 0%   other 0%   cash 0%

Largest Holdings: general obligation 21%

Unrealized Net Capital Gains: -4% of portfolio value

SHAREHOLDER INFORMATION

Minimum Investment
Initial: $10,000   Subsequent: $1,000

Minimum IRA Investment
Initial: na   Subsequent: na

Maximum Fees
Load: none   12b-1: none
Other: none

Distributions
Income: monthly   Capital Gains: Dec

Exchange Options
Number Per Year: no limit   Fee: none
Telephone: yes (money market fund available)

Services
auto invest, auto withdraw

Homestead Short-Term Bond (HOSBX)

1800 Massachusetts Ave., N.W.
Washington, DC 20036
(800) 258-3030

Corporate Bond

PERFORMANCE

fund inception date: 11/5/91

	3yr Annual	5yr Annual	10yr Annual	Bull	Bear
Return (%)	4.2	na	na	na	-1.5
Differ from Category (+/-)	-1.7 blw av	na	na	na	2.8 abv av

Total Risk	Standard Deviation	Category Risk	Risk Index	Avg Mat
low	2.2%	blw av	0.7	2.4 yrs

	1994	1993	1992	1991	1990	1989	1988	1987	1986	1985
Return (%)	0.0	6.6	6.2	—	—	—	—	—	—	—
Differ from category (+/-) . . .	2.4	-4.8	-2.7	—	—	—	—	—	—	—

PER SHARE DATA

	1994	1993	1992	1991	1990	1989	1988	1987	1986	1985
Dividends, Net Income ($) .	0.24	0.24	0.26	—	—	—	—	—	—	—
Distrib'ns, Cap Gain ($) . . .	0.00	0.00	0.01	—	—	—	—	—	—	—
Net Asset Value ($)	4.95	5.19	5.10	—	—	—	—	—	—	—
Expense Ratio (%)	0.75	0.75	0.75	—	—	—	—	—	—	—
Net Income to Assets (%). .	4.67	4.58	5.20	—	—	—	—	—	—	—
Portfolio Turnover (%).	na	14	19	—	—	—	—	—	—	—
Total Assets (Millions $)	52	36	10	—	—	—	—	—	—	—

PORTFOLIO (as of 6/30/94)

Portfolio Manager: Douglas Kern - 1991

Investm't Category: Corporate Bond

Cap Gain	Asset Allocation
Cap & Income	Fund of Funds
✔ Income	Index
	Sector
✔ Domestic	Small Cap
Foreign	Socially Conscious
Country/Region	State Specific

Portfolio: stocks 0% bonds 97%
convertibles 0% other 0% cash 3%

Largest Holdings: finance 33%, U.S. government and agencies 21%

Unrealized Net Capital Gains: -2% of portfolio value

SHAREHOLDER INFORMATION

Minimum Investment
Initial: $1,000   Subsequent: $100

Minimum IRA Investment
Initial: $250   Subsequent: $100

Maximum Fees
Load: none   12b-1: none
Other: none

Distributions
Income: monthly   Capital Gains: Dec

Exchange Options
Number Per Year: 4   Fee: none
Telephone: yes (money market fund available)

Services
IRA, pension, auto invest, auto withdraw

Homestead Value (HOVLX)
Growth & Income

1800 Massachusetts Ave., N.W.
Washington, DC 20036
(800) 258-3030

PERFORMANCE   fund inception date: 11/19/90

	3yr Annual	5yr Annual	10yr Annual	Bull	Bear
Return (%)	10.7	na	na	na	-2.2
Differ from Category (+/-)	3.6 high	na	na	na	4.1 high

Total Risk	Standard Deviation	Category Risk	Risk Index	Beta
av	7.5%	blw av	0.9	0.8

	1994	1993	1992	1991	1990	1989	1988	1987	1986	1985
Return (%)	2.4	18.7	11.6	17.1	—	—	—	—	—	—
Differ from category (+/-) . . .	3.8	5.5	1.4	-10.5	—	—	—	—	—	—

PER SHARE DATA

	1994	1993	1992	1991	1990	1989	1988	1987	1986	1985
Dividends, Net Income ($)	0.29	0.22	0.25	0.39	—	—	—	—	—	—
Distrib'ns, Cap Gain ($)	0.11	0.07	0.08	0.01	—	—	—	—	—	—
Net Asset Value ($)	14.50	14.54	12.49	11.48	—	—	—	—	—	—
Expense Ratio (%)	1.25	1.25	1.25	1.25	—	—	—	—	—	—
Net Income to Assets (%) . .	2.96	1.92	2.33	3.80	—	—	—	—	—	—
Portfolio Turnover (%)	na	2	5	26	—	—	—	—	—	—
Total Assets (Millions $)	90	54	19	10	—	—	—	—	—	—

PORTFOLIO (as of 6/30/94)

Portfolio Manager: Stuart E. Teach - 1990

Investm't Category: Growth & Income

Cap Gain	Asset Allocation
✔ Cap & Income	Fund of Funds
Income	Index
	Sector
✔ Domestic	Small Cap
Foreign	Socially Conscious
Country/Region	State Specific

Portfolio: stocks 84% bonds 0%
convertibles 0% other 0% cash 16%

Largest Holdings: basic industries 15%, consumer non-durables 13%

Unrealized Net Capital Gains: 8% of portfolio value

SHAREHOLDER INFORMATION

Minimum Investment
Initial: $1,000   Subsequent: $100

Minimum IRA Investment
Initial: $250   Subsequent: $100

Maximum Fees
Load: none   12b-1: none
Other: none

Distributions
Income: Jun, Dec   Capital Gains: Dec

Exchange Options
Number Per Year: 4   Fee: none
Telephone: yes (money market fund available)

Services
IRA, pension, auto invest, auto withdraw

Hotchkis and Wiley
Balanced Income (HWBAX)

Balanced

800 W. 6th St., 5th Fl.
Los Angeles, CA 90017
(800) 346-7301, (213) 362-8900

PERFORMANCE

fund inception date: 8/13/85

	3yr Annual	5yr Annual	10yr Annual	Bull	Bear
Return (%)	7.4	8.2	na	63.0	-3.8
Differ from Category (+/-)	1.0 abv av	0.2 av	na	-2.0 av	1.9 high

Total Risk	Standard Deviation	Category Risk	Risk Index	Beta
blw av	4.9%	low	0.8	0.5

	1994	1993	1992	1991	1990	1989	1988	1987	1986	1985
Return (%)	0.7	12.5	9.4	20.5	-0.4	17.8	14.6	3.9	13.0	—
Differ from category (+/-) . . .	2.6	-0.9	1.1	-2.9	0.1	0.5	2.8	1.5	-4.4	—

PER SHARE DATA

	1994	1993	1992	1991	1990	1989	1988	1987	1986	1985
Dividends, Net Income ($) .	0.81	0.90	0.72	0.79	0.85	0.93	0.73	0.80	0.54	—
Distrib'ns, Cap Gain ($) . . .	0.59	0.66	0.51	0.36	0.40	0.86	0.00	0.76	0.45	—
Net Asset Value ($)	15.16	16.44	16.02	15.79	14.10	15.44	14.67	13.46	14.44	—
Expense Ratio (%)	1.00	1.00	1.00	1.00	1.00	1.00	1.00	1.00	1.00	—
Net Income to Assets (%) . .	5.24	4.77	4.90	5.58	5.59	5.77	5.51	4.87	5.67	—
Portfolio Turnover (%)	97	155	36	75	78	97	112	81	27	—
Total Assets (Millions $)	34	33	16	11	9	7	6	3	1	—

PORTFOLIO (as of 6/30/94)

Portfolio Manager: Roger DeBard -1985, Laird Landmann - 1994, Tad Rivelle - 1994

Investm't Category: Balanced
- Cap Gain
- ✔ Cap & Income
- Income
- ✔ Asset Allocation
- Fund of Funds
- Index
- Sector
- ✔ Domestic
- ✔ Foreign
- Country/Region
- Small Cap
- Socially Conscious
- State Specific

Portfolio: stocks 54%   bonds 46%
convertibles 0%   other 0%   cash 0%

Largest Holdings: bonds—mortgage-backed 27%, stocks—financial services 4%

Unrealized Net Capital Gains: 0% of portfolio value

SHAREHOLDER INFORMATION

Minimum Investment
Initial: $5,000   Subsequent: $0

Minimum IRA Investment
Initial: $1,000   Subsequent: $0

Maximum Fees
Load: none   12b-1: none
Other: none

Distributions
Income: quarterly   Capital Gains: Dec

Exchange Options
Number Per Year: no limit   Fee: none
Telephone: yes (money market fund not available)

Services
IRA

Hotchkis and Wiley
Equity Income (HWEQX)

800 W. 6th St., 5th Fl.
Los Angeles, CA 90017
(800) 346-7301, (213) 362-8900

Growth & Income

PERFORMANCE

fund inception date: 6/24/87

	3yr Annual	5yr Annual	10yr Annual	Bull	Bear
Return (%)	8.3	7.0	na	101.1	-8.5
Differ from Category (+/-)	1.2 abv av	-0.9 blw av	na	25.3 high	-2.2 blw av

Total Risk	Standard Deviation	Category Risk	Risk Index	Beta
av	8.6%	abv av	1.0	0.9

	1994	1993	1992	1991	1990	1989	1988	1987	1986	1985
Return (%)	-3.5	15.7	13.9	34.6	-18.0	23.6	21.1	—	—	—
Differ from category (+/-) ..	-2.1	2.5	3.7	7.0	-12.0	2.2	4.1	—	—	—

PER SHARE DATA

	1994	1993	1992	1991	1990	1989	1988	1987	1986	1985
Dividends, Net Income ($) .	0.44	0.45	0.45	0.41	0.57	0.59	0.55	—	—	—
Distrib'ns, Cap Gain ($)....	0.36	0.53	0.23	0.00	0.30	0.25	0.02	—	—	—
Net Asset Value ($)......	14.61	15.97	14.66	13.48	10.34	13.65	11.75	—	—	—
Expense Ratio (%)........	1.00	1.00	1.00	1.00	1.00	1.00	1.00	—	—	—
Net Income to Assets (%) ..	2.90	2.99	2.95	4.23	4.42	4.68	5.11	—	—	—
Portfolio Turnover (%)	36	25	32	39	39	9	20	—	—	—
Total Assets (Millions $) ...	106	83	72	63	65	47	29	—	—	—

PORTFOLIO (as of 6/30/94)

Portfolio Manager: George Wiley - 1987, Gail Bardin - 1994

Investm't Category: Growth & Income

Cap Gain	Asset Allocation
✔ Cap & Income	Fund of Funds
Income	Index
	Sector
✔ Domestic	Small Cap
✔ Foreign	Socially Conscious
Country/Region	State Specific

Portfolio: stocks 92% bonds 0%
convertibles 4% other 0% cash 4%

Largest Holdings: financial services 12%, banks 8%

Unrealized Net Capital Gains: 10% of portfolio value

SHAREHOLDER INFORMATION

Minimum Investment
Initial: $5,000 Subsequent: $0

Minimum IRA Investment
Initial: $1,000 Subsequent: $0

Maximum Fees
Load: none 12b-1: none
Other: none

Distributions
Income: quarterly Capital Gains: Dec

Exchange Options
Number Per Year: no limit Fee: none
Telephone: yes (money market fund not available)

Services
IRA

Hotchkis and Wiley International (HWINX)

International Stock

800 W. 6th St., 5th Fl.
Los Angeles, CA 90017
(800) 346-7301, (213) 362-8900

PERFORMANCE

fund inception date: 10/1/90

	3yr Annual	5yr Annual	10yr Annual	Bull	Bear
Return (%)	11.2	na	na	na	-8.1
Differ from Category (+/-)	2.1 abv av	na	na	na	-1.1 blw av

Total Risk	Standard Deviation	Category Risk	Risk Index	Beta
high	14.6%	abv av	1.1	0.9

	1994	1993	1992	1991	1990	1989	1988	1987	1986	1985
Return (%)	-2.9	45.7	-2.6	20.3	—	—	—	—	—	—
Differ from category (+/-) . . .	0.1	7.1	0.3	7.2	—	—	—	—	—	—

PER SHARE DATA

	1994	1993	1992	1991	1990	1989	1988	1987	1986	1985
Dividends, Net Income ($) .	0.31	0.00	0.21	0.50	—	—	—	—	—	—
Distrib'ns, Cap Gain ($) . . .	0.45	0.15	0.31	1.29	—	—	—	—	—	—
Net Asset Value ($)	16.58	17.88	12.37	13.23	—	—	—	—	—	—
Expense Ratio (%)	1.00	1.00	1.00	1.00	—	—	—	—	—	—
Net Income to Assets (%). .	2.62	2.58	3.61	3.96	—	—	—	—	—	—
Portfolio Turnover (%).	23	24	88	224	—	—	—	—	—	—
Total Assets (Millions $)	27	10	4	1	—	—	—	—	—	—

PORTFOLIO (as of 6/30/94)

Portfolio Manager: D. Bouwer - 1990, S. Ketterer - 1990, H. Hartford - 1994

Investm't Category: International Stock
- ✔ Cap Gain
- Cap & Income
- Income
- Domestic
- ✔ Foreign
- Country/Region
- Asset Allocation
- Fund of Funds
- Index
- Sector
- Small Cap
- Socially Conscious
- State Specific

Portfolio: stocks 100% bonds 0%
convertibles 0% other 0% cash 0%

Largest Holdings: England 17%, Japan 16%

Unrealized Net Capital Gains: -1% of portfolio value

SHAREHOLDER INFORMATION

Minimum Investment
Initial: $5,000   Subsequent: $0

Minimum IRA Investment
Initial: $1,000   Subsequent: $0

Maximum Fees
Load: none   12b-1: none
Other: none

Distributions
Income: Jun, Dec   Capital Gains: Dec

Exchange Options
Number Per Year: no limit   Fee: none
Telephone: yes (money market fund not available)

Services
IRA

Hotchkis and Wiley Low Duration (HWLDX)

800 W. 6th St., 5th Fl.
Los Angeles, CA 90017
(800) 346-7301, (213) 362-8900

General Bond

PERFORMANCE

fund inception date: 5/18/93

	3yr Annual	5yr Annual	10yr Annual	Bull	Bear
Return (%)	na	na	na	na	1.7
Differ from Category (+/-)	na	na	na	na	5.5 high

Total Risk	Standard Deviation	Category Risk	Risk Index	Avg Mat
na	na	na	na	2.0 yrs

	1994	1993	1992	1991	1990	1989	1988	1987	1986	1985
Return (%)	5.2	—	—	—	—	—	—	—	—	—
Differ from category (+/-)	7.2	—	—	—	—	—	—	—	—	—

PER SHARE DATA

	1994	1993	1992	1991	1990	1989	1988	1987	1986	1985
Dividends, Net Income ($)	0.70	—	—	—	—	—	—	—	—	—
Distrib'ns, Cap Gain ($)	0.01	—	—	—	—	—	—	—	—	—
Net Asset Value ($)	9.84	—	—	—	—	—	—	—	—	—
Expense Ratio (%)	0.58	—	—	—	—	—	—	—	—	—
Net Income to Assets (%)	7.34	—	—	—	—	—	—	—	—	—
Portfolio Turnover (%)	254	—	—	—	—	—	—	—	—	—
Total Assets (Millions $)	70	—	—	—	—	—	—	—	—	—

PORTFOLIO (as of 6/30/94)

Portfolio Manager: Laird R. Landmann - 1993, Tad Rivelle - 1993

Investm't Category: General Bond

Cap Gain	Asset Allocation
Cap & Income	Fund of Funds
✔ Income	Index
	Sector
✔ Domestic	Small Cap
✔ Foreign	Socially Conscious
Country/Region	State Specific

Portfolio: stocks 0%   bonds 83%
convertibles 0%   other 0%   cash 17%

Largest Holdings: mortgage-backed 50%, corporate 31%

Unrealized Net Capital Gains: -1% of portfolio value

SHAREHOLDER INFORMATION

Minimum Investment
Initial: $5,000   Subsequent: $0

Minimum IRA Investment
Initial: $1,000   Subsequent: $0

Maximum Fees
Load: none   12b-1: none
Other: none

Distributions
Income: monthly   Capital Gains: Dec

Exchange Options
Number Per Year: no limit   Fee: none
Telephone: yes (money market fund not available)

Services
IRA

IAI Balanced (IABLX)

Balanced

3700 First Bank Place
P.O. Box 357
Minneapolis, MN 55440
(800) 945-3863, (612) 376-2700

PERFORMANCE

fund inception date: 4/10/92

	3yr Annual	5yr Annual	10yr Annual	Bull	Bear
Return (%)	na	na	na	na	-8.5
Differ from Category (+/-)	na	na	na	na	-2.8 low

Total Risk	Standard Deviation	Category Risk	Risk Index	Beta
na	na	na	na	na

	1994	1993	1992	1991	1990	1989	1988	1987	1986	1985
Return (%)	-1.4	4.9	—	—	—	—	—	—	—	—
Differ from category (+/-) . . .	0.5	-8.5	—	—	—	—	—	—	—	—

PER SHARE DATA

	1994	1993	1992	1991	1990	1989	1988	1987	1986	1985
Dividends, Net Income ($)	0.32	0.26	—	—	—	—	—	—	—	—
Distrib'ns, Cap Gain ($) . . .	0.38	0.20	—	—	—	—	—	—	—	—
Net Asset Value ($)	9.95	10.83	—	—	—	—	—	—	—	—
Expense Ratio (%)	1.25	1.25	—	—	—	—	—	—	—	—
Net Income to Assets (%). .	2.35	2.18	—	—	—	—	—	—	—	—
Portfolio Turnover (%). . . .	211	83	—	—	—	—	—	—	—	—
Total Assets (Millions $)	42	65	—	—	—	—	—	—	—	—

PORTFOLIO (as of 9/30/94)

Portfolio Manager: Mark Simenstad, James
Diedrich - 1993

Investm't Category: Balanced
   Cap Gain   ✔ Asset Allocation
✔ Cap & Income   Fund of Funds
   Income   Index
      · Sector
✔ Domestic   Small Cap
   Foreign   Socially Conscious
   Country/Region   State Specific

Portfolio: stocks 56%   bonds 35%
convertibles 0%   other 6%   cash 3%

Largest Holdings: bonds—corporate 20%,
stocks—cyclical consumer goods 11%

Unrealized Net Capital Gains: 3% of portfolio value

SHAREHOLDER INFORMATION

Minimum Investment
Initial: $5,000   Subsequent: $100

Minimum IRA Investment
Initial: $2,000   Subsequent: $100

Maximum Fees
Load: none   12b-1: 0.25%
Other: none

Distributions
Income: Jun, Dec   Capital Gains: Jun, Dec

Exchange Options
Number Per Year: 4   Fee: none
Telephone: yes (money market fund available)

Services
IRA, pension, auto exchange, auto invest, auto
withdraw

IAI Bond (IAIBX)

General Bond

3700 First Bank Place
P.O. Box 357
Minneapolis, MN 55440
(800) 945-3863, (612) 376-2700

PERFORMANCE

fund inception date: 8/18/77

	3yr Annual	5yr Annual	10yr Annual	Bull	Bear
Return (%)	4.4	7.4	9.2	55.2	-7.8
Differ from Category (+/-)	0.1 av	0.5 abv av	0.3 av	14.2 high	-4.0 low

Total Risk	Standard Deviation	Category Risk	Risk Index	Avg Mat
blw av	5.7%	high	1.5	10.6 yrs

	1994	1993	1992	1991	1990	1989	1988	1987	1986	1985
Return (%)	-4.9	12.3	6.7	17.3	7.0	15.8	6.3	2.0	12.1	20.0
Differ from category (+/-) . .	-2.9	3.1	0.1	2.7	-0.2	4.4	-1.1	-0.2	-2.1	0.6

PER SHARE DATA

	1994	1993	1992	1991	1990	1989	1988	1987	1986	1985
Dividends, Net Income ($) .	0.49	0.64	0.74	0.74	0.76	0.71	0.71	0.98	0.90	0.97
Distrib'ns, Cap Gain ($)	0.13	0.81	0.76	0.09	0.00	0.03	0.00	0.10	0.28	0.00
Net Asset Value ($)	8.66	9.76	9.99	10.82	10.00	10.10	9.39	9.51	10.39	10.37
Expense Ratio (%)	1.09	1.10	1.10	0.88	0.90	0.90	0.80	0.70	0.70	0.70
Net Income to Assets (%) . .	5.63	6.03	7.43	7.56	7.50	7.70	7.70	8.50	9.60	11.20
Portfolio Turnover (%)	333	160	126	43	78	115	20	35	76	22
Total Assets (Millions $)	80	98	107	109	80	50	41	46	31	22

PORTFOLIO (as of 9/30/94)

Portfolio Manager: Larry Hill - 1984

Investm't Category: General Bond

Cap Gain	Asset Allocation
Cap & Income	Fund of Funds
✔ Income	Index
	Sector
✔ Domestic	Small Cap
✔ Foreign	Socially Conscious
Country/Region	State Specific

Portfolio: stocks 0%   bonds 81%
convertibles 0%   other 0%   cash 19%

Largest Holdings: mortgage-backed 32%,
corporate 16%

Unrealized Net Capital Gains: -3% of portfolio value

SHAREHOLDER INFORMATION

Minimum Investment
Initial: $5,000   Subsequent: $100

Minimum IRA Investment
Initial: $2,000   Subsequent: $100

Maximum Fees
Load: none   12b-1: 0.25%
Other: none

Distributions
Income: monthly   Capital Gains: Jun, Dec

Exchange Options
Number Per Year: 4   Fee: none
Telephone: yes (money market fund available)

Services
IRA, pension, auto exchange, auto invest, auto withdraw

IAI Emerging Growth
(IAEGX)
Aggressive Growth

3700 First Bank Place
P.O. Box 357
Minneapolis, MN 55440
(800) 945-3863, (612) 376-2700

PERFORMANCE
fund inception date: 8/5/91

	3yr Annual	5yr Annual	10yr Annual	Bull	Bear
Return (%)	12.0	na	na	na	-18.2
Differ from Category (+/-)	3.1 abv av	na	na	na	-7.4 low

Total Risk	Standard Deviation	Category Risk	Risk Index	Beta
high	17.7%	high	1.2	1.1

	1994	1993	1992	1991	1990	1989	1988	1987	1986	1985
Return (%)	0.1	14.7	22.4	—	—	—	—	—	—	—
Differ from category (+/-)	0.8	-4.8	11.4	—	—	—	—	—	—	—

PER SHARE DATA

	1994	1993	1992	1991	1990	1989	1988	1987	1986	1985
Dividends, Net Income ($)	0.00	0.00	0.00	—	—	—	—	—	—	—
Distrib'ns, Cap Gain ($)	0.72	0.35	0.76	—	—	—	—	—	—	—
Net Asset Value ($)	14.90	15.74	14.03	—	—	—	—	—	—	—
Expense Ratio (%)	1.25	1.25	1.25	—	—	—	—	—	—	—
Net Income to Assets (%)	-0.77	-0.72	0.14	—	—	—	—	—	—	—
Portfolio Turnover (%)	76	96	127	—	—	—	—	—	—	—
Total Assets (Millions $)	317	212	38	—	—	—	—	—	—	—

PORTFOLIO (as of 9/30/94)

Portfolio Manager: Rick Leggott - 1991

Investm't Category: Aggressive Growth
- ✔ Cap Gain
- Cap & Income
- Income
- ✔ Domestic
- ✔ Foreign
- Country/Region
- Asset Allocation
- Fund of Funds
- Index
- Sector
- ✔ Small Cap
- Socially Conscious
- State Specific

Portfolio:
convertibles 0%	stocks 84%	bonds 0%
	other 4%	cash 12%

Largest Holdings: retail 21%, technology 15%

Unrealized Net Capital Gains: 12% of portfolio value

SHAREHOLDER INFORMATION

Minimum Investment
Initial: $5,000 — Subsequent: $100

Minimum IRA Investment
Initial: $2,000 — Subsequent: $100

Maximum Fees
Load: none — 12b-1: 0.25%
Other: none

Distributions
Income: Jun, Dec — Capital Gains: Jun, Dec

Exchange Options
Number Per Year: 4 — Fee: none
Telephone: yes (money market fund available)

Services
IRA, pension, auto exchange, auto invest, auto withdraw

IAI Gov't (IAGVX)
Government Bond

3700 First Bank Place
P.O. Box 357
Minneapolis, MN 55440
(800) 945-3863, (612) 376-2700

	3yr Annual	5yr Annual	10yr Annual	Bull	Bear
Return (%)	3.8	na	na	na	-4.1
Differ from Category (+/-)	-0.2 av	na	na	na	2.3 av

Total Risk	Standard Deviation	Category Risk	Risk Index	Avg Mat
low	3.5%	blw av	0.7	4.3 yrs

	1994	1993	1992	1991	1990	1989	1988	1987	1986	1985
Return (%)	-2.2	8.5	5.6	—	—	—	—	—	—	—
Differ from category (+/-) . . .	2.6	-2.4	-0.8	—	—	—	—	—	—	—

PER SHARE DATA

	1994	1993	1992	1991	1990	1989	1988	1987	1986	1985
Dividends, Net Income ($) .	0.47	0.55	0.59	—	—	—	—	—	—	—
Distrib'ns, Cap Gain ($)	0.03	0.21	0.34	—	—	—	—	—	—	—
Net Asset Value ($)	9.60	10.33	10.23	—	—	—	—	—	—	—
Expense Ratio (%)	1.10	1.10	1.10	—	—	—	—	—	—	—
Net Income to Assets (%) . .	4.40	5.40	5.16	—	—	—	—	—	—	—
Portfolio Turnover (%)	641	236	170	—	—	—	—	—	—	—
Total Assets (Millions $)	39	41	31	—	—	—	—	—	—	—

PORTFOLIO (as of 9/30/94)

Portfolio Manager: Scott Bettin - 1991

Investm't Category: Government Bond

Cap Gain	Asset Allocation
Cap & Income	Fund of Funds
✔ Income	Index
	Sector
✔ Domestic	Small Cap
Foreign	Socially Conscious
Country/Region	State Specific

Portfolio: stocks 0%   bonds 77%
convertibles 0%   other 0%   cash 23%

Largest Holdings: U.S. government 39%,
mortgage-backed 38%

Unrealized Net Capital Gains: -2% of portfolio value

SHAREHOLDER INFORMATION

Minimum Investment
Initial: $5,000   Subsequent: $100

Minimum IRA Investment
Initial: $2,000   Subsequent: $100

Maximum Fees
Load: none   12b-1: 0.25%
Other: none

Distributions
Income: monthly   Capital Gains: Jun, Dec

Exchange Options
Number Per Year: 4   Fee: none
Telephone: yes (money market fund available)

Services
IRA, pension, auto exchange, auto invest, auto withdraw

IAI Growth & Income

(IASKX)

Growth & Income

3700 First Bank Place
P.O. Box 357
Minneapolis, MN 55440
(800) 945-3863, (612) 376-2700

	3yr Annual	5yr Annual	10yr Annual	Bull	Bear
Return (%)	2.8	5.1	11.3	53.5	-7.7
Differ from Category (+/-)	-4.3 low	-2.8 low	-0.4 av	-22.3 low	-1.4 blw av

Total Risk	Standard Deviation	Category Risk	Risk Index	Beta
av	8.3%	av	1.0	0.9

	1994	1993	1992	1991	1990	1989	1988	1987	1986	1985
Return (%)	-4.7	9.9	3.9	26.7	-6.8	29.6	8.3	15.6	13.1	23.7
Differ from category (+/-) . .	-3.3	-3.3	-6.3	-0.9	-0.8	8.2	-8.7	15.0	-2.7	-2.0

PER SHARE DATA

	1994	1993	1992	1991	1990	1989	1988	1987	1986	1985
Dividends, Net Income ($) .	0.10	0.06	0.09	0.15	0.29	0.43	0.23	0.37	0.37	0.48
Distrib'ns, Cap Gain ($) . . .	0.65	1.68	0.69	0.94	1.70	2.76	1.10	1.34	1.80	0.46
Net Asset Value ($)	13.06	14.51	14.85	15.10	12.84	15.79	14.70	14.79	14.25	14.54
Expense Ratio (%)	1.25	1.25	1.25	1.05	1.00	0.90	0.80	0.80	0.70	0.70
Net Income to Assets (%). .	0.60	0.61	1.03	2.19	2.10	1.80	1.70	2.10	2.90	3.90
Portfolio Turnover (%). . . .	205	175	210	69	66	48	36	68	50	62
Total Assets (Millions $) . . .	104	123	113	91	77	77	83	84	69	60

PORTFOLIO (as of 9/30/94)

Portfolio Manager: Todd McCallister - 1993

Investm't Category: Growth & Income
- Cap Gain
- ✔ Cap & Income
- Income

- Asset Allocation
- Fund of Funds
- Index
- Sector
- ✔ Domestic
- ✔ Foreign
- Country/Region
- Small Cap
- Socially Conscious
- State Specific

Portfolio: stocks 81%   bonds 3%
convertibles 3%   other 11%   cash 2%

Largest Holdings: consumer non-cyclical 18%, consumer cyclical 14%

Unrealized Net Capital Gains: 5% of portfolio value

SHAREHOLDER INFORMATION

Minimum Investment
Initial: $5,000   Subsequent: $100

Minimum IRA Investment
Initial: $2,000   Subsequent: $100

Maximum Fees
Load: none   12b-1: 0.25%
Other: none

Distributions
Income: Jun, Dec   Capital Gains: Jun, Dec

Exchange Options
Number Per Year: 4   Fee: none
Telephone: yes (money market fund available)

Services
IRA, pension, auto exchange, auto invest, auto withdraw

IAI Int'l (IAINX)

International Stock

3700 First Bank Place
P.O. Box 357
Minneapolis, MN 55440
(800) 945-3863, (612) 376-2700

PERFORMANCE

fund inception date: 4/23/87

	3yr Annual	5yr Annual	10yr Annual	Bull	Bear
Return (%)	9.5	5.8	na	69.0	-3.6
Differ from Category (+/-)	0.4 abv av	0.9 abv av	na	5.1 abv av	3.4 abv av

Total Risk	Standard Deviation	Category Risk	Risk Index	Beta
high	12.5%	av	0.9	0.8

	1994	1993	1992	1991	1990	1989	1988	1987	1986	1985
Return (%)	0.4	39.4	-6.3	16.5	-13.0	18.3	18.0	—	—	—
Differ from category (+/-)	3.4	0.8	-3.4	3.4	-2.6	-4.2	3.6	—	—	—

PER SHARE DATA

	1994	1993	1992	1991	1990	1989	1988	1987	1986	1985
Dividends, Net Income ($)	0.00	0.34	0.04	0.22	0.00	0.30	0.10	—	—	—
Distrib'ns, Cap Gain ($)	0.88	0.05	0.42	0.33	0.14	0.63	0.00	—	—	—
Net Asset Value ($)	12.79	13.61	10.08	11.22	10.15	11.84	10.85	—	—	—
Expense Ratio (%)	1.74	1.91	2.00	1.73	1.90	2.10	2.13	—	—	—
Net Income to Assets (%)	0.87	1.42	1.39	2.79	1.00	1.20	-0.16	—	—	—
Portfolio Turnover (%)	50	28	35	41	33	71	53	—	—	—
Total Assets (Millions $)	149	122	36	34	30	16	12	—	—	—

PORTFOLIO (as of 9/30/94)

Portfolio Manager: Roy Gillson - 1990

Investm't Category: International Stock

✔ Cap Gain	Asset Allocation
Cap & Income	Fund of Funds
Income	Index
	Sector
Domestic	Small Cap
✔ Foreign	Socially Conscious
Country/Region	State Specific

Portfolio: stocks 96% bonds 3%
convertibles 0% other 0% cash 1%

Largest Holdings: Japan 27%, United Kingdom 15%

Unrealized Net Capital Gains: 7% of portfolio value

SHAREHOLDER INFORMATION

Minimum Investment
Initial: $5,000 Subsequent: $100

Minimum IRA Investment
Initial: $2,000 Subsequent: $100

Maximum Fees
Load: none 12b-1: 0.25%
Other: none

Distributions
Income: Jun, Dec Capital Gains: Jun, Dec

Exchange Options
Number Per Year: 4 Fee: none
Telephone: yes (money market fund available)

Services
IRA, pension, auto exchange, auto invest, auto withdraw

IAI MidCap Growth

(IAMCX)

Growth

3700 First Bank Place
P.O. Box 357
Minneapolis, MN 55440
(800) 945-3863, (612) 376-2700

fund inception date: 4/10/92

PERFORMANCE

	3yr Annual	5yr Annual	10yr Annual	Bull	Bear
Return (%)	na	na	na	na	-5.4
Differ from Category (+/-)	na	na	na	na	1.2 abv av

Total Risk	Standard Deviation		Category Risk	Risk Index	Beta
na	na		na	na	na

	1994	1993	1992	1991	1990	1989	1988	1987	1986	1985
Return (%)	5.6	22.8	—	—	—	—	—	—	—	—
Differ from category (+/-)	6.2	9.4	—	—	—	—	—	—	—	—

PER SHARE DATA

	1994	1993	1992	1991	1990	1989	1988	1987	1986	1985
Dividends, Net Income ($)	0.00	0.00	—	—	—	—	—	—	—	—
Distrib'ns, Cap Gain ($)	0.63	0.16	—	—	—	—	—	—	—	—
Net Asset Value ($)	14.05	13.93	—	—	—	—	—	—	—	—
Expense Ratio (%)	1.25	1.25	—	—	—	—	—	—	—	—
Net Income to Assets (%)	-0.45	0.24	—	—	—	—	—	—	—	—
Portfolio Turnover (%)	49	57	—	—	—	—	—	—	—	—
Total Assets (Millions $)	84	41	—	—	—	—	—	—	—	—

PORTFOLIO (as of 9/30/94)

Portfolio Manager: Suzanne Zak - 1993

Investm't Category: Growth

- ✔ Cap Gain
- Cap & Income
- Income
- ✔ Domestic
- ✔ Foreign
- Country/Region

- Asset Allocation
- Fund of Funds
- Index
- Sector
- Small Cap
- Socially Conscious
- State Specific

Portfolio: stocks 93% bonds 0%
convertibles 0% other 2% cash 5%

Largest Holdings: consumer cyclical 15%, technology 15%

Unrealized Net Capital Gains: 7% of portfolio value

SHAREHOLDER INFORMATION

Minimum Investment
Initial: $5,000   Subsequent: $100

Minimum IRA Investment
Initial: $2,000   Subsequent: $100

Maximum Fees
Load: none   12b-1: 0.25%
Other: none

Distributions
Income: Jun, Dec   Capital Gains: Jun, Dec

Exchange Options
Number Per Year: 4   Fee: none
Telephone: yes (money market fund available)

Services
IRA, pension, auto exchange, auto invest, auto withdraw

IAI Regional (IARGX)

Growth

3700 First Bank Place
P.O. Box 357
Minneapolis, MN 55440
(800) 945-3863, (612) 376-2700

PERFORMANCE

fund inception date: 5/20/80

	3yr Annual	5yr Annual	10yr Annual	Bull	Bear
Return (%)	4.3	8.8	15.8	68.4	-7.4
Differ from Category (+/-)	-3.4 blw av	-0.8 av	2.9 high	-23.7 blw av	-0.8 blw av

Total Risk	Standard Deviation	Category Risk	Risk Index	Beta
av	8.2%	blw av	0.8	0.8

	1994	1993	1992	1991	1990	1989	1988	1987	1986	1985
Return (%)	0.6	8.9	3.5	35.3	-0.3	31.2	18.7	5.1	24.6	38.8
Differ from category (+/-)	1.2	-4.5	-8.1	-0.4	5.4	5.1	0.7	3.3	10.0	9.6

PER SHARE DATA

	1994	1993	1992	1991	1990	1989	1988	1987	1986	1985
Dividends, Net Income ($)	0.20	0.18	0.23	0.24	0.33	0.51	0.27	0.40	0.42	0.43
Distrib'ns, Cap Gain ($)	1.19	1.82	0.52	2.08	0.82	3.97	0.57	3.21	6.45	0.40
Net Asset Value ($)	20.15	21.45	21.58	21.62	17.79	18.98	17.99	15.86	18.42	20.53
Expense Ratio (%)	1.25	1.25	1.25	1.01	1.00	1.00	0.80	0.80	0.80	0.90
Net Income to Assets (%)	0.94	1.09	1.20	2.27	2.30	2.00	1.60	1.80	3.00	2.60
Portfolio Turnover (%)	163	139	141	169	116	94	85	133	80	77
Total Assets (Millions $)	514	616	529	284	138	102	86	102	56	44

PORTFOLIO (as of 9/30/94)

Portfolio Manager: Julian Carlin - 1980

Investm't Category: Growth

✔ Cap Gain
   Cap & Income
   Income
✔ Domestic
   Foreign
   Country/Region

   Asset Allocation
   Fund of Funds
   Index
   Sector
   Small Cap
   Socially Conscious
   State Specific

Portfolio: stocks 66% bonds 0%
convertibles 0% other 6% cash 28%

Largest Holdings: consumer cyclical 17%, industrial 14%

Unrealized Net Capital Gains: 2% of portfolio value

SHAREHOLDER INFORMATION

Minimum Investment
Initial: $5,000   Subsequent: $100

Minimum IRA Investment
Initial: $2,000   Subsequent: $100

Maximum Fees
Load: none   12b-1: 0.25%
Other: none

Distributions
Income: Jun, Dec   Capital Gains: Jun, Dec

Exchange Options
Number Per Year: 4   Fee: none
Telephone: yes (money market fund available)

Services
IRA, pension, auto exchange, auto invest, auto withdraw

IAI Reserve (IARVX)

General Bond

3700 First Bank Place
P.O. Box 357
Minneapolis, MN 55440
(800) 945-3863, (612) 376-2700

PERFORMANCE

fund inception date: 1/31/86

	3yr Annual	5yr Annual	10yr Annual	Bull	Bear
Return (%)	3.1	5.1	na	18.5	0.3
Differ from Category (+/-)	-1.2 low	-1.8 low	na	-22.5 low	4.1 high

Total Risk	Standard Deviation	Category Risk	Risk Index	Avg Mat
low	0.5%	low	0.1	1.1 yrs

	1994	1993	1992	1991	1990	1989	1988	1987	1986	1985
Return (%)	2.7	3.3	3.2	7.9	8.3	8.7	6.7	5.8	—	—
Differ from category (+/-)	4.7	-5.9	-3.4	-6.7	1.1	-2.7	-0.7	3.6	—	—

PER SHARE DATA

	1994	1993	1992	1991	1990	1989	1988	1987	1986	1985
Dividends, Net Income ($)	0.46	0.38	0.39	0.59	0.80	0.78	0.69	0.70	—	—
Distrib'ns, Cap Gain ($)	0.00	0.01	0.08	0.08	0.00	0.00	0.00	0.00	—	—
Net Asset Value ($)	9.85	10.04	10.09	10.24	10.13	10.11	10.04	10.07	—	—
Expense Ratio (%)	0.85	0.85	0.85	0.85	0.85	0.80	0.80	0.80	—	—
Net Income to Assets (%)	3.95	3.49	5.63	7.09	7.90	7.20	5.90	5.60	—	—
Portfolio Turnover (%)	235	538	218	87	63	64	0	30	—	—
Total Assets (Millions $)	78	100	108	104	79	66	68	35	—	—

PORTFOLIO (as of 9/30/94)

Portfolio Manager: Timothy Palmer - 1991

Investm't Category: General Bond

Cap Gain	Asset Allocation
Cap & Income	Fund of Funds
✔ Income	Index
	Sector
✔ Domestic	Small Cap
✔ Foreign	Socially Conscious
Country/Region	State Specific

Portfolio: stocks 0% bonds 100%
convertibles 0% other 0% cash 0%

Largest Holdings: commercial paper 50%, corporate 26%

Unrealized Net Capital Gains: -1% of portfolio value

SHAREHOLDER INFORMATION

Minimum Investment
Initial: $5,000   Subsequent: $100

Minimum IRA Investment
Initial: $2,000   Subsequent: $100

Maximum Fees
Load: none   12b-1: 0.10%
Other: none

Distributions
Income: monthly   Capital Gains: Jun, Dec

Exchange Options
Number Per Year: 4   Fee: none
Telephone: yes (money market fund available)

Services
IRA, pension, auto exchange, auto invest, auto withdraw

IAI Value (IAAPX)

Growth

3700 First Bank Place
P.O. Box 357
Minneapolis, MN 55440
(800) 945-3863, (612) 376-2700

PERFORMANCE

fund inception date: 10/12/83

	3yr Annual	5yr Annual	10yr Annual	Bull	Bear
Return (%)	7.4	5.6	10.1	76.5	-5.8
Differ from Category (+/-)	-0.3 av	-4.0 low	-2.8 low	-15.6 blw av	0.8 av

Total Risk	Standard Deviation	Category Risk	Risk Index	Beta
abv av	9.5%	av	1.0	0.7

	1994	1993	1992	1991	1990	1989	1988	1987	1986	1985
Return (%)	-9.0	22.0	11.9	19.7	-11.6	22.5	24.3	14.1	1.9	12.9
Differ from category (+/-) . .	-8.4	8.6	0.3	-16.0	-5.9	-3.6	6.3	12.3	-12.7	-16.3

PER SHARE DATA

	1994	1993	1992	1991	1990	1989	1988	1987	1986	1985
Dividends, Net Income ($) .	0.03	0.13	0.00	0.15	0.17	0.18	0.10	0.17	0.18	0.20
Distrib'ns, Cap Gain ($). . . .	0.84	1.37	0.10	0.45	2.24	1.97	0.09	1.68	0.31	0.20
Net Asset Value ($).	10.18	12.11	11.18	10.09	8.94	12.60	12.08	9.87	10.18	10.45
Expense Ratio (%)	1.25	1.25	1.25	1.10	1.00	1.00	1.00	1.00	1.00	1.00
Net Income to Assets (%) . .	0.35	0.68	1.24	2.00	1.30	1.00	1.00	1.30	2.10	2.60
Portfolio Turnover (%)	191	118	125	57	70	53	63	86	85	35
Total Assets (Millions $)	34	30	32	22	26	28	21	22	24	18

PORTFOLIO (as of 9/30/94)

Portfolio Manager: Doug Platt - 1991

Investm't Category: Growth
- ✔ Cap Gain
- Cap & Income
- Income
- Asset Allocation
- Fund of Funds
- Index
- Sector
- ✔ Domestic
- ✔ Foreign
- Country/Region
- Small Cap
- Socially Conscious
- State Specific

Portfolio: stocks 84%   bonds 0%
convertibles 0%   other 8%   cash 8%

Largest Holdings: consumer cyclical 18%, industrial 17%

Unrealized Net Capital Gains: 0% of portfolio value

SHAREHOLDER INFORMATION

Minimum Investment
Initial: $5,000   Subsequent: $100

Minimum IRA Investment
Initial: $2,000   Subsequent: $100

Maximum Fees
Load: none   12b-1: 0.25%
Other: none

Distributions
Income: Jun, Dec   Capital Gains: Jun, Dec

Exchange Options
Number Per Year: 4   Fee: none
Telephone: yes (money market fund available)

Services
IRA, pension, auto exchange, auto invest, auto withdraw

International Equity

(SCIEX)

International Stock

787 Seventh Ave.
New York, NY 10019
(800) 344-8332, (212) 841-3841

PERFORMANCE

fund inception date: 12/1/85

	3yr Annual	5yr Annual	10yr Annual	Bull	Bear
Return (%)	11.7	5.2	na	65.5	-4.9
Differ from Category (+/-)	2.6 abv av	0.3 av	na	1.6 abv av	2.1 abv av

Total Risk	Standard Deviation	Category Risk	Risk Index	Beta
high	12.7%	av	1.0	0.7

	1994	1993	1992	1991	1990	1989	1988	1987	1986	1985
Return (%)	-0.2	45.7	-4.0	4.5	-11.3	22.1	19.4	3.7	49.6	—
Differ from category (+/-). . .	2.8	7.1	-1.1	-8.6	-0.9	-0.4	5.0	-10.7	-9.4	—

PER SHARE DATA

	1994	1993	1992	1991	1990	1989	1988	1987	1986	1985
Dividends, Net Income ($) .	0.00	0.08	0.12	0.23	0.25	0.44	0.04	0.00	0.02	—
Distrib'ns, Cap Gain ($) . . .	2.54	0.00	0.00	0.05	1.23	0.08	0.05	1.33	0.67	—
Net Asset Value ($)	19.44	21.94	15.11	15.86	15.44	19.10	16.07	13.52	14.37	—
Expense Ratio (%)	1.03	0.91	0.93	1.07	1.12	1.12	1.30	1.64	2.47	—
Net Income to Assets (%). .	0.37	0.84	1.62	1.59	0.83	1.27	0.38	0.42	-0.12	—
Portfolio Turnover (%).	50	56	49	51	56	72	86	85	77	—
Total Assets (Millions $) . . .	174	363	160	108	62	49	30	33	9	—

PORTFOLIO (as of 4/30/94)

Portfolio Manager: Mark J. Smith - 1989

Investm't Category: International Stock

✔ Cap Gain	Asset Allocation
Cap & Income	Fund of Funds
Income	Index
	Sector
Domestic	Small Cap
✔ Foreign	Socially Conscious
Country/Region	State Specific

Portfolio: stocks 100% bonds 0%
convertibles 0% other 0% cash 0%

Largest Holdings: Japan 31%, United Kingdom 15%

Unrealized Net Capital Gains: 19% of portfolio value

SHAREHOLDER INFORMATION

Minimum Investment
Initial: $2,500   Subsequent: $100

Minimum IRA Investment
Initial: $250   Subsequent: $100

Maximum Fees
Load: none   12b-1: 0.50%
Other: none

Distributions
Income: Dec   Capital Gains: Dec

Exchange Options
Number Per Year: none   Fee:
Telephone:

Services
IRA

INVESCO Dynamics
(FIDYX)
Aggressive Growth

P.O. Box 173706
Denver, CO 80217
(800) 525-8085, (303) 930-6300

PERFORMANCE

fund inception date: 9/15/67

	3yr Annual	5yr Annual	10yr Annual	Bull	Bear
Return (%)	9.7	15.6	14.7	149.5	-10.9
Differ from Category (+/-)	0.8 abv av	3.1 abv av	0.7 av	16.3 abv av	-0.1 av

Total Risk	Standard Deviation	Category Risk	Risk Index	Beta
high	13.7%	av	0.9	1.1

	1994	1993	1992	1991	1990	1989	1988	1987	1986	1985
Return (%)	-1.9	19.0	13.1	66.9	-6.3	22.6	9.1	3.7	6.4	29.1
Differ from category (+/-) . .	-1.2	-0.5	2.1	14.8	-0.1	-4.2	-6.1	5.9	-5.4	-3.2

PER SHARE DATA

	1994	1993	1992	1991	1990	1989	1988	1987	1986	1985
Dividends, Net Income ($)	0.00	0.00	0.00	0.00	0.12	0.12	0.09	0.02	0.06	0.09
Distrib'ns, Cap Gain ($)	2.30	0.80	0.29	1.20	0.00	0.29	0.00	1.36	2.09	0.00
Net Asset Value ($)	10.24	12.83	11.50	10.47	7.09	7.70	6.61	6.14	7.06	8.56
Expense Ratio (%)	1.17	1.20	1.18	1.15	0.98	0.98	1.02	0.92	0.90	0.78
Net Income to Assets (%)	-0.37	-0.38	-0.17	0.59	1.47	1.77	0.28	0.27	0.63	1.30
Portfolio Turnover (%)	169	144	174	243	225	237	199	234	246	152
Total Assets (Millions $) . . .	338	311	154	101	61	90	84	91	87	73

PORTFOLIO (as of 10/31/94)

Portfolio Manager: Tim Miller - 1993

Investm't Category: Aggressive Growth

✔ Cap Gain — Asset Allocation
Cap & Income — Fund of Funds
Income — Index
— Sector
✔ Domestic — Small Cap
✔ Foreign — Socially Conscious
Country/Region — State Specific

Portfolio: stocks 83% bonds 0%
convertibles 0% other 1% cash 16%

Largest Holdings: computer software 13%, retail 9%

Unrealized Net Capital Gains: 5% of portfolio value

SHAREHOLDER INFORMATION

Minimum Investment
Initial: $1,000   Subsequent: $50

Minimum IRA Investment
Initial: $250   Subsequent: $50

Maximum Fees
Load: none   12b-1: 0.25%
Other: none

Distributions
Income: Dec   Capital Gains: Dec

Exchange Options
Number Per Year: 4   Fee: none
Telephone: yes (money market fund available)

Services
IRA, pension, auto exchange, auto invest, auto withdraw

INVESCO Emerging Growth (FIEGX)

Aggressive Growth

P.O. Box 173706
Denver, CO 80217
(800) 525-8085, (303) 930-6300

PERFORMANCE

fund inception date: 12/27/91

	3yr Annual	5yr Annual	10yr Annual	Bull	Bear
Return (%)	14.3	na	na	na	-6.7
Differ from Category (+/-)	5.4 abv av	na	na	na	4.1 abv av

Total Risk	Standard Deviation	Category Risk	Risk Index	Beta
high	14.9%	av	1.0	0.8

	1994	1993	1992	1991	1990	1989	1988	1987	1986	1985
Return (%)	-3.7	23.4	25.7	—	—	—	—	—	—	—
Differ from category (+/-) . .	-3.0	3.9	14.7	—	—	—	—	—	—	—

PER SHARE DATA

	1994	1993	1992	1991	1990	1989	1988	1987	1986	1985
Dividends, Net Income ($)	0.00	0.00	0.00	—	—	—	—	—	—	—
Distrib'ns, Cap Gain ($) . . .	2.49	0.01	0.00	—	—	—	—	—	—	—
Net Asset Value ($)	9.17	12.11	9.82	—	—	—	—	—	—	—
Expense Ratio (%)	1.37	1.54	1.93	—	—	—	—	—	—	—
Net Income to Assets (%) .	-0.26	-0.70	-0.95	—	—	—	—	—	—	—
Portfolio Turnover (%)	196	153	50	—	—	—	—	—	—	—
Total Assets (Millions $) . . .	179	218	26	—	—	—	—	—	—	—

PORTFOLIO (as of 6/30/94)

Portfolio Manager: Doug Pratt - 1993

Investm't Category: Aggressive Growth

✔ Cap Gain	Asset Allocation
Cap & Income	Fund of Funds
Income	Index
	Sector
✔ Domestic	✔ Small Cap
✔ Foreign	Socially Conscious
Country/Region	State Specific

Portfolio: stocks 73% bonds 0%
convertibles 0% other 0% cash 27%

Largest Holdings: steel 8%, insurance 5%

Unrealized Net Capital Gains: 6% of portfolio value

SHAREHOLDER INFORMATION

Minimum Investment
Initial: $1,000   Subsequent: $50

Minimum IRA Investment
Initial: $250   Subsequent: $50

Maximum Fees
Load: none   12b-1: 0.25%
Other: none

Distributions
Income: May   Capital Gains: Dec

Exchange Options
Number Per Year: 4   Fee: none
Telephone: yes (money market fund available)

Services
IRA, pension, auto exchange, auto invest, auto withdraw

INVESCO Growth
(FLRFX)
Growth

P.O. Box 173706
Denver, CO 80217
(800) 525-8085, (303) 930-6300

	3yr Annual	5yr Annual	10yr Annual	Bull	Bear
Return (%)	3.4	9.2	11.6	90.6	-12.0
Differ from Category (+/-)	-4.3 low	-0.4 av	-1.3 blw av	-1.5 av	-5.4 low

Total Risk	Standard Deviation	Category Risk	Risk Index	Beta
abv av	10.3%	abv av	1.1	1.0

	1994	1993	1992	1991	1990	1989	1988	1987	1986	1985
Return (%)	-8.8	17.9	2.9	42.0	-1.1	31.2	5.8	0.0	8.1	28.4
Differ from category (+/-) ..	-8.2	4.5	-8.7	6.3	4.6	5.1	-12.2	-1.8	-6.5	-0.8

PER SHARE DATA

	1994	1993	1992	1991	1990	1989	1988	1987	1986	1985
Dividends, Net Income ($) .	0.03	0.03	0.04	0.07	0.11	0.10	0.07	0.08	0.10	0.14
Distrib'ns, Cap Gain ($)....	0.50	0.44	0.54	0.48	0.02	0.00	0.00	0.64	1.02	0.46
Net Asset Value ($).......	4.52	5.54	5.12	5.59	4.36	4.55	3.55	3.42	3.96	4.66
Expense Ratio (%)	1.03	1.04	1.04	1.00	0.78	0.82	0.81	0.77	0.71	0.68
Net Income to Assets (%) ..	0.47	0.72	0.93	1.52	2.17	2.60	1.84	1.56	4.85	5.72
Portfolio Turnover (%)	63	77	77	69	86	90	116	250	160	54
Total Assets (Millions $) ...	444	510	408	428	340	383	328	481	342	249

PORTFOLIO (as of 8/31/94)

Portfolio Manager: R. Dalton Sim - 1988

Investm't Category: Growth

✔ Cap Gain	Asset Allocation
Cap & Income	Fund of Funds
Income	Index
	Sector
✔ Domestic	Small Cap
Foreign	Socially Conscious
Country/Region	State Specific

Portfolio: stocks 89%   bonds 0%
convertibles 0%   other 0%   cash 11%

Largest Holdings: computer related 11%, utilities 7%

Unrealized Net Capital Gains: 12% of portfolio value

SHAREHOLDER INFORMATION

Minimum Investment
Initial: $1,000   Subsequent: $50

Minimum IRA Investment
Initial: $250   Subsequent: $50

Maximum Fees
Load: none   12b-1: 0.25%
Other: none

Distributions
Income: quarterly   Capital Gains: Dec

Exchange Options
Number Per Year: 4   Fee: none
Telephone: yes (money market fund available)

Services
IRA, pension, auto exchange, auto invest, auto withdraw

INVESCO Income—High Yield (FHYPX)

Corporate High-Yield Bond

P.O. Box 173706
Denver, CO 80217
(800) 525-8085, (303) 930-6300

PERFORMANCE

fund inception date: 3/1/84

	3yr Annual	5yr Annual	10yr Annual	Bull	Bear
Return (%)	7.9	8.2	10.1	66.5	-6.1
Differ from Category (+/-)	-2.0 blw av	-1.1 low	0.2 abv av	-12.8 blw av	-0.8 blw av

Total Risk	Standard Deviation	Category Risk	Risk Index	Avg Mat
low	4.7%	blw av	0.9	9.4 yrs

	1994	1993	1992	1991	1990	1989	1988	1987	1986	1985
Return (%)	-4.9	15.6	14.5	23.4	-4.5	3.6	13.4	3.6	14.5	26.5
Differ from category (+/-)	-2.2	-2.8	-1.1	-4.0	0.6	2.2	1.3	2.5	0.2	3.3

PER SHARE DATA

	1994	1993	1992	1991	1990	1989	1988	1987	1986	1985
Dividends, Net Income ($)	0.66	0.60	0.62	0.68	0.85	0.95	0.93	0.94	1.01	1.03
Distrib'ns, Cap Gain ($)	0.03	0.00	0.00	0.00	0.00	0.00	0.00	0.00	0.17	0.00
Net Asset Value ($)	6.38	7.43	6.97	6.66	6.00	7.16	7.82	7.75	8.38	8.37
Expense Ratio (%)	0.97	0.97	1.00	1.05	0.94	0.83	0.82	0.86	0.76	0.93
Net Income to Assets (%)	8.70	8.28	9.29	10.57	12.57	12.27	11.72	11.22	11.35	12.97
Portfolio Turnover (%)	195	45	120	64	28	53	42	89	134	96
Total Assets (Millions $)	210	294	212	99	40	49	61	38	46	18

PORTFOLIO (as of 8/31/94)

Portfolio Manager: Jerry Paul - 1994

Investm't Category: Corp. High-Yield Bond

Cap Gain	Asset Allocation
✔ Cap & Income	Fund of Funds
Income	Index
	Sector
✔ Domestic	Small Cap
Foreign	Socially Conscious
Country/Region	State Specific

Portfolio: stocks 0% bonds 90%
convertibles 0% other 3% cash 7%

Largest Holdings: cable television 8%, broadcasting 8%

Unrealized Net Capital Gains: -4% of portfolio value

SHAREHOLDER INFORMATION

Minimum Investment
Initial: $1,000   Subsequent: $50

Minimum IRA Investment
Initial: $250   Subsequent: $50

Maximum Fees
Load: none   12b-1: 0.25%
Other: none

Distributions
Income: monthly   Capital Gains: Dec

Exchange Options
Number Per Year: 4   Fee: none
Telephone: yes (money market fund available)

Services
IRA, pension, auto exchange, auto invest, auto withdraw

INVESCO Income— Sel Income (FBDSX)

Corporate Bond

P.O. Box 173706
Denver, CO 80217
(800) 525-8085, (303) 930-6300

PERFORMANCE

fund inception date: 11/12/76

	3yr Annual	5yr Annual	10yr Annual	Bull	Bear
Return (%)	6.7	8.6	9.9	53.1	-4.1
Differ from Category (+/-)	0.8 abv av	0.8 high	0.4 av	3.3 abv av	0.2 av

Total Risk	Standard Deviation	Category Risk	Risk Index	Avg Mat
low	3.3%	av	1.1	14.7 yrs

	1994	1993	1992	1991	1990	1989	1988	1987	1986	1985
Return (%)	-1.2	11.3	10.4	18.6	4.9	8.1	10.3	-1.5	18.8	22.6
Differ from category (+/-) ...	1.2	-0.1	1.5	1.5	0.1	-1.2	1.2	-3.6	4.0	2.9

PER SHARE DATA

	1994	1993	1992	1991	1990	1989	1988	1987	1986	1985
Dividends, Net Income ($) .	0.46	0.50	0.52	0.53	0.59	0.63	0.61	0.64	0.68	0.72
Distrib'ns, Cap Gain ($)....	0.00	0.19	0.10	0.00	0.00	0.00	0.00	0.00	0.32	0.00
Net Asset Value ($).......	6.03	6.57	6.53	6.50	5.96	6.26	6.39	6.36	7.10	6.84
Expense Ratio (%)........	1.11	1.15	1.14	1.15	1.01	0.99	1.00	0.99	0.85	0.97
Net Income to Assets (%) ..	7.22	7.40	7.97	8.57	9.67	9.92	9.47	9.36	9.19	11.10
Portfolio Turnover (%)	135	105	178	117	38	121	143	131	153	146
Total Assets (Millions $) ...	136	155	123	94	46	33	30	20	24	15

PORTFOLIO (as of 8/31/94)

Portfolio Manager: Jerry Paul - 1994

Investm't Category: Corporate Bond

Cap Gain	Asset Allocation
Cap & Income	Fund of Funds
✔ Income	Index
	Sector
✔ Domestic	Small Cap
Foreign	Socially Conscious
Country/Region	State Specific

Portfolio: stocks 0% bonds 91%
convertibles 0% other 0% cash 9%

Largest Holdings: mortgage-backed 19%, re-tail 9%

Unrealized Net Capital Gains: -3% of portfolio value

SHAREHOLDER INFORMATION

Minimum Investment
Initial: $1,000   Subsequent: $50

Minimum IRA Investment
Initial: $250   Subsequent: $50

Maximum Fees
Load: none   12b-1: 0.25%
Other: none

Distributions
Income: monthly   Capital Gains: Dec

Exchange Options
Number Per Year: 4   Fee: none
Telephone: yes (money market fund available)

Services
IRA, pension, auto exchange, auto invest, auto withdraw

INVESCO Income— US Gov't Sec (FBDGX)

Government Bond

P.O. Box 173706
Denver, CO 80217
(800) 525-8085, (303) 930-6300

PERFORMANCE

fund inception date: 1/2/86

	3yr Annual	5yr Annual	10yr Annual	Bull	Bear
Return (%)	2.6	6.0	na	46.2	-8.9
Differ from Category (+/-)	-1.4 low	-0.7 low	na	-5.0 av	-2.5 blw av

Total Risk	Standard Deviation	Category Risk	Risk Index	Avg Mat
blw av	5.7%	abv av	1.2	24.7 yrs

	1994	1993	1992	1991	1990	1989	1988	1987	1986	1985
Return (%)	-7.0	10.2	5.7	15.5	7.2	12.4	6.1	-5.0	14.2	—
Differ from category (+/-) . .	-2.2	-0.7	-0.7	0.2	1.0	-2.1	-1.8	-2.9	-6.4	—

PER SHARE DATA

	1994	1993	1992	1991	1990	1989	1988	1987	1986	1985
Dividends, Net Income ($) .	0.43	0.43	0.46	0.49	0.53	0.55	0.53	0.53	0.61	—
Distrib'ns, Cap Gain ($) . . .	0.00	0.16	0.00	0.00	0.00	0.00	0.00	0.00	0.03	—
Net Asset Value ($)	6.81	7.79	7.61	7.65	7.09	7.14	6.87	6.98	7.90	—
Expense Ratio (%)	1.32	1.40	1.27	1.27	1.07	1.04	1.19	1.29	0.74	—
Net Income to Assets (%) . .	5.46	5.36	6.08	6.78	7.58	7.98	7.75	7.06	7.53	—
Portfolio Turnover (%)	95	na	115	67	38	159	221	284	61	—
Total Assets (Millions $)	31	35	36	29	21	19	9	8	7	—

PORTFOLIO (as of 8/31/94)

Portfolio Manager: Richard Hinderlie - 1994

Investm't Category: Government Bond

Cap Gain	Asset Allocation
Cap & Income	Fund of Funds
✔ Income	Index
	Sector
✔ Domestic	Small Cap
Foreign	Socially Conscious
Country/Region	State Specific

Portfolio: stocks 0% bonds 94%
convertibles 0% other 0% cash 6%

Largest Holdings: U.S. government 59%, mortgage-backed 34%

Unrealized Net Capital Gains: 0% of portfolio value

SHAREHOLDER INFORMATION

Minimum Investment
Initial: $1,000   Subsequent: $50

Minimum IRA Investment
Initial: $250   Subsequent: $50

Maximum Fees
Load: none   12b-1: 0.25%
Other: none

Distributions
Income: monthly   Capital Gains: Dec

Exchange Options
Number Per Year: 4   Fee: none
Telephone: yes (money market fund available)

Services
IRA, pension, auto exchange, auto invest, auto withdraw

INVESCO Industrial Income (FIIIX)

P.O. Box 173706
Denver, CO 80217
(800) 525-8085, (303) 930-6300

Balanced

PERFORMANCE

fund inception date: 2/1/60

	3yr Annual	5yr Annual	10yr Annual	Bull	Bear
Return (%)	4.2	10.8	14.8	92.4	-6.4
Differ from Category (+/-)	-2.2 blw av	2.8 high	3.5 high	27.4 high	-0.7 blw av

Total Risk	Standard Deviation	Category Risk	Risk Index	Beta
av	7.3%	high	1.2	0.7

	1994	1993	1992	1991	1990	1989	1988	1987	1986	1985
Return (%)	-3.8	16.6	0.9	46.2	0.9	31.8	15.3	4.8	14.6	30.7
Differ from category (+/-) ..	-1.9	3.2	-7.4	22.8	1.4	14.5	3.5	2.4	-2.8	6.4

PER SHARE DATA

	1994	1993	1992	1991	1990	1989	1988	1987	1986	1985
Dividends, Net Income ($) .	0.41	0.43	0.30	0.31	0.38	0.42	0.36	0.36	0.42	0.48
Distrib'ns, Cap Gain ($)....	0.54	0.54	0.39	0.47	0.42	0.73	0.00	0.89	2.41	0.66
Net Asset Value ($)......	10.52	11.93	11.10	11.70	8.62	9.32	7.98	7.24	8.00	9.37
Expense Ratio (%)	0.92	0.96	0.98	0.94	0.76	0.78	0.78	0.74	0.71	0.68
Net Income to Assets (%) ..	3.11	2.94	2.75	3.92	4.14	5.08	4.29	3.96	4.85	5.72
Portfolio Turnover (%)	56	121	119	104	132	124	148	195	160	54
Total Assets (Millions $) ..	3,695	3,897	2,093	882	572	400	381	451	341	249

PORTFOLIO (as of 6/30/94)

Portfolio Manager: Charles P. Mayer - 1993, Jerry Paul - 1994

Investm't Category: Balanced
- Cap Gain
- ✔ Cap & Income
- Income
- ✔ Asset Allocation
- Fund of Funds
- Index
- Sector
- ✔ Domestic
- ✔ Foreign
- Country/Region
- Small Cap
- Socially Conscious
- State Specific

Portfolio: stocks 64% bonds 30%
convertibles 0% other 1% cash 5%

Largest Holdings: bonds—corporate 19%, stocks—oil & gas related 9%

Unrealized Net Capital Gains: 1% of portfolio value

SHAREHOLDER INFORMATION

Minimum Investment
Initial: $1,000   Subsequent: $50

Minimum IRA Investment
Initial: $250   Subsequent: $50

Maximum Fees
Load: none   12b-1: 0.25%
Other: none

Distributions
Income: quarterly   Capital Gains: Dec

Exchange Options
Number Per Year: 4   Fee: none
Telephone: yes (money market fund available)

Services
IRA, pension, auto exchange, auto invest, auto withdraw

INVESCO
Int'l—European (FEURX)
International Stock

P.O. Box 173706
Denver, CO 80217
(800) 525-8085, (303) 930-6300

PERFORMANCE   **fund inception date: 6/2/86**

	3yr Annual	5yr Annual	10yr Annual	Bull	Bear
Return (%)	3.7	3.9	na	42.1	-9.0
Differ from Category (+/-)	-5.4 low	-1.0 blw av	na	-21.8 low	-2.0 blw av

Total Risk	Standard Deviation	Category Risk	Risk Index	Beta
high	13.3%	abv av	1.0	0.9

	1994	1993	1992	1991	1990	1989	1988	1987	1986	1985
Return (%)	-3.0	24.5	-7.5	7.9	0.7	24.2	10.5	-4.5	—	—
Differ from category (+/-) . . .	0.0	-14.1	-4.6	-5.2	11.1	1.7	-3.9	-18.9	—	—

PER SHARE DATA

	1994	1993	1992	1991	1990	1989	1988	1987	1986	1985
Dividends, Net Income ($) .	0.16	0.13	0.20	0.37	0.26	0.14	0.08	0.05	—	—
Distrib'ns, Cap Gain ($) . . .	0.00	0.00	0.00	0.00	0.00	0.00	0.00	0.01	—	—
Net Asset Value ($)	12.29	12.83	10.41	11.48	10.99	11.17	9.11	8.31	—	—
Expense Ratio (%)	na	1.28	1.29	1.43	1.29	1.78	1.88	1.50	—	—
Net Income to Assets (%). . . .	na	1.76	2.23	1.83	3.38	1.57	1.08	1.44	—	—
Portfolio Turnover (%).	na	44	87	61	20	118	75	131	—	—
Total Assets (Millions $). . .	245	306	117	75	84	11	7	10	—	—

PORTFOLIO (as of 4/30/94)

Portfolio Manager: Jerry Mill - 1986; Steven Chamberlain - 1990

Investm't Category: International Stock
✔ Cap Gain   Asset Allocation
  Cap & Income   Fund of Funds
  Income   Index
                    Sector
  Domestic   Small Cap
✔ Foreign   Socially Conscious
✔ Country/Region   State Specific

Portfolio: stocks 93%   bonds 0%
convertibles 1%   other 1%   cash 5%

Largest Holdings: United Kindom 30%, France 16%

Unrealized Net Capital Gains: 11% of portfolio value

SHAREHOLDER INFORMATION

Minimum Investment
Initial: $1,000   Subsequent: $50

Minimum IRA Investment
Initial: $250   Subsequent: $50

Maximum Fees
Load: none   12b-1: none
Other: none

Distributions
Income: Oct   Capital Gains: Dec

Exchange Options
Number Per Year: 4   Fee: none
Telephone: yes (money market fund available)

Services
IRA, pension, auto exchange, auto invest, auto withdraw

464   *Guide to Low-Load Mutual Funds*

INVESCO Int'l—Int'l Growth (FSIGX)

P.O. Box 173706
Denver, CO 80217
(800) 525-8085, (303) 930-6300

International Stock

PERFORMANCE

fund inception date: 9/22/87

	3yr Annual	5yr Annual	10yr Annual	Bull	Bear
Return (%)	3.9	0.5	na	40.3	-3.8
Differ from Category (+/-)	-5.2 low	-4.4 low	na	-23.6 low	3.2 abv av

Total Risk	Standard Deviation	Category Risk	Risk Index	Beta
high	13.6%	abv av	1.0	0.8

	1994	1993	1992	1991	1990	1989	1988	1987	1986	1985
Return (%)	0.5	27.8	-12.6	7.3	-14.6	16.1	16.6	—	—	—
Differ from category (+/-) . . .	3.5	-10.8	-9.7	-5.8	-4.2	-6.4	2.2	—	—	—

PER SHARE DATA

	1994	1993	1992	1991	1990	1989	1988	1987	1986	1985
Dividends, Net Income ($) .	0.08	0.06	0.12	0.17	0.02	0.16	0.09	—	—	—
Distrib'ns, Cap Gain ($)	0.86	0.00	0.00	0.00	0.06	0.50	0.00	—	—	—
Net Asset Value ($)	15.17	16.01	12.57	14.52	13.69	16.13	14.48	—	—	—
Expense Ratio (%)	na	1.43	1.36	1.48	1.48	1.24	1.26	—	—	—
Net Income to Assets (%) . . .	na	0.94	0.83	1.17	1.85	1.18	1.14	—	—	—
Portfolio Turnover (%)	na	46	50	71	78	35	73	—	—	—
Total Assets (Millions $) . . .	108	91	35	42	39	41	12	—	—	—

PORTFOLIO (as of 4/30/94)

Portfolio Manager: W. Lindsay Davidson - 1989, Phillip Ehrman - 1993

Investm't Category: International Stock
- ✔ Cap Gain
- Cap & Income
- Income
- Asset Allocation
- Fund of Funds
- Index
- Sector
- Domestic
- ✔ Foreign
- Country/Region
- Small Cap
- Socially Conscious
- State Specific

Portfolio: stocks 92% bonds 0%
convertibles 1% other 0% cash 7%

Largest Holdings: Japan 32%, United Kingdom 16%

Unrealized Net Capital Gains: 11% of portfolio value

SHAREHOLDER INFORMATION

Minimum Investment
Initial: $1,000   Subsequent: $50

Minimum IRA Investment
Initial: $250   Subsequent: $50

Maximum Fees
Load: none   12b-1: none
Other: none

Distributions
Income: Oct   Capital Gains: Dec

Exchange Options
Number Per Year: 4   Fee: none
Telephone: yes (money market fund available)

Services
IRA, pension, auto exchange, auto invest, auto withdraw

INVESCO Int'l—Pacific Basin (FPBSX)

P.O. Box 173706
Denver, CO 80217
(800) 525-8085, (303) 930-6300

International Stock

PERFORMANCE

fund inception date: 1/19/84

	3yr Annual	5yr Annual	10yr Annual	Bull	Bear
Return (%)	8.8	1.9	14.6	54.2	2.2
Differ from Category (+/-)	-0.3 av	-3.0 low	-0.6 low	-9.7 blw av	9.2 high

Total Risk	Standard Deviation	Category Risk	Risk Index	Beta
high	15.4%	high	1.2	0.8

	1994	1993	1992	1991	1990	1989	1988	1987	1986	1985
Return (%)	4.6	42.6	-13.5	13.1	-24.4	20.1	23.1	9.7	71.8	27.3
Differ from category (+/-) . . .	7.6	4.0	-10.6	0.0	-14.0	-2.4	8.7	-4.7	12.8	-15.1

PER SHARE DATA

	1994	1993	1992	1991	1990	1989	1988	1987	1986	1985
Dividends, Net Income ($) .	0.04	0.04	0.06	0.10	0.09	0.02	0.00	0.07	0.04	0.04
Distrib'ns, Cap Gain ($) . . .	1.79	0.32	0.00	0.00	0.28	0.00	0.00	3.12	1.73	0.00
Net Asset Value ($)	14.15	15.27	10.96	12.75	11.35	15.49	12.91	10.48	12.69	8.52
Expense Ratio (%)	na	1.26	1.78	1.87	1.79	1.62	1.62	1.26	1.47	1.50
Net Income to Assets (%). . . .	na	0.60	0.66	0.99	0.36	0.13	-0.12	0.39	0.39	0.99
Portfolio Turnover (%).	na	30	123	89	93	86	69	155	199	161
Total Assets (Millions $). . .	252	270	26	28	17	24	28	36	8	2

PORTFOLIO (as of 4/30/94)

Portfolio Manager: Julian Pickstone - 1993, Doug Pratt - 1993

Investm't Category: International Stock
- ✔ Cap Gain
- Cap & Income
- Income

- Asset Allocation
- Fund of Funds
- Index
- Sector
- Domestic
- Small Cap
- ✔ Foreign
- Socially Conscious
- ✔ Country/Region
- State Specific

Portfolio: stocks 90% bonds 0%
convertibles 0% other 0% cash 10%

Largest Holdings: Japan 50%, Hong Kong 7%

Unrealized Net Capital Gains: 9% of portfolio value

SHAREHOLDER INFORMATION

Minimum Investment
Initial: $1,000   Subsequent: $50

Minimum IRA Investment
Initial: $250   Subsequent: $50

Maximum Fees
Load: none   12b-1: none
Other: none

Distributions
Income: Oct   Capital Gains: Dec

Exchange Options
Number Per Year: 4   Fee: none
Telephone: yes (money market fund available)

Services
IRA, pension, auto exchange, auto invest, auto withdraw

INVESCO Strat Port—Financial (FSFSX)

P.O. Box 173706
Denver, CO 80217
(800) 525-8085, (303) 930-6300

Growth

	3yr Annual	5yr Annual	10yr Annual	Bull	Bear
Return (%)	12.2	17.9	na	213.5	-7.1
Differ from Category (+/-)	4.5 high	8.3 high	na	121.4 high	-0.5 av

Total Risk	Standard Deviation	Category Risk	Risk Index	Beta
abv av	11.7%	high	1.2	0.9

	1994	1993	1992	1991	1990	1989	1988	1987	1986	1985
Return (%)	-5.8	18.4	26.7	74.0	-7.1	36.9	17.1	-11.0	—	—
Differ from category (+/-)	-5.2	5.0	15.1	38.3	-1.4	10.8	-0.9	-12.8	—	—

PER SHARE DATA

	1994	1993	1992	1991	1990	1989	1988	1987	1986	1985
Dividends, Net Income ($)	0.35	0.21	0.19	0.12	0.01	0.09	0.12	0.07	—	—
Distrib'ns, Cap Gain ($)	0.00	4.30	0.91	0.10	0.02	0.81	0.00	0.12	—	—
Net Asset Value ($)	14.64	15.91	17.24	14.57	8.50	9.19	7.38	6.40	—	—
Expense Ratio (%)	1.18	1.03	1.07	1.13	2.50	2.50	1.95	1.50	—	—
Net Income to Assets (%)	1.66	1.16	1.28	1.76	-0.16	1.05	1.71	1.18	—	—
Portfolio Turnover (%)	88	236	208	249	528	217	175	284	—	—
Total Assets (Millions $)	22	346	190	95	1	2	2	1	—	—

PORTFOLIO (as of 10/31/94)

Portfolio Manager: Douglas N. Pratt - 1992

Investm't Category: Growth

- ✔ Cap Gain
- Cap & Income
- Income
- ✔ Domestic
- ✔ Foreign
- Country/Region

- Asset Allocation
- Fund of Funds
- Index
- ✔ Sector
- Small Cap
- Socially Conscious
- State Specific

Portfolio: stocks 74%   bonds 0%
convertibles 0%   other 0%   cash 26%

Largest Holdings: banking 40%, insurance 13%

Unrealized Net Capital Gains: 0% of portfolio value

SHAREHOLDER INFORMATION

Minimum Investment
Initial: $1,000   Subsequent: $50

Minimum IRA Investment
Initial: $250   Subsequent: $50

Maximum Fees
Load: none   12b-1: none
Other: none

Distributions
Income: Oct   Capital Gains: Dec

Exchange Options
Number Per Year: 4   Fee: none
Telephone: yes (money market fund available)

Services
IRA, pension, auto exchange, auto invest, auto withdraw

INVESCO Strat Port—Energy (FSTEX)

Aggressive Growth

P.O. Box 173706
Denver, CO 80217
(800) 525-8085, (303) 930-6300

PERFORMANCE

fund inception date: 1/19/84

	3yr Annual	5yr Annual	10yr Annual	Bull	Bear
Return (%)	-2.0	-5.4	4.7	-16.2	-1.2
Differ from Category (+/-)	-10.9 low	-17.9 low	-9.3 low	-149.4 low	9.6 high

Total Risk	Standard Deviation	Category Risk	Risk Index	Beta
high	15.2%	abv av	1.0	0.9

	1994	1993	1992	1991	1990	1989	1988	1987	1986	1985
Return (%)	-7.2	16.7	-13.2	-3.4	-16.5	43.5	14.9	4.9	7.1	13.6
Differ from category (+/-) . .	-6.5	-2.8	-24.2	-55.5	-10.3	16.7	-0.3	7.1	-4.7	-18.7

PER SHARE DATA

	1994	1993	1992	1991	1990	1989	1988	1987	1986	1985
Dividends, Net Income ($) .	0.05	0.11	0.02	0.11	0.11	0.25	0.14	0.14	0.14	0.16
Distrib'ns, Cap Gain ($) . . .	0.00	0.00	0.00	0.00	0.00	0.00	0.00	0.64	0.17	0.00
Net Asset Value ($)	9.57	10.37	8.97	10.36	10.84	13.10	9.32	8.23	8.60	8.32
Expense Ratio (%)	1.35	1.18	1.73	1.69	1.42	1.75	1.90	1.30	1.50	1.50
Net Income to Assets (%). .	0.65	0.86	0.32	0.83	1.04	1.73	0.99	1.32	2.85	2.34
Portfolio Turnover (%). . . .	123	190	370	337	321	109	177	452	629	235
Total Assets (Millions $). . . .	73	42	17	12	20	9	6	12	1	0

PORTFOLIO (as of 10/31/94)

Portfolio Manager: Dan Leonard - 1994

Investm't Category: Aggressive Growth
- ✔ Cap Gain
- Cap & Income
- Income
- ✔ Domestic
- ✔ Foreign
- Country/Region

- Asset Allocation
- Fund of Funds
- Index
- ✔ Sector
- Small Cap
- Socially Conscious
- State Specific

Portfolio: stocks 87% bonds 0%
convertibles 2% other 1% cash 10%

Largest Holdings: exploration & production 32%, field services 10%

Unrealized Net Capital Gains: 2% of portfolio value

SHAREHOLDER INFORMATION

Minimum Investment
Initial: $1,000   Subsequent: $50

Minimum IRA Investment
Initial: $250   Subsequent: $50

Maximum Fees
Load: none   12b-1: none
Other: none

Distributions
Income: Oct   Capital Gains: Oct, Dec

Exchange Options
Number Per Year: 4   Fee: none
Telephone: yes (money market fund available)

Services
IRA, pension, auto exchange, auto invest, auto withdraw

INVESCO Strat Port—Environm'l (FSEVX)

Aggressive Growth

P.O. Box 173706
Denver, CO 80217
(800) 525-8085, (303) 930-6300

PERFORMANCE

fund inception date: 1/1/91

	3yr Annual	5yr Annual	10yr Annual	Bull	Bear
Return (%)	-11.7	na	na	na	-16.1
Differ from Category (+/-)	-20.6 low	na	na	na	-5.3 low

Total Risk	Standard Deviation	Category Risk	Risk Index	Beta
high	15.2%	abv av	1.0	0.8

	1994	1993	1992	1991	1990	1989	1988	1987	1986	1985
Return (%)	-11.3	-4.6	-18.6	16.7	—	—	—	—	—	—
Differ from category (+/-)	-10.6	-24.1	-29.6	-35.4	—	—	—	—	—	—

PER SHARE DATA

	1994	1993	1992	1991	1990	1989	1988	1987	1986	1985
Dividends, Net Income ($)	0.06	0.00	0.00	0.00	—	—	—	—	—	—
Distrib'ns, Cap Gain ($)	0.00	0.00	0.00	0.00	—	—	—	—	—	—
Net Asset Value ($)	6.36	7.24	7.60	9.34	—	—	—	—	—	—
Expense Ratio (%)	1.29	1.62	1.85	2.50	—	—	—	—	—	—
Net Income to Assets (%)	0.61	-0.40	-1.23	-1.81	—	—	—	—	—	—
Portfolio Turnover (%)	211	155	113	69	—	—	—	—	—	—
Total Assets (Millions $)	46	50	18	8	—	—	—	—	—	—

PORTFOLIO (as of 10/31/94)

Portfolio Manager: John Schroer - 1993

Investm't Category: Aggressive Growth

✔ Cap Gain
    Cap & Income
    Income
✔ Domestic
✔ Foreign
    Country/Region

    Asset Allocation
    Fund of Funds
    Index
✔ Sector
    Small Cap
    Socially Conscious
    State Specific

Portfolio: stocks 72% bonds 0%
convertibles 0% other 1% cash 27%

Largest Holdings: pollution control services 29%, medical related drugs 10%

Unrealized Net Capital Gains: 8% of portfolio value

SHAREHOLDER INFORMATION

Minimum Investment
Initial: $1,000   Subsequent: $50

Minimum IRA Investment
Initial: $250   Subsequent: $50

Maximum Fees
Load: none   12b-1: none
Other: none

Distributions
Income: Oct   Capital Gains: Dec

Exchange Options
Number Per Year: 4   Fee: none
Telephone: yes (money market fund available)

Services
IRA, pension, auto exchange, auto invest, auto withdraw

INVESCO Strat Port—Gold (FGLDX)

Gold

P.O. Box 173706
Denver, CO 80217
(800) 525-8085, (303) 930-6300

fund inception date: 1/19/84

PERFORMANCE

	3yr Annual	5yr Annual	10yr Annual	Bull	Bear
Return (%)	4.5	-3.9	1.9	38.8	-17.6
Differ from Category (+/-)	-6.3 low	-3.9 low	-3.3 low	5.9 av	-7.6 low

Total Risk	Standard Deviation	Category Risk	Risk Index	Beta
high	27.1%	abv av	1.0	0.3

	1994	1993	1992	1991	1990	1989	1988	1987	1986	1985
Return (%)	-27.8	72.6	-8.2	-7.1	-23.0	21.3	-20.0	15.9	38.6	-4.4
Differ from category (+/-).	-16.3	-14.3	7.5	-2.3	-0.5	-3.4	-1.1	-16.0	1.0	3.0

PER SHARE DATA

	1994	1993	1992	1991	1990	1989	1988	1987	1986	1985
Dividends, Net Income ($) .	0.00	0.00	0.00	0.00	0.01	0.02	0.06	0.06	0.08	0.11
Distrib'ns, Cap Gain ($) ...	0.00	0.00	0.00	0.00	0.00	0.00	0.00	0.04	0.05	0.00
Net Asset Value ($)	4.87	6.75	3.91	4.26	4.59	5.97	4.94	6.25	5.49	4.06
Expense Ratio (%)	1.07	0.97	1.41	1.47	1.32	1.63	1.58	1.15	1.50	1.50
Net Income to Assets (%).	-0.32	-0.59	-0.23	-0.25	0.26	0.69	0.62	0.98	2.35	2.72
Portfolio Turnover (%).....	97	142	101	43	107	77	47	124	232	46
Total Assets (Millions $)...	236	251	46	46	36	34	33	38	5	2

PORTFOLIO (as of 10/31/94)

Portfolio Manager: Dan Leonard - 1989

Investm't Category: Gold

✔ Cap Gain	Asset Allocation
Cap & Income	Fund of Funds
Income	Index
	✔ Sector
✔ Domestic	Small Cap
✔ Foreign	Socially Conscious
Country/Region	State Specific

Portfolio: stocks 94% bonds 0%
convertibles 4% other 0% cash 2%

Largest Holdings: exploration & mining companies 89%, metals 2%

Unrealized Net Capital Gains: -1% of portfolio value

SHAREHOLDER INFORMATION

Minimum Investment
Initial: $1,000   Subsequent: $50

Minimum IRA Investment
Initial: $250   Subsequent: $50

Maximum Fees
Load: none   12b-1: none
Other: none

Distributions
Income: Oct   Capital Gains: Dec

Exchange Options
Number Per Year: 4   Fee: none
Telephone: yes (money market fund available)

Services
IRA, pension, auto exchange, auto invest, auto withdraw

INVESCO Strat Port—Health Sci (FHLSX)

P.O. Box 173706
Denver, CO 80217
(800) 525-8085, (303) 930-6300

Aggressive Growth

PERFORMANCE

fund inception date: 1/19/84

	3yr Annual	5yr Annual	10yr Annual	Bull	Bear
Return (%)	-7.2	13.9	20.5	92.3	-14.8
Differ from Category (+/-)	-16.1 low	1.4 abv av	6.5 high	-40.9 blw av	-4.0 blw av

Total Risk	Standard Deviation	Category Risk	Risk Index	Beta
high	17.4%	high	1.2	0.9

	1994	1993	1992	1991	1990	1989	1988	1987	1986	1985
Return (%)	0.9	-8.4	-13.7	91.8	25.7	59.4	16.0	7.0	29.3	31.4
Differ from category (+/-)	1.6	-27.9	-24.7	39.7	31.9	32.6	0.8	9.2	17.5	-0.9

PER SHARE DATA

	1994	1993	1992	1991	1990	1989	1988	1987	1986	1985
Dividends, Net Income ($)	0.00	0.01	0.10	0.11	0.18	0.10	0.00	0.00	0.00	0.01
Distrib'ns, Cap Gain ($)	0.00	0.00	0.44	3.47	0.22	1.95	0.00	0.93	1.37	0.00
Net Asset Value ($)	35.47	35.14	38.38	45.17	25.63	20.76	14.39	12.40	12.50	10.69
Expense Ratio (%)	1.19	1.16	1.00	1.03	1.12	1.42	1.65	1.42	1.50	1.50
Net Income to Assets (%)	-0.57	-0.34	0.26	0.55	1.18	0.79	-0.48	-0.17	-0.28	0.19
Portfolio Turnover (%)	80	87	91	100	242	272	280	364	470	203
Total Assets (Millions $)	222	558	757	745	88	27	10	10	4	1

PORTFOLIO (as of 10/31/94)

Portfolio Manager: Barry Kurokawa - 1992,
John Schroer - 1994

Investm't Category: Aggressive Growth
- ✔ Cap Gain
- Cap & Income
- Income
- ✔ Domestic
- ✔ Foreign
- Country/Region
- Asset Allocation
- Fund of Funds
- Index
- ✔ Sector
- Small Cap
- Socially Conscious
- State Specific

Portfolio:	stocks 86%	bonds 0%
convertibles 1%	other 5%	cash 8%

Largest Holdings: medical related drugs 28%,
healthcare facilities 12%

Unrealized Net Capital Gains: 7% of portfolio value

SHAREHOLDER INFORMATION

Minimum Investment
Initial: $1,000   Subsequent: $50

Minimum IRA Investment
Initial: $250   Subsequent: $50

Maximum Fees
Load: none   12b-1: none
Other: none

Distributions
Income: Oct   Capital Gains: Dec

Exchange Options
Number Per Year: 4   Fee: none
Telephone: yes (money market fund available)

Services
IRA, pension, auto exchange, auto invest, auto withdraw

INVESCO Strat Port—Leisure (FLISX)

Aggressive Growth

P.O. Box 173706
Denver, CO 80217
(800) 525-8085, (303) 930-6300

PERFORMANCE

fund inception date: 1/19/84

	3yr Annual	5yr Annual	10yr Annual	Bull	Bear
Return (%)	16.7	16.6	19.7	186.4	-8.7
Differ from Category (+/-)	7.8 high	4.1 abv av	5.7 high	53.2 high	2.1 abv av

Total Risk	Standard Deviation	Category Risk	Risk Index	Beta
high	12.1%	blw av	0.8	0.8

	1994	1993	1992	1991	1990	1989	1988	1987	1986	1985
Return (%)	-4.9	35.6	23.4	52.7	-10.9	38.2	28.5	0.7	18.8	32.2
Differ from category (+/-)	-4.2	16.1	12.4	0.6	-4.7	11.4	13.3	2.9	7.0	-0.1

PER SHARE DATA

	1994	1993	1992	1991	1990	1989	1988	1987	1986	1985
Dividends, Net Income ($)	0.00	0.00	0.00	0.00	0.03	0.21	0.00	0.00	0.00	0.04
Distrib'ns, Cap Gain ($)	0.91	1.89	0.99	2.12	0.68	1.99	0.00	1.43	2.76	0.00
Net Asset Value ($)	21.21	23.28	18.55	15.94	11.93	14.34	11.94	9.29	10.69	11.18
Expense Ratio (%)	1.17	1.14	1.51	1.86	1.84	1.38	1.89	1.50	1.50	1.50
Net Income to Assets (%)	0.00	-0.11	-0.33	-0.24	0.10	1.44	0.16	-0.37	-0.11	0.57
Portfolio Turnover (%)	116	116	148	122	89	119	136	376	458	160
Total Assets (Millions $)	262	223	40	14	5	13	6	3	2	1

PORTFOLIO (as of 10/31/94)

Portfolio Manager: Timothy L. Miller - 1992

Investm't Category: Aggressive Growth
- ✔ Cap Gain
- Cap & Income
- Income
- Asset Allocation
- Fund of Funds
- Index
- ✔ Sector
- ✔ Domestic
- ✔ Foreign
- Country/Region
- Small Cap
- Socially Conscious
- State Specific

Portfolio: stocks 89% bonds 0%
convertibles 0% other 0% cash 11%

Largest Holdings: retail 18%, broadcasting 15%

Unrealized Net Capital Gains: 6% of portfolio value

SHAREHOLDER INFORMATION

Minimum Investment
Initial: $1,000   Subsequent: $50

Minimum IRA Investment
Initial: $250   Subsequent: $50

Maximum Fees
Load: none   12b-1: none
Other: none

Distributions
Income: Oct   Capital Gains: Dec

Exchange Options
Number Per Year: 4   Fee: none
Telephone: yes (money market fund available)

Services
IRA, pension, auto exchange, auto invest, auto withdraw

INVESCO Strat Port—Tech (FTCHX)

Aggressive Growth

P.O. Box 173706
Denver, CO 80217
(800) 525-8085, (303) 930-6300

PERFORMANCE

fund inception date: 1/19/84

	3yr Annual	5yr Annual	10yr Annual	Bull	Bear
Return (%)	12.8	22.5	18.8	191.6	-10.4
Differ from Category (+/-)	3.9 abv av	10.0 high	4.8 high	58.4 high	0.4 av

Total Risk	Standard Deviation	Category Risk	Risk Index	Beta
high	17.2%	high	1.2	1.2

	1994	1993	1992	1991	1990	1989	1988	1987	1986	1985
Return (%)	5.2	15.0	18.8	76.9	8.5	21.4	14.2	-5.2	21.7	27.3
Differ from category (+/-)	5.9	-4.5	7.8	24.8	14.7	-5.4	-1.0	-3.0	9.9	-5.0

PER SHARE DATA

	1994	1993	1992	1991	1990	1989	1988	1987	1986	1985
Dividends, Net Income ($)	0.79	0.00	0.00	0.00	0.00	0.00	0.00	0.00	0.00	0.00
Distrib'ns, Cap Gain ($)	0.00	3.22	0.00	4.39	0.00	0.00	0.00	0.01	1.06	0.00
Net Asset Value ($)	24.04	23.59	23.31	19.62	13.78	12.69	10.45	9.15	9.67	8.85
Expense Ratio (%)	1.17	1.13	1.12	1.19	1.25	1.59	1.72	1.47	1.50	1.50
Net Income to Assets (%)	-0.55	-0.69	-0.45	-0.53	-0.06	-0.62	-0.90	-0.68	-0.71	0.03
Portfolio Turnover (%)	145	184	169	307	345	259	356	556	368	175
Total Assets (Millions $)	310	248	165	63	20	9	10	9	4	2

PORTFOLIO (as of 10/31/94)

Portfolio Manager: Dan Leonard - 1985

Investm't Category: Aggressive Growth
- ✔ Cap Gain
- Cap & Income
- Income
- Asset Allocation
- Fund of Funds
- Index
- ✔ Sector
- ✔ Domestic
- ✔ Foreign
- Country/Region
- Small Cap
- Socially Conscious
- State Specific

Portfolio: stocks 84% bonds 0%
convertibles 0% other 1% cash 15%

Largest Holdings: computer services 11%, semiconductor equipment 9%

Unrealized Net Capital Gains: 11% of portfolio value

SHAREHOLDER INFORMATION

Minimum Investment
Initial: $1,000   Subsequent: $50

Minimum IRA Investment
Initial: $250   Subsequent: $50

Maximum Fees
Load: none   12b-1: none
Other: none

Distributions
Income: Oct   Capital Gains: Dec

Exchange Options
Number Per Year: 4   Fee: none
Telephone: yes (money market fund available)

Services
IRA, pension, auto exchange, auto invest, auto withdraw

INVESCO Strat Port—Utilities (FSTUX)

P.O. Box 173706
Denver, CO 80217
(800) 525-8085, (303) 930-6300

Growth & Income

PERFORMANCE

fund inception date: 6/2/86

	3yr Annual	5yr Annual	10yr Annual	Bull	Bear
Return (%)	6.5	6.8	na	86.6	-10.1
Differ from Category (+/-)	-0.6 av	-1.1 blw av	na	10.8 abv av	-3.8 low

Total Risk	Standard Deviation	Category Risk	Risk Index	Beta
av	8.2%	av	1.0	0.7

	1994	1993	1992	1991	1990	1989	1988	1987	1986	1985
Return (%)	-9.9	21.1	10.7	28.0	-10.0	31.4	14.2	-4.9	—	—
Differ from category (+/-) . .	-8.5	7.9	0.5	0.4	-4.0	10.0	-2.8	-5.5	—	—

PER SHARE DATA

	1994	1993	1992	1991	1990	1989	1988	1987	1986	1985
Dividends, Net Income ($) .	0.32	0.26	0.25	0.34	0.34	0.37	0.38	0.48	—	—
Distrib'ns, Cap Gain ($) . . .	0.00	2.00	0.78	0.00	0.00	0.72	0.00	0.01	—	—
Net Asset Value ($)	9.32	10.68	10.69	10.64	8.62	9.96	8.47	7.76	—	—
Expense Ratio (%)	1.13	1.06	1.13	1.21	1.26	1.35	1.39	1.39	—	—
Net Income to Assets (%) . .	3.33	2.66	2.73	4.19	3.48	4.07	4.93	5.07	—	—
Portfolio Turnover (%)	180	202	226	151	264	220	164	84	—	—
Total Assets (Millions $) . . .	122	178	108	69	31	24	18	16	—	—

PORTFOLIO (as of 10/31/94)

Portfolio Manager: Brian Kelly - 1993

Investm't Category: Growth & Income
- Cap Gain
- ✔ Cap & Income
- Income
- ✔ Domestic
- Foreign
- Country/Region
- Asset Allocation
- Fund of Funds
- Index
- ✔ Sector
- Small Cap
- Socially Conscious
- State Specific

Portfolio: stocks 85%   bonds 7%
convertibles 1%   other 1%   cash 6%

Largest Holdings: telephone utilities 22%, telecommunications 18%

Unrealized Net Capital Gains: -4% of portfolio value

SHAREHOLDER INFORMATION

Minimum Investment
Initial: $1,000   Subsequent: $50

Minimum IRA Investment
Initial: $250   Subsequent: $50

Maximum Fees
Load: none   12b-1: none
Other: none

Distributions
Income: quarterly   Capital Gains: Dec

Exchange Options
Number Per Year: 4   Fee: none
Telephone: yes (money market fund available)

Services
IRA, pension, auto exchange, auto invest, auto withdraw

INVESCO Tax-Free Long-Term Bond (FTIFX)

Tax-Exempt Bond

P.O. Box 173706
Denver, CO 80217
(800) 525-8085, (303) 930-6300

PERFORMANCE

fund inception date: 8/14/81

	3yr Annual	5yr Annual	10yr Annual	Bull	Bear
Return (%)	4.8	6.7	9.8	45.8	-6.0
Differ from Category (+/-)	0.3 av	0.6 abv av	1.7 high	4.0 abv av	-0.8 av

Total Risk	Standard Deviation	Category Risk	Risk Index	Avg Mat
blw av	6.0%	av	1.0	17.9 yrs

	1994	1993	1992	1991	1990	1989	1988	1987	1986	1985
Return (%)	-5.5	12.0	8.7	12.5	7.1	11.6	15.0	-4.0	22.1	22.8
Differ from category (+/-) . .	-0.3	0.3	0.4	1.2	0.8	2.6	4.8	-2.7	5.7	5.4

PER SHARE DATA

	1994	1993	1992	1991	1990	1989	1988	1987	1986	1985
Dividends, Net Income ($) .	0.81	0.85	0.90	0.93	0.98	1.00	1.00	1.03	1.18	1.24
Distrib'ns, Cap Gain ($). . . .	0.31	0.38	0.34	0.16	0.00	0.00	0.00	0.48	1.38	0.70
Net Asset Value ($).	14.52	16.54	15.90	15.81	15.09	15.05	14.42	13.46	15.59	15.00
Expense Ratio (%)	1.00	1.03	1.02	0.93	0.75	0.74	0.77	0.70	0.68	0.65
Net Income to Assets (%) . .	5.14	5.43	5.90	6.39	6.67	7.06	7.33	7.04	7.86	9.05
Portfolio Turnover (%)	28	30	28	25	27	27	41	98	92	156
Total Assets (Millions $) . . .	254	342	272	208	179	144	109	118	108	85

PORTFOLIO (as of 6/30/94)

Portfolio Manager: William Veronda - 1984

Investm't Category: Tax-Exempt Bond
Cap Gain	Asset Allocation
Cap & Income	Fund of Funds
✔ Income	Index
	Sector
✔ Domestic	Small Cap
Foreign	Socially Conscious
Country/Region	State Specific

Portfolio: stocks 0% bonds 92%
convertibles 0% other 0% cash 8%

Largest Holdings: general obligation 17%

Unrealized Net Capital Gains: 1% of portfolio value

SHAREHOLDER INFORMATION

Minimum Investment
Initial: $1,000   Subsequent: $50

Minimum IRA Investment
Initial: na   Subsequent: na

Maximum Fees
Load: none   12b-1: 0.25%
Other: none

Distributions
Income: monthly   Capital Gains: Dec

Exchange Options
Number Per Year: 4   Fee: none
Telephone: yes (money market fund available)

Services
auto exchange, auto invest, auto withdraw

INVESCO Value Trust— Interm Gov't (FIGBX)

P.O. Box 173706
Denver, CO 80217
(800) 525-8085, (303) 930-6300

Government Bond

PERFORMANCE

fund inception date: 5/19/86

	3yr Annual	5yr Annual	10yr Annual	Bull	Bear
Return (%)	4.3	7.1	na	38.6	-2.6
Differ from Category (+/-)	0.3 abv av	0.4 av	na	-12.6 blw av	3.8 abv av

Total Risk	Standard Deviation	Category Risk	Risk Index	Avg Mat
low	3.5%	blw av	0.7	5.6 yrs

	1994	1993	1992	1991	1990	1989	1988	1987	1986	1985
Return (%)	-1.5	8.7	6.0	14.1	9.1	10.5	5.4	1.2	—	—
Differ from category (+/-) . . .	3.3	-2.2	-0.4	-1.2	2.9	-4.0	-2.5	3.3	—	—

PER SHARE DATA

	1994	1993	1992	1991	1990	1989	1988	1987	1986	1985
Dividends, Net Income ($) .	0.70	0.72	0.90	0.90	0.99	1.03	0.95	0.83	—	—
Distrib'ns, Cap Gain ($) . . .	0.00	0.34	0.05	0.00	0.00	0.00	0.00	0.00	—	—
Net Asset Value ($)	11.81	12.72	12.68	12.89	12.13	12.07	11.89	12.19	—	—
Expense Ratio (%)	1.07	0.96	0.97	0.93	0.85	0.85	0.85	0.94	—	—
Net Income to Assets (%). .	5.58	5.48	6.38	7.28	8.16	8.45	7.92	7.31	—	—
Portfolio Turnover (%).	49	34	93	51	31	52	6	28	—	—
Total Assets (Millions $)	31	40	30	24	18	20	18	15	—	—

PORTFOLIO (as of 8/31/94)

Portfolio Manager: James Baker - 1993, Ralph Jenkins - 1994

Investm't Category: Government Bond

Cap Gain	Asset Allocation
Cap & Income	Fund of Funds
✔ Income	Index
	Sector
✔ Domestic	Small Cap
✔ Foreign	Socially Conscious
Country/Region	State Specific

Portfolio: stocks 0% bonds 51%
convertibles 0% other 0% cash 49%

Largest Holdings: U.S. government and agencies 39%, mortgage-backed 11%

Unrealized Net Capital Gains: -3% of portfolio value

SHAREHOLDER INFORMATION

Minimum Investment
Initial: $1,000,000 Subsequent: $50

Minimum IRA Investment
Initial: $1,000,000 Subsequent: $50

Maximum Fees
Load: none 12b-1: none
Other: none

Distributions
Income: monthly Capital Gains: Dec

Exchange Options
Number Per Year: 4 Fee: none
Telephone: yes (money market fund available)

Services
IRA, pension, auto exchange, auto invest, auto withdraw

INVESCO Value Trust— Total Return (FSFLX)

Balanced

P.O. Box 173706
Denver, CO 80217
(800) 525-8085, (303) 930-6300

PERFORMANCE

fund inception date: 9/22/87

	3yr Annual	5yr Annual	10yr Annual	Bull	Bear
Return (%)	8.1	9.5	na	70.0	-4.7
Differ from Category (+/-)	1.7 abv av	1.5 abv av	na	5.0 abv av	1.0 abv av

Total Risk	Standard Deviation	Category Risk	Risk Index	Beta
blw av	6.0%	av	1.0	0.7

	1994	1993	1992	1991	1990	1989	1988	1987	1986	1985
Return (%)	2.5	12.3	9.8	24.9	-0.3	19.1	11.5	—	—	—
Differ from category (+/-) ...	4.4	-1.1	1.5	1.5	0.2	1.8	-0.3	—	—	—

PER SHARE DATA

	1994	1993	1992	1991	1990	1989	1988	1987	1986	1985
Dividends, Net Income ($)	0.57	0.69	0.65	0.72	0.75	0.79	0.52	—	—	—
Distrib'ns, Cap Gain ($)....	0.05	0.33	0.18	0.55	0.06	0.13	0.02	—	—	—
Net Asset Value ($)......	18.10	18.26	17.18	16.43	14.21	15.08	13.46	—	—	—
Expense Ratio (%)........	0.96	0.93	0.88	0.92	1.00	1.00	1.00	—	—	—
Net Income to Assets (%) ..	3.31	3.51	4.06	4.62	5.22	5.46	5.56	—	—	—
Portfolio Turnover (%)	12	19	13	49	24	28	13	—	—	—
Total Assets (Millions $) ...	293	231	137	82	55	45	28	—	—	—

PORTFOLIO (as of 8/31/94)

Portfolio Manager: Edward Mitchell - 1987, David Griffin - 1994

Investm't Category: Balanced

Cap Gain	✔ Asset Allocation
✔ Cap & Income	Fund of Funds
Income	Index
	Sector
✔ Domestic	Small Cap
✔ Foreign	Socially Conscious
Country/Region	State Specific

Portfolio: stocks 62% bonds 22%
convertibles 0% other 0% cash 16%

Largest Holdings: bonds—U.S. government 16%, stocks—diversified companies 8%

Unrealized Net Capital Gains: 10% of portfolio value

SHAREHOLDER INFORMATION

Minimum Investment
Initial: $1,000,000 Subsequent: $50

Minimum IRA Investment
Initial: $1,000,000 Subsequent: $50

Maximum Fees
Load: none 12b-1: none
Other: none

Distributions
Income: quarterly Capital Gains: Dec

Exchange Options
Number Per Year: 4 Fee: none
Telephone: yes (money market fund available)

Services
IRA, pension, auto exchange, auto invest, auto withdraw

INVESCO Value Trust— Value Equity (FSEQX)

P.O. Box 173706
Denver, CO 80217
(800) 525-8085, (303) 930-6300

Growth & Income

	3yr Annual	5yr Annual	10yr Annual	Bull	Bear
Return (%)	6.4	9.0	na	79.7	-5.3
Differ from Category (+/-)	-0.7 av	1.1 abv av	na	3.9 av	1.0 abv av

Total Risk	Standard Deviation	Category Risk	Risk Index	Beta
av	7.8%	blw av	0.9	0.9

	1994	1993	1992	1991	1990	1989	1988	1987	1986	1985
Return (%)	4.0	10.4	4.9	35.8	-5.7	21.3	16.8	5.9	—	—
Differ from category (+/-)	5.4	-2.8	-5.3	8.2	0.3	-0.1	-0.2	5.3	—	—

PER SHARE DATA

	1994	1993	1992	1991	1990	1989	1988	1987	1986	1985
Dividends, Net Income ($)	0.31	0.37	0.34	0.40	0.47	0.49	0.42	0.50	—	—
Distrib'ns, Cap Gain ($)	1.17	0.88	0.13	1.84	0.06	0.83	0.33	0.64	—	—
Net Asset Value ($)	16.63	17.41	16.91	16.57	13.88	15.30	13.72	12.39	—	—
Expense Ratio (%)	1.01	1.00	0.91	0.98	1.00	1.00	1.00	1.00	—	—
Net Income to Assets (%)	1.80	2.07	2.19	2.39	3.00	3.29	3.48	2.95	—	—
Portfolio Turnover (%)	53	35	37	64	23	30	16	20	—	—
Total Assets (Millions $)	108	86	79	40	30	37	27	15	—	—

PORTFOLIO (as of 8/31/94)

Portfolio Manager: Michael Harhai - 1993, Terrance Irrgan - 1994

Investm't Category: Growth & Income
Cap Gain   Asset Allocation
✔ Cap & Income   Fund of Funds
Income   Index
     Sector
✔ Domestic   Small Cap
✔ Foreign   Socially Conscious
Country/Region   State Specific

Portfolio: stocks 87%   bonds 0%
convertibles 0%   other 0%   cash 13%

Largest Holdings: retail 9%, diversified companies 8%

Unrealized Net Capital Gains: 8% of portfolio value

SHAREHOLDER INFORMATION

Minimum Investment
Initial: $1,000,000   Subsequent: $50

Minimum IRA Investment
Initial: $1,000,000   Subsequent: $50

Maximum Fees
Load: none   12b-1: none
Other: none

Distributions
Income: quarterly   Capital Gains: Dec

Exchange Options
Number Per Year: 4   Fee: none
Telephone: yes (money market fund available)

Services
IRA, pension, auto exchange, auto invest, auto withdraw

Janus (JANSX)
Growth

100 Fillmore St., Suite 300
Denver, CO 80206
(800) 525-3713, (303) 333-3863

PERFORMANCE   fund inception date: 2/5/70

	3yr Annual	5yr Annual	10yr Annual	Bull	Bear
Return (%)	5.4	10.6	15.1	85.6	-6.5
Differ from Category (+/-)	-2.3 blw av	1.0 abv av	2.2 high	-6.5 av	0.1 av

Total Risk	Standard Deviation	Category Risk	Risk Index	Beta
av	7.4%	low	0.8	0.8

	1994	1993	1992	1991	1990	1989	1988	1987	1986	1985
Return (%)	-1.1	10.8	6.8	42.7	-0.7	46.3	16.5	4.1	11.2	24.5
Differ from category (+/-) . .	-0.5	-2.6	-4.8	7.0	5.0	20.2	-1.5	2.3	-3.4	-4.7

PER SHARE DATA

	1994	1993	1992	1991	1990	1989	1988	1987	1986	1985
Dividends, Net Income ($) .	0.01	0.39	0.29	0.19	0.31	0.19	0.56	0.99	0.00	0.54
Distrib'ns, Cap Gain ($)	0.39	0.93	0.90	0.91	0.01	2.50	0.00	1.61	2.20	0.73
Net Asset Value ($)	18.78	19.39	18.68	18.60	13.79	14.21	11.55	10.39	12.47	13.19
Expense Ratio (%)	0.91	0.92	0.97	0.98	1.02	0.92	0.98	1.01	1.00	1.03
Net Income to Assets (%) . .	1.12	1.55	1.54	1.77	2.11	1.68	4.99	1.55	2.82	4.01
Portfolio Turnover (%)	139	127	153	132	307	205	175	214	254	163
Total Assets (Millions $) . .	9,400	9,234	4,989	2,598	1,050	673	392	388	474	410

PORTFOLIO (as of 10/31/94)

Portfolio Manager: James P. Craig - 1986

Investm't Category: Growth

✔ Cap Gain	Asset Allocation
Cap & Income	Fund of Funds
Income	Index
	Sector
✔ Domestic	Small Cap
✔ Foreign	Socially Conscious
Country/Region	State Specific

Portfolio: stocks 80%   bonds 0%
convertibles 0%   other 1%   cash 19%

Largest Holdings: banking 7%, drugs 7%

Unrealized Net Capital Gains: 8% of portfolio value

SHAREHOLDER INFORMATION

Minimum Investment
Initial: $1,000   Subsequent: $50

Minimum IRA Investment
Initial: $250   Subsequent: $50

Maximum Fees
Load: none   12b-1: none
Other: none

Distributions
Income: Dec   Capital Gains: Dec

Exchange Options
Number Per Year: 4   Fee: none
Telephone: yes (money market fund available)

Services
IRA, pension, auto exchange, auto invest, auto withdraw

Janus Balanced (JABAX)

Balanced

100 Fillmore St., Suite 300
Denver, CO 80206
(800) 525-3713, (303) 333-3863

	3yr Annual	5yr Annual	10yr Annual	Bull	Bear
Return (%)	na	na	na	na	-2.4
Differ from Category (+/-)	na	na	na	na	3.3 high

Total Risk	Standard Deviation	Category Risk	Risk Index	Beta
na	na	na	na	na

	1994	1993	1992	1991	1990	1989	1988	1987	1986	1985
Return (%)	0.0	10.5	—	—	—	—	—	—	—	—
Differ from category (+/-)	1.9	-2.9	—	—	—	—	—	—	—	—

PER SHARE DATA

	1994	1993	1992	1991	1990	1989	1988	1987	1986	1985
Dividends, Net Income ($)	0.56	0.22	—	—	—	—	—	—	—	—
Distrib'ns, Cap Gain ($)	0.00	0.00	—	—	—	—	—	—	—	—
Net Asset Value ($)	11.63	12.19	—	—	—	—	—	—	—	—
Expense Ratio (%)	1.42	1.70	—	—	—	—	—	—	—	—
Net Income to Assets (%)	2.28	2.15	—	—	—	—	—	—	—	—
Portfolio Turnover (%)	167	131	—	—	—	—	—	—	—	—
Total Assets (Millions $)	93	78	—	—	—	—	—	—	—	—

PORTFOLIO (as of 10/31/94)

Portfolio Manager: James P. Craig - 1993

Investm't Category: Balanced

Cap Gain	✔ Asset Allocation
✔ Cap & Income	Fund of Funds
Income	Index
	Sector
✔ Domestic	Small Cap
Foreign	Socially Conscious
Country/Region	State Specific

Portfolio: stocks 53%   bonds 6%
convertibles 1%   other 21%   cash 19%

Largest Holdings: stocks—banking 11%, stocks—utilities 8%

Unrealized Net Capital Gains: 1% of portfolio value

SHAREHOLDER INFORMATION

Minimum Investment
Initial: $1,000   Subsequent: $50

Minimum IRA Investment
Initial: $250   Subsequent: $50

Maximum Fees
Load: none   12b-1: none
Other: none

Distributions
Income: quarterly   Capital Gains: Dec

Exchange Options
Number Per Year: 4   Fee: none
Telephone: yes (money market fund available)

Services
IRA, pension, auto exchange, auto invest, auto withdraw

Janus Enterprise (JAENX)

Aggressive Growth

100 Fillmore St., Suite 300
Denver, CO 80206
(800) 525-3713, (303) 333-3863

PERFORMANCE

fund inception date: 9/1/92

	3yr Annual	5yr Annual	10yr Annual	Bull	Bear
Return (%)	na	na	na	na	-6.5
Differ from Category (+/-)	na	na	na	na	4.3 abv av

Total Risk	Standard Deviation	Category Risk	Risk Index	Beta
na	na	na	na	na

	1994	1993	1992	1991	1990	1989	1988	1987	1986	1985
Return (%)	8.9	15.6	—	—	—	—	—	—	—	—
Differ from category (+/-)	9.6	-3.9	—	—	—	—	—	—	—	—

PER SHARE DATA

	1994	1993	1992	1991	1990	1989	1988	1987	1986	1985
Dividends, Net Income ($)	0.52	0.02	—	—	—	—	—	—	—	—
Distrib'ns, Cap Gain ($)	0.38	0.54	—	—	—	—	—	—	—	—
Net Asset Value ($)	22.98	21.92	—	—	—	—	—	—	—	—
Expense Ratio (%)	1.25	1.36	—	—	—	—	—	—	—	—
Net Income to Assets (%)	-0.32	0.14	—	—	—	—	—	—	—	—
Portfolio Turnover (%)	193	201	—	—	—	—	—	—	—	—
Total Assets (Millions $)	354	254	—	—	—	—	—	—	—	—

PORTFOLIO (as of 10/31/94)

Portfolio Manager: James Goff - 1992

Investm't Category: Aggressive Growth
✔ Cap Gain   Asset Allocation
  Cap & Income   Fund of Funds
  Income   Index
                    Sector
✔ Domestic   Small Cap
✔ Foreign   Socially Conscious
  Country/Region   State Specific

Portfolio: stocks 88%   bonds 0%
convertibles 1%   other 7%   cash 4%

Largest Holdings: auto related 23%, financial
services 15%

Unrealized Net Capital Gains: 14% of portfolio value

SHAREHOLDER INFORMATION

Minimum Investment
Initial: $1,000   Subsequent: $50

Minimum IRA Investment
Initial: $250   Subsequent: $50

Maximum Fees
Load: none   12b-1: none
Other: none

Distributions
Income: Dec   Capital Gains: Dec

Exchange Options
Number Per Year: 4   Fee: none
Telephone: yes (money market fund available)

Services
IRA, pension, auto exchange, auto invest, auto
withdraw

Janus Federal Tax-Exempt (JATEX)

Tax-Exempt Bond

100 Fillmore St., Suite 300
Denver, CO 80206
(800) 525-3713, (303) 333-3863

PERFORMANCE

fund inception date: 5/3/93

	3yr Annual	5yr Annual	10yr Annual	Bull	Bear
Return (%)	na	na	na	na	-7.2
Differ from Category (+/-)	na	na	na	na	-2.0 low

Total Risk	Standard Deviation	Category Risk	Risk Index	Avg Mat
na	na	na	na	na

	1994	1993	1992	1991	1990	1989	1988	1987	1986	1985
Return (%)	-7.7	—	—	—	—	—	—	—	—	—
Differ from category (+/-)	-2.5	—	—	—	—	—	—	—	—	—

PER SHARE DATA

	1994	1993	1992	1991	1990	1989	1988	1987	1986	1985
Dividends, Net Income ($)	0.36	—	—	—	—	—	—	—	—	—
Distrib'ns, Cap Gain ($)	0.00	—	—	—	—	—	—	—	—	—
Net Asset Value ($)	6.39	—	—	—	—	—	—	—	—	—
Expense Ratio (%)	0.65	—	—	—	—	—	—	—	—	—
Net Income to Assets (%)	5.20	—	—	—	—	—	—	—	—	—
Portfolio Turnover (%)	160	—	—	—	—	—	—	—	—	—
Total Assets (Millions $)	24	—	—	—	—	—	—	—	—	—

PORTFOLIO (as of 10/31/94)

Portfolio Manager: Ronald V. Speaker - 1993

Investm't Category: Tax-Exempt Bond

Cap Gain	Asset Allocation
Cap & Income	Fund of Funds
✔ Income	Index
	Sector
✔ Domestic	Small Cap
Foreign	Socially Conscious
Country/Region	State Specific

Portfolio: stocks 0% bonds 100%
convertibles 0% other 0% cash 0%

Largest Holdings: general obligations 0%

Unrealized Net Capital Gains: -5% of portfolio value

SHAREHOLDER INFORMATION

Minimum Investment
Initial: $1,000   Subsequent: $50

Minimum IRA Investment
Initial: na   Subsequent: na

Maximum Fees
Load: none   12b-1: none
Other: none

Distributions
Income: monthly   Capital Gains: Dec

Exchange Options
Number Per Year: 4   Fee: none
Telephone: yes (money market fund available)

Services
auto exchange, auto invest, auto withdraw

Janus Flexible Income
(JAFIX)
Corporate Bond

100 Fillmore St., Suite 300
Denver, CO 80206
(800) 525-3713, (303) 333-3863

PERFORMANCE

fund inception date: 7/7/87

	3yr Annual	5yr Annual	10yr Annual	Bull	Bear
Return (%)	7.8	8.5	na	75.7	-4.9
Differ from Category (+/-)	1.9 high	0.7 abv av	na	25.9 high	-0.6 av

Total Risk	Standard Deviation	Category Risk	Risk Index	Avg Mat
low	4.0%	abv av	1.3	8.9 yrs

	1994	1993	1992	1991	1990	1989	1988	1987	1986	1985
Return (%)	-2.9	15.6	11.7	25.9	-4.5	4.1	10.6	—	—	—
Differ from category (+/-) ..	-0.5	4.2	2.8	8.8	-9.3	-5.2	1.5	—	—	—

PER SHARE DATA

	1994	1993	1992	1991	1990	1989	1988	1987	1986	1985
Dividends, Net Income ($) .	0.72	0.76	0.79	0.90	0.90	0.98	0.94	—	—	—
Distrib'ns, Cap Gain ($)....	0.00	0.23	0.02	0.00	0.00	0.08	0.00	—	—	—
Net Asset Value ($).......	8.75	9.74	9.31	9.09	8.00	9.35	9.99	—	—	—
Expense Ratio (%)	0.93	1.00	1.00	1.00	1.00	1.00	1.00	—	—	—
Net Income to Assets (%) ..	7.75	7.96	8.98	9.38	11.24	10.00	9.32	—	—	—
Portfolio Turnover (%)	137	201	210	88	96	75	76	—	—	—
Total Assets (Millions $) ...	353	466	205	72	14	18	10	—	—	—

PORTFOLIO (as of 10/31/94)

Portfolio Manager: Ronald Speaker - 1991

Investm't Category: Corporate Bond

Cap Gain	Asset Allocation
Cap & Income	Fund of Funds
✔ Income	Index
	Sector
✔ Domestic	Small Cap
✔ Foreign	Socially Conscious
Country/Region	State Specific

Portfolio: stocks 0%   bonds 85%
convertibles 2%   other 7%   cash 6%

Largest Holdings: insurance 19%, food products 6%

Unrealized Net Capital Gains: -3% of portfolio value

SHAREHOLDER INFORMATION

Minimum Investment
Initial: $1,000   Subsequent: $50

Minimum IRA Investment
Initial: $250   Subsequent: $50

Maximum Fees
Load: none   12b-1: none
Other: none

Distributions
Income: monthly   Capital Gains: Dec

Exchange Options
Number Per Year: 4   Fee: none
Telephone: yes (money market fund available)

Services
IRA, pension, auto exchange, auto invest, auto withdraw

Janus Growth & Income
(JAGIX)
Growth & Income

100 Fillmore St., Suite 300
Denver, CO 80206
(800) 525-3713, (303) 333-3863

PERFORMANCE

fund inception date: 5/15/91

	3yr Annual	5yr Annual	10yr Annual	Bull	Bear
Return (%)	2.2	na	na	na	-10.2
Differ from Category (+/-)	-4.9 low	na	na	na	-3.9 low

Total Risk	Standard Deviation	Category Risk	Risk Index	Beta
abv av	9.8%	high	1.2	1.0

	1994	1993	1992	1991	1990	1989	1988	1987	1986	1985
Return (%)	-4.8	6.6	5.3	—	—	—	—	—	—	—
Differ from category (+/-). .	-3.4	-6.6	-4.9	—	—	—	—	—	—	—

PER SHARE DATA

	1994	1993	1992	1991	1990	1989	1988	1987	1986	1985
Dividends, Net Income ($) .	0.09	0.17	0.15	—	—	—	—	—	—	—
Distrib'ns, Cap Gain ($) . . .	0.00	0.33	0.00	—	—	—	—	—	—	—
Net Asset Value ($)	13.88	14.69	14.24	—	—	—	—	—	—	—
Expense Ratio (%)	1.22	1.28	1.52	—	—	—	—	—	—	—
Net Income to Assets (%). .	1.26	1.13	1.61	—	—	—	—	—	—	—
Portfolio Turnover (%). . . .	123	138	120	—	—	—	—	—	—	—
Total Assets (Millions $). . .	456	512	243	—	—	—	—	—	—	—

PORTFOLIO (as of 10/31/94)

Portfolio Manager: Thomas Marsico - 1991

Investm't Category: Growth & Income

Cap Gain	Asset Allocation
✔ Cap & Income	Fund of Funds
Income	Index
	Sector
✔ Domestic	Small Cap
✔ Foreign	Socially Conscious
Country/Region	State Specific

Portfolio: stocks 84% bonds 0%
convertibles 1% other 9% cash 6%

Largest Holdings: retail 9%, telecommunications 9%

Unrealized Net Capital Gains: 12% of portfolio value

SHAREHOLDER INFORMATION

Minimum Investment
Initial: $1,000   Subsequent: $50

Minimum IRA Investment
Initial: $250   Subsequent: $50

Maximum Fees
Load: none   12b-1: none
Other: none

Distributions
Income: quarterly   Capital Gains: Dec

Exchange Options
Number Per Year: 4   Fee: none
Telephone: yes (money market fund available)

Services
IRA, pension, auto exchange, auto invest, auto withdraw

Janus Interm Gov't Securities (JAIGX)

Government Bond

100 Fillmore St., Suite 300
Denver, CO 80206
(800) 525-3713, (303) 333-3863

PERFORMANCE

fund inception date: 7/26/91

	3yr Annual	5yr Annual	10yr Annual	Bull	Bear
Return (%)	1.5	na	na	na	-3.6
Differ from Category (+/-)	-2.5 low	na	na	na	2.8 abv av

Total Risk	Standard Deviation	Category Risk	Risk Index	Avg Mat
low	2.6%	blw av	0.5	3.2 yrs

	1994	1993	1992	1991	1990	1989	1988	1987	1986	1985
Return (%)	-2.4	2.4	4.8	—	—	—	—	—	—	—
Differ from category (+/-)	2.4	-8.5	-1.6	—	—	—	—	—	—	—

PER SHARE DATA

	1994	1993	1992	1991	1990	1989	1988	1987	1986	1985
Dividends, Net Income ($)	0.27	0.22	0.26	—	—	—	—	—	—	—
Distrib'ns, Cap Gain ($)	0.00	0.00	0.11	—	—	—	—	—	—	—
Net Asset Value ($)	4.74	5.13	5.22	—	—	—	—	—	—	—
Expense Ratio (%)	0.65	0.91	1.00	—	—	—	—	—	—	—
Net Income to Assets (%)	4.97	4.27	4.95	—	—	—	—	—	—	—
Portfolio Turnover (%)	304	371	270	—	—	—	—	—	—	—
Total Assets (Millions $)	34	56	70	—	—	—	—	—	—	—

PORTFOLIO (as of 10/31/94)

Portfolio Manager: Ronald Speaker - 1991

Investm't Category: Government Bond

Cap Gain	Asset Allocation
Cap & Income	Fund of Funds
✔ Income	Index
	Sector
✔ Domestic	Small Cap
Foreign	Socially Conscious
Country/Region	State Specific

Portfolio:	stocks 0%	bonds 100%
convertibles 0%	other 0%	cash 0%

Largest Holdings: U. S. government 100%

Unrealized Net Capital Gains: -1% of portfolio value

SHAREHOLDER INFORMATION

Minimum Investment
Initial: $1,000   Subsequent: $50

Minimum IRA Investment
Initial: $250   Subsequent: $50

Maximum Fees
Load: none   12b-1: none
Other: none

Distributions
Income: monthly   Capital Gains: Dec

Exchange Options
Number Per Year: 4   Fee: none
Telephone: yes (money market fund available)

Services
IRA, pension, auto exchange, auto invest, auto withdraw

Janus Mercury (JAMRX)

Growth

100 Fillmore St., Suite 300
Denver, CO 80206
(800) 525-3713, (303) 333-3863

PERFORMANCE
fund inception date: 5/3/93

	3yr Annual	5yr Annual	10yr Annual	Bull	Bear
Return (%)	na	na	na	na	-6.2
Differ from Category (+/-)	na	na	na	na	0.4 av

Total Risk	Standard Deviation		Category Risk	Risk Index	Beta
na	na		na	na	na

	1994	1993	1992	1991	1990	1989	1988	1987	1986	1985
Return (%)	15.8	—	—	—	—	—	—	—	—	—
Differ from category (+/-) . .	16.4	—	—	—	—	—	—	—	—	—

PER SHARE DATA

	1994	1993	1992	1991	1990	1989	1988	1987	1986	1985
Dividends, Net Income ($) .	0.16	—	—	—	—	—	—	—	—	—
Distrib'ns, Cap Gain ($) . . .	0.11	—	—	—	—	—	—	—	—	—
Net Asset Value ($)	13.61	—	—	—	—	—	—	—	—	—
Expense Ratio (%)	1.33	—	—	—	—	—	—	—	—	—
Net Income to Assets (%). .	0.25	—	—	—	—	—	—	—	—	—
Portfolio Turnover (%). . . .	283	—	—	—	—	—	—	—	—	—
Total Assets (Millions $) . . .	690	—	—	—	—	—	—	—	—	—

PORTFOLIO (as of 10/31/94)

Portfolio Manager: Warren Lammert - 1993

Investm't Category: Growth

✔ Cap Gain	Asset Allocation
Cap & Income	Fund of Funds
Income	Index
	Sector
✔ Domestic	Small Cap
✔ Foreign	Socially Conscious
Country/Region	State Specific

Portfolio: stocks 62% bonds 0%
convertibles 0% other 7% cash 31%

Largest Holdings: computer related 8%, telecommunications 6%

Unrealized Net Capital Gains: 9% of portfolio value

SHAREHOLDER INFORMATION

Minimum Investment
Initial: $1,000   Subsequent: $50

Minimum IRA Investment
Initial: $250   Subsequent: $50

Maximum Fees
Load: none   12b-1: none
Other: none

Distributions
Income: Dec   Capital Gains: Dec

Exchange Options
Number Per Year: 4   Fee: none
Telephone: yes (money market fund available)

Services
IRA, pension, auto exchange, auto invest, auto withdraw

Janus Short-Term Bond

(JASBX)

Corporate Bond

100 Fillmore St., Suite 300
Denver, CO 80206
(800) 525-3713, (303) 333-3863

PERFORMANCE   **fund inception date: 9/1/92**

	3yr Annual	5yr Annual	10yr Annual	Bull	Bear
Return (%)	na	na	na	na	-1.5
Differ from Category (+/-)	na	na	na	na	2.8 abv av

Total Risk	Standard Deviation	Category Risk	Risk Index	Avg Mat
na	na	na	na	2.2 yrs

	1994	1993	1992	1991	1990	1989	1988	1987	1986	1985
Return (%)	0.3	6.1	—	—	—	—	—	—	—	—
Differ from category (+/-)	2.7	-5.3	—	—	—	—	—	—	—	—

PER SHARE DATA

	1994	1993	1992	1991	1990	1989	1988	1987	1986	1985
Dividends, Net Income ($)	0.18	0.15	—	—	—	—	—	—	—	—
Distrib'ns, Cap Gain ($)	0.00	0.01	—	—	—	—	—	—	—	—
Net Asset Value ($)	2.83	3.00	—	—	—	—	—	—	—	—
Expense Ratio (%)	0.65	0.83	—	—	—	—	—	—	—	—
Net Income to Assets (%)	6.08	4.86	—	—	—	—	—	—	—	—
Portfolio Turnover (%)	346	372	—	—	—	—	—	—	—	—
Total Assets (Millions $)	45	53	—	—	—	—	—	—	—	—

PORTFOLIO (as of 10/31/94)

Portfolio Manager: Ronald V. Speaker - 1992

Investm't Category: Corporate Bond

Cap Gain	Asset Allocation
Cap & Income	Fund of Funds
✔ Income	Index
	Sector
✔ Domestic	Small Cap
Foreign	Socially Conscious
Country/Region	State Specific

Portfolio:	stocks 0%	bonds 97%
convertibles 0%	other 3%	cash 0%

Largest Holdings: auto related 17%, financial services 16%

Unrealized Net Capital Gains: -1% of portfolio value

SHAREHOLDER INFORMATION

Minimum Investment
Initial: $1,000   Subsequent: $50

Minimum IRA Investment
Initial: $250   Subsequent: $50

Maximum Fees
Load: none   12b-1: none
Other: none

Distributions
Income: monthly   Capital Gains: Dec

Exchange Options
Number Per Year: 4   Fee: none
Telephone: yes (money market fund available)

Services
IRA, pension, auto exchange, auto invest, auto withdraw

Janus Twenty (JAVLX)
Growth

100 Fillmore St., Suite 300
Denver, CO 80206
(800) 525-3713, (303) 333-3863

this fund is closed to new investors

PERFORMANCE

fund inception date: 4/26/85

	3yr Annual	5yr Annual	10yr Annual	Bull	Bear
Return (%)	-0.5	10.8	na	101.6	-13.5
Differ from Category (+/-)	-8.2 low	1.2 abv av	na	9.5 abv av	-6.9 low

Total Risk	Standard Deviation	Category Risk	Risk Index	Beta
abv av	11.2%	abv av	1.2	1.1

	1994	1993	1992	1991	1990	1989	1988	1987	1986	1985
Return (%)	-6.7	3.4	1.9	69.2	0.5	50.8	19.0	-11.6	12.4	—
Differ from category (+/-). .	-6.1	-10.0	-9.7	33.5	6.2	24.7	1.0	-13.4	-2.2	—

PER SHARE DATA

	1994	1993	1992	1991	1990	1989	1988	1987	1986	1985
Dividends, Net Income ($) .	0.07	0.25	0.18	0.02	0.19	0.02	0.80	0.41	0.80	—
Distrib'ns, Cap Gain ($) . . .	0.00	0.45	0.19	0.42	0.00	0.43	0.00	1.18	0.82	—
Net Asset Value ($)	22.71	24.42	24.29	24.19	14.56	14.66	10.01	9.08	12.07	—
Expense Ratio (%)	1.02	1.05	1.12	1.07	1.32	1.88	1.70	1.79	2.00	—
Net Income to Assets (%). .	0.57	0.87	1.27	1.30	1.28	0.68	3.35	2.98	3.55	—
Portfolio Turnover (%). . . .	102	99	79	163	228	220	317	202	152	—
Total Assets (Millions $). .	2,504	3,473	2,435	556	175	20	13	19	10	—

PORTFOLIO (as of 10/31/94)

Portfolio Manager: Thomas Marsico - 1988

Investm't Category: Growth

✔ Cap Gain	Asset Allocation
Cap & Income	Fund of Funds
Income	Index
	Sector
✔ Domestic	Small Cap
✔ Foreign	Socially Conscious
Country/Region	State Specific

Portfolio: stocks 95% bonds 1%
convertibles 0% other 0% cash 4%

Largest Holdings: computer related 10%, financial services 9%,

Unrealized Net Capital Gains: 14% of portfolio value

SHAREHOLDER INFORMATION

Minimum Investment
Initial: $1,000   Subsequent: $50

Minimum IRA Investment
Initial: $250   Subsequent: $50

Maximum Fees
Load: none   12b-1: none
Other: none

Distributions
Income: Dec   Capital Gains: Dec

Exchange Options
Number Per Year: 4   Fee: none
Telephone: yes (money market fund available)

Services
IRA, pension, auto exchange, auto invest, auto withdraw

Janus Venture (JAVTX)

Aggressive Growth

100 Fillmore St., Suite 300
Denver, CO 80206
(800) 525-3713, (303) 333-3863

this fund is closed to new investors

PERFORMANCE
fund inception date: 4/26/85

	3yr Annual	5yr Annual	10yr Annual	Bull	Bear
Return (%)	7.3	12.7	na	92.7	-7.7
Differ from Category (+/-)	-1.6 av	0.2 av	na	-40.5 blw av	3.1 abv av

Total Risk	Standard Deviation	Category Risk	Risk Index	Beta
abv av	8.8%	low	0.6	0.8

	1994	1993	1992	1991	1990	1989	1988	1987	1986	1985
Return (%)	5.4	9.0	7.4	47.8	-0.3	38.7	19.6	5.1	20.4	—
Differ from category (+/-)	6.1	-10.5	-3.6	-4.3	5.9	11.9	4.4	7.3	8.6	—

PER SHARE DATA

	1994	1993	1992	1991	1990	1989	1988	1987	1986	1985
Dividends, Net Income ($)	0.03	0.53	1.16	0.25	0.11	0.44	1.52	0.15	1.48	—
Distrib'ns, Cap Gain ($)	2.84	4.37	0.71	3.43	0.89	2.35	0.00	4.17	1.04	—
Net Asset Value ($)	48.68	48.88	49.30	47.63	34.71	35.85	27.85	24.55	27.45	—
Expense Ratio (%)	0.96	0.97	1.07	1.04	1.16	1.28	1.41	1.44	1.95	—
Net Income to Assets (%)	0.27	1.29	1.32	2.10	1.24	1.10	5.11	0.40	1.47	—
Portfolio Turnover (%)	114	139	124	167	184	219	299	250	248	—
Total Assets (Millions $)	1,496	1,724	1,545	893	257	58	34	46	30	—

PORTFOLIO (as of 10/31/94)

Portfolio Manager: Jim Goff - 1993, Warren Lammert - 1993

Investm't Category: Aggressive Growth

✔ Cap Gain	Asset Allocation
Cap & Income	Fund of Funds
Income	Index
	Sector
✔ Domestic	✔ Small Cap
✔ Foreign	Socially Conscious
Country/Region	State Specific

Portfolio: stocks 79% bonds 0%
convertibles 0% other 9% cash 12%

Largest Holdings: auto related 9%, railroads 6%

Unrealized Net Capital Gains: 17% of portfolio value

SHAREHOLDER INFORMATION

Minimum Investment
Initial: $1,000   Subsequent: $50

Minimum IRA Investment
Initial: $250   Subsequent: $50

Maximum Fees
Load: none   12b-1: none
Other: none

Distributions
Income: Dec   Capital Gains: Dec

Exchange Options
Number Per Year: 4   Fee: none
Telephone: yes (money market fund available)

Services
IRA, pension, auto exchange, auto invest, auto withdraw

Janus Worldwide
(JAWWX)
International Stock

100 Fillmore St., Suite 300
Denver, CO 80206
(800) 525-3713, (303) 333-3863

PERFORMANCE

fund inception date: 5/15/91

	3yr Annual	5yr Annual	10yr Annual	Bull	Bear
Return (%)	13.1	na	na	na	-7.1
Differ from Category (+/-)	4.0 high	na	na	na	-0.1 av

Total Risk	Standard Deviation	Category Risk	Risk Index	Beta
abv av	10.5%	low	0.8	0.9

	1994	1993	1992	1991	1990	1989	1988	1987	1986	1985
Return (%)	3.6	28.4	9.0	—	—	—	—	—	—	—
Differ from category (+/-) . . .	6.6	-10.2	11.9	—	—	—	—	—	—	—

PER SHARE DATA

	1994	1993	1992	1991	1990	1989	1988	1987	1986	1985
Dividends, Net Income ($) .	0.54	0.28	0.22	—	—	—	—	—	—	—
Distrib'ns, Cap Gain ($) . . .	1.01	0.38	0.00	—	—	—	—	—	—	—
Net Asset Value ($)	24.39	25.03	20.00	—	—	—	—	—	—	—
Expense Ratio (%)	1.12	1.32	1.73	—	—	—	—	—	—	—
Net Income to Assets (%). .	0.42	0.92	1.74	—	—	—	—	—	—	—
Portfolio Turnover (%). . . .	158	124	147	—	—	—	—	—	—	—
Total Assets (Millions $). .	1,542	1,022	161	—	—	—	—	—	—	—

PORTFOLIO (as of 10/31/94)

Portfolio Manager: Helen Hayes - 1992

Investm't Category: International Stock
- ✔ Cap Gain
- Cap & Income
- Income
- ✔ Domestic
- ✔ Foreign
- Country/Region
- Asset Allocation
- Fund of Funds
- Index
- Sector
- Small Cap
- Socially Conscious
- State Specific

Portfolio: stocks 76% bonds 0%
convertibles 0% other 3% cash 21%

Largest Holdings: United States 32%, Sweden 20%

Unrealized Net Capital Gains: 9% of portfolio value

SHAREHOLDER INFORMATION

Minimum Investment
Initial: $1,000 Subsequent: $50

Minimum IRA Investment
Initial: $250 Subsequent: $50

Maximum Fees
Load: none 12b-1: none
Other: none

Distributions
Income: Dec Capital Gains: Dec

Exchange Options
Number Per Year: 4 Fee: none
Telephone: yes (money market fund available)

Services
IRA, pension, auto exchange, auto invest, auto withdraw

Japan (SJPNX)

International Stock

P.O. Box 2291
Boston, MA 02107
(800) 225-2470, (617) 439-4640

	3yr Annual	5yr Annual	10yr Annual	Bull	Bear
Return (%)	4.2	-0.4	15.6	33.0	8.5
Differ from Category (+/-)	-4.9 low	-5.3 low	0.4 blw av	-30.9 low	15.5 high

Total Risk	Standard Deviation	Category Risk	Risk Index	Beta
high	21.7%	high	1.7	0.1

	1994	1993	1992	1991	1990	1989	1988	1987	1986	1985
Return (%)	10.0	23.6	-16.7	3.1	-16.3	11.6	19.4	33.0	77.5	38.8
Differ from category (+/-) ..	13.0	-15.0	-13.8	-10.0	-5.9	-10.9	5.0	18.6	18.5	-3.6

PER SHARE DATA

	1994	1993	1992	1991	1990	1989	1988	1987	1986	1985
Dividends, Net Income ($) .	0.00	0.00	0.00	0.00	0.20	0.08	0.02	0.20	0.02	0.07
Distrib'ns, Cap Gain ($)....	0.85	0.67	0.00	0.41	0.99	3.59	3.88	9.08	4.67	1.36
Net Asset Value ($)......	10.51	10.33	8.90	10.69	10.76	14.27	16.24	16.97	20.28	15.53
Expense Ratio (%)	1.12	1.25	1.42	1.26	1.05	1.02	1.01	0.90	0.70	0.64
Net Income to Assets (%) .	-0.34	-0.47	-0.31	-0.15	0.72	0.34	0.28	0.41	0.51	0.63
Portfolio Turnover (%)	76	81	47	46	53	60	39	34	38	23
Total Assets (Millions $) ...	587	431	409	335	313	401	404	394	584	360

PORTFOLIO (as of 6/30/94)

Portfolio Manager: Seung Kwak - 1989, Elizabeth J. Allen - 1990

Investm't Category: International Stock
- ✔ Cap Gain
-    Cap & Income
-    Income
-    Domestic
- ✔ Foreign
- ✔ Country/Region
-    Asset Allocation
-    Fund of Funds
-    Index
-    Sector
-    Small Cap
-    Socially Conscious
-    State Specific

Portfolio: stocks 97% bonds 0%
convertibles 0% other 0% cash 3%

Largest Holdings: Japan 97%

Unrealized Net Capital Gains: 19% of portfolio value

SHAREHOLDER INFORMATION

Minimum Investment
Initial: $1,000   Subsequent: $100

Minimum IRA Investment
Initial: $500   Subsequent: $50

Maximum Fees
Load: none   12b-1: none
Other: none

Distributions
Income: Dec   Capital Gains: Dec

Exchange Options
Number Per Year: no limit   Fee: none
Telephone: yes (money market fund available)

Services
IRA, pension, auto exchange, auto invest, auto withdraw

Jurika & Voyles Balanced

(JVBAX)

Balanced

1999 Harrison Street
Suite 700
Oakland, CA 94612
(800) 584-6878

	3yr Annual	5yr Annual	10yr Annual	Bull	Bear
Return (%)	na	na	na	na	-4.3
Differ from Category (+/-)	na	na	na	na	1.4 abv av

Total Risk	Standard Deviation	Category Risk	Risk Index	Beta
na	na	na	na	na

	1994	1993	1992	1991	1990	1989	1988	1987	1986	1985
Return (%)	-2.2	17.0	—	—	—	—	—	—	—	—
Differ from category (+/-)	-0.3	3.6	—	—	—	—	—	—	—	—

PER SHARE DATA

	1994	1993	1992	1991	1990	1989	1988	1987	1986	1985
Dividends, Net Income ($)	0.26	0.33	—	—	—	—	—	—	—	—
Distrib'ns, Cap Gain ($)	0.49	0.00	—	—	—	—	—	—	—	—
Net Asset Value ($)	11.98	13.00	—	—	—	—	—	—	—	—
Expense Ratio (%)	1.47	1.47	—	—	—	—	—	—	—	—
Net Income to Assets (%)	1.75	1.51	—	—	—	—	—	—	—	—
Portfolio Turnover (%)	na	44	—	—	—	—	—	—	—	—
Total Assets (Millions $)	31	24	—	—	—	—	—	—	—	—

PORTFOLIO (as of 4/30/94)

Portfolio Manager: William Jurika - 1992, Glen Voyles - 1992

Investm't Category: Balanced
Cap Gain	✔ Asset Allocation
✔ Cap & Income	Fund of Funds
Income	Index
	Sector
✔ Domestic	Small Cap
Foreign	Socially Conscious
Country/Region	State Specific

Portfolio: stocks 58%   bonds 33%
convertibles 2%   other 0%   cash 7%

Largest Holdings: bonds—corporate 11%, bonds—U.S. government and agencies 11%

Unrealized Net Capital Gains: 4% of portfolio value

SHAREHOLDER INFORMATION

Minimum Investment
Initial: $250,000   Subsequent: $1,000

Minimum IRA Investment
Initial: $250,000   Subsequent: $1,000

Maximum Fees
Load: none   12b-1: none
Other: none

Distributions
Income: quarterly   Capital Gains: Dec

Exchange Options
Number Per Year: no limit   Fee: none
Telephone: yes (money market fund available)

Services
IRA, auto invest, auto withdraw

Kaufmann (KAUFX)

Aggressive Growth

140 East 45th Street
New York, NY 10017
(800) 274-1520, (212) 922-0123

PERFORMANCE

fund inception date: 2/1/86

	3yr Annual	5yr Annual	10yr Annual	Bull	Bear
Return (%)	12.7	19.2	na	183.1	-10.3
Differ from Category (+/-)	3.8 abv av	6.7 high	na	49.9 high	0.5 av

Total Risk	Standard Deviation	Category Risk	Risk Index	Beta
high	15.4%	abv av	1.0	1.1

	1994	1993	1992	1991	1990	1989	1988	1987	1986	1985
Return (%)	8.9	18.2	11.3	79.4	-6.1	46.8	58.5	-37.1	—	—
Differ from category (+/-) . . .	9.6	-1.3	0.3	27.3	0.1	20.0	43.3	-34.9	—	—

PER SHARE DATA

	1994	1993	1992	1991	1990	1989	1988	1987	1986	1985
Dividends, Net Income ($) .	0.00	0.00	0.00	0.00	0.00	0.00	0.00	0.01	—	—
Distrib'ns, Cap Gain ($)	0.00	0.04	0.00	0.08	0.00	0.00	0.00	0.00	—	—
Net Asset Value ($).	3.76	3.45	2.95	2.65	1.53	1.63	1.11	0.70	—	—
Expense Ratio (%)	2.48	2.53	2.94	3.64	3.45	2.36	2.00	2.00	—	—
Net Income to Assets (%) .	-1.81	-1.34	-1.74	-1.96	-2.56	-1.41	-0.23	0.92	—	—
Portfolio Turnover (%)	na	55	51	128	195	202	343	228	—	—
Total Assets (Millions $) . .	1,620	980	314	141	40	36	6	2	—	—

PORTFOLIO (as of 6/30/94)

Portfolio Manager: Lawrence Auriana - 1986, Hans Utsch - 1986

Investm't Category: Aggressive Growth
- ✔ Cap Gain   Asset Allocation
-    Cap & Income   Fund of Funds
-    Income   Index
-     Sector
- ✔ Domestic   ✔ Small Cap
- ✔ Foreign   Socially Conscious
-    Country/Region   State Specific

Portfolio: stocks 100%   bonds 0%
convertibles 0%   other 0%   cash 0%

Largest Holdings: medical services 13%, retail 12%

Unrealized Net Capital Gains: 9% of portfolio value

SHAREHOLDER INFORMATION

Minimum Investment
Initial: $1,500   Subsequent: $100

Minimum IRA Investment
Initial: $500   Subsequent: $50

Maximum Fees
Load: 0.20% redemption   12b-1: 0.75%
Other: none

Distributions
Income: Dec   Capital Gains: Dec

Exchange Options
Number Per Year: no limit   Fee: none
Telephone: yes (money market fund available)

Services
IRA, pension, auto invest, auto withdraw

Lazard Equity (LZEQX)

Growth

1 Rockefeller Plaza
New York, NY 10020
(800) 228-0203, (212) 632-6873

PERFORMANCE

fund inception date: 6/1/87

	3yr Annual	5yr Annual	10yr Annual	Bull	Bear
Return (%)	9.1	9.5	na	83.0	-5.1
Differ from Category (+/-)	1.4 abv av	-0.1 av	na	-9.1 blw av	1.5 abv av

Total Risk	Standard Deviation	Category Risk	Risk Index	Beta
abv av	8.8%	blw av	0.9	1.0

	1994	1993	1992	1991	1990	1989	1988	1987	1986	1985
Return (%)	4.2	18.6	5.2	27.4	-4.7	23.6	20.4	—	—	—
Differ from category (+/-)	4.8	5.2	-6.4	-8.3	1.0	-2.5	2.4	—	—	—

PER SHARE DATA

	1994	1993	1992	1991	1990	1989	1988	1987	1986	1985
Dividends, Net Income ($)	0.15	0.16	0.13	0.08	0.22	0.21	0.19	—	—	—
Distrib'ns, Cap Gain ($)	0.57	1.02	0.11	2.26	0.00	0.20	0.00	—	—	—
Net Asset Value ($)	13.75	13.89	12.74	12.34	11.53	12.34	10.32	—	—	—
Expense Ratio (%)	1.05	1.05	1.05	1.93	1.77	1.78	1.84	—	—	—
Net Income to Assets (%)	1.01	1.31	1.19	0.84	1.62	1.71	1.86	—	—	—
Portfolio Turnover (%)	na	63	174	90	70	78	111	—	—	—
Total Assets (Millions $)	89	47	24	14	14	16	12	—	—	—

PORTFOLIO (as of 6/30/94)

Portfolio Manager: Herbert W. Gullquist - 1987, Michael Rome - 1991

Investm't Category: Growth

✔ Cap Gain	Asset Allocation
Cap & Income	Fund of Funds
Income	Index
	Sector
✔ Domestic	Small Cap
✔ Foreign	Socially Conscious
Country/Region	State Specific

Portfolio: stocks 93% bonds 0%
convertibles 0% other 0% cash 7%

Largest Holdings: financial services 12%, automotive 8%

Unrealized Net Capital Gains: 4% of portfolio value

SHAREHOLDER INFORMATION

Minimum Investment
Initial: $50,000   Subsequent: $5,000

Minimum IRA Investment
Initial: $50,000   Subsequent: $5,000

Maximum Fees
Load: none   12b-1: none
Other: none

Distributions
Income: quarterly   Capital Gains: Dec

Exchange Options
Number Per Year: no limit   Fee: none
Telephone: yes (money market fund not available)

Services
IRA

Lazard International Equity Portfolio (LZIEX)

1 Rockefeller Plaza
New York, NY 10020
(800) 228-0203, (212) 632-6873

International Stock

PERFORMANCE   fund inception date: 10/29/91

	3yr Annual	5yr Annual	10yr Annual	Bull	Bear
Return (%)	7.0	na	na	na	-6.3
Differ from Category (+/-)	-2.1 blw av	na	na	na	0.7 av

Total Risk	Standard Deviation	Category Risk	Risk Index	Beta
high	13.2%	abv av	1.0	0.9

	1994	1993	1992	1991	1990	1989	1988	1987	1986	1985
Return (%).............	0.2	31.0	-6.6	—	—	—	—	—	—	—
Differ from category (+/-) ..	3.2	-7.6	-3.7	—	—	—	—	—	—	—

PER SHARE DATA

	1994	1993	1992	1991	1990	1989	1988	1987	1986	1985
Dividends, Net Income ($).	0.08	0.02	0.14	—	—	—	—	—	—	—
Distrib'ns, Cap Gain ($) ...	1.05	0.08	0.00	—	—	—	—	—	—	—
Net Asset Value ($).....	11.23	12.32	9.48	—	—	—	—	—	—	—
Expense Ratio (%)	0.97	0.99	1.05	—	—	—	—	—	—	—
Net Income to Assets (%) .	1.10	1.13	2.13	—	—	—	—	—	—	—
Portfolio Turnover (%)	na	86	60	—	—	—	—	—	—	—
Total Assets (Millions $) ...	821	603	176	—	—	—	—	—	—	—

PORTFOLIO (as of 6/30/94)

Portfolio Manager: John R. Reinsberg - 1992

Investm't Category: International Stock

✔ Cap Gain	Asset Allocation
Cap & Income	Fund of Funds
Income	Index
	Sector
Domestic	Small Cap
✔ Foreign	Socially Conscious
Country/Region	State Specific

Portfolio: stocks 99%   bonds 0%
convertibles 0%   other 0%   cash 1%

Largest Holdings: Japan 18%, United Kingdom 10%

Unrealized Net Capital Gains: 7% of portfolio value

SHAREHOLDER INFORMATION

Minimum Investment
Initial: $50,000   Subsequent: $5,000

Minimum IRA Investment
Initial: $50,000   Subsequent: $5,000

Maximum Fees
Load: none   12b-1: none
Other: none

Distributions
Income: Jun, Dec   Capital Gains: Jun, Dec

Exchange Options
Number Per Year: no limit   Fee: none
Telephone: yes (money market fund not available)

Services
IRA

Lazard Small Cap Portfolio (LZSCX)

Aggressive Growth

1 Rockefeller Plaza
New York, NY 10020
(800) 228-0203, (212) 632-6873

PERFORMANCE

fund inception date: 10/30/91

	3yr Annual	5yr Annual	10yr Annual	Bull	Bear
Return (%)	18.3	na	na	na	-5.6
Differ from Category (+/-)	9.4 high	na	na	na	5.2 abv av

Total Risk	Standard Deviation	Category Risk	Risk Index	Beta
abv av	11.8%	blw av	0.8	0.9

	1994	1993	1992	1991	1990	1989	1988	1987	1986	1985
Return (%)	2.0	30.1	24.7	—	—	—	—	—	—	—
Differ from category (+/-) . . .	2.7	10.6	13.7	—	—	—	—	—	—	—

PER SHARE DATA

	1994	1993	1992	1991	1990	1989	1988	1987	1986	1985
Dividends, Net Income ($) .	0.39	0.02	0.02	—	—	—	—	—	—	—
Distrib'ns, Cap Gain ($) . . .	0.80	1.55	0.00	—	—	—	—	—	—	—
Net Asset Value ($)	14.35	15.26	12.98	—	—	—	—	—	—	—
Expense Ratio (%).	0.88	0.88	1.05	—	—	—	—	—	—	—
Net Income to Assets (%). .	0.37	0.16	0.29	—	—	—	—	—	—	—
Portfolio Turnover (%)	na	98	106	—	—	—	—	—	—	—
Total Assets (Millions $) . . .	428	350	168	—	—	—	—	—	—	—

PORTFOLIO (as of 6/30/94)

Portfolio Manager: Alexanderson - 1991, Purcell - 1991, Rome - 1991, Wilson - 1991

Investm't Category: Aggressive Growth

✔ Cap Gain	Asset Allocation
Cap & Income	Fund of Funds
Income	Index
	Sector
✔ Domestic	✔ Small Cap
Foreign	Socially Conscious
Country/Region	State Specific

Portfolio: stocks 94% bonds 0%
convertibles 0% other 0% cash 6%

Largest Holdings: retailing 11%, financial services 9%

Unrealized Net Capital Gains: 6% of portfolio value

SHAREHOLDER INFORMATION

Minimum Investment
Initial: $50,000   Subsequent: $5,000

Minimum IRA Investment
Initial: $50,000   Subsequent: $5,000

Maximum Fees
Load: none   12b-1: none
Other: none

Distributions
Income: Dec   Capital Gains: Dec

Exchange Options
Number Per Year: no limit   Fee: none
Telephone: yes (money market fund not available)

Services
IRA

Lazard Special Equity Portfolio (LZSEX)

Growth

1 Rockefeller Plaza
New York, NY 10020
(800) 228-0203, (212) 632-6873

PERFORMANCE

fund inception date: 1/16/86

	3yr Annual	5yr Annual	10yr Annual	Bull	Bear
Return (%)	7.4	8.9	na	85.4	-2.1
Differ from Category (+/-)	-0.3 av	-0.7 av	na	-6.7 av	4.5 high

Total Risk	Standard Deviation	Category Risk	Risk Index	Beta
blw av	6.4%	low	0.6	0.3

	1994	1993	1992	1991	1990	1989	1988	1987	1986	1985
Return (%)	-2.6	10.2	15.4	38.1	-10.5	16.2	28.0	-1.6	—	—
Differ from category (+/-)	-2.0	-3.2	3.8	2.4	-4.8	-9.9	10.0	-3.4	—	—

PER SHARE DATA

	1994	1993	1992	1991	1990	1989	1988	1987	1986	1985
Dividends, Net Income ($)	0.16	0.16	0.16	0.22	0.74	0.26	0.25	0.11	—	—
Distrib'ns, Cap Gain ($)	3.28	2.73	0.42	0.56	0.00	1.28	0.25	0.74	—	—
Net Asset Value ($)	11.89	15.73	16.90	15.14	11.54	13.72	13.13	10.64	—	—
Expense Ratio (%)	1.75	1.67	1.70	1.77	1.78	1.78	1.96	1.81	—	—
Net Income to Assets (%)	0.79	0.74	1.04	1.63	4.70	1.82	1.87	0.82	—	—
Portfolio Turnover (%)	na	26	10	19	27	40	64	90	—	—
Total Assets (Millions $)	66	118	150	111	76	101	74	53	—	—

PORTFOLIO (as of 6/30/94)

Portfolio Manager: Charles Dreifus - 1986

Investm't Category: Growth

✔ Cap Gain   Asset Allocation
Cap & Income   Fund of Funds
Income   Index
    Sector
✔ Domestic   ✔ Small Cap
✔ Foreign   Socially Conscious
Country/Region   State Specific

Portfolio: stocks 86%   bonds 0%
convertibles 0%   other 0%   cash 14%

Largest Holdings: services 16%, textile, shoes & apparel 14%

Unrealized Net Capital Gains: 10% of portfolio value

SHAREHOLDER INFORMATION

Minimum Investment
Initial: $50,000   Subsequent: $5,000

Minimum IRA Investment
Initial: $50,000   Subsequent: $5,000

Maximum Fees
Load: none   12b-1: none
Other: none

Distributions
Income: Jun, Dec   Capital Gains: Jun, Dec

Exchange Options
Number Per Year: no limit   Fee: none
Telephone: yes (money market fund not available)

Services
IRA

Lazard Strategic Yield Portfolio (LZSYX)

General Bond

1 Rockefeller Plaza
New York, NY 10020
(800) 228-0203, (212) 632-6873

PERFORMANCE
fund inception date: 10/1/91

	3yr Annual	5yr Annual	10yr Annual	Bull	Bear
Return (%)	6.1	na	na	na	-5.5
Differ from Category (+/-)	1.8 high	na	na	na	-1.7 blw av

Total Risk	Standard Deviation	Category Risk	Risk Index	Avg Mat
low	4.8%	high	1.2	na

	1994	1993	1992	1991	1990	1989	1988	1987	1986	1985
Return (%)	-2.3	15.5	5.9	—	—	—	—	—	—	—
Differ from category (+/-) . .	-0.3	6.3	-0.7	—	—	—	—	—	—	—

PER SHARE DATA

	1994	1993	1992	1991	1990	1989	1988	1987	1986	1985
Dividends, Net Income ($) .	0.76	0.67	1.05	—	—	—	—	—	—	—
Distrib'ns, Cap Gain ($) . . .	0.04	0.12	0.02	—	—	—	—	—	—	—
Net Asset Value ($)	9.10	10.13	9.48	—	—	—	—	—	—	—
Expense Ratio (%).	1.05	1.05	1.05	—	—	—	—	—	—	—
Net Income to Assets (%). .	7.25	6.36	10.57	—	—	—	—	—	—	—
Portfolio Turnover (%).	na	215	122	—	—	—	—	—	—	—
Total Assets (Millions $)	62	34	9	—	—	—	—	—	—	—

PORTFOLIO (as of 6/30/94)

Portfolio Manager: Eduardo Haim - 1991, Ira O. Handler - 1993

Investm't Category: General Bond
Cap Gain	Asset Allocation
Cap & Income	Fund of Funds
✔ Income	Index
	Sector
✔ Domestic	Small Cap
✔ Foreign	Socially Conscious
Country/Region	State Specific

Portfolio: stocks 0%   bonds 91%
convertibles 0%   other 0%   cash 9%

Largest Holdings: corporate 51%, foreign government 29%

Unrealized Net Capital Gains: -4% of portfolio value

SHAREHOLDER INFORMATION

Minimum Investment
Initial: $50,000   Subsequent: $5,000

Minimum IRA Investment
Initial: $50,000   Subsequent: $5,000

Maximum Fees
Load: none   12b-1: none
Other: none

Distributions
Income: monthly   Capital Gains: Dec

Exchange Options
Number Per Year: no limit   Fee: none
Telephone: yes (money market fund not available)

Services
IRA

Leeb Personal Finance

(LBPFX)

Growth

312 Walnut St., 21st Fl.
Cincinnati, OH 45202
(800) 545-0103, (513) 629-2070

fund inception date: 10/21/91

	3yr Annual	5yr Annual	10yr Annual	Bull	Bear
Return (%)	1.9	na	na	na	-4.9
Differ from Category (+/-)	-5.8 low	na	na	na	1.7 abv av

Total Risk	Standard Deviation	Category Risk	Risk Index	Beta
low	3.9%	low	0.4	0.4

	1994	1993	1992	1991	1990	1989	1988	1987	1986	1985
Return (%).	-3.0	2.8	6.2	—	—	—	—	—	—	—
Differ from category (+/-) . .	-2.4	-10.6	-5.4	—	—	—	—	—	—	—

PER SHARE DATA

	1994	1993	1992	1991	1990	1989	1988	1987	1986	1985
Dividends, Net Income ($).	0.23	0.17	0.14	—	—	—	—	—	—	—
Distrib'ns, Cap Gain ($) . . .	0.13	0.19	0.11	—	—	—	—	—	—	—
Net Asset Value ($)	10.04	10.73	10.78	—	—	—	—	—	—	—
Expense Ratio (%)	1.50	1.50	1.47	—	—	—	—	—	—	—
Net Income to Assets (%) .	1.65	1.60	2.21	—	—	—	—	—	—	—
Portfolio Turnover (%)	143	83	75	—	—	—	—	—	—	—
Total Assets (Millions $)	38	54	28	—	—	—	—	—	—	—

PORTFOLIO (as of 6/30/94)

Portfolio Manager: Stephen Leeb - 1991

Investm't Category: Growth

✔ Cap Gain	Asset Allocation
Cap & Income	Fund of Funds
Income	Index
	Sector
✔ Domestic	Small Cap
Foreign	Socially Conscious
Country/Region	State Specific

Portfolio: stocks 60%   bonds 4%
convertibles 0%   other 0%   cash 36%

Largest Holdings: finance & insurance 19%, mining 15%

Unrealized Net Capital Gains: -1% of portfolio value

SHAREHOLDER INFORMATION

Minimum Investment
Initial: $2,500   Subsequent: $0

Minimum IRA Investment
Initial: $250   Subsequent: $0

Maximum Fees
Load: none   12b-1: none
Other: none

Distributions
Income: Jun, Dec   Capital Gains: Dec

Exchange Options
Number Per Year: none   Fee:
Telephone:

Services
IRA, pension, auto invest, auto withdraw

Legg Mason American Leading Cos (LMALX)

Growth & Income

111 S. Calvert St.
Baltimore, MD 21203
(800) 822-5544, (410) 539-0000

PERFORMANCE

fund inception date: 9/1/93

	3yr Annual	5yr Annual	10yr Annual	Bull	Bear
Return (%)	na	na	na	na	-5.8
Differ from Category (+/-)	na	na	na	na	0.5 av

Total Risk	Standard Deviation	Category Risk	Risk Index	Beta
na	na	na	na	na

	1994	1993	1992	1991	1990	1989	1988	1987	1986	1985
Return (%)	-4.1	—	—	—	—	—	—	—	—	—
Differ from category (+/-)	-2.7	—	—	—	—	—	—	—	—	—

PER SHARE DATA

	1994	1993	1992	1991	1990	1989	1988	1987	1986	1985
Dividends, Net Income ($)	0.11	—	—	—	—	—	—	—	—	—
Distrib'ns, Cap Gain ($)	0.00	—	—	—	—	—	—	—	—	—
Net Asset Value ($)	9.53	—	—	—	—	—	—	—	—	—
Expense Ratio (%)	1.95	—	—	—	—	—	—	—	—	—
Net Income to Assets (%)	1.11	—	—	—	—	—	—	—	—	—
Portfolio Turnover (%)	32	—	—	—	—	—	—	—	—	—
Total Assets (Millions $)	56	—	—	—	—	—	—	—	—	—

PORTFOLIO (as of 9/30/94)

Portfolio Manager: Eric Leo - 1993

Investm't Category: Growth & Income
Cap Gain	Asset Allocation
✔ Cap & Income	Fund of Funds
Income	Index
	Sector
✔ Domestic	Small Cap
✔ Foreign	Socially Conscious
Country/Region	State Specific

Portfolio: stocks 85% bonds 2%
convertibles 0% other 2% cash 11%

Largest Holdings: multi-industry 11%, food, beverage and tobacco 9%

Unrealized Net Capital Gains: 0% of portfolio value

SHAREHOLDER INFORMATION

Minimum Investment
Initial: $1,000   Subsequent: $100

Minimum IRA Investment
Initial: $250   Subsequent: $100

Maximum Fees
Load: none   12b-1: 1.00%
Other: none

Distributions
Income: quarterly   Capital Gains: Dec

Exchange Options
Number Per Year: 4   Fee: none
Telephone: yes (money market fund available)

Services
IRA, pension, auto exchange, auto invest, auto withdraw

Legg Mason Global Gov't Trust (LMGGX)

International Bond

111 S. Calvert St.
Baltimore, MD 21203
(800) 822-5544, (410) 539-0000

PERFORMANCE

fund inception date: 4/15/93

	3yr Annual	5yr Annual	10yr Annual	Bull	Bear
Return (%)	na	na	na	na	-2.9
Differ from Category (+/-)	na	na	na	na	4.9 abv av

Total Risk	Standard Deviation	Category Risk	Risk Index	Avg Mat
na	na	na	na	7.2 yrs

	1994	1993	1992	1991	1990	1989	1988	1987	1986	1985
Return (%).............	-1.6	—	—	—	—	—	—	—	—	—
Differ from category (+/-) ..	4.7	—	—	—	—	—	—	—	—	—

PER SHARE DATA

	1994	1993	1992	1991	1990	1989	1988	1987	1986	1985
Dividends, Net Income ($).	0.59	—	—	—	—	—	—	—	—	—
Distrib'ns, Cap Gain ($) . . .	0.00	—	—	—	—	—	—	—	—	—
Net Asset Value ($)	9.52	—	—	—	—	—	—	—	—	—
Expense Ratio (%)	0.98	—	—	—	—	—	—	—	—	—
Net Income to Assets (%) .	5.39	—	—	—	—	—	—	—	—	—
Portfolio Turnover (%)	144	—	—	—	—	—	—	—	—	—
Total Assets (Millions $) . . .	145	—	—	—	—	—	—	—	—	—

PORTFOLIO (as of 6/30/94)

Portfolio Manager: Keith Gardner - 1993

Investm't Category: International Bond

Cap Gain	Asset Allocation
✔ Cap & Income	Fund of Funds
Income	Index
	Sector
✔ Domestic	Small Cap
✔ Foreign	Socially Conscious
Country/Region	State Specific

Portfolio: stocks 0%   bonds 97%
convertibles 0%   other 0%   cash 3%

Largest Holdings: United States 28%, Japan 16%

Unrealized Net Capital Gains: -2% of portfolio value

SHAREHOLDER INFORMATION

Minimum Investment
Initial: $1,000   Subsequent: $100

Minimum IRA Investment
Initial: $1,000   Subsequent: $100

Maximum Fees
Load: none   12b-1: 0.75%
Other: none

Distributions
Income: monthly   Capital Gains: Dec

Exchange Options
Number Per Year: 4   Fee: none
Telephone: yes (money market fund available)

Services
IRA, pension, auto exchange, auto invest, auto withdraw

Legg Mason Investment Grade (LMIGX)

111 S. Calvert St.
Baltimore, MD 21203
(800) 822-5544, (410) 539-0000

General Bond

PERFORMANCE

fund inception date: 8/7/87

	3yr Annual	5yr Annual	10yr Annual	Bull	Bear
Return (%)	4.1	6.7	na	46.0	-6.6
Differ from Category (+/-)	-0.2 av	-0.2 blw av	na	5.0 abv av	-2.8 low

Total Risk	Standard Deviation	Category Risk	Risk Index	Avg Mat
low	4.5%	abv av	1.1	12.2 yrs

	1994	1993	1992	1991	1990	1989	1988	1987	1986	1985
Return (%)	-4.8	11.2	6.7	15.9	5.7	12.9	7.6	—	—	—
Differ from category (+/-) . .	-2.8	2.0	0.1	1.3	-1.5	1.5	0.2	—	—	—

PER SHARE DATA

	1994	1993	1992	1991	1990	1989	1988	1987	1986	1985
Dividends, Net Income ($) .	0.60	0.62	0.66	0.76	0.88	0.82	0.78	—	—	—
Distrib'ns, Cap Gain ($) . . .	0.04	0.85	0.04	0.03	0.00	0.00	0.03	—	—	—
Net Asset Value ($)	9.27	10.40	10.71	10.71	9.97	10.29	9.88	—	—	—
Expense Ratio (%).	0.85	0.85	0.85	0.71	0.50	0.80	1.00	—	—	—
Net Income to Assets (%). .	5.80	5.60	6.10	7.30	8.30	8.10	7.70	—	—	—
Portfolio Turnover (%)	198	348	317	213	55	92	146	—	—	—
Total Assets (Millions $)	66	68	48	36	23	14	10	—	—	—

PORTFOLIO (as of 6/30/94)

Portfolio Manager: Kent S. Engel - 1987

Investm't Category: General Bond

Cap Gain	Asset Allocation
Cap & Income	Fund of Funds
✔ Income	Index
	Sector
✔ Domestic	Small Cap
✔ Foreign	Socially Conscious
Country/Region	State Specific

Portfolio: stocks 0% bonds 94%
convertibles 0% other 0% cash 6%

Largest Holdings: corporate 51%, mortgage-backed 27%

Unrealized Net Capital Gains: -5% of portfolio value

SHAREHOLDER INFORMATION

Minimum Investment
Initial: $1,000   Subsequent: $100

Minimum IRA Investment
Initial: $1,000   Subsequent: $100

Maximum Fees
Load: none   12b-1: 0.50%
Other: none

Distributions
Income: monthly   Capital Gains: Feb, Dec

Exchange Options
Number Per Year: 4   Fee: none
Telephone: yes (money market fund available)

Services
IRA, pension, auto exchange, auto invest, auto withdraw

Legg Mason Special Investment (LMASX)

Aggressive Growth

111 S. Calvert St.
Baltimore, MD 21203
(800) 822-5544, (410) 539-0000

PERFORMANCE

fund inception date: 12/30/85

	3yr Annual	5yr Annual	10yr Annual	Bull	Bear
Return (%)	7.5	11.7	na	128.1	-15.0
Differ from Category (+/-)	-1.4 av	-0.8 av	na	-5.1 av	-4.2 blw av

Total Risk	Standard Deviation	Category Risk	Risk Index	Beta
high	13.4%	av	0.9	1.1

	1994	1993	1992	1991	1990	1989	1988	1987	1986	1985
Return (%)	-13.0	24.1	15.3	39.4	0.5	32.0	19.6	-10.5	7.4	—
Differ from category (+/-)	-12.3	4.6	4.3	-12.7	6.7	5.2	4.4	-8.3	-4.4	—

PER SHARE DATA

	1994	1993	1992	1991	1990	1989	1988	1987	1986	1985
Dividends, Net Income ($)	0.00	0.03	0.11	0.03	0.27	0.08	0.01	0.08	0.02	—
Distrib'ns, Cap Gain ($)	0.23	0.14	1.10	0.08	1.32	0.00	0.00	0.89	0.22	—
Net Asset Value ($)	19.03	22.14	17.98	16.78	12.12	13.63	10.38	8.68	10.51	—
Expense Ratio (%)	1.94	2.00	2.10	2.30	2.30	2.50	2.50	2.50	2.50	—
Net Income to Assets (%)	0.00	0.20	0.08	1.40	1.00	0.70	1.00	0.00	1.20	—
Portfolio Turnover (%)	16	32	57	76	116	122	159	77	41	—
Total Assets (Millions $)	605	491	202	107	68	44	44	56	34	—

PORTFOLIO (as of 6/30/94)

Portfolio Manager: William H. Miller III - 1985

Investm't Category: Aggressive Growth

✔ Cap Gain	Asset Allocation
Cap & Income	Fund of Funds
Income	Index
	Sector
✔ Domestic	✔ Small Cap
✔ Foreign	Socially Conscious
Country/Region	State Specific

Portfolio: stocks 92% bonds 0%
convertibles 0% other 1% cash 7%

Largest Holdings: entertainment 11%, banking 9%

Unrealized Net Capital Gains: 11% of portfolio value

SHAREHOLDER INFORMATION

Minimum Investment
Initial: $1,000   Subsequent: $100

Minimum IRA Investment
Initial: $1,000   Subsequent: $100

Maximum Fees
Load: none   12b-1: 1.00%
Other: none

Distributions
Income: Dec   Capital Gains: May, Dec

Exchange Options
Number Per Year: 4   Fee: none
Telephone: yes (money market fund available)

Services
IRA, pension, auto exchange, auto invest, auto withdraw

Legg Mason Total Return
(LMTRX)
Growth & Income

111 S. Calvert St.
Baltimore, MD 21203
(800) 822-5544, (410) 539-0000

PERFORMANCE

fund inception date: 11/21/85

	3yr Annual	5yr Annual	10yr Annual	Bull	Bear
Return (%)	6.5	7.1	na	103.6	-6.8
Differ from Category (+/-)	-0.6 av	-0.8 blw av	na	27.8 high	-0.5 blw av

Total Risk	Standard Deviation	Category Risk	Risk Index	Beta
abv av	8.9%	abv av	1.1	0.9

	1994	1993	1992	1991	1990	1989	1988	1987	1986	1985
Return (%)	-7.1	14.0	14.3	40.4	-16.8	16.2	21.7	-7.7	1.4	—
Differ from category (+/-) . .	-5.7	0.8	4.1	12.8	-10.8	-5.2	4.7	-8.3	-14.4	—

PER SHARE DATA

	1994	1993	1992	1991	1990	1989	1988	1987	1986	1985
Dividends, Net Income ($) .	0.29	0.41	0.30	0.18	0.29	0.21	0.13	0.24	0.16	—
Distrib'ns, Cap Gain ($) . . .	0.60	0.34	0.00	0.00	0.07	0.18	0.00	1.39	0.04	—
Net Asset Value ($)	12.15	14.00	12.98	11.64	8.43	10.54	9.40	7.83	10.04	—
Expense Ratio (%).	1.93	1.95	2.30	2.50	2.40	2.40	2.30	2.40	2.20	—
Net Income to Assets (%). .	2.40	3.10	3.10	3.10	2.00	1.60	1.90	1.70	3.80	—
Portfolio Turnover (%)	61	40	38	62	39	26	50	83	40	—
Total Assets (Millions $) . . .	193	171	52	23	27	30	35	47	44	—

PORTFOLIO (as of 9/30/94)

Portfolio Manager: William H. Miller III - 1985, Nancy T. Dennin - 1992

Investm't Category: Growth & Income
Cap Gain	Asset Allocation
✔ Cap & Income	Fund of Funds
Income	Index
	Sector
✔ Domestic	Small Cap
✔ Foreign	Socially Conscious
Country/Region	State Specific

Portfolio: stocks 80% bonds 3%
convertibles 3% other 6% cash 8%

Largest Holdings: banking 17%, real estate 12%

Unrealized Net Capital Gains: 7% of portfolio value

SHAREHOLDER INFORMATION

Minimum Investment
Initial: $1,000   Subsequent: $100

Minimum IRA Investment
Initial: $1,000   Subsequent: $100

Maximum Fees
Load: none   12b-1: 1.00%
Other: none

Distributions
Income: quarterly   Capital Gains: May, Dec

Exchange Options
Number Per Year: 4   Fee: none
Telephone: yes (money market fund available)

Services
IRA, pension, auto exchange, auto invest, auto withdraw

Legg Mason US Gov't Interm Port (LGINX)

General Bond

111 S. Calvert St.
Baltimore, MD 21203
(800) 822-5544, (410) 539-0000

	3yr Annual	5yr Annual	10yr Annual	Bull	Bear
Return (%)	3.5	6.7	na	36.6	-2.5
Differ from Category (+/-)	-0.8 low	-0.2 blw av	na	-4.4 blw av	1.3 abv av

Total Risk	Standard Deviation	Category Risk	Risk Index	Avg Mat
low	2.8%	blw av	0.7	6.8 yrs

	1994	1993	1992	1991	1990	1989	1988	1987	1986	1985
Return (%)	-1.9	6.6	6.2	14.3	9.0	12.7	6.4	—	—	—
Differ from category (+/-)	0.1	-2.6	-0.4	-0.3	1.8	1.3	-1.0	—	—	—

PER SHARE DATA

	1994	1993	1992	1991	1990	1989	1988	1987	1986	1985
Dividends, Net Income ($)	0.51	0.53	0.60	0.72	0.79	0.80	0.74	—	—	—
Distrib'ns, Cap Gain ($)	0.00	0.46	0.10	0.22	0.00	0.00	0.01	—	—	—
Net Asset Value ($)	9.72	10.43	10.72	10.77	10.29	10.20	9.79	—	—	—
Expense Ratio (%)	0.90	0.90	0.90	0.80	0.60	0.80	1.00	—	—	—
Net Income to Assets (%)	5.20	4.80	5.50	6.70	7.70	7.90	7.40	—	—	—
Portfolio Turnover (%)	325	490	513	643	67	57	133	—	—	—
Total Assets (Millions $)	235	299	307	212	74	43	27	—	—	—

PORTFOLIO (as of 6/30/94)

Portfolio Manager: Stephen A. Walsh - 1991

Investm't Category: General Bond

Cap Gain	Asset Allocation
Cap & Income	Fund of Funds
✔ Income	Index
	Sector
✔ Domestic	Small Cap
Foreign	Socially Conscious
Country/Region	State Specific

Portfolio: stocks 0%   bonds 93%
convertibles 0%   other 0%   cash 7%

Largest Holdings: U.S. government & agencies 44%, mortgage-backed 31%

Unrealized Net Capital Gains: -2% of portfolio value

SHAREHOLDER INFORMATION

Minimum Investment
Initial: $1,000   Subsequent: $100

Minimum IRA Investment
Initial: $1,000   Subsequent: $100

Maximum Fees
Load: none   12b-1: 0.50%
Other: none

Distributions
Income: monthly   Capital Gains: Feb, Dec

Exchange Options
Number Per Year: 4   Fee: none
Telephone: yes (money market fund available)

Services
IRA, pension, auto exchange, auto invest, auto withdraw

Legg Mason Value (LMVTX)
Growth

111 S. Calvert St.
Baltimore, MD 21203
(800) 822-5544, (410) 539-0000

fund inception date: 4/16/82

	3yr Annual	5yr Annual	10yr Annual	Bull	Bear
Return (%)	7.8	7.0	10.9	87.1	-8.9
Differ from Category (+/-)	0.1 av	-2.6 low	-2.0 low	-5.0 av	-2.3 blw av

Total Risk	Standard Deviation	Category Risk	Risk Index	Beta
abv av	10.5%	abv av	1.1	1.2

	1994	1993	1992	1991	1990	1989	1988	1987	1986	1985
Return (%)	1.2	11.2	11.4	34.7	-16.9	20.0	25.7	-7.4	9.4	31.7
Differ from category (+/-)	1.8	-2.2	-0.2	-1.0	-11.2	-6.1	7.7	-9.2	-5.2	2.5

PER SHARE DATA

	1994	1993	1992	1991	1990	1989	1988	1987	1986	1985
Dividends, Net Income ($)	0.03	0.23	0.16	0.23	0.36	0.33	0.19	0.25	0.21	0.17
Distrib'ns, Cap Gain ($)	0.04	0.15	0.00	0.00	0.04	0.74	0.00	1.39	1.39	0.43
Net Asset Value ($)	19.04	18.87	17.32	15.70	11.84	14.69	13.14	10.60	13.05	13.35
Expense Ratio (%)	1.82	1.86	1.90	1.90	1.86	1.96	1.97	2.00	2.07	2.41
Net Income to Assets (%)	0.40	1.10	1.70	2.50	2.20	1.60	1.50	1.50	2.00	2.30
Portfolio Turnover (%)	12	21	39	39	31	30	48	43	32	37
Total Assets (Millions $)	967	914	746	690	809	721	666	819	599	163

PORTFOLIO (as of 9/30/94)

Portfolio Manager: William H. Miller III - 1982

Investm't Category: Growth

✔ Cap Gain	Asset Allocation
Cap & Income	Fund of Funds
Income	Index
	Sector
✔ Domestic	Small Cap
✔ Foreign	Socially Conscious
Country/Region	State Specific

Portfolio: stocks 95% bonds 0%
convertibles 0% other 2% cash 3%

Largest Holdings: banking 17%, finance 15%

Unrealized Net Capital Gains: 32% of portfolio value

SHAREHOLDER INFORMATION

Minimum Investment
Initial: $1,000   Subsequent: $100

Minimum IRA Investment
Initial: $1,000   Subsequent: $100

Maximum Fees
Load: none   12b-1: 1.00%
Other: none

Distributions
Income: quarterly   Capital Gains: May, Dec

Exchange Options
Number Per Year: 4   Fee: none
Telephone: yes (money market fund available)

Services
IRA, pension, auto exchange, auto invest, auto withdraw

Lepercq-Istel (ISTLX)
Balanced

1675 Broadway, 16th Fl.
New York, NY 10019
(800) 655-7766, (212) 698-0749

PERFORMANCE

fund inception date: 1/1/53

	3yr Annual	5yr Annual	10yr Annual	Bull	Bear
Return (%)	4.3	4.4	7.9	49.2	-4.6
Differ from Category (+/-)	-2.1 blw av	-3.6 low	-3.4 low	-15.8 blw av	1.1 abv av

Total Risk	Standard Deviation	Category Risk	Risk Index	Beta
av	8.0%	high	1.3	0.8

	1994	1993	1992	1991	1990	1989	1988	1987	1986	1985
Return (%).	-5.0	13.5	5.4	17.3	-6.6	21.7	7.0	2.2	8.1	20.0
Differ from category (+/-) . .	-3.1	0.1	-2.9	-6.1	-6.1	4.4	-4.8	-0.2	-9.3	-4.3

PER SHARE DATA

	1994	1993	1992	1991	1990	1989	1988	1987	1986	1985
Dividends, Net Income ($).	0.21	0.32	0.41	0.53	0.62	0.63	0.54	0.57	0.64	0.74
Distrib'ns, Cap Gain ($) . . .	0.71	0.92	0.22	0.00	0.00	0.37	0.23	0.85	1.08	1.47
Net Asset Value ($)	13.17	14.84	14.17	14.05	12.46	14.00	12.33	12.23	13.29	13.89
Expense Ratio (%)	na	1.49	1.53	1.54	1.50	1.48	1.50	1.44	1.67	1.12
Net Income to Assets (%) . . .	na	2.00	2.90	3.80	4.57	4.41	4.13	2.69	3.01	3.81
Portfolio Turnover (%)	na	na	20	22	24	48	72	67	44	27
Total Assets (Millions $)	18	16	17	17	19	22	20	22	23	28

PORTFOLIO (as of 6/30/94)

Portfolio Manager: Bruno Desforges - 1986

Investm't Category: Balanced

Cap Gain	✔ Asset Allocation
✔ Cap & Income	Fund of Funds
Income	Index
	Sector
✔ Domestic	Small Cap
✔ Foreign	Socially Conscious
Country/Region	State Specific

Portfolio: stocks 64% bonds 16%
convertibles 5% other 0% cash 15%

Largest Holdings: stocks—services 16%,
bonds—U.S. government 16%

Unrealized Net Capital Gains: 17% of portfolio value

SHAREHOLDER INFORMATION

Minimum Investment
Initial: $500   Subsequent: 1 share

Minimum IRA Investment
Initial: $500   Subsequent: 1 share

Maximum Fees
Load: none   12b-1: 1.00%
Other: none

Distributions
Income: Jul, Dec   Capital Gains: Dec

Exchange Options
Number Per Year: none   Fee:
Telephone:

Services
IRA, pension, auto withdraw

Lexington Global (LXGLX)

International Stock

Park 80 W. Plaza 2
P.O. Box 1515
Saddle Brook, NJ 07662
(800) 526-0056, (201) 845-7300

PERFORMANCE

fund inception date: 3/24/87

	3yr Annual	5yr Annual	10yr Annual	Bull	Bear
Return (%)	9.0	4.4	na	65.2	-3.4
Differ from Category (+/-)	-0.1 av	-0.5 av	na	1.3 av	3.6 high

Total Risk	Standard Deviation	Category Risk	Risk Index	Beta
abv av	10.9%	low	0.8	0.8

	1994	1993	1992	1991	1990	1989	1988	1987	1986	1985
Return (%)	1.8	31.8	-3.5	15.5	-16.7	25.1	16.3	—	—	—
Differ from category (+/-) ...	4.8	-6.8	-0.6	2.4	-6.3	2.6	1.9	—	—	—

PER SHARE DATA

	1994	1993	1992	1991	1990	1989	1988	1987	1986	1985
Dividends, Net Income ($) .	0.03	0.06	0.07	0.15	0.13	0.02	0.51	—	—	—
Distrib'ns, Cap Gain ($) ...	2.56	1.05	0.00	0.13	0.30	0.77	0.07	—	—	—
Net Asset Value ($)	11.17	13.51	11.09	11.57	10.26	12.83	10.89	—	—	—
Expense Ratio (%)........	1.60	1.49	1.52	1.57	1.59	1.64	1.80	—	—	—
Net Income to Assets (%)..	0.34	0.52	0.55	0.79	0.99	0.13	0.12	—	—	—
Portfolio Turnover (%).....	96	84	81	76	82	114	97	—	—	—
Total Assets (Millions $)	67	78	50	54	51	57	38	—	—	—

PORTFOLIO (as of 6/30/94)

Portfolio Manager: Richard Saler - 1994, Alan Wapnick - 1994

Investm't Category: International Stock
- ✔ Cap Gain
- Cap & Income
- Income
- ✔ Domestic
- ✔ Foreign
- Country/Region
- Asset Allocation
- Fund of Funds
- Index
- Sector
- Small Cap
- Socially Conscious
- State Specific

Portfolio: stocks 100% bonds 0%
convertibles 0% other 0% cash 0%

Largest Holdings: Japan 30%, United States 29%

Unrealized Net Capital Gains: 9% of portfolio value

SHAREHOLDER INFORMATION

Minimum Investment
Initial: $1,000   Subsequent: $50

Minimum IRA Investment
Initial: $250   Subsequent: $50

Maximum Fees
Load: none   12b-1: none
Other: none

Distributions
Income: Aug, Dec   Capital Gains: Dec

Exchange Options
Number Per Year: no limit   Fee: none
Telephone: yes (money market fund available)

Services
IRA, pension, auto exchange, auto invest, auto withdraw

Lexington GNMA Income (LEXNX)

Mortgage-Backed Bond

Park 80 W. Plaza 2
P.O. Box 1515
Saddle Brook, NJ 07662
(800) 526-0056, (201) 845-7300

PERFORMANCE

fund inception date: 8/17/73

	3yr Annual	5yr Annual	10yr Annual	Bull	Bear
Return (%)	3.6	7.0	8.7	40.3	-4.1
Differ from Category (+/-)	0.5 av	0.1 av	-0.1 blw av	2.3 abv av	0.3 blw av

Total Risk	Standard Deviation	Category Risk	Risk Index	Avg Mat
low	3.7%	abv av	1.1	na

	1994	1993	1992	1991	1990	1989	1988	1987	1986	1985
Return (%).	-2.0	7.9	5.1	15.7	9.1	15.5	6.8	1.5	11.7	17.2
Differ from category (+/-) . .	0.8	1.1	-1.0	1.3	-0.6	3.0	-0.3	-0.3	0.5	-2.4

PER SHARE DATA

	1994	1993	1992	1991	1990	1989	1988	1987	1986	1985
Dividends, Net Income ($).	0.55	0.58	0.61	0.64	0.66	0.68	0.64	0.73	0.74	0.92
Distrib'ns, Cap Gain ($) . . .	0.00	0.00	0.00	0.00	0.00	0.00	0.00	0.03	0.00	0.00
Net Asset Value ($)	7.60	8.32	8.26	8.45	7.90	7.88	7.45	7.58	8.22	8.06
Expense Ratio (%)	0.97	1.02	1.01	1.02	1.04	1.03	1.07	0.98	0.86	1.01
Net Income to Assets (%) .	6.69	6.96	7.31	7.97	8.43	8.88	8.31	8.49	9.30	11.06
Portfolio Turnover (%)	39	52	180	139	113	103	233	89	300	167
Total Assets (Millions $) . . .	132	160	132	122	98	96	97	108	141	87

PORTFOLIO (as of 6/30/94)

Portfolio Manager: Denis Jamison - 1981

Investm't Category: Mortgage-Backed Bond

Cap Gain	Asset Allocation
Cap & Income	Fund of Funds
✔ Income	Index
	Sector
✔ Domestic	Small Cap
Foreign	Socially Conscious
Country/Region	State Specific

Portfolio: stocks 0%   bonds 100%
convertibles 0%   other 0%   cash 0%

Largest Holdings: mortgage-backed 70%

Unrealized Net Capital Gains: -3% of portfolio value

SHAREHOLDER INFORMATION

Minimum Investment
Initial: $1,000   Subsequent: $50

Minimum IRA Investment
Initial: $250   Subsequent: $50

Maximum Fees
Load: none   12b-1: none
Other: none

Distributions
Income: monthly   Capital Gains: Dec

Exchange Options
Number Per Year: no limit   Fee: none
Telephone: yes (money market fund available)

Services
IRA, pension, auto exchange, auto invest, auto withdraw

Lexington GoldFund
(LEXMX)
Gold

Park 80 W. Plaza 2
P.O. Box 1515
Saddle Brook, NJ 07662
(800) 526-0056, (201) 845-7300

PERFORMANCE

fund inception date: 12/3/75

	3yr Annual	5yr Annual	10yr Annual	Bull	Bear
Return (%)	11.3	0.5	9.0	23.5	-9.7
Differ from Category (+/-)	0.5 av	0.5 blw av	3.8 high	-9.4 low	0.3 av

Total Risk	Standard Deviation	Category Risk	Risk Index	Beta
high	26.2%	av	1.0	0.4

	1994	1993	1992	1991	1990	1989	1988	1987	1986	1985
Return (%)	-7.0	86.9	-20.5	-6.1	-20.6	23.6	-15.1	46.5	32.6	12.9
Differ from category (+/-) ...	4.5	0.0	-4.8	-1.3	1.9	-1.1	3.8	14.6	-5.0	20.3

PER SHARE DATA

	1994	1993	1992	1991	1990	1989	1988	1987	1986	1985
Dividends, Net Income ($) .	0.03	0.02	0.02	0.04	0.04	0.05	0.05	0.05	0.02	0.04
Distrib'ns, Cap Gain ($) ...	0.00	0.00	0.00	0.00	0.00	0.00	0.00	0.32	0.00	0.00
Net Asset Value ($)	6.37	6.90	3.70	4.68	5.03	6.39	5.21	6.20	4.49	3.40
Expense Ratio (%)........	1.60	1.63	1.69	1.43	1.36	1.42	1.61	1.29	1.52	1.52
Net Income to Assets (%)..	0.41	0.25	0.58	0.81	0.69	1.14	0.78	0.57	1.11	0.71
Portfolio Turnover (%).....	16	28	13	22	12	16	20	14	14	30
Total Assets (Millions $) ...	158	161	72	96	106	155	93	105	24	12

PORTFOLIO (as of 6/30/94)

Portfolio Manager: Robert Radsch - 1994

Investm't Category: Gold

✔ Cap Gain	Asset Allocation
Cap & Income	Fund of Funds
Income	Index
	✔ Sector
✔ Domestic	Small Cap
✔ Foreign	Socially Conscious
Country/Region	State Specific

Portfolio:	stocks 94%	bonds 0%
convertibles 0%	other 1%	cash 5%

Largest Holdings: N. American gold mining cos. 44%, S. African gold mining cos. 31%

Unrealized Net Capital Gains: 13% of portfolio value

SHAREHOLDER INFORMATION

Minimum Investment
Initial: $1,000   Subsequent: $50

Minimum IRA Investment
Initial: $250   Subsequent: $50

Maximum Fees
Load: none   12b-1: 0.25%
Other: none

Distributions
Income: Aug, Dec   Capital Gains: Dec

Exchange Options
Number Per Year: no limit   Fee: none
Telephone: yes (money market fund available)

Services
IRA, pension, auto exchange, auto invest, auto withdraw

Lexington Growth & Income (LEXRX)

Growth & Income

Park 80 W. Plaza 2
P.O. Box 1515
Saddle Brook, NJ 07662
(800) 526-0056, (201) 845-7300

PERFORMANCE

fund inception date: 2/11/59

	3yr Annual	5yr Annual	10yr Annual	Bull	Bear
Return (%)	7.2	6.6	11.3	74.3	-7.1
Differ from Category (+/-)	0.1 av	-1.3 blw av	-0.4 av	-1.5 av	-0.8 blw av

Total Risk	Standard Deviation	Category Risk	Risk Index	Beta
av	8.5%	abv av	1.0	0.9

	1994	1993	1992	1991	1990	1989	1988	1987	1986	1985
Return (%).............	-3.1	13.2	12.3	24.8	-10.2	27.5	9.4	0.0	20.5	26.3
Differ from category (+/-) ..	-1.7	0.0	2.1	-2.8	-4.2	6.1	-7.6	-0.6	4.7	0.6

PER SHARE DATA

	1994	1993	1992	1991	1990	1989	1988	1987	1986	1985
Dividends, Net Income ($).	0.17	0.21	0.32	0.35	0.30	0.60	0.45	1.10	0.83	0.60
Distrib'ns, Cap Gain ($) ...	1.13	2.03	1.84	1.02	0.00	1.54	0.00	4.93	2.16	0.11
Net Asset Value ($)	14.36	16.16	16.25	16.39	14.24	16.19	14.39	13.57	19.16	18.62
Expense Ratio (%)	1.30	1.29	1.20	1.13	1.04	1.02	1.10	0.96	0.96	1.00
Net Income to Assets (%) .	0.79	1.20	2.57	2.19	3.91	2.82	3.20	2.37	2.52	3.52
Portfolio Turnover (%)	77	93	88	80	67	64	81	95	81	86
Total Assets (Millions $) ...	124	136	126	121	105	128	111	113	124	114

PORTFOLIO (as of 6/30/94)

Portfolio Manager: Alan Wapnick - 1991

Investm't Category: Growth & Income

Cap Gain	Asset Allocation
✔ Cap & Income	Fund of Funds
Income	Index
	Sector
✔ Domestic	Small Cap
✔ Foreign	Socially Conscious
Country/Region	State Specific

Portfolio: stocks 99% bonds 0%
convertibles 0% other 0% cash 1%

Largest Holdings: machinery 10%, electrical equipment 5%

Unrealized Net Capital Gains: 3% of portfolio value

SHAREHOLDER INFORMATION

Minimum Investment
Initial: $1,000   Subsequent: $50

Minimum IRA Investment
Initial: $250   Subsequent: $50

Maximum Fees
Load: none   12b-1: 0.25%
Other: none

Distributions
Income: quarterly   Capital Gains: Dec

Exchange Options
Number Per Year: no limit   Fee: none
Telephone: yes (money market fund available)

Services
IRA, pension, auto exchange, auto invest, auto withdraw

Lexington Tax-Exempt Bond Trust (LEBDX)

Tax-Exempt Bond

Park 80 W. Plaza 2
P.O. Box 1515
Saddle Brook, NJ 07662
(800) 526-0056, (201) 845-7300

PERFORMANCE

fund inception date: 5/20/86

	3yr Annual	5yr Annual	10yr Annual	Bull	Bear
Return (%)	3.3	5.2	na	36.6	-6.8
Differ from Category (+/-)	-1.2 low	-0.9 low	na	-5.2 low	-1.6 blw av

Total Risk	Standard Deviation	Category Risk	Risk Index	Avg Mat
blw av	5.8%	av	0.9	11.1 yrs

	1994	1993	1992	1991	1990	1989	1988	1987	1986	1985
Return (%)	-6.5	10.9	6.5	10.0	6.5	7.3	10.2	0.0	—	—
Differ from category (+/-) . .	-1.3	-0.8	-1.8	-1.3	0.2	-1.7	0.0	1.3	—	—

PER SHARE DATA

	1994	1993	1992	1991	1990	1989	1988	1987	1986	1985
Dividends, Net Income ($) .	0.45	0.55	0.61	0.67	0.71	0.63	0.63	0.86	—	—
Distrib'ns, Cap Gain ($) . . .	0.00	0.00	0.00	0.00	0.00	0.00	0.00	0.00	—	—
Net Asset Value ($)	9.80	10.95	10.39	10.35	10.05	10.12	10.03	9.69	—	—
Expense Ratio (%).	1.50	1.44	1.50	1.12	1.08	1.20	1.33	0.00	—	—
Net Income to Assets (%). .	4.80	4.83	5.92	6.64	7.20	6.22	6.33	7.95	—	—
Portfolio Turnover (%)	12	31	31	29	45	47	67	67	—	—
Total Assets (Millions $)	10	14	13	12	11	13	13	3	—	—

PORTFOLIO (as of 6/30/94)

Portfolio Manager: Denis Jamison - 1987

Investm't Category: Tax-Exempt Bond

Cap Gain	Asset Allocation
Cap & Income	Fund of Funds
✔ Income	Index
	Sector
✔ Domestic	Small Cap
Foreign	Socially Conscious
Country/Region	State Specific

Portfolio: stocks 0% bonds 100%
convertibles 0% other 0% cash 0%

Largest Holdings: general obligation 6%

Unrealized Net Capital Gains: 0% of portfolio value

SHAREHOLDER INFORMATION

Minimum Investment
Initial: $1,000   Subsequent: $50

Minimum IRA Investment
Initial: na   Subsequent: na

Maximum Fees
Load: none   12b-1: none
Other: none

Distributions
Income: monthly   Capital Gains: Dec

Exchange Options
Number Per Year: no limit   Fee: none
Telephone: yes (money market fund available)

Services
auto exchange, auto invest, auto withdraw

Lexington Worldwide Emerging Mkts (LEXGX)

International Stock

Park 80 W. Plaza 2
P.O. Box 1515
Saddle Brook, NJ 07662
(800) 526-0056, (201) 845-7300

PERFORMANCE

fund inception date: 6/17/91

	3yr Annual	5yr Annual	10yr Annual	Bull	Bear
Return (%)	13.4	na	na	na	-15.2
Differ from Category (+/-)	4.3 high	na	na	na	-8.2 low

Total Risk	Standard Deviation	Category Risk	Risk Index	Beta
high	16.9%	high	1.3	1.0

	1994	1993	1992	1991	1990	1989	1988	1987	1986	1985
Return (%)	-13.8	63.3	3.7	—	—	—	—	—	—	—
Differ from category (+/-)	-10.8	24.7	6.6	—	—	—	—	—	—	—

PER SHARE DATA

	1994	1993	1992	1991	1990	1989	1988	1987	1986	1985
Dividends, Net Income ($)	0.00	0.00	0.11	—	—	—	—	—	—	—
Distrib'ns, Cap Gain ($)	0.56	0.17	0.60	—	—	—	—	—	—	—
Net Asset Value ($)	11.47	13.96	8.66	—	—	—	—	—	—	—
Expense Ratio (%)	1.71	1.64	1.89	—	—	—	—	—	—	—
Net Income to Assets (%)	0.25	0.21	0.75	—	—	—	—	—	—	—
Portfolio Turnover (%)	67	38	91	—	—	—	—	—	—	—
Total Assets (Millions $)	288	248	30	—	—	—	—	—	—	—

PORTFOLIO (as of 6/30/94)

Portfolio Manager: Richard T. Saler - 1994

Investm't Category: International Stock

✔ Cap Gain	Asset Allocation
Cap & Income	Fund of Funds
Income	Index
	Sector
✔ Domestic	Small Cap
✔ Foreign	Socially Conscious
Country/Region	State Specific

Portfolio: stocks 100% bonds 0%
convertibles 0% other 0% cash 0%

Largest Holdings: Mexico 24%, Malaysia 10%

Unrealized Net Capital Gains: -4% of portfolio value

SHAREHOLDER INFORMATION

Minimum Investment
Initial: $1,000   Subsequent: $50

Minimum IRA Investment
Initial: $250   Subsequent: $50

Maximum Fees
Load: none   12b-1: none
Other: none

Distributions
Income: Dec   Capital Gains: Dec

Exchange Options
Number Per Year: no limit   Fee: none
Telephone: yes (money market fund available)

Services
IRA, pension, auto exchange, auto invest, auto withdraw

Lindner (LDNRX)

Growth & Income

7711 Carondelet Ave.
P.O. Box 11208
St. Louis, MO 63105
(314) 727-5305

PERFORMANCE

fund inception date: 5/24/73

	3yr Annual	5yr Annual	10yr Annual	Bull	Bear
Return (%)	10.2	7.9	12.2	71.2	-7.0
Differ from Category (+/-)	3.1 abv av	0.0 av	0.5 av	-4.6 av	-0.7 blw av

Total Risk	Standard Deviation	Category Risk	Risk Index	Beta
av	7.6%	blw av	0.9	0.7

	1994	1993	1992	1991	1990	1989	1988	1987	1986	1985
Return (%)	-0.8	19.8	12.7	23.4	-11.3	21.2	20.3	8.8	14.0	19.5
Differ from category (+/-)	0.6	6.6	2.5	-4.2	-5.3	-0.2	3.3	8.2	-1.8	-6.2

PER SHARE DATA

	1994	1993	1992	1991	1990	1989	1988	1987	1986	1985
Dividends, Net Income ($)	0.34	0.46	0.53	0.66	0.86	1.10	0.71	1.02	1.49	1.71
Distrib'ns, Cap Gain ($)	1.84	0.53	0.15	0.00	0.71	0.65	0.16	1.57	4.09	0.87
Net Asset Value ($)	20.89	23.22	20.22	18.55	15.58	19.21	17.31	15.12	16.12	19.16
Expense Ratio (%)	0.65	0.80	0.80	0.83	0.74	0.92	1.07	0.89	0.58	0.65
Net Income to Assets (%)	1.69	2.52	3.05	4.64	4.84	4.93	3.76	4.56	5.83	7.44
Portfolio Turnover (%)	37	18	11	13	19	18	21	39	32	46
Total Assets (Millions $)	1,502	1,504	979	783	716	535	404	406	390	397

PORTFOLIO (as of 6/30/94)

Portfolio Manager: R. Lange - 1977, E. Ryback - 1982, L. Callahan - 1993

Investm't Category: Growth & Income
Cap Gain	Asset Allocation
✔ Cap & Income	Fund of Funds
Income	Index
	Sector
✔ Domestic	Small Cap
✔ Foreign	Socially Conscious
Country/Region	State Specific

Portfolio: stocks 86% bonds 4%
convertibles 2% other 1% cash 7%

Largest Holdings: financial services 17%, energy 12%

Unrealized Net Capital Gains: 9% of portfolio value

SHAREHOLDER INFORMATION

Minimum Investment
Initial: $2,000 Subsequent: $100

Minimum IRA Investment
Initial: $250 Subsequent: $100

Maximum Fees
Load: 2.00% redemption 12b-1: none
Other: redemption fee applies for 60 days

Distributions
Income: Aug, Dec Capital Gains: Aug, Dec

Exchange Options
Number Per Year: none Fee:
Telephone:

Services
IRA, pension, auto withdraw

Lindner Dividend (LDDVX)

Balanced

7711 Carondelet Ave.
P.O. Box 11208
St. Louis, MO 63105
(314) 727-5305

PERFORMANCE — fund inception date: 6/22/76

	3yr Annual	5yr Annual	10yr Annual	Bull	Bear
Return (%)	10.3	9.8	11.6	77.0	-4.9
Differ from Category (+/-)	3.9 high	1.8 abv av	0.3 av	12.0 high	0.8 abv av

Total Risk	Standard Deviation	Category Risk	Risk Index	Beta
low	4.8%	low	0.8	0.4

	1994	1993	1992	1991	1990	1989	1988	1987	1986	1985
Return (%).............	-3.3	14.9	21.1	27.3	-6.5	11.8	24.2	-4.0	20.7	17.1
Differ from category (+/-) ..	-1.4	1.5	12.8	3.9	-6.0	-5.5	12.4	-6.4	3.3	-7.2

PER SHARE DATA

	1994	1993	1992	1991	1990	1989	1988	1987	1986	1985
Dividends, Net Income ($).	1.90	1.74	1.86	1.99	1.86	2.19	1.76	1.87	2.17	1.77
Distrib'ns, Cap Gain ($) ...	0.57	0.58	0.10	0.00	0.02	0.01	0.06	1.16	3.26	0.00
Net Asset Value ($).....	23.97	27.32	25.84	23.06	19.77	23.11	22.67	19.87	23.74	24.42
Expense Ratio (%)	0.64	0.74	0.80	0.87	0.87	0.97	1.04	1.00	0.95	1.14
Net Income to Assets (%) .	7.01	7.10	9.75	8.98	8.90	7.57	7.43	7.43	8.08	8.40
Portfolio Turnover (%)	43	13	24	3	5	2	17	56	26	10
Total Assets (Millions $) .	1,605	1,371	267	164	143	97	52	67	67	51

PORTFOLIO (as of 8/31/94)

Portfolio Manager: Eric Ryback - 1982

Investm't Category: Balanced

Cap Gain	Asset Allocation
✔ Cap & Income	Fund of Funds
Income	Index
	Sector
✔ Domestic	Small Cap
Foreign	Socially Conscious
Country/Region	State Specific

Portfolio: stocks 22% bonds 27%
convertibles 3% other 40% cash 8%

Largest Holdings: financial services 13%, energy 12%

Unrealized Net Capital Gains: 0% of portfolio value

SHAREHOLDER INFORMATION

Minimum Investment
Initial: $2,000   Subsequent: $100

Minimum IRA Investment
Initial: $250   Subsequent: $100

Maximum Fees
Load: 2.00% redemption 12b-1: none
Other: redemption fee applies for 60 days

Distributions
Income: quarterly   Capital Gains: Apr, Dec

Exchange Options
Number Per Year: none   Fee:
Telephone:

Services
IRA, auto withdraw

Lindner Utility (LDUTX)
Growth & Income

7711 Carondelet Ave.
P.O. Box 11208
St. Louis, MO 63105
(314) 727-5305

	3yr Annual	5yr Annual	10yr Annual	Bull	Bear
Return (%)	na	na	na	na	-9.4
Differ from Category (+/-)	na	na	na	na	-3.1 low

Total Risk	Standard Deviation	Category Risk	Risk Index	Beta
na	na	na	na	na

	1994	1993	1992	1991	1990	1989	1988	1987	1986	1985
Return (%)	-0.9	—	—	—	—	—	—	—	—	—
Differ from category (+/-)	0.5	—	—	—	—	—	—	—	—	—

PER SHARE DATA

	1994	1993	1992	1991	1990	1989	1988	1987	1986	1985
Dividends, Net Income ($)	0.15	—	—	—	—	—	—	—	—	—
Distrib'ns, Cap Gain ($)	0.09	—	—	—	—	—	—	—	—	—
Net Asset Value ($)	10.27	—	—	—	—	—	—	—	—	—
Expense Ratio (%)	1.30	—	—	—	—	—	—	—	—	—
Net Income to Assets (%)	0.76	—	—	—	—	—	—	—	—	—
Portfolio Turnover (%)	44	—	—	—	—	—	—	—	—	—
Total Assets (Millions $)	43	—	—	—	—	—	—	—	—	—

PORTFOLIO (as of 6/30/94)

Portfolio Manager: Eric Ryback - 1993

Investm't Category: Growth & Income
- Cap Gain
- Asset Allocation
- ✔ Cap & Income
- Fund of Funds
- Income
- Index
- ✔ Sector
- ✔ Domestic
- Small Cap
- ✔ Foreign
- Socially Conscious
- Country/Region
- State Specific

Portfolio: stocks 79% bonds 4%
convertibles 11% other 3% cash 3%

Largest Holdings: telecommunications 29%, utilities (gas, electric & water) 21%

Unrealized Net Capital Gains: -5% of portfolio value

SHAREHOLDER INFORMATION

Minimum Investment
Initial: $3,000   Subsequent: $100

Minimum IRA Investment
Initial: $250   Subsequent: $100

Maximum Fees
Load: 2.00% redemption   12b-1: none
Other: redemption fee applies for 60 days

Distributions
Income: quarterly   Capital Gains: Dec

Exchange Options
Number Per Year: none   Fee:
Telephone:

Services
IRA, auto withdraw

Longleaf Partners (LLPFX)

Growth

6075 Poplar Avenue
Suite 900
Memphis, TN 38119
(800) 445-9469, (901) 761-2474

PERFORMANCE
fund inception date: 4/8/87

	3yr Annual	5yr Annual	10yr Annual	Bull	Bear
Return (%)	17.0	13.3	na	122.2	5.9
Differ from Category (+/-)	9.3 high	3.7 high	na	30.1 high	12.5 high

Total Risk	Standard Deviation	Category Risk	Risk Index	Beta
av	7.7%	low	0.8	0.7

	1994	1993	1992	1991	1990	1989	1988	1987	1986	1985
Return (%)	8.9	22.2	20.5	39.1	-16.3	23.2	35.2	—	—	—
Differ from category (+/-)	9.5	8.8	8.9	3.4	-10.6	-2.9	17.2	—	—	—

PER SHARE DATA

	1994	1993	1992	1991	1990	1989	1988	1987	1986	1985
Dividends, Net Income ($)	0.16	0.09	0.07	0.06	0.15	0.15	0.06	—	—	—
Distrib'ns, Cap Gain ($)	1.14	0.95	1.29	0.79	0.23	1.53	0.00	—	—	—
Net Asset Value ($)	17.13	16.92	14.70	13.34	10.21	12.62	11.60	—	—	—
Expense Ratio (%)	1.21	1.26	1.29	1.30	1.32	1.35	1.50	—	—	—
Net Income to Assets (%)	1.08	0.63	0.50	0.42	1.13	1.37	1.40	—	—	—
Portfolio Turnover (%)	na	19	29	45	52	58	93	—	—	—
Total Assets (Millions $)	753	402	244	178	130	140	51	—	—	—

PORTFOLIO (as of 6/30/94)

Portfolio Manager: O. Mason Hawkins - 1987, Staley Cates - 1994

Investm't Category: Growth

✔ Cap Gain	Asset Allocation
Cap & Income	Fund of Funds
Income	Index
	Sector
✔ Domestic	Small Cap
✔ Foreign	Socially Conscious
Country/Region	State Specific

Portfolio: stocks 91% bonds 0%
convertibles 0% other 0% cash 9%

Largest Holdings: food 17%, publishing 10%

Unrealized Net Capital Gains: 9% of portfolio value

SHAREHOLDER INFORMATION

Minimum Investment
Initial: $10,000   Subsequent: $0

Minimum IRA Investment
Initial: $10,000   Subsequent: $0

Maximum Fees
Load: none   12b-1: none
Other: none

Distributions
Income: Dec   Capital Gains: Dec

Exchange Options
Number Per Year: no limit   Fee: none
Telephone: none

Services
IRA, pension, auto invest, auto withdraw

Longleaf Partners Small Cap (LLSCX)

Growth

6075 Poplar Avenue
Suite 900
Memphis, TN 38119
(800) 445-9469, (901) 761-2474

PERFORMANCE

fund inception date: 2/21/89

	3yr Annual	5yr Annual	10yr Annual	Bull	Bear
Return (%)	9.9	3.2	na	54.9	-4.9
Differ from Category (+/-)	2.2 abv av	-6.4 low	na	-37.2 low	1.7 abv av

Total Risk	Standard Deviation	Category Risk	Risk Index	Beta
abv av	9.4%	av	1.0	0.7

	1994	1993	1992	1991	1990	1989	1988	1987	1986	1985
Return (%)	3.7	19.8	6.8	26.3	-30.0	32.8	—	—	—	—
Differ from category (+/-) . . .	4.3	6.4	-4.8	-9.4	-24.3	6.7	—	—	—	—

PER SHARE DATA

	1994	1993	1992	1991	1990	1989	1988	1987	1986	1985
Dividends, Net Income ($) .	0.00	0.00	0.00	0.06	0.36	0.14	—	—	—	—
Distrib'ns, Cap Gain ($) . . .	0.70	0.17	0.00	0.00	0.23	0.36	—	—	—	—
Net Asset Value ($)	13.28	13.49	11.40	10.67	8.50	12.87	—	—	—	—
Expense Ratio (%)	1.38	1.45	1.45	1.43	1.43	1.50	—	—	—	—
Net Income to Assets (%) .	-0.05	-0.45	-0.03	0.60	3.48	1.63	—	—	—	—
Portfolio Turnover (%)	na	14	26	65	15	20	—	—	—	—
Total Assets (Millions $) . . .	99	85	62	60	48	44	—	—	—	—

PORTFOLIO (as of 9/30/94)

Portfolio Manager: Staley Cates - 1991, O. Mason Hawkins - 1991

Investm't Category: Growth
- ✔ Cap Gain
- Cap & Income
- Income
- ✔ Domestic
- ✔ Foreign
- Country/Region
- Asset Allocation
- Fund of Funds
- Index
- Sector
- ✔ Small Cap
- Socially Conscious
- State Specific

Portfolio:
stocks 93% bonds 0%
convertibles 0% other 0% cash 7%

Largest Holdings: business services 14%, publishing 10%

Unrealized Net Capital Gains: 9% of portfolio value

SHAREHOLDER INFORMATION

Minimum Investment
Initial: $10,000 Subsequent: $0

Minimum IRA Investment
Initial: $10,000 Subsequent: $0

Maximum Fees
Load: none 12b-1: none
Other: none

Distributions
Income: Dec Capital Gains: Dec

Exchange Options
Number Per Year: no limit Fee: none
Telephone: none

Services
IRA, pension, auto invest, auto withdraw

Loomis Sayles Bond

(LSBDX)

Corporate Bond

One Financial Center
Boston, MA 02111
(800) 626-9390, (617) 482-2450

PERFORMANCE   fund inception date: 5/16/91

	3yr Annual	5yr Annual	10yr Annual	Bull	Bear
Return (%)	10.2	na	na	na	-7.9
Differ from Category (+/-)	4.3 high	na	na	na	-3.6 blw av

Total Risk	Standard Deviation	Category Risk	Risk Index	Avg Mat
blw av	5.8%	high	1.9	20.0 yrs

	1994	1993	1992	1991	1990	1989	1988	1987	1986	1985
Return (%)	-4.0	22.2	14.2	—	—	—	—	—	—	—
Differ from category (+/-) . .	-1.6	10.8	5.3	—	—	—	—	—	—	—

PER SHARE DATA

	1994	1993	1992	1991	1990	1989	1988	1987	1986	1985
Dividends, Net Income ($).	0.86	0.81	0.76	—	—	—	—	—	—	—
Distrib'ns, Cap Gain ($) . . .	0.00	0.46	0.54	—	—	—	—	—	—	—
Net Asset Value ($)	10.05	11.37	10.36	—	—	—	—	—	—	—
Expense Ratio (%)	0.88	0.94	1.00	—	—	—	—	—	—	—
Net Income to Assets (%) .	7.33	8.26	7.50	—	—	—	—	—	—	—
Portfolio Turnover (%)	78	170	101	—	—	—	—	—	—	—
Total Assets (Millions $)	82	63	18	—	—	—	—	—	—	—

PORTFOLIO (as of 6/30/94)

Portfolio Manager: Daniel Fuss - 1991

Investm't Category: Corporate Bond

Cap Gain	Asset Allocation
Cap & Income	Fund of Funds
✔ Income	Index
	Sector
✔ Domestic	Small Cap
✔ Foreign	Socially Conscious
Country/Region	State Specific

Portfolio: stocks 0%   bonds 60%
convertibles 32%   other 8%   cash 0%

Largest Holdings: air transport 8%, steel 6%

Unrealized Net Capital Gains: -6% of portfolio value

SHAREHOLDER INFORMATION

Minimum Investment
Initial: $2,500   Subsequent: $50

Minimum IRA Investment
Initial: $250   Subsequent: $50

Maximum Fees
Load: none   12b-1: none
Other: none

Distributions
Income: quarterly   Capital Gains: Dec

Exchange Options
Number Per Year: 4   Fee: none
Telephone: yes (money market fund available)

Services
IRA, pension, auto invest, auto withdraw

Loomis Sayles Global Bond (LSGBX)

International Bond

One Financial Center
Boston, MA 02111
(800) 626-9390, (617) 482-2450

PERFORMANCE

fund inception date: 5/10/91

	3yr Annual	5yr Annual	10yr Annual	Bull	Bear
Return (%)	1.7	na	na	na	-11.4
Differ from Category (+/-)	-2.2 low	na	na	na	-3.6 blw av

Total Risk	Standard Deviation	Category Risk	Risk Index	Avg Mat
av	7.6%	high	1.3	16.4 yrs

	1994	1993	1992	1991	1990	1989	1988	1987	1986	1985
Return (%)	-8.7	14.6	0.8	—	—	—	—	—	—	—
Differ from category (+/-) . .	-2.4	1.2	-3.9	—	—	—	—	—	—	—

PER SHARE DATA

	1994	1993	1992	1991	1990	1989	1988	1987	1986	1985
Dividends, Net Income ($)	0.28	0.49	0.77	—	—	—	—	—	—	—
Distrib'ns, Cap Gain ($) . . .	0.00	0.27	0.39	—	—	—	—	—	—	—
Net Asset Value ($)	9.82	11.06	10.32	—	—	—	—	—	—	—
Expense Ratio (%).	1.34	1.50	1.50	—	—	—	—	—	—	—
Net Income to Assets (%). .	5.93	5.54	6.99	—	—	—	—	—	—	—
Portfolio Turnover (%). . . .	183	150	72	—	—	—	—	—	—	—
Total Assets (Millions $)	25	21	9	—	—	—	—	—	—	—

PORTFOLIO (as of 6/30/94)

Portfolio Manager: John de Beer - 1991

Investm't Category: International Bond

Cap Gain	Asset Allocation
Cap & Income	Fund of Funds
✔ Income	Index
	Sector
✔ Domestic	Small Cap
✔ Foreign	Socially Conscious
Country/Region	State Specific

Portfolio: stocks 0% bonds 100%
convertibles 0% other 0% cash 0%

Largest Holdings: Germany 14%, Canada 11%

Unrealized Net Capital Gains: -5% of portfolio value

SHAREHOLDER INFORMATION

Minimum Investment
Initial: $2,500 Subsequent: $50

Minimum IRA Investment
Initial: $250 Subsequent: $50

Maximum Fees
Load: none 12b-1: none
Other: none

Distributions
Income: quarterly Capital Gains: Dec

Exchange Options
Number Per Year: 4 Fee: none
Telephone: yes (money market fund available)

Services
IRA, pension, auto invest, auto withdraw

Loomis Sayles Growth
(LSGRX)
Aggressive Growth

One Financial Center
Boston, MA 02111
(800) 626-9390, (617) 482-2450

PERFORMANCE
fund inception date: 5/16/91

	3yr Annual	5yr Annual	10yr Annual	Bull	Bear
Return (%)	2.9	na	na	na	-10.8
Differ from Category (+/-)	-6.0 low	na	na	na	0.0 av

Total Risk	Standard Deviation	Category Risk	Risk Index	Beta
abv av	11.6%	blw av	0.8	1.1

	1994	1993	1992	1991	1990	1989	1988	1987	1986	1985
Return (%)	-3.6	9.2	3.8	—	—	—	—	—	—	—
Differ from category (+/-)	-2.9	-10.3	-7.2	—	—	—	—	—	—	—

PER SHARE DATA

	1994	1993	1992	1991	1990	1989	1988	1987	1986	1985
Dividends, Net Income ($)	0.00	0.00	0.00	—	—	—	—	—	—	—
Distrib'ns, Cap Gain ($)	0.05	0.60	0.00	—	—	—	—	—	—	—
Net Asset Value ($)	12.50	13.02	12.47	—	—	—	—	—	—	—
Expense Ratio (%)	1.20	1.20	1.50	—	—	—	—	—	—	—
Net Income to Assets (%)	-0.18	-0.17	-0.45	—	—	—	—	—	—	—
Portfolio Turnover (%)	42	64	98	—	—	—	—	—	—	—
Total Assets (Millions $)	36	32	24	—	—	—	—	—	—	—

PORTFOLIO (as of 6/30/94)

Portfolio Manager: Jerome Castellini - 1991

Investm't Category: Aggressive Growth
- ✔ Cap Gain
- Cap & Income
- Income
- Asset Allocation
- Fund of Funds
- Index
- Sector
- ✔ Domestic
- ✔ Foreign
- Country/Region
- Small Cap
- Socially Conscious
- State Specific

Portfolio: stocks 96%   bonds 0%
convertibles 0%   other 0%   cash 4%

Largest Holdings: independent oil producers 11%, electronic components 7%

Unrealized Net Capital Gains: 5% of portfolio value

SHAREHOLDER INFORMATION

Minimum Investment
Initial: $2,500   Subsequent: $50

Minimum IRA Investment
Initial: $250   Subsequent: $50

Maximum Fees
Load: none   12b-1: none
Other: none

Distributions
Income: Dec   Capital Gains: Dec

Exchange Options
Number Per Year: 4   Fee: none
Telephone: yes (money market fund available)

Services
IRA, pension, auto invest, auto withdraw

Loomis Sayles Growth & Income (LSGIX)

Growth & Income

One Financial Center
Boston, MA 02111
(800) 626-9390, (617) 482-2450

	3yr Annual	5yr Annual	10yr Annual	Bull	Bear
Return (%)	8.1	na	na	na	-5.0
Differ from Category (+/-)	1.0 abv av	na	na	na	1.3 abv av

Total Risk	Standard Deviation	Category Risk	Risk Index	Beta
abv av	9.0%	abv av	1.1	1.0

	1994	1993	1992	1991	1990	1989	1988	1987	1986	1985
Return (%)	-0.8	11.8	14.0	—	—	—	—	—	—	—
Differ from category (+/-)	0.6	-1.4	3.8	—	—	—	—	—	—	—

PER SHARE DATA

	1994	1993	1992	1991	1990	1989	1988	1987	1986	1985
Dividends, Net Income ($)	0.15	0.12	0.13	—	—	—	—	—	—	—
Distrib'ns, Cap Gain ($)	0.43	0.29	0.37	—	—	—	—	—	—	—
Net Asset Value ($)	11.80	12.49	11.53	—	—	—	—	—	—	—
Expense Ratio (%)	1.40	1.50	1.50	—	—	—	—	—	—	—
Net Income to Assets (%)	1.06	1.23	1.42	—	—	—	—	—	—	—
Portfolio Turnover (%)	46	53	67	—	—	—	—	—	—	—
Total Assets (Millions $)	25	20	12	—	—	—	—	—	—	—

PORTFOLIO (as of 6/30/94)

Portfolio Manager: Jeffrey Wardlow - 1991

Investm't Category: Growth & Income

Cap Gain	Asset Allocation
✔ Cap & Income	Fund of Funds
Income	Index
	Sector
✔ Domestic	Small Cap
✔ Foreign	Socially Conscious
Country/Region	State Specific

Portfolio: stocks 93%   bonds 0%
convertibles 0%   other 0%   cash 7%

Largest Holdings: communications utilities 6%, healthcare services 6%

Unrealized Net Capital Gains: 4% of portfolio value

SHAREHOLDER INFORMATION

Minimum Investment
Initial: $2,500   Subsequent: $50

Minimum IRA Investment
Initial: $250   Subsequent: $50

Maximum Fees
Load: none   12b-1: none
Other: none

Distributions
Income: Dec   Capital Gains: Dec

Exchange Options
Number Per Year: 4   Fee: none
Telephone: Yes (money market fund available)

Services
IRA, pension, auto invest, auto withdraw

Loomis Sayles International Equity (LSIEX)

International Stock

One Financial Center
Boston, MA 02111
(800) 626-9390, (617) 482-2450

	3yr Annual	5yr Annual	10yr Annual	Bull	Bear
Return (%)	8.9	na	na	na	-7.7
Differ from Category (+/-)	-0.2 av	na	na	na	-0.7 blw av

Total Risk	Standard Deviation	Category Risk	Risk Index	Beta
high	12.1%	blw av	0.9	0.7

	1994	1993	1992	1991	1990	1989	1988	1987	1986	1985
Return (%)	-1.7	38.5	-5.0	—	—	—	—	—	—	—
Differ from category (+/-)	1.3	-0.1	-2.1	—	—	—	—	—	—	—

PER SHARE DATA

	1994	1993	1992	1991	1990	1989	1988	1987	1986	1985
Dividends, Net Income ($)	0.14	0.10	0.11	—	—	—	—	—	—	—
Distrib'ns, Cap Gain ($)	0.92	0.36	0.00	—	—	—	—	—	—	—
Net Asset Value ($)	11.61	12.90	9.64	—	—	—	—	—	—	—
Expense Ratio (%)	1.50	1.50	1.50	—	—	—	—	—	—	—
Net Income to Assets (%)	2.21	1.20	1.64	—	—	—	—	—	—	—
Portfolio Turnover (%)	113	128	101	—	—	—	—	—	—	—
Total Assets (Millions $)	71	59	14	—	—	—	—	—	—	—

PORTFOLIO (as of 6/30/94)

Portfolio Manager: Frank Jedlicka - 1991

Investm't Category: International Stock

✔ Cap Gain	Asset Allocation
Cap & Income	Fund of Funds
Income	Index
	Sector
Domestic	Small Cap
✔ Foreign	Socially Conscious
Country/Region	State Specific

Portfolio: stocks 99%   bonds 0%
convertibles 0%   other 0%   cash 1%

Largest Holdings: Australia 9%, Switzerland 9%

Unrealized Net Capital Gains: 3% of portfolio value

SHAREHOLDER INFORMATION

Minimum Investment
Initial: $2,500   Subsequent: $50

Minimum IRA Investment
Initial: $250   Subsequent: $50

Maximum Fees
Load: none   12b-1: none
Other: none

Distributions
Income: Dec   Capital Gains: Dec

Exchange Options
Number Per Year: 4   Fee: none
Telephone: yes (money market fund available)

Services
IRA, pension, auto invest, auto withdraw

Loomis Sayles Small Cap

(LSSCX)

Aggressive Growth

One Financial Center
Boston, MA 02111
(800) 626-9390, (617) 482-2450

PERFORMANCE

fund inception date: 5/13/91

	3yr Annual	5yr Annual	10yr Annual	Bull	Bear
Return (%)	8.9	na	na	na	-11.7
Differ from Category (+/-)	0.0 av	na	na	na	-0.9 av

Total Risk	Standard Deviation	Category Risk	Risk Index	Beta
high	14.3%	av	1.0	0.9

	1994	1993	1992	1991	1990	1989	1988	1987	1986	1985
Return (%)	-8.3	24.6	13.1	—	—	—	—	—	—	—
Differ from category (+/-) . .	-7.6	5.1	2.1	—	—	—	—	—	—	—

PER SHARE DATA

	1994	1993	1992	1991	1990	1989	1988	1987	1986	1985
Dividends, Net Income ($) .	0.00	0.00	0.00	—	—	—	—	—	—	—
Distrib'ns, Cap Gain ($) . . .	0.11	1.90	1.22	—	—	—	—	—	—	—
Net Asset Value ($)	12.85	14.13	12.88	—	—	—	—	—	—	—
Expense Ratio (%)	1.29	1.35	1.50	—	—	—	—	—	—	—
Net Income to Assets (%) .	-0.31	-0.38	-0.79	—	—	—	—	—	—	—
Portfolio Turnover (%)	59	106	109	—	—	—	—	—	—	—
Total Assets (Millions $)	74	69	39	—	—	—	—	—	—	—

PORTFOLIO (as of 6/30/94)

Portfolio Manager: Barbara Friedman - 1991, Jeffrey Petherick - 1993

Investm't Category: Aggressive Growth

✔ Cap Gain	Asset Allocation
Cap & Income	Fund of Funds
Income	Index
	Sector
✔ Domestic	✔ Small Cap
Foreign	Socially Conscious
Country/Region	State Specific

Portfolio: stocks 90%   bonds 0%
convertibles 0%   other 0%   cash 10%

Largest Holdings: metals 8%, healthcare services 7%

Unrealized Net Capital Gains: -4% of portfolio value

SHAREHOLDER INFORMATION

Minimum Investment
Initial: $2,500   Subsequent: $50

Minimum IRA Investment
Initial: $250   Subsequent: $50

Maximum Fees
Load: none   12b-1: none
Other: none

Distributions
Income: Dec   Capital Gains: Dec

Exchange Options
Number Per Year: 4   Fee: none
Telephone: yes (money market fund available)

Services
IRA, pension, auto invest, auto withdraw

L. Roy Papp Stock
(LRPSX)
Growth

4400 North 32nd Street
Suite 280
Phoenix, AZ 85018
(800) 421-4004, (602) 956-1115

PERFORMANCE

fund inception date: 11/29/89

	3yr Annual	5yr Annual	10yr Annual	Bull	Bear
Return (%)	4.3	9.3	na	78.4	-7.0
Differ from Category (+/-)	-3.4 blw av	-0.3 av	na	-13.7 blw av	-0.4 av

Total Risk	Standard Deviation		Category Risk	Risk Index	Beta
av	8.3%		blw av	0.8	0.8

	1994	1993	1992	1991	1990	1989	1988	1987	1986	1985
Return (%).	-1.4	1.6	13.5	33.8	2.5	—	—	—	—	—
Differ from category (+/-) . .	-0.8	-11.8	1.9	-1.9	8.2	—	—	—	—	—

PER SHARE DATA

	1994	1993	1992	1991	1990	1989	1988	1987	1986	1985
Dividends, Net Income ($).	0.13	0.13	0.13	0.14	0.12	—	—	—	—	—
Distrib'ns, Cap Gain ($) . . .	0.00	0.09	0.17	0.35	0.11	—	—	—	—	—
Net Asset Value ($)	14.63	14.98	14.96	13.45	10.42	—	—	—	—	—
Expense Ratio (%)	1.25	1.25	1.25	1.25	1.25	—	—	—	—	—
Net Income to Assets (%) .	2.17	2.22	2.28	2.46	2.82	—	—	—	—	—
Portfolio Turnover (%)	9	15	11	4	28	—	—	—	—	—
Total Assets (Millions $)	36	38	22	13	6	—	—	—	—	—

PORTFOLIO (as of 6/30/94)

Portfolio Manager: L. Roy Papp - 1989, Rosellen Papp - 1989

Investm't Category: Growth

✔ Cap Gain	Asset Allocation
Cap & Income	Fund of Funds
Income	Index
	Sector
✔ Domestic	Small Cap
Foreign	Socially Conscious
Country/Region	State Specific

Portfolio: stocks 98% bonds 0%
convertibles 0% other 0% cash 2%

Largest Holdings: financial services 15%, electronics 13%

Unrealized Net Capital Gains: 8% of portfolio value

SHAREHOLDER INFORMATION

Minimum Investment
Initial: $10,000   Subsequent: $2,000

Minimum IRA Investment
Initial: $2,000   Subsequent: $2,000

Maximum Fees
Load: none   12b-1: none
Other: none

Distributions
Income: Jun, Dec   Capital Gains: Dec

Exchange Options
Number Per Year: none   Fee:
Telephone:

Services
IRA

Managers Bond (MGFIX)

General Bond

40 Richards Avenue
Norwalk, CT 06854
(800) 835-3879

PERFORMANCE

fund inception date: 6/1/84

	3yr Annual	5yr Annual	10yr Annual	Bull	Bear
Return (%)	3.7	na	na	na	-9.6
Differ from Category (+/-)	-0.6 blw av	na	na	na	-5.8 low

Total Risk	Standard Deviation	Category Risk	Risk Index	Avg Mat
blw av	5.5%	high	1.4	na

	1994	1993	1992	1991	1990	1989	1988	1987	1986	1985
Return (%)	-7.2	11.5	7.8	19.0	—	—	—	—	—	—
Differ from category (+/-) . .	-5.2	2.3	1.2	4.4	—	—	—	—	—	—

PER SHARE DATA

	1994	1993	1992	1991	1990	1989	1988	1987	1986	1985
Dividends, Net Income ($) .	1.69	1.50	1.48	1.72	—	—	—	—	—	—
Distrib'ns, Cap Gain ($) . . .	0.00	0.67	0.95	0.45	—	—	—	—	—	—
Net Asset Value ($)	18.92	22.18	21.88	22.60	—	—	—	—	—	—
Expense Ratio (%).	1.29	1.15	0.93	1.02	—	—	—	—	—	—
Net Income to Assets (%). .	7.36	6.65	6.61	7.82	—	—	—	—	—	—
Portfolio Turnover (%)	121	373	292	181	—	—	—	—	—	—
Total Assets (Millions $)	30	44	39	36	—	—	—	—	—	—

PORTFOLIO (as of 6/30/94)

Portfolio Manager: not specified

Investm't Category: General Bond

Cap Gain	Asset Allocation
Cap & Income	Fund of Funds
✔ Income	Index
	Sector
✔ Domestic	Small Cap
✔ Foreign	Socially Conscious
Country/Region	State Specific

Portfolio: stocks 0%   bonds 75%
convertibles 21%   other 4%   cash 0%

Largest Holdings: corporate 71%, foreign
government 11%

Unrealized Net Capital Gains: -9% of portfolio value

SHAREHOLDER INFORMATION

Minimum Investment
Initial: $10,000   Subsequent: $0

Minimum IRA Investment
Initial: $10,000   Subsequent: $0

Maximum Fees
Load: none   12b-1: none
Other: none

Distributions
Income: monthly   Capital Gains: Dec

Exchange Options
Number Per Year: no limit   Fee: none
Telephone: yes (money market fund available)

Services
IRA, auto exchange, auto invest, auto withdraw

Managers Capital Appreciation (MGCAX)

Aggressive Growth

40 Richards Avenue
Norwalk, CT 06854
(800) 835-3879

	3yr Annual	5yr Annual	10yr Annual	Bull	Bear
Return (%)	8.2	na	na	na	-8.7
Differ from Category (+/-)	-0.7 av	na	na	na	2.1 abv av

Total Risk	Standard Deviation	Category Risk	Risk Index	Beta
abv av	9.8%	low	0.7	1.0

	1994	1993	1992	1991	1990	1989	1988	1987	1986	1985
Return (%)	-1.5	16.5	10.4	31.9	—	—	—	—	—	—
Differ from category (+/-)	-0.8	-3.0	-0.6	-20.2	—	—	—	—	—	—

PER SHARE DATA

	1994	1993	1992	1991	1990	1989	1988	1987	1986	1985
Dividends, Net Income ($)	0.12	0.17	0.07	0.27	—	—	—	—	—	—
Distrib'ns, Cap Gain ($)	1.43	3.30	1.19	2.61	—	—	—	—	—	—
Net Asset Value ($)	23.25	25.17	24.67	23.47	—	—	—	—	—	—
Expense Ratio (%)	1.27	1.18	1.05	1.31	—	—	—	—	—	—
Net Income to Assets (%)	0.34	0.74	0.33	1.07	—	—	—	—	—	—
Portfolio Turnover (%)	124	130	175	259	—	—	—	—	—	—
Total Assets (Millions $)	84	71	56	53	—	—	—	—	—	—

PORTFOLIO (as of 6/30/94)

Portfolio Manager: not specified

Investm't Category: Aggressive Growth

✔ Cap Gain	Asset Allocation
Cap & Income	Fund of Funds
Income	Index
	Sector
✔ Domestic	Small Cap
Foreign	Socially Conscious
Country/Region	State Specific

Portfolio: stocks 73%   bonds 0%
convertibles 0%   other 0%   cash 27%

Largest Holdings: finance and insurance 12%, technology 11%

Unrealized Net Capital Gains: 1% of portfolio value

SHAREHOLDER INFORMATION

Minimum Investment
Initial: $10,000   Subsequent: $0

Minimum IRA Investment
Initial: $10,000   Subsequent: $0

Maximum Fees
Load: none   12b-1: none
Other: none

Distributions
Income: quarterly   Capital Gains: Dec

Exchange Options
Number Per Year: no limit   Fee: none
Telephone: yes (money market fund available)

Services
IRA, auto exchange, auto invest, auto withdraw

Managers Income Equity
(MGIEX)
Growth & Income

40 Richards Avenue
Norwalk, CT 06854
(800) 835-3879

	3yr Annual	5yr Annual	10yr Annual	Bull	Bear
Return (%)	7.6	na	na	na	-4.6
Differ from Category (+/-)	0.5 av	na	na	na	1.7 abv av

Total Risk	Standard Deviation	Category Risk	Risk Index	Beta
av	7.7%	blw av	0.9	0.9

	1994	1993	1992	1991	1990	1989	1988	1987	1986	1985
Return (%)	0.9	12.4	9.7	29.3	—	—	—	—	—	—
Differ from category (+/-) . . .	2.3	-0.8	-0.5	1.7	—	—	—	—	—	—

PER SHARE DATA

	1994	1993	1992	1991	1990	1989	1988	1987	1986	1985
Dividends, Net Income ($) .	0.83	0.76	1.03	1.20	—	—	—	—	—	—
Distrib'ns, Cap Gain ($) . . .	2.46	2.08	2.97	1.17	—	—	—	—	—	—
Net Asset Value ($)	24.90	27.89	27.38	28.63	—	—	—	—	—	—
Expense Ratio (%).	1.31	1.32	1.20	1.16	—	—	—	—	—	—
Net Income to Assets (%). .	2.94	2.75	3.52	4.00	—	—	—	—	—	—
Portfolio Turnover (%).	43	41	41	63	—	—	—	—	—	—
Total Assets (Millions $)	47	41	49	70	—	—	—	—	—	—

PORTFOLIO (as of 6/30/94)

Portfolio Manager: not specified

Investm't Category: Growth & Income
- Cap Gain
- ✔ Cap & Income
- Income
- ✔ Domestic
- Foreign
- Country/Region
- Asset Allocation
- Fund of Funds
- Index
- Sector
- Small Cap
- Socially Conscious
- State Specific

Portfolio: stocks 90%   bonds 0%
convertibles 3%   other 0%   cash 7%

Largest Holdings: consumer basics 21%, utilities 16%

Unrealized Net Capital Gains: 5% of portfolio value

SHAREHOLDER INFORMATION

Minimum Investment
Initial: $10,000   Subsequent: $0

Minimum IRA Investment
Initial: $10,000   Subsequent: $0

Maximum Fees
Load: none   12b-1: none
Other: none

Distributions
Income: monthly   Capital Gains: Dec

Exchange Options
Number Per Year: no limit   Fee: none
Telephone: yes (money market fund available)

Services
IRA, auto exchange, auto invest, auto withdraw

Managers Interm Mortgage (MGIGX)

Mortgage-Backed Bond

40 Richards Avenue
Norwalk, CT 06854
(800) 835-3879

fund inception date: 5/1/86

	3yr Annual	5yr Annual	10yr Annual	Bull	Bear
Return (%)	-2.6	na	na	na	-23.3
Differ from Category (+/-)	-5.7 low	na	na	na	-18.9 low

Total Risk	Standard Deviation	Category Risk	Risk Index	Avg Mat
abv av	9.5%	high	2.9	na

	1994	1993	1992	1991	1990	1989	1988	1987	1986	1985
Return (%).	-25.0	11.4	10.5	18.1	—	—	—	—	—	—
Differ from category (+/-) .	-22.2	4.6	4.4	3.7	—	—	—	—	—	—

PER SHARE DATA

	1994	1993	1992	1991	1990	1989	1988	1987	1986	1985
Dividends, Net Income ($).	1.41	2.28	2.40	2.05	—	—	—	—	—	—
Distrib'ns, Cap Gain ($) . . .	0.00	0.58	0.42	0.00	—	—	—	—	—	—
Net Asset Value ($)	14.20	20.64	21.13	21.77	—	—	—	—	—	—
Expense Ratio (%)	0.97	0.75	0.79	0.69	—	—	—	—	—	—
Net Income to Assets (%)	10.30	8.90	11.30	9.91	—	—	—	—	—	—
Portfolio Turnover (%)	241	253	278	171	—	—	—	—	—	—
Total Assets (Millions $)	56	275	115	165	—	—	—	—	—	—

PORTFOLIO (as of 6/30/94)

Portfolio Manager: not specified

Investm't Category: Mortgage-Backed Bond

Cap Gain	Asset Allocation
Cap & Income	Fund of Funds
✔ Income	Index
	Sector
✔ Domestic	Small Cap
Foreign	Socially Conscious
Country/Region	State Specific

Portfolio: stocks 0%   bonds 94%
convertibles 0%   other 0%   cash 6%

Largest Holdings: mortgage-backed 88%

Unrealized Net Capital Gains: -26% of portfolio value

SHAREHOLDER INFORMATION

Minimum Investment
Initial: $10,000   Subsequent: $0

Minimum IRA Investment
Initial: $10,000   Subsequent: $0

Maximum Fees
Load: none   12b-1: none
Other: none

Distributions
Income: monthly   Capital Gains: Dec

Exchange Options
Number Per Year: no limit   Fee: none
Telephone: yes (money market fund available)

Services
IRA, auto exchange, auto invest, auto withdraw

Managers International Equity (MGITX)

International Stock

40 Richards Avenue
Norwalk, CT 06854
(800) 835-3879

PERFORMANCE

fund inception date: 12/1/85

	3yr Annual	5yr Annual	10yr Annual	Bull	Bear
Return (%)	13.7	na	na	na	-4.5
Differ from Category (+/-)	4.6 high	na	na	na	2.5 abv av

Total Risk	Standard Deviation	Category Risk	Risk Index	Beta
abv av	9.9%	low	0.7	0.6

	1994	1993	1992	1991	1990	1989	1988	1987	1986	1985
Return (%)	2.0	38.2	4.2	18.1	—	—	—	—	—	—
Differ from category (+/-)	5.0	-0.4	7.1	5.0	—	—	—	—	—	—

PER SHARE DATA

	1994	1993	1992	1991	1990	1989	1988	1987	1986	1985
Dividends, Net Income ($)	0.08	0.40	0.22	0.36	—	—	—	—	—	—
Distrib'ns, Cap Gain ($)	0.21	0.30	0.00	0.07	—	—	—	—	—	—
Net Asset Value ($)	36.35	35.92	26.52	25.65	—	—	—	—	—	—
Expense Ratio (%)	1.45	1.47	1.45	1.69	—	—	—	—	—	—
Net Income to Assets (%)	1.13	0.78	0.97	1.50	—	—	—	—	—	—
Portfolio Turnover (%)	26	46	51	157	—	—	—	—	—	—
Total Assets (Millions $)	86	67	23	14	—	—	—	—	—	—

PORTFOLIO (as of 6/30/94)

Portfolio Manager: Willie Holzer - 1986

Investm't Category: International Stock

✔ Cap Gain	Asset Allocation
Cap & Income	Fund of Funds
Income	Index
	Sector
✔ Domestic	Small Cap
✔ Foreign	Socially Conscious
Country/Region	State Specific

Portfolio: stocks 87% bonds 0%
convertibles 1% other 0% cash 12%

Largest Holdings: Japan 14%, United States 12%

Unrealized Net Capital Gains: 14% of portfolio value

SHAREHOLDER INFORMATION

Minimum Investment
Initial: $10,000   Subsequent: $0

Minimum IRA Investment
Initial: $10,000   Subsequent: $0

Maximum Fees
Load: none   12b-1: none
Other: none

Distributions
Income: Dec   Capital Gains: Dec

Exchange Options
Number Per Year: no limit   Fee: none
Telephone: yes (money market fund available)

Services
IRA, auto exchange, auto invest, auto withdraw

Managers Short & Interm Bond (MGSIX)

General Bond

40 Richards Avenue
Norwalk, CT 06854
(800) 835-3879

PERFORMANCE

fund inception date: 6/1/84

	3yr Annual	5yr Annual	10yr Annual	Bull	Bear
Return (%)	3.4	na	na	na	-6.9
Differ from Category (+/-)	-0.9 low	na	na	na	-3.1 low

Total Risk	Standard Deviation	Category Risk	Risk Index	Avg Mat
low	3.6%	av	0.9	na

	1994	1993	1992	1991	1990	1989	1988	1987	1986	1985
Return (%).	-8.3	8.4	11.5	12.7	—	—	—	—	—	—
Differ from category (+/-) . .	-6.3	-0.8	4.9	-1.9	—	—	—	—	—	—

PER SHARE DATA

	1994	1993	1992	1991	1990	1989	1988	1987	1986	1985
Dividends, Net Income ($).	1.45	1.38	1.70	1.48	—	—	—	—	—	—
Distrib'ns, Cap Gain ($) . . .	0.00	0.00	0.00	0.00	—	—	—	—	—	—
Net Asset Value ($)	18.06	21.23	20.89	20.33	—	—	—	—	—	—
Expense Ratio (%)	1.14	0.94	0.86	0.96	—	—	—	—	—	—
Net Income to Assets (%) .	7.27	6.58	8.33	7.41	—	—	—	—	—	—
Portfolio Turnover (%)	71	126	117	536	—	—	—	—	—	—
Total Assets (Millions $)	30	112	72	52	—	—	—	—	—	—

PORTFOLIO (as of 6/30/94)

Portfolio Manager: not specified

Investm't Category: General Bond

Cap Gain	Asset Allocation
Cap & Income	Fund of Funds
✔ Income	Index
	Sector
✔ Domestic	Small Cap
✔ Foreign	Socially Conscious
Country/Region	State Specific

Portfolio: stocks 0% bonds 95%
convertibles 0% other 0% cash 5%

Largest Holdings: mortgage-backed 63%, corporate 26%

Unrealized Net Capital Gains: -8% of portfolio value

SHAREHOLDER INFORMATION

Minimum Investment
Initial: $10,000 Subsequent: $0

Minimum IRA Investment
Initial: $10,000 Subsequent: $0

Maximum Fees
Load: none 12b-1: none
Other: none

Distributions
Income: monthly Capital Gains: Dec

Exchange Options
Number Per Year: no limit Fee: none
Telephone: yes (money market fund available)

Services
IRA, auto exchange, auto invest, auto withdraw

Managers Short Gov't
(MGSGX)
Mortgage-Backed Bond

40 Richards Avenue
Norwalk, CT 06854
(800) 835-3879

PERFORMANCE

fund inception date: 10/1/87

	3yr Annual	5yr Annual	10yr Annual	Bull	Bear
Return (%)	0.4	na	na	na	-8.1
Differ from Category (+/-)	-2.7 low	na	na	na	-3.7 low

Total Risk	Standard Deviation	Category Risk	Risk Index	Avg Mat
low	3.5%	av	1.0	na

	1994	1993	1992	1991	1990	1989	1988	1987	1986	1985
Return (%)	-6.0	3.7	3.9	10.8	—	—	—	—	—	—
Differ from category (+/-) . .	-3.2	-3.1	-2.2	-3.6	—	—	—	—	—	—

PER SHARE DATA

	1994	1993	1992	1991	1990	1989	1988	1987	1986	1985
Dividends, Net Income ($) .	1.24	1.25	1.26	1.58	—	—	—	—	—	—
Distrib'ns, Cap Gain ($) . . .	0.00	0.00	0.00	0.00	—	—	—	—	—	—
Net Asset Value ($)	16.96	19.35	19.86	20.35	—	—	—	—	—	—
Expense Ratio (%)	0.94	0.87	0.76	0.58	—	—	—	—	—	—
Net Income to Assets (%) . .	7.05	8.71	6.24	6.08	—	—	—	—	—	—
Portfolio Turnover (%)	155	188	168	84	—	—	—	—	—	—
Total Assets (Millions $)	13	87	142	144	—	—	—	—	—	—

PORTFOLIO (as of 6/30/94)

Portfolio Manager: not specified

Investm't Category: Mortgage-Backed Bond
Cap Gain	Asset Allocation
Cap & Income	Fund of Funds
✔ Income	Index
	Sector
✔ Domestic	Small Cap
Foreign	Socially Conscious
Country/Region	State Specific

Portfolio: stocks 0% bonds 97%
convertibles 0% other 0% cash 3%

Largest Holdings: mortgage-backed 63%,
U.S. government 34%

Unrealized Net Capital Gains: -11% of portfolio value

SHAREHOLDER INFORMATION

Minimum Investment
Initial: $10,000   Subsequent: $0

Minimum IRA Investment
Initial: $10,000   Subsequent: $0

Maximum Fees
Load: none   12b-1: none
Other: none

Distributions
Income: monthly   Capital Gains: Dec

Exchange Options
Number Per Year: no limit   Fee: none
Telephone: yes (money market fund available)

Services
IRA, auto exchange, auto invest, auto withdraw

Managers Special Equity
(MGSEX)
Aggressive Growth

40 Richards Avenue
Norwalk, CT 06854
(800) 835-3879

PERFORMANCE

fund inception date: 6/1/84

	3yr Annual	5yr Annual	10yr Annual	Bull	Bear
Return (%)	9.9	na	na	na	-8.5
Differ from Category (+/-)	1.0 abv av	na	na	na	2.3 abv av

Total Risk	Standard Deviation	Category Risk	Risk Index	Beta
abv av	10.4%	low	0.7	0.9

	1994	1993	1992	1991	1990	1989	1988	1987	1986	1985
Return (%).	-1.9	17.3	15.6	49.2	—	—	—	—	—	—
Differ from category (+/-) . .	-1.2	-2.2	4.6	-2.9	—	—	—	—	—	—

PER SHARE DATA

	1994	1993	1992	1991	1990	1989	1988	1987	1986	1985
Dividends, Net Income ($).	0.00	0.01	0.05	0.23	—	—	—	—	—	—
Distrib'ns, Cap Gain ($) . . .	1.34	3.37	3.70	1.74	—	—	—	—	—	—
Net Asset Value ($)	36.79	38.90	36.14	34.50	—	—	—	—	—	—
Expense Ratio (%)	1.62	1.26	1.29	1.30	—	—	—	—	—	—
Net Income to Assets (%) .	-0.18	0.07	0.14	0.73	—	—	—	—	—	—
Portfolio Turnover (%)	38	45	54	69	—	—	—	—	—	—
Total Assets (Millions $) . . .	110	100	53	40	—	—	—	—	—	—

PORTFOLIO (as of 6/30/94)

Portfolio Manager: not specified

Investm't Category: Aggressive Growth

✔ Cap Gain	Asset Allocation
Cap & Income	Fund of Funds
Income	Index
	Sector
✔ Domestic	✔ Small Cap
Foreign	Socially Conscious
Country/Region	State Specific

Portfolio: stocks 94% bonds 0%
convertibles 0% other 0% cash 6%

Largest Holdings: finance & insurance 21%, general business 17%

Unrealized Net Capital Gains: 9% of portfolio value

SHAREHOLDER INFORMATION

Minimum Investment
Initial: $10,000   Subsequent: $0

Minimum IRA Investment
Initial: $10,000   Subsequent: $0

Maximum Fees
Load: none   12b-1: none
Other: none

Distributions
Income: Dec   Capital Gains: Dec

Exchange Options
Number Per Year: no limit   Fee: none
Telephone: yes (money market fund available)

Services
IRA, auto exchange, auto invest, auto withdraw

Marshall Equity Income

(MREIX)

Growth & Income

1000 North Water Street
P.O. Box 1348
Milwaukee, WI 53201
(800) 236-8554, (414) 287-8500

PERFORMANCE

fund inception date: 9/30/93

	3yr Annual	5yr Annual	10yr Annual	Bull	Bear
Return (%)	na	na	na	na	-5.9
Differ from Category (+/-)	na	na	na	na	0.4 av

Total Risk	Standard Deviation	Category Risk	Risk Index	Beta
na	na	na	na	na

	1994	1993	1992	1991	1990	1989	1988	1987	1986	1985
Return (%)	-1.6	—	—	—	—	—	—	—	—	—
Differ from category (+/-) . .	-0.2	—	—	—	—	—	—	—	—	—

PER SHARE DATA

	1994	1993	1992	1991	1990	1989	1988	1987	1986	1985
Dividends, Net Income ($) .	0.31	—	—	—	—	—	—	—	—	—
Distrib'ns, Cap Gain ($) . . .	0.00	—	—	—	—	—	—	—	—	—
Net Asset Value ($)	9.53	—	—	—	—	—	—	—	—	—
Expense Ratio (%)	1.01	—	—	—	—	—	—	—	—	—
Net Income to Assets (%) . .	3.30	—	—	—	—	—	—	—	—	—
Portfolio Turnover (%)	na	—	—	—	—	—	—	—	—	—
Total Assets (Millions $)	60	—	—	—	—	—	—	—	—	—

PORTFOLIO (as of 8/31/94)

Portfolio Manager: Bruce Hutson - 1993

Investm't Category: Growth & Income

Cap Gain	Asset Allocation
✔ Cap & Income	Fund of Funds
Income	Index
	Sector
✔ Domestic	Small Cap
Foreign	Socially Conscious
Country/Region	State Specific

Portfolio: stocks 82%   bonds 0%
convertibles 2%   other 0%   cash 16%

Largest Holdings: consumer non-durables 23%, financial 15%

Unrealized Net Capital Gains: 0% of portfolio value

SHAREHOLDER INFORMATION

Minimum Investment
Initial: $1,000   Subsequent: $50

Minimum IRA Investment
Initial: $1,000   Subsequent: $50

Maximum Fees
Load: none   12b-1: none
Other: none

Distributions
Income: quarterly   Capital Gains: Dec

Exchange Options
Number Per Year: no limit   Fee: none
Telephone: yes (money market fund available)

Services
IRA, pension, auto invest, auto withdraw

Marshall Government Income (MRGIX)

Mortgage-Backed Bond

1000 North Water Street
P.O. Box 1348
Milwaukee, WI 53201
(800) 236-8554, (414) 287-8500

PERFORMANCE

fund inception date: 12/10/92

	3yr Annual	5yr Annual	10yr Annual	Bull	Bear
Return (%)	na	na	na	na	-4.0
Differ from Category (+/-)	na	na	na	na	0.4 av

Total Risk	Standard Deviation	Category Risk	Risk Index	Avg Mat
na	na	na	na	7.4 yrs

	1994	1993	1992	1991	1990	1989	1988	1987	1986	1985
Return (%).	-2.7	5.9	—	—	—	—	—	—	—	—
Differ from category (+/-) . .	0.1	-0.9	—	—	—	—	—	—	—	—

PER SHARE DATA

	1994	1993	1992	1991	1990	1989	1988	1987	1986	1985
Dividends, Net Income ($).	0.60	0.68	—	—	—	—	—	—	—	—
Distrib'ns, Cap Gain ($) . . .	0.00	0.15	—	—	—	—	—	—	—	—
Net Asset Value ($)	8.93	9.80	—	—	—	—	—	—	—	—
Expense Ratio (%)	0.86	0.85	—	—	—	—	—	—	—	—
Net Income to Assets (%) .	6.58	6.56	—	—	—	—	—	—	—	—
Portfolio Turnover (%)	175	na	—	—	—	—	—	—	—	—
Total Assets (Millions $)	78	50	—	—	—	—	—	—	—	—

PORTFOLIO (as of 8/31/94)

Portfolio Manager: Larry Pavelec - 1992

Investm't Category: Mortgage-Backed Bond

Cap Gain	Asset Allocation
Cap & Income	Fund of Funds
✔ Income	Index
	Sector
✔ Domestic	Small Cap
Foreign	Socially Conscious
Country/Region	State Specific

Portfolio: stocks 0% bonds 95%
convertibles 0% other 0% cash 5%

Largest Holdings: mortgage-backed 85%,
U.S. government 10%

Unrealized Net Capital Gains: -2% of portfolio value

SHAREHOLDER INFORMATION

Minimum Investment
Initial: $1,000   Subsequent: $50

Minimum IRA Investment
Initial: $1,000   Subsequent: $50

Maximum Fees
Load: none   12b-1: none
Other: none

Distributions
Income: monthly   Capital Gains: Dec

Exchange Options
Number Per Year: no limit   Fee: none
Telephone: yes (money market fund available)

Services
IRA, pension, auto invest, auto withdraw

Marshall Intermediate Bond (MAIBX)

General Bond

1000 North Water Street
P.O. Box 1348
Milwaukee, WI 53201
(800) 236-8554, (414) 287-8500

fund inception date: 11/1/92

PERFORMANCE

	3yr Annual	5yr Annual	10yr Annual	Bull	Bear
Return (%)	na	na	na	na	-4.2
Differ from Category (+/-)	na	na	na	na	-0.4 av

Total Risk	Standard Deviation	Category Risk	Risk Index	Avg Mat
na	na	na	na	3.6 yrs

	1994	1993	1992	1991	1990	1989	1988	1987	1986	1985
Return (%)	-3.0	6.8	—	—	—	—	—	—	—	—
Differ from category (+/-) . .	-1.0	-2.4	—	—	—	—	—	—	—	—

PER SHARE DATA

	1994	1993	1992	1991	1990	1989	1988	1987	1986	1985
Dividends, Net Income ($) .	0.59	0.62	—	—	—	—	—	—	—	—
Distrib'ns, Cap Gain ($) . . .	0.00	0.17	—	—	—	—	—	—	—	—
Net Asset Value ($)	9.04	9.93	—	—	—	—	—	—	—	—
Expense Ratio (%).	0.71	0.70	—	—	—	—	—	—	—	—
Net Income to Assets (%). .	6.26	6.08	—	—	—	—	—	—	—	—
Portfolio Turnover (%)	228	na	—	—	—	—	—	—	—	—
Total Assets (Millions $) . . .	326	312	—	—	—	—	—	—	—	—

PORTFOLIO (as of 8/31/94)

Portfolio Manager: Larry Pavelec - 1992

Investm't Category: General Bond

Cap Gain	Asset Allocation
Cap & Income	Fund of Funds
✔ Income	Index
	Sector
✔ Domestic	Small Cap
Foreign	Socially Conscious
Country/Region	State Specific

Portfolio: stocks 0% bonds 93%
convertibles 0% other 0% cash 7%

Largest Holdings: U.S. government 67%, corporate 16%

Unrealized Net Capital Gains: -2% of portfolio value

SHAREHOLDER INFORMATION

Minimum Investment
Initial: $1,000 Subsequent: $50

Minimum IRA Investment
Initial: $1,000 Subsequent: $50

Maximum Fees
Load: none 12b-1: none
Other: none

Distributions
Income: monthly Capital Gains: Dec

Exchange Options
Number Per Year: no limit Fee: none
Telephone: yes (money market fund available)

Services
IRA, pension, auto invest, auto withdraw

Marshall Mid-Cap Stock
(MRMSX)
Aggressive Growth

1000 North Water Street
P.O. Box 1348
Milwaukee, WI 53201
(800) 236-8554, (414) 287-8500

PERFORMANCE
fund inception date: 9/30/93

	3yr Annual	5yr Annual	10yr Annual	Bull	Bear
Return (%)	na	na	na	na	-13.5
Differ from Category (+/-)	na	na	na	na	-2.7 blw av

Total Risk	Standard Deviation	Category Risk	Risk Index	Beta
na	na	na	na	na

	1994	1993	1992	1991	1990	1989	1988	1987	1986	1985
Return (%)	-5.6	—	—	—	—	—	—	—	—	—
Differ from category (+/-)	-4.9	—	—	—	—	—	—	—	—	—

PER SHARE DATA

	1994	1993	1992	1991	1990	1989	1988	1987	1986	1985
Dividends, Net Income ($)	0.01	—	—	—	—	—	—	—	—	—
Distrib'ns, Cap Gain ($)	0.00	—	—	—	—	—	—	—	—	—
Net Asset Value ($)	9.55	—	—	—	—	—	—	—	—	—
Expense Ratio (%)	1.01	—	—	—	—	—	—	—	—	—
Net Income to Assets (%)	0.23	—	—	—	—	—	—	—	—	—
Portfolio Turnover (%)	na	—	—	—	—	—	—	—	—	—
Total Assets (Millions $)	62	—	—	—	—	—	—	—	—	—

PORTFOLIO (as of 8/31/94)

Portfolio Manager: Steve Hayward - 1993

Investm't Category: Aggressive Growth
- ✔ Cap Gain
- Cap & Income
- Income
- ✔ Domestic
- Foreign
- Country/Region

- Asset Allocation
- Fund of Funds
- Index
- Sector
- Small Cap
- Socially Conscious
- State Specific

Portfolio: stocks 92% bonds 0%
convertibles 0% other 3% cash 5%

Largest Holdings: consumer non-durables 35%, financial 16%

Unrealized Net Capital Gains: 1% of portfolio value

SHAREHOLDER INFORMATION

Minimum Investment
Initial: $1,000   Subsequent: $50

Minimum IRA Investment
Initial: $1,000   Subsequent: $50

Maximum Fees
Load: none   12b-1: none
Other: none

Distributions
Income: quarterly   Capital Gains: Dec

Exchange Options
Number Per Year: no limit   Fee: none
Telephone: yes (money market fund available)

Services
IRA, pension, auto invest, auto withdraw

Marshall Short-Term Income (MSINX)

General Bond

1000 North Water Street
P.O. Box 1348
Milwaukee, WI 53201
(800) 236-8554, (414) 287-8500

PERFORMANCE

fund inception date: 11/1/92

	3yr Annual	5yr Annual	10yr Annual	Bull	Bear
Return (%)	na	na	na	na	0.0
Differ from Category (+/-)	na	na	na	na	3.8 high

Total Risk	Standard Deviation	Category Risk	Risk Index	Avg Mat
na	na	na	na	1.2 yrs

	1994	1993	1992	1991	1990	1989	1988	1987	1986	1985
Return (%)	1.8	3.6	—	—	—	—	—	—	—	—
Differ from category (+/-)	3.8	-5.6	—	—	—	—	—	—	—	—

PER SHARE DATA

	1994	1993	1992	1991	1990	1989	1988	1987	1986	1985
Dividends, Net Income ($)	0.48	0.47	—	—	—	—	—	—	—	—
Distrib'ns, Cap Gain ($)	0.00	0.00	—	—	—	—	—	—	—	—
Net Asset Value ($)	9.56	9.86	—	—	—	—	—	—	—	—
Expense Ratio (%)	0.50	0.50	—	—	—	—	—	—	—	—
Net Income to Assets (%)	4.58	4.91	—	—	—	—	—	—	—	—
Portfolio Turnover (%)	185	na	—	—	—	—	—	—	—	—
Total Assets (Millions $)	92	82	—	—	—	—	—	—	—	—

PORTFOLIO (as of 8/31/94)

Portfolio Manager: Mark Pittman - 1994

Investm't Category: General Bond

Cap Gain	Asset Allocation
Cap & Income	Fund of Funds
✔ Income	Index
	Sector
✔ Domestic	Small Cap
Foreign	Socially Conscious
Country/Region	State Specific

Portfolio: stocks 0%   bonds 88%
convertibles 0%   other 0%   cash 12%

Largest Holdings: U.S. government & agencies 31%, corporate 23%

Unrealized Net Capital Gains: 0% of portfolio value

SHAREHOLDER INFORMATION

Minimum Investment
Initial: $1,000   Subsequent: $50

Minimum IRA Investment
Initial: $1,000   Subsequent: $50

Maximum Fees
Load: none   12b-1: none
Other: none

Distributions
Income: monthly   Capital Gains: Dec

Exchange Options
Number Per Year: no limit   Fee: none
Telephone: yes (money market fund available)

Services
IRA, pension, auto invest, auto withdraw

Marshall Stock (MASTX)
Growth

1000 North Water Street
P.O. Box 1348
Milwaukee, WI 53201
(800) 236-8554, (414) 287-8500

PERFORMANCE

fund inception date: 12/10/92

	3yr Annual	5yr Annual	10yr Annual	Bull	Bear
Return (%)	na	na	na	na	-10.0
Differ from Category (+/-)	na	na	na	na	-3.4 low

Total Risk	Standard Deviation	Category Risk	Risk Index	Beta
na	na	na	na	na

	1994	1993	1992	1991	1990	1989	1988	1987	1986	1985
Return (%).............	-5.7	3.3	—	—	—	—	—	—	—	—
Differ from category (+/-) ..	-5.1	-10.1	—	—	—	—	—	—	—	—

PER SHARE DATA

	1994	1993	1992	1991	1990	1989	1988	1987	1986	1985
Dividends, Net Income ($).	0.07	0.12	—	—	—	—	—	—	—	—
Distrib'ns, Cap Gain ($) ...	0.00	0.00	—	—	—	—	—	—	—	—
Net Asset Value ($)	9.68	10.35	—	—	—	—	—	—	—	—
Expense Ratio (%)	0.99	0.94	—	—	—	—	—	—	—	—
Net Income to Assets (%) .	0.77	1.39	—	—	—	—	—	—	—	—
Portfolio Turnover (%)	86	na	—	—	—	—	—	—	—	—
Total Assets (Millions $) ...	226	265	—	—	—	—	—	—	—	—

PORTFOLIO (as of 8/31/94)

Portfolio Manager: Charles L. Mehlhouse - 1993

Investm't Category: Growth

✔ Cap Gain	Asset Allocation
Cap & Income	Fund of Funds
Income	Index
	Sector
✔ Domestic	Small Cap
Foreign	Socially Conscious
Country/Region	State Specific

Portfolio: stocks 88% bonds 0%
convertibles 0% other 0% cash 12%

Largest Holdings: consumer non-durables 30%, capital goods 24%

Unrealized Net Capital Gains: 4% of portfolio value

SHAREHOLDER INFORMATION

Minimum Investment
Initial: $1,000   Subsequent: $50

Minimum IRA Investment
Initial: $1,000   Subsequent: $50

Maximum Fees
Load: none   12b-1: none
Other: none

Distributions
Income: quarterly   Capital Gains: Dec

Exchange Options
Number Per Year: no limit   Fee: none
Telephone: yes (money market fund available)

Services
IRA, pension, auto invest, auto withdraw

Marshall Value Equity

(MRVEX)

Growth

1000 North Water Street
P.O. Box 1348
Milwaukee, WI 53201
(800) 236-8554, (414) 287-8500

PERFORMANCE

fund inception date: 9/30/93

	3yr Annual	5yr Annual	10yr Annual	Bull	Bear
Return (%)	na	na	na	na	-3.9
Differ from Category (+/-)	na	na	na	na	2.7 abv av

Total Risk	Standard Deviation	Category Risk	Risk Index	Beta
na	na	na	na	na

	1994	1993	1992	1991	1990	1989	1988	1987	1986	1985
Return (%)	2.0	—	—	—	—	—	—	—	—	—
Differ from category (+/-)	2.6	—	—	—	—	—	—	—	—	—

PER SHARE DATA

	1994	1993	1992	1991	1990	1989	1988	1987	1986	1985
Dividends, Net Income ($)	0.16	—	—	—	—	—	—	—	—	—
Distrib'ns, Cap Gain ($)	0.11	—	—	—	—	—	—	—	—	—
Net Asset Value ($)	10.13	—	—	—	—	—	—	—	—	—
Expense Ratio (%)	1.00	—	—	—	—	—	—	—	—	—
Net Income to Assets (%)	1.82	—	—	—	—	—	—	—	—	—
Portfolio Turnover (%)	na	—	—	—	—	—	—	—	—	—
Total Assets (Millions $)	195	—	—	—	—	—	—	—	—	—

PORTFOLIO (as of 8/31/94)

Portfolio Manager: Gerry Sandel - 1993

Investm't Category: Growth

✔ Cap Gain	Asset Allocation
Cap & Income	Fund of Funds
Income	Index
	Sector
✔ Domestic	Small Cap
Foreign	Socially Conscious
Country/Region	State Specific

Portfolio: stocks 86% bonds 0%
convertibles 1% other 0% cash 13%

Largest Holdings: consumer non-durables 16%, capital goods 15%

Unrealized Net Capital Gains: 3% of portfolio value

SHAREHOLDER INFORMATION

Minimum Investment
Initial: $1,000 Subsequent: $50

Minimum IRA Investment
Initial: $1,000 Subsequent: $50

Maximum Fees
Load: none 12b-1: none
Other: none

Distributions
Income: quarterly Capital Gains: Dec

Exchange Options
Number Per Year: no limit Fee: none
Telephone: yes (money market fund available)

Services
IRA, pension, auto invest, auto withdraw

Mathers (MATRX)

Growth

100 Corporate N., Suite 201
Bannockburn, IL 60015
(800) 962-3863, (708) 295-7400

	3yr Annual	5yr Annual	10yr Annual	Bull	Bear
Return (%)	-0.2	3.6	10.7	17.2	-3.6
Differ from Category (+/-)	-7.9 low	-6.0 low	-2.2 low	-74.9 low	3.0 high

Total Risk	Standard Deviation	Category Risk	Risk Index	Beta
low	4.4%	low	0.4	0.1

	1994	1993	1992	1991	1990	1989	1988	1987	1986	1985
Return (%)	-5.8	2.1	3.1	9.4	10.3	10.3	13.6	27.0	13.9	27.4
Differ from category (+/-)	-5.2	-11.3	-8.5	-26.3	16.0	-15.8	-4.4	25.2	-0.7	-1.8

PER SHARE DATA

	1994	1993	1992	1991	1990	1989	1988	1987	1986	1985
Dividends, Net Income ($).	0.68	0.23	0.51	0.74	0.84	0.97	0.33	0.88	0.81	0.55
Distrib'ns, Cap Gain ($) ...	0.00	0.00	0.00	0.55	0.24	1.73	0.50	5.97	7.38	1.82
Net Asset Value ($)	13.55	15.11	15.02	15.06	14.95	14.52	15.60	14.46	16.96	22.65
Expense Ratio (%)	0.92	0.89	0.88	0.94	0.98	1.01	0.98	0.82	0.77	0.74
Net Income to Assets (%) ...	na	1.39	3.33	5.39	6.29	5.45	2.18	2.37	1.76	3.69
Portfolio Turnover (%)	na	136	212	80	190	303	148	202	174	278
Total Assets (Millions $) ...	293	434	554	517	300	215	201	152	134	187

PORTFOLIO (as of 6/30/94)

Portfolio Manager: Henry G. Van der Eb Jr. - 1975

Investm't Category: Growth

✔ Cap Gain	Asset Allocation
Cap & Income	Fund of Funds
Income	Index
	Sector
✔ Domestic	Small Cap
✔ Foreign	Socially Conscious
Country/Region	State Specific

Portfolio: stocks 22%   bonds 70%
convertibles 0%   other 0%   cash 8%

Largest Holdings: U.S. government 70%, pollution control 7%

Unrealized Net Capital Gains: -10% of portfolio value

SHAREHOLDER INFORMATION

Minimum Investment
Initial: $1,000   Subsequent: $200

Minimum IRA Investment
Initial: $0   Subsequent: $0

Maximum Fees
Load: none   12b-1: none
Other: none

Distributions
Income: Dec   Capital Gains: Dec

Exchange Options
Number Per Year: none   Fee:
Telephone:

Services
IRA, pension, auto invest, auto withdraw

Matrix Growth (GATGX)

Growth

300 Main St
Cincinnati, OH 45202
(800) 877-3344 (513) 621-2875

PERFORMANCE

fund inception date: 5/14/86

	3yr Annual	5yr Annual	10yr Annual	Bull	Bear
Return (%)	2.9	6.9	na	75.5	-9.7
Differ from Category (+/-)	-4.8 low	-2.7 low	na	-16.6 blw av	-3.1 low

Total Risk	Standard Deviation	Category Risk	Risk Index	Beta
av	8.5%	blw av	0.9	1.0

	1994	1993	1992	1991	1990	1989	1988	1987	1986	1985
Return (%)	-4.8	9.3	4.9	34.2	-4.5	36.0	-2.0	0.7	—	—
Differ from category (+/-) . .	-4.2	-4.1	-6.7	-1.5	1.2	9.9	-20.0	-1.1	—	—

PER SHARE DATA

	1994	1993	1992	1991	1990	1989	1988	1987	1986	1985
Dividends, Net Income ($) .	0.05	0.06	0.09	0.14	0.20	0.29	0.09	0.12	—	—
Distrib'ns, Cap Gain ($) . . .	0.31	0.79	0.56	0.65	0.00	1.11	0.00	0.00	—	—
Net Asset Value ($)	13.45	14.51	14.05	14.01	11.03	11.76	9.67	9.96	—	—
Expense Ratio (%).	1.77	1.67	1.50	1.50	1.50	1.50	1.49	1.49	—	—
Net Income to Assets (%). .	0.25	0.40	0.69	1.17	1.59	2.99	0.78	0.27	—	—
Portfolio Turnover (%)	22	30	51	70	79	130	132	157	—	—
Total Assets (Millions $)	15	19	19	17	11	9	4	4	—	—

PORTFOLIO (as of 6/30/94)

Portfolio Manager: Peter Williams - 1988

Investm't Category: Growth

✔ Cap Gain	Asset Allocation
Cap & Income	Fund of Funds
Income	Index
	Sector
✔ Domestic	Small Cap
Foreign	Socially Conscious
Country/Region	State Specific

Portfolio: stocks 94% bonds 0%
convertibles 0% other 0% cash 6%

Largest Holdings: technology 20%, consumer cyclical 18%

Unrealized Net Capital Gains: 16% of portfolio value

SHAREHOLDER INFORMATION

Minimum Investment
Initial: $1,000 Subsequent: $100

Minimum IRA Investment
Initial: $1,000 Subsequent: $100

Maximum Fees
Load: none 12b-1: none
Other: none

Distributions
Income: Dec Capital Gains: Dec

Exchange Options
Number Per Year: no limit Fee: none
Telephone: yes (money market fund not available)

Services
IRA, pension, auto invest, auto withdraw

Maxus Equity (MXSEX)

Growth

28601 Chagrin Blvd.
Suite 500
Cleveland, OH 44122
(216) 292-3434

PERFORMANCE

fund inception date: 9/30/89

	3yr Annual	5yr Annual	10yr Annual	Bull	Bear
Return (%)	12.4	11.5	na	106.5	-5.2
Differ from Category (+/-)	4.7 high	1.9 abv av	na	14.4 abv av	1.4 abv av

Total Risk	Standard Deviation	Category Risk	Risk Index	Beta
abv av	8.8%	blw av	0.9	0.6

	1994	1993	1992	1991	1990	1989	1988	1987	1986	1985
Return (%)	0.6	24.5	13.5	36.4	-10.8	—	—	—	—	—
Differ from category (+/-)	1.2	11.1	1.9	0.7	-5.1	—	—	—	—	—

PER SHARE DATA

	1994	1993	1992	1991	1990	1989	1988	1987	1986	1985
Dividends, Net Income ($)	0.50	0.15	0.09	0.50	0.00	—	—	—	—	—
Distrib'ns, Cap Gain ($)	0.24	1.53	0.59	0.00	0.00	—	—	—	—	—
Net Asset Value ($)	12.95	13.60	12.28	11.41	8.73	—	—	—	—	—
Expense Ratio (%)	na	2.61	2.89	3.94	5.25	—	—	—	—	—
Net Income to Assets (%)	na	0.91	0.80	0.52	-0.19	—	—	—	—	—
Portfolio Turnover (%)	na	175	187	189	221	—	—	—	—	—
Total Assets (Millions $)	17	12	6	3	2	—	—	—	—	—

PORTFOLIO (as of 6/30/94)

Portfolio Manager: Richard Barone - 1989

Investm't Category: Growth

✔ Cap Gain	✔ Asset Allocation
Cap & Income	Fund of Funds
Income	Index
	Sector
✔ Domestic	Small Cap
Foreign	Socially Conscious
Country/Region	State Specific

Portfolio: stocks 69% bonds 6%
convertibles 9% other 6% cash 10%

Largest Holdings: information technology 12%, real estate 9%

Unrealized Net Capital Gains: 2% of portfolio value

SHAREHOLDER INFORMATION

Minimum Investment
Initial: $1,000   Subsequent: $100

Minimum IRA Investment
Initial: $1,000   Subsequent: $100

Maximum Fees
Load: none   12b-1: 0.50%
Other: none

Distributions
Income: Dec   Capital Gains: Dec

Exchange Options
Number Per Year: no limit   Fee: none
Telephone: yes (money market fund not available)

Services
IRA, pension, auto exchange, auto withdraw

Maxus Income (MXSFX)

Balanced

28601 Chagrin Blvd.
Suite 500
Cleveland, OH 44122
(216) 292-3434

PERFORMANCE

	3yr Annual	5yr Annual	10yr Annual	Bull	Bear
Return (%)	3.8	6.3	na	46.2	-4.6
Differ from Category (+/-)	-2.6 low	-1.7 blw av	na	-18.8 low	1.1 abv av

Total Risk	Standard Deviation	Category Risk	Risk Index	Beta
low	3.9%	low	0.6	0.1

	1994	1993	1992	1991	1990	1989	1988	1987	1986	1985
Return (%)	-4.4	8.7	7.8	19.2	1.7	11.4	7.8	3.5	6.5	—
Differ from category (+/-) . .	-2.5	-4.7	-0.5	-4.2	2.2	-5.9	-4.0	1.1	-10.9	—

PER SHARE DATA

	1994	1993	1992	1991	1990	1989	1988	1987	1986	1985
Dividends, Net Income ($) .	0.73	0.67	0.78	0.81	0.74	1.15	0.61	1.23	0.27	—
Distrib'ns, Cap Gain ($) . . .	0.00	0.21	0.16	0.00	0.00	0.08	0.00	0.19	0.02	—
Net Asset Value ($)	9.73	10.94	10.88	10.98	9.94	10.51	10.57	10.37	11.39	—
Expense Ratio (%)	na	1.90	1.94	2.00	2.00	2.00	2.00	2.01	2.01	—
Net Income to Assets (%) . . .	na	6.06	7.18	7.59	7.43	6.25	5.64	5.33	4.15	—
Portfolio Turnover (%)	na	88	91	108	155	145	139	168	215	—
Total Assets (Millions $)	33	36	29	18	13	13	11	11	11	—

PORTFOLIO (as of 6/30/94)

Portfolio Manager: Richard Barone - 1985

Investm't Category: Balanced
Cap Gain	✔ Asset Allocation
✔ Cap & Income	Fund of Funds
Income	Index
	Sector
✔ Domestic	Small Cap
Foreign	Socially Conscious
Country/Region	State Specific

Portfolio: stocks 2%   bonds 29%
convertibles 9%   other 60%   cash 0%

Largest Holdings: closed-end investment companies 53%, U.S. government 26%

Unrealized Net Capital Gains: -5% of portfolio value

SHAREHOLDER INFORMATION

Minimum Investment
Initial: $1,000   Subsequent: $100

Minimum IRA Investment
Initial: $1,000   Subsequent: $100

Maximum Fees
Load: none   12b-1: 0.50%
Other: none

Distributions
Income: monthly   Capital Gains: Dec

Exchange Options
Number Per Year: no limit   Fee: none
Telephone: yes (money market fund not available)

Services
IRA, pension, auto exchange, auto withdraw

Maxus Laureate (MXSPX)

Growth & Income

28601 Chagrin Blvd.
Suite 500
Cleveland, OH 44122
(216) 292-3434

	3yr Annual	5yr Annual	10yr Annual	Bull	Bear
Return (%)	na	na	na	na	-5.3
Differ from Category (+/-)	na	na	na	na	1.0 abv av

Total Risk	Standard Deviation	Category Risk	Risk Index	Beta
na	na	na	na	na

	1994	1993	1992	1991	1990	1989	1988	1987	1986	1985
Return (%).	-3.2	—	—	—	—	—	—	—	—	—
Differ from category (+/-) . .	-1.8	—	—	—	—	—	—	—	—	—

PER SHARE DATA

	1994	1993	1992	1991	1990	1989	1988	1987	1986	1985
Dividends, Net Income ($).	0.00	—	—	—	—	—	—	—	—	—
Distrib'ns, Cap Gain ($) . . .	0.00	—	—	—	—	—	—	—	—	—
Net Asset Value ($)	9.64	—	—	—	—	—	—	—	—	—
Expense Ratio (%)	na	—	—	—	—	—	—	—	—	—
Net Income to Assets (%) . . .	na	—	—	—	—	—	—	—	—	—
Portfolio Turnover (%)	na	—	—	—	—	—	—	—	—	—
Total Assets (Millions $)	2	—	—	—	—	—	—	—	—	—

PORTFOLIO (as of 6/30/94)

Portfolio Manager: Allan Miller - 1994

Investm't Category: Growth & Income

Cap Gain	Asset Allocation
✔ Cap & Income	✔ Fund of Funds
Income	Index
	Sector
✔ Domestic	Small Cap
✔ Foreign	Socially Conscious
Country/Region	State Specific

Portfolio: stocks 100%   bonds 0%
convertibles 0%   other 0%   cash 0%

Largest Holdings: general equity funds 35%,
specialty/sector funds 35%

Unrealized Net Capital Gains: -2% of portfolio value

SHAREHOLDER INFORMATION

Minimum Investment
Initial: $1,000   Subsequent: $100

Minimum IRA Investment
Initial: $1,000   Subsequent: $100

Maximum Fees
Load: none   12b-1: 0.50%
Other: none

Distributions
Income: Dec   Capital Gains: Dec

Exchange Options
Number Per Year: no limit   Fee: none
Telephone: yes (money market fund not available)

Services
IRA, pension, auto exchange, auto withdraw

Merger (MERFX)

Aggressive Growth

11 High Meadows
Mt. Kisco, NY 10549
(914) 241-3360

	3yr Annual	5yr Annual	10yr Annual	Bull	Bear
Return (%)	9.9	9.4	na	60.2	2.5
Differ from Category (+/-)	1.0 abv av	-3.1 blw av	na	-73.0 low	13.3 high

Total Risk	Standard Deviation	Category Risk	Risk Index	Beta
low	4.1%	low	0.2	0.1

	1994	1993	1992	1991	1990	1989	1988	1987	1986	1985
Return (%)	7.1	17.6	5.3	16.8	1.0	—	—	—	—	—
Differ from category (+/-) . . .	7.8	-1.9	-5.7	-35.3	7.2	—	—	—	—	—

PER SHARE DATA

	1994	1993	1992	1991	1990	1989	1988	1987	1986	1985
Dividends, Net Income ($) .	0.00	0.00	0.00	0.03	0.00	—	—	—	—	—
Distrib'ns, Cap Gain ($) . . .	0.71	1.10	0.64	0.68	0.78	—	—	—	—	—
Net Asset Value ($)	13.17	12.96	11.95	11.95	10.83	—	—	—	—	—
Expense Ratio (%).	1.76	2.19	2.75	3.05	3.26	—	—	—	—	—
Net Income to Assets (%). .	0.11	-0.57	-1.42	0.21	-1.20	—	—	—	—	—
Portfolio Turnover (%)	na	186	231	311	357	—	—	—	—	—
Total Assets (Millions $) . . .	171	27	11	10	9	—	—	—	—	—

PORTFOLIO (as of 5/31/94)

Portfolio Manager: Fredrick W. Green - 1989, Bonnie L. Smith - 1989

Investm't Category: Aggressive Growth

✔ Cap Gain	Asset Allocation
Cap & Income	Fund of Funds
Income	Index
	Sector
✔ Domestic	Small Cap
Foreign	Socially Conscious
Country/Region	State Specific

Portfolio: stocks 100%   bonds 0%
convertibles 0%   other 0%   cash 0%

Largest Holdings: banks 21%, savings & loans 19%

Unrealized Net Capital Gains: 0% of portfolio value

SHAREHOLDER INFORMATION

Minimum Investment
Initial: $2,000   Subsequent: $0

Minimum IRA Investment
Initial: $2,000   Subsequent: $0

Maximum Fees
Load: none   12b-1: 0.25%
Other: none

Distributions
Income: Dec   Capital Gains: Dec

Exchange Options
Number Per Year: none   Fee:
Telephone:

Services
IRA, pension, auto withdraw

Meridian (MERDX)
Growth

60 E. Sir Francis Drake Blvd.
Wood Island, Suite 306
Larkspur, CA 94939
(800) 446-6662, (415) 461-6237

	3yr Annual	5yr Annual	10yr Annual	Bull	Bear
Return (%)	9.5	16.5	14.9	123.1	-6.5
Differ from Category (+/-)	1.8 abv av	6.9 high	2.0 high	31.0 high	0.1 av

Total Risk	Standard Deviation	Category Risk	Risk Index	Beta
abv av	11.7%	high	1.2	0.9

	1994	1993	1992	1991	1990	1989	1988	1987	1986	1985
Return (%).............	0.5	13.0	15.5	56.8	4.6	19.5	18.0	-7.8	13.1	27.1
Differ from category (+/-) ..	1.1	-0.4	3.9	21.1	10.3	-6.6	0.0	-9.6	-1.5	-2.1

PER SHARE DATA

	1994	1993	1992	1991	1990	1989	1988	1987	1986	1985
Dividends, Net Income ($).	0.88	0.02	0.03	0.09	0.12	0.48	0.00	0.02	0.07	0.10
Distrib'ns, Cap Gain ($) ...	0.00	0.43	0.56	1.70	1.04	0.64	0.00	1.22	1.16	0.00
Net Asset Value ($).....	25.12	25.87	23.29	20.75	14.55	15.09	13.59	11.51	13.57	13.01
Expense Ratio (%)	1.22	1.47	1.75	1.68	2.08	2.01	1.85	1.72	1.91	2.00
Net Income to Assets (%) .	0.38	-0.01	0.24	0.98	0.14	2.83	-0.59	0.15	0.80	2.58
Portfolio Turnover (%)	43	61	61	85	66	62	58	88	75	156
Total Assets (Millions $) ...	256	153	18	12	11	10	11	19	18	4

PORTFOLIO (as of 6/30/94)

Portfolio Manager: Richard F. Aster Jr. - 1984

Investm't Category: Growth

- ✔ Cap Gain
- Cap & Income
- Income
- ✔ Domestic
- Foreign
- Country/Region

- Asset Allocation
- Fund of Funds
- Index
- Sector
- ✔ Small Cap
- Socially Conscious
- State Specific

Portfolio: stocks 72% bonds 1%
convertibles 0% other 0% cash 27%

Largest Holdings: cellular communications 13%, health services 11%

Unrealized Net Capital Gains: 0% of portfolio value

SHAREHOLDER INFORMATION

Minimum Investment
Initial: $1,000   Subsequent: $50

Minimum IRA Investment
Initial: $1,000   Subsequent: $50

Maximum Fees
Load: none   12b-1: none
Other: none

Distributions
Income: Sep   Capital Gains: Sep, Dec

Exchange Options
Number Per Year: no limit   Fee: none
Telephone: yes (money market fund not available)

Services
IRA, auto invest, auto withdraw

Merriman Asset Allocation (MTASX)

Balanced

1200 Westlake Ave. N.
Seattle, WA 98109
(800) 423-4893, (206) 285-8877

fund inception date: 5/1/89

	3yr Annual	5yr Annual	10yr Annual	Bull	Bear
Return (%)	5.7	6.0	na	39.8	-4.8
Differ from Category (+/-)	-0.7 av	-2.0 low	na	-25.2 low	0.9 abv av

Total Risk	Standard Deviation	Category Risk	Risk Index	Beta
blw av	5.0%	low	0.8	0.3

	1994	1993	1992	1991	1990	1989	1988	1987	1986	1985
Return (%)	-2.9	18.5	2.7	12.2	0.8	—	—	—	—	—
Differ from category (+/-) . .	-1.0	5.1	-5.6	-11.2	1.3	—	—	—	—	—

PER SHARE DATA

	1994	1993	1992	1991	1990	1989	1988	1987	1986	1985
Dividends, Net Income ($) .	0.18	0.15	0.23	0.28	0.46	—	—	—	—	—
Distrib'ns, Cap Gain ($) . . .	0.96	0.57	0.54	0.00	0.00	—	—	—	—	—
Net Asset Value ($)	10.23	11.71	10.48	10.94	10.00	—	—	—	—	—
Expense Ratio (%).	1.56	1.52	1.52	1.52	1.53	—	—	—	—	—
Net Income to Assets (%). .	1.63	0.85	2.87	3.03	5.01	—	—	—	—	—
Portfolio Turnover (%)	449	225	133	312	416	—	—	—	—	—
Total Assets (Millions $)	25	30	27	28	23	—	—	—	—	—

PORTFOLIO (as of 9/30/94)

Portfolio Manager: Paul A. Merriman - 1989

Investm't Category: Balanced

Cap Gain	✔ Asset Allocation
✔ Cap & Income	✔ Fund of Funds
Income	Index
	Sector
✔ Domestic	Small Cap
✔ Foreign	Socially Conscious
Country/Region	State Specific

Portfolio: stocks 31%   bonds 16%
convertibles 0%   other 11%   cash 42%

Largest Holdings: equity funds 31%, fixed-income funds 16%

Unrealized Net Capital Gains: 2% of portfolio value

SHAREHOLDER INFORMATION

Minimum Investment
Initial: $1,000   Subsequent: $100

Minimum IRA Investment
Initial: $250   Subsequent: $100

Maximum Fees
Load: none   12b-1: none
Other: none

Distributions
Income: quarterly   Capital Gains: Dec

Exchange Options
Number Per Year: no limit   Fee: $5 (telephone)
Telephone: yes (money market fund available)

Services
IRA, pension, auto invest, auto withdraw

Merriman Capital Appreciation (MNCAX)

Growth

1200 Westlake Ave. N.
Seattle, WA 98109
(800) 423-4893, (206) 285-8877

	3yr Annual	5yr Annual	10yr Annual	Bull	Bear
Return (%)	2.3	6.1	na	37.0	-3.7
Differ from Category (+/-)	-5.4 low	-3.5 low	na	-55.1 low	2.9 high

Total Risk	Standard Deviation	Category Risk	Risk Index	Beta
blw av	5.5%	low	0.5	0.4

	1994	1993	1992	1991	1990	1989	1988	1987	1986	1985
Return (%)	-0.6	3.6	4.1	21.8	3.1	—	—	—	—	—
Differ from category (+/-)	0.0	-9.8	-7.5	-13.9	8.8	—	—	—	—	—

PER SHARE DATA

	1994	1993	1992	1991	1990	1989	1988	1987	1986	1985
Dividends, Net Income ($)	0.15	0.07	0.13	0.23	0.45	—	—	—	—	—
Distrib'ns, Cap Gain ($)	0.71	0.46	1.14	0.00	0.00	—	—	—	—	—
Net Asset Value ($)	10.01	10.94	11.07	11.85	9.91	—	—	—	—	—
Expense Ratio (%)	1.58	1.51	1.46	1.48	1.53	—	—	—	—	—
Net Income to Assets (%)	1.70	0.04	2.48	1.73	4.79	—	—	—	—	—
Portfolio Turnover (%)	344	241	122	119	429	—	—	—	—	—
Total Assets (Millions $)	23	33	44	46	18	—	—	—	—	—

PORTFOLIO (as of 9/30/94)

Portfolio Manager: Paul A. Merriman - 1989

Investm't Category: Growth

✔ Cap Gain	Asset Allocation
Cap & Income	✔ Fund of Funds
Income	Index
	Sector
✔ Domestic	Small Cap
✔ Foreign	Socially Conscious
Country/Region	State Specific

Portfolio:	stocks 37%	bonds 0%
convertibles 0%	other 0%	cash 63%

Largest Holdings: equity funds 37%

Unrealized Net Capital Gains: 1% of portfolio value

SHAREHOLDER INFORMATION

Minimum Investment
Initial: $1,000   Subsequent: $100

Minimum IRA Investment
Initial: $250   Subsequent: $100

Maximum Fees
Load: none   12b-1: none
Other: none

Distributions
Income: quarterly   Capital Gains: Dec

Exchange Options
Number Per Year: no limit   Fee: $5 (telephone)
Telephone: yes (money market fund available)

Services
IRA, pension, auto invest, auto withdraw

Merriman Flexible Bond

(MTGVX)

General Bond

1200 Westlake Ave. N.
Seattle, WA 98109
(800) 423-4893, (206) 285-8877

PERFORMANCE

fund inception date: 1/1/89

	3yr Annual	5yr Annual	10yr Annual	Bull	Bear
Return (%)	5.1	6.9	na	41.6	-2.0
Differ from Category (+/-)	0.8 abv av	0.0 av	na	0.6 av	1.8 abv av

Total Risk	Standard Deviation	Category Risk	Risk Index	Avg Mat
low	4.5%	abv av	1.1	8.8 yrs

	1994	1993	1992	1991	1990	1989	1988	1987	1986	1985
Return (%)	-2.8	14.4	4.5	13.3	6.1	8.4	—	—	—	—
Differ from category (+/-) . .	-0.8	5.2	-2.1	-1.3	-1.1	-3.0	—	—	—	—

PER SHARE DATA

	1994	1993	1992	1991	1990	1989	1988	1987	1986	1985
Dividends, Net Income ($)	0.34	0.62	0.59	0.62	0.63	0.60	—	—	—	—
Distrib'ns, Cap Gain ($) . . .	0.00	0.66	0.46	0.00	0.00	0.18	—	—	—	—
Net Asset Value ($)	9.64	10.27	10.11	10.69	10.02	10.05	—	—	—	—
Expense Ratio (%).	1.50	1.54	1.51	1.55	1.56	1.50	—	—	—	—
Net Income to Assets (%). .	3.89	4.91	6.26	6.03	6.41	7.14	—	—	—	—
Portfolio Turnover (%). . . .	472	272	3	202	234	270	—	—	—	—
Total Assets (Millions $)	9	12	11	11	10	7	—	—	—	—

PORTFOLIO (as of 9/30/94)

Portfolio Manager: Paul A. Merriman - 1988

Investm't Category: General Bond

Cap Gain	Asset Allocation
Cap & Income	✔ Fund of Funds
✔ Income	Index
	Sector
✔ Domestic	Small Cap
Foreign	Socially Conscious
Country/Region	State Specific

Portfolio: stocks 0%   bonds 36%
convertibles 0%   other 0%   cash 64%

Largest Holdings: international bond funds 20%, high-yield corporate bond funds 15%

Unrealized Net Capital Gains: 0% of portfolio value

SHAREHOLDER INFORMATION

Minimum Investment
Initial: $1,000   Subsequent: $100

Minimum IRA Investment
Initial: $250   Subsequent: $100

Maximum Fees
Load: none   12b-1: none
Other: none

Distributions
Income: quarterly   Capital Gains: Dec

Exchange Options
Number Per Year: no limit   Fee: $5 (telephone)
Telephone: yes (money market fund available)

Services
IRA, pension, auto invest, auto withdraw

Merriman Growth & Income (MTBCX)

Growth & Income

1200 Westlake Ave. N.
Seattle, WA 98109
(800) 423-4893, (206) 285-8877

PERFORMANCE

fund inception date: 1/1/89

	3yr Annual	5yr Annual	10yr Annual	Bull	Bear
Return (%)	0.4	4.6	na	25.9	-2.8
Differ from Category (+/-)	-6.7 low	-3.3 low	na	-49.9 low	3.5 high

Total Risk	Standard Deviation	Category Risk	Risk Index	Beta
low	3.7%	low	0.4	0.3

	1994	1993	1992	1991	1990	1989	1988	1987	1986	1985
Return (%)	-0.1	2.7	-1.2	19.1	3.8	9.7	—	—	—	—
Differ from category (+/-)	1.3	-10.5	-11.4	-8.5	9.8	-11.7	—	—	—	—

PER SHARE DATA

	1994	1993	1992	1991	1990	1989	1988	1987	1986	1985
Dividends, Net Income ($)	0.20	0.09	0.18	0.19	0.43	0.31	—	—	—	—
Distrib'ns, Cap Gain ($)	0.86	0.00	1.12	0.00	0.14	0.00	—	—	—	—
Net Asset Value ($)	9.97	11.05	10.84	12.30	10.49	10.66	—	—	—	—
Expense Ratio (%)	1.90	1.69	1.60	1.71	1.83	2.00	—	—	—	—
Net Income to Assets (%)	0.87	0.93	1.64	2.47	4.16	4.12	—	—	—	—
Portfolio Turnover (%)	240	200	91	149	329	48	—	—	—	—
Total Assets (Millions $)	9	14	22	20	15	9	—	—	—	—

PORTFOLIO (as of 9/30/94)

Portfolio Manager: Paul A. Merriman - 1989

Investm't Category: Growth & Income
- Cap Gain
- ✔ Cap & Income
- Income
- ✔ Domestic
- Foreign
- Country/Region
- Asset Allocation
- ✔ Fund of Funds
- Index
- Sector
- Small Cap
- Socially Conscious
- State Specific

Portfolio: stocks 0%   bonds 0%
convertibles 0%   other 0%   cash 100%

Largest Holdings: money market funds 85%,
U. S. government securities 9%

Unrealized Net Capital Gains: 0% of portfolio value

SHAREHOLDER INFORMATION

Minimum Investment
Initial: $1,000   Subsequent: $100

Minimum IRA Investment
Initial: $250   Subsequent: $100

Maximum Fees
Load: none   12b-1: none
Other: none

Distributions
Income: quarterly   Capital Gains: Dec

Exchange Options
Number Per Year: no limit   Fee: $5 (telephone
Telephone: yes (money market fund available)

Services
IRA, pension, auto invest, auto withdraw

MIM Bond Income (MIBIX)

Balanced

4500 Rockside Rd., Suite 440
Clevland, OH 44131
(800) 233-1240, (216) 642-3000

PERFORMANCE

fund inception date: 7/25/86

	3yr Annual	5yr Annual	10yr Annual	Bull	Bear
Return (%)	1.9	4.1	na	29.1	-4.2
Differ from Category (+/-)	-4.5 low	-3.9 low	na	-35.9 low	1.5 high

Total Risk	Standard Deviation	Category Risk	Risk Index	Beta
blw av	5.7%	blw av	0.9	0.6

	1994	1993	1992	1991	1990	1989	1988	1987	1986	1985
Return (%)	-3.6	2.9	6.7	15.6	0.1	3.0	10.3	-1.1	—	—
Differ from category (+/-) . .	-1.7	-10.5	-1.6	-7.8	0.6	-14.3	-1.5	-3.5	—	—

PER SHARE DATA

	1994	1993	1992	1991	1990	1989	1988	1987	1986	1985
Dividends, Net Income ($) .	0.00	0.23	0.39	0.58	0.85	0.69	0.58	0.67	—	—
Distrib'ns, Cap Gain ($) . . .	0.00	0.00	0.00	0.00	0.00	0.00	0.00	0.00	—	—
Net Asset Value ($)	9.07	9.41	9.37	9.15	8.44	9.28	9.68	9.31	—	—
Expense Ratio (%).	3.02	2.75	2.80	2.70	2.30	2.30	2.30	2.50	—	—
Net Income to Assets (%).	-0.10	2.76	5.00	7.10	8.00	7.30	6.80	4.60	—	—
Portfolio Turnover (%)	38	95	64	25	18	42	40	50	—	—
Total Assets (Millions $)	1	3	4	4	5	10	6	1	—	—

PORTFOLIO (as of 9/30/94)

Portfolio Manager: Harvey Salkin - 1986

Investm't Category: Balanced

Cap Gain	Asset Allocation
✔ Cap & Income	Fund of Funds
Income	Index
	Sector
✔ Domestic	Small Cap
✔ Foreign	Socially Conscious
Country/Region	State Specific

Portfolio:	stocks 46%	bonds 0%
convertibles 54%	other 0%	cash 0%

Largest Holdings: stocks—drugs 12%, convertible bonds—telephone 5%

Unrealized Net Capital Gains: 0% of portfolio value

SHAREHOLDER INFORMATION

Minimum Investment
Initial: $250   Subsequent: $50

Minimum IRA Investment
Initial: $0   Subsequent: $0

Maximum Fees
Load: none   12b-1: 0.70%
Other: none

Distributions
Income: quarterly   Capital Gains: Dec

Exchange Options
Number Per Year: 6   Fee: none
Telephone: yes (money market fund available)

Services
IRA, pension, auto exchange, auto invest, auto withdraw

MIM Stock Appreciation
(MISAX)
Aggressive Growth

4500 Rockside Rd., Suite 440
Clevland, OH 44131
(800) 233-1240, (216) 642-3000

	3yr Annual	5yr Annual	10yr Annual	Bull	Bear
Return (%)	1.5	14.2	na	138.5	-14.6
Differ from Category (+/-)	-7.4 low	1.7 abv av	na	5.3 abv av	-3.8 blw av

Total Risk	Standard Deviation	Category Risk	Risk Index	Beta
high	14.2%	av	1.0	0.8

	1994	1993	1992	1991	1990	1989	1988	1987	1986	1985
Return (%).............	-10.4	10.4	5.8	76.9	5.1	16.3	-2.1	—	—	—
Differ from category (+/-) ..	-9.7	-9.1	-5.2	24.8	11.3	-10.5	-17.3	—	—	—

PER SHARE DATA

	1994	1993	1992	1991	1990	1989	1988	1987	1986	1985
Dividends, Net Income ($).	0.00	0.00	0.00	0.00	0.00	0.18	0.06	—	—	—
Distrib'ns, Cap Gain ($) ...	0.00	0.96	0.34	1.83	0.00	0.00	0.00	—	—	—
Net Asset Value ($)	13.82	15.43	14.84	14.35	9.14	8.69	7.63	—	—	—
Expense Ratio (%)	2.44	2.47	2.70	2.90	2.70	3.10	2.70	—	—	—
Net Income to Assets (%) .	-1.35	-1.85	-1.10	-1.70	-0.60	2.20	0.40	—	—	—
Portfolio Turnover (%)	254	216	288	240	185	71	207	—	—	—
Total Assets (Millions $)	5	58	29	10	4	1	2	—	—	—

PORTFOLIO (as of 9/30/94)

Portfolio Manager: Martin Weisberg - 1994

Investm't Category: Aggressive Growth
- ✔ Cap Gain   Asset Allocation
-    Cap & Income   Fund of Funds
-    Income   Index
-       Sector
- ✔ Domestic   Small Cap
-    Foreign   Socially Conscious
-    Country/Region   State Specific

Portfolio: stocks 80%   bonds 0%
convertibles 0%   other 0%   cash 20%

Largest Holdings: semiconductors 6%, tele-communications equip 6%

Unrealized Net Capital Gains: 6% of portfolio value

SHAREHOLDER INFORMATION

Minimum Investment
Initial: $250   Subsequent: $50

Minimum IRA Investment
Initial: $0   Subsequent: $0

Maximum Fees
Load: none   12b-1: 0.70%
Other: none

Distributions
Income: quarterly   Capital Gains: Dec

Exchange Options
Number Per Year: 6   Fee: none
Telephone: yes (money market fund available)

Services
IRA, pension, auto exchange, auto invest, auto withdraw

MIM Stock Growth
(MISGX)
Growth

4500 Rockside Rd., Suite 440
Clevland, OH 44131
(800) 233-1240, (216) 642-3000

PERFORMANCE
fund inception date: 7/25/86

	3yr Annual	5yr Annual	10yr Annual	Bull	Bear
Return (%)	-4.0	1.1	na	41.4	-14.6
Differ from Category (+/-)	-11.7 low	-8.5 low	na	-50.7 low	-8.0 low

Total Risk	Standard Deviation	Category Risk	Risk Index	Beta
abv av	9.2%	av	0.9	0.9

	1994	1993	1992	1991	1990	1989	1988	1987	1986	1985
Return (%)	-11.7	2.1	-1.9	26.9	-5.9	8.3	15.2	-10.9	—	—
Differ from category (+/-)	-11.1	-11.3	-13.5	-8.8	-0.2	-17.8	-2.8	-12.7	—	—

PER SHARE DATA

	1994	1993	1992	1991	1990	1989	1988	1987	1986	1985
Dividends, Net Income ($)	0.00	0.00	0.00	0.10	0.25	0.34	0.28	0.43	—	—
Distrib'ns, Cap Gain ($)	0.10	0.00	0.01	0.00	0.00	0.00	0.00	0.04	—	—
Net Asset Value ($)	9.97	11.40	11.16	11.39	9.06	9.89	9.44	8.44	—	—
Expense Ratio (%)	2.80	2.79	2.90	2.90	2.70	2.80	2.80	2.50	—	—
Net Income to Assets (%)	-1.60	-0.77	0.00	1.40	2.70	3.90	3.80	3.70	—	—
Portfolio Turnover (%)	150	137	105	67	42	38	58	50	—	—
Total Assets (Millions $)	6	9	9	7	6	7	2	1	—	—

PORTFOLIO (as of 9/30/94)

Portfolio Manager: Martin Weisberg - 1993

Investm't Category: Growth
- ✔ Cap Gain
- Cap & Income
- Income
- Asset Allocation
- Fund of Funds
- Index
- Sector
- ✔ Domestic
- Foreign
- Country/Region
- Small Cap
- Socially Conscious
- State Specific

Portfolio: stocks 86% bonds 0%
convertibles 0% other 0% cash 14%

Largest Holdings: drugs 5%, chemicals 5%

Unrealized Net Capital Gains: 5% of portfolio value

SHAREHOLDER INFORMATION

Minimum Investment
Initial: $250   Subsequent: $50

Minimum IRA Investment
Initial: $0   Subsequent: $0

Maximum Fees
Load: none   12b-1: 0.70%
Other: none

Distributions
Income: quarterly   Capital Gains: Dec

Exchange Options
Number Per Year: 6   Fee: none
Telephone: yes (money market fund available)

Services
IRA, pension, auto exchange, auto invest, auto withdraw

MIM Stock Income
(MICIX)
Growth & Income

4500 Rockside Rd., Suite 440
Clevland, OH 44131
(800) 233-1240, (216) 642-3000

PERFORMANCE

fund inception date: 7/25/86

	3yr Annual	5yr Annual	10yr Annual	Bull	Bear
Return (%)	0.8	3.4	na	36.5	-8.1
Differ from Category (+/-)	-6.3 low	-4.5 low	na	-39.3 low	-1.8 blw av

Total Risk	Standard Deviation	Category Risk	Risk Index	Beta
av	7.6%	blw av	0.9	0.8

	1994	1993	1992	1991	1990	1989	1988	1987	1986	1985
Return (%)	-1.8	-0.6	5.1	19.3	-3.3	7.8	15.8	-2.0	—	—
Differ from category (+/-)	-0.4	-13.8	-5.1	-8.3	2.7	-13.6	-1.2	-2.6	—	—

PER SHARE DATA

	1994	1993	1992	1991	1990	1989	1988	1987	1986	1985
Dividends, Net Income ($)	0.00	0.03	0.20	0.22	0.31	0.45	0.35	0.71	—	—
Distrib'ns, Cap Gain ($)	0.00	0.00	0.96	0.23	0.09	0.00	0.00	0.09	—	—
Net Asset Value ($)	10.21	10.40	10.50	11.12	9.72	10.46	10.12	9.04	—	—
Expense Ratio (%)	na	2.61	2.60	2.70	2.50	2.60	2.50	1.70	—	—
Net Income to Assets (%)	na	0.53	2.10	2.50	3.70	4.80	4.80	7.10	—	—
Portfolio Turnover (%)	na	272	222	139	86	65	78	70	—	—
Total Assets (Millions $)	41	7	12	11	10	13	5	1	—	—

PORTFOLIO (as of 9/30/94)

Portfolio Manager: Harvey Salkin - 1986

Investm't Category: Growth & Income

Cap Gain	Asset Allocation
✔ Cap & Income	Fund of Funds
Income	Index
	Sector
✔ Domestic	Small Cap
Foreign	Socially Conscious
Country/Region	State Specific

Portfolio: stocks 98% bonds 0%
convertibles 2% other 0% cash 0%

Largest Holdings: drugs 10%, tobacco 6%

Unrealized Net Capital Gains: 6% of portfolio value

SHAREHOLDER INFORMATION

Minimum Investment
Initial: $250 Subsequent: $50

Minimum IRA Investment
Initial: $0 Subsequent: $0

Maximum Fees
Load: none 12b-1: 0.70%
Other: none

Distributions
Income: quarterly Capital Gains: Dec

Exchange Options
Number Per Year: 6 Fee: none
Telephone: yes (money market fund available)

Services
IRA, pension, auto exchange, auto invest, auto withdraw

Monetta (MONTX)

Growth

1776-A S. Naperville Rd.
Suite 207
Wheaton, IL 60187
(800) 666-3882, (708) 462-9800
this fund is closed to new investors

PERFORMANCE

fund inception date: 5/5/86

	3yr Annual	5yr Annual	10yr Annual	Bull	Bear
Return (%)	-0.1	11.5	na	96.7	-9.4
Differ from Category (+/-)	-7.8 low	1.9 abv av	na	4.6 abv av	-2.8 blw av

Total Risk	Standard Deviation	Category Risk	Risk Index	Beta
abv av	10.7%	abv av	1.1	0.8

	1994	1993	1992	1991	1990	1989	1988	1987	1986	1985
Return (%)	-6.1	0.4	5.4	55.9	11.3	15.2	23.0	1.5	—	—
Differ from category (+/-) . .	-5.5	-13.0	-6.2	20.2	17.0	-10.9	5.0	-0.3	—	—

PER SHARE DATA

	1994	1993	1992	1991	1990	1989	1988	1987	1986	1985
Dividends, Net Income ($) .	0.06	0.00	0.01	0.08	0.10	0.22	0.11	0.15	—	—
Distrib'ns, Cap Gain ($) . . .	0.00	0.53	0.59	1.27	0.58	0.77	1.87	0.00	—	—
Net Asset Value ($)	14.52	15.54	15.99	15.73	10.96	10.44	9.93	9.68	—	—
Expense Ratio (%)	1.36	1.38	1.45	1.42	1.50	1.57	1.50	2.31	—	—
Net Income to Assets (%) .	-0.35	-0.19	0.16	0.93	1.09	2.18	0.96	1.33	—	—
Portfolio Turnover (%)	108	226	127	154	207	258	170	333	—	—
Total Assets (Millions $) . . .	369	524	408	57	6	4	3	2	—	—

PORTFOLIO (as of 6/30/94)

Portfolio Manager: Robert S. Bacarella - 1986

Investm't Category: Growth

✔ Cap Gain	Asset Allocation
Cap & Income	Fund of Funds
Income	Index
	Sector
✔ Domestic	✔ Small Cap
Foreign	Socially Conscious
Country/Region	State Specific

Portfolio: stocks 84% bonds 0%
convertibles 0% other 0% cash 16%

Largest Holdings: leisure, recreation products & services 9%, medical HMO services 7%

Unrealized Net Capital Gains: -7% of portfolio value

SHAREHOLDER INFORMATION

Minimum Investment
Initial: $100   Subsequent: $50

Minimum IRA Investment
Initial: $100   Subsequent: $50

Maximum Fees
Load: none   12b-1: none
Other: none

Distributions
Income: Jun, Dec   Capital Gains: Dec

Exchange Options
Number Per Year: none   Fee:
Telephone:

Services
IRA, pension, auto invest

Montgomery Emerging Markets (MNEMX)

International Stock

600 Montgomery St.
San Francisco, CA 94111
(800) 572-3863, (415) 627-2400

PERFORMANCE

fund inception date: 3/1/92

	3yr Annual	5yr Annual	10yr Annual	Bull	Bear
Return (%)	na	na	na	na	-13.2
Differ from Category (+/-)	na	na	na	na	-6.2 low

Total Risk	Standard Deviation	Category Risk	Risk Index	Beta
na	na	na	na	na

	1994	1993	1992	1991	1990	1989	1988	1987	1986	1985
Return (%).............	-7.7	58.6	—	—	—	—	—	—	—	—
Differ from category (+/-) ..	-4.7	20.0	—	—	—	—	—	—	—	—

PER SHARE DATA

	1994	1993	1992	1991	1990	1989	1988	1987	1986	1985
Dividends, Net Income ($).	0.00	0.02	—	—	—	—	—	—	—	—
Distrib'ns, Cap Gain ($)...	0.79	0.26	—	—	—	—	—	—	—	—
Net Asset Value ($).....	13.65	15.58	—	—	—	—	—	—	—	—
Expense Ratio (%).......	1.85	1.90	—	—	—	—	—	—	—	—
Net Income to Assets (%) .	-0.14	0.66	—	—	—	—	—	—	—	—
Portfolio Turnover (%)	63	21	—	—	—	—	—	—	—	—
Total Assets (Millions $) ...	878	610	—	—	—	—	—	—	—	—

PORTFOLIO (as of 6/30/94)

Portfolio Manager: Josephine Jimenez - 1992, Bryan Sudweeks - 1992

Investm't Category: International Stock

✔ Cap Gain	Asset Allocation
Cap & Income	Fund of Funds
Income	Index
	Sector
Domestic	Small Cap
✔ Foreign	Socially Conscious
Country/Region	State Specific

Portfolio: stocks 78% bonds 0%
convertibles 2% other 10% cash 10%

Largest Holdings: Brazil 10%, Malaysia 9%

Unrealized Net Capital Gains: 5% of portfolio value

SHAREHOLDER INFORMATION

Minimum Investment
Initial: $1,000   Subsequent: $100

Minimum IRA Investment
Initial: $1,000   Subsequent: $100

Maximum Fees
Load: none   12b-1: none
Other: none

Distributions
Income: Jul, Dec   Capital Gains: Jul, Dec

Exchange Options
Number Per Year: 4   Fee: none
Telephone: yes (money market fund available)

Services
IRA, pension, auto exchange, auto invest, auto withdraw

Montgomery Global Communic'ns (MNGCX)

600 Montgomery St.
San Francisco, CA 94111
(800) 572-3863, (415) 627-2400

International Stock

PERFORMANCE

fund inception date: 6/1/93

	3yr Annual	5yr Annual	10yr Annual	Bull	Bear
Return (%)	na	na	na	na	-15.7
Differ from Category (+/-)	na	na	na	na	-8.7 low

Total Risk	Standard Deviation	Category Risk	Risk Index	Beta
na	na	na	na	na

	1994	1993	1992	1991	1990	1989	1988	1987	1986	1985
Return (%)	-13.4	—	—	—	—	—	—	—	—	—
Differ from category (+/-) .	-10.4	—	—	—	—	—	—	—	—	—

PER SHARE DATA

	1994	1993	1992	1991	1990	1989	1988	1987	1986	1985
Dividends, Net Income ($) .	0.00	—	—	—	—	—	—	—	—	—
Distrib'ns, Cap Gain ($) . . .	0.03	—	—	—	—	—	—	—	—	—
Net Asset Value ($)	13.98	—	—	—	—	—	—	—	—	—
Expense Ratio (%).	1.94	—	—	—	—	—	—	—	—	—
Net Income to Assets (%) .	-0.46	—	—	—	—	—	—	—	—	—
Portfolio Turnover (%).	29	—	—	—	—	—	—	—	—	—
Total Assets (Millions $) . . .	216	—	—	—	—	—	—	—	—	—

PORTFOLIO (as of 6/30/94)

Portfolio Manager: John D. Boich - 1993, Oscar A. Castro - 1993

Investm't Category: International Stock
- ✔ Cap Gain
-   Cap & Income
-   Income
- ✔ Domestic
- ✔ Foreign
-   Country/Region
-   Asset Allocation
-   Fund of Funds
-   Index
- ✔ Sector
-   Small Cap
-   Socially Conscious
-   State Specific

Portfolio: stocks 97% bonds 0%
convertibles 0% other 3% cash 0%

Largest Holdings: United States 21%, Hong Kong 11%

Unrealized Net Capital Gains: -2% of portfolio value

SHAREHOLDER INFORMATION

Minimum Investment
Initial: $1,000 Subsequent: $100

Minimum IRA Investment
Initial: $1,000 Subsequent: $100

Maximum Fees
Load: none 12b-1: none
Other: none

Distributions
Income: Jun, Dec Capital Gains: Jun, Dec

Exchange Options
Number Per Year: 4 Fee: none
Telephone: yes (money market fund available)

Services
IRA, pension, auto exchange, auto invest, auto withdraw

Montgomery Growth
(MNGFX)
Growth

600 Montgomery St.
San Francisco, CA 94111
(800) 572-3863, (415) 627-2400

PERFORMANCE

fund inception date: 9/30/93

	3yr Annual	5yr Annual	10yr Annual	Bull	Bear
Return (%)	na	na	na	na	2.4
Differ from Category (+/-)	na	na	na	na	9.0 high

Total Risk	Standard Deviation	Category Risk	Risk Index	Beta
na	na	na	na	na

	1994	1993	1992	1991	1990	1989	1988	1987	1986	1985
Return (%)............	20.9	—	—	—	—	—	—	—	—	—
Differ from category (+/-) .	21.5	—	—	—	—	—	—	—	—	—

PER SHARE DATA

	1994	1993	1992	1991	1990	1989	1988	1987	1986	1985
Dividends, Net Income ($).	0.07	—	—	—	—	—	—	—	—	—
Distrib'ns, Cap Gain ($) . . .	0.07	—	—	—	—	—	—	—	—	—
Net Asset Value ($)	16.93	—	—	—	—	—	—	—	—	—
Expense Ratio (%)	1.49	—	—	—	—	—	—	—	—	—
Net Income to Assets (%) .	1.09	—	—	—	—	—	—	—	—	—
Portfolio Turnover (%)	110	—	—	—	—	—	—	—	—	—
Total Assets (Millions $) . . .	592	—	—	—	—	—	—	—	—	—

PORTFOLIO (as of 6/30/94)

Portfolio Manager: Roger W. Honour - 1993, Andrew Pratt - 1993

Investm't Category: Growth
- ✔ Cap Gain
- Cap & Income
- Income
- ✔ Domestic
- Foreign
- Country/Region
- Asset Allocation
- Fund of Funds
- Index
- Sector
- Small Cap
- Socially Conscious
- State Specific

Portfolio: stocks 61% bonds 0%
convertibles 1% other 0% cash 38%

Largest Holdings: computer software 8%, telecommunications 7%

Unrealized Net Capital Gains: 0% of portfolio value

SHAREHOLDER INFORMATION

Minimum Investment
Initial: $1,000   Subsequent: $100

Minimum IRA Investment
Initial: $1,000   Subsequent: $100

Maximum Fees
Load: none   12b-1: none
Other: none

Distributions
Income: Jun, Dec   Capital Gains: Jun, Dec

Exchange Options
Number Per Year: 4   Fee: none
Telephone: yes (money market fund available)

Services
IRA, pension, auto exchange, auto invest, auto withdraw

Montgomery International Small Cap

600 Montgomery St.
San Francisco, CA 94111
(800) 572-3863, (415) 627-2400

(MNISX) *International Stock*

PERFORMANCE

fund inception date: 9/30/93

	3yr Annual	5yr Annual	10yr Annual	Bull	Bear
Return (%)	na	na	na	na	-17.3
Differ from Category (+/-)	na	na	na	na	-10.3 low

Total Risk	Standard Deviation	Category Risk	Risk Index	Beta
na	na	na	na	na

	1994	1993	1992	1991	1990	1989	1988	1987	1986	1985
Return (%)	-13.2	—	—	—	—	—	—	—	—	—
Differ from category (+/-)	-10.2	—	—	—	—	—	—	—	—	—

PER SHARE DATA

	1994	1993	1992	1991	1990	1989	1988	1987	1986	1985
Dividends, Net Income ($)	0.00	—	—	—	—	—	—	—	—	—
Distrib'ns, Cap Gain ($)	0.00	—	—	—	—	—	—	—	—	—
Net Asset Value ($)	11.80	—	—	—	—	—	—	—	—	—
Expense Ratio (%)	1.99	—	—	—	—	—	—	—	—	—
Net Income to Assets (%)	0.04	—	—	—	—	—	—	—	—	—
Portfolio Turnover (%)	123	—	—	—	—	—	—	—	—	—
Total Assets (Millions $)	29	—	—	—	—	—	—	—	—	—

PORTFOLIO (as of 6/30/94)

Portfolio Manager: John D. Boich - 1993, Oscar A. Castro - 1993

Investm't Category: International Stock
✔ Cap Gain   Asset Allocation
   Cap & Income   Fund of Funds
   Income   Index
     Sector
   Domestic   ✔ Small Cap
✔ Foreign   Socially Conscious
   Country/Region   State Specific

Portfolio: stocks 96%   bonds 0%
convertibles 3%   other 0%   cash 1%

Largest Holdings: Great Britian 11%, Hong Kong 9%

Unrealized Net Capital Gains: -14% of portfolio value

SHAREHOLDER INFORMATION

Minimum Investment
Initial: $1,000   Subsequent: $100

Minimum IRA Investment
Initial: $1,000   Subsequent: $100

Maximum Fees
Load: none   12b-1: none
Other: none

Distributions
Income: Jun, Dec   Capital Gains: Jun, Dec

Exchange Options
Number Per Year: 4   Fee: none
Telephone: yes (money market fund available)

Services
IRA, pension, auto exchange, auto invest, auto withdraw

Montgomery Short Gov't Bond (MNSGX)

600 Montgomery St.
San Francisco, CA 94111
(800) 572-3863, (415) 627-2400

Mortgage-Backed Bond

PERFORMANCE

'fund inception date: 12/18/92

	3yr Annual	5yr Annual	10yr Annual	Bull	Bear
Return (%)	na	na	na	na	-1.0
Differ from Category (+/-)	na	na	na	na	3.4 high

Total Risk	Standard Deviation	Category Risk	Risk Index	Avg Mat
na	na	na	na	1.9 yrs

	1994	1993	1992	1991	1990	1989	1988	1987	1986	1985
Return (%)	1.1	8.3	—	—	—	—	—	—	—	—
Differ from category (+/-)	3.9	1.5	—	—	—	—	—	—	—	—

PER SHARE DATA

	1994	1993	1992	1991	1990	1989	1988	1987	1986	1985
Dividends, Net Income ($)	0.58	0.66	—	—	—	—	—	—	—	—
Distrib'ns, Cap Gain ($)	0.00	0.07	—	—	—	—	—	—	—	—
Net Asset Value ($)	9.63	10.10	—	—	—	—	—	—	—	—
Expense Ratio (%)	0.71	0.22	—	—	—	—	—	—	—	—
Net Income to Assets (%)	5.93	6.02	—	—	—	—	—	—	—	—
Portfolio Turnover (%)	603	213	—	—	—	—	—	—	—	—
Total Assets (Millions $)	19	27	—	—	—	—	—	—	—	—

PORTFOLIO (as of 6/30/94)

Portfolio Manager: William C. Stevens - 1994

Investm't Category: Mortgage-Backed Bond

Cap Gain	Asset Allocation
Cap & Income	Fund of Funds
✔ Income	Index
	Sector
✔ Domestic	Small Cap
Foreign	Socially Conscious
Country/Region	State Specific

Portfolio: stocks 0%   bonds 100%
convertibles 0%   other 0%   cash 0%

Largest Holdings: mortgage-backed 80%, U.S. government 20%

Unrealized Net Capital Gains: 0% of portfolio value

SHAREHOLDER INFORMATION

Minimum Investment
Initial: $1,000   Subsequent: $100

Minimum IRA Investment
Initial: $1,000   Subsequent: $100

Maximum Fees
Load: none   12b-1: none
Other: none

Distributions
Income: monthly   Capital Gains: Dec

Exchange Options
Number Per Year: 4   Fee: none
Telephone: yes (money market fund available)

Services
IRA, pension, auto exchange, auto invest, auto withdraw

Montgomery Small Cap

(MNSCX)

Aggressive Growth

600 Montgomery St.
San Francisco, CA 94111
(800) 572-3863, (415) 627-2400

this fund is closed to new investors

PERFORMANCE

fund inception date: 7/13/90

	3yr Annual	5yr Annual	10yr Annual	Bull	Bear
Return (%)	7.0	na	na	213.9	-16.9
Differ from Category (+/-)	-1.9 blw av	na	na	80.7 high	-6.1 low

Total Risk	Standard Deviation	Category Risk	Risk Index	Beta
high	15.9%	abv av	1.1	1.2

	1994	1993	1992	1991	1990	1989	1988	1987	1986	1985
Return (%)	-9.9	24.3	9.5	98.7	—	—	—	—	—	—
Differ from category (+/-)	-9.2	4.8	-1.5	46.6	—	—	—	—	—	—

PER SHARE DATA

	1994	1993	1992	1991	1990	1989	1988	1987	1986	1985
Dividends, Net Income ($)	0.00	0.00	0.00	0.00	—	—	—	—	—	—
Distrib'ns, Cap Gain ($)	0.98	1.51	0.00	3.52	—	—	—	—	—	—
Net Asset Value ($)	14.96	17.67	15.54	14.18	—	—	—	—	—	—
Expense Ratio (%)	1.35	1.40	1.50	1.45	—	—	—	—	—	—
Net Income to Assets (%)	-0.68	-0.69	-0.44	-0.45	—	—	—	—	—	—
Portfolio Turnover (%)	95	130	81	188	—	—	—	—	—	—
Total Assets (Millions $)	202	250	177	27	—	—	—	—	—	—

PORTFOLIO (as of 6/30/94)

Portfolio Manager: Stuart O. Roberts - 1990

Investm't Category: Aggressive Growth
- ✔ Cap Gain
- Cap & Income
- Income
- Asset Allocation
- Fund of Funds
- Index
- Sector
- ✔ Domestic
- Foreign
- Country/Region
- ✔ Small Cap
- Socially Conscious
- State Specific

Portfolio: stocks 86% bonds 0%
convertibles 3% other 1% cash 10%

Largest Holdings: telecommunications 16%, consumer/leisure time products 16%

Unrealized Net Capital Gains: 6% of portfolio value

SHAREHOLDER INFORMATION

Minimum Investment
Initial: $1,000   Subsequent: $100

Minimum IRA Investment
Initial: $1,000   Subsequent: $100

Maximum Fees
Load: none   12b-1: none
Other: none

Distributions
Income: Jun, Dec   Capital Gains: Jun, Dec

Exchange Options
Number Per Year: 4   Fee: none
Telephone: yes (money market fund available)

Services
IRA, pension, auto exchange, auto invest, auto withdraw

Morgan Grenfell Fixed Income (MFINX)

General Bond

680 E. Swedesford Rd.
Wayne, PA 19087
(800) 814-3401

fund inception date: 9/18/92

	3yr Annual	5yr Annual	10yr Annual	Bull	Bear
Return (%)	na	na	na	na	-4.5
Differ from Category (+/-)	na	na	na	na	-0.7 av

Total Risk	Standard Deviation	Category Risk	Risk Index	Avg Mat
na	na	na	na	5.9 yrs

	1994	1993	1992	1991	1990	1989	1988	1987	1986	1985
Return (%).	-1.9	13.6	—	—	—	—	—	—	—	—
Differ from category (+/-) . .	0.1	4.4	—	—	—	—	—	—	—	—

PER SHARE DATA

	1994	1993	1992	1991	1990	1989	1988	1987	1986	1985
Dividends, Net Income ($).	0.64	0.64	—	—	—	—	—	—	—	—
Distrib'ns, Cap Gain ($) . . .	0.00	0.11	—	—	—	—	—	—	—	—
Net Asset Value ($)	9.79	10.64	—	—	—	—	—	—	—	—
Expense Ratio (%)	0.55	0.55	—	—	—	—	—	—	—	—
Net Income to Assets (%) .	5.88	6.01	—	—	—	—	—	—	—	—
Portfolio Turnover (%)	105	196	—	—	—	—	—	—	—	—
Total Assets (Millions $) . . .	286	151	—	—	—	—	—	—	—	—

PORTFOLIO (as of 4/30/94)

Portfolio Manager: David Baldt - 1992

Investm't Category: General Bond

Cap Gain	Asset Allocation
Cap & Income	Fund of Funds
✔ Income	Index
	Sector
✔ Domestic	Small Cap
Foreign	Socially Conscious
Country/Region	State Specific

Portfolio: stocks 0% bonds 86%
convertibles 0% other 0% cash 14%

Largest Holdings: U.S. government 36%, taxable municipal bonds 22%

Unrealized Net Capital Gains: -3% of portfolio value

SHAREHOLDER INFORMATION

Minimum Investment
Initial: $250,000   Subsequent: $10,000

Minimum IRA Investment
Initial: na   Subsequent: na

Maximum Fees
Load: none   12b-1: none
Other: none

Distributions
Income: monthly   Capital Gains: Dec

Exchange Options
Number Per Year: no limit   Fee: none
Telephone: yes (money market fund not available)

Services

Morgan Grenfell Global Fixed Income (MGGFX)

680 E. Swedesford Rd.
Wayne, PA 19087
(800) 814-3401

International Bond

PERFORMANCE

fund inception date: 1/4/94

	3yr Annual	5yr Annual	10yr Annual	Bull	Bear
Return (%)	na	na	na	na	-3.1
Differ from Category (+/-)	na	na	na	na	4.7 abv av

Total Risk	Standard Deviation	Category Risk	Risk Index	Avg Mat
na	na	na	na	6.7 yrs

	1994	1993	1992	1991	1990	1989	1988	1987	1986	1985
Return (%)	-2.4	—	—	—	—	—	—	—	—	—
Differ from category (+/-)	3.9	—	—	—	—	—	—	—	—	—

PER SHARE DATA

	1994	1993	1992	1991	1990	1989	1988	1987	1986	1985
Dividends, Net Income ($)	0.00	—	—	—	—	—	—	—	—	—
Distrib'ns, Cap Gain ($)	0.00	—	—	—	—	—	—	—	—	—
Net Asset Value ($)	9.76	—	—	—	—	—	—	—	—	—
Expense Ratio (%)	0.85	—	—	—	—	—	—	—	—	—
Net Income to Assets (%)	5.01	—	—	—	—	—	—	—	—	—
Portfolio Turnover (%)	102	—	—	—	—	—	—	—	—	—
Total Assets (Millions $)	59	—	—	—	—	—	—	—	—	—

PORTFOLIO (as of 4/30/94)

Portfolio Manager: Ian Kelson - 1994, Martin Hall - 1994

Investm't Category: International Bond

Cap Gain	Asset Allocation
Cap & Income	Fund of Funds
✔ Income	Index
	Sector
✔ Domestic	Small Cap
✔ Foreign	Socially Conscious
Country/Region	State Specific

Portfolio: stocks 0% bonds 100%
convertibles 0% other 0% cash 0%

Largest Holdings: Germany 29%, United Kingdom 15%

Unrealized Net Capital Gains: 0% of portfolio value

SHAREHOLDER INFORMATION

Minimum Investment
Initial: $250,000   Subsequent: $0

Minimum IRA Investment
Initial: na   Subsequent: na

Maximum Fees
Load: none   12b-1: none
Other: none

Distributions
Income: Dec   Capital Gains: Dec

Exchange Options
Number Per Year: no limit   Fee: none
Telephone: yes (money market fund not available)

Services

Morgan Grenfell Muni Bond (MGMBX)

680 E. Swedesford Rd.
Wayne, PA 19087
(800) 814-3401

Tax-Exempt Bond

PERFORMANCE

fund inception date: 12/13/91

	3yr Annual	5yr Annual	10yr Annual	Bull	Bear
Return (%)	7.5	na	na	na	-2.6
Differ from Category (+/-)	3.0 high	na	na	na	2.6 high

Total Risk	Standard Deviation	Category Risk	Risk Index	Avg Mat
low	4.0%	low	0.6	5.8 yrs

	1994	1993	1992	1991	1990	1989	1988	1987	1986	1985
Return (%)	-1.1	12.4	11.9	—	—	—	—	—	—	—
Differ from category (+/-)	4.1	0.7	3.6	—	—	—	—	—	—	—

PER SHARE DATA

	1994	1993	1992	1991	1990	1989	1988	1987	1986	1985
Dividends, Net Income ($)	0.60	0.65	0.73	—	—	—	—	—	—	—
Distrib'ns, Cap Gain ($)	0.00	0.38	0.00	—	—	—	—	—	—	—
Net Asset Value ($)	10.27	10.98	10.71	—	—	—	—	—	—	—
Expense Ratio (%)	0.55	0.55	0.55	—	—	—	—	—	—	—
Net Income to Assets (%)	5.51	5.94	6.31	—	—	—	—	—	—	—
Portfolio Turnover (%)	57	160	143	—	—	—	—	—	—	—
Total Assets (Millions $)	151	146	94	—	—	—	—	—	—	—

PORTFOLIO (as of 4/30/94)

Portfolio Manager: David Baldt - 1991

Investm't Category: Tax-Exempt Bond
Cap Gain	Asset Allocation
Cap & Income	Fund of Funds
✔ Income	Index
	Sector
✔ Domestic	Small Cap
Foreign	Socially Conscious
Country/Region	State Specific

Portfolio: stocks 0% bonds 97%
convertibles 0% other 0% cash 3%

Largest Holdings: general obligation 1%

Unrealized Net Capital Gains: -1% of portfolio value

SHAREHOLDER INFORMATION

Minimum Investment
Initial: $250,000   Subsequent: $10,000

Minimum IRA Investment
Initial: na   Subsequent: na

Maximum Fees
Load: none   12b-1: none
Other: none

Distributions
Income: monthly   Capital Gains: Dec

Exchange Options
Number Per Year: no limit   Fee: none
Telephone: yes (money market fund not available)

Services

M.S.B. Fund (MSBFX)

Growth

330 Madison Ave.
New York, NY 10017
(212) 551-1920

PERFORMANCE

fund inception date: 4/1/63

	3yr Annual	5yr Annual	10yr Annual	Bull	Bear
Return (%)	9.4	7.3	11.6	73.9	-6.2
Differ from Category (+/-)	1.7 abv av	-2.3 blw av	-1.3 blw av	-18.2 blw av	0.4 av

Total Risk	Standard Deviation	Category Risk	Risk Index	Beta
av	8.7%	blw av	0.9	0.8

	1994	1993	1992	1991	1990	1989	1988	1987	1986	1985
Return (%)	-1.6	20.5	10.6	16.9	-7.2	27.9	9.5	4.6	12.7	27.6
Differ from category (+/-) . .	-1.0	7.1	-1.0	-18.8	-1.5	1.8	-8.5	2.8	-1.9	-1.6

PER SHARE DATA

	1994	1993	1992	1991	1990	1989	1988	1987	1986	1985
Dividends, Net Income ($) .	0.18	0.17	0.28	0.21	0.40	0.25	0.37	0.33	0.48	0.61
Distrib'ns, Cap Gain ($) . . .	2.94	1.92	0.22	2.11	1.58	2.86	2.11	3.88	3.70	1.43
Net Asset Value ($)	13.39	16.79	15.67	14.62	14.54	17.81	16.40	17.23	20.60	21.97
Expense Ratio (%).	1.14	1.12	1.13	1.86	1.39	1.20	1.19	0.98	0.94	0.79
Net Income to Assets (%). .	0.89	1.01	1.43	1.36	2.38	1.30	2.06	1.32	2.08	2.94
Portfolio Turnover (%).	na	26	13	17	31	29	19	37	8	21
Total Assets (Millions $)	35	46	41	41	42	52	49	49	50	51

PORTFOLIO (as of 6/30/94)

Portfolio Manager: Mark F. Trautman - 1993

Investm't Category: Growth

✔ Cap Gain	Asset Allocation
Cap & Income	Fund of Funds
Income	Index
	Sector
✔ Domestic	Small Cap
Foreign	Socially Conscious
Country/Region	State Specific

Portfolio: stocks 89% bonds 0%
convertibles 0% other 0% cash 11%

Largest Holdings: food 8%, speciality retail 7%

Unrealized Net Capital Gains: 18% of portfolio value

SHAREHOLDER INFORMATION

Minimum Investment
Initial: $50   Subsequent: $25

Minimum IRA Investment
Initial: na   Subsequent: na

Maximum Fees
Load: none   12b-1: none
Other: none

Distributions
Income: quarterly   Capital Gains: Dec

Exchange Options
Number Per Year: none   Fee:
Telephone:

Services
auto invest, auto withdraw

Mutual Beacon (BEGRX)

Growth & Income

51 John F. Kennedy Pkwy.
Short Hills, NJ 07078
(800) 553-3014, (201) 912-2100

PERFORMANCE

fund inception date: 1/1/85

	3yr Annual	5yr Annual	10yr Annual	Bull	Bear
Return (%)	16.8	11.5	15.4	85.9	-0.7
Differ from Category (+/-)	9.7 high	3.6 high	3.7 high	10.1 abv av	5.6 high

Total Risk	Standard Deviation	Category Risk	Risk Index	Beta
blw av	6.5%	low	0.8	0.6

	1994	1993	1992	1991	1990	1989	1988	1987	1986	1985
Return (%)	5.6	22.9	22.9	17.5	-8.1	17.4	28.9	12.7	15.4	23.3
Differ from category (+/-)	7.0	9.7	12.7	-10.1	-2.1	-4.0	11.9	12.1	-0.4	-2.4

PER SHARE DATA

	1994	1993	1992	1991	1990	1989	1988	1987	1986	1985
Dividends, Net Income ($)	0.44	0.37	0.46	0.74	1.08	1.17	0.80	0.51	0.31	0.25
Distrib'ns, Cap Gain ($)	1.36	1.82	1.10	0.33	0.26	1.55	1.41	1.04	0.94	0.00
Net Asset Value ($)	31.03	31.09	27.10	23.36	20.80	24.09	22.85	19.47	18.64	17.24
Expense Ratio (%)	0.72	0.73	0.81	0.85	0.85	0.70	0.60	0.85	1.16	1.39
Net Income to Assets (%)	2.07	1.53	1.90	3.07	4.59	5.00	3.60	2.50	2.86	1.99
Portfolio Turnover (%)	na	52	58	57	58	67	87	73	113	72
Total Assets (Millions $)	2,056	1,062	534	399	388	409	214	159	65	9

PORTFOLIO (as of 6/30/94)

Portfolio Manager: Michael F. Price - 1985

Investm't Category: Growth & Income

Cap Gain	Asset Allocation
✔ Cap & Income	Fund of Funds
Income	Index
	Sector
✔ Domestic	Small Cap
✔ Foreign	Socially Conscious
Country/Region	State Specific

Portfolio: stocks 69%   bonds 14%
convertibles 0%   other 3%   cash 14%

Largest Holdings: banking 9%, healthcare 6%

Unrealized Net Capital Gains: 8% of portfolio value

SHAREHOLDER INFORMATION

Minimum Investment
Initial: $5,000   Subsequent: $100

Minimum IRA Investment
Initial: $2,000   Subsequent: $100

Maximum Fees
Load: none   12b-1: none
Other: none

Distributions
Income: Jul, Dec   Capital Gains: Jul, Dec

Exchange Options
Number Per Year: no limit   Fee: none
Telephone: none

Services
IRA, pension, auto invest, auto withdraw

Mutual Discovery (MDISX)

Growth

51 John F. Kennedy Pkwy.
Short Hills, NJ 07078
(800) 553-3014, (201) 912-2100

this fund is closed to new investors

PERFORMANCE

fund inception date: 1/4/93

	3yr Annual	5yr Annual	10yr Annual	Bull	Bear
Return (%)	na	na	na	na	-2.1
Differ from Category (+/-)	na	na	na	na	4.5 high

Total Risk	Standard Deviation	Category Risk	Risk Index	Beta
na	na	na	na	na

	1994	1993	1992	1991	1990	1989	1988	1987	1986	1985
Return (%)	3.5	—	—	—	—	—	—	—	—	—
Differ from category (+/-)	4.1	—	—	—	—	—	—	—	—	—

PER SHARE DATA

	1994	1993	1992	1991	1990	1989	1988	1987	1986	1985
Dividends, Net Income ($)	0.16	—	—	—	—	—	—	—	—	—
Distrib'ns, Cap Gain ($)	0.81	—	—	—	—	—	—	—	—	—
Net Asset Value ($)	12.55	—	—	—	—	—	—	—	—	—
Expense Ratio (%)	0.99	—	—	—	—	—	—	—	—	—
Net Income to Assets (%)	2.35	—	—	—	—	—	—	—	—	—
Portfolio Turnover (%)	na	—	—	—	—	—	—	—	—	—
Total Assets (Millions $)	726	—	—	—	—	—	—	—	—	—

PORTFOLIO (as of 6/30/94)

Portfolio Manager: Michael Price - 1993

Investm't Category: Growth
- ✔ Cap Gain
- Cap & Income
- Income
- ✔ Domestic
- ✔ Foreign
- Country/Region
- Asset Allocation
- Fund of Funds
- Index
- Sector
- ✔ Small Cap
- Socially Conscious
- State Specific

Portfolio: stocks 77% bonds 10%
convertibles 0% other 6% cash 7%

Largest Holdings: banking 9%, food & beverages 8%

Unrealized Net Capital Gains: 7% of portfolio value

SHAREHOLDER INFORMATION

Minimum Investment
Initial: $1,000   Subsequent: $50

Minimum IRA Investment
Initial: $1,000   Subsequent: $50

Maximum Fees
Load: none   12b-1: none
Other: none

Distributions
Income: Jul, Dec   Capital Gains: Jul, Dec

Exchange Options
Number Per Year: no limit   Fee: none
Telephone: none

Services
IRA, pension, auto invest, auto withdraw

Mutual Qualified (MQIFX)

Growth & Income

51 John F. Kennedy Pkwy.
Short Hills, NJ 07078
(800) 553-3014, (201) 912-2100

PERFORMANCE

fund inception date: 9/1/80

	3yr Annual	5yr Annual	10yr Annual	Bull	Bear
Return (%)	16.7	11.6	15.1	92.3	-1.9
Differ from Category (+/-)	9.6 high	3.7 high	3.4 high	16.5 high	4.4 high

Total Risk	Standard Deviation	Category Risk	Risk Index	Beta
av	6.9%	low	0.8	0.7

	1994	1993	1992	1991	1990	1989	1988	1987	1986	1985
Return (%).............	5.7	22.7	22.6	21.1	-10.1	14.3	30.1	7.7	17.4	25.0
Differ from category (+/-) ..	7.1	9.5	12.4	-6.5	-4.1	-7.1	13.1	7.1	1.6	-0.7

PER SHARE DATA

	1994	1993	1992	1991	1990	1989	1988	1987	1986	1985
Dividends, Net Income ($).	0.43	0.37	0.49	0.67	1.23	1.36	0.83	0.88	0.85	0.61
Distrib'ns, Cap Gain ($) ...	1.43	2.56	1.02	0.37	0.38	2.39	1.62	1.44	1.56	1.17
Net Asset Value ($).....	26.67	27.00	24.43	21.18	18.37	22.21	22.71	19.37	20.06	19.15
Expense Ratio (%)	0.76	0.78	0.82	0.87	0.89	0.70	0.62	0.71	0.68	0.70
Net Income to Assets (%) .	1.77	1.65	2.10	3.09	5.40	5.61	3.96	3.43	4.55	4.27
Portfolio Turnover (%)	na	56	47	52	46	73	85	74	123	95
Total Assets (Millions $) .	1,789	1,511	1,251	1,110	1,075	1,470	1,094	686	561	432

PORTFOLIO (as of 6/30/94)

Portfolio Manager: Michael F. Price - 1980

Investm't Category: Growth & Income

Cap Gain	Asset Allocation
✔ Cap & Income	Fund of Funds
Income	Index
	Sector
✔ Domestic	Small Cap
✔ Foreign	Socially Conscious
Country/Region	State Specific

Portfolio: stocks 79%   bonds 9%
convertibles 0%   other 4%   cash 8%

Largest Holdings: consumer products & services 10%, food & beverages 7%

Unrealized Net Capital Gains: 14% of portfolio value

SHAREHOLDER INFORMATION

Minimum Investment
Initial: $1,000   Subsequent: $50

Minimum IRA Investment
Initial: $1,000   Subsequent: $50

Maximum Fees
Load: none   12b-1: none
Other: none

Distributions
Income: Jul, Dec   Capital Gains: Jul, Dec

Exchange Options
Number Per Year: no limit   Fee: none
Telephone: none

Services
IRA, pension, auto invest, auto withdraw

Mutual Shares (MUTHX)

Growth & Income

51 John F. Kennedy Pkwy.
Short Hills, NJ 07078
(800) 553-3014, (201) 912-2100

PERFORMANCE

fund inception date: 1/1/49

	3yr Annual	5yr Annual	10yr Annual	Bull	Bear
Return (%)	15.3	10.8	14.7	86.9	-2.5
Differ from Category (+/-)	8.2 high	2.9 high	3.0 high	11.1 abv av	3.8 high

Total Risk	Standard Deviation	Category Risk	Risk Index	Beta
av	7.1%	low	0.9	0.7

	1994	1993	1992	1991	1990	1989	1988	1987	1986	1985
Return (%)	4.5	20.9	21.3	20.9	-9.8	14.8	30.6	6.3	16.9	26.6
Differ from category (+/-) . . .	5.9	7.7	11.1	-6.7	-3.8	-6.6	13.6	5.7	1.1	0.9

PER SHARE DATA

	1994	1993	1992	1991	1990	1989	1988	1987	1986	1985
Dividends, Net Income ($) .	1.34	1.38	1.59	2.00	3.34	4.09	2.63	2.52	2.34	1.88
Distrib'ns, Cap Gain ($) . . .	4.56	6.31	3.16	1.63	0.89	6.55	5.05	4.09	4.52	4.12
Net Asset Value ($)	78.69	80.96	73.36	64.49	56.39	67.16	67.77	57.83	60.43	57.57
Expense Ratio (%).	0.73	0.74	0.78	0.82	0.85	0.65	0.67	0.69	0.70	0.67
Net Income to Assets (%). .	1.81	1.90	2.18	3.08	4.88	5.57	4.16	3.32	4.07	4.08
Portfolio Turnover (%)	na	48	41	48	43	72	90	78	122	91
Total Assets (Millions $) . .	3,745	3,527	2,913	2,640	2,521	3,403	2,552	1,685	1,403	1,076

PORTFOLIO (as of 6/30/94)

Portfolio Manager: Michael F. Price - 1975

Investm't Category: Growth & Income

Cap Gain	Asset Allocation
✔ Cap & Income	Fund of Funds
Income	Index
	Sector
✔ Domestic	Small Cap
✔ Foreign	Socially Conscious
Country/Region	State Specific

Portfolio: stocks 80%   bonds 10%
convertibles 0%   other 3%   cash 7%

Largest Holdings: consumer products & services 10%, insurance 7%

Unrealized Net Capital Gains: 16% of portfolio value

SHAREHOLDER INFORMATION

Minimum Investment
Initial: $5,000   Subsequent: $100

Minimum IRA Investment
Initial: $2,000   Subsequent: $100

Maximum Fees
Load: none   12b-1: none
Other: none

Distributions
Income: Jul, Dec   Capital Gains: Jul, Dec

Exchange Options
Number Per Year: no limit   Fee: none
Telephone: none

Services
IRA, pension, auto invest, auto withdraw

National Industries
(NAIDX)
Growth

5990 Greenwood Plaza Blvd.
Englewood, CO 80111
(303) 220-8500

PERFORMANCE

fund inception date: 11/1/54

	3yr Annual	5yr Annual	10yr Annual	Bull	Bear
Return (%)	0.1	6.5	9.1	48.8	-6.6
Differ from Category (+/-)	-7.6 low	-3.1 low	-3.8 low	-43.3 low	0.0 av

Total Risk	Standard Deviation	Category Risk	Risk Index	Beta
av	7.9%	low	0.8	0.8

	1994	1993	1992	1991	1990	1989	1988	1987	1986	1985
Return (%)	-0.2	1.3	-0.5	31.9	3.2	24.4	12.6	2.5	9.8	10.5
Differ from category (+/-)	0.4	-12.1	-12.1	-3.8	8.9	-1.7	-5.4	0.7	-4.8	-18.7

PER SHARE DATA

	1994	1993	1992	1991	1990	1989	1988	1987	1986	1985
Dividends, Net Income ($)	0.07	0.07	0.15	0.21	0.23	0.20	0.13	0.10	0.38	0.34
Distrib'ns, Cap Gain ($)	0.69	0.30	1.88	1.10	0.34	1.47	0.50	1.15	1.82	0.18
Net Asset Value ($)	11.92	12.71	12.90	15.01	12.37	12.53	11.41	10.69	11.64	12.66
Expense Ratio (%)	na	1.60	1.50	1.48	1.70	1.69	1.70	1.65	1.70	1.70
Net Income to Assets (%)	na	0.50	0.99	1.46	1.69	1.52	1.04	0.64	0.90	2.00
Portfolio Turnover (%)	na	56	45	22	64	83	32	68	73	70
Total Assets (Millions $)	30	33	35	34	30	32	27	24	27	27

PORTFOLIO (as of 5/31/94)

Portfolio Manager: Richard Barrett - 1984

Investm't Category: Growth

✔ Cap Gain	Asset Allocation
Cap & Income	Fund of Funds
Income	Index
	Sector
✔ Domestic	Small Cap
✔ Foreign	Socially Conscious
Country/Region	State Specific

Portfolio: stocks 81% bonds 0%
convertibles 0% other 0% cash 19%

Largest Holdings: electronics, instrumentation & computer periph'ls 8%, financial serv 7%

Unrealized Net Capital Gains: 18% of portfolio value

SHAREHOLDER INFORMATION

Minimum Investment
Initial: $250   Subsequent: $25

Minimum IRA Investment
Initial: na   Subsequent: na

Maximum Fees
Load: none   12b-1: none
Other: none

Distributions
Income: Dec   Capital Gains: Dec

Exchange Options
Number Per Year: none Fee:
Telephone:

Services
auto withdraw

Neuberger & Berman Focus (NBSSX)

Growth

605 Third Ave., 2nd Fl.
New York, NY 10158
(800) 877-9700, (212) 476-8800

PERFORMANCE

fund inception date: 10/19/55

	3yr Annual	5yr Annual	10yr Annual	Bull	Bear
Return (%)	12.4	10.7	13.0	88.2	-5.0
Differ from Category (+/-)	4.7 high	1.1 abv av	0.1 av	-3.9 av	1.6 abv av

Total Risk	Standard Deviation	Category Risk	Risk Index	Beta
abv av	9.7%	av	1.0	1.1

	1994	1993	1992	1991	1990	1989	1988	1987	1986	1985
Return (%)	0.8	16.3	21.0	24.6	-5.9	29.7	16.4	0.6	10.0	22.3
Differ from category (+/-)	1.4	2.9	9.4	-11.1	-0.2	3.6	-1.6	-1.2	-4.6	-6.9

PER SHARE DATA

	1994	1993	1992	1991	1990	1989	1988	1987	1986	1985
Dividends, Net Income ($)	0.20	0.25	0.28	0.36	0.35	0.47	0.51	0.59	0.88	0.92
Distrib'ns, Cap Gain ($)	1.48	1.70	2.13	0.87	0.38	2.57	0.54	3.35	1.66	0.93
Net Asset Value ($)	21.58	23.06	21.50	19.97	17.06	18.93	16.96	15.49	18.47	19.14
Expense Ratio (%)	0.85	0.92	0.91	0.93	0.92	0.99	1.01	0.86	0.88	0.89
Net Income to Assets (%)	0.89	1.18	1.46	2.01	2.34	2.39	2.64	2.21	4.08	4.60
Portfolio Turnover (%)	na	52	77	60	66	60	66	88	28	18
Total Assets (Millions $)	603	594	439	399	369	441	375	481	376	334

PORTFOLIO (as of 8/31/94)

Portfolio Manager: Lawrence Marx III - 1988, Kent Simons - 1988

Investm't Category: Growth

- ✔ Cap Gain
- Cap & Income
- Income
- ✔ Domestic
- ✔ Foreign
- Country/Region

- Asset Allocation
- Fund of Funds
- Index
- Sector
- Small Cap
- Socially Conscious
- State Specific

Portfolio: stocks 98% bonds 0%
convertibles 0% other 0% cash 2%

Largest Holdings: financial services 32%, media & entertainment 20%

Unrealized Net Capital Gains: 26% of portfolio value

SHAREHOLDER INFORMATION

Minimum Investment
Initial: $1,000   Subsequent: $100

Minimum IRA Investment
Initial: $250   Subsequent: $100

Maximum Fees
Load: none   12b-1: none
Other: none

Distributions
Income: Sep, Dec   Capital Gains: Sep, Dec

Exchange Options
Number Per Year: no limit   Fee: none
Telephone: yes (money market fund available)

Services
IRA, pension, auto exchange, auto invest, auto withdraw

Neuberger & Berman Genesis (NBGNX)

Aggressive Growth

605 Third Ave., 2nd Fl.
New York, NY 10158
(800) 877-9700, (212) 476-8800

fund inception date: 9/27/88

PERFORMANCE

	3yr Annual	5yr Annual	10yr Annual	Bull	Bear
Return (%)	8.9	8.9	na	99.1	-5.2
Differ from Category (+/-)	0.0 av	-3.6 blw av	na	-34.1 blw av	5.6 high

Total Risk	Standard Deviation	Category Risk	Risk Index	Beta
abv av	9.7%	low	0.6	0.7

	1994	1993	1992	1991	1990	1989	1988	1987	1986	1985
Return (%)	-1.8	13.8	15.6	41.5	-16.2	17.2	—	—	—	—
Differ from category (+/-)	-1.1	-5.7	4.6	-10.6	-10.0	-9.6	—	—	—	—

PER SHARE DATA

	1994	1993	1992	1991	1990	1989	1988	1987	1986	1985
Dividends, Net Income ($)	0.00	0.01	0.00	0.01	0.04	0.02	—	—	—	—
Distrib'ns, Cap Gain ($)	0.31	0.75	0.00	0.09	0.00	0.12	—	—	—	—
Net Asset Value ($)	7.80	8.26	7.92	6.85	4.91	5.91	—	—	—	—
Expense Ratio (%)	1.36	1.65	2.00	2.00	2.00	2.00	—	—	—	—
Net Income to Assets (%)	-0.20	0.15	-0.14	0.60	0.41	0.51	—	—	—	—
Portfolio Turnover (%)	na	54	23	46	37	10	—	—	—	—
Total Assets (Millions $)	108	122	72	28	21	18	—	—	—	—

PORTFOLIO (as of 8/31/94)

Portfolio Manager: Stephen Milman - 1988, Judy Vale - 1994

Investm't Category: Aggressive Growth

✔ Cap Gain	Asset Allocation
Cap & Income	Fund of Funds
Income	Index
	Sector
✔ Domestic	✔ Small Cap
✔ Foreign	Socially Conscious
Country/Region	State Specific

Portfolio: stocks 98% bonds 0%
convertibles 0% other 0% cash 2%

Largest Holdings: industrial & commercial products & services 19%, insurance 10%

Unrealized Net Capital Gains: 11% of portfolio value

SHAREHOLDER INFORMATION

Minimum Investment
Initial: $1,000   Subsequent: $100

Minimum IRA Investment
Initial: $250   Subsequent: $100

Maximum Fees
Load: none   12b-1: none
Other: none

Distributions
Income: Dec   Capital Gains: Dec

Exchange Options
Number Per Year: no limit   Fee: none
Telephone: yes (money market fund available)

Services
IRA, pension, auto exchange, auto invest, auto withdraw

Neuberger & Berman Guardian (NGUAX)

Growth & Income

605 Third Ave., 2nd Fl.
New York, NY 10158
(800) 877-9700, (212) 476-8800

PERFORMANCE

fund inception date: 6/1/50

	3yr Annual	5yr Annual	10yr Annual	Bull	Bear
Return (%)	11.0	11.8	14.2	110.4	-4.4
Differ from Category (+/-)	3.9 high	3.9 high	2.5 high	34.6 high	1.9 abv av

Total Risk	Standard Deviation	Category Risk	Risk Index	Beta
av	8.5%	abv av	1.0	1.0

	1994	1993	1992	1991	1990	1989	1988	1987	1986	1985
Return (%)	0.6	14.4	19.0	34.3	-4.7	21.5	28.0	-1.0	11.8	25.0
Differ from category (+/-)	2.0	1.2	8.8	6.7	1.3	0.1	11.0	-1.6	-4.0	-0.7

PER SHARE DATA

	1994	1993	1992	1991	1990	1989	1988	1987	1986	1985
Dividends, Net Income ($)	0.25	0.30	0.26	0.32	0.35	0.36	0.36	0.50	0.50	0.59
Distrib'ns, Cap Gain ($)	0.23	0.40	0.66	0.91	0.17	1.19	1.23	1.40	1.50	2.15
Net Asset Value ($)	18.23	18.60	16.87	14.97	12.08	13.22	12.17	10.74	12.71	13.10
Expense Ratio (%)	0.80	0.81	0.82	0.84	0.86	0.84	0.84	0.74	0.73	0.76
Net Income to Assets (%)	1.36	2.01	1.90	2.46	2.89	2.59	2.80	2.72	3.59	4.58
Portfolio Turnover (%)	na	27	41	59	58	52	73	91	70	57
Total Assets (Millions $)	2,430	2,000	803	629	496	569	539	461	531	388

PORTFOLIO (as of 8/31/94)

Portfolio Manager: Kent Simons - 1982

Investm't Category: Growth & Income

Cap Gain	Asset Allocation
✔ Cap & Income	Fund of Funds
Income	Index
	Sector
✔ Domestic	Small Cap
✔ Foreign	Socially Conscious
Country/Region	State Specific

Portfolio: stocks 92% bonds 1%
convertibles 1% other 1% cash 5%

Largest Holdings: media & entertainment 11%, technology 10%

Unrealized Net Capital Gains: 20% of portfolio value

SHAREHOLDER INFORMATION

Minimum Investment
Initial: $1,000   Subsequent: $100

Minimum IRA Investment
Initial: $250   Subsequent: $100

Maximum Fees
Load: none   12b-1: none
Other: none

Distributions
Income: quarterly   Capital Gains: Dec

Exchange Options
Number Per Year: no limit   Fee: none
Telephone: yes (money market fund available)

Services
IRA, pension, auto exchange, auto invest, auto withdraw

Neuberger & Berman Ltd Maturity Bond (NLMBX)

605 Third Ave., 2nd Fl.
New York, NY 10158
(800) 877-9700, (212) 476-8800

General Bond

	3yr Annual	5yr Annual	10yr Annual	Bull	Bear
Return (%)	3.8	6.3	na	30.5	-2.1
Differ from Category (+/-)	-0.5 blw av	-0.6 low	na	-10.5 low	1.7 abv av

Total Risk	Standard Deviation	Category Risk	Risk Index	Avg Mat
low	2.2%	low	0.5	2.0 yrs

	1994	1993	1992	1991	1990	1989	1988	1987	1986	1985
Return (%)	-0.3	6.7	5.1	11.8	8.7	11.1	6.7	3.6	—	—
Differ from category (+/-)	1.7	-2.5	-1.5	-2.8	1.5	-0.3	-0.7	1.4	—	—

PER SHARE DATA

	1994	1993	1992	1991	1990	1989	1988	1987	1986	1985
Dividends, Net Income ($)	0.57	0.57	0.61	0.70	0.79	0.83	0.74	0.68	—	—
Distrib'ns, Cap Gain ($)	0.00	0.06	0.05	0.00	0.00	0.00	0.00	0.00	—	—
Net Asset Value ($)	9.76	10.36	10.30	10.44	10.00	9.96	9.74	9.83	—	—
Expense Ratio (%)	0.69	0.65	0.65	0.65	0.65	0.65	0.50	0.50	—	—
Net Income to Assets (%)	5.53	5.49	6.02	7.07	8.09	8.33	6.97	6.71	—	—
Portfolio Turnover (%)	na	114	113	88	88	121	158	41	—	—
Total Assets (Millions $)	292	348	273	163	101	108	107	70	—	—

PORTFOLIO (as of 10/31/94)

Portfolio Manager: Theresa Havell - 1986

Investm't Category: General Bond

Cap Gain	Asset Allocation
Cap & Income	Fund of Funds
✔ Income	Index
	Sector
✔ Domestic	Small Cap
Foreign	Socially Conscious
Country/Region	State Specific

Portfolio: stocks 0%   bonds 98%
convertibles 0%   other 0%   cash 2%

Largest Holdings: corporate 53%, asset-backed securities 17%

Unrealized Net Capital Gains: 0% of portfolio value

SHAREHOLDER INFORMATION

Minimum Investment
Initial: $2,000   Subsequent: $100

Minimum IRA Investment
Initial: $250   Subsequent: $100

Maximum Fees
Load: none   12b-1: none
Other: none

Distributions
Income: monthly   Capital Gains: Dec

Exchange Options
Number Per Year: no limit   Fee: none
Telephone: yes (money market fund available)

Services
IRA, pension, auto exchange, auto invest, auto withdraw

Neuberger & Berman Manhattan (NMANX)

605 Third Ave., 2nd Fl.
New York, NY 10158
(800) 877-9700, (212) 476-8800

Growth

PERFORMANCE

fund inception date: 3/1/79

	3yr Annual	5yr Annual	10yr Annual	Bull	Bear
Return (%)	7.6	8.4	13.9	87.0	-10.5
Differ from Category (+/-)	-0.1 av	-1.2 blw av	1.0 abv av	-5.1 av	-3.9 low

Total Risk	Standard Deviation	Category Risk	Risk Index	Beta
high	12.2%	high	1.3	1.2

	1994	1993	1992	1991	1990	1989	1988	1987	1986	1985
Return (%)	-3.6	10.0	17.7	30.8	-8.0	29.0	18.3	0.4	16.8	37.1
Differ from category (+/-)	-3.0	-3.4	6.1	-4.9	-2.3	2.9	0.3	-1.4	2.2	7.9

PER SHARE DATA

	1994	1993	1992	1991	1990	1989	1988	1987	1986	1985
Dividends, Net Income ($)	0.01	0.02	0.05	0.11	0.16	0.18	0.16	0.26	0.08	0.11
Distrib'ns, Cap Gain ($)	0.70	2.06	1.68	0.40	0.15	1.05	0.04	0.95	1.24	0.00
Net Asset Value ($)	10.00	11.11	11.99	11.65	9.29	10.44	9.04	7.81	8.95	8.86
Expense Ratio (%)	0.96	1.04	1.07	1.09	1.14	1.12	1.18	1.00	1.10	1.43
Net Income to Assets (%)	0.16	0.20	0.57	1.28	1.44	1.60	1.55	1.60	1.34	1.76
Portfolio Turnover (%)	na	76	83	78	91	77	70	111	96	155
Total Assets (Millions $)	462	525	401	429	356	405	342	329	293	167

PORTFOLIO (as of 8/31/94)

Portfolio Manager: Mark Goldstein - 1992

Investm't Category: Growth

✔ Cap Gain	Asset Allocation
Cap & Income	Fund of Funds
Income	Index
	Sector
✔ Domestic	Small Cap
✔ Foreign	Socially Conscious
Country/Region	State Specific

Portfolio: stocks 100% bonds 0%
convertibles 0% other 0% cash 0%

Largest Holdings: financial services 16%, consumer goods & services 14%

Unrealized Net Capital Gains: 13% of portfolio value

SHAREHOLDER INFORMATION

Minimum Investment
Initial: $1,000   Subsequent: $100

Minimum IRA Investment
Initial: $250   Subsequent: $100

Maximum Fees
Load: none   12b-1: none
Other: none

Distributions
Income: Dec   Capital Gains: Dec

Exchange Options
Number Per Year: no limit   Fee: none
Telephone: yes (money market fund available)

Services
IRA, pension, auto exchange, auto invest, auto withdraw

Neuberger & Berman Muni Securities (NBMUX)

Tax-Exempt Bond

605 Third Ave., 2nd Fl.
New York, NY 10158
(800) 877-9700, (212) 476-8800

PERFORMANCE   fund inception date: 7/9/87

	3yr Annual	5yr Annual	10yr Annual	Bull	Bear
Return (%)	3.9	5.5	na	33.1	-3.7
Differ from Category (+/-)	-0.6 low	-0.6 low	na	-8.7 low	1.5 abv av

Total Risk	Standard Deviation	Category Risk	Risk Index	Avg Mat
low	4.4%	low	0.7	7.8 yrs

	1994	1993	1992	1991	1990	1989	1988	1987	1986	1985
Return (%).............	-3.9	9.5	6.9	9.0	6.8	8.2	6.7	—	—	—
Differ from category (+/-) ..	1.3	-2.2	-1.4	-2.3	0.5	-0.8	-3.5	—	—	—

PER SHARE DATA

	1994	1993	1992	1991	1990	1989	1988	1987	1986	1985
Dividends, Net Income ($).	0.46	0.46	0.54	0.57	0.63	0.63	0.60	—	—	—
Distrib'ns, Cap Gain ($) ...	0.00	0.13	0.09	0.00	0.00	0.00	0.00	—	—	—
Net Asset Value ($).....	10.12	11.01	10.61	10.53	10.21	10.17	10.00	—	—	—
Expense Ratio (%)	0.65	0.62	0.50	0.50	0.50	0.50	0.50	—	—	—
Net Income to Assets (%) .	4.24	4.33	5.16	5.61	6.28	6.26	5.90	—	—	—
Portfolio Turnover (%)	na	35	46	10	42	17	23	—	—	—
Total Assets (Millions $)	40	106	37	26	14	11	10	—	—	—

PORTFOLIO (as of 10/31/94)

Portfolio Manager: Havell - 1987, Giuliano - 1987

Investm't Category: Tax-Exempt Bond

Cap Gain	Asset Allocation
Cap & Income	Fund of Funds
✔ Income	Index
	Sector
✔ Domestic	Small Cap
Foreign	Socially Conscious
Country/Region	State Specific

Portfolio: stocks 0%   bonds 98%
convertibles 0%   other 0%   cash 2%

Largest Holdings: general obligation 32%

Unrealized Net Capital Gains: -3% of portfolio value

SHAREHOLDER INFORMATION

Minimum Investment
Initial: $2,000   Subsequent: $100

Minimum IRA Investment
Initial: na   Subsequent: na

Maximum Fees
Load: none   12b-1: none
Other: none

Distributions
Income: monthly   Capital Gains: Dec

Exchange Options
Number Per Year: no limit   Fee: none
Telephone: yes (money market fund available)

Services
auto exchange, auto invest, auto withdraw

Neuberger & Berman Partners (NPRTX)

605 Third Ave., 2nd Fl.
New York, NY 10158
(800) 877-9700, (212) 476-8800

Growth & Income

PERFORMANCE

fund inception date: 1/20/75

	3yr Annual	5yr Annual	10yr Annual	Bull	Bear
Return (%)	10.3	9.2	13.3	80.2	-7.9
Differ from Category (+/-)	3.2 abv av	1.3 abv av	1.6 abv av	4.4 abv av	-1.6 blw av

Total Risk	Standard Deviation	Category Risk	Risk Index	Beta
abv av	9.8%	high	1.2	1.1

	1994	1993	1992	1991	1990	1989	1988	1987	1986	1985
Return (%)	-1.8	16.4	17.5	22.3	-5.1	22.7	15.4	4.3	17.2	29.9
Differ from category (+/-) . .	-0.4	3.2	7.3	-5.3	0.9	1.3	-1.6	3.7	1.4	4.2

PER SHARE DATA

	1994	1993	1992	1991	1990	1989	1988	1987	1986	1985
Dividends, Net Income ($) .	0.11	0.11	0.19	0.34	0.74	0.76	0.65	0.70	0.44	0.65
Distrib'ns, Cap Gain ($) . . .	1.60	2.20	1.79	0.78	0.34	1.68	0.00	2.79	2.25	1.27
Net Asset Value ($)	18.52	20.62	19.69	18.44	16.02	18.06	16.72	15.06	17.37	17.16
Expense Ratio (%).	0.81	0.86	0.86	0.88	0.91	0.97	0.95	0.86	0.89	0.93
Net Income to Assets (%). .	0.48	0.83	1.23	2.84	4.53	3.96	3.28	2.93	3.23	4.80
Portfolio Turnover (%).	na	82	97	161	136	157	210	169	181	146
Total Assets (Millions $) . .	1,240	1,200	853	823	794	743	719	758	433	221

PORTFOLIO (as of 8/31/94)

Portfolio Manager: Michael Kassen - 1990

Investm't Category: Growth & Income

Cap Gain	Asset Allocation
✔ Cap & Income	Fund of Funds
Income	Index
	Sector
✔ Domestic	Small Cap
✔ Foreign	Socially Conscious
Country/Region	State Specific

Portfolio: stocks 94% bonds 0%
convertibles 0% other 1% cash 5%

Largest Holdings: insurance 11%, banking & financial services 9%

Unrealized Net Capital Gains: 11% of portfolio value

SHAREHOLDER INFORMATION

Minimum Investment
Initial: $1,000   Subsequent: $100

Minimum IRA Investment
Initial: $250   Subsequent: $100

Maximum Fees
Load: none   12b-1: none
Other: none

Distributions
Income: Dec   Capital Gains: Dec

Exchange Options
Number Per Year: no limit   Fee: none
Telephone: yes (money market fund available)

Services
IRA, pension, auto exchange, auto invest, auto withdraw

Neuberger & Berman Ultra Short Bond (NBMMX)

605 Third Ave., 2nd Fl.
New York, NY 10158
(800) 877-9700, (212) 476-8800

General Bond

PERFORMANCE

fund inception date: 11/7/86

	3yr Annual	5yr Annual	10yr Annual	Bull	Bear
Return (%)	3.0	4.9	na	18.1	0.0
Differ from Category (+/-)	-1.3 low	-2.0 low	na	-22.9 low	3.8 high

Total Risk	Standard Deviation	Category Risk	Risk Index	Avg Mat
low	0.7%	low	0.1	0.5 yrs

	1994	1993	1992	1991	1990	1989	1988	1987	1986	1985
Return (%)	2.2	3.2	3.6	7.4	8.3	9.3	6.8	5.5	—	—
Differ from category (+/-)	4.2	-6.0	-3.0	-7.2	1.1	-2.1	-0.6	3.3	—	—

PER SHARE DATA

	1994	1993	1992	1991	1990	1989	1988	1987	1986	1985
Dividends, Net Income ($)	0.37	0.39	0.52	0.67	0.77	0.92	0.71	0.64	—	—
Distrib'ns, Cap Gain ($)	0.00	0.00	0.00	0.00	0.00	0.00	0.00	0.00	—	—
Net Asset Value ($)	9.45	9.61	9.69	9.86	9.82	9.80	9.83	9.88	—	—
Expense Ratio (%)	0.65	0.65	0.65	0.65	0.65	0.65	0.50	0.50	—	—
Net Income to Assets (%)	3.72	4.09	5.70	6.97	8.14	9.06	6.72	6.03	—	—
Portfolio Turnover (%)	na	115	66	89	120	85	121	39	—	—
Total Assets (Millions $)	90	105	103	98	86	103	125	67	—	—

PORTFOLIO (as of 4/30/94)

Portfolio Manager: Theresa Havell - 1986

Investm't Category: General Bond

Cap Gain	Asset Allocation
Cap & Income	Fund of Funds
✔ Income	Index
	Sector
✔ Domestic	Small Cap
Foreign	Socially Conscious
Country/Region	State Specific

Portfolio: stocks 0% bonds 100%
convertibles 0% other 0% cash 0%

Largest Holdings: corporate 33%, corporate commercial paper 24%

Unrealized Net Capital Gains: 0% of portfolio value

SHAREHOLDER INFORMATION

Minimum Investment
Initial: $2,000   Subsequent: $100

Minimum IRA Investment
Initial: $250   Subsequent: $100

Maximum Fees
Load: none   12b-1: none
Other: none

Distributions
Income: monthly   Capital Gains: Dec

Exchange Options
Number Per Year: no limit   Fee: none
Telephone: yes (money market fund available)

Services
IRA, pension, auto exchange, auto invest, auto withdraw

New Century Capital Port (NCCPX)

Growth

20 William St.
Wellesley, MA 02181
(617) 239-0445

	3yr Annual	5yr Annual	10yr Annual	Bull	Bear
Return (%)	4.6	8.2	na	72.6	-6.5
Differ from Category (+/-)	-3.1 blw av	-1.4 blw av	na	-19.5 blw av	0.1 av

Total Risk	Standard Deviation	Category Risk	Risk Index	Beta
abv av	9.3%	av	1.0	0.9

	1994	1993	1992	1991	1990	1989	1988	1987	1986	1985
Return (%)	0.0	13.8	0.5	37.0	-5.1	—	—	—	—	—
Differ from category (+/-)	0.6	0.4	-11.1	1.3	0.6	—	—	—	—	—

PER SHARE DATA

	1994	1993	1992	1991	1990	1989	1988	1987	1986	1985
Dividends, Net Income ($)	0.23	0.00	0.17	0.11	0.17	—	—	—	—	—
Distrib'ns, Cap Gain ($)	0.77	0.00	1.56	0.27	0.00	—	—	—	—	—
Net Asset Value ($)	11.94	12.93	11.36	13.02	9.78	—	—	—	—	—
Expense Ratio (%)	1.60	1.54	1.58	1.76	1.90	—	—	—	—	—
Net Income to Assets (%)	-0.68	-0.53	-0.14	0.84	1.56	—	—	—	—	—
Portfolio Turnover (%)	107	133	224	156	286	—	—	—	—	—
Total Assets (Millions $)	36	38	36	36	33	—	—	—	—	—

PORTFOLIO (as of 10/31/94)

Portfolio Manager: Douglas Biggar - 1989

Investm't Category: Growth
- ✔ Cap Gain
- Cap & Income
- Income
- ✔ Domestic
- ✔ Foreign
- Country/Region
- Asset Allocation
- ✔ Fund of Funds
- Index
- Sector
- Small Cap
- Socially Conscious
- State Specific

Portfolio: stocks 99% bonds 0%
convertibles 0% other 0% cash 1%

Largest Holdings: growth funds 43%, growth and income funds 14%

Unrealized Net Capital Gains: 7% of portfolio value

SHAREHOLDER INFORMATION

Minimum Investment
Initial: $5,000 Subsequent: $100

Minimum IRA Investment
Initial: $500 Subsequent: $100

Maximum Fees
Load: none 12b-1: 0.25%
Other: none

Distributions
Income: Dec Capital Gains: Dec

Exchange Options
Number Per Year: no limit Fee: none
Telephone: yes (money market fund not available)

Services
IRA, pension, auto invest, auto withdraw

NY Muni (NYMFX)

Tax-Exempt Bond

90 Washington St.
New York, NY 10006
(800) 322-6864, (212) 635-3005

PERFORMANCE

fund inception date: 4/27/81

	3yr Annual	5yr Annual	10yr Annual	Bull	Bear
Return (%)	0.0	2.7	6.2	47.0	-12.1
Differ from Category (+/-)	-4.5 low	-3.4 low	-1.9 low	5.2 abv av	-6.9 low

Total Risk	Standard Deviation	Category Risk	Risk Index	Avg Mat
abv av	8.8%	high	1.4	17.6 yrs

	1994	1993	1992	1991	1990	1989	1988	1987	1986	1985
Return (%)	-20.5	12.5	11.7	15.8	-0.9	9.6	11.5	-7.2	17.6	20.3
Differ from category (+/-) .	-15.3	0.8	3.4	4.5	-7.2	0.6	1.3	-5.9	1.2	2.9

PER SHARE DATA

	1994	1993	1992	1991	1990	1989	1988	1987	1986	1985
Dividends, Net Income ($).	0.06	0.07	0.06	0.06	0.07	0.07	0.08	0.08	0.09	0.09
Distrib'ns, Cap Gain ($) . . .	0.01	0.11	0.00	0.00	0.00	0.00	0.00	0.03	0.05	0.00
Net Asset Value ($)	0.88	1.18	1.21	1.14	1.04	1.12	1.09	1.05	1.25	1.19
Expense Ratio (%)	2.89	2.05	1.69	1.78	1.65	1.69	1.74	2.04	1.48	1.60
Net Income to Assets (%) .	5.85	5.20	5.16	5.47	6.43	6.47	6.94	6.97	6.91	7.88
Portfolio Turnover (%)	na	404	461	365	483	386	463	549	333	424
Total Assets (Millions $) . . .	213	276	197	184	183	238	230	220	261	174

PORTFOLIO (as of 6/30/94)

Portfolio Manager: Lance Brofman - 1981

Investm't Category: Tax-Exempt Bond

Cap Gain	Asset Allocation
Cap & Income	Fund of Funds
✔ Income	Index
	Sector
✔ Domestic	Small Cap
Foreign	Socially Conscious
Country/Region	✔ State Specific

Portfolio: stocks 0% bonds 100%
convertibles 0% other 0% cash 0%

Largest Holdings: general obligation 32%

Unrealized Net Capital Gains: -13% of portfolio value

SHAREHOLDER INFORMATION

Minimum Investment
Initial: $1,000   Subsequent: $100

Minimum IRA Investment
Initial: na   Subsequent: na

Maximum Fees
Load: none   12b-1: 0.50%
Other: none

Distributions
Income: monthly   Capital Gains: Dec, Jan

Exchange Options
Number Per Year: no limit   Fee: none
Telephone: yes (money market fund available)

Services
auto invest, auto withdraw

Nicholas (NICSX)
Growth

700 N. Water St., #1010
Milwaukee, WI 53202
(800) 227-5987, (414) 272-6133

PERFORMANCE

fund inception date: 7/14/69

	3yr Annual	5yr Annual	10yr Annual	Bull	Bear
Return (%)	5.0	9.4	12.7	89.4	-5.4
Differ from Category (+/-)	-2.7 blw av	-0.2 av	-0.2 av	-2.7 av	1.2 abv av

Total Risk	Standard Deviation	Category Risk	Risk Index	Beta
av	7.9%	low	0.8	0.8

	1994	1993	1992	1991	1990	1989	1988	1987	1986	1985
Return (%)	-2.8	5.8	12.6	41.9	-4.3	24.5	17.9	-0.7	11.7	29.6
Differ from category (+/-) . .	-2.2	-7.6	1.0	6.2	1.4	-1.6	-0.1	-2.5	-2.9	0.4

PER SHARE DATA

	1994	1993	1992	1991	1990	1989	1988	1987	1986	1985
Dividends, Net Income ($) .	0.71	0.82	0.68	0.68	0.79	0.92	1.03	1.84	0.88	0.58
Distrib'ns, Cap Gain ($) . . .	3.32	1.05	2.04	0.82	0.41	1.05	0.45	4.03	0.19	0.61
Net Asset Value ($)	48.03	53.64	52.47	49.17	35.76	38.61	32.63	28.94	34.87	32.18
Expense Ratio (%)	0.80	0.76	0.78	0.81	0.82	0.86	0.86	0.86	0.86	0.82
Net Income to Assets (%) . .	1.32	1.53	1.60	2.17	2.56	2.84	3.04	3.13	4.11	3.24
Portfolio Turnover (%)	32	10	15	22	21	24	32	27	13	13
Total Assets (Millions $) . .	2,820	3,179	2,234	1,643	1,390	1,172	1,118	1,299	955	309

PORTFOLIO (as of 9/30/94)

Portfolio Manager: Albert Nicholas - 1969

Investm't Category: Growth

✔ Cap Gain	Asset Allocation
Cap & Income	Fund of Funds
Income	Index
	Sector
✔ Domestic	Small Cap
Foreign	Socially Conscious
Country/Region	State Specific

Portfolio: stocks 88% bonds 0%
convertibles 0% other 0% cash 12%

Largest Holdings: insurance 16%, banks 16%

Unrealized Net Capital Gains: 25% of portfolio value

SHAREHOLDER INFORMATION

Minimum Investment
Initial: $500   Subsequent: $100

Minimum IRA Investment
Initial: $500   Subsequent: $100

Maximum Fees
Load: none   12b-1: none
Other: none

Distributions
Income: May, Dec   Capital Gains: May, Dec

Exchange Options
Number Per Year: no limit   Fee: $5 (tel.)
Telephone: yes; 4/yr (money mkt fund available)

Services
IRA, pension, auto exchange, auto invest, auto withdraw

Nicholas II (NCTWX)

Growth

700 N. Water St., #1010
Milwaukee, WI 53202
(800) 227-5987, (414) 272-6133

PERFORMANCE

fund inception date: 10/17/83

	3yr Annual	5yr Annual	10yr Annual	Bull	Bear
Return (%)	5.5	9.0	12.9	78.3	-4.2
Differ from Category (+/-)	-2.2 blw av	-0.6 av	0.0 av	-13.8 blw av	2.4 abv av

Total Risk	Standard Deviation	Category Risk	Risk Index	Beta
av	8.4%	blw av	0.9	0.6

	1994	1993	1992	1991	1990	1989	1988	1987	1986	1985
Return (%)	1.0	6.4	9.3	39.5	-6.2	17.6	17.2	7.7	10.3	33.8
Differ from category (+/-)	1.6	-7.0	-2.3	3.8	-0.5	-8.5	-0.8	5.9	-4.3	4.6

PER SHARE DATA

	1994	1993	1992	1991	1990	1989	1988	1987	1986	1985
Dividends, Net Income ($)	0.21	0.27	0.24	0.24	0.34	0.31	0.34	0.34	0.42	0.19
Distrib'ns, Cap Gain ($)	1.89	1.40	0.80	0.40	0.14	0.67	0.08	1.30	0.51	0.03
Net Asset Value ($)	24.46	26.32	26.32	25.02	18.42	20.16	17.98	15.69	16.22	15.54
Expense Ratio (%)	0.67	0.67	0.66	0.70	0.71	0.74	0.77	0.74	0.79	1.11
Net Income to Assets (%)	0.72	0.79	1.01	1.24	1.78	1.43	1.97	1.37	2.70	3.29
Portfolio Turnover (%)	17	27	11	12	19	8	18	26	14	10
Total Assets (Millions $)	603	704	646	491	337	422	380	432	299	140

PORTFOLIO (as of 9/30/94)

Portfolio Manager: David Nicholas - 1993

Investm't Category: Growth
- ✔ Cap Gain
- Cap & Income
- Income
- Asset Allocation
- Fund of Funds
- Index
- Sector
- ✔ Domestic
- Foreign
- Country/Region
- ✔ Small Cap
- Socially Conscious
- State Specific

Portfolio: stocks 94% bonds 0%
convertibles 0% other 0% cash 6%

Largest Holdings: healthcare 20%, industrial products and services 16%

Unrealized Net Capital Gains: 32% of portfolio value

SHAREHOLDER INFORMATION

Minimum Investment
Initial: $1,000   Subsequent: $100

Minimum IRA Investment
Initial: $1,000   Subsequent: $100

Maximum Fees
Load: none   12b-1: none
Other: none

Distributions
Income: Dec   Capital Gains: Dec

Exchange Options
Number Per Year: no limit   Fee: $5 (tel.)
Telephone: yes; 4/yr (money mkt fund available)

Services
IRA, pension, auto exchange, auto invest, auto withdraw

Nicholas Income (NCINX)

Corporate High-Yield Bond

700 N. Water St., #1010
Milwaukee, WI 53202
(800) 227-5987, (414) 272-6133

PERFORMANCE

fund inception date: 1/1/29

	3yr Annual	5yr Annual	10yr Annual	Bull	Bear
Return (%)	7.5	8.5	9.2	56.0	-3.2
Differ from Category (+/-)	-2.4 low	-0.8 av	-0.7 blw av	-23.3 low	2.1 high

Total Risk	Standard Deviation	Category Risk	Risk Index	Avg Mat
low	3.1%	low	0.6	6.8 yrs

	1994	1993	1992	1991	1990	1989	1988	1987	1986	1985
Return (%)	-0.1	12.9	10.3	23.0	-1.3	3.9	11.5	2.6	11.4	21.2
Differ from category (+/-) ...	2.6	-5.5	-5.3	-4.4	3.8	2.5	-0.6	1.5	-2.9	-2.0

PER SHARE DATA

	1994	1993	1992	1991	1990	1989	1988	1987	1986	1985
Dividends, Net Income ($) .	0.30	0.29	0.30	0.35	0.39	0.38	0.37	0.47	0.38	0.42
Distrib'ns, Cap Gain ($) ...	0.00	0.00	0.00	0.00	0.00	0.00	0.00	0.00	0.00	0.00
Net Asset Value ($)	3.21	3.52	3.38	3.34	3.01	3.44	3.68	3.64	4.01	3.96
Expense Ratio (%).........	0.59	0.62	0.69	0.76	0.77	0.81	0.83	0.86	0.96	1.00
Net Income to Assets (%)..	8.68	8.42	9.23	10.70	11.74	10.46	10.03	9.79	10.22	57.00
Portfolio Turnover (%).....	36	39	56	28	40	40	12	48	20	12
Total Assets (Millions $) ...	140	159	119	80	61	75	78	70	65	35

PORTFOLIO (as of 6/30/94)

Portfolio Manager: Albert Nicholas - 1977

Investm't Category: Corp. High-Yield Bond
- Cap Gain
- ✔ Cap & Income
- Income
- Asset Allocation
- Fund of Funds
- Index
- Sector
- ✔ Domestic
- Foreign
- Country/Region
- Small Cap
- Socially Conscious
- State Specific

Portfolio: stocks 10%   bonds 86%
convertibles 1%   other 0%   cash 3%

Largest Holdings: diversified products & services 16%, food and beverages 12%

Unrealized Net Capital Gains: -3% of portfolio value

SHAREHOLDER INFORMATION

Minimum Investment
Initial: $500   Subsequent: $100

Minimum IRA Investment
Initial: $500   Subsequent: $100

Maximum Fees
Load: none   12b-1: none
Other: none

Distributions
Income: quarterly   Capital Gains: Dec

Exchange Options
Number Per Year: no limit   Fee: none
Telephone: none

Services
IRA, pension, auto exchange, auto invest, auto withdraw

Nicholas Limited Edition
(NCLEX)
Growth

700 N. Water St., #1010
Milwaukee, WI 53202
(800) 227-5987, (414) 272-6133

this fund is closed to new investors

PERFORMANCE
fund inception date: 5/18/87

	3yr Annual	5yr Annual	10yr Annual	Bull	Bear
Return (%)	7.2	11.6	na	108.7	-6.8
Differ from Category (+/-)	-0.5 av	2.0 abv av	na	16.6 abv av	-0.2 av

Total Risk	Standard Deviation	Category Risk	Risk Index	Beta
abv av	8.9%	blw av	0.9	0.6

	1994	1993	1992	1991	1990	1989	1988	1987	1986	1985
Return (%)............	-3.0	9.0	16.7	43.2	-1.7	17.3	27.2	—	—	—
Differ from category (+/-) ..	-2.4	-4.4	5.1	7.5	4.0	-8.8	9.2	—	—	—

PER SHARE DATA

	1994	1993	1992	1991	1990	1989	1988	1987	1986	1985
Dividends, Net Income ($).	0.10	0.09	0.08	0.12	0.12	0.15	0.10	—	—	—
Distrib'ns, Cap Gain ($) ...	0.91	1.68	0.83	0.24	0.12	0.62	0.25	—	—	—
Net Asset Value ($)	17.09	18.68	18.77	16.86	12.03	12.49	11.29	—	—	—
Expense Ratio (%)	0.88	0.88	0.92	0.94	1.07	1.12	1.32	—	—	—
Net Income to Assets (%) .	0.50	0.42	0.45	1.05	1.10	1.37	1.03	—	—	—
Portfolio Turnover (%)	13	24	24	13	15	31	31	—	—	—
Total Assets (Millions $) ...	142	179	190	175	71	57	33	—	—	—

PORTFOLIO (as of 6/30/94)

Portfolio Manager: David Nicholas - 1993

Investm't Category: Growth

✔ Cap Gain   Asset Allocation
Cap & Income   Fund of Funds
Income   Index
    Sector
✔ Domestic   ✔ Small Cap
Foreign   Socially Conscious
Country/Region   State Specific

Portfolio: stocks 94%   bonds 0%
convertibles 0%   other 0%   cash 6%

Largest Holdings: banks & finance 16%, healthcare 14%

Unrealized Net Capital Gains: 32% of portfolio value

SHAREHOLDER INFORMATION

Minimum Investment
Initial: $2,000   Subsequent: $100

Minimum IRA Investment
Initial: $2,000   Subsequent: $100

Maximum Fees
Load: none   12b-1: none
Other: none

Distributions
Income: Dec   Capital Gains: Dec

Exchange Options
Number Per Year: no limit   Fee: none
Telephone: none

Services
IRA, pension, auto exchange, auto invest, auto withdraw

Nomura Pacific Basin

(NPBFX)

International Stock

180 Maiden Lane
New York, NY 10038
(800) 833-0018, (212) 509-7893

PERFORMANCE

fund inception date: 7/8/85

	3yr Annual	5yr Annual	10yr Annual	Bull	Bear
Return (%)	8.5	3.8	na	65.1	2.2
Differ from Category (+/-)	-0.6 av	-1.1 blw av	na	1.2 av	9.2 high

Total Risk	Standard Deviation	Category Risk	Risk Index	Beta
high	16.5%	high	1.3	0.6

	1994	1993	1992	1991	1990	1989	1988	1987	1986	1985
Return (%)	4.2	40.4	-12.6	11.8	-15.3	22.7	16.3	33.5	74.3	—
Differ from category (+/-) . . .	7.2	1.8	-9.7	-1.3	-4.9	0.2	1.9	19.1	15.3	—

PER SHARE DATA

	1994	1993	1992	1991	1990	1989	1988	1987	1986	1985
Dividends, Net Income ($) .	0.00	0.28	0.02	0.52	0.45	0.10	0.05	0.08	0.30	—
Distrib'ns, Cap Gain ($) . . .	2.25	0.00	0.01	0.34	2.29	3.98	1.21	10.46	0.06	—
Net Asset Value ($)	15.97	17.47	12.64	14.51	13.74	19.27	19.39	17.75	21.13	—
Expense Ratio (%).	1.34	1.51	1.46	1.42	1.32	1.25	1.22	1.45	1.50	—
Net Income to Assets (%).	-0.13	0.01	0.00	0.28	0.04	0.07	0.28	0.14	0.88	—
Portfolio Turnover (%).	56	55	41	76	46	37	61	46	3	—
Total Assets (Millions $)	55	56	44	54	54	73	95	82	32	—

PORTFOLIO (as of 9/30/94)

Portfolio Manager: Takeo Nakamura - 1985

Investm't Category: International Stock

✔ Cap Gain
  Cap & Income
  Income

  Domestic
✔ Foreign
✔ Country/Region

  Asset Allocation
  Fund of Funds
  Index
  Sector
  Small Cap
  Socially Conscious
  State Specific

Portfolio: stocks 99% bonds 0%
convertibles 0% other 0% cash 1%

Largest Holdings: Japan 59%, Malaysia 8%

Unrealized Net Capital Gains: 15% of portfolio value

SHAREHOLDER INFORMATION

Minimum Investment
Initial: $1,000   Subsequent: $0

Minimum IRA Investment
Initial: $1,000   Subsequent: $0

Maximum Fees
Load: none   12b-1: none
Other: none

Distributions
Income: May, Dec   Capital Gains: Dec

Exchange Options
Number Per Year: none Fee:
Telephone:

Services
IRA

Northeast Investors Growth (NTHFX)

Growth

50 Congress St.
Boston, MA 02109
(800) 225-6704, (617) 523-3588

fund inception date: 10/27/80

PERFORMANCE

	3yr Annual	5yr Annual	10yr Annual	Bull	Bear
Return (%)	0.5	7.1	13.1	55.7	-6.6
Differ from Category (+/-)	-7.2 low	-2.5 low	0.2 av	-36.4 low	0.0 av

Total Risk	Standard Deviation	Category Risk	Risk Index	Beta
abv av	9.6%	av	1.0	1.0

	1994	1993	1992	1991	1990	1989	1988	1987	1986	1985
Return (%).	0.0	2.3	-0.7	36.9	1.3	32.9	12.8	-3.3	24.0	35.8
Differ from category (+/-) ..	0.6	-11.1	-12.3	1.2	7.0	6.8	-5.2	-5.1	9.4	6.6

PER SHARE DATA

	1994	1993	1992	1991	1990	1989	1988	1987	1986	1985
Dividends, Net Income ($).	0.19	0.20	0.21	0.36	0.26	0.28	0.27	0.12	0.13	0.05
Distrib'ns, Cap Gain ($) . . .	0.50	4.46	1.57	0.55	0.33	0.30	0.47	0.62	0.52	0.09
Net Asset Value ($)	24.40	25.11	29.11	31.12	23.44	23.70	18.27	16.84	18.20	15.24
Expense Ratio (%)	1.56	1.45	1.42	1.50	1.74	1.77	1.74	1.60	1.87	2.00
Net Income to Assets (%) .	0.61	0.62	0.71	1.02	1.19	1.11	1.25	0.60	0.53	0.92
Portfolio Turnover (%)	na	35	29	16	37	23	16	36	12	36
Total Assets (Millions $)	35	38	43	41	27	27	19	21	20	6

PORTFOLIO (as of 6/30/94)

Portfolio Manager: William Oates Jr. - 1980

Investm't Category: Growth

✔ Cap Gain	Asset Allocation
Cap & Income	Fund of Funds
Income	Index
	Sector
✔ Domestic	Small Cap
Foreign	Socially Conscious
Country/Region	State Specific

Portfolio:	stocks 99%	bonds 0%
convertibles 0%	other 0%	cash 1%

Largest Holdings: banks 17%, entertainment 10%

Unrealized Net Capital Gains: 16% of portfolio value

SHAREHOLDER INFORMATION

Minimum Investment
Initial: $1,000   Subsequent: $0

Minimum IRA Investment
Initial: $500   Subsequent: $0

Maximum Fees
Load: none   12b-1: none
Other: none

Distributions
Income: Dec   Capital Gains: Dec

Exchange Options
Number Per Year: no limit   Fee: none
Telephone: yes (money market fund not available)

Services
IRA, pension, auto exchange, auto invest, auto withdraw

Northeast Investors Trust (NTHEX)

50 Congress St.
Boston, MA 02109
(800) 225-6704, (617) 523-3588

Balanced

PERFORMANCE

fund inception date: 3/1/50

	3yr Annual	5yr Annual	10yr Annual	Bull	Bear
Return (%)	14.0	11.2	11.3	86.9	-2.2
Differ from Category (+/-)	7.6 high	3.2 high	0.0 av	21.9 high	3.5 high

Total Risk	Standard Deviation	Category Risk	Risk Index	Beta
blw av	5.6%	blw av	0.9	0.3

	1994	1993	1992	1991	1990	1989	1988	1987	1986	1985
Return (%)	2.2	23.5	17.4	26.3	-9.1	0.0	14.0	0.1	20.3	25.5
Differ from category (+/-)	4.1	10.1	9.1	2.9	-8.6	-17.3	2.2	-2.3	2.9	1.2

PER SHARE DATA

	1994	1993	1992	1991	1990	1989	1988	1987	1986	1985
Dividends, Net Income ($)	0.98	1.00	1.11	1.30	1.40	1.49	1.54	1.93	1.46	1.46
Distrib'ns, Cap Gain ($)	0.00	0.00	0.00	0.00	0.00	0.00	0.00	0.00	0.00	0.00
Net Asset Value ($)	9.55	10.29	9.21	8.83	8.14	10.43	11.89	11.83	13.70	12.68
Expense Ratio (%)	0.70	0.73	0.79	0.88	0.78	0.72	0.75	0.76	1.24	1.34
Net Income to Assets (%)	9.37	10.53	12.36	15.38	14.35	12.68	13.16	11.59	11.53	12.70
Portfolio Turnover (%)	73	75	59	34	21	32	17	52	42	22
Total Assets (Millions $)	554	562	453	311	277	386	405	348	313	217

PORTFOLIO (as of 9/30/94)

Portfolio Manager: Ernest Monrad - 1960

Investm't Category: Balanced
Cap Gain	✔ Asset Allocation
✔ Cap & Income	Fund of Funds
Income	Index
	Sector
✔ Domestic	Small Cap
Foreign	Socially Conscious
Country/Region	State Specific

Portfolio: stocks 21%   bonds 88%
convertibles 0%   other 2%   cash 0%

Largest Holdings: bonds—recreational 10%, bonds—retail food chains 9%

Unrealized Net Capital Gains: -8% of portfolio value

SHAREHOLDER INFORMATION

Minimum Investment
Initial: $1,000   Subsequent: $0

Minimum IRA Investment
Initial: $500   Subsequent: $0

Maximum Fees
Load: none   12b-1: none
Other: none

Distributions
Income: quarterly   Capital Gains: Dec

Exchange Options
Number Per Year: no limit   Fee: none
Telephone: yes (money market fund not available)

Services
IRA, pension, auto exchange, auto invest, auto withdraw

Oakmark (OAKMX)
Growth

Two N. LaSalle St.
Chicago, IL 60602
(800) 625-6275, (800) 476-9625

	3yr Annual	5yr Annual	10yr Annual	Bull	Bear
Return (%)	26.1	na	na	na	-2.7
Differ from Category (+/-)	18.4 high	na	na	na	3.9 high

Total Risk	Standard Deviation	Category Risk	Risk Index	Beta
abv av	10.0%	abv av	1.0	0.8

	1994	1993	1992	1991	1990	1989	1988	1987	1986	1985
Return (%).	3.3	30.5	48.8	—	—	—	—	—	—	—
Differ from category (+/-) . .	3.9	17.1	37.2	—	—	—	—	—	—	—

PER SHARE DATA

	1994	1993	1992	1991	1990	1989	1988	1987	1986	1985
Dividends, Net Income ($).	0.23	0.23	0.04	—	—	—	—	—	—	—
Distrib'ns, Cap Gain ($) . . .	1.47	0.77	0.21	—	—	—	—	—	—	—
Net Asset Value ($)	22.97	23.93	19.13	—	—	—	—	—	—	—
Expense Ratio (%)	1.22	1.32	1.70	—	—	—	—	—	—	—
Net Income to Assets (%) .	1.19	0.94	-0.24	—	—	—	—	—	—	—
Portfolio Turnover (%)	29	18	34	—	—	—	—	—	—	—
Total Assets (Millions $) .	1,626	1,214	115	—	—	—	—	—	—	—

PORTFOLIO (as of 10/31/94)

Portfolio Manager: Robert Sanborn - 1991

Investm't Category: Growth
- ✔ Cap Gain
- Cap & Income
- Income
- ✔ Domestic
- ✔ Foreign
- Country/Region
- Asset Allocation
- Fund of Funds
- Index
- Sector
- Small Cap
- Socially Conscious
- State Specific

Portfolio: stocks 90%   bonds 0%
convertibles 0%   other 0%   cash 10%

Largest Holdings: food & beverage 15%, other financial 9%

Unrealized Net Capital Gains: 10% of portfolio value

SHAREHOLDER INFORMATION

Minimum Investment
Initial: $2,500   Subsequent: $100

Minimum IRA Investment
Initial: $1,000   Subsequent: $100

Maximum Fees
Load: none   12b-1: none
Other: none

Distributions
Income: Dec   Capital Gains: Dec

Exchange Options
Number Per Year: no limit   Fee: $5
Telephone: yes (money market fund available)

Services
IRA, pension, auto invest, auto withdraw

Oakmark Int'l (OAKIX)

International Stock

Two N. LaSalle St.
Chicago, IL 60602
(800) 625-6275, (800) 476-9625

PERFORMANCE

fund inception date: 9/30/92

	3yr Annual	5yr Annual	10yr Annual	Bull	Bear
Return (%)	na	na	na	na	-12.9
Differ from Category (+/-)	na	na	na	na	-5.9 low

Total Risk	Standard Deviation	Category Risk	Risk Index	Beta
na	na	na	na	na

	1994	1993	1992	1991	1990	1989	1988	1987	1986	1985
Return (%)	-9.0	53.5	—	—	—	—	—	—	—	—
Differ from category (+/-) . .	-6.0	14.9	—	—	—	—	—	—	—	—

PER SHARE DATA

	1994	1993	1992	1991	1990	1989	1988	1987	1986	1985
Dividends, Net Income ($)	0.00	0.08	—	—	—	—	—	—	—	—
Distrib'ns, Cap Gain ($) . . .	1.06	0.15	—	—	—	—	—	—	—	—
Net Asset Value ($)	12.41	14.79	—	—	—	—	—	—	—	—
Expense Ratio (%).	1.37	1.26	—	—	—	—	—	—	—	—
Net Income to Assets (%). .	1.44	1.55	—	—	—	—	—	—	—	—
Portfolio Turnover (%).	55	21	—	—	—	—	—	—	—	—
Total Assets (Millions $) . .	1,079	1,108	—	—	—	—	—	—	—	—

PORTFOLIO (as of 10/31/94)

Portfolio Manager: David Herro - 1992

Investm't Category: International Stock
- ✔ Cap Gain
- Cap & Income
- Income
- Domestic
- ✔ Foreign
- Country/Region
- Asset Allocation
- Fund of Funds
- Index
- Sector
- Small Cap
- Socially Conscious
- State Specific

Portfolio: stocks 96% bonds 0%
convertibles 0% other 0% cash 4%

Largest Holdings: Great Britain 20%, Spain 9%

Unrealized Net Capital Gains: 2% of portfolio value

SHAREHOLDER INFORMATION

Minimum Investment
Initial: $2,500   Subsequent: $100

Minimum IRA Investment
Initial: $1,000   Subsequent: $100

Maximum Fees
Load: none   12b-1: none
Other: none

Distributions
Income: Dec   Capital Gains: Dec

Exchange Options
Number Per Year: no limit   Fee: $5
Telephone: yes (money market fund available)

Services
IRA, pension, auto invest, auto withdraw

Oberweis Emerging Growth (OBEGX)

Aggressive Growth

One Constitution Drive
Aurora, IL 60506
(800) 323-6166, (708) 897-7100

PERFORMANCE

fund inception date: 1/14/87

	3yr Annual	5yr Annual	10yr Annual	Bull	Bear
Return (%)	6.3	17.7	na	177.4	-19.6
Differ from Category (+/-)	-2.6 blw av	5.2 abv av	na	44.2 abv av	-8.8 low

Total Risk	Standard Deviation	Category Risk	Risk Index	Beta
high	21.2%	high	1.5	1.1

	1994	1993	1992	1991	1990	1989	1988	1987	1986	1985
Return (%)	-3.5	9.7	13.7	87.0	0.4	24.9	5.6	—	—	—
Differ from category (+/-)	-2.8	-9.8	2.7	34.9	6.6	-1.9	-9.6	—	—	—

PER SHARE DATA

	1994	1993	1992	1991	1990	1989	1988	1987	1986	1985
Dividends, Net Income ($)	0.00	0.00	0.00	0.00	0.00	0.00	0.00	—	—	—
Distrib'ns, Cap Gain ($)	0.00	0.74	0.00	4.27	0.00	0.00	0.00	—	—	—
Net Asset Value ($)	21.41	22.19	20.90	18.38	12.11	12.06	9.65	—	—	—
Expense Ratio (%)	1.78	1.80	1.99	2.13	2.15	2.00	2.46	—	—	—
Net Income to Assets (%)	-1.06	-1.04	-1.14	-1.27	-1.24	-1.19	-1.80	—	—	—
Portfolio Turnover (%)	74	70	63	114	63	112	67	—	—	—
Total Assets (Millions $)	90	104	54	20	12	13	16	—	—	—

PORTFOLIO (as of 6/30/94)

Portfolio Manager: James D. Oberweis - 1987

Investm't Category: Aggressive Growth
- ✔ Cap Gain
- Cap & Income
- Income
- Asset Allocation
- Fund of Funds
- Index
- Sector

- ✔ Domestic
- Foreign
- Country/Region
- ✔ Small Cap
- Socially Conscious
- State Specific

Portfolio: stocks 92% bonds 0%
convertibles 8% other 0% cash 0%

Largest Holdings: telecommunications 9%, computer local networks 6%

Unrealized Net Capital Gains: 2% of portfolio value

SHAREHOLDER INFORMATION

Minimum Investment
Initial: $1,000   Subsequent: $100

Minimum IRA Investment
Initial: $1,000   Subsequent: $100

Maximum Fees
Load: none   12b-1: 0.50%
Other: none

Distributions
Income: Dec   Capital Gains: Dec

Exchange Options
Number Per Year: none   Fee:
Telephone:

Services
IRA, pension, auto invest, auto withdraw

Oregon Municipal Bond

(ORBFX)

Tax-Exempt Bond

121 S.W. Morrison St.
Suite 1410
Portland, OR 97204
(800) 541-9732, (503) 295-0919

PERFORMANCE

fund inception date: 10/4/84

	3yr Annual	5yr Annual	10yr Annual	Bull	Bear
Return (%)	4.3	5.8	na	33.7	-3.9
Differ from Category (+/-)	-0.2 blw av	-0.3 blw av	na	-8.1 low	1.3 abv av

Total Risk	Standard Deviation	Category Risk	Risk Index	Avg Mat
low	4.1%	low	0.6	8.8 yrs

	1994	1993	1992	1991	1990	1989	1988	1987	1986	1985
Return (%)	-2.6	8.9	7.3	9.8	6.3	7.5	7.6	0.7	—	—
Differ from category (+/-) . . .	2.6	-2.8	-1.0	-1.5	0.0	-1.5	-2.6	2.0	—	—

PER SHARE DATA

	1994	1993	1992	1991	1990	1989	1988	1987	1986	1985
Dividends, Net Income ($) .	0.54	0.56	0.61	0.64	0.64	0.67	0.65	0.69	—	—
Distrib'ns, Cap Gain ($) . . .	0.07	0.01	0.10	0.10	0.07	0.02	0.09	0.01	—	—
Net Asset Value ($)	11.87	12.82	12.31	12.16	11.77	11.75	11.60	11.48	—	—
Expense Ratio (%).	0.98	1.05	1.11	1.21	1.38	1.04	1.21	1.31	—	—
Net Income to Assets (%). .	4.35	4.51	5.04	5.36	5.41	5.82	5.53	6.43	—	—
Portfolio Turnover (%).	na	11	25	53	58	45	31	18	—	—
Total Assets (Millions $)	26	30	20	18	18	19	20	14	—	—

PORTFOLIO (as of 4/30/94)

Portfolio Manager: Jay Willoughby - 1987

Investm't Category: Tax-Exempt Bond

Cap Gain	Asset Allocation
Cap & Income	Fund of Funds
✔ Income	Index
	Sector
✔ Domestic	Small Cap
Foreign	Socially Conscious
Country/Region	✔ State Specific

Portfolio: stocks 0%   bonds 100%
convertibles 0%   other 0%   cash 0%

Largest Holdings: general obligation 28%

Unrealized Net Capital Gains: 2% of portfolio value

SHAREHOLDER INFORMATION

Minimum Investment
Initial: $2,000   Subsequent: $500

Minimum IRA Investment
Initial: na   Subsequent: na

Maximum Fees
Load: none   12b-1: 0.25%
Other: none

Distributions
Income: monthly   Capital Gains: Dec

Exchange Options
Number Per Year: 10   Fee: none
Telephone: yes (money market fund available)

Services
auto invest, auto withdraw

Pacifica Asset Preservation (PCASX)

General Bond

237 Park Ave.
Suite 910
New York, NY 10017
(800) 662-8417, (212) 808-3937

fund inception date: 6/29/90

PERFORMANCE

	3yr Annual	5yr Annual	10yr Annual	Bull	Bear
Return (%)	3.8	na	na	23.0	0.3
Differ from Category (+/-)	-0.5 blw av	na	na	-18.0 low	4.1 high

Total Risk	Standard Deviation	Category Risk	Risk Index	Avg Mat
low	1.0%	low	0.2	0.5 yrs

	1994	1993	1992	1991	1990	1989	1988	1987	1986	1985
Return (%)	2.3	4.5	4.6	9.0	—	—	—	—	—	—
Differ from category (+/-)	4.3	-4.7	-2.0	-5.6	—	—	—	—	—	—

PER SHARE DATA

	1994	1993	1992	1991	1990	1989	1988	1987	1986	1985
Dividends, Net Income ($)	0.47	0.44	0.54	0.67	—	—	—	—	—	—
Distrib'ns, Cap Gain ($)	0.00	0.00	0.01	0.00	—	—	—	—	—	—
Net Asset Value ($)	9.96	10.19	10.18	10.26	—	—	—	—	—	—
Expense Ratio (%)	0.86	0.80	0.75	0.62	—	—	—	—	—	—
Net Income to Assets (%)	3.99	4.64	5.52	6.90	—	—	—	—	—	—
Portfolio Turnover (%)	na	49	21	30	—	—	—	—	—	—
Total Assets (Millions $)	78	144	160	73	—	—	—	—	—	—

PORTFOLIO (as of 9/30/94)

Portfolio Manager: Mark Romano - 1990

Investm't Category: General Bond

Cap Gain	Asset Allocation
Cap & Income	Fund of Funds
✔ Income	Index
	Sector
✔ Domestic	Small Cap
✔ Foreign	Socially Conscious
Country/Region	State Specific

Portfolio: stocks 0%   bonds 100%
convertibles 0%   other 0%   cash 0%

Largest Holdings: corporate 57%, commercial paper 18%

Unrealized Net Capital Gains: 0% of portfolio value

SHAREHOLDER INFORMATION

Minimum Investment
Initial: $500   Subsequent: $50

Minimum IRA Investment
Initial: $250   Subsequent: $50

Maximum Fees
Load: none   12b-1: 0.50%
Other: none

Distributions
Income: monthly   Capital Gains: Dec

Exchange Options
Number Per Year: no limit   Fee: none
Telephone: yes (money market fund available)

Services
IRA, auto invest, auto withdraw

Pacifica Short Term CA Tax-Free (PCATX)

Tax-Exempt Bond

237 Park Ave.
Suite 910
New York, NY 10017
(800) 662-8417, (212) 808-3937

PERFORMANCE

fund inception date: 1/20/93

	3yr Annual	5yr Annual	10yr Annual	Bull	Bear
Return (%)	na	na	na	na	-0.4
Differ from Category (+/-)	na	na	na	na	4.8 high

Total Risk	Standard Deviation	Category Risk	Risk Index	Avg Mat
na	na	na	na	1.9 yrs

	1994	1993	1992	1991	1990	1989	1988	1987	1986	1985
Return (%)	1.1	—	—	—	—	—	—	—	—	—
Differ from category (+/-)	6.3	—	—	—	—	—	—	—	—	—

PER SHARE DATA

	1994	1993	1992	1991	1990	1989	1988	1987	1986	1985
Dividends, Net Income ($)	0.40	—	—	—	—	—	—	—	—	—
Distrib'ns, Cap Gain ($)	0.00	—	—	—	—	—	—	—	—	—
Net Asset Value ($)	9.89	—	—	—	—	—	—	—	—	—
Expense Ratio (%)	0.54	—	—	—	—	—	—	—	—	—
Net Income to Assets (%)	3.76	—	—	—	—	—	—	—	—	—
Portfolio Turnover (%)	na	—	—	—	—	—	—	—	—	—
Total Assets (Millions $)	44	—	—	—	—	—	—	—	—	—

PORTFOLIO (as of 3/31/94)

Portfolio Manager: Keli Chaux - 1992

Investm't Category: Tax-Exempt Bond

Cap Gain	Asset Allocation
Cap & Income	Fund of Funds
✔ Income	Index
	Sector
✔ Domestic	Small Cap
Foreign	Socially Conscious
Country/Region	✔ State Specific

Portfolio: stocks 0% bonds 91%
convertibles 0% other 0% cash 9%

Largest Holdings: general obligation 7%

Unrealized Net Capital Gains: -1% of portfolio value

SHAREHOLDER INFORMATION

Minimum Investment
Initial: $500 Subsequent: $50

Minimum IRA Investment
Initial: na Subsequent: na

Maximum Fees
Load: none 12b-1: 0.50%
Other: none

Distributions
Income: monthly Capital Gains: Dec

Exchange Options
Number Per Year: no limit Fee: none
Telephone: yes (money market fund available)

Services
auto invest, auto withdraw

Pax World (PAXWX)
Balanced

224 State St.
Portsmouth, NH 03801
(800) 767-1729, (603) 431-8022

PERFORMANCE
fund inception date: 8/10/71

	3yr Annual	5yr Annual	10yr Annual	Bull	Bear
Return (%)	0.7	6.3	10.2	33.6	-3.7
Differ from Category (+/-)	-5.7 low	-1.7 blw av	-1.1 blw av	-31.4 low	2.0 high

Total Risk	Standard Deviation	Category Risk	Risk Index	Beta
blw av	5.6%	blw av	0.9	0.5

	1994	1993	1992	1991	1990	1989	1988	1987	1986	1985
Return (%)	2.6	-1.0	0.6	20.7	10.3	24.9	11.4	2.5	8.5	25.7
Differ from category (+/-)	4.5	-14.4	-7.7	-2.7	10.8	7.6	-0.4	0.1	-8.9	1.4

PER SHARE DATA

	1994	1993	1992	1991	1990	1989	1988	1987	1986	1985
Dividends, Net Income ($)	0.50	0.50	0.67	0.77	0.61	0.63	0.61	0.75	0.50	0.52
Distrib'ns, Cap Gain ($)	0.00	0.07	0.13	1.04	0.84	0.25	0.37	1.24	0.71	0.37
Net Asset Value ($)	13.39	13.55	14.27	14.99	13.97	13.98	11.92	11.58	13.19	13.34
Expense Ratio (%)	0.99	0.94	1.00	1.20	1.20	1.10	1.10	1.10	1.20	1.40
Net Income to Assets (%)	3.81	3.63	3.70	5.10	5.40	5.80	5.00	4.10	3.20	4.30
Portfolio Turnover (%)	na	22	17	26	39	37	58	124	57	48
Total Assets (Millions $)	388	464	469	270	120	93	74	66	54	33

PORTFOLIO (as of 6/30/94)

Portfolio Manager: Anthony Brown - 1971

Investm't Category: Balanced

Cap Gain	Asset Allocation
✔ Cap & Income	Fund of Funds
Income	Index
	Sector
✔ Domestic	Small Cap
Foreign	✔ Socially Conscious
Country/Region	State Specific

Portfolio: stocks 69% bonds 31%
convertibles 0% other 0% cash 0%

Largest Holdings: stocks—food 20%, bonds—U.S. government agencies 19%

Unrealized Net Capital Gains: -6% of portfolio value

SHAREHOLDER INFORMATION

Minimum Investment
Initial: $250   Subsequent: $50

Minimum IRA Investment
Initial: $250   Subsequent: $50

Maximum Fees
Load: none   12b-1: 0.25%
Other: none

Distributions
Income: Jul, Dec   Capital Gains: Dec

Exchange Options
Number Per Year: none   Fee:
Telephone:

Services
IRA, pension, auto invest, auto withdraw

PBHG Emerging Growth

(PBEGX)

Aggressive Growth

1255 Drummers Lane
Suite 300
Wayne, PA 19087
(800) 809-8008

PERFORMANCE

fund inception date: 6/15/93

	3yr Annual	5yr Annual	10yr Annual	Bull	Bear
Return (%)	na	na	na	na	-11.9
Differ from Category (+/-)	na	na	na	na	-1.1 av

Total Risk	Standard Deviation	Category Risk	Risk Index	Beta
na	na	na	na	na

	1994	1993	1992	1991	1990	1989	1988	1987	1986	1985
Return (%)	23.7	—	—	—	—	—	—	—	—	—
Differ from category (+/-) . .	24.4	—	—	—	—	—	—	—	—	—

PER SHARE DATA

	1994	1993	1992	1991	1990	1989	1988	1987	1986	1985
Dividends, Net Income ($) .	0.00	—	—	—	—	—	—	—	—	—
Distrib'ns, Cap Gain ($) . . .	0.04	—	—	—	—	—	—	—	—	—
Net Asset Value ($)	15.10	—	—	—	—	—	—	—	—	—
Expense Ratio (%)	1.45	—	—	—	—	—	—	—	—	—
Net Income to Assets (%) .	-0.77	—	—	—	—	—	—	—	—	—
Portfolio Turnover (%)	95	—	—	—	—	—	—	—	—	—
Total Assets (Millions $) . . .	177	—	—	—	—	—	—	—	—	—

PORTFOLIO (as of 10/31/94)

Portfolio Manager: Gary Pilgrim - 1993

Investm't Category: Aggressive Growth

✔ Cap Gain	Asset Allocation
Cap & Income	Fund of Funds
Income	Index
	Sector
✔ Domestic	✔ Small Cap
✔ Foreign	Socially Conscious
Country/Region	State Specific

Portfolio: stocks 79%   bonds 0%
convertibles 0%   other 0%   cash 21%

Largest Holdings: general software 11%,
healthcare services 7%

Unrealized Net Capital Gains: 16% of portfolio value

SHAREHOLDER INFORMATION

Minimum Investment
Initial: $1,000   Subsequent: $0

Minimum IRA Investment
Initial: $0   Subsequent: $0

Maximum Fees
Load: 2.00% redemption   12b-1: none
Other: redemption fee applies for 6 mos

Distributions
Income: Oct   Capital Gains: Oct

Exchange Options
Number Per Year: no limit   Fee: none
Telephone: yes (money market fund available)

Services
IRA, pension, auto invest, auto withdraw

PBHG Growth (PBHGX)

Aggressive Growth

1255 Drummers Lane
Suite 300
Wayne, PA 19087
(800) 809-8008

PERFORMANCE   fund inception date: 12/19/85

	3yr Annual	5yr Annual	10yr Annual	Bull	Bear
Return (%)	25.4	21.9	na	231.4	-18.8
Differ from Category (+/-)	16.5 high	9.4 high	na	98.2 high	-8.0 low

Total Risk	Standard Deviation	Category Risk	Risk Index	Beta
high	21.8%	high	1.5	1.3

	1994	1993	1992	1991	1990	1989	1988	1987	1986	1985
Return (%)	4.7	46.5	28.5	51.6	-9.7	29.4	6.8	11.6	23.9	—
Differ from category (+/-)	5.4	27.0	17.5	-0.5	-3.5	2.6	-8.4	13.8	12.1	—

PER SHARE DATA

	1994	1993	1992	1991	1990	1989	1988	1987	1986	1985
Dividends, Net Income ($)	0.00	0.00	0.00	0.00	0.00	0.04	0.00	0.00	0.07	—
Distrib'ns, Cap Gain ($)	0.01	0.19	2.45	2.43	0.79	2.81	0.03	4.24	0.00	—
Net Asset Value ($)	15.91	15.20	10.51	10.53	8.74	10.71	10.51	9.86	12.32	—
Expense Ratio (%)	1.55	2.39	1.52	1.50	1.32	1.19	1.21	1.31	—	—
Net Income to Assets (%)	-0.78	-1.69	-0.55	-0.09	-0.35	0.20	0.02	0.36	—	—
Portfolio Turnover (%)	94	209	114	228	219	175	208	213	—	—
Total Assets (Millions $)	745	121	7	10	18	23	28	30	—	—

PORTFOLIO (as of 3/31/94)

Portfolio Manager: Gary Pilgrim - 1985,
Harold Baxter - 1985

Investm't Category: Aggressive Growth
- ✔ Cap Gain   Asset Allocation
-   Cap & Income   Fund of Funds
-   Income   Index
                      Sector
- ✔ Domestic   ✔ Small Cap
- ✔ Foreign   Socially Conscious
-   Country/Region   State Specific

Portfolio: stocks 84%   bonds 0%
convertibles 0%   other 0%   cash 16%

Largest Holdings: computer software 13%,
medical products & services 13%

Unrealized Net Capital Gains: -1% of portfolio value

SHAREHOLDER INFORMATION

Minimum Investment
Initial: $1,000   Subsequent: $0

Minimum IRA Investment
Initial: $0   Subsequent: $0

Maximum Fees
Load: 2.00% redemption   12b-1: none
Other: redemption fee applies for 6 mos

Distributions
Income: Oct   Capital Gains: Oct

Exchange Options
Number Per Year: no limit   Fee: none
Telephone: yes (money market fund available)

Services
IRA, pension, auto invest, auto withdraw

Pennsylvania Mutual
(PENNX)
Growth

1414 Avenue of the Americas
New York, NY 10019
(800) 221-4268, (212) 355-7311

PERFORMANCE   fund inception date: 1/1/62

	3yr Annual	5yr Annual	10yr Annual	Bull	Bear
Return (%)	8.6	8.3	12.0	79.9	-5.0
Differ from Category (+/-)	0.9 av	-1.3 blw av	-0.9 blw av	-12.2 blw av	1.6 abv av

Total Risk	Standard Deviation	Category Risk	Risk Index	Beta
blw av	6.5%	low	0.7	0.5

	1994	1993	1992	1991	1990	1989	1988	1987	1986	1985
Return (%)	-0.7	11.2	16.1	31.8	-11.5	16.6	24.4	1.3	11.1	26.7
Differ from category (+/-)	-0.1	-2.2	4.5	-3.9	-5.8	-9.5	6.4	-0.5	-3.5	-2.5

PER SHARE DATA

	1994	1993	1992	1991	1990	1989	1988	1987	1986	1985
Dividends, Net Income ($)	0.11	0.11	0.10	0.12	0.16	0.22	0.12	0.33	0.13	0.09
Distrib'ns, Cap Gain ($)	0.73	0.48	0.37	0.21	0.12	0.41	0.28	1.30	1.11	0.16
Net Asset Value ($)	7.41	8.31	8.00	7.29	5.78	6.85	6.41	5.47	6.98	7.43
Expense Ratio (%)	0.97	0.98	0.91	0.95	0.96	0.97	1.01	0.99	—	—
Net Income to Assets (%)	1.22	0.12	1.48	1.73	2.62	2.93	2.35	2.02	—	—
Portfolio Turnover (%)	na	24	22	29	15	23	24	23	—	—
Total Assets (Millions $)	785	1,032	1,102	789	549	550	445	276	—	—

PORTFOLIO (as of 6/30/94)

Portfolio Manager: C. Royce - 1973, T. Ebright - 1978, J. Fockler - W. George

Investm't Category: Growth

✔ Cap Gain	Asset Allocation
Cap & Income	Fund of Funds
Income	Index
	Sector
✔ Domestic	✔ Small Cap
Foreign	Socially Conscious
Country/Region	State Specific

Portfolio: stocks 91%   bonds 7%
convertibles 0%   other 0%   cash 2%

Largest Holdings: industrial cyclicals 24%, financial 18%

Unrealized Net Capital Gains: 21% of portfolio value

SHAREHOLDER INFORMATION

Minimum Investment
Initial: $2,000   Subsequent: $50

Minimum IRA Investment
Initial: $500   Subsequent: $50

Maximum Fees
Load: 1.00% redemption   12b-1: none
Other: redemption fee applies for 1 year

Distributions
Income: Dec   Capital Gains: Dec

Exchange Options
Number Per Year: no limit   Fee: none
Telephone: yes (money market fund not available)

Services
IRA, pension, auto invest, auto withdraw

Permanent Port (PRPFX)
Balanced

P.O. Box 5847
Austin, TX 78763
(800) 531-5142, (512) 453-7558

	3yr Annual	5yr Annual	10yr Annual	Bull	Bear
Return (%)	4.7	3.6	6.3	31.0	-5.5
Differ from Category (+/-)	-1.7 blw av	-4.4 low	-5.0 low	-34.0 low	0.2 av

Total Risk	Standard Deviation	Category Risk	Risk Index	Beta
blw av	5.0%	low	0.8	0.3

	1994	1993	1992	1991	1990	1989	1988	1987	1986	1985
Return (%).............	-2.8	15.5	2.5	8.0	-3.8	6.3	1.2	13.1	13.6	12.1
Differ from category (+/-) ..	-0.9	2.1	-5.8	-15.4	-3.3	-11.0	-10.6	10.7	-3.8	-12.2

PER SHARE DATA

	1994	1993	1992	1991	1990	1989	1988	1987	1986	1985
Dividends, Net Income ($).	0.22	0.24	0.29	0.91	0.48	0.00	0.00	0.00	0.00	0.00
Distrib'ns, Cap Gain ($) ...	0.00	0.00	0.00	0.00	0.00	0.00	0.02	0.12	0.00	0.00
Net Asset Value ($).....	16.55	17.27	15.16	15.07	14.81	15.91	14.96	14.79	13.18	11.60
Expense Ratio (%)	1.25	1.25	1.27	1.36	1.17	1.17	1.15	1.17	0.90	0.90
Net Income to Assets (%) .	2.65	3.20	3.29	4.22	3.80	3.00	2.53	2.51	3.00	3.53
Portfolio Turnover (%)	45	70	8	32	61	24	22	31	17	10
Total Assets (Millions $)	23	81	72	81	94	98	90	73	72	71

PORTFOLIO (as of 7/31/94)

Portfolio Manager: Terry Coxon - 1982

Investm't Category: Balanced

Cap Gain	✔ Asset Allocation
✔ Cap & Income	Fund of Funds
Income	Index
	Sector
✔ Domestic	Small Cap
✔ Foreign	Socially Conscious
Country/Region	State Specific

Portfolio: stocks 31% bonds 19%
convertibles 0% other 35% cash 15%

Largest Holdings: stocks—gold 19%, bonds—U.S. government 19%

Unrealized Net Capital Gains: 8% of portfolio value

SHAREHOLDER INFORMATION

Minimum Investment
Initial: $1,000   Subsequent: $100

Minimum IRA Investment
Initial: $1,000   Subsequent: $100

Maximum Fees
Load: none   12b-1: none
Other: $35 start-up fee; $1.50/mo maintenance fee

Distributions
Income: Dec   Capital Gains: Dec

Exchange Options
Number Per Year: no limit   Fee: $5
Telephone: yes (money market fund available)

Services
IRA, auto withdraw

Permanent Port—
Versatile Bond (PRVBX)

Corporate Bond

P.O. Box 5847
Austin, TX 78763
(800) 531-5142, (512) 453-7558

PERFORMANCE
fund inception date: 11/12/91

	3yr Annual	5yr Annual	10yr Annual	Bull	Bear
Return (%)	3.9	na	na	na	0.0
Differ from Category (+/-)	-2.0 low	na	na	na	4.3 high

Total Risk	Standard Deviation	Category Risk	Risk Index	Avg Mat
low	1.2%	low	0.4	0.9 yrs

	1994	1993	1992	1991	1990	1989	1988	1987	1986	1985
Return (%)	2.5	3.7	5.5	—	—	—	—	—	—	—
Differ from category (+/-) . . .	4.9	-7.7	-3.4	—	—	—	—	—	—	—

PER SHARE DATA

	1994	1993	1992	1991	1990	1989	1988	1987	1986	1985
Dividends, Net Income ($) .	1.33	0.70	0.01	—	—	—	—	—	—	—
Distrib'ns, Cap Gain ($) . . .	0.02	0.00	0.00	—	—	—	—	—	—	—
Net Asset Value ($)	54.42	54.37	53.07	—	—	—	—	—	—	—
Expense Ratio (%).	0.84	0.89	1.07	—	—	—	—	—	—	—
Net Income to Assets (%) . .	3.62	3.86	4.00	—	—	—	—	—	—	—
Portfolio Turnover (%)	68	224	600	—	—	—	—	—	—	—
Total Assets (Millions $)	72	36	1	—	—	—	—	—	—	—

PORTFOLIO (as of 7/31/94)

Portfolio Manager: Terry Coxon - 1991

Investm't Category: Corporate Bond
Cap Gain	Asset Allocation
Cap & Income	Fund of Funds
✔ Income	Index
	Sector
✔ Domestic	Small Cap
Foreign	Socially Conscious
Country/Region	State Specific

Portfolio: stocks 0% bonds 100%
convertibles 0% other 0% cash 0%

Largest Holdings: utilities 13%, beverages 11%

Unrealized Net Capital Gains: -1% of portfolio value

SHAREHOLDER INFORMATION

Minimum Investment
Initial: $1,000   Subsequent: $100

Minimum IRA Investment
Initial: $1,000   Subsequent: $100

Maximum Fees
Load: none   12b-1: none
Other: $35 start-up fee; $1.50/mo maintenance fee

Distributions
Income: Dec   Capital Gains: Dec

Exchange Options
Number Per Year: no limit   Fee: $5
Telephone: yes (money market fund available)

Services
IRA, auto withdraw

Permanent Treasury Bill
(PRTBX)
Government Bond

P.O. Box 5847
Austin, TX 78763
(800) 531-5142, (512) 453-7558

PERFORMANCE   fund inception date: 9/21/87

	3yr Annual	5yr Annual	10yr Annual	Bull	Bear
Return (%)	2.8	4.1	na	12.9	1.0
Differ from Category (+/-)	-1.2 low	-2.6 low	na	-38.3 low	7.4 high

Total Risk	Standard Deviation	Category Risk	Risk Index	Avg Mat
low	0.2%	low	0.0	0.2 yrs

	1994	1993	1992	1991	1990	1989	1988	1987	1986	1985
Return (%).	3.3	2.2	2.8	5.2	7.3	8.1	6.3	—	—	—
Differ from category (+/-) . .	8.1	-8.7	-3.6	-10.1	1.1	-6.4	-1.6	—	—	—

PER SHARE DATA

	1994	1993	1992	1991	1990	1989	1988	1987	1986	1985
Dividends, Net Income ($).	0.67	1.08	2.41	1.30	0.43	0.00	0.03	—	—	—
Distrib'ns, Cap Gain ($) . . .	0.00	0.00	0.00	0.00	0.00	0.00	0.00	—	—	—
Net Asset Value ($)	66.16	64.67	64.30	64.86	62.85	58.96	54.53	—	—	—
Expense Ratio (%)	0.78	0.73	0.73	0.83	0.54	0.54	0.50	—	—	—
Net Income to Assets (%) .	3.10	2.97	4.87	6.74	7.87	6.70	5.32	—	—	—
Portfolio Turnover (%) 0	0	0	0	0	0	0	—	—	—
Total Assets (Millions $) . . . 122	139	320	208	61	31	7	—	—	—

PORTFOLIO (as of 7/31/94)

Portfolio Manager: Terry Coxon - 1987

Investm't Category: Government Bond

Cap Gain	Asset Allocation
Cap & Income	Fund of Funds
✔ Income	Index
	Sector
✔ Domestic	Small Cap
Foreign	Socially Conscious
Country/Region	State Specific

Portfolio: stocks 0% bonds 100%
convertibles 0% other 0% cash 0%

Largest Holdings: U.S. government 100%

Unrealized Net Capital Gains: 0% of portfolio value

SHAREHOLDER INFORMATION

Minimum Investment
Initial: $1,000   Subsequent: $100

Minimum IRA Investment
Initial: $1,000   Subsequent: $100

Maximum Fees
Load: none   12b-1: none
Other: $35 start-up fee; $1.50/mo maintenance fee

Distributions
Income: Dec   Capital Gains: Dec

Exchange Options
Number Per Year: no limit   Fee: $5
Telephone: yes (money market fund available)

Services
IRA, auto withdraw

Perritt Capital Growth

(PRCGX)

Aggressive Growth

680 N. Lake Shore Dr.
2038 Tower Offices
Chicago, IL 60611
(800) 338-1579, (312) 649-6940

PERFORMANCE

fund inception date: 5/11/88

	3yr Annual	5yr Annual	10yr Annual	Bull	Bear
Return (%)	2.0	4.2	na	67.5	-11.3
Differ from Category (+/-)	-6.9 low	-8.3 low	na	-65.7 low	-0.5 av

Total Risk	Standard Deviation	Category Risk	Risk Index	Beta
abv av	10.7%	low	0.7	0.6

	1994	1993	1992	1991	1990	1989	1988	1987	1986	1985
Return (%)	-5.0	5.2	6.4	38.8	-16.7	2.0	—	—	—	—
Differ from category (+/-)	-4.3	-14.3	-4.6	-13.3	-10.5	-24.8	—	—	—	—

PER SHARE DATA

	1994	1993	1992	1991	1990	1989	1988	1987	1986	1985
Dividends, Net Income ($)	0.00	0.00	0.00	0.00	0.06	0.17	—	—	—	—
Distrib'ns, Cap Gain ($)	0.60	0.54	0.36	0.12	0.00	0.00	—	—	—	—
Net Asset Value ($)	11.24	12.48	12.37	11.96	8.71	10.54	—	—	—	—
Expense Ratio (%)	2.00	1.96	2.30	2.50	2.50	2.50	—	—	—	—
Net Income to Assets (%)	-1.00	-1.10	-1.10	-0.02	0.90	1.80	—	—	—	—
Portfolio Turnover (%)	39	34	24	37	24	23	—	—	—	—
Total Assets (Millions $)	6	7	7	6	4	6	—	—	—	—

PORTFOLIO (as of 4/30/94)

Portfolio Manager: Gerald Perritt - 1988

Investm't Category: Aggressive Growth

✔ Cap Gain	Asset Allocation
Cap & Income	Fund of Funds
Income	Index
	Sector
✔ Domestic	✔ Small Cap
✔ Foreign	Socially Conscious
Country/Region	State Specific

Portfolio: stocks 94% bonds 0%
convertibles 0% other 0% cash 6%

Largest Holdings: computers 13%, consumer 12%

Unrealized Net Capital Gains: 11% of portfolio value

SHAREHOLDER INFORMATION

Minimum Investment
Initial: $1,000   Subsequent: $250

Minimum IRA Investment
Initial: $250   Subsequent: $250

Maximum Fees
Load: none   12b-1: none
Other: none

Distributions
Income: Dec   Capital Gains: Dec

Exchange Options
Number Per Year: none   Fee:
Telephone:

Services
IRA, pension, auto invest, auto withdraw

Philadelphia (PHILX)

Growth & Income

1200 N. Federal Hwy.
Suite 424
Boca Raton, FL 33432
(800) 749-9933, (407) 395-2155

PERFORMANCE

	3yr Annual	5yr Annual	10yr Annual	Bull	Bear
Return (%)	8.7	3.8	9.6	57.3	-8.7
Differ from Category (+/-)	1.6 abv av	-4.1 low	-2.1 low	-18.5 low	-2.4 low

Total Risk	Standard Deviation	Category Risk	Risk Index	Beta
av	7.9%	av	1.0	0.6

	1994	1993	1992	1991	1990	1989	1988	1987	1986	1985
Return (%).	-8.5	17.5	19.7	5.7	-11.3	32.6	15.2	3.8	7.6	21.9
Differ from category (+/-) . .	-7.1	4.3	9.5	-21.9	-5.3	11.2	-1.8	3.2	-8.2	-3.8

PER SHARE DATA

	1994	1993	1992	1991	1990	1989	1988	1987	1986	1985
Dividends, Net Income ($).	0.09	0.13	0.08	0.09	0.18	0.14	0.09	0.14	0.22	0.21
Distrib'ns, Cap Gain ($) . . .	0.03	0.62	0.08	0.00	0.00	0.89	0.16	1.77	2.35	0.82
Net Asset Value ($)	6.29	7.01	6.61	5.66	5.44	6.34	5.57	5.05	6.70	8.54
Expense Ratio (%)	1.70	1.60	1.79	1.61	1.19	0.95	0.90	0.87	0.83	0.90
Net Income to Assets (%) .	1.73	1.81	1.37	1.73	2.95	2.02	1.50	1.81	2.37	2.42
Portfolio Turnover (%)	na	24	39	49	43	9	16	152	147	60
Total Assets (Millions $)	80	94	86	82	88	110	91	89	109	108

PORTFOLIO (as of 5/31/94)

Portfolio Manager: Donald H. Baxter - 1987

Investm't Category: Growth & Income
Cap Gain	Asset Allocation
✔ Cap & Income	Fund of Funds
Income	Index
	Sector
✔ Domestic	Small Cap
✔ Foreign	Socially Conscious
Country/Region	State Specific

Portfolio: stocks 50% bonds 31%
convertibles 0% other 2% cash 17%

Largest Holdings: U.S. government bonds 31%, communications stocks 13%

Unrealized Net Capital Gains: 16% of portfolio value

SHAREHOLDER INFORMATION

Minimum Investment
Initial: $1,000 Subsequent: $0

Minimum IRA Investment
Initial: $1,000 Subsequent: $0

Maximum Fees
Load: none 12b-1: 0.25%
Other: none

Distributions
Income: quarterly Capital Gains: Dec

Exchange Options
Number Per Year: none Fee:
Telephone:

Services
IRA, pension, auto invest, auto withdraw

Portico Balanced—Retail

(POBKX)

Balanced

615 E. Michigan St.
P.O. Box 3011
Milwaukee, WI 53201
(800) 982-8909, (414) 287-3710

fund inception date: 3/30/92

	3yr Annual	5yr Annual	10yr Annual	Bull	Bear
Return (%)	na	na	na	na	-9.2
Differ from Category (+/-)	na	na	na	na	-3.5 low

Total Risk	Standard Deviation	Category Risk	Risk Index	Beta
na	na	na	na	na

	1994	1993	1992	1991	1990	1989	1988	1987	1986	1985
Return (%)	-4.2	8.2	—	—	—	—	—	—	—	—
Differ from category (+/-) . .	-2.3	-5.2	—	—	—	—	—	—	—	—

PER SHARE DATA

	1994	1993	1992	1991	1990	1989	1988	1987	1986	1985
Dividends, Net Income ($) .	0.45	0.46	—	—	—	—	—	—	—	—
Distrib'ns, Cap Gain ($) . . .	0.00	0.00	—	—	—	—	—	—	—	—
Net Asset Value ($)	21.58	23.01	—	—	—	—	—	—	—	—
Expense Ratio (%)	0.74	0.75	—	—	—	—	—	—	—	—
Net Income to Assets (%) . .	2.03	2.24	—	—	—	—	—	—	—	—
Portfolio Turnover (%)	29	72	—	—	—	—	—	—	—	—
Total Assets (Millions $) . . .	103	87	—	—	—	—	—	—	—	—

PORTFOLIO (as of 4/30/94)

Portfolio Manager: Teresa Westman - 1992,
Bart Wear - 1994

Investm't Category: Balanced
Cap Gain	Asset Allocation
✔ Cap & Income	Fund of Funds
Income	Index
	Sector
✔ Domestic	Small Cap
✔ Foreign	Socially Conscious
Country/Region	State Specific

Portfolio: stocks 60% bonds 34%
convertibles 0% other 0% cash 6%

Largest Holdings: bonds—U. S. government
20%, bonds—corporate 10%

Unrealized Net Capital Gains: 4% of portfolio value

SHAREHOLDER INFORMATION

Minimum Investment
Initial: $1,000   Subsequent: $100

Minimum IRA Investment
Initial: $100   Subsequent: $100

Maximum Fees
Load: 4.00% front   12b-1: none
Other: none

Distributions
Income: quarterly   Capital Gains: Dec

Exchange Options
Number Per Year: 4   Fee: none
Telephone: yes (money market fund available)

Services
IRA, pension, auto exchange, auto invest, auto withdraw

Portico Bond
IMMDEX—Retail (POBIX)
General Bond

615 E. Michigan St.
P.O. Box 3011
Milwaukee, WI 53201
(800) 982-8909, (414) 287-3710

PERFORMANCE

fund inception date: 12/29/89

	3yr Annual	5yr Annual	10yr Annual	Bull	Bear
Return (%)	4.9	7.8	na	48.8	-5.4
Differ from Category (+/-)	0.6 abv av	0.9 high	na	7.8 abv av	-1.6 blw av

Total Risk	Standard Deviation	Category Risk	Risk Index	Avg Mat
low	4.3%	abv av	1.1	8.4 yrs

	1994	1993	1992	1991	1990	1989	1988	1987	1986	1985
Return (%).	-3.0	10.9	7.5	16.5	8.2	—	—	—	—	—
Differ from category (+/-) . .	-1.0	1.7	0.9	1.9	1.0	—	—	—	—	—

PER SHARE DATA

	1994	1993	1992	1991	1990	1989	1988	1987	1986	1985
Dividends, Net Income ($).	1.64	1.65	1.77	1.89	1.90	—	—	—	—	—
Distrib'ns, Cap Gain ($) . . .	0.04	0.50	0.21	0.14	0.00	—	—	—	—	—
Net Asset Value ($)	25.29	27.82	27.04	27.03	25.05	—	—	—	—	—
Expense Ratio (%)	0.49	0.50	0.50	0.50	0.50	—	—	—	—	—
Net Income to Assets (%) .	5.96	6.10	6.92	7.85	8.10	—	—	—	—	—
Portfolio Turnover (%)	32	81	38	132	111	—	—	—	—	—
Total Assets (Millions $) . . .	249	258	181	90	44	—	—	—	—	—

PORTFOLIO (as of 4/30/94)

Portfolio Manager: Mary Ellen Stanek - 1989,
Teresa Westman - 1992

Investm't Category: General Bond
Cap Gain	Asset Allocation
Cap & Income	Fund of Funds
✔ Income	Index
	Sector
✔ Domestic	Small Cap
✔ Foreign	Socially Conscious
Country/Region	State Specific

Portfolio: stocks 0%   bonds 93%
convertibles 0%   other 0%   cash 7%

Largest Holdings: corporate 39%, U.S. government 35%

Unrealized Net Capital Gains: -2% of portfolio value

SHAREHOLDER INFORMATION

Minimum Investment
Initial: $1,000   Subsequent: $100

Minimum IRA Investment
Initial: $100   Subsequent: $100

Maximum Fees
Load: 2.00% front   12b-1: none
Other: 0.25% purchase adjustment

Distributions
Income: quarterly   Capital Gains: Dec

Exchange Options
Number Per Year: 4   Fee: none
Telephone: yes (money market fund available)

Services
IRA, pension, auto exchange, auto invest, auto withdraw

Portico Equity Index—Retail (POEIX)

Growth & Income

615 E. Michigan St.
P.O. Box 3011
Milwaukee, WI 53201
(800) 982-8909, (414) 287-3710

PERFORMANCE   fund inception date: 12/29/89

	3yr Annual	5yr Annual	10yr Annual	Bull	Bear
Return (%)	5.6	8.1	na	70.4	-6.6
Differ from Category (+/-)	-1.5 blw av	0.2 av	na	-5.4 blw av	-0.3 av

Total Risk	Standard Deviation	Category Risk	Risk Index	Beta
av	7.8%	blw av	0.9	1.0

	1994	1993	1992	1991	1990	1989	1988	1987	1986	1985
Return (%)	1.0	9.1	6.9	29.9	-3.2	—	—	—	—	—
Differ from category (+/-)	2.4	-4.1	-3.3	2.3	2.8	—	—	—	—	—

PER SHARE DATA

	1994	1993	1992	1991	1990	1989	1988	1987	1986	1985
Dividends, Net Income ($)	0.79	0.75	0.72	0.73	0.75	—	—	—	—	—
Distrib'ns, Cap Gain ($)	0.06	0.00	0.00	0.01	0.06	—	—	—	—	—
Net Asset Value ($)	32.38	32.91	30.87	29.57	23.37	—	—	—	—	—
Expense Ratio (%)	0.50	0.50	0.50	0.50	0.49	—	—	—	—	—
Net Income to Assets (%)	2.23	2.27	2.48	2.82	3.01	—	—	—	—	—
Portfolio Turnover (%)	3	14	6	1	9	—	—	—	—	—
Total Assets (Millions $)	106	77	81	51	36	—	—	—	—	—

PORTFOLIO (as of 4/30/94)

Portfolio Manager: D. Tranchita - 1992

Investm't Category: Growth & Income

Cap Gain	Asset Allocation
✔ Cap & Income	Fund of Funds
Income	✔ Index
	Sector
✔ Domestic	Small Cap
Foreign	Socially Conscious
Country/Region	State Specific

Portfolio: stocks 96%   bonds 0%
convertibles 0%   other 0%   cash 4%

Largest Holdings: S&P 500 stock price index

Unrealized Net Capital Gains: 20% of portfolio value

SHAREHOLDER INFORMATION

Minimum Investment
Initial: $1,000   Subsequent: $100

Minimum IRA Investment
Initial: $100   Subsequent: $100

Maximum Fees
Load: 4.00% front   12b-1: none
Other: 0.25% purchase adustment

Distributions
Income: quarterly   Capital Gains: Dec

Exchange Options
Number Per Year: 4   Fee: none
Telephone: yes (money market fund available)

Services
IRA, pension, auto exchange, auto invest, auto withdraw

Portico Growth & Income—Retail (POIGX)

Growth & Income

615 E. Michigan St.
P.O. Box 3011
Milwaukee, WI 53201
(800) 982-8909, (414) 287-3710

PERFORMANCE

fund inception date: 12/29/89

	3yr Annual	5yr Annual	10yr Annual	Bull	Bear
Return (%)	4.0	6.5	na	50.2	-4.6
Differ from Category (+/-)	-3.1 low	-1.4 blw av	na	-25.6 low	1.7 abv av

Total Risk	Standard Deviation	Category Risk	Risk Index	Beta
av	6.8%	low	0.8	0.8

	1994	1993	1992	1991	1990	1989	1988	1987	1986	1985
Return (%).............	0.1	6.6	5.4	22.2	-0.2	—	—	—	—	—
Differ from category (+/-) ..	1.5	-6.6	-4.8	-5.4	5.8	—	—	—	—	—

PER SHARE DATA

	1994	1993	1992	1991	1990	1989	1988	1987	1986	1985
Dividends, Net Income ($).	0.44	0.50	0.69	0.78	0.87	—	—	—	—	—
Distrib'ns, Cap Gain ($)...	0.60	0.59	0.18	0.00	0.00	—	—	—	—	—
Net Asset Value ($).....	22.17	23.18	22.79	22.46	19.06	—	—	—	—	—
Expense Ratio (%)	0.89	0.88	0.75	0.75	0.74	—	—	—	—	—
Net Income to Assets (%) .	1.94	2.44	3.16	3.93	4.39	—	—	—	—	—
Portfolio Turnover (%)	29	86	31	28	50	—	—	—	—	—
Total Assets (Millions $) ...	162	164	136	103	66	—	—	—	—	—

PORTFOLIO (as of 4/30/94)

Portfolio Manager: Marian Zentmyer - 1993

Investm't Category: Growth & Income

Cap Gain	Asset Allocation
✔ Cap & Income	Fund of Funds
Income	Index
	Sector
✔ Domestic	Small Cap
✔ Foreign	Socially Conscious
Country/Region	State Specific

Portfolio: stocks 81% bonds 0%
convertibles 13% other 0% cash 6%

Largest Holdings: chemicals 8%, drugs 7%

Unrealized Net Capital Gains: 5% of portfolio value

SHAREHOLDER INFORMATION

Minimum Investment
Initial: $1,000   Subsequent: $100

Minimum IRA Investment
Initial: $100   Subsequent: $100

Maximum Fees
Load: 4.00% front   12b-1: none
Other: none

Distributions
Income: quarterly   Capital Gains: Dec

Exchange Options
Number Per Year: 4   Fee: none
Telephone: yes (money market fund available)

Services
IRA, pension, auto exchange, auto invest, auto withdraw

Portico Interm Bond Market—Retail (POIMX)

General Bond

615 E. Michigan St.
P.O. Box 3011
Milwaukee, WI 53201
(800) 982-8909, (414) 287-3710

PERFORMANCE   fund inception date: 1/5/93

	3yr Annual	5yr Annual	10yr Annual	Bull	Bear
Return (%)	na	na	na	na	-3.7
Differ from Category (+/-)	na	na	na	na	0.1 av

Total Risk	Standard Deviation	Category Risk	Risk Index	Avg Mat
na	na	na	na	4.1 yrs

	1994	1993	1992	1991	1990	1989	1988	1987	1986	1985
Return (%)	-2.1	—	—	—	—	—	—	—	—	—
Differ from category (+/-)	-0.1	—	—	—	—	—	—	—	—	—

PER SHARE DATA

	1994	1993	1992	1991	1990	1989	1988	1987	1986	1985
Dividends, Net Income ($)	0.54	—	—	—	—	—	—	—	—	—
Distrib'ns, Cap Gain ($)	0.00	—	—	—	—	—	—	—	—	—
Net Asset Value ($)	9.54	—	—	—	—	—	—	—	—	—
Expense Ratio (%)	0.50	—	—	—	—	—	—	—	—	—
Net Income to Assets (%)	4.77	—	—	—	—	—	—	—	—	—
Portfolio Turnover (%)	14	—	—	—	—	—	—	—	—	—
Total Assets (Millions $)	89	—	—	—	—	—	—	—	—	—

PORTFOLIO (as of 4/30/94)

Portfolio Manager: Mary Ellen Stanek - 1993, Teresa Westman - 1993

Investm't Category: General Bond

Cap Gain	Asset Allocation
Cap & Income	Fund of Funds
✔ Income	Index
	Sector
✔ Domestic	Small Cap
Foreign	Socially Conscious
Country/Region	State Specific

Portfolio: stocks 0%   bonds 89%
convertibles 0%   other 0%   cash 11%

Largest Holdings: corporate 42%, U.S. government 34%

Unrealized Net Capital Gains: -4% of portfolio value

SHAREHOLDER INFORMATION

Minimum Investment
Initial: $1,000   Subsequent: $100

Minimum IRA Investment
Initial: $100   Subsequent: $100

Maximum Fees
Load: 2.00% front   12b-1: none
Other: 0.25% purchase adjustment

Distributions
Income: monthly   Capital Gains: Dec

Exchange Options
Number Per Year: 4   Fee: none
Telephone: yes (money market fund available)

Services
IRA, pension, auto exchange, auto invest, auto withdraw

Portico MidCore Growth—Retail (POMGX)

Growth

615 E. Michigan St.
P.O. Box 3011
Milwaukee, WI 53201
(800) 982-8909, (414) 287-3710

PERFORMANCE

fund inception date: 12/29/92

	3yr Annual	5yr Annual	10yr Annual	Bull	Bear
Return (%)	na	na	na	na	-9.6
Differ from Category (+/-)	na	na	na	na	-3.0 low

Total Risk	Standard Deviation	Category Risk	Risk Index	Beta
na	na	na	na	na

	1994	1993	1992	1991	1990	1989	1988	1987	1986	1985
Return (%)	-5.3	9.9	—	—	—	—	—	—	—	—
Differ from category (+/-)	-4.7	-3.5	—	—	—	—	—	—	—	—

PER SHARE DATA

	1994	1993	1992	1991	1990	1989	1988	1987	1986	1985
Dividends, Net Income ($)	0.06	0.11	—	—	—	—	—	—	—	—
Distrib'ns, Cap Gain ($)	0.00	0.00	—	—	—	—	—	—	—	—
Net Asset Value ($)	20.74	21.97	—	—	—	—	—	—	—	—
Expense Ratio (%)	0.86	0.89	—	—	—	—	—	—	—	—
Net Income to Assets (%)	0.33	0.57	—	—	—	—	—	—	—	—
Portfolio Turnover (%)	15	46	—	—	—	—	—	—	—	—
Total Assets (Millions $)	112	93	—	—	—	—	—	—	—	—

PORTFOLIO (as of 4/30/94)

Portfolio Manager: Bart Wear - 1992

Investm't Category: Growth

✔ Cap Gain	Asset Allocation
Cap & Income	Fund of Funds
Income	Index
	Sector
✔ Domestic	Small Cap
✔ Foreign	Socially Conscious
Country/Region	State Specific

Portfolio:	stocks 93%	bonds 0%
convertibles 0%	other 0%	cash 7%

Largest Holdings: financial services 8%, entertainment and leisure 7%

Unrealized Net Capital Gains: 8% of portfolio value

SHAREHOLDER INFORMATION

Minimum Investment
Initial: $1,000   Subsequent: $100

Minimum IRA Investment
Initial: $100   Subsequent: $100

Maximum Fees
Load: 4.00% front   12b-1: none
Other: none

Distributions
Income: quarterly   Capital Gains: Dec

Exchange Options
Number Per Year: 4   Fee: none
Telephone: yes (money market fund available)

Services
IRA, pension, auto exchange, auto invest, auto withdraw

Portico Short Term Bond Market—Retail (POSEX)

General Bond

615 E. Michigan St.
P.O. Box 3011
Milwaukee, WI 53201
(800) 982-8909, (414) 287-3710

PERFORMANCE

fund inception date: 12/29/89

	3yr Annual	5yr Annual	10yr Annual	Bull	Bear
Return (%)	4.7	6.9	na	33.4	-1.2
Differ from Category (+/-)	0.4 abv av	0.0 av	na	-7.6 blw av	2.6 high

Total Risk	Standard Deviation	Category Risk	Risk Index	Avg Mat
low	2.1%	low	0.5	2.7 yrs

	1994	1993	1992	1991	1990	1989	1988	1987	1986	1985
Return (%)	0.9	6.4	6.8	13.5	7.6	—	—	—	—	—
Differ from category (+/-) . . .	2.9	-2.8	0.2	-1.1	0.4	—	—	—	—	—

PER SHARE DATA

	1994	1993	1992	1991	1990	1989	1988	1987	1986	1985
Dividends, Net Income ($) .	0.57	0.57	0.63	0.71	0.79	—	—	—	—	—
Distrib'ns, Cap Gain ($) . . .	0.00	0.12	0.14	0.02	0.00	—	—	—	—	—
Net Asset Value ($)	9.92	10.40	10.43	10.50	9.94	—	—	—	—	—
Expense Ratio (%).	0.50	0.52	0.60	0.60	0.60	—	—	—	—	—
Net Income to Assets (%). .	5.13	5.50	6.00	7.13	7.93	—	—	—	—	—
Portfolio Turnover (%).	32	87	82	67	57	—	—	—	—	—
Total Assets (Millions $) . . .	116	138	129	63	23	—	—	—	—	—

PORTFOLIO (as of 4/30/94)

Portfolio Manager: Mary Ellen Stanek - 1989, Daniel Tranchita - 1993

Investm't Category: General Bond

Cap Gain	Asset Allocation
Cap & Income	Fund of Funds
✔ Income	Index
	Sector
✔ Domestic	Small Cap
✔ Foreign	Socially Conscious
Country/Region	State Specific

Portfolio: stocks 0%   bonds 96%
convertibles 0%   other 0%   cash 4%

Largest Holdings: corporate 48%, mortgage-backed 18%

Unrealized Net Capital Gains: -2% of portfolio value

SHAREHOLDER INFORMATION

Minimum Investment
Initial: $1,000   Subsequent: $100

Minimum IRA Investment
Initial: $100   Subsequent: $100

Maximum Fees
Load: 2.00% front   12b-1: none
Other: 0.25% purchase adjustment

Distributions
Income: monthly   Capital Gains: Dec

Exchange Options
Number Per Year: 4   Fee: none
Telephone: yes (money market fund available)

Services
IRA, pension, auto exchange, auto invest, auto withdraw

Portico Special Growth—Retail (POSGX)

Growth

615 E. Michigan St.
P.O. Box 3011
Milwaukee, WI 53201
(800) 982-8909, (414) 287-3710

PERFORMANCE

fund inception date: 12/28/89

	3yr Annual	5yr Annual	10yr Annual	Bull	Bear
Return (%)	4.3	12.6	na	108.0	-11.3
Differ from Category (+/-)	-3.4 blw av	3.0 high	na	15.9 abv av	-4.7 low

Total Risk	Standard Deviation	Category Risk	Risk Index	Beta
abv av	12.0%	high	1.2	0.9

	1994	1993	1992	1991	1990	1989	1988	1987	1986	1985
Return (%).	-2.0	8.0	7.2	57.9	1.0	—	—	—	—	—
Differ from category (+/-) . .	-1.4	-5.4	-4.4	22.2	6.7	—	—	—	—	—

PER SHARE DATA

	1994	1993	1992	1991	1990	1989	1988	1987	1986	1985
Dividends, Net Income ($).	0.02	0.07	0.18	0.21	0.30	—	—	—	—	—
Distrib'ns, Cap Gain ($) . . .	0.21	0.00	0.62	1.72	0.00	—	—	—	—	—
Net Asset Value ($)	32.46	33.37	30.96	29.67	20.16	—	—	—	—	—
Expense Ratio (%)	0.87	0.88	0.76	0.75	0.74	—	—	—	—	—
Net Income to Assets (%) .	0.20	0.24	0.65	1.10	1.41	—	—	—	—	—
Portfolio Turnover (%)	29	58	32	48	42	—	—	—	—	—
Total Assets (Millions $) . . .	388	355	205	96	39	—	—	—	—	—

PORTFOLIO (as of 4/30/94)

Portfolio Manager: J. Scott Harkness - 1989, Joseph J. Docter - 1989

Investm't Category: Growth

✔ Cap Gain
    Asset Allocation
    Cap & Income
    Fund of Funds
    Income
    Index
    Sector
✔ Domestic
    Small Cap
✔ Foreign
    Socially Conscious
    Country/Region
    State Specific

Portfolio: stocks 89%   bonds 0%
convertibles 0%   other 0%   cash 11%

Largest Holdings: healthcare service and supplies 14%, retail 10%

Unrealized Net Capital Gains: 15% of portfolio value

SHAREHOLDER INFORMATION

Minimum Investment
Initial: $1,000   Subsequent: $100

Minimum IRA Investment
Initial: $100   Subsequent: $100

Maximum Fees
Load: 4.00% front   12b-1: none
Other: none

Distributions
Income: quarterly   Capital Gains: Dec

Exchange Options
Number Per Year: 4   Fee: none
Telephone: yes (money market fund available)

Services
IRA, pension, auto exchange, auto invest, auto withdraw

Portico Tax-Exempt Interm Bond—Retail

(POTKX) *Tax-Exempt Bond*

615 E. Michigan St.
P.O. Box 3011
Milwaukee, WI 53201
(800) 982-8909, (414) 287-3710

PERFORMANCE

fund inception date: 2/8/93

	3yr Annual	5yr Annual	10yr Annual	Bull	Bear
Return (%)	na	na	na	na	-2.9
Differ from Category (+/-)	na	na	na	na	2.3 high

Total Risk	Standard Deviation	Category Risk	Risk Index	Avg Mat
na	na	na	na	5.3 yrs

	1994	1993	1992	1991	1990	1989	1988	1987	1986	1985
Return (%)	-1.6	—	—	—	—	—	—	—	—	—
Differ from category (+/-)	3.6	—	—	—	—	—	—	—	—	—

PER SHARE DATA

	1994	1993	1992	1991	1990	1989	1988	1987	1986	1985
Dividends, Net Income ($)	0.42	—	—	—	—	—	—	—	—	—
Distrib'ns, Cap Gain ($)	0.00	—	—	—	—	—	—	—	—	—
Net Asset Value ($)	9.72	—	—	—	—	—	—	—	—	—
Expense Ratio (%)	0.60	—	—	—	—	—	—	—	—	—
Net Income to Assets (%)	3.87	—	—	—	—	—	—	—	—	—
Portfolio Turnover (%)	31	—	—	—	—	—	—	—	—	—
Total Assets (Millions $)	29	—	—	—	—	—	—	—	—	—

PORTFOLIO (as of 4/30/94)

Portfolio Manager: Gary Elfe - 1993

Investm't Category: Tax-Exempt Bond

Cap Gain	Asset Allocation
Cap & Income	Fund of Funds
✔ Income	Index
	Sector
✔ Domestic	Small Cap
Foreign	Socially Conscious
Country/Region	State Specific

Portfolio: stocks 0% bonds 98%
convertibles 0% other 0% cash 2%

Largest Holdings: general obligation 22%

Unrealized Net Capital Gains: -2% of portfolio value

SHAREHOLDER INFORMATION

Minimum Investment
Initial: $1,000   Subsequent: $100

Minimum IRA Investment
Initial: na   Subsequent: na

Maximum Fees
Load: 2.00% front   12b-1: none
Other: none

Distributions
Income: monthly   Capital Gains: Dec

Exchange Options
Number Per Year: 4   Fee: none
Telephone: yes (money market fund available)

Services
auto exchange, auto invest, auto withdraw

PRA Real Estate Securities (PRREX)

Growth & Income

900 North Michigan Avenue
Suite 1000
Chicago, IL 60611
(800) 435-1405, (312) 915-3600

	3yr Annual	5yr Annual	10yr Annual	Bull	Bear
Return (%)	13.3	6.9	na	76.7	2.0
Differ from Category (+/-)	6.2 high	-1.0 blw av	na	0.9 av	8.3 high

Total Risk	Standard Deviation	Category Risk	Risk Index	Beta
high	14.5%	high	1.8	0.4

	1994	1993	1992	1991	1990	1989	1988	1987	1986	1985
Return (%)............	2.9	19.9	17.8	23.5	-22.1	—	—	—	—	—
Differ from category (+/-) ..	4.3	6.7	7.6	-4.1	-16.1	—	—	—	—	—

PER SHARE DATA

	1994	1993	1992	1991	1990	1989	1988	1987	1986	1985
Dividends, Net Income ($).	0.50	0.41	0.44	0.53	0.79	—	—	—	—	—
Distrib'ns, Cap Gain ($) ...	0.82	0.67	0.00	0.00	0.03	—	—	—	—	—
Net Asset Value ($)	8.30	9.36	8.71	7.80	6.75	—	—	—	—	—
Expense Ratio (%)	1.22	1.24	1.37	1.25	1.54	—	—	—	—	—
Net Income to Assets (%) .	2.87	4.37	5.75	7.36	7.25	—	—	—	—	—
Portfolio Turnover (%)	90	61	28	16	24	—	—	—	—	—
Total Assets (Millions $) ...	105	107	66	54	18	—	—	—	—	—

PORTFOLIO (as of 9/30/94)

Portfolio Manager: Michael Oliver - 1989, Dean Sotter - 1993

Investm't Category: Growth & Income
Cap Gain	Asset Allocation
✔ Cap & Income	Fund of Funds
Income	Index
	✔ Sector
✔ Domestic	Small Cap
Foreign	Socially Conscious
Country/Region	State Specific

Portfolio: stocks 96%   bonds 0%
convertibles 3%   other 0%   cash 1%

Largest Holdings: real estate investment trusts 96%

Unrealized Net Capital Gains: 0% of portfolio value

SHAREHOLDER INFORMATION

Minimum Investment
Initial: $2,000   Subsequent: $0

Minimum IRA Investment
Initial: $2,000   Subsequent: $0

Maximum Fees
Load: none   12b-1: none
Other: none

Distributions
Income: quarterly   Capital Gains: Dec

Exchange Options
Number Per Year: none   Fee:
Telephone:

Services
IRA

Preferred Asset Allocation (PFAAX)

Balanced

100 N.E. Adams St.
Peoria, IL 61629
(800) 662-4769, (309) 675-1000

PERFORMANCE

	3yr Annual	5yr Annual	10yr Annual	Bull	Bear
Return (%)	na	na	na	na	-8.3
Differ from Category (+/-)	na	na	na	na	-2.6 low

Total Risk	Standard Deviation	Category Risk	Risk Index	Beta
na	na	na	na	na

	1994	1993	1992	1991	1990	1989	1988	1987	1986	1985
Return (%)	-2.5	10.5	—	—	—	—	—	—	—	—
Differ from category (+/-)	-0.6	-2.9	—	—	—	—	—	—	—	—

PER SHARE DATA

	1994	1993	1992	1991	1990	1989	1988	1987	1986	1985
Dividends, Net Income ($)	0.33	0.31	—	—	—	—	—	—	—	—
Distrib'ns, Cap Gain ($)	0.08	0.21	—	—	—	—	—	—	—	—
Net Asset Value ($)	10.32	11.02	—	—	—	—	—	—	—	—
Expense Ratio (%)	1.25	1.27	—	—	—	—	—	—	—	—
Net Income to Assets (%)	2.76	3.25	—	—	—	—	—	—	—	—
Portfolio Turnover (%)	24	34	—	—	—	—	—	—	—	—
Total Assets (Millions $)	60	56	—	—	—	—	—	—	—	—

PORTFOLIO (as of 6/30/94)

Portfolio Manager: R. Jackson - 1992, T. Hazuka - 1992, E. Peters - 1992

Investm't Category: Balanced

Cap Gain	✔ Asset Allocation
✔ Cap & Income	Fund of Funds
Income	Index
	Sector
✔ Domestic	Small Cap
✔ Foreign	Socially Conscious
Country/Region	State Specific

Portfolio: stocks 58%   bonds 31%
convertibles 0%   other 0%   cash 11%

Largest Holdings: bonds—U.S. government 31%, stocks—fuel 5%

Unrealized Net Capital Gains: -1% of portfolio value

SHAREHOLDER INFORMATION

Minimum Investment
Initial: $1,000   Subsequent: $50

Minimum IRA Investment
Initial: $250   Subsequent: $50

Maximum Fees
Load: none   12b-1: none
Other: none

Distributions
Income: Jun, Dec   Capital Gains: Dec

Exchange Options
Number Per Year: 3   Fee: none
Telephone: yes (money market fund available)

Services
IRA, pension, auto invest, auto withdraw

Preferred Fixed Income

(PFXIX)

General Bond

100 N.E. Adams St.
Peoria, IL 61629
(800) 662-4769, (309) 675-1000

	3yr Annual	5yr Annual	10yr Annual	Bull	Bear
Return (%)	na	na	na	na	-4.1
Differ from Category (+/-)	na	na	na	na	-0.3 av

Total Risk	Standard Deviation	Category Risk	Risk Index	Avg Mat
na	na	na	na	11.8 yrs

	1994	1993	1992	1991	1990	1989	1988	1987	1986	1985
Return (%)	-2.3	10.3	—	—	—	—	—	—	—	—
Differ from category (+/-)	-0.3	1.1	—	—	—	—	—	—	—	—

PER SHARE DATA

	1994	1993	1992	1991	1990	1989	1988	1987	1986	1985
Dividends, Net Income ($)	0.51	0.48	—	—	—	—	—	—	—	—
Distrib'ns, Cap Gain ($)	0.00	0.30	—	—	—	—	—	—	—	—
Net Asset Value ($)	9.58	10.34	—	—	—	—	—	—	—	—
Expense Ratio (%)	0.97	1.05	—	—	—	—	—	—	—	—
Net Income to Assets (%)	4.53	4.91	—	—	—	—	—	—	—	—
Portfolio Turnover (%)	254	316	—	—	—	—	—	—	—	—
Total Assets (Millions $)	46	43	—	—	—	—	—	—	—	—

PORTFOLIO (as of 6/30/94)

Portfolio Manager: Laurence R. Smith - 1992, Paul Zemsky - 1994

Investm't Category: General Bond

Cap Gain	Asset Allocation
Cap & Income	Fund of Funds
✔ Income	Index
	Sector
✔ Domestic	Small Cap
✔ Foreign	Socially Conscious
Country/Region	State Specific

Portfolio: stocks 0%   bonds 89%
convertibles 0%   other 0%   cash 11%

Largest Holdings: U.S. government 42%, corporate 34%

Unrealized Net Capital Gains: -2% of portfolio value

SHAREHOLDER INFORMATION

Minimum Investment
Initial: $1,000   Subsequent: $50

Minimum IRA Investment
Initial: $250   Subsequent: $50

Maximum Fees
Load: none   12b-1: none
Other: none

Distributions
Income: monthly   Capital Gains: Dec

Exchange Options
Number Per Year: 3   Fee: none
Telephone: yes (money market fund available)

Services
IRA, pension, auto invest, auto withdraw

Preferred Growth (PFGRX)

Growth

100 N.E. Adams St.
Peoria, IL 61629
(800) 662-4769, (309) 675-1000

PERFORMANCE

fund inception date: 6/30/92

	3yr Annual	5yr Annual	10yr Annual	Bull	Bear
Return (%)	na	na	na	na	-13.1
Differ from Category (+/-)	na	na	na	na	-6.5 low

Total Risk	Standard Deviation	Category Risk	Risk Index	Beta
na	na	na	na	na

	1994	1993	1992	1991	1990	1989	1988	1987	1986	1985
Return (%)	-1.1	16.0	—	—	—	—	—	—	—	—
Differ from category (+/-)	-0.5	2.6	—	—	—	—	—	—	—	—

PER SHARE DATA

	1994	1993	1992	1991	1990	1989	1988	1987	1986	1985
Dividends, Net Income ($)	0.02	0.00	—	—	—	—	—	—	—	—
Distrib'ns, Cap Gain ($)	0.06	0.00	—	—	—	—	—	—	—	—
Net Asset Value ($)	13.59	13.82	—	—	—	—	—	—	—	—
Expense Ratio (%)	0.91	1.00	—	—	—	—	—	—	—	—
Net Income to Assets (%)	0.13	0.07	—	—	—	—	—	—	—	—
Portfolio Turnover (%)	51	58	—	—	—	—	—	—	—	—
Total Assets (Millions $)	241	152	—	—	—	—	—	—	—	—

PORTFOLIO (as of 6/30/94)

Portfolio Manager: Lulu C. Wang - 1992

Investm't Category: Growth

✔ Cap Gain	Asset Allocation
Cap & Income	Fund of Funds
Income	Index
	Sector
✔ Domestic	Small Cap
✔ Foreign	Socially Conscious
Country/Region	State Specific

Portfolio: stocks 100% bonds 0%
convertibles 0% other 0% cash 0%

Largest Holdings: office equipment & computers 25%, health care 8%

Unrealized Net Capital Gains: 8% of portfolio value

SHAREHOLDER INFORMATION

Minimum Investment
Initial: $1,000   Subsequent: $50

Minimum IRA Investment
Initial: $250   Subsequent: $50

Maximum Fees
Load: none   12b-1: none
Other: none

Distributions
Income: Dec   Capital Gains: Dec

Exchange Options
Number Per Year: 3   Fee: none
Telephone: yes (money market fund available)

Services
IRA, pension, auto invest, auto withdraw

Preferred Int'l (PFIFX)

International Stock

100 N.E. Adams St.
Peoria, IL 61629
(800) 662-4769, (309) 675-1000

PERFORMANCE

fund inception date: 6/30/92

	3yr Annual	5yr Annual	10yr Annual	Bull	Bear
Return (%)	na	na	na	na	-6.8
Differ from Category (+/-)	na	na	na	na	0.2 av

Total Risk	Standard Deviation	Category Risk	Risk Index	Beta
na	na	na	na	na

	1994	1993	1992	1991	1990	1989	1988	1987	1986	1985
Return (%).	3.2	41.5	—	—	—	—	—	—	—	—
Differ from category (+/-) . .	6.2	2.9	—	—	—	—	—	—	—	—

PER SHARE DATA

	1994	1993	1992	1991	1990	1989	1988	1987	1986	1985
Dividends, Net Income ($).	0.13	0.07	—	—	—	—	—	—	—	—
Distrib'ns, Cap Gain ($) . . .	0.43	0.05	—	—	—	—	—	—	—	—
Net Asset Value ($)	11.58	11.75	—	—	—	—	—	—	—	—
Expense Ratio (%)	1.38	1.60	—	—	—	—	—	—	—	—
Net Income to Assets (%) .	1.37	1.83	—	—	—	—	—	—	—	—
Portfolio Turnover (%)	27	16	—	—	—	—	—	—	—	—
Total Assets (Millions $) . . .	107	73	—	—	—	—	—	—	—	—

PORTFOLIO (as of 6/30/94)

Portfolio Manager: Peter F. Spano - 1992

Investm't Category: International Stock

✔ Cap Gain	Asset Allocation
Cap & Income	Fund of Funds
Income	Index
	Sector
Domestic	Small Cap
✔ Foreign	Socially Conscious
Country/Region	State Specific

Portfolio: stocks 94%   bonds 0%
convertibles 0%   other 0%   cash 6%

Largest Holdings: Netherlands 11%, Switzerland 11%

Unrealized Net Capital Gains: 7% of portfolio value

SHAREHOLDER INFORMATION

Minimum Investment
Initial: $1,000   Subsequent: $50

Minimum IRA Investment
Initial: $250   Subsequent: $50

Maximum Fees
Load: none   12b-1: none
Other: none

Distributions
Income: Dec   Capital Gains: Dec

Exchange Options
Number Per Year: 3   Fee: none
Telephone: yes (money market fund available)

Services
IRA, pension, auto invest, auto withdraw

Preferred Short-Term Gov't Securities (PFSGX)

General Bond

100 N.E. Adams St.
Peoria, IL 61629
(800) 662-4769, (309) 675-1000

PERFORMANCE

fund inception date: 6/30/92

	3yr Annual	5yr Annual	10yr Annual	Bull	Bear
Return (%)	na	na	na	na	-1.6
Differ from Category (+/-)	na	na	na	na	2.2 high

Total Risk	Standard Deviation	Category Risk	Risk Index	Avg Mat
na	na	na	na	1.6 yrs

	1994	1993	1992	1991	1990	1989	1988	1987	1986	1985
Return (%)	-0.6	5.5	—	—	—	—	—	—	—	—
Differ from category (+/-)	1.4	-3.7	—	—	—	—	—	—	—	—

PER SHARE DATA

	1994	1993	1992	1991	1990	1989	1988	1987	1986	1985
Dividends, Net Income ($)	0.43	0.38	—	—	—	—	—	—	—	—
Distrib'ns, Cap Gain ($)	0.00	0.02	—	—	—	—	—	—	—	—
Net Asset Value ($)	9.57	10.06	—	—	—	—	—	—	—	—
Expense Ratio (%)	0.74	0.78	—	—	—	—	—	—	—	—
Net Income to Assets (%)	3.75	3.87	—	—	—	—	—	—	—	—
Portfolio Turnover (%)	134	268	—	—	—	—	—	—	—	—
Total Assets (Millions $)	29	30	—	—	—	—	—	—	—	—

PORTFOLIO (as of 6/30/94)

Portfolio Manager: J. Orr - 1992, P. Pond - 1992, T. Sheridan - 1992

Investm't Category: General Bond
Cap Gain	Asset Allocation
Cap & Income	Fund of Funds
✔ Income	Index
	Sector
✔ Domestic	Small Cap
Foreign	Socially Conscious
Country/Region	State Specific

Portfolio: stocks 0% bonds 75%
convertibles 0% other 0% cash 25%

Largest Holdings: U.S. government 56%, mortgage-backed 19%

Unrealized Net Capital Gains: -1% of portfolio value

SHAREHOLDER INFORMATION

Minimum Investment
Initial: $1,000 Subsequent: $50

Minimum IRA Investment
Initial: $250 Subsequent: $50

Maximum Fees
Load: none 12b-1: none
Other: none

Distributions
Income: monthly Capital Gains: Dec

Exchange Options
Number Per Year: 3 Fee: none
Telephone: yes (money market fund available)

Services
IRA, pension, auto invest, auto withdraw

Preferred Value (PFVLX)

Growth & Income

100 N.E. Adams St.
Peoria, IL 61629
(800) 662-4769, (309) 675-1000

PERFORMANCE

fund inception date: 6/30/92

	3yr Annual	5yr Annual	10yr Annual	Bull	Bear
Return (%)	na	na	na	na	-4.5
Differ from Category (+/-)	na	na	na	na	1.8 abv av

Total Risk	Standard Deviation	Category Risk	Risk Index	Beta
na	na	na	na	na

	1994	1993	1992	1991	1990	1989	1988	1987	1986	1985
Return (%)	0.4	8.7	—	—	—	—	—	—	—	—
Differ from category (+/-)	1.8	-4.5	—	—	—	—	—	—	—	—

PER SHARE DATA

	1994	1993	1992	1991	1990	1989	1988	1987	1986	1985
Dividends, Net Income ($)	0.20	0.16	—	—	—	—	—	—	—	—
Distrib'ns, Cap Gain ($)	0.14	0.10	—	—	—	—	—	—	—	—
Net Asset Value ($)	11.27	11.56	—	—	—	—	—	—	—	—
Expense Ratio (%)	0.93	0.96	—	—	—	—	—	—	—	—
Net Income to Assets (%)	1.64	1.79	—	—	—	—	—	—	—	—
Portfolio Turnover (%)	11	17	—	—	—	—	—	—	—	—
Total Assets (Millions $)	148	126	—	—	—	—	—	—	—	—

PORTFOLIO (as of 6/30/94)

Portfolio Manager: John G. Lindenthal - 1992

Investm't Category: Growth & Income

Cap Gain	Asset Allocation
✔ Cap & Income	Fund of Funds
Income	Index
	Sector
✔ Domestic	Small Cap
✔ Foreign	Socially Conscious
Country/Region	State Specific

Portfolio: stocks 90% bonds 0%
convertibles 0% other 0% cash 10%

Largest Holdings: finance 20%, healthcare 10%

Unrealized Net Capital Gains: 9% of portfolio value

SHAREHOLDER INFORMATION

Minimum Investment
Initial: $1,000   Subsequent: $50

Minimum IRA Investment
Initial: $250   Subsequent: $50

Maximum Fees
Load: none   12b-1: none
Other: none

Distributions
Income: Dec   Capital Gains: Dec

Exchange Options
Number Per Year: 3   Fee: none
Telephone: yes (money market fund available)

Services
IRA, pension, auto invest, auto withdraw

Primary Trend (PTFDX)

Balanced

First Financial Centre
700 N. Water St.
Milwaukee, WI 53202
(800) 443-6544, (414) 271-2726

PERFORMANCE

fund inception date: 9/15/86

	3yr Annual	5yr Annual	10yr Annual	Bull	Bear
Return (%)	3.7	5.5	na	46.7	-5.0
Differ from Category (+/-)	-2.7 low	-2.5 low	na	-18.3 low	0.7 av

Total Risk	Standard Deviation	Category Risk	Risk Index	Beta
av	7.1%	high	1.1	0.8

	1994	1993	1992	1991	1990	1989	1988	1987	1986	1985
Return (%)	-0.1	11.4	0.2	19.5	-1.7	8.9	18.3	3.6	—	—
Differ from category (+/-) . . .	1.8	-2.0	-8.1	-3.9	-1.2	-8.4	6.5	1.2	—	—

PER SHARE DATA

	1994	1993	1992	1991	1990	1989	1988	1987	1986	1985
Dividends, Net Income ($) .	0.26	0.08	0.28	0.42	0.56	0.31	0.56	0.35	—	—
Distrib'ns, Cap Gain ($) . . .	0.40	0.13	0.86	0.29	0.68	0.30	0.10	0.07	—	—
Net Asset Value ($)	10.58	11.25	10.29	11.38	10.13	11.60	11.19	10.02	—	—
Expense Ratio (%).	1.27	1.20	1.10	1.20	1.10	1.10	1.20	1.30	—	—
Net Income to Assets (%). .	1.91	1.90	2.50	4.70	3.80	2.00	6.40	3.90	—	—
Portfolio Turnover (%). . . .	77	40	66	77	32	30	17	20	—	—
Total Assets (Millions $) . . .	20	24	32	33	39	56	45	31	—	—

PORTFOLIO (as of 6/30/94)

Portfolio Manager: David Aushwitz - 1989

Investm't Category: Balanced

Cap Gain	✔ Asset Allocation
✔ Cap & Income	Fund of Funds
Income	Index
	Sector
✔ Domestic	Small Cap
Foreign	Socially Conscious
Country/Region	State Specific

Portfolio: stocks 83% bonds 4%
convertibles 5% other 0% cash 8%

Largest Holdings: oil & gas 19%, steel 7%

Unrealized Net Capital Gains: 0% of portfolio value

SHAREHOLDER INFORMATION

Minimum Investment
Initial: $2,500   Subsequent: $100

Minimum IRA Investment
Initial: $2,000   Subsequent: $100

Maximum Fees
Load: none   12b-1: none
Other: none

Distributions
Income: Aug, Dec   Capital Gains: Aug, Dec

Exchange Options
Number Per Year: 5   Fee: $5 (telephone)
Telephone: yes (money market fund available)

Services
IRA, pension, auto exchange, auto invest, auto withdraw

Prudent Speculator
(PSLFX)
Aggressive Growth

P.O. Box 75231
Los Angeles, CA 90075
(800) 444-4778, (213) 252-9000

PERFORMANCE   fund inception date: 6/29/87

	3yr Annual	5yr Annual	10yr Annual	Bull	Bear
Return (%)	-1.7	-0.6	na	102.1	-12.2
Differ from Category (+/-)	-10.6 low	-13.1 low	na	-31.1 blw av	-1.4 blw av

Total Risk	Standard Deviation	Category Risk	Risk Index	Beta
high	19.0%	high	1.3	0.6

	1994	1993	1992	1991	1990	1989	1988	1987	1986	1985
Return (%)..............	-8.9	3.0	0.9	63.7	-37.5	-2.5	12.7	—	—	—
Differ from category (+/-) ..	-8.2	-16.5	-10.1	11.6	-31.3	-29.3	-2.5	—	—	—

PER SHARE DATA

	1994	1993	1992	1991	1990	1989	1988	1987	1986	1985
Dividends, Net Income ($).	0.00	0.00	0.00	0.00	0.00	0.00	0.05	—	—	—
Distrib'ns, Cap Gain ($) ...	0.00	0.35	0.31	0.00	0.00	0.00	0.00	—	—	—
Net Asset Value ($)	6.32	6.94	7.08	7.32	4.47	7.16	7.35	—	—	—
Expense Ratio (%)	6.03	4.41	3.83	4.09	7.42	4.26	2.81	—	—	—
Net Income to Assets (%) .	-5.69	-4.15	-3.48	-3.20	-5.90	-1.37	-.08	—	—	—
Portfolio Turnover (%)	na	71	81	107	108	88	20	—	—	—
Total Assets (Millions $)	2	na	9	16	4	8	10	—	—	—

PORTFOLIO (as of 4/30/94)

Portfolio Manager: Edwin R. Bernstein - 1989

Investm't Category: Aggressive Growth

✔ Cap Gain	Asset Allocation
Cap & Income	Fund of Funds
Income	Index
	Sector
✔ Domestic	✔ Small Cap
Foreign	Socially Conscious
Country/Region	State Specific

Portfolio: stocks 78%   bonds 0%
convertibles 0%   other 0%   cash 22%

Largest Holdings: medical products/services 15%, manufacturing 12%

Unrealized Net Capital Gains: 9% of portfolio value

SHAREHOLDER INFORMATION

Minimum Investment
Initial: $250   Subsequent: $25

Minimum IRA Investment
Initial: $50   Subsequent: $25

Maximum Fees
Load: none   12b-1: 0.25%
Other: none

Distributions
Income: Dec   Capital Gains: Dec

Exchange Options
Number Per Year: 6   Fee: none
Telephone: yes (money market fund available)

Services
IRA, pension, auto invest, auto withdraw

Prudential Gov't Securities Interm Term

(PBGVX) *Government Bond*

One Seaport Plaza
New York, NY 10292
(800) 225-1852, (908) 417-7555

PERFORMANCE

fund inception date: 9/1/82

	3yr Annual	5yr Annual	10yr Annual	Bull	Bear
Return (%)	3.5	6.3	8.1	35.7	-3.7
Differ from Category (+/-)	-0.5 blw av	-0.4 blw av	0.3 av	-15.5 low	2.7 av

Total Risk	Standard Deviation	Category Risk	Risk Index	Avg Mat
low	3.2%	blw av	0.7	na

	1994	1993	1992	1991	1990	1989	1988	1987	1986	1985
Return (%)	-2.5	7.3	6.1	13.3	7.8	11.0	6.2	2.5	13.7	17.0
Differ from category (+/-)	2.3	-3.6	-0.3	-2.0	1.6	-3.5	-1.7	4.6	-6.9	-1.5

PER SHARE DATA

	1994	1993	1992	1991	1990	1989	1988	1987	1986	1985
Dividends, Net Income ($)	0.62	0.71	0.75	0.85	0.86	0.87	1.03	0.86	0.98	1.02
Distrib'ns, Cap Gain ($)	0.00	0.00	0.00	0.00	0.00	0.00	0.00	0.08	0.23	0.00
Net Asset Value ($)	9.16	10.03	10.02	10.17	9.78	9.91	9.75	10.16	10.84	10.66
Expense Ratio (%)	0.80	0.80	0.79	0.79	0.88	0.86	0.83	0.72	0.75	0.67
Net Income to Assets (%)	5.53	6.80	7.47	8.36	8.60	9.16	9.39	8.30	8.51	8.04
Portfolio Turnover (%)	na	44	60	151	68	186	28	59	139	191
Total Assets (Millions $)	220	343	304	298	328	396	474	634	866	414

PORTFOLIO (as of 5/31/94)

Portfolio Manager: Kay Wilcox - 1991

Investm't Category: Government Bond

Cap Gain	Asset Allocation
Cap & Income	Fund of Funds
✔ Income	Index
	Sector
✔ Domestic	Small Cap
Foreign	Socially Conscious
Country/Region	State Specific

Portfolio: stocks 0% bonds 80%
convertibles 0% other 0% cash 20%

Largest Holdings: U. S. government 69%, mortgage-backed 11%

Unrealized Net Capital Gains: -1% of portfolio value

SHAREHOLDER INFORMATION

Minimum Investment
Initial: $1,000   Subsequent: $100

Minimum IRA Investment
Initial: $0   Subsequent: $0

Maximum Fees
Load: none   12b-1: 0.25%
Other: none

Distributions
Income: monthly   Capital Gains: Dec

Exchange Options
Number Per Year: no limit   Fee: none
Telephone: yes (money market fund available)

Services
IRA, pension, auto exchange, auto invest, auto withdraw

Regis C & B Balanced
(CBBAX)
Balanced

P.O. Box 2798
Boston, MA 02208
(800) 638-7983

PERFORMANCE   fund inception date: 12/29/89

	3yr Annual	5yr Annual	10yr Annual	Bull	Bear
Return (%)	3.6	8.5	na	59.4	-4.7
Differ from Category (+/-)	-2.8 low	0.5 av	na	-5.6 blw av	1.0 abv av

Total Risk	Standard Deviation	Category Risk	Risk Index	Beta
low	4.8%	low	0.8	0.5

	1994	1993	1992	1991	1990	1989	1988	1987	1986	1985
Return (%)	-0.9	6.4	5.5	25.6	7.7	—	—	—	—	—
Differ from category (+/-)	1.0	-7.0	-2.8	2.2	8.2	—	—	—	—	—

PER SHARE DATA

	1994	1993	1992	1991	1990	1989	1988	1987	1986	1985
Dividends, Net Income ($)	0.72	0.45	0.44	0.42	0.41	—	—	—	—	—
Distrib'ns, Cap Gain ($)	0.00	0.44	0.30	0.10	0.01	—	—	—	—	—
Net Asset Value ($)	11.43	12.27	12.38	12.45	10.35	—	—	—	—	—
Expense Ratio (%)	1.00	0.90	0.91	1.00	1.00	—	—	—	—	—
Net Income to Assets (%)	3.84	3.65	3.78	4.07	4.61	—	—	—	—	—
Portfolio Turnover (%)	24	22	12	11	na	—	—	—	—	—
Total Assets (Millions $)	51	41	35	26	8	—	—	—	—	—

PORTFOLIO (as of 10/31/94)

Portfolio Manager: Peter Thompson - 1994

Investm't Category: Balanced

Cap Gain	Asset Allocation
✔ Cap & Income	Fund of Funds
Income	Index
	Sector
✔ Domestic	Small Cap
Foreign	Socially Conscious
Country/Region	State Specific

Portfolio: stocks 54%   bonds 40%
convertibles 0%   other 0%   cash 6%

Largest Holdings: bonds—U.S. government
18%, stocks—financial services 7%

Unrealized Net Capital Gains: 4% of portfolio value

SHAREHOLDER INFORMATION

Minimum Investment
Initial: $250,000   Subsequent: $1,000

Minimum IRA Investment
Initial: $250,000   Subsequent: $1,000

Maximum Fees
Load: none   12b-1: none
Other: none

Distributions
Income: quarterly   Capital Gains: Oct

Exchange Options
Number Per Year: no limit   Fee: none
Telephone: yes (money market fund available)

Services
IRA, auto withdraw

Regis C & B Equity
(CBEQX)
Growth & Income

P.O. Box 2798
Boston, MA 02208
(800) 638-7983

fund inception date: 5/1/90

	3yr Annual	5yr Annual	10yr Annual	Bull	Bear
Return (%)	3.3	na	na	64.1	-4.0
Differ from Category (+/-)	-3.8 low	na	na	-11.7 blw av	2.3 high

Total Risk	Standard Deviation	Category Risk	Risk Index	Beta
blw av	6.5%	low	0.8	0.7

	1994	1993	1992	1991	1990	1989	1988	1987	1986	1985
Return (%)	1.3	4.1	4.4	31.1	—	—	—	—	—	—
Differ from category (+/-)	2.7	-9.1	-5.8	3.5	—	—	—	—	—	—

PER SHARE DATA

	1994	1993	1992	1991	1990	1989	1988	1987	1986	1985
Dividends, Net Income ($)	0.31	0.28	0.28	0.25	—	—	—	—	—	—
Distrib'ns, Cap Gain ($)	0.00	0.22	0.49	0.05	—	—	—	—	—	—
Net Asset Value ($)	12.91	13.05	13.02	13.22	—	—	—	—	—	—
Expense Ratio (%)	0.82	0.82	0.83	1.00	—	—	—	—	—	—
Net Income to Assets (%)	2.39	2.28	2.27	2.65	—	—	—	—	—	—
Portfolio Turnover (%)	46	21	45	7	—	—	—	—	—	—
Total Assets (Millions $)	208	204	112	50	—	—	—	—	—	—

PORTFOLIO (as of 10/31/94)

Portfolio Manager: Peter Thompson - 1994

Investm't Category: Growth & Income

Cap Gain	Asset Allocation
✔ Cap & Income	Fund of Funds
Income	Index
	Sector
✔ Domestic	Small Cap
Foreign	Socially Conscious
Country/Region	State Specific

Portfolio: stocks 89%   bonds 0%
convertibles 0%   other 0%   cash 11%

Largest Holdings: financial services 12%, consumer products 8%

Unrealized Net Capital Gains: 5% of portfolio value

SHAREHOLDER INFORMATION

Minimum Investment
Initial: $250,000   Subsequent: $1,000

Minimum IRA Investment
Initial: $250,000   Subsequent: $1,000

Maximum Fees
Load: none   12b-1: none
Other: none

Distributions
Income: quarterly   Capital Gains: Oct

Exchange Options
Number Per Year: no limit   Fee: none
Telephone: yes (money market fund available)

Services
IRA, auto withdraw

Regis DSI Disciplined Value (DSIDX)

Growth

P.O. Box 2798
Boston, MA 02208
(800) 638-7983

	3yr Annual	5yr Annual	10yr Annual	Bull	Bear
Return (%)	8.1	7.1	na	78.4	-6.5
Differ from Category (+/-)	0.4 av	-2.5 low	na	-13.7 blw av	0.1 av

Total Risk	Standard Deviation	Category Risk	Risk Index	Beta
av	8.4%	blw av	0.9	1.0

	1994	1993	1992	1991	1990	1989	1988	1987	1986	1985
Return (%).	-1.6	16.8	10.1	24.1	-10.0	—	—	—	—	—
Differ from category (+/-) . .	-1.0	3.4	-1.5	-11.6	-4.3	—	—	—	—	—

PER SHARE DATA

	1994	1993	1992	1991	1990	1989	1988	1987	1986	1985
Dividends, Net Income ($).	1.27	0.21	0.25	0.25	0.31	—	—	—	—	—
Distrib'ns, Cap Gain ($) . . .	0.00	1.78	0.00	0.00	0.00	—	—	—	—	—
Net Asset Value ($)	9.64	11.10	11.23	10.44	8.62	—	—	—	—	—
Expense Ratio (%)	1.09	1.04	0.99	1.05	1.01	—	—	—	—	—
Net Income to Assets (%) .	2.02	1.88	2.44	2.60	3.16	—	—	—	—	—
Portfolio Turnover (%)	184	149	74	62	75	—	—	—	—	—
Total Assets (Millions $)	44	42	37	41	33	—	—	—	—	—

PORTFOLIO (as of 10/31/94)

Portfolio Manager: McCullogh - 1989, Stephenson - 1989

Investm't Category: Growth
- ✔ Cap Gain
-   Cap & Income
-   Income
- ✔ Domestic
- ✔ Foreign
-   Country/Region

-   Asset Allocation
-   Fund of Funds
-   Index
-   Sector
-   Small Cap
-   Socially Conscious
-   State Specific

Portfolio: stocks 88% bonds 0%
convertibles 5% other 0% cash 7%

Largest Holdings: finance 19%, industrial 12%

Unrealized Net Capital Gains: -2% of portfolio value

SHAREHOLDER INFORMATION

Minimum Investment
Initial: $500,000   Subsequent: $1,000

Minimum IRA Investment
Initial: $500,000   Subsequent: $1,000

Maximum Fees
Load: none   12b-1: none
Other: none

Distributions
Income: quarterly   Capital Gains: Oct

Exchange Options
Number Per Year: no limit   Fee: none
Telephone: yes (money market fund available)

Services
IRA

Regis DSI Limited Maturity Bond (DSILX)

General Bond

P.O. Box 2798
Boston, MA 02208
(800) 638-7983

PERFORMANCE

fund inception date: 12/1/89

	3yr Annual	5yr Annual	10yr Annual	Bull	Bear
Return (%)	3.2	6.4	na	34.4	-3.5
Differ from Category (+/-)	-1.1 low	-0.5 blw av	na	-6.6 blw av	0.3 av

Total Risk	Standard Deviation	Category Risk	Risk Index	Avg Mat
low	3.3%	blw av	0.8	5.3 yrs

	1994	1993	1992	1991	1990	1989	1988	1987	1986	1985
Return (%)	-1.1	3.7	7.3	14.8	7.9	—	—	—	—	—
Differ from category (+/-) . . .	0.9	-5.5	0.7	0.2	0.7	—	—	—	—	—

PER SHARE DATA

	1994	1993	1992	1991	1990	1989	1988	1987	1986	1985
Dividends, Net Income ($) .	0.55	0.57	0.76	0.72	0.81	—	—	—	—	—
Distrib'ns, Cap Gain ($) . . .	0.00	0.00	0.43	0.18	0.00	—	—	—	—	—
Net Asset Value ($)	9.13	9.80	10.00	10.44	9.92	—	—	—	—	—
Expense Ratio (%).	0.88	0.79	0.72	0.75	0.72	—	—	—	—	—
Net Income to Assets (%). .	5.68	6.50	6.19	7.39	8.39	—	—	—	—	—
Portfolio Turnover (%). . . .	274	167	238	306	—	—	—	—	—	—
Total Assets (Millions $)	27	33	33	34	35	—	—	—	—	—

PORTFOLIO (as of 10/31/94)

Portfolio Manager: Isac Franco - 1989

Investm't Category: General Bond

Cap Gain	Asset Allocation
Cap & Income	Fund of Funds
✔ Income	Index
	Sector
✔ Domestic	Small Cap
Foreign	Socially Conscious
Country/Region	State Specific

Portfolio: stocks 0% bonds 81%
convertibles 0% other 0% cash 19%

Largest Holdings: mortgage-backed 50%, corporate 19%

Unrealized Net Capital Gains: 0% of portfolio value

SHAREHOLDER INFORMATION

Minimum Investment
Initial: $500,000 Subsequent: $1,000

Minimum IRA Investment
Initial: $500,000 Subsequent: $1,000

Maximum Fees
Load: none 12b-1: none
Other: none

Distributions
Income: quarterly Capital Gains: Oct

Exchange Options
Number Per Year: no limit Fee: none
Telephone: yes (money market fund available)

Services
IRA

Regis ICM Small Company Port (ICSCX)

Growth

P.O. Box 2798
Boston, MA 02208
(800) 638-7983

	3yr Annual	5yr Annual	10yr Annual	Bull	Bear
Return (%)	18.6	18.1	na	172.8	-7.9
Differ from Category (+/-)	10.9 high	8.5 high	na	80.7 high	-1.3 blw av

Total Risk	Standard Deviation	Category Risk	Risk Index	Beta
abv av	10.0%	abv av	1.0	0.7

	1994	1993	1992	1991	1990	1989	1988	1987	1986	1985
Return (%)	3.4	21.9	32.2	48.6	-7.3	—	—	—	—	—
Differ from category (+/-)	4.0	8.5	20.6	12.9	-1.6	—	—	—	—	—

PER SHARE DATA

	1994	1993	1992	1991	1990	1989	1988	1987	1986	1985
Dividends, Net Income ($)	0.82	0.07	0.09	0.14	0.15	—	—	—	—	—
Distrib'ns, Cap Gain ($)	0.00	2.34	1.16	0.36	0.00	—	—	—	—	—
Net Asset Value ($)	16.29	16.57	15.60	12.75	8.92	—	—	—	—	—
Expense Ratio (%)	0.93	0.95	0.95	1.02	1.14	—	—	—	—	—
Net Income to Assets (%)	0.58	0.46	0.77	1.32	1.52	—	—	—	—	—
Portfolio Turnover (%)	21	47	34	49	40	—	—	—	—	—
Total Assets (Millions $)	126	92	58	44	19	—	—	—	—	—

PORTFOLIO (as of 10/31/94)

Portfolio Manager: Robert D. McDorman Jr. - 1989

Investm't Category: Growth

✔ Cap Gain	Asset Allocation
Cap & Income	Fund of Funds
Income	Index
	Sector
✔ Domestic	✔ Small Cap
Foreign	Socially Conscious
Country/Region	State Specific

Portfolio: stocks 94% bonds 0%
convertibles 0% other 0% cash 6%

Largest Holdings: technology 19%, consumer durables 9%

Unrealized Net Capital Gains: 15% of portfolio value

SHAREHOLDER INFORMATION

Minimum Investment
Initial: $100,000   Subsequent: $1,000

Minimum IRA Investment
Initial: na   Subsequent: na

Maximum Fees
Load: none   12b-1: none
Other: none

Distributions
Income: quarterly   Capital Gains: Dec

Exchange Options
Number Per Year: no limit   Fee: none
Telephone: yes (money market fund not available)

Services

Regis Sterling Partners Balanced (SPBPX)

P.O. Box 2798
Boston, MA 02208
(800) 638-7983

Balanced

PERFORMANCE

fund inception date: 3/15/91

	3yr Annual	5yr Annual	10yr Annual	Bull	Bear
Return (%)	5.4	na	na	na	-5.9
Differ from Category (+/-)	-1.0 av	na	na	na	-0.2 blw av

Total Risk	Standard Deviation	Category Risk	Risk Index	Beta
blw av	5.2%	blw av	0.8	0.6

	1994	1993	1992	1991	1990	1989	1988	1987	1986	1985
Return (%)	-1.9	9.9	8.6	—	—	—	—	—	—	—
Differ from category (+/-)	0.0	-3.5	0.3	—	—	—	—	—	—	—

PER SHARE DATA

	1994	1993	1992	1991	1990	1989	1988	1987	1986	1985
Dividends, Net Income ($)	0.68	0.30	0.35	—	—	—	—	—	—	—
Distrib'ns, Cap Gain ($)	0.00	0.13	0.16	—	—	—	—	—	—	—
Net Asset Value ($)	10.56	11.46	10.83	—	—	—	—	—	—	—
Expense Ratio (%)	1.01	0.99	1.09	—	—	—	—	—	—	—
Net Income to Assets (%)	3.05	3.08	3.52	—	—	—	—	—	—	—
Portfolio Turnover (%)	70	49	80	—	—	—	—	—	—	—
Total Assets (Millions $)	69	54	39	—	—	—	—	—	—	—

PORTFOLIO (as of 10/31/94)

Portfolio Manager: Paul Ehrsam - 1991

Investm't Category: Balanced

Cap Gain	✔ Asset Allocation
✔ Cap & Income	Fund of Funds
Income	Index
	Sector
✔ Domestic	Small Cap
Foreign	Socially Conscious
Country/Region	State Specific

Portfolio: stocks 36% bonds 58%
convertibles 0% other 1% cash 5%

Largest Holdings: bonds—U.S. government & agencies 41%, bonds—financial services 8%

Unrealized Net Capital Gains: 1% of portfolio value

SHAREHOLDER INFORMATION

Minimum Investment
Initial: $100,000   Subsequent: $1,000

Minimum IRA Investment
Initial: $100,000   Subsequent: $1,000

Maximum Fees
Load: none   12b-1: none
Other: none

Distributions
Income: quarterly   Capital Gains: Oct

Exchange Options
Number Per Year: no limit   Fee: none
Telephone: yes (money market fund available)

Services
IRA, auto withdraw

Regis TS & W International Equity

P.O. Box 2798
Boston, MA 02208
(800) 638-7983

(TSWFX) *International Stock*

PERFORMANCE

fund inception date: 12/18/92

	3yr Annual	5yr Annual	10yr Annual	Bull	Bear
Return (%)	na	na	na	na	-5.1
Differ from Category (+/-)	na	na	na	na	1.9 abv av

Total Risk	Standard Deviation	Category Risk	Risk Index	Beta
na	na	na	na	na

	1994	1993	1992	1991	1990	1989	1988	1987	1986	1985
Return (%)	-0.7	32.7	—	—	—	—	—	—	—	—
Differ from category (+/-)	2.3	-5.9	—	—	—	—	—	—	—	—

PER SHARE DATA

	1994	1993	1992	1991	1990	1989	1988	1987	1986	1985
Dividends, Net Income ($)	0.45	0.05	—	—	—	—	—	—	—	—
Distrib'ns, Cap Gain ($)	0.00	0.00	—	—	—	—	—	—	—	—
Net Asset Value ($)	12.66	13.22	—	—	—	—	—	—	—	—
Expense Ratio (%)	1.38	1.37	—	—	—	—	—	—	—	—
Net Income to Assets (%)	0.70	1.02	—	—	—	—	—	—	—	—
Portfolio Turnover (%)	30	na	—	—	—	—	—	—	—	—
Total Assets (Millions $)	47	31	—	—	—	—	—	—	—	—

PORTFOLIO (as of 10/31/94)

Portfolio Manager: na

Investm't Category: International Stock

✔ Cap Gain	Asset Allocation
Cap & Income	Fund of Funds
Income	Index
	Sector
Domestic	Small Cap
✔ Foreign	Socially Conscious
Country/Region	State Specific

Portfolio: stocks 82% bonds 0%
convertibles 3% other 1% cash 14%

Largest Holdings: Japan 20%, United Kingdom 15%

Unrealized Net Capital Gains: 10% of portfolio value

SHAREHOLDER INFORMATION

Minimum Investment
Initial: $100,000   Subsequent: $1,000

Minimum IRA Investment
Initial: $100,000   Subsequent: $1,000

Maximum Fees
Load: none   12b-1: none
Other: none

Distributions
Income: Dec   Capital Gains: Dec

Exchange Options
Number Per Year: no limit   Fee: none
Telephone: yes (money market fund available)

Services
IRA, auto withdraw

Reich & Tang Equity

(RCHTX)

Growth

600 Fifth Avenue
New York, NY 10020
(212) 830-5200

	3yr Annual	5yr Annual	10yr Annual	Bull	Bear
Return (%)	10.4	9.3	na	86.8	-4.4
Differ from Category (+/-)	2.7 abv av	-0.3 av	na	-5.3 av	2.2 abv av

Total Risk	Standard Deviation	Category Risk	Risk Index	Beta
av	7.6%	low	0.8	0.8

	1994	1993	1992	1991	1990	1989	1988	1987	1986	1985
Return (%)	1.6	13.8	16.3	23.0	-5.8	17.8	22.8	5.1	14.6	—
Differ from category (+/-)	2.2	0.4	4.7	-12.7	-0.1	-8.3	4.8	3.3	0.0	—

PER SHARE DATA

	1994	1993	1992	1991	1990	1989	1988	1987	1986	1985
Dividends, Net Income ($)	0.24	0.21	0.23	0.37	0.36	0.45	0.45	0.40	0.28	—
Distrib'ns, Cap Gain ($)	2.28	1.43	1.04	0.03	0.00	1.93	1.53	1.78	0.63	—
Net Asset Value ($)	15.39	17.61	16.92	15.64	13.05	14.24	14.11	13.11	14.50	—
Expense Ratio (%)	1.12	1.15	1.15	1.14	1.12	1.10	1.11	1.11	1.21	—
Net Income to Assets (%)	1.58	1.15	1.35	2.33	2.56	2.68	2.87	2.07	2.51	—
Portfolio Turnover (%)	8	26	27	43	27	48	27	43	35	—
Total Assets (Millions $)	91	109	93	83	97	112	102	102	110	—

PORTFOLIO (as of 6/30/94)

Portfolio Manager: Hoerle - 1985, Wilson - 1985, Delafield - 1992, Sellecchia - 1992

Investm't Category: Growth

✔ Cap Gain	Asset Allocation
Cap & Income	Fund of Funds
Income	Index
	Sector
✔ Domestic	Small Cap
✔ Foreign	Socially Conscious
Country/Region	State Specific

Portfolio: stocks 97%   bonds 0%
convertibles 0%   other 0%   cash 3%

Largest Holdings: industrial products 19%, insurance 8%

Unrealized Net Capital Gains: 19% of portfolio value

SHAREHOLDER INFORMATION

Minimum Investment
Initial: $5,000   Subsequent: $0

Minimum IRA Investment
Initial: $250   Subsequent: $0

Maximum Fees
Load: none   12b-1: 0.05%
Other: none

Distributions
Income: quarterly   Capital Gains: Dec

Exchange Options
Number Per Year: no limit   Fee: none
Telephone: yes (money market fund available)

Services
IRA, pension, auto withdraw

Reynolds Blue Chip Growth (RBCGX)

Growth & Income

Wood Island, 3rd Fl.
80 E. Sir Francis Drake Blvd.
Larkspur, CA 94939
(800) 338-1579, (415) 461-7860

PERFORMANCE

fund inception date: 8/1/88

	3yr Annual	5yr Annual	10yr Annual	Bull	Bear
Return (%)	-1.9	5.1	na	40.8	-10.2
Differ from Category (+/-)	-9.0 low	-2.8 low	na	-35.0 low	-3.9 low

Total Risk	Standard Deviation	Category Risk	Risk Index	Beta
abv av	10.3%	high	1.3	1.1

	1994	1993	1992	1991	1990	1989	1988	1987	1986	1985
Return (%).............	-0.5	-5.2	0.0	35.9	0.0	20.6	—	—	—	—
Differ from category (+/-)..	0.9	-18.4	-10.2	8.3	6.0	-0.8	—	—	—	—

PER SHARE DATA

	1994	1993	1992	1991	1990	1989	1988	1987	1986	1985
Dividends, Net Income ($).	0.06	0.13	0.09	0.09	0.15	0.15	—	—	—	—
Distrib'ns, Cap Gain ($)...	0.17	0.00	0.00	0.00	0.00	0.05	—	—	—	—
Net Asset Value ($).....	14.50	14.82	15.78	15.86	11.74	11.88	—	—	—	—
Expense Ratio (%).......	1.50	1.40	1.50	1.70	2.10	2.00	—	—	—	—
Net Income to Assets (%).	0.50	0.80	0.60	1.20	0.80	2.70	—	—	—	—
Portfolio Turnover (%).....	43	38	0	1	66	33	—	—	—	—
Total Assets (Millions $)....	23	38	41	28	10	5	—	—	—	—

PORTFOLIO (as of 9/30/94)

Portfolio Manager: Frederick Reynolds - 1988

Investm't Category: Growth & Income

Cap Gain	Asset Allocation
✔ Cap & Income	Fund of Funds
Income	Index
	Sector
✔ Domestic	Small Cap
Foreign	Socially Conscious
Country/Region	State Specific

Portfolio: stocks 98% bonds 0%
convertibles 0% other 0% cash 2%

Largest Holdings: drugs 8%, telecommunications 5%

Unrealized Net Capital Gains: 16% of portfolio value

SHAREHOLDER INFORMATION

Minimum Investment
Initial: $1,000   Subsequent: $100

Minimum IRA Investment
Initial: $1,000   Subsequent: $100

Maximum Fees
Load: none   12b-1: none
Other: none

Distributions
Income: Dec   Capital Gains: Dec

Exchange Options
Number Per Year: no limit   Fee: none
Telephone: yes (money market fund available)

Services
IRA, pension, auto exchange, auto invest, auto withdraw

Rightime (RTFDX)
Growth

218 Glenside Ave.
Wyncote, PA 19095
(800) 242-1421, (215) 887-8111

PERFORMANCE

fund inception date: 9/17/85

	3yr Annual	5yr Annual	10yr Annual	Bull	Bear
Return (%)	4.1	8.2	na	46.2	-0.2
Differ from Category (+/-)	-3.6 blw av	-1.4 blw av	na	-45.9 low	6.4 high

Total Risk	Standard Deviation	Category Risk	Risk Index	Beta
blw av	6.1%	low	0.6	0.4

	1994	1993	1992	1991	1990	1989	1988	1987	1986	1985
Return (%)	0.8	8.0	3.6	30.8	0.6	11.8	-1.3	19.1	10.6	—
Differ from category (+/-) . . .	1.4	-5.4	-8.0	-4.9	6.3	-14.3	-19.3	17.3	-4.0	—

PER SHARE DATA

	1994	1993	1992	1991	1990	1989	1988	1987	1986	1985
Dividends, Net Income ($) .	0.44	0.00	0.05	0.17	0.61	0.35	0.14	0.67	0.24	—
Distrib'ns, Cap Gain ($) . . .	4.63	1.72	2.38	4.68	1.47	0.00	0.78	3.97	1.94	—
Net Asset Value ($)	30.53	35.32	34.29	35.43	30.93	32.79	29.64	30.97	29.80	—
Expense Ratio (%).	2.51	2.52	2.56	2.67	2.67	2.58	2.58	2.55	2.77	—
Net Income to Assets (%). .	0.78	-0.83	0.12	0.45	1.52	0.14	0.53	1.20	-1.63	—
Portfolio Turnover (%).	11	2	73	136	383	168	187	166	231	—
Total Assets (Millions $) . . .	180	165	171	163	134	167	235	211	145	—

PORTFOLIO (as of 10/31/94)

Portfolio Manager: David Rights - 1986

Investm't Category: Growth
- ✔ Cap Gain
- Cap & Income
- Income
- ✔ Domestic
- Foreign
- Country/Region
- Asset Allocation
- ✔ Fund of Funds
- Index
- Sector
- Small Cap
- Socially Conscious
- State Specific

Portfolio: stocks 23% bonds 0%
convertibles 0% other 0% cash 77%

Largest Holdings: money market funds 51%, equity funds 23%

Unrealized Net Capital Gains: 1% of portfolio value

SHAREHOLDER INFORMATION

Minimum Investment
Initial: $2,000   Subsequent: $100

Minimum IRA Investment
Initial: $2,000   Subsequent: $0

Maximum Fees
Load: none   12b-1: 0.75%
Other: none

Distributions
Income: Dec   Capital Gains: Dec

Exchange Options
Number Per Year: no limit   Fee: none
Telephone: yes (money market fund available)

Services
IRA, pension, auto withdraw

Robertson Stephens Emerging Growth (RSEGX)

Aggressive Growth

555 Califorina Street
Suite 2600
San Francisco, CA 94104
(800) 766-3863

fund inception date: 11/30/87

PERFORMANCE

	3yr Annual	5yr Annual	10yr Annual	Bull	Bear
Return (%)	4.0	14.4	na	107.0	-11.3
Differ from Category (+/-)	-4.9 blw av	1.9 abv av	na	-26.2 blw av	-0.5 av

Total Risk	Standard Deviation	Category Risk	Risk Index	Beta
high	19.6%	high	1.3	1.1

	1994	1993	1992	1991	1990	1989	1988	1987	1986	1985
Return (%)..............	7.9	7.2	-2.5	58.7	9.5	44.4	14.0	—	—	—
Differ from category (+/-) ..	8.6	-12.3	-13.5	6.6	15.7	17.6	-1.2	—	—	—

PER SHARE DATA

	1994	1993	1992	1991	1990	1989	1988	1987	1986	1985
Dividends, Net Income ($).	0.00	0.00	0.00	0.00	0.00	0.00	0.00	—	—	—
Distrib'ns, Cap Gain ($) ...	2.10	0.00	0.27	0.90	0.86	1.60	0.00	—	—	—
Net Asset Value ($).....	17.32	17.98	16.77	17.50	11.67	11.46	9.09	—	—	—
Expense Ratio (%)	1.61	1.54	1.49	1.59	1.88	2.15	2.85	—	—	—
Net Income to Assets (%) .	-0.92	-0.61	-0.92	-0.68	-0.02	-0.75	-2.44	—	—	—
Portfolio Turnover (%)	na	43	124	147	272	236	139	—	—	—
Total Assets (Millions $) ...	176	166	277	142	23	13	8	—	—	—

PORTFOLIO (as of 9/30/94)

Portfolio Manager: Bob Czepiel - 1987

Investm't Category: Aggressive Growth

✔ Cap Gain	Asset Allocation
Cap & Income	Fund of Funds
Income	Index
	Sector
✔ Domestic	✔ Small Cap
Foreign	Socially Conscious
Country/Region	State Specific

Portfolio: stocks 98% bonds 0%
convertibles 0% other 0% cash 2%

Largest Holdings: consumer products & specialty retail 14%, computer software 13%

Unrealized Net Capital Gains: 10% of portfolio value

SHAREHOLDER INFORMATION

Minimum Investment
Initial: $5,000   Subsequent: $100

Minimum IRA Investment
Initial: $1,000   Subsequent: $1

Maximum Fees
Load: none   12b-1: 0.25%
Other: none

Distributions
Income: Dec   Capital Gains: Dec

Exchange Options
Number Per Year: 4   Fee: none
Telephone: yes (money market fund not available)

Services
IRA, pension, auto invest, auto withdraw

Robertson Stephens Value + Growth (RSVPX)

Aggressive Growth

555 Califorina Street
Suite 2600
San Francisco, CA 94104
(800) 766-3863

PERFORMANCE

fund inception date: 5/12/92

	3yr Annual	5yr Annual	10yr Annual	Bull	Bear
Return (%)	na	na	na	na	-5.6
Differ from Category (+/-)	na	na	na	na	5.2 abv av

Total Risk	Standard Deviation	Category Risk	Risk Index	Beta
na	na	na	na	na

	1994	1993	1992	1991	1990	1989	1988	1987	1986	1985
Return (%)	23.1	21.6	—	—	—	—	—	—	—	—
Differ from category (+/-) . .	23.8	2.1	—	—	—	—	—	—	—	—

PER SHARE DATA

	1994	1993	1992	1991	1990	1989	1988	1987	1986	1985
Dividends, Net Income ($) .	0.08	0.00	—	—	—	—	—	—	—	—
Distrib'ns, Cap Gain ($) . . .	0.12	0.33	—	—	—	—	—	—	—	—
Net Asset Value ($)	15.88	13.06	—	—	—	—	—	—	—	—
Expense Ratio (%)	1.55	1.33	—	—	—	—	—	—	—	—
Net Income to Assets (%) .	-0.51	1.26	—	—	—	—	—	—	—	—
Portfolio Turnover (%)	250	210	—	—	—	—	—	—	—	—
Total Assets (Millions $) . . .	132	23	—	—	—	—	—	—	—	—

PORTFOLIO (as of 6/30/94)

Portfolio Manager: Ron Elijah - 1992

Investm't Category: Aggressive Growth

✔ Cap Gain	Asset Allocation
Cap & Income	Fund of Funds
Income	Index
	Sector
✔ Domestic	✔ Small Cap
Foreign	Socially Conscious
Country/Region	State Specific

Portfolio: stocks 100% bonds 0%
convertibles 0% other 0% cash 0%

Largest Holdings: semiconductors 22%,
health maintenance organizations 12%

Unrealized Net Capital Gains: 0% of portfolio value

SHAREHOLDER INFORMATION

Minimum Investment
Initial: $5,000   Subsequent: $100

Minimum IRA Investment
Initial: $1,000   Subsequent: $1

Maximum Fees
Load: none   12b-1: none
Other: none

Distributions
Income: Dec   Capital Gains: Dec

Exchange Options
Number Per Year: 4   Fee: none
Telephone: yes (money market fund not available)

Services
IRA, pension, auto invest, auto withdraw

Royce Equity Income Series (RYEQX)

Growth & Income

1414 Avenue of the Americas
New York, NY 10019
(800) 221-4268

PERFORMANCE

fund inception date: 1/2/90

	3yr Annual	5yr Annual	10yr Annual	Bull	Bear
Return (%)	9.3	7.5	na	80.3	-4.2
Differ from Category (+/-)	2.2 abv av	-0.4 av	na	4.5 abv av	2.1 abv av

Total Risk	Standard Deviation	Category Risk	Risk Index	Beta
blw av	5.8%	low	0.7	0.4

	1994	1993	1992	1991	1990	1989	1988	1987	1986	1985
Return (%).............	-3.2	13.0	19.3	30.3	-15.3	—	—	—	—	—
Differ from category (+/-) ...	-1.8	-0.2	9.1	2.7	-9.3	—	—	—	—	—

PER SHARE DATA

	1994	1993	1992	1991	1990	1989	1988	1987	1986	1985
Dividends, Net Income ($).	0.18	0.21	0.22	0.22	0.22	—	—	—	—	—
Distrib'ns, Cap Gain ($) ...	0.10	0.41	0.16	0.09	0.00	—	—	—	—	—
Net Asset Value ($)	5.12	5.58	5.49	4.93	4.03	—	—	—	—	—
Expense Ratio (%)	1.28	1.00	0.99	0.99	1.00	—	—	—	—	—
Net Income to Assets (%) .	3.12	3.79	4.31	4.58	4.74	—	—	—	—	—
Portfolio Turnover (%)	na	100	59	72	28	—	—	—	—	—
Total Assets (Millions $)	81	81	54	41	19	—	—	—	—	—

PORTFOLIO (as of 6/30/94)

Portfolio Manager: Charles Royce - 1989

Investm't Category: Growth & Income

Cap Gain	Asset Allocation
✔ Cap & Income	Fund of Funds
Income	Index
	Sector
✔ Domestic	Small Cap
Foreign	Socially Conscious
Country/Region	State Specific

Portfolio:	stocks 76%	bonds 1%
convertibles 14%	other 3%	cash 6%

Largest Holdings: industrial cyclicals 19%, financial 18%

Unrealized Net Capital Gains: -1% of portfolio value

SHAREHOLDER INFORMATION

Minimum Investment
Initial: $2,000   Subsequent: $50

Minimum IRA Investment
Initial: $1,000   Subsequent: $50

Maximum Fees
Load: 1.00% redemption   12b-1: none
Other: redemption fee applies for 1 year

Distributions
Income: quarterly   Capital Gains: Dec

Exchange Options
Number Per Year: no limit   Fee: none
Telephone: yes (money market fund not available)

Services
IRA, pension, auto invest, auto withdraw

Royce Premier (RYPRX)
Growth

1414 Avenue of the Americas
New York, NY 10019
(800) 221-4268

PERFORMANCE

fund inception date: 12/31/91

	3yr Annual	5yr Annual	10yr Annual	Bull	Bear
Return (%)	12.4	na	na	na	-1.5
Differ from Category (+/-)	4.7 high	na	na	na	5.1 high

Total Risk	Standard Deviation	Category Risk	Risk Index	Beta
blw av	5.1%	low	0.5	0.4

	1994	1993	1992	1991	1990	1989	1988	1987	1986	1985
Return (%)	3.2	19.0	15.8	—	—	—	—	—	—	—
Differ from category (+/-) . . .	3.8	5.6	4.2	—	—	—	—	—	—	—

PER SHARE DATA

	1994	1993	1992	1991	1990	1989	1988	1987	1986	1985
Dividends, Net Income ($)	0.05	0.02	0.02	—	—	—	—	—	—	—
Distrib'ns, Cap Gain ($) . . .	0.09	0.14	0.25	—	—	—	—	—	—	—
Net Asset Value ($)	6.48	6.41	5.52	—	—	—	—	—	—	—
Expense Ratio (%).	1.46	1.50	1.77	—	—	—	—	—	—	—
Net Income to Assets (%). .	0.88	0.68	0.53	—	—	—	—	—	—	—
Portfolio Turnover (%).	na	85	116	—	—	—	—	—	—	—
Total Assets (Millions $) . . .	196	47	2	—	—	—	—	—	—	—

PORTFOLIO (as of 6/30/94)

Portfolio Manager: Charles Royce - 1991

Investm't Category: Growth
- ✔ Cap Gain
- Cap & Income
- Income
- ✔ Domestic
- ✔ Foreign
- Country/Region

- Asset Allocation
- Fund of Funds
- Index
- Sector
- ✔ Small Cap
- Socially Conscious
- State Specific

Portfolio: stocks 78%   bonds 9%
convertibles 0%   other 0%   cash 13%

Largest Holdings: financial 20%, retail 13%

Unrealized Net Capital Gains: 0% of portfolio value

SHAREHOLDER INFORMATION

Minimum Investment
Initial: $2,000   Subsequent: $50

Minimum IRA Investment
Initial: $500   Subsequent: $50

Maximum Fees
Load: 1.00% redemption   12b-1: none
Other: redemption fee applies for 1 year

Distributions
Income: Dec   Capital Gains: Dec

Exchange Options
Number Per Year: no limit   Fee: none
Telephone: yes (money market fund available)

Services
IRA, pension, auto invest, auto withdraw

Rushmore American Gas Index (GASFX)

4922 Fairmont Ave.
Bethesda, MD 20814
(800) 622-1386, (301) 657-1500

Growth & Income

PERFORMANCE

fund inception date: 5/15/89

	3yr Annual	5yr Annual	10yr Annual	Bull	Bear
Return (%)	5.4	1.6	na	37.4	-10.0
Differ from Category (+/-)	-1.7 blw av	-6.3 low	na	-38.4 low	-3.7 low

Total Risk	Standard Deviation	Category Risk	Risk Index	Beta
abv av	11.1%	high	1.4	0.9

	1994	1993	1992	1991	1990	1989	1988	1987	1986	1985
Return (%)	-9.7	16.5	11.3	3.2	-10.4	—	—	—	—	—
Differ from category (+/-)	-8.3	3.3	1.1	-24.4	-4.4	—	—	—	—	—

PER SHARE DATA

	1994	1993	1992	1991	1990	1989	1988	1987	1986	1985
Dividends, Net Income ($)	0.44	0.40	0.42	0.47	0.54	—	—	—	—	—
Distrib'ns, Cap Gain ($)	0.00	0.06	0.13	0.00	0.10	—	—	—	—	—
Net Asset Value ($)	10.36	11.96	10.65	10.09	10.24	—	—	—	—	—
Expense Ratio (%)	0.84	0.85	0.85	0.79	0.75	—	—	—	—	—
Net Income to Assets (%)	3.33	3.82	4.73	5.00	4.99	—	—	—	—	—
Portfolio Turnover (%)	11	21	30	30	25	—	—	—	—	—
Total Assets (Millions $)	176	230	129	131	86	—	—	—	—	—

PORTFOLIO (as of 3/31/94)

Portfolio Manager: committee

Investm't Category: Growth & Income

Cap Gain	Asset Allocation
✔ Cap & Income	Fund of Funds
Income	✔ Index
	✔ Sector
✔ Domestic	Small Cap
Foreign	Socially Conscious
Country/Region	State Specific

Portfolio: stocks 100% bonds 0%
convertibles 0% other 0% cash 0%

Largest Holdings: American Gas Association index

Unrealized Net Capital Gains: 2% of portfolio value

SHAREHOLDER INFORMATION

Minimum Investment
Initial: $2,500   Subsequent: $0

Minimum IRA Investment
Initial: $500   Subsequent: $0

Maximum Fees
Load: none   12b-1: none
Other: none

Distributions
Income: quarterly   Capital Gains: Dec

Exchange Options
Number Per Year: 5   Fee: none
Telephone: yes (money market fund available)

Services
IRA, pension, auto exchange, auto invest, auto withdraw

Rushmore Maryland Tax-Free (RSXLX)

Tax-Exempt Bond

4922 Fairmont Ave.
Bethesda, MD 20814
(800) 622-1386, (301) 657-1500

PERFORMANCE

fund inception date: 9/1/83

	3yr Annual	5yr Annual	10yr Annual	Bull	Bear
Return (%)	4.6	5.3	7.1	40.8	-5.6
Differ from Category (+/-)	0.1 av	-0.8 low	-1.0 low	-1.0 blw av	-0.4 av

Total Risk	Standard Deviation	Category Risk	Risk Index	Avg Mat
blw av	5.7%	blw av	0.9	na

	1994	1993	1992	1991	1990	1989	1988	1987	1986	1985
Return (%)	-5.2	11.9	8.0	10.2	2.8	6.6	9.6	1.0	11.7	16.1
Differ from category (+/-) . . .	0.0	0.2	-0.3	-1.1	-3.5	-2.4	-0.6	2.3	-4.7	-1.3

PER SHARE DATA

	1994	1993	1992	1991	1990	1989	1988	1987	1986	1985
Dividends, Net Income ($) .	0.56	0.57	0.60	0.59	0.62	0.68	0.70	0.73	0.80	0.84
Distrib'ns, Cap Gain ($) . . .	0.00	0.00	0.00	0.00	0.00	0.00	0.00	0.00	0.00	0.00
Net Asset Value ($)	10.12	11.27	10.60	10.39	9.99	10.33	10.34	10.09	10.71	10.33
Expense Ratio (%).	na	0.50	0.50	0.62	0.93	0.92	0.93	0.93	0.95	0.87
Net Income to Assets (%). . .	na	5.13	5.67	5.85	6.19	6.56	6.81	7.04	7.60	8.52
Portfolio Turnover (%).	na	30	21	61	244	173	102	84	40	87
Total Assets (Millions $)	44	58	44	24	10	1	9	9	10	6

PORTFOLIO (as of 6/30/94)

Portfolio Manager: committee

Investm't Category: Tax-Exempt Bond

Cap Gain	Asset Allocation
Cap & Income	Fund of Funds
✔ Income	Index
	Sector
✔ Domestic	Small Cap
Foreign	Socially Conscious
Country/Region	✔ State Specific

Portfolio: stocks 0%   bonds 100%
convertibles 0%   other 0%   cash 0%

Largest Holdings: general obligation 43%

Unrealized Net Capital Gains: 1% of portfolio value

SHAREHOLDER INFORMATION

Minimum Investment
Initial: $2,500   Subsequent: $0

Minimum IRA Investment
Initial: na   Subsequent: na

Maximum Fees
Load: none   12b-1: none
Other: none

Distributions
Income: monthly   Capital Gains: Dec

Exchange Options
Number Per Year: no limit   Fee: none
Telephone: yes (money market fund available)

Services
auto exchange, auto invest, auto withdraw

Rushmore US Gov't Interm-Term (RSUIX)

4922 Fairmont Ave.
Bethesda, MD 20814
(800) 622-1386, (301) 657-1500

Government Bond

PERFORMANCE

fund inception date: 12/1/85

	3yr Annual	5yr Annual	10yr Annual	Bull	Bear
Return (%)	3.5	6.5	na	50.3	-8.7
Differ from Category (+/-)	-0.5 blw av	-0.2 blw av	na	-0.9 av	-2.3 blw av

Total Risk	Standard Deviation	Category Risk	Risk Index	Avg Mat
blw av	6.3%	abv av	1.4	na

	1994	1993	1992	1991	1990	1989	1988	1987	1986	1985
Return (%).	-7.3	11.8	7.0	16.3	6.4	14.8	6.8	0.7	10.4	—
Differ from category (+/-) . .	-2.5	0.9	0.6	1.0	0.2	0.3	-1.1	2.8	-10.2	—

PER SHARE DATA

	1994	1993	1992	1991	1990	1989	1988	1987	1986	1985
Dividends, Net Income ($).	0.56	0.52	0.69	0.70	0.73	0.78	0.84	0.67	0.65	—
Distrib'ns, Cap Gain ($) . . .	0.00	0.16	1.26	0.00	0.00	0.22	0.00	0.00	0.00	—
Net Asset Value ($)	8.57	9.84	9.42	10.65	9.82	9.95	9.58	9.77	10.37	—
Expense Ratio (%)	0.80	0.80	0.80	0.80	0.80	0.80	0.81	0.78	1.00	—
Net Income to Assets (%) .	5.50	5.91	6.63	7.21	7.47	7.93	8.14	6.18	6.50	—
Portfolio Turnover (%)	174	113	200	196	424	461	1,754	87	—	—
Total Assets (Millions $)	9	21	16	23	4	7	1	1	1	—

PORTFOLIO (as of 8/31/94)

Portfolio Manager: committee

Investm't Category: Government Bond

Cap Gain	Asset Allocation
Cap & Income	Fund of Funds
✔ Income	Index
	Sector
✔ Domestic	Small Cap
Foreign	Socially Conscious
Country/Region	State Specific

Portfolio: stocks 0% bonds 96%
convertibles 0% other 0% cash 4%

Largest Holdings: U.S. government 96%

Unrealized Net Capital Gains: -1% of portfolio value

SHAREHOLDER INFORMATION

Minimum Investment
Initial: $2,500   Subsequent: $0

Minimum IRA Investment
Initial: $500   Subsequent: $0

Maximum Fees
Load: none   12b-1: none
Other: none

Distributions
Income: monthly   Capital Gains: Jun, Dec

Exchange Options
Number Per Year: no limit   Fee: none
Telephone: yes (money market fund available)

Services
IRA, pension, auto exchange, auto invest, auto withdraw

Rushmore US Gov't Long-Term (RSGVX)

Government Bond

4922 Fairmont Ave.
Bethesda, MD 20814
(800) 622-1386, (301) 657-1500

PERFORMANCE

fund inception date: 12/1/85

	3yr Annual	5yr Annual	10yr Annual	Bull	Bear
Return (%)	3.2	6.0	na	60.0	-12.0
Differ from Category (+/-)	-0.8 blw av	-0.7 low	na	8.8 abv av	-5.6 low

Total Risk	Standard Deviation	Category Risk	Risk Index	Avg Mat
av	8.2%	high	1.8	na

	1994	1993	1992	1991	1990	1989	1988	1987	1986	1985
Return (%)	-9.9	15.3	6.1	16.5	4.4	18.9	7.9	0.4	8.9	—
Differ from category (+/-) . .	-5.1	4.4	-0.3	1.2	-1.8	4.4	0.0	2.5	-11.7	—

PER SHARE DATA

	1994	1993	1992	1991	1990	1989	1988	1987	1986	1985
Dividends, Net Income ($) .	0.61	0.61	0.69	0.72	0.73	0.73	0.75	0.76	0.87	—
Distrib'ns, Cap Gain ($) . . .	0.00	0.78	0.48	0.00	0.00	0.00	0.00	0.00	0.00	—
Net Asset Value ($)	8.69	10.31	10.16	10.71	9.87	10.20	9.24	9.28	10.01	—
Expense Ratio (%).	0.80	0.80	0.80	0.80	0.80	0.80	0.83	0.78	1.00	—
Net Income to Assets (%). .	5.97	6.08	6.80	7.43	7.28	7.73	8.05	7.90	8.83	—
Portfolio Turnover (%)	188	173	298	236	401	412	829	226	43	—
Total Assets (Millions $)	33	18	23	14	13	26	7	11	7	—

PORTFOLIO (as of 8/31/94)

Portfolio Manager: committee

Investm't Category: Government Bond
- Cap Gain
- Cap & Income
- ✔ Income
- ✔ Domestic
- Foreign
- Country/Region
- Asset Allocation
- Fund of Funds
- Index
- Sector
- Small Cap
- Socially Conscious
- State Specific

Portfolio: stocks 0% bonds 100%
convertibles 0% other 0% cash 0%

Largest Holdings: U.S government 100%

Unrealized Net Capital Gains: -2% of portfolio value

SHAREHOLDER INFORMATION

Minimum Investment
Initial: $2,500   Subsequent: $0

Minimum IRA Investment
Initial: $500   Subsequent: $0

Maximum Fees
Load: none   12b-1: none
Other: none

Distributions
Income: monthly   Capital Gains: Jun, Dec

Exchange Options
Number Per Year: no limit   Fee: none
Telephone: yes (money market fund available)

Services
IRA, pension, auto exchange, auto invest, auto withdraw

Rushmore Virginia Tax-Free (RSXIX)

Tax-Exempt Bond

4922 Fairmont Ave.
Bethesda, MD 20814
(800) 622-1386, (301) 657-1500

PERFORMANCE

fund inception date: 9/1/83

	3yr Annual	5yr Annual	10yr Annual	Bull	Bear
Return (%)	4.6	5.8	6.8	41.4	-5.6
Differ from Category (+/-)	0.1 av	-0.3 blw av	-1.3 low	-0.4 blw av	-0.4 av

Total Risk	Standard Deviation	Category Risk	Risk Index	Avg Mat
blw av	5.7%	blw av	0.9	na

	1994	1993	1992	1991	1990	1989	1988	1987	1986	1985
Return (%).	-5.0	11.7	8.0	10.8	4.4	7.9	7.4	-1.0	12.0	13.1
Differ from category (+/-) . .	0.2	0.0	-0.3	-0.5	-1.9	-1.1	-2.8	0.3	-4.4	-4.3

PER SHARE DATA

	1994	1993	1992	1991	1990	1989	1988	1987	1986	1985
Dividends, Net Income ($).	0.58	0.58	0.62	0.61	0.58	0.59	0.60	0.63	0.72	0.75
Distrib'ns, Cap Gain ($) . . .	0.00	0.00	0.00	0.00	0.00	0.00	0.00	0.00	0.00	0.00
Net Asset Value ($)	10.36	11.51	10.84	10.63	10.17	10.31	10.12	9.99	10.74	10.26
Expense Ratio (%)	na	0.50	0.50	0.61	0.93	0.94	0.93	0.92	0.94	0.89
Net Income to Assets (%) . . .	na	5.15	5.71	5.91	5.70	5.82	5.92	6.18	6.87	7.55
Portfolio Turnover (%)	na	43	50	74	202	150	78	125	42	67
Total Assets (Millions $)	27	34	26	17	7	7	8	8	9	6

PORTFOLIO (as of 6/30/94)

Portfolio Manager: committee

Investm't Category: Tax-Exempt Bond

Cap Gain	Asset Allocation
Cap & Income	Fund of Funds
✔ Income	Index
	Sector
✔ Domestic	Small Cap
Foreign	Socially Conscious
Country/Region	✔ State Specific

Portfolio:	stocks 0%	bonds 100%
convertibles 0%	other 0%	cash 0%

Largest Holdings: general obligation 40%

Unrealized Net Capital Gains: 1% of portfolio value

SHAREHOLDER INFORMATION

Minimum Investment
Initial: $2,500   Subsequent: $0

Minimum IRA Investment
Initial: na   Subsequent: na

Maximum Fees
Load: none   12b-1: none
Other: none

Distributions
Income: monthly   Capital Gains: Jun, Dec

Exchange Options
Number Per Year: no limit   Fee: none
Telephone: yes (money market fund available)

Services
auto exchange, auto invest, auto withdraw

Safeco CA Tax-Free Income (SFCAX)

P.O. Box 34890
Seattle, WA 98124
(800) 426-6730, (206) 545-5530

Tax-Exempt Bond

PERFORMANCE

fund inception date: 10/5/83

	3yr Annual	5yr Annual	10yr Annual	Bull	Bear
Return (%)	3.5	5.9	8.9	47.0	-7.9
Differ from Category (+/-)	-1.0 low	-0.2 blw av	0.8 abv av	5.2 abv av	-2.7 low

Total Risk	Standard Deviation	Category Risk	Risk Index	Avg Mat
av	6.9%	high	1.1	19.9 yrs

	1994	1993	1992	1991	1990	1989	1988	1987	1986	1985
Return (%)	-9.1	13.2	7.9	12.5	6.9	9.8	12.8	-2.0	19.6	21.0
Differ from category (+/-)	-3.9	1.5	-0.4	1.2	0.6	0.8	2.6	-0.7	3.2	3.6

PER SHARE DATA

	1994	1993	1992	1991	1990	1989	1988	1987	1986	1985
Dividends, Net Income ($)	0.64	0.66	0.68	0.71	0.71	0.73	0.75	0.77	0.81	0.85
Distrib'ns, Cap Gain ($)	0.10	0.34	0.13	0.08	0.06	0.18	0.00	0.43	0.11	0.00
Net Asset Value ($)	10.58	12.43	11.90	11.81	11.23	11.26	11.11	10.55	12.02	10.87
Expense Ratio (%)	0.68	0.66	0.67	0.67	0.68	0.71	0.72	0.70	0.76	0.77
Net Income to Assets (%)	5.60	5.71	6.13	6.32	6.42	6.86	6.99	6.71	7.66	8.79
Portfolio Turnover (%)	75	23	39	23	71	77	67	45	40	23
Total Assets (Millions $)	58	84	71	57	48	37	29	35	21	11

PORTFOLIO (as of 9/30/94)

Portfolio Manager: Stephen Bauer - 1983

Investm't Category: Tax-Exempt Bond

Cap Gain	Asset Allocation
Cap & Income	Fund of Funds
✔ Income	Index
	Sector
✔ Domestic	Small Cap
Foreign	Socially Conscious
Country/Region	✔ State Specific

Portfolio: stocks 0% bonds 100%
convertibles 0% other 0% cash 0%

Largest Holdings: general obligation 26%

Unrealized Net Capital Gains: 0% of portfolio value

SHAREHOLDER INFORMATION

Minimum Investment
Initial: $1,000   Subsequent: $100

Minimum IRA Investment
Initial: na   Subsequent: na

Maximum Fees
Load: none   12b-1: none
Other: none

Distributions
Income: monthly   Capital Gains: Mar, Dec

Exchange Options
Number Per Year: no limit   Fee: none
Telephone: yes (money market fund available)

Services
auto exchange, auto invest, auto withdraw

Safeco Equity (SAFQX)

Growth & Income

P.O. Box 34890
Seattle, WA 98124
(800) 426-6730, (206) 545-5530

PERFORMANCE

fund inception date: 3/14/32

	3yr Annual	5yr Annual	10yr Annual	Bull	Bear
Return (%)	16.2	12.9	16.1	107.9	-4.0
Differ from Category (+/-)	9.1 high	5.0 high	4.4 high	32.1 high	2.3 high

Total Risk	Standard Deviation	Category Risk	Risk Index	Beta
high	14.4%	high	1.8	1.4

	1994	1993	1992	1991	1990	1989	1988	1987	1986	1985
Return (%)	9.9	30.9	9.2	27.9	-8.5	35.7	25.2	-4.8	12.7	33.2
Differ from category (+/-)	11.3	17.7	-1.0	0.3	-2.5	14.3	8.2	-5.4	-3.1	7.5

PER SHARE DATA

	1994	1993	1992	1991	1990	1989	1988	1987	1986	1985
Dividends, Net Income ($)	0.26	0.18	0.13	0.18	0.20	0.40	0.20	0.25	0.29	0.40
Distrib'ns, Cap Gain ($)	0.54	0.81	0.49	0.68	0.39	0.64	0.13	1.79	2.03	1.22
Net Asset Value ($)	13.68	13.18	10.87	10.59	8.97	10.48	8.55	7.09	9.54	10.50
Expense Ratio (%)	0.85	0.94	0.96	0.98	0.97	0.96	1.00	0.97	0.88	0.68
Net Income to Assets (%)	1.72	1.50	1.34	1.70	2.19	4.13	2.16	1.92	2.55	3.97
Portfolio Turnover (%)	33	37	40	45	51	64	88	85	86	56
Total Assets (Millions $)	449	199	74	72	52	54	46	65	46	34

PORTFOLIO (as of 9/30/94)

Portfolio Manager: Doug Johnson - 1984

Investm't Category: Growth & Income

Cap Gain	Asset Allocation
✔ Cap & Income	Fund of Funds
Income	Index
	Sector
✔ Domestic	Small Cap
Foreign	Socially Conscious
Country/Region	State Specific

Portfolio: stocks 93% bonds 0%
convertibles 0% other 1% cash 6%

Largest Holdings: telephone utilities 9%, drugs & hospital supplies 8%

Unrealized Net Capital Gains: 11% of portfolio value

SHAREHOLDER INFORMATION

Minimum Investment
Initial: $1,000   Subsequent: $100

Minimum IRA Investment
Initial: $250   Subsequent: $100

Maximum Fees
Load: none   12b-1: none
Other: none

Distributions
Income: quarterly   Capital Gains: Sep, Dec

Exchange Options
Number Per Year: no limit   Fee: none
Telephone: yes (money market fund available)

Services
IRA, pension, auto exchange, auto invest, auto withdraw

Safeco GNMA (SFUSX)

Mortgage-Backed Bond

P.O. Box 34890
Seattle, WA 98124
(800) 426-6730, (206) 545-5530

PERFORMANCE

fund inception date: 7/15/86

	3yr Annual	5yr Annual	10yr Annual	Bull	Bear
Return (%)	3.0	6.4	na	38.4	-5.5
Differ from Category (+/-)	-0.1 blw av	-0.5 low	na	0.4 av	-1.1 blw av

Total Risk	Standard Deviation	Category Risk	Risk Index	Avg Mat
low	3.8%	abv av	1.1	17.6 yrs

	1994	1993	1992	1991	1990	1989	1988	1987	1986	1985
Return (%)	-4.2	7.0	6.6	14.8	8.6	12.9	7.8	0.9	—	—
Differ from category (+/-) . . .	-1.4	0.2	0.5	0.4	-1.1	0.4	0.7	-0.9	—	—

PER SHARE DATA

	1994	1993	1992	1991	1990	1989	1988	1987	1986	1985
Dividends, Net Income ($) .	0.59	0.64	0.73	0.77	0.77	0.78	0.87	0.82	—	—
Distrib'ns, Cap Gain ($) . . .	0.00	0.00	0.00	0.00	0.00	0.00	0.00	0.00	—	—
Net Asset Value ($)	8.87	9.88	9.84	9.93	9.37	9.37	9.03	9.21	—	—
Expense Ratio (%)	0.95	0.93	0.94	0.97	0.99	1.02	1.06	1.05	—	—
Net Income to Assets (%) .	6.26	6.71	7.49	8.23	8.28	8.83	9.51	8.59	—	—
Portfolio Turnover (%).	55	70	25	44	90	77	110	101	—	—
Total Assets (Millions $).	42	60	56	42	29	27	28	20	—	—

PORTFOLIO (as of 9/30/94)

Portfolio Manager: Paul Stevenson - 1988

Investm't Category: Mortgage-Backed Bond

Cap Gain	Asset Allocation
Cap & Income	Fund of Funds
✔ Income	Index
	Sector
✔ Domestic	Small Cap
Foreign	Socially Conscious
Country/Region	State Specific

Portfolio: stocks 0% bonds 97%
convertibles 0% other 0% cash 3%

Largest Holdings: mortgage-backed 97%

Unrealized Net Capital Gains: -4% of portfolio value

SHAREHOLDER INFORMATION

Minimum Investment
Initial: $1,000   Subsequent: $100

Minimum IRA Investment
Initial: $250   Subsequent: $100

Maximum Fees
Load: none   12b-1: none
Other: none

Distributions
Income: monthly   Capital Gains: Sep, Dec

Exchange Options
Number Per Year: no limit   Fee: none
Telephone: yes (money market fund available)

Services
IRA, pension, auto exchange, auto invest, auto withdraw

Safeco Growth (SAFGX)

Aggressive Growth

P.O. Box 34890
Seattle, WA 98124
(800) 426-6730, (206) 545-5530

PERFORMANCE

fund inception date: 1/1/68

	3yr Annual	5yr Annual	10yr Annual	Bull	Bear
Return (%)	5.2	10.0	11.9	119.0	-13.2
Differ from Category (+/-)	-3.7 blw av	-2.5 blw av	-2.1 blw av	-14.2 av	-2.4 blw av

Total Risk	Standard Deviation	Category Risk	Risk Index	Beta
high	18.0%	high	1.2	1.4

	1994	1993	1992	1991	1990	1989	1988	1987	1986	1985
Return (%).............	-1.6	22.1	-3.0	62.6	-14.9	19.1	22.1	7.0	1.8	20.6
Differ from category (+/-)...	-0.9	2.6	-14.0	10.5	-8.7	-7.7	6.9	9.2	-10.0	-11.7

PER SHARE DATA

	1994	1993	1992	1991	1990	1989	1988	1987	1986	1985
Dividends, Net Income ($).	0.00	0.00	0.00	0.05	0.09	0.42	0.44	0.32	0.31	0.50
Distrib'ns, Cap Gain ($) ...	2.15	0.70	0.62	1.15	1.88	0.90	0.81	1.25	1.59	2.98
Net Asset Value ($)	17.55	20.06	17.00	18.31	12.01	16.61	15.04	13.36	14.00	15.56
Expense Ratio (%)	0.95	0.91	0.91	0.90	1.01	0.94	0.98	0.92	0.85	0.63
Net Income to Assets (%) .	-0.12	-0.10	-0.10	0.36	0.88	3.27	2.37	1.46	1.90	2.94
Portfolio Turnover (%)	71	57	85	50	90	11	19	24	46	29
Total Assets (Millions $)....	150	163	128	155	59	82	74	83	68	66

PORTFOLIO (as of 9/30/94)

Portfolio Manager: Thomas M. Maguire - 1989

Investm't Category: Aggressive Growth

✔ Cap Gain	Asset Allocation
Cap & Income	Fund of Funds
Income	Index
	Sector
✔ Domestic	Small Cap
Foreign	Socially Conscious
Country/Region	State Specific

Portfolio: stocks 96% bonds 0%
convertibles 0% other 0% cash 4%

Largest Holdings: financial services 16%, leisure time 13%

Unrealized Net Capital Gains: 21% of portfolio value

SHAREHOLDER INFORMATION

Minimum Investment
Initial: $1,000   Subsequent: $100

Minimum IRA Investment
Initial: $250   Subsequent: $100

Maximum Fees
Load: none   12b-1: none
Other: none

Distributions
Income: quarterly   Capital Gains: Sep, Dec

Exchange Options
Number Per Year: no limit   Fee: none
Telephone: yes (money market fund available)

Services
IRA, pension, auto exchange, auto invest, auto withdraw

Safeco High Yield Bond
(SAFHX)
Corporate High-Yield Bond

P.O. Box 34890
Seattle, WA 98124
(800) 426-6730, (206) 545-5530

PERFORMANCE

fund inception date: 9/1/88

	3yr Annual	5yr Annual	10yr Annual	Bull	Bear
Return (%)	9.1	9.2	na	66.7	-3.5
Differ from Category (+/-)	-0.8 abv av	-0.1 av	na	-12.6 blw av	1.8 abv av

Total Risk	Standard Deviation	Category Risk	Risk Index	Avg Mat
low	4.3%	low	0.9	7.8 yrs

	1994	1993	1992	1991	1990	1989	1988	1987	1986	1985
Return (%)	-2.2	16.9	13.8	24.2	-3.5	1.9	—	—	—	—
Differ from category (+/-)	0.5	-1.5	-1.8	-3.2	.1.6	0.5	—	—	—	—

PER SHARE DATA

	1994	1993	1992	1991	1990	1989	1988	1987	1986	1985
Dividends, Net Income ($)	0.84	0.86	0.89	0.86	1.03	1.11	—	—	—	—
Distrib'ns, Cap Gain ($)	0.00	0.00	0.00	0.00	0.00	0.00	—	—	—	—
Net Asset Value ($)	8.25	9.30	8.73	8.48	7.58	8.91	—	—	—	—
Expense Ratio (%)	1.03	1.09	1.05	1.11	1.15	1.11	—	—	—	—
Net Income to Assets (%)	9.26	9.94	9.66	11.51	11.90	11.52	—	—	—	—
Portfolio Turnover (%)	63	50	40	32	18	12	—	—	—	—
Total Assets (Millions $)	25	34	19	11	7	9	—	—	—	—

PORTFOLIO (as of 9/30/94)

Portfolio Manager: Ron Spaulding - 1988

Investm't Category: Corp. High-Yield Bond

Cap Gain	Asset Allocation
Cap & Income	Fund of Funds
✔ Income	Index
	Sector
✔ Domestic	Small Cap
Foreign	Socially Conscious
Country/Region	State Specific

Portfolio: stocks 0% bonds 100%
convertibles 0% other 0% cash 0%

Largest Holdings: retail 14%, utilities 6%

Unrealized Net Capital Gains: -3% of portfolio value

SHAREHOLDER INFORMATION

Minimum Investment
Initial: $1,000   Subsequent: $100

Minimum IRA Investment
Initial: $250   Subsequent: $100

Maximum Fees
Load: none   12b-1: none
Other: none

Distributions
Income: monthly   Capital Gains: Sep, Dec

Exchange Options
Number Per Year: no limit   Fee: none
Telephone: yes (money market fund available)

Services
IRA, pension, auto exchange, auto invest, auto withdraw

Safeco Income (SAFIX)

Balanced

P.O. Box 34890
Seattle, WA 98124
(800) 426-6730, (206) 545-5530

PERFORMANCE

fund inception date: 10/1/69

	3yr Annual	5yr Annual	10yr Annual	Bull	Bear
Return (%)	7.4	6.4	11.1	68.5	-5.8
Differ from Category (+/-)	1.0 abv av	-1.6 blw av	-0.2 av	3.5 av	-0.1 blw av

Total Risk	Standard Deviation	Category Risk	Risk Index	Beta
blw av	6.6%	abv av	1.1	0.7

	1994	1993	1992	1991	1990	1989	1988	1987	1986	1985
Return (%).	-1.0	12.5	11.4	23.2	-10.7	19.1	18.9	-5.9	20.0	31.7
Differ from category (+/-). . .	0.9	-0.9	3.1	-0.2	-10.2	1.8	7.1	-8.3	2.6	7.4

PER SHARE DATA

	1994	1993	1992	1991	1990	1989	1988	1987	1986	1985
Dividends, Net Income ($).	0.81	0.78	0.78	0.80	0.86	0.81	0.79	1.00	0.78	0.75
Distrib'ns, Cap Gain ($) . . .	0.24	0.00	0.04	0.05	0.09	0.08	0.00	0.84	0.73	0.56
Net Asset Value ($)	16.54	17.77	16.50	15.58	13.37	16.03	14.23	12.64	15.28	14.03
Expense Ratio (%)	0.86	0.90	0.90	0.93	0.92	0.92	0.97	0.94	0.95	0.73
Net Income to Assets (%) .	4.59	4.55	5.06	5.58	5.59	5.28	5.58	4.53	5.08	6.41
Portfolio Turnover (%)	19	20	20	22	19	16	34	33	28	29
Total Assets (Millions $). . . .	181	202	182	181	170	233	232	313	102	31

PORTFOLIO (as of 9/30/94)

Portfolio Manager: Arley Hudson - 1978

Investm't Category: Balanced

Cap Gain	Asset Allocation
✔ Cap & Income	Fund of Funds
Income	Index
	Sector
✔ Domestic	Small Cap
Foreign	Socially Conscious
Country/Region	State Specific

Portfolio: stocks 57% bonds 0%
convertibles 41% other 0% cash 2%

Largest Holdings: stocks—banking & finance 13%, stocks—petroleum & petroleum services 11%

Unrealized Net Capital Gains: 10% of portfolio value

SHAREHOLDER INFORMATION

Minimum Investment
Initial: $1,000   Subsequent: $100

Minimum IRA Investment
Initial: $250   Subsequent: $100

Maximum Fees
Load: none   12b-1: none
Other: none

Distributions
Income: quarterly   Capital Gains: Sep, Dec

Exchange Options
Number Per Year: no limit   Fee: none
Telephone: yes (money market fund available)

Services
IRA, pension, auto exchange, auto invest, auto withdraw

Safeco Muni Bond
(SFCOX)
Tax-Exempt Bond

P.O. Box 34890
Seattle, WA 98124
(800) 426-6730, (206) 545-5530

PERFORMANCE

fund inception date: 11/18/81

	3yr Annual	5yr Annual	10yr Annual	Bull	Bear
Return (%)	3.9	6.3	9.5	48.2	-7.7
Differ from Category (+/-)	-0.6 low	0.2 av	1.4 high	6.4 high	-2.5 low

Total Risk	Standard Deviation	Category Risk	Risk Index	Avg Mat
av	7.0%	high	1.1	21.5 yrs

	1994	1993	1992	1991	1990	1989	1988	1987	1986	1985
Return (%)	-8.2	12.5	8.7	13.7	6.6	10.0	13.8	0.1	19.7	21.6
Differ from category (+/-)	-3.0	0.8	0.4	2.4	0.3	1.0	3.6	1.4	3.3	4.2

PER SHARE DATA

	1994	1993	1992	1991	1990	1989	1988	1987	1986	1985
Dividends, Net Income ($)	0.77	0.78	0.82	0.85	0.87	0.89	0.95	0.96	1.01	1.06
Distrib'ns, Cap Gain ($)	0.03	0.31	0.18	0.06	0.04	0.44	0.29	0.41	0.21	0.02
Net Asset Value ($)	12.46	14.43	13.82	13.68	12.88	12.97	13.05	12.60	13.97	12.76
Expense Ratio (%)	0.55	0.53	0.54	0.56	0.57	0.60	0.61	0.59	0.63	0.63
Net Income to Assets (%)	5.91	5.91	6.37	6.68	6.76	7.23	7.42	7.20	8.29	9.43
Portfolio Turnover (%)	32	31	25	39	66	136	72	23	21	46
Total Assets (Millions $)	434	599	428	332	286	232	184	215	161	84

PORTFOLIO (as of 9/30/94)

Portfolio Manager: Stephen Bauer - 1981

Investm't Category: Tax-Exempt Bond

Cap Gain	Asset Allocation
Cap & Income	Fund of Funds
✔ Income	Index
	Sector
✔ Domestic	Small Cap
Foreign	Socially Conscious
Country/Region	State Specific

Portfolio: stocks 0% bonds 100%
convertibles 0% other 0% cash 0%

Largest Holdings: general obligation 11%

Unrealized Net Capital Gains: 1% of portfolio value

SHAREHOLDER INFORMATION

Minimum Investment
Initial: $1,000   Subsequent: $100

Minimum IRA Investment
Initial: na   Subsequent: na

Maximum Fees
Load: none   12b-1: none
Other: none

Distributions
Income: monthly   Capital Gains: Mar, Dec

Exchange Options
Number Per Year: no limit   Fee: none
Telephone: yes (money market fund available)

Services
auto exchange, auto invest, auto withdraw

Safeco Northwest
(SFNWX)
Growth

P.O. Box 34890
Seattle, WA 98124
(800) 426-6730, (206) 545-5530

PERFORMANCE   fund inception date: 2/7/91

	3yr Annual	5yr Annual	10yr Annual	Bull	Bear
Return (%)	4.2	na	na	na	-3.0
Differ from Category (+/-)	-3.5 blw av	na	na	na	3.6 high

Total Risk	Standard Deviation	Category Risk	Risk Index	Beta
abv av	9.3%	av	1.0	0.6

	1994	1993	1992	1991	1990	1989	1988	1987	1986	1985
Return (%)...............	-1.5	1.0	14.0	—	—	—	—	—	—	—
Differ from category (+/-)...	-0.9	-12.4	2.4	—	—	—	—	—	—	—

PER SHARE DATA

	1994	1993	1992	1991	1990	1989	1988	1987	1986	1985
Dividends, Net Income ($).	0.04	0.03	0.06	—	—	—	—	—	—	—
Distrib'ns, Cap Gain ($) ...	0.10	0.24	0.31	—	—	—	—	—	—	—
Net Asset Value ($)	12.12	12.45	12.59	—	—	—	—	—	—	—
Expense Ratio (%)	1.06	1.11	1.11	—	—	—	—	—	—	—
Net Income to Assets (%) .	0.33	0.18	0.55	—	—	—	—	—	—	—
Portfolio Turnover (%)	18	14	33	—	—	—	—	—	—	—
Total Assets (Millions $).....	34	40	40	—	—	—	—	—	—	—

PORTFOLIO (as of 9/30/94)

Portfolio Manager: Charles Driggs - 1992

Investm't Category: Growth

✔ Cap Gain	Asset Allocation
Cap & Income	Fund of Funds
Income	Index
	Sector
✔ Domestic	Small Cap
Foreign	Socially Conscious
Country/Region	State Specific

Portfolio:	stocks 98%	bonds 0%
convertibles 0%	other 0%	cash 2%

Largest Holdings: banks 16%, retail 13%

Unrealized Net Capital Gains: 16% of portfolio value

SHAREHOLDER INFORMATION

Minimum Investment
Initial: $1,000   Subsequent: $100

Minimum IRA Investment
Initial: $250   Subsequent: $100

Maximum Fees
Load: none   12b-1: none
Other: none

Distributions
Income: quarterly   Capital Gains: Sep, Dec

Exchange Options
Number Per Year: no limit   Fee: none
Telephone: yes (money market fund available)

Services
IRA, pension, auto exchange, auto invest, auto withdraw

Salomon Brothers Capital (SACPX)

Aggressive Growth

7 World Trade Center
38th Floor
New York, NY 10048
(800) 725-6666, (212) 783-1301

PERFORMANCE

fund inception date: 12/19/76

	3yr Annual	5yr Annual	10yr Annual	Bull	Bear
Return (%)	1.7	5.0	9.2	78.8	-18.0
Differ from Category (+/-)	-7.2 low	-7.5 low	-4.8 low	-54.4 low	-7.2 low

Total Risk	Standard Deviation	Category Risk	Risk Index	Beta
high	13.1%	blw av	0.9	1.3

	1994	1993	1992	1991	1990	1989	1988	1987	1986	1985
Return (%)	-14.1	17.1	4.7	33.4	-9.0	39.7	-4.6	1.3	13.7	23.6
Differ from category (+/-)	-13.4	-2.4	-6.3	-18.7	-2.8	12.9	-19.8	3.5	1.9	-8.7

PER SHARE DATA

	1994	1993	1992	1991	1990	1989	1988	1987	1986	1985
Dividends, Net Income ($)	0.03	0.04	0.11	0.33	0.29	0.00	0.00	0.13	0.25	0.19
Distrib'ns, Cap Gain ($)	2.31	2.08	0.22	0.37	0.09	5.13	0.23	1.56	4.04	0.39
Net Asset Value ($)	15.62	20.80	19.64	19.06	14.86	16.75	15.58	16.58	17.87	19.75
Expense Ratio (%)	1.28	1.31	1.34	1.48	1.44	1.48	1.27	1.17	1.13	1.13
Net Income to Assets (%)	0.20	0.13	0.58	1.87	1.59	0.33	0.03	0.19	0.65	1.22
Portfolio Turnover (%)	na	104	41	94	156	362	270	395	279	162
Total Assets (Millions $)	87	114	103	89	75	72	64	91	105	116

PORTFOLIO (as of 6/30/94)

Portfolio Manager: Robert S. Salomon Jr. - 1990

Investm't Category: Aggressive Growth

✔ Cap Gain	Asset Allocation
Cap & Income	Fund of Funds
Income	Index
	Sector
✔ Domestic	Small Cap
✔ Foreign	Socially Conscious
Country/Region	State Specific

Portfolio: stocks 98% bonds 0%
convertibles 0% other 0% cash 2%

Largest Holdings: auto & auto parts 14%, retail 10%

Unrealized Net Capital Gains: 2% of portfolio value

SHAREHOLDER INFORMATION

Minimum Investment
Initial: $1,000   Subsequent: $100

Minimum IRA Investment
Initial: $250   Subsequent: $100

Maximum Fees
Load: none   12b-1: none
Other: none

Distributions
Income: Dec   Capital Gains: Feb, Dec

Exchange Options
Number Per Year: no limit   Fee: none
Telephone: yes (money market fund available)

Services
IRA, pension, auto withdraw

Salomon Brothers Investors (SAIFX)

Growth & Income

7 World Trade Center
38th Floor
New York, NY 10048
(800) 725-6666, (212) 783-1301

PERFORMANCE   fund inception date: 5/29/58

	3yr Annual	5yr Annual	10yr Annual	Bull	Bear
Return (%)	6.9	8.1	11.5	79.9	-8.5
Differ from Category (+/-)	-0.2 av	0.2 av	-0.2 av	4.1 av	-2.2 blw av

Total Risk	Standard Deviation	Category Risk	Risk Index	Beta
abv av	8.8%	abv av	1.1	1.0

	1994	1993	1992	1991	1990	1989	1988	1987	1986	1985
Return (%)	-1.2	15.1	7.4	29.3	-6.4	21.8	16.8	0.7	13.0	24.4
Differ from category (+/-)	0.2	1.9	-2.8	1.7	-0.4	0.4	-0.2	0.1	-2.8	-1.3

PER SHARE DATA

	1994	1993	1992	1991	1990	1989	1988	1987	1986	1985
Dividends, Net Income ($)	0.27	0.33	0.41	0.46	0.55	0.63	0.53	0.51	0.54	0.55
Distrib'ns, Cap Gain ($)	1.49	2.52	1.79	1.10	0.50	1.59	1.10	2.24	4.55	1.50
Net Asset Value ($)	13.63	15.60	16.10	17.10	14.54	16.65	15.55	14.77	17.37	19.86
Expense Ratio (%)	0.66	0.68	0.68	0.70	0.68	0.63	0.67	0.58	0.57	0.62
Net Income to Assets (%)	3.42	1.90	2.47	2.67	3.13	3.76	3.32	2.37	2.56	3.32
Portfolio Turnover (%)	na	79	48	44	22	36	54	80	62	46
Total Assets (Millions $)	348	392	370	378	330	393	362	352	398	403

PORTFOLIO (as of 6/30/94)

Portfolio Manager: James Fleischmann - 1992, Allan R. White III - 1992

Investm't Category: Growth & Income

Cap Gain	Asset Allocation
✔ Cap & Income	Fund of Funds
Income	Index
	Sector
✔ Domestic	Small Cap
✔ Foreign	Socially Conscious
Country/Region	State Specific

Portfolio:

	stocks 91%	bonds 4%
convertibles 1%	other 3%	cash 1%

Largest Holdings: basic industries 16%, financial services 13%

Unrealized Net Capital Gains: 9% of portfolio value

SHAREHOLDER INFORMATION

Minimum Investment
Initial: $500   Subsequent: $50

Minimum IRA Investment
Initial: $250   Subsequent: $50

Maximum Fees
Load: none   12b-1: none
Other: none

Distributions
Income: quarterly   Capital Gains: Dec

Exchange Options
Number Per Year: no limit   Fee: none
Telephone: yes (money market fund available)

Services
IRA, pension, auto withdraw

Salomon Brothers Opportunity (SAOPX)

Growth

7 World Trade Center
38th Floor
New York, NY 10048
(800) 725-6666, (212) 783-1301

PERFORMANCE

fund inception date: 2/28/79

	3yr Annual	5yr Annual	10yr Annual	Bull	Bear
Return (%)	9.0	7.2	12.0	91.3	-4.9
Differ from Category (+/-)	1.3 abv av	-2.4 blw av	-0.9 blw av	-0.8 av	1.7 abv av

Total Risk	Standard Deviation	Category Risk	Risk Index	Beta
av	8.1%	blw av	0.8	0.9

	1994	1993	1992	1991	1990	1989	1988	1987	1986	1985
Return (%)	0.8	12.8	13.8	30.5	-15.9	20.9	23.2	4.3	6.4	32.8
Differ from category (+/-)	1.4	-0.6	2.2	-5.2	-10.2	-5.2	5.2	2.5	-8.2	3.6

PER SHARE DATA

	1994	1993	1992	1991	1990	1989	1988	1987	1986	1985
Dividends, Net Income ($)	0.37	0.64	0.35	0.50	0.63	0.82	0.54	0.76	0.59	0.48
Distrib'ns, Cap Gain ($)	1.48	1.70	0.81	0.17	0.02	0.89	1.58	2.95	2.79	1.40
Net Asset Value ($)	28.39	30.01	28.70	26.24	20.65	25.35	22.40	19.91	22.60	24.29
Expense Ratio (%)	1.22	1.23	1.25	1.30	1.26	1.19	1.20	1.16	1.16	1.23
Net Income to Assets (%)	1.29	1.86	1.28	2.31	2.38	3.20	2.29	1.92	2.44	2.71
Portfolio Turnover (%)	13	10	11	11	13	15	29	25	28	24
Total Assets (Millions $)	108	115	102	103	90	119	93	114	110	71

PORTFOLIO (as of 8/31/94)

Portfolio Manager: Irving Brilliant - 1979

Investm't Category: Growth

✔ Cap Gain	Asset Allocation
Cap & Income	Fund of Funds
Income	Index
	Sector
✔ Domestic	Small Cap
✔ Foreign	Socially Conscious
Country/Region	State Specific

Portfolio: stocks 89% bonds 0%
convertibles 1% other 0% cash 10%

Largest Holdings: insurance—property & casualty 16%, banks—commercial 11%

Unrealized Net Capital Gains: 44% of portfolio value

SHAREHOLDER INFORMATION

Minimum Investment
Initial: $1,000   Subsequent: $100

Minimum IRA Investment
Initial: $250   Subsequent: $100

Maximum Fees
Load: none   12b-1: none
Other: none

Distributions
Income: Dec   Capital Gains: Dec

Exchange Options
Number Per Year: no limit   Fee: none
Telephone: yes (money market fund available)

Services
IRA, pension, auto withdraw

SBSF (SBFFX)

Growth

45 Rockefeller Plaza
New York, NY 10111
(800) 422-7273, (212) 903-1200

PERFORMANCE — fund inception date: 10/17/83

	3yr Annual	5yr Annual	10yr Annual	Bull	Bear
Return (%)	6.6	7.0	11.4	62.3	-6.1
Differ from Category (+/-)	-1.1 av	-2.6 low	-1.5 low	-29.8 low	0.5 av

Total Risk	Standard Deviation	Category Risk	Risk Index	Beta
av	7.2%	low	0.7	0.7

	1994	1993	1992	1991	1990	1989	1988	1987	1986	1985
Return (%)	-5.6	20.4	6.6	19.0	-2.6	33.9	17.1	-3.1	7.9	28.3
Differ from category (+/-)	-5.0	7.0	-5.0	-16.7	3.1	7.8	-0.9	-4.9	-6.7	-0.9

PER SHARE DATA

	1994	1993	1992	1991	1990	1989	1988	1987	1986	1985
Dividends, Net Income ($)	0.21	0.30	0.40	0.56	0.59	0.51	0.42	0.46	0.49	0.40
Distrib'ns, Cap Gain ($)	0.79	2.11	1.00	1.60	0.41	0.58	0.07	0.40	1.60	0.00
Net Asset Value ($)	13.82	15.71	15.07	15.46	14.83	16.26	12.97	11.49	12.72	13.75
Expense Ratio (%)	1.19	1.15	1.16	1.15	1.15	1.20	1.16	1.10	1.17	1.40
Net Income to Assets (%)	1.46	2.05	2.68	3.11	3.66	3.12	3.12	1.67	1.80	1.96
Portfolio Turnover (%)	22	70	45	50	42	44	47	66	65	80
Total Assets (Millions $)	115	123	105	103	93	98	81	83	90	60

PORTFOLIO (as of 5/31/94)

Portfolio Manager: Louis R. Benzak - 1983

Investm't Category: Growth

✔ Cap Gain   Asset Allocation
   Cap & Income   Fund of Funds
   Income   Index
      Sector
✔ Domestic   Small Cap
   Foreign   Socially Conscious
   Country/Region   State Specific

Portfolio: stocks 76%   bonds 16%
convertibles 8%   other 0%   cash 0%

Largest Holdings: insurance 15%, banks & bank holding companies 10%

Unrealized Net Capital Gains: 10% of portfolio value

SHAREHOLDER INFORMATION

Minimum Investment
Initial: $5,000   Subsequent: $100

Minimum IRA Investment
Initial: $500   Subsequent: $100

Maximum Fees
Load: none   12b-1: 0.25%
Other: none

Distributions
Income: Jun, Dec   Capital Gains: Dec

Exchange Options
Number Per Year: no limit   Fee: none
Telephone: yes (money market fund available)

Services
IRA, pension, auto exchange, auto invest, auto withdraw

SBSF Convertible Securities (SBFCX)

Growth & Income

45 Rockefeller Plaza
New York, NY 10111
(800) 422-7273, (212) 903-1200

PERFORMANCE

fund inception date: 3/23/88

	3yr Annual	5yr Annual	10yr Annual	Bull	Bear
Return (%)	7.7	8.6	na	77.0	-5.3
Differ from Category (+/-)	0.6 abv av	0.7 abv av	na	1.2 av	1.0 abv av

Total Risk	Standard Deviation	Category Risk	Risk Index	Beta
blw av	5.4%	low	0.6	0.4

	1994	1993	1992	1991	1990	1989	1988	1987	1986	1985
Return (%)	-6.4	20.0	11.2	27.7	-5.0	18.8	—	—	—	—
Differ from category (+/-)	-5.0	6.8	1.0	0.1	1.0	-2.6	—	—	—	—

PER SHARE DATA

	1994	1993	1992	1991	1990	1989	1988	1987	1986	1985
Dividends, Net Income ($)	0.60	0.64	0.68	0.68	0.90	0.82	—	—	—	—
Distrib'ns, Cap Gain ($)	0.43	0.24	0.23	0.16	0.03	0.19	—	—	—	—
Net Asset Value ($)	10.41	12.21	10.93	10.67	9.06	10.52	—	—	—	—
Expense Ratio (%)	1.32	1.24	1.32	1.37	1.52	1.15	—	—	—	—
Net Income to Assets (%)	5.02	4.75	5.46	7.13	9.12	8.72	—	—	—	—
Portfolio Turnover (%)	24	30	42	53	32	76	—	—	—	—
Total Assets (Millions $)	60	63	42	28	15	12	—	—	—	—

PORTFOLIO (as of 5/31/94)

Portfolio Manager: Louis R. Benzak - 1988

Investm't Category: Growth & Income

Cap Gain	Asset Allocation
✔ Cap & Income	Fund of Funds
Income	Index
	Sector
✔ Domestic	Small Cap
Foreign	Socially Conscious
Country/Region	State Specific

Portfolio: stocks 13%   bonds 4%
convertibles 78%   other 0%   cash 5%

Largest Holdings: oil & gas 16%, banks & bank holding companies 11%

Unrealized Net Capital Gains: 0% of portfolio value

SHAREHOLDER INFORMATION

Minimum Investment
Initial: $5,000   Subsequent: $100

Minimum IRA Investment
Initial: $500   Subsequent: $100

Maximum Fees
Load: none   12b-1: 0.25%
Other: none

Distributions
Income: quarterly   Capital Gains: Dec

Exchange Options
Number Per Year: no limit   Fee: none
Telephone: yes (money market fund available)

Services
IRA, pension, auto exchange, auto invest, auto withdraw

Schafer Value (SCHVX)
Growth & Income

645 5th Avenue
7th Floor
New York, NY 10022
(800) 343-0481, (212) 644-1800

PERFORMANCE   fund inception date: 8/1/85

	3yr Annual	5yr Annual	10yr Annual	Bull	Bear
Return (%)	12.0	12.2	na	127.7	-6.0
Differ from Category (+/-)	4.9 high	4.3 high	na	51.9 high	0.3 av

Total Risk	Standard Deviation	Category Risk	Risk Index	Beta
abv av	9.2%	abv av	1.1	0.9

	1994	1993	1992	1991	1990	1989	1988	1987	1986	1985
Return (%)	-4.2	23.9	18.6	40.9	-10.1	30.0	17.9	-0.3	10.0	—
Differ from category (+/-)	-2.8	10.7	8.4	13.3	-4.1	8.6	0.9	-0.9	-5.8	—

PER SHARE DATA

	1994	1993	1992	1991	1990	1989	1988	1987	1986	1985
Dividends, Net Income ($)	0.33	0.19	0.39	0.52	0.58	1.26	0.22	0.00	0.31	—
Distrib'ns, Cap Gain ($)	1.64	1.08	3.27	5.48	1.73	0.60	1.18	0.00	0.00	—
Net Asset Value ($)	33.23	36.78	30.70	28.98	24.91	30.28	24.86	22.42	22.51	—
Expense Ratio (%)	1.48	1.74	2.08	2.00	2.00	2.09	1.82	1.96	2.05	—
Net Income to Assets (%)	0.99	0.79	1.20	1.26	1.45	1.81	2.32	1.20	1.80	—
Portfolio Turnover (%)	28	33	53	55	36	42	43	47	19	—
Total Assets (Millions $)	72	25	12	10	11	14	12	20	7	—

PORTFOLIO (as of 9/30/94)

Portfolio Manager: David K. Schafer - 1985

Investm't Category: Growth & Income
Cap Gain	Asset Allocation
✔ Cap & Income	Fund of Funds
Income	Index
	Sector
✔ Domestic	Small Cap
✔ Foreign	Socially Conscious
Country/Region	State Specific

Portfolio: stocks 96% bonds 0%
convertibles 0% other 0% cash 4%

Largest Holdings: banks 12%, medical & pharmaceutical 8%

Unrealized Net Capital Gains: 2% of portfolio value

SHAREHOLDER INFORMATION

Minimum Investment
Initial: $2,000   Subsequent: $1,000

Minimum IRA Investment
Initial: $2,000   Subsequent: $1,000

Maximum Fees
Load: none   12b-1: none
Other: none

Distributions
Income: Dec   Capital Gains: Dec

Exchange Options
Number Per Year: none   Fee:
Telephone:

Services
IRA

Schroder US Equity

(SUSEX)
Growth

787 Seventh Ave.
New York, NY 10019
(800) 344-8332, (212) 841-3841

PERFORMANCE

	3yr Annual	5yr Annual	10yr Annual	Bull	Bear
Return (%)	7.1	10.2	12.2	93.4	-7.3
Differ from Category (+/-)	-0.6 av	0.6 abv av	-0.7 blw av	1.3 av	-0.7 av

Total Risk	Standard Deviation	Category Risk	Risk Index	Beta
abv av	10.0%	abv av	1.0	1.1

	1994	1993	1992	1991	1990	1989	1988	1987	1986	1985
Return (%)	-5.3	12.6	15.2	38.2	-4.0	24.4	12.0	0.4	11.9	23.7
Differ from category (+/-)	-4.7	-0.8	3.6	2.5	1.7	-1.7	-6.0	-1.4	-2.7	-5.5

PER SHARE DATA

	1994	1993	1992	1991	1990	1989	1988	1987	1986	1985
Dividends, Net Income ($)	0.05	0.05	0.04	0.12	0.13	0.26	0.14	0.36	0.24	0.23
Distrib'ns, Cap Gain ($)	0.46	2.52	1.10	0.58	0.00	0.42	0.46	5.47	0.73	0.00
Net Asset Value ($)	7.79	8.77	10.14	9.80	7.61	8.06	7.05	6.82	12.45	12.07
Expense Ratio (%)	1.27	1.18	1.40	1.39	1.34	1.49	1.60	1.30	1.16	1.16
Net Income to Assets (%)	0.38	0.51	0.42	1.30	1.59	1.99	1.89	1.60	2.25	2.66
Portfolio Turnover (%)	20	57	31	30	28	40	18	43	40	58
Total Assets (Millions $)	17	20	20	20	18	24	26	30	46	51

PORTFOLIO (as of 4/30/94)

Portfolio Manager: Fariba Talebi - 1991

Investm't Category: Growth
- ✔ Cap Gain
- Cap & Income
- Income
- Asset Allocation
- Fund of Funds
- Index
- Sector
- ✔ Domestic
- Foreign
- Country/Region
- Small Cap
- Socially Conscious
- State Specific

Portfolio: stocks 94% bonds 0%
convertibles 0% other 0% cash 6%

Largest Holdings: capital goods/construction 13%, retail 12%

Unrealized Net Capital Gains: 20% of portfolio value

SHAREHOLDER INFORMATION

Minimum Investment
Initial: $500   Subsequent: $100

Minimum IRA Investment
Initial: na   Subsequent: na

Maximum Fees
Load: none   12b-1: none
Other: none

Distributions
Income: Dec   Capital Gains: Dec

Exchange Options
Number Per Year: none   Fee:
Telephone:

Services

Schwab 1000 (SNXFX)

Growth & Income

101 Montgomery St.
San Francisco, CA 94104
(800) 566-5623

PERFORMANCE

fund inception date: 4/2/91

	3yr Annual	5yr Annual	10yr Annual	Bull	Bear
Return (%)	5.8	na	na	na	-7.2
Differ from Category (+/-)	-1.3 blw av	na	na	na	-0.9 blw av

Total Risk	Standard Deviation	Category Risk	Risk Index	Beta
av	7.9%	av	1.0	1.0

	1994	1993	1992	1991	1990	1989	1988	1987	1986	1985
Return (%)	-0.1	9.5	8.5	—	—	—	—	—	—	—
Differ from category (+/-). . .	1.3	-3.7	-1.7	—	—	—	—	—	—	—

PER SHARE DATA

	1994	1993	1992	1991	1990	1989	1988	1987	1986	1985
Dividends, Net Income ($).	0.26	0.25	0.25	—	—	—	—	—	—	—
Distrib'ns, Cap Gain ($) . . .	0.00	0.00	0.00	—	—	—	—	—	—	—
Net Asset Value ($)	12.57	12.85	11.96	—	—	—	—	—	—	—
Expense Ratio (%)	0.51	0.45	0.35	—	—	—	—	—	—	—
Net Income to Assets (%) .	2.06	2.21	2.45	—	—	—	—	—	—	—
Portfolio Turnover (%)	3	1	1	—	—	—	—	—	—	—
Total Assets (Millions $). . . .	553	na	371	—	—	—	—	—	—	—

PORTFOLIO (as of 8/31/94)

Portfolio Manager: not specified

Investm't Category: Growth & Income

Cap Gain	Asset Allocation
✔ Cap & Income	Fund of Funds
Income	✔ Index
	Sector
✔ Domestic	Small Cap
Foreign	Socially Conscious
Country/Region	State Specific

Portfolio: stocks 100% bonds 0%
convertibles 0% other 0% cash 0%

Largest Holdings: Schwab 1000 index

Unrealized Net Capital Gains: 15% of portfolio value

SHAREHOLDER INFORMATION

Minimum Investment
Initial: $1,000   Subsequent: $100

Minimum IRA Investment
Initial: $500   Subsequent: $100

Maximum Fees
Load: 0.50% redemption   12b-1: none
Other: redemption fee applies for 6 mos

Distributions
Income: Jun, Dec   Capital Gains: Dec

Exchange Options
Number Per Year: no limit   Fee: none
Telephone: yes (money market fund available)

Services
IRA, pension, auto invest

Schwab CA Long-Term Tax-Free (SWCAX)

101 Montgomery St.
San Francisco, CA 94104
(800) 566-5623

Tax-Exempt Bond

PERFORMANCE

fund inception date: 2/4/92

	3yr Annual	5yr Annual	10yr Annual	Bull	Bear
Return (%)	na	na	na	na	-7.2
Differ from Category (+/-)	na	na	na	na	-2.0 low

Total Risk	Standard Deviation	Category Risk	Risk Index	Avg Mat
na	na	na	na	17.5 yrs

	1994	1993	1992	1991	1990	1989	1988	1987	1986	1985
Return (%)	-8.9	12.8	—	—	—	—	—	—	—	—
Differ from category (+/-). . .	-3.7	1.1	—	—	—	—	—	—	—	—

PER SHARE DATA

	1994	1993	1992	1991	1990	1989	1988	1987	1986	1985
Dividends, Net Income ($) .	0.55	0.56	—	—	—	—	—	—	—	—
Distrib'ns, Cap Gain ($) . . .	0.00	0.12	—	—	—	—	—	—	—	—
Net Asset Value ($)	9.69	11.23	—	—	—	—	—	—	—	—
Expense Ratio (%)	0.60	0.60	—	—	—	—	—	—	—	—
Net Income to Assets (%) .	5.12	5.18	—	—	—	—	—	—	—	—
Portfolio Turnover (%).	48	47	—	—	—	—	—	—	—	—
Total Assets (Millions $).	87	132	—	—	—	—	—	—	—	—

PORTFOLIO (as of 8/31/94)

Portfolio Manager: Keighley - 1992, Ward - 1992

Investm't Category: Tax-Exempt Bond

Cap Gain	Asset Allocation
Cap & Income	Fund of Funds
✔ Income	Index
	Sector
✔ Domestic	Small Cap
Foreign	Socially Conscious
Country/Region	✔ State Specific

Portfolio: stocks 0% bonds 100%
convertibles 0% other 0% cash 0%

Largest Holdings: general obligation 2%

Unrealized Net Capital Gains: 0% of portfolio value

SHAREHOLDER INFORMATION

Minimum Investment
Initial: $1,000   Subsequent: $100

Minimum IRA Investment
Initial: na   Subsequent: na

Maximum Fees
Load: none   12b-1: none
Other: none

Distributions
Income: monthly   Capital Gains: Dec

Exchange Options
Number Per Year: no limit   Fee: none
Telephone: yes (money market fund available)

Services
auto invest

Schwab CA Short/Interm Tax-Free (SWCSX)

101 Montgomery St.
San Francisco, CA 94104
(800) 566-5623

Tax-Exempt Bond

PERFORMANCE

fund inception date: 4/21/93

	3yr Annual	5yr Annual	10yr Annual	Bull	Bear
Return (%)	na	na	na	na	-2.4
Differ from Category (+/-)	na	na	na	na	2.8 high

Total Risk	Standard Deviation	Category Risk	Risk Index	Avg Mat
na	na	na	na	4.1 yrs

	1994	1993	1992	1991	1990	1989	1988	1987	1986	1985
Return (%)	-2.0	—	—	—	—	—	—	—	—	—
Differ from category (+/-)	3.2	—	—	—	—	—	—	—	—	—

PER SHARE DATA

	1994	1993	1992	1991	1990	1989	1988	1987	1986	1985
Dividends, Net Income ($)	0.38	—	—	—	—	—	—	—	—	—
Distrib'ns, Cap Gain ($)	0.00	—	—	—	—	—	—	—	—	—
Net Asset Value ($)	9.60	—	—	—	—	—	—	—	—	—
Expense Ratio (%)	0.48	—	—	—	—	—	—	—	—	—
Net Income to Assets (%)	3.69	—	—	—	—	—	—	—	—	—
Portfolio Turnover (%)	35	—	—	—	—	—	—	—	—	—
Total Assets (Millions $)	40	—	—	—	—	—	—	—	—	—

PORTFOLIO (as of 8/31/94)

Portfolio Manager: Keighley, - 1992, Ward - 1992

Investm't Category: Tax-Exempt Bond

Cap Gain	Asset Allocation
Cap & Income	Fund of Funds
✔ Income	Index
	Sector
✔ Domestic	Small Cap
Foreign	Socially Conscious
Country/Region	✔ State Specific

Portfolio:

stocks 0%	bonds 100%
convertibles 0%	other 0%	cash 0%

Largest Holdings: general obligation 4%

Unrealized Net Capital Gains: -1% of portfolio value

SHAREHOLDER INFORMATION

Minimum Investment
Initial: $1,000   Subsequent: $100

Minimum IRA Investment
Initial: na   Subsequent: na

Maximum Fees
Load: none   12b-1: none
Other: none

Distributions
Income: monthly   Capital Gains: Dec

Exchange Options
Number Per Year: no limit   Fee: none
Telephone: yes (money market fund available)

Services
auto invest

Schwab International Index (SWINX)

101 Montgomery St.
San Francisco, CA 94104
(800) 566-5623

International Stock

PERFORMANCE

fund inception date: 9/9/93

	3yr Annual	5yr Annual	10yr Annual	Bull	Bear
Return (%)	na	na	na	na	-2.6
Differ from Category (+/-)	na	na	na	na	4.4 high

Total Risk	Standard Deviation	Category Risk	Risk Index	Beta
na	na	na	na	na

	1994	1993	1992	1991	1990	1989	1988	1987	1986	1985
Return (%)	3.8	—	—	—	—	—	—	—	—	—
Differ from category (+/-)	6.8	—	—	—	—	—	—	—	—	—

PER SHARE DATA

	1994	1993	1992	1991	1990	1989	1988	1987	1986	1985
Dividends, Net Income ($)	0.12	—	—	—	—	—	—	—	—	—
Distrib'ns, Cap Gain ($)	0.00	—	—	—	—	—	—	—	—	—
Net Asset Value ($)	10.31	—	—	—	—	—	—	—	—	—
Expense Ratio (%)	0.90	—	—	—	—	—	—	—	—	—
Net Income to Assets (%)	1.14	—	—	—	—	—	—	—	—	—
Portfolio Turnover (%)	6	—	—	—	—	—	—	—	—	—
Total Assets (Millions $)	138	—	—	—	—	—	—	—	—	—

PORTFOLIO (as of 10/31/94)

Portfolio Manager: not specified

Investm't Category: International Stock

✔ Cap Gain	Asset Allocation
Cap & Income	Fund of Funds
Income	✔ Index
	Sector
Domestic	Small Cap
✔ Foreign	Socially Conscious
Country/Region	State Specific

Portfolio: stocks 99%   bonds 0%
convertibles 0%   other 0%   cash 1%

Largest Holdings: Schwab international index

Unrealized Net Capital Gains: 6% of portfolio value

SHAREHOLDER INFORMATION

Minimum Investment
Initial: $1,000   Subsequent: $100

Minimum IRA Investment
Initial: $500   Subsequent: $50

Maximum Fees
Load: 0.75% redemption   12b-1: none
Other: redemption fee applies for 6 months

Distributions
Income: Dec   Capital Gains: Dec

Exchange Options
Number Per Year: no limit   Fee: none
Telephone: yes (money market fund available)

Services
IRA, pension, auto invest

Schwab Long-Term Tax-Free (SWNTX)

Tax-Exempt Bond

101 Montgomery St.
San Francisco, CA 94104
(800) 566-5623

PERFORMANCE

fund inception date: 9/11/92

	3yr Annual	5yr Annual	10yr Annual	Bull	Bear
Return (%)	na	na	na	na	-6.1
Differ from Category (+/-)	na	na	na	na	-0.9 blw av

Total Risk	Standard Deviation	Category Risk	Risk Index	Avg Mat
na	na	na	na	16.8 yrs

	1994	1993	1992	1991	1990	1989	1988	1987	1986	1985
Return (%)	-7.0	13.5	—	—	—	—	—	—	—	—
Differ from category (+/-)	-1.8	1.8	—	—	—	—	—	—	—	—

PER SHARE DATA

	1994	1993	1992	1991	1990	1989	1988	1987	1986	1985
Dividends, Net Income ($)	0.52	0.54	—	—	—	—	—	—	—	—
Distrib'ns, Cap Gain ($)	0.00	0.08	—	—	—	—	—	—	—	—
Net Asset Value ($)	9.37	10.62	—	—	—	—	—	—	—	—
Expense Ratio (%)	0.51	0.45	—	—	—	—	—	—	—	—
Net Income to Assets (%)	5.05	5.30	—	—	—	—	—	—	—	—
Portfolio Turnover (%)	62	90	—	—	—	—	—	—	—	—
Total Assets (Millions $)	67	49	—	—	—	—	—	—	—	—

PORTFOLIO (as of 8/31/94)

Portfolio Manager: Keighley - 1992, Ward - 1992

Investm't Category: Tax-Exempt Bond

Cap Gain	Asset Allocation
Cap & Income	Fund of Funds
✔ Income	Index
	Sector
✔ Domestic	Small Cap
Foreign	Socially Conscious
Country/Region	State Specific

Portfolio: stocks 0%   bonds 100%
convertibles 0%   other 0%   cash 0%

Largest Holdings: general obligation 5%

Unrealized Net Capital Gains: 1% of portfolio value

SHAREHOLDER INFORMATION

Minimum Investment
Initial: $1,000   Subsequent: $100

Minimum IRA Investment
Initial: na   Subsequent: na

Maximum Fees
Load: none   12b-1: none
Other: none

Distributions
Income: monthly   Capital Gains: Dec

Exchange Options
Number Per Year: no limit   Fee: none
Telephone: yes (money market fund available)

Services
auto invest

Schwab Short/Interm Gov't Bond (SWBDX)

101 Montgomery St.
San Francisco, CA 94104
(800) 566-5623

Government Bond

PERFORMANCE

fund inception date: 11/4/91

	3yr Annual	5yr Annual	10yr Annual	Bull	Bear
Return (%)	3.5	na	na	na	-3.9
Differ from Category (+/-)	-0.5 blw av	na	na	na	2.5 av

Total Risk	Standard Deviation	Category Risk	Risk Index	Avg Mat
low	3.2%	blw av	0.7	2.3 yrs

	1994	1993	1992	1991	1990	1989	1988	1987	1986	1985
Return (%)	-2.8	7.7	6.0	—	—	—	—	—	—	—
Differ from category (+/-). . .	2.0	-3.2	-0.4	—	—	—	—	—	—	—

PER SHARE DATA

	1994	1993	1992	1991	1990	1989	1988	1987	1986	1985
Dividends, Net Income ($) .	0.54	0.55	0.60	—	—	—	—	—	—	—
Distrib'ns, Cap Gain ($) . . .	0.00	0.12	0.03	—	—	—	—	—	—	—
Net Asset Value ($)	9.55	10.38	10.26	—	—	—	—	—	—	—
Expense Ratio (%)	0.60	0.60	0.43	—	—	—	—	—	—	—
Net Income to Assets (%) .	5.28	5.28	5.78	—	—	—	—	—	—	—
Portfolio Turnover (%).	91	107	185	—	—	—	—	—	—	—
Total Assets (Millions $). . . .	160	270	226	—	—	—	—	—	—	—

PORTFOLIO (as of 8/31/94)

Portfolio Manager: Regan - 1991, Ward - 1991

Investm't Category: Government Bond

Cap Gain	Asset Allocation
Cap & Income	Fund of Funds
✔ Income	Index
	Sector
✔ Domestic	Small Cap
Foreign	Socially Conscious
Country/Region	State Specific

Portfolio: stocks 0% bonds 93%
convertibles 0% other 0% cash 7%

Largest Holdings: U.S. government and agencies 59%, mortgage-backed 34%

Unrealized Net Capital Gains: 0% of portfolio value

SHAREHOLDER INFORMATION

Minimum Investment
Initial: $1,000   Subsequent: $100

Minimum IRA Investment
Initial: $500   Subsequent: $100

Maximum Fees
Load: none   12b-1: none
Other: none

Distributions
Income: monthly   Capital Gains: Dec

Exchange Options
Number Per Year: no limit   Fee: none
Telephone: yes (money market fund available)

Services
IRA, pension, auto invest

Schwab Short/ Intermediate Tax-Free

101 Montgomery St.
San Francisco, CA 94104
(800) 566-5623

(SWITX) *Tax-Exempt Bond*

PERFORMANCE

fund inception date: 4/21/93

	3yr Annual	5yr Annual	10yr Annual	Bull	Bear
Return (%)	na	na	na	na	-2.3
Differ from Category (+/-)	na	na	na	na	2.9 high

Total Risk	Standard Deviation	Category Risk	Risk Index	Avg Mat
na	na	na	na	3.8 yrs

	1994	1993	1992	1991	1990	1989	1988	1987	1986	1985
Return (%)	-1.1	—	—	—	—	—	—	—	—	—
Differ from category (+/-) . . .	4.1	—	—	—	—	—	—	—	—	—

PER SHARE DATA

	1994	1993	1992	1991	1990	1989	1988	1987	1986	1985
Dividends, Net Income ($) .	0.38	—	—	—	—	—	—	—	—	—
Distrib'ns, Cap Gain ($) . . .	0.00	—	—	—	—	—	—	—	—	—
Net Asset Value ($)	9.71	—	—	—	—	—	—	—	—	—
Expense Ratio (%)	0.48	—	—	—	—	—	—	—	—	—
Net Income to Assets (%) .	3.71	—	—	—	—	—	—	—	—	—
Portfolio Turnover (%)	19	—	—	—	—	—	—	—	—	—
Total Assets (Millions $)	56	—	—	—	—	—	—	—	—	—

PORTFOLIO (as of 8/31/94)

Portfolio Manager: Keighley - 1993, Ward - 1993

Investm't Category: Tax-Exempt Bond

Cap Gain	Asset Allocation
Cap & Income	Fund of Funds
✔ Income	Index
	Sector
✔ Domestic	Small Cap
Foreign	Socially Conscious
Country/Region	State Specific

Portfolio: stocks 0%   bonds 100%
convertibles 0%   other 0%   cash 0%

Largest Holdings: general obligation 11%

Unrealized Net Capital Gains: -1% of portfolio value

SHAREHOLDER INFORMATION

Minimum Investment
Initial: $1,000   Subsequent: $100

Minimum IRA Investment
Initial: na   Subsequent: na

Maximum Fees
Load: none   12b-1: none
Other: none

Distributions
Income: monthly   Capital Gains: Dec

Exchange Options
Number Per Year: no limit   Fee: none
Telephone: yes (money market fund available)

Services
auto invest

Schwab Small-Cap Index
(SWSMX)
Aggressive Growth

101 Montgomery St.
San Francisco, CA 94104
(800) 566-5623

PERFORMANCE

fund inception date: 12/3/93

	3yr Annual	5yr Annual	10yr Annual	Bull	Bear
Return (%)	na	na	na	na	-10.2
Differ from Category (+/-)	na	na	na	na	0.6 av

Total Risk	Standard Deviation	Category Risk	Risk Index	Beta
na	na	na	na	na

	1994	1993	1992	1991	1990	1989	1988	1987	1986	1985
Return (%)	-3.0	—	—	—	—	—	—	—	—	—
Differ from category (+/-)	-2.3	—	—	—	—	—	—	—	—	—

PER SHARE DATA

	1994	1993	1992	1991	1990	1989	1988	1987	1986	1985
Dividends, Net Income ($)	0.06	—	—	—	—	—	—	—	—	—
Distrib'ns, Cap Gain ($)	0.00	—	—	—	—	—	—	—	—	—
Net Asset Value ($)	9.77	—	—	—	—	—	—	—	—	—
Expense Ratio (%)	0.55	—	—	—	—	—	—	—	—	—
Net Income to Assets (%)	0.85	—	—	—	—	—	—	—	—	—
Portfolio Turnover (%)	na	—	—	—	—	—	—	—	—	—
Total Assets (Millions $)	71	—	—	—	—	—	—	—	—	—

PORTFOLIO (as of 4/30/94)

Portfolio Manager: not specified

Investm't Category: Aggressive Growth
✔ Cap Gain	Asset Allocation
Cap & Income	Fund of Funds
Income	✔ Index
	Sector
✔ Domestic	✔ Small Cap
Foreign	Socially Conscious
Country/Region	State Specific

Portfolio: stocks 95% bonds 0%
convertibles 0% other 0% cash 5%

Largest Holdings: Schwab small-cap index

Unrealized Net Capital Gains: -3% of portfolio value

SHAREHOLDER INFORMATION

Minimum Investment
Initial: $1,000   Subsequent: $100

Minimum IRA Investment
Initial: $500   Subsequent: $50

Maximum Fees
Load: 0.50% redemption   12b-1: none
Other: redemption fee applies for 6 months

Distributions
Income: Dec   Capital Gains: Dec

Exchange Options
Number Per Year: no limit   Fee: none
Telephone: yes (money market fund available)

Services
IRA, pension, auto invest

Schwartz Value (RCMFX)

Growth

3707 W. Maple Road
Bloomfield Hills, MI 48301
(810) 644-2701

PERFORMANCE

fund inception date: 7/20/93

	3yr Annual	5yr Annual	10yr Annual	Bull	Bear
Return (%)	na	na	na	na	-9.3
Differ from Category (+/-)	na	na	na	na	-2.7 blw av

Total Risk	Standard Deviation	Category Risk	Risk Index	Beta
na	na	na	na	na

	1994	1993	1992	1991	1990	1989	1988	1987	1986	1985
Return (%)	-6.7	—	—	—	—	—	—	—	—	—
Differ from category (+/-)	-6.1	—	—	—	—	—	—	—	—	—

PER SHARE DATA

	1994	1993	1992	1991	1990	1989	1988	1987	1986	1985
Dividends, Net Income ($)	0.00	—	—	—	—	—	—	—	—	—
Distrib'ns, Cap Gain ($)	1.43	—	—	—	—	—	—	—	—	—
Net Asset Value ($)	18.12	—	—	—	—	—	—	—	—	—
Expense Ratio (%)	2.13	—	—	—	—	—	—	—	—	—
Net Income to Assets (%)	-0.42	—	—	—	—	—	—	—	—	—
Portfolio Turnover (%)	84	—	—	—	—	—	—	—	—	—
Total Assets (Millions $)	41	—	—	—	—	—	—	—	—	—

PORTFOLIO (as of 6/30/94)

Portfolio Manager: George P. Schwartz - 1993

Investm't Category: Growth

✔ Cap Gain   Asset Allocation
   Cap & Income   Fund of Funds
   Income   Index
     Sector
✔ Domestic   ✔ Small Cap
   Foreign   Socially Conscious
   Country/Region   State Specific

Portfolio: stocks 75%   bonds 0%
convertibles 6%   other 0%   cash 19%

Largest Holdings: banking & thrifts 9%, consumer durables 8%

Unrealized Net Capital Gains: 1% of portfolio value

SHAREHOLDER INFORMATION

Minimum Investment
Initial: $25,000   Subsequent: $0

Minimum IRA Investment
Initial: $25,000   Subsequent: $0

Maximum Fees
Load: none   12b-1: none
Other: none

Distributions
Income: Dec   Capital Gains: Dec

Exchange Options
Number Per Year: none   Fee:
Telephone:

Services
IRA

Scudder Balanced
(SCBAX)
Balanced

P.O. Box 2291
Boston, MA 02107
(800) 225-2470, (617) 439-4640

PERFORMANCE   fund inception date: 1/4/93

	3yr Annual	5yr Annual	10yr Annual	Bull	Bear
Return (%)	na	na	na	na	-7.9
Differ from Category (+/-)	na	na	na	na	-2.2 low

Total Risk	Standard Deviation	Category Risk	Risk Index	Beta
na	na	na	na	na

	1994	1993	1992	1991	1990	1989	1988	1987	1986	1985
Return (%)	-2.3	4.1	—	—	—	—	—	—	—	—
Differ from category (+/-) . . .	-0.4	-9.3	—	—	—	—	—	—	—	—

PER SHARE DATA

	1994	1993	1992	1991	1990	1989	1988	1987	1986	1985
Dividends, Net Income ($) .	0.31	0.26	—	—	—	—	—	—	—	—
Distrib'ns, Cap Gain ($) . . .	0.00	0.00	—	—	—	—	—	—	—	—
Net Asset Value ($)	11.63	12.23	—	—	—	—	—	—	—	—
Expense Ratio (%)	1.00	1.00	—	—	—	—	—	—	—	—
Net Income to Assets (%) .	2.58	2.43	—	—	—	—	—	—	—	—
Portfolio Turnover (%)	93	99	—	—	—	—	—	—	—	—
Total Assets (Millions $)	66	65	—	—	—	—	—	—	—	—

PORTFOLIO (as of 6/30/94)

Portfolio Manager: B. F. Beaty - 1993, W. Hutchinson - 1993, H. F. Ward - 1993

Investm't Category: Balanced

Cap Gain	Asset Allocation
✔ Cap & Income	Fund of Funds
Income	Index
	Sector
✔ Domestic	Small Cap
✔ Foreign	Socially Conscious
Country/Region	State Specific

Portfolio: stocks 65% bonds 26%
convertibles 0% other 0% cash 9%

Largest Holdings: bonds—U.S. government and agencies 15%, stocks—manufacturing 8%

Unrealized Net Capital Gains: -5% of portfolio value

SHAREHOLDER INFORMATION

Minimum Investment
Initial: $1,000   Subsequent: $100

Minimum IRA Investment
Initial: $500   Subsequent: $50

Maximum Fees
Load: none   12b-1: none
Other: none

Distributions
Income: quarterly   Capital Gains: Dec

Exchange Options
Number Per Year: call fund   Fee: none
Telephone: yes (money market fund available)

Services
IRA, pension, auto exchange, auto invest, auto withdraw

Scudder CA Tax Free
(SCTFX)
Tax-Exempt Bond

P.O. Box 2291
Boston, MA 02107
(800) 225-2470, (617) 439-4640

	3yr Annual	5yr Annual	10yr Annual	Bull	Bear
Return (%)	4.8	6.7	8.8	49.5	-6.9
Differ from Category (+/-)	0.3 av	0.6 abv av	0.7 abv av	7.7 high	-1.7 low

Total Risk	Standard Deviation	Category Risk	Risk Index	Avg Mat
av	6.8%	high	1.1	11.9 yrs

	1994	1993	1992	1991	1990	1989	1988	1987	1986	1985
Return (%).............	-7.3	13.8	9.3	12.6	6.3	10.3	11.8	-1.6	16.8	18.4
Differ from category (+/-)...	-2.1	2.1	1.0	1.3	0.0	1.3	1.6	-0.3	0.4	1.0

PER SHARE DATA

	1994	1993	1992	1991	1990	1989	1988	1987	1986	1985
Dividends, Net Income ($).	0.50	0.55	0.59	0.62	0.63	0.66	0.69	0.69	0.72	0.75
Distrib'ns, Cap Gain ($) ...	0.09	0.68	0.49	0.28	0.09	0.19	0.00	0.26	0.30	0.00
Net Asset Value ($)	9.48	10.85	10.66	10.77	10.41	10.50	10.31	9.86	11.01	10.35
Expense Ratio (%)	0.78	0.79	0.81	0.84	0.83	0.89	0.88	0.84	0.88	0.99
Net Income to Assets (%) .	4.85	5.42	5.79	6.13	6.23	6.71	6.95	6.55	7.11	8.76
Portfolio Turnover (%)	126	208	143	171	70	159	52	68	92	168
Total Assets (Millions $)....	274	349	242	209	193	171	153	195	132	73

PORTFOLIO (as of 3/31/94)

Portfolio Manager: Carleton - 1983, Ragus - 1989

Investm't Category: Tax-Exempt Bond
Cap Gain	Asset Allocation
Cap & Income	Fund of Funds
✔ Income	Index
	Sector
✔ Domestic	Small Cap
Foreign	Socially Conscious
Country/Region	✔ State Specific

Portfolio: stocks 0%   bonds 96%
convertibles 0%   other 0%   cash 4%

Largest Holdings: general obligation 9%

Unrealized Net Capital Gains: -3% of portfolio value

SHAREHOLDER INFORMATION

Minimum Investment
Initial: $1,000   Subsequent: $100

Minimum IRA Investment
Initial: na   Subsequent: na

Maximum Fees
Load: none   12b-1: none
Other: none

Distributions
Income: monthly   Capital Gains: Jun, Nov

Exchange Options
Number Per Year: call fund   Fee: none
Telephone: yes (money market fund available)

Services
auto exchange, auto invest, auto withdraw

Scudder Capital Growth
(SCDUX)
Growth

P.O. Box 2291
Boston, MA 02107
(800) 225-2470, (617) 439-4640

PERFORMANCE

fund inception date: 4/5/67

	3yr Annual	5yr Annual	10yr Annual	Bull	Bear
Return (%)	5.0	6.5	14.2	104.9	-12.3
Differ from Category (+/-)	-2.7 blw av	-3.1 low	1.3 abv av	12.8 abv av	-5.7 low

Total Risk	Standard Deviation	Category Risk	Risk Index	Beta
high	12.3%	high	1.3	1.2

	1994	1993	1992	1991	1990	1989	1988	1987	1986	1985
Return (%)	-9.8	20.0	7.0	42.9	-16.9	33.8	29.7	-0.7	16.5	36.6
Differ from category (+/-). . . .	-9.2	6.6	-4.6	7.2	-11.2	7.7	11.7	-2.5	1.9	7.4

PER SHARE DATA

	1994	1993	1992	1991	1990	1989	1988	1987	1986	1985
Dividends, Net Income ($) .	0.00	0.00	0.10	0.22	0.37	0.16	0.07	0.20	0.23	0.23
Distrib'ns, Cap Gain ($) . . .	0.73	2.62	1.25	0.98	1.35	1.45	0.79	2.13	2.46	1.88
Net Asset Value ($)	18.43	21.26	19.91	19.86	14.81	19.91	16.13	13.14	15.59	15.64
Expense Ratio (%)	0.97	0.96	0.98	1.04	0.94	0.88	0.95	0.88	0.84	0.86
Net Income to Assets (%) .	-0.12	0.22	0.57	1.24	1.56	1.22	0.63	0.86	1.50	1.74
Portfolio Turnover (%).	75	92	92	93	88	56	49	58	55	57
Total Assets (Millions $). .	1,292	1,415	1,054	1,059	712	1,013	491	583	414	362

PORTFOLIO (as of 9/30/94)

Portfolio Manager: S. Aronoff - 1989, J. D. Cox - 1984, W. F. Gadsden - 1989

Investm't Category: Growth
- ✔ Cap Gain
- Cap & Income
- Income
- ✔ Domestic
- ✔ Foreign
- Country/Region
- Asset Allocation
- Fund of Funds
- Index
- Sector
- Small Cap
- Socially Conscious
- State Specific

Portfolio: stocks 95%   bonds 0%
convertibles 3%   other 0%   cash 2%

Largest Holdings: consumer discretionary 21%, media 20%

Unrealized Net Capital Gains: 8% of portfolio value

SHAREHOLDER INFORMATION

Minimum Investment
Initial: $1,000   Subsequent: $100

Minimum IRA Investment
Initial: $500   Subsequent: $50

Maximum Fees
Load: none   12b-1: none
Other: none

Distributions
Income: Dec   Capital Gains: Dec

Exchange Options
Number Per Year: call fund   Fee: none
Telephone: yes (money market fund available)

Services
IRA, pension, auto exchange, auto invest, auto withdraw

Scudder Development

(SCDVX)

Aggressive Growth

P.O. Box 2291
Boston, MA 02107
(800) 225-2470, (617) 439-4640

PERFORMANCE

fund inception date: 2/11/71

	3yr Annual	5yr Annual	10yr Annual	Bull	Bear
Return (%)	0.3	12.0	11.8	115.8	-18.8
Differ from Category (+/-)	-8.6 low	-0.5 av	-2.2 blw av	-17.4 av	-8.0 low

Total Risk	Standard Deviation	Category Risk	Risk Index	Beta
high	16.8%	abv av	1.1	1.3

	1994	1993	1992	1991	1990	1989	1988	1987	1986	1985
Return (%)	-5.3	8.8	-1.8	71.8	1.4	23.2	11.0	-1.5	7.6	19.8
Differ from category (+/-)	-4.6	-10.7	-12.8	19.7	7.6	-3.6	-4.2	0.7	-4.2	-12.5

PER SHARE DATA

	1994	1993	1992	1991	1990	1989	1988	1987	1986	1985
Dividends, Net Income ($)	0.00	0.00	0.00	0.00	0.00	0.00	0.00	0.00	0.00	0.17
Distrib'ns, Cap Gain ($)	2.12	3.07	1.70	0.96	1.23	2.28	0.42	1.90	1.33	0.92
Net Asset Value ($)	29.54	33.51	33.62	36.23	21.73	22.69	20.32	18.69	20.71	20.43
Expense Ratio (%)	1.27	1.30	1.30	1.29	1.34	1.32	1.30	1.27	1.25	1.29
Net Income to Assets (%)	-0.91	-0.83	-0.70	-0.40	-0.35	-0.47	-0.44	-0.33	-0.03	0.90
Portfolio Turnover (%)	48	49	54	71	40	32	39	24	29	25
Total Assets (Millions $)	601	749	700	476	361	275	356	387	359	254

PORTFOLIO (as of 6/30/94)

Portfolio Manager: Peter Chin - 1993, Roy C. McKay - 1988

Investm't Category: Aggressive Growth
✔ Cap Gain	Asset Allocation
Cap & Income	Fund of Funds
Income	Index
	Sector
✔ Domestic	✔ Small Cap
✔ Foreign	Socially Conscious
Country/Region	State Specific

Portfolio: stocks 92% bonds 0%
convertibles 1% other 4% cash 3%

Largest Holdings: technology 26%, consumer discretionary 17%

Unrealized Net Capital Gains: 17% of portfolio value

SHAREHOLDER INFORMATION

Minimum Investment
Initial: $1,000   Subsequent: $100

Minimum IRA Investment
Initial: $500   Subsequent: $50

Maximum Fees
Load: none   12b-1: none
Other: none

Distributions
Income: Aug, Dec   Capital Gains: Aug, Dec

Exchange Options
Number Per Year: call fund   Fee: none
Telephone: yes (money market fund available)

Services
IRA, pension, auto exchange, auto invest, auto withdraw

Scudder Emerging Markets Inc (SCEMX)

International Bond

P.O. Box 2291
Boston, MA 02107
(800) 225-2470, (617) 439-4640

PERFORMANCE

fund inception date: 1/3/94

	3yr Annual	5yr Annual	10yr Annual	Bull	Bear
Return (%)	na	na	na	na	-11.0
Differ from Category (+/-)	na	na	na	na	-3.2 blw av

Total Risk	Standard Deviation	Category Risk	Risk Index	Avg Mat
na	na	na	na	na

	1994	1993	1992	1991	1990	1989	1988	1987	1986	1985
Return (%).	-8.0	—	—	—	—	—	—	—	—	—
Differ from category (+/-). . .	-1.7	—	—	—	—	—	—	—	—	—

PER SHARE DATA

	1994	1993	1992	1991	1990	1989	1988	1987	1986	1985
Dividends, Net Income ($) .	0.77	—	—	—	—	—	—	—	—	—
Distrib'ns, Cap Gain ($) . . .	0.00	—	—	—	—	—	—	—	—	—
Net Asset Value ($)	10.27	—	—	—	—	—	—	—	—	—
Expense Ratio (%)	1.50	—	—	—	—	—	—	—	—	—
Net Income to Assets (%) .	9.17	—	—	—	—	—	—	—	—	—
Portfolio Turnover (%).	180	—	—	—	—	—	—	—	—	—
Total Assets (Millions $)	89	—	—	—	—	—	—	—	—	—

PORTFOLIO (as of 10/31/94)

Portfolio Manager: S. Gray - 1993, L. Rathnam - 1993, I. Saltzman - 1993

Investm't Category: International Bond

Cap Gain	Asset Allocation
Cap & Income	Fund of Funds
✔ Income	Index
	Sector
Domestic	Small Cap
✔ Foreign	Socially Conscious
Country/Region	State Specific

Portfolio: stocks 0%   bonds 81%
convertibles 3%   other 0%   cash 16%

Largest Holdings: Brazil 23%, Argentina 21%

Unrealized Net Capital Gains: -2% of portfolio value

SHAREHOLDER INFORMATION

Minimum Investment
Initial: $1,000   Subsequent: $100

Minimum IRA Investment
Initial: $500   Subsequent: $50

Maximum Fees
Load: none   12b-1: none
Other: none

Distributions
Income: quarterly   Capital Gains: Dec

Exchange Options
Number Per Year: call fund   Fee: none
Telephone: yes (money market fund available)

Services
IRA, pension, auto exchange, auto invest, auto withdraw

Scudder Global (SCOBX)

International Stock

P.O. Box 2291
Boston, MA 02107
(800) 225-2470, (617) 439-4640

PERFORMANCE

fund inception date: 7/23/86

	3yr Annual	5yr Annual	10yr Annual	Bull	Bear
Return (%)	9.5	7.5	na	74.8	-7.6
Differ from Category (+/-)	0.4 abv av	2.6 high	na	10.9 abv av	-0.6 blw av

Total Risk	Standard Deviation	Category Risk	Risk Index	Beta
av	8.6%	low	0.6	0.7

	1994	1993	1992	1991	1990	1989	1988	1987	1986	1985
Return (%)	-4.2	31.1	4.4	17.0	-6.4	37.3	19.1	3.0	—	—
Differ from category (+/-)	-1.2	-7.5	7.3	3.9	4.0	14.8	4.7	-11.4	—	—

PER SHARE DATA

	1994	1993	1992	1991	1990	1989	1988	1987	1986	1985
Dividends, Net Income ($)	0.11	0.24	0.16	0.31	0.62	0.11	0.14	0.06	—	—
Distrib'ns, Cap Gain ($)	0.34	0.26	0.34	0.66	0.58	0.64	0.08	0.25	—	—
Net Asset Value ($)	23.33	24.80	19.31	18.96	17.06	19.48	14.74	12.56	—	—
Expense Ratio (%)	1.45	1.48	1.59	1.70	1.81	1.98	1.71	1.84	—	—
Net Income to Assets (%)	0.97	0.90	1.09	2.21	1.77	1.22	1.23	0.63	—	—
Portfolio Turnover (%)	59	64	45	85	38	31	54	32	—	—
Total Assets (Millions $)	1,117	965	371	268	257	91	81	102	—	—

PORTFOLIO (as of 6/30/94)

Portfolio Manager: William Holzer - 1986, N. Bratt - 1993, A. Ho - 1994

Investm't Category: International Stock

✔ Cap Gain	Asset Allocation
Cap & Income	Fund of Funds
Income	Index
	Sector
✔ Domestic	Small Cap
✔ Foreign	Socially Conscious
Country/Region	State Specific

Portfolio: stocks 83% bonds 4%
convertibles 1% other 2% cash 10%

Largest Holdings: United States 20%, Japan 12%

Unrealized Net Capital Gains: 11% of portfolio value

SHAREHOLDER INFORMATION

Minimum Investment
Initial: $1,000   Subsequent: $100

Minimum IRA Investment
Initial: $500   Subsequent: $50

Maximum Fees
Load: none   12b-1: none
Other: none

Distributions
Income: Nov, Dec   Capital Gains: Nov, Dec

Exchange Options
Number Per Year: call fund   Fee: none
Telephone: yes (money market fund available)

Services
IRA, pension, auto exchange, auto invest, auto withdraw

Scudder Global Small Company (SGSCX)

International Stock

P.O. Box 2291
Boston, MA 02107
(800) 225-2470, (617) 439-4640

PERFORMANCE

fund inception date: 9/10/91

	3yr Annual	5yr Annual	10yr Annual	Bull	Bear
Return (%)	8.4	na	na	na	-7.7
Differ from Category (+/-)	-0.7 av	na	na	na	-0.7 blw av

Total Risk	Standard Deviation	Category Risk	Risk Index	Beta
abv av	10.5%	low	0.8	0.6

	1994	1993	1992	1991	1990	1989	1988	1987	1986	1985
Return (%)	-7.7	38.1	0.0	—	—	—	—	—	—	—
Differ from category (+/-). . .	-4.7	-0.5	2.9	—	—	—	—	—	—	—

PER SHARE DATA

	1994	1993	1992	1991	1990	1989	1988	1987	1986	1985
Dividends, Net Income ($) .	0.00	0.18	0.07	—	—	—	—	—	—	—
Distrib'ns, Cap Gain ($) . . .	0.08	0.15	0.12	—	—	—	—	—	—	—
Net Asset Value ($)	15.18	16.53	12.20	—	—	—	—	—	—	—
Expense Ratio (%)	1.70	1.50	1.50	—	—	—	—	—	—	—
Net Income to Assets (%) .	-0.28	0.53	0.78	—	—	—	—	—	—	—
Portfolio Turnover (%).	45	54	23	—	—	—	—	—	—	—
Total Assets (Millions $). . . .	235	216	55	—	—	—	—	—	—	—

PORTFOLIO (as of 10/31/94)

Portfolio Manager: C. L. Franklin - 1991, G. J. Moran - 1991, E. Allen - 1993

Investm't Category: International Stock

✔ Cap Gain	Asset Allocation
Cap & Income	Fund of Funds
Income	Index
	Sector
✔ Domestic	✔ Small Cap
✔ Foreign	Socially Conscious
Country/Region	State Specific

Portfolio: stocks 82% bonds 0%
convertibles 1% other 7% cash 10%

Largest Holdings: United States 23%, Japan 18%

Unrealized Net Capital Gains: 10% of portfolio value

SHAREHOLDER INFORMATION

Minimum Investment
Initial: $1,000 Subsequent: $100

Minimum IRA Investment
Initial: $500 Subsequent: $50

Maximum Fees
Load: none 12b-1: none
Other: none

Distributions
Income: Dec Capital Gains: Dec

Exchange Options
Number Per Year: call fund Fee: none
Telephone: yes (money market fund available)

Services
IRA, pension, auto exchange, auto invest, auto withdraw

Scudder GNMA (SGMSX)

Mortgage-Backed Bond

P.O. Box 2291
Boston, MA 02107
(800) 225-2470, (617) 439-4640

fund inception date: 7/5/85

PERFORMANCE

	3yr Annual	5yr Annual	10yr Annual	Bull	Bear
Return (%)	3.1	6.8	na	39.0	-5.6
Differ from Category (+/-)	0.0 blw av	-0.1 blw av	na	1.0 abv av	-1.2 low

Total Risk	Standard Deviation	Category Risk	Risk Index	Avg Mat
low	3.8%	abv av	1.1	8.7 yrs

	1994	1993	1992	1991	1990	1989	1988	1987	1986	1985
Return (%)	-3.1	6.0	6.9	15.0	10.1	12.8	6.8	1.4	11.3	—
Differ from category (+/-)	-0.3	-0.8	0.8	0.6	0.4	0.3	-0.3	-0.4	0.1	—

PER SHARE DATA

	1994	1993	1992	1991	1990	1989	1988	1987	1986	1985
Dividends, Net Income ($)	0.93	1.20	1.29	1.22	1.23	1.26	1.30	1.27	1.42	—
Distrib'ns, Cap Gain ($)	0.00	0.00	0.00	0.00	0.00	0.00	0.00	0.00	0.08	—
Net Asset Value ($)	13.66	15.06	15.36	15.62	14.72	14.56	14.09	14.43	15.50	—
Expense Ratio (%)	0.95	0.93	0.99	1.04	1.05	1.04	1.04	1.05	1.02	—
Net Income to Assets (%)	6.39	8.36	8.24	8.49	8.74	8.95	8.93	8.63	10.11	—
Portfolio Turnover (%)	117	87	147	52	71	128	92	59	123	—
Total Assets (Millions $)	417	618	350	264	251	242	252	294	153	—

PORTFOLIO (as of 9/30/94)

Portfolio Manager: Robert E. Pruyne - 1985, David H. Glen - 1985

Investm't Category: Mortgage-Backed Bond

Cap Gain	Asset Allocation
Cap & Income	Fund of Funds
✔ Income	Index
	Sector
✔ Domestic	Small Cap
Foreign	Socially Conscious
Country/Region	State Specific

Portfolio: stocks 0% bonds 99%
convertibles 0% other 0% cash 1%

Largest Holdings: mortgage-backed 96%, U.S. government 4%

Unrealized Net Capital Gains: -4% of portfolio value

SHAREHOLDER INFORMATION

Minimum Investment
Initial: $1,000   Subsequent: $100

Minimum IRA Investment
Initial: $500   Subsequent: $50

Maximum Fees
Load: none   12b-1: none
Other: none

Distributions
Income: monthly   Capital Gains: May

Exchange Options
Number Per Year: call fund   Fee: none
Telephone: yes (money market fund available)

Services
IRA, pension, auto exchange, auto invest, auto withdraw

Scudder Gold (SCGDX)
Gold

P.O. Box 2291
Boston, MA 02107
(800) 225-2470, (617) 439-4640

PERFORMANCE   fund inception date: 9/2/88

	3yr Annual	5yr Annual	10yr Annual	Bull	Bear
Return (%)	10.3	0.8	na	28.0	-8.8
Differ from Category (+/-)	-0.5 blw av	0.8 av	na	-4.9 blw av	1.2 abv av

Total Risk	Standard Deviation	Category Risk	Risk Index	Beta
high	20.7%	low	0.8	0.4

	1994	1993	1992	1991	1990	1989	1988	1987	1986	1985
Return (%)	-7.4	59.4	-9.0	-6.9	-16.6	10.6	—	—	—	—
Differ from category (+/-)	4.1	-27.5	6.7	-2.1	5.9	-14.1	—	—	—	—

PER SHARE DATA

	1994	1993	1992	1991	1990	1989	1988	1987	1986	1985
Dividends, Net Income ($)	0.25	0.24	0.00	0.00	0.00	0.06	—	—	—	—
Distrib'ns, Cap Gain ($)	0.47	0.00	0.00	0.00	0.00	0.04	—	—	—	—
Net Asset Value ($)	11.71	13.36	8.55	9.40	10.10	12.12	—	—	—	—
Expense Ratio (%)	1.69	2.17	2.54	2.54	2.60	3.00	—	—	—	—
Net Income to Assets (%)	-0.81	-0.81	-1.34	-0.59	0.34	-1.06	—	—	—	—
Portfolio Turnover (%)	50	59	58	71	81	35	—	—	—	—
Total Assets (Millions $)	129	108	31	33	17	9	—	—	—	—

PORTFOLIO (as of 6/30/94)

Portfolio Manager: Douglas D. Donald - 1988, William J. Wallace - 1988

Investm't Category: Gold

✔ Cap Gain	Asset Allocation
Cap & Income	Fund of Funds
Income	Index
	✔ Sector
✔ Domestic	Small Cap
✔ Foreign	Socially Conscious
Country/Region	State Specific

Portfolio: stocks 78% bonds 0%
convertibles 2% other 16% cash 4%

Largest Holdings: Canadian gold mining companies 43%, gold bullion 15%

Unrealized Net Capital Gains: 3% of portfolio value

SHAREHOLDER INFORMATION

Minimum Investment
Initial: $1,000   Subsequent: $100

Minimum IRA Investment
Initial: $500   Subsequent: $50

Maximum Fees
Load: none   12b-1: none
Other: none

Distributions
Income: Nov, Dec   Capital Gains: Nov, Dec

Exchange Options
Number Per Year: call fund   Fee: none
Telephone: yes (money market fund available)

Services
IRA, pension, auto exchange, auto invest, auto withdraw

Scudder Growth & Income (SCDGX)

Growth & Income

P.O. Box 2291
Boston, MA 02107
(800) 225-2470, (617) 439-4640

PERFORMANCE

fund inception date: 11/13/84

	3yr Annual	5yr Annual	10yr Annual	Bull	Bear
Return (%)	9.1	10.2	14.2	83.6	-4.4
Differ from Category (+/-)	2.0 abv av	2.3 high	2.5 high	7.8 abv av	1.9 abv av

Total Risk	Standard Deviation	Category Risk	Risk Index	Beta
av	8.1%	av	1.0	0.9

	1994	1993	1992	1991	1990	1989	1988	1987	1986	1985
Return (%)	2.5	15.5	9.5	28.1	-2.3	26.4	11.8	3.4	18.3	34.4
Differ from category (+/-). . .	3.9	2.3	-0.7	0.5	3.7	5.0	-5.2	2.8	2.5	8.7

PER SHARE DATA

	1994	1993	1992	1991	1990	1989	1988	1987	1986	1985
Dividends, Net Income ($).	0.51	0.44	0.53	0.55	0.67	0.69	0.59	0.68	0.68	0.58
Distrib'ns, Cap Gain ($) . . .	0.91	1.01	0.50	0.00	0.34	1.77	0.00	2.64	2.28	0.00
Net Asset Value ($)	16.27	17.24	16.20	15.76	12.77	14.14	13.17	12.31	15.02	15.35
Expense Ratio (%)	0.87	0.86	0.94	0.97	0.95	0.87	0.92	0.89	0.83	0.84
Net Income to Assets (%) . .	2.81	2.93	3.60	4.03	5.03	4.47	4.63	4.24	4.19	4.35
Portfolio Turnover (%)	48	36	28	45	65	77	48	60	45	73
Total Assets (Millions $). .	1,993	1,652	1,166	722	491	491	402	392	385	302

PORTFOLIO (as of 6/30/94)

Portfolio Manager: B. W. Thorndike - 1987, R. Hoffman - 1990, K. T. Millard - 1992

Investm't Category: Growth & Income

Cap Gain	Asset Allocation
✔ Cap & Income	Fund of Funds
Income	Index
	Sector
✔ Domestic	Small Cap
✔ Foreign	Socially Conscious
Country/Region	State Specific

Portfolio: stocks 87%   bonds 0%
convertibles 9%   other 0%   cash 4%

Largest Holdings: manufacturing 22%, financial 17%

Unrealized Net Capital Gains: 10% of portfolio value

SHAREHOLDER INFORMATION

Minimum Investment
Initial: $1,000   Subsequent: $100

Minimum IRA Investment
Initial: $500   Subsequent: $50

Maximum Fees
Load: none   12b-1: none
Other: none

Distributions
Income: quarterly   Capital Gains: Dec

Exchange Options
Number Per Year: call fund   Fee: none
Telephone: yes (money market fund available)

Services
IRA, pension, auto exchange, auto invest, auto withdraw

Scudder High Yield Tax-Free (SHYTX)

Tax-Exempt Bond

P.O. Box 2291
Boston, MA 02107
(800) 225-2470, (617) 439-4640

PERFORMANCE

fund inception date: 1/22/87

	3yr Annual	5yr Annual	10yr Annual	Bull	Bear
Return (%)	4.9	6.8	na	50.8	-6.9
Differ from Category (+/-)	0.4 abv av	0.7 abv av	na	9.0 high	-1.7 low

Total Risk	Standard Deviation	Category Risk	Risk Index	Avg Mat
av	6.8%	high	1.1	16.7 yrs

	1994	1993	1992	1991	1990	1989	1988	1987	1986	1985
Return (%)	-8.3	13.8	10.9	13.4	6.0	10.3	13.4	—	—	—
Differ from category (+/-)	-3.1	2.1	2.6	2.1	-0.3	1.3	3.2	—	—	—

PER SHARE DATA

	1994	1993	1992	1991	1990	1989	1988	1987	1986	1985
Dividends, Net Income ($)	0.66	0.67	0.73	0.75	0.77	0.76	0.83	—	—	—
Distrib'ns, Cap Gain ($)	0.00	0.28	0.27	0.21	0.05	0.06	0.00	—	—	—
Net Asset Value ($)	10.86	12.55	11.90	11.67	11.19	11.35	11.06	—	—	—
Expense Ratio (%)	0.80	0.92	0.98	1.00	1.00	1.00	0.67	—	—	—
Net Income to Assets (%)	5.62	5.38	6.10	6.65	6.88	6.72	7.65	—	—	—
Portfolio Turnover (%)	28	56	57	46	33	76	37	—	—	—
Total Assets (Millions $)	259	316	204	160	129	114	74	—	—	—

PORTFOLIO (as of 6/30/94)

Portfolio Manager: Condon - 1987, Manning - 1987

Investm't Category: Tax-Exempt Bond

Cap Gain	Asset Allocation
Cap & Income	Fund of Funds
✔ Income	Index
	Sector
✔ Domestic	Small Cap
Foreign	Socially Conscious
Country/Region	State Specific

Portfolio: stocks 0% bonds 100%
convertibles 0% other 0% cash 0%

Largest Holdings: general obligation 10%

Unrealized Net Capital Gains: 0% of portfolio value

SHAREHOLDER INFORMATION

Minimum Investment
Initial: $1,000   Subsequent: $100

Minimum IRA Investment
Initial: na   Subsequent: na

Maximum Fees
Load: none   12b-1: none
Other: none

Distributions
Income: monthly   Capital Gains: Dec

Exchange Options
Number Per Year: call fund   Fee: none
Telephone: yes (money market fund available)

Services
auto exchange, auto invest, auto withdraw

Scudder Income
(SCSBX)
General Bond

P.O. Box 2291
Boston, MA 02107
(800) 225-2470, (617) 439-4640

PERFORMANCE

fund inception date: 4/24/28

	3yr Annual	5yr Annual	10yr Annual	Bull	Bear
Return (%)	4.7	7.8	9.6	51.4	-7.5
Differ from Category (+/-)	0.4 abv av	0.9 high	0.7 high	10.4 high	-3.7 low

Total Risk	Standard Deviation	Category Risk	Risk Index	Avg Mat
blw av	5.0%	high	1.3	11.0 yrs

	1994	1993	1992	1991	1990	1989	1988	1987	1986	1985
Return (%).............	-4.5	12.7	6.7	17.3	8.3	12.6	8.9	0.7	14.7	21.7
Differ from category (+/-)...	-2.5	3.5	0.1	2.7	1.1	1.2	1.5	-1.5	0.5	2.3

PER SHARE DATA

	1994	1993	1992	1991	1990	1989	1988	1987	1986	1985
Dividends, Net Income ($).	0.76	0.87	0.93	0.94	1.09	1.06	1.07	1.10	1.22	1.29
Distrib'ns, Cap Gain ($) ...	0.02	0.58	0.40	0.12	0.00	0.00	0.00	0.00	0.00	0.00
Net Asset Value ($)	12.32	13.72	13.48	13.91	12.82	12.89	12.41	12.40	13.41	12.82
Expense Ratio (%)	0.96	0.92	0.93	0.97	0.95	0.93	0.94	0.94	0.88	0.91
Net Income to Assets (%) .	5.95	6.32	7.05	7.13	8.21	8.23	8.53	8.37	9.12	10.57
Portfolio Turnover (%)	39	130	121	110	48	63	20	34	24	29
Total Assets (Millions $)....	464	512	456	403	302	272	245	242	249	172

PORTFOLIO (as of 6/30/94)

Portfolio Manager: William Hutchinson - 1986, S. Wohler - 1993

Investm't Category: General Bond

Cap Gain	Asset Allocation
Cap & Income	Fund of Funds
✔ Income	Index
	Sector
✔ Domestic	Small Cap
Foreign	Socially Conscious
Country/Region	State Specific

Portfolio: stocks 0% bonds 87%
convertibles 0% other 0% cash 13%

Largest Holdings: corporate 33%, U.S. government and agencies 31%

Unrealized Net Capital Gains: -2% of portfolio value

SHAREHOLDER INFORMATION

Minimum Investment
Initial: $1,000   Subsequent: $100

Minimum IRA Investment
Initial: $500   Subsequent: $50

Maximum Fees
Load: none   12b-1: none
Other: none

Distributions
Income: quarterly   Capital Gains: Dec

Exchange Options
Number Per Year: call fund   Fee: none
Telephone: yes (money market fund available)

Services
IRA, pension, auto exchange, auto invest, auto withdraw

Scudder International
(SCINX)

International Stock

P.O. Box 2291
Boston, MA 02107
(800) 225-2470, (617) 439-4640

PERFORMANCE

fund inception date: 6/14/54

	3yr Annual	5yr Annual	10yr Annual	Bull	Bear
Return (%)	8.8	5.5	16.1	61.4	-5.2
Differ from Category (+/-)	-0.3 av	0.6 av	0.9 av	-2.5 av	1.8 abv av

Total Risk	Standard Deviation	Category Risk	Risk Index	Beta
abv av	11.7%	blw av	0.9	0.7

	1994	1993	1992	1991	1990	1989	1988	1987	1986	1985
Return (%)	-2.9	36.5	-2.6	11.7	-8.9	26.8	18.7	0.9	50.4	49.0
Differ from category (+/-)	0.1	-2.1	0.3	-1.4	1.5	4.3	4.3	-13.5	-8.6	6.6

PER SHARE DATA

	1994	1993	1992	1991	1990	1989	1988	1987	1986	1985
Dividends, Net Income ($)	0.00	0.39	0.83	0.00	0.74	0.43	0.19	0.82	0.49	0.41
Distrib'ns, Cap Gain ($)	2.42	0.39	0.86	0.40	1.98	3.15	3.00	9.39	5.93	0.13
Net Asset Value ($)	40.37	44.10	32.93	35.53	32.15	38.20	33.10	30.60	39.73	31.03
Expense Ratio (%)	1.19	1.26	1.30	1.24	1.18	1.22	1.21	1.09	0.99	1.04
Net Income to Assets (%)	0.76	1.13	1.25	2.22	1.33	1.20	1.16	1.19	2.60	2.34
Portfolio Turnover (%)	45	29	50	70	49	48	55	67	36	19
Total Assets (Millions $)	2,271	1,369	933	929	783	550	559	791	596	222

PORTFOLIO (as of 9/30/94)

Portfolio Manager: Bratt - 1976, Franklin - 1989, Cheng - 1990, Rodrigo - 1994

Investm't Category: International Stock

✔ Cap Gain	Asset Allocation
Cap & Income	Fund of Funds
Income	Index
	Sector
Domestic	Small Cap
✔ Foreign	Socially Conscious
Country/Region	State Specific

Portfolio: stocks 93% bonds 0%
convertibles 3% other 1% cash 3%

Largest Holdings: Japan 27%, United Kingdom 9%

Unrealized Net Capital Gains: 15% of portfolio value

SHAREHOLDER INFORMATION

Minimum Investment
Initial: $1,000   Subsequent: $100

Minimum IRA Investment
Initial: $500   Subsequent: $50

Maximum Fees
Load: none   12b-1: none
Other: none

Distributions
Income: Nov, Dec   Capital Gains: May, Dec

Exchange Options
Number Per Year: call fund   Fee: none
Telephone: yes (money market fund available)

Services
IRA, pension, auto exchange, auto invest, auto withdraw

Scudder International Bond (SCIBX)

International Bond

P.O. Box 2291
Boston, MA 02107
(800) 225-2470, (617) 439-4640

PERFORMANCE

fund inception date: 7/6/88

	3yr Annual	5yr Annual	10yr Annual	Bull	Bear
Return (%)	4.4	11.0	na	66.7	-9.5
Differ from Category (+/-)	0.5 abv av	2.4 high	na	6.4 abv av	-1.7 blw av

Total Risk	Standard Deviation	Category Risk	Risk Index	Avg Mat
blw av	6.2%	av	1.0	8.0 yrs

	1994	1993	1992	1991	1990	1989	1988	1987	1986	1985
Return (%)	-8.5	15.8	7.5	22.2	21.0	7.2	—	—	—	—
Differ from category (+/-)	-2.2	2.4	2.8	6.2	9.5	5.0	—	—	—	—

PER SHARE DATA

	1994	1993	1992	1991	1990	1989	1988	1987	1986	1985
Dividends, Net Income ($)	0.99	0.92	1.06	1.17	1.16	1.05	—	—	—	—
Distrib'ns, Cap Gain ($)	0.00	0.39	0.62	0.81	0.29	0.00	—	—	—	—
Net Asset Value ($)	11.38	13.50	12.83	13.53	12.90	11.97	—	—	—	—
Expense Ratio (%)	1.27	1.25	1.25	1.25	1.25	1.00	—	—	—	—
Net Income to Assets (%)	6.86	7.69	8.31	9.48	9.57	8.58	—	—	—	—
Portfolio Turnover (%)	232	249	148	260	216	104	—	—	—	—
Total Assets (Millions $)	1,086	1,377	542	144	73	13	—	—	—	—

PORTFOLIO (as of 6/30/94)

Portfolio Manager: Adam M. Greshin - 1988, Lawrence Teitelbaum - 1994

Investm't Category: International Bond

Cap Gain	Asset Allocation
Cap & Income	Fund of Funds
✔ Income	Index
	Sector
✔ Domestic	Small Cap
✔ Foreign	Socially Conscious
Country/Region	State Specific

Portfolio: stocks 0% bonds 89%
convertibles 0% other 4% cash 7%

Largest Holdings: United States 14%, Denmark 12%

Unrealized Net Capital Gains: -9% of portfolio value

SHAREHOLDER INFORMATION

Minimum Investment
Initial: $1,000   Subsequent: $100

Minimum IRA Investment
Initial: $500   Subsequent: $50

Maximum Fees
Load: none   12b-1: none
Other: none

Distributions
Income: monthly   Capital Gains: Dec

Exchange Options
Number Per Year: call fund   Fee: none
Telephone: yes (money market fund available)

Services
IRA, pension, auto exchange, auto invest, auto withdraw

Scudder Latin America
(SLAFX)
International Stock

P.O. Box 2291
Boston, MA 02107
(800) 225-2470, (617) 439-4640

PERFORMANCE

fund inception date: 12/8/92

	3yr Annual	5yr Annual	10yr Annual	Bull	Bear
Return (%)	na	na	na	na	-18.3
Differ from Category (+/-)	na	na	na	na	-11.3 low

Total Risk	Standard Deviation	Category Risk	Risk Index	Beta
na	na	na	na	na

	1994	1993	1992	1991	1990	1989	1988	1987	1986	1985
Return (%)	-9.4	74.3	—	—	—	—	—	—	—	—
Differ from category (+/-)	-6.4	35.7	—	—	—	—	—	—	—	—

PER SHARE DATA

	1994	1993	1992	1991	1990	1989	1988	1987	1986	1985
Dividends, Net Income ($)	0.00	0.06	—	—	—	—	—	—	—	—
Distrib'ns, Cap Gain ($)	0.73	0.06	—	—	—	—	—	—	—	—
Net Asset Value ($)	18.88	21.68	—	—	—	—	—	—	—	—
Expense Ratio (%)	2.01	2.00	—	—	—	—	—	—	—	—
Net Income to Assets (%)	-0.20	0.44	—	—	—	—	—	—	—	—
Portfolio Turnover (%)	22	5	—	—	—	—	—	—	—	—
Total Assets (Millions $)	649	372	—	—	—	—	—	—	—	—

PORTFOLIO (as of 10/31/94)

Portfolio Manager: Games - 1992, Truscott - 1992, Cornell - 1993

Investm't Category: International Stock
- ✔ Cap Gain
- Cap & Income
- Income
- Domestic
- ✔ Foreign
- ✔ Country/Region
- Asset Allocation
- Fund of Funds
- Index
- Sector
- Small Cap
- Socially Conscious
- State Specific

Portfolio: stocks 88% bonds 0%
convertibles 0% other 0% cash 12%

Largest Holdings: Mexico 33%, Brazil 29%

Unrealized Net Capital Gains: 16% of portfolio value

SHAREHOLDER INFORMATION

Minimum Investment
Initial: $1,000 Subsequent: $100

Minimum IRA Investment
Initial: $500 Subsequent: $50

Maximum Fees
Load: 2.00% redemption 12b-1: none
Other: redemption fee applies for 1 year

Distributions
Income: Dec Capital Gains: Dec

Exchange Options
Number Per Year: call fund Fee: none
Telephone: yes (money market fund available)

Services
IRA, pension, auto exchange, auto invest, auto withdraw

Scudder Managed Muni Bond (SCMBX)

P.O. Box 2291
Boston, MA 02107
(800) 225-2470, (617) 439-4640

Tax-Exempt Bond

	3yr Annual	5yr Annual	10yr Annual	Bull	Bear
Return (%)	5.0	6.8	9.0	47.6	-6.5
Differ from Category (+/-)	0.5 abv av	0.7 abv av	0.9 abv av	5.8 high	-1.3 blw av

Total Risk	Standard Deviation	Category Risk	Risk Index	Avg Mat
blw av	6.6%	abv av	1.1	11.7 yrs

	1994	1993	1992	1991	1990	1989	1988	1987	1986	1985
Return (%)	-6.0	13.3	9.0	12.1	6.7	11.1	12.2	0.3	16.7	17.5
Differ from category (+/-)	-0.8	1.6	0.7	0.8	0.4	2.1	2.0	1.6	0.3	0.1

PER SHARE DATA

	1994	1993	1992	1991	1990	1989	1988	1987	1986	1985
Dividends, Net Income ($)	0.46	0.48	0.51	0.53	0.55	0.59	0.60	0.61	0.60	0.60
Distrib'ns, Cap Gain ($)	0.02	0.29	0.33	0.12	0.09	0.39	0.02	0.11	0.24	0.00
Net Asset Value ($)	8.07	9.09	8.72	8.80	8.45	8.54	8.60	8.24	8.93	8.40
Expense Ratio (%)	0.63	0.63	0.63	0.64	0.61	0.62	0.61	0.63	0.58	0.58
Net Income to Assets (%)	5.29	5.21	5.76	6.16	6.61	6.78	7.13	7.20	6.88	7.27
Portfolio Turnover (%)	33	53	60	32	72	90	76	73	78	98
Total Assets (Millions $)	708	909	829	796	719	691	636	592	663	574

PORTFOLIO (as of 6/30/94)

Portfolio Manager: Carleton - 1986, Condon - 1987

Investm't Category: Tax-Exempt Bond

Cap Gain	Asset Allocation
Cap & Income	Fund of Funds
✔ Income	Index
	Sector
✔ Domestic	Small Cap
Foreign	Socially Conscious
Country/Region	State Specific

Portfolio: stocks 0%   bonds 100%
convertibles 0%   other 0%   cash 0%

Largest Holdings: general obligation 20%

Unrealized Net Capital Gains: 1% of portfolio value

SHAREHOLDER INFORMATION

Minimum Investment
Initial: $1,000   Subsequent: $100

Minimum IRA Investment
Initial: na   Subsequent: na

Maximum Fees
Load: none   12b-1: none
Other: none

Distributions
Income: monthly   Capital Gains: Dec

Exchange Options
Number Per Year: call fund   Fee: none
Telephone: yes (money market fund available)

Services
auto exchange, auto invest, auto withdraw

Scudder Mass Tax-Free
(SCMAX)
Tax-Exempt Bond

P.O. Box 2291
Boston, MA 02107
(800) 225-2470, (617) 439-4640

PERFORMANCE

fund inception date: 5/28/87

	3yr Annual	5yr Annual	10yr Annual	Bull	Bear
Return (%)	5.9	7.2	na	51.1	-6.5
Differ from Category (+/-)	1.4 high	1.1 high	na	9.3 high	-1.3 blw av

Total Risk	Standard Deviation	Category Risk	Risk Index	Avg Mat
blw av	6.6%	abv av	1.1	12.4 yrs

	1994	1993	1992	1991	1990	1989	1988	1987	1986	1985
Return (%)...............	-6.1	14.2	10.8	12.2	6.3	9.8	12.3	—	—	—
Differ from category (+/-)....	-0.9	2.5	2.5	0.9	0.0	0.8	2.1	—	—	—

PER SHARE DATA

	1994	1993	1992	1991	1990	1989	1988	1987	1986	1985
Dividends, Net Income ($) .	0.76	0.83	0.84	0.81	0.82	0.84	0.89	—	—	—
Distrib'ns, Cap Gain ($) ...	0.01	0.12	0.16	0.09	0.00	0.11	0.21	—	—	—
Net Asset Value ($)	12.57	14.21	13.31	12.96	12.39	12.46	12.24	—	—	—
Expense Ratio (%)	0.33	0.00	0.48	0.60	0.60	0.51	0.50	—	—	—
Net Income to Assets (%) .	5.76	6.36	6.38	6.72	6.60	7.23	7.55	—	—	—
Portfolio Turnover (%).......	8	29	23	27	46	111	96	—	—	—
Total Assets (Millions $)....	277	371	120	67	46	31	16	—	—	—

PORTFOLIO (as of 9/30/94)

Portfolio Manager: Condon - 1989, Meany - 1991

Investm't Category: Tax-Exempt Bond

Cap Gain	Asset Allocation
Cap & Income	Fund of Funds
✔ Income	Index
	Sector
✔ Domestic	Small Cap
Foreign	Socially Conscious
Country/Region	✔ State Specific

Portfolio:
stocks 0%   bonds 100%
convertibles 0%   other 0%   cash 0%

Largest Holdings: general obligation 21%

Unrealized Net Capital Gains: -1% of portfolio value

SHAREHOLDER INFORMATION

Minimum Investment
Initial: $1,000   Subsequent: $100

Minimum IRA Investment
Initial: na   Subsequent: na

Maximum Fees
Load: none   12b-1: none
Other: none

Distributions
Income: monthly   Capital Gains: Jun, Nov

Exchange Options
Number Per Year: call fund   Fee: none
Telephone: yes (money market fund available)

Services
auto exchange, auto invest, auto withdraw

Scudder Medium Term Tax Free (SCMTX)

Tax-Exempt Bond

P.O. Box 2291
Boston, MA 02107
(800) 225-2470, (617) 439-4640

PERFORMANCE

fund inception date: 4/12/83

	3yr Annual	5yr Annual	10yr Annual	Bull	Bear
Return (%)	5.2	6.8	na	39.9	-3.9
Differ from Category (+/-)	0.7 abv av	0.7 abv av	na	-1.9 blw av	1.3 abv av

Total Risk	Standard Deviation	Category Risk	Risk Index	Avg Mat
low	4.7%	low	0.7	6.7 yrs

	1994	1993	1992	1991	1990	1989	1988	1987	1986	1985
Return (%)	-3.5	10.9	8.9	12.1	6.3	—	—	—	—	—
Differ from category (+/-)	1.7	-0.8	0.6	0.8	0.0	—	—	—	—	—

PER SHARE DATA

	1994	1993	1992	1991	1990	1989	1988	1987	1986	1985
Dividends, Net Income ($)	0.55	0.60	0.65	0.67	0.55	—	—	—	—	—
Distrib'ns, Cap Gain ($)	0.03	0.06	0.03	0.01	0.00	—	—	—	—	—
Net Asset Value ($)	10.39	11.36	10.86	10.62	10.11	—	—	—	—	—
Expense Ratio (%)	0.56	0.14	0.00	0.00	0.97	—	—	—	—	—
Net Income to Assets (%)	5.10	5.35	6.07	6.44	5.37	—	—	—	—	—
Portfolio Turnover (%)	37	37	22	14	117	—	—	—	—	—
Total Assets (Millions $)	703	1,025	661	268	27	—	—	—	—	—

PORTFOLIO (as of 6/30/94)

Portfolio Manager: Carleton - 1986, Patton - 1987

Investm't Category: Tax-Exempt Bond

Cap Gain	Asset Allocation
Cap & Income	Fund of Funds
✔ Income	Index
	Sector
✔ Domestic	Small Cap
Foreign	Socially Conscious
Country/Region	State Specific

Portfolio: stocks 0% bonds 100%
convertibles 0% other 0% cash 0%

Largest Holdings: general obligation 28%

Unrealized Net Capital Gains: 0% of portfolio value

SHAREHOLDER INFORMATION

Minimum Investment
Initial: $1,000   Subsequent: $100

Minimum IRA Investment
Initial: na   Subsequent: na

Maximum Fees
Load: none   12b-1: none
Other: none

Distributions
Income: monthly   Capital Gains: Dec

Exchange Options
Number Per Year: call fund   Fee: none
Telephone: yes (money market fund available)

Services
auto exchange, auto invest, auto withdraw

Scudder NY Tax Free
(SCYTX)
Tax-Exempt Bond

P.O. Box 2291
Boston, MA 02107
(800) 225-2470, (617) 439-4640

	3yr Annual	5yr Annual	10yr Annual	Bull	Bear
Return (%)	4.9	6.6	8.2	51.1	-6.9
Differ from Category (+/-)	0.4 abv av	0.5 abv av	0.1 av	9.3 high	-1.7 low

Total Risk	Standard Deviation	Category Risk	Risk Index	Avg Mat
av	7.0%	high	1.1	13.1 yrs

	1994	1993	1992	1991	1990	1989	1988	1987	1986	1985
Return (%).	-7.2	12.9	10.2	14.4	4.2	9.9	10.8	-0.7	14.1	16.0
Differ from category (+/-). . .	-2.0	1.2	1.9	3.1	-2.1	0.9	0.6	0.6	-2.3	-1.4

PER SHARE DATA

	1994	1993	1992	1991	1990	1989	1988	1987	1986	1985
Dividends, Net Income ($) .	0.52	0.56	0.62	0.66	0.67	0.70	0.73	0.73	0.75	0.78
Distrib'ns, Cap Gain ($) . . .	0.05	0.73	0.61	0.25	0.00	0.09	0.00	0.19	0.15	0.00
Net Asset Value ($)	9.81	11.17	11.08	11.21	10.65	10.88	10.64	10.28	11.30	10.73
Expense Ratio (%)	0.83	0.82	0.87	0.91	0.89	0.89	0.95	0.88	0.88	1.01
Net Income to Assets (%) .	5.03	5.36	5.96	6.29	6.39	6.89	7.05	6.70	7.01	8.42
Portfolio Turnover (%).	94	201	168	225	114	132	44	72	40	166
Total Assets (Millions $). . . .	182	225	159	142	132	123	116	154	101	61

PORTFOLIO (as of 9/30/94)

Portfolio Manager: Carleton - 1986, Ragus - 1990

Investm't Category: Tax-Exempt Bond
Cap Gain	Asset Allocation
Cap & Income	Fund of Funds
✔ Income	Index
	Sector
✔ Domestic	Small Cap
Foreign	Socially Conscious
Country/Region	✔ State Specific

Portfolio: stocks 0%   bonds 100%
convertibles 0%   other 0%   cash 0%

Largest Holdings: general obligation 15%

Unrealized Net Capital Gains: -4% of portfolio value

SHAREHOLDER INFORMATION

Minimum Investment
Initial: $1,000   Subsequent: $100

Minimum IRA Investment
Initial: na   Subsequent: na

Maximum Fees
Load: none   12b-1: none
Other: none

Distributions
Income: monthly   Capital Gains: Jun, Nov

Exchange Options
Number Per Year: call fund   Fee: none
Telephone: yes (money market fund available)

Services
auto exchange, auto invest, auto withdraw

Scudder Ohio Tax-Free
(SCOHX)
Tax-Exempt Bond

P.O. Box 2291
Boston, MA 02107
(800) 225-2470, (617) 439-4640

PERFORMANCE

fund inception date: 5/28/87

	3yr Annual	5yr Annual	10yr Annual	Bull	Bear
Return (%)	4.9	6.6	na	45.8	-5.9
Differ from Category (+/-)	0.4 abv av	0.5 abv av	na	4.0 abv av	-0.7 av

Total Risk	Standard Deviation	Category Risk	Risk Index	Avg Mat
blw av	6.2%	av	1.0	13.1 yrs

	1994	1993	1992	1991	1990	1989	1988	1987	1986	1985
Return (%)	-5.5	12.3	8.8	11.8	6.6	9.5	12.8	—	—	—
Differ from category (+/-)	-0.3	0.6	0.5	0.5	0.3	0.5	2.6	—	—	—

PER SHARE DATA

	1994	1993	1992	1991	1990	1989	1988	1987	1986	1985
Dividends, Net Income ($)	0.70	0.71	0.73	0.76	0.79	0.83	0.83	—	—	—
Distrib'ns, Cap Gain ($)	0.04	0.10	0.19	0.03	0.06	0.07	0.02	—	—	—
Net Asset Value ($)	12.11	13.59	12.85	12.69	12.09	12.17	11.96	—	—	—
Expense Ratio (%)	0.50	0.50	0.50	0.50	0.50	0.50	0.50	—	—	—
Net Income to Assets (%)	5.51	5.61	6.05	6.50	6.74	7.13	7.17	—	—	—
Portfolio Turnover (%)	13	34	13	23	16	36	106	—	—	—
Total Assets (Millions $)	72	83	51	37	25	12	6	—	—	—

PORTFOLIO (as of 9/30/94)

Portfolio Manager: Condon - 1988, Manning - 1987

Investm't Category: Tax-Exempt Bond

Cap Gain	Asset Allocation
Cap & Income	Fund of Funds
✔ Income	Index
	Sector
✔ Domestic	Small Cap
Foreign	Socially Conscious
Country/Region	✔ State Specific

Portfolio: stocks 0% bonds 100%
convertibles 0% other 0% cash 0%

Largest Holdings: general obligation 27%

Unrealized Net Capital Gains: 0% of portfolio value

SHAREHOLDER INFORMATION

Minimum Investment
Initial: $1,000   Subsequent: $100

Minimum IRA Investment
Initial: na   Subsequent: na

Maximum Fees
Load: none   12b-1: none
Other: none

Distributions
Income: monthly   Capital Gains: May, Nov

Exchange Options
Number Per Year: call fund   Fee: none
Telephone: yes (money market fund available)

Services
auto exchange, auto invest, auto withdraw

Scudder Pacific Opportunities (SCOPX)

International Stock

P.O. Box 2291
Boston, MA 02107
(800) 225-2470, (617) 439-4640

PERFORMANCE

fund inception date: 12/8/92

	3yr Annual	5yr Annual	10yr Annual	Bull	Bear
Return (%)	na	na	na	na	-14.2
Differ from Category (+/-)	na	na	na	na	-7.2 low

Total Risk	Standard Deviation	Category Risk	Risk Index	Beta
na	na	na	na	na

	1994	1993	1992	1991	1990	1989	1988	1987	1986	1985
Return (%).............	-17.1	60.0	—	—	—	—	—	—	—	—
Differ from category (+/-)..	-14.1	21.4	—	—	—	—	—	—	—	—

PER SHARE DATA

	1994	1993	1992	1991	1990	1989	1988	1987	1986	1985
Dividends, Net Income ($) .	0.10	0.08	—	—	—	—	—	—	—	—
Distrib'ns, Cap Gain ($) ...	0.00	0.01	—	—	—	—	—	—	—	—
Net Asset Value ($)	15.71	19.07	—	—	—	—	—	—	—	—
Expense Ratio (%)	1.81	1.75	—	—	—	—	—	—	—	—
Net Income to Assets (%) .	0.28	1.41	—	—	—	—	—	—	—	—
Portfolio Turnover (%)......	38	10	—	—	—	—	—	—	—	—
Total Assets (Millions $)....	422	433	—	—	—	—	—	—	—	—

PORTFOLIO (as of 10/31/94)

Portfolio Manager: N. Bratt - 1992, J. Cornell 1993, Elizabeth Allen - 1994

Investm't Category: International Stock

- ✔ Cap Gain
-   Cap & Income
-   Income
-   Domestic
- ✔ Foreign
- ✔ Country/Region

-   Asset Allocation
-   Fund of Funds
-   Index
-   Sector
-   Small Cap
-   Socially Conscious
-   State Specific

Portfolio: stocks 70% bonds 0%
convertibles 6% other 0% cash 24%

Largest Holdings: Hong Kong 14%, Korea 10%

Unrealized Net Capital Gains: 11% of portfolio value

SHAREHOLDER INFORMATION

Minimum Investment
Initial: $1,000   Subsequent: $100

Minimum IRA Investment
Initial: $500   Subsequent: $50

Maximum Fees
Load: none   12b-1: none
Other: none

Distributions
Income: Dec   Capital Gains: Dec

Exchange Options
Number Per Year: call fund   Fee: none
Telephone: yes (money market fund available)

Services
IRA, pension, auto exchange, auto invest, auto withdraw

Scudder Penn Tax Free
(SCPAX)
Tax-Exempt Bond

P.O. Box 2291
Boston, MA 02107
(800) 225-2470, (617) 439-4640

PERFORMANCE

	3yr Annual	5yr Annual	10yr Annual	Bull	Bear
Return (%)	5.1	6.6	na	47.4	-6.1
Differ from Category (+/-)	0.6 abv av	0.5 abv av	na	5.6 high	-0.9 blw av

Total Risk	Standard Deviation		Category Risk	Risk Index		Avg Mat
blw av	6.0%		av	1.0		13.1 yrs

	1994	1993	1992	1991	1990	1989	1988	1987	1986	1985
Return (%)	-5.9	13.1	9.0	12.4	5.8	10.1	13.4	—	—	—
Differ from category (+/-)	-0.7	1.4	0.7	1.1	-0.5	1.1	3.2	—	—	—

PER SHARE DATA

	1994	1993	1992	1991	1990	1989	1988	1987	1986	1985
Dividends, Net Income ($)	0.74	0.75	0.77	0.78	0.82	0.84	0.84	—	—	—
Distrib'ns, Cap Gain ($)	0.03	0.09	0.21	0.07	0.00	0.01	0.06	—	—	—
Net Asset Value ($)	12.41	13.99	13.14	12.98	12.35	12.48	12.14	—	—	—
Expense Ratio (%)	0.50	0.50	0.50	0.50	0.50	0.50	0.50	—	—	—
Net Income to Assets (%)	5.67	5.47	6.05	6.67	6.78	7.09	7.16	—	—	—
Portfolio Turnover (%)	32	20	11	8	2	14	98	—	—	—
Total Assets (Millions $)	67	75	39	26	18	11	5	—	—	—

PORTFOLIO (as of 9/30/94)

Portfolio Manager: Condon - 1987, Manning - 1987

Investm't Category: Tax-Exempt Bond

Cap Gain	Asset Allocation
Cap & Income	Fund of Funds
✔ Income	Index
	Sector
✔ Domestic	Small Cap
Foreign	Socially Conscious
Country/Region	✔ State Specific

Portfolio: stocks 0%   bonds 100%
convertibles 0%   other 0%   cash 0%

Largest Holdings: general obligation 19%

Unrealized Net Capital Gains: 0% of portfolio value

SHAREHOLDER INFORMATION

Minimum Investment
Initial: $1,000   Subsequent: $100

Minimum IRA Investment
Initial: na   Subsequent: na

Maximum Fees
Load: none   12b-1: none
Other: none

Distributions
Income: monthly   Capital Gains: Jun, Nov

Exchange Options
Number Per Year: call fund   Fee: none
Telephone: yes (money market fund available)

Services
auto exchange, auto invest, auto withdraw

Scudder Quality Growth

(SCQGX)

Growth

P.O. Box 2291
Boston, MA 02107
(800) 225-2470, (617) 439-4640

PERFORMANCE

fund inception date: 5/15/91

	3yr Annual	5yr Annual	10yr Annual	Bull	Bear
Return (%)	1.7	na	na	na	-7.8
Differ from Category (+/-)	-6.0 low	na	na	na	-1.2 blw av

Total Risk	Standard Deviation	Category Risk	Risk Index	Beta
abv av	10.6%	abv av	1.1	1.1

	1994	1993	1992	1991	1990	1989	1988	1987	1986	1985
Return (%).	-1.3	0.0	6.6	—	—	—	—	—	—	—
Differ from category (+/-). . .	-0.7	-13.4	-5.0	—	—	—	—	—	—	—

PER SHARE DATA

	1994	1993	1992	1991	1990	1989	1988	1987	1986	1985
Dividends, Net Income ($) .	0.15	0.08	0.03	—	—	—	—	—	—	—
Distrib'ns, Cap Gain ($) . . .	1.09	0.24	0.00	—	—	—	—	—	—	—
Net Asset Value ($)	14.47	15.92	16.23	—	—	—	—	—	—	—
Expense Ratio (%)	1.25	1.20	1.25	—	—	—	—	—	—	—
Net Income to Assets (%) .	0.96	0.39	0.24	—	—	—	—	—	—	—
Portfolio Turnover (%).	119	111	27	—	—	—	—	—	—	—
Total Assets (Millions $). . . .	112	124	101	—	—	—	—	—	—	—

PORTFOLIO (as of 10/31/94)

Portfolio Manager: B. Beaty - 1991, H. F. Ward - 1991, M. K. Shields - 1992

Investm't Category: Growth

✔ Cap Gain	Asset Allocation
Cap & Income	Fund of Funds
Income	Index
	Sector
✔ Domestic	Small Cap
✔ Foreign	Socially Conscious
Country/Region	State Specific

Portfolio: stocks 100% bonds 0%
convertibles 0% other 0% cash 0%

Largest Holdings: food & beverage 10%, pharmaceuticals 10%

Unrealized Net Capital Gains: 4% of portfolio value

SHAREHOLDER INFORMATION

Minimum Investment
Initial: $1,000 Subsequent: $100

Minimum IRA Investment
Initial: $500 Subsequent: $100

Maximum Fees
Load: none 12b-1: none
Other: none

Distributions
Income: Dec Capital Gains: Dec

Exchange Options
Number Per Year: call fund Fee: none
Telephone: yes (money market fund available)

Services
IRA, pension, auto exchange, auto invest, auto withdraw

Scudder Short-Term Bond (SCSTX)

General Bond

P.O. Box 2291
Boston, MA 02107
(800) 225-2470, (617) 439-4640

PERFORMANCE

fund inception date: 4/2/84

	3yr Annual	5yr Annual	10yr Annual	Bull	Bear
Return (%)	3.5	6.8	8.9	35.3	-2.8
Differ from Category (+/-)	-0.8 low	-0.1 av	0.0 blw av	-5.7 blw av	1.0 abv av

Total Risk	Standard Deviation	Category Risk	Risk Index	Avg Mat
low	2.5%	blw av	0.6	0.8 yrs

	1994	1993	1992	1991	1990	1989	1988	1987	1986	1985
Return (%)	-2.8	8.2	5.4	14.3	9.8	13.2	6.3	1.2	14.6	20.9
Differ from category (+/-)	-0.8	-1.0	-1.2	-0.3	2.6	1.8	-1.1	-1.0	0.4	1.5

PER SHARE DATA

	1994	1993	1992	1991	1990	1989	1988	1987	1986	1985
Dividends, Net Income ($)	0.76	0.77	0.96	1.08	1.09	0.83	0.72	0.72	0.81	0.96
Distrib'ns, Cap Gain ($)	0.00	0.11	0.00	0.00	0.00	0.09	0.02	0.11	0.22	0.00
Net Asset Value ($)	10.92	12.01	11.93	12.25	11.72	11.71	11.19	11.23	11.92	11.35
Expense Ratio (%)	0.72	0.68	0.75	0.44	0.16	0.36	1.50	1.45	1.45	1.27
Net Income to Assets (%)	6.74	7.20	8.01	8.96	9.36	7.97	6.48	6.34	6.89	8.82
Portfolio Turnover (%)	80	66	84	41	53	40	24	29	15	58
Total Assets (Millions $)	2,138	3,196	2,862	2,248	340	72	10	10	8	5

PORTFOLIO (as of 6/30/94)

Portfolio Manager: C. Gootkind - 1989, T. Poor - 1989, S. Dolan - 1994

Investm't Category: General Bond

Cap Gain	Asset Allocation
Cap & Income	Fund of Funds
✔ Income	Index
	Sector
✔ Domestic	Small Cap
✔ Foreign	Socially Conscious
Country/Region	State Specific

Portfolio: stocks 0% bonds 95%
convertibles 0% other 0% cash 5%

Largest Holdings: mortgage-backed 37%, asset-backed 19%

Unrealized Net Capital Gains: -2% of portfolio value

SHAREHOLDER INFORMATION

Minimum Investment
Initial: $1,000   Subsequent: $100

Minimum IRA Investment
Initial: $500   Subsequent: $50

Maximum Fees
Load: none   12b-1: none
Other: none

Distributions
Income: monthly   Capital Gains: Dec

Exchange Options
Number Per Year: call fund   Fee: none
Telephone: yes (money market fund available)

Services
IRA, pension, auto exchange, auto invest, auto withdraw

Scudder Short-Term Global Income (SSTGX)

International Bond

P.O. Box 2291
Boston, MA 02107
(800) 225-2470, (617) 439-4640

PERFORMANCE

fund inception date: 3/1/91

	3yr Annual	5yr Annual	10yr Annual	Bull	Bear
Return (%)	3.6	na	na	na	-1.2
Differ from Category (+/-)	-0.3 av	na	na	na	6.6 high

Total Risk	Standard Deviation	Category Risk	Risk Index	Avg Mat
low	2.4%	low	0.4	1.9 yrs

	1994	1993	1992	1991	1990	1989	1988	1987	1986	1985
Return (%)	-1.0	6.6	5.5	—	—	—	—	—	—	—
Differ from category (+/-) . . .	5.3	-6.8	0.8	—	—	—	—	—	—	—

PER SHARE DATA

	1994	1993	1992	1991	1990	1989	1988	1987	1986	1985
Dividends, Net Income ($) .	0.87	0.93	1.06	—	—	—	—	—	—	—
Distrib'ns, Cap Gain ($) . . .	0.00	0.00	0.02	—	—	—	—	—	—	—
Net Asset Value ($)	10.54	11.53	11.70	—	—	—	—	—	—	—
Expense Ratio (%)	1.00	1.00	1.00	—	—	—	—	—	—	—
Net Income to Assets (%) .	7.76	8.10	8.94	—	—	—	—	—	—	—
Portfolio Turnover (%).	272	259	274	—	—	—	—	—	—	—
Total Assets (Millions $). . . .	496	958	1,369	—	—	—	—	—	—	—

PORTFOLIO (as of 10/31/94)

Portfolio Manager: M. Craddock - 1992, G. P. Johnson - 1992, Lawrence Teitelbaum - 1994

Investm't Category: International Bond
- Cap Gain
- Cap & Income
- ✔ Income
- ✔ Domestic
- ✔ Foreign
- Country/Region
- Asset Allocation
- Fund of Funds
- Index
- Sector
- Small Cap
- Socially Conscious
- State Specific

Portfolio: stocks 0% bonds 100%
convertibles 0% other 0% cash 0%

Largest Holdings: United States 26%, Thailand 9%

Unrealized Net Capital Gains: 0% of portfolio value

SHAREHOLDER INFORMATION

Minimum Investment
Initial: $1,000 Subsequent: $100

Minimum IRA Investment
Initial: $500 Subsequent: $50

Maximum Fees
Load: none 12b-1: none
Other: none

Distributions
Income: monthly Capital Gains: Nov, Dec

Exchange Options
Number Per Year: call fund Fee: none
Telephone: yes (money market fund available)

Services
IRA, pension, auto exchange, auto invest, auto withdraw

Scudder U.S. Government Zero Coupon 2000

(SGZTX) *Government Bond*

P.O. Box 2291
Boston, MA 02107
(800) 225-2470, (617) 439-4640

	3yr Annual	5yr Annual	10yr Annual	Bull	Bear
Return (%)	4.9	7.7	na	70.0	-9.3
Differ from Category (+/-)	0.9 high	1.0 high	na	18.8 high	-2.9 blw av

Total Risk	Standard Deviation	Category Risk	Risk Index	Avg Mat
av	7.5%	high	1.6	5.4 yrs

	1994	1993	1992	1991	1990	1989	1988	1987	1986	1985
Return (%)	-7.9	16.0	8.1	20.0	4.5	20.3	11.7	-8.0	—	—
Differ from category (+/-)	-3.1	5.1	1.7	4.7	-1.7	5.8	3.8	-5.9	—	—

PER SHARE DATA

	1994	1993	1992	1991	1990	1989	1988	1987	1986	1985
Dividends, Net Income ($)	0.31	0.83	0.93	0.94	0.83	0.52	0.63	1.22	—	—
Distrib'ns, Cap Gain ($)	0.59	0.89	1.39	0.00	0.08	0.03	0.00	0.11	—	—
Net Asset Value ($)	10.95	12.85	12.55	13.76	12.27	12.61	10.92	10.34	—	—
Expense Ratio (%)	1.00	1.00	1.00	1.00	1.00	1.00	1.00	1.00	—	—
Net Income to Assets (%)	5.05	5.29	6.38	7.12	7.62	7.10	8.10	8.13	—	—
Portfolio Turnover (%)	89	102	119	91	99	87	149	37	—	—
Total Assets (Millions $)	24	30	29	33	33	32	5	2	—	—

PORTFOLIO (as of 6/30/94)

Portfolio Manager: R. Heisler - 1988, R. Ross - 1990, S.A. Wohler - 1994

Investm't Category: Government Bond

Cap Gain	Asset Allocation
Cap & Income	Fund of Funds
✔ Income	Index
	Sector
✔ Domestic	Small Cap
Foreign	Socially Conscious
Country/Region	State Specific

Portfolio: stocks 0%   bonds 100%
convertibles 0%   other 0%   cash 0%

Largest Holdings: U.S. government 100%

Unrealized Net Capital Gains: -5% of portfolio value

SHAREHOLDER INFORMATION

Minimum Investment
Initial: $1,000   Subsequent: $100

Minimum IRA Investment
Initial: $500   Subsequent: $50

Maximum Fees
Load: none   12b-1: none
Other: none

Distributions
Income: Dec   Capital Gains: Dec

Exchange Options
Number Per Year: call fund   Fee: none
Telephone: yes (money market fund available)

Services
IRA, pension, auto exchange, auto invest, auto withdraw

Scudder Value (SCVAX)

Growth

P.O. Box 2291
Boston, MA 02107
(800) 225-2470, (617) 439-4640

PERFORMANCE

fund inception date: 12/31/92

	3yr Annual	5yr Annual	10yr Annual	Bull	Bear
Return (%)	na	na	na	na	-5.3
Differ from Category (+/-)	na	na	na	na	1.3 abv av

Total Risk	Standard Deviation	Category Risk	Risk Index	Beta
na	na	na	na	na

	1994	1993	1992	1991	1990	1989	1988	1987	1986	1985
Return (%)	1.6	11.6	—	—	—	—	—	—	—	—
Differ from category (+/-) . . .	2.2	-1.8	—	—	—	—	—	—	—	—

PER SHARE DATA

	1994	1993	1992	1991	1990	1989	1988	1987	1986	1985
Dividends, Net Income ($) .	0.12	0.11	—	—	—	—	—	—	—	—
Distrib'ns, Cap Gain ($) . . .	0.13	0.43	—	—	—	—	—	—	—	—
Net Asset Value ($)	12.82	12.85	—	—	—	—	—	—	—	—
Expense Ratio (%)	1.25	1.25	—	—	—	—	—	—	—	—
Net Income to Assets (%) .	1.16	1.56	—	—	—	—	—	—	—	—
Portfolio Turnover (%)	74	60	—	—	—	—	—	—	—	—
Total Assets (Millions $)	34	32	—	—	—	—	—	—	—	—

PORTFOLIO (as of 9/30/94)

Portfolio Manager: Donald E. Hall - 1992,
William J. Wallace - 1992

Investm't Category: Growth
✔ Cap Gain	Asset Allocation
Cap & Income	Fund of Funds
Income	Index
	Sector
✔ Domestic	Small Cap
✔ Foreign	Socially Conscious
Country/Region	State Specific

Portfolio: stocks 88% bonds 0%
convertibles 5% other 0% cash 7%

Largest Holdings: financial 28%, technology 14%

Unrealized Net Capital Gains: 0% of portfolio value

SHAREHOLDER INFORMATION

Minimum Investment
Initial: $1,000   Subsequent: $100

Minimum IRA Investment
Initial: $500   Subsequent: $50

Maximum Fees
Load: none   12b-1: none
Other: none

Distributions
Income: Dec   Capital Gains: Dec

Exchange Options
Number Per Year: call fund   Fee: none
Telephone: yes (money market fund available)

Services
IRA, pension, auto exchange, auto invest, auto withdraw

Selected American Shares (SLASX)

Growth & Income

124 East Marcy Street
Sante Fe, NM 87501
(800) 243-1575

PERFORMANCE

fund inception date: 1/30/33

	3yr Annual	5yr Annual	10yr Annual	Bull	Bear
Return (%)	2.5	8.7	13.2	86.3	-7.6
Differ from Category (+/-)	-4.6 low	0.8 abv av	1.5 abv av	10.5 abv av	-1.3 blw av

Total Risk	Standard Deviation	Category Risk	Risk Index	Beta
abv av	9.8%	high	1.2	1.1

	1994	1993	1992	1991	1990	1989	1988	1987	1986	1985
Return (%)	-3.2	5.4	5.7	46.3	-3.9	20.0	22.0	0.2	16.9	33.2
Differ from category (+/-)	-1.8	-7.8	-4.5	18.7	2.1	-1.4	5.0	-0.4	1.1	7.5

PER SHARE DATA

	1994	1993	1992	1991	1990	1989	1988	1987	1986	1985
Dividends, Net Income ($)	0.22	0.26	0.19	0.23	0.35	0.45	0.26	0.58	0.48	0.40
Distrib'ns, Cap Gain ($)	0.82	3.22	2.19	0.01	0.12	2.10	0.00	0.76	2.29	0.17
Net Asset Value ($)	13.09	14.60	17.13	18.43	12.79	13.81	13.67	11.43	12.65	13.35
Expense Ratio (%)	1.32	1.01	1.17	1.19	1.35	1.08	1.11	1.11	0.85	0.87
Net Income to Assets (%)	1.26	1.37	0.95	1.41	2.04	3.06	2.07	2.38	3.07	4.42
Portfolio Turnover (%)	na	79	50	21	48	46	35	45	40	33
Total Assets (Millions $)	502	450	581	712	401	360	285	263	160	122

PORTFOLIO (as of 6/30/94)

Portfolio Manager: Shelby M.C. Davis - 1993

Investm't Category: Growth & Income

Cap Gain	Asset Allocation
✔ Cap & Income	Fund of Funds
Income	Index
	Sector
✔ Domestic	Small Cap
Foreign	Socially Conscious
Country/Region	State Specific

Portfolio: stocks 92% bonds 0%
convertibles 8% other 0% cash 0%

Largest Holdings: insurance 15%, healthcare 7%

Unrealized Net Capital Gains: 7% of portfolio value

SHAREHOLDER INFORMATION

Minimum Investment
Initial: $1,000   Subsequent: $100

Minimum IRA Investment
Initial: $500   Subsequent: $100

Maximum Fees
Load: none   12b-1: 0.25%
Other: none

Distributions
Income: quarterly   Capital Gains: Dec

Exchange Options
Number Per Year: 4   Fee: none
Telephone: yes (money market fund available)

Services
IRA, pension, auto invest, auto withdraw

Selected Special Shares
(SLSSX)
Growth

124 East Marcy Street
Sante Fe, NM 87501
(800) 243-1575

PERFORMANCE

fund inception date: 9/15/39

	3yr Annual	5yr Annual	10yr Annual	Bull	Bear
Return (%)	5.4	6.4	10.9	66.7	-7.9
Differ from Category (+/-)	-2.3 blw av	-3.2 low	-2.0 low	-25.4 low	-1.3 blw av

Total Risk	Standard Deviation	Category Risk	Risk Index	Beta
abv av	10.1%	abv av	1.0	0.7

	1994	1993	1992	1991	1990	1989	1988	1987	1986	1985
Return (%)	-2.5	10.8	8.4	25.5	-6.8	28.9	19.5	0.3	7.3	23.9
Differ from category (+/-)	-1.9	-2.6	-3.2	-10.2	-1.1	2.8	1.5	-1.5	-7.3	-5.3

PER SHARE DATA

	1994	1993	1992	1991	1990	1989	1988	1987	1986	1985
Dividends, Net Income ($) .	0.00	0.00	0.06	0.13	0.20	0.19	0.10	0.70	0.32	0.25
Distrib'ns, Cap Gain ($) . . .	0.93	1.30	0.54	0.98	0.03	0.83	0.88	0.33	1.73	0.33
Net Asset Value ($)	9.02	10.21	10.41	10.17	9.04	9.95	8.52	7.96	8.92	10.28
Expense Ratio (%)	1.41	1.24	1.41	1.39	1.41	1.22	1.24	1.10	1.08	1.23
Net Income to Assets (%) .	-0.27	-0.07	0.56	1.11	1.81	2.11	1.09	0.85	2.47	3.23
Portfolio Turnover (%)	na	100	41	74	87	45	71	89	133	73
Total Assets (Millions $)	45	52	58	60	51	50	35	36	32	35

PORTFOLIO (as of 6/30/94)

Portfolio Manager: Elizabeth Bramwell - 1994

Investm't Category: Growth

✔ Cap Gain	Asset Allocation
Cap & Income	Fund of Funds
Income	Index
	Sector
✔ Domestic	Small Cap
Foreign	Socially Conscious
Country/Region	State Specific

Portfolio: stocks 94%   bonds 0%
convertibles 0%   other 0%   cash 6%

Largest Holdings: property & casualty insurance 17%, financial 12%

Unrealized Net Capital Gains: -5% of portfolio value

SHAREHOLDER INFORMATION

Minimum Investment
Initial: $1,000   Subsequent: $100

Minimum IRA Investment
Initial: $500   Subsequent: $100

Maximum Fees
Load: none   12b-1: 0.25%
Other: none

Distributions
Income: Dec   Capital Gains: Dec

Exchange Options
Number Per Year: 4   Fee: none
Telephone: yes (money market fund available)

Services
IRA, pension, auto invest, auto withdraw

Selected US Gov't Income (SSGTX)

Mortgage-Backed Bond

124 East Marcy Street
Sante Fe, NM 87501
(800) 243-1575

PERFORMANCE

fund inception date: 11/30/87

	3yr Annual	5yr Annual	10yr Annual	Bull	Bear
Return (%)	3.4	6.4	na	36.1	-3.1
Differ from Category (+/-)	0.3 blw av	-0.5 low	na	-1.9 blw av	1.3 abv av

Total Risk	Standard Deviation	Category Risk	Risk Index	Avg Mat
low	3.7%	abv av	1.1	21.6 yrs

	1994	1993	1992	1991	1990	1989	1988	1987	1986	1985
Return (%)	-2.4	8.0	5.0	13.5	8.5	9.1	2.9	—	—	—
Differ from category (+/-)	0.4	1.2	-1.1	-0.9	-1.2	-3.4	-4.2	—	—	—

PER SHARE DATA

	1994	1993	1992	1991	1990	1989	1988	1987	1986	1985
Dividends, Net Income ($)	0.50	0.53	0.59	0.71	0.72	0.72	0.72	—	—	—
Distrib'ns, Cap Gain ($)	0.00	0.32	0.27	0.00	0.00	0.24	0.24	—	—	—
Net Asset Value ($)	8.48	9.20	9.31	9.70	9.22	9.20	9.34	—	—	—
Expense Ratio (%)	1.35	1.34	1.44	1.41	1.44	1.50	1.50	—	—	—
Net Income to Assets (%)	5.29	5.85	6.26	6.51	6.95	6.70	6.30	—	—	—
Portfolio Turnover (%)	na	29	53	36	29	76	76	—	—	—
Total Assets (Millions $)	10	10	14	22	21	28	15	—	—	—

PORTFOLIO (as of 6/30/94)

Portfolio Manager: B. Clark Stamper - 1993

Investm't Category: Mortgage-Backed Bond
- Cap Gain
- Cap & Income
- ✔ Income
- ✔ Domestic
- Foreign
- Country/Region
- Asset Allocation
- Fund of Funds
- Index
- Sector
- Small Cap
- Socially Conscious
- State Specific

Portfolio: stocks 0% bonds 89%
convertibles 0% other 0% cash 11%

Largest Holdings: mortgage-backed 78%, U.S. government 11%

Unrealized Net Capital Gains: 0% of portfolio value

SHAREHOLDER INFORMATION

Minimum Investment
Initial: $1,000   Subsequent: $100

Minimum IRA Investment
Initial: $500   Subsequent: $100

Maximum Fees
Load: none   12b-1: 0.25%
Other: none

Distributions
Income: monthly   Capital Gains: Dec

Exchange Options
Number Per Year: 4   Fee: none
Telephone: yes (money market fund available)

Services
IRA, pension, auto invest, auto withdraw

Sentry (SNTRX)

Growth

1800 N. Point Dr.
Stevens Point, WI 54481
(800) 533-7827, (715) 346-7048

	3yr Annual	5yr Annual	10yr Annual	Bull	Bear
Return (%)	4.0	8.8	12.2	63.5	-2.1
Differ from Category (+/-)	-3.7 low	-0.8 av	-0.7 blw av	-28.6 low	4.5 high

Total Risk	Standard Deviation	Category Risk	Risk Index	Beta
av	7.2%	low	0.7	0.7

	1994	1993	1992	1991	1990	1989	1988	1987	1986	1985
Return (%)	-1.1	5.9	7.4	28.8	5.2	24.0	16.9	-5.4	14.6	32.6
Differ from category (+/-) . . .	-0.5	-7.5	-4.2	-6.9	10.9	-2.1	-1.1	-7.2	0.0	3.4

PER SHARE DATA

	1994	1993	1992	1991	1990	1989	1988	1987	1986	1985
Dividends, Net Income ($) .	0.17	0.21	0.26	0.38	0.35	0.38	0.22	0.30	0.32	0.35
Distrib'ns, Cap Gain ($) . . .	0.76	0.98	0.36	1.14	0.65	0.73	0.30	1.47	1.21	0.60
Net Asset Value ($)	13.75	14.85	15.15	14.68	12.60	12.93	11.33	10.14	12.70	12.36
Expense Ratio (%)	0.44	0.87	0.88	0.84	0.69	0.65	0.66	0.67	0.72	0.71
Net Income to Assets (%) .	0.67	1.48	1.95	2.56	2.84	2.90	1.85	1.80	2.55	2.83
Portfolio Turnover (%)	4	22	13	3	30	15	19	35	24	25
Total Assets (Millions $)	75	76	69	61	44	46	42	38	42	33

PORTFOLIO (as of 4/30/94)

Portfolio Manager: Keith Ringberg - 1977

Investm't Category: Growth

✔ Cap Gain	Asset Allocation
Cap & Income	Fund of Funds
Income	Index
	Sector
✔ Domestic	Small Cap
Foreign	Socially Conscious
Country/Region	State Specific

Portfolio: stocks 91%   bonds 0%
convertibles 0%   other 0%   cash 9%

Largest Holdings: financial 14%, retail 13%

Unrealized Net Capital Gains: 30% of portfolio value

SHAREHOLDER INFORMATION

Minimum Investment
Initial: $500   Subsequent: $50

Minimum IRA Investment
Initial: $500   Subsequent: $50

Maximum Fees
Load: none   12b-1: none
Other: none

Distributions
Income: Jun, Dec   Capital Gains: Dec

Exchange Options
Number Per Year: none   Fee:
Telephone:

Services
IRA, auto invest, auto withdraw

Sequoia (SEQUX)
Growth & Income

767 Fifth Avenue
Suite 4701
New York, NY 10153-4798
(212) 832-5280

this fund is closed to new investors

fund inception date: 7/15/70

	3yr Annual	5yr Annual	10yr Annual	Bull	Bear
Return (%)	7.7	10.9	14.0	83.4	-1.0
Differ from Category (+/-)	0.6 abv av	3.0 high	2.3 high	7.6 abv av	5.3 high

Total Risk	Standard Deviation	Category Risk	Risk Index	Beta
abv av	8.9%	abv av	1.1	0.9

	1994	1993	1992	1991	1990	1989	1988	1987	1986	1985
Return (%)	3.3	10.7	9.3	40.0	-3.8	27.7	11.0	7.4	13.3	27.9
Differ from category (+/-). . .	4.7	-2.5	-0.9	12.4	2.2	6.3	-6.0	6.8	-2.5	2.2

PER SHARE DATA

	1994	1993	1992	1991	1990	1989	1988	1987	1986	1985
Dividends, Net Income ($).	0.42	0.65	0.93	1.36	1.38	1.28	1.39	2.21	1.61	1.51
Distrib'ns, Cap Gain ($) . . .	0.67	7.20	0.63	3.58	1.78	1.43	2.23	1.59	8.54	3.77
Net Asset Value ($)	55.59	54.84	56.66	53.31	41.94	46.86	38.81	38.43	39.29	44.01
Expense Ratio (%)	1.00	1.00	1.00	1.00	1.00	1.00	1.00	1.00	1.00	1.00
Net Income to Assets (%) .	0.90	1.10	1.80	2.80	3.10	2.80	3.60	3.30	3.90	3.80
Portfolio Turnover (%)	na	24	28	36	29	44	39	43	40	44
Total Assets (Millions $). .	1,548	1,512	1,389	1,251	870	924	714	721	696	599

PORTFOLIO (as of 6/30/94)

Portfolio Manager: William Ruane - 1970

Investm't Category: Growth & Income

Cap Gain	Asset Allocation
✔ Cap & Income	Fund of Funds
Income	Index
	Sector
✔ Domestic	Small Cap
✔ Foreign	Socially Conscious
Country/Region	State Specific

Portfolio: stocks 86% bonds 11%
convertibles 0% other 0% cash 3%

Largest Holdings: financial services 22%, services 13%

Unrealized Net Capital Gains: 29% of portfolio value

SHAREHOLDER INFORMATION

Minimum Investment
Initial: na   Subsequent: $50

Minimum IRA Investment
Initial: na   Subsequent: $0

Maximum Fees
Load: none   12b-1: none
Other: none

Distributions
Income: Feb, Jun, Dec   Capital Gains: Feb, Dec

Exchange Options
Number Per Year: none   Fee:
Telephone:

Services
IRA, auto withdraw

Seven Seas Series
Growth & Income (SSGWX)
Growth & Income

Two International Place
35th Floor
Boston, MA 02110
(800) 647-7327, (617) 654-6089

PERFORMANCE

fund inception date: 9/1/93

	3yr Annual	5yr Annual	10yr Annual	Bull	Bear
Return (%)	na	na	na	na	-6.0
Differ from Category (+/-)	na	na	na	na	0.3 av

Total Risk	Standard Deviation	Category Risk	Risk Index	Beta
na	na	na	na	na

	1994	1993	1992	1991	1990	1989	1988	1987	1986	1985
Return (%)	-0.2	—	—	—	—	—	—	—	—	—
Differ from category (+/-)	1.2	—	—	—	—	—	—	—	—	—

PER SHARE DATA

	1994	1993	1992	1991	1990	1989	1988	1987	1986	1985
Dividends, Net Income ($)	0.18	—	—	—	—	—	—	—	—	—
Distrib'ns, Cap Gain ($)	0.00	—	—	—	—	—	—	—	—	—
Net Asset Value ($)	9.89	—	—	—	—	—	—	—	—	—
Expense Ratio (%)	0.95	—	—	—	—	—	—	—	—	—
Net Income to Assets (%)	1.75	—	—	—	—	—	—	—	—	—
Portfolio Turnover (%)	36	—	—	—	—	—	—	—	—	—
Total Assets (Millions $)	26	—	—	—	—	—	—	—	—	—

PORTFOLIO (as of 8/31/94)

Portfolio Manager: Brent Dickson - 1993

Investm't Category: Growth & Income

Cap Gain	Asset Allocation
✔ Cap & Income	Fund of Funds
Income	Index
	Sector
✔ Domestic	Small Cap
Foreign	Socially Conscious
Country/Region	State Specific

Portfolio: stocks 96% bonds 0%
convertibles 0% other 0% cash 4%

Largest Holdings: consumer basics 13%, finance 12%

Unrealized Net Capital Gains: 6% of portfolio value

SHAREHOLDER INFORMATION

Minimum Investment
Initial: $1,000   Subsequent: $0

Minimum IRA Investment
Initial: $1,000   Subsequent: $0

Maximum Fees
Load: none   12b-1: 0.25%
Other: none

Distributions
Income: quarterly   Capital Gains: Oct

Exchange Options
Number Per Year: no limit   Fee: none
Telephone: yes (money market fund availabe)

Services
IRA

Seven Seas Series—Matrix Equity (SSMTX)

Growth & Income

Two International Place
35th Floor
Boston, MA 02110
(800) 647-7327, (617) 654-6089

PERFORMANCE

fund inception date: 5/4/92

	3yr Annual	5yr Annual	10yr Annual	Bull	Bear
Return (%)	na	na	na	na	-7.2
Differ from Category (+/-)	na	na	na	na	-0.9 blw av

Total Risk	Standard Deviation	Category Risk	Risk Index	Beta
na	na	na	na	na

	1994	1993	1992	1991	1990	1989	1988	1987	1986	1985
Return (%)	-0.3	16.2	—	—	—	—	—	—	—	—
Differ from category (+/-)	1.1	3.0	—	—	—	—	—	—	—	—

PER SHARE DATA

	1994	1993	1992	1991	1990	1989	1988	1987	1986	1985
Dividends, Net Income ($)	0.26	0.18	—	—	—	—	—	—	—	—
Distrib'ns, Cap Gain ($)	0.06	0.18	—	—	—	—	—	—	—	—
Net Asset Value ($)	11.56	11.93	—	—	—	—	—	—	—	—
Expense Ratio (%)	0.58	0.60	—	—	—	—	—	—	—	—
Net Income to Assets (%)	2.16	2.13	—	—	—	—	—	—	—	—
Portfolio Turnover (%)	127	58	—	—	—	—	—	—	—	—
Total Assets (Millions $)	138	92	—	—	—	—	—	—	—	—

PORTFOLIO (as of 8/31/94)

Portfolio Manager: committee

Investm't Category: Growth & Income

Cap Gain	Asset Allocation
✔ Cap & Income	Fund of Funds
Income	Index
	Sector
✔ Domestic	Small Cap
Foreign	Socially Conscious
Country/Region	State Specific

Portfolio: stocks 98% bonds 0%
convertibles 0% other 0% cash 2%

Largest Holdings: consumer basics 21%, utilities 12%

Unrealized Net Capital Gains: 5% of portfolio value

SHAREHOLDER INFORMATION

Minimum Investment
Initial: $1,000   Subsequent: $250

Minimum IRA Investment
Initial: $1,000   Subsequent: $0

Maximum Fees
Load: none   12b-1: 0.25%
Other: none

Distributions
Income: quarterly   Capital Gains: Dec

Exchange Options
Number Per Year: no limit   Fee: none
Telephone: yes (money market fund available)

Services
IRA

Seven Seas Series— S&P 500 (SVSPX)

Growth & Income

Two International Place
35th Floor
Boston, MA 02110
(800) 647-7327, (617) 654-6089

PERFORMANCE

fund inception date: 12/31/92

	3yr Annual	5yr Annual	10yr Annual	Bull	Bear
Return (%)	na	na	na	na	-6.6
Differ from Category (+/-)	na	na	na	na	-0.3 av

Total Risk	Standard Deviation	Category Risk	Risk Index	Beta
na	na	na	na	na

	1994	1993	1992	1991	1990	1989	1988	1987	1986	1985
Return (%).	1.3	9.5	—	—	—	—	—	—	—	—
Differ from category (+/-). . .	2.7	-3.7	—	—	—	—	—	—	—	—

PER SHARE DATA

	1994	1993	1992	1991	1990	1989	1988	1987	1986	1985
Dividends, Net Income ($) .	0.30	0.20	—	—	—	—	—	—	—	—
Distrib'ns, Cap Gain ($) . . .	0.03	0.13	—	—	—	—	—	—	—	—
Net Asset Value ($)	10.44	10.63	—	—	—	—	—	—	—	—
Expense Ratio (%)	0.15	0.15	—	—	—	—	—	—	—	—
Net Income to Assets (%) .	2.69	3.02	—	—	—	—	—	—	—	—
Portfolio Turnover (%).	7	48	—	—	—	—	—	—	—	—
Total Assets (Millions $). . . .	302	310	—	—	—	—	—	—	—	—

PORTFOLIO (as of 8/31/94)

Portfolio Manager: committee

Investm't Category: Growth & Income
Cap Gain	Asset Allocation
✔ Cap & Income	Fund of Funds
Income	✔ Index
	Sector
✔ Domestic	Small Cap
Foreign	Socially Conscious
Country/Region	State Specific

Portfolio: stocks 96% bonds 0%
convertibles 0% other 0% cash 4%

Largest Holdings: S&P 500 stock price index

Unrealized Net Capital Gains: 4% of portfolio value

SHAREHOLDER INFORMATION

Minimum Investment
Initial: $1,000   Subsequent: $250

Minimum IRA Investment
Initial: $1,000   Subsequent: $0

Maximum Fees
Load: none   12b-1: 0.25%
Other: none

Distributions
Income: quarterly   Capital Gains: Oct

Exchange Options
Number Per Year: no limit   Fee: none
Telephone: yes (money market fund available)

Services
IRA

Seven Seas Series— Small Cap (SSMCX)

Growth

Two International Place
35th Floor
Boston, MA 02110
(800) 647-7327, (617) 654-6089

PERFORMANCE

fund inception date: 7/1/92

	3yr Annual	5yr Annual	10yr Annual	Bull	Bear
Return (%)	na	na	na	na	-9.5
Differ from Category (+/-)	na	na	na	na	-2.9 blw av

Total Risk	Standard Deviation	Category Risk	Risk Index	Beta
na	na	na	na	na

	1994	1993	1992	1991	1990	1989	1988	1987	1986	1985
Return (%)	-0.9	12.9	—	—	—	—	—	—	—	—
Differ from category (+/-)	-0.3	-0.5	—	—	—	—	—	—	—	—

PER SHARE DATA

	1994	1993	1992	1991	1990	1989	1988	1987	1986	1985
Dividends, Net Income ($)	0.23	0.23	—	—	—	—	—	—	—	—
Distrib'ns, Cap Gain ($)	0.63	0.60	—	—	—	—	—	—	—	—
Net Asset Value ($)	10.94	11.92	—	—	—	—	—	—	—	—
Expense Ratio (%)	0.30	0.25	—	—	—	—	—	—	—	—
Net Income to Assets (%)	1.73	1.85	—	—	—	—	—	—	—	—
Portfolio Turnover (%)	44	81	—	—	—	—	—	—	—	—
Total Assets (Millions $)	4	37	—	—	—	—	—	—	—	—

PORTFOLIO (as of 8/31/94)

Portfolio Manager: committee

Investm't Category: Growth

✔ Cap Gain	Asset Allocation
Cap & Income	Fund of Funds
Income	✔ Index
	Sector
✔ Domestic	✔ Small Cap
Foreign	Socially Conscious
Country/Region	State Specific

Portfolio: stocks 100%   bonds 0%
convertibles 0%   other 0%   cash 0%

Largest Holdings: S&P 400 MidCap index

Unrealized Net Capital Gains: 0% of portfolio value

SHAREHOLDER INFORMATION

Minimum Investment
Initial: $1,000   Subsequent: $250

Minimum IRA Investment
Initial: $1,000   Subsequent: $0

Maximum Fees
Load: none   12b-1: 0.25%
Other: none

Distributions
Income: quarterly   Capital Gains: Oct

Exchange Options
Number Per Year: no limit   Fee: none
Telephone: yes (money market fund available)

Services
IRA

Seven Seas Short Term Gov't Securities (SVSGX)

Government Bond

Two International Place
35th Floor
Boston, MA 02110
(800) 647-7327, (617) 654-6089

PERFORMANCE

fund inception date: 4/1/92

	3yr Annual	5yr Annual	10yr Annual	Bull	Bear
Return (%)	na	na	na	na	-1.1
Differ from Category (+/-)	na	na	na	na	5.3 high

Total Risk	Standard Deviation	Category Risk	Risk Index	Avg Mat
na	na	na	na	1.7 yrs

	1994	1993	1992	1991	1990	1989	1988	1987	1986	1985
Return (%)	0.1	4.7	—	—	—	—	—	—	—	—
Differ from category (+/-)	4.9	-6.2	—	—	—	—	—	—	—	—

PER SHARE DATA

	1994	1993	1992	1991	1990	1989	1988	1987	1986	1985
Dividends, Net Income ($)	0.45	0.69	—	—	—	—	—	—	—	—
Distrib'ns, Cap Gain ($)	0.00	0.00	—	—	—	—	—	—	—	—
Net Asset Value ($)	9.46	9.90	—	—	—	—	—	—	—	—
Expense Ratio (%)	0.70	0.64	—	—	—	—	—	—	—	—
Net Income to Assets (%)	4.58	4.62	—	—	—	—	—	—	—	—
Portfolio Turnover (%)	279	69	—	—	—	—	—	—	—	—
Total Assets (Millions $)	9	23	—	—	—	—	—	—	—	—

PORTFOLIO (as of 8/31/94)

Portfolio Manager: committee

Investm't Category: Government Bond

Cap Gain	Asset Allocation
Cap & Income	Fund of Funds
✔ Income	Index
	Sector
✔ Domestic	Small Cap
Foreign	Socially Conscious
Country/Region	State Specific

Portfolio: stocks 0%   bonds 80%
convertibles 0%   other 0%   cash 20%

Largest Holdings: U.S. government 54%, mortgage-backed 13%

Unrealized Net Capital Gains: 1% of portfolio value

SHAREHOLDER INFORMATION

Minimum Investment
Initial: $1,000   Subsequent: $250

Minimum IRA Investment
Initial: $1,000   Subsequent: $0

Maximum Fees
Load: none   12b-1: 0.25%
Other: none

Distributions
Income: monthly   Capital Gains: Oct

Exchange Options
Number Per Year: no limit   Fee: none
Telephone: yes (money market fund available)

Services
IRA

Seven Seas Yield Plus

(SSYPX)

General Bond

Two International Place
35th Floor
Boston, MA 02110
(800) 647-7327, (617) 654-6089

PERFORMANCE

fund inception date: 11/9/92

	3yr Annual	5yr Annual	10yr Annual	Bull	Bear
Return (%)	na	na	na	na	1.2
Differ from Category (+/-)	na	na	na	na	5.0 high

Total Risk	Standard Deviation	Category Risk	Risk Index	Avg Mat
na	na	na	na	0.3 yrs

	1994	1993	1992	1991	1990	1989	1988	1987	1986	1985
Return (%)	4.0	3.4	—	—	—	—	—	—	—	—
Differ from category (+/-)	6.0	-5.8	—	—	—	—	—	—	—	—

PER SHARE DATA

	1994	1993	1992	1991	1990	1989	1988	1987	1986	1985
Dividends, Net Income ($)	0.48	0.35	—	—	—	—	—	—	—	—
Distrib'ns, Cap Gain ($)	0.01	0.00	—	—	—	—	—	—	—	—
Net Asset Value ($)	9.96	10.00	—	—	—	—	—	—	—	—
Expense Ratio (%)	0.35	0.38	—	—	—	—	—	—	—	—
Net Income to Assets (%)	3.82	3.54	—	—	—	—	—	—	—	—
Portfolio Turnover (%)	142	137	—	—	—	—	—	—	—	—
Total Assets (Millions $)	1,203	1,233	—	—	—	—	—	—	—	—

PORTFOLIO (as of 8/31/94)

Portfolio Manager: committee

Investm't Category: General Bond

Cap Gain	Asset Allocation
Cap & Income	Fund of Funds
✔ Income	Index
	Sector
✔ Domestic	Small Cap
✔ Foreign	Socially Conscious
Country/Region	State Specific

Portfolio:	stocks 0%	bonds 95%
convertibles 0%	other 0%	cash 5%

Largest Holdings: asset-backed securities 41%, corporate bonds 39%

Unrealized Net Capital Gains: 0% of portfolio value

SHAREHOLDER INFORMATION

Minimum Investment
Initial: $1,000   Subsequent: $250

Minimum IRA Investment
Initial: $1,000   Subsequent: $0

Maximum Fees
Load: none   12b-1: 0.25%
Other: none

Distributions
Income: monthly   Capital Gains: Oct

Exchange Options
Number Per Year: no limit   Fee: none
Telephone: yes (money market fund available)

Services
IRA

SIT Growth (NBNGX)

Aggressive Growth

4600 Norwest Center
Minneapolis, MN 55402
(800) 332-5580, (612) 334-5888

PERFORMANCE

fund inception date: 10/1/81

	3yr Annual	5yr Annual	10yr Annual	Bull	Bear
Return (%)	1.8	11.3	15.5	104.9	-16.0
Differ from Category (+/-)	-7.1 low	-1.2 av	1.5 abv av	-28.3 blw av	-5.2 blw av

Total Risk	Standard Deviation	Category Risk	Risk Index	Beta
high	13.2%	blw av	0.9	1.2

	1994	1993	1992	1991	1990	1989	1988	1987	1986	1985
Return (%)	-0.4	8.5	-2.1	65.4	-2.0	35.0	9.7	5.6	10.2	43.6
Differ from category (+/-)	0.3	-11.0	-13.1	13.3	4.2	8.2	-5.5	7.8	-1.6	11.3

PER SHARE DATA

	1994	1993	1992	1991	1990	1989	1988	1987	1986	1985
Dividends, Net Income ($)	0.00	0.02	0.05	0.06	0.08	0.09	0.09	0.01	0.15	0.06
Distrib'ns, Cap Gain ($)	1.04	0.29	0.02	0.04	0.39	0.36	0.25	0.74	0.82	0.19
Net Asset Value ($)	11.51	12.66	11.96	12.29	7.48	8.11	6.33	6.09	6.34	6.60
Expense Ratio (%)	0.82	0.80	0.83	1.03	1.10	1.19	1.21	1.20	1.32	1.50
Net Income to Assets (%)	-0.08	0.35	0.52	0.96	0.75	1.85	0.57	0.09	0.19	2.65
Portfolio Turnover (%)	46	45	25	37	55	88	78	81	98	129
Total Assets (Millions $)	303	329	242	123	74	54	48	56	40	19

PORTFOLIO (as of 6/30/94)

Portfolio Manager: Eugene C. Sit - 1981, Erik S. Anderson - 1985

Investm't Category: Aggressive Growth

✔ Cap Gain	Asset Allocation
Cap & Income	Fund of Funds
Income	Index
	Sector
✔ Domestic	✔ Small Cap
Foreign	Socially Conscious
Country/Region	State Specific

Portfolio: stocks 89% bonds 0%
convertibles 1% other 0% cash 10%

Largest Holdings: technology 21%, financial services 14%

Unrealized Net Capital Gains: 8% of portfolio value

SHAREHOLDER INFORMATION

Minimum Investment
Initial: $2,000 Subsequent: $100

Minimum IRA Investment
Initial: $0 Subsequent: $0

Maximum Fees
Load: none 12b-1: none
Other: none

Distributions
Income: Dec Capital Gains: Dec

Exchange Options
Number Per Year: 4 Fee: none
Telephone: yes (money market fund available)

Services
IRA, pension, auto exchange, auto invest, auto withdraw

SIT Growth & Income
(SNIGX)
Growth & Income

4600 Norwest Center
Minneapolis, MN 55402
(800) 332-5580, (612) 334-5888

PERFORMANCE

fund inception date: 9/2/82

	3yr Annual	5yr Annual	10yr Annual	Bull	Bear
Return (%)	3.6	7.5	12.3	57.4	-6.8
Differ from Category (+/-)	-3.5 low	-0.4 av	0.6 av	-18.4 low	-0.5 blw av

Total Risk	Standard Deviation	Category Risk	Risk Index	Beta
abv av	8.8%	abv av	1.1	1.0

	1994	1993	1992	1991	1990	1989	1988	1987	1986	1985
Return (%)	2.8	3.0	4.9	32.7	-2.3	32.0	5.3	5.3	21.8	25.0
Differ from category (+/-)	4.2	-10.2	-5.3	5.1	3.7	10.6	-11.7	4.7	6.0	-0.7

PER SHARE DATA

	1994	1993	1992	1991	1990	1989	1988	1987	1986	1985
Dividends, Net Income ($)	0.09	0.27	0.39	0.52	0.64	0.51	0.45	0.85	0.80	0.77
Distrib'ns, Cap Gain ($)	1.41	1.38	0.54	0.54	0.68	0.91	0.00	0.90	0.64	0.24
Net Asset Value ($)	24.09	24.92	25.79	25.49	20.06	21.90	17.69	17.22	17.88	15.92
Expense Ratio (%)	1.10	1.42	1.50	1.50	1.50	1.50	1.50	1.50	—	—
Net Income to Assets (%)	0.89	1.31	1.92	2.74	2.86	2.95	2.96	2.70	—	—
Portfolio Turnover (%)	73	47	73	70	55	82	67	61	—	—
Total Assets (Millions $)	36	37	32	21	18	14	12	10	—	—

PORTFOLIO (as of 6/30/94)

Portfolio Manager: Peter Mitchelson - 1981, Eugene C. Sit - 1981

Investm't Category: Growth & Income

Cap Gain	Asset Allocation
✔ Cap & Income	Fund of Funds
Income	Index
	Sector
✔ Domestic	Small Cap
Foreign	Socially Conscious
Country/Region	State Specific

Portfolio: stocks 94% bonds 0%
convertibles 0% other 0% cash 6%

Largest Holdings: technology 18%, financial services 10%

Unrealized Net Capital Gains: 9% of portfolio value

SHAREHOLDER INFORMATION

Minimum Investment
Initial: $2,000   Subsequent: $100

Minimum IRA Investment
Initial: $0   Subsequent: $0

Maximum Fees
Load: none   12b-1: none
Other: none

Distributions
Income: quarterly   Capital Gains: Dec

Exchange Options
Number Per Year: 4   Fee: none
Telephone: yes (money market fund available)

Services
IRA, pension, auto exchange, auto invest, auto withdraw

SIT International Growth

(SNGRX)

4600 Norwest Center
Minneapolis, MN 55402
(800) 332-5580, (612) 334-5888

International Stock

PERFORMANCE

fund inception date: 11/1/91

	3yr Annual	5yr Annual	10yr Annual	Bull	Bear
Return (%)	13.9	na	na	na	-9.1
Differ from Category (+/-)	4.8 high	na	na	na	-2.1 blw av

Total Risk	Standard Deviation	Category Risk	Risk Index	Beta
high	12.8%	av	1.0	0.8

	1994	1993	1992	1991	1990	1989	1988	1987	1986	1985
Return (%).............	-2.9	48.3	2.6	—	—	—	—	—	—	—
Differ from category (+/-)...	0.1	9.7	5.5	—	—	—	—	—	—	—

PER SHARE DATA

	1994	1993	1992	1991	1990	1989	1988	1987	1986	1985
Dividends, Net Income ($)	0.04	0.10	0.03	—	—	—	—	—	—	—
Distrib'ns, Cap Gain ($) ...	0.27	0.06	0.00	—	—	—	—	—	—	—
Net Asset Value ($)	14.88	15.66	10.66	—	—	—	—	—	—	—
Expense Ratio (%)	1.65	1.85	1.85	—	—	—	—	—	—	—
Net Income to Assets (%)	-0.16	-0.29	0.67	—	—	—	—	—	—	—
Portfolio Turnover (%)......	42	52	19	—	—	—	—	—	—	—
Total Assets (Millions $).....	65	63	25	—	—	—	—	—	—	—

PORTFOLIO (as of 6/30/94)

Portfolio Manager: Andrew Kim - 1991, Eugene Sit - 1991

Investm't Category: International Stock
- ✔ Cap Gain
- Cap & Income
- Income
- Domestic
- ✔ Foreign
- Country/Region
- Asset Allocation
- Fund of Funds
- Index
- Sector
- Small Cap
- Socially Conscious
- State Specific

Portfolio: stocks 89% bonds 0%
convertibles 0% other 3% cash 8%

Largest Holdings: Japan 26%, United Kingdom 7%

Unrealized Net Capital Gains: 20% of portfolio value

SHAREHOLDER INFORMATION

Minimum Investment
Initial: $2,000 Subsequent: $100

Minimum IRA Investment
Initial: $0 Subsequent: $0

Maximum Fees
Load: none 12b-1: none
Other: none

Distributions
Income: Dec Capital Gains: Dec

Exchange Options
Number Per Year: 4 Fee: none
Telephone: yes (money market fund available)

Services
IRA, pension, auto exchange, auto invest, auto withdraw

SIT Minnesota Tax Free Income (SMTFX)

4600 Norwest Center
Minneapolis, MN 55402
(800) 332-5580, (612) 334-5888

Tax-Exempt Bond

PERFORMANCE

fund inception date: 12/1/93

	3yr Annual	5yr Annual	10yr Annual	Bull	Bear
Return (%)	na	na	na	na	-1.1
Differ from Category (+/-)	na	na	na	na	4.1 high

Total Risk	Standard Deviation	Category Risk	Risk Index	Avg Mat
na	na	na	na	16.6 yrs

	1994	1993	1992	1991	1990	1989	1988	1987	1986	1985
Return (%)	0.6	—	—	—	—	—	—	—	—	—
Differ from category (+/-)	5.8	—	—	—	—	—	—	—	—	—

PER SHARE DATA

	1994	1993	1992	1991	1990	1989	1988	1987	1986	1985
Dividends, Net Income ($)	0.55	—	—	—	—	—	—	—	—	—
Distrib'ns, Cap Gain ($)	0.00	—	—	—	—	—	—	—	—	—
Net Asset Value ($)	9.67	—	—	—	—	—	—	—	—	—
Expense Ratio (%)	0.80	—	—	—	—	—	—	—	—	—
Net Income to Assets (%)	5.50	—	—	—	—	—	—	—	—	—
Portfolio Turnover (%)	na	—	—	—	—	—	—	—	—	—
Total Assets (Millions $)	37	—	—	—	—	—	—	—	—	—

PORTFOLIO (as of 9/30/94)

Portfolio Manager: Michael C. Brilley - 1993
Debra A. Sit - 1993

Investm't Category: Tax-Exempt Bond
Cap Gain	Asset Allocation
Cap & Income	Fund of Funds
✔ Income	Index
	Sector
✔ Domestic	Small Cap
Foreign	Socially Conscious
Country/Region	✔ State Specific

Portfolio: stocks 0%   bonds 97%
convertibles 0%   other 0%   cash 3%

Largest Holdings: general obligation 1%

Unrealized Net Capital Gains: 0% of portfolio value

SHAREHOLDER INFORMATION

Minimum Investment
Initial: $2,000   Subsequent: $100

Minimum IRA Investment
Initial: na   Subsequent: na

Maximum Fees
Load: none   12b-1: none
Other: none

Distributions
Income: monthly   Capital Gains: Dec

Exchange Options
Number Per Year: 4   Fee: none
Telephone: yes (money market funds available)

Services
auto exchange, auto invest, auto withdraw

SIT Tax Free Income
(SNTIX)
Tax-Exempt Bond

4600 Norwest Center
Minneapolis, MN 55402
(800) 332-5580, (612) 334-5888

fund inception date: 9/29/88

	3yr Annual	5yr Annual	10yr Annual	Bull	Bear
Return (%)	5.7	6.7	na	33.6	-2.4
Differ from Category (+/-)	1.2 high	0.6 abv av	na	-8.2 low	2.8 high

Total Risk	Standard Deviation	Category Risk	Risk Index	Avg Mat
low	3.7%	low	0.6	14.2 yrs

	1994	1993	1992	1991	1990	1989	1988	1987	1986	1985
Return (%)	-0.6	10.4	7.6	9.1	7.2	8.3	—	—	—	—
Differ from category (+/-)	4.6	-1.3	-0.7	-2.2	0.9	-0.7	—	—	—	—

	1994	1993	1992	1991	1990	1989	1988	1987	1986	1985
Dividends, Net Income ($)	0.56	0.58	0.64	0.70	0.79	0.77	—	—	—	—
Distrib'ns, Cap Gain ($)	0.02	0.09	0.04	0.00	0.00	0.00	—	—	—	—
Net Asset Value ($)	9.43	10.08	9.76	9.72	9.57	9.68	—	—	—	—
Expense Ratio (%)	0.77	0.80	0.80	0.80	0.80	0.80	—	—	—	—
Net Income to Assets (%)	5.68	6.17	7.02	7.62	8.16	8.08	—	—	—	—
Portfolio Turnover (%)	47	58	80	74	87	132	—	—	—	—
Total Assets (Millions $)	243	340	193	87	31	13	—	—	—	—

PORTFOLIO (as of 9/30/94)

Portfolio Manager: Michael C. Brilley - 1988

Investm't Category: Tax-Exempt Bond

Cap Gain	Asset Allocation
Cap & Income	Fund of Funds
✔ Income	Index
	Sector
✔ Domestic	Small Cap
Foreign	Socially Conscious
Country/Region	State Specific

Portfolio: stocks 0% bonds 97%
convertibles 0% other 0% cash 3%

Largest Holdings: general obligation 0%

Unrealized Net Capital Gains: 0% of portfolio value

SHAREHOLDER INFORMATION

Minimum Investment
Initial: $2,000 Subsequent: $100

Minimum IRA Investment
Initial: na Subsequent: na

Maximum Fees
Load: none 12b-1: none
Other: none

Distributions
Income: monthly Capital Gains: Dec

Exchange Options
Number Per Year: 4 Fee: none
Telephone: yes (money market fund available)

Services
auto exchange, auto invest, auto withdraw

SIT US Gov't Securities
(SNGVX)
Mortgage-Backed Bond

4600 Norwest Center
Minneapolis, MN 55402
(800) 332-5580, (612) 334-5888

	3yr Annual	5yr Annual	10yr Annual	Bull	Bear
Return (%)	4.8	7.5	na	34.8	-0.5
Differ from Category (+/-)	1.7 high	0.6 abv av	na	-3.2 low	3.9 high

Total Risk	Standard Deviation	Category Risk	Risk Index	Avg Mat
low	2.0%	low	0.6	16.3 yrs

	1994	1993	1992	1991	1990	1989	1988	1987	1986	1985
Return (%)	1.7	7.3	5.4	12.8	10.9	11.0	7.8	—	—	—
Differ from category (+/-)	4.5	0.5	-0.7	-1.6	1.2	-1.5	0.7	—	—	—

PER SHARE DATA

	1994	1993	1992	1991	1990	1989	1988	1987	1986	1985
Dividends, Net Income ($)	0.64	0.68	0.71	0.80	0.78	0.85	0.84	—	—	—
Distrib'ns, Cap Gain ($)	0.00	0.05	0.15	0.17	0.00	0.00	0.00	—	—	—
Net Asset Value ($)	10.17	10.63	10.60	10.89	10.56	10.27	10.05	—	—	—
Expense Ratio (%)	0.86	0.89	0.80	0.90	1.25	1.25	1.25	—	—	—
Net Income to Assets (%)	5.79	6.60	7.28	7.60	8.02	8.33	8.27	—	—	—
Portfolio Turnover (%)	73	76	134	118	126	139	136	—	—	—
Total Assets (Millions $)	36	39	35	30	13	12	11	—	—	—

PORTFOLIO (as of 9/30/94)

Portfolio Manager: Michael C. Brilley - 1987

Investm't Category: Mortgage-Backed Bond

Cap Gain	Asset Allocation
Cap & Income	Fund of Funds
✔ Income	Index
	Sector
✔ Domestic	Small Cap
Foreign	Socially Conscious
Country/Region	State Specific

Portfolio: stocks 0%   bonds 98%
convertibles 0%   other 0%   cash 2%

Largest Holdings: mortgage-backed 93%, U.S. government 5%

Unrealized Net Capital Gains: 0% of portfolio value

SHAREHOLDER INFORMATION

Minimum Investment
Initial: $2,000   Subsequent: $100

Minimum IRA Investment
Initial: $0   Subsequent: $0

Maximum Fees
Load: none   12b-1: none
Other: none

Distributions
Income: monthly   Capital Gains: Dec

Exchange Options
Number Per Year: 4   Fee: none
Telephone: yes (money market fund available)

Services
IRA, pension, auto exchange, auto invest, auto withdraw

Skyline Special Equities II
(SPEQX)
Growth

350 North Clark Street
Chicago, IL 60610
(800) 458-5222, (312) 670-6035

PERFORMANCE

fund inception date: 2/9/93

	3yr Annual	5yr Annual	10yr Annual	Bull	Bear
Return (%)	na	na	na	na	-6.0
Differ from Category (+/-)	na	na	na	na	0.6 av

Total Risk	Standard Deviation	Category Risk	Risk Index	Beta
na	na	na	na	na

	1994	1993	1992	1991	1990	1989	1988	1987	1986	1985
Return (%)	-1.5	—	—	—	—	—	—	—	—	—
Differ from category (+/-)	-0.9	—	—	—	—	—	—	—	—	—

PER SHARE DATA

	1994	1993	1992	1991	1990	1989	1988	1987	1986	1985
Dividends, Net Income ($)	0.02	—	—	—	—	—	—	—	—	—
Distrib'ns, Cap Gain ($)	0.46	—	—	—	—	—	—	—	—	—
Net Asset Value ($)	10.14	—	—	—	—	—	—	—	—	—
Expense Ratio (%)	1.50	—	—	—	—	—	—	—	—	—
Net Income to Assets (%)	0.02	—	—	—	—	—	—	—	—	—
Portfolio Turnover (%)	84	—	—	—	—	—	—	—	—	—
Total Assets (Millions $)	100	—	—	—	—	—	—	—	—	—

PORTFOLIO (as of 6/30/94)

Portfolio Manager: Kenneth S. Kailin - 1993

Investm't Category: Growth
✔ Cap Gain	Asset Allocation
Cap & Income	Fund of Funds
Income	Index
	Sector
✔ Domestic	✔ Small Cap
Foreign	Socially Conscious
Country/Region	State Specific

Portfolio: stocks 90% bonds 0%
convertibles 0% other 0% cash 10%

Largest Holdings: retail 9%, industrial 8%

Unrealized Net Capital Gains: 1% of portfolio value

SHAREHOLDER INFORMATION

Minimum Investment
Initial: $1,000   Subsequent: $100

Minimum IRA Investment
Initial: $1,000   Subsequent: $100

Maximum Fees
Load: none   12b-1: none
Other: none

Distributions
Income: Dec   Capital Gains: Dec

Exchange Options
Number Per Year: none   Fee: none
Telephone: yes (money market fund available)

Services
IRA, pension, auto exchange, auto invest, auto withdraw

Smith Breedon Interm Duration US Gov't Series

100 Europa Drive
Suite 200
Chapel Hill, NC 27514
(919) 967-7221

(SBIDX) *Mortgage-Backed Bond*

	3yr Annual	5yr Annual	10yr Annual	Bull	Bear
Return (%)	na	na	na	na	-4.1
Differ from Category (+/-)	na	na	na	na	0.3 blw av

Total Risk	Standard Deviation	Category Risk	Risk Index	Avg Mat
na	na	na	na	na

	1994	1993	1992	1991	1990	1989	1988	1987	1986	1985
Return (%)	-1.6	11.1	—	—	—	—	—	—	—	—
Differ from category (+/-)	1.2	4.3	—	—	—	—	—	—	—	—

PER SHARE DATA

	1994	1993	1992	1991	1990	1989	1988	1987	1986	1985
Dividends, Net Income ($)	0.58	1.11	—	—	—	—	—	—	—	—
Distrib'ns, Cap Gain ($)	0.13	0.01	—	—	—	—	—	—	—	—
Net Asset Value ($)	9.47	10.36	—	—	—	—	—	—	—	—
Expense Ratio (%)	0.00	0.31	—	—	—	—	—	—	—	—
Net Income to Assets (%)	7.74	8.18	—	—	—	—	—	—	—	—
Portfolio Turnover (%)	84	42	—	—	—	—	—	—	—	—
Total Assets (Millions $)	33	4	—	—	—	—	—	—	—	—

PORTFOLIO (as of 9/30/94)

Portfolio Manager: Daniel C. Dektar - 1992

Investm't Category: Mortgage-Backed Bond

Cap Gain	Asset Allocation
Cap & Income	Fund of Funds
✔ Income	Index
	Sector
✔ Domestic	Small Cap
Foreign	Socially Conscious
Country/Region	State Specific

Portfolio: stocks 0%   bonds 100%
convertibles 0%   other 0%   cash 0%

Largest Holdings: mortgage-backed 100%

Unrealized Net Capital Gains: -1% of portfolio value

SHAREHOLDER INFORMATION

Minimum Investment
Initial: $1,000   Subsequent: $50

Minimum IRA Investment
Initial: $1,000   Subsequent: $50

Maximum Fees
Load: none   12b-1: none
Other: none

Distributions
Income: monthly   Capital Gains: Dec

Exchange Options
Number Per Year: 4   Fee: $8
Telephone: yes (money market fund available)

Services
IRA, pension, auto invest, auto withdraw

Smith Breedon Short Duration U.S. Gov't (SBSHX) *Mortgage-Backed Bond*

100 Europa Drive
Suite 200
Chapel Hill, NC 27514
(919) 967-7221

PERFORMANCE

fund inception date: 3/1/92

	3yr Annual	5yr Annual	10yr Annual	Bull	Bear
Return (%)	na	na	na	na	0.0
Differ from Category (+/-)	na	na	na	na	4.4 high

Total Risk	Standard Deviation	Category Risk	Risk Index	Avg Mat
na	na	na	na	na

	1994	1993	1992	1991	1990	1989	1988	1987	1986	1985
Return (%)	4.1	4.3	—	—	—	—	—	—	—	—
Differ from category (+/-) . . .	6.9	-2.5	—	—	—	—	—	—	—	—

PER SHARE DATA

	1994	1993	1992	1991	1990	1989	1988	1987	1986	1985
Dividends, Net Income ($) .	0.57	0.46	—	—	—	—	—	—	—	—
Distrib'ns, Cap Gain ($) . . .	0.00	0.00	—	—	—	—	—	—	—	—
Net Asset Value ($)	9.84	10.01	—	—	—	—	—	—	—	—
Expense Ratio (%)	0.29	0.27	—	—	—	—	—	—	—	—
Net Income to Assets (%) .	4.17	4.53	—	—	—	—	—	—	—	—
Portfolio Turnover (%).	112	3	—	—	—	—	—	—	—	—
Total Assets (Millions $). . . .	195	130	—	—	—	—	—	—	—	—

PORTFOLIO (as of 9/30/94)

Portfolio Manager: Daniel C. Dektar - 1992

Investm't Category: Mortgage-Backed Bond
Cap Gain	Asset Allocation
Cap & Income	Fund of Funds
✔ Income	Index
	Sector
✔ Domestic	Small Cap
Foreign	Socially Conscious
Country/Region	State Specific

Portfolio: stocks 0%   bonds 69%
convertibles 0%   other 0%   cash 31%

Largest Holdings: mortgage-backed 65%

Unrealized Net Capital Gains: -1% of portfolio value

SHAREHOLDER INFORMATION

Minimum Investment
Initial: $1,000   Subsequent: $50

Minimum IRA Investment
Initial: $1,000   Subsequent: $50

Maximum Fees
Load: none   12b-1: none
Other: none

Distributions
Income: monthly   Capital Gains: Dec

Exchange Options
Number Per Year: 4   Fee: $8
Telephone: yes (money market fund available)

Services
IRA, pension, auto invest, auto withdraw

Sound Shore (SSHFX)

Growth

P.O. Box 1810
8 Sound Shore Dr.
Greenwich, CT 06836
(800) 551-1980, (203) 629-1980

	3yr Annual	5yr Annual	10yr Annual	Bull	Bear
Return (%)	10.8	9.9	na	90.7	-4.9
Differ from Category (+/-)	3.1 abv av	0.3 abv av	na	-1.4 av	1.7 abv av

Total Risk	Standard Deviation	Category Risk	Risk Index	Beta
av	7.9%	low	0.8	0.8

	1994	1993	1992	1991	1990	1989	1988	1987	1986	1985
Return (%)	0.2	11.9	21.1	32.2	-10.6	22.3	21.1	-3.6	20.4	—
Differ from category (+/-)	0.8	-1.5	9.5	-3.5	-4.9	-3.8	3.1	-5.4	5.8	—

PER SHARE DATA

	1994	1993	1992	1991	1990	1989	1988	1987	1986	1985
Dividends, Net Income ($)	0.22	0.14	0.18	0.29	0.52	0.35	0.18	0.18	0.22	—
Distrib'ns, Cap Gain ($)	0.87	1.54	1.95	0.10	0.00	1.41	1.18	1.21	0.39	—
Net Asset Value ($)	15.46	16.50	16.24	15.17	11.77	13.73	12.67	11.58	13.31	—
Expense Ratio (%)	1.25	1.27	1.37	1.30	1.33	1.24	1.40	1.45	1.48	—
Net Income to Assets (%)	1.14	0.88	1.10	2.10	3.55	2.37	1.57	1.14	2.55	—
Portfolio Turnover (%)	42	90	88	100	105	91	134	91	82	—
Total Assets (Millions $)	15	59	40	32	29	54	29	32	14	—

PORTFOLIO (as of 6/30/94)

Portfolio Manager: Harry Burn III - 1985, Gibb Kane - 1985

Investm't Category: Growth

✔ Cap Gain	Asset Allocation
Cap & Income	Fund of Funds
Income	Index
	Sector
✔ Domestic	Small Cap
Foreign	Socially Conscious
Country/Region	State Specific

Portfolio:
stocks 81%   bonds 1%
convertibles 0%   other 0%   cash 18%

Largest Holdings: insurance 10%, banking 6%

Unrealized Net Capital Gains: 2% of portfolio value

SHAREHOLDER INFORMATION

Minimum Investment
Initial: $10,000   Subsequent: $0

Minimum IRA Investment
Initial: $250   Subsequent: $0

Maximum Fees
Load: none   12b-1: none
Other: none

Distributions
Income: Jun, Dec   Capital Gains: Dec

Exchange Options
Number Per Year: no limit   Fee: none
Telephone: yes (money market fund available)

Services
IRA, pension, auto withdraw

Standish Equity (SDEQX)

Growth

One Financial Center
Boston, MA 02111
(617) 350-6100

PERFORMANCE

fund inception date: 1/2/91

	3yr Annual	5yr Annual	10yr Annual	Bull	Bear
Return (%)	8.3	na	na	na	-8.5
Differ from Category (+/-)	0.6 av	na	na	na	-1.9 blw av

Total Risk	Standard Deviation	Category Risk	Risk Index	Beta
abv av	9.9%	abv av	1.0	1.1

	1994	1993	1992	1991	1990	1989	1988	1987	1986	1985
Return (%)	-3.7	20.8	9.5	—	—	—	—	—	—	—
Differ from category (+/-)	-3.1	7.4	-2.1	—	—	—	—	—	—	—

PER SHARE DATA

	1994	1993	1992	1991	1990	1989	1988	1987	1986	1985
Dividends, Net Income ($)	0.44	0.33	0.54	—	—	—	—	—	—	—
Distrib'ns, Cap Gain ($)	0.62	0.51	1.21	—	—	—	—	—	—	—
Net Asset Value ($)	28.66	30.89	26.28	—	—	—	—	—	—	—
Expense Ratio (%)	0.70	0.80	0.00	—	—	—	—	—	—	—
Net Income to Assets (%)	1.24	1.29	2.52	—	—	—	—	—	—	—
Portfolio Turnover (%)	na	192	92	—	—	—	—	—	—	—
Total Assets (Millions $)	84	71	14	—	—	—	—	—	—	—

PORTFOLIO (as of 6/30/94)

Portfolio Manager: David Cameron - 1991

Investm't Category: Growth

✔ Cap Gain	Asset Allocation
Cap & Income	Fund of Funds
Income	Index
	Sector
✔ Domestic	Small Cap
✔ Foreign	Socially Conscious
Country/Region	State Specific

Portfolio: stocks 92% bonds 0%
convertibles 0% other 0% cash 8%

Largest Holdings: capital goods/technology 23%, consumer stable 21%

Unrealized Net Capital Gains: 0% of portfolio value

SHAREHOLDER INFORMATION

Minimum Investment
Initial: $100,000   Subsequent: $10,000

Minimum IRA Investment
Initial: $100,000   Subsequent: $10,000

Maximum Fees
Load: none   12b-1: none
Other: none

Distributions
Income: Dec   Capital Gains: Dec

Exchange Options
Number Per Year: none   Fee:
Telephone:

Services
IRA

Standish Fixed Income
(SDFIX)
General Bond

One Financial Center
Boston, MA 02111
(617) 350-6100

PERFORMANCE   fund inception date: 3/27/87

	3yr Annual	5yr Annual	10yr Annual	Bull	Bear
Return (%)	5.2	8.4	na	53.7	-7.3
Differ from Category (+/-)	0.9 high	1.5 high	na	12.7 high	-3.5 low

Total Risk	Standard Deviation	Category Risk	Risk Index	Avg Mat
blw av	4.9%	high	1.2	8.1 yrs

	1994	1993	1992	1991	1990	1989	1988	1987	1986	1985
Return (%)	-4.8	14.6	6.8	17.6	9.2	13.7	8.5	—	—	—
Differ from category (+/-)	-2.8	5.4	0.2	3.0	2.0	2.3	1.1	—	—	—

PER SHARE DATA

	1994	1993	1992	1991	1990	1989	1988	1987	1986	1985
Dividends, Net Income ($)	1.27	1.56	1.52	1.49	1.69	1.80	1.74	—	—	—
Distrib'ns, Cap Gain ($)	0.03	0.69	0.30	0.45	0.00	0.00	0.00	—	—	—
Net Asset Value ($)	18.91	21.25	20.55	20.96	19.56	19.54	18.84	—	—	—
Expense Ratio (%)	0.39	0.40	0.41	0.46	0.49	0.53	0.54	—	—	—
Net Income to Assets (%)	6.97	7.07	7.61	8.28	9.07	9.26	8.94	—	—	—
Portfolio Turnover (%)	na	150	217	176	107	106	119	—	—	—
Total Assets (Millions $)	1,662	1,251	919	631	397	264	198	—	—	—

PORTFOLIO (as of 6/30/94)

Portfolio Manager: Caleb Aldrich - 1993

Investm't Category: General Bond

Cap Gain	Asset Allocation
Cap & Income	Fund of Funds
✔ Income	Index
	Sector
✔ Domestic	Small Cap
✔ Foreign	Socially Conscious
Country/Region	State Specific

Portfolio: stocks 0%   bonds 89%
convertibles 0%   other 2%   cash 9%

Largest Holdings: corporate 25%, mortgage-backed 24%

Unrealized Net Capital Gains: -4% of portfolio value

SHAREHOLDER INFORMATION

Minimum Investment
Initial: $100,000   Subsequent: $5,000

Minimum IRA Investment
Initial: $100,000   Subsequent: $5,000

Maximum Fees
Load: none   12b-1: none
Other: none

Distributions
Income: quarterly   Capital Gains: Dec

Exchange Options
Number Per Year: none   Fee:
Telephone:

Services
IRA

Standish Global Fixed Income (SDGIX)

One Financial Center
Boston, MA 02111
(617) 350-6100

International Bond

PERFORMANCE

fund inception date: 1/1/94

	3yr Annual	5yr Annual	10yr Annual	Bull	Bear
Return (%)	na	na	na	na	-9.4
Differ from Category (+/-)	na	na	na	na	-1.6 blw av

Total Risk	Standard Deviation	Category Risk	Risk Index	Avg Mat
na	na	na	na	11.3 yrs

	1994	1993	1992	1991	1990	1989	1988	1987	1986	1985
Return (%)	-7.0	—	—	—	—	—	—	—	—	—
Differ from category (+/-)	-0.7	—	—	—	—	—	—	—	—	—

PER SHARE DATA

	1994	1993	1992	1991	1990	1989	1988	1987	1986	1985
Dividends, Net Income ($)	0.60	—	—	—	—	—	—	—	—	—
Distrib'ns, Cap Gain ($)	0.00	—	—	—	—	—	—	—	—	—
Net Asset Value ($)	17.99	—	—	—	—	—	—	—	—	—
Expense Ratio (%)	0.67	—	—	—	—	—	—	—	—	—
Net Income to Assets (%)	7.35	—	—	—	—	—	—	—	—	—
Portfolio Turnover (%)	na	—	—	—	—	—	—	—	—	—
Total Assets (Millions $)	135	—	—	—	—	—	—	—	—	—

PORTFOLIO (as of 6/30/94)

Portfolio Manager: Richard S. Wood - 1994

Investm't Category: International Bond

Cap Gain	Asset Allocation
Cap & Income	Fund of Funds
✔ Income	Index
	Sector
✔ Domestic	Small Cap
✔ Foreign	Socially Conscious
Country/Region	State Specific

Portfolio: stocks 0%   bonds 83%
convertibles 0%   other 1%   cash 16%

Largest Holdings: United States 21%, Denmark 10%

Unrealized Net Capital Gains: -4% of portfolio value

SHAREHOLDER INFORMATION

Minimum Investment
Initial: $100,000   Subsequent: $5,000

Minimum IRA Investment
Initial: $100,000   Subsequent: $5,000

Maximum Fees
Load: none   12b-1: none
Other: none

Distributions
Income: quarterly   Capital Gains: Dec

Exchange Options
Number Per Year: none   Fee:
Telephone:

Services
IRA

Standish International Equity (SDIEX)

International Stock

One Financial Center
Boston, MA 02111
(617) 350-6100

	3yr Annual	5yr Annual	10yr Annual	Bull	Bear
Return (%)	5.0	3.2	na	54.7	-11.3
Differ from Category (+/-)	-4.1 low	-1.7 low	na	-9.2 blw av	-4.3 blw av

Total Risk	Standard Deviation	Category Risk	Risk Index	Beta
high	13.2%	abv av	1.0	1.0

	1994	1993	1992	1991	1990	1989	1988	1987	1986	1985
Return (%)	-6.9	38.2	-9.9	11.7	-9.4	18.7	—	—	—	—
Differ from category (+/-)	-3.9	-0.4	-7.0	-1.4	1.0	-3.8	—	—	—	—

PER SHARE DATA

	1994	1993	1992	1991	1990	1989	1988	1987	1986	1985
Dividends, Net Income ($)	0.15	0.59	0.21	0.31	0.82	0.69	—	—	—	—
Distrib'ns, Cap Gain ($)	1.60	0.00	0.00	0.00	0.00	0.00	—	—	—	—
Net Asset Value ($)	23.13	26.74	19.78	22.20	20.16	23.10	—	—	—	—
Expense Ratio (%)	1.16	1.34	1.53	1.54	1.60	1.60	—	—	—	—
Net Income to Assets (%)	1.20	1.09	1.18	1.30	2.19	2.29	—	—	—	—
Portfolio Turnover (%)	na	98	86	27	48	38	—	—	—	—
Total Assets (Millions $)	99	92	56	47	24	19	—	—	—	—

PORTFOLIO (as of 6/30/94)

Portfolio Manager: D. Barr Clayson - 1988, Michael Schoeck - 1994

Investm't Category: International Stock

✔ Cap Gain   Asset Allocation
   Cap & Income   Fund of Funds
   Income   Index
                    Sector
   Domestic   Small Cap
✔ Foreign   Socially Conscious
   Country/Region   State Specific

Portfolio: stocks 76% bonds 0%
convertibles 1% other 1% cash 22%

Largest Holdings: Japan 12%, United Kingdom 8%

Unrealized Net Capital Gains: 6% of portfolio value

SHAREHOLDER INFORMATION

Minimum Investment
Initial: $100,000   Subsequent: $10,000

Minimum IRA Investment
Initial: $100,000   Subsequent: $10,000

Maximum Fees
Load: none   12b-1: none
Other: none

Distributions
Income: Dec   Capital Gains: Dec

Exchange Options
Number Per Year: none Fee:
Telephone:

Services
IRA

Standish Mass Interm Tax-Exempt (SDMAX)

Tax-Exempt Bond

One Financial Center
Boston, MA 02111
(617) 350-6100

PERFORMANCE

fund inception date: 11/2/92

	3yr Annual	5yr Annual	10yr Annual	Bull	Bear
Return (%)	na	na	na	na	-4.2
Differ from Category (+/-)	na	na	na	na	1.0 abv av

Total Risk	Standard Deviation	Category Risk	Risk Index	Avg Mat
na	na	na	na	7.4 yrs

	1994	1993	1992	1991	1990	1989	1988	1987	1986	1985
Return (%)	-3.8	10.2	—	—	—	—	—	—	—	—
Differ from category (+/-)	1.4	-1.5	—	—	—	—	—	—	—	—

PER SHARE DATA

	1994	1993	1992	1991	1990	1989	1988	1987	1986	1985
Dividends, Net Income ($)	0.94	0.92	—	—	—	—	—	—	—	—
Distrib'ns, Cap Gain ($)	0.01	0.14	—	—	—	—	—	—	—	—
Net Asset Value ($)	19.55	21.31	—	—	—	—	—	—	—	—
Expense Ratio (%)	0.65	0.65	—	—	—	—	—	—	—	—
Net Income to Assets (%)	4.54	4.35	—	—	—	—	—	—	—	—
Portfolio Turnover (%)	na	94	—	—	—	—	—	—	—	—
Total Assets (Millions $)	27	29	—	—	—	—	—	—	—	—

PORTFOLIO (as of 6/30/94)

Portfolio Manager: Maria D. Furman - 1992, Raymond J. Kubiak - 1992

Investm't Category: Tax-Exempt Bond

Cap Gain	Asset Allocation
Cap & Income	Fund of Funds
✔ Income	Index
	Sector
✔ Domestic	Small Cap
Foreign	Socially Conscious
Country/Region	✔ State Specific

Portfolio: stocks 0%   bonds 93%
convertibles 0%   other 0%   cash 7%

Largest Holdings: general obligation 13%

Unrealized Net Capital Gains: -2% of portfolio value

SHAREHOLDER INFORMATION

Minimum Investment
Initial: $100,000   Subsequent: $5,000

Minimum IRA Investment
Initial: na   Subsequent: na

Maximum Fees
Load: none   12b-1: none
Other: none

Distributions
Income: monthly   Capital Gains: Dec

Exchange Options
Number Per Year: none   Fee:
Telephone:

Services

Standish Securitized
(SDSZX)
Mortgage-Backed Bond

One Financial Center
Boston, MA 02111
(617) 350-6100

PERFORMANCE   fund inception date: 8/31/89

	3yr Annual	5yr Annual	10yr Annual	Bull	Bear
Return (%)	3.8	7.6	na	41.8	-4.5
Differ from Category (+/-)	0.7 abv av	0.7 high	na	3.8 high	-0.1 blw av

Total Risk	Standard Deviation	Category Risk	Risk Index	Avg Mat
low	4.2%	high	1.3	6.5 yrs

	1994	1993	1992	1991	1990	1989	1988	1987	1986	1985
Return (%).............	-2.1	10.0	4.0	15.5	11.4	—	—	—	—	—
Differ from category (+/-)...	0.7	3.2	-2.1	1.1	1.7	—	—	—	—	—

PER SHARE DATA

	1994	1993	1992	1991	1990	1989	1988	1987	1986	1985
Dividends, Net Income ($).	1.19	1.53	1.57	1.55	1.87	—	—	—	—	—
Distrib'ns, Cap Gain ($) ...	0.00	0.36	0.08	1.04	0.00	—	—	—	—	—
Net Asset Value ($)	18.61	20.24	20.14	20.97	20.49	—	—	—	—	—
Expense Ratio (%)	0.45	0.45	0.45	0.45	0.45	—	—	—	—	—
Net Income to Assets (%) .	6.53	6.75	6.94	8.03	8.88	—	—	—	—	—
Portfolio Turnover (%)	na	130	301	324	146	—	—	—	—	—
Total Assets (Millions $).....	53	76	90	78	67	—	—	—	—	—

PORTFOLIO (as of 6/30/94)

Portfolio Manager: Dolores Driscoll - 1989

Investm't Category: Mortgage-Backed Bond

Cap Gain	Asset Allocation
Cap & Income	Fund of Funds
✔ Income	Index
	Sector
✔ Domestic	Small Cap
Foreign	Socially Conscious
Country/Region	State Specific

Portfolio: stocks 0% bonds 94%
convertibles 0% other 0% cash 6%

Largest Holdings: morgage-backed 83%, as-set-backed 9%

Unrealized Net Capital Gains: -3% of port-folio value

SHAREHOLDER INFORMATION

Minimum Investment
Initial: $1,000,000   Subsequent: $50,000

Minimum IRA Investment
Initial: $1,000,000   Subsequent: $50,000

Maximum Fees
Load: none   12b-1: none
Other: none

Distributions
Income: quarterly   Capital Gains: Dec

Exchange Options
Number Per Year: none   Fee:
Telephone:

Services
IRA

Standish Small Capitalization Equity

(SDSCX) *Aggressive Growth*

One Financial Center
Boston, MA 02111
(617) 350-6100

PERFORMANCE

	3yr Annual	5yr Annual	10yr Annual	Bull	Bear
Return (%)	10.6	na	na	176.7	-11.3
Differ from Category (+/-)	1.7 abv av	na	na	43.5 abv av	-0.5 av

Total Risk	Standard Deviation	Category Risk	Risk Index	Beta
high	13.7%	av	0.9	1.0

	1994	1993	1992	1991	1990	1989	1988	1987	1986	1985
Return (%)	-3.6	28.2	9.7	64.6	—	—	—	—	—	—
Differ from category (+/-)	-2.9	8.7	-1.3	12.5	—	—	—	—	—	—

PER SHARE DATA

	1994	1993	1992	1991	1990	1989	1988	1987	1986	1985
Dividends, Net Income ($)	0.56	0.00	0.00	0.02	—	—	—	—	—	—
Distrib'ns, Cap Gain ($)	4.42	2.10	4.05	5.39	—	—	—	—	—	—
Net Asset Value ($)	42.15	48.97	39.83	39.99	—	—	—	—	—	—
Expense Ratio (%)	0.80	0.88	1.04	0.87	—	—	—	—	—	—
Net Income to Assets (%)	-0.32	-0.18	-0.38	-0.15	—	—	—	—	—	—
Portfolio Turnover (%)	na	144	101	96	—	—	—	—	—	—
Total Assets (Millions $)	99	85	50	35	—	—	—	—	—	—

PORTFOLIO (as of 6/30/94)

Portfolio Manager: Nicholas Batelle - 1988

Investm't Category: Aggressive Growth
- ✔ Cap Gain
- Cap & Income
- Income
- Asset Allocation
- Fund of Funds
- Index
- Sector
- ✔ Domestic
- ✔ Foreign
- Country/Region
- ✔ Small Cap
- Socially Conscious
- State Specific

Portfolio: stocks 99% bonds 0%
convertibles 0% other 0% cash 1%

Largest Holdings: consumer stable 37%, consumer cyclical 21%

Unrealized Net Capital Gains: 4% of portfolio value

SHAREHOLDER INFORMATION

Minimum Investment
Initial: $100,000   Subsequent: $10,000

Minimum IRA Investment
Initial: $100,000   Subsequent: $10,000

Maximum Fees
Load: none   12b-1: none
Other: none

Distributions
Income: Dec   Capital Gains: Dec

Exchange Options
Number Per Year: none   Fee:
Telephone:

Services
IRA

SteinRoe Capital Opportunities (SRFCX)

P.O. Box 804058
Chicago, IL 60680
(800) 338-2550, (312) 368-7800

Aggressive Growth

PERFORMANCE

fund inception date: 3/31/69

	3yr Annual	5yr Annual	10yr Annual	Bull	Bear
Return (%)	9.3	8.5	12.1	129.6	-11.6
Differ from Category (+/-)	0.4 av	-4.0 blw av	-1.9 av	-3.6 av	-0.8 av

Total Risk	Standard Deviation	Category Risk	Risk Index	Beta
high	13.0%	blw av	0.9	1.1

	1994	1993	1992	1991	1990	1989	1988	1987	1986	1985
Return (%)	0.0	27.5	2.4	62.7	-29.0	36.8	-3.8	9.3	16.7	24.5
Differ from category (+/-)	0.7	8.0	-8.6	10.6	-22.8	10.0	-19.0	11.5	4.9	-7.8

PER SHARE DATA

	1994	1993	1992	1991	1990	1989	1988	1987	1986	1985
Dividends, Net Income ($)	0.02	0.01	0.08	0.20	0.16	0.11	0.10	0.09	0.20	0.29
Distrib'ns, Cap Gain ($)	0.00	0.00	0.00	0.00	0.16	5.07	0.11	6.73	0.85	0.00
Net Asset Value ($)	32.37	32.39	25.41	24.89	15.42	22.20	20.20	21.23	26.75	23.81
Expense Ratio (%)	0.97	1.06	1.06	1.18	1.14	1.09	1.01	0.95	0.95	0.95
Net Income to Assets (%)	0.04	0.09	0.42	1.19	0.43	0.42	0.34	0.18	0.19	0.94
Portfolio Turnover (%)	46	55	46	69	171	245	164	133	116	90
Total Assets (Millions $)	172	160	119	130	86	273	194	172	191	176

PORTFOLIO (as of 9/30/94)

Portfolio Manager: Gloria Santella - 1989, Bruce Dunn - 1991

Investm't Category: Aggressive Growth

✔ Cap Gain	Asset Allocation
Cap & Income	Fund of Funds
Income	Index
	Sector
✔ Domestic	Small Cap
✔ Foreign	Socially Conscious
Country/Region	State Specific

Portfolio: stocks 82% bonds 0%
convertibles 6% other 0% cash 12%

Largest Holdings: technology 13%, business services 11%

Unrealized Net Capital Gains: 19% of portfolio value

SHAREHOLDER INFORMATION

Minimum Investment
Initial: $2,500   Subsequent: $100

Minimum IRA Investment
Initial: $500   Subsequent: $50

Maximum Fees
Load: none   12b-1: none
Other: none

Distributions
Income: Dec   Capital Gains: Dec

Exchange Options
Number Per Year: no limit   Fee: none
Telephone: yes; 8/yr (money mkt fund available)

Services
IRA, pension, auto exchange, auto invest, auto withdraw

SteinRoe Gov't Income

(SRGPX)

General Bond

P.O. Box 804058
Chicago, IL 60680
(800) 338-2550, (312) 368-7800

PERFORMANCE

fund inception date: 3/5/86

	3yr Annual	5yr Annual	10yr Annual	Bull	Bear
Return (%)	3.3	6.5	na	39.9	-5.4
Differ from Category (+/-)	-1.0 low	-0.4 blw av	na	-1.1 av	-1.6 blw av

Total Risk	Standard Deviation	Category Risk	Risk Index	Avg Mat
low	4.2%	av	1.1	16.5 yrs

	1994	1993	1992	1991	1990	1989	1988	1987	1986	1985
Return (%)	-3.1	7.2	6.1	14.9	8.4	13.2	6.8	1.6	—	—
Differ from category (+/-)	-1.1	-2.0	-0.5	0.3	1.2	1.8	-0.6	-0.6	—	—

PER SHARE DATA

	1994	1993	1992	1991	1990	1989	1988	1987	1986	1985
Dividends, Net Income ($)	0.59	0.58	0.70	0.72	0.76	0.78	0.76	0.89	—	—
Distrib'ns, Cap Gain ($)	0.00	0.21	0.25	0.00	0.00	0.00	0.00	0.05	—	—
Net Asset Value ($)	9.26	10.16	10.22	10.55	9.86	9.84	9.42	9.54	—	—
Expense Ratio (%)	0.98	0.95	0.99	1.00	1.00	1.00	1.00	1.00	—	—
Net Income to Assets (%)	5.49	6.25	7.05	7.65	7.90	8.19	7.68	7.13	—	—
Portfolio Turnover (%)	167	170	139	136	181	239	237	205	—	—
Total Assets (Millions $)	44	56	59	50	47	32	27	23	—	—

PORTFOLIO (as of 6/30/94)

Portfolio Manager: Michael Kennedy - 1988

Investm't Category: General Bond

Cap Gain	Asset Allocation
Cap & Income	Fund of Funds
✔ Income	Index
	Sector
✔ Domestic	Small Cap
Foreign	Socially Conscious
Country/Region	State Specific

Portfolio: stocks 0%   bonds 86%
convertibles 0%   other 0%   cash 14%

Largest Holdings: mortgage-backed 61%,
U.S. government 24%

Unrealized Net Capital Gains: -2% of portfolio value

SHAREHOLDER INFORMATION

Minimum Investment
Initial: $2,500   Subsequent: $100

Minimum IRA Investment
Initial: $500   Subsequent: $50

Maximum Fees
Load: none   12b-1: none
Other: none

Distributions
Income: monthly   Capital Gains: Dec

Exchange Options
Number Per Year: no limit   Fee: none
Telephone: yes; 8/yr (money mkt fund available)

Services
IRA, pension, auto exchange, auto invest, auto withdraw

SteinRoe High Yield Muni (SRMFX)

Tax-Exempt Bond

P.O. Box 804058
Chicago, IL 60680
(800) 338-2550, (312) 368-7800

PERFORMANCE   fund inception date: 3/5/84

	3yr Annual	5yr Annual	10yr Annual	Bull	Bear
Return (%)	3.7	5.7	9.4	33.6	-4.1
Differ from Category (+/-)	-0.8 low	-0.4 low	1.3 high	-8.2 low	1.1 abv av

Total Risk	Standard Deviation	Category Risk	Risk Index	Avg Mat
blw av	5.3%	blw av	0.8	17.8 yrs

	1994	1993	1992	1991	1990	1989	1988	1987	1986	1985
Return (%)	-4.0	10.6	5.3	9.8	7.6	11.4	13.6	1.6	19.1	21.1
Differ from category (+/-)	1.2	-1.1	-3.0	-1.5	1.3	2.4	3.4	2.9	2.7	3.7

PER SHARE DATA

	1994	1993	1992	1991	1990	1989	1988	1987	1986	1985
Dividends, Net Income ($)	0.65	0.69	0.75	0.81	0.85	0.87	0.88	1.08	0.92	0.95
Distrib'ns, Cap Gain ($)	0.00	0.24	0.17	0.18	0.16	0.21	0.03	0.11	0.15	0.00
Net Asset Value ($)	10.64	11.76	11.49	11.80	11.68	11.82	11.61	11.06	12.06	11.09
Expense Ratio (%)	0.76	0.73	0.69	0.71	0.71	0.73	0.76	0.73	0.76	0.80
Net Income to Assets (%)	5.76	6.04	6.75	7.00	7.22	7.54	7.87	8.20	7.77	8.89
Portfolio Turnover (%)	36	75	88	195	261	208	53	110	34	46
Total Assets (Millions $)	226	348	411	374	311	278	201	182	225	99

PORTFOLIO (as of 6/30/94)

Portfolio Manager: James Grabovac - 1991

Investm't Category: Tax-Exempt Bond

Cap Gain	Asset Allocation
Cap & Income	Fund of Funds
✔ Income	Index
	Sector
✔ Domestic	Small Cap
Foreign	Socially Conscious
Country/Region	State Specific

Portfolio: stocks 0% bonds 100%
convertibles 0% other 0% cash 0%

Largest Holdings: general obligation 6%

Unrealized Net Capital Gains: -2% of portfolio value

SHAREHOLDER INFORMATION

Minimum Investment
Initial: $2,500   Subsequent: $100

Minimum IRA Investment
Initial: na   Subsequent: na

Maximum Fees
Load: none   12b-1: none
Other: none

Distributions
Income: monthly   Capital Gains: Dec

Exchange Options
Number Per Year: no limit   Fee: none
Telephone: yes; 8/yr (money market fund available)

Services
auto exchange, auto invest, auto withdraw

SteinRoe Income (SRHBX)

Corporate Bond

P.O. Box 804058
Chicago, IL 60680
(800) 338-2550, (312) 368-7800

PERFORMANCE

fund inception date: 3/5/86

	3yr Annual	5yr Annual	10yr Annual	Bull	Bear
Return (%)	5.9	8.1	na	52.8	-5.8
Differ from Category (+/-)	0.0 av	0.3 av	na	3.0 av	-1.5 blw av

Total Risk	Standard Deviation	Category Risk	Risk Index	Avg Mat
low	4.6%	abv av	1.5	6.9 yrs

	1994	1993	1992	1991	1990	1989	1988	1987	1986	1985
Return (%)	-3.8	13.3	9.1	17.1	6.1	7.1	11.5	3.8	—	—
Differ from category (+/-)	-1.4	1.9	0.2	0.0	1.3	-2.2	2.4	1.7	—	—

PER SHARE DATA

	1994	1993	1992	1991	1990	1989	1988	1987	1986	1985
Dividends, Net Income ($)	0.69	0.71	0.76	0.77	0.85	0.96	0.94	0.96	—	—
Distrib'ns, Cap Gain ($)	0.00	0.00	0.00	0.00	0.00	0.00	0.00	0.00	—	—
Net Asset Value ($)	9.06	10.14	9.60	9.53	8.85	9.17	9.47	9.37	—	—
Expense Ratio (%)	0.82	0.82	0.90	0.95	0.93	0.90	0.91	0.96	—	—
Net Income to Assets (%)	6.94	7.62	8.20	8.98	10.02	9.97	10.08	9.90	—	—
Portfolio Turnover (%)	53	39	76	77	90	94	158	153	—	—
Total Assets (Millions $)	153	162	113	94	89	110	97	92	—	—

PORTFOLIO (as of 6/30/94)

Portfolio Manager: Ann Henderson - 1990

Investm't Category: Corporate Bond

Cap Gain	Asset Allocation
✔ Cap & Income	Fund of Funds
Income	Index
	Sector
✔ Domestic	Small Cap
✔ Foreign	Socially Conscious
Country/Region	State Specific

Portfolio: stocks 0% bonds 91%
convertibles 0% other 0% cash 9%

Largest Holdings: financial 14%, utilities 10%

Unrealized Net Capital Gains: -2% of portfolio value

SHAREHOLDER INFORMATION

Minimum Investment
Initial: $2,500   Subsequent: $100

Minimum IRA Investment
Initial: $500   Subsequent: $50

Maximum Fees
Load: none   12b-1: none
Other: none

Distributions
Income: monthly   Capital Gains: Dec

Exchange Options
Number Per Year: no limit   Fee: none
Telephone: yes; 8/yr (money mkt fund available)

Services
IRA, pension, auto exchange, auto invest, auto withdraw

SteinRoe Interm Bond

(SRBFX)

General Bond

P.O. Box 804058
Chicago, IL 60680
(800) 338-2550, (312) 368-7800

PERFORMANCE

fund inception date: 12/5/78

	3yr Annual	5yr Annual	10yr Annual	Bull	Bear
Return (%)	4.6	7.1	9.5	43.0	-4.5
Differ from Category (+/-)	0.3 abv av	0.2 abv av	0.6 abv av	2.0 av	-0.7 av

Total Risk	Standard Deviation	Category Risk	Risk Index	Avg Mat
low	3.8%	av	1.0	5.7 yrs

	1994	1993	1992	1991	1990	1989	1988	1987	1986	1985
Return (%)	-2.5	9.1	7.6	15.1	7.1	12.5	7.2	2.5	16.3	22.9
Differ from category (+/-)	-0.5	-0.1	1.0	0.5	-0.1	1.1	-0.2	0.3	2.1	3.5

PER SHARE DATA

	1994	1993	1992	1991	1990	1989	1988	1987	1986	1985
Dividends, Net Income ($)	0.56	0.59	0.69	0.69	0.72	0.73	0.71	0.87	0.83	0.87
Distrib'ns, Cap Gain ($)	0.00	0.23	0.00	0.00	0.00	0.00	0.00	0.14	0.74	0.00
Net Asset Value ($)	8.19	8.98	9.00	9.02	8.48	8.63	8.35	8.46	9.26	9.36
Expense Ratio (%)	0.70	0.67	0.70	0.73	0.74	0.73	0.73	0.68	0.69	0.70
Net Income to Assets (%)	6.20	7.22	7.87	8.17	8.60	8.71	7.97	7.94	9.03	10.65
Portfolio Turnover (%)	206	214	202	239	296	197	273	230	334	286
Total Assets (Millions $)	282	326	243	185	161	165	162	189	183	134

PORTFOLIO (as of 6/30/94)

Portfolio Manager: Michael Kennedy - 1988

Investm't Category: General Bond

Cap Gain	Asset Allocation
Cap & Income	Fund of Funds
✔ Income	Index
	Sector
✔ Domestic	Small Cap
✔ Foreign	Socially Conscious
Country/Region	State Specific

Portfolio: stocks 0% bonds 91%
convertibles 0% other 0% cash 9%

Largest Holdings: corporate 58%, mortgage-backed 31%

Unrealized Net Capital Gains: -4% of portfolio value

SHAREHOLDER INFORMATION

Minimum Investment
Initial: $2,500   Subsequent: $100

Minimum IRA Investment
Initial: $500   Subsequent: $50

Maximum Fees
Load: none   12b-1: none
Other: none

Distributions
Income: monthly   Capital Gains: Dec

Exchange Options
Number Per Year: no limit   Fee: none
Telephone: yes; 8/yr (money mkt fund available)

Services
IRA, pension, auto exchange, auto invest, auto withdraw

SteinRoe Interm Muni

(SRIMX)

Tax-Exempt Bond

P.O. Box 804058
Chicago, IL 60680
(800) 338-2550, (312) 368-7800

PERFORMANCE

fund inception date: 10/9/85

	3yr Annual	5yr Annual	10yr Annual	Bull	Bear
Return (%)	4.9	6.5	na	38.4	-4.1
Differ from Category (+/-)	0.4 abv av	0.4 av	na	-3.4 blw av	1.1 abv av

Total Risk	Standard Deviation	Category Risk	Risk Index	Avg Mat
low	4.8%	blw av	0.8	7.8 yrs

	1994	1993	1992	1991	1990	1989	1988	1987	1986	1985
Return (%)	-3.4	11.0	7.6	10.5	7.5	8.1	6.1	1.8	12.1	—
Differ from category (+/-) . . .	1.8	-0.7	-0.7	-0.8	1.2	-0.9	-4.1	3.1	-4.3	—

PER SHARE DATA

	1994	1993	1992	1991	1990	1989	1988	1987	1986	1985
Dividends, Net Income ($) .	0.53	0.53	0.55	0.58	0.63	0.63	0.60	0.57	0.58	—
Distrib'ns, Cap Gain ($) . . .	0.00	0.18	0.12	0.17	0.03	0.03	0.00	0.01	0.00	—
Net Asset Value ($)	10.70	11.62	11.13	10.99	10.65	10.55	10.39	10.37	10.77	—
Expense Ratio (%)	0.71	0.72	0.79	0.80	0.80	0.80	0.80	0.80	0.80	—
Net Income to Assets (%) .	4.63	4.79	5.23	5.79	5.96	5.96	5.66	5.47	5.45	—
Portfolio Turnover (%).	55	96	109	96	141	83	22	49	10	—
Total Assets (Millions $). . . .	216	258	165	119	99	91	97	96	104	—

PORTFOLIO (as of 6/30/94)

Portfolio Manager: Joanne Costopoulos - 1991

Investm't Category: Tax-Exempt Bond

Cap Gain	Asset Allocation
Cap & Income	Fund of Funds
✔ Income	Index
	Sector
✔ Domestic	Small Cap
Foreign	Socially Conscious
Country/Region	State Specific

Portfolio: stocks 0% bonds 100%
convertibles 0% other 0% cash 0%

Largest Holdings: general obligation 25%

Unrealized Net Capital Gains: 1% of portfolio value

SHAREHOLDER INFORMATION

Minimum Investment
Initial: $2,500   Subsequent: $100

Minimum IRA Investment
Initial: na   Subsequent: na

Maximum Fees
Load: none   12b-1: none
Other: none

Distributions
Income: monthly   Capital Gains: Dec

Exchange Options
Number Per Year: no limit   Fee: none
Telephone: yes; 8/yr (money market fund available)

Services
auto exchange, auto invest, auto withdraw

SteinRoe Limited Maturity Income (SRLIX)

P.O. Box 804058
Chicago, IL 60680
(800) 338-2550, (312) 368-7800

General Bond

PERFORMANCE
fund inception date: 3/11/93

	3yr Annual	5yr Annual	10yr Annual	Bull	Bear
Return (%)	na	na	na	na	-1.6
Differ from Category (+/-)	na	na	na	na	2.2 high

Total Risk	Standard Deviation	Category Risk	Risk Index	Avg Mat
na	na	na	na	2.0 yrs

	1994	1993	1992	1991	1990	1989	1988	1987	1986	1985
Return (%)..............	0.0	—	—	—	—	—	—	—	—	—
Differ from category (+/-)...	2.0	—	—	—	—	—	—	—	—	—

PER SHARE DATA

	1994	1993	1992	1991	1990	1989	1988	1987	1986	1985
Dividends, Net Income ($).	0.51	—	—	—	—	—	—	—	—	—
Distrib'ns, Cap Gain ($) ...	0.00	—	—	—	—	—	—	—	—	—
Net Asset Value ($)	9.43	—	—	—	—	—	—	—	—	—
Expense Ratio (%)	0.45	—	—	—	—	—	—	—	—	—
Net Income to Assets (%) .	4.81	—	—	—	—	—	—	—	—	—
Portfolio Turnover (%)	122	—	—	—	—	—	—	—	—	—
Total Assets (Millions $).....	27	—	—	—	—	—	—	—	—	—

PORTFOLIO (as of 6/30/94)

Portfolio Manager: Lisa N. Wilhelm - 1993

Investm't Category: General Bond
Cap Gain	Asset Allocation
Cap & Income	Fund of Funds
✔ Income	Index
	Sector
✔ Domestic	Small Cap
✔ Foreign	Socially Conscious
Country/Region	State Specific

Portfolio: stocks 0% bonds 87%
convertibles 0% other 0% cash 13%

Largest Holdings: corporate 50%, U.S. government 19%

Unrealized Net Capital Gains: -2% of portfolio value

SHAREHOLDER INFORMATION

Minimum Investment
Initial: $10,000   Subsequent: $1,000

Minimum IRA Investment
Initial: $500   Subsequent: $50

Maximum Fees
Load: none   12b-1: none
Other: none

Distributions
Income: monthly   Capital Gains: Dec

Exchange Options
Number Per Year: no limit   Fee: none
Telephone: yes; 8/yr (money mkt fund available)

Services
IRA, pension, auto exchange, auto invest, auto withdraw

SteinRoe Managed Muni

(SRMMX)

Tax-Exempt Bond

P.O. Box 804058
Chicago, IL 60680
(800) 338-2550, (312) 368-7800

PERFORMANCE

fund inception date: 2/23/77

	3yr Annual	5yr Annual	10yr Annual	Bull	Bear
Return (%)	4.4	6.4	9.9	42.1	-5.5
Differ from Category (+/-)	-0.1 av	0.3 av	1.8 high	0.3 blw av	-0.3 av

Total Risk	Standard Deviation	Category Risk	Risk Index	Avg Mat
blw av	5.7%	blw av	0.9	16.7 yrs

	1994	1993	1992	1991	1990	1989	1988	1987	1986	1985
Return (%)	-5.3	11.2	8.2	11.8	7.0	10.6	10.8	0.9	23.3	23.4
Differ from category (+/-)	-0.1	-0.5	-0.1	0.5	0.7	1.6	0.6	2.2	6.9	6.0

PER SHARE DATA

	1994	1993	1992	1991	1990	1989	1988	1987	1986	1985
Dividends, Net Income ($)	0.51	0.51	0.54	0.55	0.58	0.61	0.61	0.66	0.79	0.69
Distrib'ns, Cap Gain ($)	0.00	0.17	0.15	0.20	0.05	0.26	0.03	0.13	0.92	0.03
Net Asset Value ($)	8.36	9.36	9.04	9.01	8.76	8.80	8.76	8.50	9.22	8.93
Expense Ratio (%)	0.65	0.64	0.64	0.66	0.66	0.65	0.65	0.65	0.65	0.65
Net Income to Assets (%)	5.45	5.65	6.17	6.39	6.66	7.00	7.03	6.99	7.04	8.11
Portfolio Turnover (%)	36	63	94	203	95	102	28	113	92	113
Total Assets (Millions $)	605	781	726	656	584	515	468	458	523	357

PORTFOLIO (as of 6/30/94)

Portfolio Manager: Jane McCart - 1991

Investm't Category: Tax-Exempt Bond
Cap Gain	Asset Allocation
Cap & Income	Fund of Funds
✔ Income	Index
	Sector
✔ Domestic	Small Cap
Foreign	Socially Conscious
Country/Region	State Specific

Portfolio: stocks 0%   bonds 100%
convertibles 0%   other 0%   cash 0%

Largest Holdings: general obligation 14%

Unrealized Net Capital Gains: 3% of portfolio value

SHAREHOLDER INFORMATION

Minimum Investment
Initial: $2,500   Subsequent: $100

Minimum IRA Investment
Initial: na   Subsequent: na

Maximum Fees
Load: none   12b-1: none
Other: none

Distributions
Income: monthly   Capital Gains: Dec

Exchange Options
Number Per Year: no limit   Fee: none
Telephone: yes; 8/yr (money market fund available)

Services
auto exchange, auto invest, auto withdraw

SteinRoe Prime Equities
(SRPEX)
Growth

P.O. Box 804058
Chicago, IL 60680
(800) 338-2550, (312) 368-7800

PERFORMANCE

fund inception date: 3/24/87

	3yr Annual	5yr Annual	10yr Annual	Bull	Bear
Return (%)	7.4	10.0	na	76.5	-4.9
Differ from Category (+/-)	-0.3 av	0.4 abv av	na	-15.6 blw av	1.7 abv av

Total Risk	Standard Deviation	Category Risk	Risk Index	Beta
av	7.3%	low	0.7	0.8

	1994	1993	1992	1991	1990	1989	1988	1987	1986	1985
Return (%)	-0.1	12.8	9.9	32.3	-1.7	30.9	9.0	—	—	—
Differ from category (+/-)	0.5	-0.6	-1.7	-3.4	4.0	4.8	-9.0	—	—	—

PER SHARE DATA

	1994	1993	1992	1991	1990	1989	1988	1987	1986	1985
Dividends, Net Income ($)	0.18	0.16	0.17	0.23	0.29	0.24	0.19	—	—	—
Distrib'ns, Cap Gain ($)	0.59	0.71	0.75	0.35	0.36	0.00	0.00	—	—	—
Net Asset Value ($)	13.78	14.58	13.71	13.32	10.54	11.39	8.89	—	—	—
Expense Ratio (%)	0.90	0.88	0.97	1.00	1.08	1.24	1.47	—	—	—
Net Income to Assets (%)	1.18	1.23	1.46	2.27	2.40	2.28	2.03	—	—	—
Portfolio Turnover (%)	85	50	40	48	51	63	105	—	—	—
Total Assets (Millions $)	122	107	71	55	43	33	23	—	—	—

PORTFOLIO (as of 9/30/94)

Portfolio Manager: Ralph Segall - 1987

Investm't Category: Growth
- ✔ Cap Gain
- Cap & Income
- Income
- ✔ Domestic
- ✔ Foreign
- Country/Region
- Asset Allocation
- Fund of Funds
- Index
- Sector
- Small Cap
- Socially Conscious
- State Specific

Portfolio: stocks 90%, bonds 1%, convertibles 2%, other 0%, cash 7%

Largest Holdings: energy 10%, banks 9%

Unrealized Net Capital Gains: 15% of portfolio value

SHAREHOLDER INFORMATION

Minimum Investment
Initial: $2,500   Subsequent: $100

Minimum IRA Investment
Initial: $500   Subsequent: $50

Maximum Fees
Load: none   12b-1: none
Other: none

Distributions
Income: quarterly   Capital Gains: Dec

Exchange Options
Number Per Year: no limit   Fee: none
Telephone: yes; 8/yr (money mkt fund available)

Services
IRA, pension, auto exchange, auto invest, auto withdraw

SteinRoe Special (SRSPX)

Aggressive Growth

P.O. Box 804058
Chicago, IL 60680
(800) 338-2550, (312) 368-7800

	3yr Annual	5yr Annual	10yr Annual	Bull	Bear
Return (%)	9.8	10.8	15.6	92.2	-8.0
Differ from Category (+/-)	0.9 abv av	-1.7 blw av	1.6 abv av	-41.0 low	2.8 abv av

Total Risk	Standard Deviation	Category Risk	Risk Index	Beta
abv av	9.2%	low	0.6	0.9

	1994	1993	1992	1991	1990	1989	1988	1987	1986	1985
Return (%)	-3.3	20.4	14.0	34.0	-5.8	37.8	20.2	4.2	14.7	29.4
Differ from category (+/-)	-2.6	0.9	3.0	-18.1	0.4	11.0	5.0	6.4	2.9	-2.9

PER SHARE DATA

	1994	1993	1992	1991	1990	1989	1988	1987	1986	1985
Dividends, Net Income ($)	0.15	0.21	0.18	0.37	0.34	0.39	0.22	0.57	0.34	0.19
Distrib'ns, Cap Gain ($)	1.31	1.77	1.16	0.31	1.32	2.08	0.06	3.90	3.80	0.54
Net Asset Value ($)	21.72	24.00	21.63	20.16	15.58	18.31	15.14	12.83	16.95	18.41
Expense Ratio (%)	0.96	0.97	0.99	1.04	1.02	0.96	0.99	0.96	0.92	0.92
Net Income to Assets (%)	0.91	0.92	0.99	2.11	2.33	2.12	1.31	1.32	1.75	2.07
Portfolio Turnover (%)	58	42	40	50	70	85	42	103	116	96
Total Assets (Millions $)	1,168	1,100	626	587	361	322	225	188	253	278

PORTFOLIO (as of 9/30/94)

Portfolio Manager: Bruce Dunn - 1991, Richard Peterson - 1991

Investm't Category: Aggressive Growth
- ✔ Cap Gain   Asset Allocation
- Cap & Income   Fund of Funds
- Income   Index
-     Sector
- ✔ Domestic   Small Cap
- ✔ Foreign   Socially Conscious
- Country/Region   State Specific

Portfolio: stocks 89%   bonds 0%
convertibles 0%   other 1%   cash 10%

Largest Holdings: business services 8%, retail 7%

Unrealized Net Capital Gains: 16% of portfolio value

SHAREHOLDER INFORMATION

Minimum Investment
Initial: $2,500   Subsequent: $100

Minimum IRA Investment
Initial: $500   Subsequent: $50

Maximum Fees
Load: none   12b-1: none
Other: none

Distributions
Income: Dec   Capital Gains: Dec

Exchange Options
Number Per Year: no limit   Fee: none
Telephone: yes; 8/yr (money mkt fund available)

Services
IRA, pension, auto exchange, auto invest, auto withdraw

SteinRoe Stock (SRFSX)

Growth

P.O. Box 804058
Chicago, IL 60680
(800) 338-2550, (312) 368-7800

PERFORMANCE

fund inception date: 7/1/58

	3yr Annual	5yr Annual	10yr Annual	Bull	Bear
Return (%)	2.3	9.5	12.8	78.3	-11.0
Differ from Category (+/-)	-5.4 low	-0.1 av	-0.1 av	-13.8 blw av	-4.4 low

Total Risk	Standard Deviation	Category Risk	Risk Index	Beta
abv av	9.8%	av	1.0	1.0

	1994	1993	1992	1991	1990	1989	1988	1987	1986	1985
Return (%)	-3.7	2.8	8.2	45.9	0.9	35.4	0.6	5.5	16.9	26.5
Differ from category (+/-)	-3.1	-10.6	-3.4	10.2	6.6	9.3	-17.4	3.7	2.3	-2.7

PER SHARE DATA

	1994	1993	1992	1991	1990	1989	1988	1987	1986	1985
Dividends, Net Income ($)	0.15	0.15	0.16	0.28	0.43	0.37	0.28	0.29	0.25	0.30
Distrib'ns, Cap Gain ($)	3.02	1.73	0.95	1.16	0.92	0.00	0.06	2.71	3.22	0.00
Net Asset Value ($)	20.29	24.39	25.59	24.67	17.97	19.14	14.43	14.67	16.97	17.43
Expense Ratio (%)	0.94	0.93	0.92	0.79	0.73	0.77	0.76	0.65	0.67	0.67
Net Income to Assets (%)	0.50	0.59	0.75	1.63	2.03	2.05	1.62	1.25	1.34	1.89
Portfolio Turnover (%)	27	29	23	34	40	47	84	143	137	114
Total Assets (Millions $)	303	368	373	292	206	206	196	233	226	224

PORTFOLIO (as of 9/30/94)

Portfolio Manager: committee

Investm't Category: Growth

✔ Cap Gain	Asset Allocation
Cap & Income	Fund of Funds
Income	Index
	Sector
✔ Domestic	Small Cap
✔ Foreign	Socially Conscious
Country/Region	State Specific

Portfolio: stocks 92% bonds 0%
convertibles 0% other 0% cash 8%

Largest Holdings: telecommunications 14%,
consumer-related 12%

Unrealized Net Capital Gains: 23% of portfolio value

SHAREHOLDER INFORMATION

Minimum Investment
Initial: $2,500   Subsequent: $100

Minimum IRA Investment
Initial: $500   Subsequent: $50

Maximum Fees
Load: none   12b-1: none
Other: none

Distributions
Income: Dec   Capital Gains: Dec

Exchange Options
Number Per Year: no limit   Fee: none
Telephone: yes; 8/yr (money mkt fund available)

Services
IRA, pension, auto exchange, auto invest, auto withdraw

SteinRoe Total Return

(SRFBX)

Balanced

P.O. Box 804058
Chicago, IL 60680
(800) 338-2550, (312) 368-7800

PERFORMANCE

fund inception date: 8/25/49

	3yr Annual	5yr Annual	10yr Annual	Bull	Bear
Return (%)	5.1	8.1	11.0	71.8	-6.9
Differ from Category (+/-)	-1.3 blw av	0.1 av	-0.3 blw av	6.8 abv av	-1.2 blw av

Total Risk	Standard Deviation	Category Risk	Risk Index	Beta
blw av	6.0%	av	1.0	0.6

	1994	1993	1992	1991	1990	1989	1988	1987	1986	1985
Return (%).	-4.1	12.3	7.8	29.5	-1.7	20.3	7.8	0.7	17.1	25.7
Differ from category (+/-). . .	-2.2	-1.1	-0.5	6.1	-1.2	3.0	-4.0	-1.7	-0.3	1.4

PER SHARE DATA

	1994	1993	1992	1991	1990	1989	1988	1987	1986	1985
Dividends, Net Income ($) .	1.19	1.23	1.30	1.32	1.07	1.40	1.31	1.63	1.35	1.42
Distrib'ns, Cap Gain ($) . . .	0.28	0.71	1.67	0.62	0.73	0.73	0.50	1.45	2.70	0.19
Net Asset Value ($)	24.30	26.85	25.69	26.62	22.16	24.41	22.15	22.25	25.07	25.04
Expense Ratio (%)	0.83	0.81	0.85	0.87	0.88	0.90	0.87	0.80	0.79	0.77
Net Income to Assets (%) .	4.53	4.69	4.94	5.50	5.36	5.83	5.68	5.12	5.21	6.30
Portfolio Turnover (%).	29	53	59	71	75	93	85	86	108	25
Total Assets (Millions $). . . .	215	226	173	151	125	145	134	140	149	128

PORTFOLIO (as of 9/30/94)

Portfolio Manager: Robert Christensen - 1981

Investm't Category: Balanced

Cap Gain	✔ Asset Allocation
✔ Cap & Income	Fund of Funds
Income	Index
	Sector
✔ Domestic	Small Cap
✔ Foreign	Socially Conscious
Country/Region	State Specific

Portfolio: stocks 40% bonds 11%
convertibles 40% other 4% cash 5%

Largest Holdings: stocks—services 5%, stocks—commercial banking 5%

Unrealized Net Capital Gains: 11% of portfolio value

SHAREHOLDER INFORMATION

Minimum Investment
Initial: $2,500   Subsequent: $100

Minimum IRA Investment
Initial: $500   Subsequent: $50

Maximum Fees
Load: none   12b-1: none
Other: none

Distributions
Income: quarterly   Capital Gains: Dec

Exchange Options
Number Per Year: no limit   Fee: none
Telephone: yes; 8/yr (money mkt fund available)

Services
IRA, pension, auto exchange, auto invest, auto withdraw

Stratton Growth (STRGX)
Growth & Income

Plymouth Mtg. Exec. Campus
610 W. Germantown Pike, # 300
Plymouth Meeting, PA 19462
(800) 634-5726, (610) 941-0255

PERFORMANCE

fund inception date: 9/30/72

	3yr Annual	5yr Annual	10yr Annual	Bull	Bear
Return (%)	6.7	6.7	11.0	49.9	-0.4
Differ from Category (+/-)	-0.4 av	-1.2 blw av	-0.7 blw av	-25.9 low	5.9 high

Total Risk	Standard Deviation	Category Risk	Risk Index	Beta
av	7.2%	low	0.9	0.8

	1994	1993	1992	1991	1990	1989	1988	1987	1986	1985
Return (%)	7.1	6.4	6.7	22.1	-6.7	23.7	22.5	-3.8	10.6	27.4
Differ from category (+/-)	8.5	-6.8	-3.5	-5.5	-0.7	2.3	5.5	-4.4	-5.2	1.7

PER SHARE DATA

	1994	1993	1992	1991	1990	1989	1988	1987	1986	1985
Dividends, Net Income ($)	0.54	0.51	0.57	0.73	0.82	0.71	0.53	0.70	0.28	0.20
Distrib'ns, Cap Gain ($)	1.28	0.91	0.82	0.44	0.46	2.49	1.49	1.53	2.07	0.61
Net Asset Value ($)	19.61	20.05	20.19	20.27	17.63	20.24	19.06	17.23	20.02	20.09
Expense Ratio (%)	1.34	1.39	1.35	1.41	1.38	1.41	1.48	1.50	1.49	1.61
Net Income to Assets (%)	2.51	2.76	3.20	3.94	4.09	2.79	2.80	1.74	1.40	1.22
Portfolio Turnover (%)	49	35	60	57	55	50	34	23	28	35
Total Assets (Millions $)	26	24	25	25	23	20	17	19	19	14

PORTFOLIO (as of 5/31/94)

Portfolio Manager: James W. Stratton - 1972,
John A. Affleck - 1979

Investm't Category: Growth & Income
Cap Gain	Asset Allocation
✔ Cap & Income	Fund of Funds
Income	Index
	Sector
✔ Domestic	Small Cap
Foreign	Socially Conscious
Country/Region	State Specific

Portfolio: stocks 85%   bonds 2%
convertibles 0%   other 0%   cash 13%

Largest Holdings: banks 18%, healthcare 12%

Unrealized Net Capital Gains: 13% of portfolio value

SHAREHOLDER INFORMATION

Minimum Investment
Initial: $2,000   Subsequent: $100

Minimum IRA Investment
Initial: $0   Subsequent: $0

Maximum Fees
Load: none   12b-1: none
Other: none

Distributions
Income: Jul, Dec   Capital Gains: Jul, Dec

Exchange Options
Number Per Year: no limit   Fee: none
Telephone: yes (money market fund not available)

Services
IRA, pension, auto invest, auto withdraw

Stratton Monthly Dividend Shares (STMDX)

Growth & Income

Plymouth Mtg. Exec. Campus
610 W. Germantown Pike, # 300
Plymouth Meeting, PA 19462
(800) 634-5726, (610) 941-0255

PERFORMANCE

fund inception date: 5/31/80

	3yr Annual	5yr Annual	10yr Annual	Bull	Bear
Return (%)	1.0	6.0	9.2	67.2	-12.7
Differ from Category (+/-)	-6.1 low	-1.9 low	-2.5 low	-8.6 blw av	-6.4 low

Total Risk	Standard Deviation	Category Risk	Risk Index	Beta
av	8.5%	abv av	1.0	0.5

	1994	1993	1992	1991	1990	1989	1988	1987	1986	1985
Return (%).	-12.1	6.5	10.3	35.0	-3.8	18.7	9.7	-11.4	20.4	29.9
Differ from category (+/-). .	-10.7	-6.7	0.1	7.4	2.2	-2.7	-7.3	-12.0	4.6	4.2

PER SHARE DATA

	1994	1993	1992	1991	1990	1989	1988	1987	1986	1985
Dividends, Net Income ($) .	1.92	1.95	1.94	1.95	2.20	2.05	2.08	2.09	2.28	2.16
Distrib'ns, Cap Gain ($) . . .	0.00	0.00	0.00	0.00	0.00	0.00	0.00	0.65	0.50	0.00
Net Asset Value ($)	23.78	29.17	29.16	28.31	22.66	25.88	23.63	23.44	29.21	26.62
Expense Ratio (%)	1.05	1.10	1.23	1.27	1.25	1.21	1.21	1.24	1.49	1.72
Net Income to Assets (%) .	7.13	6.74	7.63	8.79	8.19	8.54	7.52	6.90	8.36	9.77
Portfolio Turnover (%).	26	35	44	14	39	15	24	15	13	28
Total Assets (Millions $). . . .	121	178	46	31	33	34	36	54	21	10

PORTFOLIO (as of 7/31/94)

Portfolio Manager: Gerard E. Hefferman - 1980, James W. Stratton - 1980

Investm't Category: Growth & Income

Cap Gain	Asset Allocation
✔ Cap & Income	Fund of Funds
Income	Index
	Sector
✔ Domestic	Small Cap
Foreign	Socially Conscious
Country/Region	State Specific

Portfolio: stocks 86% bonds 4%
convertibles 5% other 4% cash 1%

Largest Holdings: utilities 62%, real estate healthcare 14%

Unrealized Net Capital Gains: -10% of portfolio value

SHAREHOLDER INFORMATION

Minimum Investment
Initial: $2,000   Subsequent: $100

Minimum IRA Investment
Initial: $0   Subsequent: $0

Maximum Fees
Load: none   12b-1: none
Other: none

Distributions
Income: monthly   Capital Gains: Dec

Exchange Options
Number Per Year: no limit   Fee: none
Telephone: yes (money market fund not available)

Services
IRA, pension, auto invest, auto withdraw

Strong Advantage
(STADX)
Corporate Bond

P.O. Box 2936
Milwaukee, WI 53201
(800) 368-1030, (414) 359-1400

PERFORMANCE   fund inception date: 11/25/88

	3yr Annual	5yr Annual	10yr Annual	Bull	Bear
Return (%)	6.5	7.3	na	31.5	0.4
Differ from Category (+/-)	0.6 abv av	-0.5 blw av	na	-18.3 low	4.7 high

Total Risk	Standard Deviation	Category Risk	Risk Index	Avg Mat
low	1.1%	low	0.3	0.2 yrs

	1994	1993	1992	1991	1990	1989	1988	1987	1986	1985
Return (%)	3.4	7.8	8.4	10.6	6.6	9.3	—	—	—	—
Differ from category (+/-)	5.8	-3.6	-0.5	-6.5	1.8	0.0	—	—	—	—

PER SHARE DATA

	1994	1993	1992	1991	1990	1989	1988	1987	1986	1985
Dividends, Net Income ($)	0.54	0.59	0.70	0.76	0.83	1.03	—	—	—	—
Distrib'ns, Cap Gain ($)	0.02	0.00	0.00	0.00	0.00	0.00	—	—	—	—
Net Asset Value ($)	9.98	10.19	10.01	9.90	9.67	9.87	—	—	—	—
Expense Ratio (%)	0.80	0.90	1.00	1.20	1.20	1.10	—	—	—	—
Net Income to Assets (%)	5.00	5.80	7.00	7.80	8.50	10.00	—	—	—	—
Portfolio Turnover (%)	241	304	316	503	274	211	—	—	—	—
Total Assets (Millions $)	910	425	272	143	119	143	—	—	—	—

PORTFOLIO (as of 6/30/94)

Portfolio Manager: Jeffrey A. Koch - 1991

Investm't Category: Corporate Bond

Cap Gain	Asset Allocation
Cap & Income	Fund of Funds
✔ Income	Index
	Sector
✔ Domestic	Small Cap
✔ Foreign	Socially Conscious
Country/Region	State Specific

Portfolio: stocks 0% bonds 83%
convertibles 0% other 0% cash 17%

Largest Holdings: corporate 54%, corporate mortgage-backed securities 23%

Unrealized Net Capital Gains: 0% of portfolio value

SHAREHOLDER INFORMATION

Minimum Investment
Initial: $1,000   Subsequent: $50

Minimum IRA Investment
Initial: $250   Subsequent: $50

Maximum Fees
Load: none   12b-1: none
Other: none

Distributions
Income: monthly   Capital Gains: Dec

Exchange Options
Number Per Year: 5   Fee: none
Telephone: yes (money market fund available)

Services
IRA, pension, auto exchange, auto invest, auto withdraw

Strong American Utilities (SAMUX)

Growth & Income

P.O. Box 2936
Milwaukee, WI 53201
(800) 368-1030, (414) 359-1400

PERFORMANCE

fund inception date: 7/1/93

	3yr Annual	5yr Annual	10yr Annual	Bull	Bear
Return (%)	na	na	na	na	-5.2
Differ from Category (+/-)	na	na	na	na	1.1 abv av

Total Risk	Standard Deviation	Category Risk	Risk Index	Beta
na	na	na	na	na

	1994	1993	1992	1991	1990	1989	1988	1987	1986	1985
Return (%)	-2.6	—	—	—	—	—	—	—	—	—
Differ from category (+/-)	-1.2	—	—	—	—	—	—	—	—	—

PER SHARE DATA

	1994	1993	1992	1991	1990	1989	1988	1987	1986	1985
Dividends, Net Income ($)	0.46	—	—	—	—	—	—	—	—	—
Distrib'ns, Cap Gain ($)	0.00	—	—	—	—	—	—	—	—	—
Net Asset Value ($)	9.46	—	—	—	—	—	—	—	—	—
Expense Ratio (%)	0.00	—	—	—	—	—	—	—	—	—
Net Income to Assets (%)	5.70	—	—	—	—	—	—	—	—	—
Portfolio Turnover (%)	105	—	—	—	—	—	—	—	—	—
Total Assets (Millions $)	37	—	—	—	—	—	—	—	—	—

PORTFOLIO (as of 6/30/94)

Portfolio Manager: not specified

Investm't Category: Growth & Income

Cap Gain	Asset Allocation
✔ Cap & Income	Fund of Funds
Income	Index
	✔ Sector
✔ Domestic	Small Cap
Foreign	Socially Conscious
Country/Region	State Specific

Portfolio: stocks 95% bonds 3%
convertibles 0% other 0% cash 2%

Largest Holdings: telecommunications 47%, electric utilities 28%

Unrealized Net Capital Gains: -7% of portfolio value

SHAREHOLDER INFORMATION

Minimum Investment
Initial: $1,000   Subsequent: $50

Minimum IRA Investment
Initial: $250   Subsequent: $50

Maximum Fees
Load: none   12b-1: none
Other: none

Distributions
Income: quarterly   Capital Gains: Dec

Exchange Options
Number Per Year: 5   Fee: none
Telephone: yes (money market fund available)

Services
IRA, pension, auto exchange, auto invest, auto withdraw

Strong Asia Pacific
(SASPX)
International Stock

P.O. Box 2936
Milwaukee, WI 53201
(800) 368-1030, (414) 359-1400

PERFORMANCE   fund inception date: 12/31/93

	3yr Annual	5yr Annual	10yr Annual	Bull	Bear
Return (%)	na	na	na	na	-7.8
Differ from Category (+/-)	na	na	na	na	-0.8 blw av

Total Risk	Standard Deviation	Category Risk	Risk Index	Beta
na	na	na	na	na

	1994	1993	1992	1991	1990	1989	1988	1987	1986	1985
Return (%)	-5.2	—	—	—	—	—	—	—	—	—
Differ from category (+/-). . . .	-2.2	—	—	—	—	—	—	—	—	—

PER SHARE DATA

	1994	1993	1992	1991	1990	1989	1988	1987	1986	1985
Dividends, Net Income ($) .	0.01	—	—	—	—	—	—	—	—	—
Distrib'ns, Cap Gain ($) . . .	0.12	—	—	—	—	—	—	—	—	—
Net Asset Value ($)	9.35	—	—	—	—	—	—	—	—	—
Expense Ratio (%)	1.90	—	—	—	—	—	—	—	—	—
Net Income to Assets (%)	-0.20	—	—	—	—	—	—	—	—	—
Portfolio Turnover (%)	123	—	—	—	—	—	—	—	—	—
Total Assets (Millions $).	57	—	—	—	—	—	—	—	—	—

PORTFOLIO (as of 6/30/94)

Portfolio Manager: Anthony L. Cragg - 1994

Investm't Category: International Stock

✔ Cap Gain	Asset Allocation
Cap & Income	Fund of Funds
Income	Index
	Sector
Domestic	Small Cap
✔ Foreign	Socially Conscious
✔ Country/Region	State Specific

Portfolio: stocks 90%   bonds 0%
convertibles 1%   other 0%   cash 9%

Largest Holdings: Japan 27%, Australia 20%

Unrealized Net Capital Gains: -4% of portfolio value

SHAREHOLDER INFORMATION

Minimum Investment
Initial: $1,000   Subsequent: $50

Minimum IRA Investment
Initial: $250   Subsequent: $50

Maximum Fees
Load: none   12b-1: none
Other: none

Distributions
Income: quarterly   Capital Gains: Dec

Exchange Options
Number Per Year: 5   Fee: none
Telephone: yes (money market fund available)

Services
IRA, pension, auto exchange, auto invest, auto withdraw

Strong Asset Allocation
(STAAX)
Balanced

P.O. Box 2936
Milwaukee, WI 53201
(800) 368-1030, (414) 359-1400

	3yr Annual	5yr Annual	10yr Annual	Bull	Bear
Return (%)	5.1	7.4	9.2	48.2	-5.7
Differ from Category (+/-)	-1.3 blw av	-0.6 blw av	-2.1 low	-16.8 low	0.0 av

Total Risk	Standard Deviation	Category Risk	Risk Index	Beta
low	4.7%	low	0.7	0.5

	1994	1993	1992	1991	1990	1989	1988	1987	1986	1985
Return (%)	-1.5	14.4	3.2	19.6	2.7	11.1	9.1	-0.3	17.6	19.3
Differ from category (+/-)	0.4	1.0	-5.1	-3.8	3.2	-6.2	-2.7	-2.7	0.2	-5.0

PER SHARE DATA

	1994	1993	1992	1991	1990	1989	1988	1987	1986	1985
Dividends, Net Income ($)	0.70	0.82	0.86	0.97	1.38	0.97	1.61	1.78	0.95	0.75
Distrib'ns, Cap Gain ($)	0.16	1.24	0.94	0.20	0.00	0.14	0.00	2.95	0.42	0.04
Net Asset Value ($)	17.91	19.06	18.49	19.68	17.50	18.41	17.57	17.60	22.18	20.12
Expense Ratio (%)	1.20	1.20	1.20	1.30	1.30	1.30	1.20	1.10	1.10	1.10
Net Income to Assets (%)	3.50	4.20	4.40	5.10	6.10	6.60	7.50	4.20	4.70	5.40
Portfolio Turnover (%)	324	348	320	418	320	207	426	337	80	143
Total Assets (Millions $)	248	257	208	215	204	241	256	273	339	220

PORTFOLIO (as of 6/30/94)

Portfolio Manager: J. Mueller - 1993, A. Stephens - 1993, B. Tank - 1993

Investm't Category: Balanced

Cap Gain	✔ Asset Allocation
✔ Cap & Income	Fund of Funds
Income	Index
	Sector
✔ Domestic	Small Cap
✔ Foreign	Socially Conscious
Country/Region	State Specific

Portfolio: stocks 30%   bonds 52%
convertibles 0%   other 1%   cash 17%

Largest Holdings: bonds—mortgage-backed 26%, bonds—corporate 18%

Unrealized Net Capital Gains: -1% of portfolio value

SHAREHOLDER INFORMATION

Minimum Investment
Initial: $1,000   Subsequent: $50

Minimum IRA Investment
Initial: $250   Subsequent: $50

Maximum Fees
Load: none   12b-1: none
Other: none

Distributions
Income: quarterly   Capital Gains: Dec

Exchange Options
Number Per Year: 5   Fee: none
Telephone: yes (money market fund available)

Services
IRA, pension, auto exchange, auto invest, auto withdraw

Strong Common Stock
(STCSX)
Aggressive Growth

P.O. Box 2936
Milwaukee, WI 53201
(800) 368-1030, (414) 359-1400

this fund is closed to new investors

	3yr Annual	5yr Annual	10yr Annual	Bull	Bear
Return (%)	14.5	18.9	na	168.8	-5.1
Differ from Category (+/-)	5.6 abv av	6.4 high	na	35.6 abv av	5.7 high

Total Risk	Standard Deviation	Category Risk	Risk Index	Beta
abv av	10.4%	low	0.7	0.9

	1994	1993	1992	1991	1990	1989	1988	1987	1986	1985
Return (%)	-0.4	25.1	20.7	57.0	0.9	—	—	—	—	—
Differ from category (+/-) . . .	0.3	5.6	9.7	4.9	7.1	—	—	—	—	—

PER SHARE DATA

	1994	1993	1992	1991	1990	1989	1988	1987	1986	1985
Dividends, Net Income ($) .	0.13	0.17	0.22	0.00	0.08	—	—	—	—	—
Distrib'ns, Cap Gain ($) . . .	0.98	0.73	0.15	2.59	0.00	—	—	—	—	—
Net Asset Value ($)	16.74	17.94	15.07	12.84	10.02	—	—	—	—	—
Expense Ratio (%)	1.30	1.40	1.40	2.00	2.00	—	—	—	—	—
Net Income to Assets (%) .	0.20	0.20	0.10	-0.50	0.90	—	—	—	—	—
Portfolio Turnover (%)	101	80	292	2,461	291	—	—	—	—	—
Total Assets (Millions $). . . .	790	788	179	49	2	—	—	—	—	—

PORTFOLIO (as of 6/30/94)

Portfolio Manager: Richard Weiss- 1991, Marina Carlson - 1993

Investm't Category: Aggressive Growth

✔ Cap Gain	Asset Allocation
Cap & Income	Fund of Funds
Income	Index
	Sector
✔ Domestic	Small Cap
✔ Foreign	Socially Conscious
Country/Region	State Specific

Portfolio: stocks 91%   bonds 0%
convertibles 0%   other 0%   cash 9%

Largest Holdings: retail 8%, telecommunications 6%

Unrealized Net Capital Gains: 5% of portfolio value

SHAREHOLDER INFORMATION

Minimum Investment
Initial: $1,000   Subsequent: $50

Minimum IRA Investment
Initial: $250   Subsequent: $50

Maximum Fees
Load: none   12b-1: none
Other: none

Distributions
Income: quarterly   Capital Gains: Dec

Exchange Options
Number Per Year: 5   Fee: none
Telephone: yes (money market fund available)

Services
IRA, pension, auto exchange, auto invest, auto withdraw

Strong Discovery (STDIX)
Growth

P.O. Box 2936
Milwaukee, WI 53201
(800) 368-1030, (414) 359-1400

PERFORMANCE   fund inception date: 12/31/87

	3yr Annual	5yr Annual	10yr Annual	Bull	Bear
Return (%)	5.5	13.8	na	121.4	-13.8
Differ from Category (+/-)	-2.2 blw av	4.2 high	na	29.3 high	-7.2 low

Total Risk	Standard Deviation	Category Risk	Risk Index	Beta
high	13.3%	high	1.4	1.1

	1994	1993	1992	1991	1990	1989	1988	1987	1986	1985
Return (%)	-5.6	22.2	1.9	67.5	-2.7	23.9	24.4	—	—	—
Differ from category (+/-)	-5.0	8.8	-9.7	31.8	3.0	-2.2	6.4	—	—	—

PER SHARE DATA

	1994	1993	1992	1991	1990	1989	1988	1987	1986	1985
Dividends, Net Income ($)	0.69	0.50	1.50	0.83	0.31	0.28	0.97	—	—	—
Distrib'ns, Cap Gain ($)	0.68	0.93	0.15	2.60	0.00	0.71	0.03	—	—	—
Net Asset Value ($)	15.67	18.05	16.01	17.49	12.51	13.18	11.44	—	—	—
Expense Ratio (%)	1.40	1.50	1.50	1.60	1.90	1.90	2.00	—	—	—
Net Income to Assets (%)	0.00	-0.02	-0.40	0.00	2.10	2.40	11.90	—	—	—
Portfolio Turnover (%)	408	668	1,259	1,060	494	550	442	—	—	—
Total Assets (Millions $)	388	304	193	162	56	58	14	—	—	—

PORTFOLIO (as of 6/30/94)

Portfolio Manager: Richard Strong - 1987

Investm't Category: Growth

✔ Cap Gain	Asset Allocation
Cap & Income	Fund of Funds
Income	Index
	Sector
✔ Domestic	✔ Small Cap
✔ Foreign	Socially Conscious
Country/Region	State Specific

Portfolio: stocks 86%   bonds 0%
convertibles 3%   other 0%   cash 11%

Largest Holdings: retail 7%, metals & mining 6%

Unrealized Net Capital Gains: -5% of portfolio value

SHAREHOLDER INFORMATION

Minimum Investment
Initial: $1,000   Subsequent: $50

Minimum IRA Investment
Initial: $250   Subsequent: $50

Maximum Fees
Load: none   12b-1: none
Other: none

Distributions
Income: quarterly   Capital Gains: Dec

Exchange Options
Number Per Year: 5   Fee: none
Telephone: yes (money market fund available)

Services
IRA, pension, auto exchange, auto invest, auto withdraw

Strong Gov't Securities
(STVSX)

General Bond

P.O. Box 2936
Milwaukee, WI 53201
(800) 368-1030, (414) 359-1400

PERFORMANCE
fund inception date: 10/29/86

	3yr Annual	5yr Annual	10yr Annual	Bull	Bear
Return (%)	5.9	8.5	na	50.7	-5.7
Differ from Category (+/-)	1.6 high	1.6 high	na	9.7 high	-1.9 low

Total Risk	Standard Deviation	Category Risk	Risk Index	Avg Mat
low	4.3%	abv av	1.1	9.7 yrs

	1994	1993	1992	1991	1990	1989	1988	1987	1986	1985
Return (%)................	-3.4	12.6	9.2	16.6	8.7	9.8	10.5	3.4	—	—
Differ from category (+/-)...	-1.4	3.4	2.6	2.0	1.5	-1.6	3.1	1.2	—	—

PER SHARE DATA

	1994	1993	1992	1991	1990	1989	1988	1987	1986	1985
Dividends, Net Income ($).	0.62	0.66	0.80	0.77	0.72	0.80	0.68	0.65	—	—
Distrib'ns, Cap Gain ($) ...	0.00	0.41	0.49	0.17	0.10	0.06	0.09	0.00	—	—
Net Asset Value ($)	9.63	10.61	10.39	10.77	10.10	10.08	9.98	9.75	—	—
Expense Ratio (%)	0.90	0.80	0.70	0.80	1.30	1.30	0.40	1.00	—	—
Net Income to Assets (%) .	5.90	6.00	7.70	7.50	7.20	7.60	6.90	6.60	—	—
Portfolio Turnover (%)	472	520	629	293	254	422	1,728	715	—	—
Total Assets (Millions $)....	276	234	82	52	41	35	25	11	—	—

PORTFOLIO (as of 6/30/94)

Portfolio Manager: Bradley C. Tank - 1990

Investm't Category: General Bond

Cap Gain	Asset Allocation
Cap & Income	Fund of Funds
✔ Income	Index
	Sector
✔ Domestic	Small Cap
✔ Foreign	Socially Conscious
Country/Region	State Specific

Portfolio: stocks 0%   bonds 93%
convertibles 0%   other 0%   cash 7%

Largest Holdings: mortgage-backed 58%,
U.S. government & agencies 19%

Unrealized Net Capital Gains: -3% of portfolio value

SHAREHOLDER INFORMATION

Minimum Investment
Initial: $1,000   Subsequent: $50

Minimum IRA Investment
Initial: $250   Subsequent: $50

Maximum Fees
Load: none   12b-1: none
Other: none

Distributions
Income: monthly   Capital Gains: Dec

Exchange Options
Number Per Year: 5   Fee: none
Telephone: yes (money market fund available)

Services
IRA, pension, auto exchange, auto invest, auto withdraw

Strong Growth (SGROX)

Growth

P.O. Box 2936
Milwaukee, WI 53201
(800) 368-1030, (414) 359-1400

PERFORMANCE

fund inception date: 12/31/93

	3yr Annual	5yr Annual	10yr Annual	Bull	Bear
Return (%)	na	na	na	na	0.0
Differ from Category (+/-)	na	na	na	na	6.6 high

Total Risk	Standard Deviation	Category Risk	Risk Index	Beta
na	na	na	na	na

	1994	1993	1992	1991	1990	1989	1988	1987	1986	1985
Return (%)	17.2	—	—	—	—	—	—	—	—	—
Differ from category (+/-) . .	17.8	—	—	—	—	—	—	—	—	—

PER SHARE DATA

	1994	1993	1992	1991	1990	1989	1988	1987	1986	1985
Dividends, Net Income ($) .	0.11	—	—	—	—	—	—	—	—	—
Distrib'ns, Cap Gain ($) . . .	0.00	—	—	—	—	—	—	—	—	—
Net Asset Value ($)	11.61	—	—	—	—	—	—	—	—	—
Expense Ratio (%)	1.60	—	—	—	—	—	—	—	—	—
Net Income to Assets (%) .	0.30	—	—	—	—	—	—	—	—	—
Portfolio Turnover (%)	628	—	—	—	—	—	—	—	—	—
Total Assets (Millions $)	106	—	—	—	—	—	—	—	—	—

PORTFOLIO (as of 6/30/94)

Portfolio Manager: Ronald C. Ognar - 1993

Investm't Category: Growth

✔ Cap Gain	Asset Allocation
Cap & Income	Fund of Funds
Income	Index
	Sector
✔ Domestic	Small Cap
Foreign	Socially Conscious
Country/Region	State Specific

Portfolio: stocks 69% bonds 0%
convertibles 3% other 0% cash 28%

Largest Holdings: banking 6%, consumer related products 5%

Unrealized Net Capital Gains: 0% of portfolio value

SHAREHOLDER INFORMATION

Minimum Investment
Initial: $1,000   Subsequent: $50

Minimum IRA Investment
Initial: $250   Subsequent: $50

Maximum Fees
Load: none   12b-1: none
Other: none

Distributions
Income: quarterly   Capital Gains: Dec

Exchange Options
Number Per Year: 5   Fee: none
Telephone: yes (money market fund available)

Services
IRA, pension, auto exchange, auto invest, auto withdraw

Strong High Yield Municipal Bond (SHYLX)

Tax-Exempt Bond

P.O. Box 2936
Milwaukee, WI 53201
(800) 368-1030, (414) 359-1400

PERFORMANCE

fund inception date: 10/1/93

	3yr Annual	5yr Annual	10yr Annual	Bull	Bear
Return (%)	na	na	na	na	-2.4
Differ from Category (+/-)	na	na	na	na	2.8 high

Total Risk	Standard Deviation	Category Risk	Risk Index	Avg Mat
na	na	na	na	20.0 yrs

	1994	1993	1992	1991	1990	1989	1988	1987	1986	1985
Return (%)	-1.0	—	—	—	—	—	—	—	—	—
Differ from category (+/-)	4.2	—	—	—	—	—	—	—	—	—

PER SHARE DATA

	1994	1993	1992	1991	1990	1989	1988	1987	1986	1985
Dividends, Net Income ($)	0.70	—	—	—	—	—	—	—	—	—
Distrib'ns, Cap Gain ($)	0.00	—	—	—	—	—	—	—	—	—
Net Asset Value ($)	9.29	—	—	—	—	—	—	—	—	—
Expense Ratio (%)	0.00	—	—	—	—	—	—	—	—	—
Net Income to Assets (%)	7.10	—	—	—	—	—	—	—	—	—
Portfolio Turnover (%)	253	—	—	—	—	—	—	—	—	—
Total Assets (Millions $)	107	—	—	—	—	—	—	—	—	—

PORTFOLIO (as of 6/30/94)

Portfolio Manager: Thomas J. Conlin - 1993, Mary Kay H. Bourbulas - 1993

Investm't Category: Tax-Exempt Bond

Cap Gain	Asset Allocation
Cap & Income	Fund of Funds
✔ Income	Index
	Sector
✔ Domestic	Small Cap
Foreign	Socially Conscious
Country/Region	State Specific

Portfolio: stocks 0% bonds 100%
convertibles 0% other 0% cash 0%

Largest Holdings: general obligation 2%

Unrealized Net Capital Gains: -2% of portfolio value

SHAREHOLDER INFORMATION

Minimum Investment
Initial: $2,500   Subsequent: $50

Minimum IRA Investment
Initial: na   Subsequent: na

Maximum Fees
Load: none   12b-1: none
Other: none

Distributions
Income: monthly   Capital Gains: Dec

Exchange Options
Number Per Year: 5   Fee: none
Telephone: yes (money market fund available)

Services
auto exchange, auto invest, auto withdraw

Strong Income (SRNCX)

General Bond

P.O. Box 2936
Milwaukee, WI 53201
(800) 368-1030, (414) 359-1400

	3yr Annual	5yr Annual	10yr Annual	Bull	Bear
Return (%)	8.0	6.2	na	48.8	-6.0
Differ from Category (+/-)	3.7 high	-0.7 low	na	7.8 abv av	-2.2 low

Total Risk	Standard Deviation	Category Risk	Risk Index	Avg Mat
low	4.8%	high	1.2	13.9 yrs

	1994	1993	1992	1991	1990	1989	1988	1987	1986	1985
Return (%)	-1.3	16.7	9.3	14.8	-6.2	0.3	12.4	4.3	29.9	—
Differ from category (+/-)	0.7	7.5	2.7	0.2	-13.4	-11.1	5.0	2.1	15.7	—

PER SHARE DATA

	1994	1993	1992	1991	1990	1989	1988	1987	1986	1985
Dividends, Net Income ($)	0.74	0.69	0.81	0.76	1.06	1.41	1.17	1.52	0.70	—
Distrib'ns, Cap Gain ($)	0.00	0.00	0.00	0.00	0.00	0.00	0.00	0.05	0.00	—
Net Asset Value ($)	9.36	10.24	9.40	9.37	8.87	10.57	11.88	11.64	12.65	—
Expense Ratio (%)	1.10	1.10	1.30	1.50	1.40	1.20	1.20	1.10	1.00	—
Net Income to Assets (%)	7.30	7.00	8.70	8.40	11.20	12.10	9.80	10.60	11.30	—
Portfolio Turnover (%)	559	666	557	392	294	207	400	245	204	—
Total Assets (Millions $)	123	123	103	92	92	195	203	138	118	—

PORTFOLIO (as of 6/30/94)

Portfolio Manager: Jeff Koch - 1992

Investm't Category: General Bond

Cap Gain	Asset Allocation
✔ Cap & Income	Fund of Funds
Income	Index
	Sector
✔ Domestic	Small Cap
✔ Foreign	Socially Conscious
Country/Region	State Specific

Portfolio: stocks 0%   bonds 98%
convertibles 0%   other 0%   cash 2%

Largest Holdings: corporate 80%, mortgage-backed securities 14%

Unrealized Net Capital Gains: -2% of portfolio value

SHAREHOLDER INFORMATION

Minimum Investment
Initial: $1,000   Subsequent: $50

Minimum IRA Investment
Initial: $250   Subsequent: $50

Maximum Fees
Load: none   12b-1: none
Other: none

Distributions
Income: monthly   Capital Gains: Dec

Exchange Options
Number Per Year: 5   Fee: none
Telephone: yes (money market fund available)

Services
IRA, pension, auto exchange, auto invest, auto withdraw

Strong Insured Muni Bond (STIMX)

P.O. Box 2936
Milwaukee, WI 53201
(800) 368-1030, (414) 359-1400

Tax-Exempt Bond

PERFORMANCE

fund inception date: 11/25/91

	3yr Annual	5yr Annual	10yr Annual	Bull	Bear
Return (%)	6.0	na	na	na	-7.1
Differ from Category (+/-)	1.5 high	na	na	na	-1.9 low

Total Risk	Standard Deviation	Category Risk	Risk Index	Avg Mat
av	7.1%	high	1.1	24.0 yrs

	1994	1993	1992	1991	1990	1989	1988	1987	1986	1985
Return (%)	-6.4	12.8	13.0	—	—	—	—	—	—	—
Differ from category (+/-)	-1.2	1.1	4.7	—	—	—	—	—	—	—

PER SHARE DATA

	1994	1993	1992	1991	1990	1989	1988	1987	1986	1985
Dividends, Net Income ($)	0.54	0.56	0.62	—	—	—	—	—	—	—
Distrib'ns, Cap Gain ($)	0.00	0.16	0.14	—	—	—	—	—	—	—
Net Asset Value ($)	10.19	11.46	10.82	—	—	—	—	—	—	—
Expense Ratio (%)	0.90	0.60	0.20	—	—	—	—	—	—	—
Net Income to Assets (%)	4.90	4.90	5.80	—	—	—	—	—	—	—
Portfolio Turnover (%)	366	110	290	—	—	—	—	—	—	—
Total Assets (Millions $)	51	61	21	—	—	—	—	—	—	—

PORTFOLIO (as of 6/30/94)

Portfolio Manager: Mary Kay Bourbulas - 1991, Tom Conlin - 1991

Investm't Category: Tax-Exempt Bond

Cap Gain	Asset Allocation
Cap & Income	Fund of Funds
✔ Income	Index
	Sector
✔ Domestic	Small Cap
Foreign	Socially Conscious
Country/Region	State Specific

Portfolio: stocks 0% bonds 86%
convertibles 0% other 0% cash 14%

Largest Holdings: general obligation 5%

Unrealized Net Capital Gains: -2% of portfolio value

SHAREHOLDER INFORMATION

Minimum Investment
Initial: $2,500   Subsequent: $50

Minimum IRA Investment
Initial: na   Subsequent: na

Maximum Fees
Load: none   12b-1: none
Other: none

Distributions
Income: monthly   Capital Gains: Dec

Exchange Options
Number Per Year: 5   Fee: none
Telephone: yes (money market fund available)

Services
auto exchange, auto invest, auto withdraw

Strong Int'l Stock (STISX)

International Stock

P.O. Box 2936
Milwaukee, WI 53201
(800) 368-1030, (414) 359-1400

fund inception date: 3/4/92

PERFORMANCE

	3yr Annual	5yr Annual	10yr Annual	Bull	Bear
Return (%)	na	na	na	na	-5.7
Differ from Category (+/-)	na	na	na	na	1.3 abv av

Total Risk	Standard Deviation	Category Risk	Risk Index	Beta
na	na	na	na	na

	1994	1993	1992	1991	1990	1989	1988	1987	1986	1985
Return (%)	-1.5	47.7	—	—	—	—	—	—	—	—
Differ from category (+/-)	1.5	9.1	—	—	—	—	—	—	—	—

PER SHARE DATA

	1994	1993	1992	1991	1990	1989	1988	1987	1986	1985
Dividends, Net Income ($)	0.27	0.02	—	—	—	—	—	—	—	—
Distrib'ns, Cap Gain ($)	1.04	0.23	—	—	—	—	—	—	—	—
Net Asset Value ($)	12.65	14.18	—	—	—	—	—	—	—	—
Expense Ratio (%)	1.60	1.90	—	—	—	—	—	—	—	—
Net Income to Assets (%)	0.10	-0.30	—	—	—	—	—	—	—	—
Portfolio Turnover (%)	162	140	—	—	—	—	—	—	—	—
Total Assets (Millions $)	257	151	—	—	—	—	—	—	—	—

PORTFOLIO (as of 6/30/94)

Portfolio Manager: Anthony Cragg - 1993

Investm't Category: International Stock

✔ Cap Gain	Asset Allocation
Cap & Income	Fund of Funds
Income	Index
	Sector
Domestic	Small Cap
✔ Foreign	Socially Conscious
Country/Region	State Specific

Portfolio: stocks 91% bonds 0%
convertibles 0% other 0% cash 9%

Largest Holdings: Japan 22%, Australia 12%

Unrealized Net Capital Gains: -1% of portfolio value

SHAREHOLDER INFORMATION

Minimum Investment
Initial: $1,000   Subsequent: $50

Minimum IRA Investment
Initial: $250   Subsequent: $50

Maximum Fees
Load: none   12b-1: none
Other: none

Distributions
Income: quarterly   Capital Gains: Dec

Exchange Options
Number Per Year: 5   Fee: none
Telephone: yes (money market fund available)

Services
IRA, pension, auto exchange, auto invest, auto withdraw

Strong Muni Bond (SXFIX)

Tax-Exempt Bond

P.O. Box 2936
Milwaukee, WI 53201
(800) 368-1030, (414) 359-1400

fund inception date: 10/28/86

PERFORMANCE

	3yr Annual	5yr Annual	10yr Annual	Bull	Bear
Return (%)	6.1	7.2	na	49.6	-5.3
Differ from Category (+/-)	1.6 high	1.1 high	na	7.8 high	-0.1 av

Total Risk	Standard Deviation	Category Risk	Risk Index	Avg Mat
blw av	5.9%	av	0.9	22.6 yrs

	1994	1993	1992	1991	1990	1989	1988	1987	1986	1985
Return (%)	-4.5	11.7	12.1	13.3	4.6	7.0	7.5	-1.7	—	—
Differ from category (+/-)	0.7	0.0	3.8	2.0	-1.7	-2.0	-2.7	-0.4	—	—

PER SHARE DATA

	1994	1993	1992	1991	1990	1989	1988	1987	1986	1985
Dividends, Net Income ($)	0.56	0.58	0.65	0.65	0.67	0.53	0.49	0.67	—	—
Distrib'ns, Cap Gain ($)	0.00	0.31	0.26	0.00	0.00	0.00	0.00	0.00	—	—
Net Asset Value ($)	9.23	10.25	10.00	9.76	9.22	9.47	9.35	9.16	—	—
Expense Ratio (%)	0.80	0.70	0.10	0.10	0.30	1.70	1.30	1.00	—	—
Net Income to Assets (%)	5.70	5.60	6.40	6.90	7.20	5.60	5.30	7.00	—	—
Portfolio Turnover (%)	271	156	324	465	586	243	344	284	—	—
Total Assets (Millions $)	279	402	290	115	32	19	18	19	—	—

PORTFOLIO (as of 6/30/94)

Portfolio Manager: Conlin - 1991, Bourbulas - 1991

Investm't Category: Tax-Exempt Bond

Cap Gain	Asset Allocation
Cap & Income	Fund of Funds
✔ Income	Index
	Sector
✔ Domestic	Small Cap
Foreign	Socially Conscious
Country/Region	State Specific

Portfolio: stocks 0% bonds 99%
convertibles 0% other 0% cash 1%

Largest Holdings: general obligation 5%

Unrealized Net Capital Gains: -1% of portfolio value

SHAREHOLDER INFORMATION

Minimum Investment
Initial: $2,500   Subsequent: $50

Minimum IRA Investment
Initial: na   Subsequent: na

Maximum Fees
Load: none   12b-1: none
Other: none

Distributions
Income: monthly   Capital Gains: Dec

Exchange Options
Number Per Year: 5   Fee: none
Telephone: yes (money market fund available)

Services
auto exchange, auto invest, auto withdraw

Strong Opportunity

(SOPFX)

Growth

P.O. Box 2936
Milwaukee, WI 53201
(800) 368-1030, (414) 359-1400

PERFORMANCE

fund inception date: 12/31/85

	3yr Annual	5yr Annual	10yr Annual	Bull	Bear
Return (%)	13.6	11.3	na	98.4	-2.9
Differ from Category (+/-)	5.9 high	1.7 abv av	na	6.3 abv av	3.7 high

Total Risk	Standard Deviation	Category Risk	Risk Index	Beta
abv av	9.5%	av	1.0	1.0

	1994	1993	1992	1991	1990	1989	1988	1987	1986	1985
Return (%)	3.1	21.1	17.3	31.6	-11.3	18.5	16.4	11.8	59.9	—
Differ from category (+/-). . .	3.7	7.7	5.7	-4.1	-5.6	-7.6	-1.6	10.0	45.3	—

PER SHARE DATA

	1994	1993	1992	1991	1990	1989	1988	1987	1986	1985
Dividends, Net Income ($) .	0.13	0.06	0.06	0.19	0.74	0.68	1.37	0.24	0.00	—
Distrib'ns, Cap Gain ($) . . .	1.28	1.57	0.16	0.00	0.04	0.16	0.18	1.80	0.00	—
Net Asset Value ($)	27.71	28.23	24.70	21.24	16.29	19.21	16.90	15.87	15.99	—
Expense Ratio (%)	1.40	1.40	1.50	1.70	1.70	1.60	1.60	1.50	1.70	—
Net Income to Assets (%) .	0.40	0.20	0.30	1.10	3.30	4.30	7.40	1.70	0.70	—
Portfolio Turnover (%).	65	109	139	271	275	306	352	371	170	—
Total Assets (Millions $). . . .	805	469	193	160	132	205	157	154	43	—

PORTFOLIO (as of 6/30/94)

Portfolio Manager: Richard T. Weiss - 1991, Marina Carlson - 1993

Investm't Category: Growth

✔ Cap Gain	Asset Allocation
Cap & Income	Fund of Funds
Income	Index
	Sector
✔ Domestic	Small Cap
✔ Foreign	Socially Conscious
Country/Region	State Specific

Portfolio: stocks 86% bonds 0%
convertibles 1% other 0% cash 13%

Largest Holdings: retail 9%, telecommunications 6%

Unrealized Net Capital Gains: 8% of portfolio value

SHAREHOLDER INFORMATION

Minimum Investment
Initial: $1,000   Subsequent: $50

Minimum IRA Investment
Initial: $250   Subsequent: $50

Maximum Fees
Load: none   12b-1: none
Other: none

Distributions
Income: quarterly   Capital Gains: Dec

Exchange Options
Number Per Year: 5   Fee: none
Telephone: yes (money market fund available)

Services
IRA, pension, auto exchange, auto invest, auto withdraw

Strong Short-Term Bond
(SSTBX)
General Bond

P.O. Box 2936
Milwaukee, WI 53201
(800) 368-1030, (414) 359-1400

	3yr Annual	5yr Annual	10yr Annual	Bull	Bear
Return (%)	4.6	6.7	na	38.7	-2.9
Differ from Category (+/-)	0.3 abv av	-0.2 blw av	na	-2.3 av	0.9 abv av

Total Risk	Standard Deviation	Category Risk	Risk Index	Avg Mat
low	2.4%	blw av	0.6	2.3 yrs

	1994	1993	1992	1991	1990	1989	1988	1987	1986	1985
Return (%)	-1.6	9.3	6.6	14.6	5.2	8.2	10.1	—	—	—
Differ from category (+/-) . . .	0.4	0.1	0.0	0.0	-2.0	-3.2	2.7	—	—	—

PER SHARE DATA

	1994	1993	1992	1991	1990	1989	1988	1987	1986	1985
Dividends, Net Income ($).	0.65	0.67	0.78	0.75	0.81	1.01	0.86	—	—	—
Distrib'ns, Cap Gain ($) . . .	0.00	0.00	0.00	0.00	0.00	0.03	0.07	—	—	—
Net Asset Value ($)	9.42	10.23	9.99	10.12	9.53	9.86	10.09	—	—	—
Expense Ratio (%)	0.90	0.80	0.60	1.00	1.30	1.10	1.00	—	—	—
Net Income to Assets (%) .	6.30	6.30	7.30	7.80	8.60	9.70	8.50	—	—	—
Portfolio Turnover (%)	311	445	353	398	314	177	461	—	—	—
Total Assets (Millions $) . .	1,041	1,569	757	165	80	130	102	—	—	—

PORTFOLIO (as of 6/30/94)

Portfolio Manager: Bradley C. Tank - 1990

Investm't Category: General Bond

Cap Gain	Asset Allocation
Cap & Income	Fund of Funds
✔ Income	Index
	Sector
✔ Domestic	Small Cap
✔ Foreign	Socially Conscious
Country/Region	State Specific

Portfolio: stocks 0%   bonds 95%
convertibles 1%   other 0%   cash 4%

Largest Holdings: corporate 45%, mortgage-backed 43%

Unrealized Net Capital Gains: -3% of portfolio value

SHAREHOLDER INFORMATION

Minimum Investment
Initial: $1,000   Subsequent: $50

Minimum IRA Investment
Initial: $250   Subsequent: $50

Maximum Fees
Load: none   12b-1: none
Other: none

Distributions
Income: monthly   Capital Gains: Dec

Exchange Options
Number Per Year: 5   Fee: none
Telephone: yes (money market fund available)

Services
IRA, pension, auto exchange, auto invest, auto withdraw

Strong Short-Term Muni Bond (STSMX)

P.O. Box 2936
Milwaukee, WI 53201
(800) 368-1030, (414) 359-1400

Tax-Exempt Bond

PERFORMANCE

fund inception date: 12/31/91

	3yr Annual	5yr Annual	10yr Annual	Bull	Bear
Return (%)	4.0	na	na	na	-1.7
Differ from Category (+/-)	-0.5 blw av	na	na	na	3.5 high

Total Risk	Standard Deviation	Category Risk	Risk Index	Avg Mat
low	2.6%	low	0.4	2.5 yrs

	1994	1993	1992	1991	1990	1989	1988	1987	1986	1985
Return (%)	-1.6	6.7	7.1	—	—	—	—	—	—	—
Differ from category (+/-)	3.6	-5.0	-1.2	—	—	—	—	—	—	—

PER SHARE DATA

	1994	1993	1992	1991	1990	1989	1988	1987	1986	1985
Dividends, Net Income ($)	0.45	0.44	0.48	—	—	—	—	—	—	—
Distrib'ns, Cap Gain ($)	0.01	0.07	0.02	—	—	—	—	—	—	—
Net Asset Value ($)	9.73	10.36	10.20	—	—	—	—	—	—	—
Expense Ratio (%)	0.70	0.60	0.20	—	—	—	—	—	—	—
Net Income to Assets (%)	4.10	4.20	4.90	—	—	—	—	—	—	—
Portfolio Turnover (%)	319	141	140	—	—	—	—	—	—	—
Total Assets (Millions $)	161	217	111	—	—	—	—	—	—	—

PORTFOLIO (as of 6/30/94)

Portfolio Manager: G. Nolan Smith - 1992

Investm't Category: Tax-Exempt Bond

Cap Gain	Asset Allocation
Cap & Income	Fund of Funds
✔ Income	Index
	Sector
✔ Domestic	Small Cap
Foreign	Socially Conscious
Country/Region	State Specific

Portfolio: stocks 0% bonds 96%
convertibles 0% other 0% cash 4%

Largest Holdings: general obligation 18%

Unrealized Net Capital Gains: -1% of portfolio value

SHAREHOLDER INFORMATION

Minimum Investment
Initial: $2,500   Subsequent: $50

Minimum IRA Investment
Initial: na   Subsequent: na

Maximum Fees
Load: none   12b-1: none
Other: none

Distributions
Income: monthly   Capital Gains: Dec

Exchange Options
Number Per Year: 5   Fee: none
Telephone: yes (money market fund available)

Services
auto exchange, auto invest, auto withdraw

Strong Total Return

(STRFX)

Growth & Income

P.O. Box 2936
Milwaukee, WI 53201
(800) 368-1030, (414) 359-1400

PERFORMANCE   fund inception date: 12/30/81

	3yr Annual	5yr Annual	10yr Annual	Bull	Bear
Return (%)	6.7	8.5	11.0	73.3	-8.9
Differ from Category (+/-)	-0.4 av	0.6 av	-0.7 blw av	-2.5 av	-2.6 low

Total Risk	Standard Deviation	Category Risk	Risk Index	Beta
abv av	9.4%	high	1.1	0.9

	1994	1993	1992	1991	1990	1989	1988	1987	1986	1985
Return (%).............	-1.3	22.5	0.5	33.5	-7.1	2.5	15.5	6.0	19.9	25.3
Differ from category (+/-)...	0.1	9.3	-9.7	5.9	-1.1	-18.9	-1.5	5.4	4.1	-0.4

PER SHARE DATA

	1994	1993	1992	1991	1990	1989	1988	1987	1986	1985
Dividends, Net Income ($).	0.34	0.33	0.17	0.22	1.14	1.32	2.21	1.65	0.70	0.58
Distrib'ns, Cap Gain ($) ...	0.00	0.05	0.00	0.00	0.00	0.51	0.00	3.17	1.04	0.20
Net Asset Value ($)	23.62	24.30	20.17	20.24	15.34	17.72	18.96	18.37	21.61	19.56
Expense Ratio (%)	1.20	1.20	1.30	1.40	1.40	1.20	1.20	1.10	1.10	1.10
Net Income to Assets (%) .	1.30	1.40	0.90	1.30	5.40	7.70	10.10	5.20	4.30	5.00
Portfolio Turnover (%)	250	271	372	426	312	305	281	224	153	304
Total Assets (Millions $)....	606	628	588	691	646	1,066	1,005	802	518	233

PORTFOLIO (as of 6/30/94)

Portfolio Manager: Ronald C. Ognar - 1993, Ian Rogers - 1994

Investm't Category: Growth & Income
- Cap Gain
- ✔ Cap & Income
- Income
- ✔ Domestic
- ✔ Foreign
- Country/Region
- Asset Allocation
- Fund of Funds
- Index
- Sector
- Small Cap
- Socially Conscious
- State Specific

Portfolio: stocks 72% bonds 4% convertibles 4% other 1% cash 19%

Largest Holdings: chemicals 8%, office equipment 6%

Unrealized Net Capital Gains: 2% of portfolio value

SHAREHOLDER INFORMATION

Minimum Investment
Initial: $250   Subsequent: $50

Minimum IRA Investment
Initial: $250   Subsequent: $50

Maximum Fees
Load: none   12b-1: none
Other: none

Distributions
Income: quarterly   Capital Gains: Dec

Exchange Options
Number Per Year: 5   Fee: none
Telephone: yes (money market fund available)

Services
IRA, pension, auto exchange, auto invest, auto withdraw

Tocqueville (TOCQX)
Growth

1675 Broadway
16th Floor
New York, NY 10019
(800) 697-3863, (212) 698-0800

PERFORMANCE
fund inception date: 1/13/87

	3yr Annual	5yr Annual	10yr Annual	Bull	Bear
Return (%)	12.4	10.1	na	76.2	-2.2
Differ from Category (+/-)	4.7 high	0.5 abv av	na	-15.9 blw av	4.4 high

Total Risk	Standard Deviation	Category Risk	Risk Index	Beta
av	7.9%	low	0.8	0.8

	1994	1993	1992	1991	1990	1989	1988	1987	1986	1985
Return (%)	-0.7	22.5	16.9	12.4	1.4	17.5	20.4	—	—	—
Differ from category (+/-) . . .	-0.1	9.1	5.3	-23.3	7.1	-8.6	2.4	—	—	—

PER SHARE DATA

	1994	1993	1992	1991	1990	1989	1988	1987	1986	1985
Dividends, Net Income ($) .	0.11	0.14	0.16	0.36	0.51	0.37	0.06	—	—	—
Distrib'ns, Cap Gain ($) . . .	1.41	0.79	0.66	0.64	0.11	0.41	0.22	—	—	—
Net Asset Value ($)	11.59	13.23	11.57	10.59	10.37	10.84	9.89	—	—	—
Expense Ratio (%)	1.53	1.58	1.74	1.96	1.61	1.70	2.09	—	—	—
Net Income to Assets (%) .	0.73	0.96	1.44	3.38	4.71	2.86	0.85	—	—	—
Portfolio Turnover (%).	49	64	89	97	125	34	65	—	—	—
Total Assets (Millions $). . . .	28	29	19	17	13	17	15	—	—	—

PORTFOLIO (as of 4/30/94)

Portfolio Manager: Francois Sicart - 1987, Robert Kleinschmidt - 1991

Investm't Category: Growth

✔ Cap Gain	Asset Allocation
Cap & Income	Fund of Funds
Income	Index
	Sector
✔ Domestic	Small Cap
Foreign	Socially Conscious
Country/Region	State Specific

Portfolio: stocks 82% bonds 10%
convertibles 0% other 2% cash 6%

Largest Holdings: survivors in depressed indus/regions 17%, revitalized behemoths 16%

Unrealized Net Capital Gains: 11% of portfolio value

SHAREHOLDER INFORMATION

Minimum Investment
Initial: $5,000   Subsequent: $1,000

Minimum IRA Investment
Initial: $2,000   Subsequent: $1,000

Maximum Fees
Load: none   12b-1: 0.25%
Other: none

Distributions
Income: na   Capital Gains: na

Exchange Options
Number Per Year: no limit   Fee: none
Telephone: yes (money market fund not available)

Services
IRA, pension

T Rowe Price Adjustable Rate US Gov't (PRARX)

Mortgage-Backed Bond

P.O. Box 89000
Baltimore, MD 21289
(800) 638-5660, (410) 547-2308

PERFORMANCE

fund inception date: 9/30/91

	3yr Annual	5yr Annual	10yr Annual	Bull	Bear
Return (%)	1.9	na	na	na	-1.0
Differ from Category (+/-)	-1.2 low	na	na	na	3.4 high

Total Risk	Standard Deviation	Category Risk	Risk Index	Avg Mat
low	1.2%	low	0.3	0.7 yrs

	1994	1993	1992	1991	1990	1989	1988	1987	1986	1985
Return (%)	-0.6	2.7	3.9	—	—	—	—	—	—	—
Differ from category (+/-)	2.2	-4.1	-2.2	—	—	—	—	—	—	—

PER SHARE DATA

	1994	1993	1992	1991	1990	1989	1988	1987	1986	1985
Dividends, Net Income ($)	0.23	0.23	0.32	—	—	—	—	—	—	—
Distrib'ns, Cap Gain ($)	0.00	0.00	0.00	—	—	—	—	—	—	—
Net Asset Value ($)	4.51	4.77	4.87	—	—	—	—	—	—	—
Expense Ratio (%)	0.55	0.25	0.00	—	—	—	—	—	—	—
Net Income to Assets (%)	5.12	5.96	7.45	—	—	—	—	—	—	—
Portfolio Turnover (%)	2	110	98	—	—	—	—	—	—	—
Total Assets (Millions $)	120	250	343	—	—	—	—	—	—	—

PORTFOLIO (as of 11/30/94)

Portfolio Manager: Heather Landon - 1993

Investm't Category: Mortgage-Backed Bond

Cap Gain	Asset Allocation
Cap & Income	Fund of Funds
✔ Income	Index
	Sector
✔ Domestic	Small Cap
Foreign	Socially Conscious
Country/Region	State Specific

Portfolio:	stocks 0%	bonds 95%
convertibles 0%	other 0%	cash 5%

Largest Holdings: mortgage-backed 95%

Unrealized Net Capital Gains: -4% of portfolio value

SHAREHOLDER INFORMATION

Minimum Investment
Initial: $2,500   Subsequent: $100

Minimum IRA Investment
Initial: $1,000   Subsequent: $50

Maximum Fees
Load: none   12b-1: none
Other: none

Distributions
Income: monthly   Capital Gains: Jan, Mar

Exchange Options
Number Per Year: 6   Fee: none
Telephone: yes (money market fund available)

Services
IRA, pension, auto exchange, auto invest, auto withdraw

T Rowe Price Balanced

(RPBAX)

Balanced

P.O. Box 89000
Baltimore, MD 21289
(800) 638-5660, (410) 547-2308

PERFORMANCE

fund inception date: 12/31/39

	3yr Annual	5yr Annual	10yr Annual	Bull	Bear
Return (%)	6.1	9.3	12.5	63.9	-6.6
Differ from Category (+/-)	-0.3 av	1.3 abv av	1.2 abv av	-1.1 av	-0.9 blw av

Total Risk	Standard Deviation	Category Risk	Risk Index	Beta
blw av	6.1%	av	1.0	0.7

	1994	1993	1992	1991	1990	1989	1988	1987	1986	1985
Return (%)	-2.0	13.3	7.7	21.9	7.2	20.6	8.9	-3.3	23.2	32.9
Differ from category (+/-)	-0.1	-0.1	-0.6	-1.5	7.7	3.3	-2.9	-5.7	5.8	8.6

PER SHARE DATA

	1994	1993	1992	1991	1990	1989	1988	1987	1986	1985
Dividends, Net Income ($)	0.43	0.39	0.51	0.61	0.66	0.68	0.48	0.78	0.76	0.76
Distrib'ns, Cap Gain ($)	0.20	0.11	0.67	0.57	0.00	0.00	0.00	2.84	3.21	0.00
Net Asset Value ($)	11.14	12.02	11.07	11.42	10.37	10.32	9.15	8.85	12.81	13.80
Expense Ratio (%)	1.00	1.00	1.03	1.10	0.94	1.15	1.25	1.18	0.98	0.74
Net Income to Assets (%)	3.67	3.45	4.07	5.61	6.82	6.27	5.19	3.81	5.76	6.93
Portfolio Turnover (%)	45	8	208	240	127	219	251	324	239	97
Total Assets (Millions $)	392	340	239	175	157	167	164	196	180	152

PORTFOLIO (as of 6/30/94)

Portfolio Manager: Richard Whitney - 1991

Investm't Category: Balanced

Cap Gain	Asset Allocation
✔ Cap & Income	Fund of Funds
Income	Index
	Sector
✔ Domestic	Small Cap
✔ Foreign	Socially Conscious
Country/Region	State Specific

Portfolio: stocks 61%   bonds 38%
convertibles 0%   other 0%   cash 1%

Largest Holdings: bonds—corporate & foreign 19%, stocks—telephone 4%

Unrealized Net Capital Gains: 2% of portfolio value

SHAREHOLDER INFORMATION

Minimum Investment
Initial: $2,500   Subsequent: $100

Minimum IRA Investment
Initial: $1,000   Subsequent: $50

Maximum Fees
Load: none   12b-1: none
Other: none

Distributions
Income: quarterly   Capital Gains: Dec

Exchange Options
Number Per Year: 6   Fee: none
Telephone: yes (money market fund available)

Services
IRA, pension, auto exchange, auto invest, auto withdraw

T. Rowe Price Blue Chip Growth (TRBCX)

P.O. Box 89000
Baltimore, MD 21289
(800) 638-5660, (410) 547-2308

Growth & Income

PERFORMANCE

fund inception date: 6/30/93

	3yr Annual	5yr Annual	10yr Annual	Bull	Bear
Return (%)	na	na	na	na	-5.6
Differ from Category (+/-)	na	na	na	na	0.7 abv av

Total Risk	Standard Deviation	Category Risk	Risk Index	Beta
na	na	na	na	na

	1994	1993	1992	1991	1990	1989	1988	1987	1986	1985
Return (%)	0.8	—	—	—	—	—	—	—	—	—
Differ from category (+/-)	2.2	—	—	—	—	—	—	—	—	—

PER SHARE DATA

	1994	1993	1992	1991	1990	1989	1988	1987	1986	1985
Dividends, Net Income ($)	0.11	—	—	—	—	—	—	—	—	—
Distrib'ns, Cap Gain ($)	0.11	—	—	—	—	—	—	—	—	—
Net Asset Value ($)	11.11	—	—	—	—	—	—	—	—	—
Expense Ratio (%)	1.25	—	—	—	—	—	—	—	—	—
Net Income to Assets (%)	0.96	—	—	—	—	—	—	—	—	—
Portfolio Turnover (%)	75	—	—	—	—	—	—	—	—	—
Total Assets (Millions $)	38	—	—	—	—	—	—	—	—	—

PORTFOLIO (as of 6/30/94)

Portfolio Manager: Thomas H. Broadus Jr. - 1993

Investm't Category: Growth & Income

Cap Gain	Asset Allocation
✔ Cap & Income	Fund of Funds
Income	Index
	Sector
✔ Domestic	Small Cap
✔ Foreign	Socially Conscious
Country/Region	State Specific

Portfolio: stocks 85% bonds 0%
convertibles 0% other 0% cash 15%

Largest Holdings: bank & trust 95, miscellaneous consumer products 7%

Unrealized Net Capital Gains: -1% of portfolio value

SHAREHOLDER INFORMATION

Minimum Investment
Initial: $2,500   Subsequent: $100

Minimum IRA Investment
Initial: $1,000   Subsequent: $50

Maximum Fees
Load: none   12b-1: none
Other: none

Distributions
Income: Dec   Capital Gains: Dec

Exchange Options
Number Per Year: no limit   Fee: none
Telephone: yes (money market fund available)

Services
IRA, pension, auto exchange, auto invest, auto withdraw

T Rowe Price CA Tax-Free Bond (PRXCX)

P.O. Box 89000
Baltimore, MD 21289
(800) 638-5660, (410) 547-2308

Tax-Exempt Bond

PERFORMANCE

fund inception date: 9/15/86

	3yr Annual	5yr Annual	10yr Annual	Bull	Bear
Return (%)	4.9	6.5	na	45.3	-6.1
Differ from Category (+/-)	0.4 abv av	0.4 av	na	3.5 abv av	-0.9 blw av

Total Risk	Standard Deviation	Category Risk	Risk Index	Avg Mat
blw av	5.9%	av	0.9	17.0 yrs

	1994	1993	1992	1991	1990	1989	1988	1987	1986	1985
Return (%)	-5.7	12.4	8.9	12.1	5.8	8.4	9.5	-6.8	—	—
Differ from category (+/-)	-0.5	0.7	0.6	0.8	-0.5	-0.6	-0.7	-5.5	—	—

PER SHARE DATA

	1994	1993	1992	1991	1990	1989	1988	1987	1986	1985
Dividends, Net Income ($)	0.54	0.56	0.58	0.59	0.59	0.59	0.57	0.57	—	—
Distrib'ns, Cap Gain ($)	0.02	0.23	0.00	0.00	0.00	0.00	0.00	0.00	—	—
Net Asset Value ($)	9.51	10.68	10.22	9.94	9.42	9.48	9.30	9.03	—	—
Expense Ratio (%)	0.60	0.60	0.60	0.73	0.93	1.00	1.00	0.85	—	—
Net Income to Assets (%)	5.41	5.69	6.07	6.29	6.25	6.23	6.19	6.10	—	—
Portfolio Turnover (%)	90	57	80	193	88	77	152	88	—	—
Total Assets (Millions $)	122	154	108	84	65	43	36	44	—	—

PORTFOLIO (as of 8/31/94)

Portfolio Manager: Mary J. Miller - 1990

Investm't Category: Tax-Exempt Bond

Cap Gain	Asset Allocation
Cap & Income	Fund of Funds
✔ Income	Index
	Sector
✔ Domestic	Small Cap
Foreign	Socially Conscious
Country/Region	✔ State Specific

Portfolio: stocks 0% bonds 100%
convertibles 0% other 0% cash 0%

Largest Holdings: general obligation 5%

Unrealized Net Capital Gains: 2% of portfolio value

SHAREHOLDER INFORMATION

Minimum Investment
Initial: $2,500   Subsequent: $100

Minimum IRA Investment
Initial: na   Subsequent: na

Maximum Fees
Load: none   12b-1: none
Other: none

Distributions
Income: monthly   Capital Gains: Jan, Mar

Exchange Options
Number Per Year: 6   Fee: none
Telephone: yes (money market fund available)

Services
auto exchange, auto invest, auto withdraw

T Rowe Price Capital Appreciation (PRWCX)

Growth

P.O. Box 89000
Baltimore, MD 21289
(800) 638-5660, (410) 547-2308

PERFORMANCE

fund inception date: 6/30/86

	3yr Annual	5yr Annual	10yr Annual	Bull	Bear
Return (%)	9.4	9.5	na	70.0	-3.1
Differ from Category (+/-)	1.7 abv av	-0.1 av	na	-22.1 blw av	3.5 high

Total Risk	Standard Deviation	Category Risk	Risk Index	Beta
blw av	5.0%	low	0.5	0.5

	1994	1993	1992	1991	1990	1989	1988	1987	1986	1985
Return (%)	3.7	15.6	9.3	21.5	-1.2	21.4	21.1	5.8	—	—
Differ from category (+/-)	4.3	2.2	-2.3	-14.2	4.5	-4.7	3.1	4.0	—	—

PER SHARE DATA

	1994	1993	1992	1991	1990	1989	1988	1987	1986	1985
Dividends, Net Income ($)	0.35	0.18	0.50	0.43	0.39	0.45	0.28	0.48	—	—
Distrib'ns, Cap Gain ($)	0.69	0.33	0.16	0.64	0.31	1.36	0.37	1.85	—	—
Net Asset Value ($)	12.10	12.66	11.39	11.02	9.98	10.82	10.42	9.15	—	—
Expense Ratio (%)	1.11	1.09	1.08	1.20	1.25	1.50	1.50	1.20	—	—
Net Income to Assets (%)	2.63	2.37	4.28	3.90	3.44	3.85	2.76	3.03	—	—
Portfolio Turnover (%)	50	39	30	51	50	99	166	291	—	—
Total Assets (Millions $)	654	534	359	216	142	133	101	64	—	—

PORTFOLIO (as of 6/30/94)

Portfolio Manager: Richard Howard - 1989

Investm't Category: Growth

- ✔ Cap Gain
- Cap & Income
- Income
- Asset Allocation
- Fund of Funds
- Index
- Sector
- ✔ Domestic
- ✔ Foreign
- Country/Region
- Small Cap
- Socially Conscious
- State Specific

Portfolio: stocks 52% bonds 5%
convertibles 16% other 3% cash 24%

Largest Holdings: integrated petroleum 6%, insurance 5%

Unrealized Net Capital Gains: 4% of portfolio value

SHAREHOLDER INFORMATION

Minimum Investment
Initial: $2,500 Subsequent: $100

Minimum IRA Investment
Initial: $1,000 Subsequent: $50

Maximum Fees
Load: none 12b-1: none
Other: none

Distributions
Income: Dec Capital Gains: Dec

Exchange Options
Number Per Year: 6 Fee: none
Telephone: yes (money market fund available)

Services
IRA, pension, auto exchange, auto invest, auto withdraw

T Rowe Price Dividend Growth (PRDGX)

Growth & Income

P.O. Box 89000
Baltimore, MD 21289
(800) 638-5660, (410) 547-2308

PERFORMANCE

fund inception date: 12/31/92

	3yr Annual	5yr Annual	10yr Annual	Bull	Bear
Return (%)	na	na	na	na	-4.3
Differ from Category (+/-)	na	na	na	na	2.0 abv av

Total Risk	Standard Deviation	Category Risk	Risk Index	Beta
na	na	na	na	na

	1994	1993	1992	1991	1990	1989	1988	1987	1986	1985
Return (%)	2.1	19.4	—	—	—	—	—	—	—	—
Differ from category (+/-)	3.5	6.2	—	—	—	—	—	—	—	—

PER SHARE DATA

	1994	1993	1992	1991	1990	1989	1988	1987	1986	1985
Dividends, Net Income ($)	0.34	0.29	—	—	—	—	—	—	—	—
Distrib'ns, Cap Gain ($)	0.34	0.15	—	—	—	—	—	—	—	—
Net Asset Value ($)	11.04	11.48	—	—	—	—	—	—	—	—
Expense Ratio (%)	1.00	1.00	—	—	—	—	—	—	—	—
Net Income to Assets (%)	2.85	2.60	—	—	—	—	—	—	—	—
Portfolio Turnover (%)	78	51	—	—	—	—	—	—	—	—
Total Assets (Millions $)	53	40	—	—	—	—	—	—	—	—

PORTFOLIO (as of 6/30/94)

Portfolio Manager: William Stromborg - 1992

Investm't Category: Growth & Income
Cap Gain	Asset Allocation
✔ Cap & Income	Fund of Funds
Income	Index
	Sector
✔ Domestic	Small Cap
✔ Foreign	Socially Conscious
Country/Region	State Specific

Portfolio: stocks 76%   bonds 5%
convertibles 4%   other 1%   cash 14%

Largest Holdings: miscellaneous consumer products 6%, pharmaceuticals 6%

Unrealized Net Capital Gains: 0% of portfolio value

SHAREHOLDER INFORMATION

Minimum Investment
Initial: $2,500   Subsequent: $100

Minimum IRA Investment
Initial: $1,000   Subsequent: $50

Maximum Fees
Load: none   12b-1: none
Other: none

Distributions
Income: quarterly   Capital Gains: Dec

Exchange Options
Number Per Year: 6   Fee: none
Telephone: yes (money market fund available)

Services
IRA, pension, auto exchange, auto invest, auto withdraw

T Rowe Price Equity Income (PRFDX)

Growth & Income

P.O. Box 89000
Baltimore, MD 21289
(800) 638-5660, (410) 547-2308

PERFORMANCE

fund inception date: 10/31/85

	3yr Annual	5yr Annual	10yr Annual	Bull	Bear
Return (%)	11.0	9.8	na	83.8	-3.7
Differ from Category (+/-)	3.9 high	1.9 high	na	8.0 abv av	2.6 high

Total Risk	Standard Deviation	Category Risk	Risk Index	Beta
blw av	6.7%	low	0.8	0.8

	1994	1993	1992	1991	1990	1989	1988	1987	1986	1985
Return (%)..............	4.5	14.8	14.1	25.2	-6.7	13.6	27.6	3.5	26.6	—
Differ from category (+/-)...	5.9	1.6	3.9	-2.4	-0.7	-7.8	10.6	2.9	10.8	—

PER SHARE DATA

	1994	1993	1992	1991	1990	1989	1988	1987	1986	1985
Dividends, Net Income ($).	0.59	0.54	0.63	0.61	0.65	0.76	0.62	0.82	0.65	—
Distrib'ns, Cap Gain ($) ...	0.81	0.72	0.39	0.10	0.19	0.39	0.38	1.35	0.26	—
Net Asset Value ($)	15.98	16.65	15.63	14.62	12.27	14.06	13.39	11.29	12.96	—
Expense Ratio (%)	0.91	0.91	0.97	1.05	1.13	1.11	1.30	1.10	1.00	—
Net Income to Assets (%) .	3.49	3.23	3.95	4.44	5.09	5.31	4.83	4.58	5.16	—
Portfolio Turnover (%)	38	31	30	34	24	34	36	80	72	—
Total Assets (Millions $)..	3,203	2,800	2,092	1,335	862	968	501	185	93	—

PORTFOLIO (as of 6/30/94)

Portfolio Manager: Brian C. Rogers - 1989

Investm't Category: Growth & Income
- Cap Gain
- ✔ Cap & Income
- Income
- ✔ Domestic
- ✔ Foreign
- Country/Region
- Asset Allocation
- Fund of Funds
- Index
- Sector
- Small Cap
- Socially Conscious
- State Specific

Portfolio: stocks 79% bonds 6%
convertibles 5% other 0% cash 10%

Largest Holdings: pharmaceuticals 10%, bank & trust 6%

Unrealized Net Capital Gains: 5% of portfolio value

SHAREHOLDER INFORMATION

Minimum Investment
Initial: $2,500   Subsequent: $100

Minimum IRA Investment
Initial: $1,000   Subsequent: $50

Maximum Fees
Load: none   12b-1: none
Other: none

Distributions
Income: quarterly   Capital Gains: Mar, Dec

Exchange Options
Number Per Year: 6   Fee: none
Telephone: yes (money market fund available)

Services
IRA, pension, auto exchange, auto invest, auto withdraw

T. Rowe Price Equity Index (PREIX)

Growth & Income

P.O. Box 89000
Baltimore, MD 21289
(800) 638-5660, (410) 547-2308

PERFORMANCE

fund inception date: 3/30/90

	3yr Annual	5yr Annual	10yr Annual	Bull	Bear
Return (%)	5.8	na	na	69.5	-6.7
Differ from Category (+/-)	-1.3 blw av	na	na	-6.3 blw av	-0.4 av

Total Risk	Standard Deviation	Category Risk	Risk Index	Beta
av	7.8%	blw av	0.9	1.0

	1994	1993	1992	1991	1990	1989	1988	1987	1986	1985
Return (%)	0.9	9.4	7.1	29.2	—	—	—	—	—	—
Differ from category (+/-)	2.3	-3.8	-3.1	1.6	—	—	—	—	—	—

PER SHARE DATA

	1994	1993	1992	1991	1990	1989	1988	1987	1986	1985
Dividends, Net Income ($)	0.36	0.32	0.31	0.34	—	—	—	—	—	—
Distrib'ns, Cap Gain ($)	0.16	0.01	0.01	0.08	—	—	—	—	—	—
Net Asset Value ($)	13.09	13.48	12.63	12.10	—	—	—	—	—	—
Expense Ratio (%)	0.45	0.45	0.45	0.45	—	—	—	—	—	—
Net Income to Assets (%)	2.63	2.40	2.57	3.07	—	—	—	—	—	—
Portfolio Turnover (%)	1	0	0	5	—	—	—	—	—	—
Total Assets (Millions $)	270	166	128	22	—	—	—	—	—	—

PORTFOLIO (as of 6/30/94)

Portfolio Manager: Richard Whitney - 1990

Investm't Category: Growth & Income
Cap Gain
✔ Cap & Income
Income
Asset Allocation
Fund of Funds
✔ Index
Sector
✔ Domestic
Foreign
Country/Region
Small Cap
Socially Conscious
State Specific

Portfolio: stocks 77% bonds 0%
convertibles 0% other 0% cash 23%

Largest Holdings: Standard & Poor's 500 composite price index

Unrealized Net Capital Gains: 4% of portfolio value

SHAREHOLDER INFORMATION

Minimum Investment
Initial: $2,500 Subsequent: $100

Minimum IRA Investment
Initial: $1,000 Subsequent: $50

Maximum Fees
Load: 0.50% redemption 12b-1: none
Other: redemption fee applies for 6 months

Distributions
Income: quarterly Capital Gains: Dec

Exchange Options
Number Per Year: no limit Fee: none
Telephone: yes (money market fund available)

Services
IRA, pension, auto exchange, auto invest, auto withdraw

T Rowe Price European Stock (PRESX)

International Stock

P.O. Box 89000
Baltimore, MD 21289
(800) 638-5660, (410) 547-2308

PERFORMANCE

fund inception date: 2/28/90

	3yr Annual	5yr Annual	10yr Annual	Bull	Bear
Return (%)	7.7	na	na	43.9	-6.8
Differ from Category (+/-)	-1.4 blw av	na	na	-20.0 low	0.2 av

Total Risk	Standard Deviation	Category Risk	Risk Index	Beta
high	12.3%	blw av	0.9	0.8

	1994	1993	1992	1991	1990	1989	1988	1987	1986	1985
Return (%)	4.0	27.2	-5.5	7.3	—	—	—	—	—	—
Differ from category (+/-)	7.0	-11.4	-2.6	-5.8	—	—	—	—	—	—

PER SHARE DATA

	1994	1993	1992	1991	1990	1989	1988	1987	1986	1985
Dividends, Net Income ($)	0.12	0.04	0.17	0.08	—	—	—	—	—	—
Distrib'ns, Cap Gain ($)	0.05	0.01	0.00	0.00	—	—	—	—	—	—
Net Asset Value ($)	12.17	11.86	9.36	10.09	—	—	—	—	—	—
Expense Ratio (%)	1.25	1.35	1.48	1.71	—	—	—	—	—	—
Net Income to Assets (%)	1.19	1.79	1.23	1.04	—	—	—	—	—	—
Portfolio Turnover (%)	24	21	52	58	—	—	—	—	—	—
Total Assets (Millions $)	366	291	174	104	—	—	—	—	—	—

PORTFOLIO (as of 10/31/94)

Portfolio Manager: M. David Testa - 1990, Martin G. Wade - 1990

Investm't Category: International Stock

✔ Cap Gain	Asset Allocation
Cap & Income	Fund of Funds
Income	Index
	Sector
Domestic	Small Cap
✔ Foreign	Socially Conscious
✔ Country/Region	State Specific

Portfolio: stocks 96% bonds 0%
convertibles 0% other 2% cash 2%

Largest Holdings: United Kingdom 30%, Netherlands 16%

Unrealized Net Capital Gains: 12% of portfolio value

SHAREHOLDER INFORMATION

Minimum Investment
Initial: $2,500   Subsequent: $100

Minimum IRA Investment
Initial: $1,000   Subsequent: $50

Maximum Fees
Load: none   12b-1: none
Other: none

Distributions
Income: Dec   Capital Gains: Dec

Exchange Options
Number Per Year: 6   Fee: none
Telephone: yes (money market fund available)

Services
IRA, pension, auto exchange, auto invest, auto withdraw

T Rowe Price Global Gov't Bond (RPGGX)

P.O. Box 89000
Baltimore, MD 21289
(800) 638-5660, (410) 547-2308

International Bond

PERFORMANCE

fund inception date: 12/30/90

	3yr Annual	5yr Annual	10yr Annual	Bull	Bear
Return (%)	3.6	na	na	na	-3.7
Differ from Category (+/-)	-0.3 av	na	na	na	4.1 av

Total Risk	Standard Deviation	Category Risk	Risk Index	Avg Mat
low	3.7%	blw av	0.6	7.4 yrs

	1994	1993	1992	1991	1990	1989	1988	1987	1986	1985
Return (%)	-3.0	10.7	3.6	11.3	—	—	—	—	—	—
Differ from category (+/-) . . .	3.3	-2.7	-1.1	-4.7	—	—	—	—	—	—

PER SHARE DATA

	1994	1993	1992	1991	1990	1989	1988	1987	1986	1985
Dividends, Net Income ($) .	0.53	0.57	0.76	0.77	—	—	—	—	—	—
Distrib'ns, Cap Gain ($) . . .	0.02	0.28	0.01	0.00	—	—	—	—	—	—
Net Asset Value ($)	9.22	10.08	9.89	10.30	—	—	—	—	—	—
Expense Ratio (%)	1.20	1.20	1.20	1.20	—	—	—	—	—	—
Net Income to Assets (%) .	5.35	5.57	7.51	8.07	—	—	—	—	—	—
Portfolio Turnover (%).	165	134	237	94	—	—	—	—	—	—
Total Assets (Millions $).	36	48	54	40	—	—	—	—	—	—

PORTFOLIO (as of 6/30/94)

Portfolio Manager: Peter B. Askew - 1994

Investm't Category: International Bond

Cap Gain	Asset Allocation
Cap & Income	Fund of Funds
✔ Income	Index
	Sector
✔ Domestic	Small Cap
✔ Foreign	Socially Conscious
Country/Region	State Specific

Portfolio: stocks 0%   bonds 96%
convertibles 0%   other 0%   cash 4%

Largest Holdings: United States 22%, Germany 13%

Unrealized Net Capital Gains: 0% of portfolio value

SHAREHOLDER INFORMATION

Minimum Investment
Initial: $2,500   Subsequent: $100

Minimum IRA Investment
Initial: $1,000   Subsequent: $50

Maximum Fees
Load: none   12b-1: none
Other: none

Distributions
Income: monthly   Capital Gains: Dec

Exchange Options
Number Per Year: 6   Fee: none
Telephone: yes (money market fund available)

Services
IRA, pension, auto exchange, auto invest, auto withdraw

T Rowe Price GNMA
(PRGMX)
Mortgage-Backed Bond

P.O. Box 89000
Baltimore, MD 21289
(800) 638-5660, (410) 547-2308

PERFORMANCE

fund inception date: 11/26/85

	3yr Annual	5yr Annual	10yr Annual	Bull	Bear
Return (%)	3.5	7.0	na	37.9	-4.3
Differ from Category (+/-)	0.4 av	0.1 av	na	-0.1 av	0.1 blw av

Total Risk	Standard Deviation	Category Risk	Risk Index	Avg Mat
low	3.1%	blw av	0.9	8.7 yrs

	1994	1993	1992	1991	1990	1989	1988	1987	1986	1985
Return (%)	-1.6	6.1	6.4	15.0	10.0	14.0	5.9	0.7	11.0	—
Differ from category (+/-)	1.2	-0.7	0.3	0.6	0.3	1.5	-1.2	-1.1	-0.2	—

PER SHARE DATA

	1994	1993	1992	1991	1990	1989	1988	1987	1986	1985
Dividends, Net Income ($)	0.68	0.69	0.76	0.80	0.83	0.85	0.91	0.90	0.92	—
Distrib'ns, Cap Gain ($)	0.00	0.00	0.00	0.00	0.00	0.00	0.00	0.02	0.00	—
Net Asset Value ($)	8.88	9.72	9.82	9.97	9.42	9.37	9.01	9.38	10.23	—
Expense Ratio (%)	0.77	0.79	0.86	0.85	0.90	0.94	0.99	1.00	1.00	—
Net Income to Assets (%)	6.93	7.65	8.25	8.94	9.19	9.75	9.56	8.82	10.06	—
Portfolio Turnover (%)	92	94	66	92	171	135	193	226	57	—
Total Assets (Millions $)	752	918	716	469	386	352	369	378	123	—

PORTFOLIO (as of 5/31/94)

Portfolio Manager: Peter Van Dyke - 1987

Investm't Category: Mortgage-Backed Bond
Cap Gain	Asset Allocation
Cap & Income	Fund of Funds
✔ Income	Index
	Sector
✔ Domestic	Small Cap
Foreign	Socially Conscious
Country/Region	State Specific

Portfolio: stocks 0%   bonds 100%
convertibles 0%   other 0%   cash 0%

Largest Holdings: mortgage-backed 92%,
U.S. government 8%

Unrealized Net Capital Gains: -1% of portfolio value

SHAREHOLDER INFORMATION

Minimum Investment
Initial: $2,500   Subsequent: $100

Minimum IRA Investment
Initial: $1,000   Subsequent: $50

Maximum Fees
Load: none   12b-1: none
Other: none

Distributions
Income: monthly   Capital Gains: Jan, Mar

Exchange Options
Number Per Year: 6   Fee: none
Telephone: yes (money market fund available)

Services
IRA, pension, auto exchange, auto invest, auto withdraw

T Rowe Price Growth & Income (PRGIX)

Growth & Income

P.O. Box 89000
Baltimore, MD 21289
(800) 638-5660, (410) 547-2308

PERFORMANCE

fund inception date: 12/21/82

	3yr Annual	5yr Annual	10yr Annual	Bull	Bear
Return (%)	9.1	8.7	10.8	90.8	-5.8
Differ from Category (+/-)	2.0 abv av	0.8 abv av	-0.9 blw av	15.0 high	0.5 av

Total Risk	Standard Deviation	Category Risk	Risk Index	Beta
av	7.4%	blw av	0.9	0.8

	1994	1993	1992	1991	1990	1989	1988	1987	1986	1985
Return (%)	-0.1	12.9	15.3	31.5	-11.0	19.2	25.0	-4.2	7.9	19.8
Differ from category (+/-)	1.3	-0.3	5.1	3.9	-5.0	-2.2	8.0	-4.8	-7.9	-5.9

PER SHARE DATA

	1994	1993	1992	1991	1990	1989	1988	1987	1986	1985
Dividends, Net Income ($)	0.49	0.47	0.60	0.56	0.57	0.64	0.49	0.88	0.71	0.61
Distrib'ns, Cap Gain ($)	0.42	0.48	0.15	0.00	0.01	0.79	0.47	1.04	1.57	0.00
Net Asset Value ($)	15.63	16.57	15.53	14.16	11.22	13.25	12.32	10.63	12.98	14.18
Expense Ratio (%)	0.83	0.83	0.85	0.93	0.97	0.96	1.04	1.03	0.96	0.94
Net Income to Assets (%)	3.02	2.91	3.75	4.23	4.68	4.70	3.94	4.80	5.26	4.53
Portfolio Turnover (%)	21	22	30	48	35	57	50	114	99	120
Total Assets (Millions $)	1,228	1,167	840	655	475	554	445	366	388	356

PORTFOLIO (as of 6/30/94)

Portfolio Manager: Stephen Boesel - 1987

Investm't Category: Growth & Income

Cap Gain	Asset Allocation
✔ Cap & Income	Fund of Funds
Income	Index
	Sector
✔ Domestic	Small Cap
✔ Foreign	Socially Conscious
Country/Region	State Specific

Portfolio: stocks 81% bonds 5%
convertibles 8% other 0% cash 6%

Largest Holdings: bank & trust 9%, consumer products 6%

Unrealized Net Capital Gains: 9% of portfolio value

SHAREHOLDER INFORMATION

Minimum Investment
Initial: $2,500   Subsequent: $100

Minimum IRA Investment
Initial: $1,000   Subsequent: $50

Maximum Fees
Load: none   12b-1: none
Other: none

Distributions
Income: quarterly   Capital Gains: Mar, Dec

Exchange Options
Number Per Year: 6   Fee: none
Telephone: yes (money market fund available)

Services
IRA, pension, auto exchange, auto invest, auto withdraw

T Rowe Price Growth Stock (PRGFX)

P.O. Box 89000
Baltimore, MD 21289
(800) 638-5660, (410) 547-2308

Growth

fund inception date: 4/11/50

PERFORMANCE

	3yr Annual	5yr Annual	10yr Annual	Bull	Bear
Return (%)	7.3	9.6	13.6	84.5	-7.1
Differ from Category (+/-)	-0.4 av	0.0 av	0.7 abv av	-7.6 av	-0.5 av

Total Risk	Standard Deviation	Category Risk	Risk Index	Beta
abv av	9.1%	av	0.9	1.0

	1994	1993	1992	1991	1990	1989	1988	1987	1986	1985
Return (%)	0.8	15.5	5.9	33.7	-4.3	25.4	6.0	3.6	21.8	35.2
Differ from category (+/-)	1.4	2.1	-5.7	-2.0	1.4	-0.7	-12.0	1.8	7.2	6.0

PER SHARE DATA

	1994	1993	1992	1991	1990	1989	1988	1987	1986	1985
Dividends, Net Income ($)	0.18	0.14	0.18	0.25	0.43	0.34	0.32	0.63	0.38	0.34
Distrib'ns, Cap Gain ($)	1.66	0.99	1.03	0.62	0.43	1.58	0.26	2.66	4.18	0.64
Net Asset Value ($)	18.75	20.42	18.66	18.75	14.71	16.27	14.55	14.27	16.96	17.95
Expense Ratio (%)	0.83	0.82	0.83	0.85	0.76	0.69	0.77	0.67	0.57	0.52
Net Income to Assets (%)	1.05	0.86	0.94	1.40	2.31	2.13	2.08	1.71	1.79	2.32
Portfolio Turnover (%)	61	35	27	32	30	39	41	51	59	68
Total Assets (Millions $)	2,067	1,980	1,946	1,846	1,397	1,516	1,295	1,268	1,273	1,158

PORTFOLIO (as of 6/30/94)

Portfolio Manager: M. David Testa - 1984

Investm't Category: Growth

✔ Cap Gain   Asset Allocation
  Cap & Income   Fund of Funds
  Income   Index
                     Sector
✔ Domestic   Small Cap
✔ Foreign   Socially Conscious
  Country/Region   State Specific

Portfolio: stocks 91%   bonds 0%
convertibles 1%   other 0%   cash 8%

Largest Holdings: financial services 8%, media & communications 8%

Unrealized Net Capital Gains: 23% of portfolio value

SHAREHOLDER INFORMATION

Minimum Investment
Initial: $2,500   Subsequent: $100

Minimum IRA Investment
Initial: $1,000   Subsequent: $50

Maximum Fees
Load: none   12b-1: none
Other: none

Distributions
Income: Dec   Capital Gains: Dec

Exchange Options
Number Per Year: 6   Fee: none
Telephone: yes (money market fund available)

Services
IRA, pension, auto exchange, auto invest, auto withdraw

T Rowe Price High Yield

(PRHYX)

Corporate High-Yield Bond

P.O. Box 89000
Baltimore, MD 21289
(800) 638-5660, (410) 547-2308

PERFORMANCE

fund inception date: 12/31/84

	3yr Annual	5yr Annual	10yr Annual	Bull	Bear
Return (%)	8.7	8.4	9.6	79.4	-9.3
Differ from Category (+/-)	-1.2 av	-0.9 blw av	-0.3 av	0.1 abv av	-4.0 low

Total Risk	Standard Deviation	Category Risk	Risk Index	Avg Mat
blw av	5.7%	high	1.1	9.0 yrs

	1994	1993	1992	1991	1990	1989	1988	1987	1986	1985
Return (%)	-8.0	21.7	14.7	30.8	-10.9	-1.4	17.9	2.9	15.0	22.4
Differ from category (+/-)	-5.3	3.3	-0.9	3.4	-5.8	-2.8	5.8	1.8	0.7	-0.8

PER SHARE DATA

	1994	1993	1992	1991	1990	1989	1988	1987	1986	1985
Dividends, Net Income ($)	0.75	0.81	0.82	0.90	1.11	1.27	1.26	1.25	1.30	1.36
Distrib'ns, Cap Gain ($)	0.00	0.00	0.00	0.00	0.00	0.00	0.00	0.14	0.13	0.00
Net Asset Value ($)	7.75	9.22	8.29	7.98	6.86	8.88	10.25	9.82	10.87	10.75
Expense Ratio (%)	0.85	0.89	0.97	1.03	1.02	0.95	0.99	0.99	1.00	1.00
Net Income to Assets (%)	8.99	9.85	11.22	14.02	13.01	12.32	12.10	11.57	13.01	16.69
Portfolio Turnover (%)	107	104	59	83	66	80	138	166	163	6
Total Assets (Millions $)	1,040	1,619	1,108	556	660	1,251	840	940	156	22

PORTFOLIO (as of 5/31/94)

Portfolio Manager: Kathy Bray - 1994

Investm't Category: Corp. High-Yield Bond

Cap Gain	Asset Allocation
✔ Cap & Income	Fund of Funds
Income	Index
	Sector
✔ Domestic	Small Cap
✔ Foreign	Socially Conscious
Country/Region	State Specific

Portfolio: stocks 9% bonds 75%
convertibles 5% other 6% cash 5%

Largest Holdings: hotels & gaming 11%,
healthcare 7%

Unrealized Net Capital Gains: -5% of portfolio value

SHAREHOLDER INFORMATION

Minimum Investment
Initial: $2,500   Subsequent: $100

Minimum IRA Investment
Initial: $1,000   Subsequent: $50

Maximum Fees
Load: 1.00% redemption   12b-1: none
Other: redemption fee applies for 1 year

Distributions
Income: monthly   Capital Gains: Jan, Mar

Exchange Options
Number Per Year: 6   Fee: none
Telephone: yes (money market fund available)

Services
IRA, pension, auto exchange, auto invest, auto withdraw

T Rowe Price Int'l Discovery (PRIDX)

International Stock

P.O. Box 89000
Baltimore, MD 21289
(800) 638-5660, (410) 547-2308

PERFORMANCE

fund inception date: 12/30/88

	3yr Annual	5yr Annual	10yr Annual	Bull	Bear
Return (%)	7.9	4.1	na	60.3	-6.5
Differ from Category (+/-)	-1.2 blw av	-0.8 av	na	-3.6 av	0.5 av

Total Risk	Standard Deviation	Category Risk	Risk Index	Beta
high	13.0%	abv av	1.0	0.7

	1994	1993	1992	1991	1990	1989	1988	1987	1986	1985
Return (%)	-7.6	49.8	-9.0	11.6	-12.8	41.7	—	—	—	—
Differ from category (+/-)	-4.6	11.2	-6.1	-1.5	-2.4	19.2	—	—	—	—

PER SHARE DATA

	1994	1993	1992	1991	1990	1989	1988	1987	1986	1985
Dividends, Net Income ($)	0.06	0.07	0.13	0.13	0.15	0.13	—	—	—	—
Distrib'ns, Cap Gain ($)	0.87	0.02	0.00	0.00	0.27	0.10	—	—	—	—
Net Asset Value ($)	15.14	17.41	11.68	12.99	11.75	13.94	—	—	—	—
Expense Ratio (%)	1.51	1.50	1.50	1.50	1.50	1.50	—	—	—	—
Net Income to Assets (%)	0.38	0.81	1.07	1.03	1.10	0.76	—	—	—	—
Portfolio Turnover (%)	57	72	38	56	44	38	—	—	—	—
Total Assets (Millions $)	503	388	166	167	137	61	—	—	—	—

PORTFOLIO (as of 10/31/94)

Portfolio Manager: M. David Testa - 1989, Martin G. Wade - 1989

Investm't Category: International Stock

- ✔ Cap Gain
- Cap & Income
- Income
- Domestic
- ✔ Foreign
- Country/Region
- Asset Allocation
- Fund of Funds
- Index
- Sector
- ✔ Small Cap
- Socially Conscious
- State Specific

Portfolio: stocks 90% bonds 2%
convertibles 0% other 7% cash 1%

Largest Holdings: Japan 18%, United Kingdom 11%

Unrealized Net Capital Gains: 9% of portfolio value

SHAREHOLDER INFORMATION

Minimum Investment
Initial: $2,500   Subsequent: $100

Minimum IRA Investment
Initial: $1,000   Subsequent: $50

Maximum Fees
Load: 2.00% redemption   12b-1: none
Other: redemption fee applies for 1 year

Distributions
Income: Dec   Capital Gains: Dec

Exchange Options
Number Per Year: 6   Fee: none
Telephone: yes (money market fund available)

Services
IRA, pension, auto exchange, auto invest, auto withdraw

T Rowe Price Int'l Stock

(PRITX)

International Stock

P.O. Box 89000
Baltimore, MD 21289
(800) 638-5660, (410) 547-2308

PERFORMANCE

fund inception date: 5/9/80

	3yr Annual	5yr Annual	10yr Annual	Bull	Bear
Return (%)	10.3	7.2	17.9	75.8	-6.3
Differ from Category (+/-)	1.2 abv av	2.3 high	2.7 high	11.9 abv av	0.7 av

Total Risk	Standard Deviation	Category Risk	Risk Index	Beta
high	12.7%	av	1.0	0.8

	1994	1993	1992	1991	1990	1989	1988	1987	1986	1985
Return (%)	-0.7	40.1	-3.4	15.8	-8.8	23.7	17.9	7.9	61.2	45.1
Differ from category (+/-) . . .	2.3	1.5	-0.5	2.7	1.6	1.2	3.5	-6.5	2.2	2.7

PER SHARE DATA

	1994	1993	1992	1991	1990	1989	1988	1987	1986	1985
Dividends, Net Income ($) .	0.12	0.09	0.16	0.15	0.16	0.16	0.16	0.24	0.11	0.15
Distrib'ns, Cap Gain ($) . . .	0.62	0.20	0.16	0.49	0.36	0.67	0.93	4.98	1.38	0.23
Net Asset Value ($)	11.32	12.16	8.89	9.54	8.81	10.24	8.97	8.54	12.89	9.04
Expense Ratio (%)	0.97	1.01	1.05	1.10	1.09	1.10	1.16	1.14	1.10	1.11
Net Income to Assets (%) .	1.11	1.52	1.49	1.51	2.16	1.63	1.78	0.93	0.89	1.54
Portfolio Turnover (%).	22	29	38	45	47	48	42	77	56	62
Total Assets (Millions $) . .	5,786	4,266	1,950	1,476	1,031	971	630	643	554	275

PORTFOLIO (as of 4/30/94)

Portfolio Manager: M. David Testa - 1980, Martin G. Wade - 1980

Investm't Category: International Stock

✔ Cap Gain	Asset Allocation
Cap & Income	Fund of Funds
Income	Index
	Sector
Domestic	Small Cap
✔ Foreign	Socially Conscious
Country/Region	State Specific

Portfolio:	stocks 92%	bonds 0%
convertibles 0%	other 2%	cash 6%

Largest Holdings: Japan 22%, United Kingdom 13%

Unrealized Net Capital Gains: 12% of portfolio value

SHAREHOLDER INFORMATION

Minimum Investment
Initial: $2,500   Subsequent: $100

Minimum IRA Investment
Initial: $1,000   Subsequent: $50

Maximum Fees
Load: none   12b-1: none
Other: none

Distributions
Income: Dec   Capital Gains: Dec

Exchange Options
Number Per Year: 6   Fee: none
Telephone: yes (money market fund available)

Services
IRA, pension, auto exchange, auto invest, auto withdraw

T Rowe Price International Bond (RPIBX)

International Bond

P.O. Box 89000
Baltimore, MD 21289
(800) 638-5660, (410) 547-2308

PERFORMANCE

fund inception date: 9/10/86

	3yr Annual	5yr Annual	10yr Annual	Bull	Bear
Return (%)	6.4	10.4	na	56.3	-3.2
Differ from Category (+/-)	2.5 high	1.8 abv av	na	-4.0 blw av	4.6 abv av

Total Risk	Standard Deviation	Category Risk	Risk Index	Avg Mat
av	7.0%	abv av	1.2	7.0 yrs

	1994	1993	1992	1991	1990	1989	1988	1987	1986	1985
Return (%)	-1.8	19.9	2.3	17.7	16.0	-3.2	-1.2	27.5	—	—
Differ from category (+/-)	4.5	6.5	-2.4	1.7	4.5	-5.4	-3.6	14.1	—	—

PER SHARE DATA

	1994	1993	1992	1991	1990	1989	1988	1987	1986	1985
Dividends, Net Income ($)	0.60	0.68	0.83	0.77	0.83	0.75	0.92	1.01	—	—
Distrib'ns, Cap Gain ($)	0.21	0.46	0.15	0.00	0.17	0.00	0.26	0.00	—	—
Net Asset Value ($)	9.34	10.34	9.61	10.35	9.53	9.15	10.25	11.60	—	—
Expense Ratio (%)	0.99	0.99	1.08	1.24	1.15	1.23	1.20	1.25	—	—
Net Income to Assets (%)	6.38	6.58	8.66	8.11	9.04	8.11	8.73	9.47	—	—
Portfolio Turnover (%)	359	395	358	296	211	293	368	284	—	—
Total Assets (Millions $)	738	749	514	414	431	304	407	400	—	—

PORTFOLIO (as of 6/30/94)

Portfolio Manager: Peter B. Askew - 1994

Investm't Category: International Bond

Cap Gain	Asset Allocation
Cap & Income	Fund of Funds
✔ Income	Index
	Sector
Domestic	Small Cap
✔ Foreign	Socially Conscious
Country/Region	State Specific

Portfolio: stocks 0%   bonds 88%
convertibles 0%   other 5%   cash 7%

Largest Holdings: Japan 17%, Germany 11%

Unrealized Net Capital Gains: 0% of portfolio value

SHAREHOLDER INFORMATION

Minimum Investment
Initial: $2,500   Subsequent: $100

Minimum IRA Investment
Initial: $1,000   Subsequent: $50

Maximum Fees
Load: none   12b-1: none
Other: none

Distributions
Income: monthly   Capital Gains: Dec

Exchange Options
Number Per Year: 6   Fee: none
Telephone: yes (money market fund available)

Services
IRA, pension, auto exchange, auto invest, auto withdraw

T Rowe Price Japan
(PRJPX)
International Stock

P.O. Box 89000
Baltimore, MD 21289
(800) 638-5660, (410) 547-2308

PERFORMANCE

	3yr Annual	5yr Annual	10yr Annual	Bull	Bear
Return (%)	6.3	na	na	na	12.7
Differ from Category (+/-)	-2.8 low	na	na	na	19.7 high

Total Risk	Standard Deviation	Category Risk	Risk Index	Beta
high	20.4%	high	1.6	0.0

	1994	1993	1992	1991	1990	1989	1988	1987	1986	1985
Return (%)	15.0	20.6	-13.4	—	—	—	—	—	—	—
Differ from category (+/-)	18.0	-18.0	-10.5	—	—	—	—	—	—	—

PER SHARE DATA

	1994	1993	1992	1991	1990	1989	1988	1987	1986	1985
Dividends, Net Income ($)	0.00	0.00	0.00	—	—	—	—	—	—	—
Distrib'ns, Cap Gain ($)	0.81	0.85	0.00	—	—	—	—	—	—	—
Net Asset Value ($)	10.24	9.61	8.66	—	—	—	—	—	—	—
Expense Ratio (%)	1.50	1.50	1.50	—	—	—	—	—	—	—
Net Income to Assets (%)	-0.68	-0.58	-0.22	—	—	—	—	—	—	—
Portfolio Turnover (%)	61	61	42	—	—	—	—	—	—	—
Total Assets (Millions $)	169	71	46	—	—	—	—	—	—	—

PORTFOLIO (as of 10/31/94)

Portfolio Manager: Martin Wade - 1991

Investm't Category: International Stock

✔ Cap Gain	Asset Allocation
Cap & Income	Fund of Funds
Income	Index
	Sector
Domestic	Small Cap
✔ Foreign	Socially Conscious
✔ Country/Region	State Specific

Portfolio: stocks 98% bonds 0%
convertibles 0% other 0% cash 2%

Largest Holdings: Japan 98%

Unrealized Net Capital Gains: 4% of portfolio value

SHAREHOLDER INFORMATION

Minimum Investment
Initial: $2,500   Subsequent: $100

Minimum IRA Investment
Initial: $1,000   Subsequent: $50

Maximum Fees
Load: none   12b-1: none
Other: none

Distributions
Income: Dec   Capital Gains: Dec

Exchange Options
Number Per Year: 6   Fee: none
Telephone: yes (money market fund available)

Services
IRA, pension, auto exchange, auto invest, auto withdraw

T Rowe Price Latin America (PRLAX)

P.O. Box 89000
Baltimore, MD 21289
(800) 638-5660, (410) 547-2308

International Stock

PERFORMANCE

fund inception date: 12/31/93

	3yr Annual	5yr Annual	10yr Annual	Bull	Bear
Return (%)	na	na	na	na	-22.5
Differ from Category (+/-)	na	na	na	na	-15.5 low

Total Risk	Standard Deviation	Category Risk	Risk Index	Beta
na	na	na	na	na

	1994	1993	1992	1991	1990	1989	1988	1987	1986	1985
Return (%)	-15.9	—	—	—	—	—	—	—	—	—
Differ from category (+/-)	-12.9	—	—	—	—	—	—	—	—	—

PER SHARE DATA

	1994	1993	1992	1991	1990	1989	1988	1987	1986	1985
Dividends, Net Income ($)	0.00	—	—	—	—	—	—	—	—	—
Distrib'ns, Cap Gain ($)	0.00	—	—	—	—	—	—	—	—	—
Net Asset Value ($)	8.45	—	—	—	—	—	—	—	—	—
Expense Ratio (%)	1.99	—	—	—	—	—	—	—	—	—
Net Income to Assets (%)	-0.35	—	—	—	—	—	—	—	—	—
Portfolio Turnover (%)	12	—	—	—	—	—	—	—	—	—
Total Assets (Millions $)	163	—	—	—	—	—	—	—	—	—

PORTFOLIO (as of 10/31/94)

Portfolio Manager: M. Edwards - 1993, John R. Ford - 1993, Martin G. Wade - 1993

Investm't Category: International Stock

✔ Cap Gain	Asset Allocation
Cap & Income	Fund of Funds
Income	Index
	Sector
Domestic	Small Cap
✔ Foreign	Socially Conscious
✔ Country/Region	State Specific

Portfolio: stocks 66%   bonds 1%
convertibles 0%   other 27%   cash 6%

Largest Holdings: Mexico 37%, Brazil 33%

Unrealized Net Capital Gains: 0% of portfolio value

SHAREHOLDER INFORMATION

Minimum Investment
Initial: $2,500   Subsequent: $100

Minimum IRA Investment
Initial: $1,000   Subsequent: $50

Maximum Fees
Load: 2.00% redemption   12b-1: none
Other: redemption applies for 1 year

Distributions
Income: Dec   Capital Gains: Dec

Exchange Options
Number Per Year: 6   Fee: none
Telephone: yes (money market fund available)

Services
IRA, pension, auto exchange, auto invest, auto withdraw

T Rowe Price Maryland Tax-Free (MDXBX)

Tax-Exempt Bond

P.O. Box 89000
Baltimore, MD 21289
(800) 638-5660, (410) 547-2308

PERFORMANCE

fund inception date: 3/31/87

	3yr Annual	5yr Annual	10yr Annual	Bull	Bear
Return (%)	5.1	6.5	na	43.8	-5.8
Differ from Category (+/-)	0.6 abv av	0.4 av	na	2.0 av	-0.6 av

Total Risk	Standard Deviation		Category Risk	Risk Index	Avg Mat
blw av	5.7%		blw av	0.9	16.4 yrs

	1994	1993	1992	1991	1990	1989	1988	1987	1986	1985
Return (%)	-5.0	12.7	8.5	11.2	6.2	9.5	8.8	—	—	—
Differ from category (+/-)	0.2	1.0	0.2	-0.1	-0.1	0.5	-1.4	—	—	—

PER SHARE DATA

	1994	1993	1992	1991	1990	1989	1988	1987	1986	1985
Dividends, Net Income ($)	0.56	0.56	0.58	0.59	0.60	0.60	0.57	—	—	—
Distrib'ns, Cap Gain ($)	0.02	0.10	0.05	0.05	0.00	0.03	0.00	—	—	—
Net Asset Value ($)	9.56	10.67	10.08	9.89	9.50	9.53	9.29	—	—	—
Expense Ratio (%)	0.57	0.61	0.64	0.68	0.85	0.92	0.85	—	—	—
Net Income to Assets (%)	5.55	5.72	6.04	6.38	6.29	6.23	6.15	—	—	—
Portfolio Turnover (%)	25	22	22	52	58	64	178	—	—	—
Total Assets (Millions $)	675	825	475	301	194	113	63	—	—	—

PORTFOLIO (as of 8/31/94)

Portfolio Manager: Mary J. Miller - 1990

Investm't Category: Tax-Exempt Bond
Cap Gain	Asset Allocation
Cap & Income	Fund of Funds
✔ Income	Index
	Sector
✔ Domestic	Small Cap
Foreign	Socially Conscious
Country/Region	✔ State Specific

Portfolio: stocks 0%   bonds 100%
convertibles 0%   other 0%   cash 0%

Largest Holdings: general obligation 13%

Unrealized Net Capital Gains: 3% of portfolio value

SHAREHOLDER INFORMATION

Minimum Investment
Initial: $2,500   Subsequent: $100

Minimum IRA Investment
Initial: na   Subsequent: na

Maximum Fees
Load: none   12b-1: none
Other: none

Distributions
Income: monthly   Capital Gains: May, Dec

Exchange Options
Number Per Year: 6   Fee: none
Telephone: yes (money market fund available)

Services
auto exchange, auto invest, auto withdraw

T Rowe Price MD Short-Term Tax-Free (PRMDX)

P.O. Box 89000
Baltimore, MD 21289
(800) 638-5660, (410) 547-2308

Tax-Exempt Bond

PERFORMANCE

fund inception date: 1/29/93

	3yr Annual	5yr Annual	10yr Annual	Bull	Bear
Return (%)	na	na	na	na	-0.8
Differ from Category (+/-)	na	na	na	na	4.4 high

Total Risk	Standard Deviation	Category Risk	Risk Index	Avg Mat
na	na	na	na	2.1 yrs

	1994	1993	1992	1991	1990	1989	1988	1987	1986	1985
Return (%)	0.6	—	—	—	—	—	—	—	—	—
Differ from category (+/-)	5.8	—	—	—	—	—	—	—	—	—

PER SHARE DATA

	1994	1993	1992	1991	1990	1989	1988	1987	1986	1985
Dividends, Net Income ($)	0.17	—	—	—	—	—	—	—	—	—
Distrib'ns, Cap Gain ($)	0.00	—	—	—	—	—	—	—	—	—
Net Asset Value ($)	4.98	—	—	—	—	—	—	—	—	—
Expense Ratio (%)	0.65	—	—	—	—	—	—	—	—	—
Net Income to Assets (%)	3.28	—	—	—	—	—	—	—	—	—
Portfolio Turnover (%)	84	—	—	—	—	—	—	—	—	—
Total Assets (Millions $)	76	—	—	—	—	—	—	—	—	—

PORTFOLIO (as of 8/31/94)

Portfolio Manager: Mary J. Miller - 1993

Investm't Category: Tax-Exempt Bond

Cap Gain	Asset Allocation
Cap & Income	Fund of Funds
✔ Income	Index
	Sector
✔ Domestic	Small Cap
Foreign	Socially Conscious
Country/Region	✔ State Specific

Portfolio: stocks 0%   bonds 100%
convertibles 0%   other 0%   cash 0%

Largest Holdings: general obligation 27%

Unrealized Net Capital Gains: 0% of portfolio value

SHAREHOLDER INFORMATION

Minimum Investment
Initial: $2,500   Subsequent: $100

Minimum IRA Investment
Initial: na   Subsequent: na

Maximum Fees
Load: none   12b-1: none
Other: none

Distributions
Income: monthly   Capital Gains: Mar, Dec

Exchange Options
Number Per Year: 6   Fee: none
Telephone: yes (money market fund available)

Services
auto exchange, auto invest, auto withdraw

T Rowe Price Mid-Cap Growth (RPMGX)

Growth

P.O. Box 89000
Baltimore, MD 21289
(800) 638-5660, (410) 547-2308

PERFORMANCE

fund inception date: 6/30/92

	3yr Annual	5yr Annual	10yr Annual	Bull	Bear
Return (%)	na	na	na	na	-7.0
Differ from Category (+/-)	na	na	na	na	-0.4 av

Total Risk	Standard Deviation	Category Risk	Risk Index	Beta
na	na	na	na	na

	1994	1993	1992	1991	1990	1989	1988	1987	1986	1985
Return (%)	0.2	26.2	—	—	—	—	—	—	—	—
Differ from category (+/-)	0.8	12.8	—	—	—	—	—	—	—	—

PER SHARE DATA

	1994	1993	1992	1991	1990	1989	1988	1987	1986	1985
Dividends, Net Income ($)	0.00	0.00	—	—	—	—	—	—	—	—
Distrib'ns, Cap Gain ($)	0.37	0.30	—	—	—	—	—	—	—	—
Net Asset Value ($)	14.85	15.18	—	—	—	—	—	—	—	—
Expense Ratio (%)	1.25	1.25	—	—	—	—	—	—	—	—
Net Income to Assets (%)	-0.07	-0.12	—	—	—	—	—	—	—	—
Portfolio Turnover (%)	40	62	—	—	—	—	—	—	—	—
Total Assets (Millions $)	100	65	—	—	—	—	—	—	—	—

PORTFOLIO (as of 6/30/94)

Portfolio Manager: Brian Berghius - 1992

Investm't Category: Growth

✔ Cap Gain	Asset Allocation
Cap & Income	Fund of Funds
Income	Index
	Sector
✔ Domestic	Small Cap
✔ Foreign	Socially Conscious
Country/Region	State Specific

Portfolio: stocks 88% bonds 0%
convertibles 0% other 0% cash 12%

Largest Holdings: machinery 8%, energy services 8%

Unrealized Net Capital Gains: 5% of portfolio value

SHAREHOLDER INFORMATION

Minimum Investment
Initial: $2,500   Subsequent: $100

Minimum IRA Investment
Initial: $1,000   Subsequent: $50

Maximum Fees
Load: none   12b-1: none
Other: none

Distributions
Income: Dec   Capital Gains: Dec

Exchange Options
Number Per Year: 6   Fee: none
Telephone: yes (money market fund available)

Services
IRA, pension, auto exchange, auto invest, auto withdraw

T Rowe Price New America Growth (PRWAX)

P.O. Box 89000
Baltimore, MD 21289
(800) 638-5660, (410) 547-2308

Growth

PERFORMANCE

fund inception date: 9/30/85

	3yr Annual	5yr Annual	10yr Annual	Bull	Bear
Return (%)	6.1	11.1	na	135.7	-10.5
Differ from Category (+/-)	-1.6 blw av	1.5 abv av	na	43.6 high	-3.9 low

Total Risk	Standard Deviation	Category Risk	Risk Index	Beta
high	14.0%	high	1.5	1.1

	1994	1993	1992	1991	1990	1989	1988	1987	1986	1985
Return (%)............	-7.4	17.4	9.8	61.9	-12.2	38.4	18.4	-9.3	14.3	—
Differ from category (+/-)...	-6.8	4.0	-1.8	26.2	-6.5	12.3	0.4	-11.1	-0.3	—

PER SHARE DATA

	1994	1993	1992	1991	1990	1989	1988	1987	1986	1985
Dividends, Net Income ($)	0.00	0.00	0.00	0.00	0.17	0.00	0.00	0.06	0.10	—
Distrib'ns, Cap Gain ($)	0.53	1.13	0.18	0.87	0.00	0.23	0.00	1.39	0.30	—
Net Asset Value ($)	25.42	28.04	24.86	22.79	14.66	16.90	12.38	10.45	13.14	—
Expense Ratio (%)	1.19	1.23	1.25	1.25	1.25	1.50	1.50	1.23	1.00	—
Net Income to Assets (%)	-0.37	-0.39	-0.44	-0.12	0.81	-0.02	-0.36	-0.08	0.38	—
Portfolio Turnover (%)	35	43	26	42	42	40	45	72	80	—
Total Assets (Millions $)	646	615	480	232	96	134	66	62	83	—

PORTFOLIO (as of 6/30/94)

Portfolio Manager: John Laporte - 1985

Investm't Category: Growth
- ✔ Cap Gain
- Cap & Income
- Income
- Asset Allocation
- Fund of Funds
- Index
- Sector
- ✔ Domestic
- Foreign
- Country/Region
- Small Cap
- Socially Conscious
- State Specific

Portfolio: stocks 93% bonds 0%
convertibles 0% other 0% cash 7%

Largest Holdings: retailing/specialty retailers 12%, healthcare services 10%

Unrealized Net Capital Gains: 17% of portfolio value

SHAREHOLDER INFORMATION

Minimum Investment
Initial: $2,500 Subsequent: $100

Minimum IRA Investment
Initial: $1,000 Subsequent: $50

Maximum Fees
Load: none 12b-1: none
Other: none

Distributions
Income: Dec Capital Gains: Dec

Exchange Options
Number Per Year: 6 Fee: none
Telephone: yes (money market fund available)

Services
IRA, pension, auto exchange, auto invest, auto withdraw

T Rowe Price New Asia

(PRASX)

International Stock

P.O. Box 89000
Baltimore, MD 21289
(800) 638-5660, (410) 547-2308

PERFORMANCE

fund inception date: 9/28/90

	3yr Annual	5yr Annual	10yr Annual	Bull	Bear
Return (%)	17.1	na	na	129.3	-15.3
Differ from Category (+/-)	8.0 high	na	na	65.4 high	-8.3 low

Total Risk	Standard Deviation	Category Risk	Risk Index	Beta
high	20.6%	high	1.6	1.1

	1994	1993	1992	1991	1990	1989	1988	1987	1986	1985
Return (%).............	-19.1	78.7	11.2	19.3	—	—	—	—	—	—
Differ from category (+/-)..	-16.1	40.1	14.1	6.2	—	—	—	—	—	—

PER SHARE DATA

	1994	1993	1992	1991	1990	1989	1988	1987	1986	1985
Dividends, Net Income ($) .	0.07	0.04	0.10	0.10	—	—	—	—	—	—
Distrib'ns, Cap Gain ($) ...	0.89	0.19	0.13	0.00	—	—	—	—	—	—
Net Asset Value ($)	8.01	11.10	6.34	5.91	—	—	—	—	—	—
Expense Ratio (%)	1.22	1.29	1.51	1.75	—	—	—	—	—	—
Net Income to Assets (%) .	0.85	1.02	1.64	1.75	—	—	—	—	—	—
Portfolio Turnover (%)......	63	40	36	49	—	—	—	—	—	—
Total Assets (Millions $)..	1,987	2,183	314	103	—	—	—	—	—	—

PORTFOLIO (as of 10/31/94)

Portfolio Manager: M. David Testa - 1990,
Martin Wade - 1990

Investm't Category: International Stock
- ✔ Cap Gain
- Cap & Income
- Income
- Domestic
- ✔ Foreign
- ✔ Country/Region
- Asset Allocation
- Fund of Funds
- Index
- Sector
- Small Cap
- Socially Conscious
- State Specific

Portfolio: stocks 90% bonds 0%
convertibles 2% other 0% cash 8%

Largest Holdings: Malaysia 22%, Hong Kong 22%

Unrealized Net Capital Gains: 8% of portfolio value

SHAREHOLDER INFORMATION

Minimum Investment
Initial: $2,500 Subsequent: $100

Minimum IRA Investment
Initial: $1,000 Subsequent: $50

Maximum Fees
Load: none 12b-1: none
Other: none

Distributions
Income: Dec Capital Gains: Dec

Exchange Options
Number Per Year: 6 Fee: none
Telephone: yes (money market fund available)

Services
IRA, pension, auto exchange, auto invest, auto withdraw

T Rowe Price New Era
(PRNEX)
Growth

P.O. Box 89000
Baltimore, MD 21289
(800) 638-5660, (410) 547-2308

PERFORMANCE   fund inception date: 1/20/69

	3yr Annual	5yr Annual	10yr Annual	Bull	Bear
Return (%)	7.3	5.3	11.5	39.8	-3.2
Differ from Category (+/-)	-0.4 av	-4.3 low	-1.4 blw av	-52.3 low	3.4 high

Total Risk	Standard Deviation	Category Risk	Risk Index	Beta
av	7.8%	low	0.8	0.8

	1994	1993	1992	1991	1990	1989	1988	1987	1986	1985
Return (%)	5.1	15.3	2.0	14.7	-8.8	24.2	10.2	17.8	15.9	23.4
Differ from category (+/-)	5.7	1.9	-9.6	-21.0	-3.1	-1.9	-7.8	16.0	1.3	-5.8

PER SHARE DATA

	1994	1993	1992	1991	1990	1989	1988	1987	1986	1985
Dividends, Net Income ($)	0.38	0.38	0.45	0.55	0.62	0.56	0.53	0.98	0.50	0.68
Distrib'ns, Cap Gain ($)	0.87	1.03	0.94	0.73	0.71	1.05	0.61	1.77	3.25	1.41
Net Asset Value ($)	20.15	20.35	18.88	19.86	18.48	21.73	18.79	18.08	17.76	18.67
Expense Ratio (%)	0.82	0.80	0.81	0.85	0.83	0.83	0.89	0.82	0.73	0.69
Net Income to Assets (%)	1.74	1.92	2.22	2.56	2.81	2.52	2.41	3.11	1.98	2.76
Portfolio Turnover (%)	21	24	17	9	9	19	16	30	32	36
Total Assets (Millions $)	979	755	700	757	707	827	727	757	496	529

PORTFOLIO (as of 6/30/94)

Portfolio Manager: George Roche - 1979

Investm't Category: Growth
✔ Cap Gain   Asset Allocation
   Cap & Income   Fund of Funds
   Income   Index
        ✔ Sector
✔ Domestic   Small Cap
✔ Foreign   Socially Conscious
   Country/Region   State Specific

Portfolio: stocks 86%   bonds 0%
convertibles 1%   other 0%   cash 13%

Largest Holdings: integrated petroleum 13%, precious metals 12%

Unrealized Net Capital Gains: 21% of portfolio value

SHAREHOLDER INFORMATION

Minimum Investment
Initial: $2,500   Subsequent: $100

Minimum IRA Investment
Initial: $1,000   Subsequent: $50

Maximum Fees
Load: none   12b-1: none
Other: none

Distributions
Income: Dec   Capital Gains: Dec

Exchange Options
Number Per Year: 6   Fee: none
Telephone: yes (money market fund available)

Services
IRA, pension, auto exchange, auto invest, auto withdraw

T Rowe Price New Horizons (PRNHX)

P.O. Box 89000
Baltimore, MD 21289
(800) 638-5660, (410) 547-2308

Aggressive Growth

PERFORMANCE

fund inception date: 6/3/60

	3yr Annual	5yr Annual	10yr Annual	Bull	Bear
Return (%)	10.6	13.2	11.9	138.7	-11.9
Differ from Category (+/-)	1.7 abv av	0.7 av	-2.1 blw av	5.5 abv av	-1.1 av

Total Risk	Standard Deviation	Category Risk	Risk Index	Beta
high	14.9%	av	1.0	1.2

	1994	1993	1992	1991	1990	1989	1988	1987	1986	1985
Return (%)	0.3	22.0	10.5	52.3	-9.6	26.1	14.0	-7.2	-0.1	24.3
Differ from category (+/-). . .	1.0	2.5	-0.5	0.2	-3.4	-0.7	-1.2	-5.0	-11.9	-8.0

PER SHARE DATA

	1994	1993	1992	1991	1990	1989	1988	1987	1986	1985
Dividends, Net Income ($) .	0.00	0.00	0.00	0.05	0.09	0.07	0.07	0.06	0.09	0.14
Distrib'ns, Cap Gain ($) . . .	1.43	2.70	1.76	0.39	0.53	1.01	0.03	1.93	2.64	0.52
Net Asset Value ($)	14.76	16.16	15.53	15.68	10.61	12.43	10.74	9.51	12.38	15.13
Expense Ratio (%)	0.95	0.93	0.93	0.92	0.82	0.79	0.84	0.78	0.73	0.70
Net Income to Assets (%) .	-0.55	-0.50	-0.32	0.35	0.72	0.58	0.67	0.23	0.10	0.63
Portfolio Turnover (%).	40	49	50	33	38	45	43	50	34	30
Total Assets (Millions $). .	1,648	1,623	1,547	1,470	855	1,043	915	856	1,033	1,474

PORTFOLIO (as of 6/30/94)

Portfolio Manager: John Laporte - 1987

Investm't Category: Aggressive Growth

✔ Cap Gain
Cap & Income
Income

Asset Allocation
Fund of Funds
Index
Sector
✔ Small Cap
Socially Conscious
State Specific

✔ Domestic
✔ Foreign
Country/Region

Portfolio: stocks 98% bonds 0%
convertibles 0% other 0% cash 2%

Largest Holdings: computer services 8%,
computer software 8%

Unrealized Net Capital Gains: 20% of portfolio value

SHAREHOLDER INFORMATION

Minimum Investment
Initial: $2,500   Subsequent: $100

Minimum IRA Investment
Initial: $1,000   Subsequent: $50

Maximum Fees
Load: none   12b-1: none
Other: none

Distributions
Income: Dec   Capital Gains: Dec

Exchange Options
Number Per Year: 6   Fee: none
Telephone: yes (money market fund available)

Services
IRA, pension, auto exchange, auto invest, auto withdraw

T Rowe Price New Income (PRCIX)

General Bond

P.O. Box 89000
Baltimore, MD 21289
(800) 638-5660, (410) 547-2308

PERFORMANCE
fund inception date: 8/31/73

	3yr Annual	5yr Annual	10yr Annual	Bull	Bear
Return (%)	3.9	7.1	8.8	41.2	-4.3
Differ from Category (+/-)	-0.4 blw av	0.2 abv av	-0.1 blw av	0.2 av	-0.5 av

Total Risk	Standard Deviation	Category Risk	Risk Index	Avg Mat
low	3.6%	av	0.9	9.4 yrs

	1994	1993	1992	1991	1990	1989	1988	1987	1986	1985
Return (%)	-2.2	9.5	4.9	15.5	8.7	12.2	7.5	2.0	13.8	17.6
Differ from category (+/-)	-0.2	0.3	-1.7	0.9	1.5	0.8	0.1	-0.2	-0.4	-1.8

PER SHARE DATA

	1994	1993	1992	1991	1990	1989	1988	1987	1986	1985
Dividends, Net Income ($)	0.57	0.54	0.59	0.67	0.71	0.76	0.81	0.75	0.77	0.90
Distrib'ns, Cap Gain ($)	0.07	0.07	0.00	0.02	0.01	0.00	0.00	0.00	0.00	0.00
Net Asset Value ($)	8.39	9.24	9.00	9.16	8.58	8.59	8.37	8.55	9.13	8.73
Expense Ratio (%)	0.82	0.84	0.87	0.88	0.86	0.91	0.80	0.65	0.66	0.64
Net Income to Assets (%)	5.77	6.36	7.64	8.33	8.85	9.50	8.77	8.22	10.39	11.53
Portfolio Turnover (%)	58	86	50	21	51	92	158	125	184	155
Total Assets (Millions $)	1,367	1,562	1,307	1,131	993	860	835	939	936	707

PORTFOLIO (as of 5/31/94)

Portfolio Manager: Charles Smith - 1986

Investm't Category: General Bond

Cap Gain	Asset Allocation
Cap & Income	Fund of Funds
✔ Income	Index
	Sector
✔ Domestic	Small Cap
✔ Foreign	Socially Conscious
Country/Region	State Specific

Portfolio: stocks 0% bonds 92%
convertibles 0% other 0% cash 8%

Largest Holdings: corporate 48%, mortgage-backed 29%

Unrealized Net Capital Gains: -1% of portfolio value

SHAREHOLDER INFORMATION

Minimum Investment
Initial: $2,500   Subsequent: $100

Minimum IRA Investment
Initial: $1,000   Subsequent: $50

Maximum Fees
Load: none   12b-1: none
Other: none

Distributions
Income: monthly   Capital Gains: Jan, Mar

Exchange Options
Number Per Year: 6   Fee: none
Telephone: yes (money market fund available)

Services
IRA, pension, auto exchange, auto invest, auto withdraw

T Rowe Price NJ Tax-Free (NJTFX)

Tax-Exempt Bond

P.O. Box 89000
Baltimore, MD 21289
(800) 638-5660, (410) 547-2308

PERFORMANCE

fund inception date: 4/30/91

	3yr Annual	5yr Annual	10yr Annual	Bull	Bear
Return (%)	5.4	na	na	na	-6.6
Differ from Category (+/-)	0.9 high	na	na	na	-1.4 blw av

Total Risk	Standard Deviation	Category Risk	Risk Index	Avg Mat
blw av	6.5%	abv av	1.0	17.3 yrs

	1994	1993	1992	1991	1990	1989	1988	1987	1986	1985
Return (%)	-6.1	13.9	9.5	—	—	—	—	—	—	—
Differ from category (+/-)	-0.9	2.2	1.2	—	—	—	—	—	—	—

PER SHARE DATA

	1994	1993	1992	1991	1990	1989	1988	1987	1986	1985
Dividends, Net Income ($)	0.56	0.56	0.58	—	—	—	—	—	—	—
Distrib'ns, Cap Gain ($)	0.01	0.14	0.07	—	—	—	—	—	—	—
Net Asset Value ($)	10.19	11.45	10.69	—	—	—	—	—	—	—
Expense Ratio (%)	0.65	0.65	0.65	—	—	—	—	—	—	—
Net Income to Assets (%)	5.20	5.47	5.86	—	—	—	—	—	—	—
Portfolio Turnover (%)	133	103	152	—	—	—	—	—	—	—
Total Assets (Millions $)	53	60	14	—	—	—	—	—	—	—

PORTFOLIO (as of 8/31/94)

Portfolio Manager: William Reynolds - 1991

Investm't Category: Tax-Exempt Bond

Cap Gain	Asset Allocation
Cap & Income	Fund of Funds
✔ Income	Index
	Sector
✔ Domestic	Small Cap
Foreign	Socially Conscious
Country/Region	✔ State Specific

Portfolio: stocks 0%   bonds 100%
convertibles 0%   other 0%   cash 0%

Largest Holdings: general obligation 9%

Unrealized Net Capital Gains: 1% of portfolio value

SHAREHOLDER INFORMATION

Minimum Investment
Initial: $2,500   Subsequent: $100

Minimum IRA Investment
Initial: na   Subsequent: na

Maximum Fees
Load: none   12b-1: none
Other: none

Distributions
Income: monthly   Capital Gains: Jan, Mar

Exchange Options
Number Per Year: 6   Fee: none
Telephone: yes (money market fund available)

Services
auto exchange, auto invest, auto withdraw

T Rowe Price NY Tax-Free (PRNYX)

Tax-Exempt Bond

P.O. Box 89000
Baltimore, MD 21289
(800) 638-5660, (410) 547-2308

PERFORMANCE

fund inception date: 8/28/86

	3yr Annual	5yr Annual	10yr Annual	Bull	Bear
Return (%)	5.5	6.8	na	47.2	-6.1
Differ from Category (+/-)	1.0 high	0.7 abv av	na	5.4 abv av	-0.9 blw av

Total Risk	Standard Deviation	Category Risk	Risk Index	Avg Mat
blw av	5.8%	av	0.9	17.1 yrs

	1994	1993	1992	1991	1990	1989	1988	1987	1986	1985
Return (%)	-5.8	13.3	10.3	12.4	5.2	8.0	10.4	-2.4	—	—
Differ from category (+/-)	-0.6	1.6	2.0	1.1	-1.1	-1.0	0.2	-1.1	—	—

PER SHARE DATA

	1994	1993	1992	1991	1990	1989	1988	1987	1986	1985
Dividends, Net Income ($)	0.58	0.60	0.63	0.62	0.62	0.62	0.61	0.60	—	—
Distrib'ns, Cap Gain ($)	0.08	0.16	0.00	0.00	0.00	0.00	0.00	0.00	—	—
Net Asset Value ($)	9.90	11.21	10.59	10.19	9.65	9.78	9.65	9.31	—	—
Expense Ratio (%)	0.60	0.60	0.60	0.73	0.96	1.00	1.00	0.85	—	—
Net Income to Assets (%)	5.52	5.91	6.33	6.43	6.40	6.40	6.44	6.16	—	—
Portfolio Turnover (%)	137	41	49	62	72	89	147	126	—	—
Total Assets (Millions $)	110	134	74	55	47	36	28	24	—	—

PORTFOLIO (as of 8/31/94)

Portfolio Manager: William T. Reynolds - 1986

Investm't Category: Tax-Exempt Bond

Cap Gain	Asset Allocation
Cap & Income	Fund of Funds
✔ Income	Index
	Sector
✔ Domestic	Small Cap
Foreign	Socially Conscious
Country/Region	✔ State Specific

Portfolio: stocks 0% bonds 100%
convertibles 0% other 0% cash 0%

Largest Holdings: general obligation 17%

Unrealized Net Capital Gains: 4% of portfolio value

SHAREHOLDER INFORMATION

Minimum Investment
Initial: $2,500   Subsequent: $100

Minimum IRA Investment
Initial: na   Subsequent: na

Maximum Fees
Load: none   12b-1: none
Other: none

Distributions
Income: monthly   Capital Gains: Jan, Mar

Exchange Options
Number Per Year: 6   Fee: none
Telephone: yes (money market fund available)

Services
auto exchange, auto invest, auto withdraw

T Rowe Price OTC
(OTCFX)
Aggressive Growth

P.O. Box 89000
Baltimore, MD 21289
(800) 638-5660, (410) 547-2308

PERFORMANCE
fund inception date: 6/1/56

	3yr Annual	5yr Annual	10yr Annual	Bull	Bear
Return (%)	10.5	8.2	10.8	95.7	-5.3
Differ from Category (+/-)	1.6 abv av	-4.3 low	-3.2 blw av	-37.5 blw av	5.5 high

Total Risk	Standard Deviation	Category Risk	Risk Index	Beta
abv av	10.0%	low	0.7	0.6

	1994	1993	1992	1991	1990	1989	1988	1987	1986	1985
Return (%)	0.0	18.4	13.9	38.6	-20.4	19.1	27.1	-12.5	4.7	35.4
Differ from category (+/-)	0.7	-1.1	2.9	-13.5	-14.2	-7.7	11.9	-10.3	-7.1	3.1

PER SHARE DATA

	1994	1993	1992	1991	1990	1989	1988	1987	1986	1985
Dividends, Net Income ($)	0.03	0.00	0.07	0.09	0.09	0.13	0.13	0.32	0.06	0.15
Distrib'ns, Cap Gain ($)	1.56	1.58	4.64	0.68	0.10	0.48	2.50	1.51	2.54	1.14
Net Asset Value ($)	13.80	15.39	14.37	16.86	12.72	16.23	14.14	13.19	17.04	18.68
Expense Ratio (%)	1.15	1.20	1.32	1.34	1.47	1.45	1.55	1.00	0.85	1.25
Net Income to Assets (%)	0.10	-0.01	0.03	0.48	0.73	0.63	0.64	0.80	0.95	0.75
Portfolio Turnover (%)	34	40	31	31	35	33	27	49	30	31
Total Assets (Millions $)	196	202	187	267	215	316	292	212	247	147

PORTFOLIO (as of 6/30/94)

Portfolio Manager: Greg McCrickard - 1992

Investm't Category: Aggressive Growth

✔ Cap Gain	Asset Allocation
Cap & Income	Fund of Funds
Income	Index
	Sector
✔ Domestic	✔ Small Cap
✔ Foreign	Socially Conscious
Country/Region	State Specific

Portfolio: stocks 88% bonds 0%
convertibles 2% other 0% cash 10%

Largest Holdings: bank & trust 8%, transportation services 7%

Unrealized Net Capital Gains: 16% of portfolio value

SHAREHOLDER INFORMATION

Minimum Investment
Initial: $2,500   Subsequent: $100

Minimum IRA Investment
Initial: $1,000   Subsequent: $50

Maximum Fees
Load: none   12b-1: none
Other: none

Distributions
Income: Dec   Capital Gains: Dec

Exchange Options
Number Per Year: 6   Fee: none
Telephone: yes (money market fund available)

Services
IRA, pension, auto exchange, auto invest, auto withdraw

T Rowe Price Science & Tech (PRSCX)

Aggressive Growth

P.O. Box 89000
Baltimore, MD 21289
(800) 638-5660, (410) 547-2308

fund inception date: 9/30/87

PERFORMANCE

	3yr Annual	5yr Annual	10yr Annual	Bull	Bear
Return (%)	19.5	21.9	na	184.5	-12.5
Differ from Category (+/-)	10.6 high	9.4 high	na	51.3 high	-1.7 blw av

Total Risk	Standard Deviation	Category Risk	Risk Index	Beta
high	17.5%	high	1.2	1.3

	1994	1993	1992	1991	1990	1989	1988	1987	1986	1985
Return (%)	15.7	24.2	18.7	60.1	-1.3	40.6	13.2	—	—	—
Differ from category (+/-)	16.4	4.7	7.7	8.0	4.9	13.8	-2.0	—	—	—

PER SHARE DATA

	1994	1993	1992	1991	1990	1989	1988	1987	1986	1985
Dividends, Net Income ($)	0.00	0.00	0.00	0.00	0.09	0.06	0.07	—	—	—
Distrib'ns, Cap Gain ($)	0.30	2.51	1.12	0.48	0.24	1.39	0.44	—	—	—
Net Asset Value ($)	21.64	18.95	17.33	15.57	10.05	10.53	8.57	—	—	—
Expense Ratio (%)	1.21	1.25	1.25	1.25	1.25	1.20	1.20	—	—	—
Net Income to Assets (%)	-0.76	-0.68	-0.81	-0.07	0.91	0.50	0.68	—	—	—
Portfolio Turnover (%)	117	163	144	148	183	203	92	—	—	—
Total Assets (Millions $)	915	494	281	166	62	24	12	—	—	—

PORTFOLIO (as of 6/30/94)

Portfolio Manager: Charles Morris - 1991

Investm't Category: Aggressive Growth

✔ Cap Gain	Asset Allocation
Cap & Income	Fund of Funds
Income	Index
	✔ Sector
✔ Domestic	Small Cap
✔ Foreign	Socially Conscious
Country/Region	State Specific

Portfolio: stocks 91%   bonds 0%
convertibles 0%   other 0%   cash 9%

Largest Holdings: computer software 24%, semiconductor related 16%

Unrealized Net Capital Gains: 4% of portfolio value

SHAREHOLDER INFORMATION

Minimum Investment
Initial: $2,500   Subsequent: $100

Minimum IRA Investment
Initial: $1,000   Subsequent: $50

Maximum Fees
Load: none   12b-1: none
Other: none

Distributions
Income: Dec   Capital Gains: Dec

Exchange Options
Number Per Year: 6   Fee: none
Telephone: yes (money market fund available)

Services
IRA, pension, auto exchange, auto invest, auto withdraw

T Rowe Price Short-Term Bond (PRWBX)

General Bond

P.O. Box 89000
Baltimore, MD 21289
(800) 638-5660, (410) 547-2308

PERFORMANCE

fund inception date: 3/2/84

	3yr Annual	5yr Annual	10yr Annual	Bull	Bear
Return (%)	2.8	5.5	7.0	29.2	-2.5
Differ from Category (+/-)	-1.5 low	-1.4 low	-1.9 low	-11.8 low	1.3 abv av

Total Risk	Standard Deviation	Category Risk	Risk Index	Avg Mat
low	2.2%	low	0.5	2.1 yrs

	1994	1993	1992	1991	1990	1989	1988	1987	1986	1985
Return (%)	-2.9	6.6	4.9	11.2	8.6	9.9	5.5	5.2	8.9	12.8
Differ from category (+/-) . . .	-0.9	-2.6	-1.7	-3.4	1.4	-1.5	-1.9	3.0	-5.3	-6.6

PER SHARE DATA

	1994	1993	1992	1991	1990	1989	1988	1987	1986	1985
Dividends, Net Income ($) .	0.28	0.32	0.34	0.35	0.40	0.42	0.41	0.39	0.42	0.47
Distrib'ns, Cap Gain ($) . . .	0.00	0.00	0.00	0.00	0.03	0.00	0.00	0.00	0.00	0.00
Net Asset Value ($)	4.63	5.05	5.04	5.13	4.95	4.97	4.92	5.06	5.19	5.16
Expense Ratio (%)	0.74	0.76	0.88	0.93	0.95	0.94	0.91	0.94	1.31	0.90
Net Income to Assets (%) .	6.00	6.59	7.07	7.90	8.43	8.27	7.85	7.58	9.12	10.73
Portfolio Turnover (%).	90	68	381	980	161	309	203	7	20	73
Total Assets (Millions $). . . .	474	680	398	219	210	232	284	218	96	41

PORTFOLIO (as of 5/31/94)

Portfolio Manager: Veena A. Kutler - 1991

Investm't Category: General Bond

Cap Gain	Asset Allocation
Cap & Income	Fund of Funds
✔ Income	Index
	Sector
✔ Domestic	Small Cap
✔ Foreign	Socially Conscious
Country/Region	State Specific

Portfolio: stocks 0%   bonds 88%
convertibles 0%   other 5%   cash 7%

Largest Holdings: mortgage-backed 32%, corporate 31%

Unrealized Net Capital Gains: -2% of portfolio value

SHAREHOLDER INFORMATION

Minimum Investment
Initial: $2,500   Subsequent: $100

Minimum IRA Investment
Initial: $1,000   Subsequent: $50

Maximum Fees
Load: none   12b-1: none
Other: none

Distributions
Income: monthly   Capital Gains: Jan, Mar

Exchange Options
Number Per Year: 6   Fee: none
Telephone: yes (money market fund available)

Services
IRA, pension, auto exchange, auto invest, auto withdraw

T Rowe Price Short-Term Global Inc (RPSGX)

P.O. Box 89000
Baltimore, MD 21289
(800) 638-5660, (410) 547-2308

International Bond

PERFORMANCE

fund inception date: 6/30/92

	3yr Annual	5yr Annual	10yr Annual	Bull	Bear
Return (%)	na	na	na	na	-3.7
Differ from Category (+/-)	na	na	na	na	4.1 av

Total Risk	Standard Deviation	Category Risk	Risk Index	Avg Mat
na	na	na	na	2.2 yrs

	1994	1993	1992	1991	1990	1989	1988	1987	1986	1985
Return (%)	-3.0	7.8	—	—	—	—	—	—	—	—
Differ from category (+/-)	3.3	-5.6	—	—	—	—	—	—	—	—

PER SHARE DATA

	1994	1993	1992	1991	1990	1989	1988	1987	1986	1985
Dividends, Net Income ($)	0.30	0.32	—	—	—	—	—	—	—	—
Distrib'ns, Cap Gain ($)	0.00	0.00	—	—	—	—	—	—	—	—
Net Asset Value ($)	4.38	4.82	—	—	—	—	—	—	—	—
Expense Ratio (%)	1.00	1.00	—	—	—	—	—	—	—	—
Net Income to Assets (%)	6.63	6.74	—	—	—	—	—	—	—	—
Portfolio Turnover (%)	116	92	—	—	—	—	—	—	—	—
Total Assets (Millions $)	56	96	—	—	—	—	—	—	—	—

PORTFOLIO (as of 6/30/94)

Portfolio Manager: Peter B. Askew - 1994

Investm't Category: International Bond

Cap Gain	Asset Allocation
Cap & Income	Fund of Funds
✔ Income	Index
	Sector
✔ Domestic	Small Cap
✔ Foreign	Socially Conscious
Country/Region	State Specific

Portfolio: stocks 0% bonds 86%
convertibles 0% other 0% cash 14%

Largest Holdings: United States 20%, France 14%

Unrealized Net Capital Gains: -1% of portfolio value

SHAREHOLDER INFORMATION

Minimum Investment
Initial: $2,500   Subsequent: $100

Minimum IRA Investment
Initial: $1,000   Subsequent: $50

Maximum Fees
Load: none   12b-1: none
Other: none

Distributions
Income: monthly   Capital Gains: Dec

Exchange Options
Number Per Year: 6   Fee: none
Telephone: yes (money market fund available)

Services
IRA, pension, auto exchange, auto invest, auto withdraw

T Rowe Price Small Cap Value (PRSVX)

P.O. Box 89000
Baltimore, MD 21289
(800) 638-5660, (410) 547-2308

Growth

this fund is closed to new investors

PERFORMANCE

fund inception date: 6/30/88

	3yr Annual	5yr Annual	10yr Annual	Bull	Bear
Return (%)	13.6	11.8	na	113.2	-3.6
Differ from Category (+/-)	5.9 high	2.2 abv av	na	21.1 abv av	3.0 high

Total Risk	Standard Deviation	Category Risk	Risk Index	Beta
av	8.3%	blw av	0.8	0.5

	1994	1993	1992	1991	1990	1989	1988	1987	1986	1985
Return (%)	-1.3	23.3	20.8	34.1	-11.3	18.0	—	—	—	—
Differ from category (+/-)	-0.7	9.9	9.2	-1.6	-5.6	-8.1	—	—	—	—

PER SHARE DATA

	1994	1993	1992	1991	1990	1989	1988	1987	1986	1985
Dividends, Net Income ($)	0.14	0.10	0.10	0.12	0.24	0.14	—	—	—	—
Distrib'ns, Cap Gain ($)	0.92	0.35	0.15	0.34	0.12	0.90	—	—	—	—
Net Asset Value ($)	13.40	14.68	12.28	10.37	8.09	9.53	—	—	—	—
Expense Ratio (%)	0.98	1.05	1.25	1.25	1.25	1.25	—	—	—	—
Net Income to Assets (%)	1.00	0.91	0.98	1.31	2.57	1.42	—	—	—	—
Portfolio Turnover (%)	17	11	12	31	33	43	—	—	—	—
Total Assets (Millions $)	408	452	264	53	26	33	—	—	—	—

PORTFOLIO (as of 6/30/94)

Portfolio Manager: Preston Athey - 1991

Investm't Category: Growth

✔ Cap Gain
  Cap & Income
  Income

  Asset Allocation
  Fund of Funds
  Index
  Sector

✔ Domestic
✔ Foreign
  Country/Region

✔ Small Cap
  Socially Conscious
  State Specific

Portfolio: stocks 92% bonds 0%
convertibles 3% other 0% cash 5%

Largest Holdings: business services 8%, consumer products 6%

Unrealized Net Capital Gains: 15% of portfolio value

SHAREHOLDER INFORMATION

Minimum Investment
Initial: $2,500 Subsequent: $100

Minimum IRA Investment
Initial: $1,000 Subsequent: $50

Maximum Fees
Load: none 12b-1: none
Other: none

Distributions
Income: Dec Capital Gains: Dec

Exchange Options
Number Per Year: 6 Fee: none
Telephone: yes (money market fund available)

Services
IRA, pension, auto exchange, auto invest, auto withdraw

T Rowe Price Spectrum Growth (PRSGX)

P.O. Box 89000
Baltimore, MD 21289
(800) 638-5660, (410) 547-2308

Growth & Income

PERFORMANCE

fund inception date: 6/30/90

	3yr Annual	5yr Annual	10yr Annual	Bull	Bear
Return (%)	9.5	na	na	87.8	-6.8
Differ from Category (+/-)	2.4 abv av	na	na	12.0 abv av	-0.5 blw av

Total Risk	Standard Deviation	Category Risk	Risk Index	Beta
av	8.5%	abv av	1.0	0.9

	1994	1993	1992	1991	1990	1989	1988	1987	1986	1985
Return (%)	1.3	20.9	7.2	29.8	—	—	—	—	—	—
Differ from category (+/-)	2.7	7.7	-3.0	2.2	—	—	—	—	—	—

PER SHARE DATA

	1994	1993	1992	1991	1990	1989	1988	1987	1986	1985
Dividends, Net Income ($)	0.17	0.16	0.20	0.21	—	—	—	—	—	—
Distrib'ns, Cap Gain ($)	0.73	0.72	0.55	0.32	—	—	—	—	—	—
Net Asset Value ($)	11.13	11.87	10.54	10.53	—	—	—	—	—	—
Expense Ratio (%)	0.00	0.00	0.00	0.00	—	—	—	—	—	—
Net Income to Assets (%)	0.82	1.57	2.15	2.77	—	—	—	—	—	—
Portfolio Turnover (%)	12	7	8	15	—	—	—	—	—	—
Total Assets (Millions $)	879	585	355	149	—	—	—	—	—	—

PORTFOLIO (as of 6/30/94)

Portfolio Manager: Peter Van Dyke - 1990

Investm't Category: Growth & Income
- Cap Gain
- ✔ Cap & Income
- Income
- Asset Allocation
- ✔ Fund of Funds
- Index
- Sector
- Small Cap
- ✔ Domestic
- ✔ Foreign
- Country/Region
- Socially Conscious
- State Specific

Portfolio: stocks 100% bonds 0%
convertibles 0% other 0% cash 0%

Largest Holdings: T. Rowe Price International Stock Fund 20%, T. Rowe Price Growth Stock 19%

Unrealized Net Capital Gains: 3% of portfolio value

SHAREHOLDER INFORMATION

Minimum Investment
Initial: $2,500 Subsequent: $100

Minimum IRA Investment
Initial: $1,000 Subsequent: $50

Maximum Fees
Load: none 12b-1: none
Other: none

Distributions
Income: Dec Capital Gains: Dec

Exchange Options
Number Per Year: 6 Fee: none
Telephone: yes (money market fund available)

Services
IRA, pension, auto exchange, auto invest, auto withdraw

T Rowe Price Spectrum Income (RPSIX)

P.O. Box 89000
Baltimore, MD 21289
(800) 638-5660, (410) 547-2308

Balanced

PERFORMANCE

fund inception date: 6/29/90

	3yr Annual	5yr Annual	10yr Annual	Bull	Bear
Return (%)	5.9	na	na	53.4	-4.8
Differ from Category (+/-)	-0.5 av	na	na	-11.6 blw av	0.9 abv av

Total Risk	Standard Deviation	Category Risk	Risk Index	Beta
low	3.5%	low	0.5	0.3

	1994	1993	1992	1991	1990	1989	1988	1987	1986	1985
Return (%).................	-1.9	12.4	7.8	19.6	—	—	—	—	—	—
Differ from category (+/-)...	0.0	-1.0	-0.5	-3.8	—	—	—	—	—	—

PER SHARE DATA

	1994	1993	1992	1991	1990	1989	1988	1987	1986	1985
Dividends, Net Income ($) .	0.68	0.70	0.76	0.83	—	—	—	—	—	—
Distrib'ns, Cap Gain ($) ...	0.10	0.19	0.08	0.06	—	—	—	—	—	—
Net Asset Value ($)	10.11	11.11	10.70	10.73	—	—	—	—	—	—
Expense Ratio (%)	0.00	0.00	0.00	0.00	—	—	—	—	—	—
Net Income to Assets (%) .	6.24	6.19	7.10	8.03	—	—	—	—	—	—
Portfolio Turnover (%)......	17	14	14	19	—	—	—	—	—	—
Total Assets (Millions $)....	624	588	377	148	—	—	—	—	—	—

PORTFOLIO (as of 6/30/94)

Portfolio Manager: Peter Van Dyke - 1990

Investm't Category: Balanced
Cap Gain	✔ Asset Allocation
✔ Cap & Income	✔ Fund of Funds
Income	Index
	Sector
✔ Domestic	Small Cap
✔ Foreign	Socially Conscious
Country/Region	State Specific

Portfolio: stocks 16% bonds 79%
convertibles 0% other 0% cash 5%

Largest Holdings: T. Rowe Price High Yield Fund 21%, T. Rowe Price New Income Fund 18%

Unrealized Net Capital Gains: -3% of portfolio value

SHAREHOLDER INFORMATION

Minimum Investment
Initial: $2,500 Subsequent: $100

Minimum IRA Investment
Initial: $1,000 Subsequent: $50

Maximum Fees
Load: none 12b-1: none
Other: none

Distributions
Income: monthly Capital Gains: Dec

Exchange Options
Number Per Year: 6 Fee: none
Telephone: yes (money market fund available)

Services
IRA, pension, auto exchange, auto invest, auto withdraw

T Rowe Price Tax-Free High Yield (PRFHX)

P.O. Box 89000
Baltimore, MD 21289
(800) 638-5660, (410) 547-2308

Tax-Exempt Bond

PERFORMANCE

fund inception date: 3/1/85

	3yr Annual	5yr Annual	10yr Annual	Bull	Bear
Return (%)	5.7	7.2	na	44.3	-4.7
Differ from Category (+/-)	1.2 high	1.1 high	na	2.5 av	0.5 abv av

Total Risk	Standard Deviation	Category Risk	Risk Index	Avg Mat
blw av	4.9%	blw av	0.8	19.0 yrs

	1994	1993	1992	1991	1990	1989	1988	1987	1986	1985
Return (%).	-4.3	12.9	9.5	11.7	7.1	10.5	11.1	0.2	20.4	—
Differ from category (+/-). . .	0.9	1.2	1.2	0.4	0.8	1.5	0.9	1.5	4.0	—

PER SHARE DATA

	1994	1993	1992	1991	1990	1989	1988	1987	1986	1985
Dividends, Net Income ($).	0.72	0.75	0.79	0.81	0.83	0.84	0.83	0.84	0.88	—
Distrib'ns, Cap Gain ($) . . .	0.04	0.23	0.10	0.10	0.03	0.06	0.00	0.25	0.00	—
Net Asset Value ($)	11.16	12.46	11.93	11.74	11.37	11.45	11.21	10.86	11.92	—
Expense Ratio (%)	0.79	0.81	0.83	0.85	0.88	0.92	0.96	0.98	1.00	—
Net Income to Assets (%) .	6.09	6.58	7.01	7.30	7.38	7.45	7.49	7.45	8.47	—
Portfolio Turnover (%)	56	34	51	51	72	62	128	111	156	—
Total Assets (Millions $). . . .	802	959	624	505	444	331	281	324	168	—

PORTFOLIO (as of 8/31/94)

Portfolio Manager: C. Stephan Wolfe - 1993

Investm't Category: Tax-Exempt Bond

Cap Gain	Asset Allocation
Cap & Income	Fund of Funds
✔ Income	Index
	Sector
✔ Domestic	Small Cap
Foreign	Socially Conscious
Country/Region	State Specific

Portfolio: stocks 0% bonds 100%
convertibles 0% other 0% cash 0%

Largest Holdings: general obligation 6%

Unrealized Net Capital Gains: 3% of portfolio value

SHAREHOLDER INFORMATION

Minimum Investment
Initial: $2,500   Subsequent: $100

Minimum IRA Investment
Initial: na   Subsequent: na

Maximum Fees
Load: none   12b-1: none
Other: none

Distributions
Income: monthly   Capital Gains: Mar, Dec

Exchange Options
Number Per Year: 6   Fee: none
Telephone: yes (money market fund available)

Services
auto exchange, auto invest, auto withdraw

T Rowe Price Tax-Free Income (PRTAX)

P.O. Box 89000
Baltimore, MD 21289
(800) 638-5660, (410) 547-2308

Tax-Exempt Bond

PERFORMANCE

fund inception date: 10/26/76

	3yr Annual	5yr Annual	10yr Annual	Bull	Bear
Return (%)	5.2	6.7	8.1	46.1	-6.2
Differ from Category (+/-)	0.7 abv av	0.6 abv av	0.0 blw av	4.3 abv av	-1.0 blw av

Total Risk	Standard Deviation	Category Risk	Risk Index	Avg Mat
blw av	6.2%	av	1.0	17.2 yrs

	1994	1993	1992	1991	1990	1989	1988	1987	1986	1985
Return (%)	-5.5	12.7	9.3	12.1	5.8	9.1	7.8	-4.1	19.8	16.9
Differ from category (+/-)	-0.3	1.0	1.0	0.8	-0.5	0.1	-2.4	-2.8	3.4	-0.5

PER SHARE DATA

	1994	1993	1992	1991	1990	1989	1988	1987	1986	1985
Dividends, Net Income ($)	0.52	0.54	0.56	0.57	0.57	0.60	0.59	0.60	0.70	0.70
Distrib'ns, Cap Gain ($)	0.04	0.18	0.00	0.00	0.00	0.00	0.00	0.54	0.00	0.00
Net Asset Value ($)	8.80	9.90	9.44	9.17	8.71	8.79	8.62	8.55	10.07	9.03
Expense Ratio (%)	0.59	0.61	0.62	0.63	0.64	0.66	0.65	0.61	0.63	0.63
Net Income to Assets (%)	5.63	5.98	6.34	6.59	6.80	6.81	6.72	6.94	8.07	7.84
Portfolio Turnover (%)	51	76	58	80	141	116	181	237	187	277
Total Assets (Millions $)	1,253	1,510	1,246	1,129	1,123	1,023	1,094	1,558	1,325	936

PORTFOLIO (as of 8/31/94)

Portfolio Manager: William T. Reynolds - 1990

Investm't Category: Tax-Exempt Bond

Cap Gain	Asset Allocation
Cap & Income	Fund of Funds
✔ Income	Index
	Sector
✔ Domestic	Small Cap
Foreign	Socially Conscious
Country/Region	State Specific

Portfolio: stocks 0% bonds 100%
convertibles 0% other 0% cash 0%

Largest Holdings: general obligation 13%

Unrealized Net Capital Gains: 2% of portfolio value

SHAREHOLDER INFORMATION

Minimum Investment
Initial: $2,500   Subsequent: $100

Minimum IRA Investment
Initial: na   Subsequent: na

Maximum Fees
Load: none   12b-1: none
Other: none

Distributions
Income: monthly   Capital Gains: Mar, Dec

Exchange Options
Number Per Year: 6   Fee: none
Telephone: yes (money market fund available)

Services
auto exchange, auto invest, auto withdraw

T Rowe Price Tax-Free Insured Interm (PTIBX)

P.O. Box 89000
Baltimore, MD 21289
(800) 638-5660, (410) 547-2308

Tax-Exempt Bond

PERFORMANCE

	3yr Annual	5yr Annual	10yr Annual	Bull	Bear
Return (%)	na	na	na	na	-3.5
Differ from Category (+/-)	na	na	na	na	1.7 abv av

Total Risk	Standard Deviation	Category Risk	Risk Index	Avg Mat
na	na	na	na	7.4 yrs

	1994	1993	1992	1991	1990	1989	1988	1987	1986	1985
Return (%)	-2.6	12.6	—	—	—	—	—	—	—	—
Differ from category (+/-)	2.6	0.9	—	—	—	—	—	—	—	—

PER SHARE DATA

	1994	1993	1992	1991	1990	1989	1988	1987	1986	1985
Dividends, Net Income ($)	0.46	0.48	—	—	—	—	—	—	—	—
Distrib'ns, Cap Gain ($)	0.03	0.06	—	—	—	—	—	—	—	—
Net Asset Value ($)	10.03	10.80	—	—	—	—	—	—	—	—
Expense Ratio (%)	0.65	0.00	—	—	—	—	—	—	—	—
Net Income to Assets (%)	4.33	5.08	—	—	—	—	—	—	—	—
Portfolio Turnover (%)	171	65	—	—	—	—	—	—	—	—
Total Assets (Millions $)	79	97	—	—	—	—	—	—	—	—

PORTFOLIO (as of 8/31/94)

Portfolio Manager: William Reynolds - 1992

Investm't Category: Tax-Exempt Bond

Cap Gain	Asset Allocation
Cap & Income	Fund of Funds
✔ Income	Index
	Sector
✔ Domestic	Small Cap
Foreign	Socially Conscious
Country/Region	State Specific

Portfolio: stocks 0% bonds 100%
convertibles 0% other 0% cash 0%

Largest Holdings: general obligation 12%

Unrealized Net Capital Gains: 0% of portfolio value

SHAREHOLDER INFORMATION

Minimum Investment
Initial: $2,500   Subsequent: $100

Minimum IRA Investment
Initial: na   Subsequent: na

Maximum Fees
Load: none   12b-1: none
Other: none

Distributions
Income: monthly   Capital Gains: Mar, Dec

Exchange Options
Number Per Year: 6   Fee: none
Telephone: yes (money market fund available)

Services
auto exchange, auto invest, auto withdraw

T Rowe Price Tax-Free Short-Interm (PRFSX)

P.O. Box 89000
Baltimore, MD 21289
(800) 638-5660, (410) 547-2308

Tax-Exempt Bond

PERFORMANCE

fund inception date: 12/23/83

	3yr Annual	5yr Annual	10yr Annual	Bull	Bear
Return (%)	4.1	5.2	5.8	24.6	-1.1
Differ from Category (+/-)	-0.4 blw av	-0.9 low	-2.3 low	-17.2 low	4.1 high

Total Risk	Standard Deviation	Category Risk	Risk Index	Avg Mat
low	2.0%	low	0.3	3.1 yrs

	1994	1993	1992	1991	1990	1989	1988	1987	1986	1985
Return (%)	0.3	6.3	6.0	7.8	6.0	6.8	4.9	2.2	9.7	8.8
Differ from category (+/-)	5.5	-5.4	-2.3	-3.5	-0.3	-2.2	-5.3	3.5	-6.7	-8.6

PER SHARE DATA

	1994	1993	1992	1991	1990	1989	1988	1987	1986	1985
Dividends, Net Income ($)	0.22	0.23	0.25	0.28	0.29	0.30	0.28	0.27	0.30	0.32
Distrib'ns, Cap Gain ($)	0.00	0.00	0.00	0.00	0.00	0.00	0.00	0.02	0.00	0.00
Net Asset Value ($)	5.18	5.38	5.28	5.22	5.11	5.10	5.06	5.09	5.27	5.09
Expense Ratio (%)	0.59	0.63	0.67	0.74	0.75	0.74	0.74	0.73	0.90	0.90
Net Income to Assets (%)	4.02	4.61	5.34	5.67	5.93	5.46	5.29	5.60	6.26	6.51
Portfolio Turnover (%)	85	38	81	190	191	53	225	120	128	300
Total Assets (Millions $)	451	530	329	233	223	249	292	405	155	68

PORTFOLIO (as of 8/31/94)

Portfolio Manager: Mary J. Miller - 1989

Investm't Category: Tax-Exempt Bond

Cap Gain	Asset Allocation
Cap & Income	Fund of Funds
✔ Income	Index
	Sector
✔ Domestic	Small Cap
Foreign	Socially Conscious
Country/Region	State Specific

Portfolio: stocks 0% bonds 100%
convertibles 0% other 0% cash 0%

Largest Holdings: general obligation 29%

Unrealized Net Capital Gains: 0% of portfolio value

SHAREHOLDER INFORMATION

Minimum Investment
Initial: $2,500   Subsequent: $100

Minimum IRA Investment
Initial: na   Subsequent: na

Maximum Fees
Load: none   12b-1: none
Other: none

Distributions
Income: monthly   Capital Gains: Mar, Dec

Exchange Options
Number Per Year: 6   Fee: none
Telephone: yes (money market fund available)

Services
auto exchange, auto invest, auto withdraw

T Rowe Price US Treasury Interm (PRTIX)

P.O. Box 89000
Baltimore, MD 21289
(800) 638-5660, (410) 547-2308

Government Bond

PERFORMANCE

fund inception date: 9/29/89

	3yr Annual	5yr Annual	10yr Annual	Bull	Bear
Return (%)	3.8	6.9	na	38.4	-3.3
Differ from Category (+/-)	-0.2 av	0.2 av	na	-12.8 blw av	3.1 abv av

Total Risk	Standard Deviation	Category Risk	Risk Index	Avg Mat
low	3.6%	av	0.8	3.9 yrs

	1994	1993	1992	1991	1990	1989	1988	1987	1986	1985
Return (%)	-2.3	7.9	6.2	14.7	8.9	—	—	—	—	—
Differ from category (+/-)	2.5	-3.0	-0.2	-0.6	2.7	—	—	—	—	—

PER SHARE DATA

	1994	1993	1992	1991	1990	1989	1988	1987	1986	1985
Dividends, Net Income ($)	0.30	0.29	0.32	0.36	0.41	—	—	—	—	—
Distrib'ns, Cap Gain ($)	0.02	0.01	0.13	0.03	0.00	—	—	—	—	—
Net Asset Value ($)	4.94	5.38	5.27	5.41	5.08	—	—	—	—	—
Expense Ratio (%)	0.79	0.80	0.80	0.80	0.80	—	—	—	—	—
Net Income to Assets (%)	5.41	5.98	6.80	7.71	8.13	—	—	—	—	—
Portfolio Turnover (%)	20	23	91	175	195	—	—	—	—	—
Total Assets (Millions $)	163	171	124	68	11	—	—	—	—	—

PORTFOLIO (as of 5/31/94)

Portfolio Manager: Charles P. Smith - 1989

Investm't Category: Government Bond

Cap Gain	Asset Allocation
Cap & Income	Fund of Funds
✔ Income	Index
	Sector
✔ Domestic	Small Cap
Foreign	Socially Conscious
Country/Region	State Specific

Portfolio: stocks 0%   bonds 100%
convertibles 0%   other 0%   cash 0%

Largest Holdings: U.S. government 86%, mortgage-backed 14%

Unrealized Net Capital Gains: 0% of portfolio value

SHAREHOLDER INFORMATION

Minimum Investment
Initial: $2,500   Subsequent: $100

Minimum IRA Investment
Initial: $1,000   Subsequent: $50

Maximum Fees
Load: none   12b-1: none
Other: none

Distributions
Income: monthly   Capital Gains: Mar, Dec

Exchange Options
Number Per Year: 6   Fee: none
Telephone: yes (money market fund available)

Services
IRA, pension, auto exchange, auto invest, auto withdraw

T Rowe Price US Treasury Long Term

P.O. Box 89000
Baltimore, MD 21289
(800) 638-5660, (410) 547-2308

(PRULX) *Government Bond*

PERFORMANCE

fund inception date: 9/29/89

	3yr Annual	5yr Annual	10yr Annual	Bull	Bear
Return (%)	4.0	6.9	na	51.7	-8.3
Differ from Category (+/-)	0.0 av	0.2 av	na	0.5 abv av	-1.9 blw av

Total Risk	Standard Deviation	Category Risk	Risk Index	Avg Mat
blw av	6.0%	abv av	1.3	17.3 yrs

	1994	1993	1992	1991	1990	1989	1988	1987	1986	1985
Return (%)	-5.7	12.9	5.8	16.2	6.6	—	—	—	—	—
Differ from category (+/-)	-0.9	2.0	-0.6	0.9	0.4	—	—	—	—	—

PER SHARE DATA

	1994	1993	1992	1991	1990	1989	1988	1987	1986	1985
Dividends, Net Income ($)	0.68	0.68	0.72	0.78	0.81	—	—	—	—	—
Distrib'ns, Cap Gain ($)	0.01	0.29	0.28	0.00	0.00	—	—	—	—	—
Net Asset Value ($)	9.41	10.71	10.36	10.78	10.01	—	—	—	—	—
Expense Ratio (%)	0.80	0.80	0.80	0.80	0.80	—	—	—	—	—
Net Income to Assets (%)	6.17	6.75	7.66	8.01	8.23	—	—	—	—	—
Portfolio Turnover (%)	59	165	162	159	316	—	—	—	—	—
Total Assets (Millions $)	58	57	53	43	11	—	—	—	—	—

PORTFOLIO (as of 5/31/94)

Portfolio Manager: Peter Van Dyke - 1989

Investm't Category: Government Bond

Cap Gain	Asset Allocation
Cap & Income	Fund of Funds
✔ Income	Index
	Sector
✔ Domestic	Small Cap
Foreign	Socially Conscious
Country/Region	State Specific

Portfolio: stocks 0% bonds 100%
convertibles 0% other 0% cash 0%

Largest Holdings: U.S. government 86%, mortgage-backed 14%

Unrealized Net Capital Gains: 0% of portfolio value

SHAREHOLDER INFORMATION

Minimum Investment
Initial: $2,500 Subsequent: $100

Minimum IRA Investment
Initial: $1,000 Subsequent: $50

Maximum Fees
Load: none 12b-1: none
Other: none

Distributions
Income: monthly Capital Gains: Mar, Dec

Exchange Options
Number Per Year: 6 Fee: none
Telephone: yes (money market fund available)

Services
IRA, pension, auto exchange, auto invest, auto withdraw

T Rowe Price Virginia Tax-Free Bond (PRVAX)

P.O. Box 89000
Baltimore, MD 21289
(800) 638-5660, (410) 547-2308

Tax-Exempt Bond

PERFORMANCE

fund inception date: 4/30/91

	3yr Annual	5yr Annual	10yr Annual	Bull	Bear
Return (%)	5.2	na	na	na	-6.0
Differ from Category (+/-)	0.7 abv av	na	na	na	-0.8 av

Total Risk	Standard Deviation	Category Risk	Risk Index	Avg Mat
blw av	6.1%	av	1.0	17.9 yrs

	1994	1993	1992	1991	1990	1989	1988	1987	1986	1985
Return (%)	-5.0	12.5	9.2	—	—	—	—	—	—	—
Differ from category (+/-)	0.2	0.8	0.9	—	—	—	—	—	—	—

PER SHARE DATA

	1994	1993	1992	1991	1990	1989	1988	1987	1986	1985
Dividends, Net Income ($)	0.56	0.57	0.58	—	—	—	—	—	—	—
Distrib'ns, Cap Gain ($)	0.01	0.15	0.03	—	—	—	—	—	—	—
Net Asset Value ($)	10.10	11.24	10.65	—	—	—	—	—	—	—
Expense Ratio (%)	0.65	0.65	0.65	—	—	—	—	—	—	—
Net Income to Assets (%)	5.29	5.53	5.80	—	—	—	—	—	—	—
Portfolio Turnover (%)	95	68	76	—	—	—	—	—	—	—
Total Assets (Millions $)	143	162	44	—	—	—	—	—	—	—

PORTFOLIO (as of 8/31/94)

Portfolio Manager: Mary J. Miller - 1991

Investm't Category: Tax-Exempt Bond

Cap Gain	Asset Allocation
Cap & Income	Fund of Funds
✔ Income	Index
	Sector
✔ Domestic	Small Cap
Foreign	Socially Conscious
Country/Region	✔ State Specific

Portfolio: stocks 0% bonds 100%
convertibles 0% other 0% cash 0%

Largest Holdings: general obligation 6%

Unrealized Net Capital Gains: 1% of portfolio value

SHAREHOLDER INFORMATION

Minimum Investment
Initial: $2,500   Subsequent: $100

Minimum IRA Investment
Initial: na   Subsequent: na

Maximum Fees
Load: none   12b-1: none
Other: none

Distributions
Income: monthly   Capital Gains: Mar, Dec

Exchange Options
Number Per Year: 6   Fee: none
Telephone: yes (money market fund available)

Services
auto exchange, auto invest, auto withdraw

Turner Growth Equity

(TRGEX)

Growth

680 East Swedesford Road
Wayne, PA 19087
(800) 932-7781

PERFORMANCE

	3yr Annual	5yr Annual	10yr Annual	Bull	Bear
Return (%)	na	na	na	na	-11.7
Differ from Category (+/-)	na	na	na	na	-5.1 low

Total Risk	Standard Deviation	Category Risk	Risk Index	Beta
na	na	na	na	na

	1994	1993	1992	1991	1990	1989	1988	1987	1986	1985
Return (%)	-6.7	15.3	—	—	—	—	—	—	—	—
Differ from category (+/-)	-6.1	1.9	—	—	—	—	—	—	—	—

PER SHARE DATA

	1994	1993	1992	1991	1990	1989	1988	1987	1986	1985
Dividends, Net Income ($)	0.10	0.09	—	—	—	—	—	—	—	—
Distrib'ns, Cap Gain ($)	0.00	0.00	—	—	—	—	—	—	—	—
Net Asset Value ($)	11.92	12.89	—	—	—	—	—	—	—	—
Expense Ratio (%)	0.95	1.00	—	—	—	—	—	—	—	—
Net Income to Assets (%)	0.86	0.80	—	—	—	—	—	—	—	—
Portfolio Turnover (%)	164	88	—	—	—	—	—	—	—	—
Total Assets (Millions $)	112	71	—	—	—	—	—	—	—	—

PORTFOLIO (as of 10/31/94)

Portfolio Manager: Robert Turner - 1992

Investm't Category: Growth
- ✔ Cap Gain
- Cap & Income
- Income
- ✔ Domestic
- Foreign
- Country/Region
- Asset Allocation
- Fund of Funds
- Index
- Sector
- Small Cap
- Socially Conscious
- State Specific

Portfolio: stocks 98% bonds 0%
convertibles 0% other 0% cash 2%

Largest Holdings: retail 7%, miscellaneous
business services 7%

Unrealized Net Capital Gains: 7% of portfolio value

SHAREHOLDER INFORMATION

Minimum Investment
Initial: $100,000   Subsequent: $10,000

Minimum IRA Investment
Initial: $0   Subsequent: $0

Maximum Fees
Load: none   12b-1: none
Other: none

Distributions
Income: quarterly   Capital Gains: Dec

Exchange Options
Number Per Year: no limit   Fee: none
Telephone: yes (money market fund not available)

Services
IRA

Tweedy Browne American Value (TWEBX)

52 Vanderbilt Avenue
New York, NY 10017
(800) 432-4789, (800) 873-8242

Growth

PERFORMANCE

fund inception date: 12/8/93

	3yr Annual	5yr Annual	10yr Annual	Bull	Bear
Return (%)	na	na	na	na	-2.9
Differ from Category (+/-)	na	na	na	na	3.7 high

Total Risk	Standard Deviation	Category Risk	Risk Index	Beta
na	na	na	na	na

	1994	1993	1992	1991	1990	1989	1988	1987	1986	1985
Return (%).	-0.5	—	—	—	—	—	—	—	—	—
Differ from category (+/-). . .	0.1	—	—	—	—	—	—	—	—	—

PER SHARE DATA

	1994	1993	1992	1991	1990	1989	1988	1987	1986	1985
Dividends, Net Income ($).	0.06	—	—	—	—	—	—	—	—	—
Distrib'ns, Cap Gain ($) . . .	0.00	—	—	—	—	—	—	—	—	—
Net Asset Value ($)	9.82	—	—	—	—	—	—	—	—	—
Expense Ratio (%)	2.26	—	—	—	—	—	—	—	—	—
Net Income to Assets (%) .	0.64	—	—	—	—	—	—	—	—	—
Portfolio Turnover (%)	na	—	—	—	—	—	—	—	—	—
Total Assets (Millions $).	35	—	—	—	—	—	—	—	—	—

PORTFOLIO (as of 9/30/94)

Portfolio Manager: C. Browne - 1993, W. Browe - 1993, Clark - 1993, Spears - 1993

Investm't Category: Growth

✔ Cap Gain	Asset Allocation
Cap & Income	Fund of Funds
Income	Index
	Sector
✔ Domestic	Small Cap
✔ Foreign	Socially Conscious
Country/Region	State Specific

Portfolio: stocks 84%   bonds 0%
convertibles 0%   other 0%   cash 16%

Largest Holdings: consumer non-durables 15%, insurance 11%

Unrealized Net Capital Gains: 2% of portfolio value

SHAREHOLDER INFORMATION

Minimum Investment
Initial: $2,500   Subsequent: $500

Minimum IRA Investment
Initial: $500   Subsequent: $500

Maximum Fees
Load: none   12b-1: none
Other: none

Distributions
Income: Dec   Capital Gains: Dec

Exchange Options
Number Per Year: no limit   Fee: none
Telephone: yes (money market fund not available)

Services
IRA, pension, auto invest, auto withdraw

Tweedy Browne Global Value (TBGVX)

52 Vanderbilt Avenue
New York, NY 10017
(800) 432-4789, (800) 873-8242

International Stock

PERFORMANCE

fund inception date: 6/15/93

	3yr Annual	5yr Annual	10yr Annual	Bull	Bear
Return (%)	na	na	na	na	-2.9
Differ from Category (+/-)	na	na	na	na	4.1 high

Total Risk	Standard Deviation	Category Risk	Risk Index	Beta
na	na	na	na	na

	1994	1993	1992	1991	1990	1989	1988	1987	1986	1985
Return (%)	4.3	—	—	—	—	—	—	—	—	—
Differ from category (+/-)	7.3	—	—	—	—	—	—	—	—	—

PER SHARE DATA

	1994	1993	1992	1991	1990	1989	1988	1987	1986	1985
Dividends, Net Income ($)	0.00	—	—	—	—	—	—	—	—	—
Distrib'ns, Cap Gain ($)	0.16	—	—	—	—	—	—	—	—	—
Net Asset Value ($)	11.88	—	—	—	—	—	—	—	—	—
Expense Ratio (%)	1.65	—	—	—	—	—	—	—	—	—
Net Income to Assets (%)	1.71	—	—	—	—	—	—	—	—	—
Portfolio Turnover (%)	na	—	—	—	—	—	—	—	—	—
Total Assets (Millions $)	565	—	—	—	—	—	—	—	—	—

PORTFOLIO (as of 9/30/94)

Portfolio Manager: Browne - 1993, Spears - 1993, Clark Jr. - 1993

Investm't Category: International Stock

✔ Cap Gain	Asset Allocation
Cap & Income	Fund of Funds
Income	Index
	Sector
✔ Domestic	✔ Small Cap
✔ Foreign	Socially Conscious
Country/Region	State Specific

Portfolio: stocks 85% bonds 0%
convertibles 0% other 0% cash 15%

Largest Holdings: France 12%, Switzerland 12%

Unrealized Net Capital Gains: 6% of portfolio value

SHAREHOLDER INFORMATION

Minimum Investment
Initial: $2,500   Subsequent: $500

Minimum IRA Investment
Initial: $500   Subsequent: $500

Maximum Fees
Load: none   12b-1: none
Other: none

Distributions
Income: Dec   Capital Gains: Dec

Exchange Options
Number Per Year: no limit   Fee: none
Telephone: yes (money market fund not available)

Services
IRA, auto invest, auto withdraw

Twentieth Century Balanced (TWBIX)

Balanced

4500 Main St.
P.O. Box 419200
Kansas City, MO 64141
(800) 345-2021, (816) 531-5575

PERFORMANCE

fund inception date: 10/20/88

	3yr Annual	5yr Annual	10yr Annual	Bull	Bear
Return (%)	0.2	8.5	na	63.7	-6.5
Differ from Category (+/-)	-6.2 low	0.5 av	na	-1.3 av	-0.8 blw av

Total Risk	Standard Deviation	Category Risk	Risk Index	Beta
av	7.7%	high	1.2	0.8

	1994	1993	1992	1991	1990	1989	1988	1987	1986	1985
Return (%)	0.0	7.2	-6.0	46.8	1.8	25.6	—	—	—	—
Differ from category (+/-)	1.9	-6.2	-14.3	23.4	2.3	8.3	—	—	—	—

PER SHARE DATA

	1994	1993	1992	1991	1990	1989	1988	1987	1986	1985
Dividends, Net Income ($)	0.43	0.38	0.34	0.36	0.42	0.42	—	—	—	—
Distrib'ns, Cap Gain ($)	0.27	0.00	0.00	0.00	0.00	0.32	—	—	—	—
Net Asset Value ($)	15.27	16.00	15.28	16.64	11.62	11.83	—	—	—	—
Expense Ratio (%)	1.00	1.00	1.00	1.00	1.00	1.00	—	—	—	—
Net Income to Assets (%)	2.70	2.40	2.40	3.10	3.80	4.20	—	—	—	—
Portfolio Turnover (%)	94	95	100	116	104	171	—	—	—	—
Total Assets (Millions $)	689	687	654	255	66	30	—	—	—	—

PORTFOLIO (as of 10/31/94)

Portfolio Manager: committee

Investm't Category: Balanced

Cap Gain	Asset Allocation
✔ Cap & Income	Fund of Funds
Income	Index
	Sector
✔ Domestic	Small Cap
✔ Foreign	Socially Conscious
Country/Region	State Specific

Portfolio: stocks 57% bonds 39%
convertibles 0% other 0% cash 4%

Largest Holdings: bonds—mortgage-backed 7%, stocks—chemicals & resins 7%

Unrealized Net Capital Gains: 7% of portfolio value

SHAREHOLDER INFORMATION

Minimum Investment
Initial: $2,500   Subsequent: $50

Minimum IRA Investment
Initial: $0   Subsequent: $50

Maximum Fees
Load: none   12b-1: none
Other: none

Distributions
Income: quarterly   Capital Gains: Dec

Exchange Options
Number Per Year: 4   Fee: none
Telephone: yes (money market fund available)

Services
IRA, pension, auto exchange, auto invest, auto withdraw

Twentieth Century Giftrust (TWGTX)

Aggressive Growth

4500 Main St.
P.O. Box 419200
Kansas City, MO 64141
(800) 345-2021, (816) 531-5575

PERFORMANCE

fund inception date: 11/25/83

	3yr Annual	5yr Annual	10yr Annual	Bull	Bear
Return (%)	20.7	21.9	25.5	215.8	-11.1
Differ from Category (+/-)	11.8 high	9.4 high	11.5 high	82.6 high	-0.3 av

Total Risk	Standard Deviation	Category Risk	Risk Index	Beta
high	19.6%	high	1.3	1.3

	1994	1993	1992	1991	1990	1989	1988	1987	1986	1985
Return (%)	13.4	31.4	17.9	84.9	-16.9	50.2	11.0	8.6	28.0	55.4
Differ from category (+/-)	14.1	11.9	6.9	32.8	-10.7	23.4	-4.2	10.8	16.2	23.1

PER SHARE DATA

	1994	1993	1992	1991	1990	1989	1988	1987	1986	1985
Dividends, Net Income ($)	0.00	0.00	0.00	0.00	0.00	0.00	0.00	0.00	0.00	0.02
Distrib'ns, Cap Gain ($)	1.09	1.91	1.43	0.70	0.03	0.92	0.21	0.86	1.43	0.00
Net Asset Value ($)	18.77	17.53	14.86	13.85	7.88	9.52	6.97	6.47	6.75	6.40
Expense Ratio (%)	1.00	1.00	1.00	1.00	1.00	1.00	1.00	1.00	1.01	1.01
Net Income to Assets (%)	-0.70	-0.70	-0.70	-0.60	-0.60	-0.50	-0.10	-0.50	-0.40	-0.30
Portfolio Turnover (%)	115	143	134	143	137	160	157	130	123	134
Total Assets (Millions $)	247	163	77	55	25	23	13	10	7	3

PORTFOLIO (as of 10/31/94)

Portfolio Manager: committee

Investm't Category: Aggressive Growth

✔ Cap Gain   Asset Allocation
   Cap & Income   Fund of Funds
   Income   Index
                  Sector
✔ Domestic   ✔ Small Cap
✔ Foreign   Socially Conscious
   Country/Region   State Specific

Portfolio: stocks 95%   bonds 0%
convertibles 0%   other 0%   cash 5%

Largest Holdings: industrial equip. & machinery 14%, electrical/electronic components 14%

Unrealized Net Capital Gains: 29% of portfolio value

SHAREHOLDER INFORMATION

Minimum Investment
Initial: $250   Subsequent: $25

Minimum IRA Investment
Initial: na   Subsequent: na

Maximum Fees
Load: none   12b-1: none
Other: none

Distributions
Income: Dec   Capital Gains: Dec

Exchange Options
Number Per Year: none   Fee:
Telephone:

Services
auto invest

Twentieth Century Growth (TWCGX)

Aggressive Growth

4500 Main St.
P.O. Box 419200
Kansas City, MO 64141
(800) 345-2021, (816) 531-5575

PERFORMANCE

fund inception date: 10/31/58

	3yr Annual	5yr Annual	10yr Annual	Bull	Bear
Return (%)	-0.7	9.7	15.4	87.9	-8.5
Differ from Category (+/-)	-9.6 low	-2.8 blw av	1.4 abv av	-45.3 low	2.3 abv av

Total Risk	Standard Deviation	Category Risk	Risk Index	Beta
abv av	11.8%	blw av	0.8	1.1

	1994	1993	1992	1991	1990	1989	1988	1987	1986	1985
Return (%)	-1.5	3.7	-4.2	69.0	-3.8	43.1	2.7	13.1	18.8	33.9
Differ from category (+/-)	-0.8	-15.8	-15.2	16.9	2.4	16.3	-12.5	15.3	7.0	1.6

PER SHARE DATA

	1994	1993	1992	1991	1990	1989	1988	1987	1986	1985
Dividends, Net Income ($)	0.05	0.06	0.00	0.01	0.11	0.08	0.32	0.13	0.18	0.15
Distrib'ns, Cap Gain ($)	3.22	2.77	0.37	0.00	0.89	0.59	0.00	3.46	5.08	0.00
Net Asset Value ($)	18.74	22.40	24.36	25.83	15.29	16.95	12.31	12.30	14.06	16.21
Expense Ratio (%)	1.00	1.00	1.00	1.00	1.00	1.00	1.00	1.00	1.01	1.01
Net Income to Assets (%)	0.30	0.20	-0.10	0.20	0.60	0.50	2.40	0.20	0.60	1.30
Portfolio Turnover (%)	100	94	53	69	118	98	143	114	105	116
Total Assets (Millions $)	4,158	4,538	4,473	3,193	1,697	1,597	1,228	1,188	964	759

PORTFOLIO (as of 10/31/94)

Portfolio Manager: committee

Investm't Category: Aggressive Growth
- ✔ Cap Gain
- Cap & Income
- Income
- ✔ Domestic
- ✔ Foreign
- Country/Region
- Asset Allocation
- Fund of Funds
- Index
- Sector
- Small Cap
- Socially Conscious
- State Specific

Portfolio: stocks 95%   bonds 0%
convertibles 0%   other 0%   cash 5%

Largest Holdings: communications equipment 10%, communications services 9%

Unrealized Net Capital Gains: 13% of portfolio value

SHAREHOLDER INFORMATION

Minimum Investment
Initial: $2,500   Subsequent: $50

Minimum IRA Investment
Initial: $0   Subsequent: $50

Maximum Fees
Load: none   12b-1: none
Other: none

Distributions
Income: Dec   Capital Gains: Dec

Exchange Options
Number Per Year: 4   Fee: none
Telephone: yes (money market fund available)

Services
IRA, pension, auto exchange, auto invest, auto withdraw

Twentieth Century Heritage (TWHIX)

Growth

4500 Main St.
P.O. Box 419200
Kansas City, MO 64141
(800) 345-2021, (816) 531-5575

PERFORMANCE

fund inception date: 11/10/87

	3yr Annual	5yr Annual	10yr Annual	Bull	Bear
Return (%)	7.5	8.9	na	93.5	-10.5
Differ from Category (+/-)	-0.2 av	-0.7 av	na	1.4 av	-3.9 low

Total Risk	Standard Deviation	Category Risk	Risk Index	Beta
abv av	11.8%	high	1.2	1.1

	1994	1993	1992	1991	1990	1989	1988	1987	1986	1985
Return (%)	-6.3	20.4	10.1	35.9	-9.1	34.9	16.4	—	—	—
Differ from category (+/-)	-5.7	7.0	-1.5	0.2	-3.4	8.8	-1.6	—	—	—

PER SHARE DATA

	1994	1993	1992	1991	1990	1989	1988	1987	1986	1985
Dividends, Net Income ($)	0.03	0.07	0.09	0.11	0.11	0.07	0.07	—	—	—
Distrib'ns, Cap Gain ($)	0.54	0.51	0.68	0.00	0.00	0.69	0.00	—	—	—
Net Asset Value ($)	9.35	10.61	9.31	9.17	6.83	7.64	6.22	—	—	—
Expense Ratio (%)	1.00	1.00	1.00	1.00	1.00	1.00	1.00	—	—	—
Net Income to Assets (%)	0.70	0.70	1.10	1.50	1.60	1.30	1.40	—	—	—
Portfolio Turnover (%)	136	116	119	146	127	159	130	—	—	—
Total Assets (Millions $)	851	725	369	269	199	117	55	—	—	—

PORTFOLIO (as of 10/31/94)

Portfolio Manager: committee

Investm't Category: Growth

✔ Cap Gain	Asset Allocation
Cap & Income	Fund of Funds
Income	Index
	Sector
✔ Domestic	Small Cap
✔ Foreign	Socially Conscious
Country/Region	State Specific

Portfolio: stocks 92% bonds 0%
convertibles 5% other 0% cash 3%

Largest Holdings: industrial equipment & machinery 10%, specialty retail 8%

Unrealized Net Capital Gains: 7% of portfolio value

SHAREHOLDER INFORMATION

Minimum Investment
Initial: $2,500   Subsequent: $50

Minimum IRA Investment
Initial: $0   Subsequent: $50

Maximum Fees
Load: none   12b-1: none
Other: none

Distributions
Income: Dec   Capital Gains: Dec

Exchange Options
Number Per Year: 4   Fee: none
Telephone: yes (money market fund available)

Services
IRA, pension, auto exchange, auto invest, auto withdraw

Twentieth Century Int'l Equity (TWIEX)

International Stock

4500 Main St.
P.O. Box 419200
Kansas City, MO 64141
(800) 345-2021, (816) 531-5575

PERFORMANCE

fund inception date: 5/9/91

	3yr Annual	5yr Annual	10yr Annual	Bull	Bear
Return (%)	12.5	na	na	na	-5.8
Differ from Category (+/-)	3.4 abv av	na	na	na	1.2 av

Total Risk	Standard Deviation	Category Risk	Risk Index	Beta
abv av	12.0%	blw av	0.9	0.7

	1994	1993	1992	1991	1990	1989	1988	1987	1986	1985
Return (%)	-4.7	42.6	4.8	—	—	—	—	—	—	—
Differ from category (+/-)	-1.7	4.0	7.7	—	—	—	—	—	—	—

PER SHARE DATA

	1994	1993	1992	1991	1990	1989	1988	1987	1986	1985
Dividends, Net Income ($)	0.00	0.00	0.19	—	—	—	—	—	—	—
Distrib'ns, Cap Gain ($)	0.37	0.40	0.00	—	—	—	—	—	—	—
Net Asset Value ($)	6.96	7.70	5.69	—	—	—	—	—	—	—
Expense Ratio (%)	1.90	1.90	1.91	—	—	—	—	—	—	—
Net Income to Assets (%)	-0.38	0.25	0.95	—	—	—	—	—	—	—
Portfolio Turnover (%)	282	255	180	—	—	—	—	—	—	—
Total Assets (Millions $)	1,272	1,023	215	—	—	—	—	—	—	—

PORTFOLIO (as of 5/31/94)

Portfolio Manager: Mark Kopinski - 1991, Ted Tyson - 1991

Investm't Category: International Stock

✔ Cap Gain
  Cap & Income
  Income

  Asset Allocation
  Fund of Funds
  Index
  Sector

  Domestic
✔ Foreign
  Country/Region

  Small Cap
  Socially Conscious
  State Specific

Portfolio: stocks 98% bonds 0%
convertibles 0% other 0% cash 2%

Largest Holdings: Japan 34%, Netherlands 10%

Unrealized Net Capital Gains: 7% of portfolio value

SHAREHOLDER INFORMATION

Minimum Investment
Initial: $2,500   Subsequent: $50

Minimum IRA Investment
Initial: $0   Subsequent: $50

Maximum Fees
Load: none   12b-1: none
Other: none

Distributions
Income: Dec   Capital Gains: Dec

Exchange Options
Number Per Year: 4   Fee: none
Telephone: yes (money market fund available)

Services
IRA, pension, auto exchange, auto invest, auto withdraw

Twentieth Century Long-Term Bond (TWLBX)

General Bond

4500 Main St.
P.O. Box 419200
Kansas City, MO 64141
(800) 345-2021, (816) 531-5575

PERFORMANCE

fund inception date: 3/2/87

	3yr Annual	5yr Annual	10yr Annual	Bull	Bear
Return (%)	3.5	6.7	na	47.7	-6.3
Differ from Category (+/-)	-0.8 low	-0.2 blw av	na	6.7 abv av	-2.5 low

Total Risk	Standard Deviation	Category Risk	Risk Index	Avg Mat
low	4.4%	abv av	1.1	10.0 yrs

	1994	1993	1992	1991	1990	1989	1988	1987	1986	1985
Return (%)	-4.4	9.9	5.6	17.4	6.0	13.9	8.3	—	—	—
Differ from category (+/-)	-2.4	0.7	-1.0	2.8	-1.2	2.5	0.9	—	—	—

PER SHARE DATA

	1994	1993	1992	1991	1990	1989	1988	1987	1986	1985
Dividends, Net Income ($) .	0.60	0.61	0.64	0.73	0.80	0.82	0.83	—	—	—
Distrib'ns, Cap Gain ($) . . .	0.00	0.19	0.16	0.00	0.00	0.00	0.00	—	—	—
Net Asset Value ($)	8.85	9.88	9.73	9.98	9.18	9.46	9.07	—	—	—
Expense Ratio (%)	0.88	1.00	0.98	0.96	1.00	1.00	1.00	—	—	—
Net Income to Assets (%) .	6.07	6.54	6.30	8.06	8.81	8.83	9.15	—	—	—
Portfolio Turnover (%)	78	113	186	219	98	216	280	—	—	—
Total Assets (Millions $)	120	157	154	114	77	62	26	—	—	—

PORTFOLIO (as of 10/31/94)

Portfolio Manager: committee

Investm't Category: General Bond

Cap Gain	Asset Allocation
Cap & Income	Fund of Funds
✔ Income	Index
	Sector
✔ Domestic	Small Cap
✔ Foreign	Socially Conscious
Country/Region	State Specific

Portfolio:	stocks 0%	bonds 98%
convertibles 0%	other 0%	cash 2%

Largest Holdings: corporate 72%, mortgage-backed 12%

Unrealized Net Capital Gains: -5% of portfolio value

SHAREHOLDER INFORMATION

Minimum Investment
Initial: $2,500   Subsequent: $50

Minimum IRA Investment
Initial: $0   Subsequent: $50

Maximum Fees
Load: none   12b-1: none
Other: none

Distributions
Income: monthly   Capital Gains: Dec

Exchange Options
Number Per Year: 4   Fee: none
Telephone: yes (money market fund available)

Services
IRA, pension, auto exchange, auto invest, auto withdraw

Twentieth Century Select (TWCIX)

Growth

4500 Main St.
P.O. Box 419200
Kansas City, MO 64141
(800) 345-2021, (816) 531-5575

PERFORMANCE

fund inception date: 10/31/58

	3yr Annual	5yr Annual	10yr Annual	Bull	Bear
Return (%)	0.2	5.7	12.7	61.0	-12.3
Differ from Category (+/-)	-7.5 low	-3.9 low	-0.2 av	-31.1 low	-5.7 low

Total Risk	Standard Deviation	Category Risk	Risk Index	Beta
abv av	9.9%	abv av	1.0	1.1

	1994	1993	1992	1991	1990	1989	1988	1987	1986	1985
Return (%)...............	-8.0	14.6	-4.4	31.5	-0.4	39.5	5.6	5.6	20.5	33.9
Differ from category (+/-)....	-7.4	1.2	-16.0	-4.2	5.3	13.4	-12.4	3.8	5.9	4.7

PER SHARE DATA

	1994	1993	1992	1991	1990	1989	1988	1987	1986	1985
Dividends, Net Income ($).	0.28	0.43	0.50	0.65	0.65	1.12	0.71	0.86	0.52	0.47
Distrib'ns, Cap Gain ($) ...	2.87	4.47	1.33	1.82	1.55	0.00	0.00	6.37	3.46	0.00
Net Asset Value ($)	33.10	39.46	38.72	42.40	34.14	36.51	26.98	26.22	31.61	29.56
Expense Ratio (%)	1.00	1.00	1.00	1.00	1.00	1.00	1.00	1.00	1.01	1.01
Net Income to Assets (%) .	1.00	1.10	1.40	1.70	1.80	3.40	2.20	1.10	1.60	2.50
Portfolio Turnover (%)	126	82	95	84	83	93	140	123	85	119
Total Assets (Millions $)..	3,995	4,908	4,535	4,163	2,953	2,721	2,367	2,417	1,978	1,143

PORTFOLIO (as of 10/31/94)

Portfolio Manager: committee

Investm't Category: Growth

✔ Cap Gain	Asset Allocation
Cap & Income	Fund of Funds
Income	Index
	Sector
✔ Domestic	Small Cap
✔ Foreign	Socially Conscious
Country/Region	State Specific

Portfolio: stocks 97% bonds 0%
convertibles 0% other 0% cash 3%

Largest Holdings: chemicals & resins 11%, electrical & electronic components 7%

Unrealized Net Capital Gains: 10% of portfolio value

SHAREHOLDER INFORMATION

Minimum Investment
Initial: $2,500   Subsequent: $50

Minimum IRA Investment
Initial: $0   Subsequent: $50

Maximum Fees
Load: none   12b-1: none
Other: none

Distributions
Income: Dec   Capital Gains: Dec

Exchange Options
Number Per Year: 4   Fee: none
Telephone: yes (money market fund available)

Services
IRA, pension, auto exchange, auto invest, auto withdraw

Twentieth Century Tax-Exempt Interm

(TWTIX) *Tax-Exempt Bond*

4500 Main St.
P.O. Box 419200
Kansas City, MO 64141
(800) 345-2021, (816) 531-5575

PERFORMANCE

fund inception date: 3/2/87

	3yr Annual	5yr Annual	10yr Annual	Bull	Bear
Return (%)	4.5	5.9	na	33.7	-3.3
Differ from Category (+/-)	0.0 av	-0.2 blw av	na	-8.1 low	1.9 high

Total Risk	Standard Deviation	Category Risk	Risk Index	Avg Mat
low	3.8%	low	0.6	6.4 yrs

	1994	1993	1992	1991	1990	1989	1988	1987	1986	1985
Return (%)	-2.0	8.9	7.1	10.0	6.2	6.6	5.9	—	—	—
Differ from category (+/-)	3.2	-2.8	-1.2	-1.3	-0.1	-2.4	-4.3	—	—	—

PER SHARE DATA

	1994	1993	1992	1991	1990	1989	1988	1987	1986	1985
Dividends, Net Income ($)	0.48	0.47	0.47	0.52	0.56	0.56	0.54	—	—	—
Distrib'ns, Cap Gain ($)	0.08	0.13	0.08	0.00	0.00	0.00	0.00	—	—	—
Net Asset Value ($)	9.88	10.66	10.35	10.19	9.76	9.73	9.67	—	—	—
Expense Ratio (%)	0.60	0.72	0.98	0.96	1.00	1.00	1.00	—	—	—
Net Income to Assets (%)	4.59	4.51	4.68	5.40	5.80	5.79	5.57	—	—	—
Portfolio Turnover (%)	74	38	36	62	102	74	86	—	—	—
Total Assets (Millions $)	77	96	77	45	26	21	14	—	—	—

PORTFOLIO (as of 10/31/94)

Portfolio Manager: committee

Investm't Category: Tax-Exempt Bond

Cap Gain	Asset Allocation
Cap & Income	Fund of Funds
✔ Income	Index
	Sector
✔ Domestic	Small Cap
Foreign	Socially Conscious
Country/Region	State Specific

Portfolio: stocks 0% bonds 96%
convertibles 0% other 0% cash 4%

Largest Holdings: general obligation 13%

Unrealized Net Capital Gains: -1% of portfolio value

SHAREHOLDER INFORMATION

Minimum Investment
Initial: $10,000   Subsequent: $50

Minimum IRA Investment
Initial: na   Subsequent: na

Maximum Fees
Load: none   12b-1: none
Other: none

Distributions
Income: monthly   Capital Gains: Dec

Exchange Options
Number Per Year: 4   Fee: none
Telephone: yes (money market fund available)

Services
auto exchange, auto invest, auto withdraw

Twentieth Century
Tax-Exempt Long (TWTLX)

Tax-Exempt Bond

4500 Main St.
P.O. Box 419200
Kansas City, MO 64141
(800) 345-2021, (816) 531-5575

PERFORMANCE

fund inception date: 3/2/87

	3yr Annual	5yr Annual	10yr Annual	Bull	Bear
Return (%)	4.4	6.2	na	43.7	-5.8
Differ from Category (+/-)	-0.1 av	0.1 av	na	1.9 av	-0.6 av

Total Risk	Standard Deviation	Category Risk	Risk Index	Avg Mat
blw av	5.7%	blw av	0.9	15.5 yrs

	1994	1993	1992	1991	1990	1989	1988	1987	1986	1985
Return (%).	-5.6	12.0	7.7	12.0	6.1	9.5	10.3	—	—	—
Differ from category (+/-). . .	-0.4	0.3	-0.6	0.7	-0.2	0.5	0.1	—	—	—

PER SHARE DATA

	1994	1993	1992	1991	1990	1989	1988	1987	1986	1985
Dividends, Net Income ($).	0.51	0.52	0.53	0.57	0.60	0.62	0.61	—	—	—
Distrib'ns, Cap Gain ($) . . .	0.04	0.34	0.16	0.09	0.00	0.09	0.00	—	—	—
Net Asset Value ($)	9.64	10.80	10.43	10.35	9.86	9.88	9.70	—	—	—
Expense Ratio (%)	0.60	0.73	0.98	0.96	1.00	1.00	1.00	—	—	—
Net Income to Assets (%) .	5.00	4.90	5.07	5.73	6.22	6.36	6.43	—	—	—
Portfolio Turnover (%)	66	81	88	110	144	120	215	—	—	—
Total Assets (Millions $).	49	67	62	39	28	20	12	—	—	—

PORTFOLIO (as of 10/31/94)

Portfolio Manager: committee

Investm't Category: Tax-Exempt Bond

Cap Gain	Asset Allocation
Cap & Income	Fund of Funds
✔ Income	Index
	Sector
✔ Domestic	Small Cap
Foreign	Socially Conscious
Country/Region	State Specific

Portfolio: stocks 0% bonds 98%
convertibles 0% other 0% cash 2%

Largest Holdings: general obligation 23%

Unrealized Net Capital Gains: -3% of portfolio value

SHAREHOLDER INFORMATION

Minimum Investment
Initial: $10,000   Subsequent: $50

Minimum IRA Investment
Initial: na   Subsequent: na

Maximum Fees
Load: none   12b-1: none
Other: none

Distributions
Income: monthly   Capital Gains: Dec

Exchange Options
Number Per Year: 4   Fee: none
Telephone: yes (money market fund available)

Services
auto exchange, auto invest, auto withdraw

Twentieth Century Tax-Exempt Short (TWTSX)

Tax-Exempt Bond

4500 Main St.
P.O. Box 419200
Kansas City, MO 64141
(800) 345-2021, (816) 531-5575

PERFORMANCE

fund inception date: 3/1/93

	3yr Annual	5yr Annual	10yr Annual	Bull	Bear
Return (%)	na	na	na	na	0.2
Differ from Category (+/-)	na	na	na	na	5.4 high

Total Risk	Standard Deviation	Category Risk	Risk Index	Avg Mat
na	na	na	na	1.1 yrs

	1994	1993	1992	1991	1990	1989	1988	1987	1986	1985
Return (%)	2.4	—	—	—	—	—	—	—	—	—
Differ from category (+/-)	7.6	—	—	—	—	—	—	—	—	—

PER SHARE DATA

	1994	1993	1992	1991	1990	1989	1988	1987	1986	1985
Dividends, Net Income ($)	0.37	—	—	—	—	—	—	—	—	—
Distrib'ns, Cap Gain ($)	0.00	—	—	—	—	—	—	—	—	—
Net Asset Value ($)	9.93	—	—	—	—	—	—	—	—	—
Expense Ratio (%)	0.00	—	—	—	—	—	—	—	—	—
Net Income to Assets (%)	3.62	—	—	—	—	—	—	—	—	—
Portfolio Turnover (%)	42	—	—	—	—	—	—	—	—	—
Total Assets (Millions $)	61	—	—	—	—	—	—	—	—	—

PORTFOLIO (as of 10/31/94)

Portfolio Manager: committee

Investm't Category: Tax-Exempt Bond

Cap Gain	Asset Allocation
Cap & Income	Fund of Funds
✔ Income	Index
	Sector
✔ Domestic	Small Cap
Foreign	Socially Conscious
Country/Region	State Specific

Portfolio: stocks 0% bonds 98%
convertibles 0% other 0% cash 2%

Largest Holdings: general obligation 28%

Unrealized Net Capital Gains: 0% of portfolio value

SHAREHOLDER INFORMATION

Minimum Investment
Initial: $10,000   Subsequent: $50

Minimum IRA Investment
Initial: na   Subsequent: na

Maximum Fees
Load: none   12b-1: none
Other: none

Distributions
Income: monthly   Capital Gains: Dec

Exchange Options
Number Per Year: 4   Fee: none
Telephone: yes (money market fund available)

Services
auto exchange, auto invest, auto withdraw

Twentieth Century Ultra
(TWCUX)
Aggressive Growth

4500 Main St.
P.O. Box 419200
Kansas City, MO 64141
(800) 345-2021, (816) 531-5575

PERFORMANCE

fund inception date: 11/2/81

	3yr Annual	5yr Annual	10yr Annual	Bull	Bear
Return (%)	5.9	19.3	18.7	186.2	-15.0
Differ from Category (+/-)	-3.0 blw av	6.8 high	4.7 high	53.0 high	-4.2 blw av

Total Risk	Standard Deviation	Category Risk	Risk Index	Beta
high	17.0%	high	1.2	1.3

	1994	1993	1992	1991	1990	1989	1988	1987	1986	1985
Return (%)	-3.6	21.8	1.2	86.4	9.3	36.9	13.3	6.6	10.2	26.1
Differ from category (+/-)	-2.9	2.3	-9.8	34.3	15.5	10.1	-1.9	8.8	-1.6	-6.2

PER SHARE DATA

	1994	1993	1992	1991	1990	1989	1988	1987	1986	1985
Dividends, Net Income ($)	0.65	0.00	0.00	0.00	0.00	0.20	0.00	0.01	0.01	0.00
Distrib'ns, Cap Gain ($)	0.00	0.00	0.00	0.00	0.03	0.95	0.00	3.26	0.00	0.00
Net Asset Value ($)	19.95	21.39	17.56	17.34	9.30	8.53	7.06	6.23	8.92	8.10
Expense Ratio (%)	1.00	1.00	1.00	1.00	1.00	1.00	1.00	1.00	1.01	1.01
Net Income to Assets (%)	-0.10	-0.60	-0.40	-0.50	-0.30	2.21	-0.30	-0.50	na	0.10
Portfolio Turnover (%)	78	53	59	42	141	132	140	137	99	100
Total Assets (Millions $)	9,850	8,353	4,275	2,148	330	347	259	236	314	385

PORTFOLIO (as of 10/31/94)

Portfolio Manager: committee

Investm't Category: Aggressive Growth
- ✔ Cap Gain
- Cap & Income
- Income
- ✔ Domestic
- ✔ Foreign
- Country/Region
- Asset Allocation
- Fund of Funds
- Index
- Sector
- ✔ Small Cap
- Socially Conscious
- State Specific

Portfolio: stocks 93% bonds 0%
convertibles 0% other 0% cash 7%

Largest Holdings: computer software & services 13%, electrical & electronic components 8%

Unrealized Net Capital Gains: 19% of portfolio value

SHAREHOLDER INFORMATION

Minimum Investment
Initial: $2,500   Subsequent: $50

Minimum IRA Investment
Initial: $0   Subsequent: $50

Maximum Fees
Load: none   12b-1: none
Other: none

Distributions
Income: Dec   Capital Gains: Dec

Exchange Options
Number Per Year: 4   Fee: none
Telephone: yes (money market fund available)

Services
IRA, pension, auto exchange, auto invest, auto withdraw

Twentieth Century US Gov't Short Term (TWUSX)

Government Bond

4500 Main St.
P.O. Box 419200
Kansas City, MO 64141
(800) 345-2021, (816) 531-5575

PERFORMANCE

fund inception date: 12/15/82

	3yr Annual	5yr Annual	10yr Annual	Bull	Bear
Return (%)	2.6	5.3	6.8	26.4	-2.0
Differ from Category (+/-)	-1.4 low	-1.4 low	-1.0 low	-24.8 low	4.4 abv av

Total Risk	Standard Deviation	Category Risk	Risk Index	Avg Mat
low	1.9%	low	0.4	1.7 yrs

	1994	1993	1992	1991	1990	1989	1988	1987	1986	1985
Return (%)	-0.4	4.1	4.4	11.6	7.5	9.9	5.6	3.8	9.8	12.9
Differ from category (+/-)	4.4	-6.8	-2.0	-3.7	1.3	-4.6	-2.3	5.9	-10.8	-5.6

PER SHARE DATA

	1994	1993	1992	1991	1990	1989	1988	1987	1986	1985
Dividends, Net Income ($)	0.44	0.33	0.42	0.60	0.78	0.83	0.82	0.80	0.84	0.99
Distrib'ns, Cap Gain ($)	0.00	0.00	0.00	0.00	0.00	0.00	0.00	0.12	0.06	0.00
Net Asset Value ($)	9.16	9.65	9.59	9.60	9.17	9.29	9.24	9.53	10.09	10.04
Expense Ratio (%)	0.81	1.00	0.99	0.99	1.00	1.00	1.00	1.00	1.01	1.01
Net Income to Assets (%)	4.17	3.73	4.62	6.88	8.64	9.10	8.60	8.10	8.54	10.10
Portfolio Turnover (%)	470	413	391	779	620	567	578	468	464	573
Total Assets (Millions $)	384	489	569	535	456	444	440	336	254	98

PORTFOLIO (as of 10/31/94)

Portfolio Manager: committee

Investm't Category: Government Bond

Cap Gain	Asset Allocation
Cap & Income	Fund of Funds
✔ Income	Index
	Sector
✔ Domestic	Small Cap
Foreign	Socially Conscious
Country/Region	State Specific

Portfolio: stocks 0% bonds 98%
convertibles 0% other 0% cash 2%

Largest Holdings: U. S. government 70%, mortgage-backed 28%

Unrealized Net Capital Gains: -1% of portfolio value

SHAREHOLDER INFORMATION

Minimum Investment
Initial: $2,500   Subsequent: $50

Minimum IRA Investment
Initial: $0   Subsequent: $50

Maximum Fees
Load: none   12b-1: none
Other: none

Distributions
Income: monthly   Capital Gains: Dec

Exchange Options
Number Per Year: 4   Fee: none
Telephone: yes (money market fund available)

Services
IRA, pension, auto exchange, auto invest, auto withdraw

Twentieth Century Value
(TWVLX)
Growth & Income

4500 Main St.
P.O. Box 419200
Kansas City, MO 64141
(800) 345-2021, (816) 531-5575

PERFORMANCE
fund inception date: 9/1/93

	3yr Annual	5yr Annual	10yr Annual	Bull	Bear
Return (%)	na	na	na	na	-3.5
Differ from Category (+/-)	na	na	na	na	2.8 high

Total Risk	Standard Deviation	Category Risk	Risk Index	Beta
na	na	na	na	na

	1994	1993	1992	1991	1990	1989	1988	1987	1986	1985
Return (%)	3.9	—	—	—	—	—	—	—	—	—
Differ from category (+/-). . .	5.3	—	—	—	—	—	—	—	—	—

PER SHARE DATA

	1994	1993	1992	1991	1990	1989	1988	1987	1986	1985
Dividends, Net Income ($).	0.12	—	—	—	—	—	—	—	—	—
Distrib'ns, Cap Gain ($) . . .	0.27	—	—	—	—	—	—	—	—	—
Net Asset Value ($)	4.92	—	—	—	—	—	—	—	—	—
Expense Ratio (%)	1.00	—	—	—	—	—	—	—	—	—
Net Income to Assets (%) .	3.37	—	—	—	—	—	—	—	—	—
Portfolio Turnover (%)	79	—	—	—	—	—	—	—	—	—
Total Assets (Millions $). . . .	153	—	—	—	—	—	—	—	—	—

PORTFOLIO (as of 3/31/94)

Portfolio Manager: Phil Davidson - 1993, Peter Zuger - 1993

Investm't Category: Growth & Income

Cap Gain	Asset Allocation
✔ Cap & Income	Fund of Funds
Income	Index
	Sector
✔ Domestic	Small Cap
✔ Foreign	Socially Conscious
Country/Region	State Specific

Portfolio: stocks 83% bonds 0%
convertibles 11% other 0% cash 6%

Largest Holdings: insurance 12%, energy (production & marketing) 11%

Unrealized Net Capital Gains: -5% of portfolio value

SHAREHOLDER INFORMATION

Minimum Investment
Initial: $2,500 Subsequent: $50

Minimum IRA Investment
Initial: $0 Subsequent: $50

Maximum Fees
Load: none 12b-1: none
Other: none

Distributions
Income: quarterly Capital Gains: Dec

Exchange Options
Number Per Year: 4 Fee: none
Telephone: yes (money market fund available)

Services
IRA, pension, auto exchange, auto invest, auto withdraw

Twentieth Century Vista
(TWCVX)
Aggressive Growth

4500 Main St.
P.O. Box 419200
Kansas City, MO 64141
(800) 345-2021, (816) 531-5575

PERFORMANCE
fund inception date: 11/25/83

	3yr Annual	5yr Annual	10yr Annual	Bull	Bear
Return (%)	2.6	9.5	14.9	100.4	-17.5
Differ from Category (+/-)	-6.3 low	-3.0 blw av	0.9 av	-32.8 blw av	-6.7 low

Total Risk	Standard Deviation	Category Risk	Risk Index	Beta
high	16.6%	abv av	1.1	1.3

	1994	1993	1992	1991	1990	1989	1988	1987	1986	1985
Return (%)	4.6	5.4	-2.1	73.6	-15.7	52.1	2.4	6.0	26.3	22.5
Differ from category (+/-)	5.3	-14.1	-13.1	21.5	-9.5	25.3	-12.8	8.2	14.5	-9.8

PER SHARE DATA

	1994	1993	1992	1991	1990	1989	1988	1987	1986	1985
Dividends, Net Income ($)	0.00	0.00	0.00	0.00	0.00	0.00	0.01	0.00	0.00	0.01
Distrib'ns, Cap Gain ($)	0.03	1.68	0.65	0.00	0.00	0.69	0.00	0.46	0.65	0.00
Net Asset Value ($)	10.72	10.27	11.35	12.28	7.07	8.39	5.97	5.84	5.95	5.22
Expense Ratio (%)	1.00	1.00	1.00	1.00	1.00	1.00	1.00	1.00	1.01	1.01
Net Income to Assets (%)	-0.80	-0.60	-0.40	-0.30	-0.10	-0.40	0.20	-0.70	-0.30	-0.20
Portfolio Turnover (%)	111	133	87	92	103	125	145	123	121	174
Total Assets (Millions $)	820	786	830	622	340	264	206	187	159	146

PORTFOLIO (as of 10/31/94)

Portfolio Manager: committee

Investm't Category: Aggressive Growth
- ✔ Cap Gain
- Cap & Income
- Income
- Asset Allocation
- Fund of Funds
- Index
- Sector
- ✔ Domestic
- ✔ Foreign
- Country/Region
- ✔ Small Cap
- Socially Conscious
- State Specific

Portfolio: stocks 97% bonds 0%
convertibles 0% other 0% cash 3%

Largest Holdings: electrical & electronic components 20%, communications equipment 13%

Unrealized Net Capital Gains: 29% of portfolio value

SHAREHOLDER INFORMATION

Minimum Investment
Initial: $2,500 Subsequent: $50

Minimum IRA Investment
Initial: $0 Subsequent: $50

Maximum Fees
Load: none 12b-1: none
Other: none

Distributions
Income: Dec Capital Gains: Dec

Exchange Options
Number Per Year: 4 Fee: none
Telephone: yes (money market fund available)

Services
IRA, pension, auto exchange, auto invest, auto withdraw

UMB Bond (UMBBX)

General Bond

Three Crown Center
2440 Pershing Rd., #G-15
Kansas City, MO 64108
(800) 422-2766, (816) 471-5200

PERFORMANCE

fund inception date: 11/18/82

	3yr Annual	5yr Annual	10yr Annual	Bull	Bear
Return (%)	3.8	6.4	8.0	35.8	-4.3
Differ from Category (+/-)	-0.5 blw av	-0.5 blw av	-0.9 low	-5.2 blw av	-0.5 av

Total Risk	Standard Deviation	Category Risk	Risk Index	Avg Mat
low	3.3%	blw av	0.8	4.6 yrs

	1994	1993	1992	1991	1990	1989	1988	1987	1986	1985
Return (%)	-3.0	8.3	6.5	13.2	8.0	11.3	5.8	2.9	12.4	16.1
Differ from category (+/-)	-1.0	-0.9	-0.1	-1.4	0.8	-0.1	-1.6	0.7	-1.8	-3.3

PER SHARE DATA

	1994	1993	1992	1991	1990	1989	1988	1987	1986	1985
Dividends, Net Income ($)	0.63	0.64	0.71	0.71	0.79	0.82	0.81	1.25	0.83	0.97
Distrib'ns, Cap Gain ($)	0.00	0.04	0.00	0.00	0.00	0.00	0.03	0.01	0.03	0.03
Net Asset Value ($)	10.46	11.44	11.20	11.19	10.54	10.50	10.19	10.42	11.37	10.94
Expense Ratio (%)	0.87	0.87	0.87	0.87	0.88	0.88	0.87	0.87	0.88	0.88
Net Income to Assets (%)	5.50	5.95	6.77	7.44	7.61	7.69	7.47	7.36	8.11	9.21
Portfolio Turnover (%)	9	19	24	21	13	8	7	12	23	51
Total Assets (Millions $)	75	89	63	43	34	28	30	31	19	10

PORTFOLIO (as of 6/30/94)

Portfolio Manager: George Root - 1982

Investm't Category: General Bond

Cap Gain	Asset Allocation
Cap & Income	Fund of Funds
✔ Income	Index
	Sector
✔ Domestic	Small Cap
Foreign	Socially Conscious
Country/Region	State Specific

Portfolio: stocks 0% bonds 98%
convertibles 0% other 0% cash 2%

Largest Holdings: corporate 41%, mortgage-backed 31%

Unrealized Net Capital Gains: -1% of portfolio value

SHAREHOLDER INFORMATION

Minimum Investment
Initial: $1,000 Subsequent: $100

Minimum IRA Investment
Initial: $250 Subsequent: $50

Maximum Fees
Load: none 12b-1: none
Other: none

Distributions
Income: monthly Capital Gains: Jun, Dec

Exchange Options
Number Per Year: no limit Fee: none
Telephone: yes (money market fund available)

Services
IRA, pension, auto exchange, auto invest, auto withdraw

UMB Heartland Fund

(UMBHX)

Growth

Three Crown Center
2440 Pershing Rd., #G-15
Kansas City, MO 64108
(800) 422-2766, (816) 471-5200

PERFORMANCE

fund inception date: 8/16/91

	3yr Annual	5yr Annual	10yr Annual	Bull	Bear
Return (%)	5.7	na	na	na	-3.0
Differ from Category (+/-)	-2.0 blw av	na	na	na	3.6 high

Total Risk	Standard Deviation	Category Risk	Risk Index	Beta
blw av	5.0%	low	0.5	0.4

	1994	1993	1992	1991	1990	1989	1988	1987	1986	1985
Return (%)	0.7	5.9	10.9	—	—	—	—	—	—	—
Differ from category (+/-)	1.3	-7.5	-0.7	—	—	—	—	—	—	—

PER SHARE DATA

	1994	1993	1992	1991	1990	1989	1988	1987	1986	1985
Dividends, Net Income ($)	0.18	0.14	0.12	—	—	—	—	—	—	—
Distrib'ns, Cap Gain ($)	0.17	0.00	0.00	—	—	—	—	—	—	—
Net Asset Value ($)	9.20	9.49	9.09	—	—	—	—	—	—	—
Expense Ratio (%)	0.91	0.92	1.06	—	—	—	—	—	—	—
Net Income to Assets (%)	1.95	1.81	1.91	—	—	—	—	—	—	—
Portfolio Turnover (%)	27	17	7	—	—	—	—	—	—	—
Total Assets (Millions $)	28	25	8	—	—	—	—	—	—	—

PORTFOLIO (as of 6/30/94)

Portfolio Manager: David Anderson - 1991

Investm't Category: Growth

✔ Cap Gain	Asset Allocation
Cap & Income	Fund of Funds
Income	Index
	Sector
✔ Domestic	✔ Small Cap
Foreign	Socially Conscious
Country/Region	State Specific

Portfolio: stocks 64% bonds 0%
convertibles 1% other 0% cash 35%

Largest Holdings: consumer staples 14%, consumer cyclical 14%

Unrealized Net Capital Gains: 0% of portfolio value

SHAREHOLDER INFORMATION

Minimum Investment
Initial: $1,000   Subsequent: $100

Minimum IRA Investment
Initial: $250   Subsequent: $50

Maximum Fees
Load: none   12b-1: none
Other: none

Distributions
Income: Jun, Dec   Capital Gains: Jun, Dec

Exchange Options
Number Per Year: no limit   Fee: none
Telephone: yes (money market fund available)

Services
IRA, pension, auto exchange, auto invest, auto withdraw

UMB Stock (UMBSX)

Growth & Income

Three Crown Center
2440 Pershing Rd., #G-15
Kansas City, MO 64108
(800) 422-2766, (816) 471-5200

PERFORMANCE

fund inception date: 11/18/82

	3yr Annual	5yr Annual	10yr Annual	Bull	Bear
Return (%)	6.7	8.2	11.3	62.2	-3.5
Differ from Category (+/-)	-0.4 av	0.3 av	-0.4 av	-13.6 blw av	2.8 high

Total Risk	Standard Deviation	Category Risk	Risk Index	Beta
blw av	6.3%	low	0.8	0.8

	1994	1993	1992	1991	1990	1989	1988	1987	1986	1985
Return (%).	2.7	10.6	7.1	24.7	-2.3	19.0	13.8	5.5	12.3	23.1
Differ from category (+/-) . .	4.1	-2.6	-3.1	-2.9	3.7	-2.4	-3.2	4.9	-3.5	-2.6

PER SHARE DATA

	1994	1993	1992	1991	1990	1989	1988	1987	1986	1985
Dividends, Net Income ($).	0.39	0.34	0.39	0.48	0.58	0.59	0.47	0.66	0.51	0.50
Distrib'ns, Cap Gain ($) . . .	1.26	0.82	0.31	0.01	0.21	0.53	0.41	1.09	1.01	0.45
Net Asset Value ($)	15.01	16.24	15.77	15.40	12.76	13.87	12.62	11.87	12.78	12.74
Expense Ratio (%)	0.87	0.87	0.86	0.85	0.88	0.87	0.86	0.87	0.87	0.88
Net Income to Assets (%) . .	2.22	2.30	2.91	4.03	4.23	4.08	3.41	3.08	3.75	4.36
Portfolio Turnover (%)	22	21	12	8	9	17	33	50	38	65
Total Assets (Millions $) . . .	120	111	76	53	48	41	43	42	32	18

PORTFOLIO (as of 6/30/94)

Portfolio Manager: David Anderson - 1982

Investm't Category: Growth & Income

Cap Gain	Asset Allocation
✔ Cap & Income	Fund of Funds
Income	Index
	Sector
✔ Domestic	Small Cap
Foreign	Socially Conscious
Country/Region	State Specific

Portfolio: stocks 74%   bonds 0%
convertibles 1%   other 0%   cash 25%

Largest Holdings: consumer staples 16%, basic materials 9%

Unrealized Net Capital Gains: 8% of portfolio value

SHAREHOLDER INFORMATION

Minimum Investment
Initial: $1,000   Subsequent: $100

Minimum IRA Investment
Initial: $250   Subsequent: $50

Maximum Fees
Load: none   12b-1: none
Other: none

Distributions
Income: Jun, Dec   Capital Gains: Jun, Dec

Exchange Options
Number Per Year: no limit   Fee: none
Telephone: yes (money market fund available)

Services
IRA, pension, auto exchange, auto invest, auto withdraw

US All American Equity

(GBTFX)

Growth & Income

P.O. Box 781234
San Antonio, TX 78278
(800) 873-8637, (210) 308-1222

PERFORMANCE

fund inception date: 3/4/81

	3yr Annual	5yr Annual	10yr Annual	Bull	Bear
Return (%)	3.2	4.3	6.8	57.9	-8.8
Differ from Category (+/-)	-3.9 low	-3.6 low	-4.9 low	-17.9 low	-2.5 low

Total Risk	Standard Deviation	Category Risk	Risk Index	Beta
av	7.8%	blw av	0.9	1.0

	1994	1993	1992	1991	1990	1989	1988	1987	1986	1985
Return (%)	-5.3	10.0	5.6	26.6	-11.2	16.7	-3.1	0.5	11.2	23.9
Differ from category (+/-) . .	-3.9	-3.2	-4.6	-1.0	-5.2	-4.7	-20.1	-0.1	-4.6	-1.8

PER SHARE DATA

	1994	1993	1992	1991	1990	1989	1988	1987	1986	1985
Dividends, Net Income ($) .	0.39	0.47	0.22	0.12	0.31	0.56	0.37	0.58	0.38	0.32
Distrib'ns, Cap Gain ($) . . .	2.17	0.31	0.00	0.00	0.00	0.00	0.00	0.00	0.00	0.00
Net Asset Value ($)	17.45	21.13	19.93	19.08	15.16	17.42	15.41	16.28	16.68	15.32
Expense Ratio (%)	0.61	1.03	2.03	2.80	2.10	1.97	1.43	1.35	1.40	1.50
Net Income to Assets (%). .	2.11	1.86	0.78	0.83	2.63	2.62	1.68	1.68	1.98	2.38
Portfolio Turnover (%). . . .	116	11	35	209	258	113	180	58	91	99
Total Assets (Millions $)	9	12	12	10	10	12	17	36	33	36

PORTFOLIO (as of 6/30/94)

Portfolio Manager: Frank Holmes - 1993

Investm't Category: Growth & Income

Cap Gain	Asset Allocation
✔ Cap & Income	Fund of Funds
Income	Index
	Sector
✔ Domestic	Small Cap
Foreign	Socially Conscious
Country/Region	State Specific

Portfolio: stocks 98% bonds 0%
convertibles 0% other 0% cash 2%

Largest Holdings: oil refining/distribution 10%, chemicals 7%

Unrealized Net Capital Gains: 2% of portfolio value

SHAREHOLDER INFORMATION

Minimum Investment
Initial: $1,000   Subsequent: $50

Minimum IRA Investment
Initial: $0   Subsequent: $0

Maximum Fees
Load: 0.10% redemption   12b-1: none
Other: redemption fee applies for 14 days; $10 close-out fee; $12/yr maintenance fee

Distributions
Income: quarterly   Capital Gains: Dec

Exchange Options
Number Per Year: no limit   Fee: $5
Telephone: yes (money market fund available)

Services: IRA, pension, auto exchange, auto invest, auto withdraw

US Global Resources
(PSPFX)
International Stock

P.O. Box 781234
San Antonio, TX 78278
(800) 873-8637, (210) 308-1222

    fund inception date: 8/3/83

	3yr Annual	5yr Annual	10yr Annual	Bull	Bear
Return (%)	1.3	-1.6	5.1	19.5	-15.7
Differ from Category (+/-)	-7.8 low	-6.5 low	-10.1 low	-44.4 low	-8.7 low

Total Risk	Standard Deviation	Category Risk	Risk Index	Beta
abv av	10.3%	low	0.8	0.8

	1994	1993	1992	1991	1990	1989	1988	1987	1986	1985
Return (%)	-9.6	18.5	-2.7	5.0	-15.9	22.0	-12.1	25.3	29.0	3.7
Differ from category (+/-)	-6.6	-20.1	0.2	-8.1	-5.5	-0.5	-26.5	10.9	-30.0	-38.7

PER SHARE DATA

	1994	1993	1992	1991	1990	1989	1988	1987	1986	1985
Dividends, Net Income ($)	0.00	0.01	0.04	0.07	0.04	0.50	0.00	0.00	0.00	0.00
Distrib'ns, Cap Gain ($)	0.31	0.15	0.00	0.16	0.42	0.40	0.40	0.70	0.00	0.00
Net Asset Value ($)	5.56	6.50	5.62	5.82	5.76	7.40	6.80	8.20	7.10	5.50
Expense Ratio (%)	2.43	2.46	2.33	2.43	2.10	2.04	-0.49	2.90	1.89	1.50
Net Income to Assets (%)	-0.34	0.17	0.61	0.58	1.37	1.78	1.78	-1.64	0.45	0.01
Portfolio Turnover (%)	57	119	55	82	70	21	27	8	83	20
Total Assets (Millions $)	20	24	25	28	32	37	45	76	61	76

PORTFOLIO (as of 6/30/94)

Portfolio Manager: Ralph Aldis - 1992

Investm't Category: International Stock
- ✔ Cap Gain
- Cap & Income
- Income
- ✔ Domestic
- ✔ Foreign
- Country/Region
- Asset Allocation
- Fund of Funds
- Index
- ✔ Sector
- Small Cap
- Socially Conscious
- State Specific

Portfolio: stocks 96%   bonds 0%
convertibles 0%   other 0%   cash 4%

Largest Holdings: petroleum refining & drilling 23%, natural gas transmission & distrib. 16%

Unrealized Net Capital Gains: -3% of portfolio value

SHAREHOLDER INFORMATION

Minimum Investment
Initial: $1,000   Subsequent: $50

Minimum IRA Investment
Initial: $0   Subsequent: $0

Maximum Fees
Load: 0.10% redemption   12b-1: none
Other: redemption fee applies for 14 days; $10 close-out fee

Distributions
Income: Dec   Capital Gains: Dec

Exchange Options
Number Per Year: no limit   Fee: $5
Telephone: yes (money market fund available)

Services: IRA, pension, auto exchange, auto invest, auto withdraw

US Gold Shares
(USERX)

Gold

P.O. Box 781234
San Antonio, TX 78278
(800) 873-8637, (210) 308-1222

PERFORMANCE

fund inception date: 7/1/74

	3yr Annual	5yr Annual	10yr Annual	Bull	Bear
Return (%)	2.3	-9.8	-1.7	-24.6	-3.0
Differ from Category (+/-)	-8.5 low	-9.8 low	-6.9 low	-57.5 low	7.0 high

Total Risk	Standard Deviation	Category Risk	Risk Index	Beta
high	34.0%	high	1.3	0.1

	1994	1993	1992	1991	1990	1989	1988	1987	1986	1985
Return (%)	-2.6	123.9	-50.8	-15.6	-34.2	64.7	-35.6	31.5	37.8	-26.8
Differ from category (+/-) . . .	8.9	37.0	-35.1	-10.8	-11.7	40.0	-16.7	-0.4	0.2	-19.4

PER SHARE DATA

	1994	1993	1992	1991	1990	1989	1988	1987	1986	1985
Dividends, Net Income ($) .	0.07	0.05	0.05	0.08	0.15	0.17	0.22	0.54	0.29	0.27
Distrib'ns, Cap Gain ($) . . .	0.00	0.00	0.00	0.00	0.00	0.00	0.00	0.00	0.00	0.00
Net Asset Value ($)	2.73	2.88	1.31	2.75	3.35	5.31	3.34	5.53	4.63	3.60
Expense Ratio (%)	1.46	1.88	1.54	1.54	1.46	1.54	1.31	1.32	1.27	1.15
Net Income to Assets (%) . .	2.61	2.58	2.52	2.71	3.80	5.46	5.10	6.45	6.90	4.47
Portfolio Turnover (%)	29	19	25	49	13	7	18	24	14	9
Total Assets (Millions $) . . .	291	305	188	343	295	239	238	408	215	390

PORTFOLIO (as of 6/30/94)

Portfolio Manager: Victor Flores - 1992

Investm't Category: Gold

✔ Cap Gain	Asset Allocation
Cap & Income	Fund of Funds
Income	Index
	✔ Sector
✔ Domestic	Small Cap
✔ Foreign	Socially Conscious
Country/Region	State Specific

Portfolio: stocks 98% bonds 0%
convertibles 0% other 0% cash 2%

Largest Holdings: long-life gold mining cos. 35%, gold/uranium mining cos. 26%

Unrealized Net Capital Gains: -9% of portfolio value

SHAREHOLDER INFORMATION

Minimum Investment
Initial: $1,000   Subsequent: $50

Minimum IRA Investment
Initial: $0   Subsequent: $0

Maximum Fees
Load: 0.10% redemption   12b-1: none
Other: redemption fee applies for 14 days; $10 close-out fee

Distributions
Income: Jun, Dec   Capital Gains: Dec

Exchange Options
Number Per Year: no limit   Fee: $5
Telephone: yes (money market fund available)

Services: IRA, pension, auto exchange, auto invest, auto withdraw

US Income (USINX)

Growth & Income

P.O. Box 781234
San Antonio, TX 78278
(800) 873-8637, (210) 308-1222

PERFORMANCE

fund inception date: 11/1/83

	3yr Annual	5yr Annual	10yr Annual	Bull	Bear
Return (%)	4.5	3.5	8.3	55.8	-11.8
Differ from Category (+/-)	-2.6 low	-4.4 low	-3.4 low	-20.0 low	-5.5 low

Total Risk	Standard Deviation	Category Risk	Risk Index	Beta
abv av	9.6%	high	1.2	0.9

	1994	1993	1992	1991	1990	1989	1988	1987	1986	1985
Return (%)	-10.2	17.7	8.0	14.3	-8.6	37.8	16.8	-4.2	5.4	15.3
Differ from category (+/-)	-8.8	4.5	-2.2	-13.3	-2.6	16.4	-0.2	-4.8	-10.4	-10.4

PER SHARE DATA

	1994	1993	1992	1991	1990	1989	1988	1987	1986	1985
Dividends, Net Income ($)	0.32	0.31	0.29	0.35	0.40	0.45	0.48	0.69	0.59	0.34
Distrib'ns, Cap Gain ($)	0.02	0.40	0.81	0.01	0.29	0.00	0.00	0.35	0.63	0.00
Net Asset Value ($)	12.30	14.08	12.57	12.66	11.41	13.25	9.98	8.97	10.43	11.05
Expense Ratio (%)	1.74	1.83	1.95	2.22	1.94	2.00	1.73	1.60	1.63	1.66
Net Income to Assets (%)	2.27	2.34	2.47	2.99	3.55	4.61	6.19	6.14	3.27	5.58
Portfolio Turnover (%)	6	44	76	110	19	18	127	174	178	271
Total Assets (Millions $)	10	14	8	7	8	5	4	4	3	2

PORTFOLIO (as of 6/30/94)

Portfolio Manager: Frank Holmes - 1993

Investm't Category: Growth & Income
- Cap Gain
- ✔ Cap & Income
- Income
- ✔ Domestic
- ✔ Foreign
- Country/Region
- Asset Allocation
- Fund of Funds
- Index
- Sector
- Small Cap
- Socially Conscious
- State Specific

Portfolio: stocks 76% bonds 0%
convertibles 5% other 0% cash 19%

Largest Holdings: electric & water utilities 28%, natural gas transmission & distrib. 25%

Unrealized Net Capital Gains: 7% of portfolio value

SHAREHOLDER INFORMATION

Minimum Investment
Initial: $1,000 Subsequent: $50

Minimum IRA Investment
Initial: $0 Subsequent: $0

Maximum Fees
Load: 0.10% redemption 12b-1: none
Other: redemption fee applies for 14 days; $10 close-out fee

Distributions
Income: quarterly Capital Gains: Dec

Exchange Options
Number Per Year: no limit Fee: $5
Telephone: yes (money market fund available)

Services: IRA, pension, auto exchange, auto invest, auto withdraw

US Real Estate (UNREX)

Growth & Income

P.O. Box 781234
San Antonio, TX 78278
(800) 873-8637, (210) 308-1222

PERFORMANCE

fund inception date: 7/2/87

	3yr Annual	5yr Annual	10yr Annual	Bull	Bear
Return (%)	-2.4	2.9	na	80.5	-10.0
Differ from Category (+/-)	-9.5 low	-5.0 low	na	4.7 abv av	-3.7 low

Total Risk	Standard Deviation	Category Risk	Risk Index	Beta
high	14.4%	high	1.8	0.8

	1994	1993	1992	1991	1990	1989	1988	1987	1986	1985
Return (%)	-11.6	0.1	4.6	55.3	-19.8	7.3	20.8	—	—	—
Differ from category (+/-) .	-10.2	-13.1	-5.6	27.7	-13.8	-14.1	3.8	—	—	—

PER SHARE DATA

	1994	1993	1992	1991	1990	1989	1988	1987	1986	1985
Dividends, Net Income ($) .	0.18	0.24	0.29	0.18	0.34	0.37	0.47	—	—	—
Distrib'ns, Cap Gain ($) . . .	0.00	0.00	0.00	0.00	0.00	0.27	0.00	—	—	—
Net Asset Value ($)	9.27	10.69	10.91	10.71	7.01	9.15	9.11	—	—	—
Expense Ratio (%)	1.59	1.40	1.63	2.63	2.51	2.14	0.00	—	—	—
Net Income to Assets (%) . .	1.96	1.55	3.17	2.66	3.50	4.70	6.76	—	—	—
Portfolio Turnover (%)	145	186	103	133	63	88	51	—	—	—
Total Assets (Millions $)	11	18	22	7	6	6	3	—	—	—

PORTFOLIO (as of 6/30/94)

Portfolio Manager: Allen Parker - 1987

Investm't Category: Growth & Income
Cap Gain	Asset Allocation
✔ Cap & Income	Fund of Funds
Income	Index
	✔ Sector
✔ Domestic	Small Cap
Foreign	Socially Conscious
Country/Region	State Specific

Portfolio: stocks 96% bonds 0%
convertibles 0% other 0% cash 4%

Largest Holdings: real estate investment trusts 85%, home builder 6%

Unrealized Net Capital Gains: -4% of portfolio value

SHAREHOLDER INFORMATION

Minimum Investment
Initial: $1,000   Subsequent: $50

Minimum IRA Investment
Initial: $0   Subsequent: $0

Maximum Fees
Load: 0.10% redemption   12b-1: none
Other: redemption fee applies for 14 days; $10 close-out fee

Distributions
Income: Jun, Dec   Capital Gains: Dec

Exchange Options
Number Per Year: no limit   Fee: $5
Telephone: yes (money market fund available)

Services: IRA, pension, auto exchange, auto invest, auto withdraw

US Tax Free (USUTX)

Tax-Exempt Bond

P.O. Box 781234
San Antonio, TX 78278
(800) 873-8637, (210) 308-1222

PERFORMANCE

fund inception date: 11/1/84

	3yr Annual	5yr Annual	10yr Annual	Bull	Bear
Return (%)	4.3	5.7	7.6	40.1	-5.0
Differ from Category (+/-)	-0.2 blw av	-0.4 low	-0.5 blw av	-1.7 blw av	0.2 abv av

Total Risk	Standard Deviation	Category Risk	Risk Index	Avg Mat
blw av	5.8%	av	0.9	19.3 yrs

	1994	1993	1992	1991	1990	1989	1988	1987	1986	1985
Return (%)	-5.2	11.7	7.1	9.9	6.0	8.2	11.9	-0.2	17.0	11.1
Differ from category (+/-)	0.0	0.0	-1.2	-1.4	-0.3	-0.8	1.7	1.1	0.6	-6.3

PER SHARE DATA

	1994	1993	1992	1991	1990	1989	1988	1987	1986	1985
Dividends, Net Income ($)	0.72	0.69	0.67	0.54	0.63	0.61	0.82	0.82	0.85	0.47
Distrib'ns, Cap Gain ($)	0.00	0.13	0.03	0.21	0.00	0.00	0.00	0.00	0.12	0.00
Net Asset Value ($)	10.89	12.24	11.71	11.60	11.26	11.24	10.97	10.56	11.42	10.63
Expense Ratio (%)	0.00	0.32	1.27	1.93	1.61	1.23	0.00	0.05	0.38	1.44
Net Income to Assets (%)	5.68	5.48	5.38	5.09	5.64	6.38	7.60	6.99	8.57	5.94
Portfolio Turnover (%)	50	93	70	54	82	110	121	37	50	67
Total Assets (Millions $)	16	22	8	7	8	10	8	8	2	1

PORTFOLIO (as of 6/30/94)

Portfolio Manager: Allen Parker - 1992

Investm't Category: Tax-Exempt Bond

Cap Gain	Asset Allocation
Cap & Income	Fund of Funds
✔ Income	Index
	Sector
✔ Domestic	Small Cap
Foreign	Socially Conscious
Country/Region	State Specific

Portfolio: stocks 0%   bonds 97%
convertibles 0%   other 0%   cash 3%

Largest Holdings: general obligation 17%

Unrealized Net Capital Gains: -3% of portfolio value

SHAREHOLDER INFORMATION

Minimum Investment
Initial: $1,000   Subsequent: $50

Minimum IRA Investment
Initial: na   Subsequent: na

Maximum Fees
Load: none   12b-1: none
Other: $10 close-out fee

Distributions
Income: monthly   Capital Gains: Dec

Exchange Options
Number Per Year: no limit   Fee: $5
Telephone: yes (money market fund available)

Services
auto exchange, auto invest, auto withdraw

US World Gold (UNWPX)

Gold

P.O. Box 781234
San Antonio, TX 78278
(800) 873-8637, (210) 308-1222

PERFORMANCE

fund inception date: 11/27/85

	3yr Annual	5yr Annual	10yr Annual	Bull	Bear
Return (%)	14.5	0.9	na	63.0	-14.4
Differ from Category (+/-)	3.7 high	0.9 abv av	na	30.1 high	-4.4 low

Total Risk	Standard Deviation	Category Risk	Risk Index	Beta
high	28.0%	high	1.0	0.5

	1994	1993	1992	1991	1990	1989	1988	1987	1986	1985
Return (%)	-16.9	89.7	-4.7	-3.3	-27.8	16.5	-18.7	31.0	38.5	—
Differ from category (+/-) . .	-5.4	2.8	11.0	1.5	-5.3	-8.2	0.2	-0.9	0.9	—

PER SHARE DATA

	1994	1993	1992	1991	1990	1989	1988	1987	1986	1985
Dividends, Net Income ($) .	0.03	0.00	0.00	0.00	0.00	0.10	0.00	0.20	0.00	—
Distrib'ns, Cap Gain ($) . . .	0.00	0.00	0.00	0.00	0.00	0.00	0.00	2.10	0.20	—
Net Asset Value ($)	14.63	17.65	9.30	9.76	10.10	14.00	12.10	14.90	13.10	—
Expense Ratio (%)	1.53	2.00	2.20	2.22	1.95	2.00	1.47	1.47	1.51	—
Net Income to Assets (%) . .	0.66	-1.15	-1.18	-0.95	-0.24	0.13	0.04	-0.05	0.01	—
Portfolio Turnover (%)	19	26	47	44	26	20	39	44	31	—
Total Assets (Millions $) . . .	182	163	58	65	73	85	104	127	27	—

PORTFOLIO (as of 6/30/94)

Portfolio Manager: Victor Flores - 1990

Investm't Category: Gold

✔ Cap Gain	Asset Allocation
Cap & Income	Fund of Funds
Income	Index
	✔ Sector
✔ Domestic	Small Cap
✔ Foreign	Socially Conscious
Country/Region	State Specific

Portfolio: stocks 94% bonds 1%
convertibles 2% other 0% cash 3%

Largest Holdings: gold producing cos. 70%,
mining—finance 12%

Unrealized Net Capital Gains: 17% of portfolio value

SHAREHOLDER INFORMATION

Minimum Investment
Initial: $1,000   Subsequent: $50

Minimum IRA Investment
Initial: $0   Subsequent: $0

Maximum Fees
Load: 0.10% redemption   12b-1: none
Other: redemption fee applies for 14 days; $10
close out fee

Distributions
Income: Dec   Capital Gains: Dec

Exchange Options
Number Per Year: no limit   Fee: $5
Telephone: yes (money market fund available)

Services: IRA, pension, auto exchange, auto
invest, auto withdraw

USAA Aggressive Growth (USAUX)

Aggressive Growth

9800 Fredericksburg Road
San Antonio, TX 78288
(800) 531-8181, (210) 498-6505

PERFORMANCE

fund inception date: 10/19/81

	3yr Annual	5yr Annual	10yr Annual	Bull	Bear
Return (%)	-0.6	8.2	9.7	100.6	-16.6
Differ from Category (+/-)	-9.5 low	-4.3 low	-4.3 low	-32.6 blw av	-5.8 low

Total Risk	Standard Deviation	Category Risk	Risk Index	Beta
high	15.6%	abv av	1.1	1.2

	1994	1993	1992	1991	1990	1989	1988	1987	1986	1985
Return (%)	-0.7	8.1	-8.5	71.6	-11.9	16.5	14.2	-0.9	5.6	23.0
Differ from category (+/-)	0.0	-11.4	-19.5	19.5	-5.7	-10.3	-1.0	1.3	-6.2	-9.3

PER SHARE DATA

	1994	1993	1992	1991	1990	1989	1988	1987	1986	1985
Dividends, Net Income ($)	0.00	0.02	0.00	0.01	0.10	0.19	0.14	0.12	0.07	0.11
Distrib'ns, Cap Gain ($)	1.55	1.25	2.14	0.00	0.00	2.62	0.47	1.86	0.35	0.00
Net Asset Value ($)	18.46	20.22	19.93	24.42	14.23	16.28	16.34	14.85	17.10	16.57
Expense Ratio (%)	0.83	0.86	0.82	0.87	0.94	0.91	1.00	0.97	1.05	1.11
Net Income to Assets (%)	-0.10	0.10	-0.05	0.17	0.68	0.78	0.82	0.54	0.37	0.66
Portfolio Turnover (%)	na	113	74	50	78	98	68	35	57	74
Total Assets (Millions $)	283	286	235	208	115	158	139	150	118	108

PORTFOLIO (as of 7/31/94)

Portfolio Manager: William Fries - 1994

Investm't Category: Aggressive Growth
✔ Cap Gain	Asset Allocation
Cap & Income	Fund of Funds
Income	Index
	Sector
✔ Domestic	✔ Small Cap
Foreign	Socially Conscious
Country/Region	State Specific

Portfolio: stocks 89% bonds 0%
convertibles 0% other 1% cash 10%

Largest Holdings: specialty retail 10%, healthcare 8%

Unrealized Net Capital Gains: 3% of portfolio value

SHAREHOLDER INFORMATION

Minimum Investment
Initial: $1,000   Subsequent: $50

Minimum IRA Investment
Initial: $1,000   Subsequent: $50

Maximum Fees
Load: none   12b-1: none
Other: none

Distributions
Income: Nov   Capital Gains: Nov

Exchange Options
Number Per Year: 6   Fee: none
Telephone: yes (money market fund available)

Services
IRA, pension, auto exchange, auto invest, auto withdraw

USAA Balanced (USBLX)

Balanced

9800 Fredericksburg Road
San Antonio, TX 78288
(800) 531-8181, (210) 498-6505

PERFORMANCE

fund inception date: 1/11/89

	3yr Annual	5yr Annual	10yr Annual	Bull	Bear
Return (%)	5.1	6.1	na	46.0	-4.4
Differ from Category (+/-)	-1.3 blw av	-1.9 low	na	-19.0 low	1.3 abv av

Total Risk	Standard Deviation	Category Risk	Risk Index	Beta
blw av	5.0%	low	0.8	0.5

	1994	1993	1992	1991	1990	1989	1988	1987	1986	1985
Return (%)	-2.6	13.7	4.9	14.6	1.3	—	—	—	—	—
Differ from category (+/-) . .	-0.7	0.3	-3.4	-8.8	1.8	—	—	—	—	—

PER SHARE DATA

	1994	1993	1992	1991	1990	1989	1988	1987	1986	1985
Dividends, Net Income ($) .	0.47	0.45	0.46	0.51	0.54	—	—	—	—	—
Distrib'ns, Cap Gain ($) . . .	0.27	0.37	0.01	0.00	0.00	—	—	—	—	—
Net Asset Value ($)	11.64	12.71	11.92	11.82	10.78	—	—	—	—	—
Expense Ratio (%)	0.84	0.86	0.92	1.00	1.00	—	—	—	—	—
Net Income to Assets (%). .	3.56	3.81	4.31	4.91	5.05	—	—	—	—	—
Portfolio Turnover (%).	na	98	107	81	106	—	—	—	—	—
Total Assets (Millions $) . . .	124	127	83	54	38	—	—	—	—	—

PORTFOLIO (as of 5/31/94)

Portfolio Manager: John W. Saunders Jr. - 1989

Investm't Category: Balanced
  Cap Gain
✔ Cap & Income
  Income

  Asset Allocation
  Fund of Funds
  Index
  Sector
✔ Domestic
  Foreign
  Country/Region

  Small Cap
  Socially Conscious
  State Specific

Portfolio: stocks 39%   bonds 61%
convertibles 0%   other 0%   cash 0%

Largest Holdings: bonds—short-term tax exempt 30%, bonds—long-term tax exempt 29%

Unrealized Net Capital Gains: 3% of portfolio value

SHAREHOLDER INFORMATION

Minimum Investment
Initial: $1,000   Subsequent: $50

Minimum IRA Investment
Initial: na   Subsequent: na

Maximum Fees
Load: none   12b-1: none
Other: none

Distributions
Income: quarterly   Capital Gains: Nov

Exchange Options
Number Per Year: 6   Fee: none
Telephone: yes (money market fund available)

Services
auto exchange, auto invest, auto withdraw

USAA Cornerstone
(USCRX)
Balanced

9800 Fredericksburg Road
San Antonio, TX 78288
(800) 531-8181, (210) 498-6505

	3yr Annual	5yr Annual	10yr Annual	Bull	Bear
Return (%)	9.2	6.5	12.3	56.1	-5.2
Differ from Category (+/-)	2.8 abv av	-1.5 blw av	1.0 abv av	-8.9 blw av	0.5 av

Total Risk	Standard Deviation	Category Risk	Risk Index	Beta
av	7.3%	high	1.2	0.6

	1994	1993	1992	1991	1990	1989	1988	1987	1986	1985
Return (%)..............	-0.9	23.7	6.3	16.2	-9.2	21.8	8.3	8.9	40.7	14.7
Differ from category (+/-) ..	1.0	10.3	-2.0	-7.2	-8.7	4.5	-3.5	6.5	23.3	-9.6

PER SHARE DATA

	1994	1993	1992	1991	1990	1989	1988	1987	1986	1985
Dividends, Net Income ($).	0.58	0.59	0.63	0.59	0.65	0.71	0.66	0.36	0.30	0.32
Distrib'ns, Cap Gain ($) ...	1.38	0.29	0.00	0.00	0.00	0.00	0.00	0.02	0.21	0.06
Net Asset Value ($).....	21.24	23.46	19.69	19.12	16.98	19.44	16.54	15.87	14.92	10.97
Expense Ratio (%)	1.11	1.18	1.18	1.18	1.21	1.21	1.21	1.07	1.50	1.50
Net Income to Assets (%) .	2.68	2.92	3.25	3.58	3.50	3.57	3.54	3.41	3.68	5.03
Portfolio Turnover (%)	na	45	33	28	41	33	28	15	70	15
Total Assets (Millions $) ...	841	770	567	580	535	522	544	823	28	13

PORTFOLIO (as of 9/30/94)

Portfolio Manager: Harry W. Miller - 1990

Investm't Category: Balanced
- Cap Gain
- ✔ Cap & Income
- Income

- ✔ Asset Allocation
- Fund of Funds
- Index
- Sector

- ✔ Domestic
- ✔ Foreign
- Country/Region

- Small Cap
- Socially Conscious
- State Specific

Portfolio: stocks 75%   bonds 25%
convertibles 0%   other 0%   cash 0%

Largest Holdings: stocks—real estate 22%, bonds—U. S. government & agencies 13%

Unrealized Net Capital Gains: 9% of portfolio value

SHAREHOLDER INFORMATION

Minimum Investment
Initial: $1,000   Subsequent: $50

Minimum IRA Investment
Initial: $1,000   Subsequent: $50

Maximum Fees
Load: none   12b-1: none
Other: none

Distributions
Income: Nov   Capital Gains: Nov

Exchange Options
Number Per Year: 6   Fee: none
Telephone: yes (money market fund available)

Services
IRA, pension, auto exchange, auto invest, auto withdraw

USAA Florida Tax-Free Income (UFLTX)

9800 Fredericksburg Road
San Antonio, TX 78288
(800) 531-8181, (210) 498-6505

Tax-Exempt Bond

PERFORMANCE

fund inception date: 10/1/93

	3yr Annual	5yr Annual	10yr Annual	Bull	Bear
Return (%)	na	na	na	na	-8.8
Differ from Category (+/-)	na	na	na	na	-3.6 low

Total Risk	Standard Deviation	Category Risk	Risk Index	Avg Mat
na	na	na	na	22.1 yrs

	1994	1993	1992	1991	1990	1989	1988	1987	1986	1985
Return (%)	-10.0	—	—	—	—	—	—	—	—	—
Differ from category (+/-) . .	-4.8	—	—	—	—	—	—	—	—	—

PER SHARE DATA

	1994	1993	1992	1991	1990	1989	1988	1987	1986	1985
Dividends, Net Income ($) .	0.48	—	—	—	—	—	—	—	—	—
Distrib'ns, Cap Gain ($) . . .	0.00	—	—	—	—	—	—	—	—	—
Net Asset Value ($)	8.51	—	—	—	—	—	—	—	—	—
Expense Ratio (%)	0.50	—	—	—	—	—	—	—	—	—
Net Income to Assets (%). .	5.34	—	—	—	—	—	—	—	—	—
Portfolio Turnover (%)	na	—	—	—	—	—	—	—	—	—
Total Assets (Millions $)	37	—	—	—	—	—	—	—	—	—

PORTFOLIO (as of 9/30/94)

Portfolio Manager: David G. Miller - 1994

Investm't Category: Tax-Exempt Bond

Cap Gain	Asset Allocation
Cap & Income	Fund of Funds
✔ Income	Index
	Sector
✔ Domestic	Small Cap
Foreign	Socially Conscious
Country/Region	✔ State Specific

Portfolio: stocks 0% bonds 100%
convertibles 0% other 0% cash 0%

Largest Holdings: general obligations 5%

Unrealized Net Capital Gains: -5% of portfolio value

SHAREHOLDER INFORMATION

Minimum Investment
Initial: $3,000   Subsequent: $50

Minimum IRA Investment
Initial: na   Subsequent: na

Maximum Fees
Load: none   12b-1: none
Other: none

Distributions
Income: monthly   Capital Gains: Nov

Exchange Options
Number Per Year: 6   Fee: none
Telephone: yes (money market fund available)

Services
auto exchange, auto invest, auto withdraw

USAA GNMA Trust
(USGNX)
Mortgage-Backed Bond

9800 Fredericksburg Road
San Antonio, TX 78288
(800) 531-8181, (210) 498-6505

PERFORMANCE   fund inception date: 2/1/91

	3yr Annual	5yr Annual	10yr Annual	Bull	Bear
Return (%)	4.3	na	na	na	-1.8
Differ from Category (+/-)	1.2 high	na	na	na	2.6 abv av

Total Risk	Standard Deviation	Category Risk	Risk Index	Avg Mat
low	3.3%	av	1.0	4.6 yrs

	1994	1993	1992	1991	1990	1989	1988	1987	1986	1985
Return (%).............	0.0	7.1	6.0	—	—	—	—	—	—	—
Differ from category (+/-) ..	2.8	0.3	-0.1	—	—	—	—	—	—	—

PER SHARE DATA

	1994	1993	1992	1991	1990	1989	1988	1987	1986	1985
Dividends, Net Income ($).	0.70	0.78	0.81	—	—	—	—	—	—	—
Distrib'ns, Cap Gain ($) ...	0.00	0.00	0.00	—	—	—	—	—	—	—
Net Asset Value ($)	9.57	10.28	10.34	—	—	—	—	—	—	—
Expense Ratio (%)	0.31	0.32	0.38	—	—	—	—	—	—	—
Net Income to Assets (%) .	7.20	7.53	7.92	—	—	—	—	—	—	—
Portfolio Turnover (%)	na	81	36	—	—	—	—	—	—	—
Total Assets (Millions $) ...	244	278	219	—	—	—	—	—	—	—

PORTFOLIO (as of 9/30/94)

Portfolio Manager: Carl W. Shirley - 1991

Investm't Category: Mortgage-Backed Bond
Cap Gain	Asset Allocation
Cap & Income	Fund of Funds
✔ Income	Index
	Sector
✔ Domestic	Small Cap
Foreign	Socially Conscious
Country/Region	State Specific

Portfolio: stocks 0%   bonds 100%
convertibles 0%   other 0%   cash 0%

Largest Holdings: mortgage-backed 70%,
U.S. government 29%

Unrealized Net Capital Gains: -2% of portfolio value

SHAREHOLDER INFORMATION

Minimum Investment
Initial: $3,000   Subsequent: $50

Minimum IRA Investment
Initial: $1,000   Subsequent: $50

Maximum Fees
Load: none   12b-1: none
Other: none

Distributions
Income: monthly   Capital Gains: Dec

Exchange Options
Number Per Year: 6   Fee: none
Telephone: yes (money market fund available)

Services
IRA, pension, auto exchange, auto invest, auto
withdraw

USAA Gold (USAGX)

Gold

9800 Fredericksburg Road
San Antonio, TX 78288
(800) 531-8181, (210) 498-6505

PERFORMANCE

fund inception date: 8/15/84

	3yr Annual	5yr Annual	10yr Annual	Bull	Bear
Return (%)	9.7	-1.5	2.6	21.3	-11.4
Differ from Category (+/-)	-1.1 low	-1.5 low	-2.6 blw av	-11.6 low	-1.4 blw av

Total Risk	Standard Deviation	Category Risk	Risk Index	Beta
high	25.2%	blw av	0.9	0.3

	1994	1993	1992	1991	1990	1989	1988	1987	1986	1985
Return (%)	-9.3	58.3	-7.9	-4.4	-26.5	18.1	-17.1	15.8	55.6	-20.6
Differ from category (+/-) . . .	2.2	-28.6	7.8	0.4	-4.0	-6.6	1.8	-16.1	18.0	-13.2

PER SHARE DATA

	1994	1993	1992	1991	1990	1989	1988	1987	1986	1985
Dividends, Net Income ($) .	0.01	0.01	0.04	0.08	0.06	0.15	0.13	0.05	0.10	0.12
Distrib'ns, Cap Gain ($) . . .	0.00	0.00	0.00	0.00	0.00	0.00	0.00	0.51	0.00	0.00
Net Asset Value ($)	8.59	9.49	6.00	6.56	6.95	9.55	8.21	10.06	9.23	6.00
Expense Ratio (%)	1.26	1.41	1.43	1.45	1.43	1.34	1.42	1.14	1.50	1.50
Net Income to Assets (%). .	0.15	0.25	1.02	1.55	0.93	1.92	0.50	0.73	1.49	3.71
Portfolio Turnover (%).	na	81	19	13	42	17	27	54	62	0
Total Assets (Millions $) . . .	158	184	114	121	157	165	174	310	29	15

PORTFOLIO (as of 9/30/94)

Portfolio Manager: Mark Johnson - 1994

Investm't Category: Gold

✔ Cap Gain	Asset Allocation
Cap & Income	Fund of Funds
Income	Index
	✔ Sector
✔ Domestic	Small Cap
✔ Foreign	Socially Conscious
Country/Region	State Specific

Portfolio: stocks 94% bonds 0%
convertibles 0% other 0% cash 6%

Largest Holdings: North American cos. 69%,
Australian gold cos. 12%

Unrealized Net Capital Gains: 5% of portfolio value

SHAREHOLDER INFORMATION

Minimum Investment
Initial: $1,000   Subsequent: $50

Minimum IRA Investment
Initial: $1,000   Subsequent: $50

Maximum Fees
Load: none   12b-1: none
Other: none

Distributions
Income: Nov   Capital Gains: Nov

Exchange Options
Number Per Year: 6   Fee: none
Telephone: yes (money market fund available)

Services
IRA, pension, auto exchange, auto invest, auto withdraw

USAA Growth (USAAX)

Growth

9800 Fredericksburg Road
San Antonio, TX 78288
(800) 531-8181, (210) 498-6505

fund inception date: 4/5/71

	3yr Annual	5yr Annual	10yr Annual	Bull	Bear
Return (%)	6.8	9.3	11.4	67.5	-5.1
Differ from Category (+/-)	-0.9 av	-0.3 av	-1.5 low	-24.6 blw av	1.5 abv av

Total Risk	Standard Deviation	Category Risk	Risk Index	Beta
abv av	9.2%	av	0.9	0.9

	1994	1993	1992	1991	1990	1989	1988	1987	1986	1985
Return (%).............	3.3	7.4	9.9	27.8	0.0	27.3	6.5	5.3	9.9	20.1
Differ from category (+/-) ..	3.9	-6.0	-1.7	-7.9	5.7	1.2	-11.5	3.5	-4.7	-9.1

PER SHARE DATA

	1994	1993	1992	1991	1990	1989	1988	1987	1986	1985
Dividends, Net Income ($).	0.27	0.16	0.32	0.41	0.46	0.46	0.34	0.37	0.19	0.28
Distrib'ns, Cap Gain ($) ...	2.51	1.99	0.27	0.00	0.00	0.00	0.00	3.88	1.59	0.31
Net Asset Value ($).....	15.63	17.69	18.51	17.40	13.96	14.45	11.72	11.32	14.76	15.03
Expense Ratio (%)	1.04	1.07	1.07	1.11	1.18	1.19	1.22	1.09	1.09	1.06
Net Income to Assets (%) .	1.33	1.07	2.27	3.18	2.95	3.02	2.40	2.14	1.37	1.86
Portfolio Turnover (%)	na	96	39	37	56	95	109	124	109	128
Total Assets (Millions $) ...	677	605	432	319	223	230	208	272	145	128

PORTFOLIO (as of 7/31/94)

Portfolio Manager: David G. Parsons - 1994

Investm't Category: Growth

✔ Cap Gain	Asset Allocation
Cap & Income	Fund of Funds
Income	Index
	Sector
✔ Domestic	Small Cap
Foreign	Socially Conscious
Country/Region	State Specific

Portfolio:	stocks 99%	bonds 0%
convertibles 0%	other 0%	cash 1%

Largest Holdings: tobacco 20%, medical products & supplies 11%

Unrealized Net Capital Gains: -1% of portfolio value

SHAREHOLDER INFORMATION

Minimum Investment
Initial: $1,000   Subsequent: $50

Minimum IRA Investment
Initial: $1,000   Subsequent: $50

Maximum Fees
Load: none   12b-1: none
Other: none

Distributions
Income: Nov   Capital Gains: Nov

Exchange Options
Number Per Year: 6   Fee: none
Telephone: yes (money market fund available)

Services
IRA, pension, auto exchange, auto invest, auto withdraw

USAA Growth & Income
(USGRX)
Growth & Income

9800 Fredericksburg Road
San Antonio, TX 78288
(800) 531-8181, (210) 498-6505

PERFORMANCE
fund inception date: 6/1/93

	3yr Annual	5yr Annual	10yr Annual	Bull	Bear
Return (%)	na	na	na	na	-6.5
Differ from Category (+/-)	na	na	na	na	-0.2 av

Total Risk	Standard Deviation	Category Risk	Risk Index	Beta
na	na	na	na	na

	1994	1993	1992	1991	1990	1989	1988	1987	1986	1985
Return (%)	1.2	—	—	—	—	—	—	—	—	—
Differ from category (+/-)	2.6	—	—	—	—	—	—	—	—	—

PER SHARE DATA

	1994	1993	1992	1991	1990	1989	1988	1987	1986	1985
Dividends, Net Income ($)	0.22	—	—	—	—	—	—	—	—	—
Distrib'ns, Cap Gain ($)	0.11	—	—	—	—	—	—	—	—	—
Net Asset Value ($)	10.18	—	—	—	—	—	—	—	—	—
Expense Ratio (%)	1.12	—	—	—	—	—	—	—	—	—
Net Income to Assets (%)	1.95	—	—	—	—	—	—	—	—	—
Portfolio Turnover (%)	na	—	—	—	—	—	—	—	—	—
Total Assets (Millions $)	150	—	—	—	—	—	—	—	—	—

PORTFOLIO (as of 7/31/94)

Portfolio Manager: R. David Ullom - 1993

Investm't Category: Growth & Income

Cap Gain	Asset Allocation
✔ Cap & Income	Fund of Funds
Income	Index
	Sector
✔ Domestic	Small Cap
Foreign	Socially Conscious
Country/Region	State Specific

Portfolio: stocks 93% bonds 0%
convertibles 0% other 1% cash 6%

Largest Holdings: telephones 8%, aerospace/defense 6%

Unrealized Net Capital Gains: 1% of portfolio value

SHAREHOLDER INFORMATION

Minimum Investment
Initial: $1,000   Subsequent: $50

Minimum IRA Investment
Initial: $1,000   Subsequent: $50

Maximum Fees
Load: none   12b-1: none
Other: none

Distributions
Income: quarterly   Capital Gains: Sep

Exchange Options
Number Per Year: 6   Fee: none
Telephone: yes (money market fund available)

Services
IRA, pension, auto exchange, auto invest, auto withdraw

USAA Income (USAIX)

Balanced

9800 Fredericksburg Road
San Antonio, TX 78288
(800) 531-8181, (210) 498-6505

	3yr Annual	5yr Annual	10yr Annual	Bull	Bear
Return (%)	4.1	7.7	9.9	52.6	-7.7
Differ from Category (+/-)	-2.3 low	-0.3 blw av	-1.4 low	-12.4 blw av	-2.0 low

Total Risk	Standard Deviation	Category Risk	Risk Index	Beta
blw av	5.2%	blw av	0.8	0.4

	1994	1993	1992	1991	1990	1989	1988	1987	1986	1985
Return (%)	-5.2	9.9	8.3	19.3	7.5	16.3	9.9	3.5	12.6	19.1
Differ from category (+/-)	-3.3	-3.5	0.0	-4.1	8.0	-1.0	-1.9	1.1	-4.8	-5.2

PER SHARE DATA

	1994	1993	1992	1991	1990	1989	1988	1987	1986	1985
Dividends, Net Income ($)	0.86	0.88	0.94	0.96	1.03	1.03	1.07	1.14	1.28	1.20
Distrib'ns, Cap Gain ($)	0.00	0.25	0.00	0.01	0.00	0.03	0.00	0.26	0.06	0.02
Net Asset Value ($)	11.19	12.71	12.61	12.55	11.41	11.62	10.96	10.97	11.98	11.89
Expense Ratio (%)	0.41	0.41	0.42	0.47	0.53	0.57	0.61	0.61	0.65	0.68
Net Income to Assets (%)	6.98	7.00	7.78	8.61	9.19	9.36	9.57	9.13	9.69	10.96
Portfolio Turnover (%)	na	44	22	15	12	14	11	36	37	78
Total Assets (Millions $)	1,611	1,546	1,359	827	435	332	285	250	213	138

PORTFOLIO (as of 7/31/94)

Portfolio Manager: John W. Saunders Jr. - 1985

Investm't Category: Balanced

Cap Gain	Asset Allocation
✔ Cap & Income	Fund of Funds
Income	Index
	Sector
✔ Domestic	Small Cap
Foreign	Socially Conscious
Country/Region	State Specific

Portfolio: stocks 14%   bonds 84%
convertibles 0%   other 0%   cash 2%

Largest Holdings: bonds—mortgage-backed 75%, stocks—electric utilities 13%

Unrealized Net Capital Gains: -4% of portfolio value

SHAREHOLDER INFORMATION

Minimum Investment
Initial: $1,000   Subsequent: $50

Minimum IRA Investment
Initial: $1,000   Subsequent: $50

Maximum Fees
Load: none   12b-1: none
Other: none

Distributions
Income: monthly   Capital Gains: Nov

Exchange Options
Number Per Year: 6   Fee: none
Telephone: yes (money market fund available)

Services
IRA, pension, auto exchange, auto invest, auto withdraw

USAA Income Stock

(USISX)

Growth & Income

9800 Fredericksburg Road
San Antonio, TX 78288
(800) 531-8181, (210) 498-6505

PERFORMANCE

fund inception date: 5/4/87

	3yr Annual	5yr Annual	10yr Annual	Bull	Bear
Return (%)	6.0	8.4	na	74.1	-6.6
Differ from Category (+/-)	-1.1 blw av	0.5 av	na	-1.7 av	-0.3 av

Total Risk	Standard Deviation	Category Risk	Risk Index	Beta
av	7.7%	blw av	0.9	0.9

	1994	1993	1992	1991	1990	1989	1988	1987	1986	1985
Return (%)	-0.7	11.5	7.7	27.3	-1.3	27.1	19.3	—	—	—
Differ from category (+/-) . . .	0.7	-1.7	-2.5	-0.3	4.7	5.7	2.3	—	—	—

PER SHARE DATA

	1994	1993	1992	1991	1990	1989	1988	1987	1986	1985
Dividends, Net Income ($) .	0.75	0.71	0.70	0.68	0.65	0.57	0.48	—	—	—
Distrib'ns, Cap Gain ($) . . .	0.22	0.19	0.09	0.00	0.00	0.58	0.00	—	—	—
Net Asset Value ($)	13.06	14.13	13.48	13.27	11.01	11.85	10.28	—	—	—
Expense Ratio (%)	0.73	0.70	0.74	0.83	1.00	1.00	1.00	—	—	—
Net Income to Assets (%) . .	5.25	5.43	5.99	6.30	5.75	5.10	4.72	—	—	—
Portfolio Turnover (%)	na	26	16	27	49	72	28	—	—	—
Total Assets (Millions $) . .	1,171	1,140	481	179	81	55	31	—	—	—

PORTFOLIO (as of 7/31/94)

Portfolio Manager: Harry Miller - 1989

Investm't Category: Growth & Income

Cap Gain	Asset Allocation
✔ Cap & Income	Fund of Funds
Income	Index
	Sector
✔ Domestic	Small Cap
Foreign	Socially Conscious
Country/Region	State Specific

Portfolio: stocks 74% bonds 0%
convertibles 25% other 0% cash 1%

Largest Holdings: real estate investment trusts 11%, electric power 10%

Unrealized Net Capital Gains: -1% of portfolio value

SHAREHOLDER INFORMATION

Minimum Investment
Initial: $1,000   Subsequent: $50

Minimum IRA Investment
Initial: $1,000   Subsequent: $50

Maximum Fees
Load: none   12b-1: none
Other: none

Distributions
Income: quarterly   Capital Gains: Nov

Exchange Options
Number Per Year: 6   Fee: none
Telephone: yes (money market fund available)

Services
IRA, pension, auto exchange, auto invest, auto withdraw

USAA International

(USIFX)

International Stock

9800 Fredericksburg Road
San Antonio, TX 78288
(800) 531-8181, (210) 498-6505

PERFORMANCE

fund inception date: 7/11/88

	3yr Annual	5yr Annual	10yr Annual	Bull	Bear
Return (%)	12.7	8.0	na	81.7	-4.9
Differ from Category (+/-)	3.6 abv av	3.1 high	na	17.8 high	2.1 abv av

Total Risk	Standard Deviation	Category Risk	Risk Index	Beta
abv av	12.0%	blw av	0.9	0.7

	1994	1993	1992	1991	1990	1989	1988	1987	1986	1985
Return (%).............	2.6	39.8	-0.1	13.4	-9.2	17.3	—	—	—	—
Differ from category (+/-) ..	5.6	1.2	2.8	0.3	1.2	-5.2	—	—	—	—

PER SHARE DATA

	1994	1993	1992	1991	1990	1989	1988	1987	1986	1985
Dividends, Net Income ($).	0.00	0.00	0.13	0.09	0.06	0.02	—	—	—	—
Distrib'ns, Cap Gain ($) ...	0.97	0.35	0.00	0.00	0.05	0.45	—	—	—	—
Net Asset Value ($)	15.56	16.10	11.79	11.94	10.61	11.82	—	—	—	—
Expense Ratio (%)	1.31	1.50	1.69	1.82	2.09	2.30	—	—	—	—
Net Income to Assets (%) .	0.04	0.72	1.05	1.26	0.81	0.48	—	—	—	—
Portfolio Turnover (%)	na	52	34	64	70	95	—	—	—	—
Total Assets (Millions $) ...	337	141	43	29	21	13	—	—	—	—

PORTFOLIO (as of 9/30/94)

Portfolio Manager: David G. Peebles - 1988

Investm't Category: International Stock

✔ Cap Gain	Asset Allocation
Cap & Income	Fund of Funds
Income	Index
	Sector
Domestic	Small Cap
✔ Foreign	Socially Conscious
Country/Region	State Specific

Portfolio:	stocks 92%	bonds 0%
convertibles 0%	other 0%	cash 8%

Largest Holdings: Japan 27%, United Kingdom 6%

Unrealized Net Capital Gains: 10% of portfolio value

SHAREHOLDER INFORMATION

Minimum Investment
Initial: $1,000   Subsequent: $50

Minimum IRA Investment
Initial: $1,000   Subsequent: $50

Maximum Fees
Load: none   12b-1: none
Other: none

Distributions
Income: Nov   Capital Gains: Nov

Exchange Options
Number Per Year: 6   Fee: none
Telephone: yes (money market fund available)

Services
IRA, pension, auto exchange, auto invest, auto withdraw

USAA Tax Exempt CA Bond (USCBX)

9800 Fredericksburg Road
San Antonio, TX 78288
(800) 531-8181, (210) 498-6505

Tax-Exempt Bond

PERFORMANCE

fund inception date: 8/1/89

	3yr Annual	5yr Annual	10yr Annual	Bull	Bear
Return (%)	3.4	5.8	na	44.4	-7.9
Differ from Category (+/-)	-1.1 low	-0.3 blw av	na	2.6 av	-2.7 low

Total Risk	Standard Deviation	Category Risk	Risk Index	Avg Mat
av	6.8%	high	1.1	22.3 yrs

	1994	1993	1992	1991	1990	1989	1988	1987	1986	1985
Return (%)	-9.3	12.7	8.3	10.9	8.1	—	—	—	—	—
Differ from category (+/-)	-4.1	1.0	0.0	-0.4	1.8	—	—	—	—	—

PER SHARE DATA

	1994	1993	1992	1991	1990	1989	1988	1987	1986	1985
Dividends, Net Income ($)	0.58	0.60	0.64	0.66	0.66	—	—	—	—	—
Distrib'ns, Cap Gain ($)	0.00	0.20	0.12	0.00	0.00	—	—	—	—	—
Net Asset Value ($)	9.36	10.94	10.44	10.36	9.97	—	—	—	—	—
Expense Ratio (%)	0.44	0.46	0.48	0.50	0.50	—	—	—	—	—
Net Income to Assets (%)	5.40	5.94	6.44	6.73	6.81	—	—	—	—	—
Portfolio Turnover (%)	102	86	51	73	136	—	—	—	—	—
Total Assets (Millions $)	335	427	306	192	108	—	—	—	—	—

PORTFOLIO (as of 9/30/94)

Portfolio Manager: David G. Miller - 1994

Investm't Category: Tax-Exempt Bond

Cap Gain	Asset Allocation
Cap & Income	Fund of Funds
✔ Income	Index
	Sector
✔ Domestic	Small Cap
Foreign	Socially Conscious
Country/Region	✔ State Specific

Portfolio: stocks 0%   bonds 100%
convertibles 0%   other 0%   cash 0%

Largest Holdings: general obligation 2%

Unrealized Net Capital Gains: 0% of portfolio value

SHAREHOLDER INFORMATION

Minimum Investment
Initial: $3,000   Subsequent: $50

Minimum IRA Investment
Initial: na   Subsequent: na

Maximum Fees
Load: none   12b-1: none
Other: none

Distributions
Income: monthly   Capital Gains: Nov

Exchange Options
Number Per Year: 6   Fee: none
Telephone: yes (money market fund available)

Services
auto exchange, auto invest, auto withdraw

USAA Tax Exempt Interm-Term (USATX)

9800 Fredericksburg Road
San Antonio, TX 78288
(800) 531-8181, (210) 498-6505

Tax-Exempt Bond

PERFORMANCE

fund inception date: 3/19/82

	3yr Annual	5yr Annual	10yr Annual	Bull	Bear
Return (%)	5.0	6.5	8.0	39.9	-4.6
Differ from Category (+/-)	0.5 abv av	0.4 av	-0.1 blw av	-1.9 blw av	0.6 abv av

Total Risk	Standard Deviation	Category Risk	Risk Index	Avg Mat
low	4.8%	blw av	0.8	8.8 yrs

	1994	1993	1992	1991	1990	1989	1988	1987	1986	1985
Return (%)	-4.0	11.4	8.4	11.1	6.7	9.2	8.6	0.9	13.1	16.3
Differ from category (+/-)	1.2	-0.3	0.1	-0.2	0.4	0.2	-1.6	2.2	-3.3	-1.1

PER SHARE DATA

	1994	1993	1992	1991	1990	1989	1988	1987	1986	1985
Dividends, Net Income ($)	0.69	0.70	0.75	0.81	0.82	0.83	0.83	0.83	0.91	0.99
Distrib'ns, Cap Gain ($)	0.03	0.13	0.00	0.00	0.00	0.00	0.00	0.02	0.00	0.00
Net Asset Value ($)	12.02	13.26	12.68	12.41	11.93	11.98	11.76	11.61	12.35	11.75
Expense Ratio (%)	0.40	0.42	0.44	0.43	0.46	0.49	0.56	0.60	0.57	0.64
Net Income to Assets (%)	5.30	5.85	6.45	6.91	6.95	7.10	7.16	7.07	8.36	9.09
Portfolio Turnover (%)	69	74	67	66	62	113	139	91	79	127
Total Assets (Millions $)	1,416	1,662	894	576	471	401	346	403	201	107

PORTFOLIO (as of 9/30/94)

Portfolio Manager: Clifford A. Gladson - 1993

Investm't Category: Tax-Exempt Bond

Cap Gain	Asset Allocation
Cap & Income	Fund of Funds
✔ Income	Index
	Sector
✔ Domestic	Small Cap
Foreign	Socially Conscious
Country/Region	State Specific

Portfolio:	stocks 0%	bonds 100%
convertibles 0%	other 0%	cash 0%

Largest Holdings: general obligation 21%

Unrealized Net Capital Gains: 0% of portfolio value

SHAREHOLDER INFORMATION

Minimum Investment
Initial: $3,000   Subsequent: $50

Minimum IRA Investment
Initial: na   Subsequent: na

Maximum Fees
Load: none   12b-1: none
Other: none

Distributions
Income: monthly   Capital Gains: May, Nov

Exchange Options
Number Per Year: 6   Fee: none
Telephone: yes (money market fund available)

Services
auto exchange, auto invest, auto withdraw

USAA Tax Exempt Long-Term (USTEX)

Tax-Exempt Bond

9800 Fredericksburg Road
San Antonio, TX 78288
(800) 531-8181, (210) 498-6505

fund inception date: 3/19/82

PERFORMANCE

	3yr Annual	5yr Annual	10yr Annual	Bull	Bear
Return (%)	4.0	6.1	8.7	44.7	-6.6
Differ from Category (+/-)	-0.5 blw av	0.0 blw av	0.6 abv av	2.9 abv av	-1.4 blw av

Total Risk	Standard Deviation	Category Risk	Risk Index	Avg Mat
blw av	6.0%	av	1.0	23.2 yrs

	1994	1993	1992	1991	1990	1989	1988	1987	1986	1985
Return (%)	-7.9	12.4	8.6	12.3	6.5	10.6	12.4	-1.8	17.2	19.6
Differ from category (+/-)..	-2.7	0.7	0.3	1.0	0.2	1.6	2.2	-0.5	0.8	2.2

PER SHARE DATA

	1994	1993	1992	1991	1990	1989	1988	1987	1986	1985
Dividends, Net Income ($) .	0.77	0.84	0.89	0.92	0.95	0.95	0.96	0.99	1.07	1.14
Distrib'ns, Cap Gain ($) ...	0.09	0.56	0.08	0.00	0.00	0.00	0.00	0.22	0.09	0.00
Net Asset Value ($)	12.22	14.18	13.90	13.73	13.09	13.21	12.84	12.31	13.79	12.81
Expense Ratio (%)	0.38	0.39	0.40	0.40	0.43	0.45	0.51	0.49	0.50	0.56
Net Income to Assets (%)..	5.69	6.35	6.83	7.22	7.23	7.58	7.75	7.64	8.94	9.78
Portfolio Turnover (%)....	109	88	76	91	92	124	169	83	122	150
Total Assets (Millions $)..	1,661	2,049	1,638	1,356	1,173	975	823	1,039	648	272

PORTFOLIO (as of 9/30/94)

Portfolio Manager: Kenneth Willmann - 1982

Investm't Category: Tax-Exempt Bond

Cap Gain	Asset Allocation
Cap & Income	Fund of Funds
✔ Income	Index
	Sector
✔ Domestic	Small Cap
Foreign	Socially Conscious
Country/Region	State Specific

Portfolio:	stocks 0%	bonds 100%
convertibles 0%	other 0%	cash 0%

Largest Holdings: general obligation 12%

Unrealized Net Capital Gains: 0% of portfolio value

SHAREHOLDER INFORMATION

Minimum Investment
Initial: $3,000   Subsequent: $50

Minimum IRA Investment
Initial: na   Subsequent: na

Maximum Fees
Load: none   12b-1: none
Other: none

Distributions
Income: monthly   Capital Gains: May, Nov

Exchange Options
Number Per Year: 6   Fee: none
Telephone: yes (money market fund available)

Services
auto exchange, auto invest, auto withdraw

USAA Tax Exempt NY Bond (USNYX)

9800 Fredericksburg Road
San Antonio, TX 78288
(800) 531-8181, (210) 498-6505

Tax-Exempt Bond

PERFORMANCE

fund inception date: 10/15/90

	3yr Annual	5yr Annual	10yr Annual	Bull	Bear
Return (%)	3.9	na	na	na	-7.8
Differ from Category (+/-)	-0.6 low	na	na	na	-2.6 low

Total Risk	Standard Deviation	Category Risk	Risk Index	Avg Mat
av	6.8%	high	1.1	21.6 yrs

	1994	1993	1992	1991	1990	1989	1988	1987	1986	1985
Return (%).	-9.0	13.4	8.9	13.7	—	—	—	—	—	—
Differ from category (+/-) . .	-3.8	1.7	0.6	2.4	—	—	—	—	—	—

PER SHARE DATA

	1994	1993	1992	1991	1990	1989	1988	1987	1986	1985
Dividends, Net Income ($).	0.61	0.63	0.66	0.70	—	—	—	—	—	—
Distrib'ns, Cap Gain ($) . . .	0.00	0.29	0.12	0.00	—	—	—	—	—	—
Net Asset Value ($)	10.17	11.83	11.27	11.09	—	—	—	—	—	—
Expense Ratio (%)	0.50	0.50	0.50	0.50	—	—	—	—	—	—
Net Income to Assets (%) .	5.24	5.79	6.32	6.73	—	—	—	—	—	—
Portfolio Turnover (%)	124	107	111	128	—	—	—	—	—	—
Total Assets (Millions $)	45	62	28	12	—	—	—	—	—	—

PORTFOLIO (as of 9/30/94)

Portfolio Manager: Kenneth E. Willmann - 1990

Investm't Category: Tax-Exempt Bond

Cap Gain	Asset Allocation
Cap & Income	Fund of Funds
✔ Income	Index
	Sector
✔ Domestic	Small Cap
Foreign	Socially Conscious
Country/Region	✔ State Specific

Portfolio: stocks 0%   bonds 100%
convertibles 0%   other 0%   cash 0%

Largest Holdings: general obligation 11%

Unrealized Net Capital Gains: -1% of portfolio value

SHAREHOLDER INFORMATION

Minimum Investment
Initial: $3,000   Subsequent: $50

Minimum IRA Investment
Initial: na   Subsequent: na

Maximum Fees
Load: none   12b-1: none
Other: none

Distributions
Income: monthly   Capital Gains: Nov

Exchange Options
Number Per Year: 6   Fee: none
Telephone: yes (money market fund available)

Services
auto exchange, auto invest, auto withdraw

USAA Tax Exempt Short-Term (USSTX)

Tax-Exempt Bond

9800 Fredericksburg Road
San Antonio, TX 78288
(800) 531-8181, (210) 498-6505

PERFORMANCE

fund inception date: 3/19/82

	3yr Annual	5yr Annual	10yr Annual	Bull	Bear
Return (%)	4.0	5.1	5.9	23.5	-0.7
Differ from Category (+/-)	-0.5 blw av	-1.0 low	-2.2 low	-18.3 low	4.5 high

Total Risk	Standard Deviation	Category Risk	Risk Index	Avg Mat
low	1.6%	low	0.2	2.7 yrs

	1994	1993	1992	1991	1990	1989	1988	1987	1986	1985
Return (%)	0.8	5.5	5.9	7.6	5.8	7.4	6.0	2.8	8.6	9.4
Differ from category (+/-)	6.0	-6.2	-2.4	-3.7	-0.5	-1.6	-4.2	4.1	-7.8	-8.0

PER SHARE DATA

	1994	1993	1992	1991	1990	1989	1988	1987	1986	1985
Dividends, Net Income ($)	0.45	0.46	0.52	0.61	0.67	0.67	0.62	0.61	0.65	0.72
Distrib'ns, Cap Gain ($)	0.00	0.00	0.00	0.00	0.00	0.00	0.00	0.04	0.00	0.00
Net Asset Value ($)	10.33	10.70	10.59	10.50	10.34	10.42	10.35	10.36	10.71	10.47
Expense Ratio (%)	0.43	0.43	0.48	0.50	0.52	0.51	0.56	0.57	0.65	0.70
Net Income to Assets (%)	4.25	4.75	5.59	6.48	6.47	6.14	5.81	5.78	6.85	7.19
Portfolio Turnover (%)	101	138	107	96	87	146	148	142	100	158
Total Assets (Millions $)	810	983	680	424	279	254	245	287	139	85

PORTFOLIO (as of 9/30/94)

Portfolio Manager: Clifford A. Gladson - 1994

Investm't Category: Tax-Exempt Bond

Cap Gain	Asset Allocation
Cap & Income	Fund of Funds
✔ Income	Index
	Sector
✔ Domestic	Small Cap
Foreign	Socially Conscious
Country/Region	State Specific

Portfolio: stocks 0%   bonds 100%
convertibles 0%   other 0%   cash 0%

Largest Holdings: general obligation 21%

Unrealized Net Capital Gains: 0% of portfolio value

SHAREHOLDER INFORMATION

Minimum Investment
Initial: $3,000   Subsequent: $50

Minimum IRA Investment
Initial: na   Subsequent: na

Maximum Fees
Load: none   12b-1: none
Other: none

Distributions
Income: monthly   Capital Gains: May, Nov

Exchange Options
Number Per Year: no limit   Fee: none
Telephone: yes (money market fund available)

Services
auto exchange, auto invest, auto withdraw

USAA Tax-Exempt Virginia Bond (USVAX)

9800 Fredericksburg Road
San Antonio, TX 78288
(800) 531-8181, (210) 498-6505

Tax-Exempt Bond

PERFORMANCE

fund inception date: 10/15/90

	3yr Annual	5yr Annual	10yr Annual	Bull	Bear
Return (%)	4.6	na	na	na	-6.4
Differ from Category (+/-)	0.1 av	na	na	na	-1.2 blw av

Total Risk	Standard Deviation	Category Risk	Risk Index	Avg Mat
blw av	5.8%	av	0.9	21.4 yrs

	1994	1993	1992	1991	1990	1989	1988	1987	1986	1985
Return (%)	-6.3	12.6	8.4	11.9	—	—	—	—	—	—
Differ from category (+/-)	-1.1	0.9	0.1	0.6	—	—	—	—	—	—

PER SHARE DATA

	1994	1993	1992	1991	1990	1989	1988	1987	1986	1985
Dividends, Net Income ($)	0.62	0.62	0.65	0.68	—	—	—	—	—	—
Distrib'ns, Cap Gain ($)	0.00	0.15	0.06	0.00	—	—	—	—	—	—
Net Asset Value ($)	10.14	11.47	10.90	10.73	—	—	—	—	—	—
Expense Ratio (%)	0.49	0.50	0.50	0.50	—	—	—	—	—	—
Net Income to Assets (%)	5.44	5.90	6.40	6.83	—	—	—	—	—	—
Portfolio Turnover (%)	92	91	87	143	—	—	—	—	—	—
Total Assets (Millions $)	215	252	132	58	—	—	—	—	—	—

PORTFOLIO (as of 9/30/94)

Portfolio Manager: David G. Miller - 1994

Investm't Category: Tax-Exempt Bond

Cap Gain	Asset Allocation
Cap & Income	Fund of Funds
✔ Income	Index
	Sector
✔ Domestic	Small Cap
Foreign	Socially Conscious
Country/Region	✔ State Specific

Portfolio: stocks 0%   bonds 100%
convertibles 0%   other 0%   cash 0%

Largest Holdings: general obligation 6%

Unrealized Net Capital Gains: 0% of portfolio value

SHAREHOLDER INFORMATION

Minimum Investment
Initial: $3,000   Subsequent: $50

Minimum IRA Investment
Initial: na   Subsequent: na

Maximum Fees
Load: none   12b-1: none
Other: none

Distributions
Income: monthly   Capital Gains: May, Nov

Exchange Options
Number Per Year: 6   Fee: none
Telephone: yes (money market fund available)

Services
auto exchange, auto invest, auto withdraw

USAA World Growth
(USAWX)

International Stock

9800 Fredericksburg Road
San Antonio, TX 78288
(800) 531-8181, (210) 498-6505

fund inception date: 10/1/92

PERFORMANCE

	3yr Annual	5yr Annual	10yr Annual	Bull	Bear
Return (%)	na	na	na	na	-6.5
Differ from Category (+/-)	na	na	na	na	0.5 av

Total Risk	Standard Deviation	Category Risk	Risk Index	Beta
na	na	na	na	na

	1994	1993	1992	1991	1990	1989	1988	1987	1986	1985
Return (%)	0.6	24.0	—	—	—	—	—	—	—	—
Differ from category (+/-)	3.6	-14.6	—	—	—	—	—	—	—	—

PER SHARE DATA

	1994	1993	1992	1991	1990	1989	1988	1987	1986	1985
Dividends, Net Income ($)	0.00	0.01	—	—	—	—	—	—	—	—
Distrib'ns, Cap Gain ($)	0.28	0.05	—	—	—	—	—	—	—	—
Net Asset Value ($)	12.50	12.70	—	—	—	—	—	—	—	—
Expense Ratio (%)	1.28	1.70	—	—	—	—	—	—	—	—
Net Income to Assets (%)	0.42	0.75	—	—	—	—	—	—	—	—
Portfolio Turnover (%)	na	45	—	—	—	—	—	—	—	—
Total Assets (Millions $)	185	100	—	—	—	—	—	—	—	—

PORTFOLIO (as of 9/30/94)

Portfolio Manager: David G. Peebles - 1992

Investm't Category: International Stock

✔ Cap Gain   Asset Allocation
   Cap & Income   Fund of Funds
   Income   Index
     Sector
✔ Domestic   Small Cap
✔ Foreign   Socially Conscious
   Country/Region   State Specific

Portfolio:	stocks 88%	bonds 1%
convertibles 0%	other 1%	cash 10%

Largest Holdings: United States 24%, Japan 20%

Unrealized Net Capital Gains: 6% of portfolio value

SHAREHOLDER INFORMATION

Minimum Investment
Initial: $1,000   Subsequent: $50

Minimum IRA Investment
Initial: $250   Subsequent: $50

Maximum Fees
Load: none   12b-1: none
Other: none

Distributions
Income: Nov   Capital Gains: Nov

Exchange Options
Number Per Year: 6   Fee: none
Telephone: yes (money market fund available)

Services
IRA, pension, auto exchange, auto invest, auto withdraw

Valley Forge (VAFGX)
Growth & Income

1375 Anthony Wayne Dr.
Wayne, PA 19087
(800) 548-1942, (610) 688-6839

PERFORMANCE   fund inception date: 1/1/71

	3yr Annual	5yr Annual	10yr Annual	Bull	Bear
Return (%)	10.6	6.7	7.4	37.1	0.7
Differ from Category (+/-)	3.5 abv av	-1.2 blw av	-4.3 low	-38.7 low	7.0 high

Total Risk	Standard Deviation	Category Risk	Risk Index	Beta
low	4.3%	low	0.5	0.3

	1994	1993	1992	1991	1990	1989	1988	1987	1986	1985
Return (%).	5.9	17.1	9.3	7.8	-5.3	12.9	6.9	4.8	5.4	10.4
Differ from category (+/-) . .	7.3	3.9	-0.9	-19.8	0.7	-8.5	-10.1	4.2	-10.4	-15.3

PER SHARE DATA

	1994	1993	1992	1991	1990	1989	1988	1987	1986	1985
Dividends, Net Income ($).	0.18	0.15	0.26	0.38	0.54	0.65	0.58	1.25	0.46	0.57
Distrib'ns, Cap Gain ($) . . .	0.48	0.88	0.01	0.33	0.02	0.56	0.15	0.27	0.59	0.06
Net Asset Value ($).	9.41	9.51	9.00	8.48	8.52	9.60	9.57	9.63	10.67	11.16
Expense Ratio (%)	1.40	1.40	1.40	1.40	1.40	1.40	1.40	1.30	1.40	1.40
Net Income to Assets (%) .	1.82	1.40	2.90	4.20	5.50	6.00	5.50	6.90	5.90	5.60
Portfolio Turnover (%)	54	22	22	46	17	50	97	56	40	87
Total Assets (Millions $)	10	10	7	7	7	8	9	9	9	10

PORTFOLIO (as of 12/31/94)

Portfolio Manager: Bernard Klawans - 1971

Investm't Category: Growth & Income

Cap Gain	Asset Allocation
✔ Cap & Income	Fund of Funds
Income	Index
	Sector
✔ Domestic	Small Cap
Foreign	Socially Conscious
Country/Region	State Specific

Portfolio: stocks 42% bonds 0%
convertibles 0% other 4% cash 54%

Largest Holdings: manufacturers 16%, retailers 6%

Unrealized Net Capital Gains: -3% of portfolio value

SHAREHOLDER INFORMATION

Minimum Investment
Initial: $1,000   Subsequent: $100

Minimum IRA Investment
Initial: $1,000   Subsequent: $100

Maximum Fees
Load: none   12b-1: none
Other: none

Distributions
Income: Dec   Capital Gains: Dec

Exchange Options
Number Per Year: none   Fee:
Telephone:

Services
IRA, pension

Value Line (VLIFX)

Growth

220 E. 42nd Street
New York, NY 10017
(800) 223-0818, (212) 907-1500

PERFORMANCE

fund inception date: 1/1/50

	3yr Annual	5yr Annual	10yr Annual	Bull	Bear
Return (%)	2.2	9.5	14.1	88.4	-12.9
Differ from Category (+/-)	-5.5 low	-0.1 av	1.2 abv av	-3.7 av	-6.3 low

Total Risk	Standard Deviation	Category Risk	Risk Index	Beta
abv av	11.4%	abv av	1.2	1.1

	1994	1993	1992	1991	1990	1989	1988	1987	1986	1985
Return (%)	-4.4	6.8	4.6	48.8	-0.7	31.4	9.6	5.2	16.5	34.5
Differ from category (+/-) . .	-3.8	-6.6	-7.0	13.1	5.0	5.3	-8.4	3.4	1.9	5.3

PER SHARE DATA

	1994	1993	1992	1991	1990	1989	1988	1987	1986	1985
Dividends, Net Income ($) .	0.10	0.08	0.17	0.24	0.27	0.35	0.32	0.27	0.23	0.20
Distrib'ns, Cap Gain ($) . . .	2.61	1.39	2.73	0.92	0.24	1.80	0.25	2.64	1.75	0.00
Net Asset Value ($)	14.36	17.90	18.16	20.17	14.42	15.06	13.15	12.51	14.68	14.27
Expense Ratio (%)	0.82	0.80	0.84	0.71	0.71	0.70	0.71	0.69	0.73	0.81
Net Income to Assets (%). .	0.33	0.41	0.90	1.35	1.83	2.00	2.67	1.53	1.44	1.62
Portfolio Turnover (%).	na	120	129	109	84	125	108	118	145	129
Total Assets (Millions $) . . .	272	332	328	321	202	195	181	205	212	206

PORTFOLIO (as of 6/30/94)

Portfolio Manager: committee

Investm't Category: Growth

✔ Cap Gain	Asset Allocation
Cap & Income	Fund of Funds
Income	Index
	Sector
✔ Domestic	Small Cap
Foreign	Socially Conscious
Country/Region	State Specific

Portfolio: stocks 87% bonds 0%
convertibles 0% other 0% cash 13%

Largest Holdings: bank 6%, retail—special lines 6%

Unrealized Net Capital Gains: 3% of portfolio value

SHAREHOLDER INFORMATION

Minimum Investment
Initial: $1,000   Subsequent: $100

Minimum IRA Investment
Initial: $1,000   Subsequent: $100

Maximum Fees
Load: none   12b-1: none
Other: none

Distributions
Income: quarterly   Capital Gains: Dec

Exchange Options
Number Per Year: 8   Fee: none
Telephone: yes (money market fund available)

Services
IRA, pension, auto invest, auto withdraw

Value Line Adjustable Rate US Gov't (VLUGX)

220 E. 42nd Street
New York, NY 10017
(800) 223-0818, (212) 907-1500

Mortgage-Backed Bond

PERFORMANCE

fund inception date: 4/10/92

	3yr Annual	5yr Annual	10yr Annual	Bull	Bear
Return (%)	na	na	na	na	-7.8
Differ from Category (+/-)	na	na	na	na	-3.4 low

Total Risk	Standard Deviation	Category Risk	Risk Index	Avg Mat
na	na	na	na	20.0 yrs

	1994	1993	1992	1991	1990	1989	1988	1987	1986	1985
Return (%).............	-9.9	6.0	—	—	—	—	—	—	—	—
Differ from category (+/-) ..	-7.1	-0.8	—	—	—	—	—	—	—	—

PER SHARE DATA

	1994	1993	1992	1991	1990	1989	1988	1987	1986	1985
Dividends, Net Income ($).	0.48	0.52	—	—	—	—	—	—	—	—
Distrib'ns, Cap Gain ($) ...	0.00	0.00	—	—	—	—	—	—	—	—
Net Asset Value ($)......	8.52	9.97	—	—	—	—	—	—	—	—
Expense Ratio (%)	0.35	0.88	—	—	—	—	—	—	—	—
Net Income to Assets (%) .	5.08	5.35	—	—	—	—	—	—	—	—
Portfolio Turnover (%)	na	126	—	—	—	—	—	—	—	—
Total Assets (Millions $)	22	na	—	—	—	—	—	—	—	—

PORTFOLIO (as of 4/30/94)

Portfolio Manager: committee

Investm't Category: Mortgage-Backed Bond

Cap Gain	Asset Allocation
Cap & Income	Fund of Funds
✔ Income	Index
	Sector
✔ Domestic	Small Cap
Foreign	Socially Conscious
Country/Region	State Specific

Portfolio:	stocks 0%	bonds 98%
convertibles 0%	other 0%	cash 2%

Largest Holdings: mortgage-backed 98%

Unrealized Net Capital Gains: -4% of portfolio value

SHAREHOLDER INFORMATION

Minimum Investment
Initial: $1,000   Subsequent: $100

Minimum IRA Investment
Initial: $1,000   Subsequent: $100

Maximum Fees
Load: none   12b-1: none
Other: none

Distributions
Income: monthly   Capital Gains: Dec

Exchange Options
Number Per Year: 8   Fee: none
Telephone: yes (money market fund available)

Services
IRA, pension, auto invest, auto withdraw

Value Line Aggressive Income (VAGIX)

220 E. 42nd Street
New York, NY 10017
(800) 223-0818, (212) 907-1500

Corporate High-Yield Bond

PERFORMANCE

fund inception date: 3/1/86

	3yr Annual	5yr Annual	10yr Annual	Bull	Bear
Return (%)	8.5	9.3	na	78.5	-5.7
Differ from Category (+/-)	-1.4 blw av	0.0 abv av	na	-0.8 av	-0.4 av

Total Risk	Standard Deviation	Category Risk	Risk Index	Avg Mat
low	4.5%	blw av	0.9	5.8 yrs

	1994	1993	1992	1991	1990	1989	1988	1987	1986	1985
Return (%)	-4.1	19.0	12.1	26.6	-3.6	2.3	6.3	-2.0	—	—
Differ from category (+/-)	-1.4	0.6	-3.5	-0.8	1.5	0.9	-5.8	-3.1	—	—

PER SHARE DATA

	1994	1993	1992	1991	1990	1989	1988	1987	1986	1985
Dividends, Net Income ($)	0.68	0.66	0.68	0.75	0.78	0.88	0.94	1.17	—	—
Distrib'ns, Cap Gain ($)	0.00	0.00	0.00	0.00	0.00	0.00	0.00	0.00	—	—
Net Asset Value ($)	6.88	7.87	7.21	7.06	6.22	7.26	7.95	8.39	—	—
Expense Ratio (%)	1.20	1.15	1.18	1.43	1.30	1.14	1.22	1.33	—	—
Net Income to Assets (%)	8.84	9.40	10.74	11.74	11.46	11.61	12.29	12.02	—	—
Portfolio Turnover (%)	320	148	59	36	129	95	134	110	—	—
Total Assets (Millions $)	30	43	31	23	29	46	54	58	—	—

PORTFOLIO (as of 7/31/94)

Portfolio Manager: committee

Investm't Category: Corp. High-Yield Bond
- Cap Gain
- Cap & Income
- ✔ Income
- ✔ Domestic
- Foreign
- Country/Region
- Asset Allocation
- Fund of Funds
- Index
- Sector
- Small Cap
- Socially Conscious
- State Specific

Portfolio: stocks 0%   bonds 88%
convertibles 1%   other 0%   cash 11%

Largest Holdings: broadcasting/cable TV 11%, financial services 9%

Unrealized Net Capital Gains: -4% of portfolio value

SHAREHOLDER INFORMATION

Minimum Investment
Initial: $1,000   Subsequent: $250

Minimum IRA Investment
Initial: $1,000   Subsequent: $250

Maximum Fees
Load: none   12b-1: none
Other: none

Distributions
Income: monthly   Capital Gains: Dec

Exchange Options
Number Per Year: 8   Fee: none
Telephone: yes (money market fund available)

Services
IRA, pension, auto invest, auto withdraw

Value Line Convertible
(VALCX)
Growth & Income

220 E. 42nd Street
New York, NY 10017
(800) 223-0818, (212) 907-1500

PERFORMANCE

fund inception date: 6/1/85

	3yr Annual	5yr Annual	10yr Annual	Bull	Bear
Return (%)	7.3	8.9	na	76.4	-6.1
Differ from Category (+/-)	0.2 av	1.0 abv av	na	0.6 av	0.2 av

Total Risk	Standard Deviation	Category Risk	Risk Index	Beta
blw av	6.3%	low	0.8	0.5

	1994	1993	1992	1991	1990	1989	1988	1987	1986	1985
Return (%)	-5.2	14.8	13.8	28.7	-3.7	10.7	15.9	-6.1	16.2	—
Differ from category (+/-) . .	-3.8	1.6	3.6	1.1	2.3	-10.7	-1.1	-6.7	0.4	—

PER SHARE DATA

	1994	1993	1992	1991	1990	1989	1988	1987	1986	1985
Dividends, Net Income ($).	0.76	0.66	0.64	0.61	0.66	0.72	0.48	0.82	0.51	—
Distrib'ns, Cap Gain ($) . . .	0.43	1.67	0.00	0.00	0.00	0.00	0.00	0.48	0.71	—
Net Asset Value ($)	11.01	12.85	13.25	12.25	10.04	11.12	10.70	9.66	11.53	—
Expense Ratio (%)	1.07	1.10	1.14	1.19	1.05	1.03	1.06	1.04	1.31	—
Net Income to Assets (%) .	5.32	4.80	5.45	5.50	5.81	6.32	4.78	5.12	5.37	—
Portfolio Turnover (%)	142	146	140	216	105	112	257	234	164	—
Total Assets (Millions $)	45	50	37	37	45	62	65	89	49	—

PORTFOLIO (as of 4/30/94)

Portfolio Manager: committee

Investm't Category: Growth & Income
Cap Gain	Asset Allocation
✔ Cap & Income	Fund of Funds
Income	Index
	Sector
✔ Domestic	Small Cap
Foreign	Socially Conscious
Country/Region	State Specific

Portfolio: stocks 0% bonds 5%
convertibles 95% other 0% cash 0%

Largest Holdings: real estate 8%, machinery 5%

Unrealized Net Capital Gains: -5% of portfolio value

SHAREHOLDER INFORMATION

Minimum Investment
Initial: $1,000   Subsequent: $250

Minimum IRA Investment
Initial: $1,000   Subsequent: $250

Maximum Fees
Load: none   12b-1: none
Other: none

Distributions
Income: quarterly   Capital Gains: Dec

Exchange Options
Number Per Year: 8   Fee: none
Telephone: yes (money market fund available)

Services
IRA, pension, auto invest, auto withdraw

Value Line Income (VALIX)

Balanced

220 E. 42nd Street
New York, NY 10017
(800) 223-0818, (212) 907-1500

PERFORMANCE

fund inception date: 1/1/52

	3yr Annual	5yr Annual	10yr Annual	Bull	Bear
Return (%)	1.7	6.6	10.3	56.2	-8.0
Differ from Category (+/-)	-4.7 low	-1.4 blw av	-1.0 blw av	-8.8 blw av	-2.3 low

Total Risk	Standard Deviation	Category Risk	Risk Index	Beta
blw av	6.5%	abv av	1.0	0.7

	1994	1993	1992	1991	1990	1989	1988	1987	1986	1985
Return (%)	-4.3	8.2	1.7	28.5	1.9	22.5	12.1	-2.3	16.7	23.8
Differ from category (+/-) . .	-2.4	-5.2	-6.6	5.1	2.4	5.2	0.3	-4.7	-0.7	-0.5

PER SHARE DATA

	1994	1993	1992	1991	1990	1989	1988	1987	1986	1985
Dividends, Net Income ($) .	0.21	0.22	0.28	0.31	0.39	0.46	0.40	0.53	0.48	0.48
Distrib'ns, Cap Gain ($) . . .	0.05	0.89	0.42	0.00	0.00	0.00	0.00	0.59	0.91	0.00
Net Asset Value ($)	6.21	6.77	7.29	7.86	6.39	6.66	5.84	5.57	6.81	7.09
Expense Ratio (%)	0.91	0.88	0.89	0.74	0.77	0.75	0.80	0.76	0.77	0.83
Net Income to Assets (%) . .	2.85	2.82	3.69	4.37	5.59	7.38	6.76	5.95	6.43	7.62
Portfolio Turnover (%)	na	165	85	67	57	108	83	96	167	148
Total Assets (Millions $) . . .	131	163	163	172	141	148	133	140	162	134

PORTFOLIO (as of 6/30/94)

Portfolio Manager: committee

Investm't Category: Balanced

Cap Gain	✔ Asset Allocation
✔ Cap & Income	Fund of Funds
Income	Index
	Sector
✔ Domestic	Small Cap
Foreign	Socially Conscious
Country/Region	State Specific

Portfolio: stocks 59% bonds 29%
convertibles 0% other 3% cash 9%

Largest Holdings: bonds—mortgage-backed 8%, bonds—U.S. government 7%

Unrealized Net Capital Gains: -1% of portfolio value

SHAREHOLDER INFORMATION

Minimum Investment
Initial: $1,000   Subsequent: $100

Minimum IRA Investment
Initial: $1,000   Subsequent: $100

Maximum Fees
Load: none   12b-1: none
Other: none

Distributions
Income: quarterly   Capital Gains: Dec

Exchange Options
Number Per Year: 8   Fee: none
Telephone: yes (money market fund available)

Services
IRA, pension, auto invest, auto withdraw

Value Line Leveraged Growth (VALLX)

Aggressive Growth

220 E. 42nd Street
New York, NY 10017
(800) 223-0818, (212) 907-1500

fund inception date: 1/1/72

PERFORMANCE

	3yr Annual	5yr Annual	10yr Annual	Bull	Bear
Return (%)	2.9	9.4	13.5	87.1	-12.8
Differ from Category (+/-)	-6.0 low	-3.1 blw av	-0.5 av	-46.1 low	-2.0 blw av

Total Risk	Standard Deviation	Category Risk	Risk Index	Beta
abv av	12.0%	blw av	0.8	1.1

	1994	1993	1992	1991	1990	1989	1988	1987	1986	1985
Return (%).............	-3.7	16.1	-2.4	46.2	-1.6	32.3	6.4	2.8	23.0	27.1
Differ from category (+/-) ..	-3.0	-3.4	-13.4	-5.9	4.6	5.5	-8.8	5.0	11.2	-5.2

PER SHARE DATA

	1994	1993	1992	1991	1990	1989	1988	1987	1986	1985
Dividends, Net Income ($).	0.11	0.06	0.15	0.23	0.36	0.39	0.44	0.45	0.34	0.13
Distrib'ns, Cap Gain ($) ...	0.45	0.98	2.69	4.61	1.18	1.45	0.00	4.93	2.60	0.00
Net Asset Value ($)	23.18	24.67	22.15	25.64	21.16	23.10	18.87	18.15	22.79	20.90
Expense Ratio (%)	0.90	0.92	0.93	0.92	0.96	0.96	0.97	0.95	0.96	0.80
Net Income to Assets (%) .	0.25	0.22	0.62	0.84	1.51	1.47	1.99	1.05	0.98	1.57
Portfolio Turnover (%)	na	80	208	250	94	122	143	148	115	121
Total Assets (Millions $) ...	264	304	291	348	236	255	235	283	290	228

PORTFOLIO (as of 6/30/94)

Portfolio Manager: committee

Investm't Category: Aggressive Growth

✔ Cap Gain   Asset Allocation
  Cap & Income Fund of Funds
  Income   Index
                Sector
✔ Domestic   Small Cap
  Foreign   Socially Conscious
  Country/Region State Specific

Portfolio: stocks 91%   bonds 4%
convertibles 0% other 0%   cash 5%

Largest Holdings: bank 10%, financial services 9%

Unrealized Net Capital Gains: 16% of portfolio value

SHAREHOLDER INFORMATION

Minimum Investment
Initial: $1,000   Subsequent: $100

Minimum IRA Investment
Initial: $1,000   Subsequent: $100

Maximum Fees
Load: none   12b-1: none
Other: none

Distributions
Income: Dec   Capital Gains: Dec

Exchange Options
Number Per Year: 8   Fee: none
Telephone: yes (money market fund available)

Services
IRA, pension, auto invest, auto withdraw

Value Line NY Tax-Exempt Trust (VLNYX)

220 E. 42nd Street
New York, NY 10017
(800) 223-0818, (212) 907-1500

Tax-Exempt Bond

PERFORMANCE

fund inception date: 7/1/87

	3yr Annual	5yr Annual	10yr Annual	Bull	Bear
Return (%)	4.8	6.5	na	47.8	-6.9
Differ from Category (+/-)	0.3 av	0.4 av	na	6.0 high	-1.7 low

Total Risk	Standard Deviation	Category Risk	Risk Index	Avg Mat
av	7.3%	high	1.2	16.0 yrs

	1994	1993	1992	1991	1990	1989	1988	1987	1986	1985
Return (%)	-7.7	13.9	9.5	14.3	4.1	7.9	10.8	—	—	—
Differ from category (+/-) . .	-2.5	2.2	1.2	3.0	-2.2	-1.1	0.6			

PER SHARE DATA

	1994	1993	1992	1991	1990	1989	1988	1987	1986	1985
Dividends, Net Income ($) .	0.52	0.58	0.59	0.66	0.71	0.71	0.75	—	—	—
Distrib'ns, Cap Gain ($) . . .	0.07	0.41	0.14	0.00	0.00	0.04	0.06	—	—	—
Net Asset Value ($)	9.32	10.73	10.32	10.12	9.47	9.79	9.78	—	—	—
Expense Ratio (%)	0.87	0.85	0.92	0.91	1.01	0.76	0.00	—	—	—
Net Income to Assets (%). .	5.21	5.82	6.50	7.46	7.16	7.51	8.15	—	—	—
Portfolio Turnover (%).	54	137	124	61	39	73	17	—	—	—
Total Assets (Millions $)	36	44	35	32	29	26	20	—	—	—

PORTFOLIO (as of 8/31/94)

Portfolio Manager: committee

Investm't Category: Tax-Exempt Bond

Cap Gain	Asset Allocation
Cap & Income	Fund of Funds
✔ Income	Index
	Sector
✔ Domestic	Small Cap
Foreign	Socially Conscious
Country/Region	✔ State Specific

Portfolio: stocks 0% bonds 91%
convertibles 0% other 0% cash 9%

Largest Holdings: general obligation 20%

Unrealized Net Capital Gains: 3% of portfolio value

SHAREHOLDER INFORMATION

Minimum Investment
Initial: $1,000 Subsequent: $250

Minimum IRA Investment
Initial: na Subsequent: na

Maximum Fees
Load: none 12b-1: none
Other: none

Distributions
Income: monthly Capital Gains: Dec

Exchange Options
Number Per Year: 8 Fee: none
Telephone: yes (money market fund available)

Services
auto invest, auto withdraw

Value Line Special Situations (VALSX)

220 E. 42nd Street
New York, NY 10017
(800) 223-0818, (212) 907-1500

Aggressive Growth

PERFORMANCE

fund inception date: 1/1/56

	3yr Annual	5yr Annual	10yr Annual	Bull	Bear
Return (%)	3.2	7.7	7.7	66.3	-18.0
Differ from Category (+/-)	-5.7 blw av	-4.8 low	-6.3 low	-66.9 low	-7.2 low

Total Risk	Standard Deviation	Category Risk	Risk Index	Beta
high	16.2%	abv av	1.1	1.0

	1994	1993	1992	1991	1990	1989	1988	1987	1986	1985
Return (%).	1.0	12.9	-3.4	38.1	-4.4	21.6	3.3	-9.0	5.1	21.0
Differ from category (+/-) . .	1.7	-6.6	-14.4	-14.0	1.8	-5.2	-11.9	-6.8	-6.7	-11.3

PER SHARE DATA

	1994	1993	1992	1991	1990	1989	1988	1987	1986	1985
Dividends, Net Income ($).	0.00	0.00	0.00	0.23	0.17	0.22	0.09	0.12	0.04	0.05
Distrib'ns, Cap Gain ($) . . .	0.96	0.75	0.15	0.86	0.00	0.00	0.00	2.56	0.00	0.00
Net Asset Value ($)	16.15	16.95	15.69	16.41	12.72	13.49	11.27	10.99	15.07	14.37
Expense Ratio (%)	1.13	1.06	1.09	1.04	1.11	1.08	1.16	1.01	1.02	1.07
Net Income to Assets (%) .	-0.73	-0.79	-0.33	0.24	0.92	1.84	0.68	0.26	0.29	0.22
Portfolio Turnover (%)	na	39	43	37	33	66	59	41	72	87
Total Assets (Millions $)	90	90	101	129	104	117	112	124	193	242

PORTFOLIO (as of 6/30/94)

Portfolio Manager: na

Investm't Category: Aggressive Growth

✔ Cap Gain	Asset Allocation
Cap & Income	Fund of Funds
Income	Index
	Sector
✔ Domestic	Small Cap
Foreign	Socially Conscious
Country/Region	State Specific

Portfolio: stocks 82% bonds 0%
convertibles 0% other 0% cash 18%

Largest Holdings: computer & peripherals 13%, drug 10%

Unrealized Net Capital Gains: 13% of portfolio value

SHAREHOLDER INFORMATION

Minimum Investment
Initial: $1,000   Subsequent: $100

Minimum IRA Investment
Initial: $1,000   Subsequent: $100

Maximum Fees
Load: none   12b-1: none
Other: none

Distributions
Income: Dec   Capital Gains: Dec

Exchange Options
Number Per Year: 8   Fee: none
Telephone: yes (money market fund available)

Services
IRA, pension, auto invest, auto withdraw

Value Line Tax Exempt High Yield (VLHYX)

220 E. 42nd Street
New York, NY 10017
(800) 223-0818, (212) 907-1500

Tax-Exempt Bond

PERFORMANCE

fund inception date: 12/1/84

	3yr Annual	5yr Annual	10yr Annual	Bull	Bear
Return (%)	3.8	6.0	8.1	42.0	-7.1
Differ from Category (+/-)	-0.7 low	-0.1 blw av	0.0 blw av	0.2 blw av	-1.9 low

Total Risk	Standard Deviation	Category Risk	Risk Index	Avg Mat
blw av	6.5%	abv av	1.0	18.0 yrs

	1994	1993	1992	1991	1990	1989	1988	1987	1986	1985
Return (%)	-6.8	11.5	7.8	12.2	6.5	8.3	10.9	0.5	13.4	19.2
Differ from category (+/-) . .	-1.6	-0.2	-0.5	0.9	0.2	-0.7	0.7	1.8	-3.0	1.8

PER SHARE DATA

	1994	1993	1992	1991	1990	1989	1988	1987	1986	1985
Dividends, Net Income ($) .	0.57	0.61	0.63	0.69	0.77	0.79	0.80	0.82	0.91	0.94
Distrib'ns, Cap Gain ($) . . .	0.04	0.20	0.00	0.00	0.00	0.00	0.00	0.05	0.34	0.00
Net Asset Value ($)	9.89	11.27	10.86	10.68	10.17	10.30	10.26	9.99	10.81	10.70
Expense Ratio (%)	0.59	0.60	0.58	0.60	0.62	0.63	0.64	0.68	0.66	0.17
Net Income to Assets (%). .	5.36	5.89	6.50	7.47	7.70	7.77	7.98	8.20	9.36	10.49
Portfolio Turnover (%). . . . . . na		101	122	122	63	73	76	79	253	186
Total Assets (Millions $) . . .	225	290	300	278	272	266	259	312	133	36

PORTFOLIO (as of 8/31/94)

Portfolio Manager: committee

Investm't Category: Tax-Exempt Bond

Cap Gain	Asset Allocation
Cap & Income	Fund of Funds
✔ Income	Index
	Sector
✔ Domestic	Small Cap
Foreign	Socially Conscious
Country/Region	State Specific

Portfolio: stocks 0%   bonds 100%
convertibles 0%   other 0%   cash 0%

Largest Holdings: general obligation 10%

Unrealized Net Capital Gains: 0% of portfolio value

SHAREHOLDER INFORMATION

Minimum Investment
Initial: $1,000   Subsequent: $250

Minimum IRA Investment
Initial: na   Subsequent: na

Maximum Fees
Load: none   12b-1: none
Other: none

Distributions
Income: monthly   Capital Gains: Dec

Exchange Options
Number Per Year: 8   Fee: none
Telephone: yes (money market fund available)

Services
auto invest, auto withdraw

Value Line US Gov't Securities (VALBX)

220 E. 42nd Street
New York, NY 10017
(800) 223-0818, (212) 907-1500

Mortgage-Backed Bond

PERFORMANCE

fund inception date: 12/1/81

	3yr Annual	5yr Annual	10yr Annual	Bull	Bear
Return (%)	1.4	6.0	8.4	43.9	-9.7
Differ from Category (+/-)	-1.7 low	-0.9 low	-0.4 low	5.9 high	-5.3 low

Total Risk	Standard Deviation	Category Risk	Risk Index	Avg Mat
low	4.8%	high	1.5	16.2 yrs

	1994	1993	1992	1991	1990	1989	1988	1987	1986	1985
Return (%)	-10.6	9.7	6.3	16.4	10.2	11.9	7.9	3.3	10.6	21.2
Differ from category (+/-)	-7.8	2.9	0.2	2.0	0.5	-0.6	0.8	1.5	-0.6	1.6

PER SHARE DATA

	1994	1993	1992	1991	1990	1989	1988	1987	1986	1985
Dividends, Net Income ($)	0.79	0.95	0.89	0.95	1.00	1.10	1.01	1.50	1.32	1.31
Distrib'ns, Cap Gain ($)	0.00	0.33	0.10	0.00	0.00	0.00	0.00	0.00	0.38	0.00
Net Asset Value ($)	10.52	12.62	12.68	12.89	11.96	11.80	11.57	11.67	12.77	13.15
Expense Ratio (%)	0.63	0.61	0.64	0.64	0.67	0.66	0.67	0.72	0.76	0.85
Net Income to Assets (%)	6.58	7.29	7.47	8.54	9.25	10.05	10.09	9.49	10.10	11.01
Portfolio Turnover (%)	100	169	130	79	59	34	54	48	72	64
Total Assets (Millions $)	289	452	424	337	258	252	247	218	112	68

PORTFOLIO (as of 8/31/94)

Portfolio Manager: committee

Investm't Category: Mortgage-Backed Bond

Cap Gain	Asset Allocation
Cap & Income	Fund of Funds
✔ Income	Index
	Sector
✔ Domestic	Small Cap
Foreign	Socially Conscious
Country/Region	State Specific

Portfolio: stocks 0%   bonds 90%
convertibles 0%   other 0%   cash 10%

Largest Holdings: mortgage-backed 77%,
U.S. government 13%

Unrealized Net Capital Gains: -5% of portfolio value

SHAREHOLDER INFORMATION

Minimum Investment
Initial: $1,000   Subsequent: $250

Minimum IRA Investment
Initial: $1,000   Subsequent: $100

Maximum Fees
Load: none   12b-1: none
Other: none

Distributions
Income: quarterly   Capital Gains: Dec

Exchange Options
Number Per Year: 8   Fee: none
Telephone: yes (money market fund available)

Services
IRA, pension, auto invest, auto withdraw

Vanguard Admiral Interm US Treas (VAITX)

Government Bond

Vanguard Financial Center
P.O. Box 2600
Valley Forge, PA 19482
(800) 662-7447, (610) 648-6000

PERFORMANCE

fund inception date: 12/14/92

	3yr Annual	5yr Annual	10yr Annual	Bull	Bear
Return (%)	na	na	na	na	-5.8
Differ from Category (+/-)	na	na	na	na	0.6 av

Total Risk	Standard Deviation	Category Risk	Risk Index	Avg Mat
na	na	na	na	7.4 yrs

	1994	1993	1992	1991	1990	1989	1988	1987	1986	1985
Return (%)	-4.2	11.3	—	—	—	—	—	—	—	—
Differ from category (+/-)	0.6	0.4	—	—	—	—	—	—	—	—

PER SHARE DATA

	1994	1993	1992	1991	1990	1989	1988	1987	1986	1985
Dividends, Net Income ($)	0.59	0.59	—	—	—	—	—	—	—	—
Distrib'ns, Cap Gain ($)	0.01	0.13	—	—	—	—	—	—	—	—
Net Asset Value ($)	9.45	10.48	—	—	—	—	—	—	—	—
Expense Ratio (%)	0.15	0.15	—	—	—	—	—	—	—	—
Net Income to Assets (%)	5.59	6.31	—	—	—	—	—	—	—	—
Portfolio Turnover (%)	84	0	—	—	—	—	—	—	—	—
Total Assets (Millions $)	319	989	—	—	—	—	—	—	—	—

PORTFOLIO (as of 7/31/94)

Portfolio Manager: Ian MacKinnon - 1992

Investm't Category: Government Bond

Cap Gain	Asset Allocation
Cap & Income	Fund of Funds
✔ Income	Index
	Sector
✔ Domestic	Small Cap
Foreign	Socially Conscious
Country/Region	State Specific

Portfolio: stocks 0% bonds 97%
convertibles 0% other 0% cash 3%

Largest Holdings: U.S. government & agencies 97%

Unrealized Net Capital Gains: -5% of portfolio value

SHAREHOLDER INFORMATION

Minimum Investment
Initial: $50,000   Subsequent: $100

Minimum IRA Investment
Initial: $50,000   Subsequent: $100

Maximum Fees
Load: none   12b-1: none
Other: none

Distributions
Income: monthly   Capital Gains: Dec

Exchange Options
Number Per Year: 2   Fee: none
Telephone: yes (money market fund available)

Services
IRA, pension, auto invest, auto withdraw

Vanguard Admiral Long US Treasury (VALGX)

Government Bond

Vanguard Financial Center
P.O. Box 2600
Valley Forge, PA 19482
(800) 662-7447, (610) 648-6000

PERFORMANCE

fund inception date: 12/14/92

	3yr Annual	5yr Annual	10yr Annual	Bull	Bear
Return (%)	na	na	na	na	-10.0
Differ from Category (+/-)	na	na	na	na	-3.6 low

Total Risk	Standard Deviation	Category Risk	Risk Index	Avg Mat
na	na	na	na	21.6 yrs

	1994	1993	1992	1991	1990	1989	1988	1987	1986	1985
Return (%)	-6.8	16.6	—	—	—	—	—	—	—	—
Differ from category (+/-)	-2.0	5.7	—	—	—	—	—	—	—	—

PER SHARE DATA

	1994	1993	1992	1991	1990	1989	1988	1987	1986	1985
Dividends, Net Income ($)	0.67	0.73	—	—	—	—	—	—	—	—
Distrib'ns, Cap Gain ($)	0.10	0.26	—	—	—	—	—	—	—	—
Net Asset Value ($)	9.22	10.71	—	—	—	—	—	—	—	—
Expense Ratio (%)	0.15	0.15	—	—	—	—	—	—	—	—
Net Income to Assets (%)	6.68	7.22	—	—	—	—	—	—	—	—
Portfolio Turnover (%)	54	17	—	—	—	—	—	—	—	—
Total Assets (Millions $)	118	831	—	—	—	—	—	—	—	—

PORTFOLIO (as of 7/31/94)

Portfolio Manager: Ian MacKinnon - 1992

Investm't Category: Government Bond

Cap Gain	Asset Allocation
Cap & Income	Fund of Funds
✔ Income	Index
	Sector
✔ Domestic	Small Cap
Foreign	Socially Conscious
Country/Region	State Specific

Portfolio: stocks 0% bonds 90%
convertibles 0% other 0% cash 10%

Largest Holdings: U.S. government 90%

Unrealized Net Capital Gains: -4% of portfolio value

SHAREHOLDER INFORMATION

Minimum Investment
Initial: $50,000   Subsequent: $100

Minimum IRA Investment
Initial: $50,000   Subsequent: $100

Maximum Fees
Load: none   12b-1: none
Other: none

Distributions
Income: monthly   Capital Gains: Dec

Exchange Options
Number Per Year: 2   Fee: none
Telephone: yes (money market fund available)

Services
IRA, pension, auto invest, auto withdraw

Vanguard Admiral Short US Treasury (VASTX)

Government Bond

Vanguard Financial Center
P.O. Box 2600
Valley Forge, PA 19482
(800) 662-7447, (610) 648-6000

PERFORMANCE

fund inception date: 12/14/92

	3yr Annual	5yr Annual	10yr Annual	Bull	Bear
Return (%)	na	na	na	na	-1.8
Differ from Category (+/-)	na	na	na	na	4.6 abv av

Total Risk	Standard Deviation	Category Risk	Risk Index	Avg Mat
na	na	na	na	2.1 yrs

	1994	1993	1992	1991	1990	1989	1988	1987	1986	1985
Return (%)	-0.3	6.4	—	—	—	—	—	—	—	—
Differ from category (+/-)	4.5	-4.5	—	—	—	—	—	—	—	—

PER SHARE DATA

	1994	1993	1992	1991	1990	1989	1988	1987	1986	1985
Dividends, Net Income ($)	0.50	0.45	—	—	—	—	—	—	—	—
Distrib'ns, Cap Gain ($)	0.02	0.01	—	—	—	—	—	—	—	—
Net Asset Value ($)	9.67	10.23	—	—	—	—	—	—	—	—
Expense Ratio (%)	0.15	0.15	—	—	—	—	—	—	—	—
Net Income to Assets (%)	4.81	4.87	—	—	—	—	—	—	—	—
Portfolio Turnover (%)	124	7	—	—	—	—	—	—	—	—
Total Assets (Millions $)	311	704	—	—	—	—	—	—	—	—

PORTFOLIO (as of 7/31/94)

Portfolio Manager: Ian MacKinnon - 1992

Investm't Category: Government Bond

Cap Gain	Asset Allocation
Cap & Income	Fund of Funds
✔ Income	Index
	Sector
✔ Domestic	Small Cap
Foreign	Socially Conscious
Country/Region	State Specific

Portfolio: stocks 0% bonds 99%
convertibles 0% other 0% cash 1%

Largest Holdings: U.S. government & agencies 99%

Unrealized Net Capital Gains: -1% of portfolio value

SHAREHOLDER INFORMATION

Minimum Investment
Initial: $50,000   Subsequent: $100

Minimum IRA Investment
Initial: $50,000   Subsequent: $100

Maximum Fees
Load: none   12b-1: none
Other: none

Distributions
Income: monthly   Capital Gains: Dec

Exchange Options
Number Per Year: 2   Fee: none
Telephone: yes (money market fund available)

Services
IRA, pension, auto invest, auto withdraw

Vanguard Asset Allocation (VAAPX)

Balanced

Vanguard Financial Center
P.O. Box 2600
Valley Forge, PA 19482
(800) 662-7447, (610) 648-6000

PERFORMANCE

fund inception date: 12/3/88

	3yr Annual	5yr Annual	10yr Annual	Bull	Bear
Return (%)	6.0	8.6	na	71.9	-8.3
Differ from Category (+/-)	-0.4 av	0.6 abv av	na	6.9 abv av	-2.6 low

Total Risk	Standard Deviation	Category Risk	Risk Index	Beta
av	6.9%	high	1.1	0.8

	1994	1993	1992	1991	1990	1989	1988	1987	1986	1985
Return (%).	-2.2	13.4	7.5	25.5	0.8	23.6	—	—	—	—
Differ from category (+/-) . .	-0.3	0.0	-0.8	2.1	1.3	6.3	—	—	—	—

PER SHARE DATA

	1994	1993	1992	1991	1990	1989	1988	1987	1986	1985
Dividends, Net Income ($).	0.57	0.48	0.59	0.59	0.62	0.51	—	—	—	—
Distrib'ns, Cap Gain ($) . . .	0.00	0.53	0.17	0.19	0.13	0.15	—	—	—	—
Net Asset Value ($)	13.54	14.45	13.64	13.41	11.35	12.01	—	—	—	—
Expense Ratio (%)	0.50	0.49	0.52	0.44	0.50	0.49	—	—	—	—
Net Income to Assets (%) .	3.68	4.07	4.95	5.28	5.53	5.53	—	—	—	—
Portfolio Turnover (%)	51	31	18	44	12	52	—	—	—	—
Total Assets (Millions $) .	1,125	1,089	502	265	160	107	—	—	—	—

PORTFOLIO (as of 9/30/94)

Portfolio Manager: Thomas Hazuka - 1988

Investm't Category: Balanced

Cap Gain	✔ Asset Allocation
✔ Cap & Income	Fund of Funds
Income	Index
	Sector
✔ Domestic	Small Cap
Foreign	Socially Conscious
Country/Region	State Specific

Portfolio: stocks 50% bonds 49%
convertibles 0% other 0% cash 1%

Largest Holdings: stocks—S&P 500 50%, bonds—U. S. government 49%

Unrealized Net Capital Gains: 1% of portfolio value

SHAREHOLDER INFORMATION

Minimum Investment
Initial: $3,000   Subsequent: $100

Minimum IRA Investment
Initial: $500   Subsequent: $100

Maximum Fees
Load: none   12b-1: none
Other: none

Distributions
Income: Apr, Dec   Capital Gains: Dec

Exchange Options
Number Per Year: 2   Fee: none
Telephone: yes (money market fund available)

Services
IRA, pension, auto exchange, auto invest, auto withdraw

Vanguard Balanced Index

(VBINX)

Balanced

Vanguard Financial Center
P.O. Box 2600
Valley Forge, PA 19482
(800) 662-7447, (610) 648-6000

PERFORMANCE

fund inception date: 9/1/92

	3yr Annual	5yr Annual	10yr Annual	Bull	Bear
Return (%)	na	na	na	na	-6.5
Differ from Category (+/-)	na	na	na	na	-0.8 blw av

Total Risk	Standard Deviation	Category Risk	Risk Index	Beta
na	na	na	na	na

	1994	1993	1992	1991	1990	1989	1988	1987	1986	1985
Return (%)	-1.5	9.9	—	—	—	—	—	—	—	—
Differ from category (+/-) . . .	0.4	-3.5	—	—	—	—	—	—	—	—

PER SHARE DATA

	1994	1993	1992	1991	1990	1989	1988	1987	1986	1985
Dividends, Net Income ($) .	0.40	0.39	—	—	—	—	—	—	—	—
Distrib'ns, Cap Gain ($) . . .	0.00	0.03	—	—	—	—	—	—	—	—
Net Asset Value ($)	10.34	10.91	—	—	—	—	—	—	—	—
Expense Ratio (%)	0.20	0.20	—	—	—	—	—	—	—	—
Net Income to Assets (%) . .	3.67	3.53	—	—	—	—	—	—	—	—
Portfolio Turnover (%)	18	25	—	—	—	—	—	—	—	—
Total Assets (Millions $) . . .	402	385	—	—	—	—	—	—	—	—

PORTFOLIO (as of 6/30/94)

Portfolio Manager: George U. Sauter - 1992

Investm't Category: Balanced

Cap Gain	Asset Allocation
✔ Cap & Income	Fund of Funds
Income	✔ Index
	Sector
✔ Domestic	Small Cap
Foreign	Socially Conscious
Country/Region	State Specific

Portfolio: stocks 60% bonds 40%
convertibles 0% other 0% cash 0%

Largest Holdings: Wilshire 5000 index 60%, Lehman aggregate bond index 40%

Unrealized Net Capital Gains: -2% of portfolio value

SHAREHOLDER INFORMATION

Minimum Investment
Initial: $3,000   Subsequent: $100

Minimum IRA Investment
Initial: $500   Subsequent: $100

Maximum Fees
Load: none   12b-1: none
Other: $10 annual account maintenance fee

Distributions
Income: quarterly   Capital Gains: Dec

Exchange Options
Number Per Year: 2   Fee: none
Telephone: none

Services
IRA, pension, auto exchange, auto invest, auto withdraw

Vanguard CA Tax-Free Insured Long (VCITX)

Tax-Exempt Bond

Vanguard Financial Center
P.O. Box 2600
Valley Forge, PA 19482
(800) 662-7447, (610) 648-6000

PERFORMANCE

fund inception date: 4/7/86

	3yr Annual	5yr Annual	10yr Annual	Bull	Bear
Return (%)	5.1	6.6	na	47.2	-5.7
Differ from Category (+/-)	0.6 abv av	0.5 abv av	na	5.4 abv av	-0.5 av

Total Risk	Standard Deviation	Category Risk	Risk Index	Avg Mat
av	8.0%	high	1.3	18.7 yrs

	1994	1993	1992	1991	1990	1989	1988	1987	1986	1985
Return (%)	-5.7	12.8	9.3	11.0	6.9	10.4	12.1	-3.8	—	—
Differ from category (+/-)	-0.5	1.1	1.0	-0.3	0.6	1.4	1.9	-2.5	—	—

PER SHARE DATA

	1994	1993	1992	1991	1990	1989	1988	1987	1986	1985
Dividends, Net Income ($)	0.60	0.60	0.63	0.64	0.66	0.67	0.68	0.67	—	—
Distrib'ns, Cap Gain ($)	0.00	0.15	0.20	0.00	0.00	0.00	0.00	0.00	—	—
Net Asset Value ($)	10.13	11.37	10.77	10.64	10.20	10.18	9.85	9.43	—	—
Expense Ratio (%)	0.20	0.19	0.24	0.25	0.26	0.24	0.30	0.31	—	—
Net Income to Assets (%)	5.43	5.38	5.92	6.24	6.57	6.67	6.83	6.86	—	—
Portfolio Turnover (%)	14	27	54	19	6	3	4	37	—	—
Total Assets (Millions $)	830	1,071	828	630	386	260	126	89	—	—

PORTFOLIO (as of 5/31/94)

Portfolio Manager: Ian MacKinnon - 1986

Investm't Category: Tax-Exempt Bond
Cap Gain	Asset Allocation
Cap & Income	Fund of Funds
✔ Income	Index
	Sector
✔ Domestic	Small Cap
Foreign	Socially Conscious
Country/Region	✔ State Specific

Portfolio: stocks 0%   bonds 100%
convertibles 0%   other 0%   cash 0%

Largest Holdings: na

Unrealized Net Capital Gains: 0% of portfolio value

SHAREHOLDER INFORMATION

Minimum Investment
Initial: $3,000   Subsequent: $100

Minimum IRA Investment
Initial: na   Subsequent: na

Maximum Fees
Load: none   12b-1: none
Other: none

Distributions
Income: monthly   Capital Gains: Dec

Exchange Options
Number Per Year: 2   Fee: none
Telephone: yes (money market fund available)

Services
auto exchange, auto invest, auto withdraw

Vanguard Convertible Securities (VCVSX)

Growth & Income

Vanguard Financial Center
P.O. Box 2600
Valley Forge, PA 19482
(800) 662-7447, (610) 648-6000

PERFORMANCE

fund inception date: 6/17/86

	3yr Annual	5yr Annual	10yr Annual	Bull	Bear
Return (%)	8.4	9.4	na	94.9	-8.2
Differ from Category (+/-)	1.3 abv av	1.5 abv av	na	19.1 high	-1.9 blw av

Total Risk	Standard Deviation	Category Risk	Risk Index	Beta
av	8.0%	av	1.0	0.7

	1994	1993	1992	1991	1990	1989	1988	1987	1986	1985
Return (%)	-5.6	13.5	18.9	34.3	-8.1	15.8	15.7	-10.6	—	—
Differ from category (+/-)..	-4.2	0.3	8.7	6.7	-2.1	-5.6	-1.3	-11.2	—	—

PER SHARE DATA

	1994	1993	1992	1991	1990	1989	1988	1987	1986	1985
Dividends, Net Income ($) .	0.51	0.53	0.53	0.54	0.57	0.56	0.57	0.56	—	—
Distrib'ns, Cap Gain ($) ...	0.18	0.91	0.00	0.00	0.00	0.00	0.00	0.12	—	—
Net Asset Value ($)	10.55	11.91	11.80	10.40	8.19	9.52	8.72	8.04	—	—
Expense Ratio (%)	0.73	0.71	0.85	0.81	0.88	0.84	0.88	0.85	—	—
Net Income to Assets (%)..	4.37	4.44	4.80	5.72	6.35	5.60	6.52	6.13	—	—
Portfolio Turnover (%).....	52	81	55	57	55	55	24	13	—	—
Total Assets (Millions $)...	170	202	120	55	44	59	69	73	—	—

PORTFOLIO (as of 5/31/94)

Portfolio Manager: Rohit Desai - 1986

Investm't Category: Growth & Income

Cap Gain	Asset Allocation
✔ Cap & Income	Fund of Funds
Income	Index
	Sector
✔ Domestic	Small Cap
Foreign	Socially Conscious
Country/Region	State Specific

Portfolio: stocks 4% bonds 0%
convertibles 86% other 0% cash 10%

Largest Holdings: banking 11%, cable and broadcasting 8%

Unrealized Net Capital Gains: -4% of portfolio value

SHAREHOLDER INFORMATION

Minimum Investment
Initial: $3,000   Subsequent: $100

Minimum IRA Investment
Initial: $500   Subsequent: $100

Maximum Fees
Load: none   12b-1: none
Other: none

Distributions
Income: quarterly   Capital Gains: Dec

Exchange Options
Number Per Year: 2   Fee: none
Telephone: yes (money market fund available)

Services
IRA, pension, auto exchange, auto invest, auto withdraw

Vanguard Equity Income

(VEIPX)

Growth & Income

Vanguard Financial Center
P.O. Box 2600
Valley Forge, PA 19482
(800) 662-7447, (610) 648-6000

PERFORMANCE

fund inception date: 3/21/88

	3yr Annual	5yr Annual	10yr Annual	Bull	Bear
Return (%)	7.1	6.3	na	70.2	-6.9
Differ from Category (+/-)	0.0 av	-1.6 blw av	na	-5.6 blw av	-0.6 blw av

Total Risk	Standard Deviation	Category Risk	Risk Index	Beta
av	7.8%	blw av	0.9	0.9

	1994	1993	1992	1991	1990	1989	1988	1987	1986	1985
Return (%)	-1.5	14.6	9.1	25.3	-11.9	26.4	—	—	—	—
Differ from category (+/-)	-0.1	1.4	-1.1	-2.3	-5.9	5.0	—	—	—	—

PER SHARE DATA

	1994	1993	1992	1991	1990	1989	1988	1987	1986	1985
Dividends, Net Income ($)	0.58	0.61	0.59	0.65	0.73	0.70	—	—	—	—
Distrib'ns, Cap Gain ($)	0.09	0.52	0.00	0.10	0.07	0.03	—	—	—	—
Net Asset Value ($)	12.77	13.66	12.92	12.40	10.54	12.86	—	—	—	—
Expense Ratio (%)	0.43	0.40	0.44	0.46	0.48	0.44	—	—	—	—
Net Income to Assets (%)	4.41	4.39	4.74	5.52	5.67	6.01	—	—	—	—
Portfolio Turnover (%)	18	15	13	9	5	8	—	—	—	—
Total Assets (Millions $)	859	1,058	778	518	353	267	—	—	—	—

PORTFOLIO (as of 9/30/94)

Portfolio Manager: Roger Newell - 1988

Investm't Category: Growth & Income

Cap Gain	Asset Allocation
✔ Cap & Income	Fund of Funds
Income	Index
	Sector
✔ Domestic	Small Cap
Foreign	Socially Conscious
Country/Region	State Specific

Portfolio: stocks 100% bonds 0%
convertibles 0% other 0% cash 0%

Largest Holdings: utilities 30%, energy 15%

Unrealized Net Capital Gains: 6% of portfolio value

SHAREHOLDER INFORMATION

Minimum Investment
Initial: $3,000   Subsequent: $100

Minimum IRA Investment
Initial: $500   Subsequent: $100

Maximum Fees
Load: none   12b-1: none
Other: none

Distributions
Income: quarterly   Capital Gains: Dec

Exchange Options
Number Per Year: 2   Fee: none
Telephone: yes (money market fund available)

Services
IRA, pension, auto exchange, auto invest, auto withdraw

Vanguard Explorer

(VEXPX)

Aggressive Growth

Vanguard Financial Center
P.O. Box 2600
Valley Forge, PA 19482
(800) 662-7447, (610) 648-6000

PERFORMANCE

fund inception date: 12/11/67

	3yr Annual	5yr Annual	10yr Annual	Bull	Bear
Return (%)	9.4	12.7	10.1	129.8	-9.1
Differ from Category (+/-)	0.5 av	0.2 av	-3.9 low	-3.4 av	1.7 abv av

Total Risk	Standard Deviation	Category Risk	Risk Index	Beta
abv av	11.9%	blw av	0.8	0.8

	1994	1993	1992	1991	1990	1989	1988	1987	1986	1985
Return (%)	0.5	15.4	12.9	55.9	-10.7	9.3	25.8	-6.9	-8.4	22.3
Differ from category (+/-) . . .	1.2	-4.1	1.9	3.8	-4.5	-17.5	10.6	-4.7	-20.2	-10.0

PER SHARE DATA

	1994	1993	1992	1991	1990	1989	1988	1987	1986	1985
Dividends, Net Income ($) .	0.17	0.14	0.13	0.26	0.34	0.37	0.32	0.11	0.02	0.33
Distrib'ns, Cap Gain ($) . . .	2.26	5.17	0.78	0.00	0.00	1.01	1.59	1.96	3.27	1.29
Net Asset Value ($)	42.86	45.11	43.84	39.62	25.58	29.06	27.85	23.66	27.66	33.73
Expense Ratio (%)	0.70	0.73	0.69	0.56	0.67	0.58	0.65	0.62	0.76	0.80
Net Income to Assets (%). .	0.37	0.32	0.38	0.85	1.11	1.24	0.99	0.28	0.05	1.02
Portfolio Turnover (%).	76	51	43	49	46	16	28	9	15	19
Total Assets (Millions $) . .	1,121	787	519	381	208	271	266	210	271	334

PORTFOLIO (as of 5/31/94)

Portfolio Manager: John Granahan - 1990, Kenneth L. Abrams - 1994

Investm't Category: Aggressive Growth

✔ Cap Gain	Asset Allocation
Cap & Income	Fund of Funds
Income	Index
	Sector
✔ Domestic	✔ Small Cap
✔ Foreign	Socially Conscious
Country/Region	State Specific

Portfolio: stocks 80% bonds 0%
convertibles 1% other 0% cash 19%

Largest Holdings: consumer services 14%, business, industrial & government services 14%

Unrealized Net Capital Gains: 10% of portfolio value

SHAREHOLDER INFORMATION

Minimum Investment
Initial: $3,000   Subsequent: $100

Minimum IRA Investment
Initial: $500   Subsequent: $100

Maximum Fees
Load: none   12b-1: none
Other: none

Distributions
Income: Dec   Capital Gains: Dec

Exchange Options
Number Per Year: 2   Fee: none
Telephone: yes (money market fund available)

Services
IRA, pension, auto exchange, auto invest, auto withdraw

Vanguard Florida Insured Tax Free (VFLTX)

Tax-Exempt Bond

Vanguard Financial Center
P.O. Box 2600
Valley Forge, PA 19482
(800) 662-7447, (610) 648-6000

PERFORMANCE

fund inception date: 8/31/92

	3yr Annual	5yr Annual	10yr Annual	Bull	Bear
Return (%)	na	na	na	na	-5.1
Differ from Category (+/-)	na	na	na	na	0.1 abv av

Total Risk	Standard Deviation	Category Risk	Risk Index	Avg Mat
na	na	na	na	18.5 yrs

	1994	1993	1992	1991	1990	1989	1988	1987	1986	1985
Return (%)	-4.7	13.4	—	—	—	—	—	—	—	—
Differ from category (+/-)	0.5	1.7	—	—	—	—	—	—	—	—

PER SHARE DATA

	1994	1993	1992	1991	1990	1989	1988	1987	1986	1985
Dividends, Net Income ($)	0.56	0.54	—	—	—	—	—	—	—	—
Distrib'ns, Cap Gain ($)	0.00	0.07	—	—	—	—	—	—	—	—
Net Asset Value ($)	9.91	10.98	—	—	—	—	—	—	—	—
Expense Ratio (%)	0.21	0.21	—	—	—	—	—	—	—	—
Net Income to Assets (%)	5.07	5.01	—	—	—	—	—	—	—	—
Portfolio Turnover (%)	54	34	—	—	—	—	—	—	—	—
Total Assets (Millions $)	328	267	—	—	—	—	—	—	—	—

PORTFOLIO (as of 5/31/94)

Portfolio Manager: Ian MacKinnon - 1992

Investm't Category: Tax-Exempt Bond

Cap Gain	Asset Allocation
Cap & Income	Fund of Funds
✔ Income	Index
	Sector
✔ Domestic	Small Cap
Foreign	Socially Conscious
Country/Region	✔ State Specific

Portfolio: stocks 0%   bonds 100%
convertibles 0%   other 0%   cash 0%

Largest Holdings: na

Unrealized Net Capital Gains: -2% of portfolio value

SHAREHOLDER INFORMATION

Minimum Investment
Initial: $3,000   Subsequent: $100

Minimum IRA Investment
Initial: na   Subsequent: na

Maximum Fees
Load: none   12b-1: none
Other: none

Distributions
Income: monthly   Capital Gains: Dec

Exchange Options
Number Per Year: 2   Fee: none
Telephone: yes (money market fund available)

Services
auto exchange, auto invest, auto withdraw

Vanguard GNMA (VFIIX)

Mortgage-Backed Bond

Vanguard Financial Center
P.O. Box 2600
Valley Forge, PA 19482
(800) 662-7447, (610) 648-6000

PERFORMANCE

fund inception date: 6/27/80

	3yr Annual	5yr Annual	10yr Annual	Bull	Bear
Return (%)	3.8	7.6	9.4	40.0	-3.2
Differ from Category (+/-)	0.7 abv av	0.7 high	0.6 high	2.0 abv av	1.2 abv av

Total Risk	Standard Deviation	Category Risk	Risk Index	Avg Mat
low	3.2%	av	1.0	8.9 yrs

	1994	1993	1992	1991	1990	1989	1988	1987	1986	1985
Return (%)	-0.9	5.8	6.8	16.7	10.3	14.7	8.8	2.1	11.5	20.6
Differ from category (+/-) . . .	1.9	-1.0	0.7	2.3	0.6	2.2	1.7	0.3	0.3	1.0

PER SHARE DATA

	1994	1993	1992	1991	1990	1989	1988	1987	1986	1985
Dividends, Net Income ($) .	0.68	0.65	0.79	0.84	0.85	0.88	0.88	0.89	0.98	1.08
Distrib'ns, Cap Gain ($) . . .	0.01	0.00	0.00	0.00	0.00	0.00	0.00	0.01	0.00	0.00
Net Asset Value ($)	9.58	10.37	10.42	10.52	9.79	9.70	9.27	9.35	10.05	9.94
Expense Ratio (%)	0.31	0.29	0.29	0.34	0.31	0.35	0.35	0.38	0.50	0.58
Net Income to Assets (%). .	6.67	7.38	8.22	8.95	9.25	9.35	9.35	9.41	10.16	11.90
Portfolio Turnover (%).	37	7	1	1	9	8	22	28	32	23
Total Assets (Millions $) . .	5,777	7,081	5,208	2,712	2,129	1,908	1,909	2,380	1,262	298

PORTFOLIO (as of 7/31/94)

Portfolio Manager: Paul Kaplan - 1994

Investm't Category: Mortgage-Backed Bond

Cap Gain	Asset Allocation
Cap & Income	Fund of Funds
✔ Income	Index
	Sector
✔ Domestic	Small Cap
Foreign	Socially Conscious
Country/Region	State Specific

Portfolio: stocks 0%   bonds 96%
convertibles 0%   other 0%   cash 4%

Largest Holdings: mortgage-backed 96%

Unrealized Net Capital Gains: -1% of portfolio value

SHAREHOLDER INFORMATION

Minimum Investment
Initial: $3,000   Subsequent: $100

Minimum IRA Investment
Initial: $500   Subsequent: $100

Maximum Fees
Load: none   12b-1: none
Other: none

Distributions
Income: monthly   Capital Gains: Dec

Exchange Options
Number Per Year: 2   Fee: none
Telephone: yes (money market fund available)

Services
IRA, pension, auto exchange, auto invest, auto withdraw

Vanguard High Yield Corporate (VWEHX)

Corporate High-Yield Bond

Vanguard Financial Center
P.O. Box 2600
Valley Forge, PA 19482
(800) 662-7447, (610) 648-6000

PERFORMANCE

fund inception date: 12/27/78

	3yr Annual	5yr Annual	10yr Annual	Bull	Bear
Return (%)	9.9	10.0	10.5	80.9	-5.9
Differ from Category (+/-)	0.0 abv av	0.7 high	0.6 high	1.6 abv av	-0.6 blw av

Total Risk	Standard Deviation	Category Risk	Risk Index	Avg Mat
blw av	5.0%	abv av	1.0	9.8 yrs

	1994	1993	1992	1991	1990	1989	1988	1987	1986	1985
Return (%)	-1.6	18.2	14.2	29.0	-5.8	1.8	13.5	2.6	16.8	21.9
Differ from category (+/-)	1.1	-0.2	-1.4	1.6	-0.7	0.4	1.4	1.5	2.5	-1.3

PER SHARE DATA

	1994	1993	1992	1991	1990	1989	1988	1987	1986	1985
Dividends, Net Income ($)	0.68	0.70	0.73	0.78	0.92	1.01	1.02	1.01	1.09	1.18
Distrib'ns, Cap Gain ($)	0.00	0.00	0.00	0.00	0.00	0.00	0.00	0.12	0.00	0.00
Net Asset Value ($)	7.20	8.02	7.41	7.16	6.22	7.55	8.39	8.32	9.20	8.86
Expense Ratio (%)	0.35	0.34	0.34	0.40	0.38	0.41	0.41	0.45	0.60	0.65
Net Income to Assets (%)	8.95	9.82	11.13	13.35	12.56	12.07	11.47	11.43	12.51	13.61
Portfolio Turnover (%)	34	83	44	61	41	48	82	67	61	71
Total Assets (Millions $)	2,120	2,518	1,594	698	829	1,235	994	1,370	634	252

PORTFOLIO (as of 7/31/94)

Portfolio Manager: Earl E. McEvoy - 1984

Investm't Category: Corp. High-Yield Bond

Cap Gain	Asset Allocation
✔ Cap & Income	Fund of Funds
Income	Index
	Sector
✔ Domestic	Small Cap
Foreign	Socially Conscious
Country/Region	State Specific

Portfolio: stocks 0% bonds 97%
convertibles 0% other 0% cash 3%

Largest Holdings: paper, chemicals, mining 15%, basic industries 13%

Unrealized Net Capital Gains: -3% of portfolio value

SHAREHOLDER INFORMATION

Minimum Investment
Initial: $3,000   Subsequent: $100

Minimum IRA Investment
Initial: $500   Subsequent: $100

Maximum Fees
Load: 1.00% redemption   12b-1: none
Other: redemption fee applies for 1 year

Distributions
Income: monthly   Capital Gains: Dec

Exchange Options
Number Per Year: 2   Fee: none
Telephone: yes (money market fund available)

Services
IRA, pension, auto exchange, auto invest, auto withdraw

Vanguard High-Yield Muni Bond (VWAHX)

Tax-Exempt Bond

Vanguard Financial Center
P.O. Box 2600
Valley Forge, PA 19482
(800) 662-7447, (610) 648-6000

PERFORMANCE

fund inception date: 12/27/78

	3yr Annual	5yr Annual	10yr Annual	Bull	Bear
Return (%)	5.5	7.3	9.9	50.8	-5.0
Differ from Category (+/-)	1.0 high	1.2 high	1.8 high	9.0 high	0.2 abv av

Total Risk	Standard Deviation	Category Risk	Risk Index	Avg Mat
blw av	6.7%	abv av	1.1	20.0 yrs

	1994	1993	1992	1991	1990	1989	1988	1987	1986	1985
Return (%)	-5.0	12.6	9.8	14.6	5.9	11.0	13.8	-1.6	19.6	21.6
Differ from category (+/-) . . .	0.2	0.9	1.5	3.3	-0.4	2.0	3.6	-0.3	3.2	4.2

PER SHARE DATA

	1994	1993	1992	1991	1990	1989	1988	1987	1986	1985
Dividends, Net Income ($) .	0.63	0.65	0.70	0.73	0.73	0.75	0.74	0.77	0.84	0.85
Distrib'ns, Cap Gain ($) . . .	0.17	0.21	0.25	0.11	0.14	0.11	0.00	0.20	0.39	0.00
Net Asset Value ($)	9.66	11.01	10.57	10.53	9.96	10.26	10.05	9.52	10.67	10.00
Expense Ratio (%)	0.20	0.20	0.23	0.25	0.25	0.27	0.29	0.26	0.33	0.39
Net Income to Assets (%). .	5.83	6.15	6.83	7.34	7.30	7.43	7.74	7.55	8.32	9.37
Portfolio Turnover (%).	50	34	64	58	82	80	40	83	38	41
Total Assets (Millions $) . .	1,572	1,873	1,506	1,215	963	866	690	791	794	451

PORTFOLIO (as of 8/31/94)

Portfolio Manager: Ian MacKinnon - 1981

Investm't Category: Tax-Exempt Bond

Cap Gain	Asset Allocation
Cap & Income	Fund of Funds
✔ Income	Index
	Sector
✔ Domestic	Small Cap
Foreign	Socially Conscious
Country/Region	State Specific

Portfolio: stocks 0% bonds 100%
convertibles 0% other 0% cash 0%

Largest Holdings: na

Unrealized Net Capital Gains: 1% of portfolio value

SHAREHOLDER INFORMATION

Minimum Investment
Initial: $3,000   Subsequent: $100

Minimum IRA Investment
Initial: na   Subsequent: na

Maximum Fees
Load: none   12b-1: none
Other: none

Distributions
Income: monthly   Capital Gains: Nov

Exchange Options
Number Per Year: 2   Fee: none
Telephone: yes (money market fund available)

Services
auto exchange, auto invest, auto withdraw

Vanguard Index Trust— Ext Market (VEXMX)

Growth

Vanguard Financial Center
P.O. Box 2600
Valley Forge, PA 19482
(800) 662-7447, (610) 648-6000

PERFORMANCE   fund inception date: 12/21/87

	3yr Annual	5yr Annual	10yr Annual	Bull	Bear
Return (%)	8.1	9.0	na	102.3	-8.3
Differ from Category (+/-)	0.4 av	-0.6 av	na	10.2 abv av	-1.7 blw av

Total Risk	Standard Deviation	Category Risk	Risk Index	Beta
abv av	9.5%	av	1.0	0.9

	1994	1993	1992	1991	1990	1989	1988	1987	1986	1985
Return (%)	-1.7	14.4	12.4	41.8	-14.0	23.9	19.7	—	—	—
Differ from category (+/-)	-1.1	1.0	0.8	6.1	-8.3	-2.2	1.7	—	—	—

PER SHARE DATA

	1994	1993	1992	1991	1990	1989	1988	1987	1986	1985
Dividends, Net Income ($)	0.28	0.23	0.25	0.25	0.33	0.23	0.20	—	—	—
Distrib'ns, Cap Gain ($)	0.29	0.20	0.18	0.20	0.16	0.23	0.16	—	—	—
Net Asset Value ($)	18.52	19.43	17.35	15.82	11.48	13.91	11.60	—	—	—
Expense Ratio (%)	0.20	0.20	0.20	0.19	0.23	0.23	0.24	—	—	—
Net Income to Assets (%)	1.44	1.48	1.73	2.14	2.68	2.92	2.90	—	—	—
Portfolio Turnover (%)	23	13	9	11	9	14	26	—	—	—
Total Assets (Millions $)	967	931	585	372	179	147	35	—	—	—

PORTFOLIO (as of 6/30/94)

Portfolio Manager: George U. Sauter - 1987

Investm't Category: Growth

✔ Cap Gain	Asset Allocation
Cap & Income	Fund of Funds
Income	✔ Index
	Sector
✔ Domestic	✔ Small Cap
Foreign	Socially Conscious
Country/Region	State Specific

Portfolio: stocks 100%   bonds 0%
convertibles 0%   other 0%   cash 0%

Largest Holdings: Wilshire 4500 index

Unrealized Net Capital Gains: 7% of portfolio value

SHAREHOLDER INFORMATION

Minimum Investment
Initial: $3,000   Subsequent: $100

Minimum IRA Investment
Initial: $500   Subsequent: $100

Maximum Fees
Load: 1.00% charge   12b-1: none
Other: $10 annual account maintenance fee

Distributions
Income: Dec   Capital Gains: Dec

Exchange Options
Number Per Year: 2   Fee: none
Telephone: none

Services
IRA, pension, auto exchange, auto invest, auto withdraw

Vanguard Index Trust—500 (VFINX)

Growth & Income

Vanguard Financial Center
P.O. Box 2600
Valley Forge, PA 19482
(800) 662-7447, (610) 648-6000

PERFORMANCE

fund inception date: 8/31/76

	3yr Annual	5yr Annual	10yr Annual	Bull	Bear
Return (%)	6.1	8.4	14.0	73.0	-6.6
Differ from Category (+/-)	-1.0 av	0.5 av	2.3 high	-2.8 av	-0.3 av

Total Risk	Standard Deviation	Category Risk	Risk Index	Beta
av	7.9%	av	1.0	1.0

	1994	1993	1992	1991	1990	1989	1988	1987	1986	1985
Return (%)	1.1	9.8	7.4	30.1	-3.3	31.3	16.2	4.7	18.0	31.2
Differ from category (+/-)	2.5	-3.4	-2.8	2.5	2.7	9.9	-0.8	4.1	2.2	5.5

PER SHARE DATA

	1994	1993	1992	1991	1990	1989	1988	1987	1986	1985
Dividends, Net Income ($)	1.17	1.13	1.12	1.15	1.17	1.20	1.10	0.69	0.89	0.91
Distrib'ns, Cap Gain ($)	0.20	0.03	0.10	0.12	0.10	0.75	0.32	0.17	2.02	1.61
Net Asset Value ($)	42.97	43.83	40.97	39.31	31.24	33.64	27.18	24.65	24.27	22.99
Expense Ratio (%)	0.19	0.19	0.19	0.20	0.22	0.21	0.22	0.26	0.28	0.28
Net Income to Assets (%)	2.68	2.65	2.81	3.07	3.60	3.62	4.08	3.15	3.40	4.09
Portfolio Turnover (%)	7	6	4	5	23	8	10	15	29	36
Total Assets (Millions $)	9,356	8,366	6,547	4,346	2,173	1,804	1,055	827	485	394

PORTFOLIO (as of 6/30/94)

Portfolio Manager: George U. Sauter - 1987

Investm't Category: Growth & Income
- Cap Gain
- ✔ Cap & Income
- Income
- ✔ Domestic
- Foreign
- Country/Region
- Asset Allocation
- Fund of Funds
- ✔ Index
- Sector
- Small Cap
- Socially Conscious
- State Specific

Portfolio: stocks 100% bonds 0%
convertibles 0% other 0% cash 0%

Largest Holdings: S&P 500 composite price index

Unrealized Net Capital Gains: 9% of portfolio value

SHAREHOLDER INFORMATION

Minimum Investment
Initial: $3,000   Subsequent: $100

Minimum IRA Investment
Initial: $500   Subsequent: $100

Maximum Fees
Load: none   12b-1: none
Other: $10 annual account maintenance fee

Distributions
Income: quarterly   Capital Gains: Dec

Exchange Options
Number Per Year: 2   Fee: none
Telephone: none

Services
IRA, pension, auto exchange, auto invest, auto withdraw

Vanguard Index Trust— Growth Port (VIGRX)

Growth

Vanguard Financial Center
P.O. Box 2600
Valley Forge, PA 19482
(800) 662-7447, (610) 648-6000

PERFORMANCE

fund inception date: 11/2/92

	3yr Annual	5yr Annual	10yr Annual	Bull	Bear
Return (%)	na	na	na	na	-6.4
Differ from Category (+/-)	na	na	na	na	0.2 av

Total Risk	Standard Deviation	Category Risk	Risk Index	Beta
na	na	na	na	na

	1994	1993	1992	1991	1990	1989	1988	1987	1986	1985
Return (%)	2.8	1.5	—	—	—	—	—	—	—	—
Differ from category (+/-)	3.4	-11.9	—	—	—	—	—	—	—	—

PER SHARE DATA

	1994	1993	1992	1991	1990	1989	1988	1987	1986	1985
Dividends, Net Income ($)	0.21	0.21	—	—	—	—	—	—	—	—
Distrib'ns, Cap Gain ($)	0.00	0.00	—	—	—	—	—	—	—	—
Net Asset Value ($)	10.28	10.20	—	—	—	—	—	—	—	—
Expense Ratio (%)	0.20	0.20	—	—	—	—	—	—	—	—
Net Income to Assets (%)	2.22	2.10	—	—	—	—	—	—	—	—
Portfolio Turnover (%)	33	36	—	—	—	—	—	—	—	—
Total Assets (Millions $)	86	50	—	—	—	—	—	—	—	—

PORTFOLIO (as of 6/30/94)

Portfolio Manager: George U. Sauter - 1992

Investm't Category: Growth
- ✔ Cap Gain
- Cap & Income
- Income
- Asset Allocation
- Fund of Funds
- ✔ Index
- Sector
- ✔ Domestic
- Foreign
- Country/Region
- Small Cap
- Socially Conscious
- State Specific

Portfolio: stocks 100% bonds 0%
convertibles 0% other 0% cash 0%

Largest Holdings: Standard & Poor's/BARRA Growth Index

Unrealized Net Capital Gains: -3% of portfolio value

SHAREHOLDER INFORMATION

Minimum Investment
Initial: $3,000   Subsequent: $100

Minimum IRA Investment
Initial: $500   Subsequent: $100

Maximum Fees
Load: none   12b-1: none
Other: $10 annual account maintenance fee

Distributions
Income: quarterly   Capital Gains: Dec

Exchange Options
Number Per Year: 2   Fee: none
Telephone: none

Services
IRA, pension, auto exchange, auto invest, auto withdraw

Vanguard Index Trust—Small Cap (NAESX)

Aggressive Growth

Vanguard Financial Center
P.O. Box 2600
Valley Forge, PA 19482
(800) 662-7447, (610) 648-6000

PERFORMANCE

fund inception date: 10/3/60

	3yr Annual	5yr Annual	10yr Annual	Bull	Bear
Return (%)	11.7	10.6	10.1	123.9	-8.6
Differ from Category (+/-)	2.8 abv av	-1.9 blw av	-3.9 low	-9.3 av	2.2 abv av

Total Risk	Standard Deviation	Category Risk	Risk Index	Beta
abv av	11.3%	blw av	0.8	0.9

	1994	1993	1992	1991	1990	1989	1988	1987	1986	1985
Return (%)	-0.5	18.7	18.2	45.2	-18.1	10.4	24.6	-6.9	0.1	23.0
Differ from category (+/-) . . .	0.2	-0.8	7.2	-6.9	-11.9	-16.4	9.4	-4.7	-11.7	-9.3

PER SHARE DATA

	1994	1993	1992	1991	1990	1989	1988	1987	1986	1985
Dividends, Net Income ($) .	0.22	0.18	0.18	0.18	0.18	0.13	0.06	0.00	0.00	0.15
Distrib'ns, Cap Gain ($) . . .	0.37	0.82	0.15	0.29	0.14	2.17	0.00	1.21	1.89	0.77
Net Asset Value ($)	14.99	15.67	14.07	12.19	8.74	11.07	11.97	9.65	11.70	13.56
Expense Ratio (%)	0.18	0.18	0.18	0.21	0.31	1.00	0.95	0.92	0.92	1.00
Net Income to Assets (%). .	1.29	1.47	1.65	2.11	1.91	0.65	0.24	-0.25	-0.06	-0.28
Portfolio Turnover (%).	48	26	26	33	40	160	68	92	92	103
Total Assets (Millions $) . . .	605	465	202	111	40	20	27	35	10	1

PORTFOLIO (as of 9/30/94)

Portfolio Manager: George U. Sauter - 1989

Investm't Category: Aggressive Growth
- ✔ Cap Gain
- Cap & Income
- Income
- ✔ Domestic
- Foreign
- Country/Region
- Asset Allocation
- Fund of Funds
- ✔ Index
- Sector
- ✔ Small Cap
- Socially Conscious
- State Specific

Portfolio:
stocks 99%	bonds 0%
convertibles 0%	other 0%	cash 1%

Largest Holdings: Russell 2000 small stock index

Unrealized Net Capital Gains: 3% of portfolio value

SHAREHOLDER INFORMATION

Minimum Investment
Initial: $3,000   Subsequent: $100

Minimum IRA Investment
Initial: $500   Subsequent: $100

Maximum Fees
Load: 1.00% charge   12b-1: none
Other: $10 annual account maintenance fee

Distributions
Income: Dec   Capital Gains: Dec

Exchange Options
Number Per Year: 2   Fee: none
Telephone: none

Services
IRA, pension, auto exchange, auto invest, auto withdraw

Vanguard Index Trust— Total Stock Mkt (VTSMX)

Growth & Income

Vanguard Financial Center
P.O. Box 2600
Valley Forge, PA 19482
(800) 662-7447, (610) 648-6000

PERFORMANCE

fund inception date: 4/28/92

	3yr Annual	5yr Annual	10yr Annual	Bull	Bear
Return (%)	na	na	na	na	-7.4
Differ from Category (+/-)	na	na	na	na	-1.1 blw av

Total Risk	Standard Deviation	Category Risk	Risk Index	Beta
na	na	na	na	na

	1994	1993	1992	1991	1990	1989	1988	1987	1986	1985
Return (%)	-0.1	10.6	—	—	—	—	—	—	—	—
Differ from category (+/-)	1.3	-2.6	—	—	—	—	—	—	—	—

PER SHARE DATA

	1994	1993	1992	1991	1990	1989	1988	1987	1986	1985
Dividends, Net Income ($)	0.27	0.26	—	—	—	—	—	—	—	—
Distrib'ns, Cap Gain ($)	0.03	0.03	—	—	—	—	—	—	—	—
Net Asset Value ($)	11.37	11.69	—	—	—	—	—	—	—	—
Expense Ratio (%)	0.20	0.20	—	—	—	—	—	—	—	—
Net Income to Assets (%)	2.31	2.31	—	—	—	—	—	—	—	—
Portfolio Turnover (%)	3	1	—	—	—	—	—	—	—	—
Total Assets (Millions $)	785	533	—	—	—	—	—	—	—	—

PORTFOLIO (as of 6/30/94)

Portfolio Manager: George U. Sauter - 1992

Investm't Category: Growth & Income

Cap Gain	Asset Allocation
✔ Cap & Income	Fund of Funds
Income	✔ Index
	Sector
✔ Domestic	Small Cap
Foreign	Socially Conscious
Country/Region	State Specific

Portfolio: stocks 99% bonds 0%
convertibles 0% other 0% cash 1%

Largest Holdings: Wilshire 5000 index

Unrealized Net Capital Gains: 1% of portfolio value

SHAREHOLDER INFORMATION

Minimum Investment
Initial: $3,000   Subsequent: $100

Minimum IRA Investment
Initial: $500   Subsequent: $100

Maximum Fees
Load: 0.25% charge   12b-1: none
Other: $10 annual account maintenance fee

Distributions
Income: quarterly   Capital Gains: Dec

Exchange Options
Number Per Year: 2   Fee: none
Telephone: none

Services
IRA, pension, auto exchange, auto invest, auto withdraw

Vanguard Index Trust—Value Port (VIVAX)

Growth & Income

Vanguard Financial Center
P.O. Box 2600
Valley Forge, PA 19482
(800) 662-7447, (610) 648-6000

PERFORMANCE

fund inception date: 11/2/92

	3yr Annual	5yr Annual	10yr Annual	Bull	Bear
Return (%)	na	na	na	na	-6.8
Differ from Category (+/-)	na	na	na	na	-0.5 blw av

Total Risk	Standard Deviation	Category Risk	Risk Index	Beta
na	na	na	na	na

	1994	1993	1992	1991	1990	1989	1988	1987	1986	1985
Return (%)	-0.7	18.3	—	—	—	—	—	—	—	—
Differ from category (+/-) . . .	0.7	5.1	—	—	—	—	—	—	—	—

PER SHARE DATA

	1994	1993	1992	1991	1990	1989	1988	1987	1986	1985
Dividends, Net Income ($) .	0.38	0.38	—	—	—	—	—	—	—	—
Distrib'ns, Cap Gain ($) . . .	0.16	0.06	—	—	—	—	—	—	—	—
Net Asset Value ($)	11.12	11.74	—	—	—	—	—	—	—	—
Expense Ratio (%)	0.20	0.20	—	—	—	—	—	—	—	—
Net Income to Assets (%). .	3.21	3.26	—	—	—	—	—	—	—	—
Portfolio Turnover (%).	32	30	—	—	—	—	—	—	—	—
Total Assets (Millions $). . .	296	192	—	—	—	—	—	—	—	—

PORTFOLIO (as of 6/30/94)

Portfolio Manager: George U. Sauter - 1992

Investm't Category: Growth & Income
- Cap Gain
- ✔ Cap & Income
- Income
- ✔ Domestic
- Foreign
- Country/Region
- Asset Allocation
- Fund of Funds
- ✔ Index
- Sector
- Small Cap
- Socially Conscious
- State Specific

Portfolio: stocks 100% bonds 0%
convertibles 0% other 0% cash 0%

Largest Holdings: Standard & Poor's/BARRA value index

Unrealized Net Capital Gains: -2% of portfolio value

SHAREHOLDER INFORMATION

Minimum Investment
Initial: $3,000   Subsequent: $100

Minimum IRA Investment
Initial: $500   Subsequent: $100

Maximum Fees
Load: none   12b-1: none
Other: $10 annual account maintenance fee

Distributions
Income: quarterly   Capital Gains: Dec

Exchange Options
Number Per Year: 2   Fee: none
Telephone: none

Services
IRA, pension, auto exchange, auto invest, auto withdraw

Vanguard Insured Long-Term Muni (VILPX)

Tax-Exempt Bond

Vanguard Financial Center
P.O. Box 2600
Valley Forge, PA 19482
(800) 662-7447, (610) 648-6000

PERFORMANCE

fund inception date: 9/30/84

	3yr Annual	5yr Annual	10yr Annual	Bull	Bear
Return (%)	5.2	7.0	9.5	48.7	-5.9
Differ from Category (+/-)	0.7 abv av	0.9 high	1.4 high	6.9 high	-0.7 av

Total Risk	Standard Deviation	Category Risk	Risk Index	Avg Mat
av	6.9%	high	1.1	17.4 yrs

	1994	1993	1992	1991	1990	1989	1988	1987	1986	1985
Return (%).	-5.6	13.0	9.1	12.4	7.0	10.5	12.7	0.0	18.6	19.3
Differ from category (+/-) . .	-0.4	1.3	0.8	1.1	0.7	1.5	2.5	1.3	2.2	1.9

PER SHARE DATA

	1994	1993	1992	1991	1990	1989	1988	1987	1986	1985
Dividends, Net Income ($).	0.70	0.71	0.75	0.78	0.79	0.83	0.82	0.84	0.89	0.91
Distrib'ns, Cap Gain ($) . . .	0.17	0.18	0.20	0.08	0.12	0.15	0.00	0.10	0.17	0.00
Net Asset Value ($)	11.23	12.81	12.14	12.03	11.50	11.64	11.45	10.92	11.86	10.94
Expense Ratio (%)	0.20	0.20	0.23	0.25	0.25	0.29	0.29	0.26	0.33	0.36
Net Income to Assets (%) .	5.62	5.77	6.34	6.77	6.99	7.50	7.50	7.35	7.99	8.70
Portfolio Turnover (%)	16	30	42	33	47	36	28	50	20	16
Total Assets (Millions $) .	1,737	2,127	1,948	1,551	1,122	934	735	793	709	335

PORTFOLIO (as of 8/31/94)

Portfolio Manager: Ian MacKinnon - 1984

Investm't Category: Tax-Exempt Bond

Cap Gain	Asset Allocation
Cap & Income	Fund of Funds
✔ Income	Index
	Sector
✔ Domestic	Small Cap
Foreign	Socially Conscious
Country/Region	State Specific

Portfolio: stocks 0% bonds 100%
convertibles 0% other 0% cash 0%

Largest Holdings: na

Unrealized Net Capital Gains: 3% of portfolio value

SHAREHOLDER INFORMATION

Minimum Investment
Initial: $3,000 Subsequent: $100

Minimum IRA Investment
Initial: na Subsequent: na

Maximum Fees
Load: none 12b-1: none
Other: none

Distributions
Income: monthly Capital Gains: Nov

Exchange Options
Number Per Year: 2 Fee: none
Telephone: yes (money market fund available)

Services
auto exchange, auto invest, auto withdraw

Vanguard Interm Term Corporate (VFICX)

Corporate Bond

Vanguard Financial Center
P.O. Box 2600
Valley Forge, PA 19482
(800) 662-7447, (610) 648-6000

PERFORMANCE

fund inception date: 11/1/93

	3yr Annual	5yr Annual	10yr Annual	Bull	Bear
Return (%)	na	na	na	na	-5.9
Differ from Category (+/-)	na	na	na	na	-1.6 blw av

Total Risk	Standard Deviation	Category Risk	Risk Index	Avg Mat
na	na	na	na	7.1 yrs

	1994	1993	1992	1991	1990	1989	1988	1987	1986	1985
Return (%)	-4.2	—	—	—	—	—	—	—	—	—
Differ from category (+/-)	-1.8	—	—	—	—	—	—	—	—	—

PER SHARE DATA

	1994	1993	1992	1991	1990	1989	1988	1987	1986	1985
Dividends, Net Income ($)	0.58	—	—	—	—	—	—	—	—	—
Distrib'ns, Cap Gain ($)	0.00	—	—	—	—	—	—	—	—	—
Net Asset Value ($)	8.95	—	—	—	—	—	—	—	—	—
Expense Ratio (%)	0.29	—	—	—	—	—	—	—	—	—
Net Income to Assets (%)	5.91	—	—	—	—	—	—	—	—	—
Portfolio Turnover (%)	92	—	—	—	—	—	—	—	—	—
Total Assets (Millions $)	151	—	—	—	—	—	—	—	—	—

PORTFOLIO (as of 7/31/94)

Portfolio Manager: Ian MacKinnon - 1993

Investm't Category: Corporate Bond

Cap Gain	Asset Allocation
Cap & Income	Fund of Funds
✔ Income	Index
	Sector
✔ Domestic	Small Cap
Foreign	Socially Conscious
Country/Region	State Specific

Portfolio: stocks 0% bonds 94%
convertibles 0% other 0% cash 6%

Largest Holdings: industrial 32%, utilities 9%

Unrealized Net Capital Gains: -4% of portfolio value

SHAREHOLDER INFORMATION

Minimum Investment
Initial: $3,000   Subsequent: $100

Minimum IRA Investment
Initial: $500   Subsequent: $100

Maximum Fees
Load: none   12b-1: none
Other: none

Distributions
Income: monthly   Capital Gains: Dec

Exchange Options
Number Per Year: 2   Fee: none
Telephone: yes (money market fund available)

Services
IRA, pension, auto exchange, auto invest, auto withdraw

Vanguard Interm-Term Muni Bond (VWITX)

Tax-Exempt Bond

Vanguard Financial Center
P.O. Box 2600
Valley Forge, PA 19482
(800) 662-7447, (610) 648-6000

PERFORMANCE

fund inception date: 9/1/77

	3yr Annual	5yr Annual	10yr Annual	Bull	Bear
Return (%)	5.9	7.3	9.1	43.3	-2.8
Differ from Category (+/-)	1.4 high	1.2 high	1.0 high	1.5 av	2.4 high

Total Risk	Standard Deviation	Category Risk	Risk Index	Avg Mat
low	4.8%	blw av	0.8	8.4 yrs

	1994	1993	1992	1991	1990	1989	1988	1987	1986	1985
Return (%)	-2.1	11.5	8.8	12.1	7.1	9.9	10.0	1.6	16.2	17.3
Differ from category (+/-)	3.1	-0.2	0.5	0.8	0.8	0.9	-0.2	2.9	-0.2	-0.1

PER SHARE DATA

	1994	1993	1992	1991	1990	1989	1988	1987	1986	1985
Dividends, Net Income ($)	0.69	0.70	0.73	0.78	0.81	0.84	0.81	0.82	0.88	0.91
Distrib'ns, Cap Gain ($)	0.16	0.08	0.12	0.08	0.09	0.07	0.00	0.09	0.02	0.00
Net Asset Value ($)	12.39	13.52	12.84	12.61	12.05	12.12	11.88	11.56	12.29	11.39
Expense Ratio (%)	0.20	0.20	0.23	0.25	0.25	0.27	0.29	0.26	0.33	0.39
Net Income to Assets (%)	5.15	5.41	5.91	6.49	6.83	7.03	6.88	6.94	7.66	8.53
Portfolio Turnover (%)	18	15	32	27	54	56	89	57	13	26
Total Assets (Millions $)	4,585	5,114	3,102	2,006	1,259	1,005	795	920	811	411

PORTFOLIO (as of 8/31/94)

Portfolio Manager: Ian MacKinnon - 1981

Investm't Category: Tax-Exempt Bond

Cap Gain	Asset Allocation
Cap & Income	Fund of Funds
✔ Income	Index
	Sector
✔ Domestic	Small Cap
Foreign	Socially Conscious
Country/Region	State Specific

Portfolio: stocks 0%   bonds 100%
convertibles 0%   other 0%   cash 0%

Largest Holdings: na

Unrealized Net Capital Gains: 3% of portfolio value

SHAREHOLDER INFORMATION

Minimum Investment
Initial: $3,000   Subsequent: $100

Minimum IRA Investment
Initial: na   Subsequent: na

Maximum Fees
Load: none   12b-1: none
Other: none

Distributions
Income: monthly   Capital Gains: Nov

Exchange Options
Number Per Year: 2   Fee: none
Telephone: yes (money market fund available)

Services
auto exchange, auto invest, auto withdraw

Vanguard Interm-Term US Treasury (VFITX)

Government Bond

Vanguard Financial Center
P.O. Box 2600
Valley Forge, PA 19482
(800) 662-7447, (610) 648-6000

PERFORMANCE

fund inception date: 10/28/91

	3yr Annual	5yr Annual	10yr Annual	Bull	Bear
Return (%)	4.7	na	na	na	-6.0
Differ from Category (+/-)	0.7 abv av	na	na	na	0.4 av

Total Risk	Standard Deviation	Category Risk	Risk Index	Avg Mat
blw av	5.1%	abv av	1.1	7.4 yrs

	1994	1993	1992	1991	1990	1989	1988	1987	1986	1985
Return (%)	-4.3	11.4	7.7	—	—	—	—	—	—	—
Differ from category (+/-)	0.5	0.5	1.3	—	—	—	—	—	—	—

PER SHARE DATA

	1994	1993	1992	1991	1990	1989	1988	1987	1986	1985
Dividends, Net Income ($)	0.59	0.63	0.67	—	—	—	—	—	—	—
Distrib'ns, Cap Gain ($)	0.03	0.41	0.02	—	—	—	—	—	—	—
Net Asset Value ($)	9.63	10.71	10.56	—	—	—	—	—	—	—
Expense Ratio (%)	0.29	0.26	0.26	—	—	—	—	—	—	—
Net Income to Assets (%)	5.58	6.44	6.47	—	—	—	—	—	—	—
Portfolio Turnover (%)	95	123	32	—	—	—	—	—	—	—
Total Assets (Millions $)	844	989	190	—	—	—	—	—	—	—

PORTFOLIO (as of 7/31/94)

Portfolio Manager: Robert Auwaerter - 1991, Ian Mackinnon - 1991

Investm't Category: Government Bond

Cap Gain	Asset Allocation
Cap & Income	Fund of Funds
✔ Income	Index
	Sector
✔ Domestic	Small Cap
Foreign	Socially Conscious
Country/Region	State Specific

Portfolio: stocks 0%   bonds 97%
convertibles 0%   other 0%   cash 3%

Largest Holdings: U.S. government & agencies 97%

Unrealized Net Capital Gains: -4% of portfolio value

SHAREHOLDER INFORMATION

Minimum Investment
Initial: $3,000   Subsequent: $100

Minimum IRA Investment
Initial: $500   Subsequent: $100

Maximum Fees
Load: none   12b-1: none
Other: none

Distributions
Income: monthly   Capital Gains: Dec

Exchange Options
Number Per Year: 2   Fee: none
Telephone: yes (money market fund available)

Services
IRA, pension, auto exchange, auto invest, auto withdraw

Vanguard Int'l Equity Index—Europe (VEURX)

International Stock

Vanguard Financial Center
P.O. Box 2600
Valley Forge, PA 19482
(800) 662-7447, (610) 648-6000

PERFORMANCE

fund inception date: 6/18/90

	3yr Annual	5yr Annual	10yr Annual	Bull	Bear
Return (%)	8.3	na	na	59.0	-6.9
Differ from Category (+/-)	-0.8 blw av	na	na	-4.9 blw av	0.1 av

Total Risk	Standard Deviation	Category Risk	Risk Index	Beta
high	12.8%	av	1.0	0.9

	1994	1993	1992	1991	1990	1989	1988	1987	1986	1985
Return (%)	1.8	29.1	-3.3	12.4	—	—	—	—	—	—
Differ from category (+/-)	4.8	-9.5	-0.4	-0.7	—	—	—	—	—	—

PER SHARE DATA

	1994	1993	1992	1991	1990	1989	1988	1987	1986	1985
Dividends, Net Income ($)	0.28	0.17	0.26	0.26	—	—	—	—	—	—
Distrib'ns, Cap Gain ($)	0.06	0.00	0.00	0.00	—	—	—	—	—	—
Net Asset Value ($)	11.76	11.88	9.33	9.92	—	—	—	—	—	—
Expense Ratio (%)	0.32	0.32	0.32	0.33	—	—	—	—	—	—
Net Income to Assets (%)	3.15	2.05	3.05	3.06	—	—	—	—	—	—
Portfolio Turnover (%)	5	4	1	15	—	—	—	—	—	—
Total Assets (Millions $)	715	616	256	161	—	—	—	—	—	—

PORTFOLIO (as of 6/30/94)

Portfolio Manager: George U. Sauter - 1990

Investm't Category: International Stock

Cap Gain	Asset Allocation
✔ Cap & Income	Fund of Funds
Income	✔ Index
	Sector
Domestic	Small Cap
✔ Foreign	Socially Conscious
✔ Country/Region	State Specific

Portfolio: stocks 99%   bonds 0%
convertibles 0%   other 0%   cash 1%

Largest Holdings: Morgan Stanley Capital International Europe index

Unrealized Net Capital Gains: 6% of portfolio value

SHAREHOLDER INFORMATION

Minimum Investment
Initial: $3,000   Subsequent: $100

Minimum IRA Investment
Initial: $500   Subsequent: $100

Maximum Fees
Load: 1.00% charge   12b-1: none
Other: $10 account maintenance fee

Distributions
Income: Dec   Capital Gains: Dec

Exchange Options
Number Per Year: 2   Fee: none
Telephone: none

Services
IRA, pension, auto exchange, auto invest, auto withdraw

Vanguard Int'l Equity Index—Pacific (VPACX)

International Stock

Vanguard Financial Center
P.O. Box 2600
Valley Forge, PA 19482
(800) 662-7447, (610) 648-6000

PERFORMANCE

fund inception date: 6/18/90

	3yr Annual	5yr Annual	10yr Annual	Bull	Bear
Return (%)	7.7	na	na	53.9	7.0
Differ from Category (+/-)	-1.4 blw av	na	na	-10.0 blw av	14.0 high

Total Risk	Standard Deviation	Category Risk	Risk Index	Beta
high	22.2%	high	1.7	0.6

	1994	1993	1992	1991	1990	1989	1988	1987	1986	1985
Return (%)	12.9	35.4	-18.1	10.7	—	—	—	—	—	—
Differ from category (+/-) . .	15.9	-3.2	-15.2	-2.4	—	—	—	—	—	—

PER SHARE DATA

	1994	1993	1992	1991	1990	1989	1988	1987	1986	1985
Dividends, Net Income ($) .	0.08	0.06	0.05	0.05	—	—	—	—	—	—
Distrib'ns, Cap Gain ($) . . .	0.06	0.05	0.10	0.00	—	—	—	—	—	—
Net Asset Value ($)	11.30	10.13	7.56	9.42	—	—	—	—	—	—
Expense Ratio (%)	0.32	0.32	0.32	0.32	—	—	—	—	—	—
Net Income to Assets (%) . .	0.80	0.75	0.92	0.70	—	—	—	—	—	—
Portfolio Turnover (%)	3	7	3	21	—	—	—	—	—	—
Total Assets (Millions $) . . .	697	500	207	84	—	—	—	—	—	—

PORTFOLIO (as of 6/30/94)

Portfolio Manager: George U. Sauter - 1990

Investm't Category: International Stock
- ✔ Cap Gain
- Cap & Income
- Income
- Domestic
- ✔ Foreign
- ✔ Country/Region
- Asset Allocation
- Fund of Funds
- ✔ Index
- Sector
- Small Cap
- Socially Conscious
- State Specific

Portfolio: stocks 99% bonds 0%
convertibles 0% other 0% cash 1%

Largest Holdings: Morgan Stanley Capital International Pacific index

Unrealized Net Capital Gains: 19% of portfolio value

SHAREHOLDER INFORMATION

Minimum Investment
Initial: $3,000   Subsequent: $100

Minimum IRA Investment
Initial: $500   Subsequent: $100

Maximum Fees
Load: 1.00% charge   12b-1: none
Other: $10 account maintenance fee

Distributions
Income: Dec   Capital Gains: Dec

Exchange Options
Number Per Year: 2   Fee: none
Telephone: none

Services
IRA, pension, auto exchange, auto invest, auto withdraw

Vanguard Int'l Growth
(VWIGX)
International Stock

Vanguard Financial Center
P.O. Box 2600
Valley Forge, PA 19482
(800) 662-7447, (610) 648-6000

PERFORMANCE
fund inception date: 9/30/81

	3yr Annual	5yr Annual	10yr Annual	Bull	Bear
Return (%)	11.1	4.8	17.1	60.2	-4.9
Differ from Category (+/-)	2.0 abv av	-0.1 av	1.9 abv av	-3.7 av	2.1 abv av

Total Risk	Standard Deviation	Category Risk	Risk Index	Beta
high	12.7%	av	1.0	0.7

	1994	1993	1992	1991	1990	1989	1988	1987	1986	1985
Return (%)	0.7	44.7	-5.7	4.7	-12.0	24.7	11.6	12.4	56.7	56.9
Differ from category (+/-)	3.7	6.1	-2.8	-8.4	-1.6	2.2	-2.8	-2.0	-2.3	14.5

PER SHARE DATA

	1994	1993	1992	1991	1990	1989	1988	1987	1986	1985
Dividends, Net Income ($)	0.18	0.11	0.21	0.19	0.20	0.15	0.16	0.13	0.07	0.09
Distrib'ns, Cap Gain ($)	0.00	0.00	0.00	0.12	0.68	0.28	1.07	2.43	0.80	0.65
Net Asset Value ($)	13.43	13.51	9.41	10.21	10.05	12.42	10.30	10.34	11.26	7.79
Expense Ratio (%)	0.46	0.59	0.58	0.67	0.68	0.64	0.67	0.66	0.52	0.56
Net Income to Assets (%)	1.37	1.27	2.04	1.80	3.01	1.27	1.39	1.00	2.65	3.11
Portfolio Turnover (%)	28	51	58	49	45	50	71	77	24	29
Total Assets (Millions $)	2,927	1,801	919	846	796	551	454	607	718	581

PORTFOLIO (as of 8/31/94)

Portfolio Manager: Richard R. Foulkes - 1981

Investm't Category: International Stock

✔ Cap Gain	Asset Allocation
Cap & Income	Fund of Funds
Income	Index
	Sector
Domestic	Small Cap
✔ Foreign	Socially Conscious
Country/Region	State Specific

Portfolio: stocks 96% bonds 0%
convertibles 0% other 0% cash 4%

Largest Holdings: Japan 30%, United Kingdom 15%

Unrealized Net Capital Gains: 19% of portfolio value

SHAREHOLDER INFORMATION

Minimum Investment
Initial: $3,000   Subsequent: $100

Minimum IRA Investment
Initial: $500   Subsequent: $100

Maximum Fees
Load: none   12b-1: none
Other: none

Distributions
Income: Dec   Capital Gains: Dec

Exchange Options
Number Per Year: 2   Fee: none
Telephone: yes (money market fund available)

Services
IRA, pension, auto exchange, auto invest, auto withdraw

Vanguard Limited-Term Muni Bond (VMLTX)

Tax-Exempt Bond

Vanguard Financial Center
P.O. Box 2600
Valley Forge, PA 19482
(800) 662-7447, (610) 648-6000

fund inception date: 8/31/87

	3yr Annual	5yr Annual	10yr Annual	Bull	Bear
Return (%)	4.2	5.8	na	27.9	-1.0
Differ from Category (+/-)	-0.3 blw av	-0.3 blw av	na	-13.9 low	4.2 high

Total Risk	Standard Deviation	Category Risk	Risk Index	Avg Mat
low	2.0%	low	0.3	2.5 yrs

	1994	1993	1992	1991	1990	1989	1988	1987	1986	1985
Return (%)	0.0	6.3	6.3	9.4	7.0	8.0	6.3	—	—	—
Differ from category (+/-) . . .	5.2	-5.4	-2.0	-1.9	0.7	-1.0	-3.9	—	—	—

PER SHARE DATA

	1994	1993	1992	1991	1990	1989	1988	1987	1986	1985
Dividends, Net Income ($) .	0.46	0.47	0.52	0.59	0.64	0.65	0.60	—	—	—
Distrib'ns, Cap Gain ($) . . .	0.00	0.02	0.05	0.06	0.01	0.01	0.01	—	—	—
Net Asset Value ($)	10.37	10.82	10.65	10.56	10.27	10.22	10.09	—	—	—
Expense Ratio (%)	0.20	0.20	0.23	0.25	0.25	0.27	0.29	—	—	—
Net Income to Assets (%). .	4.24	4.50	5.08	5.91	6.31	6.33	5.91	—	—	—
Portfolio Turnover (%).	21	20	37	57	55	89	122	—	—	—
Total Assets (Millions $) . .	1,629	1,782	873	420	245	166	162	—	—	—

PORTFOLIO (as of 8/31/94)

Portfolio Manager: Ian MacKinnon - 1987

Investm't Category: Tax-Exempt Bond

Cap Gain	Asset Allocation
Cap & Income	Fund of Funds
✔ Income	Index
	Sector
✔ Domestic	Small Cap
Foreign	Socially Conscious
Country/Region	State Specific

Portfolio: stocks 0% bonds 100%
convertibles 0% other 0% cash 0%

Largest Holdings: na

Unrealized Net Capital Gains: 0% of portfolio value

SHAREHOLDER INFORMATION

Minimum Investment
Initial: $3,000 Subsequent: $100

Minimum IRA Investment
Initial: na Subsequent: na

Maximum Fees
Load: none 12b-1: none
Other: none

Distributions
Income: monthly Capital Gains: Nov

Exchange Options
Number Per Year: 2 Fee: none
Telephone: yes (money market fund available)

Services
auto exchange, auto invest, auto withdraw

Vanguard Long Term Corp Bond (VWESX)

Corporate Bond

Vanguard Financial Center
P.O. Box 2600
Valley Forge, PA 19482
(800) 662-7447, (610) 648-6000

PERFORMANCE

fund inception date: 7/9/73

	3yr Annual	5yr Annual	10yr Annual	Bull	Bear
Return (%)	5.9	8.8	10.4	64.9	-8.1
Differ from Category (+/-)	0.0 av	1.0 high	0.9 high	15.1 high	-3.8 low

Total Risk	Standard Deviation	Category Risk	Risk Index	Avg Mat
blw av	6.1%	high	2.0	19.8 yrs

	1994	1993	1992	1991	1990	1989	1988	1987	1986	1985
Return (%).............	-5.3	14.3	9.7	20.9	6.2	15.1	9.6	0.1	14.3	21.9
Differ from category (+/-) ..	-2.9	2.9	0.8	3.8	1.4	5.8	0.5	-2.0	-0.5	2.2

PER SHARE DATA

	1994	1993	1992	1991	1990	1989	1988	1987	1986	1985
Dividends, Net Income ($).	0.61	0.63	0.68	0.71	0.72	0.73	0.74	0.77	0.89	1.01
Distrib'ns, Cap Gain ($) ...	0.07	0.26	0.15	0.00	0.00	0.00	0.00	0.12	0.00	0.00
Net Asset Value ($)	8.05	9.22	8.86	8.87	7.99	8.24	7.83	7.84	8.73	8.46
Expense Ratio (%)	0.33	0.31	0.31	0.37	0.34	0.38	0.37	0.41	0.55	0.62
Net Income to Assets (%) .	7.16	7.68	8.46	9.16	9.07	9.40	9.40	9.41	10.78	12.50
Portfolio Turnover (%)	52	50	72	62	70	60	63	47	56	55
Total Assets (Millions $) .	2,552	3,193	1,992	1,254	954	734	665	753	318	106

PORTFOLIO (as of 7/31/94)

Portfolio Manager: Earl E. McEvoy - 1994

Investm't Category: Corporate Bond

Cap Gain	Asset Allocation
Cap & Income	Fund of Funds
✔ Income	Index
	Sector
✔ Domestic	Small Cap
Foreign	Socially Conscious
Country/Region	State Specific

Portfolio: stocks 0% bonds 98%
convertibles 0% other 0% cash 2%

Largest Holdings: industrial 31%, banks & finance 22%

Unrealized Net Capital Gains: 0% of portfolio value

SHAREHOLDER INFORMATION

Minimum Investment
Initial: $3,000   Subsequent: $100

Minimum IRA Investment
Initial: $500   Subsequent: $100

Maximum Fees
Load: none   12b-1: none
Other: none

Distributions
Income: monthly   Capital Gains: Dec

Exchange Options
Number Per Year: 2   Fee: none
Telephone: yes (money market fund available)

Services
IRA, pension, auto exchange, auto invest, auto withdraw

Vanguard Long-Term Muni Bond (VWLTX)

Tax-Exempt Bond

Vanguard Financial Center
P.O. Box 2600
Valley Forge, PA 19482
(800) 662-7447, (610) 648-6000

PERFORMANCE

fund inception date: 4/7/86

	3yr Annual	5yr Annual	10yr Annual	Bull	Bear
Return (%)	5.3	7.2	9.7	50.5	-5.6
Differ from Category (+/-)	0.8 high	1.1 high	1.6 high	8.7 high	-0.4 av

Total Risk	Standard Deviation	Category Risk	Risk Index	Avg Mat
av	7.0%	high	1.1	17.8 yrs

	1994	1993	1992	1991	1990	1989	1988	1987	1986	1985
Return (%)	-5.7	13.4	9.2	13.4	6.8	11.5	12.2	-1.0	19.4	20.8
Differ from category (+/-) . .	-0.5	1.7	0.9	2.1	0.5	2.5	2.0	0.3	3.0	3.4

PER SHARE DATA

	1994	1993	1992	1991	1990	1989	1988	1987	1986	1985
Dividends, Net Income ($) .	0.61	0.62	0.68	0.73	0.72	0.76	0.74	0.79	0.84	0.86
Distrib'ns, Cap Gain ($) . . .	0.16	0.21	0.28	0.19	0.18	0.17	0.00	0.32	0.19	0.00
Net Asset Value ($)	9.88	11.29	10.71	10.72	10.31	10.53	10.31	9.88	11.12	10.23
Expense Ratio (%)	0.20	0.20	0.23	0.25	0.25	0.27	0.29	0.26	0.33	0.39
Net Income to Assets (%). .	5.56	5.81	6.52	7.09	7.04	7.33	7.48	7.40	8.09	9.13
Portfolio Turnover (%).	45	36	63	62	110	99	34	67	32	72
Total Assets (Millions $) . . .	920	1,086	962	798	684	626	531	617	627	410

PORTFOLIO (as of 8/31/94)

Portfolio Manager: Ian MacKinnon - 1981

Investm't Category: Tax-Exempt Bond

Cap Gain	Asset Allocation
Cap & Income	Fund of Funds
✔ Income	Index
	Sector
✔ Domestic	Small Cap
Foreign	Socially Conscious
Country/Region	State Specific

Portfolio: stocks 0% bonds 100%
convertibles 0% other 0% cash 0%

Largest Holdings: na

Unrealized Net Capital Gains: 3% of portfolio value

SHAREHOLDER INFORMATION

Minimum Investment
Initial: $3,000   Subsequent: $100

Minimum IRA Investment
Initial: na   Subsequent: na

Maximum Fees
Load: none   12b-1: none
Other: none

Distributions
Income: monthly   Capital Gains: Nov

Exchange Options
Number Per Year: 2   Fee: none
Telephone: yes (money market fund available)

Services
auto exchange, auto invest, auto withdraw

Vanguard Long-Term US Treasury (VUSTX)

Government Bond

Vanguard Financial Center
P.O. Box 2600
Valley Forge, PA 19482
(800) 662-7447, (610) 648-6000

PERFORMANCE

fund inception date: 5/19/86

	3yr Annual	5yr Annual	10yr Annual	Bull	Bear
Return (%)	5.2	7.6	na	64.2	-10.0
Differ from Category (+/-)	1.2 high	0.9 abv av	na	13.0 abv av	-3.6 low

Total Risk	Standard Deviation	Category Risk	Risk Index	Avg Mat
av	7.3%	high	1.6	21.6 yrs

	1994	1993	1992	1991	1990	1989	1988	1987	1986	1985
Return (%)	-7.0	16.7	7.4	17.4	5.7	17.9	9.1	-2.9	—	—
Differ from category (+/-)	-2.2	5.8	1.0	2.1	-0.5	3.4	1.2	-0.8	—	—

PER SHARE DATA

	1994	1993	1992	1991	1990	1989	1988	1987	1986	1985
Dividends, Net Income ($)	0.66	0.69	0.74	0.77	0.78	0.79	0.78	0.78	—	—
Distrib'ns, Cap Gain ($)	0.12	0.18	0.70	0.00	0.00	0.00	0.00	0.03	—	—
Net Asset Value ($)	9.05	10.57	9.82	10.54	9.70	9.96	9.16	9.13	—	—
Expense Ratio (%)	0.29	0.27	0.26	0.30	0.28	0.36	0.32	0.00	—	—
Net Income to Assets (%)	6.71	7.26	7.72	8.29	8.08	8.46	8.10	6.93	—	—
Portfolio Turnover (%)	84	170	89	147	83	387	182	182	—	—
Total Assets (Millions $)	644	831	833	722	456	172	83	35	—	—

PORTFOLIO (as of 7/31/94)

Portfolio Manager: Ian MacKinnon - 1986

Investm't Category: Government Bond

Cap Gain	Asset Allocation
Cap & Income	Fund of Funds
✔ Income	Index
	Sector
✔ Domestic	Small Cap
Foreign	Socially Conscious
Country/Region	State Specific

Portfolio:	stocks 0%	bonds 90%
convertibles 0%	other 0%	cash 10%

Largest Holdings: U.S. government & agencies 90%

Unrealized Net Capital Gains: 0% of portfolio value

SHAREHOLDER INFORMATION

Minimum Investment
Initial: $3,000   Subsequent: $100

Minimum IRA Investment
Initial: $500   Subsequent: $100

Maximum Fees
Load: none   12b-1: none
Other: none

Distributions
Income: monthly   Capital Gains: Dec

Exchange Options
Number Per Year: 2   Fee: none
Telephone: yes (money market fund available)

Services
IRA, pension, auto exchange, auto invest, auto withdraw

Vanguard Morgan Growth (VMRGX)

Growth

Vanguard Financial Center
P.O. Box 2600
Valley Forge, PA 19482
(800) 662-7447, (610) 648-6000

PERFORMANCE

fund inception date: 12/31/86

	3yr Annual	5yr Annual	10yr Annual	Bull	Bear
Return (%)	4.9	8.0	12.5	73.0	-9.1
Differ from Category (+/-)	-2.8 blw av	-1.6 blw av	-0.4 av	-19.1 blw av	-2.5 blw av

Total Risk	Standard Deviation	Category Risk	Risk Index	Beta
abv av	9.3%	av	1.0	1.0

	1994	1993	1992	1991	1990	1989	1988	1987	1986	1985
Return (%)	-1.6	7.3	9.5	29.3	-1.5	22.5	22.3	5.0	7.8	30.2
Differ from category (+/-)	-1.0	-6.1	-2.1	-6.4	4.2	-3.6	4.3	3.2	-6.8	1.0

PER SHARE DATA

	1994	1993	1992	1991	1990	1989	1988	1987	1986	1985
Dividends, Net Income ($)	0.14	0.18	0.18	0.29	0.34	0.28	0.24	0.20	0.43	0.25
Distrib'ns, Cap Gain ($)	0.31	1.35	0.52	0.86	0.80	0.59	0.98	2.45	2.88	0.60
Net Asset Value ($)	11.36	12.01	12.65	12.20	10.40	11.72	10.27	9.39	11.50	13.82
Expense Ratio (%)	0.54	0.49	0.48	0.46	0.55	0.51	0.55	0.46	0.54	0.60
Net Income to Assets (%)	1.20	1.36	1.51	2.36	2.77	2.38	2.20	1.52	1.49	1.96
Portfolio Turnover (%)	99	72	64	52	73	27	32	43	31	42
Total Assets (Millions $)	1,074	1,137	1,116	957	697	733	622	538	594	665

PORTFOLIO (as of 6/30/94)

Portfolio Manager: Nagorniak - 1990, Husic - 1993, Sauter - 1993, Rands - 1994

Investm't Category: Growth

✔ Cap Gain
  Cap & Income
  Income

  Asset Allocation
  Fund of Funds
  Index
  Sector

✔ Domestic
  Foreign
  Country/Region

  Small Cap
  Socially Conscious
  State Specific

Portfolio: stocks 93%   bonds 0%
convertibles 0%   other 0%   cash 7%

Largest Holdings: computers & services 10%, electronics 9%

Unrealized Net Capital Gains: 4% of portfolio value

SHAREHOLDER INFORMATION

Minimum Investment
Initial: $3,000   Subsequent: $100

Minimum IRA Investment
Initial: $500   Subsequent: $100

Maximum Fees
Load: none   12b-1: none
Other: none

Distributions
Income: Dec   Capital Gains: Dec

Exchange Options
Number Per Year: 2   Fee: none
Telephone: yes (money market fund available)

Services
IRA, pension, auto exchange, auto invest, auto withdraw

Vanguard NJ Tax Free Insured Long (VNJTX)

Tax-Exempt Bond

Vanguard Financial Center
P.O. Box 2600
Valley Forge, PA 19482
(800) 662-7447, (610) 648-6000

PERFORMANCE

fund inception date: 2/3/88

	3yr Annual	5yr Annual	10yr Annual	Bull	Bear
Return (%)	5.4	7.0	na	48.3	-5.6
Differ from Category (+/-)	0.9 high	0.9 high	na	6.5 high	-0.4 av

Total Risk	Standard Deviation	Category Risk	Risk Index	Avg Mat
blw av	6.6%	abv av	1.1	17.2 yrs

	1994	1993	1992	1991	1990	1989	1988	1987	1986	1985
Return (%).	-5.2	13.3	9.3	11.2	7.6	10.4	—	—	—	—
Differ from category (+/-) . .	0.0	1.6	1.0	-0.1	1.3	1.4	—	—	—	—

PER SHARE DATA

	1994	1993	1992	1991	1990	1989	1988	1987	1986	1985
Dividends, Net Income ($).	0.62	0.63	0.66	0.67	0.69	0.71	—	—	—	—
Distrib'ns, Cap Gain ($) . . .	0.00	0.06	0.13	0.01	0.01	0.01	—	—	—	—
Net Asset Value ($)	10.67	11.91	11.15	10.95	10.49	10.42	—	—	—	—
Expense Ratio (%)	0.22	0.20	0.25	0.24	0.25	0.24	—	—	—	—
Net Income to Assets (%) .	5.39	5.47	5.99	6.33	6.73	6.88	—	—	—	—
Portfolio Turnover (%)	11	12	34	18	7	17	—	—	—	—
Total Assets (Millions $) . . .	653	767	572	433	245	129	—	—	—	—

PORTFOLIO (as of 5/31/94)

Portfolio Manager: Ian MacKinnon - 1988

Investm't Category: Tax-Exempt Bond
- Cap Gain
- Cap & Income
- ✔ Income
- ✔ Domestic
- Foreign
- Country/Region
- Asset Allocation
- Fund of Funds
- Index
- Sector
- Small Cap
- Socially Conscious
- ✔ State Specific

Portfolio: stocks 0% bonds 100%
convertibles 0% other 0% cash 0%

Largest Holdings: na

Unrealized Net Capital Gains: 3% of portfolio value

SHAREHOLDER INFORMATION

Minimum Investment
Initial: $3,000   Subsequent: $100

Minimum IRA Investment
Initial: na   Subsequent: na

Maximum Fees
Load: none   12b-1: none
Other: none

Distributions
Income: monthly   Capital Gains: Dec

Exchange Options
Number Per Year: 2   Fee: none
Telephone: yes (money market fund available)

Services
auto exchange, auto invest, auto withdraw

Vanguard NY Insured Tax Free (VNYTX)

Tax-Exempt Bond

Vanguard Financial Center
P.O. Box 2600
Valley Forge, PA 19482
(800) 662-7447, (610) 648-6000

PERFORMANCE

fund inception date: 4/7/86

	3yr Annual	5yr Annual	10yr Annual	Bull	Bear
Return (%)	5.4	7.0	na	49.7	-5.3
Differ from Category (+/-)	0.9 high	0.9 high	na	7.9 high	-0.1 av

Total Risk	Standard Deviation	Category Risk	Risk Index	Avg Mat
blw av	6.6%	abv av	1.1	16.1 yrs

	1994	1993	1992	1991	1990	1989	1988	1987	1986	1985
Return (%)	-5.6	13.0	9.7	12.8	6.2	10.3	11.9	-3.4	—	—
Differ from category (+/-) . .	-0.4	1.3	1.4	1.5	-0.1	1.3	1.7	-2.1	—	—

PER SHARE DATA

	1994	1993	1992	1991	1990	1989	1988	1987	1986	1985
Dividends, Net Income ($) .	0.59	0.59	0.63	0.64	0.63	0.63	0.64	0.63	—	—
Distrib'ns, Cap Gain ($) . . .	0.00	0.01	0.14	0.00	0.00	0.00	0.00	0.00	—	—
Net Asset Value ($)	9.94	11.15	10.42	10.23	9.67	9.72	9.41	9.01	—	—
Expense Ratio (%)	0.22	0.19	0.23	0.27	0.31	0.34	0.40	0.35	—	—
Net Income to Assets (%). .	5.48	5.47	6.11	6.48	6.60	6.64	6.75	6.80	—	—
Portfolio Turnover (%).	20	10	28	19	17	10	4	31	—	—
Total Assets (Millions $) . . .	698	824	574	408	241	168	103	76	—	—

PORTFOLIO (as of 5/31/94)

Portfolio Manager: Ian MacKinnon - 1986

Investm't Category: Tax-Exempt Bond

Cap Gain	Asset Allocation
Cap & Income	Fund of Funds
✔ Income	Index
	Sector
✔ Domestic	Small Cap
Foreign	Socially Conscious
Country/Region	✔ State Specific

Portfolio: stocks 0% bonds 100%
convertibles 0% other 0% cash 0%

Largest Holdings: na

Unrealized Net Capital Gains: 1% of portfolio value

SHAREHOLDER INFORMATION

Minimum Investment
Initial: $3,000 Subsequent: $100

Minimum IRA Investment
Initial: na Subsequent: na

Maximum Fees
Load: none 12b-1: none
Other: none

Distributions
Income: monthly Capital Gains: Dec

Exchange Options
Number Per Year: 2 Fee: none
Telephone: yes (money market fund available)

Services
auto exchange, auto invest, auto withdraw

Vanguard Ohio Tax Free Insured Long (VOHIX)

Tax-Exempt Bond

Vanguard Financial Center
P.O. Box 2600
Valley Forge, PA 19482
(800) 662-7447, (610) 648-6000

PERFORMANCE   fund inception date: 6/18/90

	3yr Annual	5yr Annual	10yr Annual	Bull	Bear
Return (%)	5.4	na	na	47.2	-5.3
Differ from Category (+/-)	0.9 high	na	na	5.4 abv av	-0.1 av

Total Risk	Standard Deviation	Category Risk	Risk Index	Avg Mat
blw av	6.3%	abv av	1.0	17.6 yrs

	1994	1993	1992	1991	1990	1989	1988	1987	1986	1985
Return (%)	-5.1	12.7	9.4	11.9	—	—	—	—	—	—
Differ from category (+/-)	0.1	1.0	1.1	0.6	—	—	—	—	—	—

PER SHARE DATA

	1994	1993	1992	1991	1990	1989	1988	1987	1986	1985
Dividends, Net Income ($).	0.60	0.61	0.63	0.65	—	—	—	—	—	—
Distrib'ns, Cap Gain ($)...	0.00	0.03	0.14	0.00	—	—	—	—	—	—
Net Asset Value ($).....	10.57	11.77	11.03	10.81	—	—	—	—	—	—
Expense Ratio (%).......	0.23	0.21	0.31	0.27	—	—	—	—	—	—
Net Income to Assets (%).	5.18	5.29	5.77	6.20	—	—	—	—	—	—
Portfolio Turnover (%).....	15	10	27	20	—	—	—	—	—	—
Total Assets (Millions $)...	147	173	101	61	—	—	—	—	—	—

PORTFOLIO (as of 5/31/94)

Portfolio Manager: Ian MacKinnon - 1990

Investm't Category: Tax-Exempt Bond

Cap Gain	Asset Allocation
Cap & Income	Fund of Funds
✔ Income	Index
	Sector
✔ Domestic	Small Cap
Foreign	Socially Conscious
Country/Region	✔ State Specific

Portfolio: stocks 0%   bonds 100%
convertibles 0%   other 0%   cash 0%

Largest Holdings: na

Unrealized Net Capital Gains: 0% of portfolio value

SHAREHOLDER INFORMATION

Minimum Investment
Initial: $3,000   Subsequent: $100

Minimum IRA Investment
Initial: na   Subsequent: na

Maximum Fees
Load: none   12b-1: none
Other: none

Distributions
Income: monthly   Capital Gains: Dec

Exchange Options
Number Per Year: 2   Fee: none
Telephone: yes (money market fund available)

Services
auto exchange, auto invest, auto withdraw

Vanguard Penn Tax-Free Insured Long (VPAIX)

Tax-Exempt Bond

Vanguard Financial Center
P.O. Box 2600
Valley Forge, PA 19482
(800) 662-7447, (610) 648-6000

PERFORMANCE

fund inception date: 4/7/86

	3yr Annual	5yr Annual	10yr Annual	Bull	Bear
Return (%)	5.8	7.2	na	48.9	-4.8
Differ from Category (+/-)	1.3 high	1.1 high	na	7.1 high	0.4 abv av

Total Risk	Standard Deviation	Category Risk	Risk Index	Avg Mat
blw av	6.1%	av	1.0	18.4 yrs

	1994	1993	1992	1991	1990	1989	1988	1987	1986	1985
Return (%)	-4.5	12.7	10.1	12.2	6.9	10.5	12.2	-1.2	—	—
Differ from category (+/-) . . .	0.7	1.0	1.8	0.9	0.6	1.5	2.0	0.1	—	—

PER SHARE DATA

	1994	1993	1992	1991	1990	1989	1988	1987	1986	1985
Dividends, Net Income ($) .	0.62	0.63	0.66	0.67	0.68	0.69	0.69	0.68	—	—
Distrib'ns, Cap Gain ($) . . .	0.00	0.08	0.22	0.03	0.01	0.00	0.00	0.00	—	—
Net Asset Value ($)	10.30	11.44	10.80	10.64	10.14	10.15	9.83	9.41	—	—
Expense Ratio (%)	0.21	0.20	0.24	0.25	0.25	0.26	0.33	0.31	—	—
Net Income to Assets (%). .	5.59	5.61	6.17	6.46	6.77	6.87	6.95	7.06	—	—
Portfolio Turnover (%).	19	14	17	2	9	8	3	15	—	—
Total Assets (Millions $) . .	1,299	1,532	1,130	828	556	416	270	194	—	—

PORTFOLIO (as of 5/31/94)

Portfolio Manager: Ian MacKinnon - 1986

Investm't Category: Tax-Exempt Bond

Cap Gain	Asset Allocation
Cap & Income	Fund of Funds
✔ Income	Index
	Sector
✔ Domestic	Small Cap
Foreign	Socially Conscious
Country/Region	✔ State Specific

Portfolio: stocks 0%   bonds 100%
convertibles 0%   other 0%   cash 0%

Largest Holdings: na

Unrealized Net Capital Gains: 2% of portfolio value

SHAREHOLDER INFORMATION

Minimum Investment
Initial: $3,000   Subsequent: $100

Minimum IRA Investment
Initial: na   Subsequent: na

Maximum Fees
Load: none   12b-1: none
Other: none

Distributions
Income: monthly   Capital Gains: Dec

Exchange Options
Number Per Year: 2   Fee: none
Telephone: yes (money market fund available)

Services
auto exchange, auto invest, auto withdraw

Vanguard Preferred Stock (VQIIX)

Growth & Income

Vanguard Financial Center
P.O. Box 2600
Valley Forge, PA 19482
(800) 662-7447, (610) 648-6000

PERFORMANCE

fund inception date: 12/3/76

	3yr Annual	5yr Annual	10yr Annual	Bull	Bear
Return (%)	4.1	7.7	10.7	59.8	-7.2
Differ from Category (+/-)	-3.0 low	-0.2 av	-1.0 blw av	-16.0 blw av	-0.9 blw av

Total Risk	Standard Deviation	Category Risk	Risk Index	Beta
low	4.8%	low	0.6	0.3

	1994	1993	1992	1991	1990	1989	1988	1987	1986	1985
Return (%).	-7.9	13.0	8.4	20.9	6.3	18.7	8.0	-7.7	24.6	29.8
Differ from category (+/-) . .	-6.5	-0.2	-1.8	-6.7	12.3	-2.7	-9.0	-8.3	8.8	4.1

PER SHARE DATA

	1994	1993	1992	1991	1990	1989	1988	1987	1986	1985
Dividends, Net Income ($).	0.65	0.72	0.74	0.73	0.78	0.75	0.78	0.65	0.80	0.89
Distrib'ns, Cap Gain ($) . . .	0.00	0.14	0.00	0.00	0.00	0.00	0.00	0.12	0.05	0.00
Net Asset Value ($)	8.15	9.54	9.23	9.22	8.29	8.56	7.89	8.05	9.52	8.36
Expense Ratio (%)	0.51	0.53	0.58	0.63	0.65	0.67	0.66	0.64	0.58	0.59
Net Income to Assets (%) .	7.27	6.77	7.43	7.96	8.69	9.11	9.40	8.60	9.07	11.01
Portfolio Turnover (%)	27	45	33	18	15	42	52	67	48	34
Total Assets (Millions $) . . .	278	386	187	89	53	63	77	84	153	85

PORTFOLIO (as of 10/31/94)

Portfolio Manager: Earl E. McEvoy - 1982

Investm't Category: Growth & Income
- Cap Gain
- ✔ Cap & Income
- Income
- Asset Allocation
- Fund of Funds
- Index
- Sector
- ✔ Domestic
- Foreign
- Country/Region
- Small Cap
- Socially Conscious
- State Specific

Portfolio: stocks 0%   bonds 1%
convertibles 0%   other 99%   cash 0%

Largest Holdings: preferred stock—utilities 58%, preferred stock—financial 31%

Unrealized Net Capital Gains: -12% of portfolio value

SHAREHOLDER INFORMATION

Minimum Investment
Initial: $3,000   Subsequent: $100

Minimum IRA Investment
Initial: $500   Subsequent: $100

Maximum Fees
Load: none   12b-1: none
Other: none

Distributions
Income: quarterly   Capital Gains: Dec

Exchange Options
Number Per Year: 2   Fee: none
Telephone: yes (money market fund available)

Services
IRA, pension, auto exchange, auto invest, auto withdraw

Vanguard Primecap

(VPMCX)

Growth

Vanguard Financial Center
P.O. Box 2600
Valley Forge, PA 19482
(800) 662-7447, (610) 648-6000

	3yr Annual	5yr Annual	10yr Annual	Bull	Bear
Return (%)	12.7	13.1	15.5	105.4	-4.3
Differ from Category (+/-)	5.0 high	3.5 high	2.6 high	13.3 abv av	2.3 abv av

Total Risk	Standard Deviation	Category Risk	Risk Index	Beta
abv av	11.1%	abv av	1.1	1.1

	1994	1993	1992	1991	1990	1989	1988	1987	1986	1985
Return (%)	11.4	18.0	8.9	33.1	-2.7	21.5	14.6	-2.3	23.5	35.7
Differ from category (+/-) . .	12.0	4.6	-2.7	-2.6	3.0	-4.6	-3.4	-4.1	8.9	6.5

PER SHARE DATA

	1994	1993	1992	1991	1990	1989	1988	1987	1986	1985
Dividends, Net Income ($)	0.12	0.07	0.12	0.15	0.13	0.16	0.14	0.10	0.14	0.01
Distrib'ns, Cap Gain ($) . . .	0.41	0.59	0.41	0.68	0.12	0.61	0.21	0.24	0.18	0.00
Net Asset Value ($)	19.98	18.42	16.19	15.36	12.21	12.82	11.19	10.06	10.64	8.89
Expense Ratio (%)	0.68	0.67	0.68	0.68	0.75	0.74	0.83	0.83	0.82	0.98
Net Income to Assets (%). .	0.65	0.44	0.84	1.09	1.06	1.35	0.83	0.91	1.00	1.44
Portfolio Turnover (%)	8	16	7	24	11	15	26	21	15	14
Total Assets (Millions $) . .	1,553	815	646	486	305	279	186	165	33	13

PORTFOLIO (as of 6/30/94)

Portfolio Manager: Howard Schow - 1984

Investm't Category: Growth

- ✔ Cap Gain
- Cap & Income
- Income
- ✔ Domestic
- Foreign
- Country/Region

- Asset Allocation
- Fund of Funds
- Index
- Sector
- Small Cap
- Socially Conscious
- State Specific

Portfolio: stocks 83% bonds 0%
convertibles 0% other 0% cash 17%

Largest Holdings: technology 35%, transport & services 12%

Unrealized Net Capital Gains: 20% of portfolio value

SHAREHOLDER INFORMATION

Minimum Investment
Initial: $10,000   Subsequent: $1,000

Minimum IRA Investment
Initial: $500   Subsequent: $100

Maximum Fees
Load: none   12b-1: none
Other: none

Distributions
Income: Dec   Capital Gains: Dec

Exchange Options
Number Per Year: 2   Fee: none
Telephone: yes (money market fund available)

Services
IRA, pension, auto exchange, auto invest, auto withdraw

Vanguard Quantitative Port (VQNPX)

Growth & Income

Vanguard Financial Center
P.O. Box 2600
Valley Forge, PA 19482
(800) 662-7447, (610) 648-6000

PERFORMANCE

fund inception date: 12/10/86

	3yr Annual	5yr Annual	10yr Annual	Bull	Bear
Return (%)	6.5	8.9	na	79.1	-7.3
Differ from Category (+/-)	-0.6 av	1.0 abv av	na	3.3 av	-1.0 blw av

Total Risk	Standard Deviation	Category Risk	Risk Index	Beta
av	8.2%	av	1.0	1.0

	1994	1993	1992	1991	1990	1989	1988	1987	1986	1985
Return (%)..............	-0.6	13.8	7.0	30.2	-2.4	31.9	16.7	4.0	—	—
Differ from category (+/-) ..	0.8	0.6	-3.2	2.6	3.6	10.5	-0.3	3.4	—	—

PER SHARE DATA

	1994	1993	1992	1991	1990	1989	1988	1987	1986	1985
Dividends, Net Income ($).	0.39	0.39	0.44	0.47	0.47	0.47	0.35	0.25	—	—
Distrib'ns, Cap Gain ($) ...	0.40	1.69	0.71	0.44	0.04	0.00	0.00	0.06	—	—
Net Asset Value ($)	15.56	16.45	16.30	16.32	13.29	14.14	11.08	9.80	—	—
Expense Ratio (%)	0.51	0.50	0.40	0.43	0.48	0.53	0.64	0.64	—	—
Net Income to Assets (%) .	2.50	2.34	2.67	2.95	3.34	3.35	3.38	2.79	—	—
Portfolio Turnover (%)	65	85	51	61	81	78	50	73	—	—
Total Assets (Millions $) ...	596	539	415	335	211	175	144	149	—	—

PORTFOLIO (as of 6/30/94)

Portfolio Manager: John Nagorniak - 1986

Investm't Category: Growth & Income

Cap Gain	Asset Allocation
✔ Cap & Income	Fund of Funds
Income	Index
	Sector
✔ Domestic	Small Cap
Foreign	Socially Conscious
Country/Region	State Specific

Portfolio: stocks 97%   bonds 0%
convertibles 0%   other 0%   cash 3%

Largest Holdings: na

Unrealized Net Capital Gains: 2% of portfolio value

SHAREHOLDER INFORMATION

Minimum Investment
Initial: $3,000   Subsequent: $100

Minimum IRA Investment
Initial: $500   Subsequent: $100

Maximum Fees
Load: none   12b-1: none
Other: none

Distributions
Income: Jul, Dec   Capital Gains: Dec

Exchange Options
Number Per Year: 2   Fee: none
Telephone: none

Services
IRA, pension, auto exchange, auto invest, auto withdraw

Vanguard Short-Term Corporate (VFSTX)

Corporate Bond

Vanguard Financial Center
P.O. Box 2600
Valley Forge, PA 19482
(800) 662-7447, (610) 648-6000

PERFORMANCE

fund inception date: 10/29/82

	3yr Annual	5yr Annual	10yr Annual	Bull	Bear
Return (%)	4.6	7.2	8.4	34.8	-1.7
Differ from Category (+/-)	-1.3 blw av	-0.6 low	-1.1 low	-15.0 low	2.6 abv av

Total Risk	Standard Deviation	Category Risk	Risk Index	Avg Mat
low	2.4%	blw av	0.8	2.0 yrs

	1994	1993	1992	1991	1990	1989	1988	1987	1986	1985
Return (%)	0.0	7.0	7.1	13.0	9.2	11.4	6.9	4.4	11.3	14.8
Differ from category (+/-)	2.4	-4.4	-1.8	-4.1	4.4	2.1	-2.2	2.3	-3.5	-4.9

PER SHARE DATA

	1994	1993	1992	1991	1990	1989	1988	1987	1986	1985
Dividends, Net Income ($)	0.59	0.61	0.70	0.81	0.88	0.89	0.83	0.76	0.88	1.01
Distrib'ns, Cap Gain ($)	0.00	0.10	0.16	0.00	0.00	0.00	0.00	0.18	0.00	0.00
Net Asset Value ($)	10.30	10.90	10.86	10.97	10.47	10.43	10.20	10.33	10.82	10.55
Expense Ratio (%)	0.29	0.27	0.26	0.31	0.34	0.34	0.33	0.38	0.49	0.62
Net Income to Assets (%)	5.51	6.33	7.44	8.48	8.70	8.17	7.36	7.79	9.50	11.26
Portfolio Turnover (%)	70	71	99	107	121	165	258	278	460	270
Total Assets (Millions $)	2,905	3,473	1,912	829	597	493	429	401	198	119

PORTFOLIO (as of 7/31/94)

Portfolio Manager: Ian MacKinnon - 1982

Investm't Category: Corporate Bond
   Cap Gain   Asset Allocation
   Cap & Income   Fund of Funds
✔ Income   Index
                        Sector
✔ Domestic   Small Cap
   Foreign   Socially Conscious
   Country/Region   State Specific

Portfolio: stocks 0%   bonds 99%
convertibles 0%   other 0%   cash 1%

Largest Holdings: industrial 21%, finance—diversified 14%

Unrealized Net Capital Gains: -1% of portfolio value

SHAREHOLDER INFORMATION

Minimum Investment
Initial: $3,000   Subsequent: $100

Minimum IRA Investment
Initial: $500   Subsequent: $100

Maximum Fees
Load: none   12b-1: none
Other: none

Distributions
Income: monthly   Capital Gains: Dec

Exchange Options
Number Per Year: 2   Fee: none
Telephone: yes (money market fund available)

Services
IRA, pension, auto exchange, auto invest, auto withdraw

Vanguard Short-Term Federal (VSGBX)

General Bond

Vanguard Financial Center
P.O. Box 2600
Valley Forge, PA 19482
(800) 662-7447, (610) 648-6000

PERFORMANCE

fund inception date: 12/31/87

	3yr Annual	5yr Annual	10yr Annual	Bull	Bear
Return (%)	4.0	6.6	na	33.0	-2.1
Differ from Category (+/-)	-0.3 blw av	-0.3 blw av	na	-8.0 low	1.7 abv av

Total Risk	Standard Deviation	Category Risk	Risk Index	Avg Mat
low	2.5%	blw av	0.6	1.9 yrs

	1994	1993	1992	1991	1990	1989	1988	1987	1986	1985
Return (%).	-0.9	6.9	6.1	12.1	9.3	11.3	5.7	—	—	—
Differ from category (+/-) . .	1.1	-2.3	-0.5	-2.5	2.1	-0.1	-1.7	—	—	—

PER SHARE DATA

	1994	1993	1992	1991	1990	1989	1988	1987	1986	1985
Dividends, Net Income ($).	0.54	0.53	0.62	0.74	0.81	0.84	0.80	—	—	—
Distrib'ns, Cap Gain ($) . . .	0.01	0.11	0.16	0.07	0.00	0.00	0.00	—	—	—
Net Asset Value ($)	9.69	10.34	10.27	10.43	10.06	9.98	9.76	—	—	—
Expense Ratio (%)	0.29	0.27	0.26	0.30	0.28	0.32	0.00	—	—	—
Net Income to Assets (%) .	5.41	5.88	6.98	8.06	8.59	8.50	0.00	—	—	—
Portfolio Turnover (%)	50	70	111	141	133	228	0	—	—	—
Total Assets (Millions $) .	1,504	1,919	1,275	508	228	159	6	—	—	—

PORTFOLIO (as of 7/31/94)

Portfolio Manager: Ian MacKinnon - 1987

Investm't Category: General Bond

Cap Gain	Asset Allocation
Cap & Income	Fund of Funds
✔ Income	Index
	Sector
✔ Domestic	Small Cap
Foreign	Socially Conscious
Country/Region	State Specific

Portfolio: stocks 0%   bonds 94%
convertibles 0%   other 0%   cash 6%

Largest Holdings: U.S. government & agencies 55%, mortgage-backed 39%

Unrealized Net Capital Gains: -1% of portfolio value

SHAREHOLDER INFORMATION

Minimum Investment
Initial: $3,000   Subsequent: $100

Minimum IRA Investment
Initial: $500   Subsequent: $100

Maximum Fees
Load: none   12b-1: none
Other: none

Distributions
Income: monthly   Capital Gains: Dec

Exchange Options
Number Per Year: 2   Fee: none
Telephone: yes (money market fund available)

Services
IRA, pension, auto exchange, auto invest, auto withdraw

Vanguard Short-Term Muni Bond (VWSTX)

Tax-Exempt Bond

Vanguard Financial Center
P.O. Box 2600
Valley Forge, PA 19482
(800) 662-7447, (610) 648-6000

PERFORMANCE

fund inception date: 9/1/77

	3yr Annual	5yr Annual	10yr Annual	Bull	Bear
Return (%)	3.3	4.7	5.4	19.3	0.2
Differ from Category (+/-)	-1.2 low	-1.4 low	-2.7 low	-22.5 low	5.4 high

Total Risk	Standard Deviation	Category Risk	Risk Index	Avg Mat
low	0.9%	low	0.1	1.2 yrs

	1994	1993	1992	1991	1990	1989	1988	1987	1986	1985
Return (%)	1.6	3.8	4.7	7.1	6.5	7.0	5.6	4.1	7.3	6.9
Differ from category (+/-)	6.8	-7.9	-3.6	-4.2	0.2	-2.0	-4.6	5.4	-9.1	-10.5

PER SHARE DATA

	1994	1993	1992	1991	1990	1989	1988	1987	1986	1985
Dividends, Net Income ($)	0.55	0.58	0.67	0.82	0.91	0.90	0.81	0.77	0.87	0.95
Distrib'ns, Cap Gain ($)	0.00	0.02	0.04	0.06	0.00	0.00	0.00	0.10	0.01	0.00
Net Asset Value ($)	15.34	15.63	15.64	15.63	15.43	15.36	15.21	15.19	15.44	15.22
Expense Ratio (%)	0.20	0.20	0.23	0.25	0.25	0.27	0.29	0.26	0.33	0.39
Net Income to Assets (%)	3.42	3.88	4.58	5.55	5.90	5.77	5.13	5.12	5.81	6.47
Portfolio Turnover (%)	27	46	60	104	78	54	113	12	57	55
Total Assets (Millions $)	1,463	1,443	1,061	840	751	700	841	1,105	906	536

PORTFOLIO (as of 8/31/94)

Portfolio Manager: Ian MacKinnon - 1981

Investm't Category: Tax-Exempt Bond

Cap Gain	Asset Allocation
Cap & Income	Fund of Funds
✔ Income	Index
	Sector
✔ Domestic	Small Cap
Foreign	Socially Conscious
Country/Region	State Specific

Portfolio: stocks 0% bonds 100%
convertibles 0% other 0% cash 0%

Largest Holdings: na

Unrealized Net Capital Gains: 0% of portfolio value

SHAREHOLDER INFORMATION

Minimum Investment
Initial: $3,000 Subsequent: $100

Minimum IRA Investment
Initial: na Subsequent: na

Maximum Fees
Load: none 12b-1: none
Other: none

Distributions
Income: monthly Capital Gains: Nov

Exchange Options
Number Per Year: 2 Fee: none
Telephone: yes (money market fund available)

Services
auto exchange, auto invest, auto withdraw

Vanguard Short-Term US Treasury (VFISX)

Government Bond

Vanguard Financial Center
P.O. Box 2600
Valley Forge, PA 19482
(800) 662-7447, (610) 648-6000

PERFORMANCE

fund inception date: 10/28/91

	3yr Annual	5yr Annual	10yr Annual	Bull	Bear
Return (%)	4.1	na	na	na	-1.9
Differ from Category (+/-)	0.1 av	na	na	na	4.5 abv av

Total Risk	Standard Deviation	Category Risk	Risk Index	Avg Mat
low	2.4%	low	0.5	2.1 yrs

	1994	1993	1992	1991	1990	1989	1988	1987	1986	1985
Return (%)	-0.6	6.3	6.7	—	—	—	—	—	—	—
Differ from category (+/-)	4.2	-4.6	0.3	—	—	—	—	—	—	—

PER SHARE DATA

	1994	1993	1992	1991	1990	1989	1988	1987	1986	1985
Dividends, Net Income ($)	0.52	0.49	0.53	—	—	—	—	—	—	—
Distrib'ns, Cap Gain ($)	0.02	0.08	0.04	—	—	—	—	—	—	—
Net Asset Value ($)	9.79	10.39	10.31	—	—	—	—	—	—	—
Expense Ratio (%)	0.29	0.26	0.26	—	—	—	—	—	—	—
Net Income to Assets (%)	4.94	5.12	5.22	—	—	—	—	—	—	—
Portfolio Turnover (%)	130	71	40	—	—	—	—	—	—	—
Total Assets (Millions $)	703	704	102	—	—	—	—	—	—	—

PORTFOLIO (as of 7/31/94)

Portfolio Manager: Ian MacKinnon - 1991

Investm't Category: Government Bond

Cap Gain	Asset Allocation
Cap & Income	Fund of Funds
✔ Income	Index
	Sector
✔ Domestic	Small Cap
Foreign	Socially Conscious
Country/Region	State Specific

Portfolio: stocks 0% bonds 98%
convertibles 0% other 0% cash 2%

Largest Holdings: U.S. government & agencies 98%

Unrealized Net Capital Gains: 1% of portfolio value

SHAREHOLDER INFORMATION

Minimum Investment
Initial: $3,000   Subsequent: $100

Minimum IRA Investment
Initial: $500   Subsequent: $100

Maximum Fees
Load: none   12b-1: none
Other: none

Distributions
Income: monthly   Capital Gains: Dec

Exchange Options
Number Per Year: 2   Fee: none
Telephone: yes (money market fund available)

Services
IRA, pension, auto exchange, auto invest, auto withdraw

Vanguard Spec Port—Energy (VGENX)

Growth

Vanguard Financial Center
P.O. Box 2600
Valley Forge, PA 19482
(800) 662-7447, (610) 648-6000

PERFORMANCE

fund inception date: 5/23/84

	3yr Annual	5yr Annual	10yr Annual	Bull	Bear
Return (%)	9.7	5.4	12.0	30.7	0.1
Differ from Category (+/-)	2.0 abv av	-4.2 low	-0.9 blw av	-61.4 low	6.7 high

Total Risk	Standard Deviation	Category Risk	Risk Index	Beta
high	15.2%	high	1.6	1.1

	1994	1993	1992	1991	1990	1989	1988	1987	1986	1985
Return (%)	-1.6	26.5	6.1	0.2	-1.3	43.4	21.3	6.1	12.6	14.4
Differ from category (+/-) . .	-1.0	13.1	-5.5	-35.5	4.4	17.3	3.3	4.3	-2.0	-14.8

PER SHARE DATA

	1994	1993	1992	1991	1990	1989	1988	1987	1986	1985
Dividends, Net Income ($) .	0.24	0.29	0.36	0.42	0.46	0.36	0.37	0.76	0.44	0.14
Distrib'ns, Cap Gain ($) . . .	0.29	1.38	0.18	0.42	0.88	0.57	0.00	1.41	0.05	0.08
Net Asset Value ($)	14.29	15.06	13.28	13.03	13.84	15.40	11.39	9.69	11.18	10.46
Expense Ratio (%)	0.19	0.21	0.30	0.35	0.38	0.40	0.38	0.65	0.92	0.55
Net Income to Assets (%). .	1.67	2.47	2.78	3.24	3.05	3.07	3.70	3.43	4.40	3.75
Portfolio Turnover (%).	12	37	42	40	44	46	84	34	156	34
Total Assets (Millions $) . . .	445	250	124	114	80	44	36	29	2	1

PORTFOLIO (as of 7/31/94)

Portfolio Manager: Ernst Von Metzsch - 1984

Investm't Category: Growth

✔ Cap Gain	Asset Allocation
Cap & Income	Fund of Funds
Income	Index
	✔ Sector
✔ Domestic	Small Cap
✔ Foreign	Socially Conscious
Country/Region	State Specific

Portfolio: stocks 94%   bonds 0%
convertibles 0%   other 0%   cash 6%

Largest Holdings: foreign energy 24%, domestic integrated oil 21%

Unrealized Net Capital Gains: 5% of portfolio value

SHAREHOLDER INFORMATION

Minimum Investment
Initial: $3,000   Subsequent: $100

Minimum IRA Investment
Initial: $500   Subsequent: $100

Maximum Fees
Load: 1.00% redemption   12b-1: none
Other: redemption fee applies for 1 year

Distributions
Income: Dec   Capital Gains: Dec

Exchange Options
Number Per Year: 3   Fee: none
Telephone: yes (money market fund available)

Services
IRA, pension, auto exchange, auto invest, auto withdraw

Vanguard Spec Port—Gold & PM (VGPMX)

Gold

Vanguard Financial Center
P.O. Box 2600
Valley Forge, PA 19482
(800) 662-7447, (610) 648-6000

PERFORMANCE

fund inception date: 5/23/84

	3yr Annual	5yr Annual	10yr Annual	Bull	Bear
Return (%)	13.7	4.2	10.5	49.0	-6.5
Differ from Category (+/-)	2.9 high	4.2 high	5.3 high	16.1 high	3.5 high

Total Risk	Standard Deviation	Category Risk	Risk Index	Beta
high	25.1%	low	0.9	0.4

	1994	1993	1992	1991	1990	1989	1988	1987	1986	1985
Return (%)	-5.4	93.3	-19.4	4.3	-19.9	30.3	-14.2	38.7	49.8	-5.0
Differ from category (+/-)	6.1	6.4	-3.7	9.1	2.6	5.6	4.7	6.8	12.2	2.4

PER SHARE DATA

	1994	1993	1992	1991	1990	1989	1988	1987	1986	1985
Dividends, Net Income ($)	0.31	0.21	0.18	0.25	0.32	0.34	0.26	0.48	0.21	0.06
Distrib'ns, Cap Gain ($)	0.00	0.00	0.00	0.00	0.00	0.00	0.00	1.14	0.00	0.00
Net Asset Value ($)	12.72	13.78	7.24	9.21	9.07	11.73	9.27	11.11	9.22	6.33
Expense Ratio (%)	0.24	0.36	0.35	0.42	0.45	0.48	0.47	0.59	0.73	0.87
Net Income to Assets (%)	2.08	2.50	2.54	2.78	3.01	2.67	2.71	3.36	3.86	3.25
Portfolio Turnover (%)	7	2	3	10	17	18	44	32	40	11
Total Assets (Millions $)	639	586	178	144	223	126	128	70	30	6

PORTFOLIO (as of 7/31/94)

Portfolio Manager: David Hutchins - 1987

Investm't Category: Gold

✔ Cap Gain   Asset Allocation
   Cap & Income   Fund of Funds
   Income   Index
           ✔ Sector
✔ Domestic   Small Cap
✔ Foreign   Socially Conscious
   Country/Region   State Specific

Portfolio: stocks 89%   bonds 0%
convertibles 0%   other 6%   cash 5%

Largest Holdings: South African gold mining companies 35%, North American gold mining companies 27%

Unrealized Net Capital Gains: 17% of portfolio value

SHAREHOLDER INFORMATION

Minimum Investment
Initial: $3,000   Subsequent: $100

Minimum IRA Investment
Initial: $500   Subsequent: $100

Maximum Fees
Load: 1.00% redemption   12b-1: none
Other: redemption fee applies for 1 year

Distributions
Income: Dec   Capital Gains: Dec

Exchange Options
Number Per Year: 3   Fee: none
Telephone: yes (money market fund available)

Services
IRA, pension, auto exchange, auto invest, auto withdraw

Vanguard Spec Port— Health Care (VGHCX)

Growth

Vanguard Financial Center
P.O. Box 2600
Valley Forge, PA 19482
(800) 662-7447, (610) 648-6000

PERFORMANCE

fund inception date: 5/23/84

	3yr Annual	5yr Annual	10yr Annual	Bull	Bear
Return (%)	6.4	15.5	19.9	97.2	-8.6
Differ from Category (+/-)	-1.3 blw av	5.9 high	7.0 high	5.1 abv av	-2.0 blw av

Total Risk	Standard Deviation	Category Risk	Risk Index	Beta
high	12.9%	high	1.3	1.1

	1994	1993	1992	1991	1990	1989	1988	1987	1986	1985
Return (%)	9.5	11.8	-1.5	46.3	16.7	32.9	28.3	-0.5	21.4	45.7
Differ from category (+/-)	10.1	-1.6	-13.1	10.6	22.4	6.8	10.3	-2.3	6.8	16.5

PER SHARE DATA

	1994	1993	1992	1991	1990	1989	1988	1987	1986	1985
Dividends, Net Income ($)	0.57	0.76	0.70	0.53	0.55	0.49	0.34	0.57	0.13	0.07
Distrib'ns, Cap Gain ($)	2.31	1.97	1.20	0.53	0.84	0.72	1.29	1.39	0.80	0.11
Net Asset Value ($)	35.47	35.07	34.01	36.50	25.69	23.21	18.43	15.70	17.64	15.31
Expense Ratio (%)	0.25	0.22	0.30	0.36	0.39	0.62	0.51	0.61	0.83	0.59
Net Income to Assets (%)	1.84	2.06	1.98	2.54	2.34	1.85	1.65	1.47	1.52	2.41
Portfolio Turnover (%)	27	15	7	17	28	19	41	27	59	23
Total Assets (Millions $)	708	602	553	190	76	58	54	49	22	2

PORTFOLIO (as of 7/31/94)

Portfolio Manager: Edward Owens - 1984

Investm't Category: Growth

✔ Cap Gain	Asset Allocation
Cap & Income	Fund of Funds
Income	Index
	✔ Sector
✔ Domestic	Small Cap
✔ Foreign	Socially Conscious
Country/Region	State Specific

Portfolio: stocks 97% bonds 0%
convertibles 0% other 0% cash 3%

Largest Holdings: major pharmaceuticals 26%, international pharmaceuticals 19%

Unrealized Net Capital Gains: 13% of portfolio value

SHAREHOLDER INFORMATION

Minimum Investment
Initial: $3,000   Subsequent: $100

Minimum IRA Investment
Initial: $500   Subsequent: $100

Maximum Fees
Load: 1.00% redemption   12b-1: none
Other: redemption fee applies for 1 year

Distributions
Income: Dec   Capital Gains: Dec

Exchange Options
Number Per Year: 3   Fee: none
Telephone: yes (money market fund available)

Services
IRA, pension, auto exchange, auto invest, auto withdraw

Vanguard Spec Port— Utilities Income (VGSUX)

Growth & Income

Vanguard Financial Center
P.O. Box 2600
Valley Forge, PA 19482
(800) 662-7447, (610) 648-6000

PERFORMANCE

fund inception date: 5/15/92

	3yr Annual	5yr Annual	10yr Annual	Bull	Bear
Return (%)	na	na	na	na	-9.4
Differ from Category (+/-)	na	na	na	na	-3.1 low

Total Risk	Standard Deviation	Category Risk	Risk Index	Beta
na	na	na	na	na

	1994	1993	1992	1991	1990	1989	1988	1987	1986	1985
Return (%).............	-8.5	15.0	—	—	—	—	—	—	—	—
Differ from category (+/-) . .	-7.1	1.8	—	—	—	—	—	—	—	—

PER SHARE DATA

	1994	1993	1992	1991	1990	1989	1988	1987	1986	1985
Dividends, Net Income ($).	0.59	0.56	—	—	—	—	—	—	—	—
Distrib'ns, Cap Gain ($) . . .	0.12	0.40	—	—	—	—	—	—	—	—
Net Asset Value ($)	9.94	11.63	—	—	—	—	—	—	—	—
Expense Ratio (%)	0.44	0.45	—	—	—	—	—	—	—	—
Net Income to Assets (%) .	5.15	4.70	—	—	—	—	—	—	—	—
Portfolio Turnover (%)	41	20	—	—	—	—	—	—	—	—
Total Assets (Millions $) . . .	560	781	—	—	—	—	—	—	—	—

PORTFOLIO (as of 7/31/94)

Portfolio Manager: John R. Ryan - 1992

Investm't Category: Growth & Income
Cap Gain	Asset Allocation
✔ Cap & Income	Fund of Funds
Income	Index
	✔ Sector
✔ Domestic	Small Cap
✔ Foreign	Socially Conscious
Country/Region	State Specific

Portfolio: stocks 79% bonds 20%
convertibles 0% other 0% cash 1%

Largest Holdings: telephone 33%, electric 32%

Unrealized Net Capital Gains: -7% of portfolio value

SHAREHOLDER INFORMATION

Minimum Investment
Initial: $3,000   Subsequent: $100

Minimum IRA Investment
Initial: $500   Subsequent: $100

Maximum Fees
Load: none   12b-1: none
Other: none

Distributions
Income: quarterly   Capital Gains: Dec

Exchange Options
Number Per Year: 3   Fee: none
Telephone: yes (money market fund available)

Services
IRA, pension, auto exchange, auto invest, auto withdraw

Vanguard Star (VGSTX)

Balanced

Vanguard Financial Center
P.O. Box 2600
Valley Forge, PA 19482
(800) 662-7447, (610) 648-6000

PERFORMANCE

fund inception date: 3/29/84

	3yr Annual	5yr Annual	10yr Annual	Bull	Bear
Return (%)	6.9	7.9	na	68.0	-4.5
Differ from Category (+/-)	0.5 abv av	-0.1 blw av	na	3.0 av	1.2 abv av

Total Risk	Standard Deviation	Category Risk	Risk Index	Beta
blw av	5.5%	blw av	0.9	0.6

	1994	1993	1992	1991	1990	1989	1988	1987	1986	1985
Return (%)	-0.2	10.8	10.5	24.0	-3.6	18.7	18.9	1.6	13.7	—
Differ from category (+/-) . . .	1.7	-2.6	2.2	0.6	-3.1	1.4	7.1	-0.8	-3.7	—

PER SHARE DATA

	1994	1993	1992	1991	1990	1989	1988	1987	1986	1985
Dividends, Net Income ($)	0.52	0.47	0.51	0.62	0.73	0.77	0.69	0.85	0.86	—
Distrib'ns, Cap Gain ($) . . .	0.25	0.40	0.18	0.37	0.16	0.38	0.03	0.75	0.71	—
Net Asset Value ($)	12.61	13.41	12.89	12.29	10.73	12.05	11.12	9.98	11.34	—
Expense Ratio (%)	0.00	0.00	0.00	0.00	0.00	0.00	0.00	0.00	0.00	—
Net Income to Assets (%). .	3.29	3.67	4.36	5.48	6.65	6.42	5.87	6.08	6.08	—
Portfolio Turnover (%).	6	3	3	11	12	7	21	0	17	—
Total Assets (Millions $) . .	3,766	3,664	2,490	1,575	1,039	949	682	568	567	—

PORTFOLIO (as of 6/30/94)

Portfolio Manager: committee

Investm't Category: Balanced

Cap Gain	Asset Allocation
✔ Cap & Income	✔ Fund of Funds
Income	Index
	Sector
✔ Domestic	Small Cap
Foreign	Socially Conscious
Country/Region	State Specific

Portfolio: stocks 63% bonds 25%
convertibles 0% other 0% cash 12%

Largest Holdings: Vanguard Windsor II 42%, Vanguard Long Term Corporate 12%

Unrealized Net Capital Gains: 3% of portfolio value

SHAREHOLDER INFORMATION

Minimum Investment
Initial: $500   Subsequent: $100

Minimum IRA Investment
Initial: $500   Subsequent: $100

Maximum Fees
Load: none   12b-1: none
Other: none

Distributions
Income: Jul, Dec   Capital Gains: Dec

Exchange Options
Number Per Year: 2   Fee: none
Telephone: yes (money market fund available)

Services
IRA, pension, auto exchange, auto invest, auto withdraw

Vanguard Total Bond Market Port (VBMFX)

General Bond

Vanguard Financial Center
P.O. Box 2600
Valley Forge, PA 19482
(800) 662-7447, (610) 648-6000

PERFORMANCE

fund inception date: 12/11/86

	3yr Annual	5yr Annual	10yr Annual	Bull	Bear
Return (%)	4.5	7.4	na	44.5	-5.0
Differ from Category (+/-)	0.2 av	0.5 abv av	na	3.5 abv av	-1.2 blw av

Total Risk	Standard Deviation	Category Risk	Risk Index	Avg Mat
low	3.8%	av	1.0	8.9 yrs

	1994	1993	1992	1991	1990	1989	1988	1987	1986	1985
Return (%)	-2.6	9.6	7.1	15.2	8.6	13.6	7.3	1.5	—	—
Differ from category (+/-)	-0.6	0.4	0.5	0.6	1.4	2.2	-0.1	-0.7	—	—

PER SHARE DATA

	1994	1993	1992	1991	1990	1989	1988	1987	1986	1985
Dividends, Net Income ($)	0.62	0.64	0.70	0.77	0.80	0.80	0.81	0.87	—	—
Distrib'ns, Cap Gain ($)	0.00	0.12	0.09	0.02	0.00	0.00	0.00	0.00	—	—
Net Asset Value ($)	9.17	10.06	9.88	9.99	9.41	9.44	9.05	9.20	—	—
Expense Ratio (%)	0.18	0.18	0.20	0.16	0.21	0.24	0.30	0.14	—	—
Net Income to Assets (%)	6.28	6.24	7.06	7.95	8.60	8.49	8.84	9.01	—	—
Portfolio Turnover (%)	50	50	49	31	29	33	21	77	—	—
Total Assets (Millions $)	1,730	1,559	1,067	849	277	139	58	43	—	—

PORTFOLIO (as of 6/30/94)

Portfolio Manager: Ian MacKinnon - 1986

Investm't Category: General Bond

Cap Gain	Asset Allocation
Cap & Income	Fund of Funds
✔ Income	✔ Index
	Sector
✔ Domestic	Small Cap
Foreign	Socially Conscious
Country/Region	State Specific

Portfolio: stocks 0%   bonds 99%
convertibles 0%   other 0%   cash 1%

Largest Holdings: Lehman Brothers aggregate bond index

Unrealized Net Capital Gains: -2% of portfolio value

SHAREHOLDER INFORMATION

Minimum Investment
Initial: $3,000   Subsequent: $100

Minimum IRA Investment
Initial: $500   Subsequent: $100

Maximum Fees
Load: none   12b-1: none
Other: $10 account maintenance fee

Distributions
Income: monthly   Capital Gains: Dec

Exchange Options
Number Per Year: 2   Fee: none
Telephone: yes (money market fund available)

Services
IRA, pension, auto exchange, auto invest, auto withdraw

Vanguard Trustees' Equity—Int'l (VTRIX)

International Stock

Vanguard Financial Center
P.O. Box 2600
Valley Forge, PA 19482
(800) 662-7447, (610) 648-6000

PERFORMANCE

fund inception date: 5/16/83

	3yr Annual	5yr Annual	10yr Annual	Bull	Bear
Return (%)	7.8	3.8	16.8	45.8	-0.7
Differ from Category (+/-)	-1.3 blw av	-1.1 blw av	1.6 av	-18.1 low	6.3 high

Total Risk	Standard Deviation	Category Risk	Risk Index	Beta
abv av	11.9%	blw av	0.9	0.6

	1994	1993	1992	1991	1990	1989	1988	1987	1986	1985
Return (%)	5.2	30.4	-8.7	9.9	-12.2	25.9	18.6	23.8	50.7	40.3
Differ from category (+/-)	8.2	-8.2	-5.8	-3.2	-1.8	3.4	4.2	9.4	-8.3	-2.1

PER SHARE DATA

	1994	1993	1992	1991	1990	1989	1988	1987	1986	1985
Dividends, Net Income ($)	0.56	0.81	0.67	0.77	0.95	0.79	0.99	0.75	1.03	0.93
Distrib'ns, Cap Gain ($)	0.63	0.00	0.28	0.61	1.01	2.08	4.58	18.32	6.55	2.54
Net Asset Value ($)	31.48	31.04	24.44	27.78	26.58	32.44	28.27	28.66	38.68	30.91
Expense Ratio (%)	0.32	0.40	0.42	0.38	0.44	0.46	0.51	0.50	0.52	0.56
Net Income to Assets (%)	2.09	1.76	2.48	2.87	3.62	2.61	2.55	2.44	2.65	3.11
Portfolio Turnover (%)	na	39	51	46	18	25	14	48	24	29
Total Assets (Millions $)	1,053	1,008	679	878	796	646	467	657	718	581

PORTFOLIO (as of 6/30/94)

Portfolio Manager: Debra Miller - 1994

Investm't Category: International Stock

Cap Gain	Asset Allocation
✔ Cap & Income	Fund of Funds
Income	Index
	Sector
Domestic	Small Cap
✔ Foreign	Socially Conscious
Country/Region	State Specific

Portfolio: stocks 98% bonds 0%
convertibles 0% other 0% cash 2%

Largest Holdings: Japan 39%, United Kingdom 7%

Unrealized Net Capital Gains: 17% of portfolio value

SHAREHOLDER INFORMATION

Minimum Investment
Initial: $10,000   Subsequent: $1,000

Minimum IRA Investment
Initial: $500   Subsequent: $100

Maximum Fees
Load: none   12b-1: none
Other: none

Distributions
Income: quarterly   Capital Gains: Dec

Exchange Options
Number Per Year: 2   Fee: none
Telephone: yes (money market fund available)

Services
IRA, pension, auto exchange, auto invest, auto withdraw

Vanguard Trustees' Equity—US (VTRSX)

Growth & Income

Vanguard Financial Center
P.O. Box 2600
Valley Forge, PA 19482
(800) 662-7447, (610) 648-6000

PERFORMANCE

fund inception date: 1/31/80

	3yr Annual	5yr Annual	10yr Annual	Bull	Bear
Return (%)	6.2	6.8	11.1	80.3	-10.6
Differ from Category (+/-)	-0.9 av	-1.1 blw av	-0.6 blw av	4.5 abv av	-4.3 low

Total Risk	Standard Deviation	Category Risk	Risk Index	Beta
abv av	9.6%	high	1.2	1.0

	1994	1993	1992	1991	1990	1989	1988	1987	1986	1985
Return (%).	-3.9	17.2	6.4	26.5	-8.3	17.1	24.6	1.6	15.2	20.5
Differ from category (+/-) . .	-2.5	4.0	-3.8	-1.1	-2.3	-4.3	7.6	1.0	-0.6	-5.2

PER SHARE DATA

	1994	1993	1992	1991	1990	1989	1988	1987	1986	1985
Dividends, Net Income ($).	0.34	0.43	0.67	0.71	1.08	0.88	0.97	0.72	1.16	1.45
Distrib'ns, Cap Gain ($) . . .	0.03	2.16	0.86	0.00	0.00	3.81	1.00	5.88	6.15	4.10
Net Asset Value ($)	29.09	30.65	28.43	28.20	22.90	26.15	26.35	22.77	28.68	31.15
Expense Ratio (%)	0.76	0.90	0.65	0.44	0.52	0.51	0.58	0.52	0.52	0.48
Net Income to Assets (%) .	0.99	1.43	2.33	2.67	4.18	2.90	3.86	2.77	3.46	4.42
Portfolio Turnover (%)	na	139	209	84	81	72	90	44	19	23
Total Assets (Millions $) . . .	112	119	68	115	100	121	115	122	162	201

PORTFOLIO (as of 6/30/94)

Portfolio Manager: John Geewax - 1992

Investm't Category: Growth & Income

Cap Gain	Asset Allocation
✔ Cap & Income	Fund of Funds
Income	Index
	Sector
✔ Domestic	Small Cap
Foreign	Socially Conscious
Country/Region	State Specific

Portfolio: stocks 98%   bonds 0%
convertibles 0%   other 0%   cash 2%

Largest Holdings: consumer cyclical 21%, technology 17%

Unrealized Net Capital Gains: 1% of portfolio value

SHAREHOLDER INFORMATION

Minimum Investment
Initial: $10,000   Subsequent: $1,000

Minimum IRA Investment
Initial: $500   Subsequent: $100

Maximum Fees
Load: none   12b-1: none
Other: none

Distributions
Income: quarterly   Capital Gains: Dec

Exchange Options
Number Per Year: 2   Fee: none
Telephone: yes (money market fund available)

Services
IRA, pension, auto exchange, auto invest, auto withdraw

Vanguard US Growth

(VWUSX)

Growth

Vanguard Financial Center
P.O. Box 2600
Valley Forge, PA 19482
(800) 662-7447, (610) 648-6000

PERFORMANCE

fund inception date: 1/6/59

	3yr Annual	5yr Annual	10yr Annual	Bull	Bear
Return (%)	1.7	10.0	12.8	67.4	-5.2
Differ from Category (+/-)	-6.0 low	0.4 abv av	-0.1 abv av	-24.7 low	1.4 abv av

Total Risk	Standard Deviation	Category Risk	Risk Index	Beta
av	7.8%	low	0.8	0.8

	1994	1993	1992	1991	1990	1989	1988	1987	1986	1985
Return (%)	3.8	-1.4	2.7	46.7	4.6	37.6	8.7	-6.0	7.8	36.5
Differ from category (+/-) . . .	4.4	-14.8	-8.9	11.0	10.3	11.5	-9.3	-7.8	-6.8	7.3

PER SHARE DATA

	1994	1993	1992	1991	1990	1989	1988	1987	1986	1985
Dividends, Net Income ($) .	0.18	0.21	0.18	0.19	0.19	0.13	0.06	0.31	0.28	0.26
Distrib'ns, Cap Gain ($) . . .	0.00	0.00	0.08	0.00	0.00	0.00	0.00	3.26	1.94	0.82
Net Asset Value ($)	15.33	14.93	15.36	15.20	10.49	10.21	7.51	6.96	10.32	11.69
Expense Ratio (%)	0.52	0.49	0.49	0.56	0.74	0.95	0.88	0.65	0.80	1.04
Net Income to Assets (%). .	1.30	1.50	1.52	1.82	1.77	1.44	1.23	2.41	2.27	2.10
Portfolio Turnover (%)	47	37	24	30	49	48	38	142	77	61
Total Assets (Millions $) . .	2,109	1,821	1,441	747	339	184	130	184	187	211

PORTFOLIO (as of 8/31/94)

Portfolio Manager: J. Parker Hall III - 1987

Investm't Category: Growth

✔ Cap Gain	Asset Allocation
Cap & Income	Fund of Funds
Income	Index
	Sector
✔ Domestic	Small Cap
Foreign	Socially Conscious
Country/Region	State Specific

Portfolio: stocks 91% bonds 0%
convertibles 0% other 0% cash 9%

Largest Holdings: technology 19%, financial 17%

Unrealized Net Capital Gains: 15% of portfolio value

SHAREHOLDER INFORMATION

Minimum Investment
Initial: $3,000   Subsequent: $100

Minimum IRA Investment
Initial: $500   Subsequent: $100

Maximum Fees
Load: none   12b-1: none
Other: none

Distributions
Income: Dec   Capital Gains: Dec

Exchange Options
Number Per Year: 2   Fee: none
Telephone: yes (money market fund available)

Services
IRA, pension, auto exchange, auto invest, auto withdraw

Vanguard Wellesley Income (VWINX)

Balanced

Vanguard Financial Center
P.O. Box 2600
Valley Forge, PA 19482
(800) 662-7447, (610) 648-6000

PERFORMANCE

fund inception date: 7/1/70

	3yr Annual	5yr Annual	10yr Annual	Bull	Bear
Return (%)	6.0	8.4	11.7	65.2	-6.5
Differ from Category (+/-)	-0.4 av	0.4 av	0.4 abv av	0.2 av	-0.8 blw av

Total Risk	Standard Deviation	Category Risk	Risk Index	Beta
blw av	6.2%	abv av	1.0	0.6

	1994	1993	1992	1991	1990	1989	1988	1987	1986	1985
Return (%).............	-4.4	14.6	8.7	21.4	3.7	20.8	13.5	-1.8	18.3	27.3
Differ from category (+/-) ..	-2.5	1.2	0.4	-2.0	4.2	3.5	1.7	-4.2	0.9	3.0

PER SHARE DATA

	1994	1993	1992	1991	1990	1989	1988	1987	1986	1985
Dividends, Net Income ($).	1.11	1.14	1.21	1.27	1.30	1.31	1.23	1.04	1.33	1.38
Distrib'ns, Cap Gain ($) ...	0.24	0.40	0.21	0.00	0.08	0.24	0.00	0.38	0.47	0.10
Net Asset Value ($).....	17.05	19.24	18.16	18.07	16.02	16.82	15.26	14.57	16.27	15.31
Expense Ratio (%)	0.35	0.33	0.35	0.40	0.45	0.45	0.51	0.49	0.58	0.60
Net Income to Assets (%) .	5.94	5.79	6.50	7.08	7.77	7.68	8.14	7.83	7.74	9.36
Portfolio Turnover (%)	na	21	21	28	23	23	20	40	30	21
Total Assets (Millions $) .	5,680	6,092	3,178	1,935	1,022	788	567	495	510	224

PORTFOLIO (as of 6/30/94)

Portfolio Manager: Earl McEvoy - 1982, John Ryan - 1987

Investm't Category: Balanced
Cap Gain	Asset Allocation
✔ Cap & Income	Fund of Funds
Income	Index
	Sector
✔ Domestic	Small Cap
Foreign	Socially Conscious
Country/Region	State Specific

Portfolio: stocks 35% bonds 61%
convertibles 2% other 0% cash 2%

Largest Holdings: bonds—utility 16%, bonds—U.S. government & agencies 11%

Unrealized Net Capital Gains: -2% of portfolio value

SHAREHOLDER INFORMATION

Minimum Investment
Initial: $3,000   Subsequent: $100

Minimum IRA Investment
Initial: $500   Subsequent: $100

Maximum Fees
Load: none   12b-1: none
Other: none

Distributions
Income: quarterly   Capital Gains: Dec

Exchange Options
Number Per Year: 2   Fee: none
Telephone: yes (money market fund available)

Services
IRA, pension, auto exchange, auto invest, auto withdraw

Vanguard Wellington

(VWELX)

Balanced

Vanguard Financial Center
P.O. Box 2600
Valley Forge, PA 19482
(800) 662-7447, (610) 648-6000

PERFORMANCE

fund inception date: 7/1/29

	3yr Annual	5yr Annual	10yr Annual	Bull	Bear
Return (%)	6.8	7.9	12.4	68.8	-5.5
Differ from Category (+/-)	0.4 av	-0.1 blw av	1.1 abv av	3.8 abv av	0.2 av

Total Risk	Standard Deviation	Category Risk	Risk Index	Beta
blw av	6.5%	abv av	1.0	0.8

	1994	1993	1992	1991	1990	1989	1988	1987	1986	1985
Return (%)	-0.4	13.5	7.9	23.8	-2.9	21.6	16.1	2.2	18.4	28.5
Differ from category (+/-) . . .	1.5	0.1	-0.4	0.4	-2.4	4.3	4.3	-0.2	1.0	4.2

PER SHARE DATA

	1994	1993	1992	1991	1990	1989	1988	1987	1986	1985
Dividends, Net Income ($) .	0.88	0.92	0.94	0.96	1.01	1.02	0.96	0.98	0.94	0.92
Distrib'ns, Cap Gain ($) . . .	0.03	0.38	0.16	0.23	0.00	0.60	0.58	0.14	0.34	0.30
Net Asset Value ($)	19.39	20.40	19.16	18.81	16.24	17.78	16.01	15.15	15.85	14.50
Expense Ratio (%)	0.39	0.34	0.33	0.35	0.43	0.42	0.47	0.43	0.53	0.64
Net Income to Assets (%). .	4.21	4.55	4.98	5.39	5.99	5.77	5.88	5.56	5.88	6.84
Portfolio Turnover (%).	41	34	24	35	33	30	28	27	25	27
Total Assets (Millions $) . .	8,809	8,221	5,358	3,473	2,317	2,035	1,528	1,274	1,102	778

PORTFOLIO (as of 5/31/94)

Portfolio Manager: Vincent Bajakian - 1972, Paul Kaplan - 1994

Investm't Category: Balanced

Cap Gain	Asset Allocation
✔ Cap & Income	Fund of Funds
Income	Index
	Sector
✔ Domestic	Small Cap
✔ Foreign	Socially Conscious
Country/Region	State Specific

Portfolio: stocks 64%   bonds 33%
convertibles 2%   other 0%   cash 1%

Largest Holdings: stocks—banks & finance 10%, stocks—energy 9%

Unrealized Net Capital Gains: 11% of portfolio value

SHAREHOLDER INFORMATION

Minimum Investment
Initial: $3,000   Subsequent: $100

Minimum IRA Investment
Initial: $500   Subsequent: $100

Maximum Fees
Load: none   12b-1: none
Other: none

Distributions
Income: quarterly   Capital Gains: Dec

Exchange Options
Number Per Year: 2   Fee: none
Telephone: yes (money market fund available)

Services
IRA, pension, auto exchange, auto invest, auto withdraw

Vanguard Windsor

(VWNDX)

Growth & Income

Vanguard Financial Center
P.O. Box 2600
Valley Forge, PA 19482
(800) 662-7447, (610) 648-6000

this fund is closed to new investors

PERFORMANCE

fund inception date: 10/23/58

	3yr Annual	5yr Annual	10yr Annual	Bull	Bear
Return (%)	11.5	8.5	13.2	104.4	-3.9
Differ from Category (+/-)	4.4 high	0.6 av	1.5 abv av	28.6 high	2.4 high

Total Risk	Standard Deviation	Category Risk	Risk Index	Beta
abv av	9.8%	high	1.2	1.0

	1994	1993	1992	1991	1990	1989	1988	1987	1986	1985
Return (%)	-0.1	19.3	16.4	28.5	-15.5	15.0	28.6	1.2	20.2	28.0
Differ from category (+/-)	1.3	6.1	6.2	0.9	-9.5	-6.4	11.6	0.6	4.4	2.3

PER SHARE DATA

	1994	1993	1992	1991	1990	1989	1988	1987	1986	1985
Dividends, Net Income ($)	0.44	0.37	0.49	0.57	0.74	0.75	0.63	0.87	0.85	0.79
Distrib'ns, Cap Gain ($)	0.86	0.89	0.38	0.84	0.32	0.85	0.55	2.21	2.59	0.74
Net Asset Value ($)	12.59	13.91	12.74	11.72	10.30	13.41	13.07	11.11	13.95	14.50
Expense Ratio (%)	0.47	0.40	0.26	0.30	0.37	0.41	0.46	0.43	0.52	0.53
Net Income to Assets (%)	2.72	2.68	3.89	4.84	5.82	5.07	5.08	4.86	5.28	6.19
Portfolio Turnover (%)	38	25	32	36	21	34	24	46	51	23
Total Assets (Millions $)	10,672	10,417	8,249	7,860	5,838	8,313	5,921	4,849	4,862	3,814

PORTFOLIO (as of 4/30/94)

Portfolio Manager: John C. Neff - 1964

Investm't Category: Growth & Income
Cap Gain	Asset Allocation
✔ Cap & Income	Fund of Funds
Income	Index
	Sector
✔ Domestic	Small Cap
Foreign	Socially Conscious
Country/Region	State Specific

Portfolio: stocks 82%   bonds 1%
convertibles 1%   other 0%   cash 16%

Largest Holdings: banks 22%, oil & gas 18%

Unrealized Net Capital Gains: 5% of portfolio value

SHAREHOLDER INFORMATION

Minimum Investment
Initial: $10,000   Subsequent: $100

Minimum IRA Investment
Initial: $500   Subsequent: $100

Maximum Fees
Load: none   12b-1: none
Other: none

Distributions
Income: May, Dec   Capital Gains: Dec

Exchange Options
Number Per Year: 2   Fee: none
Telephone: yes (money market fund available)

Services
IRA, pension, auto exchange, auto invest, auto withdraw

Vanguard Windsor II
(VWNFX)
Growth & Income

Vanguard Financial Center
P.O. Box 2600
Valley Forge, PA 19482
(800) 662-7447, (610) 648-6000

PERFORMANCE

fund inception date: 6/24/85

	3yr Annual	5yr Annual	10yr Annual	Bull	Bear
Return (%)	7.9	7.8	na	85.0	-5.1
Differ from Category (+/-)	0.8 abv av	-0.1 av	na	9.2 abv av	1.2 abv av

Total Risk	Standard Deviation	Category Risk	Risk Index	Beta
av	7.7%	blw av	0.9	0.9

	1994	1993	1992	1991	1990	1989	1988	1987	1986	1985
Return (%)	-1.1	13.6	11.9	28.6	-9.9	27.8	24.7	-2.0	21.3	—
Differ from category (+/-) . . .	0.3	0.4	1.7	1.0	-3.9	6.4	7.7	-2.6	5.5	—

PER SHARE DATA

	1994	1993	1992	1991	1990	1989	1988	1987	1986	1985
Dividends, Net Income ($) .	0.55	0.51	0.52	0.61	0.73	0.74	0.57	0.61	0.43	—
Distrib'ns, Cap Gain ($) . . .	0.47	0.50	0.22	0.44	0.28	0.61	0.00	0.80	0.52	—
Net Asset Value ($)	15.82	17.04	15.91	14.89	12.46	14.96	12.81	10.75	12.39	—
Expense Ratio (%)	0.38	0.39	0.41	0.48	0.52	0.53	0.58	0.49	0.65	—
Net Income to Assets (%). .	3.10	3.11	3.72	4.51	4.93	5.29	4.94	4.11	4.33	—
Portfolio Turnover (%).	24	26	23	41	20	22	25	46	50	—
Total Assets (Millions $). .	7,958	7,467	4,879	3,297	2,087	2,161	1,486	1,323	813	—

PORTFOLIO (as of 4/30/94)

Portfolio Manager: Barrow - 1985, Ulrich - 1991, Tukman - 1991, Sauter - 1991

Investm't Category: Growth & Income
- Cap Gain
- ✔ Cap & Income
- Income
- Asset Allocation
- Fund of Funds
- Index
- Sector
- Small Cap
- Socially Conscious
- State Specific
- ✔ Domestic
- Foreign
- Country/Region

Portfolio: stocks 92% bonds 0% convertibles 0% other 0% cash 8%

Largest Holdings: banks 12%, oil 11%

Unrealized Net Capital Gains: 8% of portfolio value

SHAREHOLDER INFORMATION

Minimum Investment
Initial: $3,000   Subsequent: $100

Minimum IRA Investment
Initial: $500   Subsequent: $100

Maximum Fees
Load: none   12b-1: none
Other: none

Distributions
Income: May, Dec   Capital Gains: Dec

Exchange Options
Number Per Year: 2   Fee: none
Telephone: yes (money market fund available)

Services
IRA, pension, auto exchange, auto invest, auto withdraw

Vista Bond (TRBDX)
General Bond

P.O. Box 419392
Kansas City, MO 64179
(800) 348-4782

PERFORMANCE

fund inception date: 11/30/90

	3yr Annual	5yr Annual	10yr Annual	Bull	Bear
Return (%)	4.6	na	na	na	-5.2
Differ from Category (+/-)	0.3 abv av	na	na	na	-1.4 blw av

Total Risk	Standard Deviation	Category Risk	Risk Index	Avg Mat
low	4.2%	av	1.1	8.4 yrs

	1994	1993	1992	1991	1990	1989	1988	1987	1986	1985
Return (%).	-3.1	10.3	7.1	15.0	—	—	—	—	—	—
Differ from category (+/-) . .	-1.1	1.1	0.5	0.4	—	—	—	—	—	—

PER SHARE DATA

	1994	1993	1992	1991	1990	1989	1988	1987	1986	1985
Dividends, Net Income ($).	0.67	0.68	0.80	0.73	—	—	—	—	—	—
Distrib'ns, Cap Gain ($) . . .	0.02	0.08	0.08	0.01	—	—	—	—	—	—
Net Asset Value ($)	9.99	11.03	10.70	10.84	—	—	—	—	—	—
Expense Ratio (%)	0.31	0.31	0.30	0.29	—	—	—	—	—	—
Net Income to Assets (%) .	6.05	6.15	7.20	7.30	—	—	—	—	—	—
Portfolio Turnover (%)	na	20	31	35	—	—	—	—	—	—
Total Assets (Millions $)	50	57	41	37	—	—	—	—	—	—

PORTFOLIO (as of 4/30/94)

Portfolio Manager: Mark Buonaugurio - 1992

Investm't Category: General Bond

Cap Gain	Asset Allocation
Cap & Income	Fund of Funds
✔ Income	Index
	Sector
✔ Domestic	Small Cap
Foreign	Socially Conscious
Country/Region	State Specific

Portfolio: stocks 0% bonds 94%
convertibles 0% other 0% cash 6%

Largest Holdings: U.S. government 63%, corporate 24%

Unrealized Net Capital Gains: 0% of portfolio value

SHAREHOLDER INFORMATION

Minimum Investment
Initial: $2,500 Subsequent: $100

Minimum IRA Investment
Initial: $250 Subsequent: $25

Maximum Fees
Load: none 12b-1: 0.25%
Other: none

Distributions
Income: monthly Capital Gains: Jul, Dec

Exchange Options
Number Per Year: no limit Fee: none
Telephone: yes (money market fund available)

Services
IRA, pension, auto invest, auto withdraw

Vista Equity (TREQX)

Growth

P.O. Box 419392
Kansas City, MO 64179
(800) 348-4782

	3yr Annual	5yr Annual	10yr Annual	Bull	Bear
Return (%)	4.6	na	na	na	-6.3
Differ from Category (+/-)	-3.1 blw av	na	na	na	0.3 av

Total Risk	Standard Deviation	Category Risk	Risk Index	Beta
av	7.7%	low	0.8	1.0

	1994	1993	1992	1991	1990	1989	1988	1987	1986	1985
Return (%)	0.2	8.6	5.3	31.2	—	—	—	—	—	—
Differ from category (+/-)	0.8	-4.8	-6.3	-4.5	—	—	—	—	—	—

PER SHARE DATA

	1994	1993	1992	1991	1990	1989	1988	1987	1986	1985
Dividends, Net Income ($)	0.31	0.31	0.35	0.24	—	—	—	—	—	—
Distrib'ns, Cap Gain ($)	2.66	0.76	0.44	0.11	—	—	—	—	—	—
Net Asset Value ($)	10.06	13.00	12.96	13.12	—	—	—	—	—	—
Expense Ratio (%)	0.31	0.31	0.30	0.28	—	—	—	—	—	—
Net Income to Assets (%)	2.17	2.30	2.29	2.81	—	—	—	—	—	—
Portfolio Turnover (%)	na	33	14	19	—	—	—	—	—	—
Total Assets (Millions $)	48	117	92	95	—	—	—	—	—	—

PORTFOLIO (as of 4/30/94)

Portfolio Manager: Mark Tincher - 1993

Investm't Category: Growth

✔ Cap Gain	Asset Allocation
Cap & Income	Fund of Funds
Income	Index
	Sector
✔ Domestic	Small Cap
Foreign	Socially Conscious
Country/Region	State Specific

Portfolio: stocks 90%   bonds 0%
convertibles 1%   other 0%   cash 9%

Largest Holdings: oil & gas 9%, banking 6%

Unrealized Net Capital Gains: 9% of portfolio value

SHAREHOLDER INFORMATION

Minimum Investment
Initial: $2,500   Subsequent: $100

Minimum IRA Investment
Initial: $250   Subsequent: $25

Maximum Fees
Load: none   12b-1: 0.25%
Other: none

Distributions
Income: Jun, Dec   Capital Gains: Jun, Dec

Exchange Options
Number Per Year: no limit   Fee: none
Telephone: yes (money market fund available)

Services
IRA, pension, auto invest, auto withdraw

Vista Short-Term Bond
(TRSBX)
General Bond

P.O. Box 419392
Kansas City, MO 64179
(800) 348-4782

PERFORMANCE   fund inception date: 11/30/90

	3yr Annual	5yr Annual	10yr Annual	Bull	Bear
Return (%)	3.9	na	na	na	0.1
Differ from Category (+/-)	-0.4 blw av	na	na	na	3.9 high

Total Risk	Standard Deviation	Category Risk	Risk Index	Avg Mat
low	1.0%	low	0.2	1.0 yrs

	1994	1993	1992	1991	1990	1989	1988	1987	1986	1985
Return (%).	2.3	4.5	4.9	9.1	—	—	—	—	—	—
Differ from category (+/-) . .	4.3	-4.7	-1.7	-5.5	—	—	—	—	—	—

PER SHARE DATA

	1994	1993	1992	1991	1990	1989	1988	1987	1986	1985
Dividends, Net Income ($).	0.47	0.52	0.64	0.63	—	—	—	—	—	—
Distrib'ns, Cap Gain ($) . . .	0.00	0.00	0.00	0.00	—	—	—	—	—	—
Net Asset Value ($)	9.87	10.11	10.18	10.33	—	—	—	—	—	—
Expense Ratio (%)	0.31	0.31	0.30	0.29	—	—	—	—	—	—
Net Income to Assets (%) .	4.47	5.25	6.12	6.56	—	—	—	—	—	—
Portfolio Turnover (%)	na	17	29	1	—	—	—	—	—	—
Total Assets (Millions $)	33	67	71	71	—	—	—	—	—	—

PORTFOLIO (as of 4/30/94)

Portfolio Manager: Linda Struble - 1991

Investm't Category: General Bond

Cap Gain	Asset Allocation
Cap & Income	Fund of Funds
✔ Income	Index
	Sector
✔ Domestic	Small Cap
Foreign	Socially Conscious
Country/Region	State Specific

Portfolio: stocks 0%   bonds 88%
convertibles 0%   other 0%   cash 12%

Largest Holdings: corporate 48%, U.S. government 22%

Unrealized Net Capital Gains: 0% of portfolio value

SHAREHOLDER INFORMATION

Minimum Investment
Initial: $2,500   Subsequent: $100

Minimum IRA Investment
Initial: $250   Subsequent: $25

Maximum Fees
Load: none   12b-1: 0.25%
Other: none

Distributions
Income: monthly   Capital Gains: Jul, Dec

Exchange Options
Number Per Year: no limit   Fee: none
Telephone: yes (money market fund available)

Services
IRA, pension, auto invest, auto withdraw

Volumetric (VOLMX)
Growth

87 Violet Dr.
Pearl River, NY 10965
(800) 541-3863, (914) 623-7637

fund inception date: 9/3/87

PERFORMANCE

	3yr Annual	5yr Annual	10yr Annual	Bull	Bear
Return (%)	3.4	7.2	na	67.7	-9.3
Differ from Category (+/-)	-4.3 low	-2.4 blw av	na	-24.4 blw av	-2.7 blw av

Total Risk	Standard Deviation	Category Risk	Risk Index	Beta
abv av	9.3%	av	1.0	0.9

	1994	1993	1992	1991	1990	1989	1988	1987	1986	1985
Return (%)	-2.0	2.0	10.7	34.9	-5.0	15.9	19.9	—	—	—
Differ from category (+/-) . .	-1.4	-11.4	-0.9	-0.8	0.7	-10.2	1.9	—	—	—

PER SHARE DATA

	1994	1993	1992	1991	1990	1989	1988	1987	1986	1985
Dividends, Net Income ($) .	0.03	0.08	0.12	0.17	0.10	0.25	0.12	—	—	—
Distrib'ns, Cap Gain ($) . . .	1.40	0.63	1.11	0.00	1.24	0.69	0.00	—	—	—
Net Asset Value ($)	14.35	16.09	16.48	16.11	12.11	14.10	13.10	—	—	—
Expense Ratio (%)	1.99	2.00	2.01	2.03	2.02	2.07	2.09	—	—	—
Net Income to Assets (%) . .	0.13	0.12	0.66	0.90	1.49	0.82	1.98	—	—	—
Portfolio Turnover (%)	170	176	125	149	194	188	203	—	—	—
Total Assets (Millions $)	11	12	10	7	5	5	3	—	—	—

PORTFOLIO (as of 6/30/94)

Portfolio Manager: Gabriel Gibs - 1978

Investm't Category: Growth
- ✔ Cap Gain
- Cap & Income
- Income
- ✔ Domestic
- Foreign
- Country/Region
- Asset Allocation
- Fund of Funds
- Index
- Sector
- Small Cap
- Socially Conscious
- State Specific

Portfolio: stocks 67% bonds 0%
convertibles 0% other 0% cash 33%

Largest Holdings: drugs 5%, consumer products 4%

Unrealized Net Capital Gains: 1% of portfolio value

SHAREHOLDER INFORMATION

Minimum Investment
Initial: $500   Subsequent: $200

Minimum IRA Investment
Initial: $500   Subsequent: $200

Maximum Fees
Load: none   12b-1: none
Other: none

Distributions
Income: Jan   Capital Gains: Jan

Exchange Options
Number Per Year: none   Fee:
Telephone:

Services
IRA, pension

Vontobel EuroPacific

(VNEPX)

International Stock

450 Park Avenue
New York, NY 10022
(800) 527-9500, (212) 415-7000

PERFORMANCE — fund inception date: 7/6/90

	3yr Annual	5yr Annual	10yr Annual	Bull	Bear
Return (%)	9.1	na	na	86.1	-9.7
Differ from Category (+/-)	0.0 av	na	na	22.2 high	-2.7 blw av

Total Risk	Standard Deviation	Category Risk	Risk Index	Beta
high	12.7%	av	1.0	0.9

	1994	1993	1992	1991	1990	1989	1988	1987	1986	1985
Return (%).............	-5.3	40.8	-2.3	18.7	—	—	—	—	—	—
Differ from category (+/-) ...	-2.3	2.2	0.6	5.6	—	—	—	—	—	—

PER SHARE DATA

	1994	1993	1992	1991	1990	1989	1988	1987	1986	1985
Dividends, Net Income ($).	0.08	0.00	0.14	0.00	—	—	—	—	—	—
Distrib'ns, Cap Gain ($) ...	0.00	0.00	0.00	0.00	—	—	—	—	—	—
Net Asset Value ($)......	16.23	17.22	12.23	12.67	—	—	—	—	—	—
Expense Ratio (%)	1.64	1.77	1.98	2.71	—	—	—	—	—	—
Net Income to Assets (%) .	0.53	0.85	0.79	0.02	—	—	—	—	—	—
Portfolio Turnover (%)	na	10	27	3	—	—	—	—	—	—
Total Assets (Millions $) ...	138	138	47	25	—	—	—	—	—	—

PORTFOLIO (as of 6/30/94)

Portfolio Manager: Fabrizio Pieralini - 1994

Investm't Category: International Stock

✔ Cap Gain	Asset Allocation
Cap & Income	Fund of Funds
Income	Index
	Sector
Domestic	Small Cap
✔ Foreign	Socially Conscious
✔ Country/Region	State Specific

Portfolio: stocks 95% bonds 0%
convertibles 0% other 3% cash 2%

Largest Holdings: Japan 20%, Korea 6%

Unrealized Net Capital Gains: 17% of portfolio value

SHAREHOLDER INFORMATION

Minimum Investment
Initial: $1,000   Subsequent: $100

Minimum IRA Investment
Initial: $1,000   Subsequent: $100

Maximum Fees
Load: none   12b-1: none
Other: none

Distributions
Income: Dec   Capital Gains: Dec

Exchange Options
Number Per Year: no limit   Fee: none
Telephone: yes (money market fund not available)

Services
IRA, auto invest, auto withdraw

Vontobel US Value

(VUSVX)

Growth

450 Park Avenue
New York, NY 10022
(800) 527-9500, (212) 415-7000

	3yr Annual	5yr Annual	10yr Annual	Bull	Bear
Return (%)	7.1	na	na	86.5	-2.7
Differ from Category (+/-)	-0.6 av	na	na	-5.6 av	3.9 high

Total Risk	Standard Deviation	Category Risk	Risk Index	Beta
av	8.4%	blw av	0.9	0.9

	1994	1993	1992	1991	1990	1989	1988	1987	1986	1985
Return (%)	0.0	6.0	15.9	37.2	—	—	—	—	—	—
Differ from category (+/-) . . .	0.6	-7.4	4.3	1.5	—	—	—	—	—	—

PER SHARE DATA

	1994	1993	1992	1991	1990	1989	1988	1987	1986	1985
Dividends, Net Income ($) .	0.25	0.08	0.17	0.06	—	—	—	—	—	—
Distrib'ns, Cap Gain ($) . . .	2.14	0.00	0.99	0.74	—	—	—	—	—	—
Net Asset Value ($)	10.26	12.64	12.00	11.36	—	—	—	—	—	—
Expense Ratio (%)	1.78	1.82	1.96	2.54	—	—	—	—	—	—
Net Income to Assets (%). .	0.61	1.23	0.76	0.92	—	—	—	—	—	—
Portfolio Turnover (%).	na	137	100	166	—	—	—	—	—	—
Total Assets (Millions $)	30	33	31	22	—	—	—	—	—	—

PORTFOLIO (as of 6/30/94)

Portfolio Manager: Ed Walzack - 1990

Investm't Category: Growth

✔ Cap Gain	Asset Allocation
Cap & Income	Fund of Funds
Income	Index
	Sector
✔ Domestic	Small Cap
Foreign	Socially Conscious
Country/Region	State Specific

Portfolio: stocks 85%   bonds 0%
convertibles 0%   other 0%   cash 15%

Largest Holdings: insurance 23%, banking 14%

Unrealized Net Capital Gains: -1% of portfolio value

SHAREHOLDER INFORMATION

Minimum Investment
Initial: $1,000   Subsequent: $100

Minimum IRA Investment
Initial: $1,000   Subsequent: $100

Maximum Fees
Load: none   12b-1: none
Other: none

Distributions
Income: Dec   Capital Gains: Dec

Exchange Options
Number Per Year: no limit   Fee: none
Telephone: yes (money market fund not available)

Services
IRA, auto invest, auto withdraw

Warburg Pincus Cap Appreciation (CUCAX)

Growth

466 Lexington Ave., 10 Fl.
New York, NY 10017
(800) 257-5614, (212) 878-0600

	3yr Annual	5yr Annual	10yr Annual	Bull	Bear
Return (%)	6.5	7.6	na	70.8	-8.7
Differ from Category (+/-)	-1.2 blw av	-2.0 blw av	na	-21.3 blw av	-2.1 blw av

Total Risk	Standard Deviation	Category Risk	Risk Index	Beta
abv av	9.7%	av	1.0	1.1

	1994	1993	1992	1991	1990	1989	1988	1987	1986	1985
Return (%)	-2.8	15.8	7.6	26.2	-5.4	26.7	21.3	—	—	—
Differ from category (+/-)	-2.2	2.4	-4.0	-9.5	0.3	0.6	3.3	—	—	—

PER SHARE DATA

	1994	1993	1992	1991	1990	1989	1988	1987	1986	1985
Dividends, Net Income ($)	0.00	0.07	0.05	0.11	0.22	0.35	0.20	—	—	—
Distrib'ns, Cap Gain ($)	0.98	1.19	0.76	0.05	0.00	0.24	0.14	—	—	—
Net Asset Value ($)	12.66	14.06	13.24	13.06	10.48	11.31	9.39	—	—	—
Expense Ratio (%)	1.02	1.01	1.06	1.08	1.04	1.10	1.07	—	—	—
Net Income to Assets (%)	0.62	0.30	0.41	1.27	2.07	1.90	2.00	—	—	—
Portfolio Turnover (%)	53	48	56	40	37	37	33	—	—	—
Total Assets (Millions $)	153	169	118	115	77	57	29	—	—	—

PORTFOLIO (as of 4/30/94)

Portfolio Manager: Susan L. Black - 1994,
George U. Wyper - 1994

Investm't Category: Growth

✔ Cap Gain   Asset Allocation
   Cap & Income   Fund of Funds
   Income   Index
      Sector
✔ Domestic   Small Cap
✔ Foreign   Socially Conscious
   Country/Region   State Specific

Portfolio: stocks 94%   bonds 0%
convertibles 0%   other 0%   cash 6%

Largest Holdings: financial services 10%, communications & media 7%

Unrealized Net Capital Gains: 12% of portfolio value

SHAREHOLDER INFORMATION

Minimum Investment
Initial: $2,500   Subsequent: $500

Minimum IRA Investment
Initial: $500   Subsequent: $500

Maximum Fees
Load: none   12b-1: none
Other: none

Distributions
Income: Jun, Dec   Capital Gains: Dec

Exchange Options
Number Per Year: 36   Fee: none
Telephone: yes (money market fund available)

Services
IRA, pension, auto exchange, auto invest, auto withdraw

Warburg Pincus
Emerging Grth (CUEGX)

466 Lexington Ave., 10 Fl.
New York, NY 10017
(800) 257-5614, (212) 878-0600

Aggressive Growth

PERFORMANCE

fund inception date: 1/31/88

	3yr Annual	5yr Annual	10yr Annual	Bull	Bear
Return (%)	9.2	12.9	na	128.0	-12.8
Differ from Category (+/-)	0.3 av	0.4 av	na	-5.2 av	-2.0 blw av

Total Risk	Standard Deviation	Category Risk	Risk Index	Beta
high	13.5%	av	0.9	0.9

	1994	1993	1992	1991	1990	1989	1988	1987	1986	1985
Return (%)	-1.4	18.1	12.1	56.1	-9.8	21.7	—	—	—	—
Differ from category (+/-)	-0.7	-1.4	1.1	4.0	-3.6	-5.1	—	—	—	—

PER SHARE DATA

	1994	1993	1992	1991	1990	1989	1988	1987	1986	1985
Dividends, Net Income ($)	0.00	0.00	0.00	0.18	0.13	0.39	—	—	—	—
Distrib'ns, Cap Gain ($)	0.00	1.36	0.37	0.20	0.00	0.16	—	—	—	—
Net Asset Value ($)	21.99	22.31	20.07	18.23	11.92	13.36	—	—	—	—
Expense Ratio (%)	1.20	1.23	1.24	1.25	1.25	1.25	—	—	—	—
Net Income to Assets (%)	-0.59	-0.60	-0.25	0.32	1.05	1.38	—	—	—	—
Portfolio Turnover (%)	61	68	63	98	107	100	—	—	—	—
Total Assets (Millions $)	290	213	100	42	23	27	—	—	—	—

PORTFOLIO (as of 4/30/94)

Portfolio Manager: Elizabeth Dater - 1988,
Stephen Lurito - 1993

Investm't Category: Aggressive Growth

✔ Cap Gain	Asset Allocation
Cap & Income	Fund of Funds
Income	Index
	Sector
✔ Domestic	✔ Small Cap
✔ Foreign	Socially Conscious
Country/Region	State Specific

Portfolio: stocks 92% bonds 0%
convertibles 1% other 0% cash 7%

Largest Holdings: business services 9%, electronics 7%

Unrealized Net Capital Gains: 8% of portfolio value

SHAREHOLDER INFORMATION

Minimum Investment
Initial: $2,500   Subsequent: $500

Minimum IRA Investment
Initial: $500   Subsequent: $500

Maximum Fees
Load: none   12b-1: none
Other: none

Distributions
Income: Jun, Dec   Capital Gains: Dec

Exchange Options
Number Per Year: 36   Fee: none
Telephone: yes (money market fund available)

Services
IRA, pension, auto exchange, auto invest, auto withdraw

Warburg Pincus Fixed Income (CUFIX)

466 Lexington Ave., 10 Fl.
New York, NY 10017
(800) 257-5614, (212) 878-0600

General Bond

PERFORMANCE

fund inception date: 8/17/87

	3yr Annual	5yr Annual	10yr Annual	Bull	Bear
Return (%)	5.6	7.2	na	42.6	-3.7
Differ from Category (+/-)	1.3 high	0.3 abv av	na	1.6 av	0.1 av

Total Risk	Standard Deviation	Category Risk	Risk Index	Avg Mat
low	3.4%	av	0.8	6.6 yrs

	1994	1993	1992	1991	1990	1989	1988	1987	1986	1985
Return (%)..............	-0.6	11.1	6.6	16.8	2.8	9.2	8.6	—	—	—
Differ from category (+/-) ..	1.4	1.9	0.0	2.2	-4.4	-2.2	1.2	—	—	—

PER SHARE DATA

	1994	1993	1992	1991	1990	1989	1988	1987	1986	1985
Dividends, Net Income ($).	0.68	0.56	0.64	0.70	0.86	0.93	0.88	—	—	—
Distrib'ns, Cap Gain ($) ...	0.00	0.09	0.03	0.00	0.00	0.00	0.01	—	—	—
Net Asset Value ($)	9.49	10.24	9.82	9.86	9.09	9.69	9.75	—	—	—
Expense Ratio (%)	0.75	0.75	0.75	0.75	0.75	0.75	0.74	—	—	—
Net Income to Assets (%) .	6.40	5.99	6.82	7.85	9.35	9.34	8.80	—	—	—
Portfolio Turnover (%)	218	227	122	151	132	78	56	—	—	—
Total Assets (Millions $) ...	105	84	65	62	61	87	76	—	—	—

PORTFOLIO (as of 4/30/94)

Portfolio Manager: Dale C. Christensen - 1992, Anthony Van Daalen - 1992

Investm't Category: General Bond

Cap Gain	Asset Allocation
Cap & Income	Fund of Funds
✔ Income	Index
	Sector
✔ Domestic	Small Cap
✔ Foreign	Socially Conscious
Country/Region	State Specific

Portfolio: stocks 1%   bonds 96%
convertibles 0%   other 3%   cash 0%

Largest Holdings: corporate bonds 34%, U.S. government and agencies 33%

Unrealized Net Capital Gains: -4% of portfolio value

SHAREHOLDER INFORMATION

Minimum Investment
Initial: $2,500   Subsequent: $500

Minimum IRA Investment
Initial: $500   Subsequent: $500

Maximum Fees
Load: none   12b-1: none
Other: none

Distributions
Income: monthly   Capital Gains: Dec

Exchange Options
Number Per Year: 36   Fee: none
Telephone: yes (money market fund available)

Services
IRA, pension, auto exchange, auto invest, auto withdraw

Warburg Pincus Global Fixed Income (CGFIX)

466 Lexington Ave., 10 Fl.
New York, NY 10017
(800) 257-5614, (212) 878-0600

International Bond

PERFORMANCE

	3yr Annual	5yr Annual	10yr Annual	Bull	Bear
Return (%)	4.9	na	na	na	-6.2
Differ from Category (+/-)	1.0 abv av	na	na	na	1.6 av

Total Risk	Standard Deviation	Category Risk	Risk Index	Avg Mat
blw av	5.5%	av	0.9	5.4 yrs

	1994	1993	1992	1991	1990	1989	1988	1987	1986	1985
Return (%)	-5.4	19.6	2.1	14.7	—	—	—	—	—	—
Differ from category (+/-)	0.9	6.2	-2.6	-1.3	—	—	—	—	—	—

PER SHARE DATA

	1994	1993	1992	1991	1990	1989	1988	1987	1986	1985
Dividends, Net Income ($)	0.36	0.74	0.97	0.60	—	—	—	—	—	—
Distrib'ns, Cap Gain ($)	0.00	0.14	0.04	0.00	—	—	—	—	—	—
Net Asset Value ($)	10.16	11.13	10.06	10.84	—	—	—	—	—	—
Expense Ratio (%)	0.95	0.49	0.45	1.09	—	—	—	—	—	—
Net Income to Assets (%)	6.67	8.60	8.66	7.45	—	—	—	—	—	—
Portfolio Turnover (%)	186	109	93	186	—	—	—	—	—	—
Total Assets (Millions $)	84	69	17	12	—	—	—	—	—	—

PORTFOLIO (as of 4/30/94)

Portfolio Manager: Dale C. Christensen - 1990, Laxmi Bhandari - 1993

Investm't Category: International Bond

Cap Gain	Asset Allocation
✔ Cap & Income	Fund of Funds
Income	Index
	Sector
✔ Domestic	Small Cap
✔ Foreign	Socially Conscious
Country/Region	State Specific

Portfolio: stocks 3%   bonds 95%
convertibles 0%   other 0%   cash 2%

Largest Holdings: Germany 16%, United States 10%

Unrealized Net Capital Gains: -1% of portfolio value

SHAREHOLDER INFORMATION

Minimum Investment
Initial: $2,500   Subsequent: $500

Minimum IRA Investment
Initial: $500   Subsequent: $500

Maximum Fees
Load: none   12b-1: none
Other: none

Distributions
Income: quarterly   Capital Gains: Dec

Exchange Options
Number Per Year: 36   Fee: none
Telephone: yes (money market fund available)

Services
IRA, pension, auto exchange, auto invest, auto withdraw

Warburg Pincus Growth and Income (RBEGX)

466 Lexington Ave., 10 Fl.
New York, NY 10017
(800) 257-5614, (212) 878-0600

Growth & Income

PERFORMANCE

fund inception date: 10/1/88

	3yr Annual	5yr Annual	10yr Annual	Bull	Bear
Return (%)	16.5	13.2	na	83.3	0.6
Differ from Category (+/-)	9.4 high	5.3 high	na	7.5 abv av	6.9 high

Total Risk	Standard Deviation	Category Risk	Risk Index	Beta
abv av	10.7%	high	1.3	0.6

	1994	1993	1992	1991	1990	1989	1988	1987	1986	1985
Return (%)	7.5	35.7	8.5	13.0	4.0	20.7	—	—	—	—
Differ from category (+/-)	8.9	22.5	-1.7	-14.6	10.0	-0.7	—	—	—	—

PER SHARE DATA

	1994	1993	1992	1991	1990	1989	1988	1987	1986	1985
Dividends, Net Income ($)	0.07	0.00	0.00	0.04	0.41	0.43	—	—	—	—
Distrib'ns, Cap Gain ($)	0.22	4.09	0.17	0.39	0.55	0.31	—	—	—	—
Net Asset Value ($)	13.64	12.95	12.56	11.73	10.77	11.29	—	—	—	—
Expense Ratio (%)	1.28	1.14	1.25	1.30	1.40	1.40	—	—	—	—
Net Income to Assets (%)	0.41	0.30	1.66	3.42	3.32	4.32	—	—	—	—
Portfolio Turnover (%)	150	344	175	41	98	111	—	—	—	—
Total Assets (Millions $)	628	34	28	24	1	1	—	—	—	—

PORTFOLIO (as of 8/31/94)

Portfolio Manager: Anthony G. Orphanos - 1992

Investm't Category: Growth & Income
Cap Gain	Asset Allocation
✔ Cap & Income	Fund of Funds
Income	Index
	Sector
✔ Domestic	Small Cap
✔ Foreign	Socially Conscious
Country/Region	State Specific

Portfolio: stocks 64% bonds 3%
convertibles 0% other 0% cash 33%

Largest Holdings: metal & mining 11%, electronic computers 11%

Unrealized Net Capital Gains: 5% of portfolio value

SHAREHOLDER INFORMATION

Minimum Investment
Initial: $1,000   Subsequent: $100

Minimum IRA Investment
Initial: $500   Subsequent: $500

Maximum Fees
Load: none   12b-1: none
Other: none

Distributions
Income: quarterly   Capital Gains: Dec

Exchange Options
Number Per Year: 36   Fee: none
Telephone: yes (money market fund available)

Services
IRA, pension, auto exchange, auto invest, auto withdraw

Warburg Pincus Interm Mat Gov't (CUIGX)

466 Lexington Ave., 10 Fl.
New York, NY 10017
(800) 257-5614, (212) 878-0600

Government Bond

PERFORMANCE

fund inception date: 8/31/88

	3yr Annual	5yr Annual	10yr Annual	Bull	Bear
Return (%)	4.1	7.1	na	39.6	-3.4
Differ from Category (+/-)	0.1 av	0.4 av	na	-11.6 blw av	3.0 abv av

Total Risk	Standard Deviation	Category Risk	Risk Index	Avg Mat
low	3.6%	av	0.8	4.1 yrs

	1994	1993	1992	1991	1990	1989	1988	1987	1986	1985
Return (%)	-1.7	7.8	6.6	14.9	8.9	11.5	—	—	—	—
Differ from category (+/-) . . .	3.1	-3.1	0.2	-0.4	2.7	-3.0	—	—	—	—

PER SHARE DATA

	1994	1993	1992	1991	1990	1989	1988	1987	1986	1985
Dividends, Net Income ($) .	0.56	0.57	0.65	0.76	0.78	0.83	—	—	—	—
Distrib'ns, Cap Gain ($) . . .	0.00	0.63	0.54	0.00	0.00	0.00	—	—	—	—
Net Asset Value ($)	9.55	10.29	10.67	11.15	10.42	10.33	—	—	—	—
Expense Ratio (%)	0.60	0.60	0.60	0.57	0.50	0.50	—	—	—	—
Net Income to Assets (%). .	5.19	5.34	6.10	7.29	7.78	8.07	—	—	—	—
Portfolio Turnover (%). . . .	137	108	166	39	113	23	—	—	—	—
Total Assets (Millions $) . .	1,759	64	113	89	64	27	—	—	—	—

PORTFOLIO (as of 4/30/94)

Portfolio Manager: Dale C. Christensen - 1991, Anthony Van Daalen - 1992

Investm't Category: Government Bond

Cap Gain	Asset Allocation
Cap & Income	Fund of Funds
✔ Income	Index
	Sector
✔ Domestic	Small Cap
Foreign	Socially Conscious
Country/Region	State Specific

Portfolio: stocks 0% bonds 96%
convertibles 0% other 0% cash 4%

Largest Holdings: U.S. government and agencies 86%, mortgage-backed 10%

Unrealized Net Capital Gains: -1% of portfolio value

SHAREHOLDER INFORMATION

Minimum Investment
Initial: $2,500   Subsequent: $500

Minimum IRA Investment
Initial: $500   Subsequent: $500

Maximum Fees
Load: none   12b-1: none
Other: none

Distributions
Income: monthly   Capital Gains: Dec

Exchange Options
Number Per Year: 36   Fee: none
Telephone: yes (money market fund available)

Services
IRA, pension, auto exchange, auto invest, auto withdraw

Warburg Pincus Int'l Equity (CUIEX)

466 Lexington Ave., 10 Fl.
New York, NY 10017
(800) 257-5614, (212) 878-0600

International Stock

PERFORMANCE

fund inception date: 4/30/89

	3yr Annual	5yr Annual	10yr Annual	Bull	Bear
Return (%)	13.1	10.7	na	101.9	-6.6
Differ from Category (+/-)	4.0 high	5.8 high	na	38.0 high	0.4 av

Total Risk	Standard Deviation	Category Risk	Risk Index	Beta
high	14.6%	abv av	1.1	0.9

	1994	1993	1992	1991	1990	1989	1988	1987	1986	1985
Return (%).	0.1	51.2	-4.3	20.6	-4.5	—	—	—	—	—
Differ from category (+/-) . .	3.1	12.6	-1.4	7.5	5.9	—	—	—	—	—

PER SHARE DATA

	1994	1993	1992	1991	1990	1989	1988	1987	1986	1985
Dividends, Net Income ($).	0.11	0.03	0.06	0.32	0.39	—	—	—	—	—
Distrib'ns, Cap Gain ($) . . .	0.53	0.04	0.13	0.00	0.01	—	—	—	—	—
Net Asset Value ($)	18.38	18.98	12.60	13.36	11.35	—	—	—	—	—
Expense Ratio (%)	1.34	1.48	1.49	1.50	1.46	—	—	—	—	—
Net Income to Assets (%) .	0.26	0.38	0.88	1.19	3.73	—	—	—	—	—
Portfolio Turnover (%)	28	22	53	55	66	—	—	—	—	—
Total Assets (Millions $)	44	569	102	73	39	—	—	—	—	—

PORTFOLIO (as of 4/30/94)

Portfolio Manager: Richard King - 1989

Investm't Category: International Stock

✔ Cap Gain	Asset Allocation
Cap & Income	Fund of Funds
Income	Index
	Sector
Domestic	Small Cap
✔ Foreign	Socially Conscious
Country/Region	State Specific

Portfolio:	stocks 90%	bonds 0%
convertibles 4%	other 1%	cash 5%

Largest Holdings: Japan 24%, Mexico 7%

Unrealized Net Capital Gains: 8% of portfolio value

SHAREHOLDER INFORMATION

Minimum Investment
Initial: $2,500   Subsequent: $500

Minimum IRA Investment
Initial: $500   Subsequent: $500

Maximum Fees
Load: none   12b-1: none
Other: none

Distributions
Income: Jun, Dec   Capital Gains: Dec

Exchange Options
Number Per Year: 36   Fee: none
Telephone: yes (money market fund available)

Services
IRA, pension, auto exchange, auto invest, auto withdraw

Warburg Pincus NY Muni Bond (CNMBX)

466 Lexington Ave., 10 Fl.
New York, NY 10017
(800) 257-5614, (212) 878-0600

Tax-Exempt Bond

PERFORMANCE

fund inception date: 4/1/87

	3yr Annual	5yr Annual	10yr Annual	Bull	Bear
Return (%)	5.5	6.3	na	34.3	-2.3
Differ from Category (+/-)	1.0 high	0.2 av	na	-7.5 low	2.9 high

Total Risk	Standard Deviation	Category Risk	Risk Index	Avg Mat
low	3.9%	low	0.6	7.0 yrs

	1994	1993	1992	1991	1990	1989	1988	1987	1986	1985
Return (%)	-0.5	9.9	7.5	9.5	5.9	6.8	6.3	—	—	—
Differ from category (+/-) . . .	4.7	-1.8	-0.8	-1.8	-0.4	-2.2	-3.9	—	—	—

PER SHARE DATA

	1994	1993	1992	1991	1990	1989	1988	1987	1986	1985
Dividends, Net Income ($) .	0.45	0.47	0.49	0.56	0.59	0.59	0.55	—	—	—
Distrib'ns, Cap Gain ($) . . .	0.01	0.13	0.05	0.00	0.00	0.00	0.00	—	—	—
Net Asset Value ($)	10.03	10.55	10.16	9.97	9.64	9.68	9.63	—	—	—
Expense Ratio (%)	0.60	0.58	0.55	0.55	0.55	0.56	0.54	—	—	—
Net Income to Assets (%). .	4.34	4.50	4.99	5.84	6.21	6.14	5.70	—	—	—
Portfolio Turnover (%). . . .	169	116	48	67	70	74	145	—	—	—
Total Assets (Millions $)	76	74	54	29	22	20	28	—	—	—

PORTFOLIO (as of 4/30/94)

Portfolio Manager: Dale C. Christensen - 1992, Sharon B. Parente - 1992

Investm't Category: Tax-Exempt Bond

Cap Gain	Asset Allocation
Cap & Income	Fund of Funds
✔ Income	Index
	Sector
✔ Domestic	Small Cap
Foreign	Socially Conscious
Country/Region	✔ State Specific

Portfolio: stocks 0% bonds 94%
convertibles 0% other 0% cash 6%

Largest Holdings: general obligation 23%

Unrealized Net Capital Gains: 0% of portfolio value

SHAREHOLDER INFORMATION

Minimum Investment
Initial: $2,500   Subsequent: $500

Minimum IRA Investment
Initial: na   Subsequent: na

Maximum Fees
Load: none   12b-1: none
Other: none

Distributions
Income: monthly   Capital Gains: Dec

Exchange Options
Number Per Year: 36   Fee: none
Telephone: yes (money market fund available)

Services
auto exchange, auto invest, auto withdraw

Wasatch Aggressive Equity (WAAEX)

68 South Main Street
Salt Lake City, UT 84101
(800) 551-1700, (801) 533-0778

Aggressive Growth

fund inception date: 12/6/86

	3yr Annual	5yr Annual	10yr Annual	Bull	Bear
Return (%)	10.6	17.0	na	139.0	-9.5
Differ from Category (+/-)	1.7 abv av	4.5 abv av	na	5.8 abv av	1.3 abv av

Total Risk	Standard Deviation	Category Risk	Risk Index	Beta
high	13.4%	av	0.9	0.9

	1994	1993	1992	1991	1990	1989	1988	1987	1986	1985
Return (%).............	5.4	22.4	4.7	50.3	7.8	32.0	-1.4	-4.8	—	—
Differ from category (+/-) ..	6.1	2.9	-6.3	-1.8	14.0	5.2	-16.6	-2.6	—	—

PER SHARE DATA

	1994	1993	1992	1991	1990	1989	1988	1987	1986	1985
Dividends, Net Income ($).	0.00	0.00	0.00	0.72	0.00	0.00	0.05	0.01	—	—
Distrib'ns, Cap Gain ($) ...	1.51	1.22	0.66	0.18	0.00	0.00	0.00	1.05	—	—
Net Asset Value ($).....	19.06	19.50	16.95	16.82	11.78	10.92	8.27	8.44	—	—
Expense Ratio (%)	1.50	1.50	1.51	1.51	1.56	1.50	1.50	1.26	—	—
Net Income to Assets (%) .	-0.67	-0.77	-0.41	-0.36	0.08	-0.12	0.30	0.16	—	—
Portfolio Turnover (%)	64	70	32	41	74	82	71	58	—	—
Total Assets (Millions $)	60	26	12	7	2	1	1	1	—	—

PORTFOLIO (as of 9/30/94)

Portfolio Manager: Samuel S. Stewart - 1986

Investm't Category: Aggressive Growth

✔ Cap Gain	Asset Allocation
Cap & Income	Fund of Funds
Income	Index
	Sector
✔ Domestic	Small Cap
✔ Foreign	Socially Conscious
Country/Region	State Specific

Portfolio: stocks 95% bonds 0%
convertibles 0% other 0% cash 5%

Largest Holdings: retail 16%, computer components & software 13%

Unrealized Net Capital Gains: 5% of portfolio value

SHAREHOLDER INFORMATION

Minimum Investment
Initial: $2,000   Subsequent: $100

Minimum IRA Investment
Initial: $1,000   Subsequent: $100

Maximum Fees
Load: none   12b-1: none
Other: none

Distributions
Income: Dec   Capital Gains: Dec

Exchange Options
Number Per Year: 4   Fee: none
Telephone: yes (money market fund available)

Services
IRA, auto invest, auto withdraw

Wayne Hummer Growth
(WHGRX)
Growth

300 S. Wacker Drive
Chicago, IL 60606
(800) 621-4477, (312) 431-1700

PERFORMANCE
fund inception date: 12/30/83

	3yr Annual	5yr Annual	10yr Annual	Bull	Bear
Return (%)	4.2	8.9	12.1	68.4	-6.8
Differ from Category (+/-)	-3.5 blw av	-0.7 av	-0.8 blw av	-23.7 blw av	-0.2 av

Total Risk	Standard Deviation	Category Risk	Risk Index	Beta
av	7.0%	low	0.7	0.8

	1994	1993	1992	1991	1990	1989	1988	1987	1986	1985
Return (%)	-0.9	3.5	10.3	28.8	5.0	24.0	7.0	9.2	13.7	24.3
Differ from category (+/-) . .	-0.3	-9.9	-1.3	-6.9	10.7	-2.1	-11.0	7.4	-0.9	-4.9

PER SHARE DATA

	1994	1993	1992	1991	1990	1989	1988	1987	1986	1985
Dividends, Net Income ($)	0.31	0.28	0.29	0.39	0.44	0.24	0.22	0.31	0.24	0.34
Distrib'ns, Cap Gain ($) . . .	0.21	0.07	0.14	0.17	0.75	0.37	0.18	1.11	0.35	0.01
Net Asset Value ($)	21.34	22.06	21.64	20.02	16.00	16.41	13.74	13.22	13.33	12.25
Expense Ratio (%)	1.07	1.12	1.23	1.36	1.50	1.50	1.50	1.50	1.50	1.50
Net Income to Assets (%) . .	1.37	1.41	2.01	2.87	1.91	1.83	1.73	1.64	2.44	4.12
Portfolio Turnover (%)	5	1	3	13	3	12	10	28	27	26
Total Assets (Millions $)	87	99	56	32	25	21	21	19	10	4

PORTFOLIO (as of 9/30/94)

Portfolio Manager: Alan Bird - 1983, Thomas Rowland - 1987

Investm't Category: Growth

✔ Cap Gain	Asset Allocation
Cap & Income	Fund of Funds
Income	Index
	Sector
✔ Domestic	Small Cap
Foreign	Socially Conscious
Country/Region	State Specific

Portfolio: stocks 96%   bonds 0%
convertibles 0%   other 0%   cash 4%

Largest Holdings: chemical 17%, food, beverage & household 11%

Unrealized Net Capital Gains: 19% of portfolio value

SHAREHOLDER INFORMATION

Minimum Investment
Initial: $1,000   Subsequent: $500

Minimum IRA Investment
Initial: $500   Subsequent: $200

Maximum Fees
Load: none   12b-1: none
Other: none

Distributions
Income: quarterly   Capital Gains: Apr, Dec

Exchange Options
Number Per Year: no limit   Fee: none
Telephone: yes (money market fund available)

Services
IRA, pension, auto invest

Wayne Hummer Income
(WHICX)
General Bond

300 S. Wacker Drive
Chicago, IL 60606
(800) 621-4477, (312) 431-1700

PERFORMANCE
fund inception date: 12/1/92

	3yr Annual	5yr Annual	10yr Annual	Bull	Bear
Return (%)	na	na	na	na	-4.9
Differ from Category (+/-)	na	na	na	na	-1.1 blw av

Total Risk	Standard Deviation	Category Risk	Risk Index	Avg Mat
na	na	na	na	13.6 yrs

	1994	1993	1992	1991	1990	1989	1988	1987	1986	1985
Return (%).............	-2.4	10.7	—	—	—	—	—	—	—	—
Differ from category (+/-)..	-0.4	1.5	—	—	—	—	—	—	—	—

PER SHARE DATA

	1994	1993	1992	1991	1990	1989	1988	1987	1986	1985
Dividends, Net Income ($).	0.97	0.94	—	—	—	—	—	—	—	—
Distrib'ns, Cap Gain ($)...	0.00	0.05	—	—	—	—	—	—	—	—
Net Asset Value ($).....	14.27	15.62	—	—	—	—	—	—	—	—
Expense Ratio (%).......	0.97	1.39	—	—	—	—	—	—	—	—
Net Income to Assets (%).	6.51	5.58	—	—	—	—	—	—	—	—
Portfolio Turnover (%)	30	141	—	—	—	—	—	—	—	—
Total Assets (Millions $)	25	36	—	—	—	—	—	—	—	—

PORTFOLIO (as of 9/30/94)

Portfolio Manager: David Poitras - 1992

Investm't Category: General Bond

Cap Gain	Asset Allocation
Cap & Income	Fund of Funds
✔ Income	Index
	Sector
✔ Domestic	Small Cap
Foreign	Socially Conscious
Country/Region	State Specific

Portfolio: stocks 0% bonds 96%
convertibles 0% other 0% cash 4%

Largest Holdings: corporate 75%, mortgage-backed 20%

Unrealized Net Capital Gains: -6% of portfolio value

SHAREHOLDER INFORMATION

Minimum Investment
Initial: $2,500 Subsequent: $1,000

Minimum IRA Investment
Initial: $2,000 Subsequent: $500

Maximum Fees
Load: none 12b-1: none
Other: none

Distributions
Income: monthly Capital Gains: Apr, Dec

Exchange Options
Number Per Year: no limit Fee: none
Telephone: yes (money market fund available)

Services
IRA, pension, auto invest

Weitz Value Port (WVALX)

Growth

1125 South 103 Street
Suite 600
Omaha, NE 68124
(800) 232-4161, (402) 391-1980

PERFORMANCE

fund inception date: 5/9/86

	3yr Annual	5yr Annual	10yr Annual	Bull	Bear
Return (%)	7.1	8.2	na	82.8	-6.6
Differ from Category (+/-)	-0.6 av	-1.4 blw av	na	-9.3 blw av	0.0 av

Total Risk	Standard Deviation	Category Risk	Risk Index	Beta
av	8.5%	blw av	0.9	0.8

	1994	1993	1992	1991	1990	1989	1988	1987	1986	1985
Return (%)	-9.8	20.0	13.6	27.6	-5.2	22.0	16.4	-0.5	—	—
Differ from category (+/-) . .	-9.2	6.6	2.0	-8.1	0.5	-4.1	-1.6	-2.3	—	—

PER SHARE DATA

	1994	1993	1992	1991	1990	1989	1988	1987	1986	1985
Dividends, Net Income ($) .	0.03	0.02	0.27	0.32	0.38	0.43	0.32	0.49	—	—
Distrib'ns, Cap Gain ($) . . .	0.70	0.59	0.55	0.40	0.07	0.63	0.00	0.11	—	—
Net Asset Value ($)	14.43	16.80	14.54	13.57	11.21	12.30	10.97	9.70	—	—
Expense Ratio (%)	1.43	1.35	1.40	1.49	1.46	1.50	1.50	1.50	—	—
Net Income to Assets (%) . .	1.00	1.66	2.75	2.71	3.71	3.30	3.47	3.72	—	—
Portfolio Turnover (%)	36	23	35	28	49	25	67	54	—	—
Total Assets (Millions $) . . .	107	105	35	27	24	16	9	7	—	—

PORTFOLIO (as of 9/30/94)

Portfolio Manager: Wally Weitz - 1986

Investm't Category: Growth

✔ Cap Gain	Asset Allocation
Cap & Income	Fund of Funds
Income	Index
	Sector
✔ Domestic	Small Cap
Foreign	Socially Conscious
Country/Region	State Specific

Portfolio: stocks 73% bonds 6%
convertibles 3% other 2% cash 16%

Largest Holdings: financial services 20%, cable television 16%

Unrealized Net Capital Gains: 5% of portfolio value

SHAREHOLDER INFORMATION

Minimum Investment
Initial: $25,000 Subsequent: $5,000

Minimum IRA Investment
Initial: $10,000 Subsequent: $2,000

Maximum Fees
Load: none 12b-1: none
Other: none

Distributions
Income: Apr, Dec Capital Gains: Apr, Dec

Exchange Options
Number Per Year: no limit Fee: none
Telephone: yes (money market fund not available)

Services
IRA, pension, auto exchange, auto invest, auto withdraw

William Blair Growth Shares (WBGSX)

222 West Adams Street
Chicago, IL 60606
(800) 742-7272, (312) 364-8000

Growth

PERFORMANCE

fund inception date: 3/20/46

	3yr Annual	5yr Annual	10yr Annual	Bull	Bear
Return (%)	9.8	13.3	14.4	96.0	-5.2
Differ from Category (+/-)	2.1 abv av	3.7 high	1.5 high	3.9 abv av	1.4 abv av

Total Risk	Standard Deviation	Category Risk	Risk Index	Beta
abv av	10.3%	abv av	1.1	1.1

	1994	1993	1992	1991	1990	1989	1988	1987	1986	1985
Return (%)............	6.4	15.5	7.6	44.3	-2.0	30.4	7.1	7.9	9.7	23.7
Differ from category (+/-) ..	7.0	2.1	-4.0	8.6	3.7	4.3	-10.9	6.1	-4.9	-5.5

PER SHARE DATA

	1994	1993	1992	1991	1990	1989	1988	1987	1986	1985
Dividends, Net Income ($).	0.03	0.04	0.05	0.07	0.13	0.13	0.16	0.14	0.22	0.23
Distrib'ns, Cap Gain ($) ...	0.71	1.05	0.77	0.45	0.58	2.14	0.80	1.37	3.52	0.57
Net Asset Value ($)	9.60	9.73	9.39	9.49	6.97	7.84	7.81	8.21	9.10	11.82
Expense Ratio (%)	0.72	0.78	0.83	0.90	0.87	0.91	0.92	0.87	0.90	0.95
Net Income to Assets (%) .	0.25	0.38	1.34	0.83	1.70	1.36	1.46	1.46	1.69	1.96
Portfolio Turnover (%)	58	55	27	33	34	45	18	22	26	43
Total Assets (Millions $) ...	182	147	111	91	63	67	60	66	68	72

PORTFOLIO (as of 6/30/94)

Portfolio Manager: Rocky Barber - 1993, Mark Fuller - 1993

Investm't Category: Growth
- ✔ Cap Gain
- Cap & Income
- Income
- Asset Allocation
- Fund of Funds
- Index
- Sector
- ✔ Domestic
- Foreign
- Country/Region
- Small Cap
- Socially Conscious
- State Specific

Portfolio: stocks 88% bonds 0%
convertibles 0% other 0% cash 12%

Largest Holdings: industrial products 12%, applied technology 11%

Unrealized Net Capital Gains: 16% of portfolio value

SHAREHOLDER INFORMATION

Minimum Investment
Initial: $1,000   Subsequent: $250

Minimum IRA Investment
Initial: $500   Subsequent: $250

Maximum Fees
Load: none   12b-1: none
Other: none

Distributions
Income: Jul, Dec   Capital Gains: Dec

Exchange Options
Number Per Year: 4   Fee: none
Telephone: yes (money market fund available)

Services
IRA, pension, auto invest, auto withdraw

William Blair Income Shares (WBRRX)

222 West Adams Street
Chicago, IL 60606
(800) 742-7272, (312) 364-8000

General Bond

PERFORMANCE

fund inception date: 9/25/90

	3yr Annual	5yr Annual	10yr Annual	Bull	Bear
Return (%)	4.6	na	na	39.5	-2.9
Differ from Category (+/-)	0.3 abv av	na	na	-1.5 av	0.9 abv av

Total Risk	Standard Deviation	Category Risk	Risk Index	Avg Mat
low	3.2%	blw av	0.8	4.8 yrs

	1994	1993	1992	1991	1990	1989	1988	1987	1986	1985
Return (%)	-0.7	7.7	7.1	15.2	—	—	—	—	—	—
Differ from category (+/-) . . .	1.3	-1.5	0.5	0.6	—	—	—	—	—	—

PER SHARE DATA

	1994	1993	1992	1991	1990	1989	1988	1987	1986	1985
Dividends, Net Income ($) .	0.64	0.65	0.83	0.90	—	—	—	—	—	—
Distrib'ns, Cap Gain ($) . . .	0.00	0.18	0.09	0.00	—	—	—	—	—	—
Net Asset Value ($)	9.85	10.58	10.60	10.77	—	—	—	—	—	—
Expense Ratio (%)	0.74	0.70	0.88	0.92	—	—	—	—	—	—
Net Income to Assets (%). .	5.54	5.96	7.69	8.33	—	—	—	—	—	—
Portfolio Turnover (%).	85	114	47	64	—	—	—	—	—	—
Total Assets (Millions $) . . .	143	205	137	83	—	—	—	—	—	—

PORTFOLIO (as of 6/30/94)

Portfolio Manager: Bentley Myer - 1991

Investm't Category: General Bond

Cap Gain	Asset Allocation
Cap & Income	Fund of Funds
✔ Income	Index
	Sector
✔ Domestic	Small Cap
Foreign	Socially Conscious
Country/Region	State Specific

Portfolio: stocks 0% bonds 89%
convertibles 0% other 0% cash 11%

Largest Holdings: mortgage-backed 49%,
U.S. government & agencies 33%

Unrealized Net Capital Gains: -4% of portfolio value

SHAREHOLDER INFORMATION

Minimum Investment
Initial: $2,500   Subsequent: $250

Minimum IRA Investment
Initial: $500   Subsequent: $250

Maximum Fees
Load: none   12b-1: none
Other: none

Distributions
Income: monthly   Capital Gains: Dec

Exchange Options
Number Per Year: 4   Fee: none
Telephone: yes (money market fund available)

Services
IRA, pension, auto invest, auto withdraw

William Blair International Growth

222 West Adams Street
Chicago, IL 60606
(800) 742-7272, (312) 364-8000

(WBIGX) *International Stock*

PERFORMANCE

fund inception date: 10/1/92

	3yr Annual	5yr Annual	10yr Annual	Bull	Bear
Return (%)	na	na	na	na	-2.8
Differ from Category (+/-)	na	na	na	na	4.2 high

Total Risk	Standard Deviation	Category Risk	Risk Index	Beta
na	na	na	na	na

	1994	1993	1992	1991	1990	1989	1988	1987	1986	1985
Return (%)	0.0	33.8	—	—	—	—	—	—	—	—
Differ from category (+/-)	3.0	-4.8	—	—	—	—	—	—	—	—

PER SHARE DATA

	1994	1993	1992	1991	1990	1989	1988	1987	1986	1985
Dividends, Net Income ($)	0.02	0.00	—	—	—	—	—	—	—	—
Distrib'ns, Cap Gain ($)	0.79	0.36	—	—	—	—	—	—	—	—
Net Asset Value ($)	12.36	13.18	—	—	—	—	—	—	—	—
Expense Ratio (%)	1.88	1.71	—	—	—	—	—	—	—	—
Net Income to Assets (%)	0.09	0.11	—	—	—	—	—	—	—	—
Portfolio Turnover (%)	50	82	—	—	—	—	—	—	—	—
Total Assets (Millions $)	71	40	—	—	—	—	—	—	—	—

PORTFOLIO (as of 6/30/94)

Portfolio Manager: Norbert Truderung - 1992

Investm't Category: International Stock

✔ Cap Gain   Asset Allocation
   Cap & Income   Fund of Funds
   Income   Index
     Sector
   Domestic   Small Cap
✔ Foreign   Socially Conscious
   Country/Region   State Specific

Portfolio: stocks 92%   bonds 0%
convertibles 4%   other 0%   cash 4%

Largest Holdings: Japan 32%, United Kingdom 12%

Unrealized Net Capital Gains: 7% of portfolio value

SHAREHOLDER INFORMATION

Minimum Investment
Initial: $5,000   Subsequent: $1,000

Minimum IRA Investment
Initial: $500   Subsequent: $0

Maximum Fees
Load: none   12b-1: none
Other: none

Distributions
Income: Dec   Capital Gains: Dec

Exchange Options
Number Per Year: 4   Fee: none
Telephone: yes (money market fund available)

Services
IRA, pension, auto invest, auto withdraw

Woodward Equity Index
(WOEIX)
Growth & Income

P.O. Box 7058
Troy, MI 48007
(800) 688-3350

PERFORMANCE   fund inception date: 7/10/92

	3yr Annual	5yr Annual	10yr Annual	Bull	Bear
Return (%)	na	na	na	na	-6.7
Differ from Category (+/-)	na	na	na	na	-0.4 av

Total Risk	Standard Deviation	Category Risk	Risk Index	Beta
na	na	na	na	na

	1994	1993	1992	1991	1990	1989	1988	1987	1986	1985
Return (%)	0.9	9.0	—	—	—	—	—	—	—	—
Differ from category (+/-) . . .	2.3	-4.2	—	—	—	—	—	—	—	—

PER SHARE DATA

	1994	1993	1992	1991	1990	1989	1988	1987	1986	1985
Dividends, Net Income ($) .	0.30	0.27	—	—	—	—	—	—	—	—
Distrib'ns, Cap Gain ($) . . .	0.31	0.13	—	—	—	—	—	—	—	—
Net Asset Value ($)	10.65	11.15	—	—	—	—	—	—	—	—
Expense Ratio (%)	0.18	0.20	—	—	—	—	—	—	—	—
Net Income to Assets (%). .	2.73	2.59	—	—	—	—	—	—	—	—
Portfolio Turnover (%)	na	16	—	—	—	—	—	—	—	—
Total Assets (Millions $) . . .	329	0	—	—	—	—	—	—	—	—

PORTFOLIO (as of 6/30/94)

Portfolio Manager: Fortunate - 1992, Simmons - 1992, Neumann - 1992, Beard - 1992

Investm't Category: Growth & Income
Cap Gain	Asset Allocation
✔ Cap & Income	Fund of Funds
Income	✔ Index
	Sector
✔ Domestic	Small Cap
Foreign	Socially Conscious
Country/Region	State Specific

Portfolio: stocks 100% bonds 0%
convertibles 0% other 0% cash 0%

Largest Holdings: S&P 500 composite stock price index

Unrealized Net Capital Gains: 3% of portfolio value

SHAREHOLDER INFORMATION

Minimum Investment
Initial: $1,000   Subsequent: $100

Minimum IRA Investment
Initial: $1,000   Subsequent: $100

Maximum Fees
Load: none   12b-1: 0.35%
Other: none

Distributions
Income: quarterly   Capital Gains: Dec

Exchange Options
Number Per Year: 12   Fee: none
Telephone: yes (money market fund available)

Services
IRA, pension, auto invest, auto withdraw

WPG Gov't Securities

(WPGVX)

Government Bond

One New York Plaza, 30th Fl.
New York, NY 10004
(800) 223-3332, (212) 908-9582

	3yr Annual	5yr Annual	10yr Annual	Bull	Bear
Return (%)	2.3	5.8	na	42.2	-9.3
Differ from Category (+/-)	-1.7 low	-0.9 low	na	-9.0 av	-2.9 blw av

Total Risk	Standard Deviation	Category Risk	Risk Index	Avg Mat
low	4.6%	av	1.0	6.7 yrs

	1994	1993	1992	1991	1990	1989	1988	1987	1986	1985
Return (%)	-8.8	8.9	7.8	13.9	8.9	14.0	7.9	2.4	—	—
Differ from category (+/-)	-4.0	-2.0	1.4	-1.4	2.7	-0.5	0.0	4.5	—	—

PER SHARE DATA

	1994	1993	1992	1991	1990	1989	1988	1987	1986	1985
Dividends, Net Income ($)	0.64	0.79	0.78	0.80	0.82	0.87	0.79	0.73	—	—
Distrib'ns, Cap Gain ($)	0.02	0.15	0.41	0.00	0.00	0.00	0.00	0.07	—	—
Net Asset Value ($)	8.82	10.37	10.40	10.79	10.22	10.18	9.74	9.77	—	—
Expense Ratio (%)	0.78	0.81	0.78	0.81	0.75	0.76	0.82	0.87	—	—
Net Income to Assets (%)	6.78	7.43	7.36	7.64	8.13	8.64	7.97	7.41	—	—
Portfolio Turnover (%)	132	97	137	190	184	159	130	108	—	—
Total Assets (Millions $)	21	337	263	194	131	91	79	76	—	—

PORTFOLIO (as of 6/30/94)

Portfolio Manager: David Hoyle - 1986

Investm't Category: Government Bond

Cap Gain	Asset Allocation
Cap & Income	Fund of Funds
✔ Income	Index
	Sector
✔ Domestic	Small Cap
Foreign	Socially Conscious
Country/Region	State Specific

Portfolio: stocks 0%   bonds 98%
convertibles 0%   other 0%   cash 2%

Largest Holdings: U.S. government & agencies 73%, mortgage-backed 25%

Unrealized Net Capital Gains: -10% of portfolio value

SHAREHOLDER INFORMATION

Minimum Investment
Initial: $2,500   Subsequent: $100

Minimum IRA Investment
Initial: $250   Subsequent: $0

Maximum Fees
Load: none   12b-1: 0.05%
Other: none

Distributions
Income: monthly   Capital Gains: Dec

Exchange Options
Number Per Year: 6   Fee: none
Telephone: yes (money market fund available)

Services
IRA, pension, auto invest, auto withdraw

WPG Growth & Income
(WPGFX)
Growth & Income

One New York Plaza, 30th Fl.
New York, NY 10004
(800) 223-3332, (212) 908-9582

PERFORMANCE

fund inception date: 12/2/66

	3yr Annual	5yr Annual	10yr Annual	Bull	Bear
Return (%)	5.6	8.2	12.4	95.4	-8.6
Differ from Category (+/-)	-1.5 blw av	0.3 av	0.7 abv av	19.6 high	-2.3 blw av

Total Risk	Standard Deviation	Category Risk	Risk Index	Beta
abv av	8.9%	abv av	1.1	0.9

	1994	1993	1992	1991	1990	1989	1988	1987	1986	1985
Return (%)	-5.4	9.5	13.8	40.7	-10.3	27.6	9.4	6.8	11.4	30.3
Differ from category (+/-)	-4.0	-3.7	3.6	13.1	-4.3	6.2	-7.6	6.2	-4.4	4.6

PER SHARE DATA

	1994	1993	1992	1991	1990	1989	1988	1987	1986	1985
Dividends, Net Income ($)	0.62	0.89	0.52	0.22	0.39	0.24	0.26	0.00	0.68	0.65
Distrib'ns, Cap Gain ($)	0.09	1.93	4.69	0.00	4.11	0.47	2.84	0.38	6.02	0.00
Net Asset Value ($)	21.36	23.34	23.89	25.82	18.53	25.27	20.47	21.72	20.64	24.42
Expense Ratio (%)	1.18	1.26	1.34	1.48	1.56	1.41	1.53	1.19	1.23	1.21
Net Income to Assets (%)	2.31	2.15	1.79	1.28	1.21	1.04	0.82	0.65	1.88	2.28
Portfolio Turnover (%)	81	86	76	89	91	67	42	84	71	108
Total Assets (Millions $)	61	63	49	42	30	33	34	35	36	42

PORTFOLIO (as of 6/30/94)

Portfolio Manager: Roy Knutsen - 1992

Investm't Category: Growth & Income
Cap Gain	Asset Allocation
✔ Cap & Income	Fund of Funds
Income	Index
	Sector
✔ Domestic	Small Cap
✔ Foreign	Socially Conscious
Country/Region	State Specific

Portfolio: stocks 78%   bonds 9%
convertibles 8%   other 0%   cash 5%

Largest Holdings: real estate investment trusts—residential 7%, transportation 6%

Unrealized Net Capital Gains: 3% of portfolio value

SHAREHOLDER INFORMATION

Minimum Investment
Initial: $2,500   Subsequent: $100

Minimum IRA Investment
Initial: $250   Subsequent: $0

Maximum Fees
Load: none   12b-1: none
Other: none

Distributions
Income: quarterly   Capital Gains: Dec

Exchange Options
Number Per Year: 6   Fee: none
Telephone: yes (money market fund available)

Services
IRA, pension, auto invest, auto withdraw

WPG Quantitative Equity (WPGQX)

One New York Plaza, 30th Fl.
New York, NY 10004
(800) 223-3332, (212) 908-9582

Growth & Income

PERFORMANCE

fund inception date: 1/4/93

	3yr Annual	5yr Annual	10yr Annual	Bull	Bear
Return (%)	na	na	na	na	-7.3
Differ from Category (+/-)	na	na	na	na	-1.0 blw av

Total Risk	Standard Deviation	Category Risk	Risk Index	Beta
na	na	na	na	na

	1994	1993	1992	1991	1990	1989	1988	1987	1986	1985
Return (%)	0.3	13.9	—	—	—	—	—	—	—	—
Differ from category (+/-)	1.7	0.7	—	—	—	—	—	—	—	—

PER SHARE DATA

	1994	1993	1992	1991	1990	1989	1988	1987	1986	1985
Dividends, Net Income ($)	0.11	0.08	—	—	—	—	—	—	—	—
Distrib'ns, Cap Gain ($)	0.05	0.04	—	—	—	—	—	—	—	—
Net Asset Value ($)	5.44	5.58	—	—	—	—	—	—	—	—
Expense Ratio (%)	1.16	1.32	—	—	—	—	—	—	—	—
Net Income to Assets (%)	2.30	2.01	—	—	—	—	—	—	—	—
Portfolio Turnover (%)	64	20	—	—	—	—	—	—	—	—
Total Assets (Millions $)	73	46	—	—	—	—	—	—	—	—

PORTFOLIO (as of 6/30/94)

Portfolio Manager: Joseph Pappo - 1993

Investm't Category: Growth & Income
- Cap Gain
- ✔ Cap & Income
- Income
- ✔ Domestic
- Foreign
- Country/Region

- Asset Allocation
- Fund of Funds
- Index
- Sector
- Small Cap
- Socially Conscious
- State Specific

Portfolio: stocks 96% bonds 0%
convertibles 0% other 0% cash 4%

Largest Holdings: na

Unrealized Net Capital Gains: -1% of portfolio value

SHAREHOLDER INFORMATION

Minimum Investment
Initial: $5,000   Subsequent: $500

Minimum IRA Investment
Initial: $250   Subsequent: $0

Maximum Fees
Load: none   12b-1: none
Other: none

Distributions
Income: Dec   Capital Gains: Dec

Exchange Options
Number Per Year: 6   Fee: none
Telephone: yes (money market fund available)

Services
IRA, pension, auto invest, auto withdraw

WPG Tudor (TUDRX)

Aggressive Growth

One New York Plaza, 30th Fl.
New York, NY 10004
(800) 223-3332, (212) 908-9582

PERFORMANCE

fund inception date: 6/27/68

	3yr Annual	5yr Annual	10yr Annual	Bull	Bear
Return (%)	2.4	8.2	12.3	80.4	-17.7
Differ from Category (+/-)	-6.5 low	-4.3 low	-1.7 av	-52.8 low	-6.9 low

Total Risk	Standard Deviation	Category Risk	Risk Index	Beta
high	15.8%	abv av	1.1	1.2

	1994	1993	1992	1991	1990	1989	1988	1987	1986	1985
Return (%)	-9.8	13.3	5.1	45.8	-5.1	25.0	15.1	1.1	12.3	31.2
Differ from category (+/-) . .	-9.1	-6.2	-5.9	-6.3	1.1	-1.8	-0.1	3.3	0.5	-1.1

PER SHARE DATA

	1994	1993	1992	1991	1990	1989	1988	1987	1986	1985
Dividends, Net Income ($) .	0.00	0.00	0.00	0.29	0.24	0.16	0.03	0.00	0.07	0.37
Distrib'ns, Cap Gain ($) . . .	1.79	4.74	2.07	0.00	6.79	0.75	0.83	0.86	5.48	0.00
Net Asset Value ($)	19.34	23.40	24.85	25.68	17.85	25.97	21.65	19.64	20.08	22.75
Expense Ratio (%)	1.26	1.25	1.21	1.17	1.11	1.10	1.14	1.03	1.01	0.95
Net Income to Assets (%) .	-0.66	-0.76	-0.17	-0.11	0.84	0.76	0.22	-0.19	-0.16	0.63
Portfolio Turnover (%)	113	118	89	90	73	94	89	113	127	123
Total Assets (Millions $) . . .	144	227	273	264	162	157	157	143	163	155

PORTFOLIO (as of 6/30/94)

Portfolio Manager: Melville Straus - 1973

Investm't Category: Aggressive Growth

✔ Cap Gain	Asset Allocation
Cap & Income	Fund of Funds
Income	Index
	Sector
✔ Domestic	Small Cap
✔ Foreign	Socially Conscious
Country/Region	State Specific

Portfolio: stocks 81%   bonds 0%
convertibles 1%   other 1%   cash 17%

Largest Holdings: computer software & services 10%, retail 9%

Unrealized Net Capital Gains: 0% of portfolio value

SHAREHOLDER INFORMATION

Minimum Investment
Initial: $2,500   Subsequent: $100

Minimum IRA Investment
Initial: $250   Subsequent: $0

Maximum Fees
Load: none   12b-1: none
Other: none

Distributions
Income: quarterly   Capital Gains: Dec

Exchange Options
Number Per Year: 6   Fee: none
Telephone: yes (money market fund available)

Services
IRA, pension, auto invest, auto withdraw

Wright Int'l Blue Chip Equity (WIBCX)

1000 Lafayette Blvd.
Bridgeport, CT 06604
(800) 888-9471, (203) 333-6666

International Stock

PERFORMANCE
fund inception date: 9/14/89

	3yr Annual	5yr Annual	10yr Annual	Bull	Bear
Return (%)	6.6	5.7	na	62.2	-6.2
Differ from Category (+/-)	-2.5 blw av	0.8 abv av	na	-1.7 av	0.8 av

Total Risk	Standard Deviation	Category Risk	Risk Index	Beta
abv av	11.5%	blw av	0.9	0.7

	1994	1993	1992	1991	1990	1989	1988	1987	1986	1985
Return (%)	-1.6	28.2	-3.9	17.2	-6.9	—	—	—	—	—
Differ from category (+/-)	1.4	-10.4	-1.0	4.1	3.5	—	—	—	—	—

PER SHARE DATA

	1994	1993	1992	1991	1990	1989	1988	1987	1986	1985
Dividends, Net Income ($)	0.10	0.07	0.09	0.11	0.17	—	—	—	—	—
Distrib'ns, Cap Gain ($)	0.00	0.00	0.00	0.00	0.00	—	—	—	—	—
Net Asset Value ($)	13.09	13.41	10.52	11.04	9.52	—	—	—	—	—
Expense Ratio (%)	1.30	1.46	1.51	1.67	1.65	—	—	—	—	—
Net Income to Assets (%)	1.82	0.67	0.81	1.12	1.66	—	—	—	—	—
Portfolio Turnover (%)	na	30	15	23	13	—	—	—	—	—
Total Assets (Millions $)	199	175	74	52	19	—	—	—	—	—

PORTFOLIO (as of 6/30/94)

Portfolio Manager: committee

Investm't Category: International Stock

Cap Gain	Asset Allocation
✔ Cap & Income	Fund of Funds
Income	Index
	Sector
Domestic	Small Cap
✔ Foreign	Socially Conscious
Country/Region	State Specific

Portfolio: stocks 98% bonds 0%
convertibles 0% other 0% cash 2%

Largest Holdings: United Kingdom 18%, Japan 15%

Unrealized Net Capital Gains: 9% of portfolio value

SHAREHOLDER INFORMATION

Minimum Investment
Initial: $1,000   Subsequent: $50

Minimum IRA Investment
Initial: $1,000   Subsequent: $50

Maximum Fees
Load: none   12b-1: 0.20%
Other: none

Distributions
Income: Jun, Dec   Capital Gains: Dec

Exchange Options
Number Per Year: 8   Fee: none
Telephone: yes (money market fund available)

Services
IRA, pension, auto exchange, auto invest, auto withdraw

Yacktman (YACKX)

Growth

303 West Madison Street
Chicago, IL 60606
(800) 525-8258

PERFORMANCE

fund inception date: 7/6/92

	3yr Annual	5yr Annual	10yr Annual	Bull	Bear
Return (%)	na	na	na	na	-3.1
Differ from Category (+/-)	na	na	na	na	3.5 high

Total Risk	Standard Deviation	Category Risk	Risk Index	Beta
na	na	na	na	na

	1994	1993	1992	1991	1990	1989	1988	1987	1986	1985
Return (%)	8.7	-6.5	—	—	—	—	—	—	—	—
Differ from category (+/-) . . .	9.3	-19.9	—	—	—	—	—	—	—	—

PER SHARE DATA

	1994	1993	1992	1991	1990	1989	1988	1987	1986	1985
Dividends, Net Income ($) .	0.22	0.14	—	—	—	—	—	—	—	—
Distrib'ns, Cap Gain ($) . . .	0.12	0.00	—	—	—	—	—	—	—	—
Net Asset Value ($)	10.05	9.56	—	—	—	—	—	—	—	—
Expense Ratio (%)	1.12	1.18	—	—	—	—	—	—	—	—
Net Income to Assets (%) . .	2.34	1.61	—	—	—	—	—	—	—	—
Portfolio Turnover (%)	27	61	—	—	—	—	—	—	—	—
Total Assets (Millions $) . . .	295	145	—	—	—	—	—	—	—	—

PORTFOLIO (as of 6/30/94)

Portfolio Manager: Donald Yacktman - 1992

Investm't Category: Growth

✔ Cap Gain	Asset Allocation
Cap & Income	Fund of Funds
Income	Index
	Sector
✔ Domestic	Small Cap
✔ Foreign	Socially Conscious
Country/Region	State Specific

Portfolio: stocks 89% bonds 3%
convertibles 0% other 5% cash 3%

Largest Holdings: drugs & medical 20%, apparel shoes 14%

Unrealized Net Capital Gains: -5% of portfolio value

SHAREHOLDER INFORMATION

Minimum Investment
Initial: $2,500   Subsequent: $100

Minimum IRA Investment
Initial: $500   Subsequent: $100

Maximum Fees
Load: none   12b-1: 0.65%
Other: none

Distributions
Income: quarterly   Capital Gains: Dec

Exchange Options
Number Per Year: no limit   Fee: $5 (tel.)
Telephone: yes (money market fund available)

Services
IRA, pension, auto invest, auto withdraw

Appendix A
Special Types of Funds

ASSET ALLOCATION FUNDS

Bascom Hill Balanced
BB&K Diversa
Berwyn Income
Blanchard Global Growth
Brinson Global
CGM Mutual
Columbia Balanced
Crabbe Huson Asset Allocation
Dreyfus Asset Allocation—Total Return
Evergreen Foundation—Class Y
Fidelity Asset Manager
Fidelity Asset Manager—Growth
Fidelity Asset Manager—Income
Fidelity Balanced
Fidelity Global Balanced
Fremont Global
Galaxy Asset Allocation
Hotchkis and Wiley Balanced Income
IAI Balanced
INVESCO Industrial Income
INVESCO Value Trust—Total Return
Janus Balanced
Jurika & Voyles Balanced
Lepercq-Istel
Maxus Equity
Maxus Income
Merriman Asset Allocation
Northeast Investors Trust
Permanent Port
Preferred Asset Allocation
Primary Trend
Regis Sterling Partners Balanced

SteinRoe Total Return
Strong Asset Allocation
T Rowe Price Spectrum Income
USAA Cornerstone
Value Line Income
Vanguard Asset Allocation

FUNDS INVESTING IN FUNDS

American Pension Investors—Growth
Flex Muirfield
Maxus Laureate
Merriman Asset Allocation
Merriman Capital Appreciation
Merriman Flexible Bond
Merriman Growth & Income
New Century Capital Port
Rightime
Smith Breedon Short Duration U.S. Gov't Series
T Rowe Price Spectrum Growth
T Rowe Price Spectrum Income
Vanguard Star

GLOBAL FUNDS

Blanchard Global Growth
Blanchard Short-Term Global Inc
Brinson Global
Brinson Global Bond
Bull & Bear Global Income
Bull & Bear US & Overseas
Columbia Int'l Stock
Evergreen Global Real Estate—Class Y
Fidelity Global Balanced
Fidelity Global Bond
Fidelity Int'l Growth & Income
Fidelity New Markets Income
Fidelity Short Term World Income
Fidelity Worldwide
Flex Short Term Global Income
Founders World Wide Growth
Fremont Global
Janus Worldwide
Legg Mason Global Gov't Trust

Lexington Global
Lexington Worldwide Emerging Mkts
Loomis Sayles Global Bond
Managers International Equity
Montgomery Global Communic'ns
Morgan Grenfell Global Fixed Income
Scudder Global
Scudder Global Small Company
Scudder Short-Term Global Income
Scudder Global Fixed Income
T Rowe Price Global Gov't Bond
T Rowe Price Short-Term Global Inc
Tweedy Browne Global Value
US Global Resources
USAA World Growth
Warburg Pincus Global Fixed Income

INDEX MUTUAL FUNDS

ASM
Benham Gold Equities Index
Corefund Equity Index
Dreyfus Edison Electric Index
Dreyfus Peoples Index
Dreyfus Peoples S&P MidCap Index
Fidelity Market Index
Galaxy II Large Company Index - Retail
Galaxy II Small Company Index - Retail
Galaxy II U.S. Treasury Index - Retail
Galaxy II Utility Index - Retail
Portico Equity Index—Retail
Rushmore American Gas Index
Schwab 1000
Schwab International Index
Schwab Small-Cap Index
Seven Seas Series—S&P 500
T. Rowe Price Equity Index
Vanguard Balanced Index
Vanguard Index Trust—500
Vanguard Index Trust—Ext. Market
Vanguard Index Trust—Growth Port
Vanguard Index Trust—Small Cap
Vanguard Index Trust—Tot Stock Mkt

Vanguard Index Trust—Value Port
Vanguard Int'l Equity Index—Europe
Vanguard Int'l Equity Index—Pacific
Vanguard Total Bond Market Port
Woodward Equity Index

SECTOR FUNDS

America's Utility
Benham Gold Equities Index
Blanchard Precious Metals
Bull & Bear Gold Investors Ltd
Cappiello-Rushmore Utility Income
Century Shares Trust
Cohen & Steers Realty Shares
Dreyfus Edison Electric Index
Evergreen Global Real Estate—Class Y
Fidelity Real Estate Investment
Fidelity Sel Air Transportation
Fidelity Sel American Gold
Fidelity Sel Automotive
Fidelity Sel Biotechnology
Fidelity Sel Broker & Invest Mgmt
Fidelity Sel Chemical
Fidelity Sel Computers
Fidelity Sel Constr'n & Hous'g
Fidelity Sel Consumer Products
Fidelity Sel Defense & Aerospace
Fidelity Sel Dev'ping Communic'ns
Fidelity Sel Electronics
Fidelity Sel Energy
Fidelity Sel Energy Services
Fidelity Sel Environ'l Services
Fidelity Sel Financial Services
Fidelity Sel Food & Agriculture
Fidelity Sel Health Care
Fidelity Sel Home Finance
Fidelity Sel Industrial Equipment
Fidelity Sel Industrial Materials
Fidelity Sel Insurance
Fidelity Sel Leisure
Fidelity Sel Medical Delivery
Fidelity Sel Multimedia

Fidelity Sel Natural Gas Port
Fidelity Sel Paper & Forest Prod
Fidelity Sel Precious Metals
Fidelity Sel Regional Banks
Fidelity Sel Retailing
Fidelity Sel Software & Comp
Fidelity Sel Technology
Fidelity Sel Telecomm
Fidelity Sel Transportation
Fidelity Sel Utilities Growth
Fidelity Utilities
Galaxy II Utility Index - Retail
INVESCO Strat Port—Energy
INVESCO Strat Port—Environm'l
INVESCO Strat Port—Financial
INVESCO Strat Port—Gold
INVESCO Strat Port—Health Sci
INVESCO Strat Port—Leisure
INVESCO Strat Port—Tech
INVESCO Strat Port—Utilities
Lexington GoldFund
Lindner Utility
Montgomery Global Communic'ns
PRA Real Estate Securities
Rushmore American Gas Index
Scudder Gold
Strong American Utilities
T Rowe Price New Era
T Rowe Price Science & Tech
U.S. Global Resources
U.S. Gold Shares
U.S. Real Estate
U.S. World Gold
USAA Gold
Vanguard Spec Port—Energy
Vanguard Spec Port—Gold & PM
Vanguard Spec Port—Health Care
Vanguard Spec Port—Utilities Income

SMALL CAPITALIZATION STOCK FUNDS
Acorn
Acorn Int'l

Babson Enterprise
Babson Shadow Stock
Berger Small Company Growth
Caldwell & Orkin Aggressive Growth
Cappiello-Rushmore Emerging Growth
Columbia Special
Crabbe Huson Special
Dreyfus New Leaders
Eclipse Equity
Evergreen—Class Y
Evergreen Limited Market—Class Y
FAM Value
Fidelity Emerging Growth
Fidelity Low-Priced Stock
Fidelity New Millenium
Fifty-Nine Wall St. Small Company
Founders Discovery
Founders Frontier
Galaxy II Small Company Index - Retail
Galaxy Small Company Equity
GIT Equity—Special Growth
Gradison McDonald Opportunity Value
Heartland Value
IAI Emerging Growth
INVESCO Emerging Growth
Janus Venture
Kaufmann
Lazard Small Cap Portfolio
Lazard Special Equity Portfolio
Legg Mason Special Investment
Longleaf Partners Small Cap
Loomis Sayles Small Cap
Managers Special Equity
Meridian
Monetta
Montgomery International Small Cap
Montgomery Small Cap
Mutual Discovery
Neuberger & Berman Genesis
Nicholas II
Nicholas Limited Edition
Oberweis Emerging Growth

PBHG Emerging Growth
PBHG Growth
Pennsylvania Mutual
Perritt Capital Growth
Prudent Speculator
Regis ICM Small Company Port
Robertson Stephens Emerging Growth
Robertson Stephens Value + Growth
Royce Premier
Schwab Small-Cap Index
Schwartz Value
Scudder Development
Scudder Global Small Company
Seven Seas Series—Small Cap
SIT Growth
Skyline Special Equities II
Standish Small Capitalization Equity
Strong Discovery
T Rowe Price Int'l Discovery
T Rowe Price New Horizons
T Rowe Price OTC
T Rowe Price Small Cap Value
Tweedy Browne Global Value
Twentieth Century Giftrust
Twentieth Century Ultra
Twentieth Century Vista
UMB Heartland Fund
USAA Aggressive Growth
Vanguard Explorer
Vanguard Index Trust—Ext. Market
Vanguard Index Trust—Small Cap
Warburg Pincus Emerging Grth

SOCIALLY CONSCIOUS FUNDS

Amana Income
Domini Social Equity
Dreyfus Third Century
Pax World

STATE-SPECIFIC TAX-EXEMPT BOND FUNDS

California
Benham CA Tax-Free High-Yield

Benham CA Tax-Free Insured
Benham CA Tax-Free Interm
Benham CA Tax-Free Long-Term
Benham CA Tax-Free Short-Term
Bernstein CA Muni Port
Cal Muni
Cal Tax-Free Income
Dreyfus CA Interm Muni Bond
Dreyfus CA Tax Exempt Bond
Evergreen Short Interm Muni CA-Class Y
Fidelity CA Tax-Free High Yield
Fidelity CA Tax-Free Insured
Fidelity Spartan CA Interm Muni
Fidelity Spartan CA Muni High Yield
Fremont CA Interm Tax-Free
General CA Muni Bond
Pacifica Short Term CA Tax-Free
Safeco CA Tax-Free Income
Schwab CA Long-Term Tax-Free
Schwab CA Short/Interm Tax-Free
Scudder CA Tax Free
T Rowe Price CA Tax-Free Bond
USAA Tax Exempt CA Bond
Vanguard CA Tax-Free Insured Long

Connecticut
Dreyfus Conn Interm Muni Bond
Fidelity Spartan Conn Tax-Free High-Yield
Galaxy Connecticut Municipal Bond

Florida
Dreyfus Florida Interm Muni
Fidelity Spartan Florida Muni Income
USAA Florida Tax-Free Income
Vanguard Florida Insured Tax Free

Hawaii
First Hawaii Muni Bond

Kentucky
Dupree KY Tax-Free Income
Dupree KY Tax-Free Short to Medium

Maryland
Fidelity Spartan Maryland Muni Income

Rushmore Maryland Tax-Free
T Rowe Price Maryland Tax-Free
T Rowe Price MD Short-Term Tax-Free

Massachusetts
1784 Mass Tax-Exempt Income
Dreyfus Mass Interm Muni Bond
Dreyfus Mass Tax-Exempt Bond
Fidelity Mass Tax-Free High Yield
Scudder Mass Tax-Free
Standish Mass Interm Tax-Exempt

Michigan
Fidelity Michigan Tax-Free High Yield

Minnesota
Fidelity Minnesota Tax-Free
SIT Minnesota Tax Free Income

New Jersey
Dreyfus NJ Interm Muni Bond
Dreyfus NJ Muni Bond
Fidelity Spartan NJ Muni High Yield
T Rowe Price NJ Tax-Free
Vanguard NJ Tax Free Insured Long

New York
Bernstein NY Muni Port
Dreyfus NY Insured Tax-Exempt
Dreyfus NY Tax-Exempt
Dreyfus NY Tax-Exempt Interm
Fidelity NY Tax-Free High Yield
Fidelity NY Tax-Free Insured
Fidelity Spartan NY Interm Muni
Fidelity Spartan NY Muni High Yield
Galaxy NY Muni Bond
General NY Muni Bond
NY Muni
Scudder NY Tax Free
T Rowe Price NY Tax-Free
USAA Tax Exempt NY Bond
Value Line NY Tax-Exempt Trust
Vanguard NY Insured Tax Free
Warburg Pincus NY Muni Bond

Ohio
Fidelity Ohio Tax-Free High Yield
Scudder Ohio Tax-Free
Vanguard Ohio Tax Free Insur Long

Oregon
Oregon Municipal Bond

Pennsylvania
Fidelity Spartan Penn Muni High Yield
Scudder Penn Tax Free
Vanguard Penn Tax-Free Insur Long

Virginia
GIT Tax-Free Virginia Port
Rushmore Virginia Tax-Free
T Rowe Price Virginia Tax-Free Bond
USAA Tax-Exempt Virginia Bond

Wisconsin
Heartland Wisconsin Tax Free

Appendix B
Changes to the Funds

FUND NAME CHANGES

Former	Current
Boston Co Capital Appreciation	Dreyfus Core Value—Investor
Boston Co International	Dreyfus/Laurel International—Investor
Boston Co Special Growth	Dreyfus Special Growth—Investor
Evergreen Insured National Tax Free	Evergreen National Tax Free—Class Y
Evergreen Value Timing	Evergreen Growth & Income—Class Y
Fidelity Select Broadcast & Media	Fidelity Sel Multimedia
Fidelity Select Utilities	Fidelity Sel Utilities Growth
Fidelity Utilities Income	Fidelity Utilities
GIT Tax Free High Yield	GIT Tax-Free National Port
Maxus Prism	Maxus Laureate
Merriman Blue Chip	Merriman Growth & Income
Montgomery Short Duration Government	Montgomery Short Gov't Bond
Neuberger & Berman Selected Sectors	Neuberger & Berman Focus
Olympic Balanced Income	Hotchkis and Wiley Balanced Income
Olympic Equity Income	Hotchkis and Wiley Equity Income
Robertson Stephens Value Plus	Robertson Stephens Value + Growth
Safeco U.S. Government Securities	Safeco GNMA
Seven Seas Series—S&P MidCap Index	Seven Seas Series—Small Cap
Southeastern Asset Management Small Cap	Longleaf Partners Small Cap
Southeastern Asset Management Value Trust	Longleaf Partners
Strong Investment	Strong Asset Allocation
Twentieth Century U.S. Gov't	Twentieth Century U.S. Gov't Short-Term
Vanguard Bond Index	Vanguard Total Bond Market Portfolio
Vanguard Small Cap Stock	Vanguard Index Trust—Small Cap

INVESTMENT CATEGORY CHANGES

Fund Name	Old	New
1784 U.S. Gov't Medium Term Inc	Government Bond	Mortgage-Backed Bond

Bull & Bear U.S. Gov't Securities . .	Mortgage-Backed Bond	Government Bond
Dreyfus Peoples S&P MidCap Index	Growth & Income	Growth
Evergreen Growth & Inc—Class Y .	Growth	Growth & Income
Fidelity Spartan Short Interm Gov't	Government Bond . . .	General Bond
Flex Bond	Government Bond . . .	General Bond
Fremont Global	Balanced	International Stock
IAI Bond	Government Bond . . .	General Bond
IAI Growth & Income	Growth	Growth & Income
L. Roy Papp Stock	Growth & Income	Growth
Lazard Special Equity Portfolio . .	Aggressive Growth . . .	Growth
Maxus Income	General Bond	Balanced
Northeast Investors Trust	Corp. High-Yield Bond .	Balanced
PRA Real Estate Securities	Growth	Growth & Income
Primary Trend	Growth & Income	Balanced
Seven Seas Series—Small Cap . . .	Growth & Income	Growth
Strong Short-Term Bond	Corporate Bond	General Bond
Strong Total Return	Balanced	Growth & Income
USAA Growth	Growth & Income	Growth
Vanguard Short-Term Federal . . .	Government Bond . . .	General Bond

FUNDS DROPPED FROM THE GUIDE

Fund Name	Reason for Dropping Fund
Aetna	Added a 1% contingent deferred sales charge and a 12b-1 fee
Aetna Bond	Added a 1% contingent deferred sales charge and a 12b-1 fee
Aetna Growth & Income	Added a 1% contingent deferred sales charge and a 12b-1 fee
Aetna International Growth	Added a 1% contingent deferred sales charge and a 12b-1 fee
Alliance Bond—U.S. Gov't "C"	Multiple class structure
Alliance Mortgage Strategy "C"	Multiple class structure
Alliance Municipal Income—CA "C" . .	Multiple class structure
Alliance Municipal Income—Nat'l "C" .	Multiple class structure
Alliance World Income Trust	Multiple class structure
Beacon Hill Mutual	Total assets below $10 million for last 2 years
BNY Hamilton Equity Income	Imposed a 3% front-end sales load in addition to a 12b-1 fee
BNY Hamilton Interm Gov't	Imposed a 3% front-end sales load in addition to a 12b-1 fee
BNY Hamilton Interm NY Tax Exempt .	Imposed a 3% front-end sales load in addition to a 12b-1 fee
Boston Co Asset Allocation	Liquidated on 7/29/94
Boston Co Interm Term Gov't	Multiple class structure
Boston Co Managed Income	Multiple class structure

Boston Tax Free Muni Bond	Multiple class structure
Bruce	Total assets below $10 million for last 2 years
BT Investments—Utility	Primarily for institutional investors
Bull & Bear Financial News Composite	Merged into Bull & Bear Quality Growth
Fidelity Sel Electric Utilities	Merged into Fidelity Select Utilities Portfolio
Forty-Four Wall Street Equity	Total assets below $10 million for last 2 years
Franklin Short-Term U.S. Gov't	Imposed a 12b-1 fee in addition to a 2.25% sales charge
Gabelli Equity Income	Instituted a 4.50% sales charge
Gateway Government Bond Plus	Liquidated on 4/30/94
GE U.S. Equity	Multiple class structure
HighMark Bond	Multiple class structure
HighMark Income Equity	Multiple class structure
HighMark Special Growth Equity	Multiple class structure
Laurel Intermediate Income	Primarily for institutional investors
Laurel Stock Port	Primarily for institutional investors
LMH	Total assets below $10 million for last 2 years
Merrill Lynch Corp Interm "A"	Multiple class structure
Merrill Lynch Muni Interm "A"	Multiple class structure
Merrill Lynch Muni Ltd Mat "A"	Multiple class structure
Paine Webber Atlas Global Growth "D"	Multiple class structure
Paine Webber CA Tax-Free "D"	Multiple class structure
Paine Webber Capital Appreciation "D"	Multiple class structure
Paine Webber Dividend Growth "D"	Multiple class structure
Paine Webber Global Income "D"	Multiple class structure
Paine Webber Growth "D"	Multiple class structure
Paine Webber High Income "D"	Multiple class structure
Paine Webber Investment Inc "D"	Multiple class structure
Paine Webber Muni High Inc "D"	Multiple class structure
Paine Webber Nat'l Tax-Free Income "D"	Multiple class structure
Paine Webber N.Y. Tax Free Inc "D"	Multiple class structure
Paine Webber Small Cap Value "D"	Multiple class structure
Paine Webber U.S. Gov't Income "D"	Multiple class structure
Rainbow	Total assets below $10 million for last 2 years
Rushmore OTC Index Plus	Merged into Capiello Emerging Growth
Rushmore Stock Market Index Plus	Merged into Capiello Growth
Smith Barney—Income Return "A"	Multiple class structure
Smith Barney Muni Bond Ltd Term "A"	Multiple class structure
Smith Barney Short-Term US Treasury	Multiple class structure
US European Income	Total assets below $10 million for last 2 years
US Growth	Total assets below $10 million for last 2 years
Vanguard Spec Port—Service Econ	Merged into Vanguard Morgan Growth
Vanguard Spec Port—Tech	Merged into Vanguard Explorer
Westcore Trust Short-Term Gov't Bond	Added a 12b-1 fee in addition to a 2% sales charge

Index

1784 Growth and Income, 41, 58
1784 Mass Tax-Exempt Income, 50, 59, 943
1784 Tax-Exempt Med-Term Income, 49, 60
1784 US Gov't Medium Term Income, 47, 61

A

AARP Capital Growth, 40, 62
AARP GNMA & US Treasury, 46, 63
AARP Growth & Income, 40, 64
AARP High Quality Bond, 48, 65
AARP Insured Tax Free General Bond, 50, 66
Acorn, 24, 32, 34, 40, 56, 67, 939
Acorn Int'l, 53, 56, 68, 939
Aetna, 946
Aetna Bond, 946
Aetna Growth & Income, 946
Aetna International Growth, 946
Alliance Bond—U.S. Gov't "C", 946
Alliance Mortgage Strategy "C", 946
Alliance Municipal Income—CA "C", 946
Alliance Municipal Income—National "C", 946
Alliance World Income Trust, 946
Amana Income, 42, 69, 941
America's Utility, 43, 70, 938
American Heritage, 31, 37, 71
American Pension Investors—Growth, 39, 72, 936
AmSouth Bond, 48, 73
AmSouth Limited Maturity, 47, 74
Analytic Optioned Equity, 41, 75
Aquinas Balanced, 44, 76
Aquinas Equity Income, 42, 77
Aquinas Fixed Income, 48, 78
Ariel Appreciation, 40, 79
Armstrong Associates, 37, 80

ASM, 41, 81, 937

B

Babson Bond Trust—Port L, 48, 82
Babson Bond Trust—Port S, 48, 83
Babson Enterprise, 32, 34, 38, 55, 84, 940
Babson Enterprise II, 40, 85
Babson Growth, 41, 86
Babson Shadow Stock, 39, 56, 87, 940
Babson Tax-Free Income—Port L, 51, 89
Babson Tax-Free Income—Port S, 49, 90
Babson Value, 41, 91
Babson-Stewart Ivory Int'l, 52, 88
Baron Asset, 34, 35, 92
Bartlett Basic Value, 41, 93
Bartlett Fixed Income, 48, 94
Bartlett Value Int'l, 52, 95
Bascom Hill Balanced, 43, 96, 935
BayFunds Bond Port—Investment Shares, 48, 97
BayFunds Equity Port—Investment Shares, 39, 98
BayFunds Short-Term Yield—Investment Shares, 48, 99
BB&K Diversa, 44, 100, 935
BB&K International Equity, 53, 101
BB&K International Fixed-Income, 31, 54, 102
Beacon Hill Mutual, 946
Benham Adjustable Rate Gov't, 46, 103
Benham CA Tax-Free High-Yield, 50, 104, 941
Benham CA Tax-Free Insured, 51, 105, 942
Benham CA Tax-Free Interm, 49, 106, 942
Benham CA Tax-Free Long-Term, 51, 107, 942
Benham CA Tax-Free Short-Term, 49, 108, 942
Benham Equity Growth, 38, 109

Benham European Gov't Bond, 54, 110

Benham GNMA Income, 46, 111

Benham Gold Equities Index, 54, 112, 937, 938

Benham Income & Growth, 41, 113

Benham Long-Term Treasury & Agency, 46, 114

Benham Nat'l Tax-Free Interm Term, 49, 115

Benham Nat'l Tax-Free Long-Term, 50, 116

Benham Short-Term Treasury & Agency, 45, 117

Benham Target Mat Trust—1995, 45, 118

Benham Target Mat Trust—2000, 46, 119

Benham Target Mat Trust—2005, 46, 120

Benham Target Mat Trust—2010, 46, 121

Benham Target Mat Trust—2015, 46, 122

Benham Target Mat Trust—2020, 31, 46, 123

Benham Treasury Note, 45, 124

Benham Utilities Income, 42, 125

Berger One Hundred, 32, 33, 36, 126

Berger One Hundred & One, 42, 127

Berger Small Company Growth, 31, 35, 55, 128, 940

Bernstein CA Muni Port, 49, 129, 942

Bernstein Diversified Muni Port, 49, 130

Bernstein Gov't Short Duration, 45, 131

Bernstein Int'l Value, 52, 132

Bernstein Interm Duration, 48, 133

Bernstein NY Muni Port, 49, 134, 943

Bernstein Short Duration Plus, 47, 135

Berwyn, 34, 37, 136

Berwyn Income, 43, 137, 935

Blanchard American Equity, 39, 138

Blanchard Flexible Income, 48, 139

Blanchard Global Growth, 53, 140, 935, 936

Blanchard Precious Metals, 54, 141, 938

Blanchard Short Term Bond, 47, 142

Blanchard Short-Term Global Inc, 54, 143, 936

BNY Hamilton Equity Income, 946

BNY Hamilton Interm Gov't, 946

BNY Hamilton Interm NY Tax Exempt, 946

Boston Co Asset Allocation, 946

Boston Co Capital Appreciation, 945

Boston Co Interm Term Gov't, 946

Boston Co International, 945

Boston Co Managed Income, 946

Boston Co Special Growth, 945

Boston Tax Free Muni Bond, 947

Brandywine, 33, 38, 144

Brandywine Blue, 38, 145

Brinson Global, 53, 146, 935, 936

Brinson Global Bond, 54, 147, 936

Brinson Non-U.S. Equity, 52, 148

Brundage Story & Rose Short/Interm, 48, 149

BT Investments—Utility, 947

Bull & Bear Financial News Composite, 947

Bull & Bear Global Income, 54, 150, 936

Bull & Bear Gold Investors Ltd, 54, 151, 938

Bull & Bear Muni Income, 51, 152

Bull & Bear Special Equities, 36, 153

Bull & Bear U.S. & Overseas, 53, 154, 936

Bull & Bear U.S. Gov't Securities, 45, 155, 946

C

CA Investment Trust US Gov't, 46, 156

Cal Muni, 31, 51, 157, 942

Cal Tax-Free Income, 51, 158, 942

Caldwell & Orkin Aggressive Growth, 36, 55, 159, 940

Calvert Tax-Free Reserves Ltd Term—Class A, 49, 160

Cappiello-Rushmore Emerging Growth, 36, 56, 161, 940

Cappiello-Rushmore Utility Income, 43, 162, 938

Capstone Gov't Income, 45, 163

Century Shares Trust, 39, 164, 938

CGM Capital Development, 31, 32, 33, 37, 165

CGM Fixed Income, 44, 166

CGM Mutual, 32, 44, 167, 935

Charter Capital Blue Chip Growth, 42, 168

Chesapeake Growth, 35, 169

Clipper, 39, 170

Cohen & Steers Realty Shares, 34, 40, 171, 938

Columbia Balanced, 43, 172, 935

Columbia Common Stock, 41, 173

Columbia Fixed Income Securities, 48, 174

Columbia Growth, 32, 38, 175

Columbia Int'l Stock, 53, 176, 936

Columbia Muni Bond, 49, 177

Columbia Special, 35, 55, 178, 940

Columbia US Gov't Securities, 45, 179

Connecticut Mutual Inv Acts Income, 47, 180

Consolidated Standish Short Asset Resv, 47, 181

Copley, 42, 182

Corefund Equity Index, 41, 183, 937

Crabbe Huson Asset Allocation, 43, 184, 935

Crabbe Huson Equity, 33, 34, 38, 185

Crabbe Huson Special, 31, 33, 34, 35, 55, 186, 940

D

Dodge & Cox Balanced, 43, 187

Dodge & Cox Income, 48, 188

Dodge & Cox Stock, 32, 40, 189

Domini Social Equity, 41, 190, 941

Dreman Contrarian, 41, 191

Dreman High Return, 38, 192

Dreyfus, 42, 193

Dreyfus 100% US Treasury Interm Term, 45, 194

Dreyfus 100% US Treasury Long Term, 46, 195

Dreyfus 100% US Treasury Short Term, 45, 196

Dreyfus A Bonds Plus, 48, 197

Dreyfus Appreciation, 37, 198

Dreyfus Asset Allocation—Total Return, 43, 199, 935

Dreyfus Balanced, 43, 200

Dreyfus CA Interm Muni Bond, 50, 201, 942

Dreyfus CA Tax Exempt Bond, 51, 202, 942

Dreyfus Capital Growth, 40, 203

Dreyfus Conn Interm Muni Bond, 50, 204, 942

Dreyfus Core Value—Investor, 38, 205, 945

Dreyfus Edison Electric Index, 43, 206, 937, 938

Dreyfus Florida Interm Muni, 50, 207, 942

Dreyfus GNMA, 47, 208

Dreyfus Growth & Income, 42, 209

Dreyfus Growth Opportunity, 39, 210

Dreyfus Insured Muni Bond, 51, 211

Dreyfus Interm Muni Bond, 49, 212

Dreyfus International Equity, 53, 213

Dreyfus Investors GNMA, 46, 214

Dreyfus Mass Interm Muni Bond, 50, 216, 943

Dreyfus Mass Tax-Exempt Bond, 50, 217, 943

Dreyfus Muni Bond, 51, 218

Dreyfus New Leaders, 35, 55, 219, 940

Dreyfus NJ Interm Muni Bond, 50, 220, 943

Dreyfus NJ Muni Bond, 50, 221, 943

Dreyfus NY Insured Tax-Exempt, 51, 222, 943

Dreyfus NY Tax-Exempt, 51, 223, 943

Dreyfus NY Tax-Exempt Interm, 50, 224, 943

Dreyfus Peoples Index, 41, 225, 937

Dreyfus Peoples S&P MidCap Index, 39, 226, 937, 946

Dreyfus Short Interm Gov't, 45, 227

Dreyfus Short Term Income, 47, 228

Dreyfus Short-Interm Municipal, 49, 229

Dreyfus Special Growth—Investor, 31, 37, 230, 945

Dreyfus Third Century, 42, 231, 941

Dreyfus/Laurel International—Investor, 52, 215, 945

Dupree KY Tax-Free Income, 49, 232, 942

Dupree KY Tax-Free Short to Medium, 49, 233, 942

E

Eaton Vance Classic Gov't Obligations, 46, 234

Eaton Vance Classic Nat'l Ltd Maturity TF, 49, 235

Eaton Vance Classic National Municipals, 51, 236

Eaton Vance Short-Term Treasury, 45, 237

Eclipse Balanced, 43, 238

Eclipse Equity, 39, 56, 239, 940

Evergreen—Class Y, 35, 55, 241, 940

Evergreen American Retirement—Class Y, 43, 240

Evergreen Foundation—Class Y, 33, 43, 242, 935

Evergreen Global Real Estate—Class Y, 53, 243, 936, 938

Evergreen Growth & Income—Class Y, 41, 244, 945, 946

Evergreen Insured National Tax Free, 945

Evergreen Limited Market—Class Y, 32, 36, 56, 245, 940

Evergreen National Tax-Free—Class Y, 51, 246, 945

Evergreen Short Interm Muni CA—Class Y, 49, 247, 942

Evergreen Short-Interm Muni—Class Y, 49, 248

Evergreen Total Return—Class Y, 42, 249

Evergreen Value Timing, 945

F

Fairmont, 35, 250

FAM Value, 37, 55, 251, 940

Fidelities Utilities, 945

Fidelity Aggressive Tax-Free, 50, 252

Fidelity Asset Manager, 44, 253, 935

Fidelity Asset Manager—Growth, 44, 254, 935

Fidelity Asset Manager—Income, 43, 255, 935

Fidelity Balanced, 44, 256, 935

Fidelity Blue Chip Growth, 33, 37, 257

Fidelity CA Tax-Free High Yield, 51, 258, 942

Fidelity CA Tax-Free Insured, 51, 259, 942

Fidelity Canada, 53, 260

Fidelity Capital & Income, 33, 34, 45, 261

Fidelity Capital Appreciation Port, 34, 37, 262

Fidelity Contrafund, 32, 33, 38, 263

Fidelity Convertible Securities, 33, 42, 264

Fidelity Discipline Equity, 37, 265

Fidelity Diversified Int'l, 52, 266

Fidelity Dividend Growth, 37, 267

Fidelity Emerging Growth, 35, 55, 268, 940

Fidelity Emerging Markets, 31, 34, 53, 269

Fidelity Equity-Income, 41, 270

Fidelity Equity-Income II, 40, 271

Fidelity Europe, 52, 272

Fidelity European Capital Appreciation, 52, 273

Fidelity Fifty, 35, 274

Fidelity Fund, 41, 275

Fidelity Ginnie Mae, 46, 276

Fidelity Global Balanced, 53, 277, 935, 936

Fidelity Global Bond, 54, 278, 936

Fidelity Gov't Securities, 45, 279

Fidelity Growth & Income, 41, 280

Fidelity Growth Company, 32, 33, 36, 281

Fidelity High Yield Tax Free Port, 51, 282

Fidelity Insured Tax-Free, 51, 283

Fidelity Int'l Growth & Income, 53, 285, 936

Fidelity Interm Bond, 47, 284

Fidelity Investment Grade, 48, 286

Fidelity Japan, 31, 52, 287

Fidelity Latin America, 31, 53, 288

Fidelity Limited Term Muni, 50, 289

Fidelity Low-Priced Stock, 33, 34, 37, 55, 290, 940

Fidelity Magellan, 32, 39, 291

Fidelity Market Index, 41, 292, 937

Fidelity Mass Tax-Free High Yield, 50, 293, 943

Fidelity Michigan Tax-Free High Yield, 51, 294, 943

Fidelity Minnesota Tax-Free, 50, 295, 943
Fidelity Mortgage Securities, 46, 296
Fidelity Muni Bond, 51, 297
Fidelity New Markets Income, 54, 298, 936
Fidelity New Millenium, 35, 55, 299, 940
Fidelity NY Tax-Free High Yield, 51, 300, 943
Fidelity NY Tax-Free Insured, 51, 301, 943
Fidelity Ohio Tax-Free High Yield, 50, 302, 944
Fidelity OTC Port, 32, 36, 303
Fidelity Overseas, 32, 52, 304
Fidelity Pacific-Basin, 53, 305
Fidelity Puritan, 43, 306
Fidelity Real Estate Investment, 41, 307, 938
Fidelity Retirement Growth, 32, 38, 308
Fidelity Sel Air Transportation, 31, 37, 309, 938
Fidelity Sel American Gold, 54, 310, 938
Fidelity Sel Automotive, 33, 34, 36, 311, 938
Fidelity Sel Biotechnology, 31, 33, 37, 312, 938
Fidelity Sel Broadcast & Media, 945
Fidelity Sel Broker & Invest Mgmt, 31, 33, 37, 313, 938
Fidelity Sel Chemical, 31, 33, 37, 314, 938
Fidelity Sel Computers, 31, 33, 34, 35, 315, 938
Fidelity Sel Constr'n & Hous'g, 36, 316, 938
Fidelity Sel Consumer Products, 36, 317, 938
Fidelity Sel Defense & Aerospace, 35, 318, 938
Fidelity Sel Dev'ping Communic'ns, 31, 34, 35, 319, 938
Fidelity Sel Electric Utilities, 947
Fidelity Sel Electronics, 31, 33, 34, 35, 320, 938
Fidelity Sel Energy, 38, 321, 938
Fidelity Sel Energy Service, 35, 322, 938
Fidelity Sel Environ'l Serv, 36, 323, 938

Fidelity Sel Financial Services, 33, 34, 39, 324, 938
Fidelity Sel Food & Agriculture, 35, 325, 938
Fidelity Sel Health Care, 31, 32, 33, 35, 326, 938
Fidelity Sel Home Finance, 33, 34, 35, 327, 938
Fidelity Sel Industrial Equipment, 34, 35, 328, 938
Fidelity Sel Industrial Materials, 35, 329, 938
Fidelity Sel Insurance, 38, 330, 938
Fidelity Sel Leisure, 32, 34, 36, 331, 938
Fidelity Sel Medical Delivery, 31, 33, 35, 332, 938
Fidelity Sel Multimedia, 34, 35, 333, 938, 945
Fidelity Sel Natural Gas Port, 40, 334, 939
Fidelity Sel Paper & Forest Prod, 31, 34, 35, 335, 939
Fidelity Sel Precious Metals, 34, 54, 336, 939
Fidelity Sel Regional Banks, 33, 34, 38, 337, 939
Fidelity Sel Retailing, 33, 36, 338, 939
Fidelity Sel Software & Comp, 33, 34, 35, 339, 939
Fidelity Sel Technology, 33, 34, 35, 340, 939
Fidelity Sel Telecomm, 34, 37, 341, 939
Fidelity Sel Transportation, 33, 34, 35, 342, 939
Fidelity Sel Utilities, 945
Fidelity Sel Utilities Growth, 42, 343, 939, 945
Fidelity Short-Interm Gov't, 45, 344
Fidelity Short-Term Bond, 44, 345
Fidelity Short-Term World Income, 54, 346, 936
Fidelity Southeast Asia, 31, 53, 347
Fidelity Spartan Aggressive Municipal, 50, 348
Fidelity Spartan CA Interm Muni, 49, 349, 942

Fidelity Spartan CA Muni High Yield, 51, 350, 942

Fidelity Spartan Conn Tax-Free High-Yield, 51, 351, 942

Fidelity Spartan Florida Muni Income, 51, 352, 942

Fidelity Spartan Ginnie Mae, 46, 353

Fidelity Spartan Gov't Income, 47, 354

Fidelity Spartan High Income, 34, 45, 355

Fidelity Spartan Intermediate Municipal, 50, 356

Fidelity Spartan Investment Grade, 44, 357

Fidelity Spartan Long-Term Gov't, 46, 358

Fidelity Spartan Ltd Maturity Gov't, 46, 359

Fidelity Spartan Maryland Muni Income, 51, 360, 942

Fidelity Spartan Muni Income, 51, 361

Fidelity Spartan NJ Muni High Yield, 50, 362, 943

Fidelity Spartan NY Interm Muni, 49, 363, 943

Fidelity Spartan NY Muni High Yield, 51, 364, 943

Fidelity Spartan Penn Muni High Yield, 50, 365, 944

Fidelity Spartan Short Intermediate Gov't, 47, 366, 946

Fidelity Spartan Short-Interm Muni, 49, 367

Fidelity Spartan Short-Term Income, 44, 368

Fidelity Stock Selector, 38, 369

Fidelity Trend, 39, 370

Fidelity Utilities, 42, 371, 939, 945

Fidelity Utilities Income, 945

Fidelity Value, 34, 37, 372

Fidelity Worldwide, 34, 52, 373, 936

Fiduciary Capital Growth, 38, 374

Fifty-Nine Wall St European, 53, 375

Fifty-Nine Wall St Pacific Basin, 31, 53, 376

Fifty-Nine Wall St Small Company, 36, 56, 377

Fifty-Nine Wall St Tax-Free Short/Interm, 49, 378

Fifty-Nine Wall St Small Company, 940

First Eagle Fund of America, 34, 39, 379

First Hawaii Muni Bond, 50, 380, 942

Flex Bond, 47, 381, 946

Flex Growth, 38, 382

Flex Muirfield, 37, 383, 936

Flex Short Term Global Income, 54, 384, 936

Fontaine Capital Appreciation, 38, 385

Forty-Four Wall Street Equity, 947

Founders Balanced, 43, 386

Founders Blue Chip, 41, 387

Founders Discovery, 33, 36, 56, 388, 940

Founders Frontier, 36, 55, 389, 940

Founders Gov't Securities, 46, 390

Founders Growth, 32, 39, 391

Founders Special, 32, 36, 392

Founders World Wide Growth, 53, 393, 936

Franklin Short-Term US Gov't, 947

Fremont CA Interm Tax-Free, 50, 394, 942

Fremont Global, 53, 395, 935, 936, 946

Fremont Growth, 38, 396

Fundamental US Gov't Strat Income, 31, 46, 397

G

Gabelli Asset, 38, 398

Gabelli Equity Income, 947

Gabelli Growth, 39, 399

Galaxy Asset Allocation, 43, 400, 935

Galaxy Connecticut Municipal Bond, 51, 401, 942

Galaxy Equity Growth, 38, 402

Galaxy Equity Income, 41, 403

Galaxy Equity Value, 40, 404

Galaxy High Quality Bond, 48, 405

Galaxy II Large Company Index - Retail, 41, 406, 937

Galaxy II Small Company Index - Retail, 39, 56, 407, 937, 940

Galaxy II U.S. Treasury Index Retail, 45, 408, 937

Galaxy II Utility Index - Retail, 42, 409, 937
Galaxy Interm Bond, 48, 410
Galaxy International Equity, 53, 411
Galaxy NY Muni Bond, 51, 412, 943
Galaxy Short Term Bond, 47, 413
Galaxy Small Company Equity, 35, 55, 414, 940
Galaxy Tax-Exempt Bond, 50, 415
Gateway Government Bond Plus, 947
Gateway Index Plus, 40, 416
GE U.S. Equity, 947
General CA Muni Bond, 51, 417, 942
General Muni Bond, 51, 418
General NY Muni Bond, 51, 419, 943
Gintel, 40, 420
Gintel ERISA, 31, 43, 421
GIT Equity—Special Growth, 36, 56, 422, 940
GIT Income—Gov't Port, 45, 423
GIT Income—Maximum, 45, 424
GIT Tax Free High Yield, 945
GIT Tax-Free National Port, 51, 425, 945
GIT Tax-Free Virginia Port, 51, 426, 944
Gradison McDonald Established Value, 38, 427
Gradison McDonald Opportunity Value, 39, 55, 428, 940
Greenspring, 40, 429

H

Harbor Bond, 48, 430
Harbor Capital Appreciation, 33, 37, 431
Harbor Growth, 40, 432
Harbor Int'l, 34, 52, 433
Harbor International Growth, 53, 434
Harbor Short Duration, 47, 435
Harbor Value, 41, 436
Heartland U.S. Government Securities, 48, 437
Heartland Value, 32, 33, 34, 35, 55, 438, 940
Heartland Wisconsin Tax Free, 50, 439, 944
HighMark Bond, 947
HighMark Income Equity, 947
HighMark Special Growth Equity, 947

Homestead Short-Term Bond, 44, 440
Homestead Value, 41, 441
Hotchkis and Wiley Balanced Income, 43, 442, 935, 945
Hotchkis and Wiley Equity Income, 42, 443, 945
Hotchkis and Wiley International, 53, 444
Hotchkis and Wiley Low Duration, 47, 445

I

IAI Balanced, 43, 446, 935
IAI Bond, 48, 447, 946
IAI Emerging Growth, 35, 55, 448, 940
IAI Gov't, 45, 449
IAI Growth & Income, 42, 450, 946
IAI Int'l, 52, 451
IAI MidCap Growth, 37, 452
IAI Regional, 32, 38, 453
IAI Reserve, 47, 454
IAI Value, 40, 455
International Equity, 52, 456
INVESCO Dynamics, 32, 33, 36, 457
INVESCO Emerging Growth, 34, 36, 56, 458, 940
INVESCO Growth, 40, 459
INVESCO Income—High Yield, 45, 460
INVESCO Income—Sel Income, 44, 461
INVESCO Income—US Gov't Sec, 46, 462
INVESCO Industrial Income, 32, 44, 463, 935
INVESCO Int'l—European, 53, 464
INVESCO Int'l—Int'l Growth, 52, 465
INVESCO Int'l—Pacific Basin, 32, 52, 466
INVESCO Strat Port—Financial, 33, 39, 467
INVESCO Strat Port—Energy, 36, 468, 939
INVESCO Strat Port—Environm'l, 36, 469, 939
INVESCO Strat Port—Financial, 939
INVESCO Strat Port—Gold, 31, 54, 470, 939
INVESCO Strat Port—Health Sci, 32, 33, 35, 471, 939

INVESCO Strat Port—Leisure, 32, 33, 34, 36, 472, 939

INVESCO Strat Port—Tech, 32, 33, 35, 473, 939

INVESCO Strat Port—Utilities, 42, 474, 939

INVESCO Tax-Free Long-Term Bond, 50, 475

INVESCO Value Trust—Interm Gov't, 45, 476

INVESCO Value Trust—Total Return, 43, 477, 935

INVESCO Value Trust—Value Equity, 40, 478

J

Janus, 32, 38, 479

Janus Balanced, 43, 480, 935

Janus Enterprise, 35, 481

Janus Federal Tax-Exempt, 51, 482

Janus Flexible Income, 44, 483

Janus Growth & Income, 42, 484

Janus Interm Gov't Securities, 45, 485

Janus Mercury, 31, 37, 486

Janus Short-Term Bond, 44, 487

Janus Twenty, 40, 488

Janus Venture, 35, 55, 489, 940

Janus Worldwide, 52, 490, 936

Japan, 32, 52, 491

Jurika & Voyles Balanced, 43, 492, 935

K

Kaufmann, 33, 35, 55, 493, 940

L

L. Roy Papp Stock, 39, 525, 946

Laurel Intermediate Income, 947

Laurel Stock Port, 947

Lazard Equity, 37, 494

Lazard International Equity Portfolio, 52, 495

Lazard Small Cap Portfolio, 34, 35, 55, 496, 940

Lazard Special Equity Portfolio, 39, 55, 497, 940, 946

Lazard Strategic Yield Portfolio, 48, 498

Leeb Personal Finance, 39, 499

Legg Mason American Leading Cos., 42, 500

Legg Mason Global Gov't Trust, 54, 501, 936

Legg Mason Investment Grade, 48, 502

Legg Mason Special Investment, 36, 56, 503, 940

Legg Mason Total Return, 42, 504

Legg Mason US Gov't Interm Port, 47, 505

Legg Mason Value, 38, 506

Lepercq-Istel, 44, 507, 935

Lexington Global, 52, 508, 937

Lexington GNMA Income, 46, 509

Lexington GoldFund, 54, 510, 939

Lexington Growth & Income, 42, 511

Lexington Tax-Exempt Bond Trust, 51, 512

Lexington Worldwide Emerging Mkts, 53, 513, 937

Lindner, 42, 514

Lindner Dividend, 44, 515

Lindner Utility, 42, 516, 939

LMH, 947

Longleaf Partners, 34, 37, 517, 945

Longleaf Partners Small Cap, 37, 55, 518, 940, 945

Loomis Sayles Bond, 44, 519

Loomis Sayles Global Bond, 54, 520, 937

Loomis Sayles Growth, 36, 521

Loomis Sayles Growth & Income, 42, 522

Loomis Sayles International Equity, 52, 523

Loomis Sayles Small Cap, 36, 56, 524, 940

M

M.S.B. Fund, 39, 566

Managers Bond, 48, 526

Managers Capital Appreciation, 36, 527

Managers Income Equity, 41, 528

Managers Interm Mortgage, 31, 47, 529

Managers International Equity, 52, 530, 937

Managers Short & Interm Bond, 48, 531

Managers Short Gov't, 47, 532

Managers Special Equity, 36, 55, 533, 940

Marshall Equity Income, 42, 534
Marshall Government Income, 47, 535
Marshall Intermediate Bond, 48, 536
Marshall Mid-Cap Stock, 36, 537
Marshall Short-Term Income, 47, 538
Marshall Stock, 39, 539
Marshall Value Equity, 38, 540
Mathers, 39, 541
Matrix Growth, 39, 542
Maxus Equity, 38, 543, 935
Maxus Income, 44, 544, 935, 946
Maxus Laureate, 42, 545, 936, 945
Maxus Prism, 945
Merger, 35, 546
Meridian, 32, 33, 38, 55, 547, 940
Merrill Lynch Corp Interm "A", 947
Merrill Lynch Muni Interm "A", 947
Merrill Lynch Muni Ltd Mat "A", 947
Merriman Asset Allocation, 44, 548, 935, 936
Merriman Blue Chip, 945
Merriman Capital Appreciation, 38, 549, 936
Merriman Flexible Bond, 48, 550, 936
Merriman Growth & Income, 41, 551, 936, 945
MIM Bond Income, 44, 552
MIM Stock Appreciation, 33, 36, 553
MIM Stock Growth, 40, 554
MIM Stock Income, 42, 555
Monetta, 39, 56, 556, 940
Montgomery Emerging Markets, 53, 557
Montgomery Global Communic'ns, 53, 558, 937, 939
Montgomery Growth, 31, 37, 559
Montgomery International Small Cap, 53, 56, 560, 940
Montgomery Short Duration Government, 945
Montgomery Short Gov't Bond, 46, 561, 945
Montgomery Small Cap, 36, 56, 562, 940
Morgan Grenfell Fixed Income, 47, 563
Morgan Grenfell Global Fixed Income, 54, 564, 937
Morgan Grenfell Muni Bond, 49, 565

Mutual Beacon, 32, 34, 40, 567
Mutual Discovery, 37, 55, 568, 940
Mutual Qualified, 32, 34, 40, 569
Mutual Shares, 32, 34, 40, 570

N

National Industries, 38, 571
Neuberger & Berman Focus, 38, 572, 945
Neuberger & Berman Genesis, 36, 55, 573, 940
Neuberger & Berman Guardian, 32, 41, 574
Neuberger & Berman Ltd Maturity Bond, 47, 575
Neuberger & Berman Manhattan, 39, 576
Neuberger & Berman Muni Securities, 49, 577
Neuberger & Berman Partners, 42, 578
Neuberger & Berman Selected Sectors, 945
Neuberger & Berman Ultra Short Bond, 47, 579
New Century Capital Port, 38, 580, 936
Nicholas, 39, 582
Nicholas II, 38, 55, 583, 940
Nicholas Income, 45, 584
Nicholas Limited Edition, 39, 55, 585, 940
Nomura Pacific Basin, 52, 586
Northeast Investors Growth, 38, 587
Northeast Investors Trust, 43, 588, 935, 946
NY Muni, 31, 52, 581, 943

O

Oakmark, 34, 37, 589
Oakmark Int'l, 53, 590
Oberweis Emerging Growth, 33, 36, 56, 591, 940
Olympic Balanced Income, 945
Olympic Equity Income, 945
Oregon Municipal Bond, 49, 592, 944

P

Pacifica Asset Preservation, 47, 593
Pacifica Short Term CA Tax-Free, 49, 594, 942

Paine Webber Atlas Global Growth "D", 947

Paine Webber CA Tax-Free "D", 947

Paine Webber Capital Appreciation "D", 947

Paine Webber Dividend Growth "D", 947

Paine Webber Global Income "D", 947

Paine Webber Growth "D", 947

Paine Webber High Income "D", 947

Paine Webber Investment Inc "D", 947

Paine Webber Muni High Inc "D", 947

Paine Webber N.Y. Tax Free Inc "D", 947

Paine Webber Nat'l Tax-Free Income "D", 947

Paine Webber Small Cap Value "D", 947

Paine Webber U.S. Gov't Income "D", 947

Pax World, 43, 595, 941

PBHG Emerging Growth, 31, 35, 55, 596, 941

PBHG Growth, 33, 34, 35, 55, 597, 941

Pennsylvania Mutual, 38, 55, 598, 941

Permanent Port, 43, 599, 935

Permanent Port—Versatile Bond, 44, 600

Permanent Treasury Bill, 45, 601

Perritt Capital Growth, 36, 56, 602, 941

Philadelphia, 42, 603

Portico Balanced—Retail, 44, 604

Portico Bond IMMDEX—Retail, 48, 605

Portico Equity Index—Retail, 41, 606, 937

Portico Growth & Income—Retail, 41, 607

Portico Interm Bond Market—Retail, 48, 608

Portico MidCore Growth—Retail, 39, 609

Portico Short Term Bond Market—Retail, 47, 610

Portico Special Growth—Retail, 39, 611

Portico Tax-Exempt Intermediate Bond—Retail, 49, 612

PRA Real Estate Securities, 40, 613, 939, 946

Preferred Asset Allocation, 43, 614, 935

Preferred Fixed Income, 48, 615

Preferred Growth, 38, 616

Preferred Int'l, 52, 617

Preferred Short-Term Gov't Securities, 47, 618

Preferred Value, 41, 619

Primary Trend, 43, 620, 935, 946

Prudent Speculator, 36, 56, 621, 941

Prudential Gov't Securities Interm Term, 45, 622

R

Rainbow, 947

Regis C & B Balanced, 43, 623

Regis C & B Equity, 41, 624

Regis DSI Disciplined Value, 39, 625

Regis DSI Limited Maturity Bond, 47, 626

Regis ICM Small Company Port, 33, 34, 37, 55, 627, 941

Regis Sterling Partners Balanced, 43, 628, 935

Regis TS & W International Equity, 52, 629

Reich & Tang Equity, 38, 630

Reynolds Blue Chip Growth, 41, 631

Rightime, 38, 632, 936

Robertson Stephens Emerging Growth, 33, 35, 55, 633, 941

Robertson Stephens Value + Growth, 31, 35, 55, 634, 941, 945

Robertson Stephens Value Plus, 945

Royce Equity Income Series, 42, 635

Royce Premier, 37, 55, 636, 941

Rushmore American Gas Index, 42, 637, 937, 939

Rushmore Maryland Tax-Free, 50, 638, 943

Rushmore OTC Index Plus, 947

Rushmore Stock Market Index Plus, 947

Rushmore US Gov't Interm-Term, 46, 639

Rushmore US Gov't Long-Term, 46, 640

Rushmore Virginia Tax-Free, 50, 641, 944

S

Safeco CA Tax-Free Income, 51, 642, 942

Safeco Equity, 32, 34, 40, 643

Safeco GNMA, 47, 644, 945

Safeco Growth, 36, 645

Safeco High Yield Bond, 45, 646

Safeco Income, 43, 647

Safeco Muni Bond, 51, 648

Safeco Northwest, 39, 649
Safeco U.S. Government Securities, 945
Salomon Brothers Capital, 36, 650
Salomon Brothers Investors, 42, 651
Salomon Brothers Opportunity, 38, 652
SBSF, 39, 653
SBSF Convertible Securities, 42, 654
Schafer Value, 42, 655
Schroder US Equity, 39, 656
Schwab 1000, 41, 657, 937
Schwab CA Long-Term Tax-Free, 51, 658, 942
Schwab CA Short/Interm Tax-Free, 49, 659, 942
Schwab International Index, 52, 660, 937
Schwab Long-Term Tax-Free, 51, 661
Schwab Short/Interm Gov't Bond, 45, 662
Schwab Short/Intermediate Tax-Free, 49, 663
Schwab Small-Cap Index, 36, 55, 664, 937, 941
Schwartz Value, 40, 56, 665, 941
Scudder Balanced, 43, 666
Scudder CA Tax Free, 51, 667, 942
Scudder Capital Growth, 32, 40, 668
Scudder Development, 36, 56, 669, 941
Scudder Emerging Markets Inc, 54, 670
Scudder Global, 53, 671, 937
Scudder Global Fixed Income, 937
Scudder Global Small Company, 53, 56, 672, 937, 941
Scudder GNMA, 47, 673
Scudder Gold, 54, 674, 939
Scudder Growth & Income, 32, 41, 675
Scudder High Yield Tax-Free, 51, 676
Scudder Income, 48, 677
Scudder International, 32, 53, 678
Scudder International Bond, 54, 679
Scudder Latin America, 53, 680
Scudder Managed Muni Bond, 50, 681
Scudder Mass Tax-Free, 50, 682, 943
Scudder Medium Term Tax Free, 49, 683
Scudder NY Tax Free, 51, 684, 943
Scudder Ohio Tax-Free, 50, 685, 944
Scudder Pacific Opportunities, 31, 53, 686
Scudder Penn Tax Free, 50, 687, 944

Scudder Quality Growth, 39, 688
Scudder Short-Term Bond, 48, 689
Scudder Short-Term Global Income, 54, 690, 937
Scudder U.S. Government Zero Coupon 2000, 46, 691
Scudder Value, 38, 692
Selected American Shares, 42, 693
Selected Special Shares, 39, 694
Selected US Gov't Income, 46, 695
Sentry, 39, 696
Sequoia, 40, 697
Seven Seas Series Growth & Income, 41, 698
Seven Seas Series—Matrix Equity, 41, 699
Seven Seas Series—S&P 500, 41, 700, 937
Seven Seas Series—S&P MidCap Index, 945
Seven Seas Series—Small Cap, 38, 55, 701, 941, 945, 946
Seven Seas Short Term Gov't Securities, 45, 702
Seven Seas Yield Plus, 47, 703
SIT Growth, 32, 36, 55, 704, 941
SIT Growth & Income, 40, 705
SIT International Growth, 53, 706
SIT Minnesota Tax Free Income, 49, 707
SIT Tax Free Income, 49, 708
SIT US Gov't Securities, 46, 709
Skyline Special Equities II, 39, 55, 710, 941
Smith Barney Muni Bond Ltd Term "A", 947
Smith Barney Short-Term U.S. Treasury, 947
Smith Barney—Income Return "A", 947
Smith Breedon Interm Duration U.S. Gov't Series, 46, 711
Smith Breedon Short Duration U.S. Gov't Series, 46, 712, 936
Sound Shore, 38, 713
Southeastern Asset Management Small Cap, 945
Southeastern Asset Management Value Trust, 945
Standish Equity, 39, 714
Standish Fixed Income, 48, 715

Standish Global Fixed Income, 54, 716

Standish International Equity, 53, 717

Standish Mass Interm Tax-Exempt, 49, 718, 943

Standish Securitized, 46, 719

Standish Small Capitalization Equity, 36, 56, 720, 941

SteinRoe Capital Opportunities, 35, 721

SteinRoe Gov't Income, 48, 722

SteinRoe High Yield Muni, 49, 723

SteinRoe Income, 44, 724

SteinRoe Interm Bond, 48, 725

SteinRoe Interm Muni, 49, 726

SteinRoe Limited Maturity Income, 47, 727

SteinRoe Managed Muni, 50, 728

SteinRoe Prime Equities, 38, 729

SteinRoe Special, 32, 36, 730

SteinRoe Stock, 39, 731

SteinRoe Total Return, 44, 732, 936

Stratton Growth, 40, 733

Stratton Monthly Dividend Shares, 42, 734

Strong Advantage, 44, 735

Strong American Utilities, 42, 736, 939

Strong Asia Pacific, 53, 737

Strong Asset Allocation, 43, 738, 936, 945

Strong Common Stock, 33, 34, 36, 739

Strong Discovery, 33, 39, 56, 740, 941

Strong Gov't Securities, 48, 741

Strong Growth, 31, 37, 742

Strong High Yield Municipal Bond, 49, 743

Strong Income, 47, 744

Strong Insured Muni Bond, 51, 745

Strong Int'l Stock, 52, 746

Strong Investment, 945

Strong Muni Bond, 49, 747

Strong Opportunity, 37, 748

Strong Short-Term Bond, 47, 749, 946

Strong Short-Term Muni Bond, 49, 750

Strong Total Return, 42, 751, 946

T

T Rowe Price Adjustable Rate US Gov't, 46, 753

T Rowe Price Balanced, 43, 754

T Rowe Price Blue Chip Growth, 41, 755

T Rowe Price CA Tax-Free Bond, 50, 756, 942

T Rowe Price Capital Appreciation, 37, 757

T Rowe Price Dividend Growth, 41, 758

T Rowe Price Equity Income, 40, 759

T Rowe Price Equity Index, 41, 760, 937

T Rowe Price European Stock, 52, 761

T Rowe Price Global Gov't Bond, 54, 762, 937

T Rowe Price GNMA, 46, 763

T Rowe Price Growth & Income, 41, 764

T Rowe Price Growth Stock, 38, 765

T Rowe Price High Yield, 45, 766

T Rowe Price Int'l Discovery, 53, 56, 767, 941

T Rowe Price Int'l Stock, 32, 52, 768

T Rowe Price International Bond, 54, 769

T Rowe Price Japan, 31, 52, 770

T Rowe Price Latin America, 53, 771

T Rowe Price Maryland Tax-Free, 50, 772, 943

T Rowe Price MD Short-Term Tax-Free, 49, 773, 943

T Rowe Price Mid-Cap Growth, 38, 774

T Rowe Price New America Growth, 40, 775

T Rowe Price New Asia, 31, 34, 53, 776

T Rowe Price New Era, 37, 777, 939

T Rowe Price New Horizons, 35, 55, 778, 941

T Rowe Price New Income, 48, 779

T Rowe Price NJ Tax-Free, 50, 780, 943

T Rowe Price NY Tax-Free, 50, 781, 943

T Rowe Price OTC, 35, 55, 782, 941

T Rowe Price Science & Tech, 31, 33, 34, 35, 783, 939

T Rowe Price Short-Term Bond, 48, 784

T Rowe Price Short-Term Global Inc, 54, 785, 937

T Rowe Price Small Cap Value, 39, 55, 786, 941

T Rowe Price Spectrum Growth, 41, 787, 936

T Rowe Price Spectrum Income, 43, 788, 936
T Rowe Price Tax-Free High Yield, 49, 789
T Rowe Price Tax-Free Income, 50, 790
T Rowe Price Tax-Free Insured Interm, 49, 791
T Rowe Price Tax-Free Short-Interm, 49, 792
T Rowe Price US Treasury Interm, 45, 793
T Rowe Price US Treasury Long Term, 45, 794
T Rowe Price Virginia Tax-Free Bond, 50, 795, 944
Tocqueville, 38, 752
Turner Growth Equity, 40, 796
Tweedy Browne American Value, 38, 797
Tweedy Browne Global Value, 52, 55, 798, 937, 941
Twentieth Century Balanced, 43, 799
Twentieth Century Giftrust, 31, 32, 33, 34, 35, 55, 800, 941
Twentieth Century Growth, 32, 36, 801
Twentieth Century Heritage, 39, 802
Twentieth Century Int'l Equity, 53, 803
Twentieth Century Long-Term Bond, 48, 804
Twentieth Century Select, 40, 805
Twentieth Century Tax-Exempt Interm, 49, 806
Twentieth Century Tax-Exempt Long, 50, 807
Twentieth Century Tax-Exempt Short, 49, 808
Twentieth Century Ultra, 32, 33, 36, 56, 809, 941
Twentieth Century U.S. Gov't, 945
Twentieth Century U.S. Gov't Short Term, 45, 810, 945
Twentieth Century Value, 40, 811
Twentieth Century Vista, 32, 35, 55, 812, 941

U

UMB Bond, 48, 813
UMB Heartland Fund, 38, 55, 814, 941
UMB Stock, 41, 815

US All American Equity, 42, 816
US European Income, 947
US Global Resources, 53, 817, 937, 939
US Gold Shares, 54, 818, 939
US Income, 42, 819
US Real Estate, 42, 820, 939
US Tax Free, 50, 821
US World Gold, 34, 54, 822, 939
USAA Aggressive Growth, 36, 55, 823, 941
USAA Balanced, 43, 824
USAA Cornerstone, 43, 825, 936
USAA Florida Tax-Free Income, 51, 826, 942
USAA GNMA Trust, 46, 827
USAA Gold, 54, 828, 939
USAA Growth, 37, 829, 946
USAA Growth & Income, 41, 830
USAA Income, 44, 831
USAA Income Stock, 41, 832
USAA International, 52, 833
USAA Tax Exempt CA Bond, 51, 834, 942
USAA Tax Exempt Interm-Term, 49, 835
USAA Tax Exempt Long-Term, 51, 836
USAA Tax Exempt NY Bond, 51, 837, 943
USAA Tax Exempt Short-Term, 49, 838
USAA Tax-Exempt Virginia Bond, 50, 839, 944
USAA World Growth, 52, 840, 937

V

Valley Forge, 40, 841
Value Line, 32, 39, 842
Value Line Adjustable Rate US Gov't, 47, 843
Value Line Aggressive Income, 45, 844
Value Line Convertible, 42, 845
Value Line Income, 44, 846, 936
Value Line Leveraged Growth, 36, 847
Value Line NY Tax-Exempt Trust, 51, 848, 943
Value Line Special Situations, 35, 849
Value Line Tax Exempt High Yield, 51, 850
Value Line US Gov't Securities, 47, 851

Vanguard Admiral Interm US Treas, 45, 852

Vanguard Admiral Long US Treas, 46, 853

Vanguard Admiral Short US Treas, 45, 854

Vanguard Asset Allocation, 43, 855, 936

Vanguard Balanced Index, 43, 856, 937

Vanguard Bond Index, 945

Vanguard CA Tax-Free Insured Long, 50, 857, 942

Vanguard Convertible Securities, 42, 858

Vanguard Equity Income, 42, 859

Vanguard Explorer, 35, 55, 860, 941

Vanguard Florida Insured Tax Free, 50, 861, 942

Vanguard GNMA, 46, 862

Vanguard High Yield Corporate, 45, 863

Vanguard High-Yield Muni Bond, 50, 864

Vanguard Index Trust—500, 10, 13, 41, 866, 937

Vanguard Index Trust—Ext. Market, 39, 55, 865, 937, 941

Vanguard Index Trust—Growth Port, 37, 867, 937

Vanguard Index Trust—Small Cap, 36, 55, 868, 937, 941, 945

Vanguard Index Trust—Tot Stock Mkt, 41, 869, 937

Vanguard Index Trust—Value Port, 42, 870, 938

Vanguard Insured Long-Term Muni, 50, 871

Vanguard Int'l Equity Index—Europe, 52, 875, 938

Vanguard Int'l Equity Index—Pacific, 31, 52, 876, 938

Vanguard Int'l Growth, 32, 52, 877

Vanguard Interm Term Corporate, 44, 872

Vanguard Interm-Term Muni Bond, 49, 873

Vanguard Interm-Term US Treasury, 45, 874

Vanguard Limited-Term Muni Bond, 49, 878

Vanguard Long Term Corp Bond, 44, 879

Vanguard Long-Term Muni Bond, 50, 880

Vanguard Long-Term US Treasury, 46, 881

Vanguard Morgan Growth, 39, 882

Vanguard NJ Tax Free Insured Long, 50, 883, 943

Vanguard NY Insured Tax Free, 50, 884, 943

Vanguard Ohio Tax Free Insur Long, 50, 885, 944

Vanguard Penn Tax-Free Insur Long, 49, 886, 944

Vanguard Preferred Stock, 42, 887

Vanguard Primecap, 31, 32, 37, 888

Vanguard Quantitative Port, 41, 889

Vanguard Short-Term Corporate, 44, 890

Vanguard Short-Term Federal, 47, 891, 946

Vanguard Short-Term Muni Bond, 49, 892

Vanguard Short-Term US Treasury, 45, 893

Vanguard Small Cap Stock, 945

Vanguard Spec Port—Energy, 39, 894, 939

Vanguard Spec Port—Gold & PM, 54, 895, 939

Vanguard Spec Port—Health Care, 32, 33, 37, 896, 939

Vanguard Spec Port—Service Econ, 947

Vanguard Spec Port—Tech, 947

Vanguard Spec Port—Utilities Income, 42, 897, 939

Vanguard Star, 43, 898, 936

Vanguard Total Bond Market Port, 48, 899, 938, 945

Vanguard Trustees' Equity—Int'l, 32, 52, 900

Vanguard Trustees' Equity—US, 42, 901

Vanguard US Growth, 37, 902

Vanguard Wellesley Income, 44, 903

Vanguard Wellington, 43, 904

Vanguard Windsor, 41, 905

Vanguard Windsor II, 42, 906

Vista Bond, 48, 907

Vista Equity, 38, 908
Vista Short-Term Bond, 47, 909
Volumetric, 39, 910
Vontobel EuroPacific, 53, 911
Vontobel US Value, 38, 912

W

Warburg Pincus Cap Appreciation, 39, 913
Warburg Pincus Emerging Grth, 36, 55, 914, 941
Warburg Pincus Fixed Income, 47, 915
Warburg Pincus Global Fixed Income, 54, 916, 937
Warburg Pincus Growth and Income, 34, 40, 917
Warburg Pincus Int'l Equity, 52, 919
Warburg Pincus Interm Mat Gov't, 45, 918
Warburg Pincus NY Muni Bond, 49, 920, 943

Wasatch Aggressive Equity, 33, 35, 921
Wayne Hummer Growth, 38, 922
Wayne Hummer Income, 48, 923
Weitz Value Port, 40, 924
Westcore Trust Short-Term Gov't Bond, 947
William Blair Growth Shares, 32, 33, 37, 925
William Blair Income Shares, 47, 926
William Blair International Growth, 52, 927
Woodward Equity Index, 41, 928, 938
WPG Gov't Securities, 46, 929
WPG Growth & Income, 42, 930
WPG Quantitative Equity, 41, 931
WPG Tudor, 36, 932
Wright Int'l Blue Chip Equity, 52, 933

Y

Yacktman, 37, 934

ABOUT AAII

WHAT IS AAII?

The American Association of Individual Investors is an independent, non-profit organization that was formed in 1978 to assist individuals in becoming effective managers of their own investments.

The *AAII Journal* is the primary benefit of membership. It is published 10 times a year. The focus is on providing information and how-to articles that help the individual learn investment fundamentals. The *Journal* does not promote a specific viewpoint or recommend specific investments, and it does not accept advertising. Each March every member receives a new edition of *The Individual Investor's Guide to Low-Load Mutual Funds*.

NATIONWIDE SEMINARS

AAII holds seminars across the country taught by university finance professors on the topics of stock analysis, financial planning, retirement and estate planning, bonds, mutual funds, portfolio management and the fundamentals of investing.

LOCAL CHAPTERS

AAII sponsors over 60 local chapters throughout the U.S. AAII members organize presentations given by investment professionals. AAII members who are interested in attending these meetings also benefit from talking to like-minded members.

OTHER EDUCATIONAL PRODUCTS

Members can buy AAII educational materials at reduced prices.

FOR ONLY $49 A YEAR

Membership in AAII is $49, which includes a subscription to the *AAII Journal*, *The Individual Investor's Guide to Low-Load Mutual Funds* (published in March), a yearly tax planning guide (published in mid-November), and reduced fees for seminars and educational publications.

To join AAII or order products, call AAII at 1-800-428-2244 or 1-312-280-0170.

American Association of Individual Investors
625 North Michigan Avenue • Chicago, Illinois 60611

Fourth Quarter

		Total Return (%) Last Qrtr.	Cat. +/-	Last 2 Qrtrs.	Cat. +/-	Last 3 Qrtrs.	Cat. +/-	Annual Total Return (%) Last Year	Cat. +/-	Last 3 Years	Cat. +/-	Last 5 Years	Cat. +/-	Risk Index	Yield (%)	Exp. Ratio (%)	Max. Load (%)	Max. 12b-1 (%)	Phone
Balanced Funds																			
T Rowe Price Spectrum Income	ff	1.7	0.0	4.4	(1.1)	7.4	(0.3)	12.4	(0.9)	13.1	(2.1)	na	na	0.48	6.2	0.00	—	—	(800) 638-5660
Twentieth Century Balanced		(0.8)	(2.5)	3.4	(2.1)	6.2	(1.5)	7.2	(6.1)	13.9	(1.3)	13.6	1.4	1.85	2.3	1.00	—	—	(800) 345-2021
USAA Balanced		2.3	0.6	4.7	(0.8)	9.0	1.3	13.7	0.4	11.0	(4.2)	na	na	0.82	3.5	0.92	—	—	(800) 382-8722
USAA Cornerstone	aa	3.9	2.2	8.6	3.1	12.4	4.7	23.7	10.4	15.2	0.0	11.1	(1.1)	1.19	2.5	1.18	—	—	(800) 382-8722
USAA Income		(0.2)	(1.9)	1.9	(3.6)	4.9	(2.8)	9.9	(3.4)	12.4	(2.8)	12.2	0.0	0.68	6.9	0.42	—	—	(800) 382-8722
Value Line Income	aa	0.0	(1.7)	1.0	(4.5)	4.4	(3.3)	8.2	(5.1)	12.2	(3.0)	12.0	(0.2)	1.40	3.1	0.89	—	—	(800) 223-0818
Vanguard Asset Allocation	aa	1.2	(0.5)	5.2	(0.3)	7.4	(0.3)	13.4	0.1	15.2	0.0	13.9	1.7	1.21	3.3	0.52	—	—	(800) 662-7447
Vanguard Balanced Index	idx	0.9	(0.8)	4.4	(1.1)	5.6	(1.9)	9.9	(3.4)	na	na	na	na	na	3.5	na	—	—	(800) 662-7447
Vanguard Star	ff	0.6	(1.1)	4.6	(0.9)	5.9	(1.8)	10.8	(2.5)	15.0	(0.2)	11.7	(0.5)	1.08	3.5	0.00	—	—	(800) 662-7447
Vanguard Wellesley Income		(0.8)	(2.5)	4.1	(1.4)	7.3	(0.4)	14.6	1.3	14.8	(0.4)	13.7	1.5	0.90	5.9	0.35	—	—	(800) 662-7447
Vanguard Wellington		2.0	0.3	4.9	(0.6)	7.9	0.2	13.5	0.2	14.8	(0.4)	12.3	0.1	1.21	4.5	0.33	—	—	(800) 662-7447
BALANCED FUND AVERAGE		1.7	0.0	5.5	0.0	7.7	0.0	13.3	0.0	15.2	0.0	12.2	0.0	1.00	3.3	1.04			SD 6.2%
Corporate Bond Funds																			
➤ CGM Fixed Income		2.7	1.8	6.5	2.7	10.8	4.3	18.9	7.5	na	na	na	na	na	6.0	0.85	—	—	(800) 345-4048
Fidelity Short-Term Bond		1.6	0.7	3.6	(0.2)	5.5	(1.0)	9.1	(2.3)	10.1	(1.9)	9.3	(0.8)	0.57	5.9	0.77	—	—	(800) 544-8888
Fidelity Spartan Investment Grade Bond		(0.6)	(1.5)	4.5	0.7	8.8	2.3	15.7	4.3	na	na	na	na	na	7.3	0.65	—	—	(800) 544-8888
Fidelity Spartan Short-Term Bond		1.5	0.6	3.5	(0.3)	5.5	(1.0)	9.0	(2.4)	na	na	na	na	na	7.2	0.00	—	—	(800) 544-8888
➤ Homestead Short-Term Bond		0.5	(0.4)	2.1	(1.7)	3.4	(3.1)	6.6	(4.8)	na	na	na	na	na	4.6	0.75	—	—	(800) 258-3030
INVESCO Income—Sel Income		1.4	0.5	3.1	(0.7)	6.1	(0.4)	11.3	(0.1)	13.3	1.3	10.5		na	7.5	1.14	—	0.250	(800) 525-8085
Janus Flexible Income		1.7	0.8	5.8	2.0	9.8	3.3	15.6	4.2	17.6	5.6	10.1		1.19	7.7	1.00	—	—	(800) 525-3713
Janus Short-Term Bond		0.6	(0.3)	2.4	(1.4)	3.7	(2.8)	6.1	(5.3)	na	na	na	na	na	na	1.00	—	—	(800) 525-3713
Loomis Sayles Bond		3.2	2.3	7.7	3.9	13.5	7.0	22.2		na	na	na	na	na	7.0	1.00	—	—	(800) 633-3330
Merrill Lynch Corp Interm "A"		(0.3)	(1.2)	3.4	(0.4)	6.0	(0.5)	10.4	0.4		(0.5)	11.0		1.70	6.2	0.62	2.00f	—	(609) 282-2800
➤ Paine Webber Investment Gr Inc "D"		0.1	(0.8)	4.0	0.2	7.0	0.5	12.7		na		na	na	na	6.3	na	—	0.750	(800) 647-1568
Permanent Port—Versatile Bond		0.5	(0.4)	1.4	(2.4)	2.0	(4.1)	na		na		na	na	na	1.2	0.89	—	0.250	(800) 531-5142
SteinRoe Income		0.5	(0.4)	3.6					1.1	13.0	1.0	10.4	0.3	1.48	6.8	0.82	—	—	(800) 338-2550
Strong Advantage		1.8	0.9	3.4	(0.4)	5.2		7.7	(3.6)	9.9	(3.1)	8.5	(1.6)	0.37	5.7	1.00	—	—	(800) 368-1030
Strong Short-Term Bond		1.6	0.6	3.4	(0.4)		(1.1)	9.3	(1)	10.1	(1.9)	8.7	(1.4)	0.79	6.5	0.60	—	—	(800) 368-1030
Vanguard Long Term Corp Bond		(0.6)	(1)			(0.1)	1.1	14.3	2.9	14.9	2.9	13.1	3.0	1.96	6.8	0.31	—	—	(800) 662-7447
Vanguard Short-Term Corporate		0.6	(0.)	2.3		3.8	7)	7.0	(4.4)	9.0	(3.0)	9.5	(0.6)	0.81	5.6	0.27	—	—	(800) 662-7447
CORPORATE BOND FUND AVERA		0.9	0.0	3.8	0.0	6.5	0.0	11.4	0.0	12.0	0.0	10.1	0.0	1.00	6.1	0.72	—	—	SD 2.7%
Corporate High-Yield Bond Funds																			
Fidelity Capital & Income			0.3	6.9	0.5	14.2	3.3	24.5	6.4	27.5	7.0	14.0	3.5	1.47	8.4	0.91	1.50r	—	(800) 544-8888
Fidelity Spartan High Income		5.2	1.0	7.9	1.5	13.8	2.7	21.8	3.4	26.7	5.2	na	na	1.36	9.2	0.70	1.00r	—	(800) 544-8888
GIT Income—Maximum		4.9	0.6	6.0	(0.4)	9.1	(1.8)	15.0	(3.4)	17.4	(3.1)	9.0	(1.5)	1.14	8.0	1.54	—	—	(800) 336-3063
INVESCO Income—High Yield		3.7	(0.5)	5.2	(1.2)	9.2	(1.7)	15.6	(2.8)	17.8	(2.7)	10.1	(0.4)	0.92	8.0	1.00	—	0.250	(800) 525-8085
Nicholas Income		2.4	(1.8)	4.7	(1.7)	7.5	(3.4)	12.9	(5.5)	15.3	(5.2)	9.5	(1.0)	0.89	8.2	0.68	—	—	(800) 227-5987
Northeast Investors Trust		6.0	1.8	8.5	2.1	13.9	3.0	23.5	5.1	22.4	1.9	10.7	0.2	1.25	9.7	0.79	—	—	(800) 225-6704
➤ Paine Webber High Income "D"		3.3	(0.9)	6.3	(0.1)	8.1	(2.8)	13.5	(4.8)	na	na	na	na	na	8.7	na	—	0.750	(800) 647-1568
➤ Safeco High Yield Bond		3.0	(1.2)	5.3	(1.1)	9.7	(1.2)	16.9	(1.5)	18.2	(2.3)	10.2	(0.3)	1.03	9.2	1.05	—	—	(800) 426-6730
T Rowe Price High Yield		4.7	0.5	6.4	(0.1)	12.6	1.7	21.7	3.3	22.2	1.7	9.9	(0.5)	1.25	8.8	0.97	1.00r	—	(800) 638-5660
Value Line Aggressive Income		5.4	1.2	7.6	1.2	11.6	0.7	19.0	0.6	19.1	(1.4)	10.7	0.2	1.25	8.4	1.15	—	—	(800) 223-0818
Vanguard High Yield Corporate		3.5	(0.7)	6.0	(0.4)	10.7	(0.2)	18.2	(0.2)	20.3	(0.2)	10.8	0.3	1.14	8.6	0.34	1.00r	—	(800) 662-7447
CORPORATE HIGH-YIELD FUND AVERAGE		4.2	0.0	6.4	0.0	10.9	0.0	18.4	0.0	20.5	0.0	10.5	0.0	1.00	8.4	0.91	—	—	SD 3.6%
Government Bond Funds																			
➤ 1784 U.S. Gov't Medium Term Income		0.0	0.5	2.0	(0.7)	na	na	na	na	na	na	na	na	na	na	na	—	0.250	(800) 252-1784
Alliance Bond—U.S. Gov't "C"		(0.2)	0.3	2.2	(0.5)	na	na	na	na	na	na	na	na	na	na	na	—	1.000	(800) 221-5672
BNY Hamilton Interm Gov't		(0.6)	(0.1)	1.8	(0.9)	4.2	(1.5)	8.0	(2.4)	na	na	na	na	na	5.0	0.75	—	0.250	(800) 426-9363
➤ Benham Long Term Treasury and Agency		(1.8)	(1.3)	5.0	2.3	10.4	4.7	17.6	7.2	na	na	na	na	na	6.4	0.00	—	—	(800) 321-8321
Benham Short-Term Treasury & Agency		0.4	0.9	1.7	(1.0)	2.7	(3.0)	5.4	(5.0)	na	na	na	na	na	3.9	0.00	—	—	(800) 321-8321
Benham Target Mat Trust—1995		0.4	0.9	1.9	(0.8)	3.2	(2.5)	6.9	(3.5)	10.0	(0.8)	10.9	0.5	0.86	0.0	0.62	—	—	(800) 321-8321
Benham Target Mat Trust—2000		(1.1)	(0.6)	2.8	0.1	7.5	1.8	15.4	5.9	14.7	3.9	12.9	3.5	1.67	0.0	0.66	—	—	(800) 321-8321
Benham Target Mat Trust—2005		(2.4)	(1.9)	4.0	1.3	12.0	6.3	21.5	11.1	17.3	6.5	15.7	5.3	2.21	0.0	0.63	—	—	(800) 321-8321
Benham Target Mat Trust—2010		(2.1)	(1.6)	6.3	3.6	16.3	10.6	26.2	15.8	18.6	6.0	16.5	6.1	2.65	0.0	0.70	—	—	(800) 321-8321

MUTUAL FUNDS

Videocourse

AAII has updated its Mutual Funds Videocourse. The course was taped during a live seminar presented by John Markese, president of AAII. Dr. Markese has been presenting the mutual fund seminar for over 10 years and is both a charismatic and informative speaker. An abridged version of our full-day seminar, the videocourse still covers much of the pertinent material.

The Mutual Funds Videocourse is an ideal alternative for those people who cannot attend the live seminar as well as anyone who just wants to learn about mutual funds. The videotape format allows you to work at your own pace and to review the material whenever you wish. The topics include:

- **Mutual Funds: What They Are, How They Work, and What They Can Do For You**

- **The Importance of Tax Considerations**

- **Risk and Returns for Mutual Fund Investments**

- **Mutual Fund Selection**

- **Building and Maintaining a Mutual Fund Portfolio**

- **Mutual Fund Portfolios: Examples Using the Life Cycle Approach**

- **Questions and Answers**

The accompanying workbook expands on the points presented in the seminar and includes all of the graphics used in the videotape. It also contains a bibliography of information sources for mutual funds. The videocourse comes on two cassettes and the approximate running time is 3½ hours.

The complete videocourse with accompanying workbook is available to AAII members for $98 and to non-members for $129. For more information, contact the American Association of Individual Investors, 625 N. Michigan Avenue, Suite 1900, Chicago, Ill. 60611; (800) 428-2244 or (312) 280-0170.